편입 합격을 응원하는
해커스편입만의 특별 혜택

🎁 가입만 해도 **편입인강 무료**

해커스편입 인강(Ingang.HackersUT.com) 상단 [회원가입] 클릭 ▶ 회원가입 전 편입인강 무료 내용 확인

📄 편입영어/수학 **실력 무료진단**

해커스편입 인강(Ingang.HackersUT.com) 상단 [모의고사/이벤트]의 [실력 무료진단/맞춤인강] 클릭

🎫 해커스편입 인강 단과강의 **20% 할인쿠폰**

W52NC3T2JYS3924635342

해커스편입 인강(Ingang.HackersUT.com) 로그인 ▶
상단 [마이페이지] 클릭 ▶ 좌측 [쿠폰 확인] 클릭 ▶ 쿠폰 번호 입력

* 등록일로부터 7일간 사용 가능
* 한 ID당 1회만 사용 가능하며, 등록 후 사용기간이 만료되어 쿠폰이 소멸된 경우 재등록 불가
* 쿠폰 이용 문의: 해커스편입 02-522-1881

📧 해커스편입 학원 등록 시 **멤버십 무료**

· 편입영어 수업교재 증정 (*비매품)
· 캠퍼스 내 사물함 & 자습실 제공
· 첫 수강료 10만원 지원

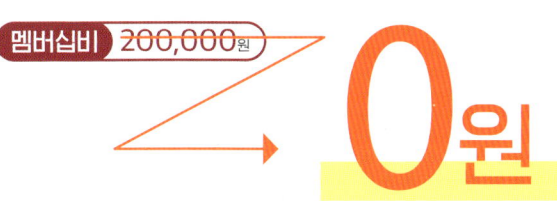

해커스편입

기출 독해 930제

주제편

문제집

해커스편입

상위권대학 편입명문 해커스편입
HackersUT.com

이제 **편입영어**도 **해커스**입니다.

영어 교재 분야에서 항상 베스트셀러의 자리를 지키는
해커스의 독보적인 노하우와 더 좋은 책을 만들겠다는 정성을 담아,
「해커스편입 기출 독해 930제 [주제편]」을 출간하였습니다.

누구나 중요하게 생각하는 기출 문제를 단순히 풀어보기만 하는 것이 아니라
고정적으로 출제되는 문제 유형과 지문의 주제를 파악하고
각각에 맞는 문제 풀이 전략을 다지는 것이 중요합니다.

「해커스편입 기출 독해 930제 [주제편]」은
주요 대학의 편입영어 최신 출제 경향을 완벽히 파악할 수 있도록
최근 6개년의 기출 문제를 수록하였으며,
고정적으로 출제되는 지문의 주제를 분야별로 모아서
한 분야씩 집중적인 문제 풀이 훈련이 가능하게 했습니다.

합격이 보이는 기출 문제 풀이,
해커스가 여러분과 함께합니다.

해커스편입 기출 독해 930제 [주제편]

CONTENTS

HackersUT.com 상위권대학 편입명문 해커스편입

「해커스편입 기출 독해 930제 [주제편]」으로 점수 잡는 비법   6
편입 전형 소개   8
편입영어 출제 경향 및 학습 전략   10

01 언어·문학   12
02 역사   38
03 예술   68
04 철학·종교   100
05 사회이슈·일상   130
06 경제·경영   158
07 정치·법   188
08 문화   220
09 교육   266
10 심리   278
11 인류학   324
12 의학·건강   338
13 물리·화학·기술·건축   364
14 생물   396
15 지구과학·천문학·환경   440
16 동·식물   466
17 기타   478

「해커스편입 기출 독해 930제 [주제편]」으로
점수 잡는 비법

01 100% 최신 기출 문제로 최신 출제 경향을 파악한다.

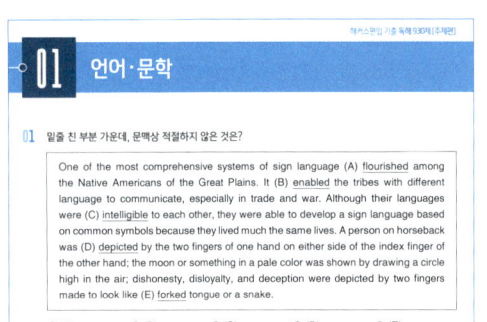

주요 대학의 편입영어 **최신 6개년** 기출 문제만을 수록하여 최신 출제 경향을 파악할 수 있게 했습니다. 각 문제가 출제된 연도와 대학은 해설집에서 쉽게 확인할 수 있습니다.

02 기출 문제를 주제별로 연습하고 실전 감각도 익힌다.

01 언어·문학
02 역사
03 예술
04 철학·종교
05 사회이슈·일상
06 경제·경영
07 정치·법
08 문화

편입영어 독해 영역에 출제되는 기출 문제를 **지문 주제에 따라 각 챕터로 구성**했습니다. 주제별로 집중 문제 풀이 훈련을 할 수 있으며, 기출 문제 풀이를 통한 실전 감각도 익힐 수 있습니다.

03 정확한 해석과 상세한 해설을 통해 약점을 극복한다.

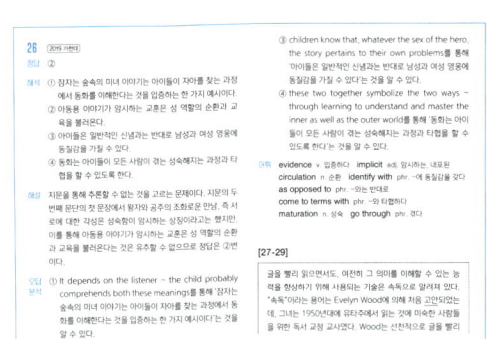

영문의 구조를 파악하기 쉽도록 **직독직해를 원칙으로 정확한 해석**을 제공했습니다. 또한, **정답에 대한 해설뿐만 아니라 어려운 오답에 대한 해설**도 제공하여 헷갈리거나 틀렸던 문제의 단서와 함정을 확인할 수 있으며, 이를 통해 자신의 약점을 파악하고 극복할 수 있습니다.

04 해커스만의 노하우가 담긴 학습자료를 200% 활용한다.

해커스편입 사이트(www.HackersUT.com)에서 **편입 시험에 관한 정보를 공유**하고 **학습 방법에 대한 조언과 자료**를 구할 수 있습니다. 또한, 본 교재에 관해 궁금한 점과 학습하면서 어려운 문제는 '편입교재Q&A'에서 해결할 수 있습니다.

편입 전형 소개

■ 편입이란?

편입이란 일정한 조건을 갖추고 있는 수험생이 새로운 대학과 전공을 선택하여 4년제 정규대학 3학년으로 이동하는 입시 제도입니다. 편입은 크게 일반편입과 학사편입으로 나뉩니다.

(1) 일반편입
- 지원 자격: 전문대 졸업(예정) 또는 4년제 대학 2학년을 수료(예정)한 대학별 지원 자격 학점 이수자
- 선발인원: 1~2학년 재적생 수와 교수확보율에 따라 정원 내 선발

(2) 학사편입
- 지원 자격: 학사학위 소지(예정)자
- 선발 인원: 입학 정원의 2% 이내, 학과 정원의 4% 이내에서 선발

■ 편입 전형 일정

편입은 매년 아래 일정에 따라 진행되며 세부 일자는 대학별로 다릅니다. 동시에 지원할 수 있는 학교 수에는 제한이 없기 때문에 필기/실기/면접 일정이 서로 겹치지 않는다면 여러 대학에 지원할 수 있습니다.

(1) 11월 말~12월 초: 대학별 모집 요강 발표
(2) 12월 중순: 원서 접수
(3) 1월: 시험 및 면접 진행
(4) 2월 초: 합격자 발표 및 등록

편입생 선발 방식

실기 시험을 실시하는 예체능 계열을 제외한 대부분의 대학, 학과에서 서류평가/필기/면접을 통해 편입생을 선발합니다.

(1) 서류평가
- 자기소개서, 학업계획서, 전적 대학 성적 증명서

(2) 필기
- 인문계: 편입영어
- 자연계: 편입영어, 편입수학

(3) 면접
- 제출 서류를 바탕으로 지원동기, 학습계획 등을 확인하며 인성 면접과 전공 면접으로 나뉨

편입을 준비해야 하는 이유!

1. 편입은 준비할 과목이 적습니다.
인문계는 편입영어 한 과목, 자연계는 편입영어와 편입수학 두 과목을 준비하면 됩니다. 일부 대학의 경우 전공 필기시험, 논술 등이 추가되기도 합니다.

2. 학교 재학 중에도 준비가 가능합니다.
방학과 주말만 잘 활용해도 재학 중에 얼마든지 준비가 가능합니다. 게다가 재학 중에 준비하여 합격할 경우, 공백 없이 3학년으로 바로 진학할 수 있다는 장점이 있습니다.

3. 계열과 전공 상관없이 지원할 수 있습니다.
대부분의 대학은 계열에 관계없이 지원이 가능합니다. 단, 일부 대학의 경우 동일 계열 출신자만 지원 가능하므로 최종 모집요강을 반드시 확인해야 합니다.

4. 전적대 성적이 크게 중요하지 않습니다.
전적대 성적도 평가 요소 중 하나지만 필기 점수가 합격 당락을 좌우하는 가장 큰 변수입니다. 전적대 성적 반영 비율이 크지 않고, 아예 반영을 하지 않는 대학도 있기 때문에 우선순위를 필기시험에 두고 학점관리를 해나가면 됩니다.

편입영어 출제 경향 및 학습 전략

편입영어 시험은 대학별로 문항 수, 제한 시간, 난이도 등이 다르지만, 보통 40~50문제로 구성되며 크게 어휘, 문법, 논리, 독해 4개 영역으로 나눌 수 있습니다. 대체로 독해 영역이 가장 큰 비중을 차지하며, 논리, 문법, 어휘 영역은 각각 10~30%의 비중을 차지합니다.

어휘

■ **출제 경향**
- 주로 밑줄 친 어휘의 동의어를 물어보는 형태가 출제됩니다.
- 일부 대학에서는 밑줄 친 어휘의 반의어를 찾는 문제와 단어 한 쌍의 관계와 비슷한 관계의 단어 한 쌍을 고르는 유추 문제가 출제되기도 합니다.
- 관용어구도 종종 출제되며, 어휘의 수준은 수능 어휘 수준에서 전문 학술 어휘까지 출제됩니다.

■ **학습 전략**
- 동의어를 찾아야 하는 문제가 주를 이루기 때문에 단어의 여러 뜻을 암기하고 이를 문맥 속에서 파악할 줄 알아야 합니다.
- 기출 어휘와 주요 동의어를 반드시 암기하고, 매일 학습한 어휘를 테스트해 보며 그날그날 자가진단을 통해 자신이 혼동하는 어휘를 파악해서 꾸준히 복습해야 합니다.

문법

■ **출제 경향**
- 지문에서 밑줄 친 부분 중 오류를 찾는 유형의 문제와 빈칸에 들어갈 문법적으로 옳은 보기를 고르는 유형이 주로 출제됩니다.
- 일부 대학에서는 보기 4개 중 어법상 틀린 보기를 고르는 문제와 옳은 보기를 고르는 문제가 출제되기도 하며 간혹 No error 보기를 포함하는 문제가 출제되기도 합니다.
- 출제 범위는 기초 문법에서부터 심화 문법까지 전반적인 문법 지식을 확인하는 문제들이 출제됩니다.

■ **학습 전략**
- 전반적인 문법 지식을 묻기 때문에 문법의 기본 개념을 반드시 꼼꼼하게 학습해야 합니다.
- 주요 대학에서 여러 문법 사항이 혼합된 형태의 고난도 문제가 출제되고 있으므로 핵심 이론을 정확하게 이해하는 것이 중요합니다.
- 시험에서 각 문법 포인트를 어떤 방식으로 출제하는지 포인트별로 모아 문제 풀이를 연습하고 실전 감각을 익혀야 합니다.

해커스편입 기출 독해 930제 [주제편]

논리

■ **출제 경향**
- 지문의 빈칸에 들어갈 적절한 보기를 고르는 문제가 출제됩니다.
- 지문의 길이는 한 문장에서 장문의 문단까지 다양하며 하나의 빈칸을 채우는 문제와 두 개 이상의 빈칸을 채우는 문제로 출제됩니다.
- 어휘의 난이도는 점점 높아지고 있는 추세이며, 단어뿐만 아니라 어구나 문장을 채우는 문제도 출제됩니다.

■ **학습 전략**
- 빈칸이 주어지는 지문의 길이가 짧은 문장부터 여러 단락으로 이루어진 장문까지 다양하게 출제되므로 처음에는 단문의 문제들로 빈칸 전후의 의미 단락을 나누는 연습부터 시작하는 것이 좋습니다.
- 그 후 차츰 지문의 길이를 늘여가며 빈칸의 단서가 되는 부분을 찾아내는 연습을 하고 나면, 두 개 이상의 빈칸 문제에서도 어느 빈칸의 단서가 더 명확한지 보다 쉽게 파악할 수 있게 됩니다.
- 기출 문제를 유형별로 풀어보며 어휘 학습과 함께 구문 독해 학습을 꾸준히 하는 것이 중요합니다.

독해

■ **출제 경향**
- 지문의 전체적인 이해를 묻는 제목, 주제, 요지 등을 묻는 문제와 글의 구조에 대한 논리적인 이해를 묻는 글의 논리성 문제, 그리고 세부적인 내용에 대한 이해를 묻는 내용일치 문제, 정보파악 문제 등의 문제 유형이 출제됩니다.
- 지문의 주제도 시사적인 내용에서 언어, 문학, 역사, 예술, 철학, 종교 등 학문적인 내용까지 다양하게 출제됩니다. 지문의 길이도 한 문단짜리 짧은 지문과 여러 문단으로 구성된 장문의 지문이 고루 출제되고 있습니다.

■ **학습 전략**
- 지문의 문장을 잘 분석하여 글의 전체적인 내용부터 세부적인 내용까지 파악할 수 있도록 연습하는 것이 중요합니다.
- 문제 유형별 풀이 전략을 익힌 뒤에는 최신 기출 지문을 통해 주제별로 어떤 내용을 다루는지 풀어보며 다양한 배경지식을 쌓는 것이 좋습니다.
- 충분한 양의 기출 문제를 풀어보며 주제별 지문에서 단서를 찾는 연습을 하며 실전 감각을 익히는 것이 중요합니다.

൦1 언어·문학

01 밑줄 친 부분 가운데, 문맥상 적절하지 않은 것은?

> One of the most comprehensive systems of sign language (A) flourished among the Native Americans of the Great Plains. It (B) enabled the tribes with different language to communicate, especially in trade and war. Although their languages were (C) intelligible to each other, they were able to develop a sign language based on common symbols because they lived much the same lives. A person on horseback was (D) depicted by the two fingers of one hand on either side of the index finger of the other hand; the moon or something in a pale color was shown by drawing a circle high in the air; dishonesty, disloyalty, and deception were depicted by two fingers made to look like (E) forked tongue or a snake.

① (A)　　　② (B)　　　③ (C)　　　④ (D)　　　⑤ (E)

Languages use rhythms composed of syllables that we mostly use unconsciously. A mother's heartbeat may be the first rhythm most of us hear. Its pattern, often described as an unstressed short sound followed by a stressed longer one is the iambic meter. This meter and many other variants, such as the trochaic (long-short) or anapaestic (short-short-long), derive from Greek and Latin, but are dominant in most European languages. Classical Chinese and Arabic poetry also use meter systems, with the latter echoing the long and short stress patterns of Latin and Greek. Stress patterns occur in everyday speech and songs, not only in high forms of literature. An interesting example is that of the Algerian artist Kamal el Oujdi, who raps in Arabic on a wonderful collaboration with British and Asian artists to combine meters and melodies across languages.

02 Which of the following is the best title for the passage?

① Patterns and Uses of Language Rhythms
② A Comparison of the Iambic and Trochaic Meter
③ A History of Rhythm in Classical Literature
④ Innovative Meters and Melodies in Music

03 According to the passage, which of the following is true?

① The iambic meter is derived from the Arabic language.
② A stressed syllable is shorter than an unstressed syllable.
③ The primary use of stress patterns is in poetry.
④ We are exposed to rhythm at a very early age.

Prior to the 1980s, U.S. presidents rarely used the word "smart," and when they did, it was typically in the traditional sense, as in "The American people are smart." [A] George H. W. Bush began using the word in its new, digital-age sense. He spoke of "smart cars," "smart freeways," "smart weapons," and "smart schools." The use of "smart" in presidential rhetoric exploded with Bill Clinton and George W. Bush, each of whom used it more than 450 times. Obama used it more than 900 times.

The same trend can be seen in general parlance. [B] In books, the use of "smart" climbed steadily from 1975 to 2008, increasing nearly threefold; the use of "stupid" doubled. In *The New York Times*, the appearance of "smart" increased fourfold from 1980 to 2000, and by 2018 had nearly doubled again.

[C] Not only did "smart" refer to digital systems and devices, it increasingly became a general term of praise, and a way of arguing for one policy rather than another. As an evaluative contrast, "smart versus dumb" began to displace ethical or ideological contrasts, such as "_____ versus _____" or "right versus wrong." [D] Both Clinton and Obama frequently argued that their favored policy was "not just the right thing to do; it's the smart thing to do." This rhetorical tick suggested that, in a meritocratic age, being smart carried more persuasive heft than being right.

04 Which of the following is most appropriate for the passage to appear in?

① a political textbook
② a newspaper article
③ a presidential address
④ a cultural review

05 Which is the most appropriate place for the sentence below?

> As a measure of meritocracy's hold on the public mind, the growing frequency of "smart" is less revealing than its changing meaning.

① [A]　　② [B]　　③ [C]　　④ [D]

06 Which of the following is most suitable for blanks?

① frugal — extravagant
② legal — illegal
③ sagacious — fabulous
④ just — unjust

07 According to the passage, which of the following is true?

① U.S presidents frequently used the word "smart" in diverse senses until the 1980s.
② The use of "stupid" increased in books from 1975 to 2008.
③ It was Bill Clinton who first used the word "smart" in its digital-age sense.
④ The use of "smart" doubled from 1980 to 2000 in books.

08~10

Until fairly recently, human beings lived in kin bands of usually no more than twenty people, loosely associated into tribes of perhaps a few hundred. Open to nature and each other, they knew each other more intimately than we can imagine today. Speech may have been (A) _____, as it often is between lovers, or between mother and baby. When we know someone that well, we know without asking what they are thinking and feeling. All the more in prelinguistic times, when our empathetic faculties were yet unclouded by the mediatory apparatus of (B) _____. (C) _____ some time alone with a person or small group in silence, and (D) _____ whether, after just a few days or even hours, you feel more intimately connected with them than if you'd been talking. The empathy and intuitive understanding of others that develops in such circumstances is amazing.

08 Which of the following best fills in the blank (A)?

① auditory
② elusive
③ analogous
④ superfluous

09 Which of the following best fills in the blank (B)?

① gesture
② kinship
③ language
④ intimacy

10 Which of the following best fills in the blanks (C) and (D)?

① Spend — observe
② Spent — observed
③ To spend — to observe
④ Spending — observing

11~13

We must also expect individual differences to manifest themselves in the form of personal styles. Messages may be short, but it is _____ possible to draw conclusions about individual users by examining the stylistic traits that they present. Evidence for this claim comes from forensic linguistics. In 2002, Stuart Campbell was found guilty of the murder of his 15 year-old niece after his text message alibi was shown to be a forgery. He had claimed that certain texts sent by the girl showed he was innocent. But a detailed comparison of the vocabulary and other stylistic features of his own text messages and those of his niece showed that he had written the critical messages himself.

11 Which choice fits best for the bank?

① nonetheless
② as such
③ although
④ necessarily
⑤ inconceivably

12 What is the core argument of the text?

① Forensic linguistics can be used to solve crimes.
② Each individual uses different vocabulary but similar stylistic features.
③ It is possible to identify writers by the way they write text messages.
④ Text messages are not an established way to provide an alibi.
⑤ A murder was discovered due to text message information.

13 What can be inferred from reading the above text?

① Text messages have been increasing in length.
② Different people use similar stylistic traits while sending text messages.
③ Stuart Campbell's niece sent the critical text messages discussed.
④ Family members will use similar vocabulary and stylistic features while writing text messages.
⑤ Forensic linguistics can be useful to solve important crimes.

14~16

A major change to revitalize the native language of New Zealand has been occurring after concerns it would die out. In 2013, only 3.7 percent of locals said they could speak the native tongue, Maori. Maori became an official language alongside English in 1987, and deaf individuals became elated when sign language became its third official language in 2006. The New Zealand government has promised to have Maori taught in every school in the country by 2025 to meet its goal of 20 percent of the country speaking the language by 2040. So far it has been a grass roots revival. Locals have started using the greeting *kia ora* (hello) or ending an email with *ngamihi* (thanks). Popular culture embraced the trend last year with the Disney film, *Moana* having a special one-day Maori-language screening. Maori is also being taught to residents of a few retirement villages. And Prime Minister Jacinda Ardern has pledged that her baby daughter will learn both Maori and English.

14 Which one is not true?

① Maori is an official language of New Zealand.
② There are only two official languages of New Zealand.
③ Maori is taught in a few retirement villages.
④ Ardern will have her daughter learn Maori and English.

15 Which one can be inferred from the passage?

① Sign language is more essential than Maori.
② Sign language is used in the film, *Moana*.
③ The Maori language has seen a resurgence from the local level.
④ Popular culture has yet to accept Maori.

16 Choose the best title.

① The Decline of Maori
② The History of New Zealand
③ The Inspiration of *Moana*
④ The Increasing Popularity of Maori

17~19

When people learn to play video games, they are learning a new literacy. Of course, this is not the way the word "literacy" is normally used. Traditionally, people think of literacy as the ability to read and write, but there are two reasons we should think of literacy more broadly. First, in the modern world, language is not the only communicational system. Today images, symbols, graphs, diagrams, artifacts, and many other visual symbols are particularly significant. Thus, the idea of different types of "visual literacy" is important. For example, knowing how to read interior designs, modernist art, and videos on MTV are other forms of visual literacy. The second reason is even though reading and writing seem so central to what literacy means traditionally, reading and writing are not such general and obvious matters. After all, we never just read or write; rather, we always read or write *something in some way*. So there are different ways to read different types of texts. Literacy is _____, then, in that the legal literacy needed for reading law books is not the same as the literacy needed for reading physics texts or superhero comic books. There are, even in regard to printed texts, different literacies.

17 Which of the following is the best title for the passage?

① The Advent of Visual Literacy
② Limits of Reading and Writing
③ Broader Perspectives of Literacy
④ A Lesson from Traditional Literacy

18 Which of the following best fits into the blank?

① confounded
② triangular
③ coherent
④ multiple

19 According to the passage, which of the following is not true?

① Traditional literacy means the ability to read and write.
② Visual literacy is needed to read diagrams and artwork.
③ Traditional writing is done in generalized and obvious ways.
④ There are different literacies for different kinds of printed texts.

20~21

Better watch your language around the _____. Babies as young as 8 months can hear and remember words — good and bad — researchers have discovered. "Little ears are listening," says Peter W. Jusczyk of Vienna University.

Jusczyk said new research shows that reading to children at such an early age, even if they don't seem to understand, can start the process of learning language.

"As you are sitting there reading out loud, the child is learning something about sound patterns of words," he said. "That is important because they learn how words are formed and it helps them to segment sound patterns out of speech."

The conclusion is based on experiments in which infants listened repeatedly to three recorded stories. Two weeks later, the babies' recognition of words from those stories was compared against words that were not in the stories. Jusczyk said it was clear the infants recognized the story words. A report on the study will be published Friday in the journal *Science*.

"This is important work," said Robin S. Chapman, a language-learning researcher at the University of Sussex. "It advances the findings of earlier work that showed children do attend to the sounds of language... and pick out those that are familiar." She said the studies showed that "a lot of language learning is happening in the first year of life. It shows that parents should talk to their children and the children will learn about the language from the talk."

20 Which is the most appropriate for the blank?

① baby shower
② kindergarten
③ cradle
④ asylum

21 According to the passage, which is not true?

① It was Chapman who conducted a research to be published in *Science*.
② Even the babies younger than one year start to learn human language.
③ There was previous research on infants' learning language.
④ In the experiment described in the passage, the subjects listened to stories.

22~23

Pidgins and creoles are the outcome of the need of people not sharing a language to communicate but differ from national and international languages in that a pidgin does not begin as an already existing language or dialect selected to serve this purpose; it is rather a particular combination of two languages. According to Loreto Todd, a pidgin is a _____ language which arises to fulfill certain restricted communication needs among people who have no common language. In the initial stages of contact the use of a pidgin is often limited to transactions where a detailed exchange of ideas is not required and where a small vocabulary, drawn almost exclusively from one language, suffices. Also, the syntactic structure of the pidgin is much less complex than the structures of the languages in contact, and though many pidgin features clearly reflect usages in the contact languages, others are unique to the pidgin. A creole arises when a pidgin becomes the mother tongue of a speech community. The simple structure that characterized the pidgin is carried over into the creole but since a creole, as a mother tongue, must be capable of expressing the whole range of human experience, the lexicon is expanded and frequently a more elaborate syntactic system evolves.

22 윗글의 내용과 가장 가까운 것은?

① A creole usually has simpler structures than a pidgin.
② The vocabulary of a pidgin is largely from two languages in contact.
③ A pidgin can be considered one of the preexisting languages in contact.
④ A pidgin has its unique features other than the ones reflecting the usages in the contact languages.
⑤ A pidgin develops as a way to facilitate communication among the groups who used to speak a common language.

23 빈칸에 들어갈 가장 적절한 것은?

① poetic
② native
③ complicated
④ marginal
⑤ rhetorical

24~26

Recently it has been claimed that the struggle against childhood dependency and for becoming oneself in fairy tales is frequently described differently for the girl than for the boy, and that this is the result of sexual (A) _____. Fairy tales do not render such one-sided pictures. Even when a girl is depicted as turning inward in her struggle to become herself, and a boy as aggressively dealing with the external world, these two together symbolize the two ways in which one has to gain selfhood: through learning to understand and master the inner as well as the outer world. In this sense the male and female heroes are again projections onto two different figures of two (artificially) separated aspects of one and the same process which everybody has to undergo in growing up. While some literal-minded parents do not realize it, children know that, whatever the sex of the hero, the story (B) _____ their own problems.

In "The Sleeping Beauty," the harmonious meeting of prince and princess, their awakening to each other, is a symbol of what maturity implies: not just harmony within oneself, but also with the other. It depends on the listener whether the arrival of the prince at the right time is interpreted as the event which causes sexual awakening or the birth of a higher ego: the child probably comprehends both these meanings.

24 Which of the following is most appropriate for the blank (A)?

① initiation
② orientation
③ reproduction
④ stereotyping

25 Which of the following is most appropriate for the blank (B)?

① contradicts
② pertains to
③ subverts
④ competes with

26 Which of the following cannot be inferred from the passage?

① The story of Sleeping Beauty is one example that evidences children's understanding of fairy tales in their finding of selfhood.
② Implicit lessons of children's story result in the circulation and education of gender roles.
③ Children can identify with both the male and female heroes as opposed to the common beliefs.
④ Fairy tales allow children to come to terms with the process of maturation that everyone goes through.

27~29

A technique used to enhance a person's ability to read text rapidly, yet still comprehend its meaning is known as speed reading. The term "speed reading" was first _____ by Evelyn Wood, a corrective reading teacher for unskilled readers in Utah back in the 1950s. Wood examined the reading habits of naturally fast readers and found that faster readers actually retained more content. She created a methodology for teaching people to read two to five times faster.

Wood pointed out poor reading habits that could be overcome and good habits that could be attained with practice. She established Evelyn Wood speed-reading schools throughout the United States and other English-speaking countries, and her system met with acclaim.

Ineffective habits that the Evelyn Wood program cites include stumbling on long words, even if the reader knows the words, regressing, or retaining a sentence or phrase, even if the reader comprehends it at the first reading, and vocalizing, or saying each word mentally. Effective reading habits identified by the program include completely focusing on the reading material, looking at groups of words instead of reading word by word, and setting a purpose for reading.

27 Which one is not appropriate for the blank?

① coined
② objected
③ created
④ devised

28 Choose the best topic.

① Evelyn Wood's speed-reading schools
② Vocalizing words mentally
③ Curbing reading speed
④ Reading groups of words

29 Which one is not true of Evelyn Wood?

① She believed reading speed was unchangeable.
② She analyzed the reading practices of quick readers.
③ She originally specialized in teaching poor readers.
④ She formulated a novel term.

30~32

Sometime in the nineteenth century, philosophy was replaced by literature in the quest for national identity. For one thing, after Immanuel Kant, the sciences were philosophy's chief preoccupation, and in the process of their incorporation, philosophy, excepting ethics, lost its taste for speculation. Novels and poems came to typify what Matthew Arnold called the "best that has been thought and said," at least in the West. What the state and most educators wanted was to imbue the student's imagination with what it was to be English, American, or French. Literature was best suited to this task because, unlike philosophy and history, which were international in scope and were assimilated into the sciences, literature was essentially national. You can read the works of, say, Dostoevsky, Flaubert, or Mann in translation, but, as everyone knows, something is always missing — chiefly, the sense of _____, that is, the specificity of the vernacular of which particular cultures are made.

30 Which does the underlined what it was to be English, American, or French refer to?

① national identity
② taste for speculation
③ western perspectives
④ philosophical preoccupation

31 Which best fits in the blank?

① place
② ethics
③ dignity
④ humanity

32 What is the passage mainly about?

① the imperialism
② the role of literature
③ the rise of science
④ the language change

33 빈칸에 들어갈 표현이 적절한 순서대로 배열된 것은?

English famously lacks a gender-neutral singular pronoun to correspond neatly with singular pronouns like *everyone* or *someone*, and as a consequence _____ has been used for this purpose for over 600 years, more recently, though, _____ has also been used to refer to one person whose gender identity is non-binary, a sense that is increasingly common in published, edited text, as well as social media and in daily personal interactions between English speakers. To take an example, we often hear "Someone left _____ phone behind."

① *they* — *he* — her
② *he* — *they* — his
③ *she* — *it* — his
④ *he* — *she* — their
⑤ *they* — *they* — their

34 다음 글의 요지로 가장 적절한 것을 고르시오.

From the beginning, rhetoric has focused on the speech act as communication. At the very least, two parties were involved, speaker and listener. The immediate and complex relationship of face-to-face communication became the model for discussing the very different situation of the writer and the reader with the introduction of a text into the situation. Reading replaces listening; but while one cannot ever re-listen (a recording is hardly the authentic performance), one can re-read a text. All of this has been obvious since Plato. The multiplicity of reading derives from, as Plato noted, the absence of the speaker, and consequently the absence of the authority that might enforce a certain understanding. Franz Kafka, we recall, seemed to see the universe from this perspective — the speaker is always absent, and, with him, any certain understanding. The "certain understanding" that has vanished with the speaker places all the burden of meaning on the reader. Hermeneutics, and therefore criticism, was born with literacy.

① Criticism starts with grasping the multiple meanings of literacy.
② An authentic performance relies on face-to-face communication.
③ Kafka gained a broader view of the world through a certain understanding.
④ It is of utmost importance to identify the rhetorical aspects of the speech act.
⑤ Reading takes on an interpretative significance with the absence of the authority.

35~36

One of the most important characteristics of the new murder mystery was the new demands it placed on readers, requiring that they play an active role in shaping the narrative and assigning guilt for the crime. Whereas execution sermons had required only that readers accept on clerical authority their official version of an uncontestable truth, the new legal narratives effectively treated readers as (A) recipients who must cast a vote for conviction or acquittal.

The anonymous reader who wrote in the margin of a convicted murderer's printed self-exculpation, "This statement is universally regarded as a lie from beginning to end," was responding to this expectation of his role as reader. But murder mysteries required that readers do more than just vote. They made readers actively shape the narrative, sifting through evidence, piecing the fragments together, tracking, detecting, probing, "unveiling" effectively taking on themselves the responsibility for crafting the master narrative of the event after (B) the withdrawal of the Providential Narrator.

To this end, the murder mystery narrative pulled readers into the (C) investigation of the crime, offering visual illustrations of key evidence, and graphic illustrations of scenes of the crime both architectural facades and interior scenes, maps aimed at assisting the readers in (D) reconstructing the crime in three-dimensional space, and architectural floor plans that paid special attention to the murderer's mode of access(the rear window, the unlocked door), sometimes tracking his path with a dotted line, increasingly noting the precise location of the victim's body.

35 위 글의 요지로서 가장 적합한 것을 고르시오.

① The readers of modern society want to know the conclusion of the mystery in advance.
② The new murder mystery has not been attractive to most readers.
③ The readers of the new murder mystery should be agile to catch the narrative.
④ The new modern mystery tends to distract the reader's interest with its narrative.

36 위 글에서 논지의 흐름상 가장 적합하지 않은 것을 고르시오.

① (A) ② (B) ③ (C) ④ (D)

37~38

On December 10, 2019, Merriam-Webster selected its word of the year, not some viral neologism like *post-truth* or *selfie* but a word that has been around since the Middle Ages: the pronoun *they*. Merriam-Webster chose the singular form of the pronoun, one that has been gaining currency and causing controversy.

There are two reasons that singular *they* is on the upswing. One is that it's a convenient way to refer to an unknown person in a gender-neutral way, versus using cumbersome constructions like "he or she." The other is that singular *they* is being used by individuals identifying themselves as transgender, non-binary, or even cisgender who don't feel like a gendered pronoun fits them. This usage of singular *they* can operate as a form of protest against some of the most fundamental ideas governing society today: namely, that _____.

While it's natural for the usage of pronouns to evolve, just as all language evolves, it can be discomfiting when the rules about how to use them start to shift. Some people balk at using singular *they* on the grounds that it is linguistically confusing (e.g., does one say "they is" or "they are"?) or that it just sounds weird. There is, however, historical precedent that proves this kind of evolution can take place. Centuries ago, the pronoun *you* was used only in a plural sense: Individuals were referred to as *thee* or *thou*. Gradually, people started to view *you* as the more polite way to refer to individuals as well. And there was similar confusion about whether to say "you is" or "you are," but today people say "you are" when referring to singles and doubles alike, with minimal fuss. We will have to wait and see whether singular *they* follows suit.

37 What is the best title for the passage?

① Singular *They* Must Be Stopped!
② Notorious Irregularities of English Pronoun System
③ Singular *They*: Why Is It Used and How Will It Evolve?
④ The Astonishing History of Singular *You* and Singular *They*

38 What is the best expression for the blank?

① language is a rule-governed system that cannot be altered easily
② every person can be identified as male or female in a clear-cut manner
③ social roles, which are inherently fixed to gender, are learned over time
④ language is a social institution, both shaping and shaped by society at large

39
~
41

A lingua franca is a language or mixture of languages used as a medium of communication by people whose native languages are different. It is also known as a trade language, contact language, and global language. The term "English as a lingua franca" refers to the teaching, learning, and use of English as a common means of communication for speakers of different native languages. The status of English is such that it has been adopted as the world's lingua franca for communication in Olympic sport, international trade, and air-traffic control. Unlike any other language, English has spread to all five continents and has become a truly global language. According to Nicholar Ostler, however, we need to draw a distinction between a language which is spread through nurture, a mother tongue, and a language that is spread through recruitment, a lingua franca. The latter is a language you consciously learn because you need to. A mother tongue is a language you learn because you can't help it. The reason English is spreading around the world at the moment is because of its utility as a lingua franca. Globish, a simplified version of English used around the world, will be there as long as it is needed, but since it's not being picked up as a mother tongue, it's not typically being spoken by people _____. It is not getting effectively to first base, the most crucial base for long-term survival of a language.

39 Which of the following is the major topic of the passage?

① Superiority of mother tongues
② English as a lingua franca
③ How to develop Globish
④ Survival of a language

40 Which of the following best fits into the blank?

① outside their own country
② for business purposes
③ in American colleges
④ to their children

41 According to the passage, a lingua franca cannot be defined as _____.

① a language used by people with different native languages
② a trade language, contact language, and global language
③ a language unconsciously learned from one's parents
④ a language that is spread through recruitment

42~44

The nature of acquiring languages is still quite mysterious. Children seem to have a natural inclination toward learning to speak from birth, and they are capable of quickly speaking intelligently. Three theories have been developed by researchers as to why children are able to learn a language with ease. These theories attempt to clarify some of the unfamiliar aspects of language acquisition. _____, they examine the behavior children exhibit during the various stages of speech development. The conditioning theory, the imitation theory, and the innateness theory all concentrate on the distinctive characteristics of this development.

No single theory is sufficient to completely explain the various characteristics of language acquisition, despite the fact that research on the subject is expanding. _____, when taken together, the conditioning, imitation, and innateness theories can provide some assistance in comprehending the subtleties of language development in children.

42 Which one cannot be inferred from the passage?

① One theory is enough to expound the acquisition of languages.
② Children learn languages effortlessly.
③ Researchers have not ceased studying language acquisition.
④ The ability to acquire languages is still enigmatic.

43 Choose the best word for the blanks.

① Specifically — However
② Specifically — Despite
③ Consequently — However
④ Consequently — Despite

44 Choose the best title.

① The Mysterious Behavior of Children
② Learning to Speak
③ Various Stages of Child Development
④ Language Acquisition Can Lead to Maturity in Adults

[45~46]

In examining writing on metaphor, it becomes helpful to consider it as existing on a continuum of linguistic conventionality. The terms "conventional metaphor" and "novel metaphor" seem to be mirrored by terms such as "dead metaphor" and "living metaphor" in academic studies. The contention stands that whereas conventional, dead metaphors are no longer noticed (e.g. the computer's memory is full), novel, living metaphors can still be perceived as a sometimes shocking act of imaginative union (e.g. depression is a cancer of the mind). Metaphors are typically codified as "A is B" relationships, whereby in the process of interpretation certain characteristics of B are transposed onto A. Although the language of metaphors often uses the word "is," the "is" represents a relationship best expressed by the term: "can be thought of as," not by "equals" or "is equivalent to."

45 Which of the following is the best title for the passage?

① Extensive Use of Metaphors in Language
② Metaphors for Language in Popular Culture
③ Ways of Categorizing and Interpreting Metaphors
④ Working Mechanism of Cognitive Operation in Metaphors

46 According to the passage, which of the following is true?

① Conventional metaphors are easily noticed by readers.
② Dead metaphors are sometimes shocking to readers.
③ "Depression is a cancer of the mind," is a novel metaphor.
④ In metaphors, the word "is" means "is equivalent to."

An important theme of Gordimer's novel, "The Moment Before the Gun Went Off", is that of paternal inheritance.

[A] The fact that Marais Van der Vyver has had no volitional control over this pivotal event in his life emphasizes that responsibility for this misdeed does not reside exclusively with him and suggests that Marais may not be entirely responsible for his other inheritances.

[B] Marais Van der Vyver's own prehistory, then, in his father's generation — the generation that created the modern apartheid system in 1948 — may be the historical "moment before" the story's findesiècle epoch. By extending the guilt for this offense transgenerationally, Gordimer implicates a whole morally corrupt society in the fate of Lucas.

[C] The story contains several references to Willem Van der Vyver, the late, great patriarchal figure whose presence seems to overshadow his son's life. Marais Van der Vyver's prominence in the community is directly related to his father's legacy; the son inherited the father's "best farm" and his employees are the children of those who worked for "old Van der Vyver." This suggests that the son inherited an entire network of social, economic, and psychological relationships.

[D] Significantly, then, we learn that it is the gun of Marais Van der Vyver's father that kills Lucas, the farmworker who is Marais's son; this legacy of violence is passed on from grandfather, to son, and finally — tragically — to grandson.

47 Which is closest in meaning to the underlined <u>implicates</u>?

① denotes
② demolishes
③ alleviates
④ incriminates

48 Which is the proper order of paragraphs [A] — [D]?

① [A] — [C] — [B] — [D]
② [B] — [C] — [A] — [D]
③ [C] — [D] — [A] — [B]
④ [D] — [B] — [C] — [A]

49 According to the passage, which is true?

① Gordimer implores the reader to forgive Marais.
② Marais criticizes the inequities built into his social system.
③ Gordimer suggests the corrupt society is responsible for Marais's murder to some extent.
④ Marais articulates a communal consciousness representing the consensus of community opinion.

50~52

African American Vernacular English (AAVE) refers to the kind of English spoken in some African American communities. The history of AAVE begins with the transatlantic slave trade. Since Africans were taken from different parts of the continent, they spoke many different languages. On American plantations, the slaves communicated with one another in a kind of pidgin English. Over generations, some characteristics of this pidgin language became fixed, and a new dialect of English emerged.

Many features of this dialect come from African languages. Some grammatical structures can be traced to West African languages. Many verbs in AAVE, for instance, are used in ways verbs are used in certain African languages. For example, *be* can be used to indicate habitual performance. When a speaker of AAVE says, "He be playing guitar," this means "He plays guitar often or all the time."

AAVE is often celebrated as a cultural heritage in African American literature. Also, African American church ministers and entertainers use AAVE for dramatic purposes. Nevertheless, many people regard AAVE as a sign of poor education. Because of this, the use of AAVE can be an impediment to socioeconomic mobility. _____, it can prevent AAVE speakers from holding high status in society.

50 Which one is not true?

① Slaves communicated in a single African language when they arrived to the United States.
② AAVE developed from a type of pidgin English.
③ Some African Americans consider AAVE as part of their proud tradition.
④ AAVE speakers can have a hard time climbing the social ladder.

51 Choose the best expression for the blank.

① However
② Otherwise
③ In other words
④ Nevertheless

52 Which one is true?

① AAVE is partially derived from African languages.
② AAVE was created by African American church ministers.
③ AAVE is only spoken and never used in literary texts.
④ All grammatical structures in AAVE can be traced to East African languages.

[A] A neologism is a recently created (or coined) word, or an existing word or phrase that has been assigned a new meaning. Neologisms are created in a number of ways, but in relation to journalism, three are of particular relevance. First, through the addition of prefixes or suffixes, new words can be created. Perhaps the most prevalent example of this in journalist discourse is the use of *-gate* as a suffix to designate a scandal. (A) Since the Watergate scandal, there has been Irangate, Lewinskygate, and Hansiegate, the result of which has been to trivialize the Watergate scandal itself.

[B] Second, neologisms can be created by shifting word meaning, either through changing grammatical function (*Google* and *eBay* used as verbs) or by developing a new euphemistic meaning. (B) Euphemisms, such as *engage* (kill), *theater* (battlefield), and *friendly fire* (being killed by your own army) are consciously used during wartime to background the uncomfortable reality that wars involve killing people. (C)

[C] Third, neologisms can be created through blending two existing words (e.g. *smog = smoke + fog*). (D) This is sometimes called a portmanteau, and of newspapers, only tabloids tend to coin new words in this way. (E) For example, an article on the designer clothes worn by certain British minor celebrities headlined Aristochavs combined *aristocracy* and *chav* — itself a derogatory neologism, applied to young adults of white working class, similar to the U.S. epithet *white trash*. Later in this same article, they reverse the portmanteau and label the 10 women pictured as Britain's *chavistocracy*. Either portmanteau is belittling, but the article also has a wider class position.

[D] We do well to remember that the middle class must work hard to achieve and maintain class position. The work of the middle class involves the (re)creation of a lifestyle that is recognizably middle class. This is tricky business because the signs of "middle classness" are easily appropriated and assimilated by the working class. Here, the newspaper is putting the identified minor celebrities in their place: that despite their expensive clothes, they are *chavs*, white working class. More than this, by labelling the people depicted *aristochavs*, the newspaper implies that they are the trashiest white trash. In doing so, the newspaper simultaneously attempts to keep its working class target audience abreast of what constitutes a middle-class lifestyle and to protect the signifiers of this middle-class lifestyle (expensive fashion) from being appropriated by the working class.

53 The following sentence was removed from the passage. In which part may it be inserted to support the argument made by the author?

> Examples of these types of neologisms are legion, particularly about the reporting of war.

① (A) ② (B) ③ (C) ④ (D) ⑤ (E)

54 According to the passage, which of the following is not true?

① The middle class tries to invent their own lifestyle.
② The use of *-gate* as a suffix has devalued the Watergate scandal itself.
③ Newspapers frequently uphold the middle class by inventing terms such as *aristochavs* and *chavistocracy*.
④ Maintaining the middle classness is challenging because it is easily copied by the working class.
⑤ Only tabloids among newspapers utilize blending as a way of coining new words.

55 Which of the following can the underlined word derogatory in paragraph [C] be best replaced with?

① pejorative
② indigenous
③ attenuated
④ tenuous
⑤ equitable

56 According to paragraph [D], what are the two goals of the newspaper when it calls minor celebrities in expensive clothes *aristochavs*?

> (a) to attract the attention of its middle-class audience with sensational terms
> (b) to coin novel expressions to survive the fierce competition among newspapers
> (c) to prevent the working class from adopting the signs of a middle-class lifestyle
> (d) to keep its working-class readers informed of a middle-class lifestyle
> (e) to appropriate the symbols of a middle-class lifestyle

① (a) & (b)
② (b) & (c)
③ (c) & (d)
④ (d) & (e)
⑤ (e) & (a)

02 역사

01 Which of the following is most appropriate for the blank?

In 1791, Olympe de Gouges wrote the "Declaration of the Rights of Woman and the Female Citizen," in which she demanded that French women be given the same rights, including the right to vote, as French men. The response from the government? Execution by guillotine. The official charge labeled her "a traitor who neglected the virtues of women giving damage to unity of the nation." Her 1791 declaration includes an apt line that is remembered by many today: "Woman has the right to mount the scaffold; she must equally have the right to mount the _____."

① podium
② gallows
③ rack
④ attic

02~03

World War I, which began nearly 100 years ago, produced its own crop of bionic men. In previous wars, severely injured soldiers often succumbed to gangrene and infection. Thanks to better surgery, many now survived. On the German side alone, there were 2 million casualties, 64 percent of them with injured limbs. Some 67,000 were amputees. In all nations involved in the war an emerging generation of so-called "_____," loomed ominously over the pension and welfare system, and many government bureaucrats, military leaders and civilians worried about their long-term fate. One solution was returning mutilated soldiers to the workforce. At last various prostheses were designed to make that possible.

02 The best expression for the blank would be _____.

① war cripples
② war veterans
③ the disabled
④ the war neurotic
⑤ the insane

03 According to the passage, World War I led to _____.

① the medical advances in surgery
② a remarkable change in welfare policy
③ advances in the technology of prosthetic limbs
④ the long-term fate of war veterans
⑤ the women's revolt against the established social system

The arrival of the Spanish conquistadors in the New World permanently and drastically reshaped the culture and the lives of the indigenous populations, leading to the disappearance of two of the greatest civilizations in the Americas, the Inca and the Maya, shortly after the Europeans discovered them. They left remarkable cities, with few records about the vanished inhabitants, forcing archaeologists to try to piece together what remains in an attempt to learn more about these lost civilizations.

The majority of the information that has been collected came from the ruins of their cities, which have withstood the passage of time since they worked primarily with stone. Yet, while both used the same material, they integrated their cities very differently into the surrounding environment. For the Inca, their skill enabled them to accomplish this almost seamlessly by sculpting nearby objects and incorporating terraces into their cities for use as farms or gardens. In comparison, Mayan urban planning appears almost haphazard. While lacking the extensive road system and organized layout of the Incans, Mayan cities tended to grow more organically from a central plaza that contained the most important buildings.

04 What can be inferred from the passage?

① All traces of the Incan and Mayan cities have vanished.
② Two of the greatest civilizations in the Americas, the Inca and the Maya, disappeared before the arrival of the Spanish conquistadors.
③ Both the Inca and the Maya used stone to build their cities.
④ The Incan and Mayan cities used similar ways to integrate their cities into the surrounding environment.
⑤ It is impossible for archaeologists to learn more about Incan and Mayan civilizations.

05 What does the underlined word, they, in paragraph 2 refer to?

① ruins
② Spanish conquistadors
③ archaeologists
④ the Inca and the Maya
⑤ the Europeans

06 The underlined word, haphazard, is closest in meaning to _____ .

① limited
② perpendicular
③ random
④ meticulous
⑤ conventional

07~10

In 1100, Henry I of England issued an edict that taxes could only be paid using tallies — wooden sticks cleaved in half between debtor and creditor. The sum of money was to be represented by a carefully prescribed abacus of notches of various sizes. For the next seven centuries, wood passed as a proxy for money and the English even evolved a sophisticated system of government financing based around tallies.

When it comes to the seemingly modern phenomenon of Bitcoin, the lessons are educational. Bitcoin supporters are everywhere. They invoke the arguments of Austrian economist, Friedrich Hayek, who noted that if given a choice, people would choose those currencies that retained their value best and were least subject to the _____ of errant policymakers.

Certainly, in an era where trust in the traditional monetary system has been shaken, Bitcoins' limited supply and freedom from human interference are powerful assets. They have transformed what was an interesting intellectual experiment into a living economy.

But history tells us that is not enough to create a sustainable currency. The reason is simple. Money retains its meaning through the polyglot of social interactions — status, social conformity and human behavior — that it encodes. Without the trust born of these, no medium of exchange can exist. Even when two nations trade, the money exchanged needs to be credible and convertible. That is why countries use U.S. dollars rather than their own currencies for many transactions.

07 Which of the following is most appropriate for the passage to appear in?

① a construction pamphlet
② a financial magazine
③ a brochure on foreign policy
④ a real estate review

08 Which of the following is the closest in meaning to cleaved?

① lifted
② adhered
③ clenched
④ split

09 Which of the following is most appropriate for the blank?

① whims
② gill
③ gaits
④ vine

10 According to the passage, which of the following is true?

① In many transactions between countries, U.S. dollars are used because of their credibility.
② The English had a sophisticated system of government financing before tallies were used.
③ Bitcoin is a sustainable currency because of its limitless supply.
④ In trade between two nations, the tallies exchanged are always credible.

11~12

The Pony Express National Historic Trail was used by young men on fast paced horses to carry the nation's mail across the country, from Missouri to California, in the unprecedented time of only ten days. Organized by private entrepreneurs, the horse-and-rider relay system became the nation's most direct and practical means of east-west communications before the telegraph. Though only in operation for 18 months, the trail proved the (A) _____ of a central overland transportation route, and played a vital role in aligning California with the Union just before the Civil War. Most of the original trail has been obliterated either by time or human activities. The trail's actual route and exact length are matters of conjecture. (B) _____, approximately 120 historic sites may eventually be available to the public, including 50 existing Pony Express stations or station ruins.

11 Which of the following is most appropriate for the blank (A)?

① tenacity
② visibility
③ mutability
④ feasibility

12 Which of the following is most appropriate for the blank (B)?

① Likewise
② Hence
③ However
④ Simultaneously

13 Choose the most appropriate one for each blank.

As late as the 1400s, native people were the only inhabitants of the western hemisphere, but following Columbus' voyage of 1492, for the next 400 years, large waves of nonnative people mostly from European countries sailed across the Atlantic Ocean to North and South America. Among them were British colonists, who settled on the East Coast of North America between what are now the states of Maine and Georgia. They came in search of opportunities for wealth, power, freedom, and adventure. _____, those who settled in the northern regions of this area did not find great riches at first; instead, they found rugged wilderness. These dangers and difficulties in the early 1600s meant the earliest colonists suffered from starvation and disease. America's abundant resources of fertile soils, abundant water supplies, and plentiful minerals had to be harnessed. Little time and energy could be squandered when there was so much work to be done just to survive. In some cases this view about idleness led to strict governmental policies. _____, the Virginia Assembly declared in 1619 that any person found idle would be condemned to prison.

① Therefore — In contrast
② Otherwise — Similarly
③ However — For example
④ Therefore — Moreover
⑤ However — Nonetheless

14~15

It took Europe some 300 years to modernize, and the process was wrenching and traumatic, involving bloody revolutions, often succeeded by reigns of terror, brutal holy wars, dictatorships, cruel exploitation of the workforce, and widespread alienation and anomie. We are now witnessing the same kind of (A) _____ in developing countries presently undergoing modernization. But some of these countries have had to attempt this difficult process far too rapidly and are forced to follow a western programme, rather than their own. (B) _____ created deep divisions in developing nations. Only an elite has a western education that enables them to understand the new modern institutions. The vast majority remains trapped in the premodern ethos.

14 Which of the following is most appropriate for the blank (A)?

① upheaval ② languor
③ seclusion ④ transcendence

15 Which of the following is most appropriate for the blank (B)?

① The regression of modernity
② This accelerated modernization
③ This intermittent modernization
④ The resistance against modernity

16~17

Although Americans have long celebrated Independence Day on July 4, technically that is not when the colonies voted to become a new nation. That honor belongs to July 2, 1776, which was not only the day the Continental Congress approved a resolution declaring independence from Britain but also the day that John Adams wrote would be celebrated by succeeding generations as the great anniversary festival with "pomp and parade." So, what happened? In a word, paperwork. According to Philip Mead, chief historian at the Museum of the American Revolution, it took two days for the Continental Congress to approve a press release explaining why the delegates had voted the way they did. That document, better known as the Declaration of Independence, arrived at the printer on July 4, 1776, which is why that date appears at the top. But though Adams might have been surprised to see Americans celebrate the Fourth of July, he did play a part in the shift. When he and Thomas Jefferson both died on July 4, 1826, that date became even more _____ in American memory.

16 Which of the following best fits into the blank?

① entertained
② estimated
③ eluded
④ enshrined

17 According to the passage, which of the following is true?

① Philip Mead belonged to the Continental Congress.
② The Declaration of Independence was printed on July 2.
③ Adams hoped independence would be celebrated on July 2.
④ Congress voted for the declaration on July 4.

18~19

The Egyptians were certainly the first civilization to preserve food on a large scale. Those narrow fertile strips on either bank of the Nile were their principal source of food, and a dry year in which the Nile failed to flood could be disastrous. To be prepared, Egyptians put up food in every way they could, including stockpiling grain in huge silos. This fixation on preserving a food supply led to considerable knowledge of curing and fermentation. Were it not for their aversion to pigs, the Egyptians would probably have invented ham, for they salt-cured meat and knew how to domesticate the pig. But Egyptian religious leadership pronounced pigs carriers of leprosy*, made pig farmers social outcasts, and never depicted the animal on the walls of tombs. They tried to domesticate for meat the hyenas that scavenged** the edge of villages looking for scraps and dead animals to eat, but most Egyptians were revolted by the idea of eating such an animal. Other failed Egyptian attempts at an animal husbandry include antelope and gazelle. But the Egyptians did succeed in domesticating fowl — ducks, geese, quail, pigeon, and pelican. Ancient walls show fowl being splayed, salted, and put into large earthen jars.

*leprosy 나병, 한센병   **to scavenge 쓰레기를 뒤지다

18 Which of the following does the passage mainly discuss?

① Preservation of food in Ancient Egypt
② Food and wall-painting in Ancient Egypt
③ Domestication of animals by the Egyptians
④ Importance of the Nile in Egyptian civilization

19 According to the passage, which of the following is true of the Egyptians?

① They managed to domesticate the hyenas.
② They knew how to preserve meat in salt.
③ They suffered from floods from the Nile.
④ They were the first civilization to invent ham.

20~21

Although Europe had experienced many serious outbreaks of disease, the most devastating of all struck in the mid-14th century, killing between one-third and half the continent's population. Known as the Black Death, the plague may have spread to Europe from Central Asia. Theories abound on what caused the disease, although it is widely supposed to have been *Yersinis pestis*, a bacterium carried by fleas on rodents. The infection has three variants: bubonic plague, which is characterized by buboes, or swellings, of the neck, groin, and armpits; pneumonic plague, which infects the lungs; and septicemic plague, or blood poisoning. The plague was transmitted via Constantinople in 1347 and reached most parts of Europe during 1348 and 1349. It caused widespread terror and panic, and most attempts to fight its spread were useless. By 1350, the Black Death had largely run its course, but with somewhere between 25 and 50 million Europeans dead, a sudden _____ of labor may have contributed to profound social changes. The peasantry found their diminished numbers led to a greater demand for their services, which meant that their living conditions and legal rights greatly improved.

20 Which of the following is most appropriate for the blank?

① shortage
② integration
③ division
④ abundance
⑤ diversification

21 Which of the following is not true according to the passage?

① Fleas are believed to have spread the plague.
② By 1350 the Black Death reached its peak.
③ The symptoms of the plague were classified into three categories.
④ The Black Death was the most catastrophic event in the history of Europe.
⑤ The Black Death made it possible for European society to change for the better.

22~24

According to Fijian legend, the great chief Lutunasobasoba led his people across the seas to Fiji. Most authorities agree that people came into the Pacific from Southeast Asia via the Malay Peninsula. On Fiji, the Melanesians and the Polynesians mixed to create a highly developed society long before the arrival of the Europeans. The European discoveries of the Fijian islands were accidental. The first of these discoveries was made in 1643 by a Dutch explorer. Major credit for the discovery and recording of the islands went to the Englishman Captain William Bligh who sailed through Fiji in 1789. The first Europeans to land and live among the Fijians were runaway convicts from the Australian penal settlements. Traders and missionaries came by the mid-19th century. Cannibalism practiced in Fiji at that time quickly disappeared as missionaries gained influence. When Ratu Seru Cakobau accepted Christianity in 1854, the rest of the country soon followed and tribal warfare came to an end. From 1879 to 1916 Indians came as indentured laborers to work on the sugar plantations. After the indentured system was abolished, many stayed on as independent farmers and businessmen.

22 According to the passage, which of the following is not true?

① The first people to land on Fiji may have come from Southeast Asia.
② Fiji was civilized even before the European arrival.
③ It was Captain William Bligh who got most of the credit for the discovery of Fiji.
④ Most Indians left Fiji once the indentured labor system ended.

23 According to the passage, where did the first European settlers come from?

① Malaysia
② The Netherlands
③ Britain
④ Australia

24 According to the passage, what happened immediately after Cakobau's religious conversion?

① Native Fijian religions were prohibited.
② Wars among tribes heightened across the country.
③ Christianity became the major religion among Fijians.
④ More missionaries arrived in the country from Europe.

25~27

Andrew Carnegie, American industrialist and philanthropist, made a fortune by manufacturing iron and steel protected by customs tariff. In 1873, on one of his frequent trips to England, he met Henry Bessemer and became convinced that the industrial future lay in steel. He built the J. Edgar Thomson Steel Mills near Pittsburgh, and from that moment on, the Carnegie empire was one of constant expansion. Later on, the Carnegie Steel Co. became an immense organization. It included all the processes of steel production from the great furnaces and finishing mills of Pittsburgh to the steamers that move the ores and the finished products. Like his grandfather, Andrew Carnegie did not abandon the radical idealism of his forebears for the benefit of the working class and the poor people. In spite of his espousal of Herbert Spencer's philosophy and the social Darwinism of the period, he believed in the social responsibility of the man of _____ to society. He must serve as a steward for the fortune he has earned and use that fortune to provide greater opportunity for all and to increase man's knowledge of himself and of his universe.

25 Which is the most appropriate for the blank?

① wealth
② sacrifice
③ religion
④ Darwinism

26 According to the passage, which is not true?

① Carnegie built his steel factory near Pittsburgh.
② Carnegie's grandfather believed in helping the poor people.
③ Carnegie's success in business was not helped at all by the government.
④ Carnegie was influenced by Bessemer in his choice of steel as his business field.

27 Which is the main topic of the passage?

① Carnegie's support of social Darwinism
② Carnegie's business success and philanthropy
③ Carnegie's business background and idealism
④ Carnegie and his grandfather's philanthropy

28 ~ 30

[A] The next wave of new immigrants came between 1870 and 1900. Among the newcomers were many Chinese, who were mostly men and lived in California. Many worked in the minefields and railroad construction sites. Others worked at menial jobs as cooks, laundrymen, or servants. However, the Chinese faced harsh racial prejudice. In 1882, the U.S. Congress passed the Chinese Exclusion Act, banning nearly all Chinese from coming into the country.

[B] The United States is a nation of immigrants. Before the 1840s, about 60,000 immigrants arrived each year. During the 1840s and 1850s, the number of people coming to the United States increased dramatically. Over three million Irish and Germans crossed the Atlantic for America at this time.

[C] Most Irish immigrants lived in extreme poverty. Most settled in the slums of Boston and New York and worked in low-paying jobs. Irish women worked as kitchen maids while men took dangerous jobs at low wages. _____, most German immigrants came with more money and training than the Irish. They were able to buy land in the Midwest. Many became farmers in states such as Ohio and Wisconsin.

28 Which one is the right order?

① [C] — [A] — [B]
② [B] — [A] — [C]
③ [B] — [C] — [A]
④ [C] — [B] — [A]

29 Which one is not true?

① The number of immigrants significantly increased around the mid-19th century in the U.S.
② Most Irish immigrants lived in the poor sections of cities.
③ All Chinese immigrants have been banned since 1882.
④ Most German immigrants came with greater wealth than Irish immigrants.

30 Choose the best expression for the blank.

① Similarly
② In contrast
③ As a result
④ As such

31~33

The material culture of the Paleo-Indians differed little from that of other Stone Age people found in Asia, Africa, and Europe. [A] In terms of human health, however, something occurred on the Beringian tundra that forever altered the history of Native Americans. For reasons that remain obscure, the members of these small migrating groups stopped hosting a number of communicable diseases — smallpox and measles being the deadliest — and although Native Americans experienced illnesses such as tuberculosis, they no longer suffered the major epidemics* that under normal conditions would have killed a large percentage of their population every year. [B] Another theory notes that epidemics* have frequently been associated with prolonged contact with domestic animals such as cattle and pigs. [C] Since the Paleo-Indians did not domesticate animals, not even horses, they may have avoided the microbes that caused virulent European and African diseases.

[D] Whatever the explanation for this curious epidemiological** record, Native Americans lost inherited immunities that later might have protected them from many contagious germs. [E] Thus, when they first came into contact with Europeans and Africans, Native Americans had no defense against the great killers of the Early Modern world.

*epidemics 전염병 **epidemiological 역학

31 위 본문의 내용과 가장 일치하지 않는 것을 고르시오.

① Genetically, Paleo-Indians lack immunities against contagious diseases.
② Indians had a material culture of the Stone Age similar to other regions.
③ Paleo-Indians had been free from pandemic microbes for a long period.
④ Because the Indians didn't domesticate livestock, they were safe from fatal epidemics.
⑤ When contacting Europeans, Indians became vulnerable to contagious germs.

32 밑줄 친 the great killers가 의미하는 바는 무엇인가?

① soldiers
② immunities
③ migrants
④ microbes
⑤ livestock

33 아래 문장을 위 본문 중에 추가할 경우, 가장 적절한 위치를 고르시오.

> The physical isolation of the various bands may have protected them from the spread of contagious diseases.

① [A]　　② [B]　　③ [C]　　④ [D]　　⑤ [E]

34~36

Numerous paintings of meals show what dining tables looked like before the seventeenth century. Forks were not included until about 1600, and very few spoons were shown. At least one knife was always depicted — an especially large one when it was the only one available for all the guests — but small individual knives were often at each place. [A] Tin disks had already replaced the large wooden plates. [B] In many other parts of the world, no utensils at all were used. [C] In the Near East, for example, it was traditional to eat with the fingers of the right hand. [D] Utensils were employed in part because of a change in the attitude toward meat. During the Middle Ages, whole sides of meat, or even an entire carcass, had been brought to the table and then carved in view of the diners. Beginning in the seventeenth century, at first in France but later elsewhere, the practice began to _____. One reason was that the family was decreasing in size and ceasing to be a production unit that did its own slaughtering; as that function was transferred to specialists outside the home, the family became essentially a consumption unit.

34 Which of the following is the best place for the sentence below?

This change in eating utensils typified the new table manners in Europe.

① [A]   ② [B]   ③ [C]   ④ [D]

35 Which of the following best fits into the blank?

① turn upside down
② make a soft landing
③ come in full swing
④ go out of fashion

36 According to the passage, which of the following is not true?

① Up to 1600 a meal scene was a frequent subject for painters.
② Forks were portrayed in paintings before knives and spoons.
③ The seventeenth century witnessed a change in the number of family members.
④ In the Middle Ages, a whole dead animal might have been served at the table.

37~38

The Celts were the first Indo-European occupants of Britain. The southern British Celts had been first subdued and thereafter ruled and sheltered by the Romans. Julius Caesar's attempt at an early invasion in 5554 BC did not result in occupation, unlike the results elsewhere in the Roman Empire, in particular Gaul (where the Latin spoken by Caesar's legions became, ultimately, Modern French). It was during the rule of the emperor Claudius (from AD 43) that the Roman invasion was followed by a more permanent occupation and military control. For about 400 years thereafter, Britain was a province of the Roman Empire. By the beginning of the fifth century, however, maintaining occupation forces in that outlying territory became too costly for the Romans, who were constantly subjected to the attacks of the Germanic tribes on the Continent. A highly simplified version of the events that followed is that when the Romans pulled out, with all of them gone by AD 410, the Celts in the south of the island were relatively defenseless. It was then that they invited Germanic mercenary soldiers to come over from northern Europe and protect them from invading Vikings, as well as from the Celts from the north and from Ireland (the Scots and the Picts).

37 Which of the following is true according to the passage?

① The Celts arrived in Britain after the Romans.
② Julius Caesar succeeded in a permanent rule of Britain.
③ The emperor Claudius made Britain part of the Roman Empire.
④ Germanic armies totally expelled the Romans from Britain.
⑤ Germanic mercenary soldiers protected the Scots as well as the Picts.

38 What does the underlined that outlying territory refer to?

① Britain
② Gaul
③ Germany
④ Europe
⑤ Ireland

[39~40]

The baleful influence of modernization after 1918 on peasants, artisans and the traditional middle classes provoked a widespread response. While there was never a concerted anti-modernist revolt across Europe, the conservative masses reacted to the crisis they faced with growing anger and desperation. In the Soviet Union the effort to modernize agriculture and village life provoked what was, in fact, a second civil war throughout rural Russia. The peasantry resisted the violent attempts to force them into collective farms by destroying their crops and livestock. The number of cattle fell from 38 million in 1928 to 7 million in 1933. Many peasants were forced into collectives at the point of a gun, and millions were denounced as rural capitalists (kulaks) by the Communists, and either killed or exiled to labour camps where chances of survival were slight.

The conflict with the peasantry produced a food crisis that led to the deaths of millions more; famine in the Ukraine, where peasant resistance in defence of their religion and distinct nationality was most marked, was deliberately engineered by Stalin to crush the anti-Soviet movement. Peasants and rural craftsmen were herded into factories where they performed poorly, trying to grapple with complex machinery and keep regular hours. The result was further terror, a wave of denunciations, accusations of sabotage and killings that reached numbers that can still only be guessed at. In the end even Stalin could see that the cost of imposing modernization from above threatened to be self-defeating. In 1935 he ordained that villagers could keep a cottage garden for themselves, and a few animals. Within a few years the value of the produce from these allotments, which constituted only 3.9 percent of the land area, almost equalled the value of everything produced on the collective farms. But this was the government's only concession. The violent reaction of the bulk of the Soviet population to Stalin's plans was crushed only at the cost of a terrible toll in lives and livelihood.

adapted from a book by Richard Overy

39 Which would be the best title for the passage above?

① The Post-War Destitution in Russia
② The Mastery over Production by the Producers
③ The Detrimental Effect of Coercive Modernization
④ The Revolutionary Potential of the Russian Peasantry
⑤ The Soviet Government Plans to Spur Economic Growth

40 Which statement can be best inferred from the passage above?

① Many peasants deplored private land ownership.
② The most persistent resistance to modernization came from urban areas.
③ Stalin's goal to vitalize the rural economy was impeded in practice.
④ The conservative masses formed an alliance to resist top-down modernization.
⑤ The Soviet government offered full support for private profit through private control of production.

41~43

Originally, election days varied by state, but in 1845 a law was passed to set a single election day for the entire country. At first, it applied only to presidential elections, but it was later extended to congressional elections as well. At that time, the United States was still a largely agrarian society. For farmers, who made up a majority of the labor force, much of the year was taken up by the planting, tending, and harvesting of crops. Early November was a good time to vote because the harvest was over but the weather was still relatively mild.

Still, some days of the week were better than others. Two days were definitely out of the question. Most Americans were devout Christians and thus set aside Sunday as a day of rest and worship. Wednesday in many areas was a market day, when farmers sold their crops in town. In addition, a travel day was sometimes required. In rural areas, the nearest polling place might have been several miles away, and, in an era before automobiles, getting there could take a while. If people couldn't use Sunday or Wednesday as their travel day, then that meant election day couldn't be on Monday or Thursday, either. And so Tuesday was perceived as the best option.

The reason that election day was specified as the Tuesday "after the first Monday" was to prevent it from falling on November 1. That day was considered unfavorable because some Christians observed it as All Saints' Day and also because merchants typically took the first day of the month to settle their books for the previous month.

41 Which of the following was not a factor to consider when the election day was decided on Tuesday?

① weather
② worship
③ sale
④ transportation

42 What does the underlined Two days refer to?

① Sunday and Wednesday
② Monday and Thursday
③ Friday and Saturday
④ Tuesday and Thursday

43 For whom was the first day of November avoided?

① workers
② farmers
③ merchants
④ politicians

44~45

Settlers from the east who traveled across the American West in the mid-nineteenth century understood that they faced a difficult journey across deserts and mountains. They knew that the trip would take years and that some people would lose their lives. However, they were optimistic.

Michael T. Simmons was one of those _____ travelers. Someone told him to go to the Pacific Northwest for new opportunities. He sold his business to pay for the supplies that he and his family needed. He knew that the area was largely unknown. He also knew that it was dangerous. This did not stop him.

When Simmons and his group reached Oregon, he announced that he was going to continue north. The Hudson's Bay Trading Company heard the news, and they _____ him. However, Simmons was certain that the trip was going to be successful, and he did not listen. Instead, he continued north as planned. After he arrived, he helped to establish the first settlement in the territory that is now known as Washington State. Documents show that Simmons built the first mill using water from the Tumwater waterfall for power. For this, he is sometimes called the father of Washington industry.

44 Which pair best fits in the blanks?

① flexible — discouraged
② determined — discouraged
③ flexible — encouraged
④ determined — encouraged

45 According to the passage, which is true?

① Many people believed Americans should proceed south.
② Many people believed westward expansion would be challenging.
③ Simmons and his group received many local supports when they headed north.
④ Simmons and his group competed with the earlier settlers in the unknown territory.

46~48

Five score years ago, a great American, in whose symbolic **shadow** we stand, signed the **Emancipation** Proclamation. This momentous (A) decree came as a great beacon light of hope to millions of Negro slaves who had been seared in the flames of withering injustice. It came as (B) a joyous daybreak to end the long night of captivity. But one hundred years later, we must face the tragic fact that the Negro is still not free. One hundred years later, the life of the Negro is still sadly crippled by the **manacles** of segregation and the chains of discrimination. One hundred years later, the Negro lives on a lonely **island** of **poverty** in the midst of a vast **ocean** of material **prosperity**. One hundred years later, the Negro is still languishing in the corners of American society and finds himself an **exile** in his own land. So we have come here today to dramatize (C) an appalling condition. In a sense we have come to our nation's capital to cash (D) a check. When the architects of our republic wrote the magnificent words of the Constitution and the Declaration of Independence, they were signing (E) a promissory note to which every American was to fall **heir**. This note was a promise that all men would be guaranteed the unalienable rights of life, liberty, and the pursuit of happiness.

46 밑줄 친 (A)~(E) 가운데 의미하는 바가 다른 것 하나를 고르시오.

① (A)　　② (B)　　③ (C)　　④ (D)　　⑤ (E)

47 위 본문의 내용과 일치하지 않는 것을 고르시오.

① Because of the shadow that an American brought over the Negro, African Americans are still suffering from the darkness and blindness.
② The Negro is granted with equal rights with the White.
③ Although the Emancipation Proclamation was declared one hundred years ago, the Negro is still under the conditions of segregation and discrimination.
④ The Negro came to the capital to request their rights.
⑤ The rights of the Negro are granted by the Declaration of Independence.

48 다음은 본문 중에 굵은 글씨로 제시된 단어들의 짝이다. 본문 중에 나타난 의미상 대조를 이루는 짝이 아닌 것을 고르시오.

① emancipation — manacle
② island — ocean
③ shadow — light
④ exile — heir
⑤ poverty — prosperity

49
~
52

Andrew Carnegie, a Scottish-American industrialist and philanthropist, was born in 1835 in Scotland, and immigrated to the United States with his parents at age 12. Carnegie started work as a telegrapher, and by the 1860s had investments in railroads, bridges, and oil derricks. He accumulated further wealth as a bond salesman. He built Pittsburgh's Carnegie Steel Company, which he sold to J. P. Morgan in 1901 for $303,450,000. After selling Carnegie Steel, he surpassed John D. Rockefeller as the richest American for the next several years.

As early as 1868, at age 33, Carnegie drafted a memo to himself. He wrote: "... The amassing of wealth is one of the worse species of idolatry. No idol more debasing than the worship of money." In order to avoid degrading himself, he wrote in the same memo he would retire at age 35 to pursue the practice of philanthropic giving for "... the man who dies thus rich dies disgraced." However, he did not begin his philanthropic work in all earnest until 1881, with the gift of a library to his hometown in Scotland.

_____ Carnegie did not comment on British imperialism, he strongly opposed the idea of American colonies. He opposed the annexation of the Philippines and tried to arrange for independence for the Philippines. As the end of the Spanish-American War neared, the United States bought the Philippines from Spain for $20 million. To counter what he perceived as imperialism on the part of the United States, Carnegie personally offered $20 million to the Philippines so that the Filipino people could buy their independence from the United States. However, nothing came of the offer.

49 Which of the following can be inferred from the passage?

① Carnegie started to invest in railroads, bridges, and oil derricks in 1860.
② Carnegie was not the richest man in America in the 1890s.
③ Carnegie idolized money so that he could accumulate his wealth.
④ Carnegie was given a library as a gift in his hometown in Scotland.

50 Which of the following is most suitable for the blank?

① But
② As
③ When
④ While

51 The third paragraph illustrates Carnegie's philosophy of _____.

① wealth
② anti-imperialism
③ the Philippines
④ idolatry

52 According to the passage, which of the following is true?

① Carnegie started to do things as a philanthropist at age 35.
② Carnegie regarded it a disgrace for a rich man to die.
③ The Philippines gained independence from America thanks to Carnegie's offering of money.
④ Carnegie opposed America's purchase of the Philippines from Spain.

53
~
57

[A] At the time of the First World War the transfer of Western ideas and institutions beyond Europe's boundaries was well under way. At the height of European imperialism, aspiring young non-Western men, commonly from privileged families, went to study in Europe or the United States. Westerners themselves established Western schools in lands under their domination. There arose a non-Western intelligentsia, its members prompted by the most advanced Western ideals and equipped with Western learning. Their sense of human dignity was patterned after that of their teachers, yet stunted because the Westerns treated them as inferior. Copying their Western masters, these uprooted and inwardly divided intellectuals became nationalists. Western-educated, they wanted to be "modern" Turks, Arabs, Indians, or Africans. They wanted their nations to be respected.

[B] These educated nationalists soon became revolutionaries as well, because colonial officials or traditional rulers generally (A) _____ open resistance. As revolutionaries they turned elitist and socialist. They believed that their people did not know how to make themselves strong. Yet the Western-trained, non-Western intelligentsia also remained dedicated — at least in the abstract — to the democratic ideal. How its eliticism and pro-Western orientation could be reconciled with its faith in the common people and its attachment to indigenous culture remained an unresolved problem for the future.

[C] (B) _____ In the dying Ottoman Empire, for instance, the Western-trained young Turks seized power in 1908. After the collapse of their ramshackle state at the end of World War 1, they created a reasonably modern and stable Turkey under the leadership of Kemal Atatürk. The transformation was achieved in relatively short order and has endured to the present.

[D] (a) The experience in India, though, was more representative of non-Western trends. British-educated Indians, with the help of a British civil servant, established in 1885 the Indian National Congress and made it the instrument of a moderate Indian nationalism. (b) Radicalized by World War 1, the Indian National Congress fell under the sway of Mohandas Gandhi, one of the most remarkable of the Westernized anticolonial leaders. (c) Under the British rule for over 150 years, India developed effective nationalist leadership and administrative, legal and economic structures suitable for nationhood. (d) Its Westernization proceeded from both above and below: from British rule and native resistance to it. When independence came in 1947, the Indian subcontinent was split into two states: India and Pakistan. (e) Independence was followed by a war of communal riots that took many hundreds of thousands of lives.

53 Which of the following would be the best title for the above passage?

① Worldwide Westernization
② Experiments in Globalism
③ The Rise of the Industrial Age
④ Obstacles to Political Developments
⑤ Global Dominance of Western Imperialism

54 Which of the following can be inserted into the blank (A) in paragraph [B]?

① deduced
② evacuated
③ conferred
④ suppressed
⑤ proclaimed

55 Which of the following would best fit in the blank (B) in paragraph [C]?

① The experiments in independence were painful, violent and marred by adversity.
② A new phase in the relationship between the West and non-Western people began.
③ The progress of this intelligentsia varied from one non-Western country to the next.
④ In some parts of the world, western penetration was much slower and more troubled.
⑤ While intellectuals were learning Western attitudes, Europeans introduced Western institutions.

56 According to the above passage, which of the following is true?

① British civil servants established the Indian National Congress.
② The western-trained Turks were led by Kemal Atatürk to create modern Turkey.
③ Non-Western people who studied in Europe constructed their own academic traditions.
④ The educated nationalists had a belief in their people's independent ability to be strong.
⑤ India formed its administrative, legal and economic systems after its independence from the U.K.

57 The following sentence is removed from paragraph [D]. In which part may it be inserted to support the argument made by the author?

> The chief flaw in Indian nationalism lay in the insurmountable religious division between Muslims and Hindus.

① (a) ② (b) ③ (c) ④ (d) ⑤ (e)

03 예술

01 Choose the most appropriate one for the blank.

> The limestone cave of Leang Bulu' Sipong 4 on the island of Sulawesi in Indonesia was occupied, more than forty thousand years ago, by early modern humans. Inside it for all that time has been a fourteen-and-a-half-foot-wide image, painted in dark-red pigment, depicting about eight tiny bipedal figures, bearing what look to be spears and ropes, bravely hunting the local wild pigs and buffalo. The discoverers, a team of archaeologists at Griffith University in Australia, call it "to our knowledge, currently the oldest _____ record of storytelling and the earliest figurative artwork in the world." The very first storytelling picture tells one of the simplest and most resonant stories we have: a tale of the hunter and the hunted, of small and easily mocked pursuers trying to bring down a scary but vulnerable beast.

① oral
② complex
③ ruined
④ Greek
⑤ pictorial

02 다음 글의 주제로 가장 적절한 것은?

> In the twenty-first century, as debates still rage over the risks and benefits of DDT as an antimalarial agent; as calls for environmental justice are heard in cities worldwide; as populations of marine organisms decline, fisheries collapse, and toxic waste washes up on our shores, Rachel Carson's work appears remarkably relevant and even prescient. Yet, Carson did not set out to be an "environmentalist" or an "environmental writer" in the modern sense. *Silent Spring*, with its detailed documentation of the dangers of pesticides and explicit warnings against their indiscriminate use, was in many ways a departure from the genre of writing Carson knew and loved best. Carson was first and foremost a nature writer, someone with an extraordinary gift for translation and an ability to evoke in rich detail the fluid boundaries, the tastes and sounds, the pains and pleasures, of the world as experienced by nonhuman forms of life.

① the use and abuse of natural resources
② Rachel Carson as a nature writer breaking new ground
③ the fame of Rachel Carson in the twenty-first century
④ the emergence of environmental writing as a new literary genre
⑤ a widening gap between environmentalist justice and realities

03~05

On ten art museum walls in Santa Fe, New Mexico, the history of Mexican-Americans, both mythical and actual, is depicted in brilliant colors and disproportionate figures. Aztec ancestor figures dance and gods protect peasants, all for the glory of the Mexican-American in the present. On some walls, the chains of bondage are being broken and the Lady of Justice, depicted as an Indian Maiden, watches over both Indians and Mexican-Americans. The expression on her face is warm and fierce at the same time, a nice dichotomy which both enlivens and nurtures visitors.

On another wall, Pancho Villa, a revolutionary leader, and Father Hidalgo, a Catholic priest who launched the revolution to free Mexico from Spanish rule, lead the Mexican peasants to freedom. But the clenched fist at the end of Pancho Villa's grotesquely muscled arms is the most (A)_____ image. It symbolizes unity, determination, ambition, and pride, all traits that are upheld as part of Mexican psychology. The figures painted are bold, upright, strong, and grasping, far from the (B)_____ of the Mexican-American with a drooping mustache and floppy sombrero hat lying in the shade of a stucco building.

03 What can be inferred from the above passage?

① Art can build unity and strength in disenfranchised communities.
② Mexican-American children are not raised to be strong and bold people.
③ The ancestral gods failed to build a positive image of Mexican-Americans.
④ Stereotypes are perpetuated by societies that do not value loyalty and leadership.
⑤ Mexican psychology is deeply rooted in a dark past.

04 Which expression does not fit (A)?

① controversial
② striking
③ predominant
④ uplifting
⑤ significant

05 Which expression best fits (B)?

① trials
② stereotype
③ fantasy
④ manifestation
⑤ synthesis

06~09

Lascaux cave, discovered in 1940, is a horizontal, wet cave covering 325 meters over its various galleries. Over 17,000 years old, it is one of the greatest concentrations of prehistoric rock paintings, pictographs, and petroglyphs in the world. [A] The grotto consists of a series of limestone-walled chambers. The Hall of the Bulls, Axial Passage, and Shaft are covered with a hard limestone forming an irregular textured surface that exhibits only paintings. [B]

The cave depicts the animal world of prehistoric people and is filled with images of galloping bulls, horses, and deer. The paintings are particularly notable because of their compositional and technical complexity. [C] Several techniques were used including the use of sharpened sticks darkened with color for outlining animals, daubing pigment using moss to produce a dappled aspect on horses, and blowing oxide through a _____ reed to provide an ephemeral quality that suggests the breath of the animal. [D]

06 What is the author's main purpose in writing this passage?

① to discuss diverse rock paintings in Lascaux cave
② to show the techniques used in constructing Lascaux cave
③ to describe the internal structure of chambers
④ to emphasize the lifestyle of prehistoric people

07 Which is the most appropriate place for the sentence below?

> Other chambers have softer walls and were easier to work into engravings, although they do contain some paintings.

① [A]   ② [B]   ③ [C]   ④ [D]

08 Which of the following is most suitable for the blank?

① hollow
② florid
③ geometrical
④ colorful

09 Which is the most appropriate tone of the passage in describing paintings in Lascaux cave?

① snobbish
② flattering
③ admiring
④ unconvincing

10~11

Philip Guston's artistic language and poetic motives seek to better understand and apprehend the illogical and paradoxical realities of human existence. The task of the painter is not "how to represent" but "how to know." Guston, having abandoned abstraction/concretion, returned to figurative painting, to a simple and direct figuration. What appears at first glance to be a difficult iconography often refers back to the pictures of his youth — light bulbs, shoe soles, and trash can lids — as if they were elements taken from the frescos of Piero della Francesca. Guston's iconography is not a simple representation that can be interpreted through a descriptive/prescriptive logic. It relates back to a more profound knowledge, to the anima of Carl Jung. Guston's illogical iconography does not speak: of a descriptive figuration, but of an underlying figuration in the mythical subconscious, an epiphany or something that manifests itself as something logically/illogically received — a divination.

10 위 글의 주제로 가장 적절한 것은?

① Philip Guston 시(詩)의 언어적 특징
② Philip Guston의 그림에 나타난 논리성
③ 추상예술과 구상예술의 철학적 배경
④ Carl Jung이 현대 예술에 미친 영향
⑤ Philip Guston 회화의 양식적 특징

11 빈칸에 들어갈 말로 바르게 짝지어진 것은?

① abstraction — descriptive — logically
② abstraction — descriptive — illogically
③ abstraction — prescriptive — logically
④ concretion — prescriptive — illogically
⑤ concretion — descriptive — logically

12~13

From the 15th century to the current day, the Renaissance maxim holds true: "Every painter paints himself." Beyond straightforward self-portraits, artists through the ages have left special signatures on their canvases, covertly inserting their own faces into their works in unusual and inventive ways. This sense of self-importance for the artist arose in the Renaissance, a period with humanist values that prized individualism and creativity. During that era, two trends for hidden self-portraits emerged in Europe. In Italy, artists tended to include their portraits on the right side of paintings or altarpieces, with their eyes looking knowingly out at the viewer. Northern Renaissance artists, however, liked to toy with dense and precise symbolism that showed off their technical skills. The self-portraits they worked into their oil paintings are usually found distorted in reflective surfaces, like mirrors. The traditions begun in this artistic golden age have persisted to this day.

12 Which of the following is the best title for the passage?

① When Did Painters Start to Work for a Patron?
② Why Did Painters Expect Appreciation of Their Work?
③ How Did Artists Hide Self-Portraits in Their Paintings?
④ What Were Art History's Greatest Unsolved Mysteries?

13 According to the passage, which of the following is true?

① Renaissance artists valued usual and conventional paintings.
② In Italy, artists drew faces that avoided the glances of viewers.
③ Northern Renaissance artists liked to insert distorted self-images.
④ Modern artists decline to include their own portraits in their paintings.

14~16

Modern sculpture has its origins in the work of Frenchman Auguste Rodin. Born into a modest family in 1840, Rodin began his creative journey in the 1860s, a journey that would lead to him being remembered as the 'bridge' between traditional and modern sculpture. Before Rodin, sculpture told stories about the past: religion, history, myth, and literature. Sculptures typically left little to the imagination. Figures tended to be idealized in some way to avoid any imperfections of the model. Rodin can be considered a realist in that he refused to improve on what he saw in front of him. He considered all of nature beautiful and if a model was old and wrinkled, he would be portrayed as such. Moreover, like much of the art that he helped inspire for later generations, his work spoke to the emotions and imagination: both his and his viewers'. The stories he told were internal and conceptual, and there was no right or wrong way to interpret them.

14 Before Rodin, which of the following was not represented in sculpture?

① myth
② beliefs
③ flaws
④ past events
⑤ literature

15 Which century is discussed in the text above?

① 17th Century
② 18th Century
③ 19th Century
④ 20th Century
⑤ 21st Century

16 Why is Rodin considered a realist?

① He created art that perfectly represented the world.
② He considered everything in the world to be beautiful.
③ He tried to make the world a more beautiful place with his art.
④ He created art that was perfect to represent the beauty of the world.
⑤ He perfected the world he saw around him in his art, even the imperfections.

17~18

In larger terms, of course, rock music has a claim to be the most representative of postmodern cultural forms. For one thing, it embodies to perfection the central paradox of contemporary mass culture, in the fact of its unifying global reach and influence on the one hand, combined with its _____ of popularity for diverse styles, media and ethnic identities on the other. Although rock music has a clearly visible and easily-evidenced history it is also characterized by a congenital impurity of means and nature. From the very beginning the importance of rock music lay in the potency of its amalgams with youth culture as a whole; with fashion, with style and street culture, with spectacle and performance art in the work of artists like The Who, Genesis, Talking Heads and Laurie Andersen, with film, and with new reproductive technologies and media.

adapted from a book by Steven Connor

17 Which expression best fits into the blank?

① annihilating
② engendering
③ oppressing
④ reforming
⑤ vaccinating

18 Which statement can not be inferred from the passage above?

① The paradox in postmodern culture is embedded in Rock music.
② Rock music is an exponent of the postmodernist's inclusive adaptation of innovative technologies.
③ Popularity, more than originality, is a highly prized value in Rock music.
④ Postmodernism is demarcated by its devaluation of youth culture.
⑤ Postmodernism can be seen as a conjecture which propagates the universal value of diversity.

19
~
20

By 1891 artists on Paris's inside loop were talking quite a lot about Paul Gauguin, a 43-year-old former stockbroker who had left job and family to commit himself to a bohemian ideal of the artistic life. This trajectory was taking him from an early Impressionist training into ever further-reaching quests after the archaic and primitive. Having already painted in rural Brittany and Provence and in Martinique in the West Indies, Gauguin was holding a farewell sale that spring before taking ship for a two-year stay in Tahiti. In 1895 he would set out again to spend the final eight years of a poverty- and disease-ridden career in the South Pacific. Gauguin's artistic direction had already been set, however, in the late 1880s, while he lodged with other hard-up artists in the Breton fishing village of Pont-Aven. It was here that a new cultural trend, which would soon be called Symbolism, catalyzed his work.

19 Which is closest in meaning to the underlined bohemian?

① visionary
② euphonious
③ conservative
④ unconventional

20 According to the passage, which is not true?

① It was in 1891 that Gauguin went to Tahiti.
② Gauguin remained devoted to Impressionism all through his career.
③ Gauguin spent his final years in deplorable conditions in the South Pacific.
④ Gauguin was a well-known figure in the inner circle of Paris's artists in the early 1890s.

21~22

The full maturity of Chinese landscape painting developed during the Tang Dynasty under the influence of a scholar and poet, Wang Wei. He expressed personal responses to nature with brush and ink largely on the basis of the Taoist view. The Taoist philosophy stressed a high value on the meaning of life by (A) respecting the law of nature. Under this tradition, the artists were supposed to be at peace with nature, free from the shackles of society and from the (B) temptation of gold, and their spirit should be deeply immersed in mountains and rivers, and other manifestations of nature. This tradition in landscape painting continued through several dynasties, and the Sung Dynasty saw its peak.

In composition, the painters achieved the effects of the landscape scene through the mastery of line and silhouette rather than the (C) rendering of light and shadow. In other words, they painted the beauty of nature from different angles and views to enhance the effects of landscape scenes, which could more intensify the magnitude of nature. Consequently, human figures were often (D) enlarged so as not to intrude on the orderly magnitude of nature. The magnitude of nature was stressed while human figures were just dependent parts of nature. It is because human beings can find the true meaning of their lives not through the shackles of society, but through the deep dependency on nature.

21 Which of the underlined words is not appropriate?

① (A) ② (B) ③ (C) ④ (D)

22 According to the passage, which is not true of the Taoist view reflected in Chinese landscape paintings?

① It encouraged people to live humbly in nature.
② It accentuated the necessity of proper social rules.
③ It depreciated the meaning of worldly possessions.
④ It recommended people to immerse their spirits in nature.

23~25

In the late nineteenth and twentieth centuries, Modernism transformed the arts and culture in several countries by rejecting the concept of certainty. For instance, Modernist art does not attempt to show a "truthful" representation of a person or a scene. For Modernists, there can never be a truthful image because what seems like _____ reality is actually a _____ viewpoint, or one person's way of seeing. Therefore, painters such as Pablo Picasso focused on how they, themselves, saw shapes and colors instead of seeing how a scene "really" looked. In music, composers embraced atonal sounds that they were interested in. In literature, writers strived to reproduce in the highly personal way an individual thought.

Postmodernists of the late twentieth century felt that Modernism did not extend far enough in emphasizing numerous perspectives. For example, Postmodernists pointed to the way that Modernist urban planners tried to solve urban problems with large uniform developments, not considering the differing desires of the intended inhabitants. Postmodernism focuses on variety, audience personalization, as well as multiculturalism. An art viewer and a Postmodern artist construct the viewing experience together. Hence, the artist does not presume to control it.

23 Which one can be inferred about Modernism?

① It considered most classical works to be lying about life.
② It presented art as an unbiased representation of reality.
③ It was not very influential because it was considered disconcerting.
④ It questioned principles that had always been viewed as being obvious.

24 Choose the best word for the blanks.

① subjective — subjective
② subjective — sedentary
③ objective — subjective
④ objective — sedentary

25 Choose the best title.

① Postmodernism vs. Modernism
② The Life of Pablo Picasso
③ The Inspiration of Classical Composers
④ How to Solve Urban Problems in the Nineteenth Century

26~27

Henri Matisse famously declared that he dreamed of an art "devoid of troubling or depressing subject matter ... a soothing, calming influence on the mind, rather like a good armchair." His close friend Picasso, who more often indulged the darker sides of human emotion, wasn't especially political in his art either. Nonetheless, in the mid-1930s, during an urgent rush of creativity, the latter painted a dramatic mural-sized protest over the bombing of Guernica in the direct black and white tones of a newspaper. The political directness of his "Guernica" may have been inspired by the revolutionary attitude of his Mexican friend Diego Rivera. The painting is an obvious example of how aesthetics and protest are not mutually exclusive. Picasso showed that painter and painting could be both.

The art world has always debated where it falls on the spectrum between _____. Do we really want art to challenge us with the conflicts and threats we find in the news every day?

If it does so, contemporary political art risks preaching to an audience comprised of a small, well-educated liberal elite that is already aligned with its message. Arguably, this art will then <u>become complicit in feeding on the same market and power structures whose hands it bites</u>.

26 The best expression for the blank would be _____.

① message and utility
② pleasure and politics
③ solace and threat
④ creativity and retro
⑤ complicity and creativity

27 The underlined phrase means _____.

① be at odds with social and political responsibility of the elite audience
② thoroughly spoil the aesthetic taste of the elite audience by damaging it
③ enthusiastically crave the high cultural taste of the elite audience
④ deny the social and political power structure in cooperation with the elite
⑤ adapt itself to the taste of the elite audience while criticizing its ideology

The first major theorization of Science Fiction (SF) occurred within a Marxist paradigm, in the work of Darko Suvin. Suvin took the ideas underlying the theatrical practice of *Verfremdungseffekt* — estrangement or alienation. [A] He wanted his audiences to think through the ideas of his plays, rather than simply empathize with his characters, and used a number of techniques to wake them up in their viewing. [B] When reading a work of SF, the reader becomes conscious that they are observing a different world from their own which is unfamiliar to them; when they are then faced with the real world, they may see it in a new way. [C] But the reader does not come to the fictional world entirely as a blank tablet to be impressed upon — the reader has a sense of the structures and interrelationships within the world they are familiar with, and comes to the fiction with the same sense of expectations. This process is known as cognition, and is associated with knowledge, especially scientific, logical knowledge. Brecht connects cognition to Galileo's ability to deduce the path of a pendulum from observation of its swing. Having seen a chandelier move, Galileo could predict the motion of a clock pendulum. [D] By analogy, the reader of SF takes their expectations of how the world works — especially in the realm of scientific knowledge — and uses them to build up a series of assumptions about the fictional world being described by the SF writer. Suvin thus defines SF as a "literary genre whose necessary and sufficient conditions are the presence and interaction of estrangement and cognition, and whose main formal device is an imaginative frame-work alternative to the author's empirical environment" — to some extent the notion of "cognition" maps on to science, the "estrangement" on to fiction, although the two impulses are connected in a sort of dialectical relationship, in the oscillation between the familiar being unrecognizable and recognizing the unfamiliar, the fictional science and scientific-flavored fiction.

28 Which is the most likely for the following sentence to be inserted?

This notion originates from the German playwright Bertolt Brecht.

① [A] ② [B] ③ [C] ④ [D]

29 Which of the following can be inferred from the passage?

① While writing plays, Brecht did his best to make his audiences sympathize with his characters.
② In reading SF, the notion of cognition and the notion of estrangement are distinguishable but intertwined.
③ When appreciating a work from SF, the reader does not have any presupposition about how the world behaves.
④ In Suvin, the notion of cognition is closely related to the imagination of the illogical and the fictional.

30 According to the passage, by reading a work from SF, a reader can _____

① identify herself with the characters.
② understand how Galileo deduces the path of a pendulum.
③ reconstruct the way of understanding her own world.
④ distinguish the familiar and the unfamiliar in terms of cognition.

31~32

Advertising techniques deployed to increase sales of retail goods can also be used to try to sell information, education, and motivation to the public. Public health campaigns have made use of developments within commercial advertising; indeed some of the best-known posters and television advertisements from recent history have been those selling health.

Abram Games was a British graphic designer who created some of the most iconic posters of the Second World War. He was born in Whitechapel in 1914 and attended St Martins School of Art, leaving after two terms to pursue his own interests in the expanding world of graphic design.

Largely _____, his talent nonetheless shone through when he won a second prize in a health care art competition in 1934. The following year, Games won a poster competition for the London County Council and became a professional graphic artist. Joining the infantry in 1940, Games was engaged by the War Office to design a recruiting poster for the Royal Armoured Corps in 1941. He served as an official war poster designer from 1942 until the end of the Second World War.

Following his design philosophy of "maximum-meaning, minimum means," Games' posters use few words and simple imagery to deliver effective messages immediately. His wartime posters reminded the population of the need to stay fit and maintain good hygiene, and of the importance of donating blood. Many of these posters encouraged people to look after their fellow citizens, while others promised rewards (such as new medical centers) once the fighting was over. He was well aware of his skill as a propagandist: he observed, "I wind the spring and the public, in looking at the poster, will have that spring _____ in its mind."

31 빈칸에 들어가기에 가장 적합한 것을 고르시오.

① self-made — retaken
② self-encouraged — stuck
③ self-taught — released
④ self-indulged — strengthened

32 위 글을 통해 추론할 수 있는 것으로 가장 적합한 것을 고르시오.

① Bored with his first job, Abram Games had hoped to be a propagandist of public health care.
② Despite his hard work at his professional job, Abram Games never felt happy due to his insufficient education.
③ Self-aware of the importance of his vocation, Abram Games tried to become an artistic painter.
④ As a public health campaigner, Abram Games pursued his own thought of design.

33
~
35

Over the past decade or two, <u>that old world</u> has been systematically blown up by a series of design mavericks. Intent on being involved from the start and taken seriously as changemakers and entrepreneurs, designers are now not only leading big businesses from the very top, but they are taking the game into their own hands. Take trailblazer Jony Ive, largely credited with turning around Apple's astonishing fortunes; or Yves Behar, who redesigned a laptop to be so cost-effective it could be distributed to children in the developing world, and then did the same with spectacles, while revolutionizing fitness trackers, wireless speakers and thermostats along the way. Marcel Wanders brought the fun back into furniture, as did Tom Dixon — who has created a lighting and furniture empire with his own name that shows no signs of slowing down. A visit to Milan's annual furniture trade fair, Salone del Mobile, is a very different experience than it used to be. Once a showcase for venerable brands, it has been taken over by superstar designers.

Consumers of everything, from fashion to furniture, have become less interested in the manufacturers than in the creator, breaking down the wall between _____.
This year, Japanese design studio Nendo exhibited a one-year retrospective of more than 100 products it had designed for commercial brands at the Museo della Permanente. When designer Jaime Hayon created a fantastical urban installation of a play cityscape to showcase the carmaker Mini's Citysurfer electric scooter, everyone came to see the 40m-long marble table with gold road markings on it and handmade copper "street lamps" he had created — rather than the actual product.

33 In the underlined that old world, designers _____.

① were more concerned with commercial value
② were supposed to do fine-tuning at best
③ were also involved in the marketing strategy
④ were highly trained by their predecessors
⑤ were fully independent from the manufacturers

34 The most appropriate expression for the blank would be _____.

① theory and practice
② dream and reality
③ past and future
④ art and commerce
⑤ school and industry

35 According to the above passage, _____.

① many entrepreneurs design their own products
② design is less important than practicality
③ any consumer can become a good designer
④ design makes the products more expensive
⑤ design matters most in modern world

36~38

It is so patently a good thing to take delight in flowers and animals that people who bring home potted plants and watch kestrels might even be surprised at the notion that these things have anything to do with virtue. When we move from beauty in nature to beauty in art, the experience of art is more easily degraded than the experience of nature. [A] A great deal of art, perhaps most art, actually is self-consoling fantasy, and even great art cannot guarantee the quality of its consumer's consciousness. [B] However, great art exists and is sometimes properly experienced and even a shallow experience of what is great can have its effect. [C] It invigorates our best faculties and inspires love in the highest part of the soul. It is able to do this partly by virtue of something which it shares with nature: a perfection of form which invites unpossessive contemplation and resists absorption into the selfish dream life of the consciousness. Art, however, considered as a sacrament or a source of good energy, possesses an extra dimension. [D] Art is less accessible than nature but also more edifying. Art is a human product and _____ as well as talents are required of the artist. The good artist, in relation to his art, is brave, truthful, patient, humble; and even in non-representational art we may receive intuitions of these qualities.

36 According to the author, what cannot be inferred about the experience of birdwatching?

① One finds a perfection of form that invites self-consoling fantasy.
② It provides delight by clearing one's mind of selfish cares.
③ It gives a self-forgetful pleasure in the independent existence of animals.
④ It inspires love in the highest part of the soul.

37 Choose the best word for blank.

① creativity   ② virtues
③ intuition   ④ experiences

38 Which will be the best place for the following sentence?

> Art, and by "art" from now on I mean good art, affords us a pure delight in the independent existence of what is excellent.

① [A]   ② [B]   ③ [C]   ④ [D]

39~40

Today of course Leonardo da Vinci is most famous for paintings like the *Mona Lisa* and *The Last Supper*. In his mind, Leonardo was not primarily _____, though. He thought of himself as _____ first. In a letter to the ruler of Milan listing his strengths, sent in the early 1480s, Leonardo mentioned 10 different skills — designing bridges, tunnels, chariots and catapults, for example — before adding at the end that he could also paint.

Leonardo was an insatiable learner, too. He studied everything he could see: the flow of water, the way smoke rises through the air, how a woodpecker uses his tongue. And he had insights that were ahead of his time. He developed a theory about the working of a certain heart valve that researchers only verified a few decades ago. He was the first person to correctly explain why you can see light between the two points of a crescent moon, the phenomenon we now call earthshine.

Scientific inquiries like these were essential to his art. He was able to give the *Mona Lisa* that mysterious look on her face because he had studied all the muscles involved in smiling. In *The Last Supper*, he could make the perspective lines work flawlessly because he had spent countless hours understanding how our eyes perceive objects at a distance. By examining his surroundings so closely, Leonardo was able to develop new techniques that advanced his field and portrayed the world in a way no one had ever seen before. In other words, he was an innovator.

39 Which is the most appropriate for the blanks?

① a scientist — a painter
② a painter — an engineer
③ an engineer — an artist
④ an artist — a biologist

40 According to the passage, which is not true?

① Leonardo was a man of various gifts.
② Leonardo applied his observations of the human body to his art.
③ Leonardo's paintings were the combinations of art and scientific techniques.
④ Leonardo abstained from revealing his painting skills to the ruler of Milan.

41~42

Critics drawn to Monet in the 1880s used two words in particular to ① characterize what set him apart from other painters, either academic or experimental. *Instantanéité* (of the instant, the moment) and enveloppe (envelope or covering) defined Monet by his ability to make ② accessible for contemplation the overall spectral qualities bathing a scene usually only for very brief periods of time. Octave Mirbeau's catalog essay for Monet's 1889 exhibition at the Georges Petit gallery defined *instantanéité* as a method for identifying the light scales that ③ allowed one to make sense of a scene. The values that constituted the scale of a scene were seeded here and there. They changed so ④ rarely that one was seldom aware of the role they played in determining one's emotional reaction. Monet's careful observation and selection allowed him to ⑤ fix the values he found "in their exact form" so that an otherwise fleeting design might become available to all for observation. Monet understood, Mirbeau assured his readers, that in order to arrive at an interpretation of nature that was at once exact and emotionally moving, one had to pierce the passing effects of time and make visible the movement of harmonic values.

41 밑줄 친 ①~⑤ 중에서 문맥상 낱말의 쓰임이 적절하지 않은 것은?

42 밑줄 친 exact and emotionally moving의 의미로 가장 적절한 것은?

① creating peace in the absence of conflict
② too complex to be comprehended through any artistic skills
③ of utmost importance to artists as a means of taming their emotional tides
④ assessing a quality that is mysterious but can be captured by artistic perception
⑤ confronting nature's capricious actions with the conviction that artists are after all incapable of intelligent replies to them

43~45

A couple of years ago, we were tasked at IDEO to design dashboard visualizations for Ford's next generation hybrid vehicle, the Ford Fusion. Hybrid cars are efficient only if the driver maximizes the car's potential; in other words, if the driver learns to make sense of the complex mechanics of two motors and regenerative braking. If the dashboard is the interface between the driver and the car, how might it coach drivers to make sense of this complexity and to adopt efficient driving habits? That is the obvious question, but it's incomplete. The missing part is, how do we design without interfering with driving and safety?

This is the key question we need to address when we put people at the center of evaluation (as Jocelyn Wyatt puts it). In this context, putting people first means recognizing that people are preoccupied with more important tasks than spending long amounts of time in front of dashboards and data visualizations. This is true in any setting, and in our case it was driving. The role of visualization should not be to demand full attention, but to support the priority task and improve it through feedback loops. The challenge is not just to display how you are doing right now, but also to figure out how you could do better. So, what does this mean for the visualization itself?

Every form of visualization should tell a story. _____ there is limited attention and time to process all the stories. _____ the gist of the story, or its immediate impact, should be visible right away. The term I like to use for this principle is "glanceability." What does a visualization tell us before we take time to analyze it?

adapted from an article by Engin Erdogan

43 What is the main purpose of this passage?

① to describe an approach to improve driver safety
② to explain a way to evaluate data visualizations
③ to outline methods of organizing dashboard displays
④ to argue that design must be human-centered
⑤ to contrast two different methods of showing data

44 Which expressions best fit into the blanks?

① And — However
② But — Or
③ But — So
④ So — Thus
⑤ Thus — Therefore

45 Which design principle does this passage focus on as most important for dashboard visualizations?

① Less is more, so keep it simple.
② Catch and hold the driver's full attention.
③ Emphasize the complex mechanics of the system.
④ Give the driver plenty of options to choose from.
⑤ Make the display an educational opportunity.

Eugène Delacroix (1798-1863) was an important artist in the French Romantic movement, and some of his greatest works, like *Massacre at Chios*, depicted the horrors of war while also supporting revolutions against oppressive governments. Many of his later paintings depicted Arabic and Jewish culture, often based on sketches that he made while traveling in Spain and North Africa. Delacroix also illustrated books by William Shakespeare, Sir Walter Scott, and Johann Wolfgang von Goethe, and he earned a reputation as a writer on art and other subjects for his *Journals*. His painting *Liberty Leading the People* commemorates France's three-day July Revolution in 1830, when the Trois Glorieuses, a coalition of workers and the middle classes, deposed King Charles X and established a constitutional monarchy under King Louis-Philippe. The July Revolution was prompted by four proclamations signed by Charles that dissolved the National Assembly, ended freedom of the press, and created an electoral system that gave the aristocracy more power. *Liberty Leading the People* combines realism and allegory, with Liberty personified as both a mythical figure, or goddess, and a woman of the people leading the rebels on the bloodiest day of the revolution. Delacroix created this painting for a May 1831 exhibit celebrating the revolution at the Salon in Paris. But because government officials feared that Delacroix's painting would encourage more insurrections, *Liberty Leading the People* was exhibited only rarely after the Salon until it entered the Louvre in 1874. Now Delacroix's painting is associated with patriotism for the French Republic, so much so that the portrait appeared on the back of the hundred-franc note for fifteen years.

46 Which does not describe Delacroix's career?

① artist
② writer
③ illustrator
④ journalist

47 According to the passage, which is true?

① France's July Revolution in 1830 ended up in abolishing monarchy permanently.
② Some of Delacroix's great works reflect the ideals of the French Romanticism.
③ In France's July Revolution in 1830 workers, the middle classes and the aristocracy joined their force to overthrow the oppressive king's regime.
④ Delacroix made his paintings on Arabic and Jewish culture directly from his memory of traveling experiences in Arabic and Jewish communities.

48 According to the passage, which is not true about *Liberty Leading the People*?

① It is particularly famous for its championing the cause of freedom.
② It describes the revolution scene on the street predominantly in the realistic mode.
③ It is so endeared by the French people that it has been displayed on money for 15 years.
④ It was seldom exhibited in France for decades even after the success of the July Revolution in 1830.

Reclining on floors and lounging on couches, Loloi's women, who weigh between 350 and 600 pounds and range in age from 23 to 50, are both demure (they hold dogs and flowers and some of them shield their breasts with their arms) as well as erotic. One model poses on an unkempt bed: red lips, tousled brown hair, stomach as large and shapeless as a pillow. Another sits modestly on a chair, wavy blond hair everywhere and stretch marks clawed into her stomach; her thighs are so vast, and jut out onto the chair at such an angle, that it's as if you're seeing a different human form. She is one of the many women featured in Italian photographer Yossi Loloi's *Full Beauty* project, a collection of photos of obese women in the nude. The work, which began in 2006, was designed to challenge our accepted notions of beauty, size, and the female body. The images offer up a corporeal exhibitionism that we rarely see in mainstream media. They are meant as provocation, an extreme end of a legitimate argument that women's bodies are beautiful and sexy at any shape and size.

The models are certainly vulnerable, but they exhibit a kind of courage that forces us to confront our assumptions about women's bodies — what we define as beautiful, ugly, fat, thin, disturbing, inspiring. Staring at their stretch marks and veins, suddenly we are the ones who are vulnerable. Our reactions to the photos say more about us than about the women we're looking at. Indeed, the impossibility of their beauty and size is at once unsettling and riveting; it's almost impossible to look away.

"The women depicted are targets of societal backlash, but they are strong," Loloi said. "They fight for acceptance in a world that doesn't approve of the slightest bulging of a love handle, let alone morbid obesity or the possibility that some people find beauty in … all those things women spend thousands of dollars on every year trying to erase."

adapted from an article by Abigail Jones

49 Which is the most accurate description of the order that the key sections of this passage are arranged in?

① main point — explanations — examples
② main point — examples — explanations
③ examples — main point — explanations
④ examples — explanations — main point
⑤ explanations — examples — main point

50 What kind of relationship does the writer establish with the reader?

① She places us on the scene of the exhibit where we can feel its impact directly.
② She establishes a friendly conversation with us to raise our interest in the exhibit.
③ She gives us information about the topic in an objective and authoritative voice.
④ She shocks us with accusations of our ignorance to challenge our assumptions.
⑤ She gathers various voices and opinions and lets each of them speak to us.

51 Which best summarizes the writer's main point about Yossi Loloi's exhibit?

① It is too provocative and extreme to change our views of female beauty.
② It is a strong affirmation of the will of the models to fight for acceptance in society.
③ It makes us think about our standards for women's bodies.
④ It makes us more critical of a world that tries to erase even small imperfections.
⑤ It makes us realize that there is an inherent eroticism in any nude female body.

52~53

The informative value of a painting or a piece of literature cannot be judged without knowing what it contains that is not easily available to the public in contemporary or earlier works. It is only independent information which is even approximately additive. The derivative information of the second-rate copyist is far from independent of what has gone before. Thus the conventional love story, the conventional detective story, the average acceptable success tale of the slicks, all are subject to the letter but not the spirit of the law of copyright. There is no form of copyright law that prevents a movie success from being followed by a stream of inferior pictures exploiting the second and third layers of the public's interest in the same emotional situation. Neither is there a way of copyrighting a new mathematical idea, or a new theory such as that of natural selection, or anything except the identical reproduction of the same idea in the same words. The prevalence of clichés is no accident, but inherent in the nature of information. Property rights in information suffer from the necessary disadvantage that a piece of information, in order to contribute to the general information of the community, must say something substantially different from the community's previous common stock of information. Even in the great classics of literature and art, much of the obvious informative value has gone out of them, merely by the fact that the public has become acquainted with their contents. Schoolboys do not like Shakespeare, because he seems to them nothing but a mass of familiar quotations. It is only when the study of such an author has penetrated to a layer deeper than that which has been absorbed into the superficial clichés of the time, that we can re-establish with him an informative *rapport*, and give him a new and fresh literary value. It is interesting from this point of view that there are authors and painters who, by their wide exploration of the aesthetic and intellectual avenues open to a given age, have an almost destructive influence on their contemporaries and successors for many years.

52 Which of the following statement is true?

① The nature of artistic communication is intercultural rather than interpersonal.
② In art, information is more a matter of process rather than of storage.
③ Once mastered, any artistic work can lose its creativity.
④ Shakespeare's achievements are exceptional in that they are immortal.

53 What would be the best title of the passage above?

① The Value of Information in Art
② The Necessity of Conventional Theme in Art
③ The Function of Intellectualism in Art
④ The Natural Delection in the Process of Generating Art

04 철학·종교

01 다음 중 내용상 성격이 나머지 넷과 다른 것은?

Pope Francis celebrated an active if low-key 80th birthday. [A] He shared breakfast with eight homeless people before celebrating Mass with cardinals as greetings poured in from around the world. [B] His predecessor, Emeritus Pope Benedict XVI, sent a "very affectionate" written greeting that the Vatican said was "particularly appreciated." [C] At breakfast, Francis chatted individually with the homeless guests at the Vatican hotel where he resides, and shared Argentinean cakes with them. [D] The guests were invited from among those staying around St. Peter's Square and at nearby showers for the homeless established by the pope's almsgiver. [E] The pope also sent enough birthday cakes for 1,500 people to kitchens serving the poor and homeless in Rome.

① [A]　　② [B]　　③ [C]　　④ [D]　　⑤ [E]

02 다음 글의 내용과 가장 거리가 먼 것을 고르시오.

> By the late eighteenth century, the discipline of natural history was dominated by so-called parson-naturalists — vicars, parsons, abbots, deacons, and monks who cultivated their gardens and collected plant and animal specimens to service the wonders of divine Creation, but generally veered away from questioning its fundamental assumptions. The result was a peculiar distortion of the field. Even as taxonomy — the classification of plant and animal species — flourished, inquiries into the origin of living beings were relegated to the forbidden sidelines. Natural history devolved into the study of nature without history. It was this static view of nature that Darwin found troubling. A natural historian should be able to describe the state of the natural world in terms of causes and effects, Darwin reasoned, just as a physicist might describe the motion of a ball in the air. The essence of Darwin's disruptive genius was his ability to think about nature not as fact but as process, as progression, as history.

① Parson-naturalists identified and classified plants and animals.
② Parson-naturalists had a static view of nature in describing nature.
③ Parson-naturalists fiercely investigated the origin of living beings.
④ Parson-naturalists celebrated the immense diversity of living beings created by an omnipotent God.
⑤ Darwin believed that a natural historian should ask how nature has progressed in terms of causes and effects.

03 Choose the one that does not fit in the passage.

> The close relationship between language and religious belief pervades cultural history. Often, a divine being is said to have invented speech, or writing, and given it as a gift to mankind. One of the first things Adam has to do, according to the Book of Genesis, is to name the acts of creation. Many other cultures have a similar story. [A] In Egyptian mythology, the god Thoth is the creator of speech and writing. [B] It is Brahma who gives the knowledge of writing to the Hindu people. [C] Odin is the inventor of runic script, according to the Icelandic sagas. [D] Literacy is often introduced into a community by the spread of a religion. [E] A heaven-sent water turtle, with marks on its back, brings writing to the Chinese. All over the world, the supernatural provides a powerful set of beliefs about the origins of language.

① [A]   ② [B]   ③ [C]   ④ [D]   ⑤ [E]

04 ~ 05

The friendship of utility and pleasure go together and are no doubt the most common. Everyone has experienced them. People are "friendly" to their business associates, neighbors, the members of their car pool, and even casual acquaintances on trains, boats, and airplanes. This kind of civility is, to some degree, a form of friendship, the friendship of utility, of mutual convenience. Similarly, people are "friendly" to their golfing partners, to others at a cocktail party, and to acquaintances who entertain them. This is also a form of friendship, the friendship of pleasure, of mutual _____.

These lower forms of friendship are not necessarily bad, but they are inadequate. One of their defects results from the fact that they depend on and vary with circumstances. This is why they can quickly arise and just as quickly disappear. By contrast, when the Book of Proverbs says, "A friend loveth at all times," it is referring to a higher form of friendship that does not depend on circumstance. In order to surmount the effect of time and happenstance, it must be based on the inherent qualities of the individuals involved. A friendship so anchored cannot be a passing friendship.

True friendship, the friendship of virtue, then surpasses (although it often includes) both utility and pleasure. For Aristotle, such a friendship must be based on a good moral character. Only in that way can it last. Further, it must develop slowly, since it presupposes familiarity, knowledge, and — eventually — mutual trust.

04 Which is the most appropriate for the blank?

① trust
② enjoyment
③ responsibility
④ reliance

05 According to the passage, which is true?

① The friendship of virtue is not a passing friendship.
② The friendship of utility is not needed.
③ The friendship of pleasure is immoral.
④ All friendships are transient.

06~08

But income and wealth would not be your only consideration. If you were rich, you might prefer the society that enabled you to bequeath your wealth and privilege to your children. This would argue for the aristocratic society. If you were poor, you might prefer the society that enabled you, or your children, a chance to rise. This would argue for the meritocratic society.

Further reflection, however, suggests a countervailing consideration in each case. People care not only about how much money they have but also about what their wealth or poverty signifies for their social standing and self-esteem. If you were born into the upper reaches of an aristocracy, you would be aware that your privilege was your good fortune, not your own doing. Whereas if you ascended, through effort and talent, to the apex of a meritocracy, you could take pride in the fact that your success was earned rather than inherited. Unlike aristocratic privilege, meritocratic success brings a sense of achievement for having earned one's place. From this point of view, it is better to be rich in a meritocracy than in an aristocracy.

_____, being poor in a meritocracy is demoralizing. If, in a feudal society, you were born into serfdom, your life would be hard, but you would not be burdened by the thought that you were responsible for your subordinate position. Nor would you labor under the belief that the landlord for whom you toiled had achieved his position by being more capable and resourceful than you. You would know he was not more deserving than you, only luckier.

06 Which of the following is most appropriate for the blank?

① To be specific
② For similar reasons
③ In general
④ In so doing

07 Which of the following can be inferred from the passage?

① A member of a lower class in a feudal society would feel satisfied as his class is inherited.
② One's hard work is always rewarded in a meritocracy whereas it is not in an aristocracy.
③ Meritocratic success or failure affects one's social esteem.
④ The gap between the rich and the poor is larger in an aristocratic society than it is in a meritocratic society.

08 Which of the following is most likely to follow the passage?

① In an aristocratic society, it is likely that you would blame the more privileged in the society for your poverty.
② In an aristocratic society, it is likely that you would attribute your affluence to your achievement.
③ In a meritocratic society, it is likely that you would attribute your poverty to your own doing.
④ In a meritocratic society, it is likely that you would be content with your social standing regardless of how rich or poor you are.

09~10

"However we analyse the difference between the regular and the irregular, we must ultimately be able to account for the most basic fact of aesthetic experience, the fact that delight lies somewhere between boredom and confusion." declares Ernst Gombrich in *A Sense of Order*. We have already seen how the human being is locked into a perpetual conflict between the need to maintain a sense of order and predictability on the one hand, whilst on the other being aware that such stability is vulnerable to dissolution and collapse. Hence, the compulsive need to draw together threads of meaning by which to maintain the wholeness of the being, to reassure oneself of one's existence. However, it is also true that to be in a constantly predictable state can lead to boredom and restlessness — even worse is experienced in the total absence of stimulation, or what might be called 'super-continuity' as in the case of sensory deprivation.

09 What would be the best title of the passage above?

① The Value of Moderation
② How to Prevent Perceptual and Conceptual Errors
③ Automated Creativity
④ The Compulsive Requirement for Continuity

10 What can be inferred from the passage above?

① In the turbulent times, people often ignore rich experience of delight.
② Accommodating the necessary degrees of simultaneous coherence and confusion is necessary.
③ Diverse juxtaposition leads to incoherence and disorder.
④ More common fragmentary experience contributes to super-continuity.

11~12

Religion can inspire people to altruism or ruthless cruelty, and can have both effects at different times. Dissecting this paradox should come naturally to Karen Armstrong. British-born and a former Roman Catholic nun, she has written more than a dozen books on religious history at its broadest, expounding her view that faith is a legitimate part of human experience, whether or not its claims are true. In her latest work, "Fields of Blood," Ms Armstrong does not add to the many existing theories on offer. Instead she presents a vast overview of religious and world history, sketching the early evolution of all global faiths. Then, with giant strokes and plenty of (not totally accurate) detail, she studies the influence of the Christian West on the world over the past 500 years. It is not obvious how all this coheres, until you realize which demons she is fighting. Ms Armstrong is not trying to prove anything; more to disprove several things. First, the idea that religion is a gratuitous cause of violence, whose elimination would promote peace. And second, the view that Islam is an egregious case of a religion that inspires violence. Her third bogeyman combines the first two: the idea that because <u>the "Christian" West has shed more religious baggage than the Muslim world has</u>, it must restrain an incorrigibly violent Islam.

11 Ms Armstrong argues in her books that _____.

① religion is fundamentally authoritarian
② religion has acted as a powerful tool for eliminating human violence
③ the dark side of religion has been exaggerated
④ a religious belief is meaningful only if its claims are proven right
⑤ faith is necessary to human life regardless of its basis in truth

12 The underlined part implies that _____.

① Islam is a religion of peace
② Christianity brings out the worst in people
③ the Christian West is more religious than the Muslim world
④ the Christian West is a more benign global force
⑤ the Christian West can learn from the Muslim world

13
~
14

Anaximander is best known for his view that the origin of the world is the apeiron, an eternal substance, boundlessly large and without any _____ features: neither hot nor cold, neither wet nor dry, neither white, black, nor any other color. Again, his reason for introducing such an unfamiliar origin for our world, in contrast to Thales' view that the origin of all things was water, can be reconstructed with some probability. The world around us is marked by contrasts: some parts of it are wet, others are dry, and so on. But if the origin of the world were wet, it is hard to account for the existence of anything that is not wet. The originating material must therefore not be either wet or dry, neither hot nor cold, and so on. It must, in fact, be _____. Also, if it is the origin of everything, it cannot have a beginning itself: hence it is eternal. The Greek philosophers are unanimous in supposing that anything that is without a beginning is also without an end. And it must be boundlessly large in order to be able to generate not only our world but also an indefinitely large number of other worlds that, according to Anaximander, come into existence and perish at different times and in different places.

13 빈칸에 들어갈 가장 알맞은 것을 고르시오.

① definite — definite
② definite — indefinite
③ indefinite — definite
④ indefinite — indefinite

14 위 글의 내용과 맞지 않는 것을 고르시오.

① According to Thales, water is the origin of everything around us.
② Anaximander had a different view from Thales on the origin of the world.
③ Thales and Anaximander believed that anything that is without a beginning is also without an end.
④ According to Anaximander, our world and other worlds are composed of identical things.

15~16

Cicero said, "A room without a book is a body without a soul." Certainly when I enter someone's home for the first time, I am likely to be drawn to the bookshelf to learn more about the personality of its owner. In a sense, books have always been more than just repositories of information. The look and feel of a book is as much a part of its appeal as its contents. There is something immensely satisfying about opening a new book: the smell of the paper, the feel of the cover, the design on the dust jacket, and the weight of the volume all contribute to the impression it makes. Books have a symbolic power. We shudder when we hear of a book burning, associated down the ages with tyranny and oppression. Books as cultural icons remind us of freedom of speech and enhanced opportunities; they remind us of the intellectual aspirations of the human race. But in the future will the book still be read? I believe it will. More books are being written and published than ever before; the book has withstood the advent of the cinema, television, and computer, and is likely to be around in centuries to come.

15 Which of the following is the best title for the passage?

① Political Roles of Books
② A History of Publication
③ The Power and Future of Books
④ Why Books Mattered in the Past

16 According to the passage, which of the following is not true?

① Books' attractiveness includes more than information.
② The cover of a book is as appealing as its contents.
③ The number of books published will gradually decline.
④ Books symbolize human aspirations to better ourselves.

[17~19]

Kant's cleavage between analytic and synthetic truths was foreshadowed in Hume's distinction between relations of ideas and matters of fact, and in Leibniz's distinction between truths of reason and truths of fact. Leibniz spoke of the truths of reason as true in all possible worlds. Picturesqueness aside, this is to say that the truths of reason are those which could not possibly be false. In the same vein we hear analytic statements defined as statements whose denials are self-contradictory. But this definition has small explanatory value; for the notion of self-contradictoriness, in the quite broad sense needed for this definition of analyticity, stands in exactly the same need of clarification as does the notion of analyticity itself. The two notions are the two sides of a single dubious coin.

Kant conceived of an analytic statement as one that attributes to its subject no more than is already conceptually contained in the subject. This formulation has two shortcomings: it limits itself to statements of subject-predicate form, and it appeals to a notion of containment which is left at a metaphorical level. But Kant's intent, evident more from the use he makes of the notion of analyticity than from his definition of it, can be restated thus: a statement is analytic when it is true by virtue of meanings and without any consideration of fact. Pursuing this line, let us examine the concept of meaning which is presupposed.

17. Which of the following is the most likely to be the main topic of the passage?

① Hume's distinction between truths of reason and truths of facts
② Leibniz's truths of reason and Kant's analytic statement
③ The relation between possible worlds and the truths of fact in Leibniz's philosophy
④ The importance of statements of subject-predicate form in Kant's philosophy

18. According to the passage, which of the following cannot be inferred?

① Leibniz's notion of truths of reason can be comparable with Kant's analytic truths.
② Kant thought that an analytic statement is always true because of its meaning by itself.
③ Kant's distinction between analytic and synthetic truths precedes Hume and Leibniz's philosophy.
④ Leibniz thought that a statement which is true by reason should be true in every possible world.

19. Which of the following is the most likely to follow the passage?

① The depiction of the notion of containment
② The critique of the definition of analyticity
③ The description of the concept of truth
④ The discussion of the notion of meaning

20~21

A stubborn old lady was walking down the middle of a street to the great confusion of the traffic and with no small danger to herself. It was pointed out to her that the sidewalk was the place for pedestrians, but she replied: "I'm going to walk where I like. We've got liberty." It did not occur to the old lady that if liberty entitled the pedestrian to walk down the middle of the road, then the end of such liberty would be universal chaos. There is a danger of the world getting liberty-drunk these days like the old lady, and it is just as well to remind ourselves of what the rules of the road mean. They mean that in order for the liberties of all to be preserved, the liberties of everybody must be _____. When a policeman at a busy intersection steps into the middle of the road and puts out his hand, he is the symbol not of tyranny, but of liberty. You may, being in a hurry, feel that your liberty has been outraged. Then, if you are a reasonable person, you will reflect that if he did not interfere with you, he would interfere with no one, and the result would be a frenzied intersection you could never cross at all. You have submitted to a _____ of private liberty in order to enjoy a social order which makes your liberty a reality.

20 Which of the following is the main theme of the passage?

① The world is too liberty-drunk these days.
② Individual liberty always leads to social chaos.
③ Policemen are necessary for unreasonable drivers.
④ You should compromise private liberty for social order.

21 Which of the following ordered pairs best fits into the blanks?

① denied — denial
② allotted — allotment
③ secured — security
④ curtailed — curtailment

22~23

There is obviously a quality about *agape* love that brings out our positive resources, making them available to the one being loved. It is this quality that makes it a commitment type of love. It is, however, more than a commitment of our best efforts — it is a commitment to what is best for the object of that love. This means it is committed to doing exactly the right thing. Doing the best or the right thing is central to the definition of *agape* love, because it allows us to see that love is not some sugar-plum notion — it is an investment in the future as well. There are times when we may not find each other attractive. A mother does not spank a child to get even with it. It is to help the child develop sufficient self-discipline to save it future heartache. _____, love is called upon to find a constructive way to point out a selfish behavior in my partner. It is not love when the concern is the fact that I am being inconvenienced, but it is when the concern is for the damage that is being done to my partner and our relationship.

22 빈칸에 들어갈 가장 알맞은 것을 고르시오.

① On the other hand
② Nevertheless
③ By the same token
④ Fortunately

23 위 글의 내용과 맞지 않는 것을 고르시오.

① *Agape* love is a commitment type of love.
② A mother with *agape* love helps her child equip itself with self-discipline for the future.
③ It is not a sort of *agape* love to point out a partner's bad behaviors in a constructive way.
④ *Agape* love is more concerned with the right type of commitment than with the commitment itself.

24~25

I believe that there are a number of questions that it is no use asking because they can never be answered. Nothing good comes from trying. Yet some people seem determined to try. I recall the story of the philosopher and the theologian. The two were engaged in disputation and the theologian said a philosopher resembles a blind man in a dark room looking for a black cat — which isn't there. "That may be," said the philosopher, "but a theologian would find it." Even in material matters of science we must learn to ask the right questions. For instance, it is no good asking the question of how animals inherit the results of their parents' experience for the simple reason that no such inheritance exists. When we come to what are usually referred to as fundamentals, the difficulty of not asking the wrong kind of question is much increased. Among some African tribes, if a person dies, the only question asked is, "Who caused his death, and by what form of magic?": _____.
Indeed, the life of the less-civilized of mankind is largely based on trying to find an answer to a wrong question: "What magical forces or powers are responsible for good or bad fortune, and how can they be avoided or calmed?"

24 Which of the following is the major topic of the passage?

① Wise answers to foolish questions
② The importance of asking good questions
③ Open questions in philosophy and theology
④ Fundamental questions in human existence

25 Which of the following best fits into the blank?

① the cause is more important than the cure
② the idea of death from natural causes is unknown
③ they do not mourn the passing of their own tribesmen
④ they show more concern for the deceased than the bereft

26~27

The idealist holds that the only things that exist are ideas. In idealism the whole structure of reality is to be understood through consciousness. All attempts to know the world in itself are futile since all data about the world must inevitably be supplied by the body's senses (which are selective) and passed to the mind for interpretation. Therefore, there is no value-free or truly objective knowledge of reality, other than what one knows about one's own thoughts. In essence, the existence of reality is subject to the existence of a conscious being. It is easy to reconcile idealism with the existence of a God since while there might not be much hard evidence of God in the real world, he can justifiably be said to exist in the form of an idea in which people believe. Most religious belief systems are idealistic in the sense that they accept a reality or existence that is outside of, and separate from, earthly reality. Idealism has gained a reputation for developing absurd propositions such as the claim that nothing existed before human consciousness, and that the thinker is the only thing that actually exists, since nothing else can satisfactorily be proved to exist — a black hole known as solipsism.

26 What would be the best title of the passage above?

① The Power of Solipsism
② The Validity of Religious Belief System
③ The Features of Idealism
④ The Existence of Absurd Reality

27 Which of the following statement is true?

① Solipsism is based on the intimate relationship between absurdity and consciousness.
② The consciousness does not distinguish nature from human consciousness.
③ Human belief system is largely dependent upon the hard evidence of God.
④ Idealism does not presuppose the reality before human consciousness.

28
~
30

Ethics may be profoundly affected by an adoption of the scientific point of view; that is to say the attitude that men of science, in their professional capacity, adopt towards the world. This attitude includes a high (perhaps an unduly high) regard for the truth, and a (A) refusal to come to unjustifiable conclusions which express itself on the plane of religion as agnosticism. And along with this is found a deliberate (B) emancipation of emotion until the last possible moment, on the ground that emotion is stumbling-block on the road to truth. So a rose and a tapeworm must be studied by the same methods and viewed from the same angle, even if the work is ultimately to lead to the killing of the tape-worms and the propagations of roses. Again, the scientific point of view involves the (C) cultivation of a scientific esthetic which rejoices in the peculiar forms of beauty which characterize scientific esthetic theory. Those who find an intimate relation between the good and the beautiful will (D) realize the importance of the fact that a group of men so influential as scientific workers are pursuing a particular kind of beauty. _____, since the scientist, as such, is contributing to an intellectual structure that belongs to humanity as a whole, his influence will inevitably fall in favour of ethical principles and practices which transcend the limits of nation, colour, and class.

28 Which is the most appropriate for the blank?

① Instead
② Finally
③ Nevertheless
④ Intriguingly

29 Which of the underlined words is not appropriate?

① (A)
② (B)
③ (C)
④ (D)

30 According to the passage, which is true?

① Science doesn't impinges upon ethics.
② Science has its own concept of the beautiful.
③ A deliberate oppression of emotion is an impetus to finding the beautiful.
④ Aesthetics has no relation with ethics.

31~33

While the mind-body problem has been around for a long time, it is no less compelling for philosophers today. This is not to say that we are in the same place with regard to understanding it as the philosophers of bygone ages. _____, there has been impressive progress. This progress has been due to great advances in the scientific understanding of the workings of the brain, and to the continual refinement of our philosophical concepts and of the questions we ask about the mind. For these reasons, can we now say that the mind-body problem is nearing a solution, and probably won't be among the open-ended puzzles of 21st century philosophy?

Judging from the remarkably hot and rather unexpected wave of controversy concerning consciousness in the last decade of the 20th century, the mind-body problem seems to be very much alive and kicking. The term 'mind-body problem' actually covers a whole cluster of philosophical issues, such as the unity of self, the intentionality of mental states, and the rationality of and agency of human beings. However, it is the problem of explaining our conscious experiences — how it is that we experience sights, colors, thoughts, emotions, as we do — that sits at the heart of this cluster, and that has generated the most vigorous controversy in recent years. In fact, the renewed interest in the question of consciousness has brought the mind-body problem into the focus of not just philosophical but also scientific debates.

Searching for the 'neural correlates of consciousness' — the types of brain activity corresponding to particular mental experiences — is now on the scientific agenda of many psychologists and neuroscientists. Philosophers, _____, are busy questioning the nature of the relationship between neural states and mental states, above and beyond a mere correlation.

31 The main theme of the passage would be '_____'.

① philosophers vs scientists
② the huge progress of modem science
③ the greatness of classic philosophers
④ how science solves the philosophical issues
⑤ where we are now with the mind-body problem

32 The most appropriate expression for the blanks would be _____.

① In fact — therefore
② On the contrary — meanwhile
③ Therefore — likewise
④ On the one hand — meanwhile
⑤ However — therefore

33 According to the passage, the mind-body problem _____.

① now belongs to the area of science
② has already been solved by philosophers
③ is not a major concern of the philosophers
④ has seen much progress due to brain scientists
⑤ is unlikely to be understood by the modem scholars

34~36

There is a difference between respect and other forms of human attachment. Love, sympathy, solidarity, and fellow feeling are moral sentiments that draw us closer to some people than to others. But the reason we must respect the dignity of persons has nothing to do with anything particular about them. Kantian respect is unlike love. It's unlike sympathy. It's unlike solidarity or fellow feeling. These reasons for caring about other people have to do with who they are in particular. We love our spouses and the members of our family. We feel sympathy for people with whom we can identify. We feel solidarity with our friends and comrades.

But Kantian respect is respect for humanity as such, for a rational capacity that resides, undifferentiated, in all of us. This explains why violating it in my own case is as objectionable as violating it in the case of someone else. It also explains why the Kantian principle of respect lends itself to doctrines of universal human rights. For Kant, justice requires us to uphold the human rights of all persons, _____ where they live or how well we know them, simply because they are human beings, capable of reason, and therefore worthy of respect.

34 Which of the following is most appropriate for the blank?

① depending on
② resulting from
③ regardless of
④ apart from

35 Which of the following is best for the title of the passage?

① Respect of Justice
② Difference Between Love and Respect
③ Respect Based on Reason
④ Respect of Emotions

36 Which of the following cannot be inferred from the passage?

① Kant does not acknowledge human capacity of love.
② Kant assumes human beings have an innate capacity of reason.
③ Kant is interested in universal human rights.
④ Kant contends that justice demands us to respect humanity capable of reason.

37~38

Today the possibilities suggested by synthetic intelligence, organic computers and genetic modification are deeply challenging to that sense of human predominance. These developments awaken deep-rooted anxieties about the threat to human existence from technology we cannot control or understand. We know we are capable of creating entities that may equal and even surpass us, and we must seriously face up to the possibility that attributes like human thought may be created in non-human forms. While this is one of our deepest fears it is also the holy grail of the computer sciences. Despite the enormous problems involved, the development of an artificially conscious entity may happen within our lifetimes. Would such an entity have human-like emotions? Would it have a sense of its own being? Such questions are difficult to answer given the redundant concepts of human existence that we have inherited from the humanist era, since many widely accepted humanist ideas about consciousness can no longer be sustained. _____, new theories about nature and the operation of the universe arising from computer modelling are starting to demonstrate the profound interconnections between all things in nature where previously we had seen separations. This has implications for traditional views of the human condition and for some of the oldest problems in philosophy.

37 Choose the words that best fill in the blank.

① However
② In addition
③ For example
④ In contrast

38 What can be inferred from the passage above?

① A new era requires to connect previously separated things without depending on synthetic intelligence.
② Human patterns take the place of non-human forms.
③ The widely accepted idea about human being is changing now.
④ Redundant concept of human being should be eliminated.

39~40

In my speech in Hay this year, I spoke about the way globalization has led to an increase in religious identities around the world. I also challenged the audience to view al-Qaida as a movement, not as an entity (to quote the great al-Qaida ideologue Abu Musab al-Suri, "al-Qaida is not an organization; it is a methodology.") And I spoke about the way al-Qaida connects the local grievances of Muslim kids living in, say, Leeds to the global grievances facing Muslims in places like Palestine and Iraq. The question that I posed to the audience was this: How, then, do you confront a movement?

Surely, not just with bombs and guns. Rather, <u>you must make the movement irrelevant</u>. In the case of al-Qaida, that means addressing the very grievances that the movement uses to rally young Muslims to its cause: the suffering of the Palestinians, American support for Arab dictators, the lack of social, political, and economic development in large parts of the Middle East, the fact that we in the west tend to treat that entire region as a giant gas station. Only by addressing these grievances can the appeal of al-Qaida be diminished.

39 According to the writer, al-Qaida _____.

① has no organization
② uses sufferings of people
③ has nothing to do with globalization
④ is the main cause of the grievances of the Arabs

40 The underlined expression means that you must _____.

① analyze the methodologies of the movement
② unite with each other to isolate the movement
③ follow the ideological aspects of the movement
④ fix the problems that motivate the movement

[A] Physical pain is exceptional in the whole fabric of psychic, somatic, and perceptual states for being the only one that has no object. Though the capacity to experience physical pain is as primal a fact about the human being as is the capacity to hear, to touch, to desire, and to fear, it differs from these events and from every other bodily and psychic event, by not having an object in the external world. Hearing and touch are of objects outside the boundaries of the body, as desire is desire of x, fear is fear of y, hunger is hunger for z; but pain is not of or for anything — it is itself alone. (A)

[B] This objectlessness, the complete absence of referential content, almost prevents it from being rendered in language. Objectless, it cannot easily be objectified in any form, material, or verbal. But it is also its objectlessness that may give rise to imagining by first occasioning the process that eventually brings forth <u>the dense sea of artifacts and symbols that we make and move about in</u>. All the other states, by precisely taking an object, at first invite one only to enter rather than to supplement the natural world. (B)

[C] The man desiring can see the rain and know it is its cessation that he is longing for, so that he can go out and find the berries he is hungry for, before the night comes that he fears. (C) Because of the inevitable bonding of his own interior states with companion objects in the outside world, he easily locates himself in that external world and has no need to invent a world to extend himself out into. The object is an extension of, an expression of, the state: the rain expresses his longing, the berries his hunger, and the night his fear. (D)

[D] The only state that is as anomalous as pain is imagination. While pain is a state remarkable for being wholly without objects, the imagination is remarkable for being the only state that is wholly its objects. There is in imagining no activity, no state, no experienceable condition or felt-occurrence separate from the objects; the only evidence that one is imagining is that imaginary objects appear in the mind. Thus, while pain is like seeing or desiring but not like seeing x or desiring y, the opposite but equally extraordinary characteristic belongs to imagining. It is like the x or the y that are objects of vision or desire but not like the felt-occurrence of seeing or desiring. (E)

41 Which of the following would be the best title for the above passage?

① Sense and Its Relation to the World
② Sense and Sensation
③ The Role of Objects in Human Perception
④ Human Desire and Physical Pain
⑤ The Uniqueness of Pain and Imagination

42 The following sentences are removed from the above passage. In which part may it be inserted to support the argument made by the author?

> But nothing expresses his physical pain. Any state that was permanently objectless would no doubt begin the process of invention. But it is especially appropriate that the very state in which he is utterly objectless is also of all states the one that makes most pressing the urge to move out and away from the body.

① (A)　　② (B)　　③ (C)　　④ (D)　　⑤ (E)

43 According to the passage, which of the following is not mentioned as the nature of pain?

① Pain is not tied to any referent in the external world.
② It is extremely hard to describe the pain that one feels.
③ Pain is a state similar to imagination in its relation to objects.
④ Five senses, unlike pain, do not add anything to the external world.
⑤ A person in pain tries hard to express his or her pain despite its difficulty.

44 Which of the following best explains the meaning of the underlined part in paragraph [B]?

① various things and words that we use to express pain
② various things and words that we experience to increase pain
③ various things and words that we create to imagine a world without pain
④ various things and words that we want to change to alleviate pain
⑤ various things and words that we use to escape from pain

45~48

Freud first became aware of the meaningfulness of certain everyday slips and lapses in 1896. In a letter to his colleague, he wrote that he had "at last grasped a little thing I had long suspected", namely, the reason why a known name sometimes eludes retrieval and wrong names are dredged up in its place. In this instance, he had been unable to recall the last name of a poet. "I was able to prove (i) that I had repressed the name because of certain associations; (ii) that material from my infancy played a part in the repression; and (iii) that the substitute names that occurred to me arose, just like a symptom, from both recent and infantile groups of material".

Having established the significance of this apparently trivial lapse, he began to collect examples of many different forms of everyday error: misreadings, slips of the tongue and pen, misquotations, bungled actions and so on. Gradually he became convinced that all of these normally _____ slips and lapses betrayed the presence within the unconscious of repressed impulses. Most of the time they remained hidden, but occasionally they seized upon an opportune moment to make themselves known through some error of 'parapraxis'.

The Psychopathology of Everyday Life first appeared as a separate volume in 1904 and was subsequently enlarged over the next 20 years. It became one of Freud's most popular books, running into many editions. The core ideas and many of the best examples were later expressed more succinctly (and more convincingly) in the *Introductory Lectures on Psychoanalysis*, given at the University of Vienna between 1915 and 1917 and later published. Thereafter, the phrase 'a Freudian slip', entered the language, and the view that errors were unconsciously determined became firmly lodged, for good and ill, in scientific and popular belief.

45 Which of the following is not appropriate for the blank?

① negligible
② unfrivolous
③ trifling
④ inconsequential

46 According to the passage, which of the following is not true?

① Both the *Introductory Lectures on psychoanalysis* and *The Psychopathology of Everyday Life* were published.
② Freud began to gather the examples of minor slips and lapses after realizing their significance.
③ The idea that errors have their roots in the unconscious mind came from Freud.
④ While the scientific community accepted Freud's theory, the public thought it was preposterous.

47 According to the passage, why was Freud unable to remember the last name of the poet?

① The poet did not have a last name since infancy, so there was no last name to begin with.
② Freud was unable to forget the substitute names due to parapraxis.
③ Freud unconsciously held back the name because of his early memories.
④ The poet's name came up as a slip of the tongue, but Freud repressed it as a trivial lapse.

48 Which of the following best represents an opportune moment in the second paragraph?

① In speech, memory retrieval or action
② A retrieval of infantile parapraxis
③ In each form of psychoanalytic disorders
④ A repressed and unconscious memory

49
~
50

The doctrine of original sin is the oldest manifestation of the rotten-to-the-core dogma, but such thinking has not died out in our democratic, secular state. Freud dragged this doctrine into twentieth-century psychology, defining all of civilization (including modern morality, science, religion, and technological progress) as just an elaborate defense against basic conflicts over infantile sexuality and aggression. We "repress" these conflicts because of the unbearable anxiety they cause and this anxiety is transmuted into the energy that generates civilization. So the reason I am sitting in front of my computer writing this preface — rather than running out to rape and kill — is that I am "compensated," zipped up and successfully defending myself against underlying savage impulses. Freud's philosophy, as bizarre as it sounds when laid out so starkly, finds its way into daily psychological and psychiatric practice, wherein patients scour their past for the negative impulses and events that have formed their identities. Thus the competitiveness of Bill Gates is really his desire to outdo his father, and Princess Diana's opposition to landmines was merely the outcome of sublimating her murderous hatred for Prince Charles and the other royals. The rotten-to-the-core doctrine also pervades the understanding of human nature in the arts and social sciences. Just one example of thousands is *No Ordinary Time*, a gripping history of Franklin and Eleanor Roosevelt written by Doris Kearns Goodwin, one of the great living political scientists. Musing on the question of why Eleanor dedicated so much of her life to helping people who were black, poor, or disabled, Goodwin decides that it was "to compensate for her mother's narcissism and her father's alcoholism." Nowhere does Goodwin consider the possibility that deep down, Eleanor Roosevelt was pursuing virtue. Motivations like exercising fairness or pursuing duty are ruled out as fundamental; there must be some covert, negative motivation that underpins goodness if the analysis is to be academically respectable. I cannot say this too strongly: In spite of the widespread acceptance of the rotten-to-the-core dogma in the religious and secular world, there is not a shred of evidence that strength and virtue _____. I believe that evolution has favored both good and bad traits, and any number of adaptive roles in the world have selected for morality, cooperation, altruism, and goodness, just as any number have also selected for murder, theft, self-seeking, and terrorism. This dual-aspect premise is the cornerstone of the second half of this book. Authentic happiness comes from identifying and cultivating your most fundamental strengths and using them every day in work, love, play, and parenting.

49 Choose the best answer to fill in the blank.

① are derived from negative motivation
② are derived from positive motivation
③ are fallacies of positive motivation
④ are fallacies of the unrevealed negative motivation

50 What would be the best title of the passage above?

① The Hidden Power of Negative Motivation
② Duel Aspects of Human Nature
③ The Illusion of Pursuing Virtuous Behaviors
④ Authentic Happiness Derived From Negative Motivation

05 사회이슈·일상

01 Choose the one that does not fit in the passage.

> There are few problems more annoying than hiccups, which can last for hours or even days. [A] According to one doctor who has studied them, hiccups are usually caused by eating or drinking too quickly. [B] People do some pretty strange things to remedy this ridiculous problem. [C] Some common remedies include holding your breath, eating a teaspoon of sugar, and putting a paper bag over your head. [D] The best exercise for a healthy heart is walking. [E] Undoubtedly, that last one is the strangest one of all.

① [A]　　② [B]　　③ [C]　　④ [D]　　⑤ [E]

02 Which of the following underlined (A), (B), (C), and (D) is not appropriately used?

> Nowadays seeing a person walking down the street talking on a cell phone has become such a (A) ubiquitous sight that a picture of modern man with one hand next to his ear should be painted next to the ape-like Cro-Magnon to (B) distort the evolution of humans. According to recent press reports, American doctors are now warning of so-called "cell phone elbow" syndrome. It seems (C) farcical that medical professionals are making such a fuss about this. Just like people who suffer daily from the constant pain of tennis elbow after playing tennis, cell phone gabbers (D) grumble about pain or numbness in the hand — especially the pinky and ring fingers.

① (A)　　② (B)　　③ (C)　　④ (D)

03 Choose the one that is inappropriate for the whole context.

> Our love of rhythm is rooted even more (A) deeply in us than our love of musical repetition. It is related to the beat of our hearts, the pulse of our blood, the intake and outflow of air from our lungs. (B) Nothing that we do naturally and gracefully we do rhythmically. There is rhythm in the way we walk, the way we swim, the way we ride a horse, the way we swing a golf club or a baseball bat. So (C) native is rhythm to us that we read it, when we can, into the (D) mechanical world around us. Our clocks go *tick-tick-tick*, but we hear *tick-tock, tick-tock*. There is a (E) strong appeal for us in language that is rhythmic.

① (A) ② (B) ③ (C) ④ (D) ⑤ (E)

04~05

> The transition from private to public can be (A) brutal, as many of us discover each morning. The moment a person leaves home, he or she is caught up in the world of work with its obligations and requirements. Punctuality is (B) inessential. Leaving home, the commuter, suddenly plunged into an alien, (C) not to say hostile, public environment, squeezes into a crowded railway car, only too happy to arrive on time. Such a journey is not a transition but a(n) _____. The workday begins with a commute, either by public transportation or, in an effort to extend private life and (D) ease the transition into the public sphere, by private automobile. The traffic jam is one consequence: even private vehicles must use public roadways, and individuals in their cars are perfectly (E) anonymous and isolated.

04 빈칸에 들어갈 가장 적절한 것은?

① termination ② concession
③ conundrum ④ leap
⑤ obstacle

05 밑줄 친 (A)~(E) 중에서 문맥상 낱말의 쓰임이 적절하지 않은 것은?

① (A) ② (B) ③ (C) ④ (D) ⑤ (E)

**06
~
07**

The near history of America's deep division can be dated from 2008, with the financial crash and the election of the country's first black president, Barack Obama. Some commentators trace Trump's election to the disaffection of the white working class with the Democratic Party, which was in power during the bailout. But there are other reasons for that disaffection. From Reconstruction to the civil rights revolution, conservatives have long felt genuinely victimized by the prospect of equality. Obama embodied that prospect, and so did the demands for racial justice that arose during his presidency. Among them was the Black Lives Matter movement, formed by three black women in 2013 in reaction to the murder of a black teenager, Trayvon Martin. It has always been dangerous for African-Americans to insist on justice or call white supremacists to account. In 2015 a young white man walked into the historic AME church in Charleston, South Carolina and gunned down nine black people gathered in prayer. Obama gave an impassioned eulogy lamenting systemic oppression and racial subjugation, and by the end of his term, reckoning with the legacy of slavery was on the national agenda. The _____ was predictably deadly. It brought Donald Trump to the White House in 2016, and a Unite the Right Rally to Charlottesville, Virginia in 2017, where white supremacist groups marched under the slogan "You will not replace us." To the shock of the nation, Trump supported his troops. And so it went.

06 윗글의 내용과 거리가 가장 먼 것은?

① Donald Trump has openly welcomed white supremacists to his base.
② Barak Obama's eulogy was occasioned by a random shooting at a church in South Carolina.
③ American conservatives have long been aggrieved by the prospect of equality and racial justice.
④ The white working class felt unfairly treated by the Democratic government during the bailout.
⑤ The overall design of Obama's policy ultimately succeeded in reducing the racial tension in American society.

07 빈칸에 들어갈 가장 적절한 것은?

① amicability
② backlash
③ complicity
④ defamation
⑤ stalemate

08~10

Recently, I've noticed something strange about what my body does while I'm flicking through apps or reading on my phone. I've become conscious of my irregular breathing patterns, and how much tension I'm holding in my back and shoulders. The technologist Linda Stone has noted something similar, describing the way her breath becomes shallow, and sometimes temporarily stops altogether, when she sits down to work on her emails in the morning. She terms the problem 'screen apnea'.

Perhaps even more striking for me, though, has been the realization that I'm often simply unaware of my body altogether. It's as if my body disappears when I enter into a digital 'space'. This perhaps explains why I've always found the narrative of online platforms competing to maximize and monetize 'eyeballs on screens' (A) _____ . The problem is not just that this paints a totally mechanistic picture of the human organism: it's also that this disembodied picture aligns all too well with how it actually feels to be totally absorbed in some 'content' on my phone for 30 minutes at a stretch.

So while we know by now that technology can hijack the mind, what do we miss when we ignore what's going on from a bodily perspective? Maurice Merleau-Ponty, the 20th-century French philosopher and influential voice within the tradition known as phenomenology, can serve as our guide here. He went further than any other Western thinker in placing our embodiment at the heart of an entire philosophical system. In our technologically mediated lives, Merleau-Ponty can help diagnose the unease we feel about the (B) _____ of the beating, pulsing body — and its reduction to the status of a mere object. Moreover, he elucidates what we overlook when we don't make the body central to our understanding of our relationships with others and to the wider ecological context we're immersed within.

To carry Merleau-Ponty's insights into our everyday lives, I suggest that we can apply the simple notion of being present — carefully attending to the here and now of experience. Doing so flips the Western cultural tendency to (C) _____ mind over body.

08 What cannot be inferred from the passage above?

① "Screen apnea" refers to the physical reactions that occur when we spend time in digital space.
② Online platforms will eventually free our bodies from spatial limits.
③ Phenomenology helps us turn to the body's presence in our everyday lives.
④ The renewed attention to the body's physical presence may make the body-mind relationship more balanced.
⑤ "Screen apnea" ironically makes us think anew the body's presence in our technologically mediated lives.

09 Which expression best fits (A)?

① vaguely unsettling
② absolutely capitalistic
③ uncomfortably ideological
④ potentially healthy
⑤ naturally vulgar

10 Which pair best fits (B) and (C)?

① awareness — reclaim
② manifestation — prefer
③ negligence — disdain
④ disappearance — privilege
⑤ emphasis — separate

11~12

Today, many people are worried that digital books and our increasingly screen-based culture herald the end of serious reading. This is nonsense. There are consequences, and sometimes drawbacks, to all new technologies, but human beings can't live without stories and poems. Young lovers will always read Sappho, Donne, and Keats. *Madame Bovary* and *The Great Gatsby* will remain irreplaceable commentaries on our proclivity for romantic illusion. Older folk, hoping to make some small sense of life before its end, will continue to study history and philosophy. Whether people turn pages or look at pixels on a screen is secondary.

But consider this: through social media, the young woman of today who discovers Sylvia Plath can quickly share her excitement with friends around the world. She might leave a comment about *Ariel* or *The Bell Jar* on Goodreads, or join an online discussion group, or post links to sites devoted to the poet's work and memory. Her enthusiasm might lead a dozen or a thousand more people to Plath.

That's just one advantage of our screen-based culture. Older and half-forgotten books are now readily available through Project Gutenberg. Entire libraries can be carried in your pocket. Digitized texts can be easily and quickly searched, or their font size enlarged for aging eyes.

_____, these real benefits create various pitfalls at the same time. Computers encourage skimming instead of focused attention and solitary engagement with a book's words and ideas. The buzzing Internet hive fosters meaningless chatter as well as meaningful dialogue. Screens themselves impose a factitious homogeneity: James Bond looks like Jane Austen and a smartphone blurs the difference in size between the Giant Bible of Mainz and a tiny miniature book.

11 Which expression best fits the blank?

① Indeed
② Alarmingly
③ Consequently
④ In addition
⑤ Nonetheless

12 What is not inferable from the passage above?

① Despite the fast change in reading habits, people will not stop reading.
② Digitized texts will altogether replace printed books.
③ Reading on screen makes us unaware of the different material and generic traits individual printed books have.
④ Screen-based culture can expand the reader's active engagements with the book.
⑤ Not all comments and dialogues in online book clubs are meaningful.

13~14

Do not wake up to the blue hue of your smartphone and immediately start working. Place it across the room, or better yet, in an adjacent one, and force yourself up and out of bed to turn off your alarm each morning. When the alarm does go off, get up and prepare for your day as you would for an office job: take a shower and get dressed. Business attire is (obviously) not required, but act as though you will be interacting with colleagues in person. After all, you never know when they may want to video chat, and you do not want to beg off because you are not wearing a shirt. This also sets the tempo for the day and discourages the sleepy notion that, perhaps, just maybe, you can crawl back into bed for a nap around lunch, although <u>there is something to be said for workday naps</u>.

13 What is the passage mainly about?

① How to manage time
② How to work from home
③ How to keep work-life balance
④ How to become successful at work

14 What does the underlined expression mean?

① You need something for workday naps.
② Workday naps might be good for you.
③ No employers will allow workday naps.
④ Workday naps are something that you can talk about.

15~16

Never call back an unknown number because you could be opening the door to scammers. You might assume calling back is safe because a number is from your area code, but (A) they are adept at faking phone numbers that come up on caller ID. Criminals purposely use familiar area codes to gain your trust. People are curious and thieves are counting on their victims to think (B) they may have missed something important. At least, answering the phone or calling back increases your vulnerability to future scams because it confirms the number is attached to a real person willing to call back an unknown number. This tells scam artists (C) they can use another ploy on another day. And at worst? Scammers could dupe you into giving out personal information. Even if (D) they simply ask, "Can you hear me?" you should hang up. A recording of your answer, "Yes," can give them access to your bank, insurance, and other financial information. Just do not answer unknown numbers; remember that vital information will be left in your voicemail.

15 According to the passage, which of the following is true?

① Criminals can record your answers to steal from you.
② The normal curiosity of people protects them from scammers.
③ People should make the effort to call back an unknown number.
④ Scammers cannot get your financial information if you answer briefly.

16 Which of the following is different from the others in what it refers to?

① (A)　　　　② (B)　　　　③ (C)　　　　④ (D)

17~19

Some Apple Card customers say the credit card issuer, Goldman Sachs, is giving women far lower credit limits, even if they share assets and accounts with their spouse. But it's impossible to know if the Apple Card — or any other credit card — discriminates against women, because creditworthiness algorithms are notoriously opaque. "It's such a mystery we are seeing," said Sara Rathner, travel and credit card expert at NerdWallet. "Because we don't know exactly what those algorithms are looking for, it can be hard to say if there might be some bias built into them." The New York Department of Financial Services is looking into the allegations of gender discrimination against users of the Apple Card. The allegations blew up on Twitter after entrepreneur David Heinmeier Hansson wrote that Apple Card offered him 20 times the credit limit as his wife, although they have shared assets and she has a higher credit score. It's common practice for credit card issuers to use algorithms when they're making lending decisions, but there's very little _____.

17 Which of the following best fits in the blank?

① credibility
② transparency
③ accuracy
④ predictability

18 According to the passage, which of the following statements is correct?

① Generally, credit card issuers discriminate against women because they do not share assets and accounts with their spouse.
② The allegations of gender discrimination against users of the Apple Card are under investigation by the entrepreneur David Hansson.
③ Usually credit card issuers are giving men higher credit limits although they share all assets and accounts with their spouse.
④ It's common practice for credit card issuers to use algorithms which are programmed to discriminate against women.

19 Which of the following can be inferred from the passage?

① Apple Card can be accused of gender bias.
② The New York Department of Financial Services blew up on twitter on the allegations of gender discrimination against users of the Apple Card.
③ Apple Card issuers will share their algorithms with other credit card issuers.
④ The allegations of gender discrimination against users of the Apple Card will be opaque.

20~21

According to experts, there are several things you can do to increase your chances of survival in an emergency, such as a fire and an earthquake. Preparation can be the key to survival. Be sure you have food, water, candles, and other supplies in your home. Having a backpack prepared for each family member is a good idea in case you have to evacuate quickly. Before going camping, hiking, or mountain climbing, make sure you have the proper equipment. Tents, sleeping bags, and a first-aid kit can save your life in case of bad weather, injury, or illness. _____ can also help you deal with any emergency situation. Swimmers, for example, sometimes get caught in strong ocean currents. If they panic, they may become exhausted and unable to swim. If they relax and swim slowly with the current, however, they will have the energy to swim to shore once they are out of the current.

20 Which is the most suitable expression for the blank?

① Acting wildly
② Keeping energetic
③ Staying calm
④ Making plans
⑤ Talking to others

21 Which is the best title for the passage?

① Various Types of Outdoor Activities
② Benefits of Learning How to Swim
③ Equipments Necessary for Surviving Emergency
④ Things to Prepare For a Family Camping
⑤ How to Cope With Emergency Situations

22~24

One morning, after I had been hanging the washing out to dry, something glistened in front of me. With the morning sun shining in my eyes, I squinted to find the most glorious masterpiece in our garden.

(A) The mini architect had meticulously spun its web across the path, from the roof to the fence. I stared in awe at the fine artistry of (B) our garden resident. Spanning about two meters, it was truly a magical sight. The web gently danced in the morning breeze, reflecting light from the sun. It was as if the spider had spun a fine web from rays of sunlight itself.

How did it weave its web from the roof to the fence? It's almost as if it built a house while enjoying extreme sports at the same time. Very carefully, I ducked my head under the web, taking great care not to ruin (C) the spider's creation.

Later that day I went back to the web to take another look. My heart sank. The beautiful web was now broken and swaying aimlessly in the breeze. It was nothing more than a few pitiful strands hanging loose. I almost choked on emotion. "Sorry, (D) little fella. It was such a splendid structure."

But the very next morning, _____, there was another castle floating in the air. The mini architect had come back to work.

22 Which is closest in meaning to the underlined meticulously?

① thoroughly
② involuntarily
③ maliciously
④ contemptuously

23 Which is different from the others in its meaning?

① (A) ② (B) ③ (C) ④ (D)

24 Which best fits in the blank?

① to my amazement
② to its disappointment
③ with high expectation
④ with immense satisfaction

> In this first decade of the twenty-first century, the world community is confronted with <u>staggering</u> problems. There are 6 billion people on our globe and forecasters project that the world population will reach 10 billion by 2050. Those people will need food, shelter, and an education that will allow them to lead fulfilled lives. The twentieth century saw great advances in many fields, but these advances did not come without costs. Acid rain, for example, polluted our vegetation, wild life, and the very bodies of millions of people. Together, the people of the world need to stop the systemic despoiling of our planet. Weaponry, such as nuclear devices and improvised explosive devices, daily threaten the world's peace and progress. Religious fanaticism, hunger, and poverty have bred a desperate terrorism in many corners of the world. It is no overstatement to say that we are in a race for global survival.

25 What would be the best title for the above passage?

① Great Advances Made in the Twentieth Century
② Global Warming, Vegetation, and Wildlife
③ Great Advances Made With Significant Costs Paid
④ How to Lead Fulfilled Religious Lives
⑤ Desperate Terrorism and Global Survival

26 Which can best replace the underlined <u>staggering</u>?

① stimulating
② suspicious
③ abundant
④ astounding
⑤ stagnant

27 Which statement is not true according to the given passage?

① The rapid growth of world population foreshadows serious problems to be dealt with.
② At a significant cost, we have made great technical advances in different areas.
③ Problems including nuclear devices and religious fanaticism are considered relatively easier to stop.
④ It is not an exaggeration to say that we need to resolve issues threatening the global community.
⑤ It is not likely that we can afford to provide enough resources to the growing population.

28~30

There are three categories of content being used to pollute the information ecosystem: disinformation, misinformation, and "malinformation." Spreaders of disinformation, false content designed to cause harm, are motivated by one of three distinct goals: to make money, to have political influence, or to cause trouble for the sake of it. Those who spread misinformation, false content shared by a person who does not realize it is false or misleading, are driven by sociopsychological factors. These people are performing their identities on social platforms in order to feel connected to others. Disinformation turns into misinformation when people share disinformation without realizing it is false. Finally, a new term, "malinformation," describes _____ information that is shared with the intent to cause harm. An example of this happened when foreign agents hacked into politician's emails and leaked personal secrets to the public to damage reputations. It must be noted that the most effective disinformation always has a kernel of truth to it, and indeed most of the content being disseminated now is not fake, but misleading. Instead of wholly fabricated stories, influence agents are reframing _____ content and using hyperbolic headlines.

28 Which of the following best fits into both the blanks?

① political
② genuine
③ imaginative
④ motivational

29 According to the passage, which of the following is not true?

① Some people spread disinformation just to cause trouble.
② People who spread misinformation are unaware it is false.
③ Sociopsychological factors aid the spread of misinformation.
④ The damage caused by malinformation is not purposeful.

30 According to the passage, which of the following is an example of spreading disinformation?

① Publishing invented stories of someone online in order to have them fired
② Hacking someone's email and then posting lurid details of their personal life to a website
③ Believing and retweeting an unverified story about someone's illegal activity
④ Investigating a story about an official engaged in illegal behavior

31~32

Google executives have responded to a 3,300-word manifesto written by one of its male engineers that argues women aren't suited for tech jobs for "biological" reasons. The document has been circulating inside Google for some time, but it was made public by Motherboard. Recode and Gizmodo published the document in full. Over the weekend, Google diversity vice president Danielle Brown and engineering VP Ari Balogh addressed the controversial document in separate messages to Google employees. _____, and defended Google's diversity efforts. The issue immediately ignited a fierce debate on social media. The author, who has not been identified by CNN Tech, is reportedly a rank-and-file software engineer at Google. He contended that Google doesn't have more female engineers because men have a "higher drive for status."

31 제목으로 다음 빈칸에 들어가기에 가장 적절한 것은?

Storm at Google Over Engineer's _____ Manifesto

① Gender
② Executive
③ Xenophobia
④ Environment
⑤ Anti-Diversity

32 빈칸에 들어가기에 가장 적절한 것은?

① They completed a fierce debate on the issue
② They rebuked Google's employment policy
③ They condemned the document's assertions
④ They are good at making a big deal out of nothing
⑤ They started their career from a mere software engineer

33~34

I asked everyone I met in South Florida who seemed at all concerned about the sea level rise the same question: _____. More than a quarter of the Netherlands is below sea level and those areas are home to millions of people, so low-elevation living is certainly possible. But the geology of South Florida is particularly intractable. Building a dike on a porous limestone is like putting a fence on top of a tunnel: It alters the route of travel, but not necessarily the amount.

"You can't build levees on the coast and stop the water" is the way John Oliver put it. "The water would just come underground."

Some people told me that they thought the only realistic response for South Florida was retreat.

"I live opposite a park." Philip Stoddard, the mayor of South Miami, told me. "And there's a low area in it that fills up when It rains. I was out there this morning walking my dog, and I saw fish in it. Where the heck did the fish come from? They came from underground. We have fish that travel underground!"

"What that means is, there's no keeping the water out," he went on. "So ultimately this area has to depopulate. What I want to work toward is a slow and graceful depopulation, rather than a sudden and catastrophic one."

33 The most appropriate expression for the blank would be _____.

① Do you live around here?
② Where do you want to live?
③ Why do you live here?
④ Are you conscious of sea level?
⑤ What could be done?

34 According to the passage, South Florida _____.

① won't attract tourists any longer
② will be an uninhabitable place
③ will develop like Netherlands
④ will be surrounded by the ocean
⑤ will be a paradise for the sea animal

35~37

TV presenter Mike Rowe wants to close America's skills gap. Right now, there are more than 7 million job openings in the U.S. with not nearly enough qualified workers to fill them. Currently, just 9 percent of high school students are planning to pursue a trade career. In order to change this, Rowe says we have to change our perception of what we consider a good job. We also need to stop telling young people to follow their passion. "We need to stop telling young people that the only way to be happy is to correctly identify your passion when you are a teenager." Rowe says that following this 'follow-your-passion mindset' typically sends young people down a long road of expensive schooling and training "in order to start feeling happy and fulfilled wherever they land." In the end, he says, many people end up swimming in student loan debt, without any good job options. Instead, Rowe advises young people <u>to follow opportunity and then to take their passion with them</u>.

35 According to the passage, which of the following is true?

① A good job is not necessarily one you are passionate about.
② Finding good job options requires passion.
③ Trade careers are increasing in popularity among students.
④ Rowe wants teens to find their passion first so they can work.

36 Which of the following can be inferred from the underlined part?

① Passion is something stationary and permanent.
② Opportunity is more important than passion.
③ You get no benefit from passion at your new job.
④ There is no need for passion in life.

37 According to the passage, which of the following is a potential consequence of following one's passion when young?

① You will not go to university.
② You may owe a lot of money.
③ You may have more job options.
④ You will be given a chance to succeed.

38~39

Would you tattoo a website address on your body? One woman from Utah did just that. A company got her to tattoo its website address on her forehead for $10,000. She wanted to do it to raise money for her son's education. The company wanted her to do it for cheap advertising space. They also got free publicity because the story was on the news. This kind of _____ advertising — known as guerrilla marketing — uses surprising ways to advertise a product and get people's attention.

A way to advertise with guerrilla marketing is to use the environment in an _____ way. For example, a few years ago, a popular candy company painted park benches so that they looked like giant chocolate bars. This creative ad strategy got consumers' attention in a positive way.

Not all guerrilla marketing works. In 2007, an ad company decided to place signs with flashing lights around different cities to advertise a television show. However, in Boston, the police thought the signs were bombs. The police tried to find and destroy all of the signs.

Unlike those who use traditional advertising strategies, guerrilla marketers are not afraid to shock people. The idea is to convince people to talk about the products. However, it is important for companies to consider how people will react. Not all publicity is always good publicity.

38 Which pair best fits in the blanks?

① safe — expected
② safe — unexpected
③ extreme — expected
④ extreme — unexpected

39 According to the passage, which is true?

① A woman tattooed the company's website address on her forehead for her own publicity.
② Guerrilla marketing uses unconventional attention-getting strategies to promote products.
③ Companies prefer guerrilla marketing because it always brings success.
④ Even bad publicity is good publicity in marketing products.

[A] Women are generally more vulnerable to extreme climate events than men, and poor women more than rich. This is due to their disproportionate involvement in climate-sensitive natural resource activities, combined with their limited access to new agricultural technologies, secure land tenure rights, decision making over natural resource use, and the opportunities for off-farm income generation.

[B] Gender exclusion is often exacerbated by the introduction of new technologies, with men capturing their benefits at much higher rates than women. For example, in a cross-technology survey of adoption rates for germplasm improvement, soil fertility management, and soil and water conservation, Kingamkono (2006) found that rates were 95 percent for men compared with only 5 percent for women and that information exchange tended to occur along gender lines. [However, there are instances of successful "gender-neutral" Natural Resource Management (NRM) innovations such as the case of improved fallow management in Zambia.] The burden on women's labor in rural communities is certain to increase given the expected climate change impacts on water and land resources. This could further impinge women's abilities to collect household fuelwood and water.

[C] Adaptation strategies need to recognize the unique vulnerabilities of women, their role in household food security, and the networks they use to access social capital. Addressing vulnerabilities along gender lines therefore requires developing policies specifically aimed at women's resource needs and capabilities, such as empowering women in NRM decision-making processes; enhancing knowledge transfer along gender lines, such as through building capacity of women extension agents; and targeting technologies and diversification activities directly at women's capabilities.

[D] The micro-finance revolution has ushered in significant progress toward empowering women through rural micro-enterprise. Sustaining and expanding this effort to include micro-finance targeted for vulnerable groups in flood- and drought-prone areas would help them diversify away from climate-sensitive activities.

40 Which of the following is the best title of the above passage?

① Factoring Gender Into Adaptation Policies
② Improving Women's Collective Actions
③ Enhancing Data Access and Knowledge Dissemination in Rural Areas
④ Improving Women's Agricultural Outcomes
⑤ Integrating Adaptation Priorities into Gender Studies

41 Which of the following can the underlined word <u>exacerbated</u> in paragraph [B] be best replaced with?

① impeded
② chastised
③ aggravated
④ meditated
⑤ retarded

42 According to the passage, which of the following is not true?

① Women's vulnerability to climate events is attributable to their limited access to natural resource activities.
② Kingamkono (2006) revealed that adoption rates for new technologies and information exchange were gender-neutral.
③ Adaptation measures need to take into consideration women's networks to get access to social capital.
④ Developing policies aimed at women's resource capabilities includes empowering women in decision-making procedures.
⑤ The micro-finance revolution for vulnerable people in flood- and drought-prone regions would help them to pursue climate-neutral activities.

43
~
44

The presence of some of the world's fastest growing economies in Africa serves as fodder for the Africa rising narrative. A walk around capital cities of Nigeria, Kenya, South Africa, Angola, and others, will put a stamp on the discourse that Africa is rising at a significant rate. The crane-filled skylines, construction of road networks and railway lines, multi-million dollar mansions and business malls erupting across major towns and cities, and growing technologies are just but a few indications of the continent's ascent to prosperity. [A] But even as people across the globe engage in discussions about how fast the continent is growing, _____, the other discourse that goes hand in hand with this narrative is the astounding number of people who are still grappling with deep-rooted poverty in the continent. One can only wonder why there is still a widening gap between the rich and the poor and why Africa is still struggling with poverty despite the fact that it is home to a major percentage of raw materials that are in hot demand around the globe. [B] During the recent World Economic Forum in Davos, African leaders argued that powering Africa will answer the continent's growth in future. According to them, powering Africa will create jobs, cause industrialization and business expansion. [C] Here, we have assorted the issues that Africa needs to pay attention to in order to be _____ the rest of the world in terms of prosperity. The argument that civil wars, like terrorism, contribute to poverty is a no-brainer. Wars disorient people and leave them destitute. They also disconnect businesses from their clients. Moreover, roads and communication networks are destroyed or barred, which further cripples these businesses. Industries collapse, people lose jobs and investors lose confidence in the affected country thus pushing the affected region down the economic slopes. [D] Then, of course, there is the trail of deaths and scores of people left injured not to mention the loss of property which adds to the increase in poverty levels in areas marred by wars and terrorism.

43 아래의 문장들이 들어갈 위치로 가장 적합한 곳을 고르시오.

> Whereas powering Africa would contribute a lot to growth on the continent, we argue that for Africa to grow sustainably, it will need to pursue comprehensive methodologies that address all the bottlenecks to development. We contend that to understand what the areas for reform are, governments will have to first understand the reasons why Africa has been held back for so long.

① [A]　　　② [B]　　　③ [C]　　　④ [D]

44 빈칸에 들어가기에 가장 적합한 것을 고르시오.

① consequently — at odds with
② ultimately — in contrast to
③ absolutely — in competition with
④ ironically — at par with

45~47

Paradoxically, the greater the amount of information that circulates, the more we rely on reputational devices to evaluate it. What makes this paradoxical is that the vastly increased access to information and knowledge we have today does not _____ us or make us more cognitively autonomous. Rather, it renders us more dependent on other people's _____ of the information we receive. We are in the middle of a fundamental paradigm shift in our relationship to knowledge: from the 'information age' to the 'reputation age'. Information will have value only if it has been already filtered, evaluated, and commented upon by others. Seen in this light, <u>reputation is the gatekeeper to knowledge, and the keys to the gate are held by others.</u> The way in which the authority of knowledge is now constructed makes us reliant on what are the inevitably biased judgments of other people, most of whom we do not know. What mature citizens of the digital age should be competent at is not spotting and confirming the veracity of the news. Rather, they should be competent at reconstructing the reputational path of the piece of information in question, evaluating the intentions of those who circulated it, and figuring out the agendas of those authorities that gave it credibility.

45 According to the passage, which of the following is true?

① Having access to more information enables better judgments.
② The role of collective intelligence is underestimated.
③ Determining the reputation and agendas of informants is crucial.
④ The change in paradigm from reputation to information is ongoing.

46 Which of the following sets of ordered pairs best fits into the blanks?

① entreat — impressions
② empower — evaluations
③ enable — premonitions
④ extricate — estimations

47 Which of the following is implied by the underlined part?

① Reputation controls the doors of knowledge, and others are more intelligent.
② Reputation, which is controlled by others, controls access to knowledge.
③ Authority over what constitutes knowledge is collectively regulated by impartial scientists.
④ Reputation keeps the gates of intelligence open by allowing access to others.

48~50

Like other industries in 2008, plastic surgery suffered a drop in revenues when the recession began to worsen. Recently, however, people have begun investing in cosmetic surgery to increase their value in the job market. For example, 56-year-old Max Seddon is aware that the weakening music industry will likely force him to begin seeking work elsewhere. He spent $17,000 on a facelift to make his appearance more youthful and to bolster his confidence when he goes job-hunting. Other middle-aged men and women have found it necessary to turn to cosmetic surgery because they are competing with younger job applicants who look young and fresh.

Plastic surgeons have noted that people now have cosmetic surgery _____ not just so they can enjoy life more, but also because they know skills are often not enough in a competitive job market. Surgeons are now offering cheaper face-lifts that use only local anesthesia to _____ the price and the recovery time. A plastic surgeon in Manhattan has considered the fact that the older yet more qualified people are being passed over for their younger, better-looking counterparts and has offered a "job-fighter package" that makes use of cosmetic surgery methods that are less invasive and much cheaper.

48 Which one is not true?

① The economy was very bad in 2008.
② Max Seddon has worked for a music company.
③ Max Seddon had cosmetic surgery to make his appearance more youthful.
④ Middle-aged people now have cosmetic surgery mainly to prolong their life.

49 Choose the best word for the blanks.

① do — increase
② do — reduce
③ done — increase
④ done — reduce

50 Which one can best replace are being passed over for?

① are being preferred to
② are being less preferred to
③ are getting closer to
④ are getting less close to

51
~
54

[A] In the global resource wars, the environmentalism of the poor is frequently triggered when an official landscape is forcibly imposed on a vernacular one. A vernacular landscape is shaped by the affective, historically textured maps that communities have devised over generations, maps replete with names and routes, maps alive to significant ecological and surface geological features. A vernacular landscape, although neither monolithic nor undisputed, is integral to the socio-environmental dynamics of community rather than being wholly externalized — treated as out there, as a separate nonrenewable resource.

[B] By contrast, an official landscape — whether government, NGO, corporate or some combination of those — is typically oblivious to such earlier maps; instead, it writes the land in a bureaucratic, externalizing, and extraction-driven manner that is often pitilessly instrumental. Lawrence Summers' scheme to export rich nation garbage and toxicity to Africa, for example, stands as a grandiose (though hardly exceptional) instance of a highly rationalized official landscape that, whether in terms of elite capture of resources and toxic disposal, has often been projected onto ecosystems inhabited by those "disposable citizens."

[C] The exponential upsurge in indigenous resource rebellion across the globe has resulted largely from a clash of temporal perspectives between the short-termers who arrive with their _____ landscape maps to extract, despoil, and depart and the long-termers who must live inside the ecological aftermath and must therefore weigh wealth differently in time's scale. More than material wealth is here at stake: imposed _____ landscapers typically discount spiritualized _____ landscape, severing webs of accumulated cultural meaning and treating the landscape as if it were uninhabited by the living, the unborn, and the animate deceased.

51 Which of the following is the best title of the above passage?

① The Best Way to Utilize Natural Resources
② The Contrast between an Official and a Vernacular Landscape
③ The Advantages and Disadvantages of Landscaping Technology
④ The Environmentalism of the Poor and Its Resistance
⑤ The Survival of the Poor in the Global Age

52 Which of the following can best fill in the blanks in the paragraph [C]?

① official — official — vernacular
② vernacular — official — vernacular
③ vernacular — vernacular — official
④ official — vernacular — official
⑤ official — official — official

53 Which of the following cannot be inferred from the above?

① If we treat an ecosystem as disposable, it amounts to treating people as disposable.
② Some developers do not calculate the long-term consequences of a destroyed ecosystem.
③ There is intensified resistance against the intensified assaults on resources in this global age.
④ A vernacular landscape reflects indigenous people's unchanging agreement on their landscape.
⑤ The idea of offloading rich-nation toxins onto the world's poorest continent is not rarely proposed.

54 Which of the following pairs includes a word that cannot replace the underlined word in the passage?

① replete, filled
② oblivious, blind
③ exponential, rapid
④ aftermath, consequence
⑤ uninhabited, prohibited

55~59

In the 16th century, Sir Thomas More described an imaginary ideal society in his book *Utopia*. His Utopians would allow only slaves to kill animals because they did not want free citizens to experience the cruelty associated with killing living things. In modern slaughterhouses, cattle have often been killed with a lot of unnecessary suffering: animals stressed by abject fear and pain.

Temple Grandin, a renowned animal behavioral scientist, is leading authority on improving conditions at processing plants, advising the U.S. government on the federal Human Slaughter Act (calling for painless killing), and writing guidelines for the American Meat Institute. [A] An example of her practical designs: slaughterhouse ramps where cattle walk single file, able to see only three animals ahead, with the walkway turning in 180 degree curves so the cattle cannot see anything unexpected that will make them balk. When there are high walls, no shadows, no loud noises, no hitting, no slippages underfoot, the animals proceed without fear, and industry efficiency improves. Although many animal welfare advocates say we should avoid eating meat entirely, livestock animals serve a human purpose. [B]

Animal activists have also alerted people to the cruel conditions of the veal industry. Deprived of their mothers at birth, male veal calves are put in tiny pens alone, chained at the neck, unable to walk — all in order to keep their meat very tender. Raised on a liquid diet, deficient in iron and fiber, full of chemicals, antibiotics, and hormones, the calves are literally dragged to the slaughter at about 4 months old. Such conditions are now banned in Britain, and many consumers and chefs in the U.S. resist buying or preparing veal raised in this way. [C]

There is also a growing switch from red meat to poultry. But chickens tightly confined in battery cages in huge factory-like warehouses are also fed antibiotics and hormones. [D] Transportation and slaughter conditions are often appalling. Consequently, consumers have become interested in stores which use only "care-free" eggs and "organic" chickens. Despite the added cost, this trend is growing, fed by consumer disgust with the treatment of animals and worries over the industrialization of the food supply.

55 According to the passage, which of the following is not true?

① Temple Grandin believes that human beings owe animals a peaceful death.
② Slaughtering veal in cruel conditions is illegal in Britain today.
③ Grandin's inventions are purely profit-oriented.
④ Many American chefs resist preparing veal raised in inhumane conditions.

56 Which of the following can be inferred from the passage?

① Consumers are gradually eating more chicken than veal because of the high-quality meat.
② Utopians believed that slaves could kill animals with greater efficiency than free men.
③ People use their buying power to show their disapproval of the veal industry.
④ Grandin's inventions make the cattle unable to see anything at all in front of them.

57 Which of the following is the closest in meaning to the underlined deficient?

① unendurable
② insufficient
③ unseemly
④ incompetent

58 The author's main purpose in writing this passage is to _____.

① emphasize the great legacy of Temple Grandin's achievements
② discuss the inhumane conditions of animals in slaughterhouses these days
③ explain how livestock animals react to Grandin's designs
④ show how the veal industry raises the young cows to make their meat tender

59 Which is the most appropriate place for the sentence below?

> And Grandin believes humans should recognize their caretaking role toward these animals.

① [A]
② [B]
③ [C]
④ [D]

06 경제·경영

01 빈칸에 들어가기에 가장 적절한 것은?

> The global stock markets used to continue the "Santa rally," where stock prices increase at the end and beginning of the year as it is a time where consumption increases and investment psychology improves. This year, _____, witnessed a "black Christmas." Negative economic outlook shrank investor psychology.

① therefore
② likewise
③ however
④ consequently
⑤ notwithstanding

02 What is this passage mainly about?

> The key to successful funding is to choose the right type of finance at each stage of a company's early growth. Start-ups usually begin modestly, with self-funding and help from friends, family, and anyone else who is prepared to take a high risk. Crowdfunders and business angels are amateurs willing the entrepreneur to succeed, while venture capitalists become interested when the level of risk goes down and they can expect a healthy profit in return for injecting substantial funds. Public markets such as stock exchanges may step in as sales soar and success looks probable. At all stages, investors will conduct credit analysis to assess a company's ability to repay its debt.

① steps for successful funding applications
② how to create a sensible investment plan
③ finance sources at different phases of a business
④ dos and don'ts for start-ups looking for funding

03 Which of the following is most appropriate for the blank?

> A "vampire economy" refers to a nation that pursues wealth accumulation that does not involve normal corporate actions or labor, or to a company that lives off the normal economic activities of others. Around four to five years ago, Wall Street made the statement that the Korean economy should have been stricter about restructuring, and called it "a vampire economy full of bad companies that will disappear the day they see sunlight." _____, the real den of vampires turned out to be in the United States. It has been discovered that the large-scale financial companies that started the financial crisis that swept the world beginning in the second half of last year accumulated their wealth by sucking the blood of the common people.

① Namely   ② Furthermore
③ Accordingly   ④ Conversely

04~06

Peering through the lens of neoliberalism, you see how, no less than the welfare state, the free market is a human invention. You see how pervasively we are now urged to think of ourselves as <u>proprietors</u> of our own talents and initiative, how glibly we are told to compete and adapt. You see the extent to which a language formerly confined to chalkboard simplifications describing commodity markets (competition, perfect information, rational behaviour) has been applied to all of society, until it has invaded the grit of our personal lives, and how the attitude of the salesman has become enmeshed in all modes of self-expression.

In short, "neoliberalism" is not simply a name for pro-market policies, or for the compromises with finance capitalism made by failing social democratic parties. It is a name for a premise that, quietly, has come to regulate all we practise and believe: that competition is the only legitimate organizing principle for human activity. (A)_____ had neoliberalism been certified as real, and (A)_____ had it made clear the universal hypocrisy of the market, (B)_____ the populists and authoritarians came to power.

04 Which of the following best describes a human being in neoliberalism society?

① calculator of profit-and-loss
② bearer of free will
③ seeker of God's grace
④ business partner
⑤ consumer of luxury products

05 Choose the most appropriate set of words for blanks (A) and (B).

① no less — than
② no more — than
③ not so much — as
④ not any more — than
⑤ no sooner — than

06 The underlined word is closest in meaning to _____.

① conductor
② creator
③ seeker
④ owner
⑤ designer

07~08

Capitalism and the economic growth it drove is what made the U.S. the world's preeminent superpower in the latter half of the 20th century. But there's the flip side to U.S.-style capitalism. This capitalist, individualist economic system generates tremendous amounts of wealth, but it has also resulted in an average American worker with less of a social safety net, not to mention a political system more prone to capture by moneyed special interests. [A] Again, this is not something new that suddenly appeared with Trump's arrival at the White House. Yet while U.S. capitalism has long allowed for inequality of outcomes, in the last thirty years we've increasingly seen the rise of inequality of opportunity as well. [B] And it's accelerating. 30 years ago, when we spoke about those who lost out from capitalism, we usually referred to a specific set of blue-collar workers left behind by free trade. [C] But now we are getting to the point where automation and AI are slowly looking to displace a far wider set of workers, and across socio-economic classes. [D] As the rise of politicians like Bernie Sanders shows, this is as much a concern for voters on the left side of the political spectrum as it is on the right. [E] The end result is a more divided electorate, fueled by fear about how they are going to survive in an American future that gives the have's more and the have-not's less, with less prospect of moving from one group to the other.

07 Choose the most appropriate place to insert the following sentence.

> This latter form is more devastating — when people feel that they never even got a shot to compete, let alone to succeed, they get angry.

① [A] ② [B] ③ [C] ④ [D] ⑤ [E]

08 Which of the following is not true according to the passage?

① The inequality of opportunity has increased in the last thirty years.
② This capitalist, individualist economic system resulted in a political system more prone to capture by moneyed special interests.
③ Automation and AI will only displace a specific set of blue-collar workers.
④ The acceleration of inequality is one reason why the U.S. is so divided at the moment.
⑤ Many American workers on both sides of the political spectrum fear for their survival.

09
~
11

Rapid industrialization in the late 1800s centralized businesses into urban centers suddenly dense with teeming masses of rural migrants attracted by the economic boom of the time. Although real estate prices skyrocketed, demand outpaced supply — a conundrum solved by _____ limited spaces with the unprecedented concept of vertically-designed buildings.

In the beginning, the construction of tall buildings was limited to certain heights because most of the technologies needed to accommodate taller ones simply did not exist. First, early elevator systems were clumsy, so the idea of running up and down dozens of flights of stairs on a daily basis seemed like _____. Next, water pressure potency at the time could only pump water to heights of about 50 feet, making high-rise plumbing facilities a pipe dream. Finally, limited awareness about the importance of structural support beams meant that most early models were entirely supported by a thick base of solid brick, load-bearing walls.

09 Which of the following best fits into the blanks?

① maximizing — fantasy
② minimizing — common sense
③ minimizing — fantasy
④ minimizing — lunacy
⑤ maximizing — lunacy

10 The underlined phrase, pipe dream, is closest in meaning to _____.

① fantastic notion   ② financial difficulty
③ technical problem   ④ structural issue
⑤ urban legend

11 Which of the following is the most appropriate title for the above passage?

① Industrialization and Real Estate
② The Development of Skyscrapers
③ The Invention of Elevators
④ Rural Migrants in Urban Centers
⑤ Understanding Urban Spaces

12~13

A Bangladeshi economist, Muhammad Yunus, and the bank he founded 30 years ago were jointly awarded the Nobel Peace Prize in 2006. Yunus founded his banking system so that tiny loans could be given to millions of people that no commercial bank would bother with, mainly the rural poor in Bangladeshi villages. Most of the low-interest microloans, as they are called, go to women, who use them to start their own profit-making enterprises, mainly in agriculture, crafts or services. Yunus' banking success in combating _____ has inspired similar schemes across the developing world.

12 Which of the following is most appropriate for the blank?

① prejudice   ② microloans
③ enterprises   ④ poverty

13 Which of the following is Not true of the passage?

① Yunus was awarded the Novel Prize for his innovation in banking system.
② The commercial bank was also ready to help the rural poor through microloans.
③ The most notable beneficiary turns out to be poor women.
④ Yunus' new economic scheme even has spread internationally.

As economists deal with quantifiable objects, such as calories consumed or miles of cable laid, the models they use in their researches are almost always mathematical constructs. They can be stated in words, but mathematics is an enormously efficient way to express the structure of a model; more interestingly, for discovering the implications of a model. Applied mathematicians and physicists have known this for a long time, but it was only in the second half of the 20th century that economists brazenly adopted that research tactic; as have related disciplines, such as ecology. The art of good modelling is to generate a lot of understanding from focusing on a very small number of causal factors. I say 'art', because there is no formula for creating a good model. The _____ of a model is whether it discriminates among alternative explanations of a phenomenon. Those that survive empirical tests are accepted — at least for a while — until further evidence comes along that casts doubt on them, in which case economists go back to their drawing board to create better (not necessarily bigger!) models.

14 Which does not fit in the blank?

① acid test
② crucial test
③ ultimate test
④ arbitrary test

15 According to the passage, which is not true?

① Economic models can be described either verbally or mathematically.
② The objects of economic researches are those that can be measured in terms of quantity.
③ Mathematics came to be widely used in economics only in the second half of the 20th century.
④ A good economic model accommodates as many causal factors as possible in explaining a phenomenon.

16~17

The rise of a handful of vast corporate powerhouses whose business models have no instructive precedent from the analogue-era forces a reappraisal of the way capitalist economies work. The top seven highest valued companies in the world are all in the technology sector. Titans such as Alphabet (which owns Google) and Facebook specialize in products that do not exist in three-dimensional space. Apple and Amazon sell real-world objects as well as concepts, but their fortunes and market dominance have been built on nebulous concepts — models, brands and algorithms. Wealth is no longer in factories, pipelines or retail outlets. Their capital is not anchored to specific fields. That makes them hard to regulate and hard to tax. These are patterns of economic globalization that pre-date the digital revolution. While some intangibles like software and data strongly rely on computers, others do not: brands, for example.

What makes the new era different is the extent to which value has become detached from the tangible, and the corresponding social and economic consequences. This is the dynamic described by Jonathan Haskell and Stian Westlake as "capitalism without capital". In their book of that title, the authors illuminate ways in which the scale of intangibility deforms the familiar mechanisms of a market economy.

16 The underlined "capitalism without capital" means _____.

① the collapse of capitalist economy
② capitalism with the intangible capital
③ the importance of global network in business
④ the inequality of wealth in capitalism
⑤ the global expansion of tangible assets in capitalism

17 The best headline of the above editorial is "_____."

① The Necessity of Globalism in Capitalism
② The Globalization of Capitalism
③ The Rise of the Intangible Wealth
④ The Changing Nature of Capitalism
⑤ The Guide to the Success in the New Era

Macroeconomics is the study of the whole market economy. Like other parts of economics, macroeconomics uses the central idea that people make purposeful decisions with scarce resources. However, instead of focusing on the workings of one market — whether the market for peanuts or the market for bicycles — macroeconomics focuses on the economy _____. Macroeconomics looks at the big picture: Economic growth, recessions, unemployment, and inflation are among its subject matter. Macroeconomics is important to you and your future since you will have a much better chance of finding a desirable job after you graduate from college during a period of economic expansion than a period of recession. Strong economic growth can help alleviate poverty, free up resources to clean up the environment, and lead to a brighter future for your generation.

18 Select the word suitable for the blank.

① as a whole
② partially
③ specifically
④ purposefully
⑤ from a specific perspective

19 Which can best replace the underlined alleviate?

① allude
② aggravate
③ reduce
④ increase
⑤ cause

20 Which of the following is true for the above passage?

① Macroeconomics uses the idea that people use enough data to reach decisions.
② Macroeconomics is selective in the sense that it focuses on a critical area.
③ Macroeconomics helps us to understand the future economic directions better.
④ Macroeconomics could result in economic recession and poverty.
⑤ Macroeconomics always provide a blue print for the bright future.

21~22

Depending on which statistics you believe, the U.S. is either the world's No. 1 or No. 2 manufacturer. In the past decade, output from American factories, adjusted for inflation, has risen by a third. Yet the success of American manufacturers has come at a cost. Factories replaced millions of workers with machines. The labor statistics are disturbing. U.S. manufacturing employment data show steady growth from the end of the 1940s until the 1980s, when the number of jobs drops slightly. Then things stay flat until 1999. After that, the numbers collapse. In the 10 years ending in 2009, factories shed workers so fast that they erased almost all the gains of the previous 70 years; roughly 6 million manufacturing jobs disappeared. Across America, many factory floors look radically different than they did 20 years ago: far fewer people, far more high-tech machines, and entirely different demands on the workers who remain.

21 According to the passage, what is implied by the underlined part?

① It is costly to manufacture in the U.S. due to the price of machines.
② American manufacturers have substituted machines with workers.
③ American manufacturing success has resulted from lost jobs.
④ The price of doing business in the U.S. has decreased slightly.

22 According to the passage, which of the following is true?

① Commencing in 2009, factories discarded workers rapidly.
② From the 1940s until the 1980s the number of workers collapsed.
③ After the turn of the century, factories sharply reduced their workforce.
④ Radical differences in modern factories require an increase in staff.

23~24

One of the strategic principles for success in the stock market is to refrain from having knee-jerk reactions to possibly deceptive fluctuations in the market's or a particular stock's performance. Before reinvesting in a rapidly falling stock, analysts and investors will often wait for the passing of one or more small upward bumps, referred to as "dead cat bounces." The term reflects the somewhat crude idea that even a dead cat will bounce if it falls from a great height. Upticks in a plummeting stock can be caused by short selling, triggered selloffs, or overly optimistic reactions to changes made by the company, such as replacing an unpopular CEO. Such a small, unimpressive rise is usually followed by another drop-off that surpasses the previous low. While almost exclusively related to the stock market, the term has found occasional use in describing other areas of misleading improvement. Poll numbers for a candidate losing ground near an election sometimes make a brief, _____ surge. In sports, losing teams that make midseason coaching changes sometimes experience a mild surge of energy that translates to one or more wins before the team reverts to form.

23. 윗글의 내용과 가장 거리가 먼 것은?

① A "dead cat bounce" can be observed in sports and politics.
② A "dead cat bounce" refers to a small surge of a stock after a rapid decline.
③ Investors usually practice patience before reinvesting when a "dead cat bounce" occurs.
④ Replacing the unpopular CEO of a company can be a cause of a "dead cat bounce" in the stock market.
⑤ A fall of the stock can be expected after a "dead cat bounce," but it typically does not exceed the previous low point.

24. 빈칸에 들어갈 가장 적절한 것은?

① sharp
② illusory
③ expected
④ impressive
⑤ inexplicable

25~27

Throughout the years, as international commerce and cargo shipping progressed, the need for common codes of conduct created the Incoterms rules. These have been published since 1923 by the International Chamber of Commerce. (A) They create a framework in which a deal is executed and determine the obligations, costs, and risks between a buyer and seller of products. Since then, one has to search very hard to find a commercial transaction between two parties that does not follow (B) them to determine who is responsible for payment and risk throughout a cargo's journey from origin to destination. The Incoterms rules are updated and amended to keep (C) them in line with current international trade practices. The eighth version was published in 2011, and consultations for a new version are ongoing, with publication expected in 2020. The Incoterms rules specify two key aspects of a transaction. First, which party, the buyer or seller, is responsible for arranging and paying for transport and associated activities, e.g. getting licenses for import and export, insuring the goods, etc.? And second, at what point in the journey does responsibility for the consignment transfer from the seller to the buyer? By agreeing to use an Incoterms rule, the buyer and seller achieve precision and clarity in defining (D) their obligations and responsibilities.

25 Which of the following is stated in or implied by the passage?

① The Incoterms rules are widespread because they clarify the responsibilities of all parties.
② International commerce could not occur without the Incoterms rules.
③ Because the Incoterms rules are so useful, they have remained unchanged since 1923.
④ Precision and clarity are no longer in line with current trade practices.

26 According to the passage, which element of a transaction would not be stated by an Incoterms rule?

① The time at which the buyer assumes responsibility for the cargo
② The party responsible for obtaining export permission
③ The amount that must be paid to the seller for the goods
④ The party that must cover the cost of insurance

27 Which of the following is different from the others in what it refers to?

① (A)　　　② (B)　　　③ (C)　　　④ (D)

28~29

The political economist Benjamin Friedman once compared modern Western society to a stable bicycle whose wheels are kept spinning by economic growth. Should that forward-propelling motion slow or cease, the pillars that define our society — democracy, individual liberties, social tolerance and more — would begin to teeter. Our world would become an increasingly ugly place, one defined by a scramble over limited resources and a rejection of anyone outside of our immediate group. Should we find no way to get the wheels back in motion, we'd eventually face total societal collapse.

Such collapses have occurred many times in human history, and no civilization, no matter how seemingly great, is immune to the vulnerabilities that may lead a society to its end. Regardless of how well things are going in the present moment, the situation can always change. Putting aside species-ending events like an asteroid strike, nuclear winter or deadly pandemic, history tells us that it's usually a plethora of factors that contribute to collapse. What are they, and which, if any, have already begun to surface? It should come as no surprise that humanity is currently on an unsustainable and uncertain path — but just how close are we to reaching the point of no return?

28
According to the passage, which one does not lead our world to its collapse?

① an interstellar collision
② the severe climatic change following a nuclear war
③ a volcanic eruption
④ the halt of economic growth
⑤ the worldwide spread of fatal epidemic disease

29
The best topic of the passage would be _____.

① the vulnerability of economic growth
② the eventual collapse of modern Western society
③ the potential doom of the ecological destruction
④ the possibility of the world collapse in the future
⑤ the sustainable model for the future society

30~32

A timely partnership with Weight Watchers International is fattening up Blue Apron's market cap days after its stock price tumbled below $1 a share. Blue Apron's stock surged back above the $1 a share level for the first time since Dec. 18. That level carries a symbolic meaning for investors — below it, an issue is considered a penny stock, a designation that deters conservative shareholders. Furthermore, the New York Stock Exchange delists stocks that trade below $1 a share for more than 30 days. The rebound in Blue Apron's stock began on Dec. 21, when the company announced it would create a new line of meal kits for Weight Watchers, now renamed WW Inc.

Blue Apron's stock hit a record low of 65 cents a share around the time the partnership was announced. As publications like the *Wall Street Journal* began writing stories about the new menu this week, the stock continued to rise. As of today's close, Blue Apron shares had risen to $1.12 a share, or 73% above its low, but remains 89% below its $10 a share offering price. This week's rebound underscores the potential opportunities ahead for the company. Some analysts have said supplying Blue Apron's meal kits to a major grocery chain like Walmart could improve the stock price.

30. Which of the following is not stated or implied about Weight Watchers?

① It changed its name.
② It helped Blue Apron's stock go up.
③ It developed a series of new meal kits.
④ It entered into a partnership with Blue Apron.

31. Which of the following is not stated or implied about Blue Apron?

① Its stock price hit a record low in December.
② Its stock rose sharply after the partnership announcement.
③ Its initial stock price on the market was $10 a share.
④ It will be purchased by Walmart.

32. Blue Apron was allowed to remain listed on the stock exchange because _____.

① it would soon be merged with a huge grocery chain
② its stock had not fallen below $1 a share for 30 days
③ its stock had not stayed below $1 for more than 30 days
④ its sales improved after a partnership with Walmart

33~35

Capital and politics influence each other to such an extent that their relations are hotly debated by economists, politicians, and the general public alike. Ardent capitalists tend to argue that capital should be free to influence politics, but politics should not be allowed to influence capital. They argue that when _____ interfere in the _____, political _____ cause them to make unwise _____ that result in slower growth. For example, a government may impose heavy taxation on industrialists and use the money to give lavish unemployment benefits, which are popular with voters. But in the view of many business people, it would be far better if the government left the money with them. They would use it, they claim, to open new factories and hire the unemployed. In this view, the wisest economic policy is to keep politics out of the economy, reduce taxation and government regulation to a minimum, and allow market forces free rein to take their course.

33 The author's presentation is most like that of:

① A researcher offering a critique of how business and government policies can interrelate.
② A blogger writing to their network of readers offering advice on the best investments.
③ A bank manager writing a brochure to attract young clients to open a new bank account.
④ A politician giving a short election speech wooing business managers to vote for them.

34 Which of the following can least be inferred from the passage?

① Industrialists are likely to vote for politicians adopting a low-tax approach to business.
② Capitalists will usually wish to see a marketplace untroubled by political interference.
③ Deregulated marketplaces give the best opportunity for businesses to turn a profit.
④ Keeping politics out of business ensures that there will always be jobs for everyone.

35 Choose the best set of words for the blanks.

① interests — investments — markets — governments
② governments — markets — interests — investments
③ investments — interests — market — governments
④ markets — governments — interests — investments

36~38

Corporations can be either public or private. The stock of a public corporation can be bought by the general public. [A] In contrast, that of a private corporation, such as Gallo Wine, Levi Strauss, or United Parcel Service, is owned by only a small group of people and is usually not sold to the general public. The controlling stockholders may be family members, a management group, or even employees of the company. [B] Corporations have several advantages. The biggest advantage is limited liability: The liability of investors is limited to the amount of money they personally invested in the company. [C] In case of failure, the courts may seize and sell a corporation's assets but cannot dispose of the investors' personal possessions at will. For example, if you invest $1,000 in a company and it goes bankrupt, you may lose no more than that amount. In other words, $1,000 is the limit of your liability. [D] Another advantage is continuity. Because it has a legal life, which is independent of the biological lives of its owners, a corporation can, _____, last forever. Shares of stock, for example, may be inherited by future generations. Finally, corporations have the upper hand in raising money. By selling more stock, for instance, they can easily increase the number of investors and the amount of funds.

36 Choose the best place for the following.

Because unknown stocks don't tend to attract buyers, most new corporations start out as private corporations.

① [A]   ② [B]   ③ [C]   ④ [D]

37 Choose the best expression for the blank.

① just like everything else in life
② at least in theory
③ never
④ by no means

38 Which is true?

① It is impossible for a private corporation to issue stock to the public.
② The liability of an investor in a corporation is virtually unlimited.
③ A corporation can continue even after the death of the initial investors.
④ An employee of a private corporation is not allowed to own its stock.

39~40

Most social policies are directly framed as attempts to maintain a given distribution of income within a social system or to redistribute income among the various social groups that make up a society. It has generally been accepted that some redistribution must take place _____ there are always those elements in a population who, by ill-luck, bad judgement, age or frailty, cannot attain an adequate standard of living through the usual means. Exactly how much redistribution of income should occur is, of course, an ethical question which different societies have answered in different ways at different times — this is the central ethical judgement which has to be made in the formulation of any social policy with respect to a city system. If we are to achieve a chosen income distribution, we must have a very clear idea of the mechanisms which generate income inequalities in the first place, for it is presumably by controlling and manipulating these mechanisms that we will achieve our given objective. It is not necessary to state any preference for a given income distribution to investigate these mechanisms, but it will probably become clear in what follows that I am generally in favour of a far more egalitarian social structure than currently exists in either American or British urban systems. It appears that the "hidden mechanisms" of income redistribution in a complex city system usually increase inequalities rather than reduce them. This has immediate implications for social policy in that it indicates the necessity for a policy of "over-kill" in direct redistribution if the general direction of hidden redistribution is to be counteracted. Another possibility is, of course, to seek to control or make use of the hidden mechanisms for redistribution, and I shall give some indications as to how this might be done. These "asides" regarding my own social policy preferences need not interfere, however, with the direct analysis of the mechanisms controlling income redistribution.

39 Which is the most appropriate for the blank?

① no matter what
② so that
③ though
④ since

40 According to the passage, which is true?

① Best forms of social policies can be found in the advanced American or British city mechanisms.
② An excessive policy in direct redistribution can be justified to achieve the equalities of a city system.
③ To maintain a given distribution of income is not the attempt of most social policies.
④ Those who live on less income than the average in the society should try harder to level up their living standards.

41
~
43

The Rhine River was the most important waterway for European trade in the Middle Ages. Merchant ships paid tolls as they passed each state along the Rhine, in return for the Holy Roman Empire's protection. But (A) in line with the decline of the empire in the 13th century, barons peppered the riverside with hundreds of castles to claim tolls from passing ships. Their toll demands became so (B) audacious that merchants gave up ventures down the Rhine altogether. The trade business along the Rhine collapsed, bringing down the sponging barons along with it.

Columbia Law School professor Michael Heller calls this effect the "tragedy of the anticommons." The waste of unclaimed property can be ruinous, but self-serving and expansive fights over a property can be (C) rarely disastrous, as seen in the Rhine River example. Heller, in his book *The Gridlock Economy: How Too Much Ownership Wrecks Markets, Stops Innovation, and Costs Lives* argued that overly fragmented property rights and broad ownership can eventually trap the industry and market in (D) a dead end.

There is an overabundance of patents in the biotech industry right now. Patents licensed over the last 30 years associated with DNA alone top 40,000 cases. Pharmaceutical companies must go through numerous patent holders and negotiate contract terms before marketing a new drug. Many tests fail to go beyond the labs _____.

41 Which of the following is best for the title of the passage?

① Conflicts Between Merchants on the Rhine and Barons
② Clash Between Ownership and Economic Development
③ Necessity of Developing New Drugs
④ Patent Issues and Progress of Medicine

42 Which of the following underlined (A), (B), (C), and (D) is not appropriately used?

① (A)   ② (B)   ③ (C)   ④ (D)

43 Which of the following is most appropriate for the blank?

① owing to political interference with new drug market
② resulting in scrambling of pharmacists and doctors for dominating market
③ despite patent holders' demanding extensive ownership
④ for fear of litigation backlashes from reclusive patent owners

44 ~ 46

Only one out of all chief executive officers (CEOs) at financial companies operating in South Korea was female, the data showed Monday, revealing much about the hard-to-crack glass ceiling for women employees in the country.

President Sohn B.O., the 61-year-old head of Prudential Life Insurance Korea Co., was the only female chief executive among the heads of all financial companies here, according to the latest industry data based on 90 major financial firms.

Sohn started her career as a bank clerk in Chase Manhattan Bank in the middle 1980s before she began working at Prudential Life in 1996. She took the helm of the Seoul-based U.S. insurance firm two years ago for the first time as a woman.

_____, the average age of financial CEOs in Korea stood at 56.4, the data showed. CEOs at brokerages had the lowest average at 54.8, followed by those at life insurers with 55.9. Financial holding companies had the highest average age of 59.3.

Chairman Lee M.J., the 46-year-old chief of Allianz Life Insurance Korea Co., was the second youngest to become the leader of a financial company here, after President Choi J.H of Hyundai Life Insurance Co., aged 45.

A large number of financial CEOs in Korea majored in either economics or business administration, accounting for 40 out of the 90 surveyed, the data showed.

Of the total, about 75 percent graduated from colleges located in Seoul and Gyeonggi areas, while the remaining 25 percent are graduates of colleges in the other regions.

44 Which is the most appropriate for the blank?

① Meanwhile
② Otherwise
③ In contrast
④ Conversely

45 According to the passage, which is true?

① The youngest CEO at Korean financial firms was 46 years old.
② Only a couple of female CEOs are found at Korean financial businesses.
③ Forty of the CEOs at Korean financial firms majored in business administration.
④ In Korean financial firms, it is hard for women to be promoted to higher positions.

46 Which is the topic of the passage?

① Gender discrimination in Korean financial businesses
② College majors of the CEOs at Korean financial firms
③ Age distribution of the CEOs at Korean financial firms
④ The characteristics of the CEOs at Korean financial firms

47 ~ 48

The standard case for _____ markets rests on two claims — one about welfare, the other about freedom. First, markets promote the welfare of society as a whole by providing incentives for people to work hard supplying the goods that other people want. (In common parlance, we often equate welfare with economic prosperity, though welfare is a broader concept that can include noneconomic aspects of social well-being.) Second, markets respect individual freedom: rather than impose a certain value on goods and services, markets let people choose for themselves what value to place on the things they exchange.

Not surprisingly, the opponents of price-gouging laws invoke these two familiar arguments for free markets. How do defenders of price-gouging laws respond? First, they argue that the welfare of society as whole is not really served by the exorbitant prices charged in hard times. _____ high prices call forth a greater supply of goods, this benefit has to be weighed against the burden such prices impose on those least able to afford them. For the affluent, paying inflated prices for a gallon of gas or a motel room in a storm may be an annoyance; but for those of modest means, such prices pose a genuine hardship, one that might lead them to stay in harm's way rather than flee to safety. Proponents of price-gouging laws argue that any estimate of the general welfare must include the pain and suffering of those who may be priced out of basic necessities during an emergency.

Second, defenders of price-gouging laws maintain that, under certain conditions, the free market is not truly free. As Crist points out, "buyers under duress have no freedom. Their purchases of necessities like safe lodging are forced." If you're fleeing a hurricane with your family, the exorbitant price you pay for gas or shelter is not really a voluntary exchange. It's something closer to extortion. So to decide whether price-gouging laws are justified, we need to assess these competing accounts of welfare and of freedom.

But we also need to consider one further argument. Much public support for price-gouging laws comes from something more visceral than welfare or freedom. People are outraged at "vultures" who prey on the desperation of others and want them punished — not rewarded with windfall profits. Such sentiments are often dismissed as atavistic emotions that should not interfere with public policy or law. As Jacoby writes, "demonizing vendors won't speed Florida's recovery." But, the outrage at price-gougers is more than mindless anger. It gestures at a moral argument worth taking seriously. Outrage is the special kind of anger you feel when you believe that people are getting things they don't deserve. Outrage of this kind is anger at injustice.

47 빈칸에 들어가기에 가장 적합한 것을 고르시오.

① untaxed — Because
② unfettered — Even if
③ unrestrained — In that
④ untapped — Whenever

48 위 글을 통해 추론할 수 있는 것으로 가장 적합한 것을 고르시오.

① Some opponents of the price-gouging laws are actually enraged at making unfair profits.
② To decide whether public policy or law is justified, natural human emotions should be restrained as much as possible.
③ The defenders to the price-gouging laws make out a case for free markets, claiming that markets improve the welfare of society and respect individual freedom.
④ The proponents of price-gouging laws want to make a good society in which people don't exploit their neighbors for financial gain in times of crisis.

Beginning with a speech in 1957, and later in a groundbreaking book called *The Human Side of Enterprise* in 1960, McGregor argued that the companies were operating from faulty assumptions about human behavior. Most leaders believed that the people in their organizations fundamentally disliked work and would avoid it if they could. These faceless minions feared taking responsibility, craved security, and badly needed direction. As a result, "most people must be coerced, controlled, directed, and threatened with punishment to get them to put forth adequate effort toward the achievement of organizational objectives." But McGregor said there was an alternative view of employees — one that offered a more accurate assessment of the human condition and a more effective starting point for running companies. This perspective held that taking an interest in work is "as natural as play or rest", that creativity and ingenuity were widely distributed in the population, and that under the proper conditions, people will accept, and even seek, responsibility. To explain these contrasting outlooks, McGregor mined the back end of the alphabet. He called the first view Theory X and the second Theory Y. If your starting point was Theory X, he said, your managerial techniques would inevitably produce limited results, or even go awry entirely. If you believed in the "mediocrity of the masses," as he put it, then mediocrity became the ceiling on what you could achieve. But if your starting point was Theory Y, the possibilities were vast — not simply for the individual's potential, but for the company's bottom line as well. The way to make business organizations work better, therefore, was to shift management thinking away from Theory X and toward Theory Y.

49 Which of the following statement is not true?

① McGregor proposed two distinct views of human behavior.
② Under Theory X, managers believe employees inherently dislike work.
③ Under Theory X, the achievement of a task depends on the nature of a task.
④ Under Theory X, employees should be directed, or even coerced into performing a task.

50 It can be inferred from the passage that _____.

① Theory X and Theory Y are based on the same assumptions about minions
② the assumption of Theory Y undermines the exercise of self-direction
③ Theory Y can overcome the mediocrity of the masses
④ Theory X can maximize an employee's job motivation

'Globalization' can mean many things. On the one hand, it is the worldwide spread of modern technologies of industrial production and communication of all kinds across frontiers — in trade, capital, production and information. This increase in movement across frontiers is itself a consequence of the spread to hitherto pre-modern societies of new technologies. To say that we live in an era of globalization is to say that nearly every society is now industrialized or embarked on industrialization.

Globalization also implies that nearly all economies are networked with other economies throughout the world. There are a few countries, such as North Korea, which seek to cut their economies off from the rest of the world. They have succeeded in maintaining independence from world markets — but at great cost, both economic and human. Globalization is a historical process. It does not require that economic life throughout the world be equally and intensively integrated. As a seminal study of the subject has put it, "Globalization is not a singular condition, a linear process or a final end-point of social change."

Nor is globalization an end-state towards which all economies are converging. A universal state of equal integration in worldwide economic activity is precisely what globalization is not. On the contrary, the increased interconnection of economic activity throughout the world accentuates _____ development between different countries. It exaggerates the dependency of 'peripheral' developing states such as Mexico on investment from economies nearer the 'center,' such as the United States. Though one consequence of a more globalized economy is to overturn or weaken some hierarchical economic relationships between states — between Western countries and China, for example — at the same time it strengthens some existing hierarchical relations and creates new ones.

Nor does the claim that we are undergoing a rapid advance in the further globalization of economic life necessarily mean that every aspect of economic activity in any one society is becoming significantly more sensitive to economic activity throughout the world. However far globalization proceeds, it will always be true that some dimensions of a society's economic life are not affected by world markets, though these may shift over time.

51 빈칸에 가장 적합한 것을 고르시오.

① unforced
② unprecedented
③ uneven
④ unflinching

52 위 글의 내용과 일치하지 않는 것을 고르시오.

① Globalization is the worldwide spread of modern industrial technologies.
② Any countries which refuse the influence of globalization should pay a high cost for their decision.
③ Globalization necessitates that the world economy should be equally integrated.
④ Globalization cannot affect every aspect of a society' economic life.

07 정치·법

01 빈칸에 들어가기에 가장 적절한 것은?

> "_____ The two powers believe that whichever leads AI technology rules the world. The 19th century where industrialized countries exploited those who lag behind can repeat itself in the 21st century with the emergence of AI technology," said a lecturer at the Hebrew University of Jerusalem. He also expressed his concerns that the rise of nationalism can pose a threat to humanity.

① The U.S.-China competition will eventually resolve humanity conflicts.
② The U.S.-China trade war is getting riskier than AI competition.
③ The U.S.-China race for AI raises more concerns than that for trade does.
④ Individuals should train themselves to revamp their lives in the U.S.-China era.
⑤ Neither the U.S. nor China can protect its people without mutual cooperation.

02~03

We see the importance of media in the fact that a camera-friendly style and appearance greatly enhance a candidate's chance of success. Looking and acting comfortable on camera can aid a candidate's cause. An early indication of the importance of appearance was the infamous presidential debate between Kennedy and Nixon in 1960. The debate was televised, but Nixon declined to wear the heavy makeup that aides recommended. On camera, he appeared haggard and in need of a shave, while Kennedy's youthful and vibrant appearance was supported by the layer of television makeup he wore. The significance of this difference in appearance became apparent after the debate. Polls showed that a slim majority of those who heard the debate on the radio thought Nixon had won, while an equally slim majority of those who watched the debate on television gave the edge to Kennedy. After this dramatic event, the fear of not performing well in televised debates so intimidated presidential hopefuls that it was 16 years before another debate was televised.

02 The underlined word, haggard, is closest in meaning to _____.

① angry
② perplexed
③ dirty
④ exhausted
⑤ sleepy

03 What is the main idea of the passage?

① The appearance of politicians is important. It is important to be telegenic in contemporary politics.
② People who watched the debate on television preferred Kennedy because he was a better speaker.
③ The presidential debate in 1960 was unsuccessful.
④ Media coverage of presidential elections is biased.
⑤ Presidential debates should not be televised because it produces unfair results.

**04
~
07**

John C. Calhoun, the great statesman of the pre-Civil War South, thought you could have responsible constitutional government without (A) <u>forcing</u> minorities to submit to the will of the majority. He advocated giving minorities the veto power over majority decisions which (B) <u>affects</u> their vital interests. The trouble with this remedy, of course, is that it makes government ineffective on all crucial issues, and gives a minority the supreme power of _____ of the majority will. The English political philosopher John Stuart Mill proposed another remedy, which has become part of electoral procedure in many countries: proportional representation. Mill (C) <u>pointed out</u> that it was possible for a minority to attain a sizable vote and yet be without any representation in the national lawmaking body. Mill felt that "minority representation" should accompany majority rule, that the minority should have a voice, though not the supreme power. He also suggested a system of "plural voting" which would grant more votes to the more highly educated or intelligent persons. There is no doubt that proportional representation gives a more just representation to various political convictions. But it (D) <u>has tended</u> to make governments unstable, with no single party able to attain a majority. I think we all agree that the majority should be prevented from taking away certain human rights. Nor should the majority (E) <u>be</u> allowed to impose its religious beliefs, political convictions, or mode of life on minorities.

04 According to the passage, which of the following is NOT true about Mill?

① granting minority to have a voice
② giving more votes to the more highly educated persons
③ sympathizing with "minority representation"
④ rectifying proportional representation
⑤ suggesting a system of "plural voting"

05 According to the passage, governments can be made unstable by _____.

① proportional representation
② supreme power
③ the majority will
④ any political unit
⑤ a political philosopher

06 Which of the following is most appropriate to fill in the blank?

① verification
② nullification
③ vindication
④ clarification
⑤ externalization

07 Which of the following underlined words is grammatically incorrect?

① (A)   ② (B)   ③ (C)   ④ (D)   ⑤ (E)

08~09

The worst Jihadist attacks on France highlighted the country's serious problems with homegrown extremism. If we try to examine what has caused this, it is tricky to decipher. France's interactions with the Middle East and North Africa have historically been violent, and its domestic Muslim community has experienced discriminatory practices and exclusion by the French. The French far-right has gained traction, using inflammatory rhetoric that is often criticized as anti-Muslim and anti-immigrant. France is a region in which jihadist recruiting can thrive due to marginalization among North African immigrants and the Islamic State presents a viable and attractive alternative to this.

08 Which of the following is closest in meaning to the underlined inflammatory?

① bilateral
② provocative
③ conspicuous
④ ostensible

09 Which of the following is not true of the passage?

① It is complicated to understand why France has so much homegrown terrorism.
② France has an ugly history with Middle Eastern and North African countries.
③ The far-right deliberately uses language that antagonizes Muslim immigrants.
④ The problems of terrorism have been exacerbated by the Islamic State's negligence to Muslim immigrants.

10~12

President Obama has forbidden federal employees from texting while driving. [A] The federal Transportation Department plans to do the same for commercial-truck and Interstate-bus drivers. [B] And support is building in Congress for legislation that would require states to outlaw texting or emailing while driving. [C] Such distractions cause tens of thousands of deaths each year. But the way to stop people from using cell phones while driving is not to make it a(n) _____. [D] A more effective way is to make it difficult or impossible to text and drive. [E]

10 빈칸에 들어갈 가장 적절한 것을 고르시오.

① standard ② crime
③ benefit ④ excuse
⑤ substitution

11 아래 문장을 위 본문 중에 추가할 경우, 가장 적절한 위치를 고르시오.

Too many drivers value convenience more than safety and would assume they wouldn't get caught.

① [A] ② [B] ③ [C] ④ [D] ⑤ [E]

12 다음 중 본문의 내용과 가장 일치하는 것을 고르시오.

① The most effective way to prohibit texting while driving is to prevent it by law.
② President Obama requested states to forbid using cell phones while driving.
③ It is illegal to send text messages while driving.
④ Using phones while driving causes mortality of thousands every year.
⑤ It is more recommended to limit the functions of phones than to enforce laws.

13~15

It is then only when suffering is considered from the standpoint of a politics of pity that the question of commitment appears as a problem. The reason for this is that a politics of pity must meet a double requirement. As a politics it aspires to generality. Its role is to detach itself from the local and so from those necessarily local situations in which events provoking compassion may arise. To do this politics may rely upon techniques for establishing equivalences, and on statistical techniques in particular. But in its reference to pity it cannot wholly free itself from the particular case. Pity is not inspired by generalities. So, for example, a picture of absolute poverty defined by means of quantitative indicators based upon existing conventions of equivalence may find its place in a macroeconomic treatise and may also help define a politics. It will not, however, inspire the sentiments which are indisputable for a politics of pity. To arouse pity, suffering and wretched bodies must be conveyed in such a way as to affect the sensibility of those more fortunate. Pity possesses the weakness of a lack of (A) _____: a suffering child fills our heart with sadness, but we greet the news of a terrible battle with indifference.

13 Which is true according to the passage?

① The death of a child is more tragic than a soldier's death.
② Statistics are irrelevant in the politics of pity.
③ Pity is less important than empathy.
④ The politics of pity requires detachment from local concerns.

14 What is the double requirement of the politics of pity?

① In order to develop an objective view of suffering, generality must not be tainted by subjective feelings.
② The politics of pity demands both a broad vision and an intimate affective response.
③ The spectator of suffering must not allow statistics to get in the way of heartfelt feelings.
④ In order to sympathize with those who suffer, one must limit statistical evidence in a way that creates empathy.

15 Choose the best word for blank.

① proportion
② lassitude
③ temerity
④ empathy

16~18

If the democratic alternative to the totalitarian one-way broadcasts is a row of separate soapboxes, then I submit that the alternative is unworkable, is unreasonable, and is humanly unattractive. It is above all a false alternative. It is not true that liberty has developed among civilized men when anyone is free (A) to set up a soapbox, is free to hire a hall where he may expound his opinions to those who are willing to listen. On the contrary, freedom of speech is established to achieve its essential purpose only when different opinions are expounded in the same hall to the same audience. For, while the right to talk may be the beginning of freedom, the necessity of listening is what makes the right important. What matters is not the utterance of opinions. What matters is the confrontation of opinions in debate. (B) No man can care profoundly that every fool should say what he likes.

16 Which is the closest meaning to the underlined part (A)?

① to say his (her) individual opinions
② to build his (her) small rooms
③ to establish his (her) own worlds
④ to make his (her) theaters

17 What is implied by the underlined part (B)?

① Every fool should be respected.
② Discussing different opinions is more important than listening to all opinions.
③ Every man has the right to say what he (she) likes.
④ Nobody likes any fool's opinions.

18 According to the passage, which is true?

① There is no actual alternative to the totalitarian broadcasts.
② To get the freedom of speech, different opinions should be exposed in the same condition.
③ Separate soapboxes are the alternatives to totalitarianism.
④ To allow the freedom to speak one's own opinions is the most important thing.

19~21

Should nations be held accountable for historic wrongdoings and be forced to apologize? Public apologies mainly exist to acknowledge the continuing effects of injustice on those wronged as well as their descendants, and to (A) <u>recompense</u> victims for past damages. In the US, the primary apology question is over the (B) <u>infamy</u> of slavery. Virginia had been the state with the most slaves, and in 2007 it became the first state to make public (C) <u>contrition</u> for slavery, after which several other states followed suit. Republican congressman Henry Hyde, however, (D) <u>substantiated</u> the entire notion of the US making an apology and reparations. He said that because he had never personally owned a slave, he did not think he should be held responsible for the actions of those generations who did prior to his birth. For political conservatives to show disdain for collective apologies from an individualist stance is _____. After all, how can one take pride in the past accomplishments of one's countrymen while insisting that we are only individuals responsible for our own actions? One must feel a degree of belonging to a timeless community in order to feel patriotic pride, and that belonging brings with it responsibility.

19 Which of the following is not true of the passage?

① Virginia was the first to decide to apologize for slavery.
② The basis of Henry Hyde's argument is individualism.
③ Conservative politicians do not take pride in their country's history.
④ Belonging to a society requires a sense of responsibility for its past.

20 Which of the following the underlined (A), (B), (C), and (D) is not appropriately used?

① (A)　　② (B)　　③ (C)　　④ (D)

21 Which of the following is most appropriate for the blank?

① baffling
② tampering
③ encouraging
④ persuading

22~23

Mosquitoes and politics have long been entwined in Florida — some counties elect dedicated mosquito commissioners — but this year, Zika and bugs that convey it have infected races across the ballot. Amid an epidemic of hyperactive credit-seeking and partisan blame, everyone criticizes Congress for failing to pass emergency funding before its summer recess. Democrats assail Rick Scott, Florida's Republican governor, for previous state budget cuts. Patrick Murphy, victor in their senatorial primary on August 30th, lambastes Marco Rubio, his confirmed Republican opponent in November. Some Tampa-area politicians are agitating for the release of genetically modified mosquitoes, currently slated for a trial in the Keys, which might cut the Zika-spreading population.

As in actual war, however, the political grandstanding is a sideshow. The real combatants are the mosquito-control operatives, whose tools include _____. As Rob Kruger of the Pinellas squad recounts, one form of surveillance involves standing in a buzzy spot and seeing how many mosquitoes land on him in a minute. "You end up with a lot of mosquito bites," he says as his boss, Jason Stuck brings in the eggs from a reserve battalion of chickens. Many diseases are carried by Florida's numerous mosquito species, but Zika is the focus of anxiety because of its impact on tourism, plus the microcephaly it can cause in infants.

22 To win the election in Florida, you need _____.

① to be exposed to mosquito bites
② to know how to get rid of mosquitoes
③ to have a basic knowledge of biotechnology
④ to criticize other politicians in Florida
⑤ to be acquainted with as many residents as possible

23 The best expression for the blank would be _____.

① their own bodies
② mosquito's predators
③ animate weapons
④ harmful insecticides
⑤ genetic mutation

24~26

Speaking after North Korea leader Kim Jong Un visited President Xi Jinping in Beijing this week, South Korea president Moon Jae-in said the next summit would include more detailed talks on how to officially end the Korean war and on sanctions relief for Pyongyang. "The second North Korea-US summit will firmly solidify peace on the Korean peninsula," he said in his new year press conference. The US president has said a meeting could take place this month or in February but talks have become deadlocked over what should come first: North Korean efforts to rein in its nuclear programme or the lifting of international sanctions against the communist state.

China has sought to cast itself as being _____ on the peninsula as Pyongyang's biggest trading partner, with Mr. Xi backing a second meeting, China's state news agency Xinhua reported. Mr. Xi said after Mr. Kim's visit: "China supports North Korea in continuing to _____ the denuclearisation of the peninsula and supports North Korea and the United States holding a summit and achieving results."

24 Which one is true?

① The leaders of North Korea and the US are scheduled to meet this month.
② Kim Jong Un met Xi this week.
③ The US president is going to lift international sanctions against North Korea soon.
④ China dislikes the second meeting between North Korea and the US.

25 Choose the best title.

① Big Deal between China and North Korea
② The US-North Korea Summit Expected Soon
③ Kim's Visit to the US
④ Denuclearisation of the US and China

26 Choose the best expression for the blanks.

① puppetry — dispatch to
② indispensable — dispatch to
③ puppetry — adhere to
④ indispensable — adhere to

27~29

Freedom of speech is best conceived by having in mind the picture of a place like the American Congress, an assembly where opposing views are represented, where ideas are not merely uttered but debated, or the British Parliament, where men who are free to speak are also compelled to answer. We may picture the true condition of freedom as existing in a place like a court of law, where witnesses testify and are cross-examined, where the lawyer argues against the opposing lawyer before the same judge and in the presence of one jury. We may picture freedom as existing in a forum where the speaker must respond to questions; in a gathering of scientists where the data, the hypothesis, and the conclusion are submitted to men competent to judge them; in a reputable newspaper which not only will publish the opinions of those who disagree but will reexamine its own opinion in the light of what they say. _____, the essence of freedom of opinions is not in mere toleration as such, but in the debate which toleration provides: it is not in the venting of opinion, but in the confrontation of opinion. That this is the practical substance can readily be understood when we remember how differently we feel and act about the censorship and regulation of opinion purveyed by different media of communication. We find then that, in so far as the medium makes difficult the confrontation of opinion in debate, we are driven towards censorship and regulation.

27 Which is the most appropriate for the blank?

① Thus
② Instead
③ Contrarily
④ Indifferently

28 Which is the closest in meaning to the underlined part?

① invention
② release
③ prevention
④ venture

29 According to the passage, which is true?

① Disagreement in opinions is not important when there is regulation.
② Toleration is more important than debate for the freedom of speech.
③ Toleration and discussion should be there for the freedom of opinions.
④ Freedom of speech should be recommended only if there is censorship.

30~31

Among the central preoccupations of Durkheim is the question of what holds societies together. His answer points to the crucial role of law in promoting and maintaining this social _____. He shows how, as society advances from religion to secularism, and from collectivism to individualism, law becomes concerned less with punishment than compensation. But punishment performs a significant role in expressing the collective moral attitudes by which social solidarity is preserved. He distinguishes between what he calls mechanical solidarity and organic solidarity. The former exists in simple, homogeneous societies which have a uniformity of values and lack any significant division of labour. These uncomplicated communities tend to be collective in nature. In advanced societies, however, where there is division of labour, a high degree of _____ exists. There is substantial differentiation, and collectivism is replaced by individualism. These forms of social solidarity are, he argues, reflected in the law: classify the different types of law and you will find the different types of social solidarity to which it corresponds. According to Durkheim, while mechanical solidarity operates in traditional and small-scale societies, organic solidarity comes from individuals' reliance on each other to perform their specified tasks.

30 위 글의 제목으로 가장 적절한 것은?

① Types of Social Solidarity, Types of Society
② Coming Full Circle?: Law and Punishment
③ Division of Labor: How Societies Have Progressed
④ Making Room for Compromise: Solidarity & Individuality

31 빈칸에 들어갈 가장 적절한 것은?

① bond — diversity
② cohesion — interdependence
③ solidarity — collectivism
④ homogeneity — distinctiveness

The neoliberal state should favor strong individual private property rights, the rule of law, and the institutions of freely functioning markets and free trade. These are the institutional arrangements considered essential to guarantee individual freedoms. The state must therefore use its monopoly of the means of violence to preserve these freedoms at all costs. By extension, the freedom of businesses and corporations (legally regarded as individuals) to operate within this institutional framework of free markets and free trade is regarded as a fundamental good. Private enterprise and entrepreneurial initiative are seen as the keys to innovation and wealth creation. Intellectual property rights are protected (for example through patents) so as to encourage technological changes.

Neoliberals are particularly assiduous in seeking the privatization of assets. Enclosure and the assignment of private property rights is considered the best way to protect against the so-called "tragedy of the commons". Sectors formerly run or regulated by the state must be turned over to the private sphere and be deregulated (freed from any state interference). Privatization and deregulation combined with competition, it is claimed, eliminate bureaucratic red tape, increase efficiency and productivity, improve quality, and reduce costs, both directly to the consumer through cheaper commodities and services and indirectly through reduction of the tax burden.

32 According to the passage, which of the following is not true?

① In situations where property rights are hard to define, it is not recommended that the state uses its power to impose or invent market systems.

② The assumption that individual freedoms are guaranteed by freedom of the market and of trade is a cardinal feature of neoliberal thinking.

③ The sanctity of contracts and the individual right to freedom of action, expression, and choice must be protected.

④ Competition — between individuals, between firms — is held to be a primary virtue.

33 Which of the following is not the characteristics of the neoliberal state?

① It seeks to transfer control of economic factors to the private sector from the public sector.

② It is a less regulatory state with regards to private life.

③ It emphasizes the efficiency of market competition and the role of individuals in determining economic outcomes.

④ It tries to protect social justice and redistribution at all costs.

34 What is the meaning of the "tragedy of the commons"?

① The tendency for markets to grow more imperfect, causing social inequality

② The tendency for individuals to irresponsibly exploit public property resources

③ The tendency for companies to ignore investing in quality-enhancing factors

④ The tendency for societies to self-protect against unregulated market exchange

35~37

A slew of factors have combined in recent years to create the impression that the world is run by plutocrats, oligarchs and semi-detached politicians in the interests of the few not the many.

A quarter of a billion people are on the move around the world, providing more ammunition than ever before for right-wing populists who argue that political elites have failed to get a handle on the kind of immigration that they say threatens jobs, wages and social cohesion.

Meanwhile, the number of billionaires has jumped fivefold in the last 20 years, to more than 2,200, according to *Forbes*, as globalization opened up new markets for entrepreneurs to tap while at the same time making it possible to shield capital, assets and income from the taxman. The world's eight richest people own as much as the poorest 3.5 billion. The amount of money gained by the financial elite is put at as much as £10 trillion.

But there are also many non-economic factors that may offer partial explanations for populism's rise: a cultural backlash against elites, a technological revolution that has rewired our politics, a convergence of now indistinguishable left and right political parties on a technocratic centre.

35 The best title of the passage would be _____.

① How Can You Spot a Populist?
② What Is Populism?
③ Who Are the Populists?
④ Why Have the Populists Emerged Now?
⑤ What's the Opposite of a Populist?

36 As a factor which has created a backdrop for populism, _____ is not mentioned in the passage.

① cultural elitism
② tax evasion
③ mass migration
④ soaring inequality
⑤ ideological confrontation

37 According to the passage, populism is against _____.

① political elites of the right
② political elites of the left
③ corrupt elites
④ the wicked businessmen
⑤ the ordinary masses

38~39

It is possible for a product to become _____. When a product is so new, so innovative, or so well marketed that it dominates the marketplace and the mindset of the consumer, it can be easy to associate the product's brand name with the product itself. When a type of product is nearly universally known or referred to by the brand name of one version of the product, the brand name becomes a victim of "genericism." Aspirin (acetylsalicylic acid), the escalator (moving stairs), and the pogo stick (hopping toy) are all former brand names whose success and popularity led to such general and widespread use of the names that the inventors or parent companies were unable to maintain their trademark protections and even lost their competitive advantage against similar products described with the term that had once been a definitive brand name. All it takes is one court ruling for a term that has shifted away from its identity as a trusted brand name to become forever identified as a generic product. When this happens, a company is likely to lose a profitable beachhead within the consumer consciousness. The loss of revenue due to a shift to genericism is compounded by the large amounts of money companies spend in an attempt to keep it from happening. Despite spending millions of dollars in legal and public relations campaigns, the company Kimberly-Clark has been fighting an uphill battle to keep people from referring to all forms of tissues as Kleenex.

38 윗글의 내용과 가장 거리가 먼 것은?

① Genericism is a by-product of a company's successful marketing of a product.
② Kimberly-Clark doesn't want people to refer to all forms of tissues as Kleenex.
③ Aspirin and the escalator are often considered brand names rather than the names of products nowadays.
④ Companies are usually unable to protect their trademarks when they become a generic term for a product.
⑤ Companies often spend a lot of money to prevent their trademarks from becoming a generic term for a product.

39 빈칸에 들어갈 가장 적절한 것은?

① a victim of its own success
② popular regardless of its quality
③ unpopular because of its brand name
④ a big success regardless of marketing strategies
⑤ nothing but a failure due to marketing strategies

40
~
42

Landlords are property owners who rent out or lease space to tenants or renters of property. [A] Eviction is the process when landlords force tenants to move out. [B] Laws dealing with eviction differ among states and communities. [C] Generally, however, a landlord is required to provide a written notice to the tenant, allowing sufficient time for locating a new property. [D] In several states, it is considered illegal for the landlord to turn off the utilities, such as electricity and water, or alter the locks until the tenant has moved out.

Landlords have a legal right to evict tenants "for cause," like nonpayment of rent. In numerous locations, they also can ask tenants to move out for no reason other than wanting to use the space for something else. Meanwhile, tenants also have legal rights. Most jurisdictions have laws requiring rental space to be "fit for habitation," or in other words, reasonably safe and clean. Tenants should notify landlords of any problems and allow a reasonable amount of time for repairs. If a landlord neglects to take any action, a tenant should make the request in writing. Furthermore, a tenant can contact local government agencies to _____ about building code enforcement.

40 Choose the best place for the following.

> If the tenant still chooses not to vacate the premises following the written notice, the landlord must then file a lawsuit and allow law enforcement officers and the courts to handle the case.

① [A] ② [B] ③ [C] ④ [D]

41 Choose the best expression for the blank.

① inquire
② discuss
③ effort
④ fuse

42 Which one is true?

① Eviction laws are standard across all states and communities.
② A landlord only needs to provide a verbal notice to tenants they want to evict.
③ Landlords can legally change locks after the tenants move out.
④ Unpaid rent is not enough to evict a tenant.

43~45

"Technology is neither good nor bad; nor is it neutral," said the late Melvin Kranzberg, one of the most influential historians of machinery. The same is true for the internet and the use of data in politics: it is neither a (A) _____ nor is it evil, yet it has an effect. But which effect? And what, if anything, needs to be done about it?

Jürgen Habermas, the German philosopher who thought up the concept of the "public sphere," has always been in two minds about the internet. Digital communication, he wrote a few years ago, has unequivocal democratic merits only in authoritarian countries, where it undermines the government's information monopoly. Yet in liberal regimes, online media, with their millions of forums for debate on a vast range of topics, could lead to a "fragmentation of the public" and a "liquefaction of politics," which would be (a) harmless to democracy.

The ups and downs of the presidential campaign in America and the political turbulences elsewhere seem to (b) support Mr. Habermas's view. Indeed, it is tempting to ask whether all this online activism is not wasted political energy that could be (c) put to better use in other ways. Indeed, the meteoric rise of many online movements appears to explain their (d) equally rapid demise: many never had time to build robust organizations.

But (B) _____. Some movements have had real impacts, either by putting an issue on the political agenda or by taking over an existing organization.

43 Which best fits in the blank (A)?

① curse
② malice
③ hostility
④ blessing

44 Which is not properly used in the context of the passage?

① (a) ② (b) ③ (c) ④ (d)

45 Which best fits in the blank (B)?

① online activism cannot be dismissed
② Mr. Habermas's view is always right
③ many online movements do not last long enough
④ digital communication is not compatible with democracy

[46~48]

Politics cannot be suppressed, whichever policy process is employed and however sensitive and respectful of differences it might be. In other words, there is no end to politics. It is wrong to think that proper institutions, knowledge, methods of consultation, or participatory mechanisms can make disagreement go away. Theories of all sorts (A) promote the view that there are ways by which disagreement can be processed or managed so as to make it disappear. The assumption behind those theories is that disagreement is wrong and consensus is the (B) desirable state of things. In fact, consensus (C) often comes without some forms of subtle coercion and the absence of fear in expressing a disagreement is a source of genuine freedom. Debates cause disagreements to evolve, often for the better, but a positively evolving debate does not have to equal a reduction in disagreement. The _____ of disagreement should never be made into a goal in political deliberation. A defense is required against any suggestion that political disagreement is not the (D) normal state of things.

46 Which of the underlined words is not appropriate?

① (A) ② (B) ③ (C) ④ (D)

47 Which is the most appropriate for the blank?

① suppression
② acknowledgement
③ refinement
④ boost

48 According to the passage, which is true?

① It is important to cultivate the skills of debate in political situations.
② People sometimes should withdraw their ideas to reach an agreement.
③ Allowing differences is the fundamental requirement of democratic societies.
④ Politicians try to negotiate with opposite parties to execute effective policies.

[A] For, whether intended or not, the effect of obedience to the law is to uphold the authority of those who make decisions about what the law should be, and how it is to be enforced. To uphold this authority is to aid in maintaining aspects of the distribution of power to make decisions for society. Similarly, all violations of the law constitute political behavior; every violation of law is ipso facto a defiance of constituted authority. It threatens the maintenance of the existing pattern of distribution of the power to make decisions for society. If the incidence of violations of law continues to increase, political authority eventually atrophies; that is axiomatic.

[B] An attempt to define political stability must begin by clarifying the concepts of politics and political structure. Political behavior is any act by any member of a society that affects the distribution of the power to make decisions for that society. Political behavior is ubiquitous. Members of society behave politically insofar as, in obeying or disobeying the laws of the society, they support or undermine the power stratification system. Obedience to the law constitutes political behavior just as much as contesting elections does.

[C] We have clearly not defined the political in the usual sense of demarcating particular acts that are political from those that are not. Nor do we intend to offer such a definition, because it is misleading to delineate the political in that fashion. Strictly speaking, there is no human act, even so simple as wearing hair long, that is intrinsically nonpolitical. This is true because the "politicalness" of an act is not a quality inherent in that act but rather a characterization of it according to the context in which we study it, and the context in which it occurs.

[D] To illustrate, we would not ordinarily consider long hair a form of political behavior. Yet a puritanical despot might decide that this act corrupts and consequently command everyone to cut his hair short. Suppose that shortly after such a decree has been widely and intensively publicized, all the men invited by the despot to a state ceremony arrive with long hair. In the circumstances, we would legitimately conclude that these men were committing a very bold act of political disobedience.

49 위 글의 단락을 논리적 흐름에 맞게 순서대로 배열한 것으로 가장 적합한 것을 고르시오.

① [D] — [B] — [C] — [A]
② [B] — [A] — [C] — [D]
③ [A] — [C] — [B] — [D]
④ [B] — [A] — [D] — [C]

50 위 글의 주제로 가장 적합한 것을 고르시오.

① Psychological effects of individual and group behaviors in organized society
② Knowing the concepts of political election and obedience
③ The contribution of cultural power to stabilize society
④ Defining the political stability in the relations between politics and political structure

[A] Historians have often seen 1898 as a clear departure from the past, the point of American emergence into world politics. Yet the extent of change can be exaggerated. There was not a sudden increase of American might; since industrialization, the U.S. had been a potential great power. Nor did 1898 mark a sudden, permanent shift in popular interest. After a flurry of arguments over imperialism, most Americans resumed, in the early twentieth century, their habitual concentration on home affairs. However, 1898 did mark a change in American commitments. From this point on, both the U.S. and the European powers assumed that America had some interest in world crises.

[B] Many reasons have been given for this change. (A) _____: the American economy had reached maturity and therefore America, like other advanced industrial countries, needed new raw materials and foreign markets. Many historians would deny any connection between American expansion abroad and internal American economic development. This connection, however, was frequently made by turn-of-the-century farmers and businessmen, who saw a relationship between domestic prosperity and foreign markets.

[C] A second explanation for the new departures in foreign policy was the revival and restatement of the traditional idea of America's "manifest destiny" of expansion. However, the change from continental to overseas expansionism needed new justification. One of the most common arguments of late nineteenth-century expansionists was the idea of Anglo-Saxon "racial" superiority. In the 1890's, some claimed superiority over southern African-Americans and new immigrants.

[D] Another less obvious cause of the change in American policy was the actual situation in great power politics. The imperial activities of the major European nations already engaged in a scramble for territory and influence in the world's underdeveloped regions (B) _____ the American appetite for expansion. Having divided up Africa, the European powers were now eyeing the last two remaining areas for expansion: the Near East and the Far East. Each of these were too important to fall to any single power so the leading nations uneasily supported the independence of both, staking out spheres of economic influence. Everywhere the situation was fluid and dangerous. When a country with a potential might of the U.S. showed an interest in world politics, the country was inevitably seen as a menace by some powers and as a potential ally by others. What happened in 1898 reflected all these forces. Against its will and without quite realizing it, the U.S. became involved in great power politics.

51 Which of the following would be the best title for the above passage?

① America's Overseas Expansion
② Forerunner of American Adventures
③ Peace and Empire in the U.S.
④ The Perils of American Imperialism
⑤ The Mature Economy of America

52 Which of the following would best fit in the blank (A) in paragraph [B]?

① The public felt that the U.S. had a special interest in the western hemisphere.
② Most believed that American freedom from foreign dangers was permanent and natural.
③ Some of the doctrines were advocated with great force by a group of able young men.
④ The most obvious suggestion embodies the traditional economic interpretation of imperialism.
⑤ Once colonial expansion was completed, public interest in foreign affairs concentrated on traditional concerns.

53 Which of the following can be inserted into the blank (B) in paragraph [D]?

① whetted
② grieved
③ vindicated
④ dangled
⑤ usurped

54 According to the above passage, which of the following is true?

① Historians have claimed that the year 1898 marks a division in American foreign policy.
② The year 1898 witnessed a sudden change in American people's interest.
③ European nations ceased to support the independence of the countries in the Near East and the Far East.
④ The idea of Anglo-Saxon racial superiority was denied in the 1890's.
⑤ Many historians believed that American overseas expansion was related to its economic crises.

55~57

As Europe confronts a rapidly escalating migration crisis driven by war, persecution and poverty in an arc of strife from West Africa to Afghanistan, even high-level European officials are beginning to admit the obvious. The region's refugee management system is broken. In Western Europe, countries are dealing with the biggest wave of asylum-seekers and refugees since the 1990s. Hundreds of thousands of asylum-seekers are streaming through Europe's _____ borders, decamping from entry nations such as Italy to countries such as Germany, where they are creating new challenges and tensions. Germany is _____ to manage the largest number of asylum-seekers in the industrialized world.

Politicians in the country are, to varying degrees, confronting a public torn between being openhearted and wanting to close off entry for migrants. A good number of the newcomers are fleeing civil war in Syria or attacks by armed groups from South Sudan to Nigeria. But a large portion, officials say, are also arriving for economic reasons, rolling the dice that appeals processes may grant them an opportunity to build an immigrant life in some of the richest nations in the world. This nation of 82 million absorbed more asylum-seekers than any other in the region last year, sheltering 173,000. So many asylum-seekers are coming that Germany has now been forced to find accomodations for them in tiny communities like Tröglitz, nestled in an area that has become the epicenter of an anti-immigrant movement.

Last year, there were significant increases in anti-immigrant attacks, including 35 incidents of arson at refugee centers. "Germany was responsible for creating so many refugees in World War II," said Markus Nierth, the former mayor of Tröglitz. "Now it is upon us to take responsibility for the refugees coming in this new great wave." But even Nierth concedes that the refugee crisis is presenting towns like Tröglitz with something that locals, used to quiet and homogeneous village life, are not accustomed to.

55 What is the most appropriate title of the passage above?

① Persecution and Poverty in Europe
② New Crisis in Coping with Refugee Problems
③ The Rise of Migration Driven by War
④ Varying Reasons to Reject Asylum-Seekers in Europe
⑤ The Epicenter of Anti-Immigrant Movement

56 Which statement can be best inferred from the passage above?

① Before 1990s, most refugees in Europe arrived from West Africa and Afghanistan.
② Some refugees arrived in Germany for economic reasons.
③ There used to live diverse people in Trölitz since World War II.
④ Germany has so far accepted 82 million asylum-seekers.
⑤ World War II caused a huge influx of refugees in Germany.

57 Which pair best fits into the blanks?

① closed — striving
② divisive — opposing
③ stalwart — navigating
④ fluid — observing
⑤ porous — straining

[A] In the type of liberal society that aspires to justice and equal opportunity for all, there are two tasks for the political cultivation of emotion. One is to engender and sustain strong commitment to worthy projects that require effort and sacrifice — such as social redistribution, the full inclusion of previously excluded or marginalized groups, the protection of the environment, foreign aid, and the national defense. Most people tend toward narrowness of sympathy. They can easily become immured in narcissistic projects and forget about the needs of those outside their narrow circle. Emotions directed at the nation and its goals are frequently of great help in getting people to think larger thoughts and recommit themselves to a larger common good.

[B] The other related task for the cultivation of public emotion is to keep at bay forces that lurk in all societies and, ultimately, in all of us: tendencies to protect the fragile self by denigrating and subordinating others. Disgust and envy, the desire to inflict shame on others — all of these are present in all societies and in every individual human life. Unchecked, they can inflict great damage. <u>The damage they do is particularly great when they are relied upon as guides in the process of lawmaking and social formation.</u>

[C] Great democratic leaders, in many times and places, have understood the importance of cultivating appropriate emotions and discouraging those that obstruct society's progress toward its goals. Liberal political philosophy, however, has said little about the topic. John Locke, defending religious toleration, acknowledged a problem of wide-spread animosity between members of different religions in the England of his time; he urged people to take up attitudes of "charity, bounty, and liberality" and recommended that churches advise their members of "the duties of peace and good-will towards all men, as well towards the erroneous as the orthodox."

[D] Locke made no attempt, however, to delve into the psychological origins of intolerance. He thus gave little guidance about the nature of the bad attitudes and how they might be combated. Nor did he recommend any official public steps to shape psychological attitudes. The cultivation of good attitudes is left to individuals and to churches. Given that it was precisely in churches that the bad attitudes festered, Locke leaves his own project in a fragile and uncertain position. In his view, however, the liberal state should confine itself to protecting people's rights to property and other political goods, when and if others assail them. In terms of his own argument, which grounds religious toleration in equal natural rights, this is intervention one step too late.

58 Which of the following is the best title for the above passage?

① The Unexpected Effects of Narrow Sympathy on the Public Goal
② How to Cultivate Political Emotions in the Liberal Society
③ The Role of Political Emotions in Sustaining a Good Liberal Society
④ Narcissism in Human Nature Against the Liberal Society
⑤ The Liberal Political Philosophy and John Locke's Theory of Emotion

59 According to the passage, which of the following is not true?

① Locke admitted that the right emotions contribute to the establishment of a decent society.
② Liberal political philosophers wanted to limit the intervening role of government as strictly as possible.
③ Patriotism sometimes helps people overcome their selfishness and widen their sympathetic feelings to include a large group of people.
④ In Locke's times, religious factions in England were the source of intense conflict, spreading the culture of hostility.
⑤ Locke believed that churches and government should be partners in cultivating citizens' toleration towards others.

60 Which of the following is the best example of *the great damage* in the underlined part The damage they do is particularly great when they are relied upon as guide in the process of lawmaking and social formation in paragraph [B]?

① The government promotes civil religion that encourages altruistic motivation in its citizens.
② The antagonism between two opposing political parties makes it impossible to reach a compromise agreement on a certain issue.
③ The statistical finding that one group of people are less capable of accomplishing a certain task is used as a valid reason for treating these people in a discriminatory way.
④ The disgust that people feel for a group of other people is used as a valid reason for treating these people in a discriminatory way.
⑤ A younger generation inherits the hatred that an older generation had towards one group of people.

61 Which of the following cannot be inferred from the above passage?

① Emotions can support the basic principles of the political culture of an aspiring yet imperfect society.

② The goal of politics in political liberalism of the past is to protect individual freedom rather than to implement justice and equality.

③ Human beings tend to prioritize the preservation of the self over the care for others.

④ The writer of the above passage believes that Locke's theory has limitations that need to be corrected with more emphasis on the role of emotions.

⑤ Cultivation of politically appropriate emotions leads to the suppression of negative emotions, which will ensure equality for all.

상위권대학 편입명문 해커스편입
HackersUT.com

08 문화

01 Choose the one that does not fit in the passage.

During adolescence, people become increasingly involved with their peer group, a group whose members are about the same age and have similar interests. The peer group, along with the family and the school, is one of the three main agents of socialization. However, the peer group is very different from the family and the school. [A] Whereas parents and teachers have more power than children and students, the peer group is made up of equals. [B] Peer groups develop among all age groups, but they are particularly important for adolescents' development. [C] There may be differences across cultures in how adolescents behave. [D] The adolescent peer group teaches its members social skills, the values of friendship among equals, and to be independent from adult authorities. [E] Sometimes this means that a peer group encourages its members to go against authorities and adults. It is important to remember, however, that this kind of rebellious behavior is partly cultural and not universal.

① [A]　　② [B]　　③ [C]　　④ [D]　　⑤ [E]

02~03

The research on African Americans is dominated by inquiries into the lives of the black poor. Contemporary ethnographies and journalistic descriptions have thoroughly described deviance, gangs, drugs, intergender relations and sexuality, stymied aspiration, and family patterns of poor neighborhoods.

Yet the majority of African Americans are _____. A significant part of the black experience, namely that of working and middle — class blacks, remains unexplored. We have little information about what black middle — class neighborhoods look like and how social life is organized within them.

02 What can be inferred from the passage above?

① Most researchers are well-educated.
② Wealthy black people do not live in black neighborhoods.
③ Researchers focus on negative aspects of African Americans because they visited their neighborhoods and witnessed such things.
④ Most black people are well-educated.
⑤ Most researchers work under stereotypical assumptions about black people.

03 Which expression best completes the blank?

① upwardly mobile
② not poor
③ well-educated
④ well-adjusted
⑤ seeking reparations

04~06

In a variety of ways, mass media turned us into the cultural schizophrenics we are today, women who rebel against yet submit to prevailing images about what a desirable, worthwhile woman should be. The mass media has engendered in many of us a kind of (A)_____. We are ambivalent toward femininity on the one hand and feminism on the other. Pulled in opposite directions — old we were equal, yet told we were subordinate; told we could change history but told we were trapped by history.

When I open *Vogue*, for example, I am simultaneously (B)_____. I adore the materialism; I despise the materialism; I want to look beautiful; I think wanting to look beautiful is about the most ridiculous goal you could have. The magazine stokes my desire; the magazine triggers my bile. And this doesn't only happen when I'm reading *Vogue*; it happens all the time. On the one hand, on the other hand — that's what it means to be a woman in America.

04 Which statement is best inferred from the passage above?

① The mass media is to blame for the low status of women.
② The media perpetuates stereotypical ideals of femininity and beauty.
③ Women should pay more attention to the media.
④ Young girls should not be allowed to watch television.
⑤ Women should seek help to control their developing identities.

05 Which expression best fits (A)?

① biased expectation
② cultural identity crisis
③ hidden opportunity
④ tragic innocence
⑤ willful wrongdoing

06 Which expression best fits (B)?

① stuck in history
② curious and passive
③ infuriated and seduced
④ mortified and aghast
⑤ captivated by the past

07~09

[A] Photography is in many ways the mechanical realization of perspective, and its effect on painting was profound. [B] With the development of a camera device that could produce realistic images of the world, the social role of painting changed dramatically. [C] _____ painting had functioned throughout most of Western history as a means to produce an idealized view of the world, specifically through the world view of the Church, it had become increasingly a tool of realism after the invention of perspective. The invention of photography was greeted by such proclamations of its verisimilitude, that some even suggested it had redefined human vision altogether. [D] Many thus felt that the camera could do a "better" job of producing realistic images of the world than a painting, and this allowed painters to think of painting in new ways not always tied to realism or to the ideology of fixed perspective. [E]

07 Where does the following sentence fit best in the passage?

> French writer Emile Zola even wrote at the time, "We cannot claim to have really seen anything before having photographed it."

① [A] ② [B] ③ [C] ④ [D] ⑤ [E]

08 Choose the best title for the above passage.

① Realism and Photography
② The Invention of Perspective
③ Painting and Western History
④ Emile Zola and Photography
⑤ The Development of Human Vision

09 Which of the following is most appropriate for the blank?

① Consequently
② Despite
③ Whereas
④ Therefore
⑤ However

10 ~ 13

In May, when the first monsoon rains sweep across the mountainous province of Yunnan, foragers throng to damp forests to hunt for wild mushrooms. Grandmothers strap wicker baskets to their backs, wielding sticks with which to rake the forest floor and hook wild mushrooms. Joining them at first light are local chefs, village children and their parents, and some migrant workers from far-flung coastal factories.

Thousands of Yunnanese families earn much of their living from the wild-fungi season, which runs until October. The 160,000 tons they collect annually in the poor south-western province generate income of about 10 billion yuan ($1.4 billion). The most valuable ones end up on posh dinner plates abroad, from Italian porcini to meaty matsutake, prized by South Koreans and Japanese. Trains are commandeered to get the mushrooms from basket to banquet in under 30 hours. A rail service launched last year has been dubbed the "high-speed matsutake express." Whatever is not sold fresh is air-dried, frozen or made into a relish.

In the summer, a forager can make 4,000 yuan a month from scouring the hills. In protected forests, where collecting is limited to local families, and so competition is less fierce, a hunter's monthly take can reach 10,000 yuan. Among the most _____ types are "goat belly" mushrooms, which can fetch up to 1,000 yuan per kilo when they appear later in the season.

10 Which of the following is most appropriate for the blank?

① lax
② cumbersome
③ egregious
④ coveted

11 According to the passage, why is the newly launched rail service named "high-speed matsutake express"?

① The rail service specializes in delivering matsutake, a mushroom prized by South Koreans and Japanese.
② The rail service delivers mushrooms from the Yunnan forests to customers in under 30 hours.
③ The rail service is faster than Yunnan's old rail service, which was named after a less sought-after mushroom.
④ The rail service runs only during the wild-fungi season, when matsutake mushrooms are harvested.

12 Which of the following is true about the Yunnan Province?

① It has coastal ports that connect to the overseas market in Europe and Asia.
② The mushroom industry makes it one of the wealthiest provinces in China.
③ It has consistent precipitation throughout the year, providing the perfect climate for mushroom growth.
④ The locals have exclusive access to collect mushrooms in the protected forests.

13 According to the passage, which of the following is NOT true?

① The wild fungi season in Yunnan province runs from May to October.
② Some mushrooms harvested during the wild-fungi season are not sold fresh.
③ Only locals are allowed to collect mushrooms in Yunnan Province.
④ Mushrooms collected in the forest can be shipped on high-speed trains.

14~15

Kabuki is a popular form of Japanese theater. It began several centuries ago and remains an important part of Japanese culture today. For this reason, many westerners who visit Japan make it a point to see at least one kabuki performance. Although western visitors usually report that the kabuki spectacle is dazzling, they are often puzzled by the tradition of the *onnagata*, a _____ actor who specializes in playing _____ roles. At one time, there was talk that the tradition of the *onnagata* should be abandoned and women should be allowed to play women, but that idea has been rejected. The *onnagata* remains a staple of the kabuki performance. In some cases, an *onnagata* can become wildly popular and be treated the way rock musicians or movie stars are treated in the United States.

14 Which is the most appropriate for the blanks?

① female — female
② male — female
③ female — male
④ male — male

15 According to the passage, which is true?

① Kabuki is no longer a Japanese cultural phenomenon.
② Some westerners are revolted by kabuki performances.
③ The tradition of the *onnagata* once became controversial.
④ An *onnagata* is popular in Japan as well as in the United States.

16~17

Origins are never merely personal, but deeply _____, and especially so for Latin Americans such as myself, who feel a strong fellowship with natives from other unfortunate countries of our region. A stubborn history of thwarted dreams has led to a shared sense of purpose and sorrow, hope and resilience, which joins us all emotionally, beyond geographic destiny or national boundaries. To stroll up and down the grocery isles of the mega-Latino supermarket is to reconnect with the people and the lands and to partake, however vicariously, in meals being planned and prepared at that very moment in millions of homes everywhere in the hemisphere.

16 Which of the following is most appropriate for the blank?

① national
② universal
③ collective
④ public

17 Which of the following is true of the passage?

① Partaking in meals with fellow Latin Americans loosens their communal bonds.
② Histories of origins are permanently erased on the passage of migration.
③ Emotional solidarity can be constructed regardless of national or geographic barriers within Latino communities.
④ National belonging can induce a fellowship beyond cultural, ethnic, and racial experiences.

18~19

Everyone has that app. The one that mocks you from your home screen. The app that lures you to the folder where you've tried to hide it. The app you've signed out of and deleted — only to download again the next morning. The app you can't quite quit. For Corey Lewis, it was Instagram, "I found myself constantly scrolling through it for no reason, all the time," the 43-year-old Seattle-based tech marketing consultant said. "Every slight pause in my brain had resulted in a pretty much subconscious reaction to open the app and start thumbing through my feed."

Making things worse were some new and unwelcome feelings. "I actually found myself getting angry and just having weird, not-very-me emotions about posts that had zero bearing on my life," he said. Lately, even as his toddler explored the world around him, Mr Lewis found himself exploring feeds on his phone.

"I found myself jamming Instagram into every single one of those times, no matter how small, which is totally selfish and the opposite of being an involved, open and present parent which I very much hope to be," he said. It was time to do something.

18 The best theme of the passage would be, _____.

① how to be a good parent
② social media addiction
③ the advantage of being connected
④ how to evaluate the app
⑤ the danger of modem technology

19 One example of the underlined to do something would be to _____.

① develop a new app
② upload the latest app
③ purchase a new app
④ spend more time with the app
⑤ sign out of and delete the app

20 Which of the following is not mentioned about Nepal?

> Nepal packs more geographical diversity into fewer square miles than any other country in the world. The people who inhabit this land mirror this diversity. In Nepal, no majority culture exists — all are minorities. One of the most famous of these cultures is the Sherpa. The Sherpa live in the high valleys in the southern shadow of Mt. Everest in the region known as the Khumbu. They are Buddhists, culturally Tibetan, and a numerically insignificant portion of the population. Their villages are situated mostly on rock, ice, and snow at altitudes between ten thousand and thirteen thousand feet, and are connected by narrow mountain footpaths. Sherpas have traditionally operated at a very low level of technology, farming potatoes, turnips, and cauliflower, weaving woolen cloth by hand, and following their yak herds to higher pastures in the summer. Community celebrations follow a pattern set mostly by the passage of the seasons and center around local monasteries.

① Sherpas' religion
② diversity in geography
③ locations of Sherpas' villages
④ prevalence of minority cultures
⑤ a woolen cloth industry by high technology

21~22

Ramadan is the ninth month of the Islamic calendar, and is observed by Muslims worldwide as a month of fasting _____ the first revelation of the Quran to Muhammad according to Islamic belief. This annual observance is regarded as one of the Five Pillars of Islam. The month lasts 29-30 days based on the visual sightings of the crescent moon, according to numerous biographical accounts compiled in the hadiths. The word, Ramadan, means scorching heat or dryness. Fasting is obligatory for adult Muslims, except those who are suffering from an illness, travelling, elderly, pregnant, breastfeeding, diabetic, chronically ill or menstruating. Muslims who live in regions with a natural phenomenon such as the midnight sun or polar night should follow the timetable of Mecca, but the more commonly accepted opinion is that Muslims in those areas should follow the timetable of the closest country to them in which night can be distinguished from day. While fasting from dawn until sunset, Muslims refrain from consuming food, drinking liquids, smoking, and engaging in sexual relations. Muslims are also instructed _____ sinful behavior that may negate the reward of fasting, such as false speech (insulting, cursing, lying, etc.) and fighting except in self-defense.

21 빈칸에 들어가기에 가장 적절한 표현의 쌍은?

① to observe — to reflect on
② to overlook — to leave off
③ to celebrate — to stand for
④ to disregard — to get around
⑤ to commemorate — to refrain from

22 윗글의 내용과 부합하지 않는 것은?

① There is a relation between Ramadan and the visibility of the crescent moon.
② Fasting during Ramadan can be optional under certain conditions.
③ The timetable of Mecca has been respected by Muslims in other countries.
④ Cursing and fighting are prohibited during Ramadan, but in some cases, they are permitted.
⑤ Muslims must not take food or liquids after sunset during Ramadan.

23~25

Asian Americans have been described in the media as "excessively, even provocatively" successful in gaining admission to universities. Asian American shopkeepers have been congratulated, as well as criticized, for their ubiquity and entrepreneurial effectiveness. If Asian Americans can make it, many politicians and pundits ask, why can't African Americans? (A) <u>Such comparisons</u> pit minorities against each other and generate African American resentment toward Asian Americans. The (B) <u>victims</u> are blamed for their plight, rather than racism and an economy that has made many young African American workers superfluous. The celebration of Asian Americans has obscured reality. For example, figures on the high earnings of Asian Americans relative to Caucasians are misleading. Most Asian Americans live in California, Hawaii, and New York — states with higher incomes and higher costs of living than the national average.

23 밑줄 친 (A)는 누구(어디)와 누구(어디) 간의 comparison인가?

① High cost areas vs. other areas
② Asian Americans vs. Caucasians
③ Caucasians vs. African Americans
④ Caucasians vs. minorities
⑤ Asian Americans vs. African Americans

24 밑줄 친 (B)의 <u>victims</u>는 누구를 가리키는가?

① African Americans
② African Americans
③ Minorities
④ Unknown
⑤ Caucasians

25 위 본문의 내용과 일치하지 않는 것을 고르시오.

① In statistics, Asian Americans have high income relative to Caucasians.
② Asian Americans are astonishingly successful in business and academics.
③ Most Asian Americans reside in areas of high costs.
④ All minorities are blamed for their plight even with their success.
⑤ Figures that show Asian American's success do not reflect the reality of them.

26 Choose the most appropriate one for the blank.

> Research itself has fallen prey to this double standard. In studies claiming that men exert power by talking more than women, women's silence is cited as evidence that they have no power. At the same time, other studies claim that men's use of silence and refusing to speak is a show of their power. A theme running through Mirra Komarovsky's classic study *Blue Collar Marriage* is that many of the wives interviewed said they talked more than their husbands ("He's tongue-tied," one woman said of her husband; "My husband has a great habit of not talking," said another). More of the wives want to talk, and have their husbands talk, about problems. In contrast, more husbands withdraw in the face of troubles, emotional stress, or a wife's "demands." Yet there is no question that these husbands are "dominant" in their marriages. _____ itself can be an instrument of power. Komarovsky quotes a mother who says of her husband, "He doesn't say much but he means what he says and the children mind him."

① Prolixity
② Frivolity
③ Solidarity
④ Volubility
⑤ Taciturnity

27~29

Vigorous debates are going on today about whether our world could sustain double its present population (along with its consumption and waste), or even whether our world's economy is sustainable at its present level. Yet those aren't the biggest risks. If, through globalization, everyone living on Earth today were to achieve the standard of living of an average American, the effect on the planet would be some 10 times what it is today, and it would certainly be unsustainable.

We can't prevent people around the world _____ aspiring to match our way of life any more than the exporters of cultures during the first wave of globalization could expect other cultures not to embrace the farming way of life. But since the world couldn't sustain even its present population if all people lived the way that those in the First World do now, we are left with a paradox. Globalization, most analysts feel, is unstoppable. But its consequences may overtax the Earth's ability to support us. That's a paradox that needs resolving.

27 위 글의 제목으로 적절한 것을 고르시오.

① Environmental Crisis Caused by Overpopulation
② Imbalance of Life Standards Between America and Farming Societies
③ Problems of Globalization
④ Increasing Living Costs in the First World
⑤ Solutions for Sustainable Development

28 빈칸에 들어갈 적절한 것을 고르시오.

① from
② as
③ while
④ in
⑤ before

29 다음 중 본문의 내용과 가장 일치하는 것을 고르시오.

① The increased population on the Earth is the most urgent problem today.
② During the first wave of globalization, the exporters of cultures wanted to spread their cultures to the other regions.
③ The current paradox has been caused by the economic gap between countries.
④ Due to the limited resources, the First World will control globalization process.
⑤ As a result of globalization, people around the world hope to raise their life standards to the level of an average American.

30~31

The latest self-help trend is *niksen*, a Dutch word for literally doing nothing or being idle. Practicing *niksen* is as simple as just hanging around looking at your surroundings, listening to music without purpose, or simply sitting in a chair. While mindfulness is about concentrating on the moment, *niksen* is more about taking time to just let your mind _____ rather than focusing on the details of life. *Niksen* has historically been dismissed as laziness; however, as stress levels climb globally and their crushing health impacts, like burnout, are getting more recognition from the medical community, doing nothing is increasingly being considered a positive, stress-fighting tactic. The research is strong when it comes to the benefits of slowing down, from emotional perks, like reducing anxiety, to physical advantages, like _____ the aging process and strengthening the body's ability to fight off a common cold. These potential health effects might be enough to encourage even the most hectic and overburdened among us to practice *niksen*.

30 Which of the following ordered pairs best fits into the blanks?

① behold — generating
② fixate — reversing
③ diverge — engaging
④ wander — curtailing

31 According to the passage, which of the following is not true?

① Traditionally, *niksen* has been viewed favorably.
② *Niksen* and mindfulness involve mental processes.
③ There are physical benefits to practicing *niksen*.
④ The advantages of *niksen* have been scientifically established.

32~33

Although there has been measurable progress in recent years in reading ability at the elementary school level, all progress appears to halt as children enter their teenage years. There is a general decline in reading among teenage and adult Americans. Most alarming, both reading ability and the habit of regular reading have greatly declined among college graduates. These negative trends have more than literary importance. The declines have demonstrable social, economic, cultural, and civic implications. How does one summarize this disturbing story? As Americans, especially younger Americans, read less, they read less well. Because they read less well, they have lower levels of academic achievement. The shameful fact that nearly one-third of American teenagers drop out of school is deeply connected to declining literacy and reading comprehension. With lower levels of reading ability, people do less well in the job market. Poor reading skills correlate heavily with lack of employment, lower wages, and fewer opportunities for advancement. And deficient readers are less likely to become active in civic and cultural life, most notably in volunteerism and voting.

32 What is the best title for the passage?

① The Future of Print Readership
② Reasons Behind Decline in Readership
③ Consequences of Declining Reading Ability
④ Reading Habit and Its Effect on Academic Performance

33 Which is true according to the passage above?

① American adults tend to read more than teenagers.
② Even college graduates tend to read less than before.
③ Once students become teenagers, their reading ability begins to soar.
④ Reading ability among elementary students has been at a standstill in recent years.

34~35

These days most people around the world dress in much the same way: the same jeans, the same sneakers, the same T-shirts. There are just a few places <u>where people hold out against the giant sartorial* blending machine</u>. One of them is rural Peru. In the mountains of the Andes, the Quechua women still wear their brightly coloured dresses and shawls and their little felt hats, pinned at jaunty angles and decorated with their tribal insignia. Except that these are not traditional Quechua clothes at all. The dresses, shawls and hats are in fact of Andalusian origin and were imposed by the Spanish Viceroy Francisco de Toledo in 1572, in the wake of Túpac Amaru's defeat. Authentically traditional Andean female attire consisted of a tunic, secured at the waist by a sash, over which was worn a mantle, which was fastened with a *tupu* pin. What Quechua women wear nowadays is a combination of these earlier garments with the clothes they were ordered to wear by their Spanish masters. The bowler hats popular among Bolivian women came later, when British workers arrived to build that country's first railways. The current fashion among Andean men for American casual clothing is thus merely the latest chapter in a long history of sartorial Westernization.

*sartorial 의복의

34 What does the underlined part imply?

① where people wear cheap clothes
② where people dislike baggy clothes
③ where people refuse mass-produced clothes
④ where people follow a current fashion trend

35 According to the passage, which of the following is not true?

① Today women in rural Peru generally wear jeans and T-shirts.
② These days many Andean men wear American casual clothing.
③ Contemporary Quechua women's attire is not authentically traditional.
④ The Spanish Viceroy forced the Quechua women to wear Andalusian-style dresses.

36~37

The _____ of humanitarianism is nowhere clearer than in the enthusiastic re-invigoration of UN celebrity advocacy — a humanitarian genre with a history of success associated with major Hollywood icons, such as Audrey Hepburn and, more recently, Angelina Jolie. The advocacy of such star figures has always relied upon a(n) _____ performativity of humanitarian discourse, which combines "impersonation," the celebrity's testimony of the suffering of others, with "personification," the infusion of such testimony with the celebrity's own distinct star aura. What differentiates contemporary from past articulations of advocacy, however, is the tendency of the former to privilege a "confessional" communicative structure of celebrity. Unlike the strict formality of earlier forms of celebrity advocacy, confessional performativity rests upon "intimacy at a distance" — a key feature of today's popular culture that refers to our _____ access to the intimate sphere of celebrity lives, rendering this sphere an inherent aspect of their public personae.

36 Which of the following can least be inferred from the passage?

① Celebrities share the suffering of others with a popular audience.
② Celebrity humanitarianism was more formal in the past.
③ Celebrities today use their public personae to confess their guilt.
④ Hollywood icons today infuse their testimony with their star power.

37 Choose the best set of words for blanks.

① spread — opaque — open
② proliferation — abstruse — free
③ conglomeration — decadent — minute
④ commodification — ambivalent — mediated

38~39

In 1950, the percentage of the world's population living in urban areas was 30%. By 2014, the figure had increased to 54% and it is predicted that, by 2050, two-thirds of us will be living in cities. This means that in just 100 years, the number of urban dwellers will have more than doubled. The overwhelming majority of this urbanization is expected to occur in Asia and Africa, as people migrate to find work, housing, and improved access to healthcare and education. London went from a population of one million to eight million in over a century. Some Asian cities have done so in 50 years or less. While many are concerned that this surge in urban populations will lead to housing shortages and increased competition for employment, there are arguably many significant benefits in terms of development. In fact, history has shown that notable developments in a country cannot take place without urbanization. This essay will therefore argue that urbanization in developing countries should _____.

38 빈칸에 들어갈 가장 알맞은 것을 고르시오.

① be gradually limited
② be actively encouraged
③ be coercively implemented
④ be observed with caution

39 위 글의 내용과 맞는 것을 고르시오.

① The percentage of urban dwellers will be less than 60% by 2050.
② Many Asians move to cities as they don't have enough land to cultivate.
③ Some Asian cities have urbanized in half the time that London did.
④ Cities should be developed with care not to break the balance with rural areas.

40~42

With free collaborative encyclopedias available to anyone online, "it's now possible for huge numbers of people to think together in ways we never imagined a few decades ago," says a researcher on collective intelligence. "No single person knows everything that's needed to deal with problems we face as a society, such as health care or climate change, but collectively _____."

Such thoughts underline an important truth about collective intelligence: Crowds are wise only if individual members act responsibly and make their own decisions. A group won't be smart if its members imitate one another, unthinkingly follow fads, or wait for someone to tell them what to do. When a group is intelligent, whether it's made up of ants or attorneys, it relies on its members to do their own part. For those of us who sometimes wonder if it's really worth recycling that extra bottle to lighten our impact on the planet, the fact is that our actions matter, even if we don't see how.

"A honeybee never sees the big picture any more than you or I do," says a bee expert. "None of us knows what society as a whole needs, but we look around and say, oh, they need someone to volunteer at school, or mow the church lawn, or help in a political campaign." If you're looking for a role model in a world of complexity, you could do worse than imitate an ant or a bee.

40 빈칸에 들어갈 가장 적절한 것은?

① there are unseen problems we need to know.
② we know much more than we've tried so far.
③ it may not be easy to work with other people.
④ an ant or a bee can be smarter than a human.
⑤ individual members need to work independently.

41 밑줄 친 recycling에 대한 예를 들은 이유는?

① Because individual actions affect the whole
② Because intelligence is only a simple matter
③ Because humans don't know the actual truth
④ Because bees and ants are important for recycling
⑤ Because humans are less perfect than bees and ants

42 윗글의 내용과 부합하지 않는 것은?

① The author mentions online collaborative encyclopedias as a case of collective intelligence.
② Collective intelligence applies not only to humans, but also to insects like ants or bees.
③ Individual members do not know what society as a whole needs, but see each social activity.
④ Individual members must be responsible and creative to make collective intelligence intelligent.
⑤ The author claims that although humans need a role model of society, we should not imitate an ant or a bee.

43~44

What we now think of as "time" is largely an invention of the industrial age. Factories and the economic system that grew around them in the 19th century depended on disconnecting workers' sense of time from the natural rhythms of day changing into night and season into season. Instead of waking more or less when the sun rose and dropping off not long after it set, sleeping more in the lean winter months and less in harvest times, and punctuating their days with naps, workers had to learn to rise consistently to the sound of a factory bell and organize their downtime accordingly. Schedules for travel, school, and commerce followed these industrial patterns of uniform clock time: a time newly homogeneous across season, region, or profession. When employers demanded too much of the workers' time, depriving them of adequate sleep, the workers advocated for sleep that was *more* standardized, rather than less. What they pictured was a time that was reserved exclusively for sleep, a time both demanded by industry and made impossible by it. The eight-hour ideal as we know it is largely a result of this push and pull between management and labor.

43 Which of the following does the passage mainly discuss?

① How research on sleep contributed to economic development
② How modern industry changed the human experience of time
③ How technology affected the nightlife of people in urban areas
④ How the fight between management and labor led to social unrest

44 According to the passage, which of the following is true?

① The industrial workers accepted uniform clock time.
② Standardized, universal time spread from schools to industry.
③ Throughout the 19th century, workers normally slept for eight hours.
④ Before the industrial age, the bedtime for workers was quite regular.

45~46

The naming of places is both a necessary means of recognition and communication but also a fundamental means of laying claim to territory. The process of naming is more than a value-free description of a point in space, _____ a means of expressing and fostering senses of place and linking these with selected aspects of the past. Using the example of rural Northern Ireland, Reid examines the relationships between identity and memory through the naming of local places. She acknowledges that naming can be part of broader processes of inclusion and exclusion when linked to particular historical narratives in a divided or unagreed society. While local names may be indicative of diverse cultural influences, they can also be subject to interpretations that reject pluralist notions of consociation in favour of singular ethnic figuring of space and place. Clearly, this does occur in Northern Ireland where the material marking of placenames in the actual landscape can be part of a broader claim to ethnic territoriality. But in her analysis of the Townlands Campaign in Northern Ireland, Reid shows, too, that the marking of local place remains of such fundamental importance that the process and its associated practices may themselves encourage divided peoples to join together in order to protect and perpetuate their named localities.

45. 윗글의 내용과 가장 가까운 것은?

① Placenames are endowed with various meanings that are self-evident.
② The naming of a place cannot be understood as a deliberate act of collective commemoration.
③ The process of naming a place is associated with how the past is identified and constructed.
④ The named locality of Northern Ireland has withered as the call for ethnic singularity mounts.
⑤ The consideration of singular ethnic figuring of place is more important than that of diverse cultural influences.

46. 빈칸에 들어갈 가장 적절한 것은?

① is
② being
③ which
④ where
⑤ of which

47~48

As more and more literature continues to emerge from America's ongoing Global War on Terror, it has become apparent that the cultural legacy of the Vietnam War has yet to wane within US military circles. If anything, the parallels between the recent wars in Iraq and Afghanistan and the war in Vietnam have helped ensure Vietnam's continued relevance, as soldiers in the Global War on Terror have looked to the culture of the Vietnam War in the hope that it would guide them in the struggle to define their own war. Plagued by questions regarding exit strategies and the legitimacy of Weapons of Mass Destruction as a *casus belli**, many soldiers in the Global War on Terror have seen a natural connection between the open-ended conflicts in Iraq and Afghanistan and their fathers' war in Vietnam. With many of those same soldiers having been brought up viewing combat through the lens of the many Vietnam-themed movies released in the mid to late 1980s, the culture of the Vietnam War has not merely been preserved into the twenty-first century — for some, it has become the _____ that soldiers look to in order to frame their own expectations about combat.

*casus belli 선전포고의 원인

47. Which is the most appropriate for the blank?

① default cultural blueprint
② after-war stress manual
③ unique nostalgic momentum
④ rigid military codebook

48. According to the passage, which is true?

① Soldiers of modern era are very confident of the cause of wars they fight.
② Americans try to forget their memory of tragic experience in Vietnam.
③ The volume of cultural products of Vietnam War themes tends to decline.
④ Many young soldiers have been exposed to the motion pictures on Vietnam War.

49~51

The present craze for cute things is motivated in part by the urge to escape from our threatening world into a garden of innocence in which childlike qualities arouse protective feelings, and bestow contentment and solace. "Cute cues" include behaviors that appear helpless, charming, and yielding, and anatomical features such as outsize heads, saucer-like eyes, and clumsy motions. Perhaps our response to cute cues evolved to motivate us to give our offspring the extensive care and nurturing that they need to prosper. But if cuteness were merely about the charming, innocent, and unthreatening; or if our attraction to it were motivated just by protective instincts, it would not be so ubiquitous. Those qualities speak only of what we might call the "sweet" end of a whole spectrum of cuteness. As we move toward the "uncanny" end of the spectrum, sweet qualities get distorted into something darker, more indeterminate, and more wounded: something like Balloon Dog, which seems at once powerful, made of stainless steel, and powerless, hollow, and lacking a face. The non-definability that pervades cute things, the erosion of borders between what used to be seen as distinct realms, such as childhood and adulthood, is also reflected in the blurred gender of many cute objects. It is reflected, too, in their frequent blending of human and nonhuman forms, as in Hello Kitty.

49 What is the purpose of this passage?

① To characterize and explain cuteness
② To promote cute and charming objects
③ To outline the production of cute objects
④ To argue for a preferred style of cuteness

50 According to the passage, which of the following is not true?

① The blurring of genders is an example of the vagueness of cuteness.
② Indeterminate and wounded characteristics pervade sweet objects.
③ The urge to escape has partly motivated the present trend for cuteness.
④ Our attraction to "uncanny" objects is due to more than evolution.

51 According to the passage, which of the following is not a cute cue?

① graceful movements
② oversize, round eyes
③ helpless appearance
④ compliance

52~54

As globalization in its current form expands, so too does the inequality that accompanies it. Rising inequality can result in an increase in racial bias which advances xenophobic and isolationist tendencies. During the days of British and French Imperialism, for example, racial bias was ingrained within culture itself. However, an element of this is still seen in today's period of globalization, with the increasing "xenophobic culture of Globalization" seen in some parts of the world.

With expanding globalization, the demand for more skilled workers, especially in North America, has led to increased efforts to attract foreign workers — but filtered, based on skill. On the other hand, it is harder to immigrate to the wealthier nations unless these citizens are part of the chosen few: highly-skilled computer wizards, doctors and nurses trained at Third World expense. Global migration management strategy saps the Third World and the former Soviet bloc of its economic lifeblood, by creaming off their most skilled and educated workforces. From the perspective of globalization the skills pool, not the genes pool, is key.

52 What is the main topic of this passage?

① the advantages and disadvantages of globalization
② how globalization helps to solve problems related to economic inequality and social injustice
③ new kinds of inequality resulting from globalization
④ the tightening of immigration policies of wealthy nations as a result of globalization

53 Which phrase is closest in meaning to the phrase "xenophobic culture of Globalization" in this passage?

① isolation of foreign culture by globalization
② excessive fear of foreign people within globalized societies
③ cultures which resist globalization
④ imported cultures through globalization

54 According to this passage, which person would most likely be allowed to enter the United States nowadays?

① a Russian person highly trained in any field
② a highly trained computer expert from any country
③ a star baseball player from Cuba
④ a person trying to escape a harsh authoritarian regime

55~57

Clothing is a general term for a variety of coverings designed to protect or adorn the human body. It may be made of woven materials or man-made fiber of animal skin or fur or even a type of paper known as "bark-cloth." To be specific, clothing is distinguished from fashion, or vogue, which signifies the prevailing mode or customary style of clothing. In present concept, clothing connotes the durable and _____ ; fashion the _____ and transitory. For example, a mother buys winter clothing for her children, and it is clear that in this context she would regard style as a secondary consideration. Her primary concern centers, rather than on fashion, on such matters as warmth of fabric, wearing qualities, ease of upkeep, and, most probably, a reasonable cost, all of which are attributes (A) relevant to the purchase of winter clothing.

On the other hand, fashion reflects the events, surroundings, and customs of its (B) era. It is influenced by laws, arts, culture, and personalities. For example, laws and regulations have had their effect on fashion as seen in early New England laws that restricted women from wearing more costly clothes than their husbands could afford. Events in the arts have influenced the effect on fashion as (C) exemplified in the tremendously successful musical comedy "My Fair Lady," based on Shaw's *Pygmalion*, which inspired feminine adaptations of 1914-1918 costumes. Culture has powerfully conditioned fashion. The splendor of the Renaissance brought the magnificence of the merchant princes in their silks, satins, velvets, and jewels. In the fabulous, extravagant courts of Louis XIV of France, headdresses soared and skirts ballooned. Personalities have had great impact on fashion ever since the days when sumptuary laws (D) assimilating nobles, farmers, and tradesmen were eliminated and when it became possible for all classes of society to dress more or less alike.

55 Which is the most appropriate for the blanks?

① substantial — novel
② permanent — revolutionary
③ imaginary — reasonable
④ enforced — voluntary

56 Which of the underlined words is not appropriate?

① (A)   ② (B)   ③ (C)   ④ (D)

57 According to the passage, which is not true?

① There were laws which restricted what to wear.
② Mothers usually pick practical clothing for their children.
③ Clothing can be made with natural and artificial materials.
④ The Renaissance emphasized the human body and simple clothing.

58~60

For six decades or more, America's political history has been driven by cultural warfare. Culture War 1.0 began in the 1950s as religious enthusiasts sought to win hearts and souls for Christ in a society that was rapidly liberalizing and secularizing. This first culture war was mostly fought over issues of _____, such as whether creationism was a viable alternative to the theory of biological evolution and whether limits should be placed on institutionalizing Christian values in the public sphere. In Culture War 2.0, the supernatural, metaphysics, and even religion have become irrelevant. Culture War 2.0 rotates around, among others, the new rules of engagement. They relate to how we deal with our disagreements. In Culture War 1.0, if an evolutionary biologist gave a public lecture about the age of the Earth based on geological dating techniques, creationists would issue a response, insist that such dating techniques are unreliable, challenge him to a debate, and ask pointed questions during the Q&A session. In Culture War 2.0, disagreements with a speaker are sometimes met with attempts at de-platforming: rowdy campaigns for the invitation to be canceled before the speech can be delivered. If this is unsuccessful, critics may resort to disrupting the speaker by screaming and shouting, engaging noise makers, or ripping out the speaker wires. The goal is not to counter the speaker with better arguments or even to insist on an alternative view, but to prevent the speaker from airing her views at all.

58 Which of the following is the best title for the passage?

① Creationism in Culture Wars
② America's Changing Culture Wars
③ Enlightenment and Cultural Revolution
④ Conservativism vs Liberalism in the Modern World

59 Which of the following best fits into the blank?

① unity and diversity
② technology and evolution
③ religious faith and values
④ traditions and innovations

60 According to the passage, Culture War 2.0, as compared with Culture War 1.0, is _____.

① more violent and intolerant
② more sophisticated and tricky
③ less friendly but more tolerant
④ less fierce and more accommodating

[61~63]

The school system is viewed by Bourdieu as an institution for the reproduction of legitimate culture through the hidden linkages between scholastic aptitude and cultural heritage. He believes that, despite ideologies of equal opportunity and meritocracy, few educational systems are called upon by the dominant classes to do anything other than reproduce the legitimate culture as it stands and produce agents capable of manipulating it legitimately.

Bourdieu has argued that it is the culture of the dominant group, which is embodied in schools. Educational differences are thus frequently misrecognized as resulting from individual giftedness, rather than from class-based differences, ignoring the fact that the abilities measured by scholastic criteria often stem not from natural "gifts" but from "the greater or lesser affinity between class cultural habits and the demands of the educational system or the criteria which define success within it."

The notion of cultural capital was proposed by Bourdieu in the early 1960s to describe familiarity with bourgeois culture, the unequal distribution of which helps to conserve social hierarchy under the cloak of individual talent and academic meritocracy. This notion includes such things as acquired knowledge (educational or otherwise), cultural codes, manner of speaking and so forth, which are embodied as a kind of "habitus" in the individual and are also objectified in cultural goods.

61 According to the passage, which of the following is not true?

① Working-class students may feel like outsiders in the middle-class habitus of higher education.
② Individuals tend to possess innate intelligence based on their social class.
③ Educational institutions ensure the profitability of the cultural capital of the dominant.
④ The dominant culture, by making itself recognized as universal, legitimizes the interests of the dominant group.

62 Which of the following statements can be inferred from the passage?

① According to Bourdieu, every culture is equally valued and equally legitimate.
② According to Bourdieu, schooling produces certain entrenched ways of recognizing that foster existing class stratification.
③ According to Bourdieu, individuals' efficacy is most strongly influenced by mastery experiences throughout all phases of their lives.
④ According to Bourdieu, cultural reproduction is a trivial mechanism through which socioeconomic polarization takes place.

63 What would be the best title of the passage above?

① The Importance of Individual Giftedness in Schooling
② The Significance of Students' Achievement in Schooling
③ The Social Responsibility of Dominant Culture in Schooling
④ The Reproduction of Inequalities in Schooling

64~66

There are certain things that, so far, social media seem to do very well. The most remarkable one is coordination. Coordinating large numbers of people to do exactly the same thing at the same time is notoriously difficult. So long as the activity is relatively simple — say, show up and protest the government — the new social media drastically reduce the costs of coordination. But if social media are good at coordinating simple events, so far they have failed at building political parties on a grander scale. In Egypt and Tunisia, the tech savvy young people who facilitated antigovernment protests have already begun to fall behind in the race to political organization. Ahead of them are Islamic democrats, political groups that have years of experience in attracting, organizing and mobilizing followers.

Why should Facebook and Twitter be good for social parties but not political parties? _____, and of course it is possible that, as technology changes and user culture evolves, more complex political organizations may come out of social media. For now, however, the answer seems to lie in the fact that they lack the kinds of contacts needed to create extended political cohesion. To show up at a social gathering, I don't need to have any close or repeated bonds with the other people. All of us can show up, enjoy ourselves and go our separate ways. The key is that our objective is simple rather than complex. Political organization, by contrast, is very complicated indeed. A successful political organization must generate beliefs about the way the world works and how it should be. It must reflect a shared ethos or morality. Above all, it must produce some sense of community.

64 Which of the following best fits in the blank?

① It's too soon to know definitively
② It's too difficult to know definitively
③ It's too late to know definitively
④ It's too early not to know definitively

65 According to the passage, which of the following is not mentioned or inferred from the passage?

① In Egypt young people who are very good at social media organized anti-government protests but failed at building political parties on a grander scale.
② More complex political organizations may come out of technological changes from social media.
③ As long as political parties seek to coordinate large numbers of people to do exactly the same thing at the same time, they should depend on social media.
④ Social media seem to do very well at such relative simple activities as showing up and protesting the government.

66 Which of the following would be the most suitable title for the passage?

① Social Media's Limitations
② Social Media vs. Political Parties
③ Advantages of Social Media
④ Ethos of Social Media

67~69

[A] "Soul Surfers" have even developed their own distinct vocabulary to discuss surfing, using words like "stoked," a verb that describes the combination of excitement and apprehension that come from surfing a giant wave. [B] Many early Californian and Australian surfers also adopted Hawaiian surf philosophies and regarded surfing as a way to connect to nature. [C] The surfing culture of the 1960s appealed mainly to teens and young adults, and it stressed romance and lack of obligations by mixing the relaxation of socializing on sunny beaches with the excitement of launching toward the shore atop a wave. [D] These practices, when combined with the time-consuming demand of searching for ideal waves, led to the "soul surfer" lifestyle, in which dedicated surfers focus their lives on discovering spiritual balance through surfing. Oftentimes, "soul surfers" will _____ school or work-related responsibilities to pursue ideal surfing conditions, leading some to consider surfers as being mainly unmotivated in school or work.

67 Which one is the right order?

① [C] — [B] — [D] — [A]
② [A] — [D] — [C] — [B]
③ [A] — [B] — [D] — [C]
④ [C] — [A] — [B] — [D]

68 Choose the best topic.

① Surfers studying at school
② Romance in socializing
③ 1960s surfing culture
④ Californian vs. Australian surfers

69 Which one is not appropriate for the blank?

① forgo
② pass up on
③ give up on
④ take on

70~72

Why would people make an adventurous journey across thousands of kilometers of ocean? Why did the pioneers cross the Great Plains, the Rocky Mountains, or the Mojave Desert to reach the American West? Why do people continue to migrate by the millions today? The hazards that many migrants have faced are a measure of the strong lure of new locations and the desperate conditions in their former homelands. A permanent move to a new location disrupts traditional cultural ties and economic patterns in one region. At the same time, when people migrate, they take with them to their new home their language, religion, ethnicity, and other cultural traits. Most people migrate for economic reasons. People think about emigrating from places that have few job opportunities, and they immigrate to places where jobs seem to be available. Because of economic restructuring, job prospects often vary from one country to another and within regions of the same country. The United States and Canada have been especially promising _____ for economic migrants. Cultural factor can be especially a compelling push factor that forces people to move out of their present location.

70. 위 글의 제목으로 가장 적절한 것을 고르시오.

① Reasons for Migrating
② How to Overcome Hazards of Immigration
③ Culture Factors Forcing People to Emigrate
④ The Increasing Number of Immigrants in the U.S.
⑤ The Effects of Immigration on the Traditional Culture

71. 밑줄 친 adventurous와 의미상 가장 유사한 것을 고르시오.

① perilous
② hilarious
③ spontaneous
④ parsimonious
⑤ monetary

72. 문맥상 빈칸에 들어갈 가장 적절한 것을 고르시오.

① stopovers
② storages
③ destinations
④ refuge
⑤ starting points

The fashion industry is a product of the modern age. Prior to the mid-19th century, virtually all clothing was handmade for individuals, either as home production or on order from dressmakers and tailors. [A] By the beginning of the 20th century — with the rise of new technologies such as the sewing machine, the rise of global capitalism and the development of the factory system of production, and the proliferation of retail outlets such as department stores — clothing had increasingly come to be mass-produced in standard sizes and sold at fixed prices. [B] Although the fashion industry developed first in Europe and America, today it is an international and highly globalized industry, with clothing often designed in one country, manufactured in another, and sold in a third. [C] The fashion industry has long been one of the largest employers in the United States, and it remains so in the 21st century. However, employment declined considerably as production increasingly moved overseas, especially to China. Because data on the fashion industry typically are reported for national economies and expressed in terms of the industry's many separate sectors, aggregate figures for world production of textiles and clothing are difficult to obtain. However, by any measure, the industry inarguably accounts for a significant share of world economic output. [D] The fashion industry consists of four levels: the production of raw materials, principally fibres and textiles but also leather and fur; the production of fashion goods by designers, manufacturers, contractors, and others; retail sales; and various forms of advertising and promotion. These levels consist of many separate but interdependent sectors, all of which are devoted to the goal of satisfying consumer demand for apparel under conditions that enable participants in the industry to operate at a profit.

73 Which of the following is not one of the factors that has contributed to the development of mass production in fashion industry?

① introduction of sewing machines
② expansion of outsourcing practices
③ expansion of retail outlets
④ rise of global capitalism

74 Which of the following is not identified as one of the levels of fashion industry?

① advertising and promotion
② employment and education
③ production of raw materials
④ production of fashion goods

75 Where should the following sentence be added?

> For example, an American fashion company might source fabric in China and have the clothes manufactured in Vietnam, finished in Italy, and shipped to a warehouse in the United States for distribution to retail outlets internationally.

① [A]   ② [B]   ③ [C]   ④ [D]

For maps, rules of inclusion also determine strategies and formal devices used to symbolize the aspects of phenomena chosen for representation. Of particular interest here are the representational strategies used to legitimate dominant interests. The primary legitimating strategy is based on the hierarchization of space, for space is not perceived isotropically, i.e., as everywhere having equal value. Because space is perceived anisotropically, the placement of visual elements becomes a way of imparting privilege. Positioning to privilege may be effected in various ways. Privileging through *centering* has not escaped notice in the cartographic literature. Thus, Mercator's 15th century mapping system, still a standard, placed the designer's homeland, Germany, at the center of the map — a Eurocentric convention quickly adopted across the continent.

Privileging can also be effected through placement on the *top*, as seen in the hierarchical representation of organizational structure in charts, where higher echelons of personnel are located above the rest. According to Mumby (1986), "the concept of hierarchy has been reified to the point where the structuring of organizations is perceived as 'naturally' occurring from the top down." In fact, readers from the Northern hemisphere may be surprised to learn that Australian children often place their continent on the top of the map.

Finally, privileging is also effected in a series through *ordering*, where the first elements gain distinction. Wood (1987) writes, for example, of the effect of map ordering in Goode's *World Atlas*, "when nation-states are given the ontogenetically privileged position of coming first — in front of . . . maps of the physical environment." Wood appraises the consequences of this privileging in terms of *naturalization*: "It imposes the impression that these nation-states have the same developmental status as landforms and climate . . . and hence are not implicatable in any different way from the rains and the winds in the fate of man" [sic].

adapted from an article by Ben F. and Marthalee S. Barton

76 Based on the examples given in the article, which is the best definition of the word "map"?

① a drawing or drawings of geographical space in two dimensions
② any type of symbolic visual representation of a concept or idea
③ a drawing that reflects the designer's perception of natural relationships among items
④ a Eurocentric convention that reinforces a hegemonic value system
⑤ a traditional representation showing the political borders of nation-states

77 Which example does not demonstrate the main point of this passage?

① ancient Chinese maps placed China, not Europe, at the center of the world
② neighborhood maps near subway stations in Korea place the direction readers are facing at the top
③ seating charts at fundraising events place the table with the guest of honor at the top
④ a dining guide to Europe, published in Paris, lists restaurants in France in Chapter 1
⑤ a company telephone directory puts the name of the company president at the top

78 Which statement can be supported by the passage?

① It is natural that some people hold more power in organizations than other people do.
② It is impossible for people making maps to legitimize dominant interests.
③ The idea of what is natural or not natural can be shown by both isotropic and anisotropic elements.
④ There is a hierarchy in map elements, with ordering privileged over centrality.
⑤ It is unavoidable for the visual elements in maps to privilege some items over others.

79~81

In Jamaica, most British and American people encounter tourism as consumers — of culture, good weather, beautiful buildings, or any of the other things that people travel in search of. During my year as a student living in Jamaica and traveling around the Caribbean, I have seen tourism through the eyes of people who live with it, and witnessed the corrupting effects of tourism on the cultures that depend on it for economic survival.

When I tell people that I was living in Jamaica on scholarship, they roll their eyes and marvel at my luck, because they have seen the ads for Jamaican tourism, showing empty beaches, clear blue skies, and the occasional smiling black face. I don't know how to respond, because the Jamaica that I lived in, and that only some tourists are privileged to see, is a poor, crowded, violent place where most people, from police officers to ganja (marijuana) peddlers, resent tourists for their leisure and their money — money that goes almost exclusively to a small elite of hotel owners and government officials.

Among the rest, who must bow, beg, sell, or steal to capture the visitors' money, tourism creates pickpockets and impostors.

It might be different if the tourists weren't so _____ in their appearance. Many things — dress, language, looks — can distinguish tourists from the native population. In Jamaica, it is skin color that sets the tourists apart, as 95 percent of Jamaicans are black, and most tourists are white. A white stranger in the streets of Jamaica is assumed to be a tourist, and therefore interested in buying trinkets, souvenirs, or drugs.

79 Which is the most appropriate for the blank?

① upbeat
② gentle
③ obvious
④ gloomy

80 Which is the tone of the passage?

① excited
② optimistic
③ analytic
④ aesthetic

81 Which is the topic of the passage?

① The reality of tourism in Jamaica
② The luring of tourists to Jamaican tourist places
③ Racism and social division in Jamaica
④ Studying as a scholarship student in Jamaica

82
~
85

The format of the Sun Dance, a traditional Native American ceremonial dance, has always varied from community to community. _____, there are certain features of the dance that many tribes share. Often, the dance must be initiated by a sponsor, someone who takes a vow in the hope of being relieved of a worry, or being blessed in the coming year. [A] It is almost always performed near the time of summer solstice. Most Sun Dances begin with the erection of a circular lodge around a solemnly chosen and cut central pole. During the next three or four days, periods of dancing, accompanied by singing and drumming, are interspersed with periods of rest and meditation. Dancers do not eat or drink during the entire period of the dance, although some do chew on bear root to keep their mouths moist. Toward the end of the dance, participants experience visions and receive blessings. [B]

Early Europeans were repulsed by some tribes' practice of self-mortification in the ceremony. [C] Dancing and straining against the ropes, they eventually tore loose from the skewers. Through this ritual, participants literally suffer on behalf of their community and call upon the Creator to pity and assist them in the fulfillment of their vows. [D] This aspect of the ritual was the main reason federal officials prohibited it between the late 1870s and 1935. Despite the ban, however, many tribes continued to hold the Sun Dance surreptitiously in remote areas of their reservations or to enact it without its objectionable features.

82 Which of the following is most suitable for the blank?

① Therefore
② Hence
③ Nevertheless
④ Meanwhile

83 Which is the most appropriate place for the sentence below?

> Male dancers had their breasts or backs skewered and tied to a central lodge pole.

① [A]　　　② [B]　　　③ [C]　　　④ [D]

84 According to the passage, which of the following is not true?

① Dancers are allowed to bite a certain plant root to moisten their mouths.
② An individual can initiate the Sun Dance as a sponsor.
③ Some aspects of the Sun Dance are common to many tribes.
④ The Sun Dance was not performed during the prohibition period.

85 According to the passage, the main objective of the self-mortification is to _____.

① test the participants' limits to endure physical sufferings
② show the participants' courage and determination to help the community
③ induce the Creator to help the participants fulfill their vows
④ experience visions of the tribal future and participants' pity toward the Creator

09 교육

01 주어진 글 다음에 이어질 순서로 가장 적절한 것을 고르시오.

> One of the key issues in any approach to initial teacher preparation is the balance to be struck between training and education.
> [A] This change in nomenclature seeks to avoid the negative associations "trainee" and "training" may be said to imply, with their connotations of the transmission of a pre-determined set of behaviors to novices who are largely seen as blank slate.
> [B] For example, novice teachers on the British PGCE program, which confers qualified teacher status and allows graduates to work in the state-school system, are more commonly referred to today as "student teachers" than as "trainee teachers."
> [C] That said, the former term has fallen out of favor somewhat over the past few years, at least among teacher educators.

① [B] — [A] — [C]　　② [C] — [B] — [A]
③ [B] — [C] — [A]　　④ [C] — [A] — [B]

02~03

American colleges in late 19th century sought to instill discipline, morality, and a curriculum heavy on mathematics and the classics; in church schools theology, along with ethics and rhetoric. History, modern languages and literature, and some science courses were tolerated, although laboratory work was usually limited to a professor's demonstration in class. The college teacher was apt to be a young man seeking temporary refuge, or a broken-down preacher seeking safe harbor. In 1871 one writer called the typical professor "nondescript, ready to teach surveying and Latin eloquence, and thankful if his salary is not docked to whitewash the college fence."

02 Which of the following is most appropriate for the underlined nondescript?

① orator
② chameleon
③ handyman
④ anonymity

03 Which of the following is true of the passage?

① In late 19th century, American colleges gave priority to modern languages and literature over classics.
② With highly equipped laboratory, students were encouraged to carry out experiments on their own.
③ Most of college teachers were prestige elderly men who majored in theology.
④ Professors didn't seem to hold themselves aloof from the worldly reward.

04 Which of the following best continues the paragraph?

> Post-secondary institutions serve students beyond the age of compulsory attendance. In the United States, post-secondary students are an extremely diverse lot of traditional — and nontraditional-age students whose goals range from very specific occupational training to more general aims such as acquiring a liberal education to highly specialized preparation for further professional study. The role and extent of bilingual approaches observed for each such student group vary considerably. Some bilingual programs for adults in the United States have been developed to provide short-term, highly focused vocational training for special populations, such as refugees who qualify for special government support. Where there are large numbers of English learners who share the same home language, native language instruction may be included as a part of relatively short programs aimed at helping participants find employment as soon as possible.

① However, the institutions are indeed bilingual in that full degree programs are offered using both English and Spanish.

② These bilingual programs including native language instruction tend to be found in areas with the largest settlement of recent immigrants.

③ A recent study indicates that most of English learners see their school as the one place of regular access to English language development.

④ Post-secondary students enrolled in degree programs may have access to academic instruction in a second language.

05~07

When Americans rediscovered teacher incompetency in the late 1970s, the media joined academic journals in tracing the problem back to teacher education. Prospective teachers were among the poorest students in colleges and universities, Americans heard repeatedly. At a time when many citizens were upset with declining scores on college entrance examinations, they learned the test scores of future teachers had fallen even faster than the scores of other students. Ranked against other undergraduates by their Scholastic Aptitude Test(SAT) and American College Testing(ACT) program scores, teacher education students consistently came in near the bottom, ahead only of students majoring in such fields as agriculture and home economics. Professors of education bore much of the blame, the media charged, _____ they had lowered their standards during the 1970s in response to declining enrollment in teacher education programs.

05 Which best fits into the blank?

① and
② for
③ whereas
④ although

06 What is the passage mainly about?

① negative impact of the mass media
② decline in teacher education program enrollment
③ declining scores on college entrance examinations
④ decline in prospective teachers' academic abilities

07 Which is true according to the passage?

① People thought that teachers were overqualified.
② The media urged professors of education to lower their standards.
③ Prospective teachers often had lower SAT scores than students in other majors.
④ Professors of education expected very high academic abilities from their students.

08~10

The idea of neurodiversity is really a paradigm shift in how we think about kids in special education. Instead of regarding these students as suffering from deficit, disease, or dysfunction, neurodiversity suggests that we speak about their strengths. Neruodiversity urges us to discuss brain diversity using the same kind of discourse that we employ when we talk about biodiversity and cultural diversity. We don't pathologize a colla lily by saying that it has a "petal deficit disorder." We simply appreciate its unique beauty. We don't diagnose individuals who have skin color that is different from our own as suffering from "pigmentation dysfunction." That would be racist. Similarly, we ought not to pathologize children who have different kinds of brains and different ways of thinking and learning.

08 What would be the best title for the above passage?

① Neurodiversity and a paradigm shift
② Neurodiversity and its relationship with biodiversity.
③ Neurodiversity as a way to diagnose personal characteristics
④ Neurodiversity to individualize children's strengths and value.
⑤ Neurodiversity as a source for a clinical treatment.

09 Which can best replace the underlined pathologize?

① diagnose
② sympathize
③ assimilate
④ evaluate
⑤ criticize

10 What does the underlined sentence mean best?

① The common principle that we use for biodiversity and cultural diversity should be applied to the area of brain diversity.
② Discourse analysis is a helpful tool that can be used in common in all those three areas.
③ Neurodiversity brings our attention back to the areas of biodiversity and cultural diversity.
④ Biodiversity and cultural diversity are more advanced areas of knowledge.
⑤ Biodiversity and cultural diversity are used as models for a psychological treatment.

11 Choose the most appropriate one for the blank.

> The growing importance of education contributed to the emergence of a separate youth culture. The idea of adolescence as a distinct period in the life of an individual was for the most part new to the twentieth century. In some measure it was a result of the influence of Freudian psychology. But it was a result, too, of society's recognition that a more extended period of training and preparation was necessary before a young person was ready to move into the workplace. Schools and colleges provided adolescents with a setting in which they could develop their own social patterns, their own hobbies, their own interests and activities. An increasing number of students saw school as a place not just for academic training but for organized athletics, other extracurricular activities, clubs, and fraternities and sororities — that is, as an institution that _____.

① led young people to look for low-paying jobs
② specialized in teaching technical skills demanded in the modern economy
③ helped many men and women make more money to support their families
④ offered both instruction and services in traditional disciplines
⑤ allowed them to define themselves more in terms of their peer group

12~13

The current academic system has fudged the distinctions between training and education. Administrations of most colleges and universities have responded to the economic and cultural uncertainties provoked by budget constraints and (A) a volatile job market by constructing their institutions on the model of the modern corporation. Consequently, many have thrust training to the fore and called it education. Lacking a unified national culture into which to socialize students and in any case lacking (B) an educational philosophy capable of steering an independent course, the academic system as a whole is caught in (C) a market logic that demands students be job-ready upon graduation. Under these imperatives colleges and universities are unable to implement an educational program that prepares students for (D) the competitive job market. _____, academic leaders chant the mantra of "excellence," which means that all of the parts of the university "perform" and are judged according to how well they deliver knowledge and qualified labor to the corporate economy and how well the administration fulfills the recruitment and funding goals needed to maintain the institution.

12 Which is least consistent with the context?

① (A)　　② (B)　　③ (C)　　④ (D)

13 Which best fits in the blank?

① Instead
② Proactively
③ Fortunately
④ Nevertheless

14~15

In higher education, we tend to focus on the needs of the human teacher — what kind of skills the human teacher needs to have, how many human teachers we need to teach the most students, what constitutes good practice for human teachers. And when we think of technology-based teaching, we tend to react in a(n) (A) _____ way. We either preach against technology, because we see online education and the various forms of artificial intelligence it might involve as threatening to the value of human contact between human teacher and human student, or we embrace the algorithm because we see technology as enabling us to be social in different ways. One way or another, when we think about what it means to teach in higher education, we tend to try very hard to keep the social and the technical separate from each other. (B) _____, the challenge over the next 20 or 50 years will be to think about the point at which the human teacher becomes the algorithm and the algorithm becomes the human teacher. At this moment, I do not think we have even started to grapple (C) _____ that significantly.

14 What is the most appropriate expression in (A)?

① binary
② negative
③ calm
④ positive
⑤ unexpected

15 What would be the most appropriate word pair to fill in (B) and (C)?

① However — with
② Nevertheless — on
③ Furthermore — at
④ Besides — in
⑤ Therefore — to

16~18

There's no coincidence that in East Asian countries, the most myopic ones all correlate with the maths league tables. Prof. Hammond says: "These kids are being pushed with very intensive education from a very young age and spend a lot of time indoors studying everything close up and very little time outdoors. [A] Therefore the concern is that all close work — like playing with smartphones — carries the potential that it could make them more short-sighted."

[B] So should we stop or limit screen use? [C] Any parent will know that youngsters are like dogs with bones when it comes to their beloved phones. [D] Trying to get them off their devices is pretty much impossible — certainly without a massive argument. Dr. Dahlmann-Noor, who is a mother of three, says trying to stop screen use is probably an unrealistic aspiration. "You can only tell them that it might make their eyes short-sighted and they should not use it as much as they like to. [E] But, hand on heart, I don't think we can get away from this because they also have to do their school homework on laptops and iPads. So I don't think we will be reducing the screen use, really, in years to come."

16 _____ is the best place which the following sentence in the box would be located in.

| Well that's much easier said than done! |

① [A] ② [B] ③ [C] ④ [D] ⑤ [E]

17 The underlined expression <u>hand on heart</u> means _____.

① sincerely
② noticeably
③ promptly
④ continually
⑤ unitedly

18 According to the passage, _____ is not a cause of myopia among East Asian kids.

① school homework using laptops
② the use of smartphones
③ excessive math study
④ sunlight exposure
⑤ indoor studies of many hours

[A] The textbook genre, irrespective of the discipline it is associated with, serves a common purpose in academic contexts, which is reflected in a number of typical features of textbook genres. Textbooks disseminate discipline-based knowledge and, at the same time, display a somewhat unequal writer-reader relationship, with the writer as the specialist and the reader as the non-initiated novice in the discipline. However, this effort to disseminate introductory uncontested knowledge is sometimes compromised by an attempt to offer what is claimed to be the 'cutting edge' theories. Textbooks nevertheless are seen as 'repositories of codified knowledge' made accessible to large audiences by the frequent use of a variety of rhetorical devices such as reporting, questioning, advance labelling and enumeration.

[B] However, _____, disciplinary cultures differ on several dimensions, some of which include constraints on patterns of membership, variation in knowledge structure and norms of inquiry, typical patterns of rhetorical intimacy associated with typical modes of expressions, specialist lexis and discourses, and distinct approaches to the teaching of these disciplines.

[C] Let me begin with two disciplines, i.e. those of economics and law, in an attempt to compare the way disciplinary knowledge is structured and communicated in instructional contexts. On the face of it, the two disciplines appear to be similar in that both of them tend to reinforce the relationship between rhetorical aspects, processes, and outcomes. Similarly, they may also create and formulate a complexity of integrated concepts and use grammatical metaphors to pack disciplinary knowledge for their specific audiences. They may also share the way they need to explain the interrelationship between various concepts by referring to facts and figures, though it is likely that in business such facts and figures have numerical values, whereas in law they consist of human acts entangled in socio-legal relations.

[D] In a number of other ways, the two disciplines appear to be very different, especially in terms of the rhetorical strategies they employ to construct knowledge. Business studies, in general, depends on aggressive innovation in the way it constructs its discourses. In fact, much of innovation in communicative practices in many other professional contexts, in the last few decades, has been inspired by changes in communicative patterns in the field of business, which is also reflected in economics textbooks. Law, on the other hand, relies on extreme conservatism in the way it constructs its discourses. This has also influenced other forms of expressions in the field. Textbook writing in law is no exception in this respect.

19 Which of the following best fits in the blank in paragraph [B]?

① in spite of these shared characteristics of textbooks across disciplines
② regardless of definitions and clarifications of technical concepts
③ with reference to a number of common disciplinary variations
④ by means of similar discursive practices in different disciplines
⑤ apart from the universal relationship between genres and specialist disciplines

20 According to the passage, which of the following is not mentioned as the characteristics of textbook genres?

① They offer state-of-the-art information.
② They involve discipline-specific knowledge.
③ They employ a range of rhetorical strategies.
④ They display a hierarchical author-reader relationship.
⑤ They contain information targeted to a limited group of readers.

21 According to the passage, which of the following is not a common feature of economics and law?

① Complicatedly integrated concepts may be constructed.
② Numerical values of facts and figures can be emphasized.
③ Metaphors can be utilized to convey discipline-based information.
④ Facts and figures may be employed to illustrate the association of concepts.
⑤ The relationship between rhetorical aspects, processes and outcomes can be consolidated.

22 According to the passage, the two key expressions "aggressive innovation" and "extreme conservatism" are mentioned because _____

① textbooks are developed according to these two goals.
② these two have influenced the way legal textbooks are written.
③ these two are the pivotal ways disciplinary knowledge is delivered.
④ they are the properties characteristic of business and law, respectively.
⑤ textbooks have changed their focused attention from conservatism to innovation.

10 심리

01 Choose the most appropriate one for each blank.

When psychologists look at the lives of the most creative people, what they find are people who are very good at exchanging ideas and advancing ideas, but who also have a serious streak of introversion in them. And this is because _____ is a crucial ingredient often to creativity. Charles Darwin took long walks alone in the woods and emphatically turned down dinner party invitations. Steve Wozniak invented the first Apple computer sitting alone in his cubicle in Hewlett-Packard where he was working at the time. And he says that he never would have become such an expert in the first place had he not been too _____ to leave the house when he was growing up.

① harmony — lonely
② solitude — extroverted
③ stubbornness — extroverted
④ solitude — introverted
⑤ stubbornness — introverted

02 밑줄 친 (A)~(E) 가운데 문맥상 적절하지 않은 것은?

Sociologists and psychologists have argued for centuries about how a person's character is formed. The argument has long been known as "nature vs. nurture," describing the two main (A) opposing theories. The first theory says that character is formed (B) genetically before birth. According to this theory, nature — through genetics — determines what a person will be like. The other theory says, on the contrary, that a newborn baby has no (C) deficient character. The child's character develops as she or he grows up, and the development of the character is (D) influenced by the child's family and social environment. Thus, according to the second theory, the most (E) important factors are cultural and social.

① (A)　　② (B)　　③ (C)　　④ (D)　　⑤ (E)

03~04

Studies show the importance of eye-to-eye contact, for instance, in real-life relationships, and indicate that the nature of one's eye-contact patterns, whether one looks another squarely in the eye or looks to the side or shifts one's gaze from side to side, may play a significant role in one's success or failure in human relationships. _____, no eye contact is possible in the child-television relationship, although in certain children's programs people purport to speak directly to the child and the camera fosters this illusion by focusing directly upon the person being filmed. How might such a distortion of real-life relationships affect a child's development of trust, of openness, of an ability to relate well to other *real* people? Children who have been taught, or conditioned, to listen passively most of the day to the warm verbal communications coming from the TV screen, to the deep emotional appeal of the so-called TV personality, are often unable to respond to real persons because they arouse so much less feeling than the skilled actor.

03 Which is the most appropriate for the blank?

① Instead
② Therefore
③ However
④ Furthermore

04 According to the passage, which is true?

① There are diverse ways of eye contact.
② TV viewers should learn how to make eye contact with skilled actors.
③ Real people arouse much more feeling than the people on the TV screen.
④ Focusing on the persons on the TV screen makes children relate well to other people.

05~07

I recently talked with a friend who is a faculty member at a well-known university. My friend travels frequently and he often chats with strangers in bars, restaurants, and airports. He says that he has learned through much experience never to use his title — professor — during these conversations. When he does, he reports, the <u>tenor</u> of the interaction changes immediately. People who have been spontaneous and interesting conversation partners for the prior half hour become respectful, accepting, and dull. His opinions that earlier might have produced a lively exchange now usually generate extended statements of accord. He says to me, "<u>I'm still the same guy they've been talking to for the past thirty minutes, right?</u>" My friend now regularly lies about his occupation in such situations.

05 What is the main idea of the passage?

① Do not boast of your occupation when you meet strangers.
② It is dangerous to give out personal information when chatting with strangers in bars, restaurants, and airports.
③ You can offend people by using your title during a conversation.
④ Even interesting conversations can become dull after thirty minutes.
⑤ Our actions are frequently more influenced by a title than by the nature of the person claiming it.

06 The underlined word, tenor, is closest in meaning to _____.

① burden
② evolution
③ atmosphere
④ theme
⑤ purpose

07 Which word best describes the tone of this underlined sentence?

① furious
② sad
③ overjoyed
④ bewildered
⑤ sentimental

08~09

Much like daydreaming, talking to yourself can help you organize your thoughts and even help you realize certain goals. "Sometimes we catch ourselves doing this in public, which can be embarrassing because we don't want to be seen as 'crazy,' but it's completely normal," says Dr. Schneberger. "Everyone does it." She explains that talking out loud to yourself "is an unfiltered unconscious response to surveying our environment" in which you're conveying what's on your mind without feeling as though you have to alter your words or be judged by them. Dr. Breur agrees, adding that talking to yourself may help you sort out the many responsibilities and pressures you face as you go throughout life. She says to be mindful of negative self-talk though. Phrases such as "I'm so stupid" can be emotionally damaging, so try to replace such statements with more positive ones. Here are some ways to stop being so hard on yourself.

08 Dr. Schneberger's point is '_____.'

① everybody is special
② you're not alone
③ there is no rule without exception
④ beauty is skin deep
⑤ every cloud has a silver lining

09 It's okay to talk to yourself in public, but it's not okay _____.

① to curse the others
② to use the dirty words
③ to interfere with the others' talk
④ to play by yourself always
⑤ to blame yourself for everything

10~12

As social beings, it's in our nature to get along with others; our survival and success depend on it. However, there is a fine line between healthy social behavior and the experience of emotional depletion caused by chronic people-pleasing. There are common signs of chronic people-pleasing and some ways to overcome it. [A]

People-pleasers want everyone around them to be happy, and they will do whatever is asked of them to keep it that way, according to Susan Newman, a social psychologist.

People-pleasers often feel like they have to say _____ when someone asks for their help. This makes them feel important and like they're contributing to someone else's life. They worry how others will view them when they say _____. People don't want to be seen as lazy, selfish, or totally egocentric. They fear they'll be disliked and cut from the group, whether it's friends, family, or co-workers. [B]

People-pleasers yearn for outside validation. Their personal feeling of security and self-confidence is based on getting the approval of others, said Linda Tillman, a clinical psychologist. Thus, at the core, people-pleasers lack confidence, she said. [C]

What many people-pleasers don't realize is that people-pleasing can have serious risks. Not only does it put a lot of pressure and stress on them, but essentially they can make themselves sick from doing too much. [D]

10 Which of the following is most suitable for blanks?

① yes — no
② yes — yes
③ no — no
④ no — yes

11 Which is the most appropriate place for the paragraph below?

> Here's a slew of strategies to help you stop being a people-pleaser. Remember that you always have a choice to say no whenever someone asks you for a favor. Set your priorities. Knowing your priorities and values helps you put the brakes on people-pleasing.

① [A]   ② [B]   ③ [C]   ④ [D]

12 Which of the following can be inferred from the passage?

① People-pleasing is one of the healthy social behaviors of humans, as social-beings.
② Susan Newman offered some tips to keep people-pleasers happy.
③ According do Linda Tillman, low self-confidence is the only reason to cause chronic people-pleasing.
④ People-pleasers tend to put much pressure and stress on themselves.

13~15

Imposter syndrome is a psychological pattern in which an individual doubts their accomplishments both in the classroom and in the workplace and has a persistent internalized fear of being exposed as a fraud. Despite _____ evidence of their competence, those experiencing this phenomenon remain convinced that they are frauds and do not deserve all they have achieved. Individuals with impostorism incorrectly attribute their success to luck or regard it as a result of deceiving others into thinking they are more intelligent than they perceive themselves to be. [A] While early research focused on the prevalence among high-achieving women, impostor syndrome has been recognized to affect both men and women equally. [B]

The term imposter phenomenon was introduced in 1978 by Dr. Pauline R. Clance and Dr. Suzanne A. Imes. They defined impostor phenomenon as an individual experience of self-perceived intellectual phoniness or fraud. The researchers investigated the prevalence of this internal experience by interviewing a sample of 150 high-achieving women. [C] Despite the consistent evidence of external validation, these women lacked the internal acknowledgement of their accomplishments. The participants explained how their success was a result of luck while others overestimated their intelligence and abilities. Clance and Imes believed that this mental framework for impostor phenomenon developed from factors such as gender stereotypes, early family dynamics, culture, and attribution style. The researchers determined that the women who experienced impostor phenomenon displayed symptoms related to depression, generalized anxiety, and low self-confidence. [D]

13 Which of the following is most suitable for the blank?

① external
② fictitious
③ constitutional
④ intestine

14 Which is the most appropriate place for the paragraph below?

> All of the participants had been formally recognized for their professional excellence by colleagues, and had displayed academic achievement through degrees earned and standardized testing scores.

① [A]　　② [B]　　③ [C]　　④ [D]

15 According to the passage, which of the following is true?

① Impostor syndrome is caused by co-workers' doubts about high-achieving women.
② Men as well as women can experience impostor phenomenon.
③ All of the 150 high-achieving female participants overcame the syndrome.
④ Those with high-self confidence tend to develop impostorism.

16
~
17

A second basic type of interference is proactive inhibition. Proactive inhibition occurs when prior learning interferes with later learning. For instance, if you cram for a psychology exam and then later the same night cram for a history exam, your memory of the second thing studied will be less accurate than it would have been if you had studied only history. Proactive inhibition is especially likely to occur when old learning conflicts with new learning. Learning to back a car with a trailer attached is a good example. Normally when you are backing a car, the steering wheel is turned in the direction you want to go. Since this is the same as normal driving, it is easily mastered.

_____, with a trailer attached, the steering wheel must be turned opposite from the direction you want the trailer to go. This causes established driving habits to interfere and makes learning to back a trailer difficult.

16 Which is the most appropriate for the blank?

① Furthermore   ② Likewise
③ However   ④ Therefore

17 According to the passage, which is not an example of proactive inhibition?

① An English-speaking person may have greater difficulty learning Chinese, applying English grammar rule to Chinese.
② When the aisles of a shopping mart are changed, you instinctively start walking towards the old shelves.
③ You move to a new place and find yourself writing your old address on a letter.
④ Some people have a hard time driving a stick shift vehicle again when they have recently started driving an automatic one.

18 위 글에서 논지의 흐름상 가장 적합하지 않은 것을 고르시오.

In the 1950s, Festinger proposed his theories of social comparison and cognitive dissonance, suggesting that others can play a (A) substantial role in the development of opinions and needs as well as reduction of dissonant cognitions. These theories focus on the fact that people look to others in their environment in order to evaluate their own opinions, beliefs, and attitudes. Through this process, one can evaluate where one stands with reference to the opinions and attitudes of an appropriate comparison group, composed of others similar to oneself. With regard to abilities, one may compare performance on a given task to (B) a standard(e.g., how fast one can run the mile can be compared to an average time for a runner of the same age). However, evaluation of one's opinions or attitudes has (C) incompatible reference and yields information that is relative only to the anchor provided by the comparison group that one chooses. Essentially, researchers have determined that individuals evaluate their opinions, beliefs, and attitudes through comparison with similar others and, partly as a result of such findings, propositions have been made that social support may (D) be derived from the social comparison process. More specifically, it is possible that the processes involved in social comparison provide a basis for the beneficial action of social support.

① (A)　　　　② (B)　　　　③ (C)　　　　④ (D)

I think that, in general, apart from expert opinion, there is too much respect paid to the opinions of others, both in great matters and in small ones. One should respect public opinion in so far as it is necessary in order to avoid starvation and to keep out of prison, but anything that goes beyond this is voluntary submission to an unnecessary tyranny, and is likely to _____ happiness in all kinds of ways. Take, for example, the matter of expenditure. Very many people spend money in ways quite different from those that their natural tastes would enjoin, merely because they feel that the respect of their neighbors depends upon their possession of a good car and their ability to give good dinners. As a matter of fact, any man who can obviously afford a car but genuinely prefers travel or a good library will in the end be much more respected than if he behaved exactly like every one else. There is of course no point in deliberately flouting public opinion; this is still to be under its domination, though in a topsy-turvy way. But to be genuinely indifferent to it is both a strength and a source of happiness.

19 Which best fits in the blank?

① indulge in
② affiliate with
③ triumph over
④ interfere with

20 Which is closest in meaning to the underlined enjoin?

① alter
② refuse
③ replace
④ demand

21~22

Fear is a great motivator; it probably motivates more people than anything else. Unfortunately, it motivates most people to hold back, to doubt themselves, to accomplish (A) much more than they could, and to hide the person they really are.

One of the biggest obstacles to reaching your potential may be your own personal fears. If you are afraid, you are not alone; (B) everyone has fears. However, our fears are learned. As a baby, you had two fears: a fear of falling and a fear of loud noises. As you got older, you probably (C) added to your list of fears. And, if you are like most people, you let your fears (D) dominate parts of your life, saying things to yourself like: "What if I try and fail?"

You have two choices where fear is concerned. You can let fear dominate your life, or you can focus on those things you really want to accomplish, put your fears (E) behind you, and go for it. The people most successful in their fields will tell you that they are afraid, but that they overcome their fear because _____. Barbra Streisand becomes physically nauseated with stage fright when she performs, yet she faces these fears and maintains her position as one of the most popular entertainers of our time.

21 (A)~(E) 가운데, 문맥상 낱말의 쓰임이 적절하지 않은 것은?

① (A)   ② (B)   ③ (C)   ④ (D)   ⑤ (E)

22 위 글의 빈칸에 들어갈 말로 가장 적절한 것은?

① they don't have to directly face it
② their potential is strong enough
③ they don't have no more choice
④ their desire to achieve is greater
⑤ it is not the biggest obstacle they face

23~24

In a study by some social psychologists, participants were asked to take part in two tasks. In the first task, they were asked to make sentences out of sets of provided words. Next, as part of what was supposedly a different study, participants played an economic game in which they were given ten $1 coins and asked to divide them up between themselves and the next participant. Only the next participant would know what they decided, and that participant wouldn't know who the givers were. Think for a moment what you would do in this situation. Here's an opportunity to make a quick 10 bucks, and there is a definite temptation to pocket all the coins. But you might feel a little guilty hoarding all the money and leaving nothing for the next person. This is one of those situations in which there is a devil on one of our shoulders ("Don't be a fool, take it all!") and an angel on the other ("Do unto others as you would have them do unto you"). In short, people want the money but this conflicts with their goal to be nice to others. Which goal wins out?

It depends in part on _____. Remember the sentence completion task people did first? In the task, half of the participants were given the words that had to do with God (spirit, divine, God, sacred, and prophet), which were designed to set the goal of acting kindly to one's neighbor. The other half got neutral words. An important detail is that the participants did not make a connection between the sentence-making task and the economic game — they thought the two tasks were completely unrelated. Even so, the people who made sentences out of words having to do with God left significantly more money for the next participant ($4.56 on average) than did people who got the neutral words ($2.56 on average).

23. What is the best expression for the blank?

① personal goals you set for yourself
② whether the person believes in God
③ which goal has been recently primed
④ prevailing norms of mainstream society

24. Which of the following is true according to the passage?

① All the participants were given the same set of words.
② Who left money to the next participant remained unknown to the recipient.
③ The participants were well aware of the connection between the two given tasks.
④ The participants were given two options — taking all the money or giving half of it to the next person.

25~26

Most of us are good at spotting overtly aggressive people. While it doesn't feel good when someone insults, criticizes, or belittles you, at least you know why you are hurting. But sometimes the people around us, including our close family, friends, and colleagues, make us feel uncomfortable, but we cannot quite put a finger on why. For example, your friend may fail to greet you in the hallway for the third time in a week. You make yourself believe that it is probably a slip, yet you feel that something is amiss.

If this happens frequently with one or more people in your life, you may be dealing with passive-aggressive behavior, which is much harder to detect than overtly aggressive behavior. Passive aggression is a tendency to engage in _____ expression of hostility through acts such as subtle insults, sullen behavior, stubbornness, or a deliberate failure to accomplish required tasks. Because passive-aggressive behavior is _____, it can be hard to spot, even when you're feeling the psychological consequences. To help you identify this type of behavior, I describe five instances of it below. These are not all of the ways a person can be passive-aggressive, but they are the most common.

25 Which of the following is most appropriate for the blanks in common?

① bold
② naive
③ implicit
④ honest
⑤ obscene

26 What will be discussed right after the passage?

① Comparison of aggressive behaviors
② Causes of passive aggression
③ Ways to deal with passive aggression
④ Effects of passive aggression
⑤ Examples of passive-aggressive behavior

27~29

The ability to poke fun at yourself is a priceless gift. People who brag about their accomplishments are bores, but the ones who invite you to laugh with them at their mistakes are a joy to be around. When you're riding high, self-deprecating humor wards off jealousy and envy. When things are not going your way, (A) it helps you keep your perspective and sense of humor. (B) It's often the essential ingredient in that mysterious intangible charm. If you work at (C) it full-time, it can even make you rich: ask Bob Hope!

Year after year, the charming Mr. Hope went on happily criticizing himself — to the _____ of millions. Audience members could not get enough of him. They adored him to no end. When he appeared as a guest on a recent television program, the subject of prize fighting came up. Mr. Hope said, "I did some boxing in my younger days," with a rapt and faraway look. "I was the only fighter in my home town who fought with a rear-view mirror. I was also the only one who had to be carried both ways — into the ring and out of (D) it!"

27 Which one can be inferred from the passage?

① Bob Hope was wealthy.
② Self-deprecating humor is offensive.
③ People who brag about their accomplishments are a joy to be around.
④ Poking fun at yourself invites jealousy and envy.

28 Which refers to a different one?

① (A)   ② (B)   ③ (C)   ④ (D)

29 Which one is not appropriate for the blank?

① delight
② amusement
③ joy
④ chagrin

> The idea that you can't buy happiness has been exposed as a myth, over and over. Richer countries are happier than poor countries. Richer people within richer countries are happier, too. The evidence is unequivocal: Money makes you happy. You just have to know what to do with it.
>
> Stop buying so much stuff, psychologist Daniel Gilbert said in an interview a few years ago, and try to spend more money on experiences. We think that experiences can be fun but leave us with nothing to show for them. But that turns out to be a good thing. Happiness, for most people, comes from sharing experiences with other people; experiences are usually shared — first when they happen and then again and again when we tell our friends.
>
> On the other hand, <u>objects wear out their welcome</u>. If you really love a rug, you might buy it. The first few times you see, you might admire it, and feel happy. But over time, it will probably reveal itself to be just a rug. Try to remember the last time an old piece of furniture made you ecstatic.

30 Which of the following does the author recommend?

① Buy experiences rather than objects.
② Be friendly to other people.
③ Change your life in a meaningful way.
④ Be satisfied with what you already have.

31 What does the underlined sentence imply?

① We can shop our way out of a bad mood.
② Objects are usually preferred to experiences.
③ Our happiness from buying things declines with time.
④ We usually buy what we want rather than what we need.

32~33

In *The Act of Creation*, the psychologist Arthur Koestler summarized his own extensive research into the human creative process by introducing the term bisociation to convey the coincidence of discontinuous ideas. He described the creative act as the perceiving of a situation or idea, L, in two self-consistent but habitually incompatible frames of reference. The event L, in which the two intersect, is made to vibrate simultaneously on two different wavelengths, as it were. While this situation lasts, L is not merely linked to one associative context, but bisociated with two. What we value in creative ideas is not just their apparent novelty. Novelty in itself induces excitement because it has the effect of opening up new connective paths, or fields, in the cognitive medium, and this may require an exceptional discharge of energy. But having had this experience the excitement may be short-lived — once opened the paths cannot be opened in the same way again. Richer creative acts lie in opening complex and far-reaching new pathways that connect disparate concepts, the more of them the greater the level of excitement; in Koestler's terms, one multiplies bisociations. If our sense of being relies, at least in part, on the presence of active mental states, it follows that more active mental states create a more expansive sense of awareness or being. And the more diverse and complex the mental states are at any one time the more corresponding energy is required to traverse them, and hence the greater the sense of physical exhilaration.

32
What would be the best title of the passage above?

① The Negative Impact of Bisociated Exhilaration
② The Birth of Novelty and Excitement
③ The Cognitive Medium and Associative Context
④ The Complex Physical Features of Energy

33
What can be inferred from the passage above?

① Human ability to connect discontinuous ideas has its own limit.
② Creativity does not necessarily consist in the production of anything that is completely new.
③ Destruction is the opposite pole of creation.
④ Creative thoughts themselves are of little use unless scientifically measured.

34~35

Is there anything a couple can do to keep the honeymoon alive? Researcher Arthur Aron says that after the thrill of a new relationship wears off, partners can combat boredom by engaging together in new and arousing activities. In an experiment, he brought randomly selected couples into a laboratory, spread gymnasium mats across the floor, tied the partners' hands together at the wrist, and had them crawl on their hands and knees, over a barrier, from one end of the room to the other — all the while carrying a pillow between their bodies. Other couples were given the simpler task of rolling a ball across the mat, one partner at a time. A third group received no assignment. Afterward, all participants were surveyed about their relationships. As Aron predicted, the couples who had struggled and laughed their way through the novel and arousing activity were reported to be _____ than the others.

34 Which of the following best fits into the blank?

① more willing to try fun and exciting moves
② more enthusiastic about their exercise routine
③ more satisfied with the quality of their relationships
④ more likely to enter a troubled marriage

35 Which of the following is the major topic of the passage?

① Signs of an unhappy marriage
② Three experiments conducted on married couples
③ Why many marriages end up in divorce
④ How to keep your marriage fresh

36~37

A century ago, Gustave Le Bon wrote about the mysterious forces that operated when people congregated to form crowds. Feelings of membership within a crowd, he argued, contributed to an enlargement of the ego (a sense of power), the release of impulses, *a sense of contagion*, and heightened suggestibility. These psychological characteristics, Le Bon argued, derived from the absorption of an individual's identity into that of the crowd. The effective crowd leader, Le Bon reasoned, relied on the affirmation of simple, imagelike ideas that point directly to action, and on the repetition of these image like ideas: The affirmation evokes the image, the image evokes a sentiment, and the sentiment leads to action. Individuals in the crowd mimic the actions of the leader, and this mimicry, once initiated, inflects all in attendance. Although Le Bon was not interested in emotional contagion per se, his observations of mob behavior may contain clues to some of the features of individuals most likely to be susceptible to emotional contagion.

36 According to Le Bon, an effective crowd leader _____.

① acts without speaking
② provides imagelike ideas
③ repeats the same action
④ listens to the people's voice

37 According to Le Bon, which of the following is not true of individuals in a crowd?

① They feel themselves to be powerful.
② They are likely to catch emotions of each other.
③ They tend to be dominated by collective identity.
④ They mimic each other before mimicking the leader.

38~39

Over the past decade behavioral scientists have come up with some intriguing insights. In one landmark experiment, conducted in an upmarket grocery store in California, researchers set up a sampling table with a display of jams. In the first test they offered a tempting array of 24 different jams to taste; on a different day they displayed just six. Shoppers who took part in the sampling were rewarded with a discount voucher to buy any jam of the same brand in the store. It turned out that more shoppers stopped at the display when there were 24 jams. But when it came to buying afterwards, fully 30% of those who stopped at the six-jam table went on to purchase a pot, against merely 3% of those who were faced with the selection of 24. As options multiply, there may be a point at which the effort required to obtain enough information to be able to distinguish sensibly between alternatives outweighs the benefit to the consumer of the extra choice. At this point, choice no longer liberates, but tyrannizes. In other words, the fact that some choice is good doesn't necessarily mean that more choice is better. Consumers find too many options debilitating because of the risk of misperception and miscalculation, of misunderstanding the available alternatives, of misreading one's own tastes, of yielding to a moment's whim and regretting it afterwards, combined with the stress of information acquisition.

38 The best title of the passage would be _____.

① Choice and Liberal Democracy
② The Paradox of Choice
③ Free Choice and Economic Growth
④ Information and Human Behavior
⑤ Being Human in a Consumer Society

39 The experiment with the shoppers in the Californian grocery store reveals that _____.

① people believe the perfect choice exists
② shoppers are not put off by more choice
③ too much choice is demotivating
④ if you can have everything in 24 varieties, making decisions becomes easy work
⑤ the more expensive an item is, the more daunting the decision becomes

40~42

Recently, as the British doctor Lord Robert Winston took a train from London to Manchester, he found himself becoming steadily enraged. A woman had picked up the phone and begun a loud conversation, which would last an unbelievable hour. Furious, Winston began to tweet about the woman, taking her picture and sending it to his more than 40,000 followers. When the train arrived at its destination, Winston bolted. The press were waiting for the woman and showed her the Lord's messages. She used just one word to describe Winston's actions: *rude*.

Studies have shown that rudeness spreads quickly and (A) virally, almost like the common cold. Just witnessing rudeness makes it far more likely that we, in turn, will be rude later on. Once infected, we are more aggressive, less creative and worse at our jobs. The only way to end a strain is to make a (B) conscious decision to do so. We must have the guts to call it out, face to face. We must say, "Just stop." For Winston, that would have meant approaching the woman, politely asking her to speak more quietly or make the call at another time.

The rage and injustice we feel at the rude behavior of a stranger can drive us to do odd things. In one research, surveying 2,000 adults, the acts of revenge people had taken ranged from the ridiculous ("I rubbed fries on their windshield") to the disturbing ("I sabotaged them at work").

We must combat rudeness head on. When we see it occur in a store, we must step up and say something. If it happens to a colleague, we must point it out. We must defend strangers in the same way we'd defend our best friends. But we can do it with grace, by handling it without a trace of aggression and without being rude ourselves. Because once rude people can see their actions through the eyes of others, they are far more likely to end that strain themselves. _____.

40 Which is the closest meaning to the underlined (A)?

① slovenly
② virtually
③ contagiously
④ heretically

41 Which is implied by the underlined (B)?

① aggressive tweeting
② outrageous injustice
③ ludicrous behavior
④ decent appeal

42 Which is the most appropriate for the blank?

① Politeness is the best policy when you meet strangers
② Increasing rudeness is fuelled by social media in our age
③ Complimenting others makes you feel superior to them
④ As this tide of rudeness rises, civilization needs civility

43~45

In one experiment participants read a story that was preceded by a title suggesting the story's schema. For example, one story was titled "Watching a Peace March from the 40th Floor." Most of the story was about crowds moving about, television cameras, and speeches. In the middle of the story, however, was the strange sentence: "The landing was gentle, and the atmosphere was such that no special suits had to be worn." Most people who read the sentence didn't really understand it because they couldn't make it fit with the rest of their schema for peace marches. (A) _____, when they were later asked to recall the story, they didn't remember that particular sentence. Another group of participants read the same story but were told its title was "A Space Trip to an Inhabited Planet." This group was perfectly able to understand the strange sentence when they read it, and they also were more likely than the participants who thought they were reading about a peace march to recall it. When you read or hear stories and when you experience events in your life, you understand them in light of the schemas you have developed over time. Not only do those schemas affect which parts of an event make sense to you, but they also influence what you remember about it. You tend to remember the details that are (B) _____. Things that don't fit often drop out of memory.

43 Which of the following is the best title of the passage?

① Planet Landing: The Forgotten Story
② Mental Schemas: The Determinant of Memory
③ Reading Experiments: Unravelling Human Mystery
④ Power of the Mind: Peace March vs. Space Exploration

44 Which of the following best fits into (A)?

① As a result
② In contrast
③ Nevertheless
④ However

45 Which of the following best fits into (B)?

① enjoyable in your mind
② consistent with your schemas
③ in line with the following sentences
④ interesting and memorable to you

46~47

I already had experimental evidence of social inhibition when I began studying yawning contagion, providing a rationale for the use of self-reporting in experiments. As my yawning studies attracted attention (the popular media have a voracious appetite for stories on this topic), I had the experience of seeing the inhibition play out.

A television news-magazine crew turned up one day to tape a segment. Against my advice, the show's producer set out to re-create my experiment in which one-half of a large lecture class read an article about yawning while the other half read a control passage about hiccupping. Normally the effect of the yawning article is robust, and it has been used as a demonstration of contagion in classes at other universities.

As I predicted, the demonstration did not _____ up-close-and-personal scrutiny by a national network television crew. With the cameras rolling as the students read, only a tiny fraction of the usual amount of yawning was observed. The video crew performed an unintentional but informative variant of my original research demonstrating the powerful effect of social inhibition on yawning. Even highly motivated and prolific yawners who volunteered to be on national television stopped yawning when placed before the camera. It is notable that the social inhibition of yawning occurred unconsciously and was not the voluntary effect of the yawner to suppress a rude or inappropriate act. A socially significant act can be either produced or inhibited by unconscious processes.

adapted from an article by Robert R. Provine

46 Which expression best fits into the blank?

① affirm
② extirpate
③ mimic
④ obliterate
⑤ survive

47 Which statement can not be inferred from the passage above?

① Intense self-awareness that you may be observed inhibits yawning.
② There is doubt in the social science community about whether you can objectively report on your own experiments.
③ People who read a passage about yawning are more likely to yawn than people who read a passage about hiccupping.
④ The experiment executed by the television show producer offers a strong evidence for social inhibition of an unconsciously controlled act.
⑤ People who are deficient in their ability to empathize with others are most susceptible to contagious yawning.

48~50

In 1874 Francis Galton, a British (A) polymath, analyzed a sample of English scientists and found the vast majority to be first-born sons. This led him to speculate that first-born children enjoyed a special level of attention from their parents that allowed them to thrive intellectually. Half a century later, Alfred Adler, an Austrian psychologist, made a similar argument relating to personality. First-born children, he thought, were more conscientious, while the later-born were more extrovert and emotionally stable. [A] Many subsequent studies have explored these ideas, but their findings have been equivocal — some supporting and some rejecting them. Now a team led by Stefan Schmukle of the University of Leipzig, in Germany, has collected the most comprehensive evidence on the matter yet. Its conclusion is that Adler was wrong, but Galton may have been right.

Birth order, they found, had no effect on personality: first-borns were no more, no less, likely than their younger sibs to be conscientious, extrovert or neurotic. But it did affect intelligence. [B] In a family with two children, the first child was more intelligent than the second 60% of the time, rather than the 50% that would be expected by chance. On average, this translated to a difference of 1.5 IQ points between first and second siblings. [C] That figure agrees with the consensus from previous studies, and thus looks confirmed. It is, nevertheless, quite a small difference — and whether it is enough to account for Galton's original observation is (B) moot. In any event, it is clearly not deterministic. [D]

48 Which is closest in meaning to the underlined (A) polymath?

① a man of great ability in mathematics
② a man of good taste in food and clothes
③ a man of much learning in various fields
④ a man of huge wealth with good manners

49 Which is closest in meaning to the underlined (B) moot?

① useless
② verified
③ debatable
④ insignificant

50 Which is the best place for the following?

| Galton was the youngest of nine. |

① [A]　　② [B]　　③ [C]　　④ [D]

51~53

The interesting thing about advice is that we often take it from the wrong people. In other words, we usually undervalue the input of normal people while we overvalue the advice from credentialed experts. One reason why taking advice is problematic is that status matters quite a lot. Optimism bias, a cognitive quirk, endows most of us with a general hopefulness that things will work out even when the odds are stacked against us. According to researchers, optimism bias gets ratcheted up when the person giving advice is viewed as an expert. The expert's advice enhances the expectation of success if we listen to them even if the expert is often proved to be wrong.

Most of us are not adept at taking advice from anyone. We typically place more stock in our own opinions than the opinions of others. This is another cognitive blind spot known as egocentric bias. It is thought to be easier to believe that our critics are too thick to grasp our genius, are just simply jealous, or have some kind of hidden _____, than to admit they may be right. The required leap of humility is a giant test. One helpful trick can be found in Eastern philosophy. According to Haemin Sunim, a Korean Zen monk, when someone is about to give you advice, that is precisely the time you need to lower your defenses, not raise them.

51 Which one is true?

① Haemin Sunim believes in egocentric bias.
② Monks love raising defenses.
③ People usually value the opinions of others more than their own.
④ Taking advice can be challenging.

52 Which one is not true?

① The majority of people are proficient at taking advice from anyone.
② Advice from normal people is sometimes undervalued.
③ Advice is not always given to us by the appropriate people.
④ Advice from experts is typically overvalued.

53 Which one is not appropriate for the blank?

① agenda
② intentions
③ extensions
④ motives

54~56

The false smile, a ubiquitous social lubricant, has been unmasked by new research that has differentiated the specific muscle patterns in smiles reflecting true delight from those masking displeasure. Psychologist Dr. Ekman and his colleagues have developed a technique for analyzing more than 100 muscle patterns of the face as a person changes expression. With their method, they have been able to determine precisely which of those muscles is at play when the face takes on a given emotional expression.

In a study on lying, real smiles differed from those that hid unhappy feelings on two counts. In spontaneous smiles, the cheeks move up and the muscles around the eyes tighten, making the lines that extend from the corners of the eyes — crow's feet, and the skin around the eyebrow droops down a bit toward the eye. In the false smile, however, the face reveals traces of unhappy feelings behind the smile that can be seen apart from the supposed expression of pleasure — for instance, a slight furrowing of the muscle between the eyebrows. The eyes will not develop crow's feet unless the smile is especially broad. And even then, the tell-tale droop of skin around the eyebrow, which is difficult to feign, will not emerge. This research may be of particular importance to those who sometimes need to rely on subtle cues to know when a person is trying to hide physical pain, emotional anguish, or evil intention behind the mask of a smile.

54 Which of the following would be the best title for the passage?

① The Anatomy of Real and Fake Smiles
② Facial Expressions and Muscle Movements
③ Reading the Facial Expression of Emotion
④ How to Tell if Someone Is Lying

55 According to the passage, which of the following is a sign of a real smile?

① Wrinkled eyelids
② Furrowed eyebrows
③ Extended eyebrow lines
④ Droopy eyebrows

56 Which of the following is not stated or implied in the passage?

① The cheeks move up in the real smile.
② There are more than 100 facial muscles.
③ This research can be used for criminal investigations.
④ Smiling falsely is a common practice.

57
~
59

If you ask any man in America, or any man in business in England, what it is that most interferes with his enjoyment of existence, he will say: "The struggle for life." He will say this in all sincerity; he will believe it. In a certain sense, it is true; yet in another very important sense, it is profoundly false. The struggle for life is a thing which does, of course, occur. It may occur to any of us if we are unfortunate. It occurred, for example, to Conrad's hero Falk, who found himself on a derelict ship, one of the two men among the crew who were possessed of firearms, with nothing to eat but the other men. When the two men had finished the meals upon which they could agree, a true struggle for life began. Falk won, but was ever after a vegetarian. Now that is not what the businessman means when he speaks (A) _____ the "struggle for life." It is an inaccurate phrase which he has picked up in order to give dignity to something essentially trivial. Ask him how many men he has known in his class of life who have died of hunger. Ask him what happened to his friends after they had been ruined. Everybody knows that a businessman who has been ruined is better (B) _____ so far as material comforts are concerned than a man who has never been rich enough to have the chance of being ruined. What people mean, therefore, by the struggle for life is really the struggle for success. What people fear when they engage in the struggle is not that they will fail to get their breakfast next morning, but that they will fail to (C) _____ .

57 According to the passage, which is true of Conrad's hero Falk?

① He had a weapon on the derelict ship.
② He found himself on a deserted island.
③ He and other crew members survived in the end.
④ He was chasing after a vegetarian who was on the ship.

58 Which pair best fits in the blanks (A) and (B)?

① of — off
② in — until
③ with — now
④ out of — than

59 Which best fits in the blank (C)?

① survive calamities
② keep themselves alive
③ prevent fatal accidents
④ outshine their neighbors

60~63

Ticked off, peeved, irritated, bothered, annoyed, no matter how you may say it, being angry is an emotion no one enjoys feeling. But _____ it's completely normal and human to experience anger, problems can come into play when we don't process our feelings in a healthy way. Anger can become a very real, chronic issue, if not handled properly and in a timely manner. You could find yourself blowing up at the smallest things, doing or saying things in the heat of the moment that you later regret.

It may sound silly, but counting to ten (or, if you're really angry, 100) is a great way to immediately relieve some built up tension. Why? Because it focuses your mind on the specific task of taking care of yourself first.

Plenty of things can cause anger but those problems can also be solved if you're willing to meet them head-on. Rather than just blowing up and storming off when your teen misbehaves, your co-worker annoys you or your spouse doesn't see eye-to-eye with you on a certain issue, work on getting to the root of the problem. Discussing differences in a way that all parties involved feel respected and letting someone you care about know how you feel are things every human being is capable of doing.

60 Which is the most appropriate place for the sentence below?

> Here are some healthy ways to process your anger.

① Before the 1st paragraph
② After the 1st paragraph
③ After the 2nd paragraph
④ After the 3rd paragraph

61 Which of the following is most suitable for the blank?

① whatever
② so
③ likewise
④ while

62 What is the best headline for the 3rd paragraph?

① Give yourself a time out
② Address the issue
③ Hit the gym
④ Find a way to endure

63 According to the passage, which of the following is true?

① Anger will be a chronic issue if it is handled properly.
② When your spouse does not see your eyes straight, you may blow up and storm off.
③ Getting to the root of the problem does not mean that you are capable of being able to let someone you care about know how you feel.
④ As a human being, you have the ability to discuss differences in a way that all parties concerned feel respected.

64~65

We are constantly subconsciously picking and choosing memories based on our current needs. This is carried out by a psychological mechanism called the 'monitoring system'. When you recall something, your monitoring system tells you whether this recollection feels like a memory based on how detailed and emotional it is and whether it fits into your current idea of yourself based on how plausible it is. If it fits, it becomes part of your story; if not, it gets neglected. However, in some cases, our 'memory' is not a recollection, but an invention. A study found that 20 percent of participants had at least one memory that they no longer believe happened. These false memories are the result of the brain's ability to imagine possible scenarios — based on something that actually happened or something completely invented. The vividness and emotional intensity of the mental images trick the monitoring system into mislabelling the image as real. So, the past we remember is not entirely truthful. But this is no bad thing. Memory provides a consistent sense of self that helps us go through life. A not-so-truthful past achieves this goal. Problems arise only when there is an extreme discrepancy between the personal narrative and reality. Most of us live extremely well with our selective memories.

64 According to the passage, which of the following is true?

① We fabricate our past in order to establish extreme discrepancies in our self.
② Research reveals that 20 percent of memories are invented.
③ Fictitious recollections that resemble the truth are not necessarily injurious to us.
④ The brain's capacity for imagining new scenarios is solely responsible for memory.

65 Which of the following can be inferred from the passage?

① Deliberate falsification is the hallmark of much of what is remembered.
② Selective memory regularly causes unfortunate predicaments.
③ The monitoring system creates memories reflecting one's self-perception.
④ Witnesses' memories of crimes are objective and reliable.

66~67

Many parents grew up with punishments, and it's understandable that they rely on them. But punishments tend to escalate conflict and shut down learning. They elicit a fight or flight response, which means that sophisticated thinking in the frontal cortex goes dark and basic defense mechanisms kick in. Punishments make us either rebel, feel shamed or angry, repress our feelings, or figure out how not to get caught. In this case, full-fledged 4-year-old resistance would be at its peak.

So rewards are the positive choice then, right? Not so fast. Over decades, psychologists have suggested that rewards can decrease our natural motivation and enjoyment. For example, kids who like to draw and are, under experimental conditions, paid to do so, draw less than those who aren't paid. This is what psychologists call the "overjustification effect" — the external reward overshadows the child's internal motivation.

_____. In one classic series of studies, people were given a set of materials (a box of pins, a candle, and a book of matches) and asked to figure out how to attach the candle to the wall. The solution requires innovative thinking — seeing the materials in a way unrelated to their purpose (the box as a candle holder). People who were told they'd be rewarded to solve this dilemma took longer, on average, to figure it out. Rewards narrow our field of view. Our brains stop puzzling freely. We stop thinking deeply and seeing the possibilities.

The whole concept of punishments and rewards is based on negative assumptions about children — that they need to be controlled and shaped by us, and that they don't have good intentions. But we can flip this around to see kids as capable, wired for empathy, cooperation, team spirit and hard work. That perspective changes how we talk to children in powerful ways. Rewards and punishments are conditional, but our love and positive regard for our kids should be unconditional. In fact, when we lead with empathy and truly listen to our kids, they're more likely to listen to us.

66 Which of the following is most appropriate for the blank?

① Rewards have also been associated with lowering creativity
② However, rewards make kids more attentive to the parents
③ Rewards have also been associated with enhancing creativity
④ Rewards and punishments are vital to enhancing creativity
⑤ Rewards were more effective than punishments in enhancing creativity

67 Which of the following is true according to the passage?

① Neither rewards nor punishments are good solutions.
② First punishments and then rewards are better solutions.
③ First rewards and then punishments are better solutions.
④ More rewards and less punishments are good solutions.
⑤ More punishments and less rewards are better solutions.

Human error is defined as any deviance from "appropriate" behavior. The word appropriate is in quotes because in many circumstances, the appropriate behavior is not known or is only determined after the fact. But still, error is defined as deviance from the generally accepted correct or appropriate behavior. Error is the general term for all wrong actions. There are two major classes of error: slips and mistakes. Slips are further divided into two major classes and mistakes into three. These categories of errors all have different implications for design. I now turn to a more detailed look at these classes of errors and their design implications. A slip occurs when a person intends to do one action and ends up doing something else. With a slip, the action performed is not the same as the action that was intended. There are two major classes of slips: action-based and memory-lapse. In action-based slips, the wrong action is performed. In lapses, memory fails, so the intended action is not done or its results not evaluated. Action-based slips and memory lapses can be further classified according to their causes. A mistake occurs when the wrong goal is established or the wrong plan is formed. From that point on, even if the actions are executed properly they are part of the error, because the actions themselves are inappropriate; they are part of the wrong plan. With a mistake, the action that is performed matches the plan: it is the plan that is wrong. Mistakes have three major classes: rule-based, knowledge-based, and memory-lapse. In a rule-based mistake, the person has appropriately diagnosed the situation, but then decided upon an erroneous course of action: the wrong rule is being followed. In a knowledge-based mistake, the problem is misdiagnosed because of erroneous or incomplete knowledge. Memory-lapse mistakes take place when there is forgetting at the stages of goals, plans, or evaluation.

68 Which of the following statement is not true?

① Errors have two major forms.
② Slips occur when the goal is correct, but the required actions are not done properly.
③ Memory lapses can lead to either slips or mistakes.
④ Slips can be further divided based upon their results.

69 It can be inferred from the passage that to pour some milk into coffee and then put the coffee cup into the refrigerator is an example of _____.

① knowledge-based mistake
② memory-lapse mistake
③ action-based slip
④ memory-lapse slip

70~72

_____ kilos is harder than putting on, which is why the weight-loss industry is so big. Its latest manifestation is online weight-management sites: social networks for the plump in which participants can set a target weight and monitor their progress towards it.

[A] As with other social networks, they can also get their help from friends — either real-life ones who sign up to the same site, or else digital ones whom they have befriended on the internet. Those friendships are likely to be important. Other studies of weight-loss programs have suggested that having the support or chivying of friends helps people stick to their diets and exercise regimes.

[B] But she and her colleagues are quick to point out that a study like this can establish only that two things — in this case, friends and weight-loss — are correlated. It cannot show which causes which. Working this out requires controlled experiments.

[C] Their results are, nonetheless, encouraging. Weight-management websites have the potential to reach many more people much more cheaply than real-world support groups do. Moreover, if it turns out that friendship networks are a magic wand for weight loss, then it may be easier to nudge people into such networks electronically than if they actually had to meet each other in a sweaty gym. Given the medical consequences of rising levels of obesity, that would be well worth doing.

[D] Those studies, however, have all been done with groups of people who knew each other in the real world. A team of researchers led by Julia Poncela-Casanovas of Northwestern University, in Illinois, decided to check if the same was true of groups in cyberspace. Their results suggest that it is.

70 Which best fits in the blank?

① Shedding
② Controlling
③ Increasing
④ Calculating

71 Which is closest in meaning to the underlined chivying?

① nagging
② praising
③ embracing
④ recommending

72 Which is the proper order of paragraphs [A] — [D]?

① [A] — [B] — [C] — [D]
② [A] — [D] — [B] — [C]
③ [B] — [D] — [C] — [A]
④ [B] — [C] — [D] — [A]

Dave Balter worked in advertising, and he knew that most people don't like ads. They avoid watching them, reading them, or listening to them. He also knew that people do pay attention when they hear about goods and services from people they know. So he said to himself, "If no one pays attention to advertising, but they *do* pay attention to the opinions of their friends and family, let's focus our attention there."

What Balter came up with was a website where consumers could sign up to receive free products. _____, they promised that if they liked the products, they would tell their friends. In most cases, the volunteers also got coupons to give to their friends. All Balter asked was that they report back on two questions: what did you think of the product, and who did you talk to about it?

After four years, Balter had 65,000 volunteers trying products and telling people about the ones they liked. Then a reporter heard about Balter's idea and wrote a story on it for a major magazine. Free advertising! Within a year after that story appeared, Balter had 130,000 volunteers. Today, the company he started has over one million people spreading the word about a wide variety of products. They are doing word-of-mouth advertising, perhaps the best kind of advertising there is.

There may be a risk to advertising by word of mouth, however, according to George Silverman, the author of *The Secrets of Word-of-Mouth Marketing*. What's the danger? Studies have shown that a customer who likes a product or service will tell an average of three people about it. But when customers don't like it, on average they'll tell eleven.

73 빈칸에 들어갈 가장 알맞은 것을 고르시오.

① Similarly
② In return
③ Consequently
④ In fact

74 위 글의 내용과 맞지 않는 것을 고르시오.

① Even though most people don't like ads, they pay attention to their friends' opinions of products.
② Balter set up a website where a person could put his or her name on a list to get free products.
③ Within a year after his story appeared in a magazine, Balter had twice as many volunteers as before.
④ Silverman's studies found that dissatisfied customers tell fewer people than satisfied ones do.

75~77

The term normal or healthy can be defined in two ways. Firstly, from the standpoint of a functioning society, one can call a person normal or healthy if he is able to fulfill the social role he is to take in that given society. More concretely, this means that he is able to work in the fashion which is required in that particular society, and furthermore that he is able to participate in the reproduction of society that he can raise a family. Secondly, from the standpoint of the individual, we look upon health or normalcy as the optimum of growth and happiness of the individual. If the structure of a given society were such that it offered the optimum possibility for individual happiness, both view-points would coincide. However, this is not the case in most societies we know, including our own. Although they differ in the degree to which they promote the aims of individual growth, there is a discrepancy between the aims of the smooth functioning of society and of the full development of the individual. [A] This fact makes it imperative to differentiate sharply between the two concepts of health. The one is governed by social necessities, the other by values and norms concerning the aim of individual existence. Unfortunately, this differentiation is often neglected. [B] Most psychiatrists take the structure of their own society so much for granted that to them the person who is not well adapted assumes the stigma of being less valuable. On the other hand, the well-adapted person is supposed to be the more valuable person in terms of a scale of human values. If we differentiate the two concepts of normal and neurotic, we come to the following conclusion: the person who is normal in terms of being well adapted is often less healthy than the neurotic person in terms of human values. Often he is well adapted only at the expense of having given up his self in order to become more or less the person he believes he is expected to be. [C] On the other hand, the neurotic person can be characterized as somebody who was not ready to surrender completely in the battle for his self. [D] To be sure, his attempt to save his individual self was not successful, and instead of expressing his self productively he sought salvation through neurotic symptoms and by withdrawing into a phantasy life. Nevertheless, from the standpoint of human values, he is less crippled than the kind of normal person who has lost his individuality altogether.

75 Which of the following statement is true?

① Neurotics are great threats to human happiness and self-realization.
② Adapting oneself to one's own society provides a stable ground for being a healthy person.
③ In a functioning society, the conflict between the neurotic and the normal is invaluable.
④ Commonly labeled as neurotics can be meaningful in terms of human values.

76 Which one is the above passage mainly about?

① The discrepancy between the two definitions of health, and the significance of the neurotic.
② The malfunction of the neurotic in comparison with the healthy and the normal.
③ The harmonious relationship of the normal, the healthy, and the neurotic in a normal society.
④ The reductionism of the unhealthy and the neurotic in relation to individuality in an abnormal society.

77 Choose the most appropriate place for the sentence below.

> All genuine individuality and spontaneity may have been lost.

① [A]　　　② [B]　　　③ [C]　　　④ [D]

11 인류학

01 빈칸에 들어가기에 가장 적절한 표현의 쌍은?

> Sapiens came to dominate the world because it is the only animal that can cooperate flexibly in large numbers. Prehistoric Sapiens were a key cause of the extinction of other human species such as the Neanderthals. The ability of Sapiens to _____ in large numbers arises from its unique capacity to believe in things existing purely in the imagination, such as gods, nations, money, and human rights. All large-scale human cooperation systems, including religions, political structures, trade networks, and legal institutions, _____ their emergence to Sapiens' distinctive cognitive capacity for fiction.

① access — appreciate
② inhabit — process
③ dominate — expend
④ harmonize — secure
⑤ cooperate — owe

02 Which of the following underlined (A), (B), (C), and (D) is not appropriately used?

> How does anthropology apply to the real world? It's a question often posed by new anthropologists. One practical application is in the aftermath of natural catastrophes, when a variety of people from different cultural groups need to be (A) <u>relocated</u>. In this process, communities with disparate backgrounds and values have no choice but to co-exist, with (B) <u>clashes</u> often resulting. Anthropologists can lend their knowledge and insight to (C) <u>aggravate</u> these situations. Their value lies in demonstrating how a cultural system can be dynamic, paving the way for communities with a mix of cultures that are at once (D) <u>resilient</u> and adaptable.

① (A) ② (B) ③ (C) ④ (D)

03 Choose the most appropriate one for the blank.

> The most significant event of all human migrations began around 50,000 years ago during the last Ice Age. This period saw the spread of *Homo Sapiens* out of Africa, until they settled on the whole of mainland Eurasia and crossed land bridges into the Americas. *Homo Sapiens* had also mastered tropical waters with canoes or rafts, which allowed them to drift to New Guinea and Australia. Colonizing the world was not a deliberate project, but a consequence of their ceaseless search for new animals to hunt, new food plants to gather, and new places to live in. Once they moved on to the next place, they made themselves at home. The _____ of *Homo Sapiens* as a species made them capable of exploiting a vast range of new environments.

① ferocity   ② exclusivity
③ adaptability   ④ immovability
⑤ meticulousness

What is phenomenology? And why should anthropologists, as well as students of history, psychology, education, or political economy be interested in it? Within philosophy, phenomenology is as diverse as its practitioners. Indeed, an introduction to philosophical traditions of phenomenology finds it important to warn readers [A] to overstate the degree to which phenomenology "coheres into an agreed method, or accepts one theoretical outlook, or one set of philosophical theses about consciousness, knowledge, and the world." Some of this diversity continues [B] to be a feature of anthropological uses of phenomenology. Yet we also argue for a heuristic narrowing of the range of its meanings. We do so in order to widen its potential applicability, making it more instructive to anthropology as well as to aligned disciplines. What might appear to be a paradox — restricting meaning in order to expand its use — is in fact in keeping with phenomenology's own teachings. For preliminary purposes, we offer a serviceable definition of phenomenology: phenomenology is [C] an investigation of how humans perceive, experience, and comprehend the sociable, materially assembled world that they inherit at infancy and in which they dwell.

Framed in this way, phenomenology in anthropology is a theory of perception and experience that pertains to every man, woman, and child in every society. As such, it is relevant not just to locals in the fieldwork sites that anthropologists step into and out of, but also to anthropologists and philosophers in their own regional lives, surrounded like everyone everywhere by significant others, human and non-human. Phenomenology therefore has a decidedly universalistic dimension. But it is also determinedly particularistic. The phenomenology we privilege sets out [D] to show how experience and perception are constituted through social and practical engagements. There is a temporal, cumulative dimension to phenomenological descriptions of people's activities and concerns, which comes through most profoundly in phenomenology's subtle vocabulary of the orientations that inhabit our bodies and guide people's actions and perspectives.

04 Which of the following is most likely to be the topic of this passage?

① How one can distinguish between phenomenology and anthropology
② How we can identify anthropological approach in phenomenology
③ How phenomenological methods can be applied to anthropology
④ How social sciences can ignore non-empirical methodologies such as phenomenology

05 According to the passage, which of the following is true?

① Phenomenology can be defined as a philosophical discipline based on a unified methodology.
② Phenomenology mainly focuses on people's perception, experience, and understanding of the world.
③ By adopting phenomenological methodologies in anthropology, researchers narrowly focus on locals in fieldwork.
④ Phenomenological anthropology emphasizes universal aspects of human lives, without considering particular aspects.

06 Which of the following is the most appropriate place for the word "not" to be inserted in?

① [A]　　　② [B]　　　③ [C]　　　④ [D]

07~08

It is impossible to calculate how many tribes of uncontacted people survive in the world's jungle. The best guess of experts is that around 100 small groups remain, mostly in the Amazonian rainforest.

How many of these tribes are genuinely unaware of the modern world is also unknown. What is certain, though, is that contact almost always ends in disaster. A decade ago, "first contact" was made with the Murunahua group that was living in an area in the Peruvian jungle.

They were forcibly contacted by illegal loggers, who shoot to kill. Some were shot, but most died from diseases such as the flu, which Westerners have natural defenses against, can prove fatal to tribes that have always lived in isolation.

07 Which one is not true?

① Experts roughly estimate that about 100 uncontacted tribes now survive in the world.
② It is not certain how many of those tribes have actually never contacted the modern world.
③ The Murunahua group did not have the first contact with the outside world on their own.
④ Illegal loggers' shooting was the biggest reason for the deaths of many Murunahuan people.

08 What does natural defenses refer to?

① arms
② immunities
③ diseases
④ rainforests

09~10

The switch from hunting and gathering to farming was a gradual one from the perspective of individual farmers, despite being very rapid within the grand scheme of human history. For just as wild crops and domesticated crops occupy a continuum, there is a range from pure hunter-gatherer to relying entirely on farmed foods. Hunter-gatherers sometimes manipulate ecosystems to increase the availability of food, though such behavior falls far short of the deliberate large-scale cultivation we call farming. Using fire to clear land and prompt new growth, for example, is a practice that goes back at least 35,000 years. Australian aborigines, one of the few remaining groups of hunter-gatherers to have survived into modern times, plant seeds on occasion to increase the availability of food when they return to a particular site a few months later. It would be an exaggeration to call this farming, since such food makes up only a tiny fraction of their diet. But the deliberate manipulation of the ecosystem means they are not exclusively hunter-gatherers either.

09 According to the passage, which of the following is true of Australian aborigines?

① Most of their food comes from domesticated crops.
② They use fire to clear land and prompt new growth.
③ They deliberately manipulate the ecosystem on occasion.
④ They have rapidly evolved from hunting and gathering to farming.

10 Why does the writer refer to Australian aborigines in the passage?

① To emphasize the long history of Australian aborigines
② To inform people that Australian aborigines are nomadic
③ To show that hunting-gathering and farming occupy a continuum
④ To warn people of environmental problems caused by agricultural chemicals

11
~
12

Writing helps us to record and communicate ideas. It is a definitive and essential part of daily human experience. Whether we write a shopping list or a great novel, we use a tool without which we would find ourselves isolated. Without writing we cut ourselves off from vital processes like the expression of political opinions, the description of medical emergencies, and the examination of our feelings in diaries and letters.

Writing crosses many cultures. Whether we consider historic cave drawings or the transmission of fax messages after the World Trade Center disaster, we find evidence of the human instinct to communicate to other people.

[A] In the past, writing brought about change. [B] African American slaves were frequently forbidden to learn to read or write, but some managed to find ways to gain literacy anyway. [C] Women in the nineteenth century used writing to advance the cause of suffrage, winning votes with passionate speeches and articles in newspapers. [D] Immigrants struggled to learn English in order to find a better life in the New World. [E]

11 윗글이 제시하거나 암시하는 내용과 일치하는 것을 고르시오.

① As we write something, we usually stay alone, separated from others.
② Before the abolition of slavery, none of African Americans could read or write.
③ While drawings are universal communication tools across various cultures, writing is confined in a certain culture.
④ Women were not allowed to vote before the 19th century.
⑤ To write a brief note or long prose, we need a tool.

12 다음 문장이 들어갈 가장 알맞은 위치를 고르시오.

> Their narratives of slave life helped fire the abolition movement.

① [A]　　② [B]　　③ [C]　　④ [D]　　⑤ [E]

13~15

The posthuman subject is an amalgam, a collection of heterogeneous components, a material-informational entity whose boundaries undergo continuous construction and reconstruction. Consider the six-million-dollar man, a paradigmatic citizen of the posthuman regime. As his name implies, the parts of the self are indeed owned, but they are owned precisely because they were purchased, not because ownership is a natural condition preexisting market relations. Similarly, the presumption that there is an agency, desire, or will belonging to the self and clearly distinguished from the wills of others is undercut in the posthuman, for the posthuman's collective heterogenous quality implies a distributed cognition located in disparate parts. We have only to recall Robocop's memory flashes that interfere with his programmed directives to understand how the distributed cognition of the posthuman complicates individual agency. If human essence is freedom from the wills of others, the posthuman is "post" not because it is necessarily unfree but because there is no a priori way to identify a self-will that can be clearly distinguished from an other-will. Although these examples foreground the cybernetic aspect of the posthuman, it is important to recognize that the construction of the posthuman does not require the subject to be a literal cyborg. Whether or not interventions have been made on the body, new models of subjectivity emerging from such fields as cognitive science and artificial life imply that even a biologically unaltered *Homo sapiens* count as posthuman. The defining characteristics involve the construction of subjectivity, not the presence of nonbiological components.

13 Which of the following is not the characteristic of the posthuman?

① an entity of hybrid components
② an agency of the distributed cognition
③ a model of a new subjectivity
④ a species of biologically altered parts

14 Which of the following can be inferred from the passage?

① There is a humanist presumption that is never weakened in the posthuman.
② The posthuman is represented only through bodily interventions.
③ The construction of the posthuman subjectivity is not altogether artificial.
④ The posthuman gives way to the biological aspect of *Homo sapiens*.

15 Why does the author mention Robocop in the passage?

① To put an emphasis on the mechanism of artificial intelligence
② To put the case that cognition is distributed and complicated
③ To give a further example of the current market relations
④ To offer an in-depth analysis of the posthuman anxiety

16~17

The misfortunes of human beings may be divided into two classes: first, those inflicted by the non-human environment, and, second, those inflicted by other people. As mankind have progressed in knowledge and technique, the second class has become a continually increasing percentage of the total. In olden times, famine, for example, was due to natural causes, and, although people did their best to combat it, large numbers of them died of starvation. At the present moment large parts of the world are still faced with the threat of famine, but although natural causes have contributed to the situation, the principal causes are human.

For a long time the civilized nations of the world devoted all their best energies to killing each other, and they find it difficult suddenly to switch over to keeping each other alive. It is now man that is _____. Nature, it is true, still sees to it that we are mortal, but with the progress in medicine it will become more and more common for people to live until they have had their fill of life. We are supposed to wish to live for ever and to look forward to the unending joys of heaven. But in fact, if you question any candid person who is no longer young, he is very likely to tell you that, having tasted life in this world, he has no wish to begin again as a "new boy" in another. For the future, therefore, it may be taken that much the most important evils that mankind have to consider are those which they inflict upon each other through stupidity or malevolence or both.

16 빈칸에 들어갈 가장 적합한 표현을 고르시오.

① defender of nature
② man's worst enemy
③ environment's friend
④ creator of civilization

17 위 글의 내용과 맞지 않는 것을 고르시오.

① Human problems created by humans themselves exceed all others.
② Though we must all die some time, medicine has made it possible for people to live longer than before.
③ There is no one who would refuse the opportunity, if offered, to begin a new life again in another world.
④ The most important problem for man in the future will probably be himself because of his maliciousness and lack of wisdom.

18~20

If there is a preponderance among mankind of rational opinions and rational conduct, it is owing to a quality of the human mind, the source of everything respectable in man either as an intellectual or as a moral being, namely, that his errors are corrigible. He is capable of rectifying his mistakes, by discussion and experience. Not by experience alone. There must be discussion, to show how experience is to be interpreted.

Wrong opinions and practices gradually yield to fact and argument: but facts and arguments, to produce any effect on the mind, must be brought before it. Very few facts are able to tell their own story, without comments to bring out their meaning. Then, reliance can be placed on the whole strength and value of human judgement only when the means of setting it right are kept constantly at hand. In the case of any person whose judgement is really deserving of confidence, how has it become so? Because he has kept his mind open to criticism of his opinions and conduct. The steady habit of correcting and completing his own opinion by collating it with those of others is the only stable foundation for a just reliance on it. For, being cognisant of all that can, at least obviously, be said against him, and having taken up his positions against all _____, he has a right to think his judgement better than that of any person, or any multitude, who have not gone through a similar process.

18 Which is the closest in meaning to the underlined part?

① criticism
② rationality
③ superiority
④ reflection

19 Which is the most appropriate for the blank?

① gainsayers
② supporters
③ votaries
④ apostates

20 According to the passage, which is not true?

① Facts will determine the reliance of opinions.
② Opinions are not reliable without being put to discussion.
③ Criticism is not to be avoided to strengthen the confidence of opinions.
④ The intellectual quality of human mind is found in the ability to correct errors.

21~22

In the ant community, each worker performs its proper functions. There may be a separate caste of soldiers. Certain highly specialized individuals perform the functions of king and queen. If man were to adopt this community as a pattern, he would live in a fascist state, in which ideally each individual is conditioned from birth for his proper occupation: in which rulers are perpetually rulers, soldiers perpetually soldiers, the peasant is never more than a peasant, and the worker is doomed to be a worker. This aspiration of the fascist for a human state based on the model of the ant results from a profound misapprehension both of the nature of the ant and of the nature of man. I wish to point out that the very physical development of the insect conditions it to be an essentially stupid and unlearning individual, cast in a mold which cannot be modified to any great extent. I also wish to show how these physiological conditions make it into a cheap mass-produced article, of no more individual value than a paper pie plate to be thrown away after it is once used. On the other hand, I wish to show that the human individual, capable of vast learning and study, which may occupy almost half of his life, is physically equipped, as the ant is not, for this capacity. Variety and possibility are inherent in the human sensorium — and are indeed the key to man's most noble flights — because variety and possibility belong to the very structure of the human organism. While it is possible to throw away this enormous advantage that we have over the ants, and to organize the fascist ant-state with human material, I certainly believe that this is a degradation of man's very nature, and economically a waste of the great human values which man possesses.

21 Which of the following statement is true?

① The ant community has a hard organizational structure which cannot be properly analyzed by human reasoning.
② The organizational structure of an ant can be widely used in the apprehension of human beings.
③ A misapprehension of the nature of the ant and the nature of man may produce a human fascist society.
④ An ant has more developmental possibilities and potentials than human beings.

22 What would be the best title of the passage above?

① The degradation of human nature
② The vulnerability of human organism
③ The quirks and eddies found in ants and humans
④ The inherent noble structure of human beings

12 의학·건강

01 Reorder the following sentences in the best way to form a coherent passage for the question.

> [A] Indeed, the evidence for fiber's benefits extends beyond any particular ailment.
> [B] But while the benefits are clear, it's not so clear why fiber is so great.
> [C] A diet of fiber-rich foods reduces the risk of developing diabetes, heart disease and arthritis.
> [D] That's why experts are always saying how good dietary fiber is for us.

① [B] — [A] — [D] — [C]   ② [C] — [B] — [A] — [D]
③ [C] — [A] — [D] — [B]   ④ [B] — [D] — [A] — [C]

02 Choose the best place for the sentence in the box.

> The challenge for health-conscious consumers is to determine which ones fit easily into a nutritious diet.

> Frozen dinners have become part of the American diet. [A] Consumers spend $4 billion a year on them, and food manufacturers are constantly turning out new lines. [B] In a study of frozen foods, strict criteria were used to identify entrees that are suitable for people wanting to limit their intake of fat, calories, and sodium while including essential vitamins and minerals. [C] The results were encouraging. [D] A total of 173 frozen dishes had less than 20% of calories from fat, 73 contained less than 200 milligrams of sodium per 100 calories, and 50 had at least 30% of the recommended daily allowance for vitamins A and/or C. [E] Since some meals are likely to be deficient in some nutrients, foods that will compensate must be added.

① [A]   ② [B]   ③ [C]   ④ [D]   ⑤ [E]

03~04

When older people can no longer remember names at a cocktail party, they tend to think that their brainpower is declining. But a growing number of studies suggest that this assumption is often wrong. _____, the research finds, the aging brain is simply taking in more data and trying to sift through a clutter of information, often to its long-term benefit. Some brains do deteriorate with age. Alzheimer's disease, _____, strikes 13 percent of Americans 65 and older. But for most aging adults, the authors say, much of what occurs is a gradually widening focus of attention that makes it more difficult to <u>latch onto</u> just one fact, like a name or a telephone number. Although that can be frustrating, it is often useful.

03 빈칸에 들어갈 말로 가장 적절한 것은?

① Namely — in contrast
② Moreover — however
③ Instead — for example
④ What is worse — in conclusion
⑤ Therefore — however

04 밑줄 친 <u>latch onto</u>와 의미가 가장 가까운 것은?

① ignore
② forget
③ overstate
④ minimize
⑤ comprehend

05~07

Severe depression is not something people can pull themselves out of _____ they can pull themselves out of congestive heart failure, kidney disease, or gallstones. When patients with congestive heart failure develop difficulty breathing, they are usually grateful for (A)_____ that relieves their distress. They rarely believe they can handle such illnesses themselves because they have no sense of being in control over the workings of their heart. We also do not sense our brains at work, but we feel in control of our minds. This sense of being in control of our minds allows those with depression to believe they can pull themselves out of the severe depression. In my experience once older adults understand that depression is a disease of the brain, and not something they have control over, they become more open to considering (A)_____. It's not that they can't handle their problems any longer; rather, their brain has let them down. I often say to my patients, (B) _____.

05 Which of the following best fills in the blank?

① less than
② any more than
③ no more than
④ no less than

06 Which of the following best fills in the blank (A)?

① contentment
② treatment
③ refreshment
④ requirement

07 What would the doctor say to his patients in the blank (B)?

① "It's not you; it's your brain."
② "It's not your brain; it's you."
③ "It's not you; it's your depression."
④ "It's not your depression; it's you."

08~09

It is not wise to study soon after a big meal. Since the digestive organs are heavily burdened at this time, they take a large supply of blood from the brain and the other parts of the body. And, since there cannot be a proper supply of blood in both places at the same time, either the digestive organs will be robbed of their supply, with the result that digestion cannot be carried out properly, or the brain will be so impoverished that it will do poor work. <u>For this reason</u> at least a half-hour after a big meal should be spent either in the enjoyment of music or light reading, or in some form of _____ physical exercise.

08
Which of the following is closest to what is referred to by <u>For this reason</u>?

① The brain becoming acutely active after a meal
② There being not enough blood for both organs
③ Digestive functions being severely handicapped
④ Blood supply working only on a schedule

09
Which of the following best fits into the blank?

① agreeable and easy
② hard and sweaty
③ familiar but demanding
④ mental as well as

10 다음 글의 빈칸에 들어갈 말로 가장 적절한 것은?

Optimists get the last laugh and their hearts stay healthy longer than those of the grump. People who described themselves as highly _____ a decade ago had lower rates of death from cardiovascular disease and lower overall death rates than strong pessimists. Nine years ago a study group — 999 men and women aged 65 to 85 — completed a questionnaire on health, self-respect, morale, optimism and relationships. Since then, 397 of them have died. _____ participants had a 55 percent lower risk of death from all causes and 23 percent lower risk of death from heart failure. The study notes that _____ people may be more prone to developing habits and problems that cut life short, such as smoking, obesity and hypertension. A predisposition toward optimism seemed to provide a survival benefit in subjects with relatively short life expectancies otherwise.

① optimistic — Optimistic — pessimistic
② optimistic — Pessimistic — pessimistic
③ pessimistic — Optimistic — optimistic
④ pessimistic — Optimistic — pessimistic
⑤ optimistic — Pessimistic — optimistic

11~12

(A) _____. For decades the (B) _____ brain was understood to be incapable of growing new neurons. Once an individual reached adulthood, the thinking went, the brain began losing neurons rather than gaining them. But evidence was building that the (C) _____ brain could, in fact, generate new neurons. In one particularly (D) _____ experiment with mice, scientists found that simply running on a wheel led to the birth of new neurons in the hippocampus, a brain structure that is associated with memory. Since then, other studies have established that exercise also has positive effects on the brains of humans, especially as we age, and that it may even help reduce the risk of Alzheimer's disease and other neurodegenerative conditions.

11 Choose the best set of words for blanks (B), (C), and (D).

① human — elderly — precipitous
② mammal — immature — astounding
③ adolescent — fully developed — definitive
④ mature — adult — striking

12 Choose the best sentence for blank (A).

① Recent research confirms what we have long suspected to be true about the brain.
② Researchers recently announced a series of discoveries that would upend a bedrock tenet of neuroscience.
③ Researchers have recently found an exciting new treatment for neurodegenerative conditions.
④ Recent research suggests that exercise can double the total mass of the adult brain by generating new neurons.

13~14

It's not uncommon for young women like Maya to be repeatedly misdiagnosed. Because autism is at least three times as common in boys as in girls, scientists routinely include only boys in their research. The result is that we know shockingly little about whether and how autism might be different in girls and boys. What we do know is grim: on average, girls who have mild symptoms of autism are diagnosed two years later than boys. There's some debate about why this might be so. From the start, girls' restricted interests seem more socially acceptable — dolls or books, perhaps, rather than train schedules — and may go unnoticed. But the fact that diagnostic tests are based on observations of boys with autism almost certainly contributes to errors and delays.

As they enter teens, girls struggle to keep up with the elaborate rules of social relationships. Cribbing notes on what to say and how to say it, many try to blend in, but at great cost to their inner selves. Starting in adolescence, they have high rates of depression and anxiety. A few studies have also found an intriguing overlap between autism and eating disorders such as anorexia, although the studies are too small to estimate how many women have both.

13 The autism in girls is not well-known because _____.

① there were not many autistic girls
② parents of autistic girls hide their kids
③ It is not different from that in boys
④ autistic girls only stay at home
⑤ girls' autism didn't get much attention

14 Which one is not a symptom of autism in teenage girls?

① depression
② anxiety
③ gaining weight
④ thin figure
⑤ eating little

15~16

Depression is a serious problem. Its causes include work or academic pressures, environmental impacts, family history and disease/medication side effects, among others. _____ can play a role in the prevention and treatment of depression. The disease may occur due to hormonal imbalances or vitamin deficiencies. To prevent these situations, shifting your diet to contain more vitamin-rich foods may be beneficial. For example, Brazil nuts, brown rice and seafood are high in selenium, an element that protects against free radicals and may decrease the likelihood of developing depression. Furthermore, B vitamins have been shown to help produce important chemicals in the brain that combat depression. Dietary sources of B vitamins include milk, bananas, leafy greens, eggs and clams. There are foods you may want to avoid, such as coffee or alcohol. Caffeine may keep your brain active, but it may also increase anxiety or nervousness, while alcohol may interfere with antidepressant medications and decrease their effectiveness.

15 Which of the following is most appropriate for the blank?

① Food
② Family
③ Exercise
④ Hormones
⑤ Medication

16 Which of the following is not implied or stated in the passage?

① Depression can be caused by genes.
② Hormones need to be balanced to prevent depression.
③ Brazil nuts and brown rice may help prevent depression.
④ Bananas, eggs and clams may be good for depressed people.
⑤ Coffee and Alcohol can be used in the treatment of depression.

17~18

We talk about food in the negative: What we shouldn't eat, what we'll regret later, what's evil, dangerously tempting, unhealthy. (A) The effects are more insidious than any overindulgent amount of "bad food" can ever be. By fretting about food, we turn occasions for comfort and joy into sources of fear and anxiety. And when we avoid certain foods, we usually compensate by consuming too much of others. All of this happens under the guise of science. But a closer look at the research behind our food fears shows that many of our most demonized foods are actually fine for us. Consider salt. It's true that, if people with high blood pressure consume a lot of salt, it can lead to cardiovascular events like heart attacks. It's also true that salt is overused in processed foods. But the average American consumes just over three grams of sodium per day, which is actually in the sweet spot for health. Eating too little salt may be just as dangerous as eating too much. This is especially true for the majority of people who don't have high blood pressure. Regardless, (B) experts continue to push for lower recommendations. (C) Many of the doctors and nutritionists who recommend avoiding certain foods fail to properly explain the magnitude of their risks. In some studies, processed red meat in large amounts is associated with an increased relative risk of developing cancer. The absolute risk, however, is often quite small.

17 What does the underlined (A) mean?

① The effects of food fears
② The effects of "bad food"
③ The effects of eating too much
④ The effects of eating processed food

18 The author agrees _____.

① with both (B) and (C)
② with (B), but not with (C)
③ with (C), but not with (B)
④ with neither (B) nor (C)

19~20

A surgical technique known as 'keyhole surgery' has become more common in recent years. This technique eliminates the need for surgeons to make large incisions. _____, a couple of small incisions, each measuring about one centimeter, are made around the area to be operated on. Long instruments, which look a bit like chopsticks, are inserted through the tiny incisions and into the patient's body. At the end of these instruments are small tools that resemble standard surgical tools. A tiny camera, called an endoscope, is also inserted into the body through one of the incisions. The camera relays an image of what is happening inside the patient's body to a large computer monitor, so doctors are able to see what is going on, and where to place the tools. The awkward part of the keyhole surgery is that it is counterintuitive; if a surgeon wants to move the tool to the left, he or she must push it to the right, and vice versa.

19 Which is the most appropriate for the blank?

① Instead
② However
③ Likewise
④ In particular

20 According to the passage, which is not true for the keyhole surgery?

① It requires the use of long, thin tools and a small camera.
② A doctor views the inside of a patient's body on a computer screen.
③ It would leave rather smaller scars.
④ It needs long chopsticks to be inserted through the incisions.

21
~
22

If you are feeling numbness, tingling, or weakness in your hand, consider asking your doctor to check you for carpal tunnel syndrome. It's caused by pressure on your median nerve, which runs the length of the arm, goes through a passage in the wrist called the carpal tunnel, and ends in the hand. The median controls the movement and feeling of your thumb, and also the movement of all your fingers except your pinky. The carpal tunnel is narrowed as a result of the pressure on the median, usually from swelling. Carpal tunnel syndrome can happen due to _____, movements that you perform over and over such as typing. This is especially true of actions when your hands are lower than your wrist. As it becomes more severe, you may have less grip strength because the muscles in your hand shrink. For prevention, you should keep your wrists straight, and take more frequent breaks while working. Certain stretching and exercises could help, too.

21 According to the passage, which of the following is not true?

① Symptoms of carpal tunnel syndrome include numbness and tingling of the hand.
② The movement and feeling of the thumb are controlled by the median.
③ Carpal tunnel syndrome may cause the muscles in the hand to shrink.
④ Keeping the hand above the wrist increases chances of carpal tunnel syndrome.

22 Which of the following best fits into the blank?

① repetitive motions
② slow contractions
③ minuscule flexing
④ irregular tapping

23~24

Vitamin D is also known as the 'sunshine vitamin', as it is produced by our bodies when we are exposed to sunlight. It is vital to our health to consume a sufficient amount of Vitamin D. Vitamin D helps us maintain healthy bones and teeth, and also supports our immune system, brain, and nervous system. In addition, it also protects us against a wide range of diseases such as cancer, diabetes, and sclerosis. Though we may be fooled by the name, Vitamin D _____ but a type of pro-hormone. Vitamins are defined as nutrients that cannot be produced by the body and must be obtained through our diet. However, our bodies are capable of creating 'Vitamin' D if exposed to direct sunlight for five to ten minutes, two or three times a week. Experts warn that in the winter, when we are generally exposed to less sunlight, Vitamin D can break down very quickly. They recommend that in order to prevent stores from running low, we should increase our intake of Vitamin D through food or nutritional supplements.

23 According to the passage, which of the following is not true of Vitamin D?

① A sufficient amount of Vitamin D is necessary for a healthy skeletal structure.
② Vitamin D is a type of pro-hormone that can be produced by our bodies.
③ Daily exposure to sunlight is necessary to produce enough Vitamin D.
④ Nutritional supplements of Vitamin D are recommended in the winter.

24 Which of the following best fits into the blank?

① is not only a vitamin
② is a rare type of vitamin
③ has several different forms
④ is actually not a vitamin

25~28

Until recently, pioneers of _____ health innovation had remained at the margins of our biomedical research and regulatory establishment. Yet in the last two months alone, two individuals widely shared videos in which they injected themselves with unregulated gene therapies. Josiah Zayner is one of the self-experimenters and the CEO of the Odin, a start-up that sells gene-editing kits for home use. [A] Is self-experimentation with gene-editing techniques something we should herald as a new form of "permissionless" innovation? Or will self-proclaimed biohackers, by testing the regulatory framework, harm the emerging ecosystem of citizens who contribute to biomedical innovation? [B] _____ banning the sale of gene-editing kits is only a weak, temporary solution. What we need is to foster an ethos of responsible innovation outside of traditional research institutions. We must recognize the urgent need to build legitimacy, but also tailored regulatory support for new forms of health research. [C] The path forward is not to promote radical, unregulated science, but to develop engagement channels that force citizens, patients, ethicists and regulators to rethink and design an adaptive oversight system. [D]

25 Choose the words that fit best for blanks.

① transnational — Furthermore
② democratized — Yet
③ ecological — For instance
④ optimal — Nevertheless

26 The author's presentation is most like that of a _____.

① researcher offering a scholarly analysis
② daily journalist reporting on a news story
③ motivational speaker giving an inspiring talk
④ public intellectual presenting an opinion on an ethical dilemma

27 Which of the following cannot be inferred from the passage?

① Biotechnologies have progressed to a point where individuals can experiment with gene therapies at home.
② The U.S. government recently approved self-experimentation by a practitioner outside of a traditional research institution.
③ A recent development in health research involves entrepreneurship.
④ Despite the potential for citizens to take a proactive role outside of medical practices, many ethical issues remain unresolved.

28 Which would be the best place for the following sentence?

> Self-experimentation with gene therapies raises troubling safety and ethical questions, from the potential for infections and immunological reactions to lack of understanding of the risks involved and unrealistic expectations from patients.

① [A]　　　② [B]　　　③ [C]　　　④ [D]

[29~30]

_____. More than 50,000 years ago, stone-age, cave-dwelling humans first crushed and infused herbs for their curative properties. Traditional forms of medicine — few of which, sadly, are known to written history — evolved on all continents, from the deserts and jungles of Africa to North American plains, South American rain forests, and balmy Pacific islands. Earliest records in West Asia, the Middle East, North Africa, China, and India document myriad diseases, healing plants, and surgical procedures. Ancient Egyptians had complex, hierarchical methods of medicine integrated into their religious beliefs. Gods and spirits were in charge of mortal disease, and priest-physicians — Imhotep is one of the first great names in medical history — mediated with the supernatural realm to ease human suffering. The civilizations of Greece and Rome had their respective medical giants in Hippocrates and Galen. Hippocrates set standards for patient care and the physician's attitudes and philosophy that persist today. Galen wrote so extensively and authoritatively that his theories and practices attained quasi-religious status and effectively stalled medical progress in Europe for 1,400 years. After the Roman Empire ended, the murky arts of alchemy, sorcery, exorcism, and miracle cures flourished in Western Europe. Ancient India and China also developed sophisticated medical systems with outstanding contributors. In India, in the centuries before and after Hippocrates, Susruta and Chakara produced encyclopedic founding works of Ayurvedic medicine. Chinese physician Zhang Zhongjing, a contemporary of Galen, also compiled works that described hundreds of diseases and prescribed thousands of remedies.

29 Choose the one that would best fill in the blank.

① Medicine is as old as humankind
② Good medicine always tastes bitter
③ Medicine and religion converge after all
④ The medical profession is not what it used to be

30 Choose the one that is not true according to the passage.

① Ancient Egyptian priest-physicians are recognized in medical history.
② Galen's practices advanced medicine after the fall of the Roman Empire.
③ In the past, medicine was thought to be tied to matters of faith.
④ Europe and China developed medical systems around the same time.

31~32

Penicillin is effective against many serious bacterial infections. Alexander Fleming, a Scottish scientist, discovered penicillin in 1928. However, he did not immediately understand what he had discovered. At the time he was observing several fungi that could destroy bacteria. However, Fleming was not a very neat scientist. He often left trays of bacteria around his lab. In August 1928, he went away for a vacation. When he returned, he found that something strange had happened to one of the trays. A fungus had grown on the bacteria and killed them. At first, Fleming did not understand why this had happened, but he later realized what he had discovered. He realized that the fungus was powerful and could be useful in curing bacterial infections, but he still had not understood how important it was. He doubted whether the fungus could be effective long enough to kill bacteria inside a human body. The penicillin he grew in the first few years was too slow in taking effect, so he stopped working on it. After a few years, he returned to it. Fleming and other scientists discovered ways to make the _____ work more rapidly, and it soon became the most effective antibiotic in existence. This discovery has saved millions of lives.

31 Which best fits in the blank?

① substance
② substitute
③ subsidiary
④ subthreshold

32 Which is the best title for the passage?

① An Accidental Discovery
② An Expensive Discovery
③ A Catastrophic Discovery
④ A Controversial Discovery

33~35

At the University of Pennsylvania Hospital in Philadelphia, 17-year-old Amy Salinger and her parents listened to the diagnosis of Dr. Smith, a kidney specialist. He told them that Amy had an unusual inflammation known as acute nephritis and that her kidneys were 95 percent destroyed. Amy's face went blank as she heard the horrific news. A few minutes later, Amy composed herself and asked about treatment options. The doctor told her that her condition was _____ and she would soon have to go on dialysis. Amy was stunned once again. However, Dr. Smith mentioned there was still a sliver of hope for Amy. A compatible donor would have to be found so that a transplant could be performed.

A short time later, Dr. Smith privately consulted with Amy's parents and told them that transplant options are limited as the wait for a cadaver kidney was over three years. _____, her foster parents had no idea where Amy's birth parents were since Amy was adopted. Also, tragically, Amy's foster parents are far from being compatible. Dr. Smith told them that it was imperative that they find Amy's birth parents as soon as possible if Amy was to have any chance of surviving.

33 Choose the best word for the blanks.

① reversible — Unfortunately
② irreversible — Unfortunately
③ irreversible — Fortunately
④ reversible — Fortunately

34 Which one is true?

① Amy is in her twenties.
② Amy's foster parents are not ideal donors.
③ Cadaver kidneys are readily available.
④ Dr. Smith specializes only in liver transplants.

35 Choose the best title.

① Adopting Amy
② The History of Acute Nephritis
③ Waiting for a Diagnosis
④ Saving Amy

In 2006, researchers at Cornell University released results of a long-term study containing some hypotheses about the reorganization of television in the 1980s. The research project assembled data to suggest a correlation between television viewing by very young children and autism. One of the most urgent problems in autism studies has been to explain the extraordinary and anomalous rise in its frequency beginning in the mid to late 1980s. From the late 1970s, when autism occurred in one out of 2,500 children, the rate of incidence has risen so fast that, as of a few years ago, it affected approximately one in 150 children, and showed no sign of leveling off. Obviously, television had been pervasive in North American homes since the 1950s: Why then might it have markedly different consequences beginning in the 1980s? The study proposes that a new coalescence of factors occurred in that decade — in particular, the widespread availability of cable TV, the growth of dedicated children's channels and video cassettes, and the popularity of VCRs, as well as huge increases in households with two or more television sets. Thus conditions were, and continue to be, in place for the exposure of very young children to television for extended periods of time on a daily basis. Their specific conclusions were relatively cautious: that extended television viewing before the age of three can trigger the onset of the disorder in "at risk" children.

36 What led the researchers at Cornell University to take interest in television was _____.

① the increase of the cases of autism in the 1980s
② the nationwide spread of television sets in the 1950s
③ the emergence of new visual instruments such as VCRs
④ new evidence of the relation between television and autism

37 According to the passage, which of the following is true?

① In North America, dedicated children's channels were already popular in the 1950s.
② In the late 1970s, the rate of child autism incidence was no higher than one in 2,500 children.
③ Watching TV for an extended period of time tends to cause autism in adults as well as in children.
④ A few years ago, the rate of child autism incidence stabilized with approximately one in 150 children affected.

38 ~ 40

"Mental illness" is no longer a breach of the self but a neurochemical event happening to — but separate from — the self. Like hypertension, it happens in our cells, and we swallow pills to get rid of it. This is more or less how grown-ups talked about what was wrong with me for several years after I was diagnosed with OCD(Obsessive Compulsive Disorder) at thirteen. I was, clinically, a nervous wreck, and many of my fears were about the transformation of my own mind. Was I insane? Was I doomed? Was this who I really was? Therapists and my parents were ready with reassurances that what was happening was only an accident of serotonin, a mysterious but correctable "imbalance" no more essential to who I was than a flu or a sunburn. I balked at taking medication, worried it would change who I was. "You have an illness, and this is just medicine to correct that illness," I was told. "It's like having diabetes. You wouldn't refuse insulin because your body's 'authentic' state is to have diabetes." In the end, I couldn't take the panic attacks, so I took the Prozac and, with it, this narrative of what was happening. _____. The pills made my hands shake, but my mind was transformed back, more or less, to the healthy, stable state I remembered.

(*Prozac: medicine for depression, OCD, etc.)

38 The adults around the author wanted to make sure that _____.

① everybody has a sort of illness
② all human beings are doomed
③ the author's illness could be cured
④ there is no cure for a flu or a sunburn
⑤ the disease will go away when the author grows up

39 The most appropriate expression for the blank would be '_____.'

① It worked
② It's a big mistake
③ I didn't mean it
④ I was wrong
⑤ Too bad

40 The author hesitated to take the medicine because _____.

① she hated the medical treatment
② she didn't believe in the doctors
③ she knew the side-effects of the drugs
④ she wanted to remain as she was
⑤ she was afraid she could not make it

41~43

Facebook's CEO Mark Zuckerberg pledged to invest at least $3 billion to "cure, manage, and prevent all disease." Many others followed suit, seeking a legacy in the realm of health and medicine with a heavy emphasis on gene modification. But there is a disconnect. Comparing the body to a machine, complete with bugs to be fixed by means of gene modification tools, conflicts with Charles Darwin's theory of evolution: machines and computers do not evolve, but organisms do. Evolution matters here because bits of code that compromise one function often enhance a second function, or can be repurposed for a new function when the environment shifts. In evolution, everything is grasping for its purpose. Parts that break down can become the next best thing. In evolution, nothing comes for free. Stress can both trigger creativity and compound a raft of chronic maladies. Genetic variants that cause cystic fibrosis can protect against cholera. Gene transfer can effectively treat diseases caused by a single errant gene. However, this gene's existing risk variants that influence diseases won't go away because they often provide advantages as time goes on. From Darwin's perspective we don't progress to a more perfect form, but adapt to local environments. If humans are machines, then we can simply repair the broken parts. But we are not, and there is something more fundamental to the crisis of life than mere mechanisms of biology. Thus, risk and an element of danger will _____.

41 From the context, which of the following is closest in meaning to the underlined sentence?

① Gene modification therapy costs more than evolutionary intervention.
② Advantageous evolutionary features are accompanied by disadvantageous ones.
③ All organisms are the product of extremely long evolutionary processes.
④ Evolutionary processes require tremendous effort on the part of the organisms.

42 Which of the following best fits into the blank?

① always be with us
② never emerge again
③ be completely eradicated
④ be negligible in magnitude

43 Which of the following is the author's stance?

① Identifying defective genes is the top priority.
② Fixing genes is a long but desirable process.
③ Gene modification methods will not succeed.
④ Cataloging adaptive gene interactions is imperative.

44
~
47

As you get older, little growths called skin tags might start popping up on your body. You'll recognize them because they're thinner at the base and get wider at the top. They aren't painful or dangerous like cancerous moles, but there's a very good reason you'll want them removed. People have used all kinds of crazy methods to try removing skin tags on their own, says Dr. Rossi, MD, dermatologic surgeon. He's heard of people tying strings around them, burning them, trying to pick them off with their fingers, and even slamming books against them. A dermatologist, on the other hand, can snip away skin tags quickly and cleanly.

For one thing, dermatologists have sterile instruments, but using your own could lead to an infection. [A] Plus, while dermatologists can use local anesthesia and have supplies to stop the blood, you could bleed uncontrollably with at-home methods. [B] Even hospital medications claiming to dissolve the skin tags could be bad news, says Dr. Rossi. "You could burn the skin or make marks," he says. "There could be unintended consequences."

But there's an even bigger reason you should visit an expert. [C] After dermatologists remove a growth, they'll look at it under a microscope. "There are things that look like skin tags but are cancerous," says Dr. Rossi. That doesn't mean you should freak out if you do find a skin tag. [D] Plus, checking a skin tag is a "_____" to get your doctor to check the rest of your body for skin cancer and atypical or malignant growths, says Dr. Rossi.

44 Choose the best title.

① How to Handle Skin Tags
② The Consequences of Skin Tags
③ The Benefits of Home-Treatment of Skin Tags
④ The Cause of Skin Tags

45 Which one is not true?

① Skin tags have a circular cone shape.
② People try a variety of ways to remove skin tags.
③ Most skin tags are cancerous.
④ It is good to get your body checked when a skin tag is found.

46 Choose the best place for the following.

> Most will just be benign, but you won't know for sure until you've asked.

① [A]　　　② [B]　　　③ [C]　　　④ [D]

47 Choose the best expression for the blank.

① good excuse　　　② dangerous process
③ useless method　　④ necessary evil

48~50

There are several pro tips for long and healthy life. First, diet. Weight loss likely explains many of the positive changes, such as lower blood pressure and better blood-sugar levels. But some experts speculate that fasting also makes the body more resistant to stress, which can have beneficial effects at the cellular level. One expert says, "Diet is by far the most powerful intervention to delay aging and age-related diseases."

In the past couple of years, scientists have shown that (A) _____ behavior, like sitting all day, is a risk factor for earlier death. They found that hours spent sitting are linked to increased risks of Type 2 diabetes and nonalcoholic fatty liver disease. You can't exercise away all the bad effects of sitting too much. But the good news is that doing anything but sitting still — even fidgeting counts — can add up. People who logged the least physical activity had the highest risk of a heart event in the next ten years, which isn't shocking. But to the surprise of the researchers, moving just a little bit more during the day — like doing chores around the house — was enough to lower the risk of a heart event.

By now it's clear to scientists that our emotions affect our biology. Studies have shown for years that anger and stress can release stress hormones like adrenaline into our blood, which trigger the heart to beat faster and harder. Stress may even have an effect on how well our brains hold up against Alzheimer's disease. The researchers found that people who held more negative views of aging earlier in life had greater loss in the volume of their hippocampus, a region of the brain whose loss is linked to Alzheimer's disease. This is not the first time research has suggested that (B) _____.

48 Which best fits in the blank (A)?

① active
② abrupt
③ sedentary
④ vociferous

49 According to the passage, which is not one of the pro tips for long and healthy life?

① not sitting still for long
② doing excessive exercise
③ keeping to a regimen of diet
④ having an optimistic attitude

50 Which best fits in the blank (B)?

① how we feel about aging can affect how we age
② stress and exercise are interrelated with each other
③ Alzheimer's disease is linked to positive views of aging
④ anger and stress have no direct bearing on Alzheimer's disease

13 물리·화학·기술·건축

01~02

The Aristotelian tradition held that one could work out all the laws that govern the universe by pure thought: it was not necessary to check by observation. So no one until Galileo bothered to see whether bodies of different weight did in fact fall at different speeds. It is said that Galileo demonstrated that Aristotle's belief was false by dropping weights from the leaning tower of Pisa. The story is almost certainly untrue, but Galileo did do something equivalent: he rolled balls of different weights down a smooth slope. The situation is similar to that of heavy bodies falling vertically, but it is easier to observe because _____. Galileo's measurements indicated that each body increased its speed at the same rate, no matter what its weight. For example, if you let go of a ball on a slope that drops by one meter for every ten meters you go along, the ball will be traveling down the slope at a speed of about one meter per second after one second, two meters per second after two seconds, and so on.

01 윗글의 내용과 거리가 가장 먼 것은?

① An object falls with uniform acceleration.
② The story of the Leaning Tower of Pisa is probably not true.
③ A heavy object falls faster than a lighter one, in direct proportion to its weight.
④ In Galileo's experiment, an inclined plane was used to measure falling objects.
⑤ In the Aristotelian tradition, a scientific law could be a result of pure thought rather than observation.

02 빈칸에 들어갈 가장 적절한 것은?

① the speeds are smaller
② objects with different weight are used
③ objects accelerate at different rates
④ objects are dropped from the same height
⑤ the speed at which an object falls depends on the mass

The word *cyborg* — a short form of "cybernetic organism" — was first used in a 1960 paper on space travel. A cyborg was defined as an organism "to which external components have been added for the purpose of adapting to new environments." According to this definition, an astronaut in a spacesuit is an example of a cyborg, as the spacesuit helps the astronaut adapt to a new environment — space. More recently, the word has evolved to refer to human beings who have mechanical body parts that make them more than human.

Although super-humans like RoboCop are not yet a reality, advances in real-life cyborg technology allow some people to compensate for abilities they have lost, and give other people new and unusual abilities. An example is filmmaker Rob Spence and his bionic eye. Spence injured one of his eyes in an accident. _____ replacing his damaged eye with the typical glass eye, Spence had a prosthetic eye with a camera implanted in his eye socket. The eye is not connected to Spence's brain or optic nerve, but it can record what Spence sees. Spence has used his camera eye to record interviews for a documentary about people with bionic body parts.

03 Which is the most appropriate for the blank?

① Instead of
② Thanks to
③ In addition to
④ Despite

04 According to the passage, which is true?

① Spence can see things thanks to his prosthetic eye.
② Spence injured his two eyes in an accident.
③ An astronaut in a spacesuit can be considered a cyborg.
④ Super-humans are a reality nowadays.

05~06

Combustion is just one example of many different types of chemical reactions. Three others are decomposition, combination, and replacement. During decomposition, compounds in matter split apart to form smaller compounds or even individual elements. In the case of combination, the opposite process takes place; here, compounds join together to create new compounds. In a replacement chemical reaction, one or more compounds split apart and swap parts with others. Throughout all chemical reactions, it is important to understand that matter is neither created nor destroyed. Matter simply changes from one form to another.

05 According to the passage, what process occurs during decomposition?

① Energy is released in the form of heat and light.
② Compounds separate to form smaller compounds.
③ Molecules join together to form new compounds.
④ Substances split apart and swap parts.

06 According to the author's description of matter, which of the following is true?

① It is created during chemical reactions.
② It is detectable in the presence of chemical reactions.
③ It is destroyed during chemical reactions.
④ It is changed from one form to another during chemical reactions.

07~08

Whereas the discovery of the double-helical structure of DNA was originally revered, it is now thought to have opened a door to an uncertain future. The scientists were able to put new DNA parts into living cells; immediately, those activities were looked upon _____. It was considered that human civilization could be destroyed by some disease that could be engineered into cells. People realized that calls needed to be made for strict rules to control such research. Because of this, it took a while before scientists discovered recombinant-DNA technology. The controlling rules did not get put into action, fortunately, so when the fears about DNA technology went unfounded, all attempts at regulation, even moderate, dissipated.

07 Which of the following is most appropriate for the blank?

① suspiciously
② favorably
③ impartially
④ approvingly

08 Which of the following is best for the main idea of the passage?

① Successful attempts at regulations on DNA technology
② The unreliability of biology technology
③ Groundless fear of DNA technology
④ The potential of biological advances

09~10

There was, actually, an important statistical reservation implicit in Newton's work, though the eighteenth century, which lived by Newton, ignored it. No physical measurements are ever precise; and what we have to say about a machine or other dynamic system really concerns not what we must expect when the initial positions and momenta are given with perfect accuracy (which never occurs), but what we are to expect when they are given with attainable accuracy. This merely means that we know, not the complete initial conditions, but something about their distribution. The functional part of physics, in other words, cannot escape considering uncertainty and the contingency of events. It was the merit of Gibbs to show for the first time a clean-cut scientific method for taking this contingency into consideration. The historian of science looks in vain for a single line of development. Gibbs' work, while well cut out, was badly sewed, and it remained for others to complete the job that he began.

09 It can be inferred from the passage that _____.

① in Newton's age, the implication of statistics was not fully discovered
② the function of physics is irrelevant to contingency and accuracy of events
③ the function of physics depends largely upon Gibbs' clear-cut tool of finding the complete initial conditions
④ in Newton's age, the same physical laws did not apply to a variety of systems

10 What would be the best title of the passage above?

① The completeness of dynamic system
② Newton's contribution to physics
③ The irreversible position of Newton's theory
④ The benefit of Gibbs' theory

[11~12]

The most important scientific tools for astronomers are telescopes. This is proven by the fact that the first major discoveries about the solar system, those of Galileo, accompanied the invention of the telescope. As telescopes have increased in power over the centuries, they have allowed astronomers to make more discoveries about the nature of the universe. The first telescopes used glass lenses to focus their light, but most modern telescopes now use mirrors as their major light collectors. In a lens telescope, the light must pass through the lens, so the lens must be entirely perfect. But in a mirror telescope, the light simply bounces off the mirror. This means that only the surface of the mirror must be perfect, making it much easier to manufacture large mirrors. Making larger and larger mirrors for telescopes is important because a telescope's power is directly proportional to the size of its mirror. Therefore, the primary concern for astronomers is to get the largest mirror possible for their telescope.

11 Which of the following is true of lens telescopes?

① They were easier to make.
② They were more powerful.
③ They capture light more effectively.
④ The lens needs to be flawless.

12 According to the passage, which of the following statements is not true?

① In modern days, mirrors are used to gather lights instead of lenses.
② Lens telescopes present no problems in manufacturing.
③ Mirror telescopes require a mirror with a perfect surface.
④ The power of mirror telescopes increases with the size of the mirror.

13~15

Virtual reality and self-driving cars have been talked about a lot in recent years, and they will still be talked about this year. But these two technologies are still nascent or premature. Over the last two years, tech companies like Facebook, Google and Samsung have flooded the market with virtual reality headsets and plenty of software and games. Yet people have not exactly embraced the products. "The industry has been plagued by high-cost hardware, (A) _____," said Martin Kabila, an analyst for the research firm eMarketer, in a recent post.

Self-driving cars are also still many years from becoming mainstream, Even though some companies have permits to test autonomous cars in California, Arizona and elsewhere, several of the leaders in the technology — such as Google and Amazon — have refrained from committing to a release date for self-driving vehicles. "There's going to be a lot of noise about automotive technology, (B) _____ nothing distinct or specific," Kabila said.

13 Choose the best title.

① Still Long Way to Go for High-Techs
② Bright Future of High-Techs
③ A Good Area to Invest
④ Advantages of Virtual Reality and Autonomous Vehicle

14 Which one is not appropriate for (A)?

① motion sickness
② a dearth of compelling content
③ a general lack of consumer interest
④ a series of convenient utilities

15 Choose the best word for (B).

① or
② but
③ so
④ then

16~18

The Great Hanoi Rat Massacre of 1902 is a classic reminder of why we need to be wary of Big Data. The French colonial government of the time, alarmed by the spread of rodents through the city, offered local rat-catchers a bounty for each animal killed. They paid one cent for every rat tail submitted as proof of elimination. Initially, the data looked promising because substantial numbers were reported killed, but the plan went awry. Crafty Vietnamese entrepreneurs set up rodent farms to boost their income. Soon, bubonic plague broke out in Hanoi.

The data we generate on our smartphones today may seem far removed from colonial statistics on Hanoi's rat infestation, but the dangers of misinterpreting the data remain the same. Incentives will invariably be gamed. Correlations are sometimes spurious. Stripped of context, data can be misleading because there is a significant difference between Big Data and strong data. Statistical models do not necessarily apply across different contexts. "Will a plagiarizing student also commit fraud?" Statistics might assume a positive relationship, even though other factors led to the plagiarism. Using the same model in future cases will therefore be problematic.

16 What is the main theme of the passage?

① Because data can be misleading, we should dispense with it.
② Data from smartphones are similar to strong data.
③ Rodent farming used to be a profitable endeavor.
④ Using data for predictions requires consideration of context.

17 According to the passage, which of the following is true?

① Games will provide good data.
② The data regarding rat kills were misleading.
③ Administrators were alarmed by entrepreneurs.
④ Rat catchers paid for each rat they killed.

18 According to the passage, which of the following is not true?

① The rat catchers took advantage of the reward system.
② The difference between Big Data and strong data is important.
③ Predictive models using smartphone data are accurate.
④ Paying a bounty did not solve the rat problem in Hanoi.

19~20

Today we are confronted with an expanding array of technical means for making acts of seeing themselves into objects of observation. The most advanced forms of surveillance and data analysis used by intelligence agencies are now equally indispensable to the marketing strategies of large businesses. Widely employed are screens or other forms of display that track eye movements, as well as durations and fixations of visual interest in sequences or streams of graphic information. One's casual perusal of a single web page can be minutely analyzed and quantified in terms of how the eye scans, pauses, moves, and gives attentive priority to some areas over others. Even in the ambulatory* space of big department stores, eye-tracking scanners provide detailed information about individual behavior — for example, determining how long one looked at items that one did not buy. A generously funded research field of optical ergonomics** has been in place for some time. Passively and often voluntarily, one now collaborates in one's own surveillance and data-mining.

*ambulatory 보행의   **ergonomics 인체공학

19 Which of the following does the passage mainly discuss?

① Technological innovations in the process of production
② New methodologies of data analysis in management science
③ The ways an observer is turned into an object of observation
④ The prison surveillance system utilizing inmates' optical activities

20 Which of the following is not mentioned in the passage?

① Internet searching habits
② People's behaviors in shopping
③ Instruments for tracking eye movements
④ Government funds for intelligence agencies

21~22

One key question for the United States in the 21st century is whether noncoastal towns and rural communities will be able to participate in the digital revolution. We know that almost all Americans are avid consumers of technology, but many lack the opportunity to do the creative work that fuels our digital economy. (A) At stake is the dignity of millions of people. Within the next 10 years, nearly 60 percent of jobs could have a third of their tasks automated by artificial intelligence. Many traditional industries are becoming digital. Recently, a senior hotel executive described his business as essentially a digital one, explaining that his profit margins were contingent on the effectiveness of his software architects. Today's hospitality vendors, precision farmers and electricians spend significant time on digital work. Economists keep telling those left out of our digital future to move to the tech hubs. If they visit places like Lincoln, NE or Tacoma, WA, they will realize that many people there are not looking to move. They are proud of their small-town values and enjoy being close to family. They brag that their town doesn't need many traffic lights. (B) The choice facing small towns should not be binary — it should not be "adopt the Silicon name or miss out on the tech future."

21 밑줄 친 (A)의 원인은?

① A great number of people in the rural areas have become unemployed although the economy started to recover.
② Americans spend way too much money to purchase the latest technologies with artificial intelligence.
③ Although America undergoes technological development, many people fail to be productive with such a change.
④ Companies started to replace traditional human labors avidly with modern technologies with artificial intelligence.
⑤ As companies in the United States relocate to other areas, many people who can't move may lose their jobs.

22 밑줄 친 (B)의 내용과 가장 부합하는 것은?

① Small towns should adopt the Silicone name or miss out on the tech future.
② Small towns must delimit the growth to protect the populations to move out.
③ Small towns may move toward the digital future as changing to tech hubs.
④ Small towns can protect their community value as creating various tech jobs there.
⑤ Small towns need to encourage their people to be more aware of the digital economy.

23~25

Legend and history mix in the story of India's Taj Mahal, one of the world's most beautiful buildings. In 1631, Mumtaz Mahal, the beloved third wife of Mughal emperor Shah Jahan, died giving birth to their 14th child. When the emperor emerged from mourning, he started to build a great tomb for her: the Taj Mahal.

From 1632 to 1653, the white marble mausoleum arose on the banks of the Yamuna River in Agra. Twenty thousand artisans working under a team of architects assembled the symmetrical domed building and gardens. It is a masterpiece of careful construction; for instance, the tall towers that flank the central building lean outward slightly but appear to be upright in a feat of _____.

Stories arose that afterward, the building's artisans had their hands struck off and their eyes gouged out so that they would never be able to raise a rival building. Yet another tale says that the brooding emperor built a dark mirror of the tomb, the Black Taj, on the opposite bank of the Yamuna. Neither of these stories has been substantiated. What is true is that the emperor spent his last years imprisoned by his own son in Agra Fort, from which he could gaze upon the Taj but never enter it again.

23 Which one is true?

① The Taj Mahal is a tomb of an emperor.
② The towers around the main building seem to stand vertically.
③ Artisans worked independently to build the Taj Mahal.
④ Mahal built the Taj in honor of his wife.

24 Choose the best expression for the blank.

① color effect
② great tomb
③ optical trickery
④ Mumtaz Mahal

25 Which one is not true?

① According to a story, the artisans went blind after completing the building.
② According to a tale, the Black Taj was built on the Yamuna.
③ There is no verified evidence of the Black Taj.
④ Shah Jahan spent time in Agra Fort.

26~28

Many fields are going to find their landscapes greatly altered by virtual reality. Educators, for one, will be presented with a vast array of new opportunities through which to pass on knowledge. _____ the next five to ten years, teachers may become able to move completely away from the course book or flat screen — even the classroom itself — and into an immersive world of instruction and learning. By way of example, history students could be taken into the epicenter of the world's greatest battles and conflicts, experiencing and understanding the machinations of victory first-hand. Medical students may be provided with the opportunity to travel through the human body as if they were themselves the size of a blood cell, building their comprehension of how veins and arteries, or nerve systems, are interconnected. Music students will be able to watch a VR orchestra perform their new composition in a venue of their choice, whether that be the local concert hall or even the Sydney Opera House. A student of Mandarin should one day be able to 'walk' the streets of Beijing, conversing with the local native speakers, and practicing the regional pronunciation.

26 What would be an appropriate title for the text above?

① How Could Virtual Reality Change Education?
② The Future of Virtual Reality
③ How Virtual Reality Helps Students
④ Case Studies of Virtual Reality and Students
⑤ Immersive Education Today!

27 What would best fit in the blank _____?

① About
② Since
③ On
④ As
⑤ Within

28 Which of the following is not an example used in the text above?

① Students learning a Chinese language
② Students studying to be doctors
③ Students of history
④ Students composing new music
⑤ Students learning ballet

[A] Developments in computing technologies have allowed scientists to make vast advancements in AI even though the simulated reconstruction of a human brain is still unattainable. [B] People expect machines that act human should look human as well. [C] For instance, Honda revealed in 2000, ASIMO, a 130-centimeter humanoid robot. ASIMO, which stands for Advanced Step in Innovative Mobility, was created to assist individuals who have difficulty with mobility to complete common everyday tasks. ASIMO is bipedal, and it can navigate unbalanced terrain like stairs, attaining a top speed of six kilometers per hour. With its two camera "eyes," the robot is programmed to ascertain direction and distance, respond to human gestures, and recognize and name up to ten individuals. [D]

However, the prospect of designing machines capable of possessing human qualities has also engendered many fears and anxieties. In the 1968 dystopian novel by Philip K. Dick entitled, *Do Androids Dream of Electric Sheep?*, androids appear human and have implanted human memories, but are devoid of empathy. They are forced to do difficult or dangerous work _____ humans. When six of these androids start a rebellion, a bounty hunter is called upon to track them down and destroy them. The novel begs the questions, "What distinguishes machines from humans?" and "Is it moral to destroy a machine that believes that it is human?"

29 Choose the best place for the following.

> To promote interest in the sciences, ASIMO often makes appearances in public in which he performs choreographed dances and displays his understanding of voice commands.

① [A]   ② [B]   ③ [C]   ④ [D]

30 Why does the author mention but are devoid of empathy?

① To persuade readers that androids possess morals
② To claim that empathy is the most important characteristic in androids
③ To criticize Philip K. Dick's depiction of non-human intelligence
④ To point out what differentiates humans and androids

31 Which one is true?

① People generally imagine that machines with human-like abilities also have a human-like appearance.
② ASIMO's design is based on the design of the androids from Philip K. Dick's novel.
③ Implanted human memories are the critical factors dividing robots like ASIMO from humans.
④ Philip K. Dick's anxieties about the creation of ASIMO have been brought into existence with the advent of empathetic androids.

32 Which one does not appropriately replace the blank?

① instead of
② in place of
③ in hopes of
④ in lieu of

33~34

Strivr works with companies to make personalized virtual experiences that can be created quickly, with 360° cameras and software, and then used to help all kinds of employees hone skills that can be applied in a store, on a playing field, or somewhere else entirely. These days Strivr, which sits midway between Facebook's headquarters and Stanford on a busy corner in Menlo Park, has branched out far beyond football. In addition to Walmart and various NFL and other sports teams, it's working with United Rentals, two car makers, and numerous other customers. At Walmart, at least, Brock McKeel, senior director of digital operations, thinks it's helpful. He says the company uses Strivr in about 187 employee training centers, for three types of training: preparing for situations like Black Friday or emergencies where you can't set up a simulation in a store, learning customer service, and teaching operational stuff like how produce should be stacked and arranged. In the future, Strivr wants to bring its focus to more types of jobs, says Brian Meek, the company's chief technology officer. He envisions training employees in virtual reality (VR) on how to deal with hazardous situations, as well as teaching so-called soft skills like empathy and hospitality. Strivr has also recently worked with a technical college to produce a VR experience that shows what it's like to work on a construction site, including safety basics. That will be rolling out soon, Meek says.

33 Choose the best title for the passage.

① Training People the VR Way
② The Uncertain Future of Strivr
③ Strivr Comes to Walmart's Rescue
④ Correlation between Location and VR Usage

34 Choose the one that is not true according to the passage.

① Football is an original big part of Strivr's customer base.
② Walmart uses Strivr to teach how to arrange goods in the store.
③ Strivr can teach employees how to deal with dangerous situations.
④ Thanks to Strivr, robots can now simulate human emotions.

Fermat furthered the study of optics with his principle of minimization which says that over any sufficiently short part of its course, light follows the path which it takes the least time to traverse. Huygens developed the primitive form of what is now known as "Huygens' Principle" by saying that light spreads from a source by forming around that source something like a small sphere consisting of secondary sources which in turn propagate light just as the primary sources do. Leibnitz, in the meantime, saw the whole world as a collection of beings called "monads" whose activity consisted in the perception of one another on the basis of a pre-established harmony laid down by God, and it is fairly clear that he thought of this interaction largely in optical terms. Apart from this perception, the monads had no "windows," so that in his view all mechanical interaction really becomes nothing more than a subtle consequence of optical interaction. A preoccupation with optics and with message, which is apparent in this part of Leibnitz's philosophy, runs through its whole texture. It plays a large part in two of his most original ideas: that of the *Characteristica Universalis*, or universal scientific language, and that of the *Calculus Ratiocinator*, or calculus of logic. This Calculus Ratiocinator, imperfect as it was, was the direct ancestor of modern mathematical logic. Dominated by ideas of communication, Leibnitz is an intellectual ancestor in more than one way, for he was also interested in machine computation and in automata. My views are very far from being Leibnitzian, but the problems with which I am concerned are most certainly Leibnitzian. Leibnitz's computing machines were only an offshoot of his interest in a computing language, a reasoning calculus which again was in his mind, merely an extension of his idea of a complete artificial language.

35 Which of the following statement is not true?

① Unlike Fermat, Leibnitz was interested in optics.
② Leibnitz's conception of monads is based upon the ready-made divine harmony.
③ According to Leibnitz, monads interact optically.
④ After Leibnitz, some scientists studied machine computation.

36 What would be the best title of the passage above?

① The Imperfectness of a Reasoning Calculus
② The Unstable Traits of Computing Language
③ The Relation Between Optics and Computing Language
④ The Negative Influence of Leibnitz in Automata

37 Which of the following sentence is likely to follow the passage above?

① Thus, the machine which is conditioned by its relation to the external world is with us and has been with us for some time.
② Thus, even in his computing machine, Leibnitz's preoccupations were mostly linguistic and communicational.
③ Thus, to live effectively is to live with adequate information.
④ Thus, communication and control belong to the essence of man's inner life.

38~40

While some women experience pregnancy and childbirth as joyful, natural, and fulfilling, others find themselves recoiling in horror at the physical demands of carrying and sustaining a child in their womb, and even more so at the potential brutality of giving birth. Some might view the blood, sweat, and tears as a necessary and unavoidable part of life. Others assume a less forgiving view of the process as "barbaric." Most oscillate between the (A) <u>two positions</u>, or else sit somewhere in between. Whatever one's position on the matter of the "naturalness" of pregnancy, it can't be denied that the development of artificial-womb technology would radically change the debate. First, there are the therapeutic benefits it promises: women prone to risky pregnancies could transfer the fetus to an artificial womb, thereby allowing fetal development to continue at little cost to their own physical health; likewise, fetuses at risk of premature birth could be transferred to artificial wombs to complete their development as required. The blood, sweat, and tears, it seems, might not be so intrinsic to the process after all. Second, the technology could have important social benefits for women. Artificial wombs would eliminate a crucial condition that currently ensures women's oppression by neutralizing (B) <u>the heavily gendered roles played in reproduction</u>. But if fetuses were to develop in artificial wombs, women would finally be free to pursue their interests and desires.

38 Which of the following is the major topic of the passage?

① Females' liberation from homekeeping
② Mental and physical health for females
③ Planned pregnancies and physical health
④ Potential benefits of artificial-womb technology

39 Which of the following closest to what (A) refers to?

① Pros and cons of artificial wombs
② Brutal and horrific views on pregnancy
③ Proponents of artificial and natural wombs
④ Positive and negative views on pregnancy and childbirth

40 Which of the following is implied by (B)?

① Social pressure on women for reproduction
② Health risks of childbearing and nursing
③ Child-raising demands on women
④ Workplace handicaps for females

41~44

[A] They can also darken light that helps you see better. [B] This superior lens technology was first discovered when NASA scientists looked to nature for a means to superior eye protection — specifically, by studying the eyes of eagles, known for their extreme visual acuity. [C] But now, independent research conducted by scientists from NASA's Jet Propulsion Laboratory has brought forth ground-breaking technology to help protect human eyesight from the harmful effects of solar radiation light. [D] Some ordinary sunglasses can obscure your vision by exposing your eyes to harmful UV rays, blue light, and reflective glare.

This discovery resulted in what is now known as Eagle Eyes. Eagle Eyes features the most advanced eye protection technology ever created. It offers triple-filter polarization to block 99.9% UVA and UVB as well as the added benefit of blue-light eye protection. Eagle Eyes is the only optic technology that _____ official recognition from the Space Certification Program for this remarkable technology.

41 Which one is the right order?

① [D] — [A] — [C] — [B]
② [A] — [B] — [C] — [D]
③ [D] — [A] — [B] — [C]
④ [A] — [B] — [D] — [C]

42 Choose the best topic.

① Splendid lens technology
② Solar radiation light
③ Blue-light protection
④ NASA scientists

43 Which one is true?

① Some sunglasses can be dangerous.
② Eagles lack visual acuity.
③ Eagle Eyes completely blocks all light.
④ Blue light is more harmful than UV rays.

44 Which one is not appropriate for the blank?

① has earned
② has garnered
③ has qualified
④ has attained

45~46

Expressionist architecture is particularly difficult to characterize. Ian Boyd Whyte, in speaking of Expressionism, noted that "the movement has usually been defined in terms of what it is not (rationalist, functionalist, and so on) rather than what it is". Despite (A) the lack of any clear definition, the concerns of the movement are patent: expression of angst, subordination of objectivity and realism in favour of symbolic expression of inner experience, abstraction, and a critical position vis-à-vis Modernism. The impulse to distort reality for subjective or emotional effect is exhibited in all art forms. The underlying objective of any art is to achieve a new and visionary dimension which Expressionism pursued more than most other avantgarde movements.

In the pictorial arts, the movement focused on capturing vivid reactions through powerful color, dynamic composition, formal distortion, and the desire for expression. In architecture, (B) on the other hand, Expressionism emphasized form, abstraction, repudiation of modernist rationalist ideals, and the traditional classical box. The recurring formal themes were often inspired by (C) natural phenomena, such as caves, crystal, rocks, and organic, non-geometric forms. The reason for focusing on the organic rather than the geometric was to produce an architecture of motion and emotion, ambiance, (D) classicism, and sweeping change. This encouraged expression of subjective interpretation rather than the reproduction of aesthetically pleasing subject matter. The loss of design restraints implied an inevitable dismantling of the immediate past.

45 위 글의 제목으로 가장 적합한 것을 고르시오.

① The Characteristics and Subjectivity of Expressionist Architecture
② The Upheaval of Revivalist Styles of Arts
③ The Importance of the Precedents' Authority in Arts
④ Historical Trajectory of Expressionism: Past and Future

46 위 글에서 논지의 흐름상 가장 적합하지 않은 것을 고르시오.

① (A)   ② (B)   ③ (C)   ④ (D)

[A] The object called the Möbius strip has fascinated environmentalists, artists, engineers, mathematicians and many others ever since its discovery in 1858 by August Möbius, a German mathematician. Möbius seems to have encountered the Möbius strip while working on the geometric theory of polyhedra, solid figures composed of vertices, edges, and flat faces. (A) A Möbius strip can be created by taking a strip of paper, giving it an odd number of half-twists, then taping the ends back together to form a loop. If you take a pencil and draw a line along the center of the strip, you'll see that the line runs along both sides of the loop.

[B] The concept of a onesided object inspired artists like Dutch graphic designer M.C. Escher, whose woodcut "Möbius Strip II" shows red ants crawling one after another along a Möbius strip. (B) The Möebius strip has more than just one surprising property. For instance, try taking a pair of scissors and cutting the strip in half along the line you just drew. You may be astonished to find that you are left not with two smaller one-sided Möbius strips, but instead with one long two-sided loop.

[C] (C) A topologist studies properties of objects that are preserved when moved, bent, stretched or twisted, without cutting or gluing parts together. For example, a tangled pair of earbuds is in a topological sense the same as an untangled pair of earbuds, because changing one into the other requires only moving, bending and twisting. Another pair of objects that are topologically the same are a coffee cup and a doughnut. (D) Because both objects have just one hole, one can be _____ into the other through just stretching and bending. The number of holes in an object is a property which can be changed only through cutting or gluing. This property — called the "genus" of an object — allows us to say that a pair of earbuds and a doughnut are topologically different, since a doughnut has one hole, whereas a pair of earbuds has no holes.

[D] Unfortunately, a Möbius strip and a two-sided loop, like a typical silicone awareness wristband, both seem to have one hole, so this property is insufficient to tell them apart — at least from a topologist's point of view. Instead, the property that distinguishes a Möbius strip from a two-sided loop is called orientability. Like its number of holes, an object's orientability can only be changed through cutting or gluing. (E) Imagine writing yourself a note on a see-through surface, then taking a walk around on that surface. The surface is orientable if, when you come back from your walk, you can always read the note. On a nonorientable surface, you may come back from your walk only to find that the words you wrote have apparently turned into their mirror image and can be read only from right to left. On the two-sided loop, the note will always read the same, no matter where your journey took you. Since the Möbius strip is nonorientable, whereas the two-sided loop is orientable, the Möubius strip and the two-sided loop are topologically different.

47 Which of the following is the best title of the above passage?

① The Mathematical Implication of Möbius Strips and Other One-Sided Objects
② The Critical Differences between One-Sided Objects and Two-Sided Objects
③ The Academic Usability of Möbius Strips
④ The Unexpected Effects of the Discovery of Möbius Strips
⑤ The Distinguishing Characteristics of Möbius Strips and Other One-Sided Objects

48 Which of the following can best fill in the blank in paragraph [C]?

① deformed
② conformed
③ performed
④ preformed
⑤ thermoformed

49 Which of the following is not true about orientability in paragraph [D]?

① A two-sided loop is orientable.
② It can be a "genus" of a group of objects.
③ Twisting an object can affect its orientability.
④ It has mainly been investigated in the field of topology.
⑤ It can distinguish a silicon awareness bracelet from a Möbius strip.

50 The following paragraph is removed from the passage. In which part may it be inserted to support the argument made by the author?

> While the strip certainly has visual appeal, its greatest impact has been in mathematics, where it helped to spur on the development of an entire field called topology.

① (A) ② (B) ③ (C) ④ (D) ⑤ (E)

51~52

I am not sure when I first became aware of the Singularity. I'd have to say it was a progressive awakening. In the almost half century that I've immersed myself in computer and related technologies. I've sought to understand the meaning and purpose of the continual upheaval that I have witnessed at many levels. Gradually, I've become aware of a transforming event looming in the first half of the twenty-first century. Just as a black hole in space dramatically alters the patterns of matter and energy accelerating toward its event horizon, this impending Singularity in our future is increasingly transforming every institution and aspect of human life, from sexuality to spirituality.

What, then, is the Singularity? It's a future period during which the pace of technological change will be so rapid, its impact so deep, that human life will be irreversibly transformed. Although neither utopian nor dystopian, this epoch will transform the concepts that we rely on to give meaning to our lives, from our business models to the cycle of human life, including death itself. Understanding the Singularity will alter our perspective on the significance of our past and the ramifications for our future. To truly understand it inherently changes one's view of life in general and one's own particular life. I regard someone who understands the Singularity and who has reflected on its implications for his or her own life as a "singularitarian."

I can understand why many observers do not readily embrace the obvious implications of what I have called the law of accelerating returns (the inherent acceleration of the rate of evolution, with technological evolution as a continuation of biological evolution). After all. it took me forty years to be able to see what was right in front of me. and I still cannot say that I am entirely comfortable with all of its consequences.

The key idea _____ the impending Singularity is that the pace of change of our human-created technology is _____ and its powers are _____ at an exponential pace. Exponential growth is deceptive. It starts out almost imperceptibly and then explodes with unexpected fury — unexpected, that is, if one does not take care to follow its trajectory.

51 빈칸에 들어가기에 가장 적합한 것을 고르시오.

① accelerating — underlying — expanding
② accelerating — expanding — underlying
③ underlying — accelerating — expanding
④ underlying — expanding — accelerating

52 위 글을 통해 추론할 수 있는 것으로 가장 적합한 것을 고르시오.

① At Singularity, humans will be evolved into an irreversible human species by technology.
② The author is afraid that a dystopian future will come along with the development of technology.
③ Our traditional concept of the past and future could be changed if we comprehend Singularity.
④ Despite the rapid development of technology, the author is skeptical of the impending Singularity.

53~56

[A] Salt is often used in ice cream makers to make the water surrounding the inside container cold enough to freeze the cream. Salt works to (A) _____ the freezing point of water so the water can become colder than 32 degrees Fahrenheit (zero degrees Celsius) before it turns to ice. In fact, water containing salt can reach temperatures of nearly minus 6 degrees F.

[B] When ice cream is made, cream is placed into a canister and rotated within an ice bath. If no salt is added to the ice bath, the lowest temperature it can reach is 32 degrees F. While the cream can freeze at this temperature, it can do so more quickly at a lower temperature. When salt is added to the ice bath (usually rock salt in ice cream making), it comes into contact with the thin layer of water on the surface of the melting ice. The salt dissolves and the water becomes salty. This salt water has a lower freezing point, so the temperature of the ice bath can get even colder, thus freezing the ice cream more quickly.

[C] The principle of salt lowering the freezing point of water is used frequently to keep roads safe in winter. During snow and ice events, trucks spread a thin layer of salt on roadways. This causes snow and ice to melt on impact rather than freeze and makes the roads wet rather than icy and dangerous. However, there is a limit to how cold water can become before freezing; in extremely frigid temperatures, applying sand to the roads to increase friction is more useful than applying salt. Types of salt other than sodium chloride can be used in colder temperatures. Calcium chloride and magnesium chloride, for example, can melt ice at low temperatures. However, some of these compounds can be detrimental to the environment and are used only occasionally.

[D] Does adding salt lower the boiling point of water? While salt will lower the freezing point of water, it does not lower the boiling point. Actually, (B) _____. Adding salt to water results in a phenomenon called boiling point elevation. The boiling point of water is increased slightly, but no enough that you would notice the temperature difference.

53 Which of the following would be the best title for the above passage?

① Why Is Salt Most Valued?
② How Does Salt Work on Water?
③ How Can We Utilize Salt in Our Daily Life?
④ What Are the Scientific Effects Made Possible by Salt?
⑤ How Are Temperature and the Physical States of Water Related?

54 Which of the following cannot be inserted into the blank (A) in paragraph [A]?

① decrease
② depress
③ distend
④ drop
⑤ reduce

55 Which of the following would best flt in the blank (B) in paragraph [D]?

① Salt will not affect the boiling point
② Salt will interfere boiling point elevation
③ Salty water will boil at a lower temperature
④ Salty water will boil at a higher temperature
⑤ Salt will substantially increase the boiling point

56 According to the above passage, which of the following is not true?

① Sodium chloride can make water colder.
② Sodium chloride can lower the freezing point of water.
③ Sodium chloride can increase the boiling point of water.
④ Sodium chloride is more effective in producing friction than sand.
⑤ Sodium chloride and magnesium chloride can be used interchangeably.

57~58

After running a plastic comb through your hair, you will find that the comb attracts bits of paper. The attractive force is often strong enough to suspend the paper from the comb, defying the gravitational pull of the entire Earth. The same effect occurs with other rubbed materials, such as glass and hard rubber. Another simple experiment is to rub an inflated balloon against wool. On a dry day, the rubbed balloon will then stick to the wall of a room, often for hours. These materials have become electrically charged. You can give your body an electric charge by vigorously rubbing your shoes on a wool rug or by sliding across a car seat. You can then surprise and annoy a friend or co-worker with a light touch on the arm, delivering a slight shock to both yourself and your victim. These experiments work best on a dry day because excessive moisture can facilitate a leaking away of the charge. Experiments also demonstrate that there are two kinds of electric charge, which Benjamin Franklin named positive and negative. A hard rubber or a plastic rod that has been rubbed with fur is suspended by a piece of string. When a glass rod that has been rubbed with silk is brought near the rubber rod, the rubber rod is attracted toward the glass rod. If two charged rubber rods or two charged glass rods are brought near each other, the force between them is repulsive. These observations may be explained by assuming that the rubber and glass rods have acquired different kinds of excess charge. We use the convention suggested by Franklin, where the excess electric charge on the glass rod is called positive and that on the rubber rod is called negative. On the basis of observations such as these, we conclude that like charges repel one another and unlike charges attract one another. Objects usually contain equal amounts of positive and negative charge — electrical forces between objects arise when those objects have net negative or positive charges. Nature's basic carriers of positive charge are protons, which, along with neutrons, are located in the nuclei of atoms. The nucleus is surrounded by a cloud of negatively charged electrons about ten thousand times larger in extent. An electron has the same magnitude charge as a proton, but the opposite sign. In a gram of matter there are approximately 1023 positively charged protons and just as many negatively charged electrons, so the net charge is zero. Because the nucleus of an atom is held firmly in place inside a solid, protons never move from one material to another. Electrons are far lighter than protons and hence more easily accelerated by forces. Furthermore, they occupy the outer regions of the atom. _____, objects become charged by gaining or losing electrons. Charge transfers readily from one type of material to another. Rubbing the two materials together serves to increase the area of contact, facilitating the transfer process. An important characteristic of charge is that electric charge is always conserved. Charge isn't created when two neutral objects are rubbed together; rather, the objects become charged because negative charge is transferred from one object to the other. One object gains a negative charge while the other loses an equal amount of negative charge and hence is left with a net positive charge. When a glass rod is rubbed with silk, electrons are transferred from the rod to the silk. As a result, the glass rod carries a net positive charge, the silk a net negative charge. Likewise, when rubber is rubbed with fur, electrons are transferred from the fur to the rubber.

57 Choose the most appropriate one for the blank.

① In contrast
② Consequently
③ However
④ Nevertheless

58 Which of the following statement is not true?

① A negatively charged rubber rod is attracted to a positively charged glass rod.
② A negatively charged rubber rod is repelled by a negatively charged glass rod.
③ When rubber is rubbed with fur, the fur is left with a net positive charge.
④ When a glass rod is rubbed with silk, electrons and protons are transferred from the glass to the silk.

14 생물

01 Choose the most appropriate one for the blank.

> Discussions on human genome modifications to eliminate disease genes and/or for human enhancement are not new and have been commonplace since the first discussions on sequencing the human genome occurred in the 1980s. Many a(n) _____ has made their careers from such discussions, and currently on Amazon there are dozens of books on a wide range of human enhancement topics including those that predict that editing our genes will lead to the end of humanity.

① bioethicist
② gynecologist
③ physicist
④ orthodontist
⑤ radiologist

02 Reorder the following sentences to form the most coherent passage.

> [A] The genetically engineered salmon might also have an advantage surviving in the wild because they grow faster, and this could cause all of the natural salmon to die out.
> [B] Some fish farmers also see these new salmon as an unnecessary risk for the industry, as there is already too much salmon on the world market.
> [C] If these salmon escape into the wild, they may breed with natural salmon and pollute the gene pool of the natural salmon.
> [D] Environmentalists worry that genetically engineered salmon might be unhealthy to eat.

① [B] — [C] — [A] — [D]
② [B] — [D] — [C] — [A]
③ [C] — [A] — [D] — [B]
④ [D] — [C] — [A] — [B]

03~04

Evolutionary biology has always been controversial. This is largely because Darwin's theory directly contradicted the supernatural accounts of human origins rooted in religious tradition and replaced them with fully natural ones. The philosopher Daniel Dennett has described evolution as a sort of "universal acid" that "eats through just about every traditional concept, and leaves in its wake a revolutionized worldview, with most of the old landmarks still recognizable, but transformed in fundamental ways." Fearing this _____ idea, opposition in the U.S. to evolution mainly came from Rightwing evangelical Christians who believed God created life in its present form, as described in Genesis.

03 내용상 빈칸에 들어가기에 가장 적절한 것은?

① corrosive
② constructivist
③ collaborative
④ contemporary
⑤ contemptuous

04 윗글의 내용과 가장 잘 부합하는 것은?

① Christians in the U.S. no longer believe that Darwin is right.
② Darwin was praised by Right-wing evangelists for some time.
③ Dennett accounted for the origin of human beings via chemistry.
④ Darwin's theory turned out to support the supernatural accounts of human origins.
⑤ According to Dennett, "universal acid" transforms old concepts to a completely new world-view.

05~08

Humans naturally develop patterns of thinking modeled _____ repetitive activities and commonly accessed knowledge. These assist us in quickly applying the same actions and knowledge in similar or familiar situations, but they also have the potential to prevent us from quickly and easily accessing or developing new ways of seeing, understanding, and solving problems. These patterns of thinking are often referred to as schemas, which are organized sets of information and relationships between things, actions, and thoughts that are stimulated and initiated in the human mind when we encounter some environmental stimuli. A single schema can contain a vast amount of information. For example, we have a schema for dogs which encompasses the presence of four legs, fur, sharp teeth, a tail, paws, and a number of other perceptible characteristics. When the environmental stimuli match this schema — even when there is a <u>tenuous</u> link or only a few of the characteristics are present — the same pattern of thought is brought _____ the mind. As these schemas are stimulated automatically, this can obstruct a more fitting impression of the situation or prevent us from seeing a problem in a way that will enable a new problem-solving strategy.

05 Which of the following pairs is most appropriate to fill the blanks?

① on — into
② on — about
③ with — into
④ with — about
⑤ at — on

06 What is the closest in meaning to the underlined tenuous?

① circumspect
② implacable
③ reckless
④ weak
⑤ stout

07 What is the most appropriate title of the passage?

① The Problem with Ingrained Patterns of Thinking
② Teaching Patterns of Critical Thinking
③ The Benefit of the Conventional Problem-Solving Practices
④ Generating Creative Ideas by a Holistic Approach
⑤ How to Apply a Schema in Teaching and Learning

08 Which of the following is NOT true about "the repetitive activities and commonly accessed knowledge"?

① They are naturally developed by humans.
② They potentially interfere with solving problems.
③ Extremely large quantitiy of information is a part of them.
④ Schemas are produced without conscious intention.
⑤ They encourage us to develop a new way of problem solving.

09
~
12

Pachyrhynchus weevils are found on most islands in the eastern Pacific Ocean. If these weevils could fly, that would not be surprising. But they cannot. Why they are so _____ is therefore a mystery. But it is one that Wen-San Huang of the National Museum of Natural Science in Taiwan thinks he has solved.

One theory, which dates back to 1923, is that the beetles drift from place to place, buoyed up by a tiny air cavity each has beneath its outer shell, which allows the insects to float. When Dr. Huang put it to the test, he discovered that the beetles do, indeed, float. However, floating in seawater does not do them much good: all 57 adults he tried it with died within two days. Clearly, adult weevils are not good sailors.

That does not, however, mean that weevil young are not. [A] Pachyrhynchus weevils have a predilection for laying their eggs inside the fruit of a mangrove-dwelling plant called the fish-poison tree. The tree drops its fruits into the ocean, which carries them away to germinate on distant beaches. Chemicals in fish-poison-tree fruits protect them from being eaten by hungry sea creatures. [B]

Dr. Huang wondered how beetle larvae would fare if they were deep inside a piece of fruit floating in seawater. So he tested this as well. His experiment revealed that such larvae are tolerant of saline conditions. [C] Moreover, these larvae went on to develop into healthy adults. [D]

09 Which of the following is most appropriate for the blank?

① adamant
② widespread
③ regressive
④ shrewd

10 Which is the most appropriate place for the sentence below?

> Specifically, of 18 grubs thrown into seawater inside a piece of fruit, two survived for six days.

① [A]   ② [B]   ③ [C]   ④ [D]

11 Which of the following can be inferred from the passage?

① Pachyrhynchus weevils are found in most tropical islands around the world.
② Pachyrhynchus weevil larvae can swim between islands, while adults cannot.
③ Fish-poison tree has a physical protection against sea creatures.
④ Once the beetle matures, it stays on the same island for the rest of its life.

12 Which of the following cannot be inferred about the fish-poison tree?

① The tree can be found in more than one eastern Pacific Ocean island.
② The fruit of the fish-poison tree can float in saline water.
③ The chemical from the tree's fruit is poisonous for adult beetles, but not for beetle larvae.
④ The fruit of the fish-poison tree can be penetrated by Pachyrhynchus weevils.

13
~
16

[A] After famine, humanity's second great enemy was plagues and infectious diseases. Bustling cities linked by a ceaseless stream of merchants, officials and pilgrims were both the bedrock of human civilization and an ideal breeding ground for pathogens. People consequently lived their lives in ancient Athens or medieval Florence knowing that they might fall ill and die next week, or that an epidemic might suddenly erupt and destroy their entire family in one swoop.

The most famous outbreak, the so-called Black Death, began in the 1330s, somewhere in East or Central Asia, when the flea-dwelling bacterium Yersinia pestis started infecting humans bitten by the fleas. [B] From there, riding on an army of rats and fleas, the plague quickly spread all over Asia, Europe, and North Africa, taking less than twenty years to reach the shores of the Atlantic Ocean. [C] Between 75 million and 200 million people died. In England, four out of ten people died. The city of Florence lost 50,000 of its 100,000 inhabitants. [D] Except for organizing mass prayers and processions, they had no idea how to stop the spread of the epidemic, _____ how to cure it. Until the modern era, humans blamed diseases on bad air, malicious demons, and angry gods, and did not suspect the existence of bacteria and viruses. People readily believed in angels and fairies, but they could not imagine that a tiny flea or a single drop of water might contain an entire armada of deadly predators.

13 Which of the following is most appropriate to describe the purpose of the author?

① to admire
② to encourage
③ to persuade
④ to inform

14 Which of the following is most suitable for the blank?

① only alone
② let alone
③ rather than
④ more than

15 Which is the most appropriate place for the sentence below?

> The authorities were completely helpless in the face of the calamity.

① [A]   ② [B]   ③ [C]   ④ [D]

16 According to the passage, which of the following is true?

① Half of the inhabitants died of the Black Death in the city of Florence.
② The most serious challenge faced by humanity was plagues and infectious diseases.
③ The so-called Black Death originated from humans bitten by rats.
④ Until the modern era, people were suspicious of the existence of angels and fairies.

17~18

Why don't we run out of oxygen to breathe or water to drink? Many organisms produce oxygen during a process called photosynthesis, which constantly replenishes the oxygen consumed by all aerobic organisms. The physical materials on which life depends are limited to what is presently on earth. Water, for example, is naturally recycled from the atmosphere to the surface of Earth, through food webs and back to the atmosphere. Nitrogen, carbon, and other essential substances are cycled in a _____ manner. A natural resource that is replaced or recycled by natural processes is called a renewable resource. Other examples of renewable resources include plants, animals, food crops, sunlight, and soil.

17 위 글의 제목으로 가장 적절한 것은?

① Limits of Natural Processes
② Preservation or Consumption
③ Recycling Natural Resources
④ What If Oxygen is Run Out
⑤ Substances Essential for Life

18 위 글의 빈칸에 들어갈 말로 가장 적절한 것은?

① positive
② transitive
③ dramatic
④ unpredictable
⑤ similar

19~20

An emerging field of neuroscience concerns how one person's emotion may affect another's. Central to this field are "mirror neurons," a class of brain cells that appear to help us sense what others might feel. When we perceive or sense the emotion or even intentions of another person, these neurons _____ the parts of our brain associated with what we have perceived or sensed. In a way, the behavior of others is replicated or "mirrored" within our own minds by these neurons. Mirror neurons may explain our feelings of empathy and our understanding of the feelings of another person.

19 Which of the following is most appropriate for the blank?

① arrest
② congeal
③ stimulate
④ reflect

20 Which of the following is not true of the passage?

① Studying how brain works toward empathy is an emerging field.
② People control others' feelings through mirror neurons.
③ Neuroscientists are much concerned with how people are affected by others' feelings.
④ Mirror neurons may help us empathize with others.

21~22

Madagascar, which separated from India 80 million to 100 million years ago before eventually settling off the southeastern coast of Africa, is in many ways an Earth apart. All that time in geographic isolation made Madagascar a Darwinian playground, its animals and plants evolving into forms utterly original. Some 90% of the island's plants and about 70% of its animals are (A) _____, meaning that they are found only in Madagascar. But what makes life on the island unique also makes it uniquely (B) _____. If we lose these animals on Madagascar, they're gone forever.

21 Which best fits into the blank (A)?

① edible
② endemic
③ prolific
④ carnivorous

22 Which best fits into the blank (B)?

① sacred
② vulnerable
③ flourishing
④ prestigious

23 다음 글의 빈칸에 들어갈 말로 가장 적절한 것은?

Here are a few interesting points about the brain and learning. A key idea behind exercise is getting the right amount of oxygen to the brain. This can also be done through breathing exercises. Just taking the time to breathe deeply and slowly for a few minutes before taking a test or before starting homework can have a positive impact on concentration and motivation. This is why it's often a good idea to have your child get some exercise before leaping into homework. Chewing gum is another way to exercise your brain. Studies also show that like exercise, chewing _____ blood circulation in the brain, _____ memory, and _____ anxiety — as long as the gum doesn't contain a high percentage of sugar. For this reason, some kids with attention issues are given an accommodation to chew gum during school.

① improves — increases — increases
② improves — increases — decreases
③ improves — decreases — increases
④ deteriorates — decreases — decreases
⑤ deteriorates — decreases — increases

24
~
25

A "biological annihilation" of wildlife in recent decades means <u>a sixth mass extinction</u> in Earth's history is under way and is more severe than previously feared, according to research. Scientists analyzed both common and rare species and found billions of regional or local populations have been lost. They blame human overpopulation and overconsumption for the crisis and warn that it threatens the survival of human civilization, with just a short window of time in which to act.

Previous studies have shown species are becoming extinct at a significantly faster rate than for millions of years before, but even so extinctions remain relatively rare giving the impression of _____. The new work instead takes a broader view, assessing many common species which are losing populations all over the world as their ranges shrink, but remain present elsewhere.

24 According to the passage, which of the following is not correct about <u>a sixth mass extinction</u>?

① It is partly caused by human overpopulation.
② It is in progress, but its speed becomes slower.
③ It is seriously happening all over the world.
④ It endangers the continuation of human civilization.
⑤ It means a disappearance of regional bio-species from the earth.

25 Which of the following is most appropriate for the blank?

① a gradual loss of biodiversity
② a sudden disappearance of species
③ a whole extinction of human race
④ a partial end of biological types
⑤ an enduring continuity of biological variety

26~27

Today we think of the brain as the organ controlling the nervous system, one of the 10 or so interacting functional systems the body is divided into by biologists — along with the skeletal system, circulatory system, digestive system, and so on. The nervous system is preeminent because of its two functions. First, it directs the body's interactions with the _____ world by controlling behavior on the one hand, and by processing environmental sensory information through the eyes, ears, nose, tongue, and skin on the other. Thinking or cognition is a basic function of the brain in this interaction of the nervous system with the environment. And second, the nervous system controls the _____ state of the body and processes visceral sensory information from the heart, stomach, genitals, and so on. Feeling or affect is a basic function of the brain in this control of the viscera by the nervous system. In short, the brain is a biological organ within the nervous system as a whole, the mind is a product of brain activity, and thinking and feeling are components of the mind.

26 Which pair best fits in the blanks?

① stable — unstable
② sensory — receptive
③ external — internal
④ concrete — abstract

27 What is the passage mainly about?

① What does the brain do?
② What constitutes the body system?
③ How do the body and mind compete?
④ How are thinking and feeling different?

28~29

The status of a character trait depends on the reference point. For instance, for an ape fingernails are considered primitive in relation to other primates because all other primates have fingernails. Thus, fingernails would not serve to distinguish apes from, for example, monkeys. Fingernails are a derived character for primates as a whole, however, because no other mammals have them. Thus, fingernails serve to distinguish primates from other mammals. The second character illustrated here — brow ridges — is found only in hominoids, not in other primates, and is therefore derived for hominoids. This character distinguishes apes from monkeys. In a chimpanzee, however, brow ridges would be considered to be primitive with respect to other hominoids; that is, the character would not distinguish a chimpanzee from, for example, a gorilla.

28 글의 제목으로 가장 알맞은 것을 고르시오.

① Relative Status of Species
② Absolute Status of Species
③ Relative Status of Characters
④ Absolute Status of Characters

29 글의 내용과 맞지 않는 것을 고르시오.

① All primates have fingernails.
② Some primates have brow ridges.
③ Neither apes nor monkeys belong to hominoids.
④ Both chimpanzees and gorillas belong to hominoids.

30~31

Processing written material — from the letters to the words to the sentences to the stories themselves — snaps the neurons to attention as they start the work of transmitting all that information. That happens when we process spoken language, too, but the very nature of (A) _____ encourages the brain to work harder and better. "Typically, when you read, you have more time to think," says Maryanne Wolf, director of the UCLA Center for Dyslexia in Los Angeles. "Reading gives you a unique pause button for comprehension and insight. (B) _____, with oral language — when you watch a film or listen to a tape — you don't press pause in general."

30 Which best fits in the blank (A)?

① reading
② learning
③ watching
④ speaking

31 Which best fits in the blank (B)?

① Likewise
② Correctly
③ However
④ Additionally

32~33

Until recently, scientists believed that the human brain was fully developed by the age of three. According to this theory, the teen behaviors that most concern parents — risk-taking, a lack of sensitivity to how their actions affect both themselves and others, increased aggression, reduced concentration, or a negative attitude — were thought to be due to bad parenting or changes in body chemistry. However, new technology has allowed researchers to examine the healthy brain at work, and what they have discovered _____. Not only does the brain continue to grow past the age of three, but the brain of a teenager is larger than that of an adult.

As teen brains are flooded with chemicals during adolescence, the brain grows. However, at the same time, the cells of the brain that are used more compete with those that are used less. Only the cells and the connections between the cells that are used the most will survive the competition. Those that are used less begin to die off until the brain reaches what will be its adult size.

32 빈칸에 들어갈 가장 알맞은 것을 고르시오.

① causes them to fear
② might surprise you
③ is disappointing to them
④ might make you understood

33 위 글의 내용과 맞는 것을 고르시오.

① Human brains stop developing after the age of three.
② Teens' bad behaviors are mostly caused by bad parents.
③ Brain size becomes the largest in one's teen years.
④ The brain cells most actively used kill those unused.

34
~
35

Invasive species are a scientific puzzle. Humans transport animals and plants thousands of miles from where they first evolved. Many of those species die off in their new homes. Some barely eke out an existence. But some become ecological nightmares, outcompeting natives. Scientists aren't certain why species like these are proving superior so far from home, and ask: "If natives are adapted to their environment and exotics are from somewhere else, why are they able to invade?" Ecologists have observed that many alien species in the northeastern United States invaded from East Asia. But the opposite is not true. This is not a coincidence. It has to do with the habitats in which invasive species evolve. There is evidence that some parts of the world have been evolutionary incubators, producing superior competitors primed to thrive in other environments. Invasive plants are more likely to have evolved in habitats with a great diversity of competing species. These species continue to grow more diverse, to evolve, and eventually to become _____ — ready to invade.

34 According to the passage, which of the following could be the answer to the underlined sentence?

① It depends on where the exotics evolved.
② It has to do with the natural enemies in the habitat.
③ Exotics tend to be mutations with superior genetic makeup.
④ Exotics fast evolve on the way to a new environment.

35 Which of the following best fits into the blank?

① extinct in no time
② evolutionary niches
③ superior competitors
④ too complicated to survive

36~37

Archaeopteryx, a toothy, feathered fossil found in Germany in the 19th century, hinted at a crucial moment in the history of life — the point when dinosaurs took to the skies, and birds were thus born. [A] There are not many evolutionary journeys that can rival this, but that made by the descendants of some small, terrestrial mammals, which turned into the gigantic aquatic krill-eaters called baleen whales, is one such. [B] Baleen whales suck in large volumes of water and then force it out of their mouths through fibrous outgrowths known as baleen plates, to filter out small animals for consumption. [C] These plates sit where other mammals have teeth, but rather than robust dentine, the principal ingredient of teeth, they are composed of keratin, a flexible material that also makes up hair and fingernails. [D] Some researchers theorize that suction-filter feeding in whales began with teeth that could be gnashed together to form a simple sieve, and that only subsequently were these teeth replaced by baleen.

36 아래 주어진 문장이 들어갈 가장 알맞은 곳을 고르시오.

Analysis of a newly discovered toothy, finned baleen fossil from North America promises to illuminate one part of this remarkable journey.

① [A]　　　② [B]　　　③ [C]　　　④ [D]

37 밑줄 친 표현의 설명으로 가장 가까운 것을 고르시오.

① mesh for separating solids from liquids
② firm flesh around the roots of the teeth
③ apparatus for grinding any solid to powder
④ bony structures used for biting and chewing

38~39

The Red Cross estimates that 6.8 million people donate blood in the U.S. every year, giving approximately 13.6 million units of blood. The earliest known human-to-human blood donation came in 1818, before humans even knew what blood types were, when obstetrician James Blundell transferred blood to a woman who had just given birth. Having watched many patients die in childbirth, Blundell wrote that his experimental procedure stemmed from being appalled at his own helplessness. For the rest of the century, scientists experimented with blood transfer. Not all of these ideas were successful — some advocated infusing humans with cow's milk, which was considered superior to actual blood. From 1873 through 1880, the milk-for-blood trend swept through the U.S. Thankfully, soon an Austrian biologist would make a discovery that would change everything. In 1901, Karl Landsteiner realized that foreign bodies were broken up in the human bloodstream by hemoglobin in human-to-human blood transfers. In 1909, when Landsteiner first classified human blood into types, his work really took off. These groups are what are known today as A, B, AB, and O.

38 According to the passage, which of the following is true?

① Nearly fourteen million Americans donate blood every year.
② Landsteiner took off work in 1909 in order to develop transfers.
③ Blundell felt aghast at his inability to prevent women from dying in childbirth.
④ Blood transfers currently disregard the groups that Landsteiner discovered.

39 Which of the following is closest to what discovery refers to?

① Hemoglobin destroys unnatural things in blood.
② Successful blood transfers depend on blood type.
③ Blood is superior to milk in transfusions.
④ Blood transfers break up the hemoglobin.

40~42

Since humans are among the most populous mammals on Earth, one would expect humans to possess one of the largest genetic variances. Paradoxically, humans have even less genetic variance than their closest living relatives, primates. This startling discovery has led many scientists to conclude that all humans today come from a relatively small gene pool that might be the result of a population bottleneck or the founder effect.

[A] A population bottleneck happens when a catastrophic event, like a flood, overhunting, or famine, causes a significant decrease in the overall population of a species. [B] Because such an event forces random groups of a population to die, allele frequencies change, making a major genetic shift more likely to occur. [C] Some researchers claim that humans experienced a population bottleneck during the Toba catastrophe. [D] About 70,000 years ago, at Lake Toba in Indonesia, the eruption of a gigantic volcano may have plunged the Earth into a decade-long "volcanic winter," when volcanic ash blocked the Sun's light and destroyed much of the Earth's animal and vegetation population. Estimates place the human population at approximately 3,000 to 10,000 individuals shortly following the eruption. Therefore, humankind's current genetic diversity could have been the result of small, isolated groups drawing from a limited genetic pool to repopulate the Earth after the eruption.

40 Why does the author use Paradoxically?

① To argue that other primates are better suited to their environment
② To summarize the contents of the previous sentence
③ To point out a surprising fact regarding human genetics
④ To compare similar traits in humans and primates

41 Choose the best place for the following.

> For example, overhunting made the population of animals like the American bison drop to fewer than 1,000 individuals by the early 20th century.

① [A]   ② [B]   ③ [C]   ④ [D]

42 Which one can be inferred about the outcome of the Toba catastrophe?

① Human survivors frequently fought with bisons for resources.
② Most humans died out because of insufficient food supplies.
③ Indonesia was not affected by the eruption.
④ Allele frequencies did not change.

43~44

In the late 1890s two German psychologists, Georg Müler and Alfons Pilzecker, found out that it takes an hour or so for memories to become fixed, or "consolidated", in the brain. Subsequent studies confirmed the existence of short-term and long-term forms of memory and provided further evidence of the importance of the consolidation phase during which the former are turned into the latter. In the 1960s, University of Pennsylvania neurologist Louis Flexner made a particularly intriguing discovery. After injecting mice with an antibiotic drug that prevented their cells from producing proteins, he found that the animals were unable to form long-term memories but could continue to store short-term ones. The implication was clear: long-term memories are not just stronger forms of short-term memories. [A] Storing long-term memories requires the synthesis of new proteins. Storing short-term memories does not. More recent research turned to the issue of the physical workings of both short-term and long-term memory. [B] The results demonstrated that the more times an experience is repeated, the longer the memory of the experience lasts. Repetition encourages consolidation. Particularly, when researchers examined the physiological effects of repetition on neuronal signals, they discovered something amazing. [C] Not only did the concentration of neurotransmitters in synapses change, altering the strength of the existing connections between neurons, but the neurons grew entirely new synaptic terminals. The formation of long-term memories, in other words, involves not only biochemical changes but anatomical ones. [D] That explains why memory consolidation requires new proteins. Proteins play an essential role in producing structural changes in cells.

43 아래의 문장이 들어갈 위치로 가장 적합한 곳을 고르시오.

The two types of memory entail different biological processes.

① [A]   ② [B]   ③ [C]   ④ [D]

44 윗글을 통해 추론할 수 있는 것으로 가장 적합한 것을 고르시오.

① Use of antibiotic drugs prevents humans from recalling even quite recent experiences.
② Short-term memory is a key predictor for how long we can hold consolidated information in mind in an active manner.
③ Relatively fewer neurotransmitters are expected to be released in the brain synapses when long-term memory is formed.
④ Retaining information in the brain for a longer period is most likely to be accompanied by anatomical changes of synapses.

45~47

[A] How can you stop these tiny invaders from making you sick? Your skin is the first defense against germs. One of the easiest ways to prevent some illnesses is simply by washing with soap and water. But germs can still enter the body through small cuts in the skin or through the mouth, eyes, and nose.

[B] There are two types of germs: viruses and bacteria. Viruses use the cells inside animals or plants to live and multiply. Viruses cause illnesses such as influenza, or the flu. Bacteria are tiny creatures. Some bacteria are good. They can help your stomach digest food. Other bacteria aren't as good. They can cause sore throats and ear infections.

[C] A germ is a bit of living matter capable of growth and development into an organism. Germs can cause many problems, including disease. The germs that make people sick are everywhere. You can't see them, but they're there. They're sitting on your desk. They're hiding on your computer's keyboard. They're even in the air that you are breathing.

45 Which one is the right order?

① [B] — [C] — [A]
② [B] — [A] — [C]
③ [C] — [B] — [A]
④ [C] — [A] — [B]

46 Which one is true?

① Germs are too small to see with our own eyes.
② Some viruses can have a positive impact on a human body.
③ Bacteria can cause illnesses such as influenza, or the flu.
④ Bacteria can grow and multiply only in living cells.

47 Choose the best title.

① How to Protect your Skin
② Skin, the First Line of Defense
③ Tiny Invaders
④ Germ Industry

48~51

The ability to experience pain is one of nature's gifts to humankind and the rest of the animal kingdom. Without it, we would not _____ recoil our hand upon touching a hot object or know to avoid walking barefoot over broken glass. Those actions, motivated by an immediate or remembered experience of pain, allow us to minimize the risk of bodily harm. We evolved to feel pain because the sensation serves as an alarm system that is vital to self-preservation.

The sentries in this system are a special category of sensory neurons called nociceptors, which are placed close to the spine, with (A) their fibers extending into the skin, the lungs, the gut, and other areas of the body. (B) They are equipped to sense different kinds of harmful stimuli: a knife's cut, burning acid, and the heat of molten wax. When nociceptors detect any of these threats, (C) they send electrical signals to the spinal cord, which transmits (D) them via other neurons to the brain. Higher order neurons in the cortex — the next destination of this ascending pain pathway — translate this input into the perception of pain.

Upon registering the pain, the brain attempts to counteract it. Neural networks in the brain send electrical signals back down the spinal cord along what is called the descending pain pathway, triggering the release of endorphins and other natural opioids. These biochemicals inhibit ascending pain signals, _____ reducing the amount of pain perceived.

48 Which one is not true?

① Feeling pain is a key bodily function for survival.
② Without certain neurons in the brain, we wouldn't be able to perceive pain.
③ Nociceptors are like guards that protect our body against the infiltration of external pain.
④ The signals of pain travel up and down the body through a network of neurons.

49 Choose the best word for the blanks.

① reflectively — effectively
② reflectively — affectively
③ reflexively — affectively
④ reflexively — effectively

50 Which refers to a different one?

① (A)   ② (B)   ③ (C)   ④ (D)

51 Choose the best title.

① How Our Body Handles Pain
② How to Minimize Pain
③ The Final Destination of Pain Signals
④ The Evolution of Opioids

[A] Breakthroughs in genetics present us with a promise and a predicament. The promise is that we may soon be able to treat and prevent a host of debilitating diseases. The predicament is that our newfound genetic knowledge may also enable us to manipulate our own nature — to enhance our muscles, memories, and moods; to choose the sex, height, and other genetic traits of our children; to improve our physical and cognitive capacities; to make ourselves "better than well." Most people find at least some forms of genetic engineering disquieting. But it is not easy to articulate the source of our unease. The familiar terms of moral and political discourse make it difficult to say what is wrong with reengineering our nature.

[B] Consider again the question of cloning. The birth of Dolly the cloned sheep in 1997 brought a torrent of worry about the prospect of cloned human beings. There are good medical reasons to worry. Most scientists agree that cloning is unsafe and likely to produce offspring with serious abnormalities and birth defects. Dolly died a _____ death. But suppose cloning technology improves to the point where the risks are no greater than with natural pregnancy. Would human cloning still be (A) objectionable? What exactly is wrong with creating a child who is a genetic twin of his or her parent?

[C] Some say cloning is wrong because it violates the child's right to autonomy. By choosing in advance the genetic makeup of the child, the parents consign her to a life in the shadow of someone who had gone before, and so deprive the child of her right to an open future. (B) The autonomy objection can be raised not only against cloning but also against any form of bioengineering that allows parents to choose their child's genetic characteristics.

52 Which of the following would be the best title for the above passage?

① The Breakthroughs in Genetic Engineering and Genetic Engineering's Promising Future
② The Need for Moral Discourse to Support Reengineering Our Nature
③ Articulating Our Anxiety about Genetic Engineering
④ The Significance of Autonomy and Parental Care in Child Rearing
⑤ The Growth of the Medical Industry due to the Proliferation of Debilitating Disease

53 Which word best fits the blank in paragraph [B]?

① premature
② blissful
③ covetous
④ placid
⑤ excusable

54 Which of the following can the underlined word (A) objectionable in paragraph [B] be best replaced with?

① curable
② undesirable
③ comprehensible
④ workable
⑤ understandable

55 According to the underlined part (B) the autonomy objection in paragraph [C], the problem with genetic engineering is that "designer children" are not completely free because even favorable genetic enhancements _____.

① do make them perfect beings who are immune to all diseases
② are not able to inculcate in them the capacity to reflect and create a well-made life plan
③ would force them to follow values and norms of mainstream society without respecting the autonomy of others
④ would cause them to object to their own autonomy and constantly depend on their parents' assistance
⑤ would point children toward particular life choices, violating their right to choose their life plan for themselves

56~57

The nervous system of vertebrates is characterized by a hollow, dorsal nerve cord that ends in the head region as an enlargement, the brain. Even in its most primitive form this cord and its attached nerves are the result of evolutionary specialization, and their further evolution from lower to higher vertebrate classes is a process that is far from fully understood. Nevertheless, the basic arrangements are similar in all vertebrates, and the study of lower animals gives insight into the form and structure of the nervous system of higher animals. Moreover, for any species, the study of the embryological development of the nervous system is indispensable for an understanding of adult morphology. In any vertebrate two chief parts of the nervous system may be distinguished. These are the central nervous system consisting of the brain and spinal cord, and the peripheral nervous system, consisting of the cranial, spinal, and peripheral nerves, together with their motor and sensory endings. The term "autonomic nervous system" refers to the parts of the central and peripheral systems that supply and regulate the activity of cardiac muscle, smooth muscle, and many glands. The nervous system is composed of many millions of nerve and glial cells, together with blood vessels and a small amount of connective tissue. The nerve cells, or "neurons," are characterized by many processes and are specialized in that they exhibit to a great degree the phenomena of irritability and conductivity. The glial cells of the central nervous system are supporting cells collectively termed "neuroglia." They are characterized by short processes that have special relationships to neurons, blood vessels, and connective tissue. The comparable cells in the peripheral nervous system are termed "neurilemmal" cells.

*vertebrate 척추가 있는, 척추동물

56 위 글의 주제로 가장 적절한 것은?

① the evolution of nerve cells
② the advancement of bioengineering
③ the nervous system of vertebrates
④ the functions of the automatic nervous system

57 The author implies that a careful investigation of a biological structure in an embryo may lead to _____.

① improved research of the same structure in other species
② a better understanding of the fully developed structure
③ a method by which scientists can diagnose nervous disease
④ discovering ways in which poor development can be corrected

58~60

Genus Homo's position in the food chain was, until recently, solidly in the middle. For millions of years, humans hunted smaller creatures and gathered what they could, all the while being hunted by larger predators. It was only 400,000 years ago that several species of man began to hunt large game on a regular basis, and only in the last 100,000 years — with the rise of Homo sapiens — that man jumped to the top of the food chain.

That spectacular leap from the middle to the top had enormous consequences. Other animals at the top of the pyramid, such as lions and sharks, evolved into that position very gradually, over millions of years. This enabled the ecosystem to develop _____ that prevent lions and sharks from wreaking too much havoc. As lions became deadlier, so gazelles evolved to run faster, hyenas to cooperate better, and rhinoceroses to be more bad-tempered. In contrast, humankind ascended to the top so quickly that the ecosystem was not given enough time to adjust. Moreover, humans themselves failed to adjust. Most top predators of the planet are majestic creatures. Millions of years of domination have filled them with confidence. Sapiens by contrast is more like a banana-republic dictator.

58 Which is the most appropriate for the blank?

① disposition and reproduction
② competition and coexistence
③ checks and balances
④ privilege and regulation

59 According to the passage, which best explains the underlined part?

① Sapiens first evolved from the apes, being dependent on staple food crops, bananas.
② Homo sapiens accomplished immense power based on unique political structures.
③ Humans are anxious about their position, which makes them brutal and dangerous.
④ Humankind accomplished agricultural revolution to make the original affluent society.

60 According to the passage, which is true?

① Homo sapiens subsisted by domesticating animals and plants 400,000 years ago.
② Lions and sharks are in the middle of food chain for millions of years.
③ Most top predators destroyed the ecosystem by hunting other animals.
④ The ecosystem changed as predators evolved to be more powerful.

61~62

A person watching and analysing the behaviour of a computer whose program had been lost might, in principle, be able to reconstruct the program or its functional equivalent. But there is no way of knowing in which language the program was originally written. The end result is the same in any case: the computer performs some useful task such as calculating square roots. A biologist looking at an animal is in somewhat the same position as an engineer looking at a computer running a lost program. The animal is behaving in what appears to be an organized, purposeful way, as if it was obeying a program, an orderly sequence of imperative instructions.

The animal's program has not actually been lost, for it never was written out. Rather, natural selection <u>cobbled together</u> the equivalent of a hard-wired machine code program, by favouring mutations that altered successive generations of nervous systems to behave. Nevertheless, it is convenient for us to think of the animal as 'obeying' a program 'written' in some easily understood language such as English. One of the things we can then do is to imagine alternative programs or subroutines which might 'compete' with each other for 'computer time' in the nervous systems of the population.

61 위 글의 내용과 일치하지 않는 것은?

① Natural selection acts on a pool of alternative programs or subroutines.
② There are many ways of knowing in which of the genes an animal's program was originally written.
③ The animal is behaving in an apparently effective and well-planed way as if it was obeying the program.
④ In explaining animal behavior mechanisms, the author uses the analogy of a computer running a lost program.

62 The author uses the words "cobbled together" to imply that the equivalent of a hard-wired machine code program natural section made is something _____.

① firmly fastened
② lost permanently
③ useful but not perfect
④ translated into a set of rules

63~64

The behavior of an organism is its tendency to react in a particular fashion to a specific situation or stimulus. But while any one animal may behave in a consistent way, different individuals will vary in their behavior. To see this variation, you need only approach a squirrel in your yard. At some point you will get too close, and the animal will bolt for a tree. Now approach another. And another. You'll find that some squirrels willl allow you to get close, whereas others will flee quickly. This kind of variation ubiquitous in animals. Some individuals are more aggressive than others. Some are more <u>inquisitive</u>. Some react swiftly, while others hold back. Variation in behavior can mean life or death. A bold squirrel might end up as a coyote's lunch. A shy squirrel may fail to discover enough food to survive the winter. Variation in the expression of behavior thus influences individual fitness.

63 위 글의 제목으로 가장 알맞은 것을 고르시오.

① Special Behaviors of Squirrels
② Behaviors and Individual Fitness
③ Inconsistency of Individual Behaviors
④ Aggressiveness and Chances of Survival

64 밑줄 친 부분의 의미와 가장 가까운 것을 고르시오.

① curious   ② indifferent
③ suspicious   ④ defensive

65~66

Over millennia, prolonged seasonal freezing of Lake Baikal has caused most of the lake's flora and fauna to adapt to life on and under the ice. Phytoplankton, microscopic organisms that live in fresh- or saltwater environments, are the basis of the lake's food web. Lake Baikal is the only lake in the world in which both the dominant primary producers (phytoplankton) and the top predator (the Baikal seal) require ice for reproduction.

Baikal's phytoplankton include green algae, which can grow explosively in "blooms" that may last days and weeks. Ice thickness and transparency determine the amount of light reaching the water, a critical factor for phytoplankton growth. Because these unique algae have adapted to specific under-ice conditions, recent changes in the ice, which was caused by warming air temperature, have decreased algae growth rates and slowed spring algal blooms. The effects of this decrease then move up the food chain, from the enormous quantities of tiny crustaceans that eat the algae to the fish that eat the crustaceans to the seals that depend on fish as their main food source.

The Baikal seal, smallest of the world's seals and the only species exclusively living in freshwater, mates and gives birth on the lake ice. The seals require ice in early spring for shelter. If ice melt occurs early, the seals are forced into the water, and the extra energy expended affects female fertility and nurturing ability.

65 According to the passage above, what is the best expression for the blank in the following sentence?

> Recent changes in water temperature and ice over at Lake Baikal exemplify _____.

① that global warming may lead to beneficial changes in some areas around the globe
② that living things display remarkable resilience in the face of environmental changes
③ how flora and fauna can protect the freshwater environment from climate change
④ how changes in the atmosphere link to changes in the hydrosphere and biosphere

66 Which of the following is not true according to the passage?

① Ice at Lake Baikal creates a crucial environment for algae to reproduce.
② Recent warm weather caused an increase in phytoplankton living in Lake Baikal.
③ Among seals, the Baikal seal is a unique species living only in water that is not salty.
④ Premature ice melting reduces the Baikal seal's fertility.

67~70

[A] Mammals and birds regularly express mate preferences and make mate choices. Data on mate choice among mammals suggest that this behavioral 'attraction system' is associated with dopaminergic reward pathways in the brain. It has been proposed that intense romantic love, a human cross-cultural universal, is a developed form of this attraction system.

[B] To begin to determine the neural mechanisms associated with romantic attraction in humans, we used functional magnetic resonance imaging (fMRI) to study 17 people who were intensely 'in love.' Activation specific to the beloved occurred in the brainstem right ventral tegmental area and right postero-dorsal body of the caudate nucleus. These and other results suggest that dopaminergic reward and motivation pathways contribute to aspects of romantic love.

[C] We also used fMRI to study 15 men and women who had just been rejected in love. Preliminary analysis showed activity specific to the beloved in related regions of the reward system associated with monetary gambling for uncertain large gains and losses, and in regions of the lateral orbito frontal cortex associated with theory of mind, obsessive/compulsive behaviors and controlling anger, revealed in recently abstinent cocaine-dependent individuals.

[D] These data contribute to our view that romantic love is one of the three primary brain systems that evolved in avian and mammalian species to direct reproduction. The sex drive evolved to motivate individuals to seek a range of mating partners; attraction evolved to motivate individuals to prefer and pursue specific partners; and attachment evolved to motivate individuals to remain together long enough to complete species-specific parenting duties. These three behavioral repertoires appear to be based on brain systems that are largely distinct yet interrelated, and they interact in specific ways to orchestrate reproduction, using both hormones and monoamines. Romantic attraction in humans and its antecedent in other mammalian species play a primary role: this neural mechanism motivates individuals to focus their courtship energy on specific others, thereby conserving valuable time and metabolic energy, and _____.

67 Which of the following would be the best title for the above passage?

① Romantic Love: Absolute Human Faculty
② Romantic Love: A Mammalian Brain System for Mate Choice
③ No Romantic Love: What the Brain Lies about in Mate Choices
④ No Romantic Love: Another Word for Sex Drive
⑤ Human Brain Demystified

68 According to the above passage, which of the following is not true?

① When mammals choose their mates, it is likely that dopamine is released in their brains.
② fMRI helps us to measure and map brain activity.
③ The brains of those rejected in love show patterns similar to those of drug-addicts.
④ Romantic love is related to mammals' brains that control reproduction.
⑤ The word "attachment" connotes more durability than the word "attraction."

69 Which of the following would best fit in the blank in the paragraph [D]?

① helping them to focus on more important things in life
② interfering with mate choice
③ preventing them from focusing on more important things in life
④ facilitating mate choice
⑤ helping them to fall in love

70 According to the passage, the author suggests that some animals stay with their mates for a long time mainly to _____.

① feel dopamine-induced happiness
② consummate their relationship in a more stable way
③ cooperate to raise their children
④ protect themselves against hostile environment
⑤ experience marital bliss

71~73

You may have felt sick when traveling in a car, train, or airplane. If so, you should take comfort because the queasiness you feel indicates your brain is functioning properly. Motion sickness researchers have found that while we are moving, our brains respond the same way they do when we are poisoned. It appears that because high-speed travel is a recent addition to human behavior, our brains have not adapted to it. As you travel at high speed, usually you are sitting down. Your brain gets signals from your body including your feet, buttocks, and back, that you are stationary. But your brain also gets signals from the balance sensors, little tubes of liquid in your inner ears, that you are moving forward at high speed. The mixed messages lead your brain to the incorrect assumption that you have perceived things incorrectly, and in the natural world, the only things that can make you perceive incorrectly are poisons. So, just to be safe, the body, believing you have been poisoned, automatically tries to flush out the toxin. In short, you get sick. However, if you stare out the window, the increased visual stimulation tells your brain that you are in fact moving, and this should make the nausea pass.

71 According to the passage, what is the cure for motion sickness?

① Stimulating your balance tubes
② Taking an antidote
③ Looking out the window
④ Having something to drink

72 According to the passage, what does having motion sickness imply?

① Your brain has adapted to travel.
② Your body is too weak from travel.
③ You have been poisoned by toxic liquids.
④ Your body is functioning naturally.

73 According to the passage, which of the following is true?

① Mind and body work in complete coordination.
② Illness is the result of staring out the window.
③ Car sickness is an old problem caused by adaptation.
④ Conflicting sensory information causes car sickness.

74~76

If you were to enter the baby's room in a typical American home today, you would probably see a crib full of stuffed animals and colorful toys dangling directly over the infant. Some of these toys may light up, move, or play music. What do you suppose is the parents' reasoning behind providing infants with so much to see and do? Aside from the fact that babies seem to enjoy and respond positively to these toys, most parents believe that children need a stimulating environment for optimal brain development.

The question of whether certain experiences produce physical changes in the brain has been a topic of research among scientists for centuries. In 1785, Vincenzo Malacarne, _____, studied pairs of dogs from the same litter and pairs of birds from the same batches of eggs. For each pair, he would train one participant over a long period of time while the other would be equally cared for but untrained. He discovered later, in his autopsies of the animals, that the brains of the trained animals appeared more complex, with a greater number of folds and fissures. In the 19th century, attempts were made to relate the circumference of the human head with the amount of learning a person had experienced. Although some early findings claimed such a relationship, later research determined that this was not a valid measure of brain development.

74. Which occupation best describes Vincenzo Malacarne in the blank?

① a physicist ② an anatomist
③ an optometrist ④ a biostatistician

75. According to the passage, which of the following is not a reason why you would find stuffed animals and colorful toys in a baby's room?

① Because babies appear to like them
② Because parents believe that babies disregard optimal brain development
③ Because babies seem to react affirmatively to them
④ Because parents suppose that babies need stimulating surroundings

76. Which of the following best describes the purpose of writing the above passage?

① to introduce a line of scientific research
② to advertise a new line of toys for children
③ to advise parents about the best child-rearing practices
④ to report a problematic phenomenon in society

77~79

Many people had never even heard the word "clone" until they read about a sheep named Dolly. By the time newspapers around the world carried the story of how scientists had successfully cloned Dolly in the laboratory, it seemed everybody was talking about cloning. People talked about cloning as if it were something completely new that had never happened before. Actually, (A) _____ scientists cloned Dolly, there had already been a lot of small cloning successes in research laboratories. What made Dolly different was that scientists had cloned her from an adult sheep cell, not an (B) _____ one.

When people learned about Dolly's cloning, they thought the idea was very controversial. A debate began about whether cloning is a good thing to do or not. When Dolly was born, most people had only heard about someone creating life in a laboratory in books like *Frankenstein*, by Mary Shelley. As soon as Dolly was born, however, people had to think very hard about what cloning might mean in the future.

When Dolly died in 2003, she had only lived for six years, but (C) _____ she died, she had been a completely normal sheep, except for having no father!

77 Which pair best fits in the blanks (A) and (C)?

① although — after
② before — by the time
③ although — by the time
④ before — after

78 Which best fits in the blank (B)?

① emotive
② embroiled
③ emollient
④ embryonic

79 According to the passage, which is not true?

① Dolly was not the first success story of cloning.
② The birth of Dolly led people to think about the future of cloning.
③ Dolly was unique because she was created outside the laboratory.
④ Not everyone welcomed the idea of duplicating living things.

80
~
83

[A] The first brains appeared on earth about 500 million years ago, spent a leisurely 430 million years evolving into the brains of the earliest primates and another 70 million years evolving into the brains of the first protohumans. Then, something happened and the soon-to-be-human brain experienced an unprecedented growth spurt that more than doubled its mass in a little over two million years, transforming it from the one-and-a-quarter-pound brain of Homo habilis to the nearly three-pound brain of Homo sapiens. (A)

[B] Now if you were put on a hot-fudge diet and managed to double your mass in a very short time, we would not expect all of your various body parts to share equally in the gain. (B) Similarly, the dramatic increase in the size of the human brain did not democratically double the mass of every part so that modern people ended up with new brains that were structurally identical to the old ones, only bigger. Rather a disproportionate share of the growth centered on a particular part of the brain known as the frontal lobe. (C)

[C] Scientists noticed that although patients with frontal lobe damage often performed well on standard intelligence tests, they showed severe impairment on any test that involved planning. They even found it practically impossible to say what they would do later that afternoon. (D) This finding helps us assume that the frontal lobe is a time machine that allows each of us to vacate the present and experience the future before it happens. No other animals have a frontal lobe quite like ours, which is why we are the only animal that thinks about the future as we do. (E) If the story of the frontal lobe tells us how people conjure their imaginary tomorrows, it doesn't tell us why.

80 Which of the following is the best title for the above passage?

① The Steady Evolution of the Human Brain
② The Importance of Brain Size
③ Amazing Human Brain Power Demystified
④ Future-Planning Brain Areas
⑤ Impact of Brain Damage on Time-Concept

81 Which of the following cannot be inferred from the passage?

① The size of the protohuman's brain is less than half the size of the human brain.
② It is still unknown what caused the rapid growth of the human brain.
③ The human brain has disproportionately evolved.
④ Patients with frontal lobe damage cannot understand how time proceeds.
⑤ The human brain is different from other brains not only in size but in structure.

82 The following sentence is removed from the passage. In which part may it be inserted to support the argument made by the author?

> Your belly and buttocks would probably be the major recipients of newly acquired flab, while your tongue and toe would remain relatively svelte and unaffected.

① (A)   ② (B)   ③ (C)   ④ (D)   ⑤ (E)

83 Which of the following would most likely to be discussed after the above passage?

① Why we should study the human brain.
② Why people should prepare for the unexpected future.
③ Why animal brains work differently from human brains.
④ Why the severely impaired frontal lobe cannot be easily treated.
⑤ Why people think about the consequences of their actions in advance.

15 지구과학·천문학·환경

01 Choose the most appropriate one for the blank.

Desertification is the accumulated result of ill-adapted land use and the effects of a harsh climate. Four human activities represent the most immediate causes: over-cultivation exhausts the soil, overgrazing removes the vegetation cover that protects it from erosion, deforestation destroys the trees that bind the soil to the land and poorly drained irrigation systems turn croplands salty. _____, the lack of education and knowledge, the movement of refugees in the case of war, the unfavourable trade conditions of developing countries and other socio-economic and political factors enhance the effects of desertification. The causes are multiple and interact in a complex manner.

① By contrast
② Consequently
③ For example
④ In return
⑤ Moreover

02 전체 글의 의미가 통하도록 [A]~[C]의 순서를 알맞게 배열한 것을 고르시오.

Navigation is the science of accurately determining one's location and then planning and following a route. The earliest form of navigation was land navigation. This relied on physical landmarks to chart the journey from one place to another. Away from land, one must use other markers in order to navigate successfully.

[A] Latitude is distance north or south of Earth's equator.
[B] These are two kinds of imaginary lines drawn on maps or globes representing the Earth.
[C] One modern way to do this is to keep track of one's position using longitude and latitude.

Longitude is distance east or west of the Greenwich Meridian, an imaginary line that runs from the North Pole to the South Pole and through Greenwich, England.

① [A] — [B] — [C]
② [B] — [C] — [A]
③ [C] — [B] — [A]
④ [C] — [A] — [B]

03~04

Urban floods make the news with alarming regularity. Just in the past few months, Hurricane Harvey submerged Houston, and the seasonal monsoon crippled cities in South Asia. Dramatic floods from increasingly severe storms come with a steep cost, both human and financial, and the problem will only get worse with climate change. Urbanization is one of the biggest culprits for the deadly toll these floods wreak.

As cities develop, miles of impervious pavement are laid over forest or wetlands, displacing the natural flood management systems like creeks, underground streams, or bogs. In a completely uninhabited landscape, rainfall integrates into the natural water cycle in four different ways: it either soaks all the way into the ground and becomes groundwater; runs down valleys into bodies of water and finds its way to the sea; is taken up by plants; or just evaporates. In urban or suburban sprawls with paved roads, highways, and parking lots, water has nowhere to go, so every heavy rain can turn into a flood.

But now there's a movement around the world to build smarter and "spongier" cities that can absorb rainwater instead of letting it flow through miles of pavement and cause damaging floods. From Iowa to Vermont and from San Francisco to Chicago, urban infrastructure is getting a reboot. Creating better stormwater management systems requires using green infrastructure elements in urban planning and restoring some of _____ that cities have lost to urbanization. These elements can be roughly broken into two categories: the man-made engineered replacements of the natural water pathways and the restorations of the original water routes that existed before a city was developed.

03 Which expression best fits the blank?

① the uninhabited areas
② the rain-retention capacity
③ the natural hydration
④ the amount of groundwater
⑤ the value of ecosystem

04 What is the most appropriate title of the passage above?

① How to Make Urban Life More Ecofriendly
② The Problem of Urbanization Kills Innocent Lives
③ How to Make Amends for the Rash Technological Urbanization
④ How to Solve Urban Floods by Making Cities Spongier
⑤ The Man-Made Disaster: The Consequences of Urbanization

05~07

Suppose you want to know how many fish are in a huge body of water. Obviously you can't count them all. You get your rod and reel and pull out a fish, tag it, release it, and give it time to swim away. Then you catch another fish, tag it and release it, then another, and so on, noting for each fish whether you had caught it before. If the body of water contains a small number of fish, at some point you'll keep catching the same few fish again and again. If it has an enormous number, most fish you pull out will not have been caught before. If the number is open-ended, or essentially (A)_____ — if the fish breed faster than you can catch them — you will never catch the same fish twice. After a million tries, you can write down the number of fish that you have caught once, the number you caught twice, and so on. The larger the proportion of the catch that consists of fish caught only once, you may conclude, (B)_____.

05 What is the most suitable expression for the blank (A)?

① consummate
② penultimate
③ definite
④ ultimate
⑤ infinite

06 According to the passage, which of the following is most likely if a few fish were caught repeatedly?

① Not a few fish will be caught in the long term.
② Tagged fish are easy to catch.
③ The total number of fish in the water is small.
④ There must be the same number of fishes in the water as that caught.
⑤ None of the above

07 What is the most suitable expression for the blank (B)?

① the more fish are caught faster
② the more fish are out there in the water
③ the slimmer become the chances of fish being alive
④ the less fish will breed in the water
⑤ the less frequent is the appearance of tagged fish

08~09

Sustainable development is the current philosophy in the resource industries in this time of environmental concern. Its main premise is to make certain that there are enough resources for the human race today and the future while concurrently ensuring the needs of the natural environment are being met. To do this, companies are always on the lookout to cut down the energy they consume, reduce their carbon footprint, and find new ways to minimize other types of waste. Companies taking a longer term view of profit with the idea of being socially responsible through sustainable development are being _____ both with government support and by consumers as they make their purchases.

08 Which of the following is closest in meaning to the underlined premise?

① profit
② probity
③ proposition
④ propaganda

09 Which of the following is most appropriate for the blank?

① rewarded
② countered
③ denounced
④ penalized

[10~11]

As you near the equator, the weather becomes more permanently summery. There are flowers and green leaves all year long, which is why the tropics are considered a kind of paradise by many. Think about this: If we can escape to a tropical island during a northern winter, we owe our vacation to the round shape and sideways tilt of our planet. Why? The northern and southern hemispheres, as they curve away, bear the brunt of the Earth's tilt. For part of the year, New York broils in the sun. For another part, it shivers under a load of snow and freezing rain and wind. In between, it enjoys the milder weather of spring and fall. _____, those near the Earth's bulging middle aren't as affected by the tilt. The middle of the Earth doesn't lean sharply away from the sun for part of the year and toward it the next. Places near the equator get good strong sunlight year round.

10 Which is the most appropriate for the blank?

① However ② Thus
③ Besides ④ Similarly

11 According to the passage, which is true?

① Tropical regions can have freezing weather frequently.
② Temperate zones are regarded as paradises by most people.
③ Places in the torrid zone have permanently summery weather.
④ New York's weather is relatively invariable throughout the year.

12~14

Birds are everywhere. We see them every day flying over our heads or hopping around our backyards. But scientists say that bird populations are declining rapidly, especially in North America. Approximately 29% of the continent's total bird population has been lost since 1970. _____, it has been found that common bird species, such as sparrows and blackbirds, are disappearing at an alarming rate, even faster than rare bird species. According to a new study, almost every group of birds is facing difficulty. Grassland bird populations have suffered the greatest loss, having declined by 53%. Forest-dwelling birds, which outnumber grassland birds, are also disappearing fast. One billion have been lost. Shorebirds, which migrate over entire hemispheres, are also showing sharp, consistent population losses. Their total population has dropped by 37% within the past 50 years. Even invasive species, which are often able to adapt to different environments, have not been able to escape this fate. As birds are indicator animals, whose well-being can reflect an ecosystem's overall health, scientists say that this massive population loss should be taken as a warning about the state of North American ecosystems in general.

12 Which of the following is most appropriate for blank?

① Finally
② Therefore
③ However
④ Moreover

13 Which bird group has experienced the largest decline in percentage terms in North America?

① shorebirds
② invasive birds
③ grassland birds
④ forest-dwelling birds

14 What can be inferred from the passage?

① The fate of birds points to potential threats posed to other animals.
② Bird species are declining mainly because of invasive species.
③ The most common bird species are proving the best able to adapt.
④ Bird numbers are falling most along common bird migration routes.

15 Which of the following is true according to the passage?

> The aurora borealis (aka the Northern Lights) is a spectacular natural phenomenon caused by particles of solar wind as they hurtle towards Earth and interact with chemicals in the atmosphere. Less well known but equally trippy is the aurora australis (or the Southern Lights), visible from the southernmost regions of the Southern Hemisphere. The reason the northern (and southern) lights exist exclusively around the poles is due to the Earth's magnetic field, which causes the solar particles to converge at the northernmost and southernmost latitudes. Here, they mingle with oxygen and nitrogen particles, releasing the photons that form the famously exuberant rainbow-colored auroras. Interactions with oxygen typically cause either yellow and green light, whereas interactions with nitrogen result in purplish-red, violet, and (slightly less frequently) blue colors. The brightness of the lights at any one time correlates to the movement of the solar wind particles and the oscillating magnetic field lines.

① Solar particles mingle with oxygen to form violet auroras.
② The aurora australis can be observed at the North Pole.
③ Solar particles converge at the poles due to the Earth's magnetic field.
④ The Earth's magnetic field lines are regular and stable.

16~17

Carl Bosch made it possible to produce huge quantities of ammonia, much of which is made into nitrogen-rich ammonium nitrate fertilizer. Careful estimates suggest that synthetic fertilizers feed about half of the world's population. Plants rely upon nitrogen compounds for building proteins and DNA. In nature, nitrates come from decaying plant and animal matter and from certain bacteria, which fix nitrogen from the air. Bosch's lasting legacy is double-edged, however. Artificial fertilizers saved millions from starvation, but the huge increases in population they allowed, from nearly 1.8 billion in 1910 to nearly 7 billion a century later, have put a strain on the world's resources. Their manufacture accounts for about one percent of the world's total energy consumption and their use causes pollution; agricultural run-off creates 'harmful algal blooms' in lakes and estuaries due to the extra nitrogen.

16 Carl Bosch made it possible _____.

① to reduce water pollution
② to manufacture synthetic fertilizers
③ to get nitrogen from the water
④ to prevent the creation of algal blooms

17 According to the passage, which of the following is true?

① Agricultural run-off causes bacterial infection when animals take it.
② Carl Bosch was actively engaged in establishing a starvation relief fund.
③ Decaying plant and animal matter is a major cause of pollution in lakes.
④ The manufacture of ammonia enabled the production of fertilizers on a large scale.

18~19

"When we say 'potentially habitable' exoplanets, that's a term that refers to measurable qualities of a planet that are necessary for habitable conditions," says Prof. Abel Mendez, from the University of Puerto Rico at Arecibo.

These are, then, promising targets where nothing is guaranteed. But two criteria dominate popular discussions of planetary habitability: first, whether it is within Earth's general size range (and therefore has a chance of being rocky) and, second, whether it resides in what's known as the habitable zone.

This is the range of distances around a host star where there's just enough starlight to keep water in liquid form on a planet's surface. Too close to the star, and the heat will cause water to boil off; too far away and any water will freeze.

These are useful rules of thumb, but a host of factors influence how hospitable planets are. And some are excluded from the conversation because of limitations in technology.

18

'_____' is not included in necessary conditions for a habitable exoplanet.

① Water
② Size
③ Distance
④ Starlight
⑤ Sun

19

The underlined rules of thumb means _____.

① standards based on practical experience
② procedures drawn by theoretical inference
③ best rules induced from scientific observations
④ prime standards built on the expenditures
⑤ easy procedures made by elaborate calculation

20~21

A recent study in the journal *Lancet Planetary Health* found that airborne pollen counts have been increasing around the world as average temperatures climbed. The majority of the 17 sites studied showed an increase in the amount of pollen and longer pollen seasons over 20 years. And the faster the climate changes, the worse it gets. That's why residents of Alaska, which is warming twice as fast as the global average, now face especially high allergy risks.

Taken together over the long term, seasonal allergies present one of the most robust examples of how global warming is increasing risks to health. Allergies are already a major health burden, and they will become an even larger drain on the economy. "It's very strong. In fact, I think there's irrefutable data," said Jeffrey Demain, director of the Allergy, Asthma, and Immunology Center of Alaska. "It's become the model of health impacts of _____." And since so many are afflicted — some estimates say up to 50 million Americans have nasal allergies — scientists and health officials are now trying to tease out the climate factors driving these risks in the hopes of bringing some relief in the wake of growing pollen avalanches.

20 Which of the following is most appropriate for the blank?

① climate change
② moral hazard
③ economic crisis
④ decreasing pollen counts
⑤ environmental destruction

21 What is the main idea of this passage?

① Allergies are going to get controlled.
② Pollen is becoming impossible to avoid.
③ Alaska is too cold to suffer from pollen allergies.
④ Seasonal allergies play an important role in national economy.
⑤ Pollen allergy seasons get longer and more intense as temperatures rise.

22~23

Landscape ecology focuses on the ecological relationships at the landscape scale. According to ecologists Richard Forman and Michel Godron, landscape ecology is "a study of the structure, function, and change in a heterogeneous land area composed of interacting ecosystems." European scientists advanced landscape ecology before their American counterparts. The landscapes of Europe have been more _____ settled than in North America, and, as a result, the human influence was recognized quickly by European scientists. American ecologists are more accustomed to studying relatively pristine landscapes. The refinement of the landscape ecology discipline, coupled with increased suburban sprawl nationwide, has changed this situation as more American ecologists acknowledge human interactions with natural systems. As landscape ecology has evolved through multiple interactions among European, American, and Australian contributors, it has crystallized into something new and powerful. Richard Forman observes that human settlements form mosaic-like patterns on landscapes and that this land mosaic vision makes the landscape readily accessible to scientists, especially ecologists.

*landscape ecology 경관 생태학

22 위 글의 빈칸에 들어갈 말로 가장 적절한 것은?

① perfectly
② safely
③ densely
④ lightly
⑤ precisely

23 위 글의 내용과 일치하지 않는 것은?

① 유럽 과학자들은 미국 과학자들에 앞서 경관 생태학을 발전시켰다.
② 유럽 과학자들은 자연에 미치는 인간의 영향력을 일찍이 인식하였다.
③ 미국 생태학자들은 비교적 원시적 경관을 연구하는 데 더 익숙하다.
④ 많은 미국 생태학자들은 인간과 자연의 독립성을 인정한다.
⑤ 생태학자들은 땅의 모자이크식 패턴 덕분에 경관에 쉽게 접근한다.

24~25

Gervase describes in his book how, in June of 1178, a group of Canterbury monks were outside one night looking at the new moon. As they were watching it, one end of the (A) _____ moon seemed to split into two. Flames and sparks burst from it and the rest of the moon seemed to shake.

Gervase admits that he didn't see the event himself, but was told about it by some of the men who did see it. He says that the men swore they were telling the truth.

For many years historians have puzzled over what the monks might have seen. Some think it was something simple like a cloud passing in front of the moon. Others believe that it was just a story, and not a real event.

However, one scientist, Dr. Jack Hartung, believes he may have found the answer. When Dr. Hartung read Gervase's account, he thought it sounded like some sort of explosion on the moon's surface. He thought that if (B) _____, the view from Earth would be similar to the event the monks saw.

24 빈칸 (A)에 들어갈 가장 알맞은 것을 고르시오.

① waning
② half
③ full
④ crescent

25 글의 내용상 빈칸 (B)에 들어갈 가장 알맞은 것을 고르시오.

① a meteor crashed into the moon's surface
② aliens from another planet invaded the moon
③ the Earth's gravity was stronger than usual
④ the moon drifted out of orbit by accident

26~27

The effects of an earthquake are strongest in a broad zone surrounding the epicenter. Surface ground cracking often occurs, with horizontal and vertical displacements of several yards. Such movement does not usually occur during a major earthquake: slight periodic movements called 'fault creep' can be accompanied by microearthquakes, too small to be felt. The extent of earthquake vibration and subsequent damage to a region is partly dependent on characteristics of the ground. For example, earthquake vibrations last longer and are of greater wave amplitudes in unconsolidated surface material, _____ poorly compacted fill or river deposits; bedrock areas receive fewer effects. The worst damage occurs in _____ populated urban areas where structures are not built to withstand intense shaking.

26 Which of the following is not true for the above passage?

① During a major earthquake, horizontal and vertical earthquake usually occur.
② The characteristics of the ground partly affect the extent of earthquake vibration.
③ Densely populated urban areas could have the worst damage.
④ Horizontal and vertical earthquake do not usually occur during a major earthquake.
⑤ Earthquake vibrations may last shorter in consolidated surface material than unconsolidated one.

27 Which would be the most appropriate pair for the blanks?

① such as — clearly
② such as — rarely
③ as for — scarcely
④ for instance — scarcely
⑤ such as — densely

28~29

Plastic bags were found in the digestive systems of more than 400 leatherback turtles. The leatherback turtle is a critically endangered species. Jellyfish is their main diet. Mistaking the increased amounts of plastic bag drifting in the currents for drifting jellyfish is causing the leatherbacks harm. Plastic bags account for 12 percent of all marine debris, and plastic bottles and plastic caps and lids are also prevalent at six and eight percent respectively. Marine litter is one of the most pervasive and solvable pollution problems plaguing the world's oceans and waterways. A simple solution to the plastic bag issue is reusable shopping bags. An increased awareness of the effects of plastic bags has caused many states and countries to _____ _____. For example, when Ireland imposed a fee on each plastic bag used by consumers, single-use plastic bag consumption dropped by 90 percent.

28 위 글의 빈칸에 들어갈 말로 가장 적절한 것은?

① emphasize the usefulness of plastic bags
② implement plastic bag related legislation
③ recognize the state of many endangered animals
④ acknowledge the civil rights for better environment
⑤ ban manufacturers from producing plastic products

29 위 글의 내용과 일치하지 않는 것은?

① 바다 장수거북의 소화기관에서 플라스틱이 발견되었다.
② 바다 장수거북은 멸종 위기종에 속한다.
③ 플라스틱병은 전체 해양 쓰레기의 6퍼센트를 차지한다.
④ 해양 오염은 해결이 거의 불가능하다.
⑤ 아일랜드에서는 플라스틱 봉투를 사용할 때 수수료를 내야 한다.

30~32

Sustainable living deals with the practice of decreasing your demand on natural resources by ensuring you recycle what you use to the best of your ability. Sometimes that can mean not choosing to _____ a product that is made using practices that don't promote sustainability, and sometimes it means altering how you do things so that you can start playing more of an active part in the cycle of life.

People know that global warming, climate change, depletion of the ozone layer, and resource depletion are real and their _____ on human and animal lives can be catastrophic. It is time for individuals to adopt actions for sustainable living by changing their lifestyle. For example, basic measures such as using public transportation more frequently, reducing energy consumption, and becoming more eco-friendly can go a long way in minimizing your environmental impact and making this planet a safe and clean place.

30 Which one is not true?

① Sustainable living involves changing your lifestyle to minimize your environmental impact.
② Sustainable living involves using more natural resources by buying more products.
③ Sustainable living involves trying your best to recycle what you use.
④ Sustainable living involves using less energy.

31 Which one cannot be inferred from the passage?

① You can help promote sustainability by walking or biking to work more often.
② You can reduce your energy consumption by using more natural light than light bulbs.
③ You can become eco-friendly by reusing or repurposing items for different uses.
④ You can help reduce carbon footprint by increasing your imprint on the world.

32 Choose the best word for the blanks.

① consume — affect
② consume — impact
③ consult — affect
④ consult — impact

33~36

After traveling 300 million miles through the solar system, NASA's InSight spacecraft descended through the Martian sky and touched down safely on the smooth surface of Elysium Planitia. [A]

Using a robotic arm, the lander will first install a super-sensitive seismometer on the Martian surface, where it will listen for meteorite impacts and Marsquakes. [B] The seismic waves from these events will give scientists a clearer picture of the planet's internal structure. InSight will then release its heat probe, a self-hammering 16-inch nail that will burrow down as deep as 16 feet over the course of several weeks. The instrument will measure how much heat escapes from Mars' interior, which will reveal the amount of heat-producing radioactive elements it contains and how _____ active the planet is today. [C] The spacecraft also has two X-band antennas on its deck that make up a third instrument, called RISE. [D] Radio signals from RISE will be used to track the wobble of Mars' orbit. This will help researchers understand the size and state of the Martian core. Together, these experiments will crack open Mars and spill the planetary secrets scientists have sought for decades.

33 The author's main purpose in writing this passage is to _____.

① discuss Martian internal structure and heat-producing radioactive elements
② emphasize the safe landing of InSight on Mars after a long journey
③ explain the experiments InSight will perform to reveal Mars' secrets
④ show how the wobble in the rotation of Mars is related to its magnetic field

34 Which is the most appropriate place for the sentence below?

> Unlike the space agency's rovers, InSight is a lander designed to study an entire planet from just one spot.

① [A]   ② [B]   ③ [C]   ④ [D]

35 Which of the following is most suitable for the blank?

① astronomically
② geologically
③ geometrically
④ astronautically

36 According to the passage, which of the following is true?

① NASA managed to land spacecraft safely on the surface of Mars three times.
② The deck of InSight spacecraft has a total of five instruments that can reveal Martian secrets.
③ The seismic waves will be used in tracking the wobble in the rotation of Mars.
④ A self-hammering nail will measure the amount of heat coming from the inside of Mars.

37~38

The scientific consensus on global warming comes from the Intergovernmental Panel on Climate Change (IPCC). It was established in 1988 by the World Meteorological Organization and the United Nations Environment Program to assess the science of climate change, determine its impacts on the environment and society, and formulate strategies to respond. More than 900 scientists from 40 countries have participated as authors or expert reviewers in the IPCC's latest report, published in 1995.

"It's a look at the state of the art — what we know about the climate system," says Gerald Meehl of the National Center for Atmospheric Research, a lead author for one of the report's chapters. "Literally thousands of people wind up reading these things.... It's the consensus view of just about everyone who's chosen to become involved." In June, some 2,400 scientists signed a letter saying they _____ the findings. The basics of global warming are simple. So-called greenhouse gases — including carbon dioxide and methane — build up in the atmosphere. Carbon dioxide is the most important of the greenhouse gases generated by human activity. The gases trap the sun's heat, like a car parked in the sun with the windows closed. Couple that with a basic fact: The amount of carbon dioxide in the atmosphere has risen by 30% since pre-industrial times (about 1750). The implication is that temperatures are rising, and that's what the IPCC was charged with studying.

37 Which is the topic of the passage?

① Scientific and social consensus of global warming
② The causes and results of global warming
③ IPCC's report and the basics of global warming
④ The political view of IPCC on global warming

38 Which is the most appropriate for the blank?

① endorsed
② disputed
③ rebuked
④ denounced

39~40

Astronomers all over the world were waiting in excitement as August 1993 approached. Mars Observer, the American spacecraft, was scheduled to move into orbit around Mars and began sending new information back to Earth. In addition to mapping the planet, Mars Observer was going to study the Martian atmosphere and surface. (A) Unfortunately, scientists lost contact with Mars Observer on August 24. The Mars Observer mission, which cost $845 million, failed.

In contrast, the United States' (B) previous mission to Mars was a great success. In 1976, two American spacecraft landed on Mars in order to search for signs of life. The tests that the Viking landers performed had negative results. However, scientists still had questions about our close neighbor in space. They wanted to investigate further into the possibility of life on Mars. This was the purpose of the Mars Observer mission.

Scientists were (C) satisfied with the Viking mission. The two sites where the spacecraft landed provided safe landing places, but they were no particularly interesting locations. Scientists believe there are other areas on Mars that are similar to specific places on Earth that support life. For example, an area in Antarctica, southern Victoria land, which is not covered by ice, (D) resembles an area on Mars. In the dry valleys of southern Victoria Land, the temperature averages below zero, yet biologists found simple life forms in rocks and frozen lakes. Perhaps this is also true of places on Mars.

Scientists want another investigation of Mars. They want to map the planet's surface and land a spacecraft in a more promising location. They want to search for fossils, the ancient remains of life. If life ever existed on Mars, scientists believe that future missions might find records of it under sand, or in the ice. They are very (E) disappointed in the failure of the Mars Observer mission and want to start a new mission.

39 (A)~(E) 가운데, 문맥상 낱말의 쓰임이 적절하지 않은 것은?

① (A)   ② (B)   ③ (C)   ④ (D)   ⑤ (E)

40 위 글의 제목으로 가장 적절한 것은?

① Missions to Find Life on Mars
② The Disaster of Mars Observer
③ Astronomers' Challenge in Mars
④ How Earth and Mars are Similar
⑤ Future Spacecraft for Space Travel

41~43

For years, attention has focused on the role of China, the largest emitter of greenhouse gases, and the United States, one of the largest emitter of per capita emitters. In November 2014 the two nations promised substantial limits on greenhouse gas emissions for the first time; China has pledged that its carbon dioxide output would fall after 2030, while the US has vowed to cut its output by more than a quarter in about the same time frame. Indeed, China's emissions have fallen so fast in the past year that many believe it may achieve its target ahead of time — the biggest stride yet in the fight against the climate change.

India's carbon output, _____, is growing faster than any other country's. Should that trend continue — and there is reason to think that it will — India could surpass China in 25 years to become the world's greatest emitter. Conceivably, its increasing emissions could offset all the efforts at curtailment in the rest of the world, leading to catastrophe. "India is the biggest piece of the puzzle," says John Coequyt, Sierra Club's director of international climate campaigns. "Is there a way for that rapid growth to happen quickly and pull people out of poverty using more renewable energy than has ever been used before? Or will they build more of what they have with almost no pollution controls?" The latter of course, he says, would be "a disaster for everyone."

41 According to the passage, _____.

① China is reluctant to keep the promise with the US
② the US pressed China to obey the global rule
③ India will be the largest emitter of gases
④ the US had to compete with China
⑤ India will follow the Chinese way

42 The most appropriate expression for the blank would be _____.

① by contrast
② however
③ on the one hand
④ in fact
⑤ by the way

43 Which one would be an example of what they have?

① solar energy
② wind power
③ hydrogen energy
④ coal plants
⑤ reforestation project

44~47

Nature challenges humans in many ways, through disease, weather, and famine. For those living along the coast, one unusual phenomenon capable of catastrophic destruction is the tsunami. A tsunami is a series of waves generated in a body of water by an impulsive disturbance. Earthquakes, landslides, volcanic eruptions, explosions, and even the impact of meteorites can generate tsunamis. Starting at sea, a tsunami slowly approaches land, growing in height and losing energy through bottom friction and turbulence. Still, just like any other water waves, tsunamis unleash tremendous energy as they plunge onto the shore. They have great erosion potential, stripping beaches of sand, undermining trees, and flooding hundreds of meters inland. They can easily crush cars, homes, vegetation, and anything they collide with. To minimize the devastation of a tsunami, scientists are constantly trying to anticipate them more accurately and more quickly. Because many factors come together to produce a life-threatening tsunami, foreseeing them is not easy. _____ this, researchers in meteorology persevere in studying and predicting tsunami behavior.

44 In the first sentence, why does the author mention weather?

① because tsunamis are caused by bad weather
② because tsunamis are more destructive than weather phenomena
③ as an example of a destructive natural force
④ as an introduction to the topic of coastal storms

45 Which of the following is closest in meaning to the underlined word unleash?

① release
② consume
③ contain
④ sustain

46 Which of the following is most appropriate for blank?

① In line with
② Despite
③ Contrary to
④ Compared with

47 Which sentence best expresses the essential information of this passage?

① Tsunamis could become a new source of usable energy in the near future.
② Tsunamis do more damage to the land than flooding.
③ Tsunamis can have an especially catastrophic impact on coastal communities.
④ Scientists can predict and track tsunamis with a fair degree of accuracy, reducing their potential impact.

48 ~ 51

Dr. Pickett, a Canadian entomologist, and his associates struck out on a new road instead of going along with other entomologists who continued to pursue the will-o'-the-wisp of the ever more toxic chemical. [A] Recognizing that they had a strong ally in nature, they devised a program that makes maximum use of natural controls and minimum use of insecticides. Whenever insecticides are applied only minimum dosages are used — barely enough to control the pest without avoidable harm to beneficial species. Proper timing also enters in. [B]

How well has this program worked? Nova Scotia orchardists who are following Dr. Pickett's _____ spray program are producing as high a share proportion of first-grade fruit as are those who are using _____ chemical applications. They are also getting as good production. They are getting these results, moreover, at a substantially lower cost. [C]

More important than even these excellent results is the fact that Dr. Pickett's program is not doing violence to nature's balance. [D] It is well on the way to realizing the philosophy stated by G. C. Ullyett a decade ago: "We must change our philosophy, abandon our attitude of human superiority and admit that in many cases in natural environments we find ways of limiting populations of organisms in a more economical way than we can do it ourselves."

48 Which of the following is most suitable for the blanks?

① prolific — resilient
② unvaried — varied
③ indiscreet — discreet
④ modified — intense

49 Which is the most appropriate place for the sentence below?

> Thus if nicotine sulphate is applied before rather than after the apple blossoms turn pink one of the important predators is spared, probably because it is still in the egg stage.

① [A]　　② [B]　　③ [C]　　④ [D]

50 What are the two most important factors in applying insecticides in Dr. Pickett's program?

① maximum dosages and proper timing
② proper dosages and early timing
③ sufficient dosages and early timing
④ minimum dosages and proper timing

51 Which of the following can not be inferred from the passage?

① Dr. Pickett and his associates believed that they had a strong ally in nature.
② One of the advantages of the Dr. Pickett's program was that it produced positive results at a lower cost.
③ G. C. Ullyett and Dr. Pickett saw eye to eye about ways to use nature.
④ Dr. Pickett and his associates did not believe in the need to limit populations of organisms.

16 동·식물

01~02

After a long day at the beach being out in the sun too long, many of us reach for a soothing lotion to cool our sunburn. The main ingredient of these ointments is usually Aloe vera, a plant <u>indigenous</u> to Africa with a long and well-documented history of human use. Aloe vera is one of 299 species of Aloe and has nearly as many uses. It has abundant, broad, fleshy leaves that comprise its rosette and grows in tropical as well as arid regions. Aloe vera has proven medicinal properties and can be used both externally and internally. Not only does it give immediate _____ from sunburns, but it also provides a thin layer over cuts and wounds that prevents infection.

01 Which of the following is the closest in meaning to the underlined <u>indigenous</u>?

① aboriginal
② genuine
③ infiltrated
④ immaculate

02 Which of the following is most appropriate for the blank?

① aggravation
② incipience
③ hostage
④ relief

03 Choose the one that is not mentioned in the passage.

> The Thai wildlife authorities found 40 dead tiger cubs in a freezer on Wednesday at the Tiger Temple and were investigating whether the carcasses were evidence of the temple's involvement in the illegal wildlife trade. The discovery came as Thai wildlife rangers were removing adult tigers from the temple in an effort to shut down the attraction after receiving complaints that the temple was trafficking in endangered species. The temple has long been accused by conservationists and animal rights activists of exploiting and abusing the animals, accusations the temple has denied. Wildlife officials said that only one of the dead cubs found on Wednesday had been reported to the government as required by law. Tiger parts, while illegal to sell, are in high demand in Asia for use in traditional medicine. There is even a market for frozen tiger cubs, as the arrest last month of a Vietnamese man carrying four of them attests.

① How many carcasses of baby tigers were found in a freezer
② Why the Thai wildlife rangers were removing adult tigers from the temple
③ How the tiger Temple obtained the tiger cubs
④ Why tiger parts are in high demand in Asia

04 Cranberry에 관한 다음 글의 내용과 일치하지 않는 것은?

> The cranberry is a North American fruit that grows on a bush. The settlers from England in the 1600s liked the berries and called them "crane berries" because birds called cranes ate them. The cranberry bush does not grow everywhere in the United States. In fact, it grows in only five states. These states have the special conditions that the cranberry bush needs. Cranberries ripen when the weather starts to become cold. We see cranberries in the stores in the fall. Cranberry growers separate the best cranberries from all the rest. It's hard to recognize the best cranberries just by looking. So cranberry growers use a special method. They use a seven-step test to separate berries. The best cranberries are the ones that bounce down seven steps!

① 덤불에서 자라는 북아메리카 과일이다.
② 이름의 유래가 그것을 먹는 새와 관련이 있다.
③ 미국의 5개 주에서만 자란다.
④ 날씨가 추워지기 시작하면 열매가 익는다.
⑤ 제품의 품질을 육안으로 구별할 수 있다.

05~06

The giant panda has an insatiable appetite for bamboo. A typical animal eats half the day — a full 12 out of every 24 hours — and relieves itself dozens of times a day. It takes 28 pounds of bamboo to satisfy a giant panda's daily dietary needs, and it hungrily plucks the stalks with elongated wrist bones that function rather like thumbs. Pandas will sometimes eat birds or rodents as well.

Wild pandas live only in remote, mountainous regions in central China. These high bamboo forests are cool and wet, just as pandas like it. They may climb as high as 13,000 feet to feed on higher slopes in the summer season. They are skilled tree-climbers and efficient swimmers.

Giant pandas are solitary. They have a highly developed sense of smell that males use to avoid each other and to find females for mating in the spring. After a five-month pregnancy, females give birth to a cub or two, though they cannot care for both twins. The blind infants weigh only 5 ounces at birth and cannot crawl until they reach three months of age. They are born white, and develop their much loved coloring later.

05 Which of the following is not mentioned about giant pandas?

① diet
② habitat
③ population
④ reproduction

06 Which of the following is true about giant pandas?

① They only feed on plants.
② They do not live in groups.
③ They only see black and white at birth.
④ They have black-and-white fur at birth.

My next-door neighbor had a pure-bred corgi that he was planning to breed from, but a fox terrier got into the act, and before long a litter of five corgi-fox terriers were born. I was fortunate enough to be offered one of the pups, and when I went to view them, one tottered over and laid its head squarely on my foot. This was the one I wanted. I eventually named him Max.

With a white blaze down the front of his head and chest, Max became an integral part of the family in no time. He gave my wife and two boys years of happiness and excitement, but in later years developed arthritis, which made moving extremely painful. The vet prescribed pills, which proved to be of no use, so as hard as it was to deal with losing him, I decided that it was time to have Max euthanized to prevent _____ the pain. However, the vet recommended that we try another set of pills, to which I agreed. The new pills proved to be amazing and in about two weeks, Max was back to running and playing with no sign of pain. Initially, it was a challenge to give Max his pills, but he soon realized that they were doing him some good. I only had to say, "Come on Max, pill time" and he would trot over, lay down and roll onto his back, open his mouth and swallow the pills when I dropped them in. Then he would stand up with a huge grin.

07 Choose the best word for the blank.

① curtailing
② shortening
③ minimizing
④ prolonging

08 Which one is not true?

① Max is a pure-breed corgi.
② Max enjoys running and playing.
③ Giving Max his pills has not always been easy.
④ Putting Max to sleep for good was an option Max's owner pondered.

09 Choose the best title.

① Recovering From Cancer
② How to Adopt Pure-Breeds
③ Max's Second Chance at Life
④ Choosing the Right Dog

10~12

The next time your pup starts pacing during a thunderstorm, or you have to leave for a day and you know separation anxiety may ensue, consider turning on your radio or sound system. The sound of a human voice can be reassuring to pets, so you could tune into a talk station. However, according to a new Scottish study, dogs also like music — especially the sounds of reggae and soft rock.

In the study, researchers from the University of Glasgow played six hours of music in five different genres (classical, soft rock, reggae, pop and Motown) to shelter dogs. While the dogs were listening, researchers took note of their heart rate variability, cortisol levels and behaviours that measure stress levels, such as barking or lying down.

It turns out that dogs were generally 'less stressed' when they heard music — and were most chilled when listening to reggae or soft rock. Motown got the paws down, though not by much.

However, like humans, it seems dogs possibly have a(n) _____ as different dogs in the study responded differently to particular types of music. Based on the results, shelters and dog owners could benefit from playing music to their canines during high-stress situations.

A previous study on the effects of classical music on dogs, by the same team, discovered they barked less and showed other signs of relaxation. However, after six days of classical music the dogs became restless. The solution? Mix up the music playlist you play to your dog.

10 Which is closest in meaning to the underlined ensue?

① follow
② growl
③ descend
④ disappear

11 Which best fits into the blank?

① unique voice trait
② superb olfactory sense
③ unusual life experience
④ individual music preference

12 Which is the best title for the passage?

① Music, A Way to Calm Dogs
② Motown, The Music Dogs Like Best
③ Separation Anxiety, A Silent Killer of a Dog
④ Classical Music, A Stress Reliever for a Dog

13 Which of the following is the best order for a passage starting with the given sentences in the box?

> If you're shopping for a live Christmas tree this year, you may have to search harder than in the past. Over the last five years Christmas tree shortages have been reported in many parts of the U.S.

[A] Collectively, these trends don't bode well for Christmas tree lovers, the growers, or the industry. However, there are opportunities for younger farmers to enter this market, either full- or part-time.

[B] One factor is that growers sold off land and planted fewer trees during and after the 2008 recession. In the lifespan of Christmas trees, the decade from 2008 to the present is roughly a single generation of plantings. However, in my research on the human dimensions of farming and food systems, I also see other factors at play.

[C] If new and beginning growers live in an area with appropriate environmental conditions, Christmas trees are a high-quality complementary crop that farmers can use to diversify their operations and provide off-season income.

[D] Christmas trees take 6 to 12 years to mature, and consumer preferences often change more quickly than farmers can adjust. Climate change is altering temperature and rainfall patterns, which severely affects growers' ability to produce high-quality trees and the varieties that customers seek.

① [A] — [C] — [B] — [D]
② [B] — [D] — [A] — [C]
③ [B] — [C] — [D] — [A]
④ [D] — [A] — [C] — [B]
⑤ [D] — [C] — [A] — [B]

14~15

One reason for the rising interest in protecting whales is the opportunity many people have had to observe them firsthand. Indeed, whale watching has become an important tourist enterprise in coastal areas. Stellwagen Bank, within easy reach of boats from Boston, Massachusetts, has become the center of the U.S. whale-watching industry estimated to be worth more than $78 million annually. Operating from spring through fall, scores of boats venture offshore daily to watch the whales that congregate over the bank. Many of the humpback whales seem to enjoy entertaining the visitors and often frolic alongside the boats for hours. Besides having aesthetic and entertainment value, whale-watching is of scientific value. Whale-watching tour boats usually carry a biologist who identifies the whale species and interprets the experience for the visitors. The biologists are often associated with research groups that have studied the whales of Stellwagen Bank and have published many papers on the humpback whale.

14 Which of the following is not addressed in the passage?

① The popularity of whale watching
② The value of the U.S. whale-watching industry
③ The endangered status of humpback whales
④ The role of biologists on whale-watching trips

15 According to the passage, Stellwagen Bank is not _____.

① a valuable tourist destination
② close to Boston, Massachusetts
③ the center of a multi-million dollar industry
④ open for whale watching in winter

16~18

Bamboo is one of the world's most important plants. For one thing, a stand of bamboo benefits humans by releasing into our atmosphere 35 percent more oxygen than a stand of trees the same size. Bamboo also cleanses the atmosphere by absorbing a great deal of carbon dioxide. In addition, bamboo is a very hardy, fast-growing plant. Some bamboo species grow at the rate of two inches per hour, so they can quickly regreen a deforested area, preventing damaging erosion and providing protection from the sun. The plant's amazing growth rate, along with a strength that _____ that of mild steel, makes bamboo an excellent building material. And bamboo has also provided humans with a wide range of other products from foods and medicines to paper and fuel. Thomas Edison used a bamboo filament in his first light bulb, which still burns at the Smithsonian Museum in Washington, D.C., and Alexander Graham Bell's first phonograph needle was made of bamboo.

16 Which is the most appropriate for the blank?

① overcomes
② surpasses
③ reinforces
④ dissipates

17 According to the passage, which is not true?

① Bamboo is one of the fastest-growing plants on earth.
② Bamboo could play a major role in preventing soil loss.
③ Bamboo was used for Edison's light bulbs and Bell's telephones.
④ Bamboo releases much more oxygen than an equivalent stand of trees.

18 Which is the best title of this passage?

① Bamboo as a Green Solution
② Why Bamboo?
③ Planting Bamboo
④ Fascinating Bamboo Foods

19
~
23

Beavers are famously busy, and they turn their talents to reengineering the landscape as few other animals can. When sites are available, beavers burrow in the banks of rivers and lakes. But they also transform less suitable habitats by building dams. Felling and gnawing trees with their strong teeth and powerful jaws, they create massive log, branch, and mud structures to block streams and turn fields and forests into the large ponds that beavers love. [A]

Domelike beaver homes, called lodges, are also constructed of branches and mud. They are often _____ located in the middle of ponds and can only be reached by underwater entrances. These dwellings are home to extended families of monogamous parents, young kits, and the yearlings born in the previous spring. [B]

Beavers are among the largest of rodents. They are herbivores and prefer to eat leaves, bark, twigs, roots, and aquatic plants.

These large rodents move with an ungainly waddle on land but are graceful in the water, where they use their large, webbed rear feet like swimming fins, and their paddle-shaped tails like rudders. [C] They can remain underwater for 15 minutes without surfacing, and have a set of transparent eyelids that function much like goggles. Their fur is naturally oily and waterproof.

Beavers are known for their danger signal which a beaver makes when the beaver is startled or frightened. A swimming beaver will rapidly dive while forcefully slapping the water with its broad tail. This means that the beaver creates a loud slapping noise, which can be heard over large distances above and below water. This beaver warning noise serves as a warning to beavers in the area. [D] Once a beaver has made this danger signal, nearby beavers dive and may not come back up for some time.

There are two species of beavers, which are found in the forests of North America, Europe, and Asia. These animals are active all winter, swimming and foraging in their ponds even when a layer of ice covers the surface.

19 Which of the following is most appropriate for the passage to appear in?

① a wildlife magazine
② a financial report
③ an environment pamphlet
④ a paper on omnivores

20 Which of the following is most likely to be the author's attitude toward beavers?

① indignant
② sympathetic
③ uninterested
④ adoring

21 Which is the most appropriate place for the sentence below?

> These attributes allow beavers to swim at speeds of up to five miles an hour.

① [A]   ② [B]   ③ [C]   ④ [D]

22 Which of the following is most suitable for the blank?

① inalienably
② strategically
③ indiscreetly
④ indescribably

23 According to the passage, which of the following is true?

① Beavers are mid-sized rodents that eat all plants and roots.
② Beavers can create a loud slapping noise by using their paddle-shaped tails.
③ Yearlings of beavers leave their lodges permanently in the spring.
④ Beavers do not swim when the surface of their ponds is covered with ice.

01 Choose the best order after the sentences given in the box.

> Much of the appeal of soccer lies in the fact that it can be played without special equipment.

> [A] Understandably so, a bladder alone did not last very long, so as time passed people began to protect the bladders in a shell made of animal skin properly cured to turn it into leather.
> [B] Children everywhere know that a tin can, some bound-up rags, or a ball from a different sport entirely can be satisfyingly kicked around. This ingenuity was first displayed hundreds of years ago when people discovered that an animal's bladder could be inflated and knotted to provide a light, bouncy ball.
> [C] This design worked so well that it is still used to this day, but with modern, synthetic materials rather than animal products.

① [A] — [C] — [B] ② [B] — [A] — [C]
③ [B] — [C] — [A] ④ [C] — [A] — [B]

02~03

The international press has dubbed us YAPs ("Young Americans in Prague"). The cheap cost of living, the many job opportunities, and the electric atmosphere have attracted tens of thousands of young Americans and other Westerners since the 1989 revolution. Relatively rich, Westerners in Prague can afford to live in the center of town, use the excellent public transport system, wander through the teeming streets. In Prague you don't see the beggars that have become so familiar in the doorways of cities both west and east of here. It is safe to walk around town at night. We have watched new buildings go up and old ones cleared of grime. We have soaked up Prague's revived cafe society, its Art Nouveau splendor, jazz clubs, opera houses. We have not had any difficulty finding at least one job, and many of us have two or three. The major Western companies have been happy to employ YAPs for above-average Czech wages, _____ we lack Czech language skills, for we are honest, efficient, and diligent.... In the early 1990s, where else could an inexperienced young American walk into the offices of the world's top advertising agencies or law firms and gain employment without showing a réumé?

02 Which is the most appropriate for the blank?

① no matter what
② so that
③ though
④ since

03 According to the passage, which is NOT true?

① Czech businesses were willing to employ young Americans because of the latter's efficiency and industry.
② Generally young Americans living in Prague liked the city's atmosphere and low living costs.
③ There was a revolution in Czechoslovakia at the end of the 1980s.
④ Quite a large number of young Americans in Prague were able to get more than one job.

04~06

There is an old television commercial from the seventies that shows a Native American walking along a polluted river. The garbage floats to the top and onto the river banks as a tear flows down his cheek. There are no words spoken by the man but it is clear that he is ashamed and appalled at what we have done to the beautiful land that was once his ancestors'. Every day, we fail to realize that our actions have an impact on the future. If we pull up our stakes and move the family to Florida, they will grow up as Southerners and not as New Englanders. They will live in a world devoid of snow and cold and be reliant on fans and air conditioners for their comfort. If you work eighteen hours a day and your children are raised by baby sitters and other child care providers, do not be surprised at the people _____. Every action has a reaction. You may not realize it today, but someone will in the future.

04 The underlined expression pull up our stakes means _____.

① take a risk
② invest all the money
③ restore the land
④ move away

05 Which of the following best fills in the blank?

① they grow up to be
② they would meet in the future
③ who treat the beautiful nature
④ who get used to the weather

06 What is the main idea of the passage?

① We should protect nature before it is too late.
② We are subject to weather conditions.
③ You should be careful when you raise your children.
④ Future consequences are inevitably shaped by present actions.

07~08

Most of us mistakenly think that speed of reading is a measure of intelligence. There is no such thing as the right speed for intelligent reading. Some things should be read quickly and effortlessly and some should be read slowly and carefully. The sign of intelligence in reading is the ability to read different things differently according to their worth. In the case of good books, the point is not to see how many of them you can get through, but rather how many can get through you, that is, how many you can _____. A few friends are better than a thousand acquaintances. If this is your aim, as it should be, you will not be impatient if it takes more time and effort to read a great book than it does a newspaper.

07 Which of the following is the major topic of the passage?

① How to choose a good book
② How to read great books
③ How to increase reading speed
④ How to measure book qualities

08 Which of the following best fits into the blank?

① make your own
② recall from memory
③ write your own books
④ read within a limited time

The purpose of the résumé is to get you a job interview. Employers use résumés to _____ undesirable, or less desirable, candidates. Your résumé should summarize your skills and experience, and convince employers of the value they will gain in hiring you. It's an advertisement for yourself, and as with all ads, it should generate interest and motivate the reader.

Before you prepare your résumé, take a few moments to consider your marketable skills. Identify the strengths and accomplishments that are relevant to the position you are seeking, and present them as succinctly and as clearly as possible. You'll need to organize all of this information in no more than two pages, in an easy-to-read, attractive format. Beyond this, there are no hard-and-fast rules about writing résumés.

09 Which best fits in the blank?

① put out
② take on
③ catch on
④ screen out

10 Which is not mentioned in the passage?

① purpose of the résumé
② variations of the résumé format
③ necessary contents of the résumé
④ guiding principles in writing résumés

11
~
12

The unique feature of judo is using your opponents' force against them. For instance, you can bear-hug an opponent charging you at full speed, use your own body as a lever and throw them over your shoulder to the ground. This is how smaller judokas beat bigger ones, which is the essence of judo. Just when your opponent tries to mount an attack, you can duck and make them lose their balance. Just as David beat Goliath, big guys can be surprised by smaller ones in judo, ensuring plenty of tactical battles during a five-minute match. For instance, going all out on offense often leaves one vulnerable to counterattack. But you can't afford to sit back all the time, either; a passive approach will get you a warning and may cost you a point. This is why judo, for all its physicality, is known as _____.

11 Which of the following is implied by the underlined part?

① You are required to sit down after each round.
② You should be both aggressive and defensive.
③ You have to keep a standing position.
④ You had better change to a front seat.

12 Which of the following best fits into the blank?

① a matter of time   ② a war of strength
③ a game of chance   ④ a battle of wits

13 Which of the following is not true according to the passage?

> The history of chocolate can be traced to the ancient Mayans. Mayans not only consumed chocolate, but they revered it. The Mayan written history mentions chocolate drinks being used in celebrations and to finalize important transactions. Despite chocolate's importance in Mayan culture, it wasn't reserved for the wealthy and powerful but readily available to almost everyone. In many Mayan households, chocolate was enjoyed with every meal. Mayan chocolate was thick and frothy and often combined with chili peppers, honey or water.
>
> The Aztecs took chocolate admiration to another level. They believed cacao was given to them by their gods. Like the Mayans, they enjoyed the caffeinated kick of hot or cold, spiced chocolate beverages in ornate containers, but they also used cacao beans as currency to buy food and other goods. In Aztec culture, cacao beans were considered more valuable than gold. Aztec chocolate was mostly an upper-class extravagance, although the lower classes enjoyed it occasionally at weddings or other celebrations.

① In Maya, chocolate was consumed by people from all walks of life.
② Chocolate was considered divine in Aztec culture.
③ Chocolate beverages consumed in Maya and Aztec differed considerably.
④ The Aztecs used cacao beans as money.

14~15

All my life I've been registering exceptional scores with tests, so that I have the complacent feeling that I'm highly intelligent. Actually, though, don't such scores simply mean that I am good at answering the type of academic questions that are considered worthy of answers by the people making up the intelligence tests — people with an intellectual bent similar to mine?

In a world where I could not use my academic training and my verbal talents, I would do poorly. My intelligence, then, is not absolute but is a function of the society I live in and of the fact that a small subsection of that society has managed to foist itself on the rest as a _____ of matters of intelligence.

14 Which of the following is closest in meaning to the underlined bent?

① endowment   ② investment
③ propensity   ④ property

15 Which of the following most appropriate for the blank?

① layman   ② judge
③ dissenter   ④ recluse

16~17

Good afternoon Kathy, it was good chatting with you this morning. As promised, attached is a copy of the confidential mediation letter we submitted on your behalf to the mediator. The mediation will take place at the Arbitration & Mediation Service Center located in Union Plaza, 1200 University Avenue, Suite 700, Seattle from 9 a.m. to 1p.m. Your attorney, Mr. Rawlins, will meet you there. In case you are wondering, please dress "business casual." You may wish to bring with you reading material or other electronic devices (tablet, laptop) to the mediation, as long intervals are expected throughout the meeting. Also, light refreshments will be provided. Please let me know if you have any other questions prior to the mediation.

Sincerely,
Sandra

Sandra J. Kelly, Litigation Paralegal
J. Rawlins Law Group

16. What is the relationship between the sender and the recipient of the letter?

① legal office — client
② court office — mediator
③ plaintiff — defendant
④ prosecutor — the accused

17. Which of the following is true according to the passage?

① The attached letter is open to the public.
② The meeting is a formal event with a strict dress code.
③ The meeting is unlikely to involve intense non-stop discussions.
④ Food and drinks will not be provided at the meeting.

18
~
20

I still believe, many years after coming to Johnson University from my native Canada, that teaching is a noble calling and that professors are obligated to serve their students. Yet, no professor can be all things to all students, so one must be prepared to temper one's aspirations with practicality. For me, this balancing act has led me to focus my working life primarily on assisting my students in the development of their English as a foreign language speaking and listening skills by endeavoring to be an effective classroom teacher and a useful researcher. In the classroom, I understand the importance of motivating learners to exceed their English language limits without setting unreasonable goals for them to achieve. If I were to abandon reason and set impractical learning goals, the result would likely be failure, which would in turn negatively impact motivation. So I have sought to invoke passion in my students for learning while at the same time being practical about the expectations that I have for them.

18 According to the passage, which is not true?

① The writer has a singular aim with regard to students.
② Professors cannot meet every student's needs.
③ The writer has tried to increase students' enthusiasm for learning English.
④ Failure decreases motivation.

19 Which of the following words is closest in meaning to the underlined word temper?

① abandon   ② examine
③ confound   ④ moderate

20 Which of the following is the most appropriate title for this passage?

① Balance in an Academic Context
② Practicality is the Key to Effective Instruction
③ Teaching Is a Noble Profession
④ Daily Life at Johnson University

21~22

As for the pigs, they could already read and write perfectly. The dogs learned to read fairly well, but were not interested in reading anything except the Seven Commandments. Muriel, the goat, could read somewhat better than the dogs, and sometimes used to read to the others in the evenings. Benjamin could read as well as any pig, but never exercised his faculty. So far as he knew, he said, there was nothing worth reading. Clover learnt the whole alphabet, but could not put words together. Boxer could not get beyond the letter D. He would trace out A, B, C, D, in the dust with his great hoof, and then would stand staring at the letters, trying with all his might to remember what came next and never succeeding. On several occasions, indeed, he did learn E, F, G, H, but by the time he knew them, it was always discovered that he had forgotten A, B, C, and D. Finally he decided to be _____ with the first four letters, and used to write them out once or twice every day to refresh his memory.

21 Which of the following is most appropriate for the blank?

① content ② neutral
③ indifferent ④ resolute

22 Which of the following is not true of the passage?

① The dogs are pretty smart in learning.
② Benjamin has no motivation to learn.
③ Clover is slower in learning than Boxer.
④ Boxer is an industrious learner.

23~24

According to *The Newbury House Dictionary of American English*, gossip is "talk or writing about other people's actions or lives, sometimes untruthful." For example, if someone sees a friend crying, and then tells someone else that the friend was crying and has emotional problems, this is gossip. At first, gossip might not seem bad. One person tells a second person something private about someone else, and that second person tells a third, and so on. The information passes from person to person. (A) _____, gossip is much more than just information. The gossip can grow and change. People often do not know all the facts. They may add something untrue, either on purpose or not. (B) _____, the person who is the subject of the gossip may be hurt. Because the results (C) _____ from making the person feel bad to destroying his or her career, gossip is much worse than just "talk or writing."

23 Which pair best fits in the blanks (A) and (B)?

① However — In addition
② Moreover — For example
③ However — As a result
④ Moreover — By the way

24 Which best fits in the blank (C)?

① range
② deliver
③ connect
④ alternate

25 Which of the following is not mentioned about sepak takraw?

> Sepak takraw is a popular sport in Southeast Asia. It resembles volleyball, except that it uses a rattan ball and only allows players to use their feet, knee, chest, and head to touch and move the ball over a high net. The game is likely based on the Chinese game of *cuju*, a term that means "kick ball." By the early 1400s the game had been brought into Malaysia and Thailand through trade. Back then the game was played mainly by men and boys standing in a circle, kicking the ball back and forth between them. The game remained in its circle form for hundreds of years, and the modern version of sepak takraw began taking shape sometime during the early 1800s. By 1829 the Siam Sports Association had drafted the first rules and introduced the volleyball-style net. Within a few years, sepak takraw was introduced to the curriculum in Thai and Malaysian schools, and became such a cherished local custom that exhibitions were staged as part of the celebrations of independence for both countries. By the 1940s, the game had spread throughout Southeast Asia, and today play is governed by the International Sepak Takraw Federation.

① The difference from volleyball
② The regions where it is popular
③ The link to a Chinese game *cuju*
④ The institution that established the rules first
⑤ The reason for being introduced to the school curriculum

26~28

As a teenager I got into the habit of listening to the string quartets of Béla Bartók — which I found slightly cacophonous but still enjoyed — while doing my homework. Somehow tuning out those discordant tones helped me focus on, say, the chemical equation for ammonium hydroxide.

Years later, when I found myself writing articles on deadline for the *New York Times*, I remembered that early drill in ignoring Bartók. At the *Times* I labored away in the midst of the science desk, which in those years occupied a classroom-sized cavern into which were crammed desks for the dozen or so science journalists and a half dozen editors. There was always a Bartók-ish hum of cacophony. Nearby there might be three or four people chatting; you'd overhear the near end of a phone conversation — or several — as reporters interviewed sources; editors shouted across the room to ask when an article would be ready for them. There were rarely, if ever, the sounds of silence. And yet we science writers, myself among them, would reliably deliver our ready-to-edit copy right on time, day after day. No one ever pleaded, *Everyone please be quiet*, so we could concentrate. We all just redoubled our focus, tuning out the roar.

That focus in the midst of a din indicates selective attention, the neural capacity to beam in on just one target while _____.

26 What is the most appropriate title of the passage above?

① Why Noise Is So Crucial to Productivity
② The Noisy Work Environment of a Journalist
③ How to Endure Everyday Noise
④ The Function of Noise in Improving Concentration
⑤ Why Silence Harms Our Ability to Focus

27 Which statement can be best inferred from the passage above?

① The work space for the journalists described above is large.
② The typical work environment for journalists is appropriate for those who want to increase productivity.
③ Journalists are not usually bothered by the noise they hear.
④ Bartók is notorious for the poor quality of his music.
⑤ Music can be used as noise that helps you to be attentive to the work you do.

28 Which expression best completes the blank?

① processing the information you receive
② ignoring incoming stimuli
③ turning up the volume of noise
④ increasing the level of attentiveness
⑤ maintaining healthy partnership with colleagues

29~30

Science works for two reasons. First, its results are based on experiments: extracting Mother Nature's secrets by asking her directly, rather than by armchair philosophising. And a culture of openness and replications means that scientists are policed by their peers. Scientific papers include sections on methods so that others can repeat the experiments and check that they reach the same conclusions.

That, at least, is the theory. In practice, checking old results is much less good for a scientist's career than publishing exciting new ones. Without such checks, dodgy results can sneak into the literature. In recent years medicine, psychology and genetics have all been put under the microscope and found wanting. One analysis of 100 psychology papers, published last year, for instance, was able to replicate only 36% of their findings. And a study conducted in 2012 by Amgen, an American pharmaceutical company, could replicate only 11% of the 53 papers it reviewed.

29 The main theme of the passage would be "_____."

① The importance of cross-checking in scientific papers
② Difference between scientific papers and editorials
③ How to write a scientific article
④ What makes the best scientific experiments
⑤ What motivates the scientific study of human beings

30 According to the above article, the experiment methods are important because without them _____.

① you cannot complete your experiments
② you don't get the result you want
③ you may mislead the fellow scientists
④ you cannot verify the scientific experiments
⑤ you would get the unreliable outcome

31~33

Pepsi and Coca-Cola may be one of the most controversial drink debates of all time. A strong divide between diehard Coke drinkers and Pepsi enthusiasts has always existed. Yet, the two drinks are practically identical in every way from their caramel syrup color to their ingredients. Both sodas contain sodium, sugar, carbonated water, high fructose corn syrup, phosphoric acid, caffeine, and natural flavors.

Despite their numerous similarities, Pepsi and Coca-Cola still give people two vastly different flavor experiences, which explains why people prefer one over the other. In *Blink*, a book about decision making and thinking, by author and journalist, Malcolm Gladwell, he writes, "Pepsi is sweeter than Coke and is also characterized by a citrusy flavor burst, unlike the more raisiny-vanilla taste of Coke." In fact, a 12 ounce can of Pepsi contains one thing Coke does not — citric acid. In addition, Pepsi also has two more grams of sugar than Coke. These two subtle differences give Pepsi its sweet, citrus-like flavor that people either love or loathe. Plus, the additional 1.5 mg of sodium in a can of Coke may explain why it tastes more like a club soda with a _____ sweetness.

31 Choose the best title.

① The Benefits of Sodium and Sugar
② The Sweeter Pepsi
③ The Difference in Taste Between Pepsi and Coca-Cola
④ The Ingredients of Soda

32 Which one is true?

① Coca-Cola is more flavorful than Pepsi.
② Coca-Cola has more diehards than Pepsi does.
③ Coca-Cola is as sweet as Pepsi.
④ Coca-Cola enthusiasts do not love the citrusy flavor.

33 Choose the best expression for the blank.

① strong
② toned-down
③ sour
④ citrus-like

34~36

Sports facilities built in the late 1970s, 80s, and early 90s were routinely designed to enhance in-facility experiences but routinely ignored the potential for (A) <u>harnessing</u> associated economic activity that could take place on adjacent real estate. Facilities built during this time period were constructed with substantial public investments. The failure to (B) <u>diminish</u> property values and capitalize on the economic activity taking place within the venue generated substantial levels of discontent with the decision to support a team's effort to secure a new venue. _____, all of the benefits from the building of venues (C) <u>accrued</u> to team owners and others linked to the sports industry. There was little if any financial return to the public sector partners. The situation was made worse when team owners were allowed to (D) <u>retain</u> most, if not all, of the revenue streams that were created in these new state-of-the-art facilities.

34 Which of the underlined words is not appropriate?

① (A) ② (B) ③ (C) ④ (D)

35 Which is the most appropriate for the blank?

① As a result
② Nevertheless
③ Otherwise
④ In contrast

36 According to the passage, which is true?

① The benefits from building new sports facilities are not fairly distributed.
② It is difficult for sports teams to find new facilities.
③ Financial management is the most significant in modern sports industry.
④ Team owners contributed to the development of public-invested sports industry.

37~38

A special case of time deepening is multitasking. The term multitasking (and multiprocessing) was originally applied to a computer's ability to execute more than one task or program at the same time. In contemporary parlance it applies the concept of time deepening to work tasks. Multitasking typically involves juggling phone calls, emails, instant messages, and computer work all at once in order to be more productive. Several research reports, _____, provide evidence that multitasking doesn't actually increase productivity. The findings of neuroscientists, psychologists and management professors suggest multitasking slows you down and increases the chances of mistakes. Doing more than one task at a time prohibits our ability to process information. The young, according to conventional wisdom, are the most adept multitaskers; emailing, instant messaging, listening to iPods, and studying at the same time. _____, in one recent study of young Microsoft workers, it took them 15 minutes to be able to return to serious mental tasks, like writing reports or computer code, after responding to incoming emails or instant messages. It is estimated that the cost of such lost productivity to the U.S. economy is nearly $650 billion a year.

37 What does the passage mainly discuss?

① Tips for how to encourage multitasking
② Effects of multitasking on work productivity
③ Positive influence of multitasking on time saving
④ Importance of connecting multitaskers to computer work
⑤ Ways that technology-enabled communication thrives in workplace

38 Which of the following is most appropriate for each blank?

① however — Likewise
② for example — As a result
③ therefore — Nonetheless
④ however — Yet
⑤ for example — In contrast

39~40

The only way to really know whether an idea is reasonable is to test it. Build a quick prototype or mock-up of each potential solution. In the early stages of this process, the mock-ups can be pencil sketches, foam and cardboard models, or simple images made with simple drawing tools. I have made mock-ups with spreadsheets, PowerPoint slides, and with sketches on index cards or sticky notes. Sometimes ideas are best conveyed by skits, especially if you're developing services or automated systems that are difficult to prototype. One popular prototype technique is called "Wizard of Oz", after the wizard in L. Frank Baum's classic book *The Wonderful Wizard of Oz*. The wizard was actually just an ordinary person but, through the use of smoke and mirrors, he managed to appear mysterious and omnipotent. In other words, it was all a fake: the wizard had no special powers. The Wizard of Oz method can be used to mimic a huge, powerful system _____.

39 Choose the phrase that best fills in the blank.

① as soon as it is built
② without consideration of its building time
③ after it is built
④ before it can be built

40 Which of the following is true?

① Prototyping is remarkably effective in the early stages of creating omnipotent images.
② Automated systems can be represented through PowerPoint slides.
③ Prototyping method is a test system of checking the validity of an idea.
④ Wizard of Oz technique represents the virtual power of real products.

41~42

Doctors Without Borders (Médecins Sans Frontieres, or MSF) is an international medical humanitarian organization. The doctors, nurses, and other medical specialists who work with MSF are dedicated to helping people in crisis situations regardless of their race, religion, or political affiliation. Since 1971, MSF teams have been responsible for providing quality medical care in nearly 60 countries. The teams have well-qualified specialists who are familiar with working in difficult, even dangerous, circumstances and the majority of MSF's aid workers are from the communities where the crises are occurring. The work of MSF teams is not limited to offering direct medical care; they also share a commitment about serving as witnesses to the crises of the people they assist. However, as an organization, MSF is _____. It has a reputation for not taking sides in armed conflicts and for being concerned with providing care on the basis of need alone. This belief in operating independently of government or other parties and obtaining independent funding is the key to MSF's ability to conduct its aid efforts.

41 빈칸에 들어갈 가장 알맞은 것을 고르시오.

① neutral
② aggressive
③ professional
④ humanitarian

42 위 글의 내용과 맞지 않는 것을 고르시오.

① MSF aims to provide qualified medical care to people in crisis.
② Most MSF members are volunteers from communities in peaceful situations.
③ MSF aims to obtain funding independently of government or other parties.
④ MSF offers direct medical care but stays away from political matters.

43
~
45

My aunt Marti calls me at home tonight and asks what I am doing. "Just hitting the books," I say. That doesn't go over so well. She scolds me for the violent metaphor — no need to use the word "hit." "Okay, I'm performing gentle acupressure on the books," I say. She seems to like that better. I love Marti, but a conversation with her always includes a list of what I'm doing and saying wrong, and how it supports the phallocentric power structure. She's got some opinions, my aunt. There's liberal, there's really liberal, then there's Marti, a few miles farther to the left. She lives out near Berkeley, appropriately enough — though even Berkeley is a bit too fascist for her.

[A] You'd think she'd like soy, but she believes the soy industry is corrupt. She recently took her diet to a new level by becoming a raw foodist, meaning she eats only food that's uncooked, because it's more natural.

[B] I haven't talked to Marti since Julie got pregnant. I break the news to her as gently as I can, and apologize to her for contributing to the overpopulation problem. "That's okay," she says. She'll forgive me. But, she points out, I can help minimize the damage to the environment by raising the child vegan.

[C] Marti herself is beyond vegan. Animal rights are her passion (even if she thinks the concept of rights is too Western), and she spends a good part of the year flying around the country attending vegetarian conferences. I could take up quite a bit of space listing the things that Marti doesn't eat meat, of course, and chicken, fish, eggs, dairy (she likes to call ice cream "solidified mucus"), but also honey — she won't eat honey because the bees are oppressed, not paid union scale or something.

43 Choose the best order of paragraphs after the given passage.

① [B] — [A] — [C]
② [B] — [C] — [A]
③ [C] — [A] — [B]
④ [C] — [B] — [A]

44 Choose the one that best describes the author's demeanor.

① enraged and flabbergasted
② calm and nonchalant
③ excited but critical
④ humorous but candid

45 Which of the following is true of Marti?

① She lives in the town left of Berkeley.
② Her daughter is pregnant at the moment.
③ She finds the author's language euphemistic.
④ She advocates an extreme vegetarian lifestyle.

46~48

Jane Walden's eyes widened. "You're, you're not suspecting that Mike had anything to do with it?"

"Well, Jane, somehow, somebody who wasn't supposed to be able to, disarmed that alarm system. And naturally suspicion falls on anyone who had access to that code." Jane Walden looked like she might start to cry, then composed herself. "Mike is almost seventy years old." "Then he's probably in need of a nice little nest egg. You understand what I'm telling you is to be held in the strictest confidence of course?"

She nodded and at the same time wiped her nose. The coffee, untouched, was now sipped in quick little bursts.

Frank continued. "And until someone can explain to me how that security system was accessed, then I'm going to have to explore the avenues that make the most sense to me."

46 Frank appears to be _____.

① a suspect
② a plaintiff
③ a detective
④ a burglar
⑤ a defendant

47 The underlined nest egg means _____.

① a bait to attract the victim
② a sum of money saved for the future
③ a close friend to depend upon
④ a marginal egg left in a nest
⑤ a new gadget never shown before

48 The underlined explore the avenues means _____.

① justify the cause of the action
② find out the case
③ testify against the evidence
④ search for the new witness
⑤ investigate the possibility

49~51

Thousands of years ago, people used ancient types of wheat and other grains to make flat bread on the hot rocks of their campfires. At some point in time, early cooks started putting other kinds of food on the bread — using the bread as a plate. It was the world's first _____ crust!

Over time, _____ began to look more like the food we know today. When European explorers arrived in the Americas, they saw Native American people eating tomatoes. When they brought (A) them back to Europe, however, people there wouldn't eat (B) them. They thought eating tomatoes could make (C) them ill.

Slowly, however, Europeans discovered that tomatoes were delicious and safe to eat. Cooks in Naples, an Italian city, began putting (D) them on their flat bread. The world's first true _____ shop opened in Naples in 1830. People there ate _____ for lunch and dinner. They even ate it for breakfast!

49 Choose the best word for the blank.

① hamburger
② pizza
③ pasta
④ sandwich

50 Which one is true about the food introduced above?

① It was first introduced to Native Americans.
② It was first invented by Native Americans.
③ Tomatoes began to be added only after Europeans came to Americas.
④ People in Naples preferred it for breakfast.

51 Which refers to a different one?

① (A)   ② (B)   ③ (C)   ④ (D)

52~54

Louise suffers from muscular dystrophy. While trying to exit a train station one day, she found herself facing a large flight of stairs without an elevator or escalator. On the verge of tears, Louise saw a woman suddenly appear, pick up her bag, and gently help her up the stairs. When she turned to thank her, she was gone. Michael was late for a meeting. Already stressed from a relationship breakdown, he started battling London's traffic only to get a flat tire. As he stood helplessly in the rain, a man stepped out of the crowd, opened the trunk, jacked up the car, and changed the tire. When Michael turned to thank him, he was gone. Who were these mysterious helpers: kind strangers or something more? The popular image we have of angels as radiant or winged creatures is only half true. While some appear this way, others come with dirty feet and are easily mistaken for everyday people. We don't know if Louise's and Michael's helpers were angels, but they could have been. Angels are at work right now, and they can appear _____.

52 Which of the following is the main theme of the passage?

① Devils bring distresses and angels remove them.
② As society changes, so does the concept of angel.
③ Angels appear in many different forms in our daily life.
④ Angels are radiant creatures appearing in moments of distress.

53 Which of the following is closest to what this way refers to?

① As supernatural beings
② As a herald of good news
③ As helpers for the distressed
④ As human and non-human benefactors

54 Which of the following best fits into the blank?

① as radiant as radiant can be
② as often as one wishes to see them
③ as ordinary as a person on the street
④ as miraculously as told in religious scriptures

55~56

PRE-CONFERENCE EVENT
FIBERS FOR HIGH PERFORMANCE TEXTILES TUTORIAL
2:00-5:15p.m Tuesday, March 6
Presenter: Dr. Seshardri Ramkumar, Professor of Advanced Materials, Nonwovens & Advanced Materials Laboratory, Texas Tech University

High performance textiles are basically functional textiles that provide added value to the textiles in addition to common attributes of clothing materials. The functionality is achieved due to the starting material, i.e., fibers, structural aspects and finishing imparted to the final product.

This tutorial will focus on the first pillar, which is the raw material for advanced textile products. The seminar is aimed at beginners in this field as well as those who have the basic understanding of textiles and industrial textiles in particular. Subject areas covered will include: an outline of high performance textiles, classification of fibers, fibers that provide different functionality, functionality provided by 3-dimensional and structural fibers such as bi-component, sustainability aspects, micro and nano structural fibers, and what's next?

The tutorial is not included with the conference registration. A discounted tutorial registration fee will be available to individuals attending the conference.

55 Who is most likely to have interest in this information?

① accountants of clothing companies
② researchers in fiber materials
③ laborers working at energy plants
④ teachers engaging in kindergartens

56 According to the passage, which is true?

① The tutorial will take place after the conference.
② For tutorial registration, conference participants will be charged less than the regular fee.
③ The pre-conference event will be held for two days.
④ People cannot take part in both the tutorial event and the conference presentations.

57~58

Ground beef has likely been served on some form of bread since time immemorial, but that does not make a hamburger. A hamburger is defined as much by the use of a purposefully baked bread — universally called a "hamburger bun" — as by the beef patty. You can add as many toppings as you like to this combination or cook the beef in a myriad of ways and you will still have a hamburger. But replace the bread or use a different type of meat and you have something other than a hamburger.

The modern hamburger, as we enjoy it today was first conceived in 1916 in Wichita, Kansas when Walter A. Anderson combined a beef patty with a custom-made bun designed to encapsulate it. In fact, it was just another type of sandwich until 1921 when Anderson partnered with Edgar Waldo Ingram and founded White Castle.

In this restaurant, the hamburger was commoditized and standardized for a defined, universally recognizable American dish. In addition to creating the modern hamburger, White Castle also set up the first fast food "system," creating the blueprint for all fast food chains to come. The hamburger existed on restaurant menus before White Castle, but it was listed within the sandwich section. After White Castle, the hamburger became separate and distinct from other sandwiches, with its own section on the menu.

The first hamburgers were small in size — about two to three ounces of beef. But it did not remain stagnant. Innovations came quick and fast. The first cheeseburger was reputedly created in 1926 at the Rite Spot in Pasadena, CA as a "cheese hamburger." In the post World War II era, the nation enjoyed an explosion of cheap beef and cheap steel, as well as a burgeoning interstate highway system. This allowed the hamburger to move out of the industrial park and onto Main Street. The hamburger that emerged after the war spoke to America's rapid rise — they became _____.

57 Which of the following is most appropriate for the blank?

① out of fashion
② more European
③ local and isolated
④ bigger and more diverse
⑤ something other than a hamburger

58 Which of the following is true according to the passage?

① Chicken breast on top of corn bread can be called a hamburger.
② White Castle takes up an important place in the history of a hamburger.
③ The hamburger was listed in the hamburger section on the menu in 1916.
④ Walter A. Anderson and Edgar Waldo Ingram created the first cheeseburger.
⑤ American people were poor and starved after the war.

Controversy over the soccer star Alex Morgan's tea-drinking victory dance during a World Cup game has died down, but it has reignited debate among readers of The Times of London, Britain's second-starchiest broadsheet, over a matter that has long troubled the British people: When pouring tea into a teacup, what should be poured first? The tea? Or the milk?

The dueling letters to the editor began on July 4, when Bob Maddams, of Brighton, mused aloud about whether Ms Morgan, the American soccer player, pours her milk in first. This inspired a response from Tom Howe, from Surrey, which was printed on July 5:

"Sir, Bob Maddams' letter (July 4) on Alex Morgan's tea celebration at the Women's World Cup suggests that it is correct to put the milk in first. I was always led to believe that the milk first or second question was originally a signal of social standing. Cheap porcelain cracked when hot tea was poured into it, so the milk was poured in first to lower the temperature and avoid such a disaster."

Mr Howe's letter really set them off. On July 6, The Times printed not one but four responses. Peter Sergeant wrote from Leicestershire to point out that "tea stains porcelain, so putting the milk in first mitigates this." The second response, sent from Oxfordshire, argued that tea must be poured first so as to determine how much milk is necessary. The third referred to the Boston Tea Party. And the fourth, from Catherine Money, of Surrey, provided important cultural context of social class, as well as an acronym for "milk-in-first."

"Sir," she wrote. *"Tom Howe is correct in his recollection of the message given by pouring milk into a cup before the tea. Describing someone as 'rather MIF' told one all one needed to know."*

The letters pages of Britain's newspapers are a sensitive instrument, which can be used to detect waves of dismay emanating from the heartland. This spring, for example, the editor of a weekly newspaper in Oxfordshire decided to phase out "Sir" as the form of address for letters to the editor and was so inundated with angry letters that he promptly reversed the decision.

59 According to the passage, _____ claims that 'milk-in-first' is not right.

① Bob Maddams
② Tom Howe
③ the second response
④ the forth response
⑤ Peter Sergent

60 What does the underlined the decision mean?

① to pour the milk first
② not to use the expression "Sir"
③ to remove the letters-to-the-editor section
④ not to take sides with one of the writers
⑤ not to respond to the letters to the editor

61 According to Catherine Money, the so-called MIF refers to _____.

① the upper class who knew the manners
② the rich who could afford the tea culture
③ the royal family who used the chinese porcelain
④ the poor people who used the cheap teacup
⑤ the middle class who drank more tea than milk

62
~
64

To go into solitude, a man needs to retire as much from his chamber as from society. I am not solitary whilst I read and write, though nobody is with me. But if a man would be alone, let him look at the stars. The rays that come from those heavenly worlds will separate between him and what he touches. One might think the atmosphere was made transparent with this design, to give man, in the heavenly bodies, the perpetual presence of the sublime. Seen in the streets of cities how great they are! If the stars should appear one night in a thousand years, how would men believe and adore; and preserve for many generations the remembrance of the city of God which had been shown! But every night come out these envoys of beauty, and light the universe with their admonishing smile.

The stars awaken a certain reverence, because though always present, they are inaccessible; but all natural objects make a kindred impression, when the mind is open to their influence. Nature never wears a mean appearance. Neither does the wisest man extort her secret, and lose his curiosity by finding out all her perfection. Nature never became a toy to a wise spirit. The flowers, the animals, the mountains, reflected the wisdom of his best hour, as much as they had delighted the simplicity of his childhood.

When we speak of nature in this manner, we have a distinct but most poetical sense in the mind. We mean the integrity of impression made by manifold natural objects. It is this which distinguishes the stick of timber of the wood-cutter from the tree of the poet. The charming landscape which I saw this morning is indubitably made up of some twenty or thirty farms. Miller owns this field, Locke that, and Manning the woodland beyond. But none of them owns the landscape. There is a property in the horizon which no man has but he whose eye can integrate all the parts, that is, the poet. This is the best part of these men's farms, yet to this their warranty-deeds give no title.

62 According to the passage, which of the following is not mentioned as a way of appreciating nature?

① to make a solitary time for looking at the stars
② to train oneself to have the poet's eye
③ to guarantee oneself possession of several farms
④ to keep one's curiosity about the perfection of nature

63 According to the passage, which of the following is true?

① The stars are likened to the envoys of beauty.
② A wise man has looked upon nature as a toy.
③ The tree of the poet is as valuable as that of the woodcutter.
④ The more inaccessible the stars are, the more sublime they become.

64 Which of the following is the purpose of the passage?

① to inform his readers of the hidden rule of the heavenly bodies
② to persuade his readers to go into a quiet retirement
③ to encourage his readers to participate in an environmental movement
④ to remind his readers of the wonderful values of nature

**65
~
67**

When Annette Poitras _____, winded and dazed, two sets of canine eyes were peering back into hers. Moments before — or was it hours? — the professional dog-walker had been working her way along a familiar gravel trail that snakes across Eagle Mountain, a ten-minute drive from her home.

She had three charges with her: Roxy (a boxer), Bubba (a 3-year-old puggle) and Chloe (her own black-and-white border collie). When the quartet came across a fallen tree — its trunk, thick as a barrel, stretching over an expanse of soggy moss a metre below — Poitras clambered up to cross over it. That morning, after a walk in the rain, she had exchanged her soaked hiking boots for gum-boots. As she trod on the slick wood, she'd slipped, slamming into the log. Hitting her head on the way down, Poitras had plummeted to the forest floor below.

Now, as she lay on the ground, pain shot from her left armpit all the way down to her calf and she wondered, dizzily, if she'd cracked a rib. She hadn't broken her back, she figured, because she was able to stand up and carefully climb back onto firm terrain. Looking around past Roxy and Chloe, unleashed at her side, Poitras realised that Bubba had bolted. She didn't know what time it was or how long she'd been knocked out. But she knew she needed to find that puggle before she could get off the mountain. She adored the dogs — leaving one behind was unthinkable.

65 Which does not fit in the blank?

① saw to
② came to
③ woke up
④ came round

66 Which is closest in meaning to the underlined soaked and unleashed?

① wet — untied
② seared — left
③ sturdy — set loose
④ worn out — relieved

67 According to the passage, which is true?

① It was her boots that caused Poitras' accident.
② Poitras didn't realize that she had cracked a rib.
③ While Poitras was unconscious, her own dog ran away.
④ Poitras' job ethic wouldn't allow her to come down without the missing dog.

[68~69]

For the past 48 hours the 280-foot vessel *Knorr*, temporary if not harmonious home to some 30 engineers, scientists, and academics, as well as a rotating roster of friends and financial supporters, has been lashed to a pier in the northern Turkish city of Sinop, kept from its appointed mission by the lack of research visas. The American ship and crew have come to the Black Sea to investigate ancient shipwrecks, but the local media are skeptical. During the day packs of journalists scramble up and down the stone dock, aiming their cameras and questions at anyone on the deck within earshot.

"Why are you really here? Are you searching for oil? Are you on a secret mission for the U.S. military? Are you looking for Noah's ark?"

Hundreds of residents, curious to see for themselves, stroll arm in arm to the waterfront in the lovely late July evenings to marvel at the great ship stuffed with high-tech wizardry bobbing in the bay of their historic walled city.

But for expedition leader Robert D. Ballard, who is spending $40,000 a day on the project and is losing priceless research time — having invested millions in a state-of-the-art remotely controlled submersible, deep-sea high-definition cameras, and a futuristic high-bandwidth satellite communications system — there's nothing magical about the nightly carnival on the dock.

"We're bleeding to death," he says. "We're hemorrhaging money."

Nor has this latest delay been the only setback of the summer. Ballard's original itinerary called for testing his machines on a series of Greek and Byzantine wrecks off Bulgaria and Turkey before moving on to a pair of 2,700-year-old Phoenician wrecks off Egypt. But weeks earlier, just before the *Knorr* left its home port at Woods Hole, Massachusetts, complications in his negotiations with the Bulgarian Academy of Sciences forced Ballard to cancel that part of the cruise for now. Later, after the expedition was under way, Ballard also got words that Egyptian security had denied him permission to explore the Phoenician ships.

68 According to the passage, why did the ship *Knorr* come to Turkey?

① To search for oil
② To accomplish a military mission
③ To investigate ancient shipwrecks
④ To look for the remains of Noah's ark
⑤ To rescue the crew from a sunken ship

69 Which is not a problem that Ballard has faced?

① No research visas to Turkey
② Troubles with Turkish journalists
③ Heavy expenditures for the project
④ No permission to explore shipwrecks from Egypt
⑤ Difficulties in negotiations with the Bulgarian Academy of Sciences

70~74

Einstein was a physicist who challenged some of basic principles in physics that had been accepted by scientists for almost 300 years, since the work of Isaac Newton. He was also an accomplished writer, violinist and one of the most influential political voices of the 20th century.

(A) _____, during and after his lifetime, what ordinary people enjoyed most about Einstein was his legendary image rather than his theories and other accomplishments. For instance, his somewhat disorganized appearance — wide, open eyes, messy hair and careless clothing — intrigued people. In fact, there are many stories surrounding his extraordinary personality and behavior. When he was still a boy, his teacher at school told Einstein's father, "It does not matter what fields he goes into, he'll never make a success of anything." During his college years, his wife and best friends had to keep reminding him to do basic things, such as to eat and go to class. After he became famous, he began charging people who asked for his autograph. He would ask for a dollar before signing and gave the money to charities.

Another legendary incident further showed his (B) _____. At Princeton one day, Einstein was on his way back to his office after having lunch. While walking, he began to sit quietly and think on the problems of space and time, which were two of his favorite subjects. When he returned to his office, he read his own sign, "Gone to Lunch. Be back in 10 minutes." Later he was found by his fellow professors sitting outside his office waiting for himself to come back.

70 Which of the following is most suitable for the blank (A)?

① However
② Therefore
③ Similarly
④ Consequently

71 Which of the following can be inferred from the passage?

① People criticized Einstein's intriguing appearance.
② Einstein was poorer at field sports than any other area when he was a young boy.
③ Some of the principles in physics Isaac Newton established were challenged by Einstein.
④ Ordinary people were not interested in the physical theories of Einstein.

72 According to the passage, which of the following is true about Einstein?

① Einstein asked for a dollar after he gave his autograph.
② Einstein used to forget to go to class in the college years.
③ Einstein gave charities money throughout his lifetime.
④ Einstein was meticulous and punctual in doing things.

73 Which of the following is most appropriate for the blank (B)?

① genius
② forgetfulness
③ languidness
④ fame

74 Which of the following does not describe the incident at Princeton correctly?

① Einstein mistook his own office for someone else's office.
② He waited outside someone else's office, mistaking it for his office.
③ Einstein read a sign on the door and thought that the occupant of the office was gone.
④ Einstein did not realize that he was the person who wrote the sign on the door.

75
~
78

[A] Steve Jobs and Lee Clow agreed that Apple was one of the great brands of the world, probably in the top five based on emotional appeal, but they need to remind folks what was distinctive about it. So they wanted a brand image campaign, not a set of advertisements featuring products. It was designed to celebrate not what the computers could do, but what creative people could do with the computers. "This wasn't about processor speed or memory," Jobs recalled. "It was about creativity. That was the genesis of that campaign."

[B] Clow and his team tried a variety of approaches that praised the "crazy ones" who "think different." Eventually they decided they needed to write their own text; their draft began, "Here's to the crazy ones." In its original sixty-second version it read: Here's to the crazy ones. The misfits. The rebels. The troublemakers. The round pegs in the square holes. The ones who see things differently. They're not fond of rules. And they have no respect for the status quo. You can quote them, disagree with them, glorify or vilify them. About the only thing you can't do is ignore them. Because they change things. They push the human race forward. And while some may see them as the crazy ones, we see genius. Because the people who are crazy enough to think they can change the world are the ones who do.

[C] Jobs, who could identify with each of those sentiments, wrote some of the lines himself, including "They push the human race forward." By the time of the Boston Macworld in early August, they had produced a rough version. They agreed it was not ready, but Jobs used the concepts, and the "think different" phrase, in his keynote speech there. "There's a germ of a brilliant idea there." He said at the time. "Apple is about people who think outside the box, _____."

[D] They debated the grammatical issue: If "different" was supposed to modify the verb "think," it should be an adverb, as in "think differently." But Job insisted he wanted "different" to be used as a noun, as in "think victory" or "think beauty." Also, it echoed colloquial use, as in "think big." Jobs later explained, "We discussed whether it was correct before we ran it. It's grammatical, if you think about what we're trying to say. It's not think *the same*, it's think *different*. Think a little different, think a lot different, think different. 'Think differently' wouldn't hit the meaning for me."

75 Which of the following can the underlined word <u>genesis</u> in paragraph [A] be best replaced with?

① completion
② origination
③ grandeur
④ cessation
⑤ omega

76 Which of the following best matches the underlined expression <u>The round pegs in the square holes</u> in paragraph [B]?

① the rivals
② the peacemakers
③ the advocates
④ the puritans
⑤ the nonconformists

77 Which of the following would best fit in the blank in paragraph [C]?

① who aim to produce a computer that is second to none in terms of yielding economic profits
② who long to invent the most stylish metal boxes in the history of the box industry
③ who attempt to drastically improve computing power, memory, and storage
④ who want to use computers to help them change the world
⑤ who aspire to create a supercomputer that demonstrates technology's superiority over the humanities

78 The way in which Steve Job decided to choose "Think Different" as the key phrase in the Apple advertisement campaign proves that _____.

① he was quite a dogmatic leader, who ignored the advice of his colleagues while disregarding the grammar issue
② he preferred "think different" to "think differently" although he realized that "think different" does not conform to colloquial use
③ he was very sensitive toward and fastidious in following orthodox grammar rules
④ it is, in itself, a good example of "think different"
⑤ it is absolutely essential for advertisement designers to violate the traditional grammar rules to write compelling advertisement copy

Memo

종로 특별반 **최종합격률 100%**
최상위권 진학에 특화된
해커스편입 특별반

전과목 1타
스타강사진 지도

상위권으로만 구성된
선발고사 필수반

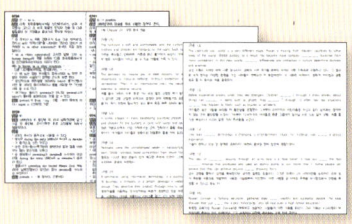

매달 최대 2,000제의
상위권 전용문제로 수업

심층 토론 스터디로
학습능률 극대화

[100%] 2019년 12월 종각 본원 특별반 등록생 기준 16명 중 16명 합격
[강우진 1위] 해커스편입 강남/종각/수원 편입논리 강의평가 평균 1위(2020년 1월~6월)
[공재웅 1위] 해커스편입 종각 본원 편입문법 강의평가 평균 1위(2020년 3월~6월)
[유익재 1위] 해커스편입 수원역캠퍼스 편입독해 독해 수강생 수 1위(2020년 3월~6월)

성적우수자 장학 혜택! 선발고사 무료 응시하기 ▶

상담 및 문의전화
[종 각 본원] 02-735-1881
[강남역캠퍼스] 02-522-1881
[수원역캠퍼스] 031-243-3333

해커스편입 HackersUT.com

편입 합격을 응원하는
해커스편입만의 특별 혜택

🎁 가입만 해도 **편입인강 무료**

해커스편입 인강(Ingang.HackersUT.com) 상단 [회원가입] 클릭 ▶ 회원가입 전 편입인강 무료 내용 확인

📄 편입영어/수학 **실력 무료진단**

해커스편입 인강(Ingang.HackersUT.com) 상단 [모의고사/이벤트]의 [실력 무료진단/맞춤인강] 클릭

🎟️ 해커스편입 인강 단과강의 **20% 할인쿠폰**

W52NC3T2JYS3924635342

해커스편입 인강(Ingang.HackersUT.com) 로그인 ▶
상단 [마이페이지] 클릭 ▶ 좌측 [쿠폰 확인] 클릭 ▶ 쿠폰 번호 입력

* 등록일로부터 7일간 사용 가능
* 한 ID당 1회만 사용 가능하며, 등록 후 사용기간이 만료되어 쿠폰이 소멸된 경우 재등록 불가
* 쿠폰 이용 문의: 해커스편입 02-522-1881

📧 해커스편입 학원 등록 시 **멤버십 무료**

· 편입영어 수업교재 증정 (*비매품)
· 캠퍼스 내 사물함 & 자습실 제공
· 첫 수강료 10만원 지원

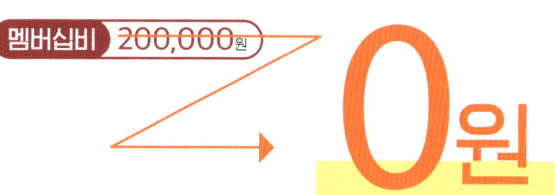

멤버십비 200,000원 → **0원**

2022 대비 최신판

해커스편입
기출 독해 930제

주제편

초판 1쇄 발행 2021년 8월 4일

지은이	해커스편입연구소
펴낸곳	해커스편입
펴낸이	해커스편입 출판팀
주소	서울특별시 서초구 서초대로 77길 27 해커스편입
고객센터	02-522-1881
교재 관련 문의	publishingUT@hackers.com
	카카오톡 플러스 친구 [해커스편입]
학원 강의	HackersUT.com
동영상강의	Ingang.HackersUT.com
ISBN	979-11-5657-625-9 (13740)
Serial Number	01-01-01

저작권자 ⓒ 2021, 해커스편입

이 책의 모든 내용, 이미지, 디자인, 편집 형태는 저작권법에 의해 보호받고 있습니다.
서면에 의한 저자와 출판사의 허락 없이 내용의 일부 혹은 전부를 인용, 발췌하거나 복제, 배포할 수 없습니다.

편입학원 1위,
HackersUT.com
해커스편입

· 최신 편입정보·가이드 및 대학별 출제경향 제공
· 편입 인강 및 교수님의 1:1 질의응답 서비스 제공
· 최신 경향의 적중률 높은 <전국단위 모의고사> 실시
· 편입 보카테스트 및 무료 학습자료 제공

한국소비자포럼 선정 '올해의 브랜드 대상' 6년 지속 편입학원 부문 1위(10',12'~16')

해커스편입
기출독해 930제 주제편 해설집

CONTENTS

- 01 언어·문학 — 2
- 02 역사 — 21
- 03 예술 — 42
- 04 철학·종교 — 62
- 05 사회이슈·일상 — 81
- 06 경제·경영 — 103
- 07 정치·법 — 123
- 08 문화 — 146
- 09 교육 — 177
- 10 심리 — 185
- 11 인류학 — 213
- 12 의학·건강 — 222
- 13 물리·화학·기술·건축 — 239
- 14 생물 — 260
- 15 지구과학·천문학·환경 — 288
- 16 동·식물 — 306
- 17 기타 — 314

해커스편입

01 언어·문학

01-56
문제집 p.12

01 ③	02 ①	03 ④	04 ④	05 ③
06 ④	07 ②	08 ②	09 ③	10 ①
11 ①	12 ③	13 ⑤	14 ②	15 ③
16 ④	17 ③	18 ④	19 ④	20 ③
21 ①	22 ④	23 ④	24 ④	25 ②
26 ②	27 ②	28 ②	29 ①	30 ②
31 ①	32 ②	33 ⑤	34 ⑤	35 ③
36 ①	37 ③	38 ②	39 ②	40 ④
41 ③	42 ①	43 ①	44 ②	45 ③
46 ③	47 ④	48 ③	49 ③	50 ①
51 ③	52 ①	53 ②	54 ①	55 ①
56 ③				

01 [2019 건국대]
정답 ③

해석 수화의 가장 광범위한 체계들 중 하나는 대초원 지대의 북미 원주민들 사이에서 (A)번성했다. 수화는 다른 언어를 가진 부족들이 특히 무역과 전쟁에서 의사소통을 (B)할 수 있게 했다. 부족들의 언어들은 서로 (C)이해할 수 있긴 하지만, 부족들은 거의 같은 삶을 살았기 때문에 공통된 상징에 근거하여 수화를 발전시킬 수 있었다. 말을 탄 사람은 한 손의 두 손가락을 다른 손의 집게손가락의 양쪽에 올리는 모양으로 (D)묘사되었다. 창백한 색깔의 달과 같은 것은 하늘 높이 떠 있는 원을 그려서 나타냈다. 부정직, 불성실, 사기는 (E)갈라진 모양의 혀 또는 뱀처럼 보이도록 만든 두 손가락으로 묘사되었다.

해설 밑줄 친 단어들 중에서 문맥상 적절하지 않은 어휘를 고르는 문제이다. 언어들이 서로 이해할 수 없었지만 거의 같은 삶을 살았기 때문에 수화를 발전시킬 수 있었다는 내용이므로 (C)에는 '이해할 수 있는'을 의미하는 intelligible이 아니라 '이해할 수 없는'을 의미하는 unintelligible이 들어가는 것이 자연스럽다. 따라서 ③번이 정답이다.

어휘 comprehensive adj. 광범위한, 포괄적인
sign language phr. 수화 flourish v. 번성하다, 번영하다
Great Plains phr. 대초원 지대
on horseback phr. 말을 타고, 말을 이용하여
index finger phr. 집게손가락 pale adj. 창백한
dishonesty n. 부정직 disloyalty n. 불성실
deception n. 사기, 속임 forked adj. 갈라진 모양의

[02-03]

언어는 우리가 주로 무의식적으로 사용하는 음절로 구성된 박자를 사용한다. 어머니의 심장 박동이 우리들 대부분이 처음 듣는 박자일 것이다. 하나의 강세가 없는 짧은소리에 강세가 있는 긴소리가 뒤따르는 것으로 종종 묘사되는 그 패턴을 약강격이라고 한다. 그리스어와 라틴어에서 파생된 이 보격과 강약격(긴소리-짧은소리), 약약강격(짧은소리-짧은소리-긴소리)과 같이 다른 많은 변형은 대부분의 유럽 언어에서 지배적이다. 고전 중국어 시와 아랍어 시에서 또한 보격 체계를 이용하고 있으며, 아랍 시에서는 라틴어와 그리스어의 길고 짧은 강세 패턴을 그대로 따라 한다. 강세 패턴은 문학의 고상한 형태만이 아니라 일상적인 발화나 노래에서도 일어난다. 한 가지의 흥미로운 예는 알제리의 예술가인 Kamal el Oujdi의 예인데, 그는 언어 간의 보격과 선율을 결합하기 위해 영국과 아시아의 예술가들과 환상적으로 협업하며 아랍어로 랩을 한다.

rhythm n. 박자, 리듬 **composed of** phr. ~로 구성된
syllable n. 음절 **unconsciously** adv. 무의식적으로
heartbeat n. 심장 박동 **unstressed** adj. 강세가 없는
stressed adj. 강세가 있는 **iambic** adj. 약강격의
meter n. 보격(운율의 단위) **variant** n. 변종, 이형
trochaic adj. 강약격의 **anapaestic** adj. 약약강격의
derive from phr. ~에서 유래하다
dominant adj. 지배적인, 우세한
echo v. 따라 하다, 메아리치다
collaboration n. 협업, 공동 작업 **combine** v. 결합하다
melody n. 선율, 멜로디

02 [2019 한국외대]
정답 ①

해석 ① 언어 박자의 패턴과 사용
② 약강격과 강약격의 비교
③ 고전 문학 속 박자의 역사
④ 음악 속의 혁신적인 박자와 선율

해설 지문의 제목을 묻는 문제이다. 지문의 전반에 걸쳐 언어는 박자를 사용하고 있으며, 그 박자를 문학과 예술에서 사용하고 있다는 것을 예시와 함께 설명하고 있다. 따라서 이 지문의 제목을 '언어 박자의 패턴과 사용'이라고 표현한 ①번이 정답이다.

어휘 comparison n. 비교 innovative adj. 혁신적인

03 [2019 한국외대]
정답 ④

해설 ① 약강격은 아랍어에서 유래했다.
② 강세가 있는 음절은 강세가 없는 음절보다 더 짧다.
③ 강세 패턴은 시에서 주로 사용된다.
④ 우리는 매우 어린 나이부터 박자에 노출되어 있다.

해설 지문의 내용과 일치하는 것을 묻는 문제이다. 지문의 중간에서 A mother's heartbeat may be the first rhythm most of us hear의 내용을 통해 우리가 매우 어린 나이부터 박자에 노출되어 있다는 것을 알 수 있다. 따라서 ④번이 지문의 내용과 일치한다.

오답 분석
① 그리스어와 라틴어에서 파생된 약강격의 보격과 강약격, 약약강격과 같이 다른 많은 변형은 대부분의 유럽 언어에서 지배적이라고 했으므로, 약강격이 아랍어에서 유래했다는 것은 지문의 내용과 다르다.
② 약강격이 하나의 강세가 없는 짧은소리에 강세가 있는 긴 소리가 뒤따르는 것으로 종종 묘사된다고 했으므로, 강세가 있는 음절이 강세가 없는 음절보다 더 짧다는 것은 지문의 내용과 다르다.
③ 강세 패턴은 문학의 고상한 형태만이 아니라 일상적인 발화나 노래에서도 일어난다고 했으므로, 강세 패턴이 시에서 주로 사용된다는 것은 지문의 내용과 다르다.

어휘 primary adj. 주요한, 주된 expose v. 노출시키다

[04-07]

1980년대 이전에는, 미국 대통령들이 "스마트"라는 단어를 거의 사용하지 않았고, 대통령들이 "스마트"를 사용했을 때는, 일반적으로 "미국인들은 스마트하다(똑똑하다)"에서처럼 전통적인 느낌이었다. [A] 조지 H. W. 부시 대통령은 "스마트"라는 단어를 새롭고, 디지털 시대의 느낌으로 사용하기 시작했다. 조지 H. W. 부시 대통령은 "스마트 자동차", "스마트 고속도로", "스마트 무기" 그리고 "스마트 학교"라고 말했다. 대통령의 미사여구로 "스마트"의 사용은 빌 클린턴 대통령과 조지 W. 부시 대통령 재임 당시에 폭발적으로 증가했고, 빌 클린턴 대통령과 조지 W. 부시 대통령은 각각 "스마트"를 450번 이상 사용했다. 오바마 대통령은 "스마트"를 900번 이상 사용했다. 똑같은 추세를 일반적인 말투에서도 발견할 수 있다. [B] 책에서, "스마트"의 사용은 1975년부터 2008년까지 꾸준히 증가했으며, 거의 3배 증가했다. "어리석은"의 사용은 2배 증가했다. The New York Times에서, "스마트"의 등장은 1980년에서 2000년까지 4배 증가했고, 2018년까지는 거의 다시 2배가 되었다. [C] 대중의 마음에 대한 성과주의적 척도로서, "스마트"의 점점 늘어나는 사용 빈도는 "스마트"의 변화보다 덜 드러난다. "스마트"는 디지털 시스템과 기기를 나타낼 뿐만 아니라, 점점 더 칭찬을 나타내는 일반적인 말이 되었고, 다른 방침보다 어떤 하나의 방침에 찬성하는 방식이 되었다. 평가에 대한 대조로서, "스마트 대 어리석은"은 "정당한 대 부당한" 또는 "옳은 대 잘못된"과 같은 윤리적 혹은 이념적인 대조를 대체하기 시작했다. [D] 클린턴 대통령과 오바마 대통령은 둘 다 자주 자신들의 선호 정책이 "옳은 일을 하는 것뿐만 아니라, 스마트한 일을 하는 것"이라고 주장했다. 이런 진드기 같은 미사여구 단어는, 성과주의 시대에, 스마트한 것이 옳은 것을 추구

하는 것보다 더 설득력 있는 중요성을 가져다주었다고 시사했다.

typically adv. 일반적으로, 보통 rhetoric n. 미사여구
parlance n. 말투 displace v. 대체하다, 대신하다
ethical adj. 윤리적인 ideological adj. 이념적인
meritocratic adj. 성과주의의
persuasive adj. 설득력 있는 heft n. 중요성

04 2021 세종대

정답 ④

해석 ① 정치 교과서 ② 신문 기사
③ 대통령 연설 ④ 문화 평론

해설 지문의 종류를 묻는 문제이다. 지문의 첫 번째 문단에서 1980년대 이전에는 미국 대통령들이 "스마트"라는 단어를 거의 사용하지 않았으나, 조지 H. W. 부시 대통령 때부터 빈번히 사용되기 시작했다고 하였고, 두 번째 문단에서 "스마트" 단어의 의미가 어떻게 바뀌어 왔는지 설명하고 있다. 따라서 이 지문의 종류를 '문화 평론'이라고 표현한 ④번이 정답이다.

05 2021 세종대

정답 ③

해석 대중의 마음에 있어서 성과주의적 척도로서, "스마트"의 점점 늘어나는 사용 빈도는 "스마트"의 의미 변화보다 덜 드러난다.

해설 지문의 흐름상 주어진 문장이 들어가기에 가장 적절한 위치를 고르는 문제이다. 주어진 문장은 '대중의 마음에 있어서 성과주의적 척도로서, "스마트"의 점점 늘어나는 사용 빈도는 "스마트"의 의미 변화보다 덜 드러난다'라는 의미이다. 이 문장을 [C] 자리에 넣는다면, 대중의 마음에 있어서 성과주의적 척도로서 "스마트"의 변화가 디지털 시스템과 기기뿐만 아니라 칭찬을 나타내고 찬성하는 방식이 되었다는 "스마트"의 의미적 변화에 대한 내용으로 이어지므로 글의 흐름이 자연스럽게 연결된다. 따라서 ③번이 정답이다.

어휘 meritocracy n. 성과주의

06 2021 세종대

정답 ④

해석 ① 절약하는 — 낭비하는 ② 합법적인 — 불법적인
③ 현명한 — 엄청난 ④ 정당한 — 부당한

해설 지문의 빈칸을 채우는 문제이다. 세 번째 문단의 평가에 대한 대조로서, "스마트 대 어리석은"은 "_____ 대 _____" 또는 "옳은 대 잘못된"과 같은 윤리적 혹은 이념적 대조를 대체하기 시작했다는 것으로 보아, 첫 번째 빈칸에는 '스마트'와 '옳은'을 대신할 수 있는 윤리적 혹은 이념적 단어가 나

와야 하므로, '정당한'이라는 의미의 just가 들어가는 것이 자연스럽다. 또한, 두 번째 빈칸에는 '어리석은'과 '잘못된'을 대신할 수 있는 윤리적 혹은 이념적 단어가 나와야 하므로, '부당한'이라는 의미의 unjust가 들어가는 것이 자연스럽다. 따라서 ④번이 정답이다.

07 [2021 세종대]

정답 ②

해석 ① 미국 대통령들은 1980년대까지 다양한 느낌으로 자주 "스마트" 단어를 사용했다.
② "어리석은"은 1975년부터 2008년까지 책에서 사용되는 빈도가 늘어났다.
③ 디지털 시대의 느낌으로 "스마트" 단어를 처음으로 사용했던 사람은 빌 클린턴 대통령이었다.
④ "스마트"는 1980년부터 2000년까지 책에서 2배로 사용되었다.

해설 지문의 내용과 일치하는 것을 묻는 문제이다. 지문의 두 번째 문단의 In books, the use of "smart" climbed steadily from 1975 to 2008, ~; the use of "stupid" doubled의 내용을 통해 "어리석은"은 1975년부터 2008년까지 책에서 사용되는 빈도가 늘어났다는 것을 알 수 있다. 따라서 ②번이 지문의 내용과 일치한다.

오답분석 ① 1980년대 이전에 미국 대통령들이 "스마트"라는 단어를 거의 사용하지 않았다고 했으므로, 미국 대통령들이 1980년대까지 다양한 느낌으로 자주 "스마트" 단어를 사용했다는 것은 지문의 내용과 다르다.
③ 조지 H. W. 부시 대통령이 "스마트"라는 단어를 새롭고 디지털 시대의 느낌으로 사용하기 시작했다고 했으므로, 디지털 시대의 느낌으로 "스마트" 단어를 처음으로 사용했던 사람이 빌 클린턴 대통령이었다는 것은 지문의 내용과 다르다.
④ 책에서 "스마트"의 사용은 1975년부터 2008년까지 꾸준히 올랐으며 거의 3배 증가했다고는 했지만, "스마트"가 1980년부터 2000년까지 책에서 2배로 사용되었는지는 알 수 없다.

[08-10]

꽤 최근까지, 인류는 느슨하게 연결된 아마 몇백 명 정도 되었을 부족들로 나뉘어 보통 20명을 넘지 않는 친족 무리에서 살았다. 자연과 서로에게 개방된 채, 그 당시 사람들은 우리가 오늘날 상상할 수 있는 것보다 더 서로와 가까운 사이였다. 말은 보통 연인, 또는 엄마와 아기 사이이기 때문에, (A)찾아보기 어려웠을 수 있다. 우리가 어떤 사람을 그만큼 잘 안다면, 우리는 그 사람들이 무엇을 생각하고 느끼는지 물어보지 않아도 안다. (B)언어라는 중재 도구에 의해 우리의 감정이입 능력이 아직 또렷해지지 않았던 언어 이전의 시기에는 더욱더 그러했다.

침묵 속에서 한 사람이나 작은 집단과 단독으로 시간을 (C)보내보며, 겨우 며칠 또는 심지어 몇 시간 안에, 당신이 그 사람들과 대화를 했을 때보다 더 마음속으로부터 친해진 것을 느끼는지 어떤지 (D)지켜보아라. 이 침묵 상황 속에서 발달하는 다른 사람에 대한 감정 이입과 직감적인 이해는 놀랄 만하다.

kin adj. 친족인   loosely adv. 대략, 막연히, 느슨하게
intimately adv. 친밀히, 마음속으로부터
prelinguistic adj. 언어 이전의
empathetic adj. 감정이입의   faculty n. 능력
unclouded adj. 구름이 끼지 않은, 맑은
mediatory adj. 중재의   apparatus n. 도구, 장치
silence n. 침묵, 고요   intuitive adj. 직감적인, 직관적인
circumstance n. 상황, 환경

08 [2021 동국대]

정답 ②

해석 ① 청각적이었을   ② 찾아보기 어려웠을
③ 유사했을   ④ 불필요했을

해설 지문의 빈칸을 채우는 문제이다. 지문의 중간에서 우리가 어떤 사람을 잘 안다면 그 사람들이 무엇을 생각하고 느끼는지 물어보지 않아도 알고, 언어에 의해 감정이입 능력이 아직 또렷해지기 전에는 더욱더 그러했다고 했으므로, 빈칸에는 말은 보통 연인, 또는 엄마와 아기 사이이기 때문에 찾아보기 어려웠을 수 있다는 내용이 나오는 것이 자연스럽다. 따라서 '찾아보기 어려웠을'이라고 한 ②번이 정답이다.

09 [2021 동국대]

정답 ③

해석 ① 몸짓   ② 친족
③ 언어   ④ 친밀함

해설 지문의 빈칸을 채우는 문제이다. 지문의 중간에서 어떤 사람을 잘 안다면 그 사람들이 무엇을 생각하고 느끼는지 물어보지 않아도 알고 언어 이전의 시기에는 더욱더 그러했다고 했으므로, 빈칸에는 언어라는 중재 도구에 의해 우리의 감정이입 능력이 아직 또렷해지지 않았을 때라는 내용이 나오는 것이 자연스럽다. 따라서 ③번이 정답이다.

10 [2021 동국대]

정답 ①

해설 빈칸 (C), (D)는 명령문의 동사 자리이다. 명령문은 주어를 생략하고 동사원형으로 문장을 시작한다. 따라서 동사원형 ① Spend — observe가 정답이다.

[11-13]

우리는 또한 개인의 차이들이 개인의 문체들의 형태로서 스스로 나타내길 기대해야 한다. 메시지는 짧을 수 있지만, 그럼에도 불구하고, 개별적 사용자들이 보여주는 문체적 특성을 조사함으로써 그들에 대한 결론을 도출하는 것은 가능하다. 이 주장에 대한 증거는 법의학적 언어학에서 나온다. 2002년에, Stuart Campbell은 그의 문자 메시지 알리바이가 위조라는 것이 밝혀진 후, 자신의 15세 조카딸을 살인한 죄로 유죄판결을 받았다. Stuart Campbell은 그 소녀가 보낸 특정 문자 메시지들이 그가 결백하다는 것을 보여준다고 주장했었다. 그러나 그 자신의 문자 메시지들과 그의 조카딸의 문자 메시지의 어휘와 다른 문체적 특징들에 대한 자세한 비교는 Stuart Campbell이 직접 대단히 중요한 메시지들을 썼다는 것을 보여 주었다.

expect v. 기대하다 individual adj. 개인의
manifest v. 나타내다 personal style phr. 생활양식
draw v. 도출하다, 이끌어내다 conclusion n. 결론
examine v. 조사하다 stylistic adj. 문체의 trait n. 특성
evidence n. 증거 forensic adj. 법의학의
linguistics n. 언어학 guilty adj. 유죄 murder n. 살인
alibi n. 알리바이 forgery n. 위조 innocent adj. 결백한
detailed adj. 자세한 comparison n. 비교
vocabulary n. 어휘 feature n. 특징
critical adj. 대단히 중요한

11 2020 상명대

정답 ①

해석 ① 그럼에도 불구하고 ② 보통 말하는 그런
③ ~이긴 하지만 ④ 필연적으로
⑤ 믿을 수 없을 정도로

해설 빈칸에 적절한 연결어를 넣는 문제이다. 빈칸 앞은 메시지는 짧다는 내용이고, 빈칸 뒤에서 메시지는 개별적 사용자들이 보여주는 문체적 양식을 조사함으로써 그들에 대한 결론을 도출하는 것은 가능하다는 내용이다. 따라서 양보의 의미를 나타내는 연결어인 ① nevertheless가 정답이다.

어휘 nonetheless adv. 그럼에도 불구하고
as such phr. 보통 말하는 그런
necessarily adv. 필연적으로
inconceivably adv. 믿을 수 없을 정도로

12 2020 상명대

정답 ③

해석 ① 법의학적 언어학은 범죄를 해결하기 위해 사용될 수 있다.
② 각 개인은 다른 어휘를 사용하지만 유사한 문체적 특징을 사용한다.
③ 필자들이 쓰는 문자 메시지 방식으로 그들을 확인할 수 있다.
④ 문자 메시지는 알리바이를 제공하는 확립된 방식이 아니다.
⑤ 한 살인 사건은 문자 메시지 정보로 인해 밝혀졌다.

해설 지문의 요지를 묻는 문제이다. 지문 처음에서 메시지는 짧을 수 있지만, 개별적 사용자들이 보여주는 문체적 양식을 조사함으로써 그들에 대한 결론을 도출하는 것이 가능하다고 하고, 문자 메시지의 문체적 특징을 통해 유죄가 밝혀진 Stuart Campbell의 예를 보여주고 있다. 따라서 이 지문의 요지를 '필자들이 쓰는 문자 메시지 방식으로 그들을 확인할 수 있다'라고 표현한 ③번이 정답이다.

어휘 feature n. 특징 identify v. 확인하다
established adj. 확립된

13 2020 상명대

정답 ⑤

해석 ① 문자 메시지 길이가 증가해오고 있다.
② 서로 다른 사람들은 문자 메시지를 보내는 동안 비슷한 문체적 특성을 사용한다.
③ Stuart Campbell의 조카딸은 논의되었던 대단히 중요한 문자 메시지를 보냈다.
④ 가족 구성원들은 문자 메시지를 보내는 동안 유사한 어휘와 문체적 특징을 사용할 것이다.
⑤ 법의학적 언어학은 중요한 범죄를 해결하는 데 유용할 수 있다.

해설 지문을 통해 추론할 수 있는 것을 고르는 문제이다. 지문 처음에서 개인들이 메시지에서 보여주는 문체적 특성으로 그들에 대한 결론을 도출하는 것이 가능하다는 주장에 대한 증거는 법의학적 언어학에서 나온다고 하고, Stuart Campbell의 예시를 통해 법의학적 언어학이 범죄 해결에 도움이 된다는 것을 알 수 있으므로, 법의학적 언어학은 중요한 범죄를 해결하는 데 유용할 수 있다는 것을 추론할 수 있다. 따라서 정답은 ⑤번이다.

오답분석 ① 메시지는 짧을 수 있다고 했으므로, 문제 메시지 길이가 증가해오고 있다는 것은 추론할 수 없다.
② 개별적 사용자들이 보여주는 문체적 특성으로 그들에 대한 결론 도출이 가능하다고 했으므로, 서로 다른 사람들은 문자 메시지를 보내는 동안 비슷한 문체적 특성을 사용한다는 것은 추론할 수 없다.
③ Stuart Campbell과 그의 조카딸 문자 메시지를 비교한 결과, 조카딸이 아닌 그가 직접 메시지들을 썼음을 보여주었다고 했으므로, Stuart Campbell의 조카딸이 논의되었던 대단히 중요한 문자 메시지를 보냈다는 것은 추론할 수 없다.
④ Stuart Campbell의 문자 메시지들과 그의 조카딸의 문제 메시지 사이의 다른 어휘 및 문체적 특징으로 범죄를 해결한 것이므로, 가족 구성원들은 문자 메시지를 보내는 동안 유사한 어휘와 문체적 특징을 사용하리라는 것은 추론할 수 없다.

어휘 in length phr. 길이에 있어서

[14-16]

원주민의 언어가 사라질지도 모른다는 염려가 생긴 이후에 뉴질랜드에서 원주민의 언어를 되살리기 위한 큰 도전이 생겨났다. 2013년에, 단지 3.7퍼센트의 지역민들만이 모국어인 마오리어를 말할 수 있다고 말했다. 마오리어는 1987년에 영어와 함께 공용어가 되었고, 2006년에 수화가 세 번째 공용어로 지정되었을 때에는 청각장애인들이 매우 기뻐했다. 뉴질랜드 정부는 2040년까지 국가의 20퍼센트의 사람이 마오리어를 말할 수 있도록 하는 목표를 달성하기 위해 2025년까지 국내의 모든 학교에서 마오리어를 가르칠 것을 약속했다. 지금까지 그것은 보통 사람들에 의한 부흥 운동이었다. 지역민들은 'kia ora'(안녕하세요)와 같은 인사말을 사용하거나 이메일의 마지막을 'ngamihi'(감사합니다)로 끝내기 시작했다. 대중문화도 지난해에는 이러한 추세를 받아들여, 디즈니의 영화인 '모아나'도 하루 동안 마오리어로 특별 상영회를 했다. 마오리어는 또한 일부 실버타운의 거주자에게 가르쳐지고 있다. 총리인 Jacinda Ardern은 자신의 딸이 마오리어와 영어를 모두 배울 것이라고 약속했다.

revitalize v. 되살리다, 재활성화하다
alongside prep. ~와 함께 **elated** adj. 행복해하는
sign language phr. 수화 **grass roots** phr. 보통 사람들
revival n. 부흥, 부활 **greeting** n. 인사말
embrace v. 받아들이다, 포옹하다 **trend** n. 추세
resident n. 거주자 **retirement village** phr. 실버타운
prime minister phr. 총리 **pledge** v. 약속하다, 맹세하다

14 [2019 한성대]

정답 ②

해석 ① 마오리어는 뉴질랜드의 공용어다.
② 뉴질랜드에는 두 개의 공용어만이 있다.
③ 마오리어는 일부 실버타운에서 가르쳐진다.
④ Ardern은 딸이 마오리어와 영어를 배우게 할 것이다.

해설 지문의 내용과 일치하지 않는 것을 묻는 문제이다. ②번의 키워드인 official languages(공용어)와 관련된 지문의 official language(공용어) 주변에서 2006년에 수화가 세 번째 공용어로 지정되었다고 했으므로, 뉴질랜드에는 두 개의 공용어만이 있다는 것은 지문의 내용과 다르다. 따라서 ②번이 지문의 내용과 일치하지 않는다.

오답분석
① Maori became an official language alongside English in 1987을 통해 '마오리어는 뉴질랜드의 공용어다'라는 것을 알 수 있다.
③ Maori is also being taught to residents of a few retirement villages를 통해 '마오리어는 일부 실버타운에서 가르쳐진다'라는 것을 알 수 있다.
④ Prime Minister Jacinda Ardern has pledged that her baby daughter will learn both Maori and English를 통해 'Ardern은 딸이 마오리어와 영어를 배우게 할 것이다'라는 것을 알 수 있다.

15 [2019 한성대]

정답 ③

해석 ① 수화는 마오리어보다 더 필수적이다.
② 수화는 영화 '모아나'에서 사용되었다.
③ 마오리어는 지역 수준에서 부활했다.
④ 대중문화는 아직 마오리어를 받아들이지 않았다.

해설 지문을 통해 추론할 수 있는 것을 고르는 문제이다. 지문 중간에서 마오리어를 사용하는 것이 보통 사람들에 의한 부흥 운동이었다고 했으므로, 마오리어가 지역 수준에서 부활했다는 것을 추론할 수 있다. 따라서 정답은 ③번이다.

오답분석
① 마오리어와 수화가 모두 뉴질랜드의 공용어가 되었다고는 했지만, 수화가 마오리어보다 더 필수적인지는 알 수 없다.
② 마오리어로 영화 '모아나'의 특별 상영회가 열렸다고는 했지만, 수화가 영화 '모아나'에서 사용되었다는 것은 추론할 수 없다.
④ 사람들이 이메일로 마오리어를 사용하고 있으며, 영화 '모아나' 또한 마오리어로 상영되었다고 했으므로, 대중문화가 아직 마오리어를 받아들이지 않았다는 것은 추론할 수 없다.

어휘 **essential** adj. 필수적인 **resurgence** n. 부활

16 [2019 한성대]

정답 ④

해석 ① 마오리어의 쇠퇴
② 뉴질랜드의 역사
③ 영화 '모아나'의 영감
④ 마오리어의 증가하는 인기

해설 지문의 제목을 묻는 문제이다. 지문의 중간에서 사람들이 마오리어를 인사나 이메일에서 사용하고 있으며, 대중문화에서도 마오리어가 사용된다고 설명하고 있다. 따라서 지문의 제목을 '마오리어의 증가하는 인기'라고 표현한 ④번이 정답이다.

어휘 **decline** n. 쇠퇴 **inspiration** n. 영감, 자극
increasing adj. 증가하는, 늘어나는 **popularity** n. 인기

[17-19]

비디오 게임을 하는 법을 배울 때, 사람들은 새로운 문해력도 습득하게 된다. 물론, 그 방식은 "문해력"이라는 단어가 일반적으로 사용될 때의 방식과는 다르다. 전통적으로, 사람들은 문해력을 읽고 쓸 줄 아는 능력으로만 생각해 왔지만, 문해력을 조금 더 넓은 범위로 생각해야만 하는 두 가지 이유가 있다. 첫 번째로, 현대 사회에서, 언어는 유일한 의사소통 체계가 아니라는 것이다. 오늘날에는 이미지와 상징, 그래프, 도표, 공예품을 비롯하여 또 다른 수많은 시각적 상징들이 특히 중요하다.

그러므로, "시각적 문해력"이라는 다른 유형의 개념이 중요한 것이다. 예를 들어, 실내 디자인, 현대 미술, MTV의 비디오를 이해하는 법을 아는 것은 여러 형태의 시각적 문해력이라고 할 수 있다. 두 번째 이유는 비록 읽기와 쓰기가 전통적으로 문해력이 의미하는 것의 중심인 것 같지만, 읽기와 쓰기가 그렇게 일반적이고 명백한 것이 아니라는 것이다. 결국, 우리는 단순히 읽고 쓰는 것이 아니라, 무언가를 어떤 방식으로 읽고 쓰는 것이다. 그래서 다양한 유형의 텍스트를 읽는 다양한 방법이 존재한다. 문해력은 다양한데, 법률서를 읽는 데 필요한 법률적인 문해력은 물리학 서적이나 슈퍼히어로 만화책을 읽는데 필요한 문해력과는 다른 것이다. 이처럼, 심지어 인쇄된 텍스트를 읽는 것에 있어서도, 다양한 문해력이 존재한다.

literacy n. 문해력 **modern** adj. 현대의
communicational adj. 의사소통의 **diagram** n. 도표
artifact n. 공예품 **visual** adj. 시각의
particularly adv. 특히 **significant** adj. 중요한
legal adj. 법적인 **law book** phr. 법률서
in regard to phr. ~에 관해

17 2020 한국외대

정답 ③

해석 ① 시각적 문해력의 도래
② 읽기와 쓰기의 한계
③ 문해력에 대한 넓은 관점
④ 전통적인 문해력의 교훈

해설 지문의 제목을 묻는 문제이다. 지문의 세 번째 문장에서, 사람들은 문해력을 읽고 쓸 줄 아는 능력으로만 생각하고 있지만, 문해력을 조금 더 넓은 범위로 생각해야만 하는 두 가지 이유가 있다고 했고, 그 이후의 부분에서 두 가지 이유를 하나씩 설명하고 있다. 따라서 이 지문의 제목을 '문해력에 대한 넓은 관점'이라고 표현한 ③번이 정답이다.

어휘 **advent** n. 도래 **lesson** n. 교훈

18 2020 한국외대

정답 ④

해석 ① 당황한 ② 삼각의
③ 일관성 있는 ④ 다양한

해설 지문의 빈칸을 채우는 문제이다. 빈칸이 포함된 문장의 앞 문장에서 다양한 유형의 텍스트를 읽기 위한 다양한 방법이 있다고 했다. 여기에서 읽기 위한 방법은 문해력을 의미하므로, 빈칸에는 문해력이 다양하다는 내용이 들어가야 한다. 따라서 ④번이 정답이다.

19 2020 한국외대

정답 ③

해석 ① 전통적인 문해력은 읽고 쓰는 능력을 의미한다.
② 시각적 문해력은 도표와 미술품을 이해하는 데 필요하다.
③ 전통적인 글쓰기는 일반화되고 명백한 방식으로 수행된다.
④ 다양한 종류의 인쇄된 텍스트들을 위한 다양한 문해력이 존재한다.

해설 지문의 내용과 일치하지 않는 것을 묻는 문제이다. 지문의 여덟 번째 문장에서, 전통적으로 문해력이 의미하는 것의 중심에 읽기와 쓰기가 있기는 하지만, 읽기와 쓰기가 그렇게 일반적이고 명백한 것이 아니라고 했으므로, 전통적인 글쓰기는 일반화되고 명백한 방식으로 수행된다는 것은 지문의 내용과 다르다. 따라서 ③번이 정답이다.

어휘 **artwork** n. 미술품 **generalized** adj. 일반화된

[20-21]

아기 침대 근처에서는 당신이 하는 말을 조심해야 한다. 연구원들이 알아낸 바에 따르면, 8개월 정도의 어린 아기들은 좋은 단어와 나쁜 단어를 듣고 기억할 수 있다. Vienna 대학교의 Peter W. Jusczyk는 "어린아이들도 들을 수 있다."라고 말한다.
Jusczyk는 새로운 연구에서 그렇게 어린 나이의 아이들에게 책을 읽어주는 것은 아이들이 이해하지 못하는 것처럼 보일지라도, 그들이 말을 배우는 과정을 시작할 수 있다는 것을 보여준다고 말했다.
Jusczyk는 "당신이 거기에 앉아서 크게 소리 내어 읽으면, 아이는 단어들의 소리 패턴에 대해 어떤 것을 배우고 있는 것이며, 단어들이 어떻게 만들어지는지 배우고 그렇게 배움으로써 말에서 소리 패턴을 나누도록 도와주기 때문에 중요하다."라고 말했다.
결론은 아기들이 세 개의 녹음된 이야기를 반복적으로 들었던 실험에 근거한다. 2주 후에, 아기들이 그 이야기들에 나온 단어들과 안 나온 단어들을 다르게 인식하는지 비교되었다. Jusczyk는 아기들은 분명하게 이야기에 나온 단어들을 인식했다고 말했다. 그 연구에 따른 보고서는 금요일에 *Science*지에 실릴 것이다.
Sussex 대학교의 언어 학습 연구원인 Robin S. Chapman은 "이것은 중요한 연구이고, 아이들이 말소리에 주목하고... 익숙한 소리를 고른다는 내용의 이전 연구 결과들을 진척시켰다."라고 말했다.
Chapman은 그 연구들이 "많은 언어 학습이 생애 첫해에 일어나는데, 그것은 부모가 아이들에게 이야기를 하면 아이들이 그 이야기에서 말을 배울 것이라는 것을 보여준다."라고 말했다.

read out loud phr. 크게 소리 내어 읽다
pattern n. 패턴, 양상 **conclusion** n. 결론
experiment n. 실험 **infant** n. 아기, 유아

repeatedly adv. 반복적으로, 되풀이하여
publish v. 싣다, 출판하다
advance v. 진척시키다, 전진시키다
finding n. (조사·연구 등의) 결과, 결론 attend v. 주목하다
pick out phr. 고르다 familiar adj. 익숙한, 친숙한
happen v. 일어나다

20 [2019 단국대]

정답 ③

해석 ① 베이비 샤워 ② 유치원
③ 아기 침대 ④ 보호 시설

해설 지문의 빈칸을 채우는 문제이다. 두 번째 문장에서 연구원들이 알아낸 바에 따르면, 8개월 정도의 어린 아기들은 좋은 단어와 나쁜 단어를 듣고 기억할 수 있다고 했으므로, 빈칸에는 아기 침대 근처에서는 당신이 하는 말을 조심해야 한다는 내용이 나와야 적절하다는 것을 알 수 있다. 따라서 '아기 침대'라고 한 ③번이 정답이다.

21 [2019 단국대]

정답 ①

해석 ① Chapman이 *Science*지에 실릴 연구를 수행했다.
② 한 살이 안 된 아기들도 인간의 말을 배우기 시작한다.
③ 아기들의 언어 학습에 대한 이전 연구가 있었다.
④ 지문에 서술된 실험에서, 연구 대상들은 이야기를 들었다.

해설 지문의 내용과 일치하지 않는 것을 묻는 문제이다. ①번의 키워드인 *Science*(*Science*지)와 관련된 지문의 네 번째 문단에서 *Science*지에 실릴 연구를 수행한 것은 Juszcyk라고 했으므로, Chapman이 *Science*지에 실릴 연구를 수행했다는 것은 지문의 내용과 다르다. 따라서 ①번이 지문의 내용과 일치하지 않는다.

오답분석
② 첫 번째 문단 Babies as young as 8 months can hear and remember words를 통해 '한 살이 안 된 아기들도 인간의 말을 배우기 시작한다'는 것을 알 수 있다.
③ 다섯 번째 문단 It advances the findings of earlier work that showed children do attend to the sounds of language를 통해 '아기들의 언어 학습에 대한 이전 연구가 있었다'는 것을 알 수 있다.
④ 네 번째 문단 The conclusion is based on experiments in which infants listened repeatedly to three recorded stories를 통해 '지문에 서술된 실험에서, 연구 대상들이 이야기를 들었다'는 것을 알 수 있다.

어휘 conduct v. 수행하다, 시행하다 subject n. 연구(실험) 대상

[22-23]

피진과 크레올은 언어를 공유하지 않는 사람들이 의사소통하기 위한 요구에서 나온 결과물이지만, 피진이 이러한 목적에 알맞도록 선택된 방언이나 이미 존재하는 언어로 시작되지 않는다는 점에서 국어나 국제어와는 다르다. 오히려 그것은 두 개의 언어의 독특한 조합이다. Loreto Todd에 따르면, 피진은 공통 언어가 없는 사람들 사이에서 어떠한 제한받는 의사소통의 요구를 만족시키기 위해서 생긴 주변 언어이다. 접촉의 초기 단계에서 피진의 사용은 종종 생각의 세부적인 교환이 필요하지 않거나 거의 오로지 한 언어로부터 온 적은 어휘로도 충분한 거래로 제한된다. 또한, 피진의 통사적인 구조는 만나는 두 언어의 구조보다 훨씬 덜 복잡하고, 많은 피진의 특징이 접촉하는 언어들의 사용을 반영하지만 다른 것들은 피진의 고유의 것이다. 크레올은 언어 집단에서 피진이 모국어로 될 때 생긴다. 피진의 특징인 간단한 구조는 크레올에도 전해지지만, 모국어로서의 크레올이 인간 경험의 모든 영역을 표현할 수 있어야 하므로, 어휘는 확장되고 더 정교한 통사적 체계로 빈번하게 진화한다.

pidgin n. 피진(언어가 서로 다른 사람들이 제한된 의사소통을 위해 서로의 언어를 혼합하여 쓰는 제한적인 언어)
creole n. 크레올(피진을 모국어로 쓰는 언어 집단이 사용하는 언어)
dialect n. 방언, 사투리 particular adj. 독특한, 특별한
combination n. 조합 fulfill v. 만족시키다, 수행하다
restricted adj. 제한된 initial adj. 초기의, 처음의
transaction n. 거래, 매매 detailed adj. 세부적인
exclusively adv. 오로지, 배타적으로 suffice v. 충분하다
syntactic adj. 통사적인, 문장 구조의
in contact phr. 만나는, 접촉하는 feature n. 특징
reflect v. 반영하다 unique adj. 고유한, 독특한
mother tongue phr. 모국어
speech community phr. 언어 집단
characterize v. 특징짓다
carry over phr. 전하다, 이어지다 lexicon n. 어휘
elaborate adj. 정교한

22 [2019 한양대]

정답 ④

해석 ① 크레올은 보통 피진보다 더 간단한 구조로 되어 있다.
② 피진의 어휘는 대체로 접촉하는 두 언어에서 나온다.
③ 피진은 이미 존재하는 접촉하는 언어 중의 하나로 생각할 수 있다.
④ 피진은 접촉 언어의 사용을 반영하는 언어들의 특징들 외에도 다른 독특한 특징을 가지고 있다.
⑤ 피진은 공통의 언어를 말하는데 익숙한 집단 사이에서 의사소통을 쉽게 만들려는 방법으로 발달한다.

해설 지문을 통해 추론할 수 있는 것을 고르는 문제이다. 지문의 처음중반에서 피진은 접촉 언어의 사용을 반영하지만, 피진만이 갖는 고유한 특징도 있다고 했으므로, 피진은 접촉 언어의 사

용을 반영하는 언어들의 특징들 외에도 다른 독특한 특징을 가지고 있다는 것을 추론할 수 있다. 따라서 정답은 ④번이다.

오답 분석
① 피진의 간단한 구조가 크레올에도 전해지지만, 모국어로서의 크레올은 어휘는 확장되고 더 정교한 통사적 체계를 가진다고 했으므로, 크레올은 보통 피진보다 더 간단한 구조로 되어 있다는 것은 추론할 수 없다.
② 피진의 어휘는 거의 오로지 한 언어에서 나온 적은 어휘로도 충분한 거래에서 사용하는 어휘로 제한된다고 했으므로, 피진의 어휘는 대체로 접촉하는 두 언어에서 나온다는 것은 추론할 수 없다.
③ 피진이 목적에 알맞도록 선택된 방언이나 이미 존재하는 언어로 시작되지 않는다는 점에서 국어나 국제어와는 다르다고 했으므로, 피진은 이미 존재하는 접촉하는 언어 중의 하나로 생각할 수 있다는 것은 추론할 수 없다.
⑤ 피진과 크레올은 언어를 공유하지 않는 사람들이 의사소통하기 위한 요구에서 나온 결과라고 했으므로, 피진은 공통의 언어를 말하는데 익숙한 집단 사이에서 의사소통을 쉽게 만들려는 방법으로 발달한다는 것은 추론할 수 없다.

어휘 largely adv. 대체로 facilitate v. 쉽게 만들다, 용이하게 하다

23 [2019 한양대]

정답 ④

해석 ① 시적인 ② 토박이의
③ 복잡한 ④ 주변부의
⑤ 수사적인

해설 지문의 빈칸을 채우는 문제이다. 빈칸이 포함된 문장에서 음악적 피진이 공통된 언어를 가지고 있지 않은 사람들 사이에서 제한된 의사소통을 하기 위한 목적으로 나온 언어라고 했으므로, 빈칸에는 주요한 언어가 아니라는 내용이 나와야 한다는 것을 알 수 있다. 따라서 '주변부의'라고 한 ④번이 정답이다.

어휘 poetic adj. 시적인 native adj. 토박이의, 태어난 곳의
complicated adj. 복잡한
marginal adj. 주변부의, 중요하지 않은
rhetorical adj. 수사적인, 미사여구의

[24-26]

최근에는 동화 속에서 어린 시절의 의존을 반대하고 자기 자신이 되기 위한 투쟁이 자주 소년과 소녀에게 다르게 묘사되며, 이것은 성적 (A)고정관념의 결과라고 주장되어 왔다. 동화는 그런 일방적인 그림을 만들지 않는다. 소녀가 자기 자신이 되기 위한 투쟁에서 내면으로 들어가고, 소년은 외부 세계를 공격적으로 다룰 때도, 이 두 가지가 함께 사람이 자아를 얻어야 하는 두 가지 방식, 즉 바깥세상뿐만이 아닌 내면의 세계도 이해하고 정복하는 것을 배우는 방법을 상징한다. 이런 의미에서, 남성과 여성 영웅은 (인공적으로) 분리된 두 관점의 다른 두 가지 모습과 모든 사람이 성장하면서 겪어야 하는 같은 과정을 투영한다. 어떤 상상력이 없는 부모는 그것을 깨닫지 못하지만, 아이들은 영웅의 성별이 무엇이든 간에 이야기가 자신이 가진 문제와 (B)관련이 있다는 것을 안다.
"잠자는 숲속의 미녀"에서, 왕자와 공주의 조화로운 만남, 즉 서로에 대한 각성은 성숙함이 암시하는 상징이다. 그것은 자신 안에서의 조화만이 아닌 다른 사람 간의 조화도 암시한다. 적절한 시기에 왕자가 도착한 것이 성적인 각성을 유발하는 사건으로 해석되는지 또는 높은 자아의 탄생으로 해석되는지는 듣는 사람에 달려있다. 아이는 아마도 이 두 가지 의미를 모두 이해할 것이다.

---

struggle n. 투쟁 dependency n. 의존
fairy tale phr. 동화 frequently adv. 자주, 빈번하게
render v. 만들다 depict v. 묘사하다, 그리다
aggressively adv. 공격적으로
external adj. 외부의, 바깥의 symbolize v. 상징하다
projection n. 투영, 투사 figure n. 모습, 모양
artificially adv. 인공적으로 separated adj. 분리된
aspect n. 관점, 측면 undergo v. 겪다
literal-minded adj. 상상력이 없는, 무미건조한
harmonious adj. 조화로운 awakening n. 각성
maturity n. 성숙함 interpret v. 해석하다 ego n. 자아
comprehend v. 이해하다

24 [2019 가천대]

정답 ④

해석 ① 시작 ② 방향
③ 번식 ④ 고정관념

해설 지문의 빈칸을 채우는 문제이다. 지문의 빈칸이 포함된 문장에서 어린 시절의 의존이나 자기 자신이 되기 위한 투쟁을 동화에서 소년과 소녀를 다르게 묘사하고 있다고 설명하고 있으므로, 빈칸에는 성별에 대한 고정관념에 대한 내용이 나와야 적절하다는 것을 알 수 있다. 따라서 '고정관념'이라고 한 ④번이 정답이다.

어휘 initiation n. 시작 orientation n. 방향
reproduction n. 번식 stereotyping n. 고정관념

25 [2019 가천대]

정답 ②

해석 ① 모순되다 ② 관련이 있다
③ 뒤집다 ④ 경쟁하다

해설 지문의 빈칸을 채우는 문제이다. 지문의 빈칸이 포함된 문장의 이전 문장에서 남성과 여성 영웅이 두 가지의 다른 모습을 투영한다고 설명하고 있으므로, 빈칸에는 아이들이 영웅의 이야기를 자신의 문제에 투영한다는 대한 내용이 나와야 적절하다는 것을 알 수 있다. 따라서 '관련이 있다'라고 한 ②번이 정답이다.

어휘 contradict v. 모순되다 pertain to phr. ~와 관련이 있다
subvert v. 뒤집다 compete v. 경쟁하다

26 2019 가천대
정답 ②

해석 ① 잠자는 숲속의 미녀 이야기는 아이들이 자아를 찾는 과정에서 동화를 이해한다는 것을 입증하는 한 가지 예시이다.
② 아동용 이야기가 암시하는 교훈은 성 역할의 순환과 교육을 불러온다.
③ 아이들은 일반적인 신념과는 반대로 남성과 여성 영웅에 동질감을 가질 수 있다.
④ 동화는 아이들이 모든 사람이 겪는 성숙해지는 과정과 타협을 할 수 있도록 한다.

해설 지문을 통해 추론할 수 없는 것을 고르는 문제이다. 지문의 두 번째 문단의 첫 문장에서 왕자와 공주의 조화로운 만남, 즉 서로에 대한 각성은 성숙함이 암시하는 상징이라고는 했지만, 이를 통해 아동용 이야기가 암시하는 교훈은 성 역할의 순환과 교육을 불러온다는 것은 유추할 수 없으므로 정답은 ②번이다.

오답 분석
① It depends on the listener ~ the child probably comprehends both these meanings를 통해 '잠자는 숲속의 미녀 이야기는 아이들이 자아를 찾는 과정에서 동화를 이해한다는 것을 입증하는 한 가지 예시이다'는 것을 알 수 있다.
③ children know that, whatever the sex of the hero, the story pertains to their own problems를 통해 '아이들은 일반적인 신념과는 반대로 남성과 여성 영웅에 동질감을 가질 수 있다'는 것을 알 수 있다.
④ these two together symbolize the two ways ~ through learning to understand and master the inner as well as the outer world를 통해 '동화는 아이들이 모든 사람이 겪는 성숙해지는 과정과 타협을 할 수 있도록 한다'는 것을 알 수 있다.

어휘 evidence n. 입증하다 implicit adj. 암시하는, 내포된
circulation n. 순환 identify with phr. ~에 동질감을 갖다
as opposed to phr. ~와는 반대로
come to terms with phr. ~와 타협하다
maturation n. 성숙 go through phr. 겪다

[27-29]

글을 빨리 읽으면서도, 여전히 그 의미를 이해할 수 있는 능력을 향상하기 위해 사용되는 기술은 속독으로 알려져 있다. "속독"이라는 용어는 Evelyn Wood에 의해 처음 고안되었는데, 그녀는 1950년대에 유타주에서 읽는 것에 미숙한 사람들을 위한 독서 교정 교사였다. Wood는 선천적으로 글을 빨리 읽는 사람들의 독서 습관을 조사했고 빨리 글을 읽는 사람들이 실제로 더 많은 내용을 머리에 남겨둔다는 사실을 밝혀냈다. 그래서 그녀는 두 배에서 다섯 배까지 글을 빨리 읽을 수 있도록 사람들을 가르치기 위한 한 가지 방법론을 고안했다. Wood는 나쁜 독서 습관은 극복될 수 있고, 좋은 독서 습관은 연습을 통해 습득될 수 있다고 지적했다. 그녀는 Evelyn Wood 속독 학교를 미국 전역과 영어를 사용하는 나라에 설립했고, 그녀의 체계는 찬사를 받게 되었다. Evelyn Wood의 프로그램에서 언급하는 비효율적인 독서 습관은 독자가 그 단어를 알고 있다고 하더라도, 긴 단어를 더듬거리며 읽는 것, 읽는 사람이 처음 읽었을 때의 의미를 알고 있음에도 그 문장이나 어구로 돌아가 그 문장이나 문단에 머물러 있는 것, 그리고 마음속으로 각각의 단어를 발음하거나 말하는 것을 포함한다. 반면 이 프로그램에서 확인된 효과적인 독서 습관은 전적으로 읽어야 할 자료에 집중하는 것, 단어 하나하나를 읽기보다는 단어를 집단으로 묶어 보는 것, 읽기의 목적을 설정하는 것을 포함한다.

enhance v. 높이다 comprehend v. 이해하다
speed reading phr. 속독 corrective adj. 교정하는
unskilled adj. 미숙한 retain v. 남겨두다
methodology n. 방법론 overcome v. 극복하다
attain v. 얻다 acclaim n. 찬사
stumble v. 더듬거리며 말하다 regress v. 회귀하다
vocalize v. 발음하다

27 2020 한성대
정답 ②

해석 ① (새로운 낱말 어구가) 만들어지다
② 반대되다
③ 창조되다
④ 고안되다

해설 문맥상 빈칸에 적절하지 않은 어휘를 묻는 문제이다. 빈칸이 포함된 문장은 "속독"이라는 용어가 Evelyn Wood에 의해 만들어졌다는 내용이므로, '반대되다'라는 의미의 objected는 빈칸에 적절하지 않다. 따라서 ②번이 정답이다.

28 2020 한성대
정답 ①

해석 ① Evelyn Wood의 속독 학교
② 단어를 마음속으로 발음하는 것
③ 글 읽는 속도를 억제하는 것
④ 단어를 집단으로 묶어 읽는 것

해설 지문의 주제를 묻는 문제이다. 지문 전체적으로 Evelyn Wood가 만들어 낸 속독의 방법론과 그녀가 설립한 속독 학교에 관해 설명하고 있으므로, 이 지문의 요지를 'Evelyn Wood의 속독 학교'라고 표현한 ①번이 정답이다.

어휘 curb v. 억제하다

29 2020 한성대

정답 ①

해석 ① 그녀는 글 읽는 속도가 변하지 않는다고 믿었다.
② 그녀는 빠르게 읽는 사람의 독서 습관을 분석했다.
③ 그녀는 원래 읽는 것이 미숙한 이들을 가르치는 일을 전문으로 했다.
④ 그녀는 새로운 단어를 만들어냈다.

해설 Evelyn Wood에 관해 일치하지 않는 것을 묻는 문제이다. 지문의 두 번째 문단에서, Wood가 나쁜 독서 습관은 극복할 수 있고, 좋은 독서 습관은 습득할 수 있다고 지적했다고 했으므로, 그녀가 글 읽는 속도가 변하지 않는다고 믿었다는 것은 지문의 내용과 다르다. 따라서 ①번이 정답이다.

오답 분석
② 지문의 첫 번째 문단에서, Wood는 선천적으로 빨리 읽는 사람들의 독서 습관을 조사했다고 했으므로, 그녀가 빠르게 읽는 사람의 독서 습관을 분석했다는 것은 지문의 내용과 일치한다.
③ 지문의 첫 번째 문단에서, Wood가 유타주에서 읽는 것이 미숙한 사람들을 위한 독서 교정 교사였다고 했으므로, 그녀가 원래 읽는 것이 미숙한 이들을 가르치는 일을 전문으로 했다는 것은 지문의 내용과 일치한다.
④ 지문의 첫 번째 문단에서, Wood가 "속독"이라는 용어를 처음 고안했다고 했으므로, 그녀가 새로운 단어를 만들어냈다는 것은 지문의 내용과 일치한다.

[30-32]

19세기의 어느 때, 철학은 민족 주체성 추구의 측면에서 문학으로 대체되었다. 우선 Immanuel Kant 이후, 과학은 철학이 최고로 몰두하는 것이었고, 그것들의 결합 과정에서 윤리를 제외한 철학은 사색에 대한 가치관을 상실했다. 소설과 시는 적어도 서양에서만큼은 Matthew Arnold가 말하는 "생각되고 말해지는 최상의 것"의 전형이 되었다. 국가와 대부분의 교육 전문가들이 원했던 것은 학생의 생각을 <u>영국인, 미국인, 프랑스인이 되는 것</u>으로 고취시키는 것이었다. 문학이 이 과제에 가장 적합했던 것은 그 범위가 국제적이고 과학에 동화되었던 철학이나 역사학과는 달리, 문학은 본질적으로 국가적인 것이었기 때문이다. 번역 작품으로 물론 Dostoevsky, Flaubert, 혹은 Mann 등의 작품을 읽을 수 있지만, 모두가 알고 있듯이 뭔가가 항상 부족한데, 주로 <u>장소</u>감이며, 즉, 어떤 특정 문화를 구성하는 자국어의 특수함이 그것이다.

philosophy n. 철학 replace v. 대체하다, 대신하다
quest n. 추구, 탐구 national identity phr. 민족 주체성
chief adj. 최고의, 주된 preoccupation n. 몰두, 열중
incorporation n. 결합, 합동 ethics n. 윤리
taste n. 가치관, 기호 speculation n. 사색, 숙고
typify v. ~의 전형이 되다, ~을 대표하다
state n. 국가, 나라 educator n. 교육 전문가
imbue v. 고취하다, 불어 넣다 international adj. 국제적인
scope n. 범위 assimilate v. 동화하다, 융화하다
essentially adv. 본질적으로
in translation phr. 번역 작품으로 chiefly adv. 주로
specificity n. 특별함, 특수함 vernacular n. 자국어, 토착어
particular adj. 특정한

30 2020 국민대

정답 ①

해석 ① 민족 주체성 ② 사색에 대한 가치관
③ 서양의 관점 ④ 철학의 몰두

해설 밑줄 친 부분의 의미를 추론하는 문제이다. 밑줄 친 what it was to be English, American, or French는 '영국인, 미국인, 프랑스인이 되는 것'이라는 의미이다. 주변의 내용을 살펴보면 이것이 민족의 주체성을 가지는 것임을 알 수 있다. 따라서, 이를 '민족 주체성'이라고 표현한 ①번이 정답이다.

어휘 perspective n. 관점 philosophical adj. 철학의

31 2020 국민대

정답 ①

해석 ① 장소 ② 윤리
③ 위엄 ④ 인간성

해설 지문의 빈칸을 채우는 문제이다. 지문의 마지막 문장에서 문학 작품은 번역본으로 읽을 수도 있지만, 이 경우, 이 감각이 부족한 데, 이것은 특정 문화를 구성하는 자국어의 특수함이라고 했으므로, 빈칸에는 자국어의 특수함을 느낄 수 있는 조건에 관한 내용이 나와야 적절하다는 것을 알 수 있다. 따라서 '장소'라고 한 ①번이 정답이다.

어휘 dignity n. 위엄, 품위 humanity n. 인간성, 인간애

32 2020 국민대

정답 ②

해석 ① 제국주의 ② 문학의 역할
③ 과학의 진보 ④ 언어 변화

해설 지문의 요지를 묻는 문제이다. 지문 처음에서 19세기의 어느 때, 철학은 민족 주체성 추구의 측면에서 문학으로 대체되었다고 하고, 이어서 문학이 철학, 과학, 역사학보다 이에 적합한 이유들에 대해 설명하고 있다. 따라서 이 지문의 요지를 '문학의 역할'이라고 표현한 ②번이 정답이다.

어휘 imperialism n. 제국주의 rise n. 진보, 향상

33 2020 광운대

정답 ⑤

해석 영어는 everyone이나 someone과 같은 단수 대명사와 적절하게 부합하는 성 중립적 단수 대명사가 없는 것으로 잘 알려져 있으며, 그 결과 they가 600년 넘는 동안 이러한 목적으로 사용되어 왔으며, 최근에는 they가 성 정체성이 여성도 남성도 아닌 사람을 지칭하기 위해 사용되어 왔는데, 이러한 관념은 소셜 미디어와 영어 사용자들 간 매일 매일의 사적 대화에서뿐만 아니라 출판되고 편집되는 글에서 점점 더 일반적인 것이 되고 있다. 예를 들면, 우리는 종종 "누군가가 그들의 핸드폰을 두고 갔다"는 말을 듣는다.

① they — he — 그녀의
② he — they — 그의
③ she — it — 그의
④ he — she — 그들의
⑤ they — they — 그들의

해설 지문의 빈칸을 채우는 문제이다. 첫 번째 빈칸이 있는 문장에서 영어에는 성 중립적 단수 대명사가 없어서 _____를 이러한 목적으로 사용해 왔다고 했으므로 첫 번째 빈칸에는 성 중립적 성격의 단어가 나와야 적절하다는 것을 알 수 있다. 따라서 'they'가 들어가야 한다. 두 번째 빈칸이 있는 문장에서 _____이 성 정체성이 여성도 남성도 아닌 사람을 지칭하는 데 사용되어 왔다고 했으므로 두 번째 빈칸에도 성 중립적 성격의 단어가 나와야 적절하다는 것을 알 수 있다. 따라서 'they' 또는 'it'이 들어가야 한다. 지문의 첫 번째 문장에서 someone에 부합하는 성 중립적 대명사로 they가 사용되어 왔다고 했으므로, 세 번째 빈칸에서 Someone을 받는 소유격 대명사로 their가 적절하다는 것을 알 수 있다. 따라서 ⑤ they — they — their가 정답이다.

어휘 gender-neutral adj. 성 중립적인 singular adj. 단수형의
pronoun n. 대명사 correspond with phr. ~와 부합하다
neatly adv. 적절하게, 깔끔하게
as a consequence phr. ~의 결과
gender identity phr. 성 정체성
non-binary adj. 여성도 남성도 아닌
increasingly adv. 점점 더
publish v. 출판하다 personal adj. 사적인, 개인적인
interaction n. 대화, 상호 작용
leave behind phr. 두고 가다

34 2020 한양대

정답 ⑤

해석 처음부터, 수사학은 의사소통으로서의 발화 행위에 초점을 맞추었다. 적어도, 두 명의 당사자인 화자와 청자가 수반되었다. 대면하는 의사소통의 즉각적이고 복잡한 관계는 글을 상황 속으로 도입하여 작가와 독자의 매우 다른 상황을 논의하는 모델이 되었다. 읽기는 듣기를 대체하지만, 사람은 절대 다시 들을 수 없는 반면 (녹음은 완전히 진정한 행위는 아니다), 사람은 글을 다시 읽을 수 있다. 이 모든 것은 플라톤 이후로 분명해졌다. 플라톤이 언급했듯이, 읽기의 중복성은 화자의 부재에서 유래하며, 결과적으로 특정한 이해를 강요하는 권위자의 부재에서 유래하는 것이다. 우리가 상기하기에 Franz Kafka는 이러한 관점에서 우주를 보는 것 같았다. 이해도 화자는 항상 부재하며, 그에게 있어서 어떤 특정한 이해도 부재하다. 화자가 사라진 "특정한 이해"는 의미라는 모든 짐을 독자에게 둔다. 해석학, 따라서 비평은 글을 읽고 쓸 줄 아는 능력과 함께 생겨났다.

① 비평은 읽고 쓸 줄 아는 능력의 다양한 의미를 이해하는 데서 시작한다.
② 진정한 행위는 대면하는 의사소통을 필요로 한다.
③ Kafka는 특정한 이해를 통해 더 넓은 세계관을 획득했다.
④ 발화 행위의 수사적 측면을 알아보는 것이 가장 중요하다.
⑤ 읽기는 권위자의 부재로 인해 해석상 중요성을 띤다.

해설 지문의 요지를 묻는 문제이다. 지문 중간에서 플라톤의 말을 통해 읽기에서 화자는 특정한 이해를 강요하는 권위자임을 알 수 있고, 지문 마지막에서 화자(권위자)가 사라진 "특정한 이해"는 의미라는 모든 짐을 독자에게 두며, 해석학은 글을 읽고 쓸 줄 아는 능력과 함께 생겨났다는 것을 설명하고 있다. 따라서 이 지문의 요지를 '읽기는 권위자의 부재로 인해 해석상 중요성을 띤다'라고 표현한 ⑤번이 정답이다.

어휘 rhetoric n. 수사학 speech act phr. 발화 행위
face-to-face adj. 대면하는 authentic adj. 진정한
multiplicity n. 중복 absence n. 부재
authority n. 권위자 enforce v. 강요하다
absent adj. 부재한 vanish v. 사라지다
hermeneutics n. 해석학 criticism n. 비평
literacy n. 글을 읽고 쓸 줄 아는 능력
grasp v. 완전히 이해하다 multiple adj. 다양한
rely on phr. ~을 필요로 하다 utmost adj. 최고의
rhetorical adj. 수사적인 interpretative adj. 해석상의
significance n. 중요성

[35-36]

현대 살인 추리소설의 가장 중요한 특징 중 하나는 그것이 독자들에게 부여한 새로운 요구였고, 독자들이 이야기를 구체화하고 범행에 죄를 지우는 데 적극적인 역할을 하도록 요구했다. Execution Sermons는 오직 독자들이 성직자의 권위로 명백히 공식적인 진실의 형태만을 수용하도록 요구했었지만, 현대 법정 소설은 사실상 독자들을 유죄 혹은 무죄 선고에 투표해야 하는 (A)수용자로 취급했다.

유죄를 선고받은 살인자의 자기변호가 쓰인 페이지의 여백에 "이 진술은 처음부터 끝까지 모두 거짓말로 생각된다"고 적었던 익명의 독자는 독자로서 자신의 역할에 대한 이 기대에 응하고 있었다. 하지만 현대 살인 추리소설은 독자들이 의견을 내놓는 것 그 이상을 하도록 요구했다. 현대 살인 추리소설은 독자들이 적극적으로 이야기를 구체화하면서, 증거를 꼼꼼하게 살펴 추려내고, 단편적인 것들을 종합하고, 추적하고, 알아내고, 탐색하고, "밝혀내고", 운 좋은 서술자라는 생각은

(B)거두고 사건의 거대 서사를 정교하게 만들어내는 일을 효과적으로 떠맡도록 했다.

이것을 위해, 현대 살인 추리소설 이야기는 독자들을 범행에 대한 (C)수사로 끌어당기면서, 핵심 증거의 시각적 삽화, 건축상의 외관과 내부 상황 모두를 포함한 현장의 그림 삽화, 독자들이 3차원적 공간에서 범죄를 (D)재구성하도록 돕는 것을 목적으로 한 지도, 살인자의 접근 방식(뒤 창문, 잠기지 않은 문)에 특히 주의를 기울이고, 때로는 점선으로 된 살인자의 경로를 쫓고, 점차 희생자 시체의 정확한 위치를 나타내는 건축상 평면도를 제공한다.

---

narrative n. 이야기, 담화　assign v. 지정하다, 할당하다
Execution Sermons phr. 미국 뉴잉글랜드 식민지에서 17~18세기에 두드러졌던 범죄 소설의 형태
uncontestable adj. 명백한　cast a vote phr. 투표하다
conviction n. 유죄 선고　acquittal n. 무죄 선고
anonymous adj. 익명의　exculpation n. 변호, 변명
vote v. 의견을 내놓다
sift through phr. 꼼꼼하게 살펴 추려내다
piece together phr. 종합하다　probe v. 탐색하다
unveil v. 밝히다　take on phr. 떠맡다, (책임을) 지다
craft v. 정교하게 만들다
withdrawal n. 도로 거두기, 철회, 취소
providential adj. 운 좋은　narrator n. 서술자
investigation n. 수사, 조사　facade n. 외관, 겉보기
reconstruct v. 재구성하다　floor plan phr. 평면도
precise adj. 정확한

35　2019 중앙대

정답　③

해석　① 현대 사회의 독자들은 추리소설의 결말을 미리 알고 싶어 한다.
② 현대 살인 추리소설은 대다수 독자의 마음을 끌지 못했다.
③ 현대 살인 추리소설의 독자들은 이야기를 이해하기 위해 기민해야 한다.
④ 최신 형태의 현대 추리소설은 이야기에 관한 독자들의 관심을 흩뜨리는 경향이 있다.

해설　지문의 요지를 묻는 문제이다. 두 번째 문단 중간에서 살인 추리소설은 독자들이 의견을 내놓는 것 그 이상을 하도록 요구했다고 하고, 이어서 독자들은 이야기를 구체화하면서, 증거를 꼼꼼하게 살펴 추려내고, 단편적인 것들을 종합하고, 추적하는 등의 태도가 요구된다는 것을 설명하고 있다. 따라서 이 지문의 요지를 '현대 살인 추리소설의 독자들은 이야기를 이해하기 위해 기민해야 한다'라고 표현한 ③번이 정답이다.

어휘　conclusion n. 결말, 결론　in advance phr. 미리
attractive adj. 마음을 끄는　agile adj. 기민한, 민첩한
distract v. 흩뜨리다

36　2019 중앙대

정답　①

해설　지문의 흐름에 적합하지 않은 것을 고르는 문제이다. 지문은 현대 살인 추리소설이 이야기를 구체화하는 데 독자들의 적극적인 역할을 요구한다는 내용이므로, (B) 독자들은 자신이 운 좋은 서술자라는 생각은 '거두어야' 한다는 내용, (C) 살인 추리소설 이야기는 독자들을 범행에 대한 '수사'로 끌어당긴다는 내용, (D) 소설에서 제공되는 지도는 독자들이 3차원적 공간에서 범죄를 '재구성하도록' 돕는다는 내용은 모두 지문 내용과 관련이 있다. 그러나 (A)는 독자들을 '받아들이는 사람'으로 취급했다는 내용이므로, 현대 살인 추리소설에서의 적극적인 독자의 역할과 관련이 없다. 따라서 ①번이 정답이다.

[37-38]

2019년, 12월 10일, 메리엄-웹스터 사전은 올해의 단어를 선정하였는데, *post-truth* 혹은 *selfie*와 같이 널리 유행한 신조어가 아닌 중세시대 이후로 존재해온, 대명사 *they*라는 단어였다. 메리엄-웹스터 사전은 단수대명사 *they*를 올해의 단어로 선정했는데, 이 대명사는 널리 통용되면서, 동시에 논란을 일으키고 있다.

단수대명사 *they*가 상승세에 있는 이유에는 두 가지가 있다. 한 가지 이유는 단수대명사 *they*가 모르는 사람을 성 중립적인 방식으로 지칭하는 방식으로, "그 또는 그녀"와 같이 성가신 구문을 사용하는 것에 비해 편리한 방식이기 때문이다. 다른 이유는 단수대명사 *they*가 스스로를 트랜스젠더, 논 바이너리, 혹은 심지어 시스젠더라고 여기는 개인에 의해 사용되기 때문인데, 이들은 성별이 정해진 대명사가 자신들에게 맞지 않는다고 생각한다. 단수대명사 *they*의 사용은 오늘날 사회를 규정하고 있는 가장 근본적인 생각들의 일부에 대항하는 항의의 형태로 작용할 수 있는데, 즉, 단수대명사 *they*가 모든 사람은 명백한 방식으로 남성 혹은 여성으로 식별될 수 있다는 것에 대항한다.

대명사의 용법이 진화하는 것은, 모든 언어가 진화하는 것처럼, 자연스러운 일이지만, 대명사를 어떻게 사용해야 하는지에 대한 규칙이 바뀌기 시작하면 혼란이 야기될 수 있다. 어떤 사람들은 단수대명사 *they*를 사용하는 것을 망설이는데 그 이유는 단수대명사 *they*의 사용이 언어학적으로 혼란을 야기할 수 있기 때문이거나 단수대명사 *they*가 단지 이상하게 들리기 때문이다. 그러나, 이런 종류의 진화가 일어날 수 있음을 증명해주는 역사적인 선례가 있다. 수 세기 전에, 대명사 *you*는 복수의 의미로만 사용되었는데, 개인은 *thee*나 *thou*로 지칭되었다. 점차, 사람들이 *you*를 개개인을 지칭하는 보다 정중한 방법으로 보기 시작했다. 그래서 "you is"라고 말할지 혹은 "you are"라고 말할지에 대한 유사한 혼동이 있는데, 오늘날 사람들은 한 명이나 다수나 똑같이 "you are"라고 언급하여, 소란을 최소화했다. 우리는 단수대명사 *they*가 이런 선례를 따를 것인지 여부를 지켜보아야 할 것이다.

neologism n. 신조어 pronoun n. 대명사
singular adj. 단수형의 cumbersome adj. 성가신
discomfit v. 혼란스럽게 만들다
on the grounds that phr. ~라는 이유로
precedent n. 선례 plural adj. 복수의
fuss n. 야단법석, 소동 follow suit phr. 선례를 따르다

어휘 alter v. 변하다 clear-cut adj. 명백한
at large phr. 전반적인

37 2020 가톨릭대

정답 ③

해석 ① 단수대명사 they의 사용을 멈춰야만 한다!
② 영어 대명사 체계의 악명 높은 불규칙성
③ 단수대명사 they는 왜 사용되며 어떻게 진화할까?
④ 단수대명사 you와 they의 정말 놀라운 역사

해설 지문의 제목을 묻는 문제이다. 첫 번째 지문에서 메리엄-웹스터 사전이 단수대명사 they를 올해의 단어로 선정했다고 하고, 두 번째 지문에서 단수대명사 they를 사용하는 두 가지 이유로, 하나는 단수대명사 they의 사용이 성중립적인 방식이라는 점과, 또 하나는 스스로를 트랜스젠더, 논바이너리, 혹은 심지어 시스젠더라고 여기는 개인이 he 또는 she 사용을 꺼린다는 점을 말했다. 세 번째 지문에서 대명사의 용법의 진화 가능성을 언급하며 대명사 you가 진화한 선례를 말했다. 따라서 이 지문의 제목을 '단수대명사 they는 왜 사용되며 어떻게 진화할까?'라고 표현한 ③번이 정답이다.

어휘 notorious adj. 악명 높은 irregularity n. 불규칙성
astonishing adj. 정말 놀라운, 믿기 힘든

38 2020 가톨릭대

정답 ②

해석 ① 언어는 쉽게 변할 수 없는 규칙적으로 통제된 시스템이다
② 모든 사람은 명백한 방식으로 남성 혹은 여성으로 식별될 수 있다
③ 성에 본질적으로 고정된 사회적 역할은, 오랜 시간에 걸쳐 학습된다
④ 언어는 사회 제도, 전반적인 사회를 형성하거나, 전반적인 사회에 의해 형성된다

해설 지문의 빈칸을 채우는 문제이다. 두 번째 문단의 처음에서 단수명사 they를 사용하는 이유 중의 하나로 일부의 사람들은 "그 또는 그녀"와 같은 특정한 성의 사용을 원치 않기 때문이라고 했고, 빈칸 앞 문장에서 단수대명사 they의 사용은 오늘날 사회를 규정하고 있는 가장 근본적인 생각들의 일부에 대항하는 항의의 형태로 작용할 수 있다고 했으므로, 빈칸에는 성과 관련하여 오늘날 사회를 규정하는 생각에 대한 내용이 나와야 적절하다는 것을 알 수 있다. 따라서 '모든 사람은 명백한 방식으로 남성 혹은 여성으로 식별될 수 있다'라고 한 ②번이 정답이다.

[39-41]

국제어는 모국어가 다른 사람들에 의해 의사소통의 도구로 사용되는 언어이거나 혹은 언어들의 혼합물이다. 국제어는 또한 통상어나, 접촉어, 혹은 세계어로도 알려져 있다. "국제어로서의 영어"라는 용어는 다른 모국어를 사용하는 사람들을 위한 의사소통의 수단으로써 영어를 가르치고, 배우고, 사용하는 것을 말한다. 영어의 지위는 올림픽의 스포츠 경기나, 국제적인 무역, 항공 교통 통제 등에서 의사소통을 위한 세계의 국제어로 채택되었다는 것에서 드러나는 것 같다. 다른 어떠한 언어들과는 다르게, 영어는 5개 모든 대륙에 퍼져 있고, 점차 진정한 세계어가 되어가고 있다. 하지만, Nicholar Ostler에 따르면, 우리는 양육에 의해 퍼져나가는 언어인, 모국어와 부족한 부분을 보충하기 위해 퍼져나가는 언어인, 국제어 사이의 구분선을 그어야 할 필요가 있다. 후자의 것은 의식적으로 당신이 필요하기 때문에 배우는 언어이다. 모국어는 당신이 어쩔 수 없기 때문에 배우는 언어이다. 영어가 이 시기에 세계의 주위로 퍼져나가는 이유는 영어의 국제어로서의 유용성 때문이다. 전 세계에서 사용되고 있는 간소화한 영어인, 글로비시는 영어가 필요한 그동안만큼은 존재할 것이지만, 이것은 모국어로 선택되는 언어가 아니기 때문에, 전형적으로 사람들이 아이들에게 말을 할 때 사용되는 언어는 아니다. 글로비시는 언어가 장기 생존을 위해 무엇보다도 중요한 첫 번째 근거지로 효과적으로 나아가지 못하고 있다.

lingua franca phr. 국제어 mixture n. 혼합물
medium n. 도구 trade language phr. 통상어
be adopt as phr. ~로 채택되다 nurture n. 양육
recruitment n. 보충 consciously adv. 의식적으로
utility n. 유용성 Globish n. 글로비시
simplified adj. 간소화한 typically adv. 전형적으로
crucial adj. 중요한

39 2020 한국외대

정답 ②

해석 ① 모국어의 우월성
② 국제어로서의 영어
③ 어떻게 글로비시를 발전시킬 것인가
④ 언어의 생존

해설 지문의 주제를 묻는 문제이다. 지문 전체적으로 영어가 국제어로 사용되는 이유와 국제어로서의 영어가 갖는 한계점 등의 내용을 다루고 있다. 따라서 이 지문의 주제를 '국제어로서의 영어'라고 표현한 ②번이 정답이다.

어휘 superiority n. 우월성

40 2020 한국외대

정답 ④

해석 ① 그들 나라의 바깥에서 ② 사업적인 목적을 위해
③ 미국 대학에서 ④ 아이들에게

해설 지문의 빈칸을 채우는 문제이다. 지문의 여섯 번째 문장에서 모국어는 아이들을 양육하는 과정을 통해 퍼져나가는 언어라고 했고, 지문이 포함된 문장에서 글로비시는 모국어로 선택되는 언어가 아니라고 했으므로 빈칸에는 양육과 관련된 내용이 들어가야 자연스럽다. 따라서 '아이들에게'라는 의미의 ④번이 정답이다.

41 2020 한국외대

정답 ③

해석 ① 다양한 모국어를 가진 사람들에 의해 사용되는 언어
② 통상어, 접촉어, 그리고 세계어
③ 부모에 의해 무의식적으로 배우는 언어
④ 보충을 통해 퍼져나가는 언어

해설 국제어가 어떻게 정의될 수 없는지를 파악하는 문제이다. 지문의 열 번째 문장에서 국제어로 활용되고 있는 글로비시가 사람들이 그들의 아이들에게 사용하는 언어는 아니라고 했으므로, 국제어는 부모에 의해 무의식적으로 배우는 언어로 정의될 수 없다. 따라서 ③번이 정답이다.

[42-44]

언어를 습득한다는 것의 본질은 여전히 꽤 신비롭다. 아이들은 태어났을 때부터 말하는 것을 배우려는 타고난 성향이 있는 것 같으며, 아이들은 지능적으로 빨리 말할 수 있는 능력이 있다. 연구가들은 아이들이 언어를 쉽게 배울 수 있는 이유에 관한 세 가지 이론을 개발했다. 이 이론들은 언어 습득에 관한 익숙하지 않은 일부 측면을 명확하게 하려고 시도한다. 구체적으로, 연구가들은 발화의 다양한 발달단계 동안 아이들이 보이는 행동을 연구한다. 조건형성 이론, 모방 이론, 그리고 선천성 이론은 모두 이 언어 발달의 독특한 특징을 집중적으로 다루고 있다.
이 주제에 대한 연구가 확장되고 있다는 사실에도 불구하고, 어떠한 하나의 이론으로는 언어 습득의 다양한 특징을 완벽하게 설명하기에 충분하지 않다. 하지만, 조건형성 이론, 모방 이론, 그리고 선천성 이론을 함께 적용할 때, 그것은 아이들의 언어 발달에 관한 미묘함을 이해하는 데 어느 정도 도움을 줄 수 있다.

> acquire v. 습득하다 mysterious adj. 신비로운
> inclination n. 성향, 경향 intelligently adv. 지능적으로
> theory n. 이론 with ease phr. 쉽게
> clarify v. 명확하게 하다 exhibit v. 보이다, 전시하다
> conditioning n. 조건형성 imitation n. 모방
> innateness n. 선천성 concentrate on phr. ~에 집중하다
> distinctive adj. 독특한, 구별되는 characteristic n. 특징
> sufficient adj. 충분한 assistance n. 도움, 지원
> comprehend v. 이해하다 subtlety n. 미묘함

42 2019 한성대

정답 ①

해석 ① 언어 습득을 자세히 설명하려면 한 가지 이론으로 충분하다.
② 아이들은 언어를 힘들이지 않고 배운다.
③ 연구원들은 언어 습득에 관한 연구를 끊임없이 하고 있다.
④ 언어를 습득하는 능력은 여전히 불가사의하다.

해설 지문을 통해 추론할 수 없는 것을 고르는 문제이다. 지문의 두 번째 문단의 첫 번째 문장에서 어떠한 하나의 이론으로는 언어 습득의 다양한 특징을 완벽하게 설명하기에 충분하지 않다고 했으므로, 언어 습득을 자세히 설명하려면 한 가지 이론으로 충분하다는 것은 유추할 수 없다. 따라서 정답은 ①번이다.

오답분석
② Three theories have been developed by researchers as to why children are able to learn a language with ease를 통해 '아이들은 언어를 힘들이지 않고 배운다'는 것을 알 수 있다.
③ despite the fact that research on the subject is expanding을 통해 '연구원들은 언어 습득에 관한 연구를 끊임없이 하고 있다'는 것을 알 수 있다.
④ The nature of acquiring languages is still quite mysterious를 통해 '언어를 습득하는 능력은 여전히 불가사의하다'는 것을 알 수 있다.

어휘 expound v. 자세히 설명하다
effortlessly adv. 힘들이지 않고, 노력하지 않고
cease v. 중단하다 enigmatic adj. 불가사의한

43 2019 한성대

정답 ①

해석 ① 구체적으로 — 하지만
② 구체적으로 — ~에도 불구하고
③ 결과적으로 — 하지만
④ 결과적으로 — ~에도 불구하고

해설 빈칸에 적절한 연결어를 넣는 문제이다. 첫 번째 빈칸의 앞 문장은 세 가지의 이론이 언어 습득의 익숙하지 않은 측면을 분명하게 해준다는 내용이고, 빈칸 뒤 문장은 연구원들이 발화의 발달단계에서 아이들이 보이는 행동을 연구한다는 내용이다. 따라서 구체적인 내용을 설명하는 연결어인 Specifically(구체적으로)가 들어가야 한다. 두 번째 빈칸의 앞 문장은 한 가지 이론으로 언어 습득의 다양한 특징을 완벽하게 설명하기에는 충분하지 않다는 내용이고, 빈칸 뒤 문

장은 세 가지 이론을 함께 적용하면 아이들의 언어 발달을 이해하는 데 도움을 준다는 내용이다. 따라서 역접을 나타내는 연결어인 However(하지만)가 들어가야 한다. 따라서 ① Specifically – However가 정답이다.

어휘 **specifically** adv. 구체적으로, 특히 **however** adv. 하지만
despite prep. ~에도 불구하고
consequently adv. 결과적으로

44 [2019 한성대]

정답 ②

해석 ① 아이들의 신비로운 행동
② 말의 학습
③ 다양한 아동 발달 단계
④ 어른의 성숙함을 부르는 언어 습득

해설 지문의 제목을 묻는 문제이다. 지문의 전체적으로 아이들이 언어를 습득하는 것은 매우 신비로운 일이며 이를 연구하기 위한 세 가지 이론이 있다고 설명하고 있다. 따라서 지문의 제목을 '말의 학습'이라고 표현한 ②번이 정답이다.

어휘 **maturity** n. 성숙함

[45-46]

비유에 대한 글을 살필 때, 비유가 언어적 관습의 연속성 위에 존재한다는 것을 고려하는 것은 도움이 될 수 있다. "관습적인 비유"라는 용어와 "새로운 비유"라는 용어는 학문적 연구에서 "죽은 비유"와 "살아있는 비유"라는 용어를 반영하고 있는 것 같다. 관습적이고, 죽은 비유는 더 이상 인식되지 않지만(예를 들어, 컴퓨터의 메모리가 다 찼다는 비유), 새롭고, 살아있는 비유는 여전히 때때로 놀랄만한 상상적 결합 행위로 인식되고 있다(예를 들어, 우울증은 마음의 암이다)는 견해가 있다. 비유는 전형적으로 "A는 B이다"의 관계로 성문화되는데, 이는 해석 과정에서 B의 어떤 특징이 A로 옮겨지는 관계이다. 비록 비유의 언어에서 "is"라는 단어를 사용하기는 하지만, 여기에서 "is"는 "~이다" 혹은 "~와 동등하다"의 의미가 아니라 "~라고 생각될 수 있다"는 의미로 가장 잘 표현된다.

metaphor n. 비유 **continuum** n. 연속체
linguistic adj. 언어의 **conventionality** n. 관습
mirror v. 반영하다 **contention** n. 견해
perceive v. 인식하다 **imaginative** adj. 상상의
codify v. 성문화하다 **interpretation** n. 해석
characteristic n. 특성 **transpose** v. 이동시키다

45 [2020 한국외대]

정답 ③

해석 ① 언어에서의 광범위한 비유의 사용
② 대중문화 언어를 위한 비유
③ 비유를 분류하고 해석하는 방법
④ 비유의 인식적 작용의 작동 기제

해설 지문의 제목을 묻는 문제이다. 지문의 전반부에서, 학문적 연구에서 비유가 죽은 비유와 살아있는 비유로 구분되고 있다고 설명하고 있고, 지문의 후반부에서 "A is B"로 성문화되는 비유를 어떻게 해석하는지 설명하고 있다. 따라서 지문의 제목을 '비유를 분류하고 해석하는 방법'이라고 표현한 ③번이 정답이다.

어휘 **extensive** adj. 광범위한 **mechanism** n. 기제
cognitive adj. 인식의

46 [2020 한국외대]

정답 ③

해석 ① 관습적인 비유는 독자들에 의해 쉽게 인식된다.
② 죽은 비유는 때때로 독자들에게 충격을 준다.
③ "우울증은 마음의 암이다"는 새로운 비유이다.
④ 비유에서, "is"는 "~와 동등하다"의 의미이다.

해설 지문의 내용과 일치하는 것을 묻는 문제이다. 지문의 세 번째 문장에서 새로운 비유에 대한 예시로 "우울증은 마음의 암이다"라는 표현이 쓰였다. 따라서 ③번이 정답이다.

오답 분석
① 지문의 세 번째 문장에서, 관습적이고, 죽은 비유는 더 이상 인식되지 않는다고 했으므로, 관습적인 비유가 독자들에 의해 쉽게 인식된다는 것은 지문의 내용과 다르다.
② 지문의 세 번째 문장에서, 독자들에게 때때로 충격을 주는 비유는 죽은 비유가 아니라 새롭고, 살아있는 비유라는 것을 알 수 있으므로, 죽은 비유가 때때로 독자들에게 충격을 준다는 것은 지문의 내용과 다르다.
④ 지문의 마지막 문장에서, 비유에서 사용되는 is는 '~와 동등하다' 혹은 '~이다'의 의미가 아니라 '~라고 생각될 수 있다'는 의미로 가장 잘 표현된다고 했으므로, 비유에서, "is"는 "~와 동등하다"의 의미라는 것은 지문의 내용과 다르다.

[47-49]

Gordimer의 소설 "The Moment Before the Gun Went Off"의 중요한 주제는 부계 상속에 관한 것이다.
[C] 그 이야기에는 Willem Van der Vyver에 대한 언급이 여러 번 들어가 있는데, 그는 자신의 존재가 아들의 삶에 그림자를 드리우는 것 같이 보였던 이미 고인이 된 위대한 가장의 모습이다. 지역 사회에서 Marais Van der Vyver의 명성은 직접적으로 그의 아버지의 유산과 관련되는데, 아들은 아버지의 "최고의 농장"을 상속받았고 그의 직원들은 "이전 Van der Vyver"를 위해 일했던 사람들의 자식들이다. 이것은 아들이 사회적, 경제적, 심리적 관계의 전체 네트워크를 상속받았다는 것을 암시한다.

[D] 그리고 중요하게, 우리는 Marais의 아들이자 농장 일꾼인 Lucas를 죽이는 것이 Marais Van der Vyver의 아버지의 총이라는 것을 알게 되는데, 이 폭력의 유산은 할아버지에서 아들로, 마지막으로 비극적이게도 손자까지 전해진다.

[A] Marais Van der Vyver가 자신의 삶에서 중심이 되는 이 사건을 의지로 통제할 수 없었다는 사실은 이 나쁜 짓에 대한 책임이 전적으로 그에게만 있는 것이 아니라는 것을 강조하며, Marais가 그의 다른 상속에 대해 전부 책임이 있지 않을 수도 있다는 것을 암시한다.

[B] 그리고 1948년에 근대 아파르트헤이트 제도를 만들어 냈던 아버지 세대 내 Marais Van der Vyver 자신의 이전 단계는 그 이야기의 세기말 시대 "이전의" 역사적인 "시기"일 수도 있다. 세대를 초월하여 이 죄에 대한 죄책감을 연장함으로써, Gordimer는 Lucas의 운명을 통해 도덕적으로 타락한 모든 사회가 연루되었음을 보여준다.

theme n. 주제, 테마 **paternal** adj. 부계의
inheritance n. 상속, 유산 **reference to** phr. ~에의 언급
the late phr. 고인이 된
patriarchal adj. 가장의, 가부장제의 **figure** n. 모습, 형상
presence n. 존재 **overshadow** v. 그림자를 드리우다
prominence n. 명성, 중요성 **community** n. 지역 사회
legacy n. 유산 **inherit** v. 상속받다 **entire** adj. 전체의
psychological adj. 심리적인 **relationship** n. 관계
significantly adv. 중요하게
tragically adv. 비극적으로, 비참하게 **grandson** n. 손자
volitional adj. 의지에 의한, 결단력이 있는
pivotal adj. 중심이 되는 **misdeed** n. 악행, 비행
reside v. 있다 **exclusively** adv. 전적으로, 독점적으로
inheritance n. 유산, 상속 **prehistory** n. 전 단계, 과정
apartheid n. 아파르트헤이트(예전 남아프리카공화국의 인종 차별정책) **fin-de-siecle** adj. (19세기의) 세기말의
epoch n. 시대, 세 **extend** v. 연장하다
guilt n. 죄책감 **offense** n. 죄, 공격
implicate v. (나쁜 것의) 원인임을 보여주다
morally adv. 도덕적으로 **corrupt** adj. 타락한, 부패한
fate n. 운명

47 2019 국민대

정답 ④

해설 implicate(연루시키다)와 비슷한 의미를 가진 어휘를 묻고 있다. ①번 denote는 '~을 나타내다', ②번 demolish는 '파괴하다, 철거하다', ③번 alleviate는 '경감하다, 완화하다', ④번 incriminate는 '(남에게) 죄를 씌우다, 연루시키다'라는 의미이다. 따라서 ④번이 정답이다.

48 2019 국민대

정답 ③

해설 주어진 지문 다음에 이어질 [A], [B], [C], [D]의 적절한 순서를 파악하는 문제이다. 주어진 지문은 Gordimer의 소설의 주제가 부계 상속에 관한 것이라는 내용이므로, 소설 속 구체적인 부계 상속을 설명하는 [C]가 먼저 와야 한다. 그다음에 [D]에서 부계 상속의 또 다른 예시로 폭력에 대해 설명하고, 그다음에 [A]에서 이 폭력 사건에 대한 책임을 설명하고, 마지막으로 [B]에서 세대를 초월한 죄에 대한 죄책감에 대해 설명하는 것이 자연스럽다. 따라서 주어진 지문 다음에 이어질 순서는 ③ [C] — [D] — [A] — [B]다.

49 2019 국민대

정답 ③

해석 ① Gordimer는 독자가 Marais를 용서하도록 간청한다.
② Marais는 자신의 사회 제도에 들어가 있는 불공평을 비판한다.
③ Gordimer는 타락한 사회가 Marais의 살인에 어느 정도는 책임이 있다는 것을 시사한다.
④ Marais는 지역 사회의 의견에 대한 합의를 나타내는 공동 의식을 분명히 표현한다.

해설 지문의 내용과 일치하는 것을 묻는 문제이다. 지문의 중간에서 By extending the guilt ~, Gordimer ~ morally corrupt society in the fate of Lucas의 내용을 통해 Gordimer는 타락한 사회가 Marais의 살인에 어느 정도는 책임이 있다는 것을 시사한다는 것을 알 수 있다. 따라서 ③번이 지문의 내용과 일치한다.

오답분석 ① 지문의 초반에서 Marais에게 폭력 사건에 대해 전적으로 책임이 있지 않으며, 다른 상속에 대해서도 전부 책임이 있지 않을 수 있다고는 했지만, Gordimer는 독자가 Marais를 용서하도록 간청하는지는 알 수 없다.
② 지문의 중간에서 아버지 세대에서 아파르트헤이트(예전 남아프리카공화국의 인종 차별정책)를 만들어 냈다고는 했지만, Marais는 자신의 사회 제도에 들어가 있는 불공평을 비판하는지는 알 수 없다.
④ 지문의 중간에서 세대를 초월하여 죄에 대한 죄책감을 연장함으로써 Gordimer는 Lucas의 운명을 통해 도덕적으로 타락한 모든 사회가 원인임을 보여준다고는 했지만, Marais는 지역 사회의 의견에 대한 합의를 나타내는 공동 의식을 분명히 표현하는지는 알 수 없다.

어휘 **implore** v. 간청하다, 애원하다
criticize v. 비판하다, 비평하다 **inequity** n. 불공평
built into phr. ~에 들어가 있는 **murder** n. 살인
articulate v. 분명히 표현하다, 설명하다
communal adj. 공동의 **consciousness** n. 의식
represent v. 나타내다 **consensus** n. 합의, 의견 일치

[50-52]

AAVE(African American Vernacular English)는 몇몇 아프리카계 미국인 공동체 사이에서 사용되는 영어의 한 종류를 지칭한다. AAVE의 역사는 대서양을 횡단했던 노예 거래에서 시작되었다. 아프리카인들은 아프리카 대륙의 여러 지역에서 데려왔기 때문에, 그들은 다양하게 많은 언어를 사용할 수밖에 없었다. 미국의 농장에서, 노예들은 피진 영어의 한 갈래를 활용해 서로 의사소통하게 되었다. 그리고 여러 세대가 지나가면서, 노예들이 사용한 이 피진 영어의 특징은 고착화되어, 이것이 새로운 영어 방언의 등장으로 이어졌다.

이 방언의 많은 특징은 아프리카의 언어에서 유래했다. 일부 문법적인 구조는 서아프리카의 언어에서 온 것으로 추적될 수 있다. 예컨대, AAVE의 많은 동사는 특정한 아프리카 언어에서 사용되는 방식으로 사용된다. 가령, AAVE에서 *be*는 습관적인 행위를 지칭하기 위해 사용될 수 있다. 따라서 이 언어를 사용하는 이가 "He be playing guitar"라는 말을 한다면, 이것은 "그는 기타를 자주 혹은 항상 연주한다"라는 의미이다. AAVE는 종종 아프리카계 미국인의 문학에서 문화적인 유산으로 찬양받는다. 또한, 아프리카계 미국인 목사나 연예인들은 AAVE를 극적인 의도를 위해 활용한다. 그런데도, 많은 사람이 AAVE를 교육받지 못했다는 것의 증거라고 생각하고 있다. 이러한 이유로, AAVE를 사용하는 것은 사회 경제적인 이동에 장애가 될 수 있다. 다시 말해서, 이 언어를 사용하는 것은 AAVE를 사용하는 화자가 사회적으로 높은 위치를 차지하는 것을 막을 가능성이 있다.

vernacular n. 말, 토착어 **refer to** phr. 지칭하다
transatlantic adj. 대서양 횡단의 **plantation** n. 농장
pidgin English phr. 피진 영어 **dialect** n. 방언
grammatical adj. 문법적인 **trace** v. 추적하다
habitual adj. 습관적인 **celebrate** v. 찬양하다
heritage n. 유산 **minister** n. 목사
impediment n. 장애물
socioeconomic adj. 사회 경제적인 **mobility** n. 이동

50 2020 한성대

정답 ①

해석 ① 노예들은 그들이 미국에 도착했을 때 하나의 아프리카 언어만을 활용해 의사소통했다.
② AAVE는 피진 영어의 한 종류에서부터 발전했다.
③ 몇몇 아프리카계 미국인들은 AAVE를 그들의 자랑스러운 전통이라고 생각한다.
④ AAVE를 사용하는 화자는 사회 계층을 올라가기에 어려움을 겪을 수 있다.

해설 지문의 내용과 일치하지 않는 것을 묻는 문제이다. 지문의 첫 번째 문단에서, 아프리카인들이 아프리카 대륙의 여러 지역에서 데려와 졌기 때문에, 그들은 다양하고 많은 언어를 사용할 수밖에 없다고 했으므로, 노예들이 미국에 도착했을 때 하나의 아프리카 언어를 활용해 의사소통했다는 것은 지문의 내용과 다르다. 따라서 ①번이 정답이다.

오답분석 ② 지문의 첫 번째 문단에서, 미국 농장에서 노예들이 처음 사용하기 시작한 것은 피진 영어의 한 종류였고, 이 언어의 특징이 고착화되면서 새로운 영어의 방언이 등장했다고 했으므로, AAVE가 피진 영어의 한 종류에서부터 발전했다는 것은 지문의 내용과 일치한다.
③ 지문의 두 번째 문단에서, AAVE가 종종 아프리카계 미국 문학에서 문화적 유산으로 찬양받는다고 했으므로, 몇몇 아프리카계 미국인들은 AAVE를 그들의 자랑스러운 전통이라고 생각한다는 것은 지문의 내용과 일치한다.
④ 지문의 마지막에서, 많은 사람이 AAVE를 교육받지 못한 증거로 간주한다고 했고, 이러한 이유로 AAVE가 AAVE를 사용하는 화자가 사회 경제적으로 이동하는 데 걸림돌이 될 수 있다고 했으므로, AAVE를 사용하는 화자는 사회 계층을 올라가기에 어려움을 겪을 수 있다는 것은 지문의 내용과 일치한다.

어휘 **social ladder** phr. 사회 계층

51 2020 한성대

정답 ③

해석 ① 그러나   ② 그렇지 않으면
③ 다시 말해서   ④ 그럼에도 불구하고

해설 빈칸에 적절한 연결어를 넣는 문제이다. 빈칸 앞부분은 AAVE를 사용하는 것은 사회 경제적인 이동에 장애가 될 수 있다는 내용이고, 빈칸 뒤 문장은 AAVE를 사용하는 것은 화자가 사회적으로 높은 위치를 차지하는 것을 막을 가능성이 있다는 내용이다. 따라서 내용을 보충하는 연결어인 ③ in other words(다시 말해서)가 정답이다.

52 2020 한성대

정답 ①

해석 ① AAVE는 부분적으로 아프리카 언어에서 파생되었다.
② AAVE는 아프리카계 미국인 목사에 의해 만들어졌다.
③ AAVE는 회화를 할 때만 쓰이며, 문학적인 글에서는 사용되지 않는다.
④ AAVE의 모든 문법적 구조는 동아프리카 언어에서 온 것으로 추적될 수 있다.

해설 지문의 내용과 일치하는 것을 묻는 문제이다. 지문의 두 번째 문단에서 AAVE의 많은 특징이 아프리카 언어에서 유래했다고 했으므로, AAVE가 부분적으로 아프리카 언어에서 파생되었다는 것은 지문의 내용과 일치한다. 따라서 ①번이 정답이다.

오답분석 ② 지문의 첫 번째 문단에서, AAVE는 미국으로 건너온 노예들이 사용하던 피진 영어의 한 갈래의 특징이 굳어지면서 만들어졌다고 했으므로, AAVE가 아프리카계 미국인 목사에 의해 만들어졌다는 것은 지문의 내용과 다르다.

③ 지문의 마지막 문단에서, AAVE가 종종 아프리카계 미국 문학에서 그들만의 문화적 유산으로 찬양받고 있다고 했으므로, AAVE가 회화에서만 쓰이고, 문학적인 글에서는 사용되지 않는다는 것은 지문의 내용과 다르다.

④ 지문의 두 번째 문단에서, AAVE의 일부 문법적인 구조가 서아프리카언어에서 유래되었다고 했으므로, AAVE의 모든 문법적 구조가 동아프리카 언어에서 온 것으로 추적될 수 있다는 것은 지문의 내용과 다르다.

어휘 partially adv. 부분적으로

[53-56]

[A] 신조어란 최근에 만들어진 단어, 또는 존재하는 단어나 구에 새로운 의미가 부여된 것이다. 신조어는 여러 가지 방법으로 만들어지는데, 언론과 관련해서는 특히 세 가지가 관련이 있다. 첫째는, 접두사나 접미사의 추가를 통해 새로운 단어가 만들어진다. 언론적 담화에서 이것의 가장 널리 알려진 예는 아마도 스캔들을 지명하기 위해 접미사로 "~게이트"라는 말을 사용하는 것이다. (A) 워터게이트 사건을 시작해, 이란게이트, 르윈스키게이트, 그리고 한지게이트가 있었는데, 그것의 결과는 워터게이트 사건 자체를 하찮아 보이게 만들게 되었다.

[B] 둘째로, 신조어는 문법적 기능을 바꾸는 것을 통하거나(Google과 eBay를 동사로 사용) 새로운 완곡한 의미를 만들어 내는 것으로 단어의 의미를 바꾸어 만들어질 수 있다. (B) <u>이러한 종류의 신조어들의 예는 다양한데, 특히 전쟁을 보도하는 것에 관해 그렇다.</u> engage(죽이다), theater(전장), 그리고 friendly fire(자신의 군대에게 살해당함)와 같은 완곡어법들은 전쟁 중에 사람들을 죽이던 불편한 현실의 배경을 설명하고자 전시에 의식적으로 사용되었다. (C)

[C] 셋째로, 신조어는 존재하는 두 단어를 섞어 만들 수 있다(smog = smoke + fog). (D) 이것은 때때로 혼성어라고 불리는데, 신문 중에서도 타블로이드 신문만이 이런 방법으로 새로운 단어를 만드는 경향이 있다. (E) 예를 들어, 어떤 영국의 미성년 유명인사가 입은 디자이너의 의상에 관한 기사는 aristocracy(귀족)와 chav(유행 추종자)를 결합하여 Aristochavs라는 단어로 헤드라인을 장식했는데, 그 자체가 백인 노동자 계급의 청년에게 적용되는, 미국에서의 별칭인 "가난한 백인"과 비슷한 <u>폄하하는</u> 신조어였다. 후에 같은 기사에서, 그들은 그 혼성어를 거꾸로 뒤집어 그들이 묘사한 열 명의 여성에게 영국의 chavistocracy라는 꼬리표를 붙였다. 어느 쪽의 혼성어도 업신여기고 있긴 하지만, 그 기사는 또한 더 넓은 계층적 위치도 가지고 있다.

[D] 우리는 중산층이 계층적 위치를 달성하고 유지하기 위해 반드시 열심히 일해야 한다는 것을 기억하는 것이 당연하다. 중산층의 일은 중산층으로 알아볼 수 있는 생활방식을 (재)창조하는 것을 포함한다. 이것은 "중산층"의 징조가 노동자 계급에 의해 쉽게 도용되고 동화되기 때문에 어려운 일이다. 여기서, 신문은 확인된 미성년 유명인사들을 그들의 신문에 싣고 있는데, 그들의 비싼 옷에도 불구하고, 그들은 유행을 추종하는, 백인 노동자 계급이다. 이보다 더하게, 묘사된 사람들에게 aristochavs라는 꼬리표를 붙임으로써, 신문은 그들이 가장 가난한 백인이라는 것을 암시한다. 그렇게 해서, 신문은 동시에 중산층의 생활양식을 구성하는 것과 병행하여 그들이 대상으로 하는 노동자 계급의 독자를 계속하여 유지하고 이 중산층의 생활양식(비싼 옷)의 의미를 노동자 계급에 도용당하는 것으로부터 지키려고 시도한다.

---

neologism n. 신조어 coin v. (단어를) 만들다
assign v. 부여하다 journalism n. 언론
relevance n. 관련 prefix n. 접두사 suffix n. 접미사
discourse n. 담화 designate v. 지명하다
trivialize v. 하찮게 만들다 grammatical adj. 문법적인
euphemistic adj. 완곡어법의 battlefield n. 전장
consciously adv. 의식적으로 wartime n. 전시
blend v. 섞다 portmanteau n. 혼성어
tabloid n. 타블로이드(가십거리나 오락적 소재를 다루는 신문)
minor adj. 미성년의 derogatory adj. 폄하하는
epithet n. 별칭 reverse v. 뒤집다 belittle v. 업신여기다
do well to phr. ~하는 것이 당연하다
recognizably adv. 알아볼 수 있게 tricky adj. 어려운
appropriate v. 도용하다 assimilate v. 동화시키다
depict v. 묘사하다 imply v. 암시하다
simultaneously adv. 동시에 attempt v. 시도하다
abreast of phr. ~와 병행하여 constitute v. 구성하다
signifier n. 의미, 기표

53 [2020 아주대]

정답 ②

해설 지문의 흐름상 주어진 문장이 들어가기에 가장 적절한 위치를 고르는 문제이다. (B)의 뒤 문장에서 단어 engage, theater, friendly fire가 전쟁 중에 사람들이 죽는 상황의 배경을 완곡하게 표현하기 위해 사용되었다고 했으므로, (B) 자리에 주어진 문장 '이러한 종류의 신조어들의 예는 다양한데, 특히 전쟁을 보도하는 것에 관해 그렇다'가 들어가야 글의 흐름이 자연스럽게 연결된다. 따라서 ②번이 정답이다.

어휘 legion adj. 다양한

54 [2020 아주대]

정답 ①

해석 ① 중산층은 자신들만의 생활양식을 만들기 위해 노력했다.
② 게이트라는 단어를 접미사로 사용하는 것은 워터게이트 사건 자체의 가치를 낮추었다.
③ 신문들은 빈번하게 aristochavs와 chavistocracy와 같은 용어를 개발함으로써 중산층을 옹호한다.

④ 중산층임을 유지하는 것은 노동자 계급이 쉽게 따라 할 수 있기 때문에 힘들다.
⑤ 신문 중에 타블로이드만이 새로운 단어를 만드는 방법으로 혼합을 사용한다.

해설 지문의 내용과 일치하지 않는 것을 묻는 문제이다. ①번의 키워드인 lifestyle(생활양식)과 관련된 지문의 a middle-class lifestyle(중산층의 생활양식) 주변에서 중산층의 일은 중산층으로 알아볼 수 있는 생활방식을 (재)창조하는 것을 포함한다고는 했지만, 중산층은 자신들만의 생활양식을 만들기 위해 노력했다는 것은 알 수 없다. 따라서 ①번이 지문의 내용과 일치하지 않는다.

오답 분석
② the result of which has been to trivialize the Watergate scandal itself를 통해 '게이트라는 단어를 접미사로 사용하는 것은 워터게이트 사건 자체의 가치를 낮추었다'라는 것을 알 수 있다.
③ to protect the signifiers of this middle-class lifestyle (expensive fashion) from being appropriated by the working class를 통해 '신문들은 빈번하게 aristochavs와 chavistocracy와 같은 용어를 개발함으로써 중산층을 옹호한다'는 것을 알 수 있다.
④ This is tricky business because the signs of "middle classness" are easily appropriated를 통해 '중산층임을 유지하는 것은 노동자 계급이 쉽게 따라 할 수 있기 때문에 힘들다'는 것을 알 수 있다.
⑤ only tabloids tend to coin new words in this way를 통해 '신문 중에 타블로이드판만이 새로운 단어를 만드는 방법으로 혼합을 사용한다'는 것을 알 수 있다.

어휘 devalue v. 가치를 낮추다   uphold v. 옹호하다
challenging adj. 힘드는   utilize v. 사용하다

---

55 [2020 아주대]

정답 ①

해석 ① 경멸적인   ② 토착의
③ 약화된   ④ 미약한
⑤ 공정한

해설 밑줄 친 derogatory를 대신할 수 있는 동의어를 고르는 문제이다. derogatory는 '폄하하는'이라는 의미이다. 따라서 '경멸적인'을 의미하는 ①번 pejorative가 정답이다.

---

56 [2020 아주대]

정답 ③

해석 (a) 중산층의 독자들의 관심을 자극적인 용어로 끌기 위해
(b) 신문사들 사이의 격렬한 경쟁에서 살아남기 위한 참신한 표현들을 만들기 위해
(c) 노동자 계급이 중산층의 생활양식의 징조를 채택하는 것을 막기 위해
(d) 노동자 계급 독자들이 중산층의 생활양식을 계속 알도록 하기 만들기 위해
(e) 중산층의 생활양식의 상징을 도용하기 위해

해설 문단 [D]를 바탕으로 비싼 옷을 입고 있는 미성년 유명인사를 aristochavs라고 부를 때 신문이 목표하는 두 가지가 무엇인지를 파악하는 문제이다. 지문 마지막에서 신문은 동시에 중산층의 생활양식을 구성하는 것과 병행하여 그들이 대상으로 하는 노동자 계급의 독자를 계속하여 유지하고 이 중산층의 생활양식(비싼 옷)의 의미를 노동자 계급에 도용당하는 것으로부터 지키려고 시도한다고 했으므로, (c)의 '노동자 계급이 중산층의 생활양식의 징조를 채택하는 것을 막'는 것, 그리고 (d)의 '노동자 계급 독자들이 중산층의 생활양식을 계속 알도록 하'는 것의 두 가지가 목표임을 알 수 있다. 따라서 정답은 ③번이다.

어휘 sensational adj. 자극적인, 관심을 끄는   novel adj. 참신한
fierce adj. 격렬한   competition n. 경쟁
adopt v. 채택하다

02 역사

01-57
문제집 p.38

01 ①	02 ①	03 ③	04 ③	05 ④
06 ③	07 ②	08 ④	09 ①	10 ①
11 ④	12 ③	13 ③	14 ①	15 ②
16 ④	17 ②	18 ①	19 ②	20 ①
21 ③	22 ④	23 ④	24 ③	25 ①
26 ③	27 ②	28 ②	29 ③	30 ②
31 ①	32 ④	33 ②	34 ②	35 ④
36 ②	37 ③	38 ①	39 ③	40 ②
41 ①	42 ①	43 ③	44 ②	45 ②
46 ③	47 ①	48 ③	49 ②	50 ④
51 ②	52 ④	53 ①	54 ④	55 ③
56 ②	57 ⑤			

01 2019 가천대

정답 ①

해석 1791년, 올랑프 드 구주는 "여성과 여성 시민의 권리 선언"을 저술하였는데, 그 안에서 그녀는 프랑스의 여성이 투표권을 포함하여 프랑스 남성과 같은 권리를 받아야 한다고 요구했다. 정부의 대응은 어땠을까? 그녀를 단두대에 처형시켜버렸다. 그녀에게는 "국가의 단결을 훼손해가며 여성의 미덕을 도외시한 반역자"라는 공식적인 혐의가 붙었다. 그녀의 1791년 선언은 오늘날 많은 사람에 의해 기억되는 적절한 구절을 포함하고 있다. "여성에게 처형대에 올라갈 권리가 있다면, 연설대에 올라갈 권리도 반드시 동등하게 가지고 있어야 할 것이다."
① 연설대   ② 교수대
③ 받침대   ④ 다락

해설 지문의 빈칸을 채우는 문제이다. 지문의 전체에서 올랑프 드 구주가 프랑스의 여성도 남성과 동일하게 투표권과 같은 권리를 받아야 한다는 것을 요구했다고 설명하고 있으므로, 빈칸에는 투표권과 같은 정치적인 것을 상징하는 내용이 나와야 적절하다는 것을 알 수 있다. 따라서 '연설대'라고 한 ①번이 정답이다.

어휘 declaration n. 선언   execution n. 처형
guillotine n. 단두대   charge n. 혐의, 기소
label v. (꼬리표를) 붙이다   traitor n. 반역자, 배반자
neglect v. 도외시하다, 등한하다   virtue n. 미덕
unity n. 단결, 일치   apt adj. 적절한   mount v. 오르다
scaffold n. 처형대   equally adv. 동등하게
podium n. 연설대   gallow n. 교수대   rack n. 받침대
attic n. 다락

[02-03]

거의 100년 전에 시작되었던 제1차 세계 대전은 자체적으로 생체 공학적인 사람들을 만들어 냈다. 이전 전쟁들에서는, 심하게 부상을 입은 군인들은 흔히 괴저와 감염으로 죽었다. 더 나아진 수술 덕분에, 많은 사람들이 이제 살아남았다. 독일 쪽에서만, 2백만 명의 사상자가 있었고, 사상자 중 64퍼센트는 팔다리에 부상을 입었다. 약 6만 7천 명은 팔다리 절단 수술을 받은 사람이었다. 전쟁에 참여했던 모든 국가에서 흔히 "전쟁 장애인"이라고 일컬어지는 세대가 연금과 복지 시스템에 불길하게 등장했고, 많은 정부 관료, 군 지도자와 민간인들은 그들의 장기적인 운명을 걱정하게 되었다. 하나의 해결책은 불구가 된 군인들을 노동 인구로 돌려보내는 것이었다.

bionic adj. 생체 공학적인   severely adv. 심하게
succumb v. (병·부상·노령 등으로) 죽다, 쓰러지다
gangrene n. 괴저   infection n. 감염, 전염병
surgery n. 수술   casualty n. 사상자   limb n. 팔다리, 사지
amputee n. 팔다리 절단 수술을 받은 사람
generation n. 세대
loom over phr. (불길하게) 다가오다, 떠오르다
ominously adv. 불길하게, 기분 나쁘게   pension n. 연금
welfare n. 복지, 행복   bureaucrat n. (정부) 관료
civilian n. 시민   fate n. 운명   mutilate v. 불구로 만들다
workforce n. 노동 인구, 노동력

02 2019 성균관대

정답 ①

해석 ① 전쟁 장애인
② 전쟁 참전 용사
③ 장애인
④ 전쟁 신경증 환자
⑤ 정신 이상자

해설 지문의 빈칸을 채우는 문제이다. 지문의 중반에서 독일 쪽에서만, 2백만 명의 사상자가 있었고, 사상자 중 64퍼센트는 팔다리에 부상을 입었으며, 약 6만 7천 명은 팔다리 절단 수술을 받은 사람이었다고 했으므로, 빈칸에는 전쟁 때문에 팔다리 절단 수술을 받은 사람에 대한 내용이 나와야 적절하다는 것을 알 수 있다. 따라서 '전쟁 장애인'이라고 한 ①번이 정답이다.

어휘 cripple n. 신체장애인, 불구자
veteran n. 참전 용사, 베테랑   disabled adj. 장애를 가진
neurotic n. 신경증 환자   insane adj. 정신 이상의

03 2019 성균관대

정답 ③

해석
① 수술의 의학적 진보
② 복지 정책에서의 놀랄 만한 변화
③ 보철 팔다리 기술에서의 진보
④ 전쟁 참전 용사의 장기적인 운명
⑤ 정착된 사회 시스템에 반대하는 여성들의 저항

해설 지문을 통해 제1차 세계 대전이 이끈 것에 대해 추론할 수 있는 것을 고르는 문제이다. 첫 문장에서 제1차 세계 대전은 자체적으로 생체 공학적인 사람들을 만들어 냈다고 했고, 다섯 번째 문장에서 팔다리 절단 수술을 받은 사람을 언급하고 있으므로, 제1차 세계 대전이 보철 팔다리 기술에서의 진보를 이끌었다는 것을 추론할 수 있다. 따라서 ③번이 정답이다.

오답분석
① 세 번째 문장에서 더 나아진 수술 덕분에, 많은 사람들이 이제 살아남았다고는 했지만, 제1차 세계 대전이 수술의 의학적 진보를 이끌었는지는 추론할 수 없다.
② 여섯 번째 문장에서 전쟁에 참여했던 모든 국가에서 흔히 "전쟁 장애인"이라고 일컬어지는 세대가 연금과 복지 시스템에 불길하게 등장했다고는 했지만, 제1차 세계 대전이 복지 정책에서의 놀랄 만한 변화를 이끌었는지는 추론할 수 없다.
④ 여섯 번째 문장에서 많은 정부 관료, 군 지도자와 민간인들은 그들의 장기적인 운명을 걱정하게 되었다고는 했지만, 제1차 세계 대전이 전쟁 참전 용사의 장기적인 운명을 이끌었는지는 추론할 수 없다.
⑤ 정착된 사회 시스템에 반대하는 여성들의 저항에 대해서는 언급되지 않았다.

어휘 remarkable adj. 놀랄 만한 prosthetic adj. 보철의
revolt n. 저항, 반란 established adj. 정착된

[04-06]

스페인 정복자의 신대륙 도착은 영구히 그리고 철저하게 토착 인구의 문화와 삶을 새로운 형태로 만들었고, 미대륙의 가장 위대한 두 문명, 잉카와 마야의 소멸을 이끌었는데, 이는 그 유럽인들이 그들을 발견한 지 얼마 지나지 않아서였다. 그들은 사라진 주민들에 대한 극히 적은 기록들과 함께 주목할 만한 도시들을 남겼고, 이것이 고고학자들로 하여금 그 사라진 문명들에 대해 알아내기 위한 시도로써 남아있는 것들을 종합하게 만들었다.

수집되어온 정보의 대다수가 그들 도시의 유적에서 나왔는데, 그 도시들은 시간의 경과를 견뎌내 왔고 이는 그들이 주로 돌을 가지고 작업했기 때문이었다. 그러나, 양측이 똑같은 재료를 사용하기는 했지만, 그들은 도시를 매우 다른 식으로 주변 환경과 통합시켰다. 잉카에서, 그들의 기술은 주변의 물체를 조각하거나 농지나 정원의 용도로 도시에 단구를 포함함으로써 그들이 그것을 거의 균일하게 완수할 수 있도록 했다. 그에 비해, 마야의 도시 계획은 거의 무계획적으로 보인다. 잉카 대규모의 도로 설비와 체계적인 배치는 없지만, 마야의 도시들은 대부분의 건물들을 포함하는 중앙의 광장으로부터 보다 유기적으로 성장하는 경향이 있었다.

conquistador n. 정복자 **permanently** adv. 영구히
drastically adv. 철저하게
reshape v. 새로운 형태로 만들다
indigenous population phr. 토착 인구
disappearance n. 소멸 **remarkable** adj. 주목할 만한
vanished adj. 사라진 **inhabitant** n. 주민
archaeologist n. 고고학자 **piece together** phr. 종합하다
collect v. 수집하다 **withstand** v. 견뎌내다
primarily adv. 주로 **integrate** v. 통합시키다
seamlessly adv. 균일하게 **sculpt** v. 조각하다
terrace n. 단구(계단형 지형) **extensive** adj. 광범위한
organically adv. 유기적으로 **plaza** n. 광장

---

04 2021 경희대

정답 ③

해석
① 잉카와 마야의 도시들의 모든 흔적이 사라졌다.
② 미 대륙의 가장 위대한 두 개의 문명, 잉카와 마야는, 스페인 정복자의 도착 이전에 사라졌다.
③ 잉카와 마야 모두 그들의 도시를 짓기 위해 돌을 사용했다.
④ 잉카와 마야의 도시들은 유사한 방식으로 그들의 도시를 주변 환경과 통합시켰다.
⑤ 고고학자들이 잉카와 마야 문명에 대해 더 알아내는 것은 불가능하다.

해설 지문을 통해 추론할 수 있는 것을 고르는 문제이다. ③번 보기의 키워드인 'stone(돌)'이 등장한 지문의 두 번째 단락의 첫 문장을 통해 잉카와 마야 모두 그들의 도시를 짓기 위해 돌을 사용했다는 것을 추론할 수 있다. 따라서 정답은 ③번이다.

오답분석
① 지문의 중간에서 수집되어온 정보의 대다수가 그들 도시의 유적에서 나왔다고 했으므로, 잉카와 마야의 도시들의 모든 흔적이 사라졌다는 것은 잘못된 추론이다.
② 첫 번째 단락에 그 유럽인들이 그들(잉카와 마야 문명)을 발견한 지 얼마 지나지 않아서 잉카와 마야가 소멸되었다는 내용이 있으므로, 잉카와 마야가 스페인 정복자의 도착 이전에 사라졌다는 것은 잘못된 추론이다.
④ 두 번째 단락에서 잉카와 마야 문명이 같은 재료를 사용하기는 했지만, 그들의 도시를 매우 다른 식으로 주변 환경과 통합시켰다고 했으므로, 잉카와 마야 문명이 유사한 방식으로 그들의 도시를 주변 환경과 통합시켰다는 것은 잘못된 추론이다.
⑤ 첫 번째 단락에서, 사라진 주민들에 대한 기록이 극히 적었다고는 했지만, 고고학자들이 잉카와 마야 문명에 대해 더 알아내는 것이 불가능한지는 추론할 수 없다.

05 [2021 경희대]

정답 ④

해석 ① 유적 ② 스페인 정복자들
③ 고고학자들 ④ 잉카와 마야
⑤ 유럽인들

해설 두 번째 단락에서 밑줄 친 they가 지칭하고 있는 대상이 무엇인지를 묻는 문제이다. 주어진 지문이 잉카와 마야가 남긴 도시들에 관한 내용이고, 밑줄 친 they를 포함하는 문장이 '그러나, 양측이 똑같은 재료를 사용하기는 했지만, 그들은 도시를 매우 다른 식으로 주변 환경과 통합시켰다'라는 의미이므로 they가 잉카와 마야를 지칭하고 있음을 알 수 있다. 따라서 ④번이 정답이다.

06 [2021 경희대]

정답 ③

해설 주어진 지문에서 '무계획적인'이라는 의미로 사용된 haphazard의 동의어를 묻는 문제이다. ①번 limited는 '제한된', ②번 perpendicular는 '직각의', ③번 random은 '무계획적인', ④번 meticulous는 '꼼꼼한', ⑤번 conventional은 '관습적인'이라는 의미이므로, ③번이 정답이다.

[07-10]

1100년에, 영국의 헨리 1세는 채무자와 채권자 사이에서 반으로 쪼갠 나무 막대기인 부신을 사용하는 방법으로 세금을 납부할 수 있다는 포고령을 내렸다. 총금액은 다양한 크기의 등급이 새겨지고 고심해서 미리 정해진 주판으로 볼 수 있었다. 다음 7세기 동안, 나무는 돈의 대용품처럼 유통되었고, 영국인들은 심지어 부신을 바탕으로 하는 정교한 정부 자금 조달 체계를 발달시켰다.

언뜻 보기에 현대의 비트코인 현상에 관해서라면, 좀 더 쉽게 이해할 수 있을 것이다. 비트코인 지지자들은 어디에나 있다. 비트코인 지지자들은 선택권이 주어진다면 사람들이 최고 가치를 계속 유지하는 그 통화(비트코인)를 선택할 것이고 잘못된 정책 입안자들의 변덕에 휘둘리지 않을 것이라는 점에 주목했던 오스트리아의 경제학자인 Friedrich Hayek의 주장을 언급한다.

분명히, 전통적인 통화 제도에서의 신뢰가 뒤흔들린 시대에서는, 비트코인의 한정된 공급과 인간의 간섭으로부터의 자유가 강력한 자산이다. 비트코인은 흥미로운 지적 실험이었던 것을 생활 경제로 바꾸어 놓았다. 하지만 역사는 지속 가능한 통화를 만들어 내기에는 충분하지 않다는 것을 보여준다. 이유는 단순하다. 돈은 암호화하는 돈의 지위, 사회적 순응, 인간 행동과 같은 사회적 상호 작용 속에서 여러 언어를 하는 사람들을 통해 돈 자체의 의미를 계속 유지한다. 사회적 상호 작용에서 생긴 신뢰가 없다면, 교환 수단은 존재할 수 없다. 두 나라가 무역을 하는 동안에도, 교환되는 통화는 믿을 수 있고 교환할 수 있어야 한다. 국가들이 많은 거래를 위해 자국 통화보다 미국 달러를 사용하는 이유이다.

---

edict n. 포고령, 칙령 tally n. 부신(나무에 금액을 새기고 그것을 둘로 갈라 후일의 증거로 쌍방이 하나씩 가진 것)
cleaved adj. 쪼개진 debtor n. 채무자
creditor n. 채권자 represent v. 보여주다, 나타내다
abacus n. 주판 notch n. 등급, 단계
proxy n. 대용품, 대리인 sophisticated adj. 정교한, 복잡한
when it comes to phr. ~에 관해서라면, ~에 관한 한
phenomenon n. 현상 errant adj. 잘못된
currency n. 통화 retain v. 계속 유지하다
policymaker n. 정책 monetary adj. 통화의
interference n. 간섭 asset n. 자산
intellectual adj. 지적인
polyglot n. 여러 나라 말을 아는 사람
interaction n. 상호 작용 conformity n. 순응
encode v. 암호화하다
medium of exchange phr. 교환 수단, 화폐
transaction n. 거래

07 [2021 세종대]

정답 ②

해석 ① 건축 팸플릿 ② 금융 잡지
③ 외교 정책에 관한 책자 ④ 부동산 평가

해설 지문의 종류를 묻는 문제이다. 지문의 첫 번째 문단에서 영국의 헨리 1세가 내렸던 세금 납부 포고령에 설명하면서 영국인들이 정교한 정부 자금 조달 체계를 발달시켰다고 하였고, 두 번째 문단과 세 번째 문단에서 현대의 비트코인 현상과 통화 제도에 관해 설명하고 있다. 따라서 이 지문의 종류를 '금융 잡지'라고 표현한 ②번이 정답이다.

어휘 construction n. 건축, 건설 brochure n. 책자

08 [2021 세종대]

정답 ④

해설 주어진 지문에서 '쪼개다'라는 의미로 사용된 과거분사 cleaved의 동의어를 묻는 문제이다. ①번 lift는 '들어 올리다', ②번 adhere는 '들러붙다', ③번 clench는 '꽉 쥐다', ④번 split은 '나누다'라는 의미이므로, ④번이 정답이다.

09 [2021 세종대]

정답 ①

해석 ① 변덕 ② 아가미
③ 걸음걸이 ④ 덩굴

해설 지문의 빈칸을 채우는 문제이다. 지문의 두 번째 문단에서 비트코인 지지자들은 선택권이 주어진다면 사람들이 비트코인을 선택할 것이라고 했으므로, 빈칸에는 잘못된 정책 입안자

들의 변덕에 휘둘리지 않을 것이라는 내용이 나오는 것이 자연스럽다. 따라서 '변덕'이라고 한 ①번이 정답이다.

10 2021 세종대

정답 ①

해석
① 국가들 간의 많은 거래에서, 신용을 이유로 미국 달러가 사용된다.
② 영국인들은 부신이 사용되기 전에 정교한 정부 자금 조달 체계를 가지고 있었다.
③ 비트코인은 무한한 공급량 때문에 지속 가능한 통화이다.
④ 두 나라 사이의 무역에서, 교환되는 부신은 항상 믿을 수 있다.

해설 지문의 내용과 일치하는 것을 묻는 문제이다. 지문의 네 번째 문단의 Even when two nations trade, the money exchanged needs to be credible and convertible ~ countries use U.S. dollars라는 내용을 통해 국가들 간의 많은 거래에서, 신용을 이유로 미국 달러가 사용된다는 것을 알 수 있다. 따라서 ①번이 지문의 내용과 일치한다.

오답 분석
② 영국인들이 부신을 바탕으로 하는 정교한 정부 자금 조달 체계를 발달시켰다고 했으므로, 영국인들이 부신이 사용되기 전에 정교한 정부 자금 조달 체계를 가지고 있었다는 것은 지문의 내용과 다르다.
③ 비트코인의 공급이 한정되었다고 했으므로, 비트코인이 무한한 공급량 때문에 지속 가능한 통화라는 것은 지문의 내용과 다르다.
④ 영국인들이 부신을 바탕으로 하는 정교한 정부 자금 조달 체계를 발달시켰다고는 했지만, 두 나라 사이의 무역에서 교환되는 부신이 항상 믿을 수 있는지는 알 수 없다.

[11-12]

포니 익스프레스 국립역사 트레일은 빠른 속도의 말에 탄 청년들이 미주리주에서 캘리포니아주까지 전국의 국내 우편을 단 10일이라는 전례 없는 시간 안에 나르기 위해 사용되었다. 민간 사업자들이 조직한 말-기수 중계 체계는 전신이 나오기 전 국가에서 가장 직통이면서 실용적인 동부와 서부 간 소통 수단이 되었다. 단 18개월 동안만 사용되었음에도, 그 트레일은 가장 중요한 육상 수송로의 (A)실현 가능성을 입증했고, 미국 남북 전쟁 직전에 캘리포니아주가 북부 주와 제휴하는 데 필수적인 역할을 했다. 본래의 트레일 대부분은 시간이나 인간 활동에 의해 그 흔적이 없어졌다. 트레일의 실제 경로와 정확한 길이는 추측의 문제. (B)하지만, 기존 50여 개의 포니 익스프레스 역이나 역 폐허를 비롯한 대략 120개의 사적은 결국 대중이 이용할 수 있게 될 것이다.

unprecedented adj. 전례 없는 organize v. 조직하다
entrepreneur n. 사업가 relay n. 중계
telegraph n. 전신 in operation phr. 사용 중인
overland adj. 육상의 transportation route phr. 수송로
vital adj. 필수적인 align with phr. ~와 제휴하다
obliterate v. (흔적을) 없애다 conjecture n. 추측
approximately adv. 대략 historic site phr. 사적
ruins n. 폐허

11 2020 가천대

정답 ④

해석
① 고집   ② 가시성
③ 변덕   ④ 실현 가능성

해설 지문의 빈칸을 채우는 문제이다. 지문의 두 번째 문장에서 말-기수 중계 체계는 전신이 나오기 전 국가에서 가장 직통이면서 실용적인 동부와 서부 간 소통 수단이 되었다고 했으므로, 빈칸에는 트레일이 가장 중요한 육상 수송로의 무엇을 입증했는지에 대한 내용이 나와야 적절하다는 것을 알 수 있다. 따라서 '실현 가능성'이라고 한 ④번이 정답이다.

어휘 tenacity n. 고집 visibility n. 가시성 mutability n. 변덕
feasibility n. 실현 가능성

12 2020 가천대

정답 ③

해석
① 비슷하게   ② 이런 이유로
③ 하지만   ④ 동시에

해설 빈칸에 적절한 연결어를 넣는 문제이다. 빈칸 앞부분은 본래의 트레일 대부분은 흔적이 없어져서 트레일의 실제 경로와 정확한 길이는 추측의 문제라는 내용이고, 빈칸 뒤 문장은 기존 50여 개의 포니 익스프레스 역이나 역 폐허를 비롯한 대략 120개의 사적은 결국 대중이 이용할 수 있게 될 것이라는 대조적인 내용이다. 따라서 대조를 나타내는 연결어인 ③ However가 정답이다.

13 2019 인하대

정답 ③

해설 1400년대까지 원주민이 서반구의 유일한 거주민이었지만, 후술할 1492년 콜럼버스의 항해부터 그다음 400년 동안, 대부분 유럽 국가에서 온 비원주민의 거대한 물결이 대서양을 가로질러 북아메리카와 남아메리카로 항해해 왔다. 그들 중에는 영국 식민지 개척자도 있었는데, 그들은 지금의 메인주와 조지아주 사이의 북아메리카 동쪽 해안에 자리 잡았다. 그 개척자들은 부, 권력, 자유, 그리고 모험의 기회를 찾아서 왔다. 그러나, 처음에 이 지역의 북쪽 지방에 자리 잡은 사람들은 큰 부를 찾지 못했다. 그 대신에, 그 사람들은 바위투성이의 황무지를 발견했다. 1600년대 초반의 이러한 위험과 어려움은 초기 개척자들이 굶주림과 질병으로 고생했다는 것을 의미한다. 아메리카의 비옥한 토양, 풍부한 물 공급, 그리고 많

은 양의 광석이라는 풍부한 자원을 활용했어야 했다. 오로지 살아남기 위해서 해야 할 일이 많았을 때는 시간과 에너지가 거의 낭비되지 않아야 했다. 몇몇 경우에는 나태함에 대한 이러한 관점이 엄격한 정부 정책으로 이끌었다. 예를 들어, 버지니아 주의회는 1619년에 어떠한 사람이든지 나태하게 지내는 것이 발견되면 징역형을 선고받을 것이라고 선언했다.

① 따라서 — 대조적으로
② 그렇지 않으면 — 유사하게
③ 그러나 — 예를 들어
④ 따라서 — 게다가
⑤ 그러나 — 그렇기는 하지만

해설 빈칸에 적절한 연결어를 넣는 문제이다. 첫 번째 빈칸 앞 문장은 사람들이 부, 권력, 자유, 그리고 모임의 기회를 찾아왔다는 내용이고, 빈칸 뒤 문장은 정착하고 나서 황무지를 발견했고 위험과 어려움으로 고생했다는 내용이므로, 대조를 나타내는 연결어인 However가 들어가야 한다. 두 번째 빈칸 앞 문장은 나태함에 대한 관점이 엄격한 정부 정책으로 이끌었다는 내용이고, 빈칸 뒤 문장은 엄격한 정부 정책에 대한 예시에 대한 내용이므로, 예시를 나타내는 연결어인 For example이 들어가야 한다. 따라서 ③ However — For example이 정답이다.

어휘 inhabitant n. 거주민 hemisphere n. 반구
voyage n. 항해, 여행 Atlantic Ocean phr. 대서양
colonist n. 식민지 개척자 settle v. 자리 잡다, 정착하다
rugged adj. 바위투성이의, 울퉁불퉁한
wilderness n. 황무지 starvation n. 굶주림, 기근
abundant adj. 풍부한 fertile adj. 비옥한
plentiful adj. 많은 양의 mineral n. 광석
harness v. 활용하다; n. 마구(馬具)
squander v. 낭비하다 idleness n. 나태함, 실업 상태
declare v. 선언하다, 공표하다 idle adj. 나태한, 쉬고 있는
condemn v. 선고하다; 비난하다

[14-15]

유럽이 근대화되기까지 300여 년의 시간이 걸렸고, 그 과정은 고통스럽고 충격적이며, 피비린내 나는 혁명을 수반했고, 종종 그 뒤를 공포 정치, 잔혹한 성전, 독재 정부, 노동력의 잔인한 착취, 그리고 광범위한 소외와 사회적 무질서 상태가 이어갔다. 우리는 현재 근대화를 겪고 있는 개발도상국에서 같은 종류의 (A)격변을 목격하고 있다. 하지만 이 나라들의 일부는 이 어려운 과정을 꽤 빨리 시도해야 했고, 그들이 가지고 있는 계획보다 서양의 계획을 따르길 강요받았다. (B)이 가속된 근대화는 개발도상국에 깊은 분열을 만들었다. 오로지 지식인만 새로운 현대식 제도를 이해할 수 있도록 하는 서양의 교육을 받는다. 광범위한 다수는 전근대적 정신에 갇힌 채로 남아있다.

modernize v. 근대화하다, 현대화하다
wrenching adj. 고통스러운
traumatic adj. 충격적인, 트라우마가 남는

revolution n. 혁명 reign of terror phr. 공포 정치
holy war phr. 성전(聖戰) dictatorship n. 독재 정부
exploitation n. 착취; 개발, 이용
widespread adj. 광범위한, 널리 퍼진 alienation n. 소외
anomie n. (사회적, 도덕적인) 무질서 witness v. 목격하다
undergo v. 겪다 division n. 분열, 분할
institution n. 제도, 관습 trap v. 가두다, (덫으로) 잡다
premodern adj. 전근대적인 ethos n. 정신, 기풍

14 2019 가천대

정답 ①

해석 ① 격변 ② 나른함
③ 호젓함 ④ 초월

해설 지문의 빈칸을 채우는 문제이다. 빈칸 이전의 부분에서 유럽이 근대화되기까지 공포 정치, 성전, 독재 정부, 노동력 착취, 무질서와 같은 고통스럽고 충격적인 과정을 겪었다고 설명하고 있으므로, 빈칸에는 이러한 혼돈의 과정에 대한 내용이 나와야 적절하다는 것을 알 수 있다. 따라서 '격변'이라고 한 ①번이 정답이다.

어휘 upheaval n. 격변, 대변동 languor n. 나른함
seclusion n. 호젓함 transcendence n. 초월

15 2019 가천대

정답 ②

해석 ① 현대성의 퇴보 ② 이 가속된 근대화
③ 이 간헐적인 근대화 ④ 현대성에 대한 저항

해설 지문의 빈칸을 채우는 문제이다. 빈칸 이전의 문장에서 지금 근대화를 겪고 있는 개발도상국에서는 이전에 유럽이 겪었던 근대화보다 더 빨리 겪고 있다고 설명하고 있으므로, 빈칸에는 근대화의 속도가 빨라졌다는 내용이 나와야 적절하다는 것을 알 수 있다. 따라서 '이 가속된 근대화'라고 한 ②번이 정답이다.

어휘 regression n. 퇴보, 퇴행 modernity n. 현대성
accelerated adj. 가속된 intermittent adj. 간헐적인
resistance n. 저항

[16-17]

비록 미국인들이 오랫동안 7월 4일에 독립기념일을 기념해왔지만, 엄밀히 말하면 7월 4일은 (미국의) 콜로니들이 새 국가가 되기 위해 투표를 한 날이 아니다. 그 명예는 1776년 7월 2일의 것인데, 그날은 대륙회의가 영국으로부터의 독립을 선언하는 결의안을 승인한 날일뿐만 아니라 다음 세대들에 의해 위대한 기념일 축제로서 '화려함과 행진'으로 기념될 것이라고 존 애덤스(John Adams)가 기록한 날이다. 그런데 무슨 일이 일어난 것인가? 한마디로 하자면, 문서작업 때문이었다. 미국

혁명 박물관의 최고 역사학자인 필립 미드(Philip Mead)에 따르면, 대륙회의가 대표자들이 그렇게 투표한 이유를 설명하는 언론 발표를 승인하는 데 이틀이 걸렸다. <독립선언문(the Declaration of Independence)>으로 더 유명한, 그 문서가 1776년 7월 4일 인쇄소에 도착했으며, 그것이 바로 그날짜(7월 4일)가 맨 위에 나타나게 된 이유다. 그러나 비록 미국인들이 7월 4일을 기념하고 있는 것을 보면 애덤은 깜짝 놀랐겠지만, 그는 사실 그 전환(기념일이 7월 2일에서 7월 4일로 바뀐 것)에 어느 정도 역할을 했다. 1826년 7월 4일 그와 토마스 제퍼슨(Thomas Jefferson) 두 사람이 사망하자, 그 날짜는 미국인의 기억 속에서 훨씬 더 소중한 것이 되었다.

technically adv. 엄밀히 말하면
the colonies phr. 미국 독립 당시의 동부 13주
the Continental Congress phr. 대륙회의(미국 독립 혁명 당시 미국 13개 식민지의 대표자 회의) resolution n. 결의안
succeeding generation phr. 다음 세대
pomp n. 장관; 화려함
press release phr. 대언론 공식 발표(성명), 보도 자료
delegate n. 대표(자)

16 [2018 한국외대]

정답 ④

해석 ① 즐거워하는   ② 추정되는
     ③ 기피되는   ④ 소중한

해설 지문의 빈칸을 채우는 문제이다. 빈칸 앞 문장에서 미국의 독립기념일이 본래 7월 2일이어야 하는데 7월 4일로 바뀌게 된 것(the shift)에 존 애덤스도 어느 정도 역할을 했다(did play a part)고 했으므로, '1826년 7월 4일에 그와 토마스 제퍼슨이 둘 다 사망했을 때, 그 날짜는 미국인의 기억 속에 훨씬 더 소중한 것이 되었다'라고 해야 적절하다는 것을 알 수 있다. 따라서 '소중한'이라고 한 ④번이 정답이다.

어휘 elude v. 회피하다, (교묘히) 빠져나가다
enshrine v. 소중히 간직하다

17 [2018 한국외대]

정답 ③

해석 ① 필립 미드는 대륙회의의 일원이었다.
     ② 독립선언문은 7월 2일에 인쇄되었다.
     ③ 애덤은 독립이 7월 2일에 기념되기를 희망했다.
     ④ 대륙회의는 7월 4일에 독립선언문을 위한 투표를 했다.

해설 지문의 내용과 일치하는 것을 찾는 문제이다. 지문의 두 번째 문장 That honor belongs to July 2 ~ with pomp and parade.에서 '존 애덤스는 7월 2일이 후손들에 의해 기념될 것이라고 적었다'고 했다. 따라서 ③번은 지문의 내용과 일치한다.

오답분석 ① 다섯 번째 문장에서 필립 미드는 미국 혁명 박물관의 최고 역사학자(chief historian at the Museum of the American Revolution)라고 했으므로, '필립 미드가 대륙회의의 일원이었다'는 것은 지문의 내용과 다르다.
② 여섯 번째 문장에서 독립선언문으로 더 유명한 그 문서가 인쇄소에 도착한 것은 7월 4일(That document ~ arrived at the printer on July 4)이라고 했으므로, '독립선언문이 7월 2일에 인쇄되었다'는 것은 지문의 내용과 다르다.
④ 두 번째 문장에서 7월 2일이 대륙회의가 영국으로부터의 독립을 선언하는 결의문을 승인한 날(That honor belongs to July 2 ~ from Britain)이라고 했으므로, '대륙회의가 7월 4일에 독립선언문을 위한 투표를 했다'는 것은 지문의 내용과 다르다.

[18-19]

이집트인들은 대규모로 음식을 저장했던 확실한 첫 번째 문명이었다. 나일강 양쪽 둑에 있는 그 좁고 비옥한 긴 땅 조각이 그들의 음식의 주된 공급원이었고, 나일강이 범람하지 못했던 가뭄 해에는 상황이 처참했다. 이것에 대비하기 위해서, 이집트인들은 커다란 저장고에 곡식을 비축하는 것을 포함해서 그들이 할 수 있는 모든 방법으로 음식을 저장했다. 식량 공급의 보존에 대한 이와 같은 집착은 건조와 발효에 관한 상당한 지식으로 이어졌다. 이집트인들은 고기를 염장했으며 돼지를 사육하는 방법도 알았기 때문에, 그들이 돼지에 대한 혐오감만 없었다면 이집트인들은 아마도 햄을 발명했을 것이다. 하지만, 이집트 종교의 지도자는 돼지를 나병의 매개체라고 선언하고, 돼지 농장주를 사회적으로 추방된 사람으로 취급했으며, 그 동물을 무덤의 벽에 절대로 묘사하지 않았다. 그들은 먹을 수 있는 남은 음식이나 죽은 동물들을 찾아 마을 변두리에서 쓰레기를 뒤지는 하이에나를 고기를 위해 사육하려고 시도했지만, 대부분의 이집트인은 그런 동물을 먹는다는 생각에 반기를 들었다. 이집트인들의 축산업에 대한 다른 실패한 시도는 영양과 가젤을 포함한다. 하지만 이집트인들은 오리, 거위, 메추라기, 비둘기, 그리고 펠리컨과 같은 조류를 사육하는 데에 성공했다. 고대의 벽은 조류의 다리가 벌려지고, 소금에 절여지고, 커다란 토기 안에 넣어지는 것을 보여준다.

civilization n. 문명   preserve v. 보존하다
fertile adj. 비옥한   strip n. 긴 조각   bank n. 둑
principal adj. 주된, 주요한   flood v. 범람하다, 넘치다
disastrous adj. 처참한   stockpile v. 비축하다
grain n. 곡식   silo n. 저장고   fixation n. 집착
considerable adj. 상당한   cure v. 말리다
fermentation n. 발효   aversion n. 혐오감
salt-cure v. 염장하다   domesticate v. 사육하다
pronounce v. 선언하다   carrier n. 질병의 매개체
outcast n. 추방된 사람, 따돌림받는 사람
scraps n. 남은 음식, 음식물 쓰레기
revolt v. 반기를 들다, 반란을 일으키다

```
animal husbandry  phr. 축산업   antelope  n. (동물) 영양
fowl  n. 조류, 가금류   quail  n. 메추라기
splay  v. (팔다리를) 벌리다   earthen  adj. 흙으로 된
```

18 2019 서울여대

정답 ①

해석
① 고대 이집트의 식량 보존
② 고대 이집트의 식량과 벽화
③ 이집트인들에 의한 동물 사육
④ 이집트 문명에서 나일강의 중요성

해설 지문의 주제를 묻는 문제이다. 지문의 처음에서 이집트인들은 대규모로 음식을 저장한 첫 번째 문명이라고 하였다. 따라서 이 지문의 주제를 '고대 이집트의 식량 보존'이라고 표현한 ①번이 정답이다.

어휘 preservation n. 보존   wall-painting n. 벽화
domestication n. 사육

19 2019 서울여대

정답 ②

해석
① 그들은 간신히 하이에나를 사육해냈다.
② 그들은 소금에 고기를 보존하는 법을 알았다.
③ 그들은 나일강의 범람으로 인해 고생했다.
④ 그들은 햄을 발명한 첫 번째 문명이었다.

해설 지문의 내용과 일치하는 것을 묻는 문제이다. 지문의 중간에서 이집트인들이 고기를 염장하고 돼지를 사육하는 방법을 알았다는 내용을 통해 그들은 소금에 고기를 보존하는 법을 알았다는 것을 알 수 있다. 따라서 ②번이 지문의 내용과 일치한다.

오답 분석
① 하이에나를 사육하려고 시도했지만, 이집트 사람들이 반기를 들었다고 했으므로, 그들이 간신히 하이에나를 사육했다는 것은 지문의 내용과 다르다.
③ 나일강이 범람하지 못했던 가뭄 해에는 처참했다고는 했지만, 나일강이 범람해서 이집트인들이 고생했는지는 알 수 없다.
④ 이집트인들이 돼지에 대한 혐오감을 갖지 않았다면 아마도 햄을 발명했을 것이라고 했으므로, 그들이 햄을 발명한 첫 번째 문명이라는 것은 지문의 내용과 다르다.

어휘 manage to phr. 간신히 ~ 하다
suffer from phr. ~로 인해 고생하다

[20-21]

유럽은 여러 심각한 질병의 발발을 경험해왔지만, 14세기 중반에 가장 파괴적인 질병이 덮쳐 유럽 대륙 인구의 1/3에서 절반이 사망했다. 흑사병으로 알려진 이 전염병은 중앙아시아에서 유럽으로 퍼졌을 수 있다. 설치류에 있는 벼룩에 의해 옮겨지는 박테리아인 *Yersinis pestis*로 널리 알려져 있지만, 이 질병의 원인에 대한 이론은 아주 많다. 감염에는 세 가지 변종이 있다. 목, 사타구니 및 겨드랑이의 서혜선종 또는 부종으로 특징지어지는 림프절 페스트, 폐를 감염시키는 폐 페스트, 그리고 패혈성 페스트, 또는 패혈증이다. 이 전염병은 1347년에 콘스탄티노플을 통해 전염되어 1348년과 1349년 동안 유럽 대부분 지역에 도달했다. 이는 광범위한 두려움과 공포를 유발하였고, 이 확산에 대응하는 대부분의 시도들은 소용이 없었다. 1350년까지 흑사병은 대체로 갈 데까지 갔지만 2,500만에서 5천만 명 사이의 유럽인이 사망하면서 갑작스러운 노동력 부족이 심각한 사회 변화의 원인이 되었을 수 있다. 소작농들의 수가 줄어듦에 따라 그들의 노동에 대한 수요가 커졌고, 이는 그들의 생활 환경과 법적 권리가 크게 향상되었다는 것을 의미했다.

```
outbreak  n. 발발, 발생   devastating  adj. 파괴적인, 강력한
strike  v. (병·죽음 등이) ~을 덮치다, 쓰러뜨리다
continent  n. 유럽 대륙   population  n. 인구
Black Death  phr. 흑사병   plague  n. 전염병
abound  v. 아주 많다   bacterium  n. 박테리아, 세균
flea  n. 벼룩   rodent  n. 설치류   infection  n. 감염
variant  n. 변종   bubonic plague  phr. 림프절 페스트
characterize  v. 특징짓다   buboes  n. 서혜선종
swelling  n. 종기, 부기   groin  n. 사타구니
armpit  n. 겨드랑이   infect  v. 감염시키다
pneumonic  adj. 폐의, 폐렴의   lung  n. 폐
septicemic  adj. 패혈증의   blood poisoning  phr. 패혈증
transmit  v. 전염시키다   via  prep. ~을 통하여, 경유하여
widespread  adj. 광범위한, 널리 퍼진   terror  n. 두려움
panic  n. 공포   spread  n. 확산, 전파
run one's course  phr. 갈 데까지 가다
contribute to  phr. ~의 원인이 되다   profound  adj. 심오한
peasantry  n. 소작농   diminish  v. 줄어들다
condition  n. 환경, 상태   legal  adj. 법적인   right  n. 권리
```

20 2020 인하대

정답 ①

해석
① 부족   ② 통합
③ 분할   ④ 풍부
⑤ 다양화

해설 지문의 빈칸을 채우는 문제이다. 지문의 빈칸이 있는 일곱 번째 문장에서 2,500만에서 5천만 명 사이의 유럽인이 흑사병으로 사망했다고 했으므로, 빈칸에는 인구가 감소한 것에 대한 내용이 나와야 적절하다는 것을 알 수 있다. 따라서 노동력 '부족'이 심각한 사회변화의 원인이 되었을 수 있다고 한 ①번이 정답이다.

어휘 integration n. 통합   division n. 분할, 분배
abundance n. 풍부   diversification n. 다양화, 다양성

21 [2020 인하대]

정답 ③

해석
① 벼룩이 전염병을 퍼뜨린 것으로 여겨진다.
② 1350년까지 흑사병이 절정에 달했다.
③ 그 전염병의 증상은 세 가지 범주로 분류되었다.
④ 흑사병은 유럽 역사상 가장 비극적인 사건이었다.
⑤ 흑사병으로 인해 유럽 사회가 더 나은 방향으로 변화할 수 있었다.

해설 지문의 내용과 일치하지 않는 것을 묻는 문제이다. ③번의 키워드인 three categories(세 가지 범주)와 관련된 지문의 three variants(세 가지 변종) 주변에서 이 질병에는 림프절 페스트, 폐 페스트, 패혈성 페스트로 세 가지 변종이 있다고는 했지만, 증상이 세 가지 범주로 분류되었다는 것은 알 수 없다. 따라서 ③번이 지문의 내용과 일치하지 않는다.

오답분석
① ~ although it is widely supposed to have been *Yersinis pestis*, a bacterium carried by fleas on rodents를 통해 '벼룩이 전염병을 퍼뜨린 것으로 여겨진다'는 것을 알 수 있다.
② By 1350, the Black Death had largely run its course ~를 통해 '1350년까지 흑사병이 절정에 달했다'는 것을 알 수 있다.
④ ~ the most devastating of all struck in the mid-14th century, killing between one-third and half the continent's population을 통해 '흑사병은 유럽 역사상 가장 비극적인 사건이었다'는 것을 알 수 있다.
⑤ The peasantry found their diminished numbers led to a greater demand for their services, which meant that their living conditions and legal rights greatly improved를 통해 '흑사병으로 인해 유럽 사회가 더 나은 방향으로 변화할 수 있었다'는 것을 알 수 있다.

어휘 peak n. 절정, 정점 symptom n. 증상
classify v. 분류하다 category n. 범주
catastrophic adj. 비극적인, 큰 재앙의

[22-24]

피지 전설에 따르면, 최고의 족장이었던 Lutunasobasoba는 그의 사람들을 이끌고 바다를 건너 피지로 향했다. 대부분의 족장은 사람들이 동남아시아에서 말레이반도를 거쳐 태평양으로 들어오는 것에 동의했다. 피지에서, 멜라네시아 사람과 폴리네시아 사람들이 섞여 유럽인들이 도착하기 오래전에 이미 고도로 발전된 사회를 만들어 냈다. 유럽인들이 피지섬을 발견한 것은 우연한 일이었다. 첫 번째 발견은 1643년 어느 네덜란드 탐험가에 의해 이루어졌다. 하지만 발견의 주된 공과 섬에 대한 기록의 작성은 영국의 선장이었던 William Bligh에게 돌아갔는데, 그는 1789년에 피지를 통해 항해한 사람이었다. 처음 이 섬에 정착하고 피지 사람들과 어울려 살아가기 위해 들어온 유럽인들은 호주의 범죄자 식민지로부터 도망친 재소자들이었다. 상인들과 선교사들도 19세기 중반 무렵에 들어왔다. 그 시기에는 인육을 먹는 풍습이 피지에서 시행되고 있었는데 선교사들이 영향력을 얻게 되자 빠르게 사라졌다. Ratu Seru Cakobau가 1854년에 기독교를 받아들이자, 나라의 다른 사람들도 곧이어 따르게 되었으며, 부족 간의 전쟁도 종결되었다. 1879년과 1916년 사이에는 인도인들이 연기계약 노동자들로 설탕 농장에서 일하기 위해 들어왔다. 그리고 연기계약 제도가 폐지된 이후에도, 많은 이들이 독립된 농부 혹은 사업가로서 피지에 머물게 되었다.

Chief n. 족장, 추장 authority n. 권위자
Malay Peninsula phr. 말레이반도
Melanesian n. 멜라네시아 사람
Polynesian n. 폴리네시아 사람 accidental adj. 우연한
credit n. 공 runaway adj. 달아난
convict n. 재소자 penal settlement phr. 범죄자 식민지
trader n. 상인 missionary n. 선교사
cannibalism n. 인육을 먹는 풍습 christianity n. 기독교
warfare n. 전쟁 indentured labor phr. 연기계약 노동자
plantation n. (대)농장

22 [2020 한국외대]

정답 ④

해석
① 피지에 처음 정착한 사람들은 아마도 동남아시아에서 왔을 것이다.
② 피지는 유럽인들이 도착하기 이전에도 문명화되어 있었다.
③ 피지의 발견에 대한 공의 대부분을 차지한 사람은 선장 William Bligh였다.
④ 대부분의 인도인은 연기계약 제도가 종결된 이후 피지를 떠났다.

해설 지문의 내용과 일치하지 않는 것을 묻는 문제이다. 지문의 마지막 문장에서 연기계약 제도가 폐지된 이후에도, 많은 이들이 독립된 농부 혹은 사업가로서 피지에 머물게 되었다고 했으므로, 대부분의 인도인은 연기계약 제도가 종결된 이후 피지를 떠났다는 것은 지문의 내용과 다르다. 따라서 ④번이 지문의 내용과 일치하지 않는다.

오답분석
① 지문의 처음에서 최고 족장이었던 Lutunasobasoba와 족장들이 동남아시아에서부터 말레이반도를 거쳐 피지에 도착했다는 내용이 있으므로, '피지에 처음 정착한 사람들은 아마도 동남아시아에서 왔을 것이다'는 지문의 내용과 일치한다.
② 지문의 세 번째 문장에서 멜라네시아 사람과 폴리네시아 사람들이 섞여 유럽인들이 도착하기 오래전에 이미 고도로 발전된 사회를 만들어 냈다고 했으므로, '피지는 유럽인들이 도착하기 이전에도 문명화되어 있었다'는 지문의 내용과 일치한다.
③ 지문의 여섯 번째 문장에서 발견의 주된 공과 섬에 대한 기록의 작성은 영국의 선장이었던 William Bligh에게 돌아갔다고 했으므로, '피지의 발견에 대한 공의 대부분을

차지한 사람은 선장 William Bligh였다'는 지문의 내용과 일치한다.

어휘 civilize v. 문명화하다

23 [2020 한국외대]

정답 ④

해석 ① 말레이시아 ② 네덜란드
③ 영국 ④ 호주

해설 첫 번째 유럽 정착민들이 어디에서 왔는지를 파악하는 문제이다. 지문의 일곱 번째 문장에서 처음 이 섬에 정착해서 피지 사람들과 어울려 살아가기 위해 들어온 유럽인들은 호주의 범죄자 식민지로부터 도망친 재소자들이었다고 했으므로, ④번이 정답이다.

24 [2020 한국외대]

정답 ③

해석 ① 피지 원주민들의 종교가 금지되었다.
② 부족 간의 전쟁이 나라 전체적으로 고조되었다.
③ 기독교가 피지인들 사이에서 주요한 종교가 되었다.
④ 더 많은 선교사가 유럽에서부터 도착했다.

해설 Cakobau의 개종 이후 무슨 일이 일어났는지를 파악하는 문제이다. 지문의 열 번째 문장에서 Cakobau가 기독교를 받아들이자, 나라의 다른 사람들도 곧이어 따르게 되었다고 했으므로, 기독교가 피지인들 사이에서 주요한 종교가 되었다는 것을 추론할 수 있다. 따라서 ③번이 정답이다.

어휘 prohibit v. 금하다 heighten v. 고조되다

[25-27]

미국의 기업가 겸 박애주의자인 앤드루 카네기는 관세 표에 의해 보호를 받는 철강을 제조하여 큰돈을 벌었다. 1873년, 그가 영국으로 빈번하게 떠났던 여행 중 하나에서, 그는 Henry Bessemer를 만나 산업의 미래가 철강에 달려 있다는 것을 확신하게 되었다. 그는 피츠버그 인근에 J. Edgar Thomson 제철소를 건설했고, 그 순간부터 카네기 제국은 끊임없이 팽창하게 되었다. 나중에, 카네기 철강 회사는 거대한 조직이 되었다. 그것은 피츠버그의 큰 용광로와 마감 공장에서부터 광석과 완제품을 옮기는 증기선까지 모든 철강 생산 공정을 포함했다. 앤드루 카네기는 그의 할아버지와 마찬가지로 노동자 계급과 가난한 사람들의 이익을 위해 그의 선조가 가졌던 급진적인 이상주의를 버리지 않았다. 허버트 스펜서의 철학과 그 시대의 사회적 다윈주의를 옹호함에도 불구하고, 그는 <u>부</u>를 가진 사람이 사회에 가져야 하는 사회적인 책임을 믿었던 것이다. 그는 자신이 벌어들인 재산의 관리인 역할을 해야 하며, 모두에게 더 큰 기회를 제공하고 자신과 우주에 대한 인간의 지식을 늘

려기 위해 그 재산을 써야 한다.

---

industrialist n. 기업가 philanthropist n. 박애주의자
manufacture v. 제조하다 customs tariff phr. 관세 표
frequent adj. 빈번한 convinced adj. 확신한
empire n. 제국 constant adj. 끊임없는
immense adj. 거대한 furnace n. 용광로
finish v. 마감 처리를 하다 steamer n. 증기선
radical adj. 급진적인 idealism n. 이상주의
forebear n. 선조 espousal n. 지지
responsibility n. 책임 steward n. 관리인
universe n. 우주

25 [2020 단국대]

정답 ①

해석 ① 부 ② 희생
③ 종교 ④ 다윈주의

해설 지문의 빈칸을 채우는 문제이다. 빈칸이 포함된 문장 다음에 모두에게 더 큰 기회를 제공하고 자신과 우주에 대한 인간의 지식을 늘리기 위해 그 재산을 써야 한다고 설명하고 있으므로, 재산과 비슷한 의미의 단어가 와야 한다는 것을 알 수 있다. 따라서 '부'라고 한 ①번이 정답이다.

어휘 wealth n. 부 sacrifice n. 희생 religion n. 종교
Darwinism n. 다윈주의(자연 선택에 의한 생물의 진화를 주장한 이론)

26 [2020 단국대]

정답 ③

해석 ① 카네기는 피츠버그 인근의 그의 철강 공장을 지었다.
② 카네기의 할아버지는 가난한 사람들을 돕는 것이 옳다고 생각했다.
③ 카네기의 사업 성공은 정부에 의해 도움을 받은 것이 전혀 아니었다.
④ 카네기는 그의 사업 분야에서 철강을 선택한 것에 Bessemer의 영향을 받았다.

해설 지문의 내용과 일치하지 않는 것을 묻는 문제이다. ③번의 키워드인 the government(정부)와 관련된 지문의 customs tariff(관세 표) 주변에서 앤드루 카네기는 관세 표에 의해 보호를 받는 철강을 제조하여 큰돈을 벌었다고 했으므로, 카네기의 사업 성공은 정부에 의해 도움을 받은 것이 전혀 아니었다는 것은 지문의 내용과 다르다. 따라서 ③번이 지문의 내용과 일치하지 않는다.

오답분석
① He built the J. Edgar Thomson Steel Mills near Pittsburgh를 통해 '카네기는 피츠버그 인근의 그의 철강 공장을 지었다'는 것을 알 수 있다.
② the radical idealism of his forebears for the benefit of the working class and the poor people

을 통해 '카네기의 할아버지는 가난한 사람들을 돕는 것이 옳다고 생각했다'는 것을 알 수 있다.

④ he met Henry Bessemer and became convinced that the industrial future lay in steel을 통해 '카네기는 그의 사업 분야에서 철강을 선택한 것에 Bessemer의 영향을 받았다'는 것을 알 수 있다.

어휘 government n. 정부 influence v. 영향을 주다

27 [2020 단국대]

정답 ②

해석 ① 사회적 다윈주의에 대한 카네기의 지지
② 카네기의 사업 성공과 박애주의
③ 카네기의 사업 배경과 이상주의
④ 카네기와 그의 할아버지의 박애주의

해설 지문의 제목을 묻는 문제이다. 지문의 전반에 걸쳐 카네기가 철강 산업에서 성공을 거두었고, 그것으로 번 돈을 통해 노동자 계급과 가난한 사람들의 이익을 위해 써야 한다는 이상주의를 가졌다고 했다. 따라서 이 지문의 제목을 '카네기의 사업 성공과 박애주의'라고 표현한 ②번이 정답이다.

어휘 philanthropy n. 박애주의 background n. 배경

[28-30]

> [B] 미국은 이민자의 나라이다. 1840년대 이전에는, 매해 대략 60,000명의 이민자들이 도착했다. 1840년대와 1850년대에는 미국으로 들어오는 사람의 숫자가 급격하게 증가했다. 이 시기에 무려 300만 명이 넘는 아일랜드인과 독일인이 대서양을 건너 미국으로 들어왔다.
>
> [C] 대부분의 아일랜드계 이민자들은 극심한 빈곤 속에 살았다. 그들 중 대부분은 보스턴과 뉴욕의 빈민가에 정착했고, 보수가 낮은 일을 하게 되었다. 아일랜드계 여성들은 주로 식모로 일하게 되었는데, 그에 반해 남성들은 저임금의 위험한 일을 해야만 했다. 대조적으로, 독일계 이민자들은 아일랜드계 이민자에 비해 많은 돈을 가지고, 교육도 더 받은 상태에서 이민을 왔다. 그들은 미국 중서부의 땅을 살 수 있었다. 그래서 그들은 오하이오와 위스콘신 같은 주에서 농부가 되었다.
>
> [A] 그다음 이민의 물결은 1870년과 1900년 사이에 있었다. 새로운 이민자 중에는 중국인이 가장 많았는데, 대다수가 남자였으며 주로 캘리포니아주에서 살았다. 그들 중 많은 이들이 철광이나 철도 건설 현장에서 일했다. 그리고 몇몇은 요리사, 세탁부 혹은 하인 같은 천한 일을 하게 되었다. 하지만, 중국인들은 가혹한 인종적 편견을 마주하게 되었다. 1882년, 미국 의회는 중국인 입국 금지법을 통과시켰고, 중국인들이 미국으로 들어오는 것을 금지하였다.
>
> immigrant n. 이민자
> dramatically adv. 급격하게, 극적으로
> Irish n. 아일랜드인 German n. 독일인 poverty n. 빈곤
> slum n. 빈민가 kitchen maid phr. 식모
> minefield n. 광석 매장 구역 menial adj. 천한
> laundrymen n. 세탁부 racial adj. 인종의
> the Chines Exclusion Act phr. 중국인 입국 금지법

28 [2020 한성대]

정답 ③

해설 [A], [B], [C]의 적절한 순서를 파악하는 문제이다. 미국이 이민자들의 나라이고, 1840년대와 1850년대에 아일랜드와 독일에서 많은 이민자가 들어왔다는 내용의 [B]가 가장 먼저 와야 한다. 그다음에 [C]에서 아일랜드계 이민자와 독일계 이민자가 미국에서 어떻게 살게 되었는지를 설명한 다음, 마지막으로 [A]에서 새로운 이민자의 물결인 중국인 이민자에 관한 내용이 이어지는 것이 자연스럽다. 따라서 주어진 지문 다음에 이어질 순서는 ③ [B] ― [C] ― [A]이다.

29 [2020 한성대]

정답 ③

해석 ① 미국에서 이민자들의 숫자는 19세기 중반 무렵 상당히 증가했다.
② 대부분의 아일랜드계 이민자들은 도시의 궁핍한 지역에서 살았다.
③ 1882년 이후 모든 중국계 이민자는 금지되어 있다.
④ 대부분의 독일계 이민자들은 아일랜드계 이민자들과 비교해 더 많은 재산을 가지고 왔다.

해설 지문의 내용과 일치하지 않는 것을 묻는 문제이다. 지문의 세 번째 문단에서, 중국계 이민자들이 심한 인종 차별에 직면했고, 미국 의회가 중국인 이민 금지법을 통과시켰다고는 했지만, 이 법안이 현재까지 이어지고 있는지는 알 수 없으므로, 1882년 이후 모든 중국계 이민자가 금지되어 있다는 것은 지문의 내용과 다르다. 따라서 ③번이 정답이다.

오답분석 ① 지문의 첫 번째 문단에서, 1840년대와 1850년대에 미국에 이민한 이민자의 숫자가 급격하게 증가했다고 했으므로, 미국에서 이민자들의 숫자가 19세기 중반 무렵에 상당히 증가했다는 것은 지문의 내용과 일치한다.
② 지문의 두 번째 문단에서, 대부분의 아일랜드계 이민자들이 극심한 빈곤 속에 살았고, 보스턴과 뉴욕의 빈민가에 정착했다고 했으므로, 아일랜드계 이민자들이 도시의 가난한 궁핍한 지역에서 살았다는 것은 지문의 내용과 일치한다.
④ 지문의 두 번째 문단에서, 아일랜드계 이민자와 비교해 독일계 이민자들은 더 많은 교육을 받고, 많은 재산을 가지고 미국으로 이민 왔다고 했으므로, 대부분의 독일계 이민자가 아일랜드계 이민자에 비해 더 많은 재산을 가지고 왔다는 것은 지문의 내용과 일치한다.

어휘 significantly adv. 상당히 section n. 구역, 부문

30 [2020 한성대]

정답 ②

해석
① 유사하게 ② 대조적으로
③ 그 결과 ④ 그것으로써

해설 빈칸에 적절한 연결어를 넣는 문제이다. 빈칸 앞부분은 아일랜드계 여성과 남성들이 식모나 저임금의 위험한 일을 하게 되었다는 내용이고, 빈칸 뒤 문장은 독일계 이민자들은 아일랜드계 이민자들에 비해 많은 돈을 가지고, 교육도 더 받은 상태에서 이민을 왔다는 내용이다. 따라서 대조를 나타내는 연결어인 ② In contrast(대조적으로)가 정답이다.

[31-33]

고 아메리카 인디언의 물질문화는 아시아, 아프리카와 유럽에서 발견된 다른 석기 시대 사람들의 문화와 조금 달랐다. [A] 하지만, 인간의 건강이라는 면에서, 베링 툰드라에서 발생한 것은 아메리카 원주민의 역사를 영원히 바꾸었다. 이유는 잘 알려지지 않았지만, 이 작은 이주 집단의 구성원들은 가장 치명적인 천연두와 홍역 같은 많은 전염병에 더 이상 걸리지 않았고, 아메리카 원주민들이 결핵과 같은 병에 걸리긴 했지만, 그들은 더 이상 일반적으로 매년 인구의 큰 비율의 사람들을 죽였을 주요 전염병으로 고통받지 않았다. [B] <u>다양한 무리들이 물리적으로 고립되었던 것이 전염병의 확산으로부터 그들을 보호했을지도 모른다.</u> 다른 이론은 전염병이 흔히 소와 돼지 같은 가축들과의 장기적인 접촉과 관련된다는 점에 주목한다. [C] 고 아메리카 인디언은 심지어, 말을 포함하여 어떤 동물도 길들이지 않았기 때문에, 그들은 유럽과 아프리카에 치명적인 질병을 일으켰던 병원균을 피할 수 있었을지도 모른다. [D] 이 호기심을 끄는 역학 기록에 대한 설명이 무엇이든 간에, 아메리카 원주민은 나중에 많은 전염성 병원균으로부터 그들을 보호해주었을지도 모르는 유전된 면역력을 잃었다. [E] 따라서, 유럽인과 아프리카인과 처음 접촉했을 때, 아메리카 원주민은 초기 현대의 <u>엄청난 사망 원인들</u>을 방어할 수 없었다.

material culture phr. 물질문화
Paleo-Indian n. 고 아메리카 인디언
differ from phr. ~와 다르다 Stone Age phr. 석기 시대
in terms of phr. ~면에서 tundra n. 툰드라, 동토대
alter v. 바꾸다 Native American phr. 아메리카 원주민
remain v. 계속 ~이다
obscure adj. 잘 알려지지 않은, 이해하기 힘든, 모호한
communicable disease phr. 전염병
communicable adj. 전염성인, 쉽게 전달될 수 있는
disease n. 병, 질환 smallpox n. 천연두
measles n. 홍역 deadly adj. 치명적인, 생명을 앗아가는
illness n. 병, 질환 tuberculosis n. 결핵
population n. 인구, 주민
prolonged adj. 장기적인, 오래 계속되는 contact n. 접촉
domestic animal phr. 가축 cattle n. 소
domesticate v. 길들이다, 사육하다 avoid v. 피하다
microbe n. 병원균, 미생물 virulent adj. 치명적인, 악성의
explanation n. 설명 inherited adj. 유전의, 상속한
immunity n. 면역력, 면제 germ n. 병균, 세균, 미생물
defense n. 방어

31 [2019 상명대]

정답 ①

해석
① 유전적으로, 고 아메리카 인디언은 전염병에 대한 면역력이 부족하다.
② 인디언들은 다른 지역과 비슷한 석기 시대의 물질문화를 가지고 있었다.
③ 고 아메리카 인디언은 오랜 기간 동안 전국적으로 퍼지는 병원균으로부터 자유로웠다.
④ 인디언들은 가축을 길들이지 않았기 때문에, 치명적인 전염병으로부터 안전했다.
⑤ 유럽인들과 접촉했을 때, 인디언들은 전염성 세균에 취약해졌다.

해설 지문의 내용과 일치하지 않는 것을 묻는 문제이다. ①번의 키워드인 immunities(면역력)과 관련된 두 번째 문단에서 아메리카 원주민이 나중에 많은 전염성 병원균으로부터 그들을 보호해주었을지도 모르는 유전된 면역력을 잃었다고 했으므로, 유전적으로, 고 아메리카 인디언이 전염병에 대한 면역력이 부족하다는 것은 지문의 내용과 다르다. 따라서 ①번이 지문의 내용과 일치하지 않는다.

오답 분석
② 첫 번째 문단 The material culture of the ~ and Europe을 통해 '인디언들은 다른 지역과 비슷한 석기 시대의 물질문화를 가지고 있었다'는 것을 알 수 있다.
③ 첫 번째 문단 For reasons ~ population every year를 통해 '고 아메리카 인디언은 오랜 기간 동안 전국적으로 퍼지는 병원균으로부터 자유로웠다'는 것을 알 수 있다.
④ 첫 번째 문단 Since the ~ African diseases를 통해 '인디언들은 가축을 길들이지 않았기 때문에, 치명적인 전염병으로부터 안전했다'는 것을 알 수 있다.
⑤ 두 번째 문단 Thus, when they ~ Early Modern world를 통해 '유럽인들과 접촉했을 때, 인디언들은 전염성 세균에 취약해졌다'는 것을 알 수 있다.

어휘 genetically adv. 유전적으로
pandemic adj. (전염병이) 전국적으로 퍼지는, 광역 유행의
livestock n. 가축 fatal adj. 치명적인, 죽음을 초래하는
vulnerable adj. 취약한, 연약한

32 [2019 상명대]

정답 ④

해설 밑줄 친 the great killers의 의미를 추론하는 문제이다. 두 번째 문단에서 아메리카 원주민은 나중에 많은 전염성 병원균으로부터 그들을 보호해주었을지도 모르는 유전된 면역력을

잃었다고 했다. 따라서, the great killers의 의미를 '병원균'이라고 한 ④번이 정답이다.

어휘 **migrant** n. 이주자

33 (2019 상명대)

정답 ②

해설 지문의 흐름상 주어진 문장이 들어가기에 가장 적절한 위치를 고르는 문제이다. [B]의 앞 문장에서 이 작은 이주 집단의 구성원들은 가장 치명적인 천연두와 홍역 같은 많은 전염병에 더 이상 걸리지 않았고, 아메리카 원주민들이 결핵과 같은 병에 걸리긴 했지만, 그들은 더 이상 일반적으로 매년 인구의 큰 비율의 사람들을 죽였을 주요 전염병으로 고통받지 않았다고 했으므로, [B] 자리에 물리적 고립이 전염병의 확산으로부터 아메리카 원주민들을 보호했을지도 모른다고 설명하는 주어진 문장 '다양한 무리들이 물리적으로 고립되었던 것이 전염병의 확산으로부터 그들을 보호했을지도 모른다'가 들어가야 글의 흐름이 자연스럽게 연결된다. 따라서 ②번이 정답이다.

어휘 **isolation** n. 고립, 분리
contagious disease phr. (접촉) 전염병

[34-36]

수많은 식사 그림들은 17세기 이전에 식탁이 어떻게 생겼는지를 보여준다. 1600년경까지 포크는 포함되지 않았으며, 숟가락도 겨우 몇 개밖에 보이지 않았다. 최소한 한 개의 나이프가 항상 그려져 있었지만 — 모든 손님들이 이용할 수 있는 유일한 나이프인 경우엔 특히 큰 나이프가 그려져 있었지만 — 작은 개인용 나이프가 종종 각자의 자리에 있었다. [A] 양철 원판이 이미 큰 나무 접시를 대체했다. [B] 식사 도구의 이런 변화는 유럽에서의 새로운 식사 예법을 나타낸다. 세계의 많은 다른 지역에서는, 도구가 전혀 사용되지 않았다. [C] 예를 들어, 근동 지역에서는, 오른손 손가락으로 식사를 하는 것이 전통이었다. [D] 부분적으로는 고기에 대한 태도의 변화 때문에 도구가 사용되었다. 중세시대에는, 고기의 모든 부위 또는 심지어 죽은 동물 전체를 식탁에 가져온 다음 식사하는 사람들이 보는 데서 고기를 잘랐다. 17세기부터, 처음엔 프랑스에서 하지만 나중엔 다른 곳에서도, 그 관행은 유행하지 않기 시작했다. 그렇게 된 한 가지 이유는 가족의 규모가 감소하고 있었고 가족이 더 이상 스스로 도축을 하는 생산 단위가 아니었기 때문이었다. 그런 역할(도축)은 집 밖의 전문가들에게 이전되었기 때문에, 가족은 본질적으로 소비 단위가 되었다.

tin n. 양철   **disk** n. 원판   **utensil** n. 도구, 용구
Near East phr. 근동 (아라비아와 북동 아프리카 등을 포함한 지역)   **carcass** n. (식용으로 쓸) 죽은 동물
carve v. (큰 고깃덩이를) 자르다   **cease** v. 그치다, 그만두다
slaughtering n. 도살, 도축

34 (2018 한국외대)

정답 ②

해설 지문의 흐름상 주어진 문장이 들어가기에 가장 적합한 위치를 고르는 문제이다. 주어진 문장은 '식사 도구의 이런 변화는 유럽에서의 새로운 식사 예법을 나타낸다'는 의미이므로, 지문에서 '식사 도구의 이런 변화(This change in eating utensils)'에 해당하는 것을 찾아야 하며 [B] 앞의 두 문장에 있는 '각자의 자리에 작은 개인용 나이프가 있었으며 양철 원판이 이미 큰 나무 접시를 대체했다'는 것이 '식사 도구의 이런 변화'에 해당한다. 따라서 ②번이 정답이다.

어휘 **typify** v. 대표하다, 상징하다, 나타내다

35 (2018 한국외대)

정답 ④

해석 ① 엉망으로 만들다   ② 연착륙하다
③ 최고조에 이르다   ④ 유행하지 않게 되다

해설 지문의 빈칸을 채우는 문제이다. 지문의 후반부에서 식사 도구의 사용은 부분적으로는 고기에 대한 태도의 변화 때문이라고 했으며 중세시대에는 고기를 통째로 식탁에 가져와서 잘랐다고 했다. 그리고 빈칸 뒤 문장에서는 가족이 더 이상 직접 도축을 하는 생산의 단위가 아니었으며 소비의 단위가 되었다고 했다. 따라서 그 관행(고기를 통째로 식탁에 가져와서 자르던 관행)은 '사라져갔다'는 내용이 들어가야 적절하다는 것을 알 수 있다. 따라서 '유행하지 않게 되다'라고 한 ④번이 정답이다.

어휘 **turn upside down** phr. 뒤집어엎다, 엉망으로 만들다
full swing phr. 대활약, 최대 활동

36 (2018 한국외대)

정답 ②

해석 ① 1600년까지 식사 장면은 화가들에게 빈번한 소재였다.
② 나이프와 숟가락보다 이전에 포크가 그림에 그려졌다.
③ 17세기에 가족 수의 변화가 있었다.
④ 중세시대에는, 죽은 동물을 통째로 식탁에 가져왔던 것 같다.

해설 지문의 내용과 일치하지 않는 것을 찾는 문제이다. 지문의 두 번째 문장 Forks were not included ~ were shown.에서 '그림에 포크는 포함되지 않았지만, 숟가락은 몇 개 보였다'고 했으며, 세 번째 문장 At least one knife ~ at each place.에서 '나이프는 최소한 한 개 그려져 있었다'고 했으므로, '나이프와 숟가락보다 이전에 포크가 그림에 그려졌다'고 한 ②번은 지문의 내용과 일치하지 않는다.

오답분석 ① 지문의 첫 문장 Numerous paintings of meals ~ before the seventeenth century.를 통해 '1600년까지

식사 장면은 화가들에게 빈번한 소재였다'는 것을 알 수 있다.
③ 지문의 마지막 문장 중 the family was decreasing in size를 통해 '17세기에 가족 수의 변화가 있었다'는 것을 알 수 있다.
④ 지문의 여덟 번째 문장 During the Middle Ages, ~ and then carved in view of the diners.를 통해 '중세시대에는, 죽은 동물을 통째로 식탁에 가져왔다'는 것을 알 수 있다.

[37-38]

켈트인은 영국 최초의 인도·유럽 거주자였다. 영국 남부의 켈트인은 로마인에 의해 처음으로 진압되었으며 그 후로 로마인에게 통치되고 보호받았다. 기원전 55년에서 54년에 있었던 초기 침략에서 율리우스 카이사르의 시도는 로마 제국의 다른 곳들, 특히 골(카이사르의 군단에 의해 말해졌던 라틴어가 궁극적으로 현대 프랑스어가 된 곳)에서의 결과와는 다르게 점령으로 이어지지 않았다. 로마의 침략에 더 영구적인 점령과 군사적 통치가 뒤따랐던 것은 바로 서기 43년부터의 클라우디우스 황제의 통치 중이었다. 그 이후로 약 400년 동안, 영국은 로마 제국의 한 지방이었다. 하지만 5세기의 초반부터, 그 외딴 영토에서 점령군을 유지하는 것은 로마인들에게 너무 큰 비용이 들게 되었는데, 그들은 끊임없이 대륙에 있는 게르만족으로부터 공격의 대상이었다. 뒤따른 사건들의 상당히 간소화된 형태는 서기 410년까지 모든 로마인이 사라지면서 철수했을 때, 섬의 남부에 있던 켈트인은 비교적 무방비 상태였다는 것이다. 그들이 북쪽과 아일랜드로부터 온 켈트인(스코틀랜드인과 픽트인) 뿐만이 아니라, 침략해오는 바이킹으로부터 자신들을 지키기 위해 게르만 용병들을 북유럽으로부터 건너오도록 초청한 것도 그때였다.

---

occupant n. 거주자 subdue v. 진압하다
thereafter adv. 그 후에 shelter v. 보호하다
invasion n. 침략 occupation n. 점령
elsewhere adv. 다른 곳에서 legion n. 군단
ultimately adv. 궁극적으로 emperor n. 황제
permanent adj. 영구적인 province n. 지방, 지역
occupation force phr. 점령군 outlying adj. 외딴, 외진
territory n. 영토 costly adj. 큰 비용이 드는
constantly adv. 끊임없이 be subject to phr. ~의 대상인
continent n. 대륙 simplified adj. 간소화된, 간략화된
pull A out phr. A를 철수시키다
defenseless adj. 무방비 상태의
mercenary soldier phr. 용병

---

37 2019 인하대

정답 ③

해석 ① 켈트인은 로마인 다음으로 영국에 도착했다.
② 율리우스 카이사르는 영국의 영구적인 통치에 성공했다.
③ 클라우디우스 황제는 영국을 로마 제국의 일부로 만들었다.
④ 게르만 군대는 영국으로부터 로마인을 완전히 추방했다.
⑤ 게르만 용병들은 픽트인 뿐만 아니라 스코틀랜드인도 보호했다.

해설 지문의 내용과 일치하는 것을 묻는 문제이다. 지문의 중간에서 로마의 침략에 더 영구적인 점령과 군사적 통치가 뒤따랐던 것은 클라우디우스 황제의 통치 중이었고, 그 이후로 400년 동안 영국은 로마 제국의 한 지방이었다는 내용을 통해 클라우디우스 황제는 영국을 로마 제국의 일부로 만들었다는 것을 알 수 있다. 따라서 ③번이 지문의 내용과 일치한다.

오답분석 ① 켈트인은 영국 최초의 유럽 거주자였고, 이들은 로마인에 의해 처음으로 진압되었다고 했으므로, 켈트인이 로마인 다음으로 영국에 도착했다는 것은 지문의 내용과 다르다.
② 율리우스 카이사르가 침략을 시도했을 때에는 그것이 점령으로 이어지지 않았다고 했으므로, 율리우스 카이사르가 영국의 영구적인 통치에 성공했다는 것은 지문의 내용과 다르다.
④ 서기 410년까지 영국에서 모든 로마인이 철수했다고는 했지만, 게르만 군대가 영국으로부터 로마인을 완전히 추방했는지는 알 수 없다.
⑤ 게르만 용병들은 스코틀랜드인과 픽트인을 포함한 켈트인뿐만이 아니라 바이킹으로부터도 로마인을 보호하기 위해 초청되었다고 했으므로, 게르만 용병들이 픽트인 뿐만이 아니라 스코틀랜드인도 보호했다는 것은 지문의 내용과 다르다.

어휘 succeed in phr. ~에 성공하다 expel v. 추방하다

38 2019 인하대

정답 ①

해석 ① 영국 ② 골
③ 독일 ④ 유럽
⑤ 아일랜드

해설 밑줄 친 that outlying territory의 의미를 추론하는 문제이다. 지문의 밑줄 친 단어가 있는 문장의 바로 앞에서 영국은 로마 제국의 한 지방이라고 했다. 따라서, that outlying territory의 의미를 '영국'이라고 한 ①번이 정답이다.

[39-40]

1918년 이후 소작농, 장인과 전통적인 중류 계급에 대한 근대화의 해로운 영향은 광범위한 반응을 유발했다. 유럽 전역에 걸쳐 합심한 반근대주의자의 반란은 없었던 한편, 보수적인 대중은 자신들이 직면했던 위기에 고조되는 분노와 절망으로 대처했다. 소비에트 연방에서 농업과 시골 마을 생활을 근대화하기 위한 노력은 사실상 러시아 시골 도처에 두 번째 내전을 유발했다. 소작농은 농작물과 가축을 말살함으로써 자신들을 집단 농장에 억지로 들어가게 하려는 폭력적인 공격에 저항했다.

소의 수는 1928년 3천 8백만 마리에서 1933년 7백만 마리로 감소했다. 많은 소작농은 총을 들이대고 집단 농장으로 억지로 들어갔고, 다수가 공산당원에 의해 시골의 자본주의자(부농)로 맹렬히 비난받았으며, 죽거나 생존 가능성이 얼마 안 되는 강제 노동 수용소로 추방되거나 둘 중 하나였다.

소작농과의 갈등은 수백만 명 이상의 죽음으로 이어졌던 식량 위기를 야기했다. 종교와 다른 국적을 지키기 위한 소작농의 저항이 가장 두드러졌던 우크라이나에서의 기근은 반 소비에트 운동을 탄압하기 위해 스탈린에 의해 의도적으로 교묘하게 처리되었다. 소작농과 시골의 장인은 자신들이 형편없이 일을 해냈던 공장으로 이동했고, 복잡한 기계와 씨름하고 규칙적인 생활을 하기 위해 노력했다. 결과는 한층 더한 공포, 맹렬한 비난의 물결, 사보타주와 여전히 짐작만 할 수 있는 수에 이르렀던 죽음에 대한 비난의 말이었다. 결국 스탈린조차도 위에서부터의 강요된 근대화의 희생은 자멸적인 조짐을 보였다는 것을 알 수 있었다. 1935년에 스탈린은 주민들이 자신을 위한 정원이 있는 작은 집과 약간의 동물을 가질 수 있다고 규정했다. 몇 년 안에 육지 면적의 3.9퍼센트만 구성했던 이 시민 농장의 생산물의 가치는 거의 집단 농장에서 생산되었던 모든 것의 가치와 맞먹었다. 하지만 시민 농장은 정부의 특권일 뿐이었다. 스탈린의 계획에 대한 소비에트 인구 대부분의 폭력적인 반응은 오직 목숨과 생계의 끔찍한 희생의 대가로 진압되었다.

baleful adj. 해로운, 악의적인   peasant n. 소작농
artisan n. 장인, 기능공   provoke v. 유발하다
concerted adj. 합심한   revolt n. 반란, 저항
conservative adj. 보수적인
react to the crisis phr. 위기에 대처하다
desperation n. 절망   Soviet Union phr. 소비에트 연방
village life phr. 시골 마을 생활   civil war phr. 내전
peasantry n. 소작농   resist v. 저항하다, 반대하다
collective farm phr. 집단 농장   livestock n. 가축
cattle n. 소   at the point of a gun phr. 총을 들이대고
denounce v. 맹렬히 비난하다   capitalist n. 자본주의자
kulak n. 부농   Communist n. 공산당원
exile v. 추방하다   labour camp phr. 강제 노동 수용소
slight adj. 얼마 안 되는   conflict n. 갈등, 충돌
famine n. 기근   distinct adj. 별개의, 다른
nationality n. 국적   marked adj. 두드러진, 현저한
deliberately adv. 의도적으로, 고의로
engineer v. ~을 교묘하게 처리하다, 공작하다
crush v. (폭력으로) 탄압하다, 진압하다   craftsman n. 장인
herd v. 이동시키다   perform v. 일을 해내다, 수행하다
grapple v. (~과) 씨름하다, 해결하려고 노력하다
machinery n. 기계
keep regular hours phr. 규칙적인 생활을 하다
further adj. 한층 더한   terror n. 공포
denunciation n. 맹렬한 비난
accusation n. 비난의 말, 고발
sabotage n. 사보타주(고의로 공장의 기계·설비를 손상하여 생산을 지연시키는 행위), 방해 행위   cost n. 희생, 손실
self-defeating adj. (행위·계획·논의 등이) (예상과는 달리) 자멸적인   ordain v. 규정하다, 명하다   cottage n. 작은 집
allotment n. 시민 농장   constitute v. ~을 구성하다, 이루다
equal v. ~와 맞먹다, 필적하다
concession n. (정부에서 받는) 특권, 이권   toll n. 희생
livelihood n. 생계

39 2019 이화여대

정답 ③

해석 ① 러시아에서의 전후의 빈곤
② 생산국에 의한 생산에 대한 지배
③ 강압적인 근대화의 해로운 영향
④ 러시아의 소작농의 혁명적인 가능성
⑤ 경제 성장에 박차를 가하려는 소비에트 정부 계획

해설 지문의 제목을 묻는 문제이다. 첫 문단에서 1918년 이후 소작농, 장인과 전통적인 중류 계급에 대한 근대화의 해로운 영향은 광범위한 반응을 유발했다(The baleful influence of modernization after 1918 on peasants, artisans and the traditional middle classes provoked a widespread response)고 했으며, 두 번째 문단에서 결국 스탈린조차도 위에서부터의 강요된 근대화의 희생은 자멸적인 조짐을 보였다는 것을 알 수 있었다(In the end even Stalin could see that the cost of imposing modernization from above threatened to be self-defeating)고 했으므로, 지문의 제목을 '강압적인 근대화의 해로운 영향'이라고 표현한 ③번이 정답이다.

어휘 destitution n. 빈곤, 결핍   mastery n. 지배
detrimental adj. 해로운   revolutionary adj. 혁명적인
potential n. 가능성

40 2019 이화여대

정답 ③

해석 ① 많은 소작농이 토지 사유권을 비난했다.
② 근대화에 대한 가장 끈질긴 저항은 도시 지역에서 비롯되었다.
③ 시골 경제에 활력을 주기 위한 스탈린의 목표는 실제로는 방해받았다.
④ 보수적인 대중은 상의하달식의 근대화에 저항하기 위해 동맹을 결성했다.
⑤ 소비에트 정부는 생산의 사적인 통제를 통해 개인의 이익을 위한 전적인 지원을 제공했다.

해설 지문을 통해 추론할 수 있는 것을 고르는 문제이다. 1935년에 스탈린은 주민들이 자신을 위한 정원이 있는 작은 집과 약간의 동물을 가질 수 있다고 규정했다(In 1935 he ordained that villagers could keep a cottage garden ~ animals)고 했고, 스탈린의 계획에 대한 소비에트 인구 대부분의 폭력적인 반응은 오직 목숨과 생계의 끔찍한 희생의 대가로 진압되었다(The violent reaction ~ at the cost of a terrible toll in lives and livelihood.)고 했으므로,

시골 경제에 활력을 주기 위한 스탈린의 목표는 실제로는 방해받았다는 것을 추론할 수 있다. 따라서 ③번이 정답이다.

오답분석
① 첫 번째 문단의 Many peasants ~ were denounced as rural capitalists (kulaks) by the Communists, and ~ slight에서 많은 소작농이 총을 들이대고 집단 농장으로 억지로 들어갔고, 다수가 공산당원에 의해 시골의 자본주의자(부농)로 맹렬히 비난받았으며, 죽거나 생존 가능성이 얼마 안 되는 강제 노동 수용소로 추방되거나 둘 중 하나였다고 했으므로, 많은 소작농이 토지 사유권을 비난했다는 것은 지문의 내용과 다르다.
② 첫 번째 문단의 In the Soviet Union ~ throughout rural Russia. The peasantry resisted ~ by destroying their crops and livestock에서 소비에트 연방에서 농업과 시골 마을 생활을 근대화하기 위한 노력은 사실상 러시아 시골 도처에 두 번째 내전을 유발했고, 소작농은 농작물과 가축을 말살함으로써 자신들을 집단 농장에 억지로 들어가게 하려는 폭력적인 공격에 저항했다고 했으므로, 근대화에 대한 가장 끈질긴 저항이 도시 지역에서 비롯되었다는 것은 지문의 내용과 다르다.
④ 두 번째 문장의 While there was never ~, the conservative masses reacted to the crisis they faced with growing anger and desperation에서 유럽 전역에 걸쳐 합심한 반근대주의자의 반란은 없었던 한편, 보수적인 대중은 자신들이 직면했던 위기에 고조되는 분노와 절망으로 대처했다고 했으므로, 보수적인 대중이 상의하달식의 근대화에 저항하기 위해 동맹을 결성했다는 것은 지문의 내용과 다르다.
⑤ 두 번째 문단의 Within a few years ~ everything produced on the collective farms. But this was the government's only concession. The violent reaction ~ a terrible toll in lives and livelihood에서 몇 년 안에 육지 면적의 3.9퍼센트만 구성했던 이 시민 농장의 생산물의 가치는 거의 집단 농장에서 생산되었던 모든 것의 가치와 맞먹었지만, 시민 농장은 정부의 특권일 뿐이었고, 스탈린의 계획에 대한 소비에트 인구 대부분의 폭력적인 반응은 오직 목숨과 생계의 끔찍한 희생의 대가로 진압되었다고 했으므로, 소비에트 정부가 생산의 사적인 통제를 통해 개인의 이익을 위한 전적인 지원을 제공했다는 것은 지문의 내용과 다르다.

어휘
deplore v. 비난하다, 개탄하다
private land ownership phr. 토지 사유권
persistent adj. 끈질긴   vitalize v. ~에 활력을 주다
impede v. 방해하다   in practice phr. 실제로는
form an alliance phr. 동맹을 결성하다
top-down adj. 상의하달식의, 통제가 잘 되어 있는

[41-43]

원래, 선거일은 주마다 달랐지만, 1845년에 단 하나의 전국 선거일을 설정하기 위한 법이 통과되었다. 처음에, 그것은 대통령 선거에만 적용되었으나, 이후에 의회 선거로도 확대되었다. 그 당시, 미국은 여전히 대체로 농업사회였다. 노동 인구의 대다수를 구성했던 농부들의 경우, 한 해의 대부분이 심기, 관리, 그리고 작물 수확으로 이루어져 있었다. 11월 초는 수확이 끝나 선거하기에 좋은 시기였지만, 날씨는 여전히 비교적 포근했다.

하지만, 한 주 중 어떤 날들은 다른 날들보다 더 좋았다. 이틀은 확실히 불가능했다. 대부분의 미국인들은 독실한 기독교도였기 때문에 일요일을 휴식과 예배의 날로 따로 잡아두었다. 많은 지역에서 수요일은 장날이었고, 그날 농부들은 마을에서 그들의 작물을 팔았다. 게다가, 때로는 이동하는 날도 필요했다. 시골 지역에서는, 가장 가까운 투표소가 여러 마일 떨어져 있었을지도 모르고, 자동차가 있기 전 시대에 투표소로 가는 것은 시간이 걸렸을 것이다. 만약 사람들이 일요일이나 수요일을 이동하는 날로 사용하지 못했다면, 그것은 선거일이 월요일이나 목요일이 될 수 없었음을 의미했다. 그리하여 화요일이 최고의 선택권으로 여겨졌다.

선거일이 '첫 번째 월요일 다음' 화요일로 명시된 이유는 11월 1일에 해당되지 않도록 하기 위함이었다. 그날은 일부 기독교도가 만성절로 알고 있는 날이고, 상인들이 보통 달의 첫 번째 날을 지난달 회계 장부를 정리하기 위해 사용했기 때문에 적합하지 않은 것으로 간주되었다.

presidential adj. 대통령의   congressional adj. 의회의
agrarian adj. 농업의   majority n. 다수   tending n. 관리
harvest v. 수확하다   relatively adv. 비교적
devout adj. 독실한
set aside phr. (돈·시간을) 따로 떼어 두다
worship n. 예배   market day phr. 장날
polling place phr. 투표소   era n. 시대
perceive v. ~을 여기다   specify v. 명시하다
fall on phr. ~에 해당되다   unfavorable adj. 적합하지 않은
merchant n. 상인   books n. 회계 장부
previous adj. 이전의

41 2020 서울여대

정답 ①

해석
① 날씨   ② 예배
③ 판매   ④ 이동

해설 선거일이 화요일로 결정되었을 때 고려해야 할 요소가 아니었던 것을 파악하는 문제이다. 지문 중간에서 대부분의 미국인들은 일요일을 예배의 날로 따로 잡아두었고, 수요일에 농부들은 작물을 팔았으며, 때로는 이동하는 날도 필요했기 때문에 화요일이 최고의 선택권으로 여겨졌다고 했다. 한편, 첫 번째 문단에서 11월 초에 날씨가 여전히 포근했다는 내용이 있지만, 이것이 선거일 결정에서 고려된 요소는 아니다. 따라서 정답은 ①번이다.

어휘 transportation n. 이동 (수단)

42 2020 서울여대

정답 ①

해석 ① 일요일과 수요일   ② 월요일과 목요일
      ③ 금요일과 토요일   ④ 화요일과 목요일

해설 밑줄 친 이틀이 지칭하는 것이 무엇인지 파악하는 문제이다. 지문 중간에서 대부분의 미국인들은 일요일을 휴식과 예배의 날로 따로 잡아두었고, 많은 지역에서 수요일은 장날이었다고 했다. 따라서, Two days가 지칭하는 것을 '일요일과 수요일'이라고 한 ①번이 정답이다.

43 2020 서울여대

정답 ③

해석 ① 근로자   ② 농부
      ③ 상인   ④ 정치인

해설 누구를 위해 11월의 첫째 날이 배제되었는지를 파악하는 문제이다. 마지막 문장에서 상인들이 보통 달의 첫 번째 날을 지난달 회계 장부를 정리하기 위해 사용했기 때문에 11월 1일이 적합하지 않은 것으로 간주되었다고 했으므로, 11월의 첫째 날이 배제된 것은 '상인'을 위해서이다. 따라서 정답은 ③번이다.

[44-45]

19세기 중반에 미국 서부를 횡단한 동부의 정착민들은 그들이 사막과 산을 가로지르는 힘든 여정에 직면했다는 것을 알게 되었다. 그들은 그 여행이 몇 년이 걸릴 것이고 어떤 사람들은 목숨을 잃을 것이라는 것을 알고 있었다. 하지만 그들은 낙관적이었다.
Michael T. Simmons는 결연한 여행자 중 한 명이었다. 누군가가 그에게 새로운 기회를 얻기 위해 태평양 북서부로 가라고 말했다. 그는 자신과 가족에게 필요한 물품의 대금을 지불하기 위해 그의 가게를 팔았다. 그는 그 지역이 거의 알려지지 않았다는 것을 알았다. 그는 또한 그것이 위험하다는 것을 알았다. 이것은 그를 막지 못했다.
Simmons와 그의 일행이 오리건주에 도착했을 때, 그는 북쪽으로 계속 갈 것이라고 알렸다. Hudson's Bay 무역회사는 그 소식을 듣고 그를 말렸다. 그러나 Simmons는 그 여행이 성공할 것이라고 확신했고, 그는 듣지 않았다. 대신 계획대로 북쪽으로 계속 갔다. 그가 도착한 후, 그는 현재 워싱턴 주로 알려진 지역에 최초의 정착지를 세우는 것에 기여했다. Simmons가 텀워터 폭포에서 나온 물을 동력으로 삼아 최초의 방앗간을 세웠다는 기록이 있다. 이로 인해, 그는 때때로 워싱턴 산업의 아버지로 불리기도 한다.

settler n. 정착민   face v. 직면하다, 마주치다
optimistic adj. 낙관적인   opportunity n. 기회
sell one's business phr. 가게를 팔다, 점포의 권리를 팔다
supply n. 물품, 비축물자   announce v. 알리다, 발표하다
certain adj. 확신하는   establish v. 세우다, 설립하다
settlement n. 정착지   territory n. 지역, 영토
mill n. 방앗간   waterfall n. 폭포   power n. 동력, 에너지

44 2020 국민대

정답 ②

해석 ① 유연한 – 말렸다   ② 결연한 – 말렸다
      ③ 유연한 – 권장했다   ④ 결연한 – 권장했다

해설 지문의 빈칸을 채우는 문제이다. 두 번째 문단 마지막에서 여행이 위험하다는 것을 알았지만 이것이 그를 막지 못했다고 했으므로, 첫 번째 빈칸에는 Simmons가 의지가 확고한 사람이라는 내용이 나와야 적절하다는 것을 알 수 있다. 따라서 '결연한'이 들어가야 한다. 세 번째 문단 세 번째 문장에서 Simmons는 무역회사의 말을 듣지 않고, 계획대로 했다고 했으므로 두 번째 빈칸에는 무역회사가 그의 계획에 반대했다는 내용이 나와야 적절하다는 것을 알 수 있다. 따라서 '말렸다'가 들어가야 한다. 따라서 ② determined(결연한) – discouraged(말렸다)가 정답이다.

어휘 flexible adj. 유연한, 융통성 있는
      determined adj. 결연한, 완강한
      discourage v. 말리다, 막다

45 2020 국민대

정답 ②

해석 ① 많은 사람들은 미국인들이 남쪽으로 가야 한다고 믿었다.
      ② 많은 사람들은 서쪽으로 확장하는 것이 힘들 거라고 생각했다.
      ③ Simmons와 그의 일행은 북쪽으로 향할 때 많은 현지의 지원을 받았다.
      ④ Simmons와 그의 일행은 미지의 영토에서 초기 정착민들과 경쟁했다.

해설 지문의 내용과 일치하는 것을 묻는 문제이다. 지문 첫 번째 문장에서 미국 서부를 횡단한 사람들은 그들이 힘든 여정에 직면한 걸 알게 되었다는 내용을 통해 많은 사람들은 서쪽으로 확장하는 것이 힘들 거라고 생각했다는 것을 알 수 있다. 따라서 ②번이 지문의 내용과 일치한다.

오답분석 ① 누군가가 Simmons에게 새로운 기회를 위해 태평양 북서부로 가라고 했고, Simmons도 북쪽으로 계속 갈 것이라고 알렸다고 했으므로, 많은 사람들은 미국인들이 남쪽으로 가야 한다고 믿었다는 것은 지문의 내용과 다르다.
③ Simmons가 북쪽으로 계속 간다고 했을 때, Hudson's Bay 무역회사가 그를 말렸다고는 했지만, Simmons와 그의 일행은 북쪽으로 향할 때 많은 현지의 지원을 받았는지는 알 수 없다.

④ Simmons가 현재 워싱턴 주로 알려진 지역에 최초의 정착지를 세우는 것에 기여했다고 했으므로, Simmons와 그의 일행이 미지의 영토에서 초기 정착민들과 경쟁했다는 것은 지문의 내용과 다르다.

어휘 proceed v. 나아가다, 이동하다 westward adv. 서쪽으로
expansion n. 확장 local adj. 현지의

[46-48]

100년 전에, 한 위대한 미국인이 노예 해방령에 서명했고, 우리는 그의 상징적인 그림자 위에 서 있다. 이 중대한 (A)법령은 위축시키는 불평등의 불꽃 속에서 무감각해진 수백만 명의 흑인 노예들에게 엄청난 희망의 불빛으로 다가왔다. 노예 해방령은 긴 밤 같은 감금의 시간을 끝낼 (B)즐거운 새벽처럼 다가왔다. 하지만 100년 후에, 우리는 흑인이 여전히 자유롭지 않다는 비극적인 사실을 직시해야 한다. 100년 후, 흑인의 삶은 여전히 슬프게도 차별의 족쇄와 차별의 굴레로 인해 무력하다. 100년 후, 흑인은 물질적 번영의 방대한 바다의 한가운데에 있는 외로운 가난의 섬에서 살고 있다. 100년 후에도, 흑인은 여전히 미국 사회의 모퉁이에서 비참하게 살고 있으며 자기 나라에서 스스로 추방된 사람이라는 것을 깨닫는다. 그래서 우리는 (C)소름 끼치는 상황을 극적으로 표현하기 위해 오늘 여기에 온 것이다. 어떤 의미에서 우리는 우리나라의 수도에 (D)수표를 현금으로 바꾸기 위해 온 것이다. 우리 공화국의 건축가들이 헌법과 독립선언문에서 훌륭한 말을 썼을 때, 그들은 모든 미국인이 상속인이 된다는 (E)약속 어음에 서명하고 있었다. 이 어음은 모든 사람이 양도할 수 없는 삶, 자유에 대한 권리와 행복 추구권을 보장받는다는 약속이었다.

score n. 20 symbolic adj. 상징적인, 상징하는
Emancipation Proclamation phr. 노예 해방령
emancipation n. (노예 등의) 해방
proclamation n. 선언(서), 성명서
momentous adj. 중대한, 중요한
decree n. 법령, (법원의) 결정 beacon n. 불빛, 신호등
sear v. 무감각하게 하다 withering adj. 위축시키는
injustice n. 불평등, 부당함 flame n. 불꽃, 정열
joyous adj. 즐거운 daybreak n. 새벽, 동틀 녘
captivity n. 감금, 포로(의 기간)
face v. (힘든 사실을) 직시하다, 받아들이다
tragic adj. 비극적인, 안타까운 manacle n. 족쇄, 수갑
segregation n. 차별, 분리 discrimination n. 차별
lonely adj. 외로운, 쓸쓸한 poverty n. 가난, 빈곤
in the midst of phr. ~의 한가운데에
vast adj. 방대한, 막대한
material prosperity phr. 물질적 번영
languish v. 비참하게 살다, 괴로워하다, 시들다
exile n. 추방자, 유배자
dramatize v. 극적으로 표현하다, 각색하다
appalling adj. 소름 끼치는, 오싹해지는
condition n. 상황, 조건 in a sense phr. 어떤 의미에서는
capital n. 수도, 자산

cash v. 수표를 현금으로 바꾸다, 현금화하다 check n. 수표
architect n. 건축가 republic n. 공화국
magnificent adj. 훌륭한, 감명 깊은 constitution n. 헌법
Declaration of Independence phr. 독립선언문
promissory note phr. 약속 어음
promissory adj. 약속하는, 약속을 포함한
fall heir phr. 상속인이 되다 promise n. 약속
guarantee v. 보장하다 unalienable adj. 양도할 수 없는
liberty n. 자유 pursuit n. 추구

46 [2019 상명대]

정답 ③

해설 (A)~(E) 가운데 의미하는 바가 다른 것을 파악하는 문제이다. (A), (B), (D), (E)는 모두 노예 해방령을 의미하는데, (C)는 흑인의 외롭고 비참한 삶을 의미하므로, (A)~(E) 가운데 의미하는 바가 다른 것은 (C)이다. 따라서 ③번이 정답이다.

47 [2019 상명대]

정답 ①

해석 ① 흑인에게 드리운 한 미국인의 그림자 때문에, 아프리카계 미국인들은 여전히 어둠과 무지 속에서 고통받고 있다.
② 흑인은 백인과 동등한 권리를 받는다.
③ 노예 해방령이 100년 전에 선언되었음에도 불구하고, 흑인은 여전히 차별당하는 상황 아래에 있다.
④ 흑인은 그들의 권리를 요구하기 위해 수도에 왔다.
⑤ 흑인의 권리는 노예 해방령에 의해 부여된다.

해설 지문의 내용과 일치하지 않는 것을 묻는 문제이다. ①번의 키워드인 shadow(그림자)와 관련된 첫 번째 문장에서 100년 전에, 한 위대한 미국인이 노예 해방령에 서명했고, 우리는 그의 상징적인 그림자 위에 서 있다고 했으므로, 흑인에게 드리운 한 미국인의 그림자 때문에, 아프리카계 미국인들이 여전히 어둠과 무지 속에서 고통받고 있다는 것은 지문의 내용과 다르다. 따라서 ①번이 지문의 내용과 일치하지 않는다.

오답 분석
② 두 번째 문장 This momentous decree ~ withering injustice를 통해 '흑인은 백인과 동등한 권리를 받는다'는 것을 알 수 있다.
③ 다섯 번째 문장 One hundred years later, ~ chains of discrimination을 통해 '노예 해방령이 100년 전에 선언되었음에도 불구하고, 흑인은 여전히 차별당하는 상황 아래에 있다'는 것을 알 수 있다.
④ 아홉 번째 문장 In a sense ~ a check를 통해 '흑인은 그들의 권리를 요구하기 위해 수도에 왔다'는 것을 알 수 있다.
⑤ 두 번째 문장 This momentous decree ~ withering injustice를 통해 '흑인의 권리는 노예 해방령에 의해 부여된다'는 것을 알 수 있다.

어휘 darkness n. 어둠, 암흑 blindness n. 무지, 맹목

48 2019 상명대

정답 ③

해석 ① 해방 — 족쇄　　② 섬 — 바다
　　③ 그림자 — 불빛　④ 추방자 — 상속인
　　⑤ 가난 — 번영

해설 본문 중에 나타난 의미상 대조를 이루는 짝이 아닌 것을 파악하는 문제이다. 첫 번째 문장의 '그림자'는 노예 해방령에 서명한 위대한 미국인의 영향력을 의미하고, 두 번째 문장의 '불빛'은 흑인 노예들에게 다가온 희망을 의미하므로, 의미상 대조를 이루는 짝이 아닌 것은 '그림자 — 불빛'이다. 따라서 ③번이 정답이다.

어휘　prosperity n. 번영

[49-52]

앤드류 카네기라는, 스코틀랜드계 미국인 기업가이자 자선가는, 1835년 스코틀랜드에서 태어나, 12세에 그의 부모님과 미국으로 이민을 갔다. 카네기는 전신 기사로 일을 시작했는데, 1860년대에 이미 철도, 다리, 석유 기중기에 투자하고 있었다. 카네기는 채권 판매원으로서 더 많은 부를 축적했다. 그는 피츠버그의 카네기 철강회사를 지었는데, 1901년 존 피어폰 모건에게 그 회사를 3억 345만 달러에 팔았다. 카네기 철강회사를 매각한 뒤, 그는 몇 년간 가장 부유한 미국인으로 존 D. 록펠러를 능가했다.
일찍이 1868년, 33세였던, 카네기는 스스로 메모를 작성했다. 그는, "... 부를 축적하는 것은 우상 숭배의 나쁜 종류 중 하나이다. 돈을 숭배하는 것보다 인격을 떨어뜨리는 우상은 없다."라고 썼다. 자신의 품위를 떨어뜨리는 것을 피하고자, 카네기는 똑같은 메모에 자신이 35세에 은퇴할 것이며 "... 부자인 채로 죽는 것은 수치이기" 때문에 박애주의적인 기부를 할 것이라고 썼다. 하지만, 카네기는 자신의 고향인 스코틀랜드에 도서관을 선물한 1881년까지 자선 사업을 본격적으로 시작하지 않았다.
반면에 카네기는 영국의 제국주의에 대해 아무런 언급도 하지 않았지만, 미국의 식민지 사상에 대해서는 강하게 반대했다. 카네기는 필리핀의 합병을 반대했으며 필리핀의 독립을 주선하려고 노력했다. 스페인-미국 전쟁의 끝이 다가오자, 미국은 스페인으로부터 2천만 달러에 필리핀을 사들였다. 카네기는 자신이 미국의 제국주의라고 인식한 것에 반대하기 위해, 필리핀인들이 미국으로부터 독립을 쟁취할 수 있도록 개인적으로 필리핀인들에게 2천만 달러를 주겠다고 제의했다. 하지만, 그 제안은 아무런 성과가 없었다.

---

industrialist n. 기업가　philanthropist n. 자선가
immigrate to phr. ~로 이주하다　telegrapher n. 전신 기사
derrick n. 기중기　accumulate v. 축적하다, 모으다
bond n. 채권　surpass v. 능가하다
amass v. 모으다, 축적하다　idolatry n. 우상 숭배
debase v. (품성·인격 등을) 떨어뜨리다

degrade v. ~의 품위를 떨어뜨리다
philanthropic adj. 박애(주의)의; 자선(사업, 기금)의
disgrace v. 망신시키다
in earnest phr. 본격적으로; 진심으로
imperialism n. 제국주의　oppose v. 반대하다, 대항하다
colony n. 식민지　annexation n. 합병
arrange for phr. 준비하다, 계획을 짜다
near v. 접근하다, 다가오다　counter v. 반대하다, 거스르다
perceive v. 지각하다, 인식하다

49 2020 세종대

정답 ②

해석 ① 카네기는 1860년대에 철도, 다리, 석유 기중기에 투자를 시작했다.
② 카네기는 1890년대에 미국에서 가장 부유한 사람이 아니었다.
③ 카네기는 부를 축적하기 위해 돈을 우상화했다.
④ 카네기는 그의 고향인 스코틀랜드에서 도서관을 선물로 받았다.

해설 지문을 통해 추론할 수 있는 것을 고르는 문제이다. 지문 처음에서 카네기가 존 피어폰 모건에게 카네기 철강회사를 매각한 1901년부터 몇 년 동안 가장 부유한 미국인이었다고 했으므로, 카네기는 1890년대에 미국에서 가장 부유한 사람이 아니었다는 것을 추론할 수 있다. 따라서 정답은 ②번이다.

오답 분석
① 카네기는 1860년대에 이미 철도와, 다리, 석유 기중기에 투자하고 있었다고 했으므로, 1860년대에 시작한 건 지는 추론할 수 없다.
③ 카네기는 부를 축적하는 것은 우상 숭배의 나쁜 종류 중 하나라고 했으므로, 부를 축적하기 위해 돈을 우상화했다는 것은 추론할 수 없다.
④ 카네기가 자신의 고향인 스코틀랜드에 도서관을 선물했다고 했으므로, 선물 받았다는 것은 추론할 수 없다.

50 2020 세종대

정답 ④

해석 ① 그러나　　　　② ~ 때문에
　　③ ~때　　　　　④ 반면에

해설 빈칸에 적절한 연결어를 넣는 문제이다. 빈칸이 있는 문장은 카네기가 영국의 제국주의에 대해 아무런 언급을 하지 않았다는 내용이고, 빈칸 뒤 문장은 미국의 식민지 사상에 대해 강하게 반대했다는 내용으로 카네기가 영국의 제국주의와 미국의 식민지 사상에 대해 각기 다른 태도를 보인다는 내용이다. 따라서 역접을 나타내는 연결어인 ④ While(반면에)이 정답이다.

51 [2020 세종대]

정답 ②

해석 ① 부 ② 반제국주의
③ 필리핀 ④ 우상 숭배

해설 지문의 세 번째 문단의 주제를 묻는 문제이다. 지문의 세 번째 문단에서 카네기가 미국의 식민지 사상에 대해 강하게 반대했으며, 자신이 미국의 제국주의라고 인식한 것에 반대하기 위해 필리핀을 도우려 했다고 하였다. 따라서 이 지문의 주제를 카네기의 '반제국주의' 철학이라고 표현한 ②번이 정답이다.

52 [2020 세종대]

정답 ④

해석
① 카네기는 35세에 자선가로 활동하기 시작했다.
② 카네기는 부자가 죽는 것을 수치스럽게 여겼다.
③ 필리핀은 카네기의 자금 제공 덕분에 미국으로부터 독립을 얻었다.
④ 카네기는 미국이 스페인으로부터 필리핀을 사는 것에 반대했다.

해설 지문의 내용과 일치하는 것을 묻는 문제이다. 지문의 마지막 문단 he strongly opposed the idea of American colonies. He opposed ~ 의 내용을 통해 카네기가 미국의 식민지 사상에 강하게 반대하며, 필리핀의 합병을 반대했고 필리핀의 독립을 주선하려고 노력했다는 것을 알 수 있다. 따라서 ④번이 지문의 내용과 일치한다.

오답 분석
① 카네기는 자신의 고향인 스코틀랜드에 도서관을 선물한 1881년부터 자선가로 활동하기 시작했는데, 1835년에 태어난 카네기의 나이는 당시 46세였으므로, 35세에 자선가로 활동하기 시작했다는 것은 지문의 내용과 다르다.
② 카네기는 기부를 하지 않고 부자인 채로 죽는 것이 수치라고는 했지만, 그가 부자가 죽는 것을 수치스럽게 여겼는지는 알 수 없다.
③ 필리핀인들이 미국으로부터 독립할 수 있도록 2천만 달러를 주겠다고 제의했지만 아무런 성과가 없었다고 했으므로, 카네기의 자금 제공 덕분에 필리핀이 미국으로부터 독립을 얻었다는 것은 지문의 내용과 다르다.

[53-57]

[A] 제1차 세계대전 시기에, 유럽 대륙의 경계를 넘어 서구 사상과 제도의 전달은 순조로이 진행되고 있었다. 유럽 제국주의가 한창일 때, 대망을 품은 젊은 비서양 사람들은 보통 특권 계급에 속한 가정 출신이었고, 공부를 위해 유럽이나 미국으로 갔다. 서양 사람들은 직접 그들의 지배하에 있는 지역들에 서양식 학교를 설립했다. 그곳에서 비서양 지식인들이 생겨났고, 그 구성원들은 가장 선진의 서구 사상에 자극받고 서양 학문을 갖추었다. 인간 존엄성에 대한 그들의 의식은 자신들의 교사를 거울로 삼은 것이었지만, 서양 사람들이 비서양 지식인들을 열등하게 취급하여 그 의식은 발달하지 못했다. 떠나게 되고 내부적으로 분열된 이 지식인들은 자신들의 서양인 교사를 따라 민족주의자가 되었다. 서구식 교육을 받은 그들은 "현대" 터키인, 아랍인, 인도인, 혹은 아프리카인이 되고 싶어 했다. 그들은 그들의 나라가 존경받기를 원했다.

[B] 이러한 교육을 받은 민족주의자들은 곧 혁명가가 되기도 했는데, 식민지 당국이나 전통적인 통치자들이 대개 공개적인 저항을 (A)진압했기 때문이다. 혁명가로서, 그들은 엘리트주의자와 사회주의자에서 돌아섰다. 그들은 민족이 그들 자신을 강하게 만드는 방법을 모른다고 생각했다. 하지만 서구식 교육을 받은 비서양 지식인들은 적어도 개략적으로는 민주적 이상에 계속 헌신하기도 했다. 어떻게 엘리트주의와 친서방 성향이 민중에 대한 신뢰와 미래에 해결되지 않은 문제로 남아있던 토착문화에 대한 애착과 조화될 수 있었을까?

[C] (B)이 지식인들의 진보는 비서양 국가들에 따라 다양했다. 예를 들어, 멸망해 가는 오스만 제국에서, 서구식 교육을 받은 젊은 터키인들이 1908년 정권을 잡았다. 제1차 세계대전 말미에 금방이라도 무너질 듯한 그들의 제국이 붕괴한 후, 그들은 Kernal Atatürk의 지도로 상당히 현대적이고 안정적인 터키를 만들었다. 그 변화는 비교적 빨리 이루어졌으며 현재까지 지속되고 있다.

[D] (a) 하지만, 인도의 경험은 비서양 국가의 추세를 더 전형적으로 나타냈다. 영국식 교육을 받은 인도인들은 영국 공무원의 도움으로 1885년에 인도 국민 회의를 설립했고 이 기관을 온건한 인도 민족주의 기관으로 만들었다. (b) 제1차 세계대전으로 인해 급진적으로 된 인도 국민 회의는 마하트마 간디의 영향력 아래에 있었는데, 간디는 가장 주목할 만한 서구화된 반식민주의 지도자 중 한 명이었다. (c) 150년이 넘는 영국의 통치하에서, 인도는 효과적인 민족주의 지휘부와 독립국의 지위에 적합한 행정적, 법적, 그리고 경제적 구조를 발달시켰다. (d) 인도의 서구화는 상위층과 하위층 모두에서, 영국의 통치와 그에 대한 원주민의 저항에서 비롯되었다. 1947년에 독립이 왔을 때, 인도 아대륙은 인도와 파키스탄이라는 두 개의 국가로 갈라졌다. (e) 인도 민족주의의의 가장 큰 결함은 이슬람교도와 힌두교 신자 간의 극복할 수 없는 종교적 분열에 있었다. 독립은 수십만 명의 목숨을 앗아간 주민 폭동 전쟁으로 이어졌다.

---

institution n. 제도 **imperialism** n. 제국주의
privileged adj. 특권 계급에 속하는 **domination** n. 지배
intelligentsia n. 지식인들 **prompt** v. 자극하다
pattern after phr. 거울로 삼다 **stunt** v. 발달을 저해하다
nationalist n. 민족주의자 **revolutionary** n. 혁명가
resistance n. 저항 **elitist** n. 엘리트주의자
dedicate v. 헌신하다 **orientation** n. 성향
reconcile v. 조화시키다 **indigenous** adj. 토착의
ramshackle adj. 금방이라도 무너질 듯한

endure v. 지속되다   instrument n. 기관
proceed from phr. ~에서 비롯되다
subcontinent n. 아대륙   communal riot phr. 주민 폭동
radicalize v. 급진적으로 하다
anticolonial adj. 반식민주의의
administrative adj. 행정의   nationhood n. 독립국의 지위

53 2019 아주대

정답 ①

해석
① 전 세계적인 서구화
② 세계 통합주의의 시도
③ 산업 시대의 출현
④ 정치적 발달에 대한 장애물
⑤ 서양 제국주의의 세계적 지배

해설 지문의 제목을 묻는 문제이다. [A] 문단과 [B] 문단에서는 제1차 세계대전 시기에 서구식 교육을 받은 비서양 지식인들이 그들의 나라가 존경받기를 원했고, 혁명가가 되었다고 했다. [C] 문단과 [D] 문단에서는 비서양 지식인들에 의해 서구화가 일어난 두 국가의 예시를 보여주고 있다. 따라서 이 지문의 제목을 '전 세계적인 서구화'라고 표현한 ①번이 정답이다.

어휘 globalism n. 세계 통합주의   obstacle n. 장애물
dominance n. 지배

54 2019 아주대

정답 ④

해석
① 추론했다   ② 비웠다
③ 수여 했다   ④ 진압했다
⑤ 선포했다

해설 지문의 빈칸을 채우는 문제이다. 빈칸이 있는 문장에서 이러한 교육을 받은 민족주의자들은 곧 혁명가가 되기도 했다고 했으므로, 빈칸에는 이들이 혁명가가 된 이유에 대한 내용이 나와야 적절하다는 것을 알 수 있다. 따라서 '식민지 당국이나 전통적인 통치자들이 대개 공개적인 저항을 _____ 때문이다'라는 문맥의 빈칸에는 '진압했다'가 들어가는 것이 자연스럽다. 따라서 ④번이 정답이다.

어휘 deduce v. 추론하다   evacuate v. 비우다
confer v. 수여 하다   suppress v. 진압하다
proclaim v. 선포하다

55 2019 아주대

정답 ③

해석
① 독립의 시도는 고통스럽고, 폭력적이며, 역경으로 인해 실패했다.
② 서양과 비서양 사람 간 관계에서 새로운 국면이 시작됐다.
③ 이 지식인들의 진보는 비서양 국가들에 따라 다양했다.
④ 세계의 일부 지역에서, 서양의 침투는 더 더디면서 문제가 많았다.
⑤ 지식인들이 서양의 사고방식을 배우고 있는 동안, 유럽인들은 서양 제도를 도입했다.

해설 지문의 빈칸을 채우는 문제이다. 빈칸 앞부분에서 서구식 교육을 받은 비서양 지식인들이 혁명가가 되었다고 하고, 빈칸 뒤에서 터키와 인도에서의 실제 사례를 차례대로 설명하고 있으므로, 빈칸에는 '이 지식인들의 진보는 비서양 국가들에 따라 다양했다'가 들어가는 것이 자연스럽다. 따라서 ③번이 정답이다.

어휘 mar v. 망치다   adversity n. 역경   penetration n. 침투
intellectual n. 지식인   attitude n. 사고방식

56 2019 아주대

정답 ②

해석
① 영국 공무원들은 인도 국민 회의를 설립했다.
② 서구식 교육을 받은 터키인들은 Kernal Atatürk의 지도를 받아 현대의 터키를 만들었다.
③ 유럽에서 공부한 비서양 사람들은 그들만의 학문적 전통을 세웠다.
④ 교육받은 민족주의자들에게는 그들의 민족의 독립 능력이 강해질 거라는 믿음이 있었다.
⑤ 인도는 영국으로부터 독립한 이후 행정적, 법적, 그리고 경제적 제도를 형성했다.

해설 지문의 내용과 일치하는 것을 묻는 문제이다. [C] 문단의 두 번째 문장 After the collapse ~ Kemal Atatürk의 내용을 통해 서구식 교육을 받은 터키인들이 Kernal Atatürk의 지도를 받아 현대의 터키를 만들었다는 것을 알 수 있다. 따라서 ②번이 지문의 내용과 일치한다.

오답 분석
① 영국식 교육을 받은 인도인들은 영국 공무원의 도움으로 1885년에 인도 국민 회의를 설립했다고 했으므로, 영국 공무원들이 인도 국민 회의를 설립했다는 것은 지문의 내용과 다르다.
③ 인간 존엄성에 대한 비서양 지식인들의 의식은 서양 사람들이 그들을 열등하게 취급하여 발달하지 못했다고 했으므로, 유럽에서 공부한 비서양 사람들이 그들만의 학문적 전통을 세웠다는 것은 지문의 내용과 다르다.
④ 서구식 교육을 받은 민족주의자들은 민족이 그들 자신을 강하게 만드는 방법을 모른다고 생각했다고 했으므로, 교육받은 민족주의자들에게 그들의 민족의 독립 능력이 강해질 거라는 믿음이 있었다는 것은 지문의 내용과 다르다.
⑤ 150년이 넘는 영국의 통치하에서, 행정적, 법적, 그리고 경제적 구조를 발달시켰다고 했으므로, 인도가 영국으로부터 독립한 이후 행정적, 법적, 그리고 경제적 제도를 형성했다는 것은 지문의 내용과 다르다.

어휘 construct v. 세우다, 구성하다

57 2019 아주대

정답 ⑤

해설 지문의 흐름상 주어진 문장이 들어가기에 가장 적절한 위치를 고르는 문제이다. (e)의 앞 문장에서 1947년에 독립이 왔을 때, 인도 아대륙은 인도와 파키스탄이라는 두 개의 국가로 갈라졌다고 했으므로, (e) 자리에 두 개의 국가로 갈라진 것에 대해 구체적으로 설명하는 주어진 문장 '인도 민족주의의의 가장 큰 결함은 이슬람교도와 힌두교 신자 간의 극복할 수 없는 종교적 분열에 있었다'가 들어가야 글의 흐름이 자연스럽게 연결된다. 따라서 ⑤번이 정답이다.

어휘 flaw n. 결함   insurmountable adj. 극복할 수 없는

03 예술

01-53
문제집 p.68

01 ⑤	02 ②	03 ①	04 ①	05 ②
06 ①	07 ②	08 ①	09 ③	10 ⑤
11 ②	12 ③	13 ③	14 ③	15 ③
16 ①	17 ②	18 ④	19 ④	20 ②
21 ④	22 ②	23 ④	24 ③	25 ①
26 ②	27 ⑤	28 ①	29 ②	30 ③
31 ③	32 ④	33 ②	34 ④	35 ⑤
36 ①	37 ②	38 ③	39 ②	40 ④
41 ④	42 ④	43 ④	44 ③	45 ①
46 ④	47 ②	48 ②	49 ⑤	50 ③
51 ③	52 ②	53 ①		

01 [2020 인하대]

정답 ⑤

해석 인도네시아 술라웨시섬에 있는 Leang Bulu' Sipong 4의 석회암 동굴은 4만 년도 더 전에 초기 현대인들에 의해 사용되었다. 그 안에는 짙은 붉은 색으로 칠해진 약 14.5피트 너비의 그림이 있었는데, 약 8개의 작은 두발 달린 모습이 그려져 있는데, 창과 밧줄처럼 보이는 것을 지니고 있으며, 현지 야생멧돼지와 물소를 용감하게 사냥하고 있다. 호주의 그리피스 대학교의 고고학자 팀인 발견자들은 이것을 "틀림없이, 현재 세계에서 가장 오래된 이야기 그림 기록이며 최초의 회화적 예술작품"이라고 한다. 가장 첫 번째 이야기 그림은 우리가 알고 있는 가장 단순하고 가장 공감을 불러일으키는 이야기 중 하나이다. 사냥꾼과 사냥감에 대한 이야기인데, 작고 쉽게 무시당하는 추격자는 무섭지만 연약한 짐승을 쓰러뜨리려 한다.
① 구전의
② 복잡한
③ 멸망한
④ 그리스의
⑤ 그림의

해설 지문의 빈칸을 채우는 문제이다. 지문의 빈칸이 있는 문장 바로 앞 문장에서 동굴 안에 그림이 있다고 했고, 빈칸이 있는 문장에서 이것을 최초의 회화적 예술 작품이라고 했으므로, 빈칸에는 그림 관련 기록이라는 내용이 나와야 적절하다는 것을 알 수 있다. 따라서 '그림' 기록이라고 한 ⑤번이 정답이다.

어휘 limestone n. 석회암 occupy v. 사용하다, 거주하다
pigment n. 색소 bipedal adj. 두발 달린, 두발의
figure n. 모습, 인물 bear v. 지니다, 가지다
spear n. 창 bravely adv. 용감하게, 훌륭하게
buffalo n. 물소 discoverer n. 발견자, 창안자
archaeologist n. 고고학자
to one's knowledge phr. 틀림없이, 확실히
currently adv. 현재, 지금 storytelling adj. 이야기하는
figurative adj. 회화적 표현의 artwork n. 예술 작품
resonant adj. 공감을 불러일으키는 tale n. 이야기
mock v. 조롱하다, 무시하다 pursuer n. 추격자
bring down phr. 쓰러뜨리다, 콧대를 꺾다
vulnerable adj. 연약한, 취약한 oral adj. 구전의, 구술의
ruined adj. 멸망한, 파멸한 pictorial adj. 그림의, 회화의

02 [2019 한양대]

정답 ②

해석 21세기에, DDT가 항말라리아제로서 그 위험과 이점을 둘러싸고 여전히 논쟁이 격렬해지고, 전 세계의 도시에서 환경의 정의에 대한 요구가 들려오고, 해양 생물의 개체 수가 줄어들고, 수산업이 붕괴하고, 유독성 폐기물이 우리의 해안가를 휩쓸면서, Rachel Carson의 연구가 상당히 관계있고 심지어는 선견지명이 있는 것처럼 보인다. 그러나, Carson은 현대적인 의미에 있어 "환경론자"나 "환경 작가"로서 출발한 것은 아니다. 살충제의 위험성과 그것을 무분별하게 사용하는 것에 반대하는 명시적인 경고에 대한 자세한 문서가 담긴 Silent Spring은 여러 방면에서 Carson이 알고 가장 사랑했던 글의 장르에서 벗어난 것이었다. Carson은 무엇보다도 자연 작가였으며, 번역에 대한 탁월한 재능과 인간이 아닌 삶의 형태가 경험하는 세사의 유동적 경계, 맛과 소리, 고통과 즐거움의 풍부한 세심함을 환기하는 능력을 갖춘 사람이었다.
① 천연자원의 사용과 남용
② 새로운 영역을 개척하는 자연 작가로서의 Rachel Carson
③ 21세기의 Rachel Carson의 명성
④ 새로운 문학 장르로서의 환경적 글의 출현
⑤ 환경론자의 정의와 현실 사이의 벌어지는 격차

해설 지문의 주제를 묻는 문제이다. 지문의 중반에서 Rachel Carson은 원래 "환경론자"나 "환경 작가"로서 출발한 것이 아니며, 자신이 사랑했던 글의 장르에서 벗어났다고 설명하고 있다. 따라서 이 지문의 주제를 '새로운 영역을 개척하는 자연 작가로서의 Rachel Carson'이라고 표현한 ②번이 정답이다.

어휘 rage v. 격렬해지다
antimalarial agent phr. 항말라리아제
environmental adj. 환경의 justice n. 정의
worldwide adv. 전 세계적으로 population n. 개체 수, 인구
marine adj. 해양의 organism n. 생명체
fishery n. 수산업, 어업 collapse v. 붕괴하다
shore n. 해안가 remarkably adv. 상당히, 현저하게
prescient adj. 선견지명이 있는
documentation n. 문서, 서류 pesticide n. 살충제
explicit adj. 명시적인 indiscriminate adj. 무분별한
departure n. 벗어남 first and foremost phr. 무엇보다도
extraordinary adj. 탁월한, 대단한 translation n. 번역

evoke v. 환기하다, 떠올리다 **fluid** adj. 유동적인
boundary n. 경계 **abuse** n. 남용
break new ground phr. 새로운 영역을 개척하다
emergence n. 출현 **widen** v. 벌어지다, 넓어지다

[03-05]

뉴멕시코 샌타페이에 있는 10개 미술관 벽에는 멕시코계 미국인의 역사가 신화 속에 나오는 버전뿐만 아니라 실제 버전으로도 선명한 색상과 불균형적인 모습으로 묘사되어 있다. 아즈텍 조상은 춤추고 신들은 소작농을 보호하는데, 이 모든 것은 현재의 멕시코계 미국인의 영광을 위한 것이다. 일부 벽에는, 속박의 사슬이 깨지고, 인디언 아가씨로 묘사된 정의의 여인이, 인디언과 멕시코계 미국인을 지켜보고 있다. 인디언 아가씨의 표정은 따뜻하면서도 동시에 험악한데, 이는 더 생동감 있게 만들면서 방문자들도 보살펴주는 좋은 이분법이다.

또 다른 벽에는, 혁명적인 지도자인 Pancho Villa와 멕시코를 스페인 지배에서 해방시키려는 혁명을 일으켰던 가톨릭 신부인 Hidalgo 신부가 멕시코 소작농들을 자유로 이끌고 있다. 하지만 Pancho Villa의 기괴하게 근육이 있는 팔 끝에 꽉 쥔 주먹은 가장 (A)논란이 많은 그림이다. Pancho Villa의 그림은 멕시코인의 심리 상태를 대변하며 지켜지고 있는 모든 특징들인 단결, 투지, 야망, 그리고 자부심을 상징한다. 그려진 인물들은 용감하고, 올바르고, 강하며, 욕심 많은 느낌인데, 이는 늘어진 콧수염과 헐렁한 솜브레로 모자를 쓰고 치장용 벽토를 바른 건물의 그늘에 누워 있는 멕시코계 미국인에 대한 (B)고정관념과는 거리가 멀다.

disproportionate adj. 불균형의 **peasant** n. 소작농
bondage n. 속박 **maiden** n. 아가씨
fierce adj. 험악한, 사나운 **dichotomy** n. 이분법
enliven v. 더 생동감 있게 만들다 **nurture** v. 보살피다
revolutionary adj. 혁명적인 **priest** n. 신부, 사제
clenched adj. 꽉 쥔 **fist** n. 주먹
grotesquely adv. 기괴하게 **symbolize** v. 상징하다
unity n. 단결, 통합 **determination** n. 투지, 결단(력)
ambition n. 야망 **uphold** v. 지키다, 유지하다
psychology n. 심리 상태, 심리학 **grasping** adj. 욕심 많은
drooping adj. 늘어진 **mustache** n. 콧수염
floppy adj. 헐렁한
sombrero n. 솜브레로(챙이 넓은 멕시코 모자)
stucco n. 치장용 벽토

03 [2021 이화여대]

정답 ①

해석 ① 예술은 권리를 빼앗긴 지역 사회에서 통합과 힘을 만들어 낼 수 있다.
② 멕시코계 미국인 아이들은 강하고 용감한 사람들로 길러지지 않는다.
③ 조상신들은 멕시코계 미국인들에 대한 긍정적인 이미지를 만드는 데 실패했다.
④ 고정관념들은 충성심과 지도력을 가치 있게 생각하지 않는 사회에서 영속된다.
⑤ 멕시코인의 심리 상태는 어두운 과거에 깊이 뿌리박혀 있다.

해설 지문을 통해 추론할 수 있는 것을 고르는 문제이다. ①번 보기의 키워드인 'art(예술)'와 관련된 지문의 후반을 통해, 예술은 권리를 빼앗긴 지역 사회에서 통합과 힘을 만들어 낼 수 있다는 것을 추론할 수 있다. 따라서 정답은 ①번이다.

오답분석
② 멕시코계 미국인들을 묘사한 그림들이 용감하고, 올바르고, 강하며, 욕심 많은 느낌이라고 했으므로, 멕시코계 미국인 아이들이 강하고 용감한 사람들로 길러지지 않는다는 것은 지문의 내용과 다르다.
③ 아즈텍 조상이 춤추고 신들은 소작농을 보호하는 모든 것이 현재 멕시코계 미국인의 영광을 위한 것이라고 했으므로, 조상신들이 멕시코계 미국인들에 대한 긍정적인 이미지를 만드는 데 실패했다는 것은 지문의 내용과 다르다.
④ 고정관념들이 충성심과 지도력을 가치 있게 생각하지 않는 사회에서 영속되는지에 대해서는 언급되지 않았다.
⑤ 멕시코인의 심리 상태가 어두운 과거에 깊이 뿌리박혀 있는지에 대해서는 언급되지 않았다.

어휘 **disenfranchised** adj. 권리를 빼앗긴
ancestral adj. 조상의 **perpetuate** v. 영속시키다

04 [2021 이화여대]

정답 ①

해석 ① 논란이 많은 ② 눈에 띄는
③ 지배적인 ④ 희망을 주는
⑤ 중요한

해설 지문의 빈칸에 들어갈 수 없는 것을 고르는 문제이다. 빈칸 (A)는 Pancho Villa의 기괴하게 근육이 있는 팔 끝에 꽉 쥔 주먹이 어떤 그림인지에 대한 내용으로 빈칸 (A)가 있는 뒤 문장에 Pancho Villa의 그림이 멕시코인의 심리 상태를 대변하며 지켜지고 있는 모든 특징들인 단결, 투지, 야망, 그리고 자부심을 상징한다고 했으므로, 그림이 논란이 많다는 내용을 나타내는 'controversial'은 빈칸에 적합하지 않다. 따라서 ①번이 정답이다.

05 [2021 이화여대]

정답 ②

해석 ① 재판, 시도 ② 고정관념
③ 환상 ④ 징후
⑤ 종합

해설 지문의 빈칸을 채우는 문제이다. 지문의 후반에서 그려진 인물들은 용감하고, 올바르고, 강하며, 욕심 많은 느낌이라고 했으므로, 빈칸 (B)에는 늘어진 콧수염과 헐렁한 솜브레로 모자

를 쓰고 치장용 벽토를 바른 건물의 그늘에 누워 있는 멕시코계 미국인에 대한 고정관념과는 거리가 멀다는 내용이 나오는 것이 자연스럽다. 따라서 '고정관념'이라고 한 ②번이 정답이다.

[06-09]

1940년에 발견된 라스코 동굴은 다양한 미술품으로 325m를 뒤덮은 수평으로 된 젖은 동굴이다. 17,000년이 넘은 라스코 동굴은 세계에서 선사 시대 암벽화, 상형 문자와 암석 조각들의 가장 위대한 집합물 중의 하나이다. [A] 작은 동굴은 석회석 벽으로 둘러싼 일련의 공간으로 이루어져 있다. 들소의 전당, 자연의 중심과 새로운 길, 깊은 샘은 벽화만을 전시하는 불규칙적인 질감을 살린 표면을 형성하는 단단한 석회석으로 덮여 있다. [B] 다른 공간들에 더 부드러운 벽이 있어서 조각하기에는 더 쉬웠지만, 그것들은 몇몇 벽화를 가지고 있다.
동굴은 선사 시대 사람들의 동물 세계를 묘사하고 전속력으로 달리는 황소, 말과 사슴의 이미지로 가득 차 있다. 벽화들은 특히 벽화들의 구도의 복잡성과 기술적인 복잡성 때문에 주목할 만하다. [C] 동물들의 윤곽을 그리기 위해 색을 어둡게 한 뾰족한 막대기의 사용, 말의 얼룩덜룩한 면을 만들어 내기 위해 이끼를 사용하여 색소를 바르는 것, 그리고 동물의 숨결을 나타내는 찰나적 특징을 주기 위해 속이 빈 갈대를 통해 산화물을 부는 것을 포함하여 여러 기법들이 사용되었다. [D]

horizontal adj. 수평의   concentration n. 집합물, 집중
prehistoric adj. 선사 시대의   pictograph n. 상형 문자
petroglyph n. 암석 조각   grotto n. 작은 동굴
limestone n. 석회석   chamber n. 공간
textured adj. 질감을 살린   gallop v. 전속력으로 달리다
compositional adj. 구도의   complexity n. 복잡성
outline v. 윤곽을 그리다   daub v. 바르다
pigment n. 색소   moss n. 이끼
dappled adj. 얼룩덜룩한   oxide n. 산화물
reed n. 갈대, 막대기   ephemeral adj. 잠시 동안의, 덧없는

06 [2021 세종대]

정답 ①

해석 ① 라스코 동굴의 다양한 암벽화를 논하기 위해
② 라스코 동굴을 구성하는 데 사용된 기법을 보여주기 위해
③ 공간의 내부 구조를 묘사하기 위해
④ 선사 시대 사람들의 생활 방식을 강조하기 위해

해설 지문의 목적을 묻는 문제이다. 지문의 첫 번째 문단에서 17,000년이 넘은 라스코 동굴은 세계에서 선사 시대 암벽화, 상형 문자와 암석 조각들의 가장 위대한 집합물 중의 하나라고 하였고, 두 번째 문단에서 벽화들은 특히 벽화들의 구도의 복잡성과 기술적인 복잡성 때문에 주목할 만하다고 설명하고 있다. 따라서 이 지문의 목적을 '라스코 동굴의 다양한 암벽화를 논하기 위해'라고 표현한 ①번이 정답이다.

07 [2021 세종대]

정답 ②

해석 다른 공간들에 더 부드러운 벽이 있어서 조각하기에는 더 쉬웠지만, 그것들은 몇몇 벽화를 가지고 있다.

해설 지문의 흐름상 주어진 문장이 들어가기에 가장 적절한 위치를 고르는 문제이다. 주어진 문장은 '다른 공간들에 더 부드러운 벽이 있어서 조각하기 쉬운 공간도 있지만 단단한 석회석으로 덮여 있는 공간에도 벽화가 있다는 내용이 나오므로 글의 흐름이 자연스럽게 연결된다. 따라서 ②번이 정답이다.

어휘 engraving n. 조각

08 [2021 세종대]

정답 ①

해석 ① 속이 빈   ② 화려한
③ 기하학적인   ④ 알록달록한

해설 지문의 빈칸을 채우는 문제이다. 지문의 후반에서 동물의 숨결을 나타내는 찰나적 특징을 주기 위해 갈대를 통해 산화물을 분다고 했으므로, 빈칸에는 동물들을 그리기 위해 막대기를 사용하고, 이끼를 사용하여 색소를 바르고, 속이 빈 갈대를 통해 산화물을 불었다는 내용이 나오는 것이 자연스럽다. 따라서 '속이 빈'이라고 한 ①번이 정답이다.

09 [2021 세종대]

정답 ③

해석 ① 속물적인   ② 아첨하는
③ 감탄하는   ④ 설득력이 없는

해설 라스코 동굴 벽화를 묘사하는 글의 어조를 묻는 문제이다. 지문의 초반에서 1940년에 발견된 라스코 동굴이 다양한 미술품으로 가득 차 있다고 하였고 지문의 후반에서 벽화들의 구도의 복잡성과 기술적인 복잡성 때문에 주목할 만하다고 한 것에서 동굴 벽화에 감탄하고 있음을 짐작할 수 있다. 따라서 라스코 동굴 벽화를 묘사하는 글의 어조를 '감탄하는'이라고 표현한 ③번이 정답이다.

[10-11]

필립 거스턴의 예술적인 언어와 시적인 동기는 인간 존재의 비논리적이고 역설적인 현실을 더 잘 이해하고 파악하려고 했다. 이 화가의 업무는 "표현의 방법"이 아니라 "이해하는 방법"이다. 거스턴은 추상화를 포기하고 구상화로 돌아갔는데, 이는 단순하고 직접적인 형상이었다. 언뜻 보기에 어려운 도상학으

로 보이는 것은 종종 전구, 신발 밑창, 쓰레기통의 뚜껑과 같은 요소들이 피에로 델라 프란체스카의 프레스코화에서 차용한 요소인 것처럼 그의 어린 시절의 그림들로 돌아갔다. 거스턴의 도상학은 <u>서술적</u> 논리를 통해 이해될 수 있는 단순한 표현이 아니다. 이것은 더욱 심오한 지식과 칼 융의 아니마와 연관이 있다. 거스턴의 비논리적 도상학은 서술적 형상에 관해 이야기하지 않고, 신화적 잠재의식의 근본적인 형상이나, 직관 또는 예지와 같이 무언가 그 자신을 <u>비논리적</u>으로 받아들여지는 것으로 나타나는 것을 말한다.

apprehend v. 파악하다 **illogical** adj. 비논리적인
paradoxical adj. 역설적인, 모순된
abstraction n. 추상화 **concretion** n. 구체화
figurative adj. 구상의 **iconography** n. 도상화
fresco n. 프레스코화 **descriptive** adj. 서술적인
prescriptive adj. 지시적인 **profound** adj. 엄청난
epiphany n. 직관, 통찰 **manifest** v. 명백히 하다
divination n. 예지

10 2020 건국대
정답 ⑤

해설 지문의 주제를 묻는 문제이다. 지문의 네 번째 문장에서 필립 거스턴의 그림의 양식적인 특징인 도상학에 관해 설명하고 있다. 또 마지막 문장에서 거스턴의 비논리적인 도상학의 특징에 관해 설명하고 있다. 따라서 이 지문의 요지를 'Philip Guston 회화의 양식적 특징'이라고 한 ⑤번이 정답이다.

11 2020 건국대
정답 ②

해석 ① 추상화 ─ 서술적인 ─ 논리적인
② 추상화 ─ 서술적인 ─ 비논리적인
③ 추상화 ─ 지시적인 ─ 논리적인
④ 구체화 ─ 지시적인 ─ 비논리적인
⑤ 구체화 ─ 서술적인 ─ 논리적인

해설 지문의 빈칸을 채우는 문제이다. 첫 번째 빈칸 뒤에 필립 거스턴은 단순하고 직접적인 형상의 구상화로 돌아갔다고 했으므로 첫 번째 빈칸에는 이와 반대되는 내용인 '추상화'라고 한 abstraction이 들어가는 것이 자연스럽다. 두 번째 빈칸 뒤에 거스턴의 비논리적인 도상학은 서술적인 형상에 대해 말하는 것이 아니라 했으므로 두 번째 빈칸에는 서술적 논리를 통해 해석될 수 없다는 내용이 나와야 적절하므로 두 번째 빈칸에는 '서술적인'이라고 한 descriptive가 들어가는 것이 자연스럽다. 세 번째 빈칸 뒤에는 직관이나 예지와 같이 비논리적인 것을 지칭해야 하므로 '비논리적인'이라고 한 illogically가 들어가는 것이 자연스럽다. 따라서 ② abstraction ─ descriptive ─ illogically가 정답이다.

[12-13]

15세기에서 오늘에 이르기까지, 르네상스 시대의 격언 중 "모든 화가는 자화상을 그린다"라는 격언은 여전히 사실이다. 단순한 자화상을 넘어서, 화가들은 모든 시대에 걸쳐 자신의 화폭 위에 특별한 서명을 남겼고, 그들의 얼굴을 특이하고 독창적인 방식으로 그들의 작품 안에 끼워 넣었다. 화가들의 이런 자존감은 르네상스 시기에서 비롯됐는데, 르네상스 시기는 개인주의와 창조성을 중히 여기는 인본주의적 가치로 가득 찬 시기였다. 르네상스 시기 동안, 숨겨진 자화상의 두 가지 트렌드가 유럽에서 등장했다. 이탈리아에서는, 화가들이 그들의 자화상을 그림이나 제단 뒤의 장식 오른편에 포함시키는 경향이 있었는데, 이런 방식으로 그들은 그림 속 그들의 눈이 마치 모든 걸 알고 있다는 듯이 관람객을 바라보게 만들고 있었다. 반면, 북부의 르네상스 화가들은 자신의 기술적 솜씨를 자랑하는 난해하고 정밀한 상징을 활용한 장난을 치는 것을 좋아했다. 그들이 그린 유화에 그려 넣은 자화상은 거울처럼 반사된 표면 위에서 왜곡된 형태로 발견된다. 이 전통은 미술의 황금기에 시작되어 현재까지 지속되어 왔다.

Renaissance n. 르네상스 **maxim** n. 격언
straightforward adj. 간단한 **self-portrait** n. 자화상
signature n. 서명 **canvas** n. 화폭 **insert** v. 끼워 넣다
inventive adj. 독창적인 **self-importance** n. 자존
humanist n. 인본주의 **altarpiece** n. 제단 뒤의 장식
toy v. 장난을 치다 **dense** adj. 난해한
precise adj. 정밀한 **distort** v. 왜곡하다
reflective adj. 반사하는

12 2020 한국외대
정답 ③

해석 ① 화가들이 언제부터 후원자들을 위해 작업하기 시작했는가?
② 왜 화가들이 그들의 작품에 대해 찬사를 예측했는가?
③ 어떻게 화가들이 그들의 그림 안에 자화상을 숨겨두었는가?
④ 예술의 역사에서 가장 큰 미스터리는 무엇인가?

해설 지문의 제목을 묻는 문제이다. 지문 전체적으로 르네상스 시기에 시작되어 지금까지 지속되고 있는 화가들이 자화상을 자신의 작품 안에 끼워 넣는 두 가지 트렌드에 관해 설명하고 있다. 따라서 지문의 제목을 '어떻게 화가들이 그들의 그림 안에 자화상을 숨겨 두었는가?'라고 표현한 ③번이 정답이다.

어휘 **patron** n. 후원자 **appreciation** n. 찬사

13 2020 한국외대
정답 ③

해석 ① 르네상스의 화가들은 평범하고 관습적인 그림을 가치 있게 생각했다.
② 이탈리아에서는, 화가들이 관객의 시선을 피하는 얼굴을 그렸다.

③ 북부 르네상스 화가들은 왜곡된 자아상을 끼워 넣는 것을 좋아했다.
④ 그림 속에 자화상을 끼워 넣는 화가들이 줄어들고 있다.

해설 지문의 내용과 일치하는 것을 묻는 문제이다. 지문의 일곱 번째 문장에서 북부 르네상스 화가들이 그린 유화에 그려 넣은 자화상은 거울처럼 반사된 표면 위에서 왜곡된 형태로 발견된다고 했으므로, 북부 르네상스 화가들이 왜곡된 자아상을 끼워 넣는 것을 좋아했다는 내용은 지문과 일치한다. 따라서 ③번이 정답이다.

오답 분석
① 지문의 세 번째 문장에서, 르네상스 시기는 창조성과 개인주의가 중히 여겨지는 시기였다고 했으므로, 르네상스 화가들이 평범하고 관습적인 그림을 가치 있게 생각했다는 것은 지문의 내용과 다르다.
② 지문의 다섯 번째 문장에서, 이탈리아 화가들이 관람객을 바라보게 만들기 위해 자화상을 그림이나 제단 뒤의 장식에 오른편에 끼워 넣는다고 했으므로, 이탈리아 화가들이 관람객의 시선을 피하는 얼굴을 그렸다는 것은 지문의 내용과 다르다.
④ 지문의 마지막 문장에서, 미술의 황금 시기에 시작된 이 전통이 현재까지도 이어지고 있다고 했으므로, 자화상을 그림에 끼워 넣는 화가들이 줄어들고 있다는 것은 지문의 내용과 다르다.

어휘 conventional adj. 관습적인   glance n. 흘끗 봄, 시선

[14-16]

현대 조각품은 프랑스인 오귀스트 로댕의 작품에 기원을 두고 있다. 1840년 보통의 가정에서 태어나, 로댕은 그의 창조적인 여정을 1860년대에 시작했는데, 이 여정은 그가 그를 전통적인 조각품과 현대적인 조각품 사이의 '다리'로 기억되도록 이끌었다. 로댕 이전에, 조각품은 종교, 역사, 신화 그리고 문학과 같은 과거에 대한 이야기를 들려주었다. 조각품들은 일반적으로 상상력을 거의 남기지 않았다. 형태는 모델의 어떠한 결함도 피하기 위해 어떠한 방식으로 이상화하는 경향이 있었다. 로댕은 자신 눈앞에서 본 것을 개선하기를 거부했다는 점에서 사실주의 화가라고 여겨질 수 있다. 그는 있는 그대로의 모습이 아름답다고 여겼고 만약 모델이 늙고 주름이 있다면, 그는 그렇게 묘사했을 것이다. 더 나아가, 후세대를 위해 영감을 주도록 도왔던 많은 예술처럼, 그의 작품은 그의 그리고 그의 관객들의 감정과 상상력에 이야기를 걸었다. 그가 말한 이야기들은 내면적이고 개념적이었으며, 그 이야기들을 해석하는 데에는 옳고 그른 방법이 없었다.

sculpture n. 조각품, 조각   modest adj. 보통의
journey n. 여정, 여행   myth n. 신화   literature n. 문학
figure n. 형태   idealize v. 이상화하다   avoid v. 피하다
imperfection n. 결함   wrinkled adj. 주름이 있는
portray v. 묘사하다   internal adj. 내면의
conceptual adj. 개념의   interpret v. 해석하다

14 [2020 상명대]
정답 ③

해석
① 신화
② 신앙
③ 결함
④ 과거 사건들
⑤ 문학

해설 로댕 전의 조각품들에서 보여지지 않는 것을 파악하는 문제이다. 지문의 중간에서 로댕 이전에, 조각품은 종교, 역사, 신화 그리고 문학과 같은 과거에 대한 이야기를 들려주었으며, 형태는 모델의 어떠한 결함도 피하기 위해 어떠한 방식으로 이상화하는 경향이 있었다고 했으므로, 로댕 전의 조각품들에서 보여지지 않는 것은 '결함'이다. 따라서 정답은 ③번이다.

어휘 myth n. 신화   flaw n. 결함

15 [2020 상명대]
정답 ③

해석
① 17세기
② 18세기
③ 19세기
④ 20세기
⑤ 21세기

해설 지문에서 어느 세기가 논의되고 있는지를 파악하는 문제이다. 지문의 처음에서 로댕은 그의 창조적인 여정을 1860년대에 시작했는데, 이 여정은 그가 그를 전통적인 조각품과 현대적인 조각품 사이의 '다리'로 기억되도록 이끌었다고 했으므로, 지문에서 논의되고 있는 세기는 '19세기'이다. 따라서 정답은 ③번이다.

16 [2020 상명대]
정답 ①

해석
① 그는 세상을 정확히 표현하는 예술을 창조했다.
② 그는 세상의 모든 것들을 아름답다고 여겼다.
③ 그는 자신의 예술로 세상을 더 아름다운 곳으로 만들기 위해 노력했다.
④ 그는 세상의 아름다움을 표현하기에 완벽한 예술을 창조했다.
⑤ 그는 자신의 예술로 그의 주변에서 본 세상, 심지어는 결함들까지도 완벽하게 만들었다.

해설 로댕이 사실주의 화가로 여겨지는 이유를 파악하는 문제이다. 지문의 중간에서 로댕은 자신 눈앞에서 본 것을 개선하기를 거부했다는 점에서 사실주의 화가라고 여겨질 수 있으며, 그는 있는 그대로의 모습이 아름답다고 여겼고 만약 모델이 늙고 주름이 있다면, 그렇게 묘사했을 것이라고 했으므로, '그는 세상을 정확히 표현하는 예술을 창조했다'라는 점에서 로댕이 사실주의 화가로 여겨진다고 할 수 있다. 따라서 정답은 ①번이다.

어휘 perfectly adv. 정확하게   perfect v. 완벽하게 하다

[17-18]

더 큰 의미로, 물론, 록 음악이 포스트모던의 문화 형태의 가장 대표적인 것이라는 주장이 있다. 우선 첫째로, 록 음악은 동시대 대중문화의 중심적인 모순을 완전히 구현하는데, 한편으로는 록 음악이 세계적인 범위를 통합하고 영향력을 미치고 있다는 사실에서 그렇고, 다른 한편으로는 다양한 스타일, 매체와 민족 정체성에 대한 록 음악의 인기의 발생과 결합되어 있다. 록 음악이 분명히 보이고 쉽게 입증되는 역사를 가지고 있긴 하지만, 록 음악은 또한 수단과 특성의 기질적인 외설로 특징지어질 수 있다. 맨 처음부터 록 음악의 중요성은 전체적으로 보아서는 젊은이 문화, 즉 패션, 스타일과 거리의 문화, The Who, Genesis, Talking Heads and Laurie Andersen과 같은 예술가들의 작품 속 구경거리와 공연, 영화, 새로운 재현 기술과 매체와 록 음악의 결합물의 잠재력에 있었다.

claim n. 주장　representative n. 대표
to perfection phr. 완전히, 더할 나위 없이
central adj. 중심적인　paradox n. 모순, 역설
contemporary adj. 동시대의　reach n. 범위
diverse adj. 다양한　ethnic adj. 민족의
identity n. 정체성
congenital adj. 타고난, 기질적인, 성격상의
impurity n. 외설, 불순, 불결　means n. 수단, 방법
nature n. 특성, 성격　importance n. 중요성
potency n. 잠재력, 영향력　amalgam n. 결합물, 혼합물
spectacle n. 구경거리　performance n. 공연
reproductive adj. 재현의, 재생의

17 (2019 이화여대)

정답 ②

해석　① 전멸　　　② 발생
　　　③ 억압　　　④ 개혁
　　　⑤ 예방 접종

해설　지문의 빈칸을 채우는 문제이다. 두 번째 문장에서 록 음악은 동시대 대중문화의 중심적인 모순을 완전히 구현한다고 했으므로, '다양한 스타일, 매체와 민족 정체성에 대한 록 음악의 인기의 _____과 결합되어 있다'라는 문맥에서, 빈칸에는 '발생'을 의미하는 engendering이 들어가는 것이 자연스럽다. 따라서 ②번이 정답이다.

어휘　annihilate v. 전멸하다　engender v. 발생하다
　　　oppress v. 억압하다　reform v. 개혁하다
　　　vaccinate v. 예방 접종하다

18 (2019 이화여대)

정답 ④

해석　① 포스트모던 문화의 모순은 록 음악에 박혀 있다.
　　　② 록 음악은 혁신적인 기술에 대한 포스트모더니즘주의자의 폭넓은 각색물의 대표이다.
　　　③ 록 음악에서는 독창성보다도 인기가 매우 소중한 가치이다.
　　　④ 포스트모더니즘은 청년 문화에 대한 포스트모더니즘의 평가 절하에 의해 경계가 정해졌다.
　　　⑤ 포스트모더니즘은 다양성의 보편적인 가치를 전달하는 추측으로 보일 수 있다.

해설　지문을 통해 추론할 수 없는 것을 고르는 문제이다. 록 음악이 포스트모던 문화 형태의 가장 대표적인 것이라는 주장이 있으며, 록 음악이 동시대 대중문화의 중심적인 모순을 완전히 구현한다는 내용이므로, 포스트모더니즘이 청년 문화에 대한 포스트모더니즘의 평가 절하에 의해 경계가 정해졌는지는 유추할 수 없다. 따라서 ④번이 정답이다.

오답분석
① 두 번째 문장에서 록 음악은 동시대 대중문화의 중심적인 모순을 완전히 구현한다(it embodies to perfection the central paradox of contemporary mass culture)고 했으므로, 포스트모던 문화의 모순은 록 음악에 박혀 있다는 것을 알 수 있다.
② 첫 번째 문장에서 록 음악이 포스트모던의 문화 형태의 가장 대표적인 것이라는 주장이 있다(rock music has a claim to be the most representative of postmodern cultural forms)고 했으므로, 록 음악은 혁신적인 기술에 대한 포스트모더니즘주의자의 폭넓은 각색물의 대표라는 것을 알 수 있다.
③ 두 번째 문장에서 록 음악이 동시대 대중문화의 중심적인 모순을 완전히 구현하는 것이 다양한 스타일, 매체와 민족 정체성에 대한 록 음악의 인기의 발생과 결합되어 있다(it embodies to perfection the central paradox of contemporary mass culture, ~ combined with its ~ popularity for diverse styles, media and ethnic identities on the other)고 했으므로, 록 음악에서는 독창성보다도 인기가 매우 소중한 가치라는 것을 알 수 있다.
⑤ 첫 번째 문장에서 록 음악이 포스트모던의 문화 형태의 가장 대표적인 것이라는 주장이 있다(rock music has a claim to be the most representative of postmodern cultural forms)고 했으므로, 포스트모더니즘은 다양성의 보편적인 가치를 전달하는 추측으로 보일 수 있다는 것을 알 수 있다.

어휘　exponent n. 대표자, 주창자
　　　inclusive adj. 폭넓은, 포괄적인
　　　adaptation n. 각색(물), 개작(물)
　　　demarcate v. 경계를 정하다　conjecture n. 추측
　　　propagate v. 전달하다, 전파하다

[19-20]

1891년까지 파리의 내부 실세 그룹의 예술가들은 예술적 삶의 자유분방한 이상에 전념하기 위해 직업과 가족을 떠난, 43세의 전 증권 중개인 폴 고갱에 대해 꽤 많은 이야기를 하고 있었다. 이 궤도는 고갱을 초기 인상주의자 교육에서 구식의 초기 화가 작품 이후 더 멀리까지 이르는 탐구까지 데려갔

다. 이미 브르타뉴와 프로방스 지방과 서인도 제도의 마르티니크에서 그린 후에, 고갱은 타히티섬에서의 2년 체류를 위해 배를 타기 전 그 봄에 작별 할인 판매를 하고 있었다. 1895년에 고갱은 남태평양에서 가난과 질병에 시달리는 생활의 마지막 8년을 보내기 위해 다시 출발했다. 그러나, 1880년대 후반에 고갱이 퐁타방의 브르타뉴어 어촌에서 다른 결핍한 예술가들과 기숙하는 동안, 고갱의 예술적 목표는 이미 정해졌다. 그 목표는 곧 상징주의라 불릴 새로운 문화적 추세가 고갱의 작품을 촉진시켰던 시점이었다.

loop n. 실세 집단   stockbroker n. 증권 중개인
commit v. 전념하다   artistic adj. 예술적인
trajectory n. 궤도   quest n. 탐구, 탐색
archaic adj. 구식의   primitive n. 초기 화가 작품
farewell n. 작별   ridden adj. 시달리는
lodge v. 기숙하다, 하숙하다   hard-up adj. 결핍한
catalyze v. 촉진시키다

19 2019 국민대

정답 ④

해설 bohemian(자유분방한)과 비슷한 의미를 가진 어휘를 묻고 있다. ①번 visionary는 '공상적인', ②번 euphonious는 '듣기 좋은', ③번 conservative는 '보수적인', ④번 unconventional은 '자유로운, 관습에 얽매이지 않는'이라는 의미이다. 따라서 ④번이 정답이다.

20 2019 국민대

정답 ②

해석 ① 고갱이 타히티섬으로 갔던 것은 1891년이었다.
② 고갱은 전 생애 동안 변함없이 인상주의에 전념했다.
③ 고갱은 남태평양에서 비참한 상태로 마지막 몇 년을 보냈다.
④ 고갱은 1890년대 초에 파리 예술가들의 실세 집단에서 잘 알려진 인물이었다.

해설 지문의 내용과 일치하지 않는 것을 묻는 문제이다. ②번의 키워드인 Impressionism all through his career(전 생애 동안 인상주의)와 관련된 지문의 new cultural trend ~ called Symbolism, catalyzed his work의 문장에서 상징주의라 불릴 새로운 문화적 추세가 그의 작품을 촉진시켰다고 했으므로, 고갱은 전 생애 동안 변함없이 인상주의에 전념했다는 것은 지문의 내용과 다르다. 따라서 ②번이 지문의 내용과 일치하지 않는다.

오답 분석
① 지문의 첫 번째 문장 By 1891~과 세 번째 문장 Having already ~ holding a farewell sale that spring before taking ship for a two-year stay in Tahiti를 통해 '고갱이 타히티섬으로 갔던 것은 1891년이었다'는 것을 알 수 있다.

③ 지문의 마지막에서 세 번째 문장 In 1895 he would set out again to spend the final eight years of a poverty- and disease-ridden career를 통해 '고갱은 남태평양에서 비참한 상태로 마지막 몇 년을 보냈다'는 것을 알 수 있다.
④ 지문의 첫 번째 문장 By 1891 artists on Paris's inside loop were talking quite a lot about Paul Gauguin을 통해 '고갱은 1890년대 초에 파리 예술가들의 실세 집단에서 잘 알려진 인물이었다'는 것을 알 수 있다.

어휘   deplorable adj. 비참한

[21-22]

중국 산수화의 완전한 성숙함은 학자이자 시인이었던 왕위의 영향 아래에 있던 당나라 왕조 동안 발전했다. 그는 주로 도교적 관점에 기초하여 붓과 먹으로 자연에 대한 개인적인 반응을 표현했다. 도교 철학은 자연의 법칙을 (A)존중함으로써 삶의 의미에 높은 가치를 둘 것을 강조했다. 이러한 전통 아래, 예술가들은 자연 속에서 평화롭고 사회의 족쇄와 금전의 (B)유혹으로부터 자유로워야 했으며, 그들의 정신은 산과 강, 그리고 다른 자연의 발현에 깊이 잠겨 있어야 했다. 산수화의 이런 전통은 여러 왕조를 거쳐 계속되었으며, 성나라 왕조에 그 정점을 보았다.

창작에서, 화가들은 빛과 그림자를 (C)만들기보다 선과 윤곽을 통달하는 것을 통해 풍경화의 효과를 얻어냈다. 즉, 그들은 자연의 아름다움을 풍경화의 효과를 높이기 위해 다른 각도와 시점으로 그렸는데, 이는 자연의 웅장함을 더 강하게 만들 수 있었다. 결과적으로, 인간의 형상은 자연의 질서정연한 웅장함을 해치지 않기 위해 (D)확대되었다. 인간의 형상은 그저 자연에 종속적인 부분인 반면 자연의 웅장함은 강조되었다. 이는 인간이 그들의 삶의 진정한 의미를 사회의 족쇄를 통해서가 아닌 자연에 깊이 의존하는 것을 통해 찾을 수 있기 때문이다.

maturity n. 성숙   landscape n. 풍경   dynasty n. 왕조
scholar n. 학자   Taoist adj. 도교의   shackle n. 족쇄
temptation n. 유혹   immersed adj. 잠긴
manifestation n. 발현   peak n. 정점
composition n. 창작   mastery n. 통달
silhouette n. 윤곽   intensify v. 강하게 하다
consequently adv. 결과적으로
intrude v. 해치다, 침범하다   figure n. 형상
orderly adj. 질서정연한   dependency n. 의존

21 2020 단국대

정답 ④

해설 밑줄 친 단어들 중에서 문맥상 적절하지 않은 어휘를 고르는 문제이다. 자연의 웅장함을 강조하기 위해 자연을 중점적으로 표현했다는 내용이므로 ④번에는 '확대하다'를 의미하는 enlarged가 아니라 '축소하다'를 의미하는 reduced가 들어가는 것이 자연스럽다. 따라서 ④번이 정답이다.

22 [2020 단국대]

정답 ②

해석
① 사람들이 자연 속에서 겸손하게 살아가기를 장려했다.
② 적합한 사회적 규칙의 필요성을 강조했다.
③ 세속적인 소유의 의미를 보잘것없이 만들었다.
④ 사람들이 그들의 정신을 자연 속에 잠기게 하는 것을 추천했다.

해설 중국 산수화에 담긴 도교의 관점과 일치하지 않는 것을 묻는 문제이다. ②번의 키워드인 the proper social rules(적합한 사회적 규칙)와 관련된 지문의 the law(법칙) 주변에서 도교 철학은 자연의 법칙을 존중했다고는 했지만, 적합한 사회적 규칙의 필요성을 강조했는지는 알 수 없다. 따라서 ②번이 지문의 내용과 일치하지 않는다.

오답분석
① the artists were supposed to be at peace with nature를 통해 '사람들이 자연 속에서 겸손하게 살아가기를 장려했다'는 것을 알 수 있다.
③ free from the shackles of society and from the temptation of gold를 통해 '세속적인 소유의 의미를 보잘것없이 만들었다'는 것을 알 수 있다.
④ their spirit should be deeply immersed in mountains and rivers, and other manifestations of nature를 통해 '사람들이 그들의 정신을 자연 속에 잠기게 하는 것을 추천했다'는 것을 알 수 있다.

어휘
humbly adv. 겸손하게 accentuate v. 강조하다
depreciate v. 보잘것없이 만들다, 가치를 떨어뜨리다
worldly adj. 세속적인 possession n. 소유

[23-25]

> 19세기 후반에서 20세기까지, 몇몇 나라에서 모더니즘은 확실성이라는 개념을 거부함으로써 미술과 문화를 변화시켰다. 예를 들어, 모더니즘 회화는 사람이나 풍경에 대한 "진실한" 표현을 보여주기 위한 시도를 하지 않았다. 모더니스트에게, 진실한 이미지라는 것은 존재할 수 없는 것이었는데 객관적인 현실로 보이는 것이 실제로는 주관적인 관점이나 한 사람이 사물을 보는 방식에 의한 결과였기 때문이다. 그러므로, 파블로 피카소와 같은 화가들은 풍경이 실제로 어떻게 보이는지를 보는 대신 그들이 스스로 모양과 색을 어떻게 보고 있는지에 초점을 맞추었다. 더불어 음악계에서는, 작곡가들이 흥미를 느끼고 있었던 무조의 소리를 받아들이게 되었다. 그리고 문학계에서는, 작가들이 개인의 생각을 매우 개인적인 방식으로 재생산하기 위해 고군분투했다.
> 20세기 후반의 포스트모더니스트들은 모더니즘이 수많은 관점을 강조하는 면에서 충분히 넓게 확장되지 않는다고 느꼈다. 예를 들어, 포스트모더니스트들은 모더니스트 도시 설계자들이 개발의 목표였던 거주민들의 서로 다른 욕구를 고려하지 않은 채, 대규모의 획일화 된 개발을 통해 도시 문제를 해결하려고 시도했던 방식을 지적했다. 포스트모더니즘은 다문화주의만큼 다양성, 청중의 개인화에도 초점을 맞추고 있다. 예술을 관람하는 사람과 포스트모던 예술가들은 감상 경험을 함께 구축해나간다. 요컨대, 이 예술가들은 주제넘게 관람자의 감상 경험을 통제하려 들지 않는다.

---

modernism n. 모더니즘 certainty n. 확실성
representation n. 표현 embrace v. 받아들이다
atonal adj. 무조의 urban adj. 도시의
intended adj. 의도된 personalization n. 개인화
multiculturalism n. 다문화 presume v. 주제넘게 굴다

23 [2020 한성대]

정답 ④

해석
① 이것은 대부분의 고전 작품들이 삶에 관해 거짓말을 하고 있다고 생각했다.
② 이것은 예술을 실제에 관한 편견 없는 표현으로 나타났다.
③ 이것은 당황스러운 것으로 여겨져서 그렇게 크게 영향력이 있지는 않았다.
④ 이것은 객관적이라 여겨져 왔던 원칙들에 의문을 제기했다.

해설 지문의 내용을 통해 모더니즘에 대해 추론할 수 있는 것을 고르는 문제이다. 지문의 첫 번째 문장에서, 모더니스트들은 확실성의 개념을 거부함으로써, 많은 나라의 문화와 예술을 변화시켰다고 했으므로, 이것이 객관적이라 여겨져 왔던 원칙들에 의문을 제기했다는 것을 추론할 수 있다. 따라서 ④번이 정답이다.
① 모더니즘이 고전 작품들이 삶에 관해 거짓말을 하고 있다고 생각했다는 것은 지문의 내용에서 근거를 찾을 수 없다.
② 모더니즘은 '객관적인 실제'라는 것이 존재할 수 없다고 보았으며, 물체를 바라보는 주관적인 관점과 방식이 작용하는 결과라 생각했다. 따라서 모더니즘이 실제에 관한 편견 없는 표현으로 나타났다는 것은 지문의 내용과 다르다.
③ 모더니즘이 19세기 후반에서 20세기까지 세계 여러 나라의 문화와 예술을 변화시켰다고 했으므로, 이것이 크게 영향력이 있지 않았다는 것은 지문의 내용과 다르다.

어휘 unbiased adj. 편견 없는 influential adj. 영향력이 큰
disconcerting adj. 당황케 하는

24 [2020 한성대]

정답 ③

해석
① 주관적인 — 주관적인
② 주관적인 — 앉아서 하는
③ 객관적인 — 주관적인
④ 객관적인 — 앉아서 하는

해설 지문의 빈칸을 채우는 문제이다. 지문의 첫 번째 문단에서, 모더니스트들은 확실성이라는 개념을 거부하고 사람이나 풍경에 대한 "진실한" 표현을 보여주기 위한 시도를 하지 않았다

고 했다. 이러한 맥락에서, '모더니스트에게, 진실한 이미지라는 것은 존재할 수 없는 것이었는데 _____ 현실로 보이는 것이 실제로는 _____ 관점이나 한 사람이 사물을 보는 방식에 의한 결과였기 때문이다'라는 문장의 두 빈칸에는 '주관적인'이라는 의미의 subjective와 '객관적인'이라는 의미의 objective가 각각 들어가는 것이 자연스럽다. 따라서 ③번이 정답이다.

25 [2020 한성대]

정답 ①

해석 ① 포스트모더니즘 vs. 모더니즘
② 파블로 피카소의 일생
③ 고전적 작곡가들의 영감
④ 19세기의 도시 문제를 해결하는 방법

해설 지문의 제목을 묻는 문제이다. 지문의 첫 번째 문단에서는 모더니즘에 관해 설명하고 있고, 지문의 두 번째 문단에서는 모더니즘의 한계를 지적한 포스트모더니즘에 대해 설명하고 있으므로, 이 지문의 제목을 '포스트모더니즘 vs. 모더니즘'이라고 표현한 ①번이 정답이다.

어휘 inspiration n. 영감

[26-27]

앙리 마티스는 유명하게 자신은 예술이 "귀찮게 하거나 우울하게 만드는 주제가 없는 ... 좋은 안락의자같이 마음을 달래고, 진정시키는 효과가 있는" 꿈을 꿨다고 단언했다. 앙리 마티스의 친한 친구인 더 자주 인간 감정의 더 어두운 면에 빠졌던 피카소도 앙리 마티스의 예술에 특별히 정치적인 것은 아니었다. 그럼에도 불구하고, 1930년대 중반 창조성이 급박하게 밀려오던 시기에, 피카소는 게르니카를 폭격하는 극적인 벽화 크기의 시위 모습을 신문 느낌의 직접적인 흑백 색상으로 그렸다. 피카소의 "게르니카"에 대한 정치적 직접성은 피카소의 멕시코인 친구인 디에고 리베라의 혁명적인 태도가 영감을 주었을지도 모른다. 그 그림은 어떻게 미학과 시위가 서로 배타적일 수 없는지를 분명하게 보여주는 예시이다. 피카소는 화가와 그림이 둘 다일 수 있다는 것을 보여주었다.
예술은 즐거움과 정치 사이의 스펙트럼 어디에 떨어지는지에 관해 항상 논쟁해왔다. 우리는 정말로 예술이 우리가 매일 뉴스에서 보는 갈등과 위협을 가지고 우리에게 도전하기를 원하는가?
만약 예술이 우리에게 도전한다면, 현대의 정치적인 예술은 이미 그 메시지에 맞추어 조정된 소수의 잘 교육 받은 진보적인 엘리트로 이루어진 관객들을 설교하는 위험을 무릅쓰는 것이다. 거의 틀림없이, 이 예술은 그렇다면 <u>그것이 물고 있는 영향력을 가진 같은 시장과 권력 구조 때문에 더 강해지도록 연루될</u> 것이다.

famously adv. 유명하게   declare v. 단언하다, 나타내다
dream of phr. ~을 꿈꾸다   devoid of phr. ~이 없는

trouble v. 귀찮게 하다   depress v. 우울하게 만들다
subject matter phr. 주제, 소재   soothing adj. 달래는
calming adj. 진정시키는   armchair n. 안락의자
indulge v. 빠지다, 탐닉하다   emotion n. 감정
political adj. 정치적인   urgent adj. 급박한
creativity n. 창조성   dramatic adj. 극적인, 인상적인
mural adj. 벽화의   protest n. 시위   direct adj. 직접적인
directness n. 직접성   revolutionary adj. 혁명적인
attitude n. 태도   obvious adj. 분명한
aesthetics n. 미학   mutually adv. 서로, 상호 간에
exclusive adj. 배타적인, 독립적인   debate v. 논쟁하다
challenge v. 도전하다   conflict n. 충돌
threat n. 위협, 협박   contemporary adj. 현대의, 동시대의
preach v. 설교하다, 전하다   comprise v. 구성하다
liberal adj. 진보적인   align with phr. ~에 맞추어 조정되다
arguably adv. 거의 틀림없이, 주장하건대
complicit adj. 연루된, 공모한   structure n. 구조

26 [2019 성균관대]

정답 ②

해석 ① 메시지와 유용성   ② 즐거움과 정치
③ 위안과 위협   ④ 창조성과 복고풍
⑤ 공모와 창조성

해설 지문의 빈칸을 채우는 문제이다. 첫 번째 문단에서 피카소의 "게르니카"가 미학과 시위가 서로 배타적일 수 없는지를 분명하게 보여주는 예시이며, 피카소는 화가와 그림이 둘 다일 수 있다는 것을 보여주었다고 했으므로, 빈칸에는 예술은 즐거움과 정치 사이의 스펙트럼 어디에 떨어지는지에 관해 항상 논쟁해왔다는 내용이 나와야 적절하다는 것을 알 수 있다. 따라서 '즐거움과 정치'라고 한 ②번이 정답이다.

어휘 utility n. 유용성   solace n. 위안, 위로   retro n. 복고풍
complicity n. 공모

27 [2019 성균관대]

정답 ⑤

해석 ① 엘리트 관객들의 사회적 정치적 책임과 불화한다
② 엘리트 관객들의 미적 취향을 손상시켜서 완전히 망친다
③ 엘리트 관객들의 높은 문화적 취향을 열광적으로 갈망한다
④ 엘리트와 협력한 사회적 정치적 권력 구조를 부정한다
⑤ 이념을 비난하면서 엘리트 관객들의 취향에 맞춘다

해설 밑줄 친 become complicit in feeding on the same market and power structures whose hands it bites의 의미를 추론하는 문제이다. 세 번째 문단에서 만약 예술이 우리에게 도전한다면, 현대의 정치적인 예술은 이미 그 메시지에 맞추어 조정된 소수의 잘 교육 받은 진보적인 엘리트로 이루어진 관객들을 설교하는 위험을 무릅쓰는 것이라고 했다. 따라서, become complicit in feeding on the same market and power structures whose hands it bites의 의미를 '이념을 비난하면서 엘리트 관객들의 취향에 맞춘다'라고 한 ⑤번이 정답이다.

어휘 be at odds with phr. ~와 불화하다
responsibility n. 책임
enthusiastically adv. 열광적으로   crave v. 갈망하다
deny v. 부정하다, 부인하다   adapt v. 맞추다

[28-30]

공상 과학 작품의 최초 주요 이론화는 마르크스주의 패러다임 내의 Darko Suvin의 작품에서 일어났다. Suvin은 *Verfremdungseffekt*(소외효과), 즉 소원 또는 소외의 연극적 실행의 밑바탕에 깔린 사상들을 받아들였다. [A] 이 개념은 독일의 극작가 베르톨트 브레히트에서 시작되었다. 베르톨트 브레히트는 관객들이 단순히 자신의 등장인물들에 공감하기보다는 그의 연극의 사상을 통해 생각하기를 원했고, 관객들의 관람 중에 활기를 불어넣기 위해 여러 가지 기법들을 사용했다. [B] 공상 과학 작품을 읽을 때, 독자는 자신에게는 생소한 자신의 세계와 다른 세계를 관찰하고 있다는 것을 의식하게 되고, 이후 자신들이 현실 세계와 마주했을 때, 독자들은 세계를 새로운 방식으로 바라볼지도 모른다. [C] 그러나 독자는 새로 새겨질 수 있는 완전한 백지상태로 허구의 세계로 들어오지 않는다. 독자는 그들에게 익숙한 세계 내의 구조와 상호관계들에 대한 의식을 가지고 있으며, 동일한 기대감을 가지고 소설에 다가간다. 이 과정은 인식이라고 알려져 있으며, 지식, 특히 과학적이고 논리적인 지식과 연관되어 있다. 브레히트는 인지를 추 진동의 관찰로부터 추의 경로를 추론하는 갈릴레오의 능력과 연결시킨다. 샹들리에의 움직임을 관찰함으로써, 갈릴레오는 시계추의 움직임을 예측할 수 있었다. [D] 유추에 의해, 공상 과학 소설의 독자는 어떻게 세계가 작용하는가에 대한 기대감을, 특히 과학적 지식의 영역에서 가지며, 공상 과학 작가에 의해 묘사되는 허구의 세계에 대한 일련의 가정들을 쌓는 데 그 기대감을 이용한다. 따라서 Suvin은 공상 과학을 "현존과 소원의 상호작용과 인식이 필요충분조건인 문학 장르이며, 공상 과학의 주요한 형식적 장치는 작가의 경험적 환경에 대한 대안을 제시하는 상상력이 풍부한 이야기 틀"이라고 정의한다. 비록 인식과 소원, 이 두 가지의 자극은 변증법적인 관계 즉, 익숙하지만 인식할 수 없는 것과 익숙하지 않은 것을 인식하는 것 사이 그리고 허구적인 과학과 과학적 특성을 가진 허구 사이의 진동 속 관계이지만, 어느 정도까지는 "인식"의 개념은 과학과 연결되며, "소원"의 개념은 소설과 관련지어진다.

theorization n. 이론화
Science Fiction(SF) phr. 공상 과학, 공상 과학 소설(영화)
occur v. 일어나다, 발생하다   Marxist n. 마르크스주의
paradigm n. 패러다임, 사고의 틀   theatrical adj. 연극적인
Verfremdungseffekt n. (문학) 소외효과 [독일어]
estrangement n. 소원   alienation n. 소외
empathize v. 공감하다   conscious adj. 의식의

observe v. 관찰하다   unfamiliar adj. 생소한, 익숙하지 않은
fictional adj. 허구의, 소설의   impress v. 새기다
structure n. 구조   interrelationship n. 상호관계
expectation n. 기대   process n. 과정
cognition n. 인식   associate v. 연관시키다
logical adj. 논리적인   deduce v. 추론하다
path n. 경로   pendulum n. 추   observation n. 관찰
swing n. 진동   chandelier n. 샹들리에
predict v. 예측하다   realm n. 영역   assumption n. 가정
define v. 정의하다   literary adj. 문학의
necessary and sufficient condition phr. 필요충분조건
presence n. 현존   alternative n. 대안
empirical adj. 경험적인   map on phr. 연결시키다
impulse n. 충동   dialectical adj. 변증법적인

28 2020 홍익대

정답 ①

해설 지문의 흐름상 주어진 문장이 들어가기에 가장 적절한 위치를 고르는 문제이다. [A]의 앞 문장에서 Suvin은 *Verfremdungseffekt*(소외효과), 즉 소원 또는 소외의 연극적 실행의 밑바탕에 깔린 사상들을 받아들였다고 했으므로, [A] 자리에 이 소외 이론의 개념이 누구로부터 시작되었는지를 설명하는 주어진 문장 '이 개념은 독일의 극작가 베르톨트 브레히트에서 시작되었다'가 들어가야 글의 흐름이 자연스럽게 연결된다. 따라서 ①번이 정답이다.

어휘 originate v. 시작하다, 비롯하다   playwright n. 극작가

29 2020 홍익대

정답 ②

해석 ① 작품을 쓰면서, 브레히트는 그의 관객들이 그의 등장인물들에 공감할 수 있게 하기 위해 최선을 다했다.
② 공상 과학 소설을 읽을 때, 인식의 개념과 소원의 개념은 구별할 수 있지만 뒤얽혀있다.
③ 공상 과학 소설의 작품을 감상할 때, 독자는 어떻게 세계가 행동할지에 대한 어떠한 전제도 가지고 있지 않다.
④ Suvin에 따르면, 인식의 개념은 비논리적이고 허구적인 상상력과 밀접하게 관련 있다.

해설 지문을 통해 추론할 수 있는 것을 고르는 문제이다. 지문의 후반부에서 Suvin은 공상 과학을 현존과 소원의 상호작용과 인식이 필요충분조건인 문학 장르이며 인식과 소원, 이 두 가지의 자극은 변증법적인 관계 즉, 익숙하지만 인식할 수 없는 것과 익숙하지 않은 것을 인식하는 것 사이 그리고 허구적인 과학과 과학적 특성을 가진 허구 사이의 진동 속 관계를 가지고 있다고 했으므로, 공상 과학 소설을 읽을 때, 인식의 개념과 소원의 개념은 구별할 수 있지만 뒤얽혀있다는 것을 추론할 수 있다. 따라서 정답은 ②번이다.

오답
분석
① 베르톨트 브레히트는 관객들이 단순히 자신의 등장인물들에 공감하기보다는 그의 연극의 사상을 통해 생각하기를 원했다고 했으므로, 작품을 쓰면서, 브레히트는 그의 관객들이 그의 등장인물들에 공감할 수 있게 하기 위해 최선을 다했다는 것은 지문의 내용과 다르다.
③ 독자는 새로 새겨질 수 있는 완전한 백지상태로 허구의 세계로 들어오지 않는다고 했으므로, 공상 과학 소설의 작품을 감상할 때, 독자는 어떻게 세계가 행동할지에 대한 어떠한 전제도 가지고 있지 않다는 것은 지문의 내용과 다르다.
④ 독자는 그들에게 익숙한 세계 내의 구조와 상호관계들에 대한 의식을 가지고 있으며, 동일한 기대감을 가지고 소설에 다가간다. 이 과정은 인식이라고 알려져 있고 특히 과학적이고 논리적인 지식과 연관되어 있다고 했으므로, 인식의 개념은 비논리적이고 허구적인 상상력과 밀접하게 관련 있다는 것은 지문의 내용과 다르다.

어휘 sympathize v. 공감하다
distinguishable adj. 구별할 수 있는
intertwine v. 뒤얽히다, 밀접하게 관련 있다
appreciate v. 감상하다 presupposition n. 전제
illogical adj. 비논리적인

30 [2020 홍익대]

정답 ③

해석 ① 등장인물들과 자신을 동일시할 수 있다.
② 갈릴레오가 어떻게 추의 경로를 추론했는지 이해할 수 있다.
③ 자신의 세계를 이해하는 방식을 재구성할 수 있다.
④ 익숙한 것과 생소한 것을 인식의 면에서 구별할 수 있다.

해설 지문을 통해 공상 과학 작품을 읽음으로써 독자들이 무엇을 할 수 있는지를 파악하는 문제이다. 지문 중간에서 공상 과학 작품을 읽을 때, 독자는 자신에게는 생소한 자신의 세계와는 다른 세계를 관찰하고 있다는 것을 의식하게 되고, 이후 자신들이 현실 세계와 마주했을 때, 독자들은 세계를 새로운 방식으로 바라볼지도 모른다고 했으므로, 독자들은 공상 과학 작품을 읽음으로써 '자신의 세계를 이해하는 방식을 재구성할 수 있다.' 따라서 정답은 ③번이다.

어휘 identify v. 동일시하다 reconstruct v. 재구성하다
in terms of phr. ~의 면에서

[31-32]

소매품 판매를 증대하기 위해 알맞게 사용되는 광고 기법은 대중에게 정보, 교육, 그리고 동기 부여를 선전하려고 하는 데 사용될 수도 있다. 공중 보건 캠페인은 상업 광고의 발달로 덕을 보았다. 실제로 근대 역사에서 가장 잘 알려진 몇몇 포스터와 텔레비전 광고는 건강을 알리는 것들이었다.

Abram Games는 제2차 세계대전의 가장 상징이 되는 포스터 몇 개를 만들어낸 영국의 그래픽 디자이너였다. 그는 1914년에 화이트채플에서 태어났으며 St Martins 예술학교에 다녔는데, 그래픽 디자인 세계의 확장에 대한 자신의 관심사를 추구하기 위해 두 학기 이후 학교를 떠났다.

주로 독학을 했지만, 그럼에도 불구하고 그의 재능은 그가 1934년에 건강 관리 예술 경연 대회에서 2등을 했을 때 빛을 발했다. 이듬해, Games는 런던 시의회의 포스터 경연 대회에서 우승했고 전문적인 그래픽 예술가가 되었다. 1940년에 보병대에 들어간 Games는 육군부로 인해 1941년에 왕실 기갑부대를 위한 징집 포스터를 만드는 것에 관여했다. 그는 1942년부터 제2차 세계대전의 종식 때까지 당국으로부터 공인받은 전쟁 포스터 디자이너의 역할을 했다.

"최대의 의미, 최소의 수단"이라는 자신의 디자인 철학을 따라, Games의 포스터는 효과적인 메시지를 즉각 전달하기 위해 언어를 거의 사용하지 않고 단순한 이미지를 사용한다. 그의 전시 포스터는 사람들에게 건강을 유지하고 적절한 위생을 유지할 필요성, 혈액 기부의 중요성을 상기시켰다. 이 여러 포스터는 사람들이 그들의 동료 시민을 돌보도록 장려하는 한편, 다른 포스터들은 일단 전쟁이 끝나면 새로운 의료 시설과 같은 보상을 줄 것을 약속했다. 그는 선전원으로서 자신의 기량을 잘 알고 있었다. 그는 다음과 같이 말했다. "나는 동기를 불어넣고 대중은 포스터를 보면서 마음속에 그 동기를 뿜어낼 것이다."

advertising n. 광고 deploy v. 알맞게 사용하다
sell v. 선전하다, 알리다 commercial adj. 상업용의
pursue v. 추구하다 infantry n. 보병대
engage v. 관여시키다 recruit v. 징집하다
philosophy n. 철학 hygiene n. 위생
propagandist n. 선전원 observe v. 말하다, 진술하다
wind v. 불어넣다 spring n. 동기, 원동력

31 [2019 중앙대]

정답 ③

해석 ① 자수성가한 — 탈환된
② 스스로 고무되는 — 갇힌
③ 독학한 — 뿜어진
④ 스스로 충족시키는 — 강화된

해설 지문의 빈칸을 채우는 문제이다. 첫 번째 빈칸의 경우, 빈칸 뒤 문장에서 그럼에도 불구하고(nonetheless) 그의 재능은 그가 건강 관리 예술 경연 대회에서 2등을 했을 때 빛을 발했다고 했으므로, 빈칸에는 이와 양보적인 내용이 나와야 적절하다는 것을 알 수 있다. 따라서 첫 번째 빈칸에는 '독학한'이라는 의미의 self-taught가 들어가는 것이 자연스럽다. 두 번째 빈칸의 경우, 지문의 마지막 문단 중간에서 Games의 전시 포스터는 사람들에게 전달하고자 하는 메시지를 상기시키고 장려했다고 했으므로, 빈칸에는 대중은 포스터를 보면서 그 동기를 어떻게 하는지에 대한 내용이 나와야 적절하다는 것을 알 수 있다. 따라서 두 번째 빈칸에는 '뿜어진'이라는

의미의 released가 들어가는 것이 자연스럽다. 따라서 ③번이 정답이다.

어휘 retake v. 탈환하다 stuck adj. 갇힌
indulge v. 충족시키다

32 2019 중앙대

정답 ④

해석 ① Abram Games는 첫 직업에 권태를 느껴, 공중 보건 관리의 선전원이 되기를 희망했었다.
② 본업에서 그의 노력에도 불구하고, Abram Games는 불충분한 교육으로 인해 결코 행복하지 않았다.
③ Abram Games는 그의 직업의 중요성에 대해 자각하여, 예술적 화가가 되기 위해 노력했다.
④ 공중 보건 운동가로서, Abram Games는 디자인에 대한 그 자신의 생각을 추구했다.

해설 지문을 통해 추론할 수 있는 것을 고르는 문제이다. 지문 마지막 문단에서 Abram Games는 "최대의 의미, 최소의 수단"이라는 자신의 디자인 철학을 따랐고, 사람들에게 건강을 유지하고 적절한 위생을 유지할 필요, 혈액 기부의 중요성을 상기시켰다고 했으므로, 공중 보건 운동가로서, Abram Games는 디자인에 대한 그 자신의 생각을 추구했다는 것을 추론할 수 있다. 따라서 정답은 ④번이다.

오답 분석 ① Abram Games가 첫 직업에 권태를 느껴, 공중 보건 관리의 선전원이 되기를 희망했었는지에 대해서는 언급되지 않았다.
② Abram Games는 그래픽 디자인 세계의 확장에 대한 자신의 관심사를 추구하기 위해 두 학기 이후 예술학교를 떠났다고 했으므로, 본업에서 그의 노력에도 불구하고, Abram Games는 불충분한 교육으로 인해 결코 행복하지 않았다는 것은 추론할 수 없다.
③ Abram Games가 그의 직업의 중요성에 대해 자각하여, 예술적 화가가 되기 위해 노력했는지에 대해서는 언급되지 않았다.

어휘 professional adj. 본업의, 전문의
insufficient adj. 불충분한, 부족한 vocation n. 직업
campaigner n. 운동가

[33-35]

지난 10년 내지 20년간, 그 구세계는 일련의 개성 강한 디자이너들에 의해 체계적으로 무너졌다. 처음부터 참여하여 변화를 만들어내는 기업가로 진지하게 간주되는 것에 몰두하는, 디자이너들이 이제 바로 최고위직에서 대기업을 이끌 뿐만 아니라 사업을 자신의 손아귀에 넣고 있다.
예를 들면, 개척자 조니 아이브(Jony Ive)는 애플의 놀라운 운명을 반전시킨 공을 크게 인정받고 있으며, 이브 베하(Yves Behar)는 노트북 컴퓨터를 비용대비 효율성이 있도록 다시 디자인하여 개발도상국의 아이들에게 나누어줄 수 있게 했고, 그런 다음 안경을 가지고도 똑같은 일을 했으며, 그러는 동안 건강 추적기와 무선 스피커 및 온도조절장치에도 혁신을 일으켰다. 톰 딕슨(Tom Dixon)이 침체의 기미를 전혀 보여주지 않는 자기 이름의 조명 및 가구 제국(대기업)을 창조했듯이, 마르셀 반더스(Marcel Wanders)는 가구에 재미를 다시 불어넣었다. 밀라노에서 해마다 열리는 가구 무역 박람회인 살로네 델 모빌레를 방문하는 것은 과거와는 아주 다른 경험이다. 한 때 신망 있는 브랜드를 위한 공개행사였던 살로네 델 모빌레 박람회는 유명 디자이너들이 접수했다.
패션부터 가구에 이르기까지 모든 것의 소비자들은 제조업자보다 창조자에 관심을 더 갖게 되었으며, 예술과 상업 사이의 벽을 허물었다. 올해 일본의 디자인 스튜디오 넨도는 상업 브랜드를 위해 디자인했던 100개 이상의 제품들로 페르마넨테 박물관에서 1년간의 회고전을 열었다. 디자이너 하이메 아온(Jamie Heyon)가 자동차 제조사 미니의 전기 스쿠터 시티서퍼를 소개하기 위해 놀이용 도시경관인 환상적인 도시 시설을 만들었을 때, 모두 와서 40미터 길이의 대리석 테이블을 보았는데 그 위에는 실제 제품이 아니라 금으로 만든 도로 표시와 구리로 만든 '가로등'이 있었다.

---

blow up phr. 폭파하다, 날려버리다
maverick n. 개성이 강한 사람; 독불장군
intent on phr. ~에 열중(몰두)한
be involved in phr. ~에 개입하다, 참여하다
take v. ~을 예로 들다 trailblazer n. 개척자, 선구자
turn around phr. (경제 등을) 호전시키다
spectacles n. 안경 fitness tracker phr. 건강 추적기
thermostat n. 온도조절 장치
along the way phr. 그 과정에서
trade fair phr. 무역 박람회
showcase n. 공개행사; 진열장; v. (신제품을) 소개하다
venerable adj. 공경할만한; 덕망(신망) 있는
retrospective n. (화가 등의) 회고전
installation n. 설치; 시설
cityscape n. 도시경관, 도시 풍경

33 2018 성균관대

정답 ②

해석 ① 상업적 가치에 더 관심이 있었다
② 기껏해야 미세 조정만 하기로 되어 있었다
③ 또한 마케팅 전략에도 관여했다
④ 전임자에 의해 고도로 훈련을 받았다
⑤ 제조업자들로부터 완전히 독립되어 있었다

해설 밑줄 친 그 구세계(that old world)에서 디자이너들은 어떠했는지를 유추하는 문제이다. 첫 문단에서 구세계는 개성 강한 디자이너들에 의해 무너졌는데, 그들은 처음부터 참여하여 변화를 만들어내는 기업가로 진지하게 간주되는 것에 몰두하며, 최고위직에서 대기업을 이끌 뿐만 아니라 사업을 자신의 손아귀에 넣고 있는 사람들이라고 했으므로, 구세계에서

의 디자이너들은 역할이 미미했다는 것을 알 수 있다. 따라서 ②번이 정답이다.

어휘 at best phr. 기껏해야

34 (2018 성균관대)

정답 ④

해석 ① 이론과 실제　　② 꿈과 현실
③ 과거와 미래　　④ 예술과 상업
⑤ 학교와 산업

해설 지문의 빈칸을 채우는 문제이다. 빈칸 앞에서 패션에서부터 가구에 이르기까지 모든 것의 소비자들은 제조업자(상업)보다 창조자(예술)에 관심을 더 갖게 되었다고 했으므로, 이런 소비자들이 '예술과 상업' 사이의 벽을 허물었다는 것을 알 수 있다. 따라서 ④번이 정답이다.

35 (2018 성균관대)

정답 ⑤

해석 ① 많은 기업가들이 자신의 제품을 디자인한다
② 디자인은 실용성보다 덜 중요하다
③ 어떤 소비자든 훌륭한 디자이너가 될 수 있다
④ 디자인은 제품을 더 비싸게 만든다
⑤ 현대 세계에서는 디자인이 가장 중요하다

해설 지문의 내용과 일치하는 것을 묻는 문제이다. 지난 10~20년간 개성 강한 디자이너들에 의해 구세계는 무너졌으며 이들이 산업 전반의 변화를 주도하며 혁신을 가져오고 있다는 내용이므로 '현대 세계에서는 디자인이 가장 중요하다'는 것을 알 수 있다. 따라서 ⑤번이 지문의 내용과 일치한다.

오답분석 ① 첫 문단의 Intent on being involved from the start and taken seriously as changemakers and entrepreneurs에서 디자이너들이 변화를 만들어내는 기업가로 진지하게 간주되고 싶어 한다고 했을 뿐이므로, 많은 기업가들이 자신의 제품을 디자인한다는 것은 지문의 내용과 다르다.
② 디자인과 실용성을 비교하는 내용은 언급하지 않았다.
③ 세 번째 문단 Consumers of everything ~ in the creator에서 소비자들이 제조업자보다 창조자에게 더 관심을 갖게 되었다고 했을 뿐이므로, 어떤 소비자든 훌륭한 디자이너가 될 수 있다는 것은 지문의 내용과 다르다.
④ 디자인이 제품을 더 비싸게 만드는지 여부는 언급하지 않았다.

[36-38]

동식물에서 기쁨을 얻는 것은 아주 명백히 좋은 일이라서 화분에 심은 식물을 집으로 가져오고 황조롱이를 관찰하는 사람들은 이러한 것들이 미덕과 어떠한 관련이 있다는 개념에 놀라기까지 할 수도 있다. 우리가 자연의 아름다움에서 예술의 아름다움으로 이동하면, 예술에 대한 경험은 자연에 대한 경험보다 더 쉽게 질적으로 저하된다. [A] 많은 예술, 아마도 대부분의 예술이 사실상 자기 위안적 예술이고, 위대한 예술조차도 그 예술을 소비하는 사람의 의식의 질을 보장할 수 없다. [B] 하지만, 위대한 예술은 존재하고 때때로 적절하게 경험되며, 위대한 것에 대한 얕은 경험이라도 효과가 있을 수 있다. [C] <u>예술, 즉 지금부터 본인이 "예술"로 의미하고자 하는 훌륭한 예술은 우리에게 탁월한 것의 독립적인 존재에서 얻는 순수한 기쁨을 준다.</u> 그것은 우리의 최고 능력을 활성화하고 영혼의 가장 고귀한 부분에 사랑을 불어넣는다. 예술이 이렇게 할 수 있는 것은 부분적으로 예술이 자연과 공유하는 어떤 미덕 때문인데, 이것은 바로 무소유적 사색을 불러일으키고 이기적인 꿈속 생활로 의식이 몰두하는 것을 막는 완벽함의 형태이다. 하지만, 신성한 것, 또는 좋은 에너지의 원천으로 여겨지는 예술은 특별한 차원을 갖추고 있다. [D] 예술은 자연보다 이해하기 어렵지만, 의식을 더욱 고양시키기도 한다. 예술은 인간의 산물이고 재능뿐만 아니라 <u>미덕</u>도 예술가에게 요구된다. 훌륭한 예술가는 자신의 예술과 관련하여 용감하고, 진실하고, 끈기 있고, 겸손하며, 추상적인 예술에서조차도 우리는 이러한 자질에 대해 직관할 수도 있다.

patently adv. 명백히　kestrel n. 황조롱이
notion n. 개념　virtue n. 미덕
degrade v. (특히 질적으로) 저하시키다
a great deal of phr. 많은　console v. 위안을 주다
guarantee v. 보장하다　consciousness n. 의식
shallow adj. 얕은　invigorate v. 활성화하다
faculty n. 능력　inspire v. 불어넣다　perfection n. 완벽
unpossessive adj. 무소유의　contemplation n. 사색
absorption n. 몰두, 흡수　sacrament n. 신성한 것
possess v. 갖추고 있다　dimension n. 차원
accessible adj. 이해하기 쉬운　edify v. (의식을) 고양시키다
truthful adj. 진실한　humble adj. 겸손한
non-representational adj. 추상적인　intuition n. 직관

36 (2020 서강대)

정답 ①

해석 ① 사람은 자기 위안적인 환상을 불러일으키는 완벽함의 형태를 찾는다.
② 그것은 사람의 마음에서 이기적인 사항을 없앰으로써 기쁨을 준다.
③ 그것은 동물의 독립적인 존재에서 사심 없는 기쁨을 준다.
④ 그것은 영혼의 가장 고귀한 부분에 사랑을 불어넣는다.

해설 새를 관찰하는 경험에 대해서 지문을 통해 추론할 수 없는 것을 고르는 문제이다. 지문의 세 번째 문장에서 대부분의 예술이 사실상 자기 위안적 예술이라고 했으므로, 새를 관찰하는 자연에 대한 경험에서 사람이 자기 위안적인 환상을 불러일

으키는 완벽함의 형태를 찾는다는 것은 추론할 수 없다. 따라서 정답은 ①번이다.

오답 분석
② 지문의 여섯 번째 문장 It is able to ~ dream life of the consciousness.를 통해 '그것은 사람의 마음에서 이기적인 사항을 없앰으로써 기쁨을 준다'는 것을 알 수 있다.
③ [C]에 들어갈 문장 Art ~ what is excellent.를 통해 '그것은 동물의 독립적인 존재에서 사심 없는 기쁨을 준다'는 것을 알 수 있다.
④ 지문 다섯 번째, 여섯 번째 문장의 It invigorates ~ shares with nature를 통해 '그것은 영혼의 가장 고귀한 부분에 사랑을 불어넣는다'는 것을 알 수 있다.

어휘 perfection n. 완벽 console v. 위안을 주다
self-forgetful adj. 사심 없는 independent adj. 독립적인
existence n. 존재 inspire v. 불어넣다

37 [2020 서강대]
정답 ②

해석 ① 창조성 ② 미덕
③ 직관 ④ 경험

해설 지문의 빈칸을 채우는 문제이다. 빈칸 뒤 문장에서 훌륭한 예술가는 자신의 예술과 관련하여 용감하고, 진실하고, 끈기 있고, 겸손하다고 했으므로, 빈칸에는 재능뿐만 아니라 무엇이 예술가에게 요구되는지에 대한 내용이 나와야 적절하다는 것을 알 수 있다. 따라서 '미덕'이라고 한 ②번이 정답이다.

어휘 virtue n. 미덕 intuition n. 직관

38 [2020 서강대]
정답 ③

해설 지문의 흐름상 주어진 문장이 들어가기에 가장 적절한 위치를 고르는 문제이다. [C]의 앞 문장에서 위대한 예술에 대한 얕은 경험이라도 효과가 있을 수 있다고 했으므로, [C] 자리에 훌륭한 예술이 우리에게 구체적으로 어떤 효과를 주는지 설명하는 주어진 문장 '예술, 즉 지금부터 본인이 "예술"로 의미하고자 하는 훌륭한 예술은 우리에게 탁월한 것의 독립적인 존재에서 얻는 순수한 기쁨을 준다'가 들어가야 글의 흐름이 자연스럽게 연결된다. 따라서 ③번이 정답이다.

어휘 independent adj. 독립적인 existence n. 존재

[39-40]

물론 오늘날 레오나르도 다빈치는 '모나리자'와 '최후의 만찬' 같은 그림들로 가장 유명하다. 하지만, 레오나르도는 애초에 마음속으로는 화가가 아니었다. 그는 처음에 자신을 기술자로 생각했다. 레오나르도는 1480년대 초에 밀라노의 통치자에게 보내는 그의 힘을 열거한 한 편지에서, 예를 들어 다리, 터널, 마차, 그리고 투석기를 설계한 것과 같이 열 가지의 다른 기술들을 언급하고, 마지막에는 그림도 그릴 수 있다고 덧붙였다. 레오나르도는 배우는 데에 만족하지 못했던 사람이기도 했다. 그는 물의 흐름, 공기 중으로 연기가 피어오르는 모습, 딱따구리가 혀를 사용하는 방법과 같이 그가 볼 수 있었던 모든 것을 배웠다. 그리고 그는 시대를 앞서 보는 통찰력을 가지고 있었다. 그는 연구원들이 수십 년 전에서야 밝혀냈던 심장 판막의 원리에 관한 이론을 발전시켰다. 그는 우리가 현재 지구 반사광이라고 부르는 현상인 초승달의 두 지점 사이에 있는 빛을 볼 수 있는 이유를 정확하게 설명했던 최초의 사람이었다. 이와 같은 과학적 탐구는 그의 예술에 있어 필수적이었다. 그는 미소와 관련된 모든 근육을 연구했기 때문에 '모나리자'의 얼굴에 그렇게나 신비로운 모습을 담을 수 있었다. 그가 우리의 눈이 멀리 떨어져 있는 물체를 어떻게 인식하는지를 이해하는 데에 수많은 시간이 들었기 때문에, 그는 '최후의 만찬'에서 투시선이 완벽하게 작용할 수 있도록 했다. 그의 환경을 자세하게 조사함으로써, 레오나르도는 그의 분야를 향상시킬 새로운 기술을 개발하고, 전에는 아무도 보지 못했던 방법으로 세상을 그려낼 수 있었다. 다른 말로, 그는 혁신가였다.

primarily adv. 애초에 chariot n. 마차
catapult n. 투석기 insatiable adj. 만족하지 못하는
woodpecker n. 딱따구리 insight n. 통찰력
theory n. 이론 heart valve phr. 심장 판막
verify v. 밝히다, 확인하다 crescent moon phr. 초승달
phenomenon n. 현상 inquiry n. 탐구, 조사
essential adj. 필수적인 mysterious adj. 신비로운
perspective adj. 투시도법의 flawlessly adv. 완벽하게
countless adj. 수많은 perceive v. 인식하다, 감지하다
at a distance phr. 멀리에 surroundings n. 환경
portray v. 그리다 innovator n. 혁신가

39 [2020 단국대]
정답 ②

해석 ① 과학자 — 화가 ② 화가 — 기술자
③ 기술자 — 예술가 ④ 예술자 — 생물학자

해설 지문의 빈칸을 채우는 문제이다. 첫 번째 빈칸이 포함된 문장 이전에 레오나르도 다빈치는 그림으로 유명했다고 했으므로, 첫 번째 빈칸에는 그림과 관련된 의미의 단어가 와야 한다는 것을 알 수 있다. 두 번째 빈칸이 포함된 문장 이후에 그가 다리, 터널, 마차, 투석기와 같은 기구들을 설계했다는 것을 언급한 편지를 보냈다고 했으므로, 두 번째 빈칸에는 설계와 관련된 의미의 단어가 와야 한다는 것을 알 수 있다. 따라서 '화가 — 기술자'라고 한 ②번이 정답이다.

40 [2020 단국대]
정답 ④

해석 ① 레오나르도는 다양한 재능을 가진 사람이었다.
② 레오나르도는 그가 인체를 관찰한 것을 예술에 적용했다.

③ 레오나르도의 그림들은 예술과 과학 기술의 결합이었다.
④ 레오나르도는 밀라노의 통치자에게 그의 그림 실력을 밝히는 것을 삼갔다.

해설 지문의 내용과 일치하지 않는 것을 묻는 문제이다. ④번의 키워드인 the ruler of Milan(밀라노의 통치자)과 관련된 지문의 a letter to the ruler of Milan(밀라노의 통치자에게 보내는 편지) 주변에서 밀라노의 통치자에게 보내는 그의 힘을 열거한 한 편지에서 마지막에는 그림도 그릴 수 있다고 덧붙였다고 했으므로 레오나르도는 밀라노의 통치자에게 그의 그림 실력을 밝히는 것을 삼갔다는 것은 지문의 내용과 다르다. 따라서 ④번이 지문의 내용과 일치하지 않는다.

오답 분석
① Leonardo mentioned 10 different skills를 통해 '레오나르도는 다양한 재능을 가진 사람이었다'라는 것을 알 수 있다.
② He was able to give the *Mona Lisa* that mysterious look on her face because he had studied all the muscles involved in smiling을 통해 '레오나르도는 그가 인체를 관찰한 것을 예술에 적용했다'는 것을 알 수 있다.
③ Scientific inquiries like these were essential to his art를 통해 '레오나르도의 그림들은 예술과 과학 기술의 결합이었다'는 것을 알 수 있다.

어휘 gift n. (천부적인) 재능 observation n. 관찰
combination n. 결합, 조합
abstain from phr. ~를 삼가다

[41-42]

1880년대에 모네에게 끌린 비평가들은 학술적이든 실험적이든 그를 다른 화가들과 차별화되는 것을 ①특징짓기 위해 특별한 두 단어를 사용했다. *Instantanéité*(순간성)와 *enveloppe*(둘러싼 공간)의 개념은 보통 매우 짧은 시간 동안에만 전체적인 광질이 풍경을 휩싸는 사색에 모네가 ②접근할 수 있도록 만드는 능력으로 정의했다. George Petit 미술관에서 열린 모네의 1889년 전시회를 위한 Octave Mirbeau의 작품 수필에서, 장면을 이해할 수 있도록 ③만드는 빛의 규모를 확인하는 수단을 순간성으로 정의했다. 장면의 규모를 구성하는 가치들은 여기저기에 뿌려져 있었다. 그 가치들은 매우 ④드물게 변해서 그것들이 감적적인 반응을 결정하는 데에 한 역할을 알아차린 사람이 거의 없었다. 모네의 세심한 관찰과 선택은 그가 "정확한 형태"에서 발견한 가치들로 ⑤고정할 수 있게 만들어서, 그렇게 하지 않았다면 순간적이었을 디자인을 모두가 관찰을 위해서 이용할 수 있게 되었다. 모네는 빈틈이 없는 동시에 정서적으로 감동하게 하는 자연에 대한 해석에 도달하기 위해서 시간이 지나가는 효과를 꿰뚫고 조화를 이루는 가치들의 움직임을 가시적으로 만들어야 한다는 것을 이해했다고 Mirbeau는 그의 독자에게 확신했다.

particular adj. 특별한, 특정한 characterize v. 특징짓다
set apart phr. 차별화하다, 구별 짓다, 떼어놓다
academic adj. 학술적인 experimental adj. 실험적인
instant n. 순간 envelope n. 봉투 define v. 정의하다
accessible adj. 접근할 수 있는 contemplation n. 사색
spectral quality phr. 광질 bathe v. 휩싸다; 목욕하다
brief adj. 짧은, 간결한 catalog n. (목록에 기재된) 작품
essay n. 수필 exhibition n. 전시회 method n. 방법
identify v. 확인하다 scale n. 규모
make sense of phr. ~를 이해하다 constitute v. 구성하다
seed v. 씨를 뿌리다 be aware of phr. ~를 알아차리다
observation n. 관찰 value n. 가치
otherwise adv. 그렇지 않으면 fleeting adj. 순간간의
available adj. 이용할 수 있는, 구할 수 있는
assure v. 확신하다, 장담하다
interpretation n. 해석 at once phr. 동시에
emotionally adv. 정서적으로 moving adj. 감동적인
pierce v. 꿰뚫다 visible adj. 가시적인, 보이는
harmonic adj. 조화의

41 [2019 한양대]

정답 ④

해설 밑줄 친 단어들 중에서 문맥상 적절하지 않은 어휘를 고르는 문제이다. 모네의 작품의 특징으로 언급되는 순간성과 둘러싼 공간은 매우 짧은 시간 동안 빛이 풍경을 휩싸기 때문에 그 가치에 쉽게 접근할 수 없다는 내용이므로 ④번에는 '드물게'를 의미하는 rarely가 아니라 '빈번하게'를 의미하는 frequently가 들어가는 것이 자연스럽다. 따라서 ④번이 정답이다.

42 [2019 한양대]

정답 ④

해석 ① 갈등이 없는 평화를 만드는
② 어떠한 예술적 기술로도 이해하기에 너무 복잡한
③ 감정적인 물결을 다스리는 수단으로서의 예술가에게 극도로 중요한
④ 신비하지만, 예술가의 지각으로 포착할 수 있는 자질을 평가하는
⑤ 변덕스러운 자연의 행동에 예술가는 결국 자연에 지적인 답변을 할 수 없다는 확신으로 맞서는

해설 밑줄 친 exact and emotionally moving의 의미를 추론하는 문제이다. 밑줄 친 부분의 앞에서 모네는 감정적인 반응을 결정하는 데에 있어 자연의 역할을 알아차리기 위해 세심한 관찰과 선택을 통해 정확한 형태로 가치들을 고정했다고 말하고 있다. 따라서, 밑줄 친 문장의 의미를 '신비하지만 예술가의 지각으로 포착할 수 있는 자질을 평가하는'이라고 한 ④번이 정답이다.

어휘 absence n. 부재 conflict n. 갈등
complex adj. 복잡한 comprehend v. 이해하다
artistic adj. 예술적인 utmost adj. 극도의
tame v. 다스리다, 길들이다 tide n. 물결, 파도
mysterious adj. 신비한, 기이한 perception n. 지각
confront v. 맞서다 capricious adj. 변덕스러운
conviction n. 확신 incapable adj. 하지 못하는
intelligent adj. 지적인

[43-45]

몇 년 전에, 우리는 IDEO사에서 Ford사의 다음 세대 하이브리드 자동차인 Ford Fusion을 위한 계기판 시각화를 디자인하는 일을 맡았다. 하이브리드 자동차는 운전자가 그 차의 잠재력을 최대한 활용해야만, 즉 운전자가 두 모터와 회생 제동의 복잡한 구조를 이해하는 것을 배워야만 효율적이다. 만약 계기판이 운전자와 자동차 사이의 경계면이라면, 계기판은 어떻게 운전자에게 이 복잡성을 이해하고 효율적인 운전 습관을 취하도록 지도하는가? 그것은 분명한 질문이지만, 불완전하다. 빠진 부분은, 우리는 어떻게 운전과 안전에 지장을 주지 않고 디자인할 수 있는가?

이는 우리가 사람들을 평가의 중심에 둘 때 (Jocelyn Wyatt가 그랬던 것처럼) 다뤄야 하는 중요한 질문이다. 이 맥락에서, 사람들을 먼저 두는 것은 사람들이 게시판과 데이터 시각화 앞에서 오랜 시간을 보내는 것보다 더 중요한 일에 정신이 팔렸다는 것을 알아차리는 것을 의미한다. 이것은 어떤 장소에서도 사실이고, 우리의 경우 사람을 중심에 두는 것은 운전하는 것이었다. 시각화의 역할은 완전한 주목을 요구하는 것이 아니라, 우선하는 일을 지원하고 피드백 회로를 통해 개선하는 것이 되어야 한다. 문제는 당신이 지금 어떻게 지내는지를 보여주는 것뿐만 아니라 당신이 어떻게 더 나아질 수 있는지 알아내는 것이다. 그럼, 이것은 시각화 자체에 상응하여 무엇을 의미하는가?

모든 시각화 형태는 이야기되어야 한다. 그러나 모든 이야기들을 처리하기에는 관심과 시간이 한정되어 있다. 그래서 이야기의 요지, 혹은 즉각적인 영향은 곧바로 보여야 한다. 내가 이 원리를 위해 사용하기 좋아하는 용어는 "글랜스어빌리티(힐끗 보고 파악하기 쉬운 속성)"이다. 시각화는 우리가 시각화를 분석하기 위한 시간을 갖기 전에 우리에게 무엇을 말하는가?

task v. 일을 맡기다 dashboard n. 계기판
visualization n. 시각화, 구상화
maximize v. 최대한 활용하다 potential n. 잠재력, 가능성
mechanics n. 구조, 역학
regenerative braking phr. 회생 제동, 재생 제동
interface n. 경계면, 공유 영역 coach v. 지도하다, 코치하다
complexity n. 복잡성 adopt v. 취하다, 채택하다
obvious adj. 분명한 incomplete adj. 불완전한, 미완성의
interfere with phr. ~에 지장을 주다, ~을 방해하다
address v. 다루다, 처리하다 evaluation n. 평가
context n. 맥락 recognize v. 알아차리다
preoccupied adj. 정신이 팔린 attention n. 주목, 주의

priority n. 우선 feedback loop phr. 피드백 회로
figure out phr. ~을 알아내다 gist n. 요지
glanceability n. 글랜스어빌리티(힐끗 보고 파악하기 쉬운 속성)
analyze v. 분석하다

43 [2019 이화여대]

정답 ④

해석 ① 운전자 안전을 개선하기 위한 접근법을 설명하기 위해
② 데이터 시각화를 평가하는 방법을 설명하기 위해
③ 계기판 화면을 구성하는 방법을 약술하기 위해
④ 디자인이 인간 중심이어야 한다는 것을 주장하기 위해
⑤ 데이터를 보여주는 두 가지 다른 방법을 대조하기 위해

해설 지문의 목적을 묻는 문제이다. 두 번째 문단에서 사람들을 먼저 두는 것은 사람들이 게시판과 데이터 시각화 앞에서 오랜 시간을 보내는 것보다 더 중요한 일에 정신이 팔렸다는 것을 알아차리는 것을 의미한다고 한 후, 사람을 중심에 두는 것은 운전하는 것이었다고 설명하고 있다. 따라서 이 지문의 목적을 '디자인이 인간 중심이어야 한다는 것을 주장하기 위해'라고 표현한 ④번이 정답이다.

어휘 describe v. 설명하다, 서술하다 approach n. 접근법
outline v. 약술하다, ~의 윤곽을 그리다
contrast v. 대조하다 method n. 방법

44 [2019 이화여대]

정답 ③

해설 빈칸에 적절한 접속사를 넣는 문제이다. 첫 번째 빈칸의 앞 문장에서 모든 시각화 형태는 이야기되어야 한다고 했고, 빈칸 뒤 문장에서 모든 이야기들을 처리하기에는 관심과 시간이 한정되어 있다는 내용이므로, 역접을 나타내는 접속사 But이 들어가는 것이 자연스럽다. 두 번째 빈칸의 앞 문장에서 모든 이야기들을 처리하기에는 관심과 시간이 한정되어 있다고 했고, 빈칸 뒤 문장에서 이야기의 요지, 혹은 즉각적인 영향은 곧바로 보여야 한다는 내용이므로, 인과관계를 나타내는 접속사 So가 들어가는 것이 자연스럽다. 따라서 ③ But — So가 정답이다.

45 [2019 이화여대]

정답 ①

해석 ① 적은 것이 더 좋은 것이니, 단순하게 하라.
② 운전자의 완전한 주의를 잡아서 유지해라.
③ 그 시스템의 복잡한 구조를 강조해라.
④ 운전자에게 고를 많은 선택권을 주어라.
⑤ 화면을 교육의 기회로 만들어라.

해설 지문에서 계기판 시각화를 위해 가장 중점을 두는 디자인 원리를 파악하는 문제이다. 모든 시각화 형태는 이야기되어야

하며, 이야기의 요지, 혹은 즉각적인 영향은 곧바로 보여야 한다고 했고, 이 원리를 위한 용어가 "글랜스어빌리티(힐끗 보고 파악하기 쉬운 속성)"라고 했으므로, 계기판 시각화를 위해 가장 중점을 두는 디자인 원리는 '적은 것이 더 좋은 것이니, 단순하게 하라'이다. 따라서 정답은 ①번이다.

어휘 **emphasize** v. 강조하다　**plenty of** phr. 많은
option n. 선택권　**educational** adj. 교육의, 교육적인
opportunity n. 기회

[46-48]

Eugène Delacroix(1798년~1863년)는 프랑스 낭만주의 운동의 중요한 화가였으며, *Massacre at Chios* 같은 그의 위대한 작품들 중 일부는 전쟁의 참상을 묘사하면서 억압적인 정부에 대항하는 혁명을 지지하기도 했다. 그의 후기 그림들 중 많은 것들이 아랍과 유대인 문화를 묘사했는데, 보통 그가 스페인과 북아프리카를 여행하면서 그린 스케치에 바탕을 두고 있다. Delacroix는 또한 윌리엄 셰익스피어, 월터 스콧 경, 요한 볼프강 폰 괴테 책의 삽화를 작업했으며, 그의 *Journals*에서 예술과 다른 주제에 관한 작가로서의 명성을 얻었다. 그의 그림 *Liberty Leading the People*은 노동자와 중산층의 연합인 Trois Glorieuses가 찰스 10세를 폐위시키고 Louis-Philippe 왕 아래에서 입헌 군주 체제를 수립한 1830년 3일간의 프랑스의 7월 혁명을 기념하고 있다. 프랑스 7월 혁명은 찰스가 서명한 4대 선언으로 촉발되었는데, 이 선언은 국민 의회를 해산하고 언론의 자유를 종식시키며 귀족들에게 더 많은 권력을 부여하는 선거제도를 만들었다. *Liberty Leading the People*은 사실주의와 풍자가 결합되어 있으며, 자유는 신화적 인물이나 여신 그리고 혁명 중 가장 피비린내 나는 날에 반란군을 이끈 사람들의 여성으로 의인화되었다. Delacroix는 1831년 5월 파리 살롱에서의 혁명을 기념하는 전시를 위해 이 그림을 만들었다. 그러나 정부 관리들이 Delacroix의 그림이 더 많은 반란을 부추길 것을 우려했기 때문에, 1874년 루브르 박물관에 들어갈 때가 되어서야 *Liberty Leading the People*은 살롱에 전시될 수 있었다. 지금 Delacroix의 그림은 프랑스 공화국에 대한 애국심과 관련되어 있기 때문에 그 초상화는 15년 동안 100프랑 지폐의 뒷면에 등장했다.

---

depict v. 묘사하다　**horror** n. ~의 참상, 공포
revolution n. 혁명　**oppressive** adj. 억압적인
Jewish adj. 유대인의, 유대교의　**illustrate** v. 삽화를 넣다
reputation n. 명성　**commemorate** v. 기념하다
July Revolution phr. 프랑스 7월 혁명
coalition n. 연합, 연합체　**middle class** phr. 중산층
depose v. 폐위시키다, 물러나게 하다　**establish** v. 수립하다
constitutional monarchy phr. 입헌 군주 체제, 입헌 군주국
prompt v. 촉발하다　**proclamation** n. 선언, 성명서
dissolve v. 해산하다
National Assembly phr. 국민 의회, 국회　**press** n. 언론
electoral system phr. 선거 제도　**aristocracy** n. 귀족
combine v. 결합하다　**realism** n. 사실주의
allegory n. 풍자, 우화　**personify** v. 의인화하다
mythical adj. 신화적인　**figure** n. 인물
exhibit n. 전시, 전시품　**celebrate** v. 기념하다
salon n. 살롱(과거 상류 가정 응접실에서 흔히 열리던 작가, 예술가들을 포함한 사교 모임)
government officials phr. 정부 관리, 공무원
insurrection n. 반란, 폭동
associated with phr. ~와 관련된　**patriotism** n. 애국심

46 [2020 국민대]

정답　④

해석　① 화가　　② 작가
　　　③ 삽화가　④ 기자

해설　Delacroix의 직업이 아닌 것을 고르는 문제이다. 지문의 세 번째 문장에서 그의 *Journals*에서 예술과 다른 주제에 관한 작가로서의 명성을 얻었다고는 했지만, 그가 기자인지는 알 수 없다. 따라서 정답은 ④번이다.

오답 분석
① Eugene Delacroix (1798-1863) was an important artist in the French Romantic movement~를 통해 그가 '화가'임을 알 수 있다.
② ~ he earned a reputation as a writer n art and other subjects for his Journals를 통해 그가 '작가' 임을 알 수 있다.
③ Delacroix also illustrated books~를 통해 그가 '삽화가'임을 알 수 있다.

어휘　**illustrator** n. 삽화가　**journalist** n. 기자, 저널리스트

47 [2020 국민대]

정답　②

해석　① 1830년 프랑스의 7월 혁명은 결국 군주제를 영구히 폐지했다.
② Delacroix의 위대한 작품들 중 일부는 프랑스 낭만주의의 이상을 반영한다.
③ 1830년 프랑스의 7월 혁명에서는 중산층과 귀족이 힘을 합쳐 억압적인 왕의 정권을 전복시켰다.
④ Delacroix는 아랍과 유대인 지역사회에서의 여행 경험에 대한 기억에서부터 바로 아랍과 유대인 문화에 대한 그림을 그렸다.

해설　지문의 내용과 일치하는 것을 묻는 문제이다. 지문의 처음에서 Delacroix는 프랑스 낭만주의 운동의 중요한 화가였다는 내용을 통해 Delacroix의 위대한 작품들 중 일부는 프랑스 낭만주의의 이상을 반영한다는 것을 알 수 있다. 따라서 ②번이 지문의 내용과 일치한다.

오답 분석
① 찰스 10세를 폐위시키고 Louis-Philippe 왕 아래에서 입헌 군주 체제를 수립한 1830년 3일간의 프랑스의 7월 혁명이라고 했으므로, 1830년 프랑스의 7월 혁명은 결국 군주제를 영구히 폐지했다는 것은 지문의 내용과 다르다.
③ 노동자와 중산층의 연합인 Trois Glorieuses가 입헌 군주 체제를 수립한 1830년 3일간의 프랑스의 7월 혁명이라고 했으므로, 1830년 프랑스의 7월 혁명에서는 중산층과 귀족이 힘을 합쳐 억압적인 왕의 정권을 전복시켰다는 것은 지문의 내용과 다르다.
④ 그의 후기 그림들 중 많은 것들이 아랍과 유대인 문화를 묘사했는데, 보통 그가 스페인과 북아프리카를 여행하면서 그린 스케치에 바탕을 두고 있다고 했으므로, Delacroix는 아랍과 유대인 지역사회에서의 여행 경험에 대한 기억에서부터 바로 아랍과 유대인 문화에 대한 그림을 그렸다는 것은 지문의 내용과 다르다.

어휘
abolish v. 폐지하다   monarchy n. 군주제
permanently adv. 영구히   ideal n. 이상
overthrow v. 전복시키다, 타도하다
oppressive adj. 억압적인   regime n. 정권, 체제

48 [2020 국민대]

정답 ②

해석
① 그것은 특히 자유의 대의명분을 옹호하는 것으로 유명하다.
② 그것은 거리에서의 혁명 장면을 주로 사실주의적 방식으로 묘사하고 있다.
③ 그것은 프랑스 사람들에 의해 매우 사랑받아서 15년 동안 화폐에 전시되었다.
④ 그것은 1830년 프랑스 7월 혁명의 성공 이후에도 수십 년간 프랑스에서는 거의 전시되지 않았다.

해설 Liberty Leading the People에 관해 사실이 아닌 것을 고르는 문제이다. Liberty Leading the People은 사실주의와 풍자가 결합되어 있다고 했으므로, Liberty Leading the People이 거리에서의 혁명 장면을 주로 사실주의적 방식으로 묘사하고 있다는 것은 지문의 내용과 다르다. 따라서 ②번이 정답이다.

오답 분석
① Liberty personified as both a mythical figure or goddess ~를 통해 Liberty Leading the People이 '특히 자유의 대의명분을 옹호하는 것으로 유명하다'는 것을 알 수 있다.
③ Now Delacroix's painting is associated ~ that the portrait appeared on the back of the hundred-franc note for fifteen years를 통해 Liberty Leading the People이 '프랑스 사람들에 의해 매우 사랑받아서 15년 동안 화폐에 전시되었다'는 것을 알 수 있다.
④ ~ Liberty Leading the People was exhibited only rarely after the Salon until it entered the Louvre in 1874를 통해 Liberty Leading the People이 '1830년 프랑스 7월 혁명의 성공 이후에도 수십 년간 프랑스에서는 거의 전시되지 않았다'는 것을 알 수 있다.

어휘
particularly adv. 특히
champion v. ~을 옹호하다, ~을 위해 싸우다
cause n. 대의명분   predominantly adv. 주로
endear v. 사랑받게 하다   seldom adv. 거의 ~ 않는

[49-51]

바닥에 기대어 있고 소파에 늘어져 앉아있는, 몸무게가 350에서 650파운드 사이이며 나이는 23세에서 50세까지인 Loloi의 여자들은 (그들은 강아지와 꽃들을 들고 있으며, 그들 중 일부는 그들의 팔로 가슴을 가린다.) 얌전할 뿐만 아니라 에로틱하기까지 하다. 한 모델은 흐트러진 침대 위에서 포즈를 취하는데, 붉은 입술, 헝클어진 갈색 머리, 베개처럼 크고 형체가 없는 배를 가지고 있다. 다른 모델은 의자에 얌전히 앉아있는데, 온통 물결치는 금발머리에 그녀의 배에는 살이 튼 자국이 남겨져 있고, 그녀의 허벅지는 너무 넓으며 그러한 각도로 의자에서 돌출되어 있는 것을 보면, 마치 다른 인간의 형체를 보는 것 같다.

그녀는 이탈리아의 사진가인 Yossi Loloi가 비만 여성들을 나체로 찍은 사진을 모은 완전한 아름다움이라는 프로젝트에서 다루는 많은 여자들 중의 한 명이다. 2006년에 시작된 이 작업은 아름다움, 체구, 그리고 여성의 몸에 대해 일반적으로 인정된 우리의 개념에 저항하기 위해 기획되었다. 그 사진들은 주류 매체에서 우리가 거의 보지 못하는 육체적인 노출을 제공한다. 그것들은 도발, 여성의 몸은 어느 형태나 크기에서도 아름답고 섹시하다는 정당한 논쟁의 한 쪽 극단을 위한 것이다. 모델들은 확실히 연약하지만 그들은 우리를 우리가 아름답고, 추하고, 뚱뚱하고, 말랐고, 충격적이고, 고무적이라고 정의하는 여성의 몸에 대한 추정에 맞서게 하는 용기를 보여준다. 그들의 살이 튼 자국과 정맥을 보고 있으면, 갑자기 우리가 연약한 존재가 되어버린다. 사진에 대한 우리의 반응은 우리가 보고 있는 여성에 관한 것보다 우리에 관해 더 많은 것을 말해준다. 정말로, 그들의 아름다움과 크기의 불가능은 한순간 불안하고 관심을 사로잡는다. 그것은 거의 눈을 돌리기 힘든 것이다. Loloi는 "묘사된 여성은 사회의 반발의 대상이지만, 그들은 강합니다."라고 말했다. "병적인 비만이나 매년 수천 달러를 여성들이 없애려고 쓰는 그런 것들에서 아름다움을 찾는 일부 사람들의 가능성은커녕 아주 작은 허리의 군살의 튀어나옴도 인정하지 않는 세상에서 그들은 받아들여지기 위해 싸운다."

recline v. 기대다   lounge v. 늘어지다
demure adj. 얌전한   unkempt adj. 흐트러진
tousled adj. 헝클어진   pillow n. 베개
stretch mark phr. (살이) 튼 자국   thigh n. 허벅지
jut out phr. 돌출하다   obese adj. 비만인
accepted adj. 일반적으로 인정된   notion n. 개념
corporeal adj. 육체적인   exhibitionism n. 노출
mainstream n. 주류   provocation n. 도발

extreme end phr. 극단　legitimate adj. 정당한
vulnerable adj. 연약한　assumption n. 추정
disturbing adj. 충격적인　inspiring adj. 고무하는
vein n. 정맥　impossibility n. 불가능
unsettling adj. 불안한　riveting adj. 관심을 사로잡는
look away phr. 눈을 돌리다　depict v. 묘사하다
societal adj. 사회의　backlash n. 반발
bulging adj. 튀어나온　love handle phr. 허리의 군살
let alone phr. ~는커녕　morbid adj. 병적인

49 2020 이화여대

정답 ③

해석
① 요지 — 설명 — 예시
② 요지 — 예시 — 설명
③ 예시 — 요지 — 설명
④ 예시 — 설명 — 요지
⑤ 설명 — 예시 — 요지

해설 지문의 단락들이 배열된 순서를 가장 정확하게 묘사한 것을 찾는 문제이다. 맨 앞의 두 단락은 Yossi Loloi의 *완전한 아름다움* 프로젝트에 포함된 몇몇 사진을 묘사하며 예시로 보여주고 있다. 두 번째 단락에서는 여성의 몸은 어느 형태나 크기에서도 아름답고 섹시하다는 정당한 논쟁의 한 쪽 극단을 위한 것이라며 프로젝트에 대한 요지를 제시하고 있고, 뒤의 두 단락에서는 이 프로젝트에 대한 부연 설명을 하고 있다. 따라서 이 글의 배열 순서를 예시 — 요지 — 설명이라고 한 ③번이 정답이다.

50 2020 이화여대

정답 ③

해석
① 그녀는 우리가 그 충격을 직접 느낄 수 있는 전시회의 장면에 우리를 놓는다.
② 그녀는 그 전시회에 대한 우리의 관심을 높이기 위해 우리와 친근한 대화를 만든다.
③ 그녀는 객관적이고 권위적인 목소리로 우리에게 그 주제에 관한 정보를 준다.
④ 그녀는 우리의 추정에 저항하기 위해 우리의 무지함을 비난하여 충격을 준다.
⑤ 그녀는 다양한 목소리와 의견을 모아 그것들 각자가 우리에게 말하도록 한다.

해설 필자가 독자와 만들고자 하는 관계의 종류를 찾는 문제이다. 지문 중간에서 필자는 *완전한 아름다움* 프로젝트에 관해 설명하고, 이 프로젝트가 사람들이 기존에 여성의 몸에 관해 생각하는 관념에 저항하기 위한 의미를 담고 있다는 것을 프로젝트에 관해 분석하면서 전달하고 있다. 따라서 필자가 만들고자 하는 관계의 종류를 '그녀는 객관적이고 권위적인 목소리로 우리에게 그 주제에 관한 정보를 준다'고 한 ③번이 정답이다.

어휘 exhibit n. 전시회　establish v. 만들다, 세우다
objective adj. 객관적인　authoritative adj. 권위적인
accusation n. 비난　ignorance n. 무지함

51 2020 이화여대

정답 ③

해석
① 여성의 아름다움에 관한 우리의 관점을 바꾸기에는 그것이 너무 도발적이고 극단적이다.
② 그것은 사회의 포용에 맞서 싸우기 위한 모델들의 의지의 강한 긍정이다.
③ 그것은 우리를 여성의 신체의 기준에 관해 생각하게 한다.
④ 그것은 우리를 작은 결점이라도 지우려고 하는 세상에 관해 더 비판적으로 만든다.
⑤ 그것은 우리가 어떠한 여성의 나체에도 내재되어 있는 에로티시즘이 있다는 것을 깨닫게 한다.

해설 Yossi Loloi의 전시회에 관한 필자의 요지를 묻는 문제이다. 지문의 네 번째 단락에서 필자는 모델들이 우리가 정의하는 여성의 몸에 대한 추정에 맞서게 하는 용기를 보여준다고 설명하고 있다. 따라서 이 전시회에 관한 필자의 요지를 '그것은 우리를 여성의 신체의 기준에 관해 생각하게 한다'라고 표현한 ③번이 정답이다.

어휘 affirmation n. 긍정　will n. 의지　standard n. 기준
imperfection n. 결함　inherent adj. 내재된

[52-53]

그림이나 문학 작품의 지식적 가치는 동시대의 혹은 그 이전의 작품들에서 대중들이 쉽게 알 수 없는, 내재된 무언가를 이해하지 않고서는 평가될 수 없다. 내재된 그것은 대체로 누적되고 독립적인 유일한 정보이다. 이류 모방자가 모방하는 지식은 이전에 있었던 것에서 별개가 되는 것과는 거리가 멀다. 따라서, 진부한 연애 소설, 진부한 탐정 소설, 사기꾼들의 일반적이고 평범한 성공 소설 모두는 저작권법에 대한 사조가 아니라 문학의 대상이다. 한 영화의 성공이 동일한 감정적 상황에 대한 대중의 두 번째, 세 번째 감흥을 이용하려는 저급한 영화들로 이어지는 것을 막는 저작권법은 없다. 새로운 수학적 개념이나 자연 선택에 대한 개념과 같은 새로운 이론, 또는 동일한 말로 동일한 개념을 담는 동일한 복제품 이외의 것의 저작권을 보호하는 방법도 없다. 상투적 수법의 만연은 우연이 아니라, 지식의 본질에 내재된 것이다. 지적 재산권은 지식이 공동체의 총체적 지성에 기여하려면 공동체가 이전에 가지고 있던 보편적 많은 지식과는 확연히 다른 무언가를 전달해야 한다는 불가피한 불리함을 겪고 있다. 단지 대중이 작품 내용들에 익숙해졌다는 사실에 의하여 위대한 고전 문학 및 예술 작품들에서도 명백한 지식적 가치의 대부분이 그 작품들에서 없어졌다. 남학생들에게 셰익스피어 작품은 유명한 인용구들의 모음일 뿐이기 때문에 남학생들은 셰익스피어를 좋아하지 않는다. 그런 작가에 대한 연구가 당대의 무의미한 상투적 수법으로 흡

수된 층보다 더 아래를 파고들었을 때만 우리는 작가와 지식적 관계를 재확립하고 그에게 새롭고 신선한 문학적 가치를 부여할 수 있다. 특정한 시대로 나아가는 미적, 지적 방안에 대한 폭넓은 탐구를 통해 다년간 동시대인들이나 후대인들에게 거의 파괴적인 영향을 미쳤던 작가들과 화가들이 있다는 것은 이러한 관점에서 흥미롭다.

---

contemporary adj. 동시대의   derivative adj. 모방한
second-rate adj. 이류의   copyist n. 모방자
conventional adj. 진부한   slick n. 사기꾼   letter n. 문학
prevalence n. 만연   cliché n. 상투적인 문구
general adj. 총체적인   go out of phr. ~에서 없어지다
penetrate v. 파고들다   superficial adj. 무의미한
rapport n. 관계   successor n. 후임자

---

52 [2020 한국항공대]

정답 ②

해석 ① 예술적 의사소통의 본질은 사람 사이에 존재하기보다는 다른 문화 간에 있다.
② 예술에서, 지식은 축적보다는 과정의 문제이다.
③ 예술 작품은 통달 되면 작품의 창조성을 잃을 수 있다.
④ 셰익스피어의 업적들은 영원히 기억된다는 점에서 뛰어나다.

해설 지문의 내용과 일치하는 것을 묻는 문제이다. 지문의 중간에서 지적 재산권은 지식이 공동체의 총체적 지성에 기여하려면 공동체가 이전에 가지고 있던 보편적인 많은 지식과는 확연히 다른 무언가를 전달해야 한다는 내용을 통해 예술에서, 지식은 축적보다는 과정의 문제라는 것을 알 수 있다. 따라서 ②번이 지문의 내용과 일치한다.

오답 분석
① 특정한 시대로 나아가는 미적, 지적 방안에 대한 폭넓은 탐구를 통해 다년간 동시대인들이나 후대인들에게 거의 파괴적인 영향을 미쳤던 작가들과 화가들이 있다는 것은 이러한 관점에서 흥미롭다고 했으므로, 예술적 의사소통의 본질은 사람 사이에 존재하기보다는 다른 문화 간에 있다는 것은 지문의 내용과 다르다.
③ 단지 대중이 작품 내용들에 익숙해졌다는 사실에 의하여 위대한 고전 문학 및 예술 작품들에서도 명백한 지식적 가치의 대부분이 그 작품들에서 없어졌다고는 했지만, 예술 작품은 통달 되면 작품의 창조성을 잃을 수 있다는 것은 지문에서 알 수 없다.
④ 남학생들에게 셰익스피어 작품은 유명한 인용구들의 모음일 뿐이기 때문에 남학생들은 셰익스피어를 좋아하지 않는다고 했으므로, 셰익스피어의 업적들은 영원히 기억된다는 점에서 뛰어나다는 것은 지문의 내용과 다르다.

어휘 storage n. 저장

53 [2020 한국항공대]

정답 ①

해석 ① 예술에서의 지식의 가치
② 예술에서의 진부한 주제의 필요성
③ 예술에서의 지성 주의의 역할
④ 예술을 창조하는 과정에서의 자연적 선택

해설 지문의 제목을 묻는 문제이다. 지문의 처음에서 그림이나 문학 작품의 지식적 가치는 동시대의 혹은 그 이전의 작품들에서 대중들이 쉽게 알 수 없는, 내재된 무언가를 이해하지 않고서는 평가될 수 없다고 말하고 있다. 따라서 이 지문의 제목을 '예술에서의 지식의 가치'라고 표현한 ①번이 정답이다.

어휘 intellectualism n. 지성 주의

04 철학·종교

01-50
문제집 p.100

01 ②	02 ③	03 ④	04 ②	05 ①
06 ②	07 ③	08 ③	09 ①	10 ②
11 ⑤	12 ④	13 ②	14 ④	15 ③
16 ③	17 ③	18 ③	19 ③	20 ④
21 ④	22 ③	23 ②	24 ②	25 ②
26 ②	27 ④	28 ②	29 ③	30 ②
31 ⑤	32 ②	33 ④	34 ③	35 ③
36 ①	37 ③	38 ②	39 ②	40 ④
41 ⑤	42 ④	43 ④	44 ①	45 ②
46 ④	47 ③	48 ①	49 ①	50 ②

01 [2017 광운대]

정답 ②

해석 프란치스코 교황(Pope Francis)은 적극적이지만 절제된 80회 생일 축하 행사를 가졌다. [A] 그는 전 세계로부터 축하 인사가 쏟아져 들어오는 가운데 추기경들과 미사를 올리기 전에 8명의 노숙인과 아침 식사를 함께했다. [B] 그의 전임자인, 명예 교황 베네딕트 16세(Benedict XVI)는 '매우 애정 어린' 인사말을 보냈는데, 바티칸(교황청)은 '특히 감사드린다'고 말했다. [C] 아침 식사를 하면서, 프란치스코는 그가 거주하는 바티칸 호텔에서 노숙인 손님들과 개인적으로 대화를 나누었고, 아르헨티나에서 보낸 케이크를 그들과 함께 먹었다. [D] 그 손님들은 성 베드로 광장 주변에 머무는 노숙인들 중에서 그리고 교황의 자선단체가 인근에 세운 노숙인들을 위한 샤워 시설에 있던 사람들 중에서 초대를 받은 사람들이었다. [E] 교황은 또한 로마에서 가난한 사람들과 노숙인들에게 식사를 제공하는 급식소에 1천5백 명분의 충분한 생일 케이크를 보냈다.

해설 지문의 흐름과 무관한 문장을 고르는 문제이다. 이 지문은 교황의 80회 생일과 관련하여 어떤 일이 있었는지를 소개하고 있는데, [A], [C], [D]는 교황이 생일날의 아침 식사를 광장의 노숙인들과 함께하며 개인적으로 대화도 하고 케이크도 함께 나누어 먹었다는 내용이며, [E]도 무료급식소에 충분한 케이크를 보냈다는 것이므로 글의 흐름상 일관성이 있다. 그러나 [B]는 '전임 교황이 애정 어린 인사말을 보냈다'는 내용이므로 글의 흐름과 관련이 없다. 따라서 ②번이 정답이다.

어휘 celebrate v. 기념(축하)하다; 미사를 올리다
low-key adj. (사람들의 이목을 끌지 않도록) 절제된
cardinal n. 추기경   emeritus adj. 명예직의
affectionate adj. 다정한, 애정 어린
reside v. 살다, 거주하다   almsgiver n. 자선가, 자선단체

02 [2019 한양대]

정답 ③

해석 18세기 후반까지 자연사의 규율은 목사, 사제, 수도원장, 집사, 그리고 수도사와 같은 소위 교구 자연주의자에 의해 지배되었는데, 이들은 신성한 창조의 놀라움을 제공하기 위해 자신들의 정원을 가꾸고 식물과 동물 표본을 수집했지만, 일반적으로 근본적인 추정에 대한 의문을 제기하는 것으로부터 방향이 벗어나지 않았다. 그 결과는 그 분야의 특이한 왜곡이었다. 식물과 동물의 종을 분류하는 분류학이 번창함과 동시에, 살아있는 생명체의 기원에 대한 탐구는 금지된 구석으로 밀려났다. 자연사는 역사가 없는 자연의 연구가 되었다. 다윈을 괴롭혔던 것이 바로 이런 정적인 자연관이었다. 다윈은 마치 물리학자가 공기 중의 공이 움직이는 것을 묘사할 수 있는 것처럼 자연사학자는 자연계의 상태를 원인과 결과라는 용어를 사용해 묘사할 수 있어야 한다고 판단했다. 다윈의 파괴적인 천재성의 본질은 자연을 사실로써 생각하는 것이 아닌 과정, 진보, 그리고 역사로써 생각하는 그의 능력이었다.

① 교구 자연주의자는 식물과 동물을 확인하고 분류했다.
② 교구 자연주의자는 자연을 묘사하는 데에 있어 정적인 자연관을 갖고 있었다.
③ 교구 자연주의자는 살아있는 생명체의 기원에 대해 맹렬하게 조사했다.
④ 교구 자연주의자는 전능한 신이 창조한 살아있는 생명체의 어마어마한 다양성을 찬양했다.
⑤ 다윈은 자연사학자는 원인과 결과의 용어를 이용해 자연이 어떻게 진보했는지를 물어야 한다고 믿었다.

해설 지문의 내용과 일치하지 않는 것을 묻는 문제이다. 지문에서 ③번의 키워드인 the origin of living beings(살아있는 생명체의 기원)이 나온 부분에서 살아있는 생명체의 기원에 대한 탐구는 금지된 구석으로 밀려났다고 했으므로, 교구 자연주의자는 살아있는 생명체의 기원에 대해 맹렬하게 조사했다는 것은 지문의 내용과 다르다. 따라서 ③번이 지문의 내용과 일치하지 않는다.

오답분석
① who cultivated their gardens and collected plant and animal specimens to service the wonders of divine Creation을 통해 '교구 자연주의자는 식물과 동물을 확인하고 분류했다'는 것을 알 수 있다.
② It was this static view of nature that Darwin found troubling을 통해 '교구 자연주의자는 자연을 묘사하는 데에 있어 정적인 자연관을 갖고 있었다'는 것을 알 수 있다.
④ who cultivated their gardens and collected plant and animal specimens to service the wonders of divine Creation을 통해 '교구 자연주의자는 전지전능한 신이 창조한 살아있는 생명체의 어마어마한 다양성을 찬양했다'는 것을 알 수 있다.
⑤ A natural historian should be able to describe the state of the natural world in terms of causes and effects, Darwin reasoned를 통해 '다윈은 자연사학자는

원인과 결과의 용어를 이용해 자연이 어떻게 진보했는지를 물어야 한다고 믿었다'는 것을 알 수 있다.

어휘 discipline n. 규율　natural history phr. 자연사
dominated adj. 지배된
parson-naturalist n. 교구 자연주의자
cultivate v. 가꾸다, 경작하다　specimen n. 표본, 견본
wonder n. 놀라움　veer v. 방향을 바꾸다
fundamental adj. 근본적인　assumption n. 추측, 가정
peculiar adj. 독특한　distortion n. 왜곡
taxonomy n. 분류학　classification n. 분류
inquiry n. 탐구, 문의　relegate v. 밀어내다, 좌천시키다
forbidden adj. 금지된　reason v. 판단하다, 추리하다
physicist n. 물리학자　essence n. 본질, 정수
disruptive adj. 파괴적인, 방해하는
progression n. 진보, 진행　classify v. 분류하다
fiercely adv. 맹렬하게　investigate v. 조사하다
celebrate v. 찬양하다　immense adj. 어마어마한
omnipotent adj. 전능한

03 2019 인하대
정답 ④

해석 언어와 종교적 믿음 사이의 긴밀한 관계는 문화사에 널리 퍼져있다. 종종, 신성한 존재가 말이나 글을 발명하였고 그것을 인류에게 선물로 주었다고 한다. 창세기에 따르면, 아담이 해야 하는 것 중에 첫 번째는 창조 활동에 이름을 붙이는 것이다. 다른 많은 문화도 비슷한 이야기를 가지고 있다. [A] <u>이집트 신화에서, 토트 신은 말과 글의 창시자이다.</u> [B] <u>힌두교 사람들에게 글의 지식을 전해준 것은 브라마 신이다.</u> [C] <u>아이슬란드의 영웅 전설에 따르면, 오딘은 룬 문자의 창안자이다.</u> [D] <u>글을 읽고 쓸 줄 아는 능력은 보통 종교의 전파에 의해 공동체에 도입되었다.</u> [E] <u>등에 표식을 가진 하늘이 주신 민물 거북은 중국인들에게 글을 가져다주었다.</u> 전 세계에서, 초자연적 현상이 언어의 기원에 대한 믿음의 강한 집합체를 제공하였다.

해설 지문의 흐름과 무관한 문장을 고르는 문제이다. 지문은 오래 전부터 신성한 존재가 말이나 글을 발명하여 인류에게 전해줬다는 것에 대한 내용이므로, ① 이집트 신화에서 토트 신은 말과 글의 창시자이다, ② 힌두교 사람들에게 글의 지식을 전해준 것은 브라마 신이다, ③ 아이슬란드의 영웅 전설에 따르면 오딘은 룬 문자의 창시자이다, ⑤ 등에 표식을 가진 민물 거북이 중국 사람들에게 글을 가져다주었다는 것은 모두 지문 내용과 관련이 있다. 그러나 ④는 '글을 읽고 쓸 줄 아는 능력은 보통 종교의 전파에 의해 공동체에 도입되었다'라는 내용이므로, 신성한 존재가 말과 글을 발명하여 인류에게 전해줬다는 것과 관련이 없다. 따라서 ④번이 정답이다.

어휘 pervade v. 널리 퍼지다, 고루 미치다　divine adj. 신성한
mankind n. 인류　the Book of Genesis phr. 창세기
name v. 이름을 붙이다　mythology n. 신화
runic adj. 룬 문자(고대 문자의 일종)로 쓰여진
script n. 문자, 글　saga n. 영웅 전설

literacy n. 글을 읽고 쓸 줄 아는 능력
introduce v. 도입하다, 소개하다
community n. 공동체, 지역 사회
heaven-sent adj. 하늘이 주신, 신의 뜻인
supernatural n. 초자연적 현상; adj. 초자연적인

[04-05]

유용성의 우정과 기쁨의 우정은 동반되며 의심의 여지 없이 가장 일반적이다. 모두가 그것들을 경험한 적 있다. 사람들은 그들의 동료, 이웃, 그들의 카풀 멤버, 그리고 심지어는 열차, 배, 그리고 비행기에서 만나는 조금 아는 사람에게조차 "친절하다". 이러한 종류의 정중함은 어느 정도는 우정의 한 형태로, 유용성의 우정, 즉 상호 편의에 관한 것이다. 유사하게, 사람들은 그들의 골프 파트너, 칵테일 파티에서 만난 다른 사람들, 그리고 그들을 즐겁게 해주는 지인들에게 "친절하다". 이것 역시 우정의 한 형태인데, 이는 기쁨의 우정, 즉의 상호 간의 즐거움에 관한 것이다.

우정의 이러한 하위 형태들이 꼭 나쁜 것만은 아니지만, 그것들은 불충분하다. 그것들의 결점 중 하나는 그것들이 상황에 달려있고 상황마다 다르다는 사실에서 기인한다. 이것은 우정의 하위 형태들이 빠르게 발생하고 그만큼 빠르게 사라지는 이유이다. 대조적으로, 성경의 잠언에는 "친구는 사랑이 끊이지 아니한다"라고 쓰여있는데, 이는 상황에 의존하지 않는, 더 상위 형태의 우정을 가리키고 있다. 시간과 우연의 영향을 극복하기 위해, 우정은 관련된 사람들의 고유의 특성들을 기반으로 해야 한다. 단단히 고정되어 있는 우정은 일시적인 우정이 될 수 없다.

진정한 우정, 즉 미덕의 우정은, 따라서 (비록 우정이 그것들을 포함하지만) 유용성과 기쁨 모두를 능가한다. 아리스토텔레스에게, 그러한 우정은 선한 품성이 기반되어야만 했다. 오직 그렇게 하는 것만이 우정을 오래 지속하게 할 수 있다. 더 나아가서 우정은 친밀감, 지식, 그리고 결국에는 상호 신뢰를 전제로 하기 때문에, 천천히 발전해야 한다.

utility n. 유용성　associate n. 동료
acquaintance n. 아는 사람, 지인　civility n. 정중함
inadequate adj. 불충분한
Book of Proverbs phr. 잠언(구약성경)
surmount v. 극복하다　happenstance n. 우연
inherent adj. 고유의, 내재된
anchored adj. 단단히 고정된, 닻을 내린
passing adj. 일시적인　surpass v. 능가하다, 뛰어넘다
Aristotle n. 아리스토텔레스　moral character phr. 품성
presuppose v. 전제로 하다　familiarity n. 친밀감

04 2021 단국대
정답 ②

해석 ① 신뢰　② 즐거움
③ 책임　④ 의존

해설 지문의 빈칸을 채우는 문제이다. 빈칸 앞 문장에서 사람들은 그들을 즐겁게 해주는 사람들에게 친절하다고 했으므로, 빈칸에는 이것 역시 우정의 한 형태인데 이는 기쁨의 우정, 즉 상호 간의 즐거움에 관한 것이라는 내용이 나오는 것이 자연스럽다. 따라서 '즐거움'이라고 한 ②번이 정답이다.

05 2021 단국대
정답 ①

해석 ① 미덕의 우정은 일시적인 우정이 아니다.
② 유용성의 우정은 필요하지 않다.
③ 기쁨의 우정은 비도덕적이다.
④ 모든 우정은 일시적이다.

해설 지문의 내용과 일치하는 것을 묻는 문제이다. 지문의 후반에서 True friendship, the friendship of virtue ~의 내용을 통해 미덕의 우정은 선한 품성을 기반으로 하는 방식으로만 우정을 오래 지속하게 할 수 있다는 것을 알 수 있다. 따라서 ①번이 지문의 내용과 일치한다.

오답 분석
② 우정의 하위 형태들(유용성의 우정과 기쁨의 우정)이 꼭 나쁜 것만은 아니라고 했으므로, 유용성의 우정이 필요하지 않다는 것은 지문의 내용과 다르다.
③ 우정의 하위 형태들이 불충분하다고는 했지만, 그것들이 비도덕적인지는 알 수 없다.
④ 미덕의 우정은 오래 지속한다고 했으므로, 모든 종류의 우정이 일시적이라는 것은 지문의 내용과 다르다.

어휘 transient adj. 일시적인

[06-08]

하지만 소득과 부가 당신의 유일한 고려사항은 아닐 것이다. 만약 당신이 부유하다면, 당신은 당신의 부와 특권을 자녀에게 물려줄 수 있는 사회를 선호할 것이다. 이것은 귀족 사회에 찬성하는 것이다. 당신이 가난하다면, 당신은 당신이나 당신의 자녀에게 출세할 기회가 있는 사회를 선호할 것이다. 이것은 능력주의 사회에 찬성하는 것이다.
그러나, 그 이상의 숙고는 각 사례를 상쇄하는 생각을 떠오르게 한다. 사람들은 그들이 얼마의 돈을 가지고 있는지 뿐만 아니라 그들의 부 혹은 가난이 그들의 사회적 지위와 자부심을 나타내는지 관심을 갖는다. 만약 당신이 귀족의 상류 계급으로 태어났다면, 당신은 당신의 특권이 행운이며, 당신이 직접 이룬 것이 아니라는 것을 알고 있을 것이다. 반면에 당신이 노력과 재능을 통해 능력주의 사회의 정점으로 올라섰다면, 당신은 당신의 성공이 물려받았다기보다는 얻어낸 것이라는 사실을 자랑스러워할 수 있다. 귀족적 특권과는 달리, 능력주의적 성공은 그 자리를 얻어낸 것에 대한 성취감을 불러일으킨다. 이러한 관점에서, 귀족 사회보다 능력주의 사회에서 부자가 되는 것이 더 낫다.

비슷한 이유에서, 능력주의 사회에서 가난한 것은 의기소침하게 만든다. 봉건사회에서, 만약 당신이 농노의 신분으로 태어났다면, 당신의 삶은 힘들겠지만, 당신이 당신의 종속적 지위에 대한 책임이 있다는 생각 때문에 고민하지 않을 것이다. 당신은 또한 당신이 주인을 위해 힘껏 일해도, 주인이 당신보다 더 유능하고 기략이 풍부해서 그의 자리를 성취했다는 믿음으로 일하지는 않을 것이다. 당신은 그가 당신보다 자격이 있는 것이 아니라, 단지 운이 더 좋았을 뿐임을 알 것이다.

bequeath v. 물려주다, 남기다
aristocratic adj. 귀족의, 귀족적인
rise v. 출세하다, 승진하다, 치솟다
meritocratic adj. 능력주의의
countervailing adj. 상쇄하는, 대항하는   standing n. 지위
self-esteem n. 자부심
reach n. 계급, 지위; v. ~에 도착하다   apex n. 정점, 꼭대기
demoralize v. 의기소침하게 하다, 사기를 꺾다
feudal adj. 봉건의, 봉건적인
serfdom n. 농노의 신분, 농노제도
subordinate adj. 종속적인, 하층의
toil v. 힘들게 일하다   resourceful adj. 기략이 풍부한

06 2021 홍익대
정답 ②

해석 ① 분명히 말하자면   ② 비슷한 이유에서
③ 보통, 일반적으로   ④ 그렇게 하면서

해설 빈칸에 적절한 연결어를 넣는 문제이다. 빈칸 앞 내용은 능력주의 사회에서 부자가 되는 것이 더 낫다는 것이고, 빈칸 뒤 내용은 능력주의 사회에서 가난한 것은 의기소침하게 만든다는 것으로 서로 같은 맥락에서 부가적인 설명을 덧붙이고 있다는 것을 알 수 있다. 따라서 ② For similar reasons(비슷한 이유에서)가 정답이다.

07 2021 홍익대
정답 ③

해석 ① 봉건사회에서 하층 계급의 사람은 그의 계급을 물려받았기 때문에 만족감을 느낀다.
② 능력주의 사회에서 한 사람의 노고는 항상 보상받는 반면 귀족 사회에서는 그렇지 않다.
③ 능력 중심의 성공이나 실패는 한 사람의 사회적 평판에 영향을 미친다.
④ 부자와 가난한 사람의 차이는 능력주의 사회에서보다 귀족 사회에서 더 크다.

해설 지문을 통해 추론할 수 있는 것을 고르는 문제이다. ③번 보기의 키워드인 'social esteem'(사회적 평판)의 유의어인 'social standing'(사회적 지위)이 등장한 지문의 초반과 지문의 중간의 'meritocratic success'(능력주의적 성공)가 등장한 부분에서 능력 중심의 성공이나 실패는 한 사람의 사회

적 평판에 영향을 미친다는 것을 추론할 수 있다. 따라서 정답은 ③번이다.

오답분석
① 봉건사회에서 농노의 신분으로 태어났다면 본인의 위치에 대한 책임 때문에 고민하지 않는다고 했지만, 봉건사회에서 하층 계급의 사람들이 그의 계급을 물려받았기 때문에 만족감을 느낀다는 것은 추론할 수 없다.
② 능력주의 사회에서의 성공은 노력으로 인해 얻은 자리이므로 성취감을 얻을 수 있다고는 했지만, 능력주의 사회에서의 한 사람의 노고는 항상 보상받고 귀족 사회에서는 아니라는 내용은 알 수 없다.
④ 능력주의 사회에서 부자가 되는 것은 성취감을 얻고, 가난한 것은 의기소침하게 만든다고는 했지만, 부자와 가난한 사람의 차이는 능력주의 사회에서보다 귀족 사회에서 더 크다는 내용은 알 수 없다.

어휘 esteem n. 평판, 존중

08 [2021 홍익대]

정답 ③

해석
① 귀족 사회에서, 당신은 당신의 가난을 더 특권을 가진 사람들을 탓할 것이다.
② 귀족 사회에서, 당신은 당신의 부를 당신의 성취 덕분으로 돌릴 것이다.
③ 능력주의 사회에서, 당신은 당신의 가난을 자신의 탓으로 돌릴 것이다.
④ 능력주의 사회에서, 당신이 얼마나 부자인지 혹은 가난한지와 상관없이 당신의 사회적 지위에 만족할 것이다.

해설 주어진 지문의 뒤에 올 내용을 고르는 문제이다. 지문의 마지막에서 능력주의 사회에서 가난한 것은 의기소침하게 만든다고 하고 봉건사회의 농노 신분을 예로 들어 설명하고 있으므로 '능력주의 사회에서, 당신은 당신의 가난을 자신의 탓으로 돌릴 것이다'와 관련된 내용이 지문의 뒤에 나올 것임을 알 수 있다. 따라서 ③번이 정답이다.

어휘 attribute to phr. ~의 덕분으로 돌리다, ~의 탓으로 돌리다
affluence n. 부, 풍족

[09-10]

Ernst Gombrich는 A Sense of Order에서 "우리가 어떻게 일정한 것과 일정하지 않은 것 간의 차이를 분석한다고 하더라고, 우리는 궁극적으로는 심미적 경험의 가장 기본적인 사실, 즉 즐거움은 지루함과 혼란 사이의 어딘가에 있다는 사실을 설명할 수 있어야 한다"고 분명히 말한다. 우리는 어떻게 인간이 한편으로 질서 유지에 대한 욕구와 예측 가능함 사이의 계속되는 갈등 속에 갇혀있는지, 반면에 다른 한편에서는 그러한 안정감이 소멸과 붕괴에 취약하다는 것을 인지하고 있는지를 이미 알고 있다. 따라서, 강제력은 존재의 완전함을 유지하고 누군가의 존재를 스스로에게 확고히 하려는 의도를 한데 모아야 한다. 하지만, 계속해서 예측 가능한 상태에 있는 것은 지루함과 쉬지 않음으로 이어질 수 있고, 자극의 완전한 부재 또는 지각 상실의 경우와 같이 '초연속성'이라고 불리는 무언가 속에서 더 나쁜 것을 경험하게 된다는 것도 사실이다.

ultimately adv. 결국   **account for** phr. 설명하다
aesthetic adj. 심미적인   **perpetual** adj. 계속해서 반복되는
stability n. 안정감

09 [2020 한국항공대]

정답 ①

해석
① 중용의 중요성
② 지각적 오류와 개념적 오류를 막는 방안
③ 자동적인 창조력
④ 지속성을 위한 강제적 요구 조건

해설 지문의 제목을 묻는 문제이다. 지문의 처음에서 우리는 궁극적으로는 심미적 경험의 가장 기본적인 사실, 즉 즐거움은 지루함과 혼란 사이의 어딘가에 있다는 사실을 설명할 수 있어야 한다고 했다. 따라서 이 지문의 제목을 '중용의 중요성'이라고 표현한 ①번이 정답이다.

어휘 moderation n. 중용

10 [2020 한국항공대]

정답 ②

해석
① 격변의 시기에, 사람들은 종종 즐거움에 대한 값진 경험을 간과한다.
② 동시에 존재하는 일관성과 혼란이 필요한 정도를 받아들이는 것은 필수적이다.
③ 다양한 병치는 모순과 무질서로 이어진다.
④ 더 일상적인 단편적 경험은 초연속성에 기여한다.

해설 지문을 통해 추론할 수 있는 것을 고르는 문제이다. 지문의 초반에서 즐거움은 지루함과 혼란 사이의 어딘가에 있다는 사실을 설명할 수 있어야 한다고 했으므로, 동시에 존재하는 일관성과 혼란이 필요한 정도를 받아들이는 것은 필수적이라는 것을 추론할 수 있다. 따라서 정답은 ②번이다.

오답분석
① 계속해서 예측 가능한 상태에 있는 것은 지루함과 쉬지 않음으로 이어질 수 있다고는 했지만, 격변의 시기에, 사람들은 종종 즐거움에 대한 값진 경험을 간과한다는 것은 알 수 없다.
③ 다양한 병치는 모순과 무질서로 이어진다는 것은 지문에서 알 수 없다.
④ 자극의 완전한 부재 또는 지각 상실의 경우와 같은 것을 '초연속성'이라고 부른다고 했으므로, 더 일상적인 단편적 경험은 초연속성에 기여한다는 것은 지문의 내용과 다르다.

어휘 turbulent adj. 격변의 accommodate v. 받아들이다
simultaneous adj. 동시에 존재하는
coherence n. 일관성 juxtaposition n. 병치
fragmentary adj. 단편적인

[11-12]

종교는 사람이 이타심이나 무자비한 잔인함을 갖도록 고무할 수 있으며, 여러 경우에 두 가지 모두의 효과를 가질 수 있다. 이 역설을 분석하는 것은 Karen Armstrong에게 손쉽다. 영국에서 태어나 과거 로마 가톨릭 수녀였던 그녀는 가장 광범위한 종교 역사에 대해 12권 이상의 책을 썼고, 신앙의 주장이 진실이든 아니든, 신앙은 인간 경험의 타당한 부분이라는 그녀의 견해를 자세히 설명했다. 그녀의 최신작 "Fields of Blood"에서, Armstrong 씨는 거론되고 있는 기존의 많은 이론들에 내용을 더하지 않는다. 대신에, 그녀는 종교 및 세계 역사에 대한 방대한 개요를 제시하면서, 세계 모든 신앙의 초기 발전에 대한 개요를 제시한다. 그러고 나서, 위대한 필치와 많은 (완전히 정확하지는 않은) 세부 사항과 함께, 그녀는 지난 500년 동안 전 세계에 미친 기독교도 서양의 영향을 연구한다. 그녀가 어떤 악령과 싸우고 있는지 당신이 깨달아야 이 모든 것이 어떻게 논리 정연한지 명확해진다. Armstrong 씨는 어떤 것도 입증하려고 하지 않고, 오히려 여러 가지 것들을 반증하려고 한다. 첫 번째는, 종교가 폭력의 불필요한 이유이고, 종교를 없애는 것이 평화를 증진할 것이라는 생각이다. 그리고 두 번째는 이슬람교가 폭력을 고무하는 악명 높은 종교의 사례라는 생각이다. 그녀의 세 번째 악령은 앞선 두 가지의 생각과 결합되는데, 이것은 "기독교도" 서양이 이슬람교도 세계보다 더 많은 낡은 종교적 생각을 없애왔기 때문에, 기독교도 서양이 고질적으로 폭력적인 이슬람교를 억눌러야 한다는 생각이다.

altruism n. 이타심 ruthless adj. 무자비한
cruelty n. 잔인함 dissect v. 분석하다 paradox n. 역설
nun n. 수녀 broad adj. 광범위한
expound v. 자세히 설명하다 faith n. 신앙
legitimate adj. 타당한 existing adj. 기존의
vast adj. 방대한 overview n. 개요
sketch v. 개요를 제시하다 evolution n. 발전
stroke n. 필치(글에 나타나는 맛이나 개성)
Christian adj. 기독교도의 cohere adj. 논리 정연한
demon n. 악령 prove v. 입증하다 disprove v. 반증하다
gratuitous adj. 불필요한 elimination n. 제거
egregious adj. 악명 높은 bogeyman n. 귀신
baggage n. 낡은 생각 restrain v. 억누르다
incorrigibly adv. 고질적으로

11 [2020 성균관대]

정답 ⑤

해설 ① 종교는 근본적으로 권위주의적이다
② 종교는 인류의 폭력을 없애기 위한 강력한 수단으로 역할을 해왔다
③ 종교의 어두운 면이 과장되어왔다
④ 종교적 신념은 그 주장이 옳다고 입증될 때만 의미 있다
⑤ 신앙은 진실의 기반과는 상관없이 인간의 삶에 필수적이다

해설 Armstrong 씨가 그녀의 책에서 무엇을 주장하는지 파악하는 문제이다. 지문의 세 번째 문장에서 신앙의 주장이 진실이든 아니든, 신앙은 인간 경험의 타당한 부분이라는 그녀의 견해를 자세히 설명했다고 했으므로, Armstrong 씨가 책에서 주장한 것은 '신앙은 진실의 기반과는 상관없이 인간의 삶에 필수적이다'라는 것이다. 따라서 정답은 ⑤번이다.

어휘 fundamentally adv. 근본적으로
authoritarian adj. 권위주의적인 eliminate v. 없애다
exaggerate v. 과장하다 meaningful adj. 의미 있는
prove v. 입증하다 regardless of phr. ~에 상관없이

12 [2020 성균관대]

정답 ④

해석 ① 이슬람교는 평화의 종교이다
② 기독교는 사람들 안의 가장 악한 것을 드러내게 한다
③ 기독교도 서양은 이슬람교도 세계보다 더 신앙심이 깊다
④ 기독교도 서양은 더 유순한 국제적 세력이다
⑤ 기독교도 서양은 이슬람교도 세계로부터 배울 수 있다

해설 밑줄 친 부분의 의미를 추론하는 문제이다. 밑줄 친 the "Christian" West has shed more religious baggage than the Muslim world has는 '"기독교도" 서양이 이슬람교도 세계보다 더 많은 낡은 종교적 생각을 없애왔다'라는 의미이다. 주변의 내용을 살펴보면 이것이 고질적으로 폭력적인 이슬람교와 반대되는 의미임을 알 수 있다. 따라서 이를 '기독교도 서양은 더 유순한 국제적 세력이다'라고 표현한 ④번이 정답이다.

어휘 Christianity n. 기독교 bring out phr. 드러내게 하다
benign adj. 유순한

[13-14]

Anaximander는 세계의 근원이 영원한 실체이자 무한히 크고 어떠한 명확한 특징도 없는 아페이론이라는 그의 견해로 가장 잘 알려져 있다. 아페이론은 뜨겁지도 차갑지도, 습하거나 건조하지도, 백색, 흑색, 또는 무언가 다른 색깔이지도 않다. 다시 말해서, 우리의 세계에 대한 이러한 익숙하지 않은 근원을 소개하는 그의 근거는 모든 것의 근원이 물이라는 Thales의 견해와는 대조적으로, 다소 개연성을 갖고 재구성될 수 있다. 우리를 둘러싼 세계는 대조로 특징지어진다. 일부분은 습하고, 다른 부분은 건조한 것 등과 같이 말이다. 하지만 세계의 근원이 습하다면, 습하지 않은 모든 것의 존재를 설명하기 어렵다. 따라서 태생 물질은 습하거나 건조하지도, 뜨겁거나 차갑지도 않아야 한다. 사실, 태생 물질은 분명히 규정되지 않아

야 한다. 또한, 태생 물질이 모든 것의 근원이라면, 그것에는 처음 그 자체가 있을 수 없으므로, 그것은 영원하다. 그리스 철학자들은 처음이 없는 모든 것에는 끝도 없다는 것을 가정하는데 모두 의견이 같다. 그리고 태생 물질은 우리의 세계뿐만 아니라 Anaximander에 따르면 서로 다른 시간과 장소에서 생겨나고 소멸되는 무한정으로 많은 다른 세계를 만들어낼 수 있기 위해 무한히 커야 한다.

---

origin n. 근원 eternal adj. 영원한, 끊임없는
substance n. 실체, 물질 boundlessly adv. 무한히
feature n. 특징 unfamiliar adj. 익숙지 않은
contrast n. 대조, 차이 reconstruct v. 재구성하다
probability n. 개연성 account for phr. ~을 설명하다
existence n. 존재 originate v. 유래하다
philosopher n. 철학자 unanimous adj. 모두 의견이 같은
suppose v. 가정하다 generate v. 만들어내다
a large number of phr. 다수의 indefinitely adv. 무한정
come into existence phr. 생기다 perish v. 소멸되다

13 2020 한양대에리카

정답 ②

해석 ① 명확한 — 명확한
② 명확한 — 분명히 규정되지 않은
③ 분명히 규정되지 않은 — 명확한
④ 분명히 규정되지 않은 — 분명히 규정되지 않은

해설 지문의 빈칸을 채우는 문제이다. 첫 번째 빈칸 뒤 문장에서 아페이론은 뜨겁지도 차갑지도, 습하거나 건조하지도, 백색, 흑색, 또는 무언가 다른 색깔이지도 않다고 했으므로, 첫 번째 빈칸에는 아페이론이 어떠한 특징이 없는지에 대한 내용이 나와야 적절하다는 것을 알 수 있다. 따라서 '명확한'이 들어가야 적절하다. 두 번째 빈칸 앞 문장에서 태생 물질은 습하거나 건조하지도, 뜨겁거나 차갑지도 않아야 한다고 했으므로, 두 번째 빈칸에는 태생 물질이 어떠해야 하는지에 대한 내용이 나와야 적절하다는 것을 알 수 있다. 따라서 '분명히 규정되지 않은'이 들어가야 적절하다. 따라서 ②번이 정답이다.

어휘 definite adj. 명확한 indefinite adj. 분명히 규정되지 않은

14 2020 한양대에리카

정답 ④

해석 ① Thales에 따르면, 물은 우리를 둘러싼 모든 것의 근원이다.
② Anaximander는 세계의 근원에 대해 Thales와 다른 견해를 갖고 있었다.
③ Thales와 Anaximander는 처음이 없는 모든 것은 끝도 없다고 믿었다.
④ Anaximander에 따르면, 우리 세계와 다른 세계들은 동일한 것들로 구성되어 있다.

해설 지문의 내용과 일치하지 않는 것을 묻는 문제이다. ④번의 키워드인 other worlds(다른 세계들)가 언급된 지문 주변에서 태생 물질은 우리의 세계뿐만 아니라 서로 다른 시간과 장소에서 생겨나고 소멸되는 무한정으로 많은 다른 세계를 만들어낼 수 있기 위해 무한히 커야 한다고 했으므로, Anaximander에 따르면, 우리 세계와 다른 세계들은 동일한 것들로 구성되어 있다는 것은 지문의 내용과 다르다. 따라서 ④번이 지문의 내용과 일치하지 않는다.

오답분석 ① 지문의 두 번째 문장 Thales' view that the origin of all things was water를 통해 'Thales에 따르면, 물은 우리를 둘러싼 모든 것의 근원이다'라는 것을 알 수 있다.
② 지문의 두 번째 문장 his reason ~ in contrast to Thales' view ~ some probability를 통해 'Anaximander는 세계의 근원에 대해 Thales와 다른 견해를 갖고 있었다'는 것을 알 수 있다.
③ 지문의 여덟 번째 문장 The Greek philosophers are ~ without an end.를 통해 'Thales와 Anaximander는 처음이 없는 모든 것은 끝도 없다고 믿었다'는 것을 알 수 있다.

어휘 compose v. 구성하다

[15-16]

키케로가 말했다, "책이 없는 방은 영혼 없는 몸이다." 확실히 내가 누군가의 집에 처음 방문했을 때, 나는 그 집주인의 성격에 대해 알기 위해 책 선반으로 이끌리는 것 같았다. 어느 정도는, 책들은 항상 정보의 보고 이상의 것이었다. 책을 보고 느끼는 것은 책의 내용만큼 책이 가진 매력 일부를 보고 느끼는 것이다. 새로운 책을 펴는 것에는 굉장히 만족을 주는 무언가가 있는데, 책의 냄새, 표지의 감촉, 책 커버의 디자인, 책의 무게와 같은 모든 것들이 책이 만들어내는 인상에 이바지한다. 책은 어떤 상징적인 힘도 가지고 있다. 우리는 독재와 억압의 시대의 아래에 연결된 어떤 책이 불타고 있다는 것을 듣게 되면 몸서리를 치게 된다. 문화적인 상징으로서의 책들은 우리에게 표현의 자유와 높아진 기회를 상기시키며, 더불어 책들은 우리에게 인류의 지적인 열망에 대해서도 상기시킨다. 그러나 미래에도 책이 읽혀질 것인가? 나는 그렇다고 믿는다. 지금까지에 비해 더 많은 책이 쓰이고 출판되고 있으며, 책들은 영화와 텔레비전, 컴퓨터의 도입을 견뎌내 왔던 것처럼, 앞으로 올 몇 세기에도 책은 우리 주변에 존재하고 있을 것이다.

---

draw v. 끌어당기다 bookshelf n. 책 선반
personality n. 성격 repository n. 보고, 보관소
appeal n. 매력 immensely adv. 굉장하게
dust jacket phr. 책 커버 symbolic adj. 상징적인
shudder v. 몸서리치다 tyranny n. 독재
oppression n. 억압 icon n. 상징
freedom of speech phr. 표현의 자유
enhanced adj. 향상된 intellectual adj. 지적인
aspiration n. 열망 publish v. 출판하다
withstand v. 견뎌 내다

15 [2020 한국외대]

정답 ③

해석
① 책의 정치적 역할
② 출판의 역사
③ 책의 힘과 미래
④ 왜 책은 과거에 문제가 되었는가

해설 지문의 제목을 묻는 문제이다. 지문의 여섯 번째 문장에서 책은 상징적인 힘을 가지고 있다고 했고, 지문의 마지막 문장에서 책들이 지금까지 영화와 텔레비전, 컴퓨터의 도입을 견뎌내 왔던 것처럼 앞으로 올 몇 세기 동안에도 존재할 것이라고 했으므로, 지문의 제목을 '책의 힘과 미래'라고 표현한 ③번이 정답이다.

어휘 matter v. 문제가 되다

16 [2020 한국외대]

정답 ③

해석
① 책의 매력은 정보 이상의 것을 포함한다.
② 책의 표지는 책의 내용만큼 매력적이다.
③ 출간되는 책의 숫자는 점진적으로 감소할 것이다.
④ 책은 더 나은 스스로가 되기를 바라는 사람들의 열망을 상징한다.

해설 지문의 내용과 일치하지 않는 것을 묻는 문제이다. 지문의 마지막 문장에서 지금까지에 비해 더 많은 책이 쓰이고 출판되고 있다고 했으므로, 출간되는 책의 숫자는 점진적으로 감소하리라는 것은 지문의 내용과 다르다. 따라서 ③번이 지문의 내용과 일치하지 않는다.

오답 분석
① 세 번째 문장에서 책들은 항상 정보의 보고 이상의 것이었다고 했으므로, '책의 매력은 정보 이상의 것을 포함한다'는 지문의 내용과 일치한다.
② 다섯 번째 문장에서 책의 냄새, 커버의 감촉, 책 커버의 디자인, 책의 무게와 같은 모든 것들이 책이 만들어내는 인상에 이바지한다고 했으므로 '책의 표지는 책의 내용만큼 매력적이다'는 지문의 내용과 일치한다.
④ 여덟 번째 문장에서 책들은 우리에게 인류의 지적인 열망에 대해서도 상기시킨다고 했으므로 '책은 더 나은 스스로가 되기를 바라는 사람들의 열망을 상징한다'는 지문의 내용과 일치한다.

어휘 attractiveness n. 매력

[17-19]

칸트가 말한 분석적 진리와 종합적 진리 사이의 차이는 흄이 제시한 관념들의 관계와 사실들의 문제 사이의 구분과 라이프니츠가 제시한 이성의 진리와 사실의 진리 사이의 구분에서 미리 암시되었다. 라이프니츠는 이성의 진리를 모든 가능한 세계에서 참인 것이라고 말했다. 사실적인 것은 둘째치고, 이는 이성의 진리가 거짓일 수가 없다고 말하는 것이다. 같은 맥락에서 우리는 분석명제가 그것을 부정하면 자기모순이 되는 진술로 정의된다고 받아들인다. 그러나, 이 정의는 작은 설명적 가치를 가질 뿐인데, 이 분석성의 정의를 위해 필요한 상당히 넓은 의미에서 자기모순의 개념도 분석성의 개념 자체와 마찬가지로 정확히 동일한 명확성이 필요하기 때문이다. 이 두 개념은 의심스러운 하나의 동전의 양면성이다.

칸트는 분석명제를 그 주어에 이미 개념적으로 포함되어 있는 것 외에는 주어에 속성을 주는 것이 없는 것으로 여겼다. 이 공식화에는 두 가지 단점이 있는데, 이 공식화가 스스로를 주어-술어 형식의 명제로만 한정시키며, 은유적인 수준에 남겨진 포함의 개념에 호소한다는 것이다. 그러나 칸트의 의도는, 분석성에 대한 자신의 정의로부터 보다는 그가 분석성의 개념을 사용하는 용도에서 더 분명하게 드러나며, 다음과 같이 재진술될 수 있다. 하나의 명제는 그것이 어떠한 사실에 대한 고려 없이 의미의 덕목에 의해서 참일 때 분석적이다. 이 입장을 따라, 전제된 의미의 개념을 검토해보자.

---

cleavage n. 의견의 불일치, 분열 analytic adj. 분석적인
synthetic adj. 종합적인 foreshadow v. ~을 미리 암시하다
distinction n. 구분 picturesqueness n. 사실적임, 생생함
aside adv. 둘째치고 in the same vein phr. 같은 맥락에서
self-contradictory adj. 자기모순의
explanatory adj. 설명적인
self-contradictoriness n. 자기모순
analyticity n. 분석성 clarification n. 명확성
conceive v. 여기다, 생각하다
conceptually adv. 개념적으로 formulation n. 공식화
predicate n. 술부 appeal v. 호소하다 notion n. 개념
containment n. 속박, 봉쇄 metaphorical adj. 은유적인
intent n. 의도 evident adj. 분명한 virtue n. 덕목
presuppose v. 전제로 하다

17 [2020 홍익대]

정답 ②

해석
① 이성의 진리와 사실의 진리 간의 흄의 구분
② 라이프니츠의 이성의 진리와 칸트의 분석명제
③ 라이프니츠 철학에서 가능한 세계와 사실의 진리 사이의 관계
④ 칸트 철학에서 주어-술부 형식의 진술의 중요성

해설 지문의 주제를 묻는 문제이다. 지문의 첫 번째 문단에서 이성의 진리에 대한 라이프니츠의 정의와 분석명제에 대한 설명이 나오며, 이어지는 두 번째 문단에서 분석명제에 대한 칸트의 생각이 구체적으로 설명되고 있다. 따라서 이 지문의 주제를 '라이프니츠의 이성의 진리와 칸트의 분석적 진술'이라고 표현한 ②번이 정답이다.

어휘 philosophy n. 철학

18 (2020 홍익대)

정답 ③

해석
① 라이프니츠의 이성의 진리 개념은 칸트의 분석적 진리와 비슷하다.
② 칸트는 분석명제가 그 자체로서의 의미 때문에 항상 참이라고 생각했다.
③ 칸트의 분석적 진리와 종합적 진리 사이의 구분은 흄과 라이프니츠의 철학을 앞선다.
④ 라이프니츠는 이성에 의해 참인 진술은 모든 가능한 세계에서 참이어야 한다고 생각했다.

해설 지문을 통해 추론할 수 없는 것을 고르는 문제이다. 지문의 첫 번째 단락에서 칸트가 말한 분석적 진리와 종합적 진리 사이의 차이는 흄이 제시한 관념들의 관계와 사실들의 문제 사이의 구분과 라이프니츠가 제시한 이성의 진리와 사실의 진리 사이의 구분에서 미리 암시되었다고 했기 때문에, 이를 통해 칸트의 분석적 진리와 종합적 진리 사이의 구분이 흄과 라이프니츠의 철학보다 앞섰다는 것은 유추할 수 없으므로 정답은 ③번이다.

오답분석
① 지문의 첫 번째 문단 this is to say that the truths of reason ~ possibly be false. In the same vein ~ are self-contradictory.를 통해 '라이프니츠의 이성의 진리 개념은 칸트의 분석적 진리와 비슷하다'는 것을 알 수 있다.
② 지문의 두 번째 문단 a statement is analytic when it is true by virtue of meanings and without any consideration of fact.를 통해 '칸트는 분석명제가 그 자체로서의 의미 때문에 항상 참이라고 생각했다'는 것을 알 수 있다.
④ 지문의 첫 번째 문단 Leibniz spoke of the truths of reason as true in all possible worlds.를 통해 '라이프니츠는 이성에 의해 참인 진술은 모든 가능한 세계에서 참이어야 한다고 생각했다'는 것을 알 수 있다.

어휘 comparable adj. 비슷한 precede v. 앞서다

19 (2020 홍익대)

정답 ④

해석
① 포함의 개념에 대한 묘사
② 분석성의 개념에 대한 비판
③ 진리 개념에 대한 설명
④ 의미 개념에 대한 논의

해설 주어진 지문의 뒤에 올 내용을 고르는 문제이다. 지문의 마지막 문장에서 이 입장을 따라, 전제된 의미의 개념을 검토해보자라고 했으므로, '의미 개념에 대한 논의'에 대한 내용이 지문의 뒤에 나올 것임을 알 수 있다. 따라서 ④번이 정답이다.

어휘 depiction n. 묘사 containment n. 포함
critique n. 비판 description n. 설명 notion n. 개념

[20-21]

한 고집스러운 노년의 여성이 그녀 스스로도 작지 않은 위험에 처하면서 길 가운데를 가로질러 차량이 매우 혼잡한 곳으로 내려가고 있었다. 그녀는 인도가 보행자를 위한 곳이라고 지적받았지만, 그녀는 응했다: "나는 내가 좋아하는 곳에서 걷는 중이에요, 우리에겐 자유가 있습니다." 이 노년 여성의 생각 속에는 만약 자유가 보행자들에게 길 가운데를 가로질러 걸어 다닐 수 있는 자격을 준다면, 이런 자유의 결과는 보편적인 혼란으로 이어지리라는 것이 떠오르지 않는 것 같았다. 오늘날에는 이 나이 든 여성처럼 세상이 자유에 취할 위험이 있으므로, 우리 스스로가 도로의 규칙이 무엇을 의미하는지 상기하는 편이 적절하다. 이 규칙들은 질서 안에서 모든 자유가 보존되기 위해서는, 모든 이들의 자유가 축소되어야만 한다는 것을 의미한다. 어떤 경찰관이 부산한 교차로의 길 가운데로 걸어가 그의 손을 뻗으면, 그는 독재를 상징하는 것이 아니라 자유를 상징하는 것이다. 당신이 서두르는 중이면, 당신은 아마 당신의 자유가 침해되고 있다고 느낄지도 모른다. 이 경우에, 만약 당신이 합리적인 사람이라면, 당신은 경찰관이 당신을 방해하지 않으면, 다른 누구도 방해할 수 없을 것이고, 그 결과가 혼란으로 가득 찬 교차로로 당신이 절대 건널 수 없을 것이라는 결과로 이어지리라는 것을 생각해 낼 수 있을 것이다. 당신은 당신의 자유를 실제로 만드는 사회적 질서를 즐기기 위해 당신은 사적 자유의 축소를 감수하고 있다.

stubborn adj. 고집스러운 confusion n. 혼란
traffic n. (특정 시간대의) 차량들 sidewalk n. 인도
pedestrian n. 보행자 liberty n. 자유
occur v. 머릿속에 떠오르다 entitle v. 자격을 주다
intersection n. 교차로 tyranny n. 독재
outrage v. (권리를) 침해하다 reasonable adj. 합리적인
reflect v. 생각하다 interfere v. 방해하다
frenzied adj. 광란한 submit v. ~을 감수하다

20 (2020 한국외대)

정답 ④

해석
① 세계는 오늘날 너무 자유에 취해 있다.
② 개인의 자유는 항상 사회적 혼란을 이끈다.
③ 경찰은 비합리적인 운전자들 때문에 필요하다.
④ 당신은 사회적 질서를 위해 사적 자유를 양보해야 한다.

해설 지문의 주제를 묻는 문제이다. 지문의 마지막 문장에서 당신은 당신의 자유를 실제로 만드는 사회적 질서를 즐기기 위해 당신은 사적 자유의 축소를 감수하고 있다고 했다. 따라서 이 지문의 주제를 '당신은 사회적 질서를 위해 사적 자유를 양보해야 한다'고 표현한 ④번이 정답이다.

어휘 unreasonable adj. 비합리적인
compromise v. 양보하다

21 [2020 한국외대]

정답 ④

해석 ① 거부되다 – 거부 ② 할당되다 – 할당
③ 보장되다 – 보장 ④ 축소되다 – 축소

해설 지문의 빈칸을 채우는 문제이다. 지문 전체적으로 사적 자유를 실제로 만드는 사회적 질서를 위해 사적 자유가 일부 양보되어야 한다고 설명하고 있으므로, 첫 번째 빈칸과 두 번째 빈칸 모두 자유가 축소되어야 한다는 내용이 들어가야 한다. 따라서 '축소되다 – 축소'라고 표현한 ④번이 정답이다.

[22-23]

우리의 긍정적인 자질들을 끌어내는 *아가페적* 사랑에 대한 특성이 분명히 있고, 이것은 긍정적인 자질들을 사랑받는 사람에게 사용할 수 있게 한다. 이 특성이 *아가페적* 사랑을 헌신의 형태를 띠는 사랑이 되게 만든다. 하지만, 그것은 우리가 전력을 다하는 헌신 그 이상이다. 그것은 사랑의 대상을 위해 최선인 것에 헌신하는 것이다. 이것은 정확히 올바른 일을 하는 것에 전념하는 것을 의미한다. 최선의 혹은 올바른 일을 하는 것은 *아가페적* 사랑에 대한 정의에서 가장 중요한데, 그것은 사랑이 뭔가 캔디처럼 달콤한 개념이 아니라는 것을 알게 해준다. 그것은 미래에 대한 투자이기도 하다. 우리는 서로 매력적이라 생각하지 않을 때가 있다. 어머니는 자녀에게 복수하기 위해 자녀의 엉덩이를 때리지 않는다. 그것은 자녀가 충분한 자기 수양을 발달 시켜 미래의 심적 고통을 면할 수 있도록 돕기 위함이다. 마찬가지로, 사랑은 내 상대의 이기적인 행동을 지적하기 위한 건설적인 방법을 찾기 위해 요구된다. 만약 내가 불편을 느끼고 있다는 사실이 걱정이라면 그것은 사랑이 아니고, 내 상대와 우리 관계에 가해지고 있는 악영향이 걱정이라면 그것이 사랑이다.

obviously adv. 분명히, 확실히 bring out phr. ~을 끌어내다
resource n. 자질, 자원 commitment n. 헌신, 약속
be committed to phr. ~에 전념하다
central adj. 가장 중요한 definition n. 정의
sugar-plum n. 캔디 notion n. 개념
investment n. 투자 spank v. 엉덩이를 때리다
get even with phr. ~에 복수하다 sufficient adj. 충분한
self-discipline n. 자기 훈련 heartache n. 심적 고통
call upon phr. 요구하다 constructive adj. 건설적인
concern n. 걱정, 우려 inconvenience v. 불편하게 하다

22 [2020 한양대에리카]

정답 ③

해석 ① 반면에 ② 그럼에도 불구하고
③ 마찬가지로 ④ 다행스럽게도

해설 빈칸에 적절한 연결어를 넣는 문제이다. 빈칸 앞 문장은 어머니가 자녀를 때리지 않는 이유는 자녀가 충분한 자기 수양을 발달 시켜 미래의 심적 고통을 면할 수 있도록 돕기 위한

다는 내용이고, 빈칸 뒤 문장은 사랑은 상대의 이기적인 행동을 지적하기 위한 건설적인 방법을 찾기 위해 요구된다는 내용이다. 따라서 유사한 내용을 나타내는 연결어인 ③ By the same token(마찬가지로)이 정답이다.

어휘 by the same token phr. 마찬가지로, 같은 이유로

23 [2020 한양대에리카]

정답 ③

해석 ① *아가페적* 사랑은 헌신의 형태를 띠는 사랑이다.
② *아가페적* 사랑을 지닌 어머니는 그녀의 자녀가 미래를 위해 스스로 자기 수양을 갖추도록 돕는다.
③ 상대의 나쁜 행동을 건설적인 방법으로 지적하는 것은 *아가페적* 사랑의 유형이 아니다.
④ *아가페적* 사랑은 헌신 그 자체보다 올바른 유형의 헌신에 더 관심을 둔다.

해설 지문의 내용과 일치하지 않는 것을 묻는 문제이다. ③번의 키워드인 a constructive way(건설적인 방법)가 언급된 지문 주변에서 사랑은 내 상대의 이기적인 행동을 지적하기 위한 건설적인 방법을 찾기 위해 요구된다고 했으므로, 상대의 나쁜 행동을 건설적인 방법으로 지적하는 것이 *아가페적* 사랑의 유형이 아니라는 것은 지문의 내용과 다르다. 따라서 ③번이 지문의 내용과 일치하지 않는다.

오답 분석
① 지문의 두 번째 문장 It is this quality that makes it a commitment type of love.를 통해 '*아가페적* 사랑은 헌신의 형태를 띠는 사랑이다'라는 것을 알 수 있다.
② 지문의 여덟 번째 문장 It is to help the child develop sufficient self-discipline to save it future heartache.를 통해 '*아가페적* 사랑을 지닌 어머니는 그녀의 자녀가 미래를 위해 스스로 자기 수양을 갖추도록 돕는다'는 것을 알 수 있다.
④ 지문의 세 번째 문장 It is ~ more than a commitment of our best efforts.와 네 번째 문장 This means it is committed to doing exactly the right thing.을 통해 '*아가페적* 사랑은 헌신 그 자체보다 올바른 유형의 헌신에 더 관심을 둔다'는 것을 알 수 있다.

어휘 equip with phr. ~을 갖게 하다

[24-25]

우리는 절대로 답을 할 수 없기 때문에 물어보는 것이 소용없는 많은 질문들이 있다는 것을 믿는다. 시도해도 아무것도 좋을 것이 없다. 하지만 몇몇 사람들은 시도하기로 결정한 것 같다. 나는 철학자와 신학자의 이야기를 떠올려본다. 그 두 사람은 논쟁에 참여했고 신학자는 철학자가 어두운 방에서 존재하지 않는 검은 고양이를 찾는 장님과 닮았다고 말했다. 철학자는 "그럴 수도 있겠지만, 신학자는 그 고양이를 찾아내겠죠."라고 말했다. 심지어 과학의 물질 문제에서도 우리는 올바른 질문을

하도록 배워야 한다. 예를 들어, 그러한 계승이 존재하지 않는다는 단순한 이유로 동물들이 어떻게 부모의 경험을 계승하는지를 물어보는 것은 소용이 없다. 우리가 흔히 기초라고 부르는 것들에 도달하게 되면, 잘못된 종류의 질문을 하지 않는 어려움은 더 늘어나게 된다. 몇몇 아프리카 부족들 사이에는, 만약 사람이 죽으면, 오로지 "누가, 그리고 어떤 형태의 마법으로 그의 죽음을 초래했는가?"라는 질문만을 물어보기 때문에, 자연적인 원인의 죽음에 대한 생각은 알려지지 않는다. 실제로, 덜 문명화된 인류의 삶은 "행운이나 불운의 원인은 어떤 마법적인 힘이나 능력인지, 그리고 어떻게 그 힘들을 피하거나 잠재울 수 있는지"와 같은 잘못된 질문에 대한 대답을 찾기 위해 노력하는 것에 크게 기반하고 있다.

---

it is no use -ing phr. ~해도 소용이 없다
determine v. 결정하다   philosopher n. 철학자
theologian n. 신학자   be engaged in phr. ~에 참여하다
disputation n. 논쟁   inherit v. 계승하다
experience v. 경험하다   fundamental n. 기초
increase v. 늘어나다   less-civilized adj. 덜 문명화된
mankind n. 인류
be responsible for phr. ~의 원인이 되다, ~에 책임이 있다
fortune n. 운   calm v. 잠재우다, 진정시키다

---

24 [2019 한국외대]

정답 ②

해석 ① 어리석은 질문에 대한 현명한 대답
② 좋은 질문을 하는 것의 중요성
③ 철학과 신학의 열린 질문
④ 인간 존재에 대한 기초적인 질문

해설 지문의 제목을 묻는 문제이다. 지문의 전반에 걸쳐 어리석은 질문에 대한 예시를 언급하며 올바른 질문을 하는 방법을 배워야 한다고 말하고 있다. 따라서 이 지문의 제목을 '좋은 질문을 하는 것의 중요성'이라고 표현한 ②번이 정답이다.

어휘 foolish adj. 어리석은, 바보 같은   importance n. 중요성
philosophy n. 철학   theology n. 신학
fundamental adj. 기초적인   existence n. 존재

25 [2019 한국외대]

정답 ②

해석 ① 원인이 치유보다 더 중요하다
② 자연적인 죽음의 원인에 대한 생각은 알려지지 않는다
③ 그들은 부족 구성원의 죽음에 애도하지 않는다
④ 그들은 유족들보다 사망한 사람에게 더 많은 관심을 보인다

해설 지문의 빈칸을 채우는 문제이다. 빈칸이 있는 문장에서 한 아프리카 부족에서 사람이 죽으면 오로지 "누가, 그리고 어떤 형태의 마법으로 그의 죽음을 초래했는가?"라는 질문만을 물어본다고 했으므로, 빈칸에는 자연적인 원인이 아닌 누군가에 의해서 죽는 원인만을 생각한다는 것을 알 수 있다. 따라서 '자연적인 죽음의 원인에 대한 생각은 알려지지 않는다'라고 한 ②번이 정답이다.

어휘 cure n. 치유   mourn v. 애도하다   passing n. 죽음
tribesman n. 부족 구성원   deceased adj. 사망한
bereave v. 사별하다

[26-27]

관념론자들은 존재하는 것들만이 관념이라고 간주한다. 관념론에서 현실의 전반적인 구조는 인식을 통해 이해된다. 세상에 대한 모든 데이터는 반드시 신체의 감각들에 의해 제공되는데 이 감각들은 선별적이고, 이해를 위해 생각으로 연결되어야 하므로 세상을 이해하려는 모든 시도는 그 자체만으로는 소용없다. 따라서, 우리들의 사고에 대해 우리가 아는 것 외에, 현실과 관련하여 가치가 개입되지 않거나 완전히 객관적인 지식은 없다. 본질적으로, 현실의 존재는 인식을 하는 인간의 존재에 종속된다. 실제 세상에서 신에 대한 확실한 증거가 많지 않지만 신은 사람들이 믿는 관념의 형태 내에서 존재한다고 정당화되어 이야기될 수 있으므로 관념론을 신의 존재와 융화시키기는 어렵지 않다. 대부분의 종교적 신념 체계는 사람들이 세속적 현실 밖에 있거나 세속적 현실에서 동떨어져 있는 현실이나 존재를 받아들인다는 점에서 관념적이다. 관념론은 인간의 자각 이전에 아무것도 존재하지 않았고 다른 어느 것도 존재한다고 납득할 만큼 증명될 수 없으므로 사상가만이 실제로 존재하는 유일한 것이라는 주장과 같은 불합리한 명제, 즉 유아론으로 알려진 블랙홀을 발전시켰다는 명성을 쌓아왔다.

---

idealist n. 관념론자   inevitably adv. 반드시
in essence phr. 본질적으로   reconcile v. 융화시키다
justifiably adv. 정당화되어   earthly adj. 세속적인
absurd adj. 불합리한   proposition n. 명제
satisfactorily adv. 납득이 가도록   solipsism n. 유아론

---

26 [2020 한국항공대]

정답 ③

해석 ① 유아론의 영향력
② 종교적 신념 체계의 타당성
③ 관념론의 특징들
④ 부조리한 현실의 존재

해설 지문의 제목을 묻는 문제이다. 지문 전반적으로 관념론이 현실의 구조를 이해하는 방법, 관념론과 종교적 신념 체계의 관계, 관념론의 영향을 받은 명제와 같은 것들을 나열하며 설명하고 있다. 따라서 이 지문의 제목을 '관념론의 특징들'이라고 표현한 ③번이 정답이다.

어휘 validity n. 타당성

27 [2020 한국항공대]

정답 ④

해석
① 유아론은 불합리와 의식 간의 밀접한 관계에 근거를 둔다.
② 인식은 천지 만물과 인간의 의식을 구별하지 않는다.
③ 인간의 신념 체계는 신에 대한 확실한 증거에 크게 의존한다.
④ 관념론은 인간의 의식 이전의 현실을 전제로 하지 않는다.

해설 지문의 내용과 일치하는 것을 묻는 문제이다. 지문의 초반에서 관념론에서 현실의 전반적인 구조는 인식을 통해 이해된다는 내용을 통해 관념론은 인간의 의식 이전의 현실을 전제로 하지 않는다는 것을 알 수 있다. 따라서 ④번이 지문의 내용과 일치한다.

오답 분석
① 유아론은 인간의 자각 이전에 아무것도 존재하지 않았고 다른 어느 것도 존재한다고 납득할 만큼 증명될 수 없으므로 사상가만이 실제로 존재하는 유일한 것이라는 주장이라고는 했지만, 유아론은 불합리와 의식 간의 밀접한 관계에 근거를 둔다는 것은 알 수 없다.
② 현실의 존재는 인식을 하는 인간의 존재에 종속된다고 했으므로, 인식은 천지 만물과 인간의 의식을 구별하지 않는다는 것은 지문의 내용과 다르다.
③ 실제 세상에서 신에 대한 확실한 증거가 많지 않지만 신은 사람들이 믿는 관념의 형태 내에서 존재한다고 정당화되어 이야기될 수 있다고 했으므로, 인간의 신념 체계는 신에 대한 확실한 증거에 크게 의존한다는 것은 지문의 내용과 다르다.

어휘 intimate adj. 밀접한   presuppose v. 전제로 하다

[28-30]

윤리학은 과학적인 관점의 채택에 깊이 영향을 받을 것인데, 바꾸어 말하자면 과학적인 관점이란 과학자가 전문적인 능력으로 세계에 대해 취하는 사고방식이다. 이 사고방식은 사실에 대한 높은 (아마도 지나치게 높은) 관심, 그리고 종교적 차원에서 불가지론으로 표현하는 정당성 없는 결론에 이르는 것에 대한 (A)거부를 포함한다. 이것과 함께, 감정이 사실로 향하는 길에 장애물이라는 이유로 가능한 마지막 순간까지 감정을 의도적으로 (B)해방하는 것이 발견된다. 그래서 장미와 조충에 대한 연구가 궁극적으로 조충을 죽이고 장미의 증식으로 이어지는 것일지라도, 장미와 조충은 같은 방법으로 연구되어야 하고 같은 관점에서 고려되어야 한다. 다시 말해, 과학적인 관점은 과학적 미학 이론을 특징짓는 특유한 형태의 아름다움을 즐기는 과학적 미학의 (C)함양을 수반한다. 선과 아름다움 사이의 밀접한 관계를 발견한 사람들은 과학자와 같이 매우 영향력 있는 집단의 사람들이 특정한 종류의 아름다움을 추구하고 있다는 사실의 중요성을 (D)깨달을 것이다. 결국, 이처럼 과학자는 인류 전체에 있는 지적 구조에 기여하고 있기 때문에, 과학자의 영향력은 틀림없이 국가, 피부색, 그리고 계층의 한계를 초월하는 윤리 원칙과 실천을 위한 것이 될 것이다.

---

ethics n. 윤리학   profoundly adv. 깊이
adoption n. 채택   attitude n. 사고방식
unduly adv. 지나치게   regard n. 관심   refusal n. 거부
unjustifiable adj. 정당성 없는   plane n. 차원
agnosticism n. 불가지론(초 경험적인 것의 존재나 본질은 인식 불가능하다고 하는 철학상의 입장)
deliberate adj. 의도적인   emancipation n. 해방
stumbling-block n. 장애물   tape-worm n. 조충
propagation n. 증식   cultivation n. 함양
esthetic n. 미학; adj. 미학의   intimate adj. 밀접한
influential adj. 영향력 있는   pursue v. 추구하다
contribute v. 기여하다   transcend v. 초월하다

28 [2019 단국대]

정답 ②

해석
① 대신에   ② 결국
③ 그럼에도 불구하고   ④ 흥미롭게도

해설 빈칸에 적절한 연결어를 넣는 문제이다. 빈칸 앞 문장은 선과 아름다움 사이의 밀접한 관계를 발견한 사람들은 과학자와 같이 매우 영향력 있는 집단의 사람들이 특정한 종류의 아름다움을 추구하고 있다는 사실의 중요성을 깨달을 것이라는 내용이고, 빈칸 뒤 문장은 이처럼 과학자는 인류 전체에 있는 지적 구조에 기여하고 있기 때문에, 과학자의 영향력은 틀림없이 국가, 피부색, 그리고 계층의 한계를 초월하는 윤리 원칙과 실천을 위한 것이 될 것이라는 내용이다. 따라서 그 중간의 연결어로는 '결국'을 의미하는 Finally가 들어가는 것이 자연스럽다. 따라서 ②번이 정답이다.

29 [2019 단국대]

정답 ②

해설 지문의 흐름과 무관한 단어를 고르는 문제이다. 지문은 윤리학과 과학적인 관점 사이의 밀접한 관련성에 대한 내용이고, 지문에서 과학적인 관점의 특징으로 사실에 대한 높은 관심 및 감정에 대한 부정적인 인식을 언급하고 있으므로, (A) 정당성 없는 결론에 이르는 것에 대한 '거부', (C) 과학적인 관점은 과학적 미학의 '함양'을 수반한다는 것, (D) 과학자와 같은 집단이 특정한 종류의 아름다움을 추구하고 있다는 사실의 중요성을 '깨닫는다'는 내용은 모두 지문 내용과 관련이 있다. 그러나 (B)는 감정을 의도적으로 '해방'한다는 내용이므로, 감정에 대해 부정적으로 생각하는 과학적인 관점의 특징과 관련이 없다. 지문에서 감정은 사실로 향하는 길에 장애물이라고 했으므로, 문맥상 감정을 의도적으로 '억압(suppression)'한다는 내용이 들어가야 지문의 흐름이 자연스럽게 연결된다. 따라서 ②번이 정답이다.

30 [2019 단국대]

정답 ②

해석 ① 과학은 윤리학에 악영향을 미치지 않는다.
② 과학은 아름다움에 대한 그것만의 개념을 갖고 있다.
③ 의도적인 감정 억압은 아름다움을 발견하는 자극제이다.
④ 미학은 윤리학과 관련이 없다.

해설 지문의 내용과 일치하는 것을 묻는 문제이다. 지문의 다섯 번째 문장 Again, the scientific point ~를 통해 과학은 아름다움에 대한 그것만의 개념을 갖고 있다는 것을 알 수 있다. 따라서 ②번이 지문의 내용과 일치한다.

오답분석 ① 윤리학은 과학적인 관점의 채택에 깊이 영향을 받을 것이라고는 했지만, 과학이 윤리학에 악영향을 미치지 않는지는 알 수 없다.
③ 감정이 사실로 향하는 길에 장애물이라고는 했지만, 의도적인 감정 억압이 아름다움을 발견하는 자극제인지는 알 수 알 수 없다.
④ 선과 아름다움 사이의 밀접한 관계를 발견한 사람들은 과학자와 같이 매우 영향력 있는 집단의 사람들이 특정한 종류의 아름다움을 추구하고 있다는 사실의 중요성을 깨달을 것이라고 했으므로, 미학이 윤리학과 관련이 없다는 것은 지문의 내용과 다르다.

어휘 impinge v. 악영향을 미치다   oppression n. 억압
impetus n. 자극제   aesthetics n. 미학

[31-33]

심신 관계 문제가 오랫동안 있어왔지만, 이것은 오늘날 철학자들에게도 역시 흥미진진하다. 이는 우리가 심신 관계 문제를 이해하는 것에 관해 지난날의 철학자들과 같은 위치에 있다고 말하는 것이 아니다. <u>그와는 반대로</u>, 인상적인 진척이 있어 왔다. 이 진척은 뇌의 작용에 대한 과학적 이해의 큰 발전, 철학적 개념과 마음에 대해 우리가 하는 질문들의 끊임없는 개선 때문이었다. 이러한 이유들 때문에, 지금 우리는 심신 관계 문제가 해답에 가까워지고 있다고, 그리고 아마 21세기 철학의 정해진 답이 없는 수수께끼에 속한 것이 아닐 것이라 말할 수 있는가?

20세기의 마지막 10년 동안 의식과 관련된 매우 치열하고 다소 예기치 못했던 논쟁의 물결로 미루어 보아, 심신 관계 문제는 매우 왕성한 것처럼 보인다. '심신 관계 문제'라는 용어는 사실상 자아 통합, 정신 상태의 지향성, 그리고 인간의 합리성과 작용과 같은 철학 관련 문제들의 전체 무리를 포함한다. 하지만, 이 문제들의 전체 무리의 핵심에 있는 것, 그리고 최근 가장 격렬한 논쟁을 발생시켰던 것은, '우리가 경험하는 것처럼, 우리는 어떻게 광경, 색상, 사고, 감정을 경험하는가'와 같이 우리의 의식 경험을 설명하는 것에 대한 문제이다.

사실, 의식에 대한 질문에서 새로운 관심은 심신 관계 문제를 단지 철학적 논쟁이 아닌 과학적 논쟁으로 이동시켰다. '의식의 신경 상관물', 즉 특정한 정신적 경험에 상응하는 뇌 활동 유형을 찾는 것은 현재 많은 심리학자와 신경 과학자들의 과학적 의제이다. <u>그 사이에</u>, 철학자들은 단순한 상관관계에 더하여, 신경 상태와 정신 상태 간 관계의 본질에 대해 질문하느라 바쁘다.

compelling adj. 흥미진진한, 주목하지 않을 수 없는
philosopher n. 철학자   with regard to phr. ~에 관해
bygone adj. 지나간   impressive adj. 인상적인
progress n. 진척   advance n. 발전
continual adj. 끊임없는   refinement n. 개선
philosophical adj. 철학의   concept n. 개념
open-ended adj. 정해진 답이 없는   philosophy n. 철학
remarkably adv. 매우   controversy n. 논쟁
concerning prep. ~에 관련된   consciousness n. 의식
alive and kicking phr. 원기 왕성한   cluster n. 무리
intentionality n. 지향성, 고의성   rationality n. 합리성
agency n. 작용   conscious adj. 의식하는
generate v. 발생시키다   vigorous adj. 격렬한
renewed adj. 새로워진   neural adj. 신경의
correlate n. 상관물; v. 상관관계가 있다
corresponding adj. 상응하는   agenda n. 의제
psychologist n. 심리학자   neuroscientist n. 신경 과학자
above and beyond phr. ~에 더하여
mere adj. 단순한, 단지   correlation n. 상관관계

31 [2020 성균관대]

정답 ⑤

해석 ① 철학자 vs 과학자
② 현대 과학의 큰 진척
③ 일류 철학자들의 위대함
④ 과학이 철학적 문제를 해결하는 방법
⑤ 우리는 현재 심신 관계 문제의 어디에 위치해 있는가

해설 지문의 주제를 묻는 문제이다. 첫 번째 문단에서 지금 우리는 심신 관계 문제가 해답에 가까워지고 있는지, 정해진 답이 없는 수수께끼에 속한 것이 아닐 것이라 말할 수 있는지 의문을 제기한 후, 뒤 문단들에서 심신 관계 문제는 심리학자와 신경 과학자, 그리고 철학자들에게 지금도 매우 왕성하다는 것을 설명하고 있다. 따라서 이 지문의 주제를 '우리는 현재 심신 관계 문제의 어디에 위치해 있는가'라고 표현한 ⑤번이 정답이다.

어휘 philosopher n. 철학자   progress n. 진척
classic adj. 일류의   philosophical adj. 철학의

32 [2020 성균관대]

정답 ②

해석 ① 사실 — 따라서
② 그와는 반대로 — 그 사이에
③ 따라서 — 비슷하게

④ 한편으로 — 그 사이에
⑤ 그러나 — 따라서

해설 빈칸에 적절한 연결어를 넣는 문제이다. 첫 번째 빈칸 앞 문장은 우리가 심신 관계 문제를 이해하는 것에 관해 지난날의 철학자들과 같은 위치에 있는 것은 아니라는 내용이고, 첫 번째 빈칸 뒤 문장은 인상적인 진척이 있어왔다는 내용이다. 따라서 대조를 나타내는 연결어인 On the contrary(그와는 반대로)가 나와야 적절하다. 두 번째 빈칸 앞 문장은 특정한 정신적 경험에 상응하는 뇌 활동 유형을 찾는 것은 현재 많은 심리학자와 신경 과학자들의 과학적 의제라고 설명하는 내용이고, 두 번째 빈칸 뒤 문장은 철학자들이 단순한 상관관계에 더하여, 신경 상태와 정신 상태 간 관계의 본질에 대해 질문한다는 내용이다. 따라서 서로 다른 일이 일어나고 있는 상황을 나타내는 연결어인 meanwhile(그 사이에)이 나와야 적절하다. 따라서 ② On the contrary — meanwhile이 정답이다.

33 [2020 성균관대]

정답 ④

해설 ① 현재 과학 분야에 속한다
② 이미 철학자들에 의해 해결되었다
③ 철학자들의 주요 관심사가 아니다
④ 뇌 과학자들로 인해 많은 발전을 보았다
⑤ 현대 학자들에 의해 이해되기 어렵다

해설 심신 관계 문제에 대해 파악하는 문제이다. 첫 번째 문단에서 우리가 심신 관계 문제를 이해하는 것에 관한 진척은 뇌의 작용에 대한 과학적 이해의 큰 발전 때문이라고 했으므로, 심신 관계 문제는 '뇌 과학자들로 인해 많은 발전을 보았다'. 따라서 정답은 ④번이다.

어휘 philosopher n. 철학자 major adj. 주요한
progress n. 진척

[34-36]

존중과 다른 형태의 인간 애착 사이에는 차이가 있다. 사랑, 동정, 연대, 그리고 동포애는 우리가 다른 사람보다 몇몇 사람에게 더 가까이 끌리게 하는 도덕적 감정이다. 하지만 우리가 사람의 존엄성을 존중해야 하는 이유는 도덕적 감정에 대한 어떤 특별한 것과도 관계가 없다. 칸트의 존중은 사랑과 다르다. 그것은 동정과 다르다. 그것은 연대나 동포애와 다르다. 다른 사람들에 관심을 가지는 이러한 이유들은 그들이 특히 누구인지와 관련된다. 우리는 배우자와 가족 구성원을 사랑한다. 우리는 우리가 동일시할 수 있는 사람들에게 동정을 느낀다. 우리는 친구와 전우에게 연대감을 느낀다.

하지만 칸트의 존중은 인간성 그 자체에 대한 존중, 즉 우리 모두의 안에 획일적으로 존재하는 이성적인 능력에 대한 존중이다. 이것은 나 자신의 경우에서 인간성을 어기는 것이 왜 어떤 다른 사람의 경우에서 인간성을 어기는 것만큼 무례한 것인지를 설명한다. 이것은 또한 칸트의 존중 원칙이 보편적 인권 원칙에 도움이 되는지를 설명한다. 칸트에게, 공평성은 사람들이 어디에 사는지, 혹은 우리가 그들을 얼마나 잘 아는지와 관계없이, 단지 그들이 이성적 능력이 있는 사람이고, 그 결과 존중받을 자격이 있기 때문에 우리가 모든 사람의 인권을 옹호하도록 요구한다.

attachment n. 애착 sympathy n. 동정
solidarity n. 연대 fellow feeling phr. 동포애
sentiment n. 감정 dignity n. 존엄성
Kantian adj. 칸트의 identify v. 동일시하다
comrade n. 전우 humanity n. 인간성
rational adj. 이성적인 capacity n. 능력
reside v. 존재하다 undifferentiated adj. 획일적인
objectionable adj. 무례한
lend oneself to phr. ~에 도움이 되다
doctrine n. 원칙 uphold v. 옹호하다
capable adj. 능력 있는 worthy adj. 자격이 있는

34 [2020 가천대]

정답 ③

해설 ① ~에 의존하여   ② ~에서 기인하여
③ ~와 관계없이   ④ ~을 제외하고

해설 지문의 빈칸을 채우는 문제이다. 지문의 두 번째 문단 처음에서 칸트의 존중은 우리 모두의 안에 획일적으로 존재하는 이성적인 능력에 대한 존중이라고 했으므로, 빈칸에는 칸트에게, 공평성이 무엇을 의미하는지에 대한 내용이 나와야 적절하다는 것을 알 수 있다. 따라서 사람들이 어디에 사는지, 혹은 우리가 그들을 얼마나 잘 아는지와 '관계없이' 우리가 모든 사람의 인권을 옹호해야 한다고 한 ③번이 정답이다.

어휘 regardless of phr. ~와 관계없이
apart from phr. ~을 제외하고

35 [2020 가천대]

정답 ③

해설 ① 공평성 존중   ② 사랑과 존중의 차이
③ 이성에 근거한 존중   ④ 감정 존중

해설 지문의 제목을 묻는 문제이다. 첫 번째 문단에서 칸트의 존중은 사랑, 동정 등과 다르다고 하고, 두 번째 문단 마지막에서 칸트에게, 공평성은 사람들이 어디에 사는지, 혹은 우리가 그들을 얼마나 잘 아는지와 관계없이, 단지 그들이 이성적 능력이 있는 사람이고, 그 결과 존중받을 자격이 있기 때문에 우리가 모든 사람의 인권을 옹호하도록 요구한다고 설명하고 있다. 따라서 이 지문의 제목을 '이성에 근거한 존중'이라고 표현한 ③번이 정답이다.

36 2020 가천대

정답 ①

해석 ① 칸트는 사랑할 수 있는 인간의 능력을 인정하지 않는다.
② 칸트는 인간에게 선천적인 이성적 능력이 있다고 추정한다.
③ 칸트는 보편적 인권에 관심을 둔다.
④ 칸트는 공평성이 우리로 하여금 이성적 능력이 있는 인간성을 존중하도록 요구한다고 주장한다.

해설 지문을 통해 추론할 수 없는 것을 고르는 문제이다. 지문의 네 번째 문장에서 칸트의 존중은 사랑과 다르다고 했지만, 이를 통해 칸트가 사랑할 수 있는 인간의 능력을 인정하지 않는지는 유추할 수 없으므로 정답은 ①번이다.

오답 분석
② 두 번째 문단의 첫 번째 문장 But Kantian respect ~ a rational capacity that reside, undifferentiated, in all of us.를 통해 '칸트는 인간에게 선천적인 이성적 능력이 있다고 추정한다'는 것을 알 수 있다.
③ 두 번째 문단의 세 번째 문장 It also explains why the Kantian principle of respect ~ universal human rights.를 통해 '칸트는 보편적 인권에 관심을 둔다'는 것을 알 수 있다.
④ 지문의 마지막 문장 For Kant, justice requires us to uphold the human rights ~ worthy of respect.를 통해 '칸트는 공평성이 우리로 하여금 이성적 능력이 있는 인간성을 존중하도록 요구한다고 주장한다'는 것을 알 수 있다.

어휘 acknowledge v. 인정하다 capacity n. 능력
assume v. 추정하다 innate adj. 선천적인
contend v. 주장하다 capable adj. 능력 있는

[37-38]

오늘날, 인공 지능, 생물학적 컴퓨터, 그리고 유전자 변형이 암시하는 가능성들은 인간의 우위 의식에 교묘히 도전하고 있다. 이러한 발전들은 우리가 통제하거나 이해할 수 없는 기술에서 오는, 인간의 존재에 대한 뿌리 깊은 불안을 일깨운다. 우리와 동일하거나 심지어 우리를 능가할 수 있는 존재를 우리가 만들어 낼 수 있다는 것을 우리는 알고 있고, 우리는 인간의 사고와 같은 속성이 비인간의 형체에서 만들어질 수 있다는 가능성들을 진지하게 직시해야 한다. 이는 우리의 가장 뿌리 깊은 두려움이지만, 컴퓨터 공학의 성배이다. 수반되는 엄청난 문제들에도 불구하고, 인공적으로 자각을 하는 존재의 개발은 우리의 생애 중에 일어날 수 있다. 그런 존재가 인간과 같은 감정들을 가질 것인가? 그 존재물은 자신의 존재에 대한 의식을 가질 것인가? 인간 존재에 대해 우리가 인본주의 시대에서 계승한 중복적인 관념들을 고려하면, 인식에 대해 널리 용인되는 많은 인본주의 개념들이 더 이상 입증될 수 없기 때문에 그러한 질문들은 답하기가 어렵다. 게다가, 세계와 우주의 작용에 관해 컴퓨터 모델링에서 비롯되는 새로운 이론들은 이전에 우리가 분리를 봐왔던 세계에서의 모든 것들 간의 깊은 상호연결을 입증하기 시작하고 있다. 이는 인간의 지위에 관한 전통적인 시각과 철학에서의 가장 오래된 문제들 중 일부에 영향을 미친다.

synthetic adj. 인조의
genetic modification phr. 유전자 변형
predominance n. 우위 surpass v. 능가하다
attribute n. 속성 holy grail phr. 성배
inherit v. 물려받다 humanist n. 인본주의자
interconnection n. 상호연결 implication n. 영향

37 2020 한국항공대

정답 ②

해석 ① 그렇지만 ② 게다가
③ 예를 들어 ④ 대조적으로

해설 빈칸에 적절한 연결어를 넣는 문제이다. 빈칸 앞 문장은 인간 존재에 대해 인본주의에서 계승한 관념들을 고려하면 많은 인본주의 개념들이 입증될 수 없기 때문에 답하기 어렵다는 내용이고, 빈칸 뒤 문장은 컴퓨터 모델링에서 비롯되는 새로운 이론들이 모든 것들 간의 깊은 상호연결을 입증하기 시작하고 있다는 내용이다. 따라서 추가를 나타내는 연결어인 ② In addition(게다가)이 정답이다.

38 2020 한국항공대

정답 ③

해석 ① 새로운 시대는 인조 지능에 의존하지 않고 이전에 분리되어 있던 것들을 연결하는 것을 요한다.
② 인간의 패턴은 비인간의 존재를 대신한다.
③ 인간에 관해 널리 용인되는 관념들이 이제 바뀌고 있다.
④ 인간에 대한 중복적인 관념들은 제거되어야 한다.

해설 지문을 통해 추론할 수 있는 것을 고르는 문제이다. 지문의 후반에서 인식에 대해 널리 용인되는 많은 인본주의 개념들이 더 이상 입증될 수 없기 때문에 그러한 질문들은 답하기가 어렵지만, 컴퓨터 모델링에서 비롯되는 새로운 이론들은 이전에 우리가 분리를 봐왔던 세계에서의 모든 것들 간의 깊은 상호연결을 입증하기 시작하고 있다고 했으므로, 인간에 관해 널리 용인되는 관념들이 이제 바뀌고 있다는 것을 추론할 수 있다. 따라서 정답은 ③번이다.

오답 분석
① 세계와 우주의 작용에 관해 컴퓨터 모델링에서 비롯되는 새로운 이론들은 이전에 우리가 분리를 봐왔던 세계에서의 모든 것들 간의 깊은 상호연결을 입증하기 시작하고 있다고 했으므로, 새로운 시대는 인조 지능에 의존하지 않고 이전에 분리되어 있던 것들을 연결하는 것을 요한다는 것은 지문의 내용과 다르다.
② 인간 존재에 대해 우리가 인본주의 시대에서 계승한 중복적인 관념들을 고려하면 인식에 대해 널리 용인되는 많은

인본주의 개념들이 더 이상 입증될 수 없다고 했으므로, 인간의 패턴은 비인간의 존재를 대신한다는 것은 지문의 내용과 다르다.

④ 인간 존재에 대해 우리가 인본주의 시대에서 계승한 중복적인 관념들을 고려하면 인식에 대해 널리 용인되는 많은 인본주의 개념들이 더 이상 입증될 수 없다고는 했지만, 인간에 대한 중복적인 관념들은 제거되어야 한다는 것은 지문에서 알 수 없다.

[39-40]

올해 Hay에서의 연설에서, 나는 세계화가 전 세계에서 종교적 독자성의 증가로 귀결되어 온 방식에 관해 말했다. 나는 또한 청중들에게 al-Qaida를 한 독립체가 아니라 하나의 사회 운동으로 보라는 도전적 요구를 했다. (al-Qaida의 이념적 대 지도자 Abu Musab al-Suri의 말을 인용하자면 이렇다, "al-Qaida는 조직이 아니라 방법론이다.") 그리고 나는 al-Qaida가, 예를 들어 Leeds에 사는 이슬람교도 아이들의 국부적 불만들을 Palestine과 Iraq와 같은 장소에 사는 이슬람교도들에게 직면하는 세계적인 불만들과 연결시키는 방식에 관해 말했다. 내가 청중들에게 제기했던 질문은 이것이었다: 그렇다면 당신은 사회 운동에 어떻게 맞설 것인가?

분명, 폭탄과 총만으로는 안 된다. 차라리, 당신은 그 운동을 무의미한 것으로 만들어야만 한다. al-Qaida의 경우에, 이 말은 젊은 이슬람교도들을 대의명분으로 결집시키기 위해 사회 운동이 이용하는 바로 그 불만 — 팔레스타인 거주자들의 고통, 아랍 독재자들에 대한 미국의 지원, 중동의 많은 지역에서의 사회적 정치적 경제적 발달의 부족, 그리고 우리 서방세계가 중동 지역 전체를 커다란 주유소로 여기는 경향이 있다는 사실 등 — 을 해결하려 고심하는 것을 뜻한다. 이러한 불만들을 해결하려 고심함으로써만 al-Qaida의 호소력이 약해질 수 있다.

identity n. 정체성; 독자성
challenge v. (도전이 될 일) 요구하다
movement n. 사회적 운동   entity n. 독립체
ideologue n. 이념적 지도자   organization n. 조직
methodology n. 방법론   local adj. 지역의; 국부적인
grievance n. 불만; 고충   confront v. 맞서다
rather adv. 오히려, 차라리   irrelevant adj. 무의미한; 무관한
address v. 다루다, (해결하려) 고심하다
rally A to B phr. A를 B로 결집시키다
cause n. 대의명분   treat A as B phr. A를 B로 여기다
appeal n. 호소(력), 매력   diminish v. 줄어들다, 약해지다

39 [2018 서울여대]

정답 ②

해석 ① 조직을 가지지 않는다
② 사람들의 고통을 이용한다
③ 세계화와 관계가 없다
④ 아랍 사람들 불만의 주원인이다

해설 지문의 내용과 일치하는 것을 묻는 문제이다. 지문 중에서 In the case of al-Qaida, that means addressing the very grievances that the movement uses to rally young Muslims to its cause: the suffering of the Palestinians ~의 내용을 통해 al-Qaida가 사람들의 고통을 이용한다는 것을 알 수 있다. 따라서 ②번이 지문의 내용과 일치한다.

오답 분석 ① 지문의 내용에서 저자는 not as an entity라는 자신의 표현과 not an organization이라는 인용을 통한 부연 설명에서 al-Qaida가 개념적으로 조직이 아니라는 점을 강조하고 있는데, 그렇다고 실질 조직을 가지고 있는지 아닌지는 알 수 없는 내용이다. 즉, is no organization인 것을 강조하지만 has no organization인지는 알 수 없다.

40 [2018 서울여대]

정답 ④

해석 ① 그 운동의 방법론을 분석해야만 한다
② 그 운동을 고립시키기 위해서 서로 연합해야 한다
③ 그 운동의 이념적 측면을 따라야 한다
④ 그 운동에 동기를 부여하는 문제들을 바로 잡아야 한다

해설 밑줄 친 부분의 의미를 추론하는 문제이다. 밑줄 친 you must make the movement irrelevant는 '당신은 그 운동을 무의미한 것으로 만들어야만 한다'라는 의미이다. 주변의 내용을 살펴보면 Qaida의 경우에, 이 말은 젊은 이슬람교도들을 결집시키기 위해 그 운동이 이용하는 불만을 해결해 주는 것임을 알 수 있다. 따라서 이를 '그 운동에 동기를 부여하는 문제들을 바로 잡아야 한다'라고 표현한 ④번이 정답이다.

어휘 methodology n. 방법론   isolate v. 고립시키다

[41-44]

[A] 육체적 고통은 대상이 없는 유일한 존재라는 점에서 심리적, 신체적, 그리고 지각적 상태의 전체적인 구조에서 특별하다. 육체적 고통을 경험할 수 있는 능력은 듣고, 만지고, 원하고, 두려워하는 능력만큼 인간에 관한 원시적인 사실이지만, 그것은 외부 세계에 어떠한 대상을 갖지 않음으로써 모든 다른 육체적, 정신적 작용과는 다르다. 청각과 촉각은 몸의 경계 바깥의 물체에 관한 것이며, 욕망은 X에 대한 욕망이고, 두려움은 Y에 대한 두려움이며, 배고픔은 Z에 대한 배고픔이다. 그러나 고통은 무언가의 고통이 아니라 그냥 고통 그 자체이다. (A)

[B] 이렇게 대상이 없는 성질, 지시하는 내용의 완벽한 부재는 그것을 언어로 표현하는 것을 거의 하지 못하게 막는다. 대상이 없이는, 어떠한 형태로든, 내용으로든, 말로든 쉽게 대상화될 수 없다. 하지만, 처음으로 결국에는 우리가 만들고 옮겨 다니는 인공물과 상징이 가득한 바다를 생산하는 과정을 불러일으킴으로써 상상력을 발휘할 수 있는

것 또한 그러한 대상이 없는 성질이다. 다른 모든 상태들은 처음에 한 가지 대상을 정확하게 취하면서 자연계를 보완하기보다는 단 하나만을 들어오도록 만든다. (B)

[C] 갈망하는 사람은 비를 보면서 그가 갈망하는 것이 비가 그치는 것임을 알 수 있기 때문에 두려운 밤이 오기 전에 그는 밖으로 나가 배고픔을 위한 열매를 찾을 수 있다. (C) 자신의 내적 상태들이 바깥세상에 동반하는 대상과 불가피하게 묶여있기 때문에, 그는 바깥세상에 쉽게 자신을 위치시키고 자신을 확장시킬 세상을 만들 필요가 없다. 대상은 비가 그의 갈망을 표현하고, 열매는 배고픔을, 그리고 밤은 무서움을 표현하는 상태의 연장이자 표출이다. (D) 하지만 육체적인 고통을 표현할 수 있는 것은 아무것도 없다. 영구적으로 대상이 없던 어느 상태도 확실히 창조하는 과정을 시작할 것이다. 하지만 특히 철저히 대상이 없는 바로 그 상태 또한 그가 육체로부터 벗어나려는 충동을 가장 압박하게 만드는 모든 상태 중의 하나라는 것이 적절하다.

[D] 고통만큼 변칙적인 유일한 상태는 상상이다. 고통은 완전히 대상이 없다는 점에서 주목할 만한 상태지만, 상상은 완전히 대상이 존재하는 유일한 상태라는 점에서 주목할 만하다. 상상에는 활동도, 상태도, 경험할 수 있는 상황이나 대상과 분리되어 느껴지는 발생도 존재하지 않으며, 누군가 상상하고 있다는 유일한 증거는 상상의 대상이 마음속에 나타난다는 것이다. 그러므로, 고통이 X를 보거나 Y를 바라는 것이 아닌 그냥 보고 바라는 것인 반면, 상상에는 반대이지만 똑같이 놀라운 특징이 속한다. 그것은 시야나 욕망의 대상인 X나 Y 같은 것이며, 보는 것과 바라는 것이 느낌으로 일어나는 것이 아니다. (E)

exceptional adj. 특별한 psychic adj. 심리적인
somatic adj. 신체적인 perceptual adj. 지각적인
primal adj. 원시적인 boundary n. 경계
absence n. 부재 referential adj. 지시적인
render v. 만들다 objectify v. 객관화하다
occasion v. 불러일으키다 eventually adv. 결국에는
bring forth phr. 생산하다 artifact n. 유물
supplement v. 보완하다 cessation n. 중단
inevitable adj. 불가피한 extension n. 연장
expression n. 표출, 표현 long v. 바라다
anomalous adj. 변칙의 remarkable adj. 주목할 만한
wholly adv. 완전히 occurrence n. 발생
separate adj. 분리된 evidence n. 증거
opposite adj. 반대의 extraordinary adj. 놀라운

41 2020 아주대

정답 ⑤

해설 ① 감각과 그것이 세상과 맺는 관계
② 감각과 느낌
③ 인간 지각에서 대상의 역할
④ 인간의 욕망과 육체적 고통
⑤ 고통과 상상의 독특함

지문의 제목을 묻는 문제이다. 지문의 전반에 걸쳐 고통은 대상이 없기 때문에 다른 심리적, 신체적, 지각적 상태와 달리 특별하며 이와 달리 상상은 완전하게 대상이 존재하는 유일한 상태라는 것을 설명하고 있다. 따라서 이 지문의 제목을 '고통과 상상의 독특함'이라고 표현한 ⑤번이 정답이다.

어휘 sensation n. 느낌 perception n. 지각

42 2020 아주대

정답 ④

해설 지문의 흐름상 주어진 문장이 들어가기에 가장 적절한 위치를 고르는 문제이다. (D)의 앞 문장에서 갈망과 배고픔과 무서움과 같은 상태를 비, 열매, 그리고 밤이라는 대상을 통해 상태를 표출하는 것을 예시를 들며 설명하고 했으므로, (D)의 자리에 주어진 문장 '하지만 육체적인 고통을 표현할 수 있는 것은 아무것도 없다. 영구적으로 대상이 없던 어느 상태도 확실히 만드는 과정을 시작할 것이다. 하지만 특히 그가 철저히 대상이 없는 바로 그 상태 또한 육체로부터 벗어나려는 충동을 가장 압박하게 만드는 모든 상태 중의 하나라는 것이 적절하다'가 들어가야 글의 흐름이 자연스럽게 연결된다. 따라서 ④번이 정답이다.

어휘 permanently adv. 영구적으로 appropriate adj. 적절한
utterly adv. 철저히 urge n. 충동

43 2020 아주대

정답 ④

해석 ① 고통은 바깥세상에 있는 어떠한 지시 대상과도 연결되어 있지 않다.
② 사람이 느끼는 고통을 묘사하는 것은 극도로 어렵다.
③ 고통은 대상과의 관계에서 상상과 비슷한 상태이다.
④ 고통과는 다르게, 오감은 외부 세상에 아무것도 더하지 않는다.
⑤ 고통을 겪는 사람은 그 어려움에도 불구하고 자신의 고통을 표현하기 위해 열심히 노력한다.

해설 고통의 본질로써 언급되지 않은 것을 고르는 문제이다. '이렇게 대상이 없는 성질, 지시하는 내용의 완벽한 부재는 그것을 언어로 표현하는 것을 거의 하지 못하게 막는다'라는 내용에서 ①번과 ②번이, '고통은 완전히 대상이 없다는 점에서 주목할 만한 상태지만, 상상은 완전히 대상이 존재하는 유일한 상태라는 점에서 주목할 만하다'라는 내용에서 ③번이, '하지만 특히 철저히 대상이 없는 바로 그 상태 또한 그가 육체로부터 벗어나려는 충동을 가장 압박하게 만드는 모든 상태 중의 하나라는 것이 적절하다'라는 내용에서 ⑤번이 언급되었음을 알 수 있지만, ④번은 지문에서 언급되지 않았다. 따라서 정답은 ④번이다.

어휘 referent n. 지시 대상 describe v. 묘사하다

44 [2020 아주대]

정답 ①

해석 ① 우리가 고통을 표현하기 위해 쓰는 많은 것과 단어들
② 우리가 고통을 증가시키기 위해 경험하는 많은 것과 단어들
③ 우리가 고통이 없는 세상을 상상하기 위해 만드는 많은 것과 단어들
④ 우리가 고통을 완화하기 위해 바꾸고 싶어 하는 많은 것과 단어들
⑤ 우리가 고통으로부터 달아나기 위해 사용하는 많은 것과 단어들

해설 밑줄 친 the dense sea of artifacts and symbols that we make and move about in의 의미를 추론하는 문제이다. 밑줄 이전에서 지시하는 대상이 없이는 그것을 어떠한 형태로든 쉽게 표현할 수 없다고 했다. 따라서, 밑줄 친 부분의 의미를 '우리가 고통을 표현하기 위해 쓰는 많은 것과 단어들'이라고 한 ①번이 정답이다.

어휘 alleviate v. 완화하다

[45-48]

프로이트는 일상의 특정한 실수와 착오에 큰 의미가 있음을 1896년에 처음 인지하였다. 그의 동료에게 쓴 편지에서, 프로이트는 "내가 오랫동안 의심해왔던 사소한 문제를 마침내 이해했는데", 즉, 알고 있는 이름이 가끔 생각나지 않고 대신에 엉뚱한 이름들이 떠오르는 이유를 이해했다고 적었다. 이에 대한 사례로, 프로이트는 한 시인의 성을 기억할 수 없었다. "(i) 나는 특정한 연상 때문에 그 이름을 억눌러왔고, (ii) 나의 유아기에 있었던 일이 그 이름의 억누름에 일부 역할을 했으며, (iii) 나에게 떠올랐던 대체 이름들은, 마치 어떤 증상처럼, 최근에 있었던 일과 유아기에 있었던 일들 모두로부터 생겨났다는 사실을 입증할 수 있게 되었다."
이처럼 겉보기에는 사소한 착오의 중요성을 확증하며, 프로이트는 일상의 여러 가지 형태의 오류의 예시들을 수집하기 시작했는데, 여기에는 잘못 읽거나, 말이나 글의 실수, 잘못된 인용, 실수로 한 행동 등이 있다. 그는 보통 사소하다고 할 만한 이 모든 실수와 착오는 무의식 속에 억압된 충동이 존재한다는 것을 드러내는 것이라고 점차 확신하게 되었다. 실수와 착오는 대부분의 경우에 숨어있지만, 가끔 적절한 순간을 포착하여 '착오행위'라는 실수들을 통해 밖으로 알려진다.
*The Psychopathology of Everyday Life*는 1904년 단행본으로 처음 나왔으며, 이후 20년에 걸쳐 증보판이 나왔다. 이 책은 프로이트의 가장 인기 있는 책 중 하나가 되었으며, 여러 차례에 걸쳐 중판을 계속했다. 핵심 개념들과 많은 최고의 사례들이 후에 *Introductory Lectures on Psychoanalysis* 속에 보다 간결하게 (그리고 보다 설득력 있게) 표현되었는데, 이는 1915년에서 1917년 사이에 빈 대학에서 한 강의 내용을 나중에 책으로 출판한 것이다. 그 후, '프로이트식 실수'라는 표현은 언어로 들어가게 되었고, 실수가 무의식적으로 결정된다는 견해는 좋든 나쁘든, 과학계와 대중들의 믿음에 확고하게 자리 잡게 되었다.

---

meaningfulness n. 의미 있음; 중요함 slip n. 과실, 잘못
lapse n. 착오; 실수 colleague n. 동료
at last phr. 마침내 grasp v. 완전히 이해하다
elude v. 피하다; 이해하기 어렵다
retrieval n. 만회, 복구; 검색
dredge up phr. (과거 일을) 기억해내다
instance n. 사례, 경우 poet n. 시인
repress v. 억누르다, 억압하다 association n. 연상
infancy n. 유아기 substitute adj. 대체의
symptom n. 증상 infantile adj. 유아의
apparently adv. 겉보기에 trivial adj. 사소한, 하찮은
misreading n. 잘못 읽음 slip of tongue phr. 말실수, 실언
misquotation n. 잘못된 인용
bungle v. 실수하다, 서투른 방식으로 하다
gradually adv. 점차 convinced adj. 확신하는
betray v. 드러내다, 무심코 노출시키다
impulse n. 충동; 욕구
seize upon phr. 포착하다, 잘 이용하다
opportune adj. 적절한 parapraxis n. 착오행위
psychopathology n. 정신 병리학
separate volume phr. 단행본
subsequently adv. 나중에
enlarge v. 크게 하다, 확대하다; (책을) 증보하다
succinctly adv. 간결하게 psychoanalysis n. 정신분석
thereafter adv. 그 후에 phrase n. 표현법; 구
unconsciously adv. 무의식적으로 lodge v. ~에 꽂히다

45 [2020 세종대]

정답 ②

해석 ① 하찮은   ② 하찮지 않은
③ 시시한   ④ 중요하지 않은

해설 지문의 빈칸을 채우는 문제이다. 지문의 두 번째 문단 처음에서 사소한 착오라는 말이 나왔으므로, 빈칸에도 비슷한 뜻의 단어가 나와야 적절하다는 것을 알 수 있다. ①번, ③번, ④번은 trivial과 같은 의미인 것에 반해, ②번은 반대의 의미이다. 따라서 '하찮지 않은'이라고 한 ②번이 정답이다.

46 [2020 세종대]

정답 ④

해석 ① *Introductory Lectures on Psychoanalysis*와 *The Psychopathology of Everyday Life*는 둘 다 출판되었다.
② 프로이트는 사소한 실수와 착오의 중요성을 깨달은 후에 그것들의 사례를 모으기 시작했다.
③ 실수가 무의식 속에 뿌리를 내리고 있다는 생각은 프로이트로부터 나왔다.

④ 과학계는 프로이트의 이론을 받아들인 반면, 대중은 그것이 터무니없다고 생각했다.

해설 지문의 내용과 일치하지 않는 것을 묻는 문제이다. ④번의 키워드인 public(대중)과 관련된 지문의 세 번째 문단의 마지막 문장에서 주변에서 프로이트의 이론은 과학계와 대중들의 믿음에(popular belief) 확고하게 자리 잡게 되었다고 했으므로, 과학계는 프로이트의 이론을 받아들인 반면, 대중은 그것이 터무니없다고 생각했는지는 알 수 없다. 따라서 ④번이 지문의 내용과 일치하지 않는다.

오답분석
① 지문의 세 번째 문단 The Psychopathology of ~ 20 years.와 The core ideas ~ later published.를 통해 'Introductory Lectures on Psychoanalysis와 The Psychopathology of Everyday Life는 둘 다 출판되었다'는 것을 알 수 있다.
② 지문의 두 번째 문단 he began to collect ~ everyday error를 통해 '프로이트는 사소한 실수와 착오의 중요성을 깨달은 후에 그것들의 사례를 모으기 시작했다'는 것을 알 수 있다.
③ 지문의 두 번째 문단 Gradually he ~ impulses.를 통해 '실수가 무의식 속에 뿌리를 내리고 있다는 생각은 프로이트로부터 나왔다'라는 것을 알 수 있다.

어휘 preposterous adj. 터무니없는

47 [2020 세종대]

정답 ③

해석
① 그 시인은 유년기 이래로 성이 없었기에, 애초에 성이 없었다.
② 프로이트는 착오행위 때문에 대체 이름들을 잊어버릴 수 없었다.
③ 프로이트는 그의 어린 시절 기억 때문에 무의식적으로 그 이름을 억눌렀다.
④ 그 시인의 이름은 말실수로 나왔지만, 프로이트는 사소한 착오라고 생각하고 억눌렀다.

해설 프로이트가 왜 한 시인의 성을 기억할 수 없었는지에 대한 이유를 파악하는 문제이다. 지문의 첫 문단 (ii)에서 프로이트의 유아기에 있었던 일이 그 시인의 이름의 억누름에 일부 역할을 했다고 했으므로, 시인의 성을 기억할 수 없었던 이유는 '프로이트는 그의 어린 시절 기억 때문에 무의식적으로 그 이름을 억눌렀다.'이다. 따라서 정답은 ③번이다.

48 [2020 세종대]

정답 ①

해석
① 말하거나, 기억을 회상하거나, 행동을 할 때
② 유년 시절의 착오행위를 떠올림
③ 정신분석적 장애 각각의 형태에 있어서
④ 억압되고 무의식적인 기억

해설 밑줄 친 an opportune moment의 의미를 추론하는 문제이다. 두 번째 지문에서 잘못 읽거나, 말이나 글의 실수, 잘못된 인용, 실수로 한 행동 등 일상에서 저지르는 여러 가지 형태의 오류, 즉 '착오행위'를 통해 나타난다고 했다. 따라서, an opportune moment의 의미를 '말하거나, 기억을 회상하거나, 행동을 할 때'라고 한 ①번이 정답이다.

어휘 disorder n. 장애

[49-50]

원죄 교리는 완전히 타락한 신조를 보여주는 가장 오래된 징후이지만, 이러한 사고는 민주주의와 세속 국가에서 사라지지 않았다. 프로이트는 이 교리를 20세기 심리학으로 끌어들이면서, 현대의 도덕, 과학, 종교, 그리고 기술적 진보를 포함한 모든 문명을 단지 유아 성욕과 공격성을 둘러싼 분쟁을 막는 정교한 방어물로서 정의했다. 우리는 그 분쟁이 유발하는 견딜 수 없는 불안 때문에 이러한 분쟁을 "억압하고" 이 불안은 문명을 발생시키는 원동력으로 변화한다. 따라서 내가 밖으로 뛰어나가 강간과 살인을 하기보다 컴퓨터 앞에서 이 서문을 작성하며 앉아있는 이유는 내가 "보상을 받고", 침묵하고, 잠재하고 있는 야만적인 충동에 대해 나 자신을 성공적으로 방어하고 있기 때문이다. 프로이트의 철학은 정말 완전하게 제시될 때 기이하긴 하지만, 매일 일어나는 심리학 및 정신의학적 실제에 자리매김하고 있는데, 그 실제에서 환자들은 자신들의 정체성을 형성한 부정적인 충동과 사건에 대한 과거를 찾아 헤맨다. 따라서 빌 게이츠의 경쟁력은 실제로 자신의 아버지를 능가하려는 그의 욕망이고, 지뢰에 대한 다이애나 공주의 반대는 그저 찰스 왕자와 다른 왕족에 대한 그녀의 지독한 증오를 승화한 것의 결과였을 뿐이었다. 완전히 타락한 그 교리는 또한 미술과 사회과학에 있는 인간의 본성에 대한 이해에 스며들어 있다. 수천 개의 예시 중 하나가 No Ordinary Time인데, 이것은 현존하는 위대한 정치학자 중 한 명인 Doris Kearns Goodwin이 쓴 프랭클린 루스벨트와 엘리너 루스벨트에 대한 시선을 사로잡는 연대기이다. 엘리너가 흑인, 가난한 사람, 혹은 장애인을 돕는 데 그녀의 삶 대부분을 헌신한 이유에 대한 질문을 곰곰이 생각하면서, Goodwin은 그것이 "그녀 어머니의 자기중심주의와 아버지의 알코올 중독을 보상하기 위한" 것이었다고 결정 내린다. 책 어디에서도 Goodwin은 엘리너 루스벨트가 사실 선을 추구하고 있었을 가능성을 고려하지 않는다. 공정성을 발휘하거나 의무를 추구하는 것과 같은 동기 부여는 원칙에서 배제되고, 그 분석이 학문적으로 인정받으려면 선을 지지하는 무언가 은밀하고, 부정적인 동기 부여가 있어야 한다. 나는 이것을 아주 강력하게 주장할 수는 없다. 종교계와 세속적인 세계에서의 완전히 타락한 신조에 대한 일반적인 인정에도 불구하고, 용기와 선은 부정적인 동기 부여에서 기인한다는 증거가 전혀 없다. 나는 진화가 선하고 악한 특성 모두를 촉진해왔으며, 세상의 많은 적응적 역할이 살인, 절도, 이기적임, 그리고 테러를 선택했듯이, 도덕, 협력, 이타주의, 그리고 선도 선택했다고 믿는다. 이러한 양면성을 가진 전제는 이 책 후반부의 초석이다. 진짜 행복은 당신의 가장 근본적인 용기를 발견하고 기르고 그 용기를 일, 사랑, 놀이, 그리고 육아에서 매일 활용하는 것에서 생겨난다.

doctrine n. 교리 original sin phr. 원죄
manifestation n. 징후, 표명
rotten-to-the-core adj. 완전히 타락한 dogma n. 신조
secular adj. 세속의 elaborate adj. 정교한
infantile adj. 유아의 aggression n. 공격성
repress v. 억압하다, 억누르다 transmute v. 변화시키다
compensate v. 보상하다 savage adj. 야만적인
impulse n. 충동 bizarre adj. 기이한
starkly adv. 완전히 scour v. 찾아 헤매다
landmine n. 지뢰 sublimate v. 승화시키다
pervade v. 스며들다 gripping adj. 사로잡는
muse on phr. 곰곰이 생각하다 dedicate v. 헌신하다
narcissism n. 자기중심주의 deep down phr. 사실은
pursue v. 추구하다 virtue n. 선 rule out phr. 배제하다
fundamental n. 원칙, 기본; adj. 근본적인
covert adj. 은밀한 underpin v. 지지하다
adaptive adj. 적응성의 altruism n. 이타주의
dual-aspect adj. 양면성을 가진 premise n. 전제
identify v. 발견하다 cultivate v. 기르다

49 2019 한국항공대

정답 ①

해석 ① 부정적 동기 부여에서 기인한다
② 긍정적 동기 부여에서 기인한다
③ 긍정적 동기 부여의 오류이다
④ 숨겨진 부정적 동기 부여의 오류이다

해설 지문의 빈칸을 채우는 문제이다. 빈칸 앞부분에서 선을 지지하는 무언가 은밀하고, 부정적인 동기 부여가 있어야 한다는 것을 저자가 강력하게 주장할 수는 없다고 했으므로, 빈칸에는 저자가 강력하게 주장할 수 없는 이유를 부연 설명하는 내용이 나와야 적절하다는 것을 알 수 있다. 따라서 용기와 선이 '부정적 동기 부여에서 기인한다'는 증거가 전혀 없다고 한 ①번이 정답이다.

어휘 derive v. 유래하다 fallacy n. 오류
unrevealed adj. 숨겨진

50 2019 한국항공대

정답 ②

해석 ① 부정적 동기 부여의 숨겨진 영향력
② 인간 본성의 양면성
③ 도덕적인 행동을 추구하는 것에 대한 오해
④ 부정적 동기 부여에서 기인하는 진짜 행복

해설 지문의 제목을 묻는 문제이다. 지문 후반부에서 용기와 선이 부정적인 동기 부여에서 기인한다는 증거는 없으며, 저자는 진화가 선하고 악한 특성을 모두 촉진해왔다고 믿는다고 하였다. 따라서 이 지문의 제목을 '인간 본성의 양면성'이라고 표현한 ②번이 정답이다.

어휘 illusion n. 오해, 착각

05 사회이슈·일상

01-59   문제집 p.130

01 ④	02 ②	03 ②	04 ④	05 ②
06 ⑤	07 ②	08 ②	09 ①	10 ④
11 ⑤	12 ②	13 ②	14 ②	15 ①
16 ②	17 ②	18 ②	19 ①	20 ③
21 ⑤	22 ①	23 ③	24 ①	25 ②
26 ④	27 ②	28 ②	29 ④	30 ①
31 ⑤	32 ③	33 ⑤	34 ②	35 ①
36 ②	37 ②	38 ②	39 ②	40 ②
41 ③	42 ②	43 ③	44 ④	45 ②
46 ④	47 ②	48 ④	49 ④	50 ②
51 ④	52 ①	53 ④	54 ⑤	55 ③
56 ③	57 ②	58 ③	59 ②	

01 [2019 인하대]

정답 ④

해석 딸꾹질보다 더 짜증 나는 문제는 거의 없는데, 그것은 몇 시간이나 심지어는 며칠 동안 지속할 수 있다. [A] 딸꾹질을 연구한 한 박사에 따르면, 딸꾹질은 주로 너무 빨리 먹거나 마시는 것으로 유발된다. [B] 사람들은 이 우스꽝스러운 문제를 고치기 위해 꽤나 이상한 것들을 한다. [C] 몇 가지 일반적인 방안은 숨을 참고 있기, 설탕 한 티스푼을 먹기, 그리고 머리에 종이 가방을 뒤집어쓰기를 포함한다. [D] 건강한 심장을 위한 가장 좋은 운동은 걷기이다. [E] 의심할 여지가 없이, 마지막이 모든 것 중에 가장 이상한 것이다.

해설 지문의 흐름과 무관한 문장을 고르는 문제이다. 지문은 딸꾹질의 원인과 그것을 해결하기 위한 이상한 방법들에 대한 내용이므로, ① 딸꾹질은 주로 너무 빨리 먹거나 마시는 것으로 유발된다, ② 사람들을 이 우스꽝스러운 문제를 고치기 위해 꽤나 이상한 것들을 한다, ③ 몇 가지 일반적인 방안은 숨을 참고 있기, 설탕 한 티스푼을 먹기, 머리에 종이 가방을 뒤집어쓰기 등이다, ⑤ 마지막 방법이 가장 이상한 것이라는 것은 모두 지문 내용과 관련이 있다. 그러나 ④는 '건강한 심장을 위한 가장 좋은 운동은 걷기이다'라는 내용이므로, 딸꾹질의 원인과 해결하기 위한 방법과 관련이 없다. 따라서 ④번이 정답이다.

어휘 annoying adj. 짜증 나는   hiccup n. 딸꾹질
remedy v. 고치다, 치료하다; n. 방안, 해결책
ridiculous adj. 우스꽝스러운, 웃기는   hold v. (숨을) 참다
undoubtedly adv. 의심할 여지가 없이

02 [2020 가천대]

정답 ②

해석 오늘날 거리를 걸으며 휴대폰으로 통화하는 사람을 보는 것은 정말 (A)아주 흔한 모습이 되어서 한 손을 귀 옆에 댄 현대인의 그림을 유인원 같은 크로마뇽인 옆에 그려야 인간의 진화를 (B)왜곡할 수 있다. 최근 언론 보도에 따르면, 미국 의사들은 현재 소위 "휴대전화 엘보" 증후군을 경고하고 있다. 전문 의료진들이 이것을 두고 야단을 떨고 있는 것이 (C)터무니없는 것처럼 여겨진다. 테니스를 친 후 테니스 엘보의 끊임없는 고통을 매일 겪는 사람들처럼, 휴대폰 수다쟁이들은 손, 특히 새끼손가락과 넷째 손가락의 아픔이나 무감각에 대해 (D)투덜거린다.

해설 밑줄 친 낱말의 쓰임이 적절하지 않은 것을 묻는 문제이다. (B) 앞 문장에서 '오늘날 거리를 걸으며 휴대폰으로 통화하는 사람을 보는 것은 정말 아주 흔한 모습이 되었다'고 했으므로, '한 손을 귀 옆에 댄 현대인의 그림을 유인원 같은 크로마뇽인 옆에 그려야 인간의 진화를 묘사할(depict) 수 있다'라고 하는 것이 문맥에 알맞다. (B)의 distort를 depict로 고쳐야 한다. 따라서 ②번이 정답이다.

어휘 ubiquitous adj. 아주 흔한   ape-like adj. 유인원 같은
Cro-Magnon n. 크로마뇽인   distort v. 왜곡하다
evolution n. 진화
cell phone elbow phr. 휴대전화 엘보(휴대전화로 오래 통화하고 나면 팔꿈치가 아픈 현상)
syndrome n. 증후군   farcical adj. 터무니없는
medical professional phr. 전문 의료진   fuss n. 야단
constant adj. 끊임없는   gabber n. 수다쟁이
grumble v. 투덜거리다   numbness n. 무감각
pinky n. 새끼손가락   ring finger phr. 넷째 손가락

03 [2019 성균관대]

정답 ②

해석 리듬에 대한 우리의 사랑은 음악적 반복에 대한 우리의 사랑보다 더 (A)깊이 우리에게 뿌리박혀 있다. 그것은 우리 심장의 고동 소리, 피의 리듬, 폐로 들이쉬고 내쉬는 공기와 관련된다. 우리가 자연스럽고 우아하게 하는 (B)아무것도 아닌 것을 리드미컬하게 한다. 우리가 걷고, 수영하고, 말을 타고, 골프채나 야구 방망이를 휘두르는 방식에 리듬이 있다. 리듬은 우리에게 (C)자연스러운 것이라서, 우리는 (D)기계로 작동되는 우리 주변의 세계에서도 리듬을 알아챌 수 있다. 우리의 시계는 똑똑똑 거리면서 가지만, 우리는 똑딱똑딱으로 듣는다. 리드미컬한 언어에는 우리의 관심을 끄는 (E)강한 매력이 있다.

해설 밑줄 친 단어들 중에서 문맥상 적절하지 않은 어휘를 고르는 문제이다. 우리가 걷고, 수영하고, 말을 타고, 골프채나 야구 방망이를 휘두르는 방식과 같은 모든 일상에 리듬이 있다는 내용이므로 (B)에는 '아무것도 아닌 것'을 의미하는

Nothing이 아니라 '모든 것'을 의미하는 Everything이 들어가는 것이 자연스럽다. 따라서 ②번이 정답이다.

어휘 **repetition** n. 반복, 되풀이 **intake** n. (특히 숨을) 들이쉬기
outflow n. 유출 **naturally** adv. 자연스럽게, 저절로
gracefully adv. 우아하게, 품위 있게
rhythmically adv. 리드미컬하게, 율동적으로
mechanical adj. 기계로 작동되는

[04-05]

우리 중 많은 이가 각각의 아침에 발견하듯, 사적인 곳에서 공적인 곳으로의 이동은 (A)혹독할 수 있다. 한 사람이 집을 떠나는 그 순간에, 그 혹은 그녀는 의무와 필요를 가지고 일의 세계에 사로잡힌다. 시간 엄수가 (B)꼭 필요한 것은 아니다. 집을 떠나면서, 통근자는 적대적이라고 (C)말할 수는 없지만, 이질적이고 공적인 환경에 돌연히 뛰어들어, 붐비는 철도 차량에 비집고 들어가지만, 제시간에 도착하는 것이 너무 행복할 뿐이다. 이러한 여정은 이동이 아니라 도약이다. 평일은 대중교통이나 사적인 삶의 확장을 위한 시도 혹은 공적인 영역으로의 이동을 (D)쉽게 하기 위한 시도로써, 개인 자동차를 통해 통근하는 것으로 시작한다. 교통 체증이 하나의 결과인데, 개인 자동차조차 공용 도로를 이용하기 때문이며, 그들의 차 안에 있는 개인들은 완전하게 (E)익명으로 고립되어 있다.

transition n. 이동 **private** n. 사적인 곳
public n. 공적인 곳 **brutal** adj. 혹독한
obligation n. 의무 **requirement** n. 필요
punctuality n. 시간 엄수 **inessential** n. 꼭 필요하지 않은
commuter n. 통근자 **plunge into** phr. 뛰어들다
alien adj. 이질적인 **hostile** adj. 적대적인
squeeze v. 비집고 들어가다 **extend** v. 확장하다
automobile n. 자동차 **sphere** n. 영역
traffic jam phr. 교통 체증 **anonymous** adj. 익명의
isolated adj. 고립된

04 [2021 한양대]

정답 ④

해석 ① 종료 ② 양보
③ 난문제 ④ 도약
⑤ 장애물

해설 지문의 빈칸을 채우는 문제이다. 지문 전체적으로 사적인 곳에서 공적인 곳으로 이동하는 것이 힘든 일이라는 것을 설명하고 있다. 지문의 후반에서 개인 자동차를 통해 통근하는 사람들이 그들의 차 안에서 완전하게 익명으로 고립된다고 하였는데, 이것은 어떤 개인이 사적인 곳에서 공적인 곳으로 움직일 때 타인 혹은 주변 환경과 단절된다는 것을 의미하는 것이므로, 지문의 빈칸에는 '도약'이라는 의미의 leap이 들어가는 것이 자연스럽다. 따라서 ④번이 정답이다.

05 [2021 한양대]

정답 ②

해설 밑줄 친 낱말의 쓰임이 적절하지 않은 것을 묻는 문제이다. (B)의 뒤 문장에서 '통근자는 적대적이지는 않을지언정, 이질적이고 공적인 환경에 돌연히 뛰어들어, 붐비는 철도 차량에 비집고 들어가지만, 제시간에 도착하는 것이 너무 행복할 뿐이다'라고 하고 있으므로, '시간 엄수가 꼭 필요하다'고 하는 것이 문맥에 알맞다. (B)의 inessential을 essential로 고쳐야 한다. 따라서 ②번이 정답이다.

[06-07]

미국의 깊은 분열에 대한 최근의 역사는 금융 붕괴와 첫 흑인 대통령인, 버락 오바마의 당선이 일어난 2008년도로 거슬러 올라갈 수 있다. 몇몇 시사평론가들은 트럼프의 당선이 구제 금융 당시 집권했던, 민주당에 대한 미국 백인 노동 계층의 불만족에 근거하고 있다고 추적한다. 그러나 이 불만족에는 다른 이유들이 있다. 재건기에서 시민 혁명기까지, 보수주의자들은 오랫동안 평등의 전망에 의해 진정하게 희생된다고 느껴왔다. 오바마는 그 전망을 구체화했고, 그의 대통령 재임 기간 일어난 인종적 정의에 대한 요구도 마찬가지였다. 그것들 사이에 Trayvon Martin이라는, 10대 흑인 소녀의 살해에 대한 반발로 2013년에 세 흑인 여성에 의해 형성된, 흑인 민권 운동이 있었다. 아프리카계 미국인들이 정의를 주장하거나 미국 우월주의자들의 책임을 묻는 것은 항상 위험한 일이었다. 2015년에 사우스캐롤라이나주 찰스턴에 위치한 역사적인 AME 교회 안으로 걸어 들어간 젊은 백인 남성이, 모여서 기도를 하고 있던 9명의 흑인을 쏘아 쓰러뜨렸다. 오바마는 제도적인 억압과 인종적 예속에 대해 한탄하며 열정적인 추도사를 남겼고, 그의 임기 말에는, 노예제도의 유산을 국가적 의제로 생각했다. 그 반발은 예상대로 치명적이었다. 그것은 2016년 도널드 트럼프가 백악관에 입성하게 했고, 2017년 백인 우월주의자 집단이 "당신은 우리를 대신하지 않을 것이다."라는 슬로건 아래 행진했던 버지니아주 샬러츠빌에서 Unite the Right Rally를 이끌었다. 그 나라에는 충격적이게도, 트럼프는 그의 지지자들을 지지했다. 그래서 그것은 그렇게 되었다.

division n. 분열 **date** v. 거슬러 올라가다
financial crash phr. 금융 붕괴 **election** n. 당선
commentator n. 시사평론가 **trace** v. 추적하다
disaffection n. 불만족 **bailout** n. 구제금융
Reconstruction n. 재건기 **conservative** n. 보수주의자
genuinely adv. 진정으로 **victimize** v. 희생시키다
embody v. 구체화하다 **racial** adj. 인종적인
presidency n. 대통령 재임 기간
Black Live Matter movement phr. 흑인 민권 운동
murder n. 살해 **insist** v. 주장하다
supremacist n. 우월주의자
gun down phr. 쏘아 쓰러뜨리다
eulogy n. 추도사 **lament** v. 한탄하다
subjugation n. 예속 **march** v. 행진하다 **troop** n. 지지자

06 2021 한양대

정답 ⑤

해석
① 도널드 트럼프는 백인 우월주의자들을 그의 지지기반으로 드러내 놓고 환영했다.
② 버락 오바마의 연설이 사우스캐롤라이나주의 교회에서 무차별 총격에 의해 야기됐다.
③ 미국의 보수주의자들은 인종적 정의와 평등의 전망에 의해 오랜 기간 고통받아 왔다.
④ 백인 노동 계급은 금융 구제 기간 당시의 민주당 정부에게 부당하게 대우받았다고 느꼈다.
⑤ 오바마 정책의 전체적인 디자인은 궁극적으로 미국 사회에서의 인종적 긴장을 줄이는 데 성공했다.

해설 지문의 내용과 일치하지 않는 것을 묻는 문제이다. 지문의 후반에 오바마는 제도적인 억압과 인종적 예속에 대해 한탄하며 열정적인 추도사를 남겼고, 그의 임기 말에는 노예제도의 유산을 국가적 의제로 생각했지만, 그에 대한 반발이 예상대로 치명적이었다는 내용이 있으므로, 오바마 정책의 전체적인 디자인이 궁극적으로 미국 사회에서의 인종적 긴장을 줄이는 데 성공했다는 것은 지문의 내용과 다르다. 따라서 ⑤번이 지문의 내용과 거리가 멀다.

오답분석
① 지문의 후반에서 도널드 트럼프가 백악관에 입성하고 버지니아주 샬러츠빌에서 백인 우월주의자들의 행진이 있었으며, 트럼프가 그의 지지자들을 지지했다는 내용이 있으므로 지문의 내용과 일치한다.
② 2015년 한 역사적인 AME 교회에서 한 백인이 9명의 흑인들을 쏴 쓰러뜨린 후, 오바마가 열정적인 추도사를 남겼다고 했으므로 지문의 내용과 일치한다.
③ conservatives have long felt genuinely victimized by the prospect of equality를 통해 미국의 보수주의자들이 평등의 전망에 의해 오랜 기간 고통받아 왔다는 것을 알 수 있다.
④ 지문의 초반에서 몇몇 시사평론가들은 트럼프의 당선이 구제금융 당시 집권했던 민주당에 대한 미국 백인 노동 계층의 불만족에 근거하고 있다고 추적한다고 했으므로 지문의 내용과 일치한다.

어휘 occasion v. 야기하다   aggrieve v. 고통을 주다

07 2021 한양대

정답 ②

해석
① 우호   ② 반발
③ 공모   ④ 중상
⑤ 고착

해설 지문의 빈칸을 채우는 문제이다. 빈칸 앞의 내용은 오바마가 노예제도의 유산을 국가적 의제로 생각했다는 내용이고, 빈칸 뒤의 내용은 그것이 2016년 도널드 트럼프가 백악관에 입성하게 했고, 2017년 백인 우월주의자 집단이 "당신은 우리를 대신하지 않을 것이다."라는 슬로건 아래 버지니아주 샬러츠빌에서 행진을 했다고 하였다는 내용이다. 따라서 지문의 빈칸에는 '반발'이라는 의미의 backlash가 들어가는 것이 자연스러우므로 ②번이 정답이다.

[08-10]

최근에, 나는 앱을 획획 넘겨보거나 핸드폰으로 읽는 동안 내 몸이 뭔가 이상하다는 것을 알아챘다. 나는 나의 불규칙한 호흡 패턴과 내 등과 어깨가 얼마나 긴장하고 있는지를 알게 되었다. 과학 기술자인 Linda Stone은 뭔가 비슷한 것에 주목했는데, 아침에 이메일을 확인하기 위해 앉을 때 자신의 호흡이 얕아지고, 때때로 일시적으로 완전히 멈추는 방식을 설명했다. Linda Stone은 그 문제를 '스크린 무호흡'이라고 부른다. 어쩌면 내가 더 훨씬 더 놀랐던 건, 내가 그야말로 내 몸을 전혀 모른다는 걸 깨달아서인 것 같다. 내가 디지털 '공간'에 들어가면 마치 내 몸은 사라져버리는 것 같았다. 이는 아마도 내가 왜 '스크린을 보는 눈'을 극대화하고 이를 이용해 돈을 벌기 위해 경쟁을 벌이는 온라인 플랫폼의 이야기가 (A)약간 불안하다고 항상 생각했는지를 설명해줄 것이다. 문제는 단순히 인체를 완전히 기계로 취급하여 그린다는 것이 아니다. 이 실체 없는 그림은 모든 것을 실제로 어떻게 느끼는지에 맞춰 너무도 잘 조정해서 내 핸드폰의 어떤 '콘텐츠'에 단번에 30분 동안 완전히 몰두하게 한다.

그래서 이제 우리는 기술이 정신을 빼앗을 수 있다는 것을 알긴 하지만, 몸의 입장이 되어서 무슨 일이 일어나고 있는지를 무시한다면 우리는 뭘 놓치고 있는 것일까? 20세기 프랑스 철학자이자 현상학으로 알려진 전통 안에서 영향력 있는 대변인인, Maurice Merleau-Ponty는 여기서 우리의 가이드가 되어 줄 수 있다. Maurice Merleau-Ponty는, 전 철학 체계의 중심에 우리의 구체화를 맡기는 데 있어서 서양의 어떤 사상가보다도 더 나아갔다. 기술로 조정되는 우리의 삶에서, Merleau-Ponty는 심장이 뛰고 활기가 넘치는 몸이 (B)사라지는 것, 그리고 물건에 불과한 지위로 떨어지는 것에서 우리가 느끼는 불안감을 진단하도록 도와줄 수 있다. 게다가, Merleau-Ponty는 다른 사람들과의 관계에 대해 우리가 이해하는 것과 우리가 몰두해있는 더 광범위한 생태학적 맥락에 맞춰 우리 몸이 중심이 되게 만들지 못할 때 간과하고 있는 것을 설명해준다.

Merleau-Ponty의 통찰력을 우리의 일상생활로 가져오려면, 현재를 경험하고 있다는 사실을 주의 깊게 생각하면서 우리가 존재하고 있다는 간단한 개념을 적용할 수 있을 것이라고 생각한다. 그렇게 하는 것은 몸보다 정신에 (C)특권을 주는 서양의 문화적 경향을 뒤집어 볼 수 있다.

flick through phr. ~을 획획 넘겨보다
become conscious of phr. ~을 알고 있다, 자각하다
tension n. 긴장   **apnea** n. 무호흡
disembodied adj. 실체 없는, 알 수 없는 곳에서 나오는
align with phr. ~에 맞추어 조정하다
at a stretch phr. 단번에   **hijack** v. 빼앗다, 강탈하다

| phenomenology n. 현상학 philosophical adj. 철학의
| elucidate v. 설명하다 immerse v. ~에 몰두하다
| insight n. 통찰력

08 2021 이화여대

정답 ②

해석
① "스크린 무호흡"은 우리가 디지털 공간에서 시간을 보낼 때 발생하는 신체적 반응을 지칭한다.
② 온라인 플랫폼은 결국 우리의 몸을 공간적인 한계로부터 자유롭게 해줄 것이다.
③ 현상학은 우리의 일상생활에서 몸의 존재에 의지할 수 있게 도와준다.
④ 몸의 물리적 존재에 대한 새로운 관심은 몸과 정신의 관계를 더 균형 잡히게 만들어 줄지도 모른다.
⑤ "스크린 무호흡"은 역설적이게도 기술로 조정되는 우리의 삶에서 몸의 존재를 다시 생각하게 해준다.

해설 지문을 통해 추론할 수 없는 것을 고르는 문제이다. 지문의 중간에서 내가 디지털 '공간'에 들어가면 마치 내 몸이 사라져버리는 것 같았다고는 했지만, 이를 통해 온라인 플랫폼이 결국 우리의 몸을 공간적인 한계로부터 자유롭게 해줄 것이라는 내용을 추론해 내기에는 무리가 있다. 따라서 정답은 ②번이다.

오답 분석
① 보기의 키워드인 'Screen apnea'(스크린 무호흡)가 등장한 지문의 초반에서, "스크린 무호흡"이 우리가 디지털 공간에서 시간을 보낼 때 발생하는 신체적 반응을 지칭한다는 것을 추론할 수 있다.
③ 보기의 키워드인 'Phenomenology'(현상학)가 등장한 지문의 중간에서, 현상학이 우리의 일상생활에서 몸의 존재에 의지할 수 있게 도와준다는 것을 추론할 수 있다.
④ 보기의 키워드인 'body-mind'(몸과 신체)와 관련된 'privilege mind over body'(몸보다 정신에 특권을 주다)가 등장한 지문의 후반에서, 몸의 물리적 존재에 대한 새로운 관심이 몸과 정신의 관계를 더 균형 잡히게 만들어 줄지도 모른다는 것을 추론할 수 있다.
⑤ 보기의 키워드인 'Screen apnea'(스크린 무호흡)가 등장한 지문의 초반에서, "스크린 무호흡"은 역설적이게도 기술로 조정되는 우리의 삶에서 몸의 존재를 다시 생각하게 해준다는 것을 추론할 수 있다.

어휘 presence n. 존재 anew adv. (처음부터) 다시, 새로

09 2021 이화여대

정답 ①

해석
① 약간 불안한
② 전적으로 자본주의적인
③ 불편하게 이념적인
④ 잠재적으로 건강한
⑤ 자연스럽게 상스러운

해설 지문의 빈칸을 채우는 문제이다. 지문의 초반에서 '스크린 무호흡'이라는 몸의 이상한 증상에 대해 언급하고, 지문의 중간에서 내가 디지털 '공간'에 들어가면 마치 내 몸은 사라져버리는 것 같았다고 했으므로, 빈칸 (A)에는 아마도 내가 왜 '스크린을 보는 눈'을 극대화하고 이를 이용해 돈을 벌기 위해 경쟁을 벌이는 온라인 플랫폼의 이야기가 약간 불안하다고 항상 생각했는지를 설명해줄 것이라는 내용이 나오는 것이 자연스럽다. 따라서 '약간 불안한'이라고 한 ①번이 정답이다.

어휘 vaguely adv. 약간, 모호하게
unsettling adj. 불안하게 만드는
absolutely adv. 전적으로 capitalistic adj. 자본주의적인
potentially adv. 잠재적으로 vulgar adj. 상스러운

10 2021 이화여대

정답 ④

해석
① 의식 — 되찾다   ② 징후 — 선호하다
③ 태만 — 경멸하다   ④ 사라짐 — 특권을 주다
⑤ 강조 — 분리하다

해설 지문의 빈칸을 채우는 문제이다. 지문의 중간에서 Maurice Merleau-Ponty가 전 철학 체계의 중심에 우리의 구체화를 맡기는 데 있어서 서양의 어떤 사상가보다도 더 나아갔다고 했으므로, 빈칸 (B)에는 기술로 조정되는 우리의 삶에서, Merleau-Ponty는 심장이 뛰고 활기가 넘치는 몸이 물건에 불과한 지위로 떨어지는 것에서 우리가 느끼는 불안감을 진단하도록 도와줄 수 있다고 했으므로, 빈칸 (B)에는 '사라짐'이라고 한 disappearance가 적절하다. 지문의 후반에서 Merleau-Ponty의 통찰력을 우리의 일상생활로 가져오려면, 현재를 경험하고 있다는 사실을 주의 깊게 생각하면서 우리가 존재하고 있다는 간단한 개념을 적용할 수 있을 것이라고 생각한다고 했으므로, 빈칸 (C)에는 '특권을 주는'이라고 한 privilege가 적절하다. 따라서 ④ disappearance — privilege가 정답이다.

어휘 manifestation n. 징후 disdain v. 경멸하다

[11-12]

오늘날, 많은 사람들은 디지털 책과 점점 더 스크린을 기반으로 하는 문화가 진지한 독서의 끝을 예고하는 것을 걱정하고 있다. 이것은 말도 안 된다. 모든 새로운 기술에는 성과가 있고 때로는 문제점도 있지만, 인간은 이야기와 시 없이는 살 수 없다. 젊은 연인들은 항상 Sappho, Donne 그리고 Keats의 작품을 읽을 것이다. *Madame Bovary*와 *The Great Gatsby*는 낭만적인 환상을 추구하는 우리의 성향을 반영한 대체할 수 없는 기록으로 남을 것이다. 낭만적 환상이 끝나기 전에 조금이라도 삶을 이해하고 싶어 하는 나이 든 사람들은 계속해서 역사와 철학을 공부할 것이다. 사람들이 페이지를 넘기든 스크린 위로 픽셀을 보든 그건 부수적인 문제이다. 하지만 Sylvia

Plath를 알게 되는 오늘날 젊은 여성들은 소셜 미디어를 통해 전 세계 친구들과 빠르게 자신의 즐거움을 공유할 수 있다는 것을 생각해보아라. 그녀는 Goodreads 사이트에 *Ariel*이나 *The Bell Jar*에 대해 코멘트를 남길 수도 있고, 온라인 토론 그룹에 가입할 수도 있으며, 또는 그 시인(Sylvia Plath)의 작품과 추억으로 가득한 사이트의 링크를 게시할 수도 있다. 그녀의 열정은 십여 명 혹은 천 명의 사람들을 Plath에게로 이끌지도 모른다.

그것은 스크린을 기반으로 한 문화의 한 가지 장점일 뿐이다. 더 오래되고 절반은 잊힌 책들은 이제 손쉽게 Project Gutenberg를 통해 이용할 수 있다. 도서관 전체가 당신의 주머니로 옮겨질 수 있는 것이다. 디지털화된 텍스트는 쉽고 빠르게 검색할 수 있으며, 노화된 눈을 위해 글꼴 크기 또한 확대할 수 있다.

그럼에도 불구하고, 이 실질적인 이익들은 동시에 다양한 문제들도 만들어 낸다. 컴퓨터는 책에 담긴 단어들과 생각에 대한 온전한 집중과 고독한 참여 대신에 대충 읽는 것을 조장한다. 윙윙거리는 인터넷 벌집은 의미 있는 대화뿐만 아니라 의미 없는 수다도 조장한다. 스크린 그 자체는 꾸며낸 동종성을 강요한다. James Bond가 Jane Austen처럼 보이고 스마트폰은 Mainz의 거대한 성경과 아주 작은 책의 크기 차이를 모호하게 만들고 있다.

increasingly adv. 점점 더, 갈수록 더
herald v. 예고하다, 알리다 **drawback** n. 문제점, 단점
irreplaceable adj. (다른 것과) 대체할 수 없는
commentary n. 기록, 해설 **proclivity** n. 성향
philosophy n. 철학 **secondary** adj. 부수적인, 부차적인
excitement n. 즐거움, 흥분 **enlarge** v. 확대하다
pitfall n. 문제, 함정 **skim** v. ~을 대충 읽다
buzzing adj. 윙윙거리는 **foster** v. 조장하다
factitious adj. 꾸며낸, 인위적인
homogeneity n. 동종성, 균질성

11 [2021 이화여대]

정답 ⑤

해석 ① 실제로 ② 놀랍게도
③ 결과적으로 ④ 게다가
⑤ 그럼에도 불구하고

해설 빈칸에 적절한 연결어를 넣는 문제이다. 빈칸 앞 내용은 스크린을 기반으로 한 문화의 장점이고, 빈칸 뒤 내용은 이 실질적인 이익(스크린을 기반으로 한 문화의 장점)이 동시에 다양한 문제를 만들어 낸다는 것이므로 서로 대조적이라는 것을 알 수 있다. 따라서 '역접'을 나타내는 연결어인 ⑤ Nonetheless(그럼에도 불구하고)가 정답이다.

12 [2021 이화여대]

정답 ②

해석 ① 독서 습관의 빠른 변화에도 불구하고, 사람들은 독서를 멈추지 않을 것이다.
② 디지털화된 텍스트는 인쇄된 책을 완전히 대체할 것이다.
③ 스크린으로 읽는 것은 개개의 인쇄된 책들이 가진 다른 요소와 일반적인 특징을 우리가 알지 못하게 만든다.
④ 스크린을 기반으로 하는 문화는 책에 대한 독자의 활발한 참여를 늘릴 수 있다.
⑤ 온라인 독서 모임에 있는 모든 코멘트와 대화가 의미 있는 것은 아니다.

해설 지문을 통해 추론할 수 없는 것을 고르는 문제이다. 지문의 초반에서 많은 사람들이 디지털 책과 스크린 기반으로 하는 문화가 독서의 끝을 예고하는 것을 걱정하지만 이것은 말도 안 된다고 했으므로, 디지털화된 텍스트가 인쇄된 책을 완전히 대체할 것이라는 내용은 지문의 내용과 다르다. 따라서 정답은 ②번이다.

오답분석 ① 보기의 키워드인 'reading'(독서)이 등장한 지문의 초반을 통해, 독서 습관의 빠른 변화에도 불구하고 사람들이 독서를 멈추지 않을 것이라는 것을 추론할 수 있다.
③ 보기의 키워드인 'different'(다른)와 관련된 'difference'(차이)가 등장한 지문의 후반을 통해, 스크린으로 읽는 것은 개개의 인쇄된 책들이 가진 다른 요소와 일반적인 특징을 우리가 알지 못하게 만든다는 것을 추론할 수 있다.
④ 보기의 키워드인 'Screen-based culture'(스크린을 기반으로 하는 문화)가 등장한 지문의 중간을 통해, 스크린을 기반으로 하는 문화가 독자의 활발한 책 참여를 늘릴 수 있다는 것을 추론할 수 있다.
⑤ 보기의 키워드인 'dialogue'(대화)가 등장한 지문의 후반을 통해, 온라인 독서 모임에 있는 모든 코멘트와 대화가 의미 있는 것은 아니라는 것을 추론할 수 있다.

어휘 **altogether** adv. 완전히 **unaware** adj. 알지 못하는
generic adj. 일반적인

[13-14]

당신 핸드폰의 푸른빛에 잠이 깨서 곧바로 일을 시작하지 마라. 핸드폰은 떨어진 곳에, 혹은 더 낫게는, 옆방에 두고서 억지로라도 알람을 끄기 위해 매일 아침 침대에서 몸을 일으켜 나오도록 만들라. 알람이 꺼질 때, 직장에서 일하기 위해 그럴 것처럼, 일어나서 하루를 준비하라. 즉, 샤워하고 옷을 입어라. 업무용 정장이 (명백히) 필수 사항은 아니지만, 마치 당신이 직장 동료를 직접 만나 소통할 것처럼 행동하라. 어쨌든, 당신은 언제 그들이 화상채팅을 원할지 모르는데, 셔츠를 입고 있지 않기 때문에 못 하겠다고 하고 싶지는 않다. 이것은 또한 하루를 위한 박자를 설정하고, 어쩌면, 물론 그럴 리는 없겠지만, 당신이 점심 전후로 침대로 다시 기어들어 갈 수 있다는 나

른한 생각을 막아준다. 비록 근무시간에 잠깐 자는 것에는 뭔가 좋은 점이 있을지라도 말이다.

---

hue n. 색조, 색, 빛깔   adjacent adj. 인접한
go off phr. (불, 전기) 나가다, 꺼지다
interact v. 소통하다, 교류하다; 상호작용하다
in person phr. 몸소, 직접 대면하여
beg off phr. 못하겠다고 하다   tempo n. 속도; 박자
discourage v. 막다, 좌절시키다   crawl v. 기다, 기어가다
sleepy adj. 졸린; 나른한   notion n. 개념, 생각
workday n. 근무일, 근무시간
there is something to be said for ~ phr. ~에는 뭔가 좋은 점이 있다

13 [2018 서울여대]

정답 ②

해석 ① 시간 관리법
② 재택 근무하는 법
③ 일과 삶의 균형을 맞추는 법
④ 직장[일]에서 성공하는 법

해설 지문의 주제를 묻는 문제이다. 지문 전체적으로 재택 근무시 어떻게 하라는 내용을 명령문으로 전달하고 있다.

14 [2018 서울여대]

정답 ②

해석 ① 근무 시간에 잠깐 자기 위해서 당신은 뭔가가 필요하다.
② 근무 시간에 잠깐 자는 것은 당신에게 좋을지도 모른다.
③ 어떤 고용주도 근무시간에 잠깐 자는 것을 허락하지 않을 것이다.
④ 근무 시간에 잠깐 자는 것은 당신이 말할 수 있는 어떤 것이다.

해설 밑줄 친 부분의 의미를 추론하는 문제이다. 밑줄 친 there is something to be said for workday naps는 '근무시간에 잠깐 자는 것에는 뭔가 좋은 점이 있다'는 의미이다. 따라서, 이를 '근무 시간에 잠깐 자는 것은 당신에게 좋을지도 모른다'라고 표현한 ②번이 정답이다.

오답분석 ④ 숙어 표현의 뜻을 묻는 문제인데, ④번은 직역해서 다른 의미가 된 보기이다.

[15-16]

절대 모르는 번호에 답신 전화를 해서는 안 되는데 그 이유는 이 행동이 당신이 사기꾼에게 문을 열어주는 행위일 수도 있기 때문입니다. 당신은 번호가 당신이 사는 곳의 지역 번호이기 때문에 답신 전화를 하는 것이 안전하다고 추정할지도 모르지만, (A)사기꾼들은 발신자의 계정에 나타나는 가짜 전화번호에 능숙합니다. 범인들은 고의로 당신의 신뢰를 얻기 위해 친숙한 지역번호를 활용하고 있습니다. 사람들은 호기심이 많고, 절도범들은 (B)피해자들이 중요한 무언가를 놓쳤을지도 모른다고 생각하기를 기대하고 있습니다. 적어도, 전화에 응답하거나 답신을 하는 것은 미래의 사기 사건에 대한 당신의 취약성을 늘리게 되는데 이 같은 행동이 이 번호가 모르는 번호에도 답신하려고 하는 실제 사람에게 연결되어 있다는 것을 확인시켜주기 때문입니다. 이것은 사기꾼들에게 (C)그들이 다른 계획 혹은 다른 날짜에 이용할 수 있다는 것을 말해줍니다. 최악은 무엇일까요? 사기꾼들이 당신이 개인정보를 보내도록 속일 수 있다는 것입니다. 심지어 (D)사기꾼들이 간단하게, "제 말 들려요?"라는 질문을 할 때도, 당신은 전화를 끊어야 합니다. "네"라는, 당신의 응답 소리를 녹음하는 것이 사기꾼들에게 당신의 은행, 보험, 그리고 또 어떤 금융 정보들에 접근하도록 할 수 있기 때문입니다. 그저 모르는 번호에 응답하지 마시고, 필수적인 정보가 당신의 음성 메시지에 남아 있으리라는 것만 기억해 두십시오.

---

scammer n. 사기꾼   assume v. 추정하다
area code phr. 지역 번호   adept at phr. 능숙한
faking adj. 허위의   come up phr. 나오다
criminal n. 범죄자   purposely adv. 고의로
familiar adj. 친숙한   victim n. 피해자
vulnerability n. 취약성   confirm v. 확인해 주다
dupe v. 속이다   recording n. 녹음   insurance n. 보험
vital adj. 필수적인   voicemail n. 음성 메시지

15 [2020 한국외대]

정답 ①

해석 ① 범죄자들은 당신으로부터 도둑질하기 위해 당신의 응답을 녹음할 수 있다.
② 사람들의 일반적인 호기심은 그들을 사기꾼들로부터 보호한다.
③ 사람들은 모르는 번호에 답신 전화를 걸기 위해 노력해야 한다.
④ 당신이 대답을 간략하게 하면, 사기꾼들은 당신의 금융 정보를 얻을 수 없다.

해설 지문의 내용과 일치하는 것을 묻는 문제이다. 지문의 열 번째 문장에서 당신의 음성을 녹음하는 것이 사기꾼들에게 당신의 은행, 보험, 그리고 또 다른 금융 정보에 접근하도록 할 수 있다고 했으므로, 범죄자들은 당신으로부터 도둑질하기 위해 당신의 응답을 녹음할 수 있다가 지문의 내용과 일치한다. 따라서 ①번이 정답이다.

오답분석 ② 지문의 네 번째 문장에서, 사람들은 호기심이 많고 절도범들은 피해자들이 중요한 무언가를 놓쳤다고 생각하기를 기대한다고 했으므로, 사람들의 호기심이 사기꾼들을 예방하는 데에 좋지 않다는 것을 알 수 있다. 따라서 '사람들의 일반적인 호기심은 그들을 사기꾼들로부터 보호한다'는 지문의 내용과 다르다.

③ 지문의 첫 번째 문장에서, 모르는 번호에 답신 전화를 하지 말라고 했으므로, '사람들은 모르는 번호에 답신 전화를 걸기 위해 노력해야 한다'는 지문의 내용과 다르다.

④ 지문의 열 번째 문장에서, "네"라는 간단한 응답의 녹음만으로도 사기꾼이 금융 정보에 접근할 수 있도록 한다고 했으므로, '당신이 대답을 간략하게 하면, 사기꾼들은 당신의 금융 정보를 얻을 수 없다'는 지문의 내용과 다르다.

어휘 steal v. 도둑질하다   briefly adv. 간략하게

16   2020 한국외대

정답 ②

해설 (A)~(D) 가운데 의미하는 바가 다른 것을 파악하는 문제이다. (A), (C), (D)는 모두 사기꾼을 의미하는데, (B)는 사기꾼들의 피해자를 의미하므로, (A)~(D) 가운데 의미하는 바가 다른 것은 (B)이다. 따라서 ②번이 정답이다.

[17-19]

일부 애플 카드 소비자들은 해당 신용 카드의 발행자, 골드만삭스사가 여성들에게, 심지어 여성들이 그들의 배우자와 자산과 계좌를 공유하고 있다고 하더라도, 더 낮은 신용 한도를 제공하고 있다고 이야기한다. 그러나, 애플 카드나 다른 신용 카드사가 여성을 차별하는지 아닌지 아는 것은 불가능한데, 신용도 알고리즘이 악명 높게 불투명하기 때문이다. "이것이 우리가 지금 보고 있는 수수께끼이다"라고 NerdWallet의 여행 및 신용 카드 전문가인 Sara Rathner는 이야기한다. "왜냐하면 우리는 정확히 신용도 알고리즘이 무엇을 위한 것인지 알 수 없고, 어떤 편견이 그 알고리즘 안에 내장되어 있을 수 있다고 이야기하기도 어려울 수 있기 때문이다." 뉴욕 금융당국은 애플 카드 이용자들에 대한 성적 차별의 혐의를 찾는 중이다. 이 혐의는 트위터상에서 폭발했는데, 이 폭발은 사업가인 David Heinmeier Hansson이 그의 부인과 자산을 공유하고 있고, 부인이 더 높은 신용 점수를 가지고 있음에도 불구하고, 애플 카드가 그의 부인보다 그에게 20배나 높은 신용한도를 제공했다고 글을 쓴 직후에 일어났다. 신용카드 발행사가 대출 결정을 할 때, 알고리즘을 이용하는 것은 일반적인 관습이지만, 이 알고리즘에는 <u>투명성</u>이 거의 없다.

credit card phr. 신용 카드   issuer n. 발행인
credit limit phr. 신용 한도   asset n. 자산
account n. 계좌   spouse n. 배우자
discriminate v. 차별하다   creditworthiness n. 신용도
algorithm n. 알고리즘   notoriously adv. 악명 높게
opaque adj. 불투명한   bias n. 편견   allegation n. 혐의
gender discrimination phr. 성차별
entrepreneur n. 사업가   practice n. 관습
lending n. 대출   decision n. 결정

17   2020 덕성여대

정답 ②

해석 ① 신뢰성   ② 투명성
③ 정확도   ④ 예측 가능성

해설 지문의 빈칸을 채우는 문제이다. 두 번째 문장에서 애플 카드나 다른 카드사가 여성을 차별하는지 아닌지 아는 것은 불가능한데, 그 이유는 신용도 알고리즘이 악명 높게 불투명하기 때문이라고 했으므로, 빈칸에는 빈칸의 앞에 쓰인 부정어 little과 함께 opaque(불투명한)과 같은 의미를 갖는 단어가 와야 한다. 따라서 '투명성'이라는 의미의 ②번이 정답이다.

18   2020 덕성여대

정답 ③

해석 ① 일반적으로, 신용 카드 발행자들은 여성을 차별하는데, 여성들이 그들의 배우자와 자산과 계좌를 공유하지 않기 때문이다.
② 애플 카드 이용자들에 대한 성차별 혐의는 사업가 David Hansson에 의한 조사하에 있다.
③ 일반적으로 카드 발행자들은 비록 남성들이 그들의 배우자와 자산과 계좌를 공유하고 있다고 할지라도, 남성에게 더 높은 신용 한도를 제공한다.
④ 신용 카드 발행사가 여성에 대한 차별이 프로그램된 알고리즘을 사용하는 것은 일반적인 관습이다.

해설 지문의 내용과 일치하는 것을 묻는 문제이다. 첫 번째 문장에서 애플 카드의 발행인인 골드만삭스가 여성들이 남성과 재산과 계좌를 공유하고 있음에도 불구하고 더 낮은 신용 한도를 제공한다고 주장하는 사람들이 있다고 했고, 여섯 번째 문장에서 사업가인 David Hansson의 부인이 David Hansson과 자산을 공유하고 있고, 더 높은 신용 점수를 가지고 있음에도 그가 부인보다 20배 높은 신용한도를 가지고 있다고 했으므로, 일반적으로 카드 발행사들은 남성들이 그들의 배우자와 자산과 계좌를 공유하고 있다고 할지라도, 남성에게 더 높은 신용 한도를 제공하고 있다는 것을 알 수 있다. 따라서 ③번이 정답이다.

오답분석 ① 지문의 첫 번째 문장에서 여성들이 남성과 재산과 계좌를 공유하고 있음에도 불구하고 여성에게 더 낮은 신용 한도를 제공한다고 주장하는 사람들이 있다고 했으므로, 여성들이 배우자와 자산과 계좌를 공유하지 않기 때문에 여성을 차별한다는 것은 지문의 내용과 다르다.
② 다섯 번째 문장에서 뉴욕 금융당국이 애플 카드 이용자들에 대한 성적 차별의 혐의를 찾는 중이라고 했으므로, 사업가 David Hansson이 성적 차별 혐의를 조사하고 있다는 것은 지문의 내용과 다르다.
④ 네 번째 문장에서 Sara Rathner가 이야기한 바에 따르면, 신용도 알고리즘에 어떤 편견이 내장되어 있다고 말하기 어렵다고 했으므로, 신용 카드 발행사가 여성에 대한 차

별이 프로그램된 알고리즘을 사용하는 것이 일반적인 관습이라는 것은 지문의 내용과 다르다.

어휘 investigation n. 조사 programmed adj. 프로그램된

19 2020 덕성여대

정답 ①

해석 ① 애플 카드는 성 편견으로 비난받을 수 있다.
② 뉴욕 금융당국이 트위터상에서 애플 카드 이용자에 대한 성차별 혐의를 폭발시켰다.
③ 애플 카드 발행사는 그들의 알고리즘을 다른 신용 카드 발행사와 공유할 것이다.
④ 애플 카드 이용자에 대한 성차별 혐의는 불투명해질 것이다.

해설 지문을 통해 추론할 수 있는 것을 고르는 문제이다. 지문의 여섯 번째 문장에서 David Heinmeier Hansson이 자신의 사례를 쓴 이후에 트위터상에서 애플 카드 이용자에 대한 성적 차별 혐의가 폭발했다는 내용이 있으므로, 애플 카드가 성 편견으로 비난받을 수 있다는 것을 추론할 수 있다. 따라서 ①번이 정답이다.

오답 분석
② 지문의 여섯 번째 문장에서 트위터상에서 해당 혐의를 폭발시킨 것은 David Hansson이라고 언급되었으므로, 뉴욕 금융당국이 트위터상에서 애플 카드 이용자에 대한 성차별 혐의를 폭발시켰다는 것은 지문의 내용과 일치하지 않는다.
③ 골드먼 삭스 사가 자사의 알고리즘을 공유하고 있는지에 대해서는 언급되지 않았다.
④ 다섯 번째 문장에서 뉴욕 금융 당국이 애플 카드 이용자에 대한 성차별 혐의가 있는지 찾는 중이라고 했지만, 그 결과에 대해서는 언급되지 않았으므로, 애플 카드 이용자에 대한 성차별 혐의가 불투명해질 것인지는 알 수 없다.

어휘 be accuse of phr. ~로 비난받다 share v. 공유하다

[20-21]

전문가들에 따르면, 화재나 지진과 같은 비상시에 당신의 생존 가능성을 늘리기 위해 할 수 있는 몇 가지가 있다. 준비가 생존의 핵심이 될 수 있다. 당신이 식량, 물, 양초 및 기타 저장품을 집에 갖고 있도록 하라. 당신이 빨리 피난해야 하는 경우를 대비해서 각 가족 구성원을 위해 준비된 배낭을 갖고 있는 것도 좋은 생각이다. 캠핑, 하이킹, 또는 등산을 가기 전에, 당신이 적절한 장비를 갖도록 하라. 텐트, 침낭 및 구급상자는 악천후, 부상, 또는 질병이 발생하는 경우에 당신의 생명을 구할 수 있다. 침착함을 유지하는 것 또한 당신이 어떤 비상 상황이라도 대처하도록 도울 수 있다. 예를 들어, 수영하는 사람들은 때때로 강한 해류를 만난다. 만약 그들이 공황 상태에 빠지면, 그들은 기진맥진하여 수영할 수 없게 될지도 모른다. 하지만, 그들이 진정하고 해류를 따라 천천히 수영한다면, 일단 해류에서 빠져나오기만 하면 그들은 해변을 향해 수영할 기력이 있을 것이다.

survival n. 생존 preparation n. 준비, 대비
supplies n. 저장품 in case phr. ~할 경우에 대비해서
evacuate v. 피난하다 first-aid kit phr. 구급상자
current n. 해류, 흐름

20 2020 숙명여대

정답 ③

해석 ① 극도로 행동하는 것
② 계속 활동적인 것
③ 침착함을 유지하는 것
④ 계획을 세우는 것
⑤ 다른 사람들에게 이야기하는 것

해설 지문의 빈칸을 채우는 문제이다. 지문 마지막에서 수영하는 사람들은 때때로 강한 해류를 만나지만, 진정하고 해류를 따라 천천히 수영한다면, 해변을 향해 수영할 수 있을 것이라고 했으므로, 빈칸에는 어떤 것이 비상 상황에 대처하도록 도울 수 있는지에 대한 내용이 나와야 적절하다는 것을 알 수 있다. 따라서 '침착함을 유지하는 것'이라고 한 ③번이 정답이다.

어휘 wildly adv. 극도로 energetic adj. 활동적인

21 2020 숙명여대

정답 ⑤

해석 ① 다양한 야외활동 유형
② 수영하는 방법을 배우는 것의 이점
③ 비상시 살아남는 데 필수적인 장비
④ 가족 캠핑을 위해 준비해야 할 것
⑤ 비상 상황에 대처하는 방법

해설 지문의 제목을 묻는 문제이다. 지문 처음에서 전문가들에 따르면, 화재나 지진과 같은 비상시에 생존 가능성을 늘리기 위해 할 수 있는 몇 가지가 있다고 하고, 지문 전반적으로 그 방법들을 차례로 제시하고 있다. 따라서 이 지문의 제목을 '비상 상황에 대처하는 방법'이라고 표현한 ⑤번이 정답이다.

어휘 cope with phr. ~에 대처하다

[22-24]

어느 날 아침, 빨랫감을 말리기 위해 밖에 널어놓고 난 뒤, 내 앞에서 무엇인가가 반짝였다. 아침 햇살이 내 눈에 비쳐서, 나는 우리 정원에서 가장 눈부시게 아름다운 걸작을 찾기 위해 눈을 가늘게 떴다.
(A)그 작은 건축가는 지붕에서 울타리까지 길을 가로질러 꼼꼼하게 거미줄을 쳤다. 나는 (B)우리 정원 거주자의 훌륭한

예술성을 경외심을 가지고 응시했다. 약 2미터에 걸쳐 이어지는 이 광경은 정말 마법 같은 광경이었다. 그 거미줄은 햇빛을 반사하며 아침 산들바람에 살랑살랑 춤을 추었다. 마치 거미가 햇빛의 빛살 그 자체로부터 고운 거미줄을 친 것 같았다. 어떻게 지붕에서 울타리까지 거미줄을 짰을까? 익스트림 스포츠를 즐기면서 동시에 집을 지은 것이나 다름없다. 아주 조심스럽게, 나는 (C)거미의 창조물을 망치지 않도록 대단히 신경을 쓰면서 거미줄 밑으로 머리를 숙였다.

그날 늦게 나는 다시 한번 살펴보기 위해 거미줄로 갔다. 내 심장은 주저앉았다. 그 아름다운 거미줄은 이제 부서져서 산들바람 속에서 정처 없이 흔들거리고 있었다. 그것은 초라한 몇 가닥이 느슨하게 늘어져 있는 것에 지나지 않았다. 나는 감정에 겨워 목이 멜 뻔했다. "안됐구나, (D)작은 친구. 너무나 멋진 건축물이었어."

그런데 바로 다음 날 아침, 놀랍게도, 또 다른 성이 공중에 떠 있었다. 그 작은 건축가는 다시 일터로 돌아와 있었다.

---

hang out phr. (세탁물 등을) 밖에 널다, 줄에 널다
washing n. 빨랫감, 세탁물   glisten v. 반짝이다
squint v. 눈을 가늘게 뜨고 보다
glorious adj. 눈부시게 아름다운
masterpiece n. 걸작, 명작   architect n. 건축가, 설계자
meticulously adv. 꼼꼼하게, 세심하게
spin a web phr. 거미줄을 치다, 거미집을 짓다
path n. 길   fence n. 울타리   stare at phr. ~을 응시하다
awe n. 경외심   fine adj. 훌륭한, 고운, 섬세한
artistry n. 예술성   resident n. 거주자
span v. 걸쳐 이어지다   sight n. 광경, 경치
breeze n. 산들바람   ray n. 빛살, 광선
weave v. 짜다, 엮다   duck v. (머리·몸 등을) 휙 숙이다
creation n. 창조물, 창조   sway v. 흔들거리다
aimlessly adv. 정처 없이, 목적 없이
pitiful adj. 초라한, 가련한   strand n. 가닥, 줄
loose adj. 느슨한, 풀린   choke v. (목이) 메다, 잠기다
fella n. 친구, 남자   splendid adj. 멋진, 훌륭한
structure n. 건축물, 구조물

22 2020 국민대

정답 ①

해설 meticulously(꼼꼼하게)와 비슷한 의미를 가진 어휘를 묻고 있다. ①번 thoroughly는 '철저히, 철두철미하게', ②번 involuntarily는 '모르는 사이에, 본의 아니게', ③번 maliciously는 '악의를 갖고', ④번 contemptuously는 '모욕적으로'라는 의미이다. 따라서 ①번이 정답이다.

23 2020 국민대

정답 ③

해설 밑줄 친 부분의 의미를 추론하는 문제이다. 밑줄 친 (A)The mini architect, (B)our garden resident, (D)little fella의 경우, 모두 거미와 관련된 단어이지만, (C)the spider's creation의 경우 거미줄을 의미하므로 나머지와 의미가 일치하지 않는다. 따라서 ③번이 정답이다.

24 2020 국민대

정답 ①

해석 ① 놀랍게도   ② 실망스럽게도
③ 큰 기대를 가지고   ④ 대단히 만족하여

해설 지문의 빈칸을 채우는 문제이다. 빈칸이 있는 문장에서 다음 날 아침에 공중에 성이 떠 있었다(거미줄이 쳐져 있었다)고 했으므로, 빈칸에는 하루 만에 거미줄이 다시 쳐진 것에 대한 놀라움을 표현하는 내용이 나와야 적절하다는 것을 알 수 있다. 따라서 '놀랍게도'라고 한 ①번이 정답이다.

어휘 amazement n. 놀라움   disappointment n. 실망
satisfaction n. 만족

[25-27]

21세기의 첫 10년 동안, 세계 사회는 충격적인 문제들에 직면해 있다. 우리 지구에는 60억 명의 사람이 있으며 예측가들은 세계의 인구가 2050년까지 100억 명에 달할 것이라고 예상한다. 이 사람들은 음식, 주거지, 그리고 충실한 삶을 살도록 자신들을 이끌게 할 교육이 필요할 것이다. 20세기는 많은 분야에서 대단한 진보를 이루었지만, 이 진보들이 아무런 비용 없이 나온 것은 아니었다. 예를 들어, 산성비는 우리의 초목, 야생 동물, 그리고 수백만 명의 사람들의 몸을 오염시켰다. 이와 함께, 세계의 사람들은 우리 지구에 전체적인 훼손을 멈추어야 한다. 핵무기와 사제 폭발물과 같은 무기들이 세계의 평화와 진보를 매일 위협한다. 종교적 광신주의, 굶주림, 그리고 가난은 세계 곳곳에서 극심한 테러를 낳았다. 우리는 세계적인 생존 경쟁을 하고 있다고 말해도 과언이 아니다.

---

decade n. 10년   community n. (지역) 사회
confront v. 맞서다   staggering adj. 충격적인
globe n. 지구, 세계   forecaster n. 예측가
project v. 예상하다, 전망하다   population n. 인구
shelter n. 주거지   fulfilled adj. 충실한, 성취감을 느끼는
acid rain phr. 산성비   vegetation n. 초목, 식물
systemic adj. 전체에 영향을 주는
despoil v. 훼손하다, 빼앗다   weaponry n. 무기
nuclear device phr. 핵폭탄
improvised explosive device phr. 사제 폭발물
threaten v. 위협하다   fanaticism n. 광신주의, 광신
poverty n. 가난   breed v. 낳다
desperate adj. 극심한, 발악하는   terrorism n. 테러
overstatement n. 과언, 과장   race n. 경쟁

25 2019 숙명여대

정답 ③

해석
① 20세기에 만들어진 위대한 진보
② 지구 온난화, 초목, 그리고 야생 동물
③ 상당한 비용이 들어간 위대한 진보
④ 충실한 종교적 삶을 이끄는 방법
⑤ 극심한 테러와 세계의 생존

해설 지문의 제목을 묻는 문제이다. 지문의 중간에서 20세기는 많은 분야에서 진보를 이루었지만 이것이 아무런 비용 없이 나온 것은 아니라고 설명하고 있다. 따라서 이 지문의 제목을 '상당한 비용이 들어간 위대한 진보'라고 표현한 ③번이 정답이다.

어휘 global warming phr. 지구 온난화 significant adj. 상당한

26 2019 숙명여대

정답 ④

해석
① 자극하는   ② 의심스러운
③ 풍부한   ④ 경악스러운
⑤ 침체된

해설 밑줄 친 staggering의 의미를 추론하는 문제이다. 지문의 중반부터 후반에 걸쳐 산성비, 지구에 대한 훼손, 무기, 극심한 테러 등의 심각한 문제들에 관해 설명하고 있다. 따라서, staggering의 의미를 '경악스러운'이라고 한 ④번이 정답이다.

어휘 stimulating adj. 자극하는   suspicious adj. 의심스러운
abundant adj. 풍부한   astounding adj. 경악스러운
stagnant adj. 침체된

27 2019 숙명여대

정답 ③

해석
① 세계 인구의 급속한 성장은 다뤄져야 할 심각한 문제의 조짐을 보인다.
② 상당한 비용으로, 우리는 다른 영역들에서 위대한 기술의 진보를 이뤄냈다.
③ 핵폭탄과 종교적 광신주의를 포함한 문제가 비교적 더 멈추기 쉽다고 간주한다.
④ 우리는 세계 사회를 위협하는 문제들을 풀어야 할 필요가 있다고 하는 것은 과장이 아니다.
⑤ 우리는 늘어나는 인구에 충분한 자원을 제공할 수 있을 것 같지 않다.

해설 지문의 내용과 일치하지 않는 것을 묻는 문제이다. 지문의 후반에 핵무기와 사제 폭발물과 같은 무기들이 세계의 평화와 진보를 매일 위협하고 있다고 설명하고 있지만, 핵폭탄과 종교적 광신주의를 포함한 문제가 비교적 더 멈추기 쉽다고 간주한다는 내용은 지문에서 알 수 없다. 따라서 ③번이 정답이다.

오답 분석
① 지문의 In this first decade of the twenty-first century, the world community is confronted with staggering problems를 통해 세계 인구의 급속한 성장이 심각한 문제를 만들고 있음을 알 수 있다.
② 지문의 The twentieth century saw great advances in many fields, but these advances did not come without costs를 통해 상당한 비용을 통해 우리가 여러 영역에서 위대한 기술의 진보를 이루어 냈음을 알 수 있다.
④ 지문의 the people of the world need to stop the systemic despoiling of our planet을 통해 우리가 세계 사회를 위협하는 문제들을 풀어야 할 필요가 있다고 하는 것은 과장이 아니라는 것을 알 수 있다.
⑤ 지문의 Those people will need food, shelter, and an education that will allow them to lead fulfilled lives를 통해 늘어나는 사람들에게 충분한 자원을 제공할 수 있을 것 같지 않다는 것을 알 수 있다.

어휘 rapid adj. 급속한, 신속한   foreshadow v. 조짐을 보이다
deal with phr. 다루다   technical adj. 기술적인
relatively adv. 비교적으로   exaggeration n. 과장
resolve v. 풀다, 해결하다   issue n. 문제
resource n. 자원

[28-30]

정보 생태계를 오염시키는 데 이용되는 세 가지 범주의 콘텐츠가 있는데, 각각 허위정보, 오보, "유해 정보"이다. 피해를 야기하기 위해 고안된 거짓된 정보를 포함하는 허위 정보를 퍼뜨리는 사람은 보통 세 가지 목적 중 하나의 이유를 가지고 있는데, 이 세 가지 목적은 돈을 버는 것, 정치적 영향력을 얻는 것, 단순히 문제 유발 자체를 위한 것의 세 가지이다. 사람들이 그 정보가 거짓이거나 오해하게 하는 것인 줄 모르게 만드는 정보를 포함하는 오류정보의 유포자는 사회 심리학적 요인 때문에 정보를 유포하도록 이끌리게 된다. 이들은 소셜네트워크 플랫폼상에서 다른 사람들과의 유대감을 느끼기 위해 자신의 정체성을 내보이고 있다. 앞의 허위 정보는 사람들이 그것이 거짓인 줄 모른 채 공유하게 되면 오류 정보로 바뀌게 된다. 마지막으로, 새로운 용어인, "유해 정보"는 남들에게 피해를 주기 위해 공유되는 진짜 정보이다. 유해 정보의 사례에는 외국 첩보원들이 정치인들의 평판을 떨어뜨리기 위해 이메일을 해킹하여 사적인 비밀을 대중에 공개한 것과 같은 것들이 있다. 가장 효과적인 허위정보는 언제나 진실의 알맹이를 포함하고 있고, 실제로 지금 유포되고 있는 대부분의 정보는 거짓이 아니지만, 오해의 소지가 있는 정보이다. 영향을 미치는 첩보원들은 전체가 조작된 정보 대신에, 진짜 정보를 재가공하고 과장된 표제를 활용하고 있다.

disinformation n. 허위정보   misinformation n. 오보
malinformation n. 유해 정보
for the sake it phr. ~을 위해서
misleading adj. 오해의 소지가 있는

sociopsychological adj. 사회 심리학적인 intent n. 의도
agent n. 첩보원 leak v. 유출하다 reputation n. 평판
kernel n. 알맹이 disseminate v. 퍼뜨리다
fabricated adj. 조작된 reframe v. 다시 구성하다
hyperbolic adj. 과장법을 쓴

28 [2020 한국외대]

정답 ②

해석 ① 정치적인 ② 진짜의
③ 상상의 ④ 동기의

해설 빈칸에 들어갈 내용을 묻고 있다. 지문의 일곱 번째 문장에서, 유해 정보의 사례를 정치인의 이메일을 해킹하여 대중에 유출 시킨 사건으로 들고 있고, 바로 다음 문장에서, 가장 효과적인 허위정보는 항상 진실의 알맹이를 포함하고 있다고 했으므로, 빈칸에는 '진짜의'라는 의미의 genuine이 들어가는 것이 자연스럽다. 따라서 ②번이 정답이다.

29 [2020 한국외대]

정답 ④

해석 ① 일부 사람들은 허위정보를 단순히 문제를 유발하기 위해 퍼뜨린다.
② 오보를 퍼뜨리는 사람들은 그 정보가 거짓인 것을 인지하지 못한다.
③ 사회 심리학적 요인들이 오보의 유포를 돕고 있다.
④ 유해 정보에 의한 피해는 고의적이지 않다.

해설 지문의 내용과 일치하지 않는 것을 묻고 있다. 지문의 일곱 번째 문장에서 외국 첩보원들이 정치인의 평판을 떨어뜨리기 위해 이메일을 해킹하여 대중에 유출한 사례가 나와 있다. 이 사례를 통해 사람들이 특정한 의도를 가지고 유해 정보를 퍼뜨린다는 사실을 알 수 있으므로, 유해 정보에 의한 피해가 고의적이지 않다는 것은 지문의 내용과 다르다. 따라서 ④번이 정답이다.

오답 분석
① 지문의 두 번째 문장에서, 허위정보를 퍼뜨리는 사람들의 세 가지 목적 중 하나를 단순히 문제 유발 자체를 위해서라고 했으므로, 일부 사람들은 허위정보를 단순히 문제를 유발하기 위해 퍼뜨린다는 것은 지문의 내용과 일치한다.
② 지문의 세 번째 문장에서, 오보는 그 정보가 거짓이거나 오해의 여지가 있는 정보인 줄 모르는 사람들에 의해 공유된다고 했으므로, 오보를 퍼뜨리는 사람들은 그 정보가 거짓인 것을 인지하지 못한다는 것은 지문의 내용과 일치한다.
③ 지문의 세 번째 문장에서, 사람들은 사회 심리학적 요인 때문에 오보를 유포하도록 이끌린다고 했으므로, 사회 심리학적 요인들이 오보의 유포를 돕고 있다는 것은 지문의 내용과 일치한다.

어휘 unaware adj. 인지하지 못하는 purposeful adj. 고의적인

30 [2020 한국외대]

정답 ①

해석 ① 어떤 사람들을 해고하도록 만들기 위해 거짓된 이야기를 발표하기
② 누군가의 이메일을 해킹하고 그들의 사생활에서 충격스러운 사항들을 인터넷에 게재하기
③ 어떤 사람의 불법 활동에 대한 입증되지 않은 이야기를 믿고 트위터에 올리기
④ 불법 활동에 연루된 공직자에 대한 이야기를 조사하기

해설 허위정보의 사례로 적절한 것을 고르는 문제이다. 지문의 두 번째 문장에서, 피해를 야기하기 위해 고안된 거짓의 정보를 포함하는 정보를 허위정보라고 했으므로, 허위정보의 사례를 '어떤 사람들을 해고하도록 만들기 위해 거짓된 이야기를 발표하기'라고 표현한 ①번이 정답이다.

어휘 invented adj. 거짓된 lurid adj. 충격스러운
unverified adj. 입증되지 않은 investigate v. 조사하다
illegal adj. 불법적인

[31-32]

구글의 경영진은 여성이 생물학적인 이유로 기술적인 업무에는 적합하지 않다고 주장한 한 남성 기술자에 작성된 3,300자의 성명서에 대한 답변을 내놓았다. 그 문서는 한동안 구글사의 내부에서 회자되고 있었지만, Motherboard(온라인 매체)에 의해 공개되었다. Record(IT전문매체)와 Gizmodo(IT웹블로그)는 그 문서의 전체를 공개했다. 주말 동안, 구글사의 다양성 부사장인 Danielle Brown과 기술 담당 부사장인 Ari Balogh는 구글사의 직원들에게 보내는 개별 메시지에 그 논란이 되는 문서를 언급했다. 그들은 그 문서의 주장을 비난했고, 그리고 구글의 다양성을 위한 노력을 옹호했다. 그 문제는 즉시 소셜미디어상에서 치열한 논쟁을 불러일으켰다. CNN 기술팀의 신원을 밝히지 않은 그 문서의 작성자는 소문에 의하면 구글에서 일하는 소프트웨어 기술직의 평사원인 것으로 알려졌다. 그는 구글에 여성 기술자들이 더 많지 않은 것은 남자들이 "신분 상승에 대한 더 높은 욕구"가 있기 때문이라고 주장했다.

executive n. 임원, 고위 간부 manifesto n. 성명서, 포고문
suited adj. 적당한 biological adj. 생물학적인
circulate v. 순환하다, 퍼지다
diversity n. 다양성, 차이, 변화
address v. 말을 걸다, 편지를 보내다, 중점적으로 다루다
controversial adj. 논쟁이 되는
ignite v. 불을 붙이다, 점화하다 fierce adj. 사나운, 치열한
reportedly adv. 소문에 의하면
rank-and-file adj. 평사원의, 일반인의
contend v. 주장하다, 옹호하다 status n. 자격, 지위, 신분

31 2018 광운대

정답 ⑤

해석 기술직원의 반다양성 성명서에 대한 구글의 폭풍
① 성 ② 임원
③ 외국인에 대한 혐오 ④ 환경
⑤ 반다양성

해설 지문의 제목을 묻는 문제이다. 주어진 글은 여성이 생물학적인 이유로 기술직에 부적합하다는 글에 대한 구글사의 반대 입장을 나타낸 글인데, 단순히 여성에 대한 성차별에 관한 것이 아니라 사내에서 다양성(diversity)을 추구하는 구글사의 노력에 대한 전반적인 제목이 되는 것이 자연스럽다. 또한 지문에서 성(sex)차별에 대한 말보다는 다양성(diversity) 추구라는 말이 더 자주 언급되므로 Gender보다 Anti-Diversity가 빈칸에 더 적절하다. 따라서 빈칸에 '반다양성'을 넣어 이 지문이 제목을 '기술직원의 반다양성 성명서에 대한 구글의 폭풍'이라고 한 ⑤번이 정답이다.

어휘 xenophobia n. 외국인에 대한 혐오

32 2018 광운대

정답 ③

해석 ① 그들은 그 문제에 대한 치열한 논쟁을 마무리 지었다.
② 그들은 구글사의 고용정책을 비난했다.
③ 그들은 그 문서의 주장을 비난했다.
④ 그들은 아무것도 아닌 것에서 큰 거래(타협)을 하는 데 능숙하다
⑤ 그들은 단순한 소프트웨어 기술자로 자신들의 경력을 시작했다.

해설 지문의 빈칸을 채우는 문제이다. 빈칸의 뒤에 순접의 접속사 'and'가 있으므로, 뒤의 다양성을 위한 구글의 노력을 옹호했다는 내용이 있으므로, 빈칸에는 그 성명서의 내용을 비판하는 문장이 들어가는 것이 자연스럽다. 따라서 '그들은 그 문서의 주장을 비난했다'고 한 ③번이 정답이다.

[33-34]

나는 남부 플로리다에서 내가 만났던 해수면 상승에 대해 전혀 걱정하지 않는 것처럼 보였던 모든 사람들에게 물었다. 어떻게 하는 게 좋을까? 네덜란드의 4분의 1 이상이 해수면 아래에 있고 그 지역들은 수백만 명의 고향이라서, 낮은 고도에서의 생활은 분명히 있음 직하다. 하지만 남부 플로리다의 지질은 특히 다루기 어렵다. 다공성 석회석에 제방을 짓는 것은 터널 위에 울타리를 놓는 것과 같다. 그것은 이동 경로는 바꾸지만, 꼭 양을 바꾸는 것은 아니다.
John Oliver는 "당신은 해안에 제방을 짓고 물을 막을 수는 없어요. 물은 그냥 지하로 올 거예요."라고 표현한다.
몇몇 사람들은 나에게 남부 플로리다에 대한 현실적인 조치는 철수라고 말했다.
남부 마이애미의 시장인 Philip Stoddard는 "저는 공원 맞은편에 살아요. 그리고 그곳에는 비가 올 때 가득 차는 저지대가 있어요. 저는 오늘 아침에 그곳에서 개를 산책시키다가 그 안에 있는 물고기를 보았어요. 도대체 그 물고기가 어디서 왔겠어요? 지하에서 온 거예요. 우리에게 지하에서 돌아다니는 물고기가 있는 거죠!"라고 나에게 말했다.
Philip Stoddard는 계속 이어서 "그게 의미하는 건 물이 들어가지 않게 할 수는 없다는 거예요. 그러니까 결국 이 지역에서 인구를 줄여야 하는 거죠. 저는 갑작스럽고 비극적인 인구 감소 대신에 천천히 우아한 인구 감소를 위해 노력하고 싶어요."라고 말했다.

---

sea level phr. 해수면 elevation n. 고도
geology n. 지질 intractable adj. 다루기 어려운
dike n. 제방, 둑 porous adj. 다공성의, 투과성의
limestone n. 석회석 fence n. 울타리, 장애물
alter v. 바꾸다 not necessarily phr. 꼭 ~은 아닌
levee n. (강가의) 제방, 부두 underground adv. 지하에서
realistic adj. 현실적인 retreat n. 철수, 후퇴
mayor n. 시장 ultimately adv. 궁극적으로
depopulate v. 인구를 줄이다 graceful adj. 우아한
depopulation n. 인구 감소
catastrophic adj. 비극적인, 대변동의

33 2019 성균관대

정답 ⑤

해석 ① 이 주변에 사세요?
② 어디서 살고 싶으세요?
③ 왜 여기서 사세요?
④ 해수면을 알고 계세요?
⑤ 어떻게 하는 게 좋을까요?

해설 지문의 빈칸을 채우는 문제이다. 첫 번째 문장에서 남부 플로리다에서 만났던 모든 사람들이 해수면 상승에 대해 전혀 걱정하지 않는 것처럼 보였다고 했으므로, 빈칸에는 어떻게 하는 게 좋을지에 대해 묻는 내용이 나와야 적절하다는 것을 알 수 있다. 따라서 '어떻게 하는 게 좋을까요?'라고 한 ⑤번이 정답이다.

어휘 be conscious of phr. ~을 알고 있다, 자각하다

34 2019 성균관대

정답 ②

해석 ① 더 이상 관광객들을 끌어모으지 못할 것이다
② 사람이 살 수 없는 곳이 될 것이다
③ 네덜란드처럼 개발할 것이다
④ 바다에 둘러싸일 것이다
⑤ 바다 동물들에게 천국이 될 것이다

해설 지문을 통해 남부 플로리다에 대해 추론할 수 있는 것을 고르는 문제이다. 지문의 후반에서 남부 마이애미의 시장인 Philip Stoddard가 결국 이 지역에서 인구를 줄여야 한다고 했으므로, 남부 플로리다는 사람이 살 수 없는 곳이 될 것이라는 것을 추론할 수 있다. 따라서 ②번이 정답이다.

오답 분석
① 남부 플로리다가 더 이상 관광객들을 끌어모으지 못할 것인지에 대해서는 언급되지 않았다.
③ 첫 번째 문단에서 네덜란드의 4분의 1 이상이 해수면 아래에 있고 그 지역들은 수백만 명의 고향이라서, 낮은 고도에서의 생활은 분명히 있음직하다고는 했지만, 남부 플로리다를 네덜란드처럼 개발할 것인지는 알 수 없다.
④ 남부 플로리다가 바다에 둘러싸일 것인지에 대해서는 언급되지 않았다.
⑤ 남부 플로리다가 바다 동물들에게 천국이 될 것인지에 대해서는 언급되지 않았다.

어휘 uninhabitable adj. 사람이 살 수 없는, 주거하기에 부적합한
paradise n. 천국, 낙원

[35-37]

텔레비전 진행자인 Mike Rowe는 미국의 기술 격차를 줄이길 원한다. 지금 당장, 미국에는 7백만 개 이상의 일자리가 있고 그 일자리들을 채울 수 있는 웬만큼 충분히 자격을 갖춘 노동자가 없다. 현재, 고등학생의 겨우 9퍼센트만이 무역 관련 직업을 찾으려고 한다. 이것을 바꾸기 위해, Rowe는 우리가 좋은 직업이라고 생각하는 것에 대한 인식을 바꿔야 한다고 말한다. 우리는 또한 젊은 사람들에게 자신의 열정을 따르라고 말하지 말아야 한다. "우리는 젊은 사람들에게 10대에 너의 열정을 확실하게 찾는 것이 행복해질 수 있는 유일한 길이라고 말하지 말아야 합니다." Rowe는 이런 '열정을 따르는 사고방식'을 따르는 것은 일반적으로 "젊은 사람들이 어디에 도착하든지 행복과 성취감을 느끼기 시작하도록" 값비싼 학업과 훈련의 기나긴 길 아래로 보낸다. 그가 말하길, 많은 사람은 아무런 좋은 직업 선택도 가지지 못한 채, 결국 학자금 대출의 빚에 허덕이게 된다. 대신에, Rowe는 기회를 찾고 나서 그 안으로 열정을 가져가라고 젊은 사람들에게 조언한다.

presenter n. 진행자, 사회자, 발표자
job opening phr. (빈) 일자리   qualified adj. 자격을 갖춘
currently adv. 현재   pursue v. 찾다, 추구하다
mindset n. 사고방식   typically adv. 일반적으로, 전형적으로
fulfilled adj. 성취감을 느끼는   land v. 도착하다, 착륙하다
student loan phr. 학자금 대출   debt n. 빚

35 2019 한국외대

정답 ①

해석
① 좋은 직업은 반드시 자신이 열정적이어야 하는 것은 아니다.
② 좋은 직업을 찾는 것은 열정이 필요하다.
③ 무역 관련 직업은 학생들 사이에서 인기가 늘어나고 있다.
④ Rowe는 10대들이 일하기 위해 먼저 열정을 찾기를 원한다.

해설 지문의 내용과 일치하는 것을 묻는 문제이다. 지문의 마지막에서 We also need to stop telling young people to follow their passion의 내용을 통해 좋은 직업은 반드시 자신이 열정적이어야 하는 것은 아니라는 것을 알 수 있다. 따라서 ①번이 지문의 내용과 일치한다.

오답 분석
② 우리는 또한 젊은 사람들에게 자신의 열정을 따르라고 말하지 말아야 한다고 했으므로, 좋은 직업을 찾는 것은 열정이 필요하다는 것은 지문의 내용과 다르다.
③ 고등학생의 겨우 9퍼센트만이 무역 관련 직업을 찾으려고 한다고 했으므로, 무역 관련 직업은 학생들 사이에서 인기가 늘어나고 있다는 것은 지문의 내용과 다르다.
④ Rowe는 기회를 찾고 나서 그 안으로 열정을 가져가라고 젊은 사람들에게 조언한다고 했으므로, Rowe가 10대들이 일하기 위해 먼저 열정을 찾기를 원한다는 것은 지문의 내용과 다르다.

어휘 not necessarily phr. 반드시 ~인 것은 아니다
passionate adj. 열정적인   popularity n. 인기

36 2019 한국외대

정답 ②

해석
① 열정은 고정적이고 영원한 것이다.
② 기회는 열정보다 더 중요하다.
③ 새로운 직장에서 열정으로 아무런 이익을 볼 수 없다.
④ 인생에서 열정은 필요가 없다.

해설 밑줄 친 to follow opportunity and then to take their passion with them의 의미를 추론하는 문제이다. 밑줄이 포함된 문장의 앞 문장에서 돈을 많이 벌기 위해 열정만을 따르다 보면 학업이나 훈련에 큰 비용이 들고 결국에는 학자금 대출의 빚에 허덕인다고 말하고 있다. 따라서, 밑줄 친 문장의 의미를 '기회는 열정보다 더 중요하다'라고 한 ②번이 정답이다.

어휘 stationary adj. 고정적인, 움직이지 않는
permanent adj. 영원한, 영구적인   benefit n. 이익, 이득

37 2019 한국외대

정답 ②

해석
① 대학교에 가지 못할 것이다.
② 많은 돈을 빚지게 될 것이다.
③ 더 많은 직업 선택이 있을 것이다.
④ 성공할 기회가 주어질 것이다.

해설 어린 나이에 열정을 쫓는 것의 잠재적인 결과를 찾는 문제이다. 지문 마지막에 열정을 쫓는 사고방식은 많은 사람을 아무

런 좋은 직업 선택도 가지지 못한 채, 결국 학자금 대출의 빚에 허덕이게 만든다고 설명하고 있다. 따라서 정답은 ②번이다.

어휘 university n. 대학교   owe v. 빚지다
succeed v. 성공하다

[38-39]

당신의 몸에 웹사이트 주소에 문신을 새기시겠습니까? 유타에서 온 한 여자가 바로 그렇게 했다. 한 회사가 그녀에게 1만 달러에 그들의 웹사이트 주소를 그녀의 이마에 문신을 새겼다. 그녀는 아들의 교육비를 마련하기 위해 그렇게 하기를 원했다. 그 회사는 값싼 광고 지면을 위해 그녀가 그렇게 하기를 원했다. 뉴스에 그 이야기가 나왔기 때문에 그들은 또한 무료로 광고를 한 것이다. 게릴라 마케팅으로 알려진 이런 종류의 <u>극단적인</u> 광고는 상품을 광고하고 사람들의 관심을 끌기 위해 놀라운 방법들을 이용한다.

게릴라 마케팅으로 광고하는 방법은 <u>예상치 못한</u> 방법으로 환경을 이용하는 것이다. 예를 들어, 몇 년 전에 한 유명 사탕 회사는 공원 벤치를 칠해서 거대한 초콜릿 바처럼 보이게 했다. 이 창의적인 광고 전략은 긍정적인 방식으로 소비자들의 관심을 끌었다.

모든 게릴라 마케팅이 효과가 있는 것은 아니다. 2007년, 한 광고 회사는 텔레비전 쇼를 광고하기 위해 여러 도시들 주변에 번쩍이는 전구가 있는 표지판을 설치하기로 결정했다. 하지만 보스턴에서 경찰은 그 표지판이 폭탄이라고 생각했다. 경찰은 모든 표지판을 찾아내서 없애버리려고 했다.

전통적인 광고 전략을 쓰는 사람들과 달리 게릴라 마케팅 담당자들은 사람들에게 충격을 주는 것을 두려워하지 않는다. 그 아이디어는 사람들이 제품에 대해 이야기하도록 설득하기 위함이다. 하지만 사람들이 어떻게 반응할지에 대해 고민하는 것이 기업들에 중요하다. 모든 광고가 항상 좋은 광고인 것은 아니다.

tattoo v. 문신을 새기다   forehead n. 이마
advertising space phr. 광고지면   publicity n. 광고, 홍보
attention n. 관심, 주목   environment n. 환경
strategy n. 전략   flash v. 번쩍이다
traditional adj. 전통적인   convince v. 설득하다

38 [2020 국민대]

정답 ④

해석 ① 안전한 — 예상한
② 안전한 — 예상치 못한
③ 극단적인 — 예상한
④ 극단적인 — 예상치 못한

해설 지문의 빈칸을 채우는 문제이다. 첫 번째 빈칸의 앞 문장들은 이마에 웹사이트 주소를 문신으로 새긴 광고의 예시이므로, 첫 번째 빈칸에는 이러한 예시와 같은 광고의 종류인 게릴라 마케팅의 성격이 어떠한지에 대한 내용이 나와야 적절하다는 것을 알 수 있다. 따라서 '극단적인'이 들어가야 한다. 두 번째 빈칸의 뒤 문장들은 공원 벤치를 초콜릿 바로 보이게 칠해서 광고한 예시이므로 두 번째 빈칸에는 이러한 예시와 같은 게릴라 마케팅의 광고 방법이 어떠한지에 관한 내용이 나와야 적절하다는 것을 알 수 있다. 따라서 '예상치 못한'이 들어가야 한다. 따라서 ④ extreme — unexpected가 정답이다.

39 [2020 국민대]

정답 ②

해석 ① 한 여성이 자신의 홍보를 위해 회사의 웹사이트 주소를 이마에 문신을 새겼다.
② 게릴라 마케팅은 제품을 홍보하기 위해 틀에 박히지 않은 이목을 끄는 전략들을 사용한다.
③ 회사들은 항상 성공을 가져오기 때문에 게릴라 마케팅을 선호한다.
④ 나쁜 광고조차도 제품을 광고하는 데 있어서는 좋은 광고이다.

해설 지문의 내용과 일치하는 것을 묻는 문제이다. 지문 첫 문단의 마지막 문장에서 게릴라 마케팅으로 알려진 광고는 상품을 광고하고 사람들의 관심을 끌기 위해 놀라운 방법들을 이용한다는 내용을 통해 게릴라 마케팅은 제품을 홍보하기 위해 틀에 박히지 않은 이목을 끄는 전략들을 사용한다는 것을 알 수 있다. 따라서 ②번이 지문의 내용과 일치한다.

오답 분석
① 그녀는 아들의 교육비를 마련하기 위해 그렇게 하기(자신의 이마에 회사 웹사이트 주소를 문신으로 새긴 것)를 원했다고 했으므로, 한 여성이 자신의 홍보를 위해 회사의 웹사이트 주소를 이마에 문신을 새겼다는 것은 지문의 내용과 다르다.
③ 모든 게릴라 마케팅이 효과가 있는 것은 아니라고 했으므로, 회사들은 항상 성공을 가져오기 때문에 게릴라 마케팅을 선호한다는 것은 지문의 내용과 다르다.
④ 모든 광고가 항상 좋은 광고인 것은 아니라고 했으므로, 나쁜 광고조차도 제품을 광고하는 데 있어서는 좋은 광고라는 것은 지문의 내용과 다르다.

어휘 promote v. 홍보하다
unconventional adj. 틀에 박히지 않은, 독특한
attention-getting adj. 이목을 끄는   market v. 광고하다

[40-42]

[A] 여성은 일반적으로 남성보다 극심한 기후 사건에 더욱 취약하고, 부유한 여성보다 가난한 여성이 더 취약하다. 이것은 기후에 민감한 천연자원 활동에의 그들의 불균형적인 관여 때문이고, 이는 새로운 농업 기술, 안정적인 토지 소유권, 천연자원 사용에 대한 의사 결정, 그리고 농업 외 소득 창출을 위한 가능성에 제한적인 접근 기회와 결합되어 있다.

[B] 성별 배제는 보통 새로운 기술의 도입으로 인해 악화되고, 남성은 여성보다 더 높은 비율로 이익을 손에 넣는다. 예를 들어, 생식질 향상, 토양 비옥도 관리, 그리고 토양과 용수 보존법 적용 비율에 관한 상호 기술 설문 조사에서, Kingamkono는 고작 5퍼센트를 차지하는 여성과 비교하여 비율의 95퍼센트가 남성이었고, 정보 교환이 성별을 따라 발생하는 경향이 있다는 것을 발견했다. [하지만, 잠비아에서의 개선된 휴한지 관리 사례와 같이, "성 중립적인" 천연자원 관리(NRM) 혁신의 성공적인 사례가 있다.] 기후 변화가 용수와 토지 자원에 미칠 예상되는 영향을 고려하면 농촌에서의 여성 노동 부담이 틀림없이 늘어날 것이다. 이것은 더 나아가 가정용 장작과 용수를 모으는 여성의 능력에 악영향을 미칠 수 있다.

[C] 적응 전략들은 여성의 고유한 취약성, 가정용 식량 확보에서의 여성의 역할, 그리고 사회적 자본에 접근하기 위해 여성이 사용하는 네트워크를 알아야 한다. 따라서 성별에 따른 취약성을 해결하는 것은 특별히 여성의 자원 수요와 능력을 겨냥한 정책을 만들도록 요구하는데, 예를 들자면, 천연자원 관리에 관한 의사결정 과정에 있어서 여성에게 권한을 부여하고, 여성 농업 연구원의 역량을 기르는 것과 같이 성별에 따른 지식 전달을 개선하고, 기술과 다양화 활동을 여성의 능력에 직접 맞추는 것이다.

[D] 소액금융 지원 혁명은 농촌의 소기업을 통해 여성에게 권한을 부여하는 상당한 진보에 선도 역을 해왔다. 홍수와 가뭄이 발생하기 쉬운 지역의 취약한 집단을 겨냥한 소액금융 지원을 포함하기 위한 이 노력을 지속하고 확장해나가는 것은 취약한 집단이 기후에 민감한 활동에서 벗어나 가지각색의 작물을 생산하도록 도울 것이다.

vulnerable adj. 취약한 disproportionate adj. 불균형인
natural resource phr. 천연자원 agricultural adj. 농업의
tenure n. 소유 generation n. 발생, 생성
exclusion n. 배제 exacerbate v. 악화시키다
germplasm n. 생식질 fertility n. 비옥도
fallow n. 휴한지(일정 기간 경작을 하지 않고 있는 토지)
impinge v. 악영향을 미치다 fuelwood n. 장작
social capital phr. 사회적 자본 empower v. 권한을 주다
capacity n. 역량, 능력 extension agent phr. 농업 연구원
diversification n. 다양화 micro-finance n. 소액금융 지원
usher v. 선도 역을 하다 sustain v. 지속하다
diversify v. 가지각색의 작물을 생산하다

40 [2019 아주대]

정답 ①

해석 ① 적응 정책에 성별을 요인으로 포함하기
② 여성의 단체 행위 개선하기
③ 시골 지역에서 정보에의 접근과 지식 보급 향상하기
④ 여성의 농업 성과 개선하기
⑤ 적응에 관한 우선 사항들을 성 연구에 통합시키기

해설 지문의 제목을 묻는 문제이다. 지문 전체적으로 여성이 남성보다 기후에 민감한 천연자원 활동에서 취약하므로, 적응 전략들은 여성의 고유한 취약성을 겨냥하여 만들어져야 한다고 설명하고 있다. 따라서 이 지문의 제목을 '적응 정책에 성별을 요인으로 포함하기'라고 표현한 ①번이 정답이다.

어휘 factor into phr. ~을 요인으로 포함하다
dissemination n. 보급 integrate v. 통합시키다
priority n. 우선 사항

41 [2019 아주대]

정답 ③

해석 ① 지연되다 ② 심하게 비난받다
③ 악화되다 ④ 계획되다
⑤ 지연되다

해설 밑줄 친 exacerbated를 대신할 수 있는 동의어를 고르는 문제이다. exacerbate는 '악화시키다'라는 의미이다. 따라서 '악화시키다'를 의미하는 aggravate의 과거분사형인 ③번 aggravated가 정답이다.

어휘 impede v. 지연시키다 chastise v. 심하게 비난하다
aggravate v. 악화시키다 meditate v. 계획하다
retard v. 지연시키다

42 [2019 아주대]

정답 ②

해석 ① 기후 사건들에 대한 여성의 취약성은 천연자원 활동에 대한 제한된 접근 기회가 원인이다.
② Kingamkono는 신기술과 정보 교환 적용 비율이 성 중립적이라는 것을 밝혔다.
③ 적응 정책은 사회 자본에 접근하기 위한 여성의 네트워크를 고려해야 한다.
④ 여성의 자원 능력을 겨냥한 정책을 만드는 것은 의사결정 과정에서 여성에게 권한을 부여하는 것을 포함한다.
⑤ 홍수와 가뭄이 발생하기 쉬운 지역의 취약한 사람들을 위한 소액금융 지원 혁명은 그들이 기후 중립적인 활동을 추구할 수 있도록 도울 것이다.

해설 지문의 내용과 일치하지 않는 것을 묻는 문제이다. ②번의 키워드인 adoption rates(적용 비율)가 그대로 언급된 지문 주변에서, 새로운 기술 적용 비율에 관한 상호 기술 설문 조사에서, Kingamkono는 고작 5퍼센트를 차지하는 여성과 비교하여 비율의 95퍼센트가 남성이었고, 정보 교환이 성별을 따라 발생하는 경향이 있다는 것을 발견했다고 했으므로, Kingamkono가 신기술과 정보 교환 적용 비율이 성 중립적이라는 것을 밝혔다는 것은 지문의 내용과 다르다. 따라서 ②번이 지문의 내용과 일치하지 않는다.

오답 분석 ① [A] 문단의 두 번째 문장 This is due to their disproportionate involvement in climate-sensitive natural resource activities를 통해 '기후 사건들에 대한 여성의 취약성은 천연자원 활동에 대한 제한된 접근 기회가 원인이다'라는 것을 알 수 있다.

③ [C] 문단의 첫 번째 문장 Adaptation strategies need to recognize ~ the networks they use to access social capital.을 통해 '적응 정책은 사회 자본에 접근하기 위한 여성의 네트워크를 고려해야 한다'는 것을 알 수 있다.

④ [C] 문단의 두 번째 문장 Addressing vulnerabilities ~ such as empowering women in NRM decision-making processes를 통해 '여성의 자원 능력을 겨냥한 정책을 만드는 것은 의사결정 과정에서 여성에게 권한을 부여하는 것을 포함한다'는 것을 알 수 있다.

⑤ [D] 문단의 마지막 문장 Sustaining and ~ climate-sensitive activities.를 통해 '홍수와 가뭄이 발생하기 쉬운 지역의 취약한 사람들을 위한 소액금융 지원 혁명은 그들이 기후 중립적인 활동을 추구할 수 있도록 도울 것이다'라는 것을 알 수 있다.

어휘 vulnerability n. 취약성 attributable v. ~가 원인이다
take into consideration phr. ~을 고려하다
pursue v. 추구하다

[43-44]

아프리카에 있는 세계에서 가장 빠르게 성장하는 몇몇 국가의 존재는 아프리카에 생기고 있는 담화 소재이다. 나이지리아, 케냐, 남아프리카, 앙골라 등의 수도를 걸어 다니는 것은 아프리카가 상당한 속도로 부흥하고 있다는 그 담화를 사람들에게 각인시킬 것이다. 크레인으로 가득한 지평선, 도로망과 철도선 건설, 주요 마을과 도시 전역에서 생기고 있는 수억 달러의 저택과 상점가, 그리고 증가하는 기술은 아프리카 대륙의 번영을 향한 오르막의 그저 몇 가지 암시일 뿐이다. [A] 그러나 전 세계의 사람들이 아프리카 대륙이 얼마나 빠르게 성장하고 있는지에 대한 논의에 참여하는 바로 그 순간에, 반어적으로, 이 담화와 관련된 다른 담화는 아프리카 대륙에 깊이 뿌리박힌 가난을 해결하려고 여전히 노력하고 있는 놀랄 만한 사람들의 수이다. 한 사람은 아프리카에 아직도 부자와 가난한 사람 간의 큰 격차가 있는 이유와 아프리카가 전 세계에서 수요가 많은 원자재의 상당 비율을 차지하는 생산지라는 사실에도 불구하고 여전히 가난과 고군분투하고 있는 이유를 궁금해할 뿐이다. [B] 다보스에서 열린 세계 경제포럼 중에, 아프리카의 지도자들은 아프리카 강화가 미래에 아프리카 대륙의 성장에 도움이 될 것이라고 주장했다. 지도자들에 따르면, 아프리카 강화는 일자리를 만들고, 산업화와 산업 확장을 일으킬 것이다. [C] 아프리카 강화는 그 대륙의 성장에 많은 기여를 할 수 있겠지만, 우리는 아프리카가 장기적으로 성장하려면 발전에 대한 모든 장애물을 해결하는 종합적인 방안들을 추구해야 할 것이라고 주장한다. 우리는 정부가 개혁 분야가 무엇인지를 알기 위해서 우선 아프리카가 오랫동안 발전을 저지당한 이유를 알아야 할 것이라고 주장한다. 여기서, 우리는 아프리카가 번영에 관해서 세계의 다른 나라들과 동등해지기 위해 주의를 기울여야 하는 사안들을 분류했다. 테러와 같은 내전이 가난의 한 원인이 된다는 주장은 이해하기 쉽다. 전쟁은 사람들을 혼란시키고 빈곤하게 한다. 전쟁은 또한 산업을 고객으로부터 단절시킨다. 게다가, 도로와 통신망은 파괴되거나 막히고, 이것은 이러한 산업들이 더욱 제대로 기능을 못 하게 한다. 산업은 붕괴하고, 사람들은 직업을 잃고, 투자자들은 타격을 입은 국가에 대한 확신을 잃기 때문에 피해를 입은 그 지역을 경기 후퇴로 끌어내린다. [D] 그러고 나면, 당연히, 아프리카에는 죽음의 흔적과 전쟁과 테러로 망가진 지역들의 빈곤선 상승에 보태는 재산의 상실은 물론이고 부상한 채로 남겨진 많은 사람이 있게 된다.

fodder n. 소재 narrative n. 담화 discourse n. 담화
significant adj. 상당한 erupt v. 발발하다, 폭발하다
ascent n. 오르막, 진보, 향상 prosperity n. 번영
go hand in hand phr. 관련되다
astounding adj. 놀랄 만한
grapple with phr. ~을 해결하려고 노력하다
raw materials phr. 원자재 industrialization n. 산업화
assort v. 분류하다, 구분하다
contribute v. ~의 한 원인이 되다
no-brainer n. 알기 쉬운 것 disorient v. 혼란시키다
destitute adj. 빈곤한 bar v. 막다, 금하다
cripple v. 제대로 기능을 못 하게 하다
affected adj. 피해를 입은
economic slope phr. 경기 후퇴, 불경기 property n. 재산
poverty level phr. 빈곤선 mar v. 망치다, 손상시키다

43 2019 중앙대

정답 ③

해설 지문의 흐름상 주어진 문장이 들어가기에 가장 적절한 위치를 고르는 문제이다. [C]의 앞 문장에서 아프리카 강화는 일자리를 만들고, 산업화와 산업 확장을 일으킬 것이라고 했으므로, [C] 자리에 아프리카 강화가 성장에 많은 기여를 할 수 있겠지만, 아프리카가 장기적인 성장을 하고 개혁 분야가 무엇인지 알기 위해 해야 할 일을 설명하는 주어진 문단이 들어가야 글의 흐름이 자연스럽게 연결된다. 따라서 ③번이 정답이다.

어휘 sustainably adv. 장기적으로
comprehensive adj. 종합적인 methodology n. 방안
bottleneck n. 장애물 contend v. 주장하다
reform n. 개혁, 개선 hold back phr. 저지하다, 억제하다

44 2019 중앙대

정답 ④

해석 ① 따라서 ― ~와 불화하여
② 궁극적으로 ― ~와 대조적으로
③ 전적으로 ― ~와 경쟁하여
④ 반어적으로 ― ~와 동등한

해설 지문의 빈칸을 채우는 문제이다. 첫 번째 빈칸의 경우, 빈칸 앞 문장은 전 세계의 사람들이 아프리카 대륙이 얼마나 빠르게 성장하고 있는지에 대한 논의에 참여한다는 내용이고, 빈칸 뒤 문장은 이 담화와 관련된 다른 담화는 아프리카 대륙에 깊게 뿌리박힌 가난을 해결하려고 여전히 노력하고 있는 놀라운 사람들의 수라는 내용이다. 따라서 역설적인 상황을 나타내는 '역설적으로'라는 의미의 ironically가 들어가는 것이 자연스럽다. 두 번째 빈칸의 경우, 빈칸 앞부분에서 장기적인 성장과 개혁을 위해 아프리카가 해야 할 일을 언급했으므로, 빈칸에는 앞 내용이 아프리카가 세계의 다른 나라들과 어떤 관계가 되기 위해 주의를 기울여야 하는 사안들인지에 대한 내용이 나와야 적절하다는 것을 알 수 있다. 따라서 '~와 동등한'이라는 의미의 at par with가 들어가는 것이 자연스럽다. 따라서 ④ ironically — at par with가 정답이다.

어휘 consequently adv. 따라서 ultimately adv. 궁극적으로
absolutely adv. 전적으로
ironically adv. 역설적으로, 얄궂게도

[45-47]

역설적으로, 더 많은 양의 정보가 순환할수록, 우리는 그 정보를 평가하기 위한 세평적인 장치에 더 많이 의존한다. 이것을 역설적으로 만드는 것은 바로 우리가 오늘날 가지고 있는 엄청나게 증가한 정보와 지식의 접근 권한이 우리에게 능력을 주거나 인지적으로 우리를 더 자율적으로 만들지 않는다는 것이다. 오히려, 우리가 받는 다른 사람들이 내린 정보의 평가에 우리를 더 의존적으로 만든다. 우리는 지식에 대한 관계의 근본적인 인식 체계의 변환인 '정보의 시대'로부터 '평판의 시대'로 이어지는 가운데에 있다. 정보는 다른 사람에 의해 이미 걸러지고, 평가되고, 언급되었을 때에만 가치가 있을 것이다. 이 점에 비추어 보면, 평판이라는 것은 지식에 대한 문지기이고, 그 문을 열 수 있는 열쇠는 다른 사람이 쥐고 있다. 이제 지식의 권위가 구축되는 방법은 우리 대부분이 모르고 있는 다른 사람의 불가피하게 편향된 판단에 우리를 의존하게 만든다. 디지털 시대의 성숙한 시민이 능숙해야 하는 것은 뉴스의 진실성을 비추고 확인하는 것이 아니다. 오히려, 사람들은 질문에 대한 정보의 평판 경로를 재구성하고, 그 정보를 순환시킨 사람의 의도를 평가하고, 그 정보에 신뢰성을 부여한 권위들의 의제를 알아내는 것에 능숙해야 한다.

paradoxically adv. 역설적으로 circulate v. 순환시키다
rely on phr. ~에 의존하다
reputational adj. 세평적인, 평판의 device n. 장치
evaluate v. 평가하다 vastly adv. 엄청나게, 대단히
cognitively adv. 인지적으로 autonomous adj. 자율적인
render v. 만들다 dependent adj. 의존적인
fundamental adj. 근본적인, 기초적인
paradigm shift phr. 인식 체계의 변화
comment v. 언급하다 gatekeeper n. 문지기
authority n. 권위, 권력, 당국
construct v. 구축하다, 건설하다 reliant adj. 의존하는

inevitably adv. 불가피하게
biased adj. 편향된, 선입견이 있는 judgment n. 판단
mature adj. 성숙한 competent adj. 능숙한
confirm v. 확인하다 veracity n. 진실성
figure out phr. 알아내다 agenda n. 의제
credibility n. 신뢰성

45 2019 한국외대

정답 ③

해석 ① 더 많은 정보에 접근 권한을 가지는 것은 더 나은 판단을 가능하게 한다.
② 집단지성의 역할은 과소평가되고 있다.
③ 정보원의 평판과 의제를 알아내는 것은 중요하다
④ 평판으로부터 정보로의 인식체계의 변화는 진행 중이다.

해설 지문의 내용과 일치하는 것을 묻는 문제이다. 지문의 마지막에서 they should be competent at reconstructing the reputational path ~ figuring out the agendas of those authorities that gave it credibility의 내용을 통해 사람들이 정보원의 평판과 의제를 알아내는 것이 중요한 것이라는 것을 알 수 있다. 따라서 ③번이 지문의 내용과 일치한다.

오답 ① 더 많은 양의 정보가 순환할수록 그 정보를 평가하기 위해서 우리가 세평적인 장치에 더 많이 의존한다고는 했지만, 더 많은 정보에 접근 권한을 가지는 것이 더 나은 판단을 가능하게 하는지는 알 수 없다.
② 우리는 다른 사람들이 내린 정보의 평가에 더 의존적으로 된다고는 했지만, 집단지성의 역할이 과소평가되고 있는지는 알 수 없다.
④ 우리는 지식에 대한 관계의 근본적인 인식 체계의 변환인 '정보의 시대'로부터 '평판의 시대'로 이어지는 가운데에 있다고 했으므로, 평판으로부터 정보로의 인식체계의 변화는 진행 중이라는 것은 지문의 내용과 다르다.

어휘 collective intelligence phr. 집단지성
underestimate v. 과소평가하다
determine v. 알아내다, 결정하다
informant n. 정보원, 정보 제공자 ongoing adj. 진행 중인

46 2019 한국외대

정답 ②

해석 ① 간청하다 — 인상
② 능력을 주다 — 평가
③ 가능하게 하다 — 예감
④ 해방시키다 — 판단

해설 지문의 빈칸을 채우는 문제이다. 첫 번째 빈칸의 경우 다음 문장에서 우리가 다른 사람들에 의한 정보에 훨씬 더 의존적으로 된다고 했으므로, '우리가 오늘날 가지고 있는 엄청나게 증가한 정보와 지식의 접근 권한이 우리에게 _____

인지적으로 우리를 더 자율적으로 만들지 않는다는 것이다' 라는 문맥에서 첫 번째 빈칸에는 '능력을 주다'라는 의미의 empower가 적합하다. 두 번째 빈칸의 경우 지문의 중간에서 정보는 다른 사람에 의해 이미 걸러지고, 평가되고, 언급되었을 때에만 가치가 있을 것이라고 했으므로, '우리가 받는 다른 사람들이 내린 정보의 _____ 에 우리를 더 의존적으로 만든다'라는 문맥에서 두 번째 빈칸에는 '평가'라는 의미의 evaluations가 적합하다. 따라서 ②번이 정답이다.

어휘 entreat v. 간청하다 empower v. 능력을 주다, 권한을 주다
 enable v. 가능하게 하다 premonition n. 예감
 extricate v. 해방시키다 estimation n. 판단

47 [2019 한국외대]

정답 ②

해석 ① 평판은 지식의 문을 통제하며, 다른 사람들은 더 똑똑하다.
② 평판은 다른 사람들에 의해 통제되는데, 지식의 접근 권한을 통제한다.
③ 지식을 구성하는 것 이상의 권위는 공정한 과학자들에 의해 집단으로 규제된다.
④ 평판은 다른 사람들에게 접근할 수 있도록 함으로써 지식의 문을 계속 열어있게 한다.

해설 밑줄 친 reputation is the gatekeeper to knowledge, and the keys to the gate are held by others의 의미를 추론하는 문제이다. 지문의 밑줄 친 단어가 있는 문장 이전에서 정보는 다른 사람에 의해 이미 걸러지고, 평가되고, 언급되었을 때에만 가치가 있을 것이라고 했다. 따라서, 밑줄 친 절의 의미를 '평판은 다른 사람들에 의해 통제되는데, 지식의 접근 권한을 통제한다'라고 한 ②번이 정답이다.

어휘 intelligent adj. 똑똑한 constitute v. 구성하다
 collectively adv. 집단으로 impartial adj. 공정한

[48-50]

2008년의 다른 산업과 비슷하게, 성형수술은 불경기가 더 나빠지기 시작했을 때 수입 감소를 겪었다. 하지만, 최근에는 사람들이 구직 시장에서 자신의 가치를 높이기 위해 미용 성형수술에 투자하기 시작했다. 예를 들어, 56세의 Max Seddon은 약화해가는 음악 산업이 자신이 다른 일을 찾기 시작하게 할 것 같다는 것을 알게 되었다. 그는 주름 제거 수술에 17,000달러를 써서 자신의 외모를 더 젊어 보이게 만들고 직업을 구하러 갈 때 자신감을 키웠다. 다른 중년의 남성과 여성들은 미용 성형수술에 의지하는 것이 필요하다는 것을 알게 되었는데, 더 젊고 생기로워 보이는 더 젊은 구직자들과 경쟁하기 때문이다. 성형외과 의사는 사람들이 이제 인생을 더 즐기기 위해서뿐만 아니라 경쟁이 심한 구직 시장에서 기술로는 충분하지 않다는 것을 알았기 때문에 성형수술을 받는다는 사실에 주목했다. 의사들은 이제 가격과 회복 시간을 낮출 수 있도록 국소마취만을 사용한 주름 제거 수술을 더 저렴하게 제공하고 있다. 맨해튼의 한 성형외과 의사는 나이가 더 많지만 자격을 더 갖춘 사람들이 더 젊고 더 잘생긴 경쟁자들보다 무시당하고 있다는 사실을 고려하여, 몸에 칼을 덜 대면서도 더 저렴한 성형수술 방법을 활용하는 "취직 전용 패키지" 상품을 제공하고 있다.

industry n. 산업 plastic surgery phr. 성형수술
revenue n. 수입 recession n. 불경기, 경기 침체
invest v. 투자하다 cosmetic adj. 미용의
job market phr. 구직 시장 facelift n. 주름 제거 수술
appearance n. 외모 bolster v. 키우다, 북돋우다
confidence n. 자신감 compete v. 경쟁하다
applicant n. 지원자 surgeon n. (외과)의사
competitive adj. 경쟁이 심한, 경쟁력이 있는
anesthesia n. 마취
qualified adj. 자격을 갖춘, 능력이 있는
pass over phr. 무시하다 counterpart n. 경쟁자, 상대방
method n. 방법 invasive adj. 몸에 칼을 대는, 외과적인

48 [2019 한성대]

정답 ④

해석 ① 2008년에 경제가 매우 나빴다.
② Max Seddon은 음악 회사에서 일했다.
③ Max Seddon은 그의 외모를 더 젊게 만들기 위해서 성형수술을 했다.
④ 중년의 사람들은 주로 그들의 삶을 연장하기 위해서 성형수술을 받는다.

해설 지문의 내용과 일치하지 않는 것을 묻는 문제이다. ②번의 키워드인 Middle-aged people(중년의 사람들)과 관련된 지문의 middle-aged men and women(중년의 남성과 여성들) 주변에서 더 젊고 생기로워 보이는 더 젊은 구직자들과 경쟁하기 때문에 미용 성형수술에 의지하는 것이 필요하다는 것을 알게 되었다고 했으므로, 중년의 사람들은 주로 그들의 삶을 연장하기 위해서 성형수술을 받는다는 것은 지문의 내용과 다르다. 따라서 ④번이 지문의 내용과 일치하지 않는다.

오답 분석
① Like other industries in 2008, plastic surgery suffered a drop in revenues when the recession began to worsen을 통해 '2008년에 경제가 매우 나빴다'라는 것을 알 수 있다.
② 56-year-old Max Seddon is aware that the weakening music industry will likely force him to begin seeking work elsewhere를 통해 'Max Seddon은 음악 회사에서 일했다'는 것을 알 수 있다.
③ He spent $17,000 on a facelift to make his appearance more youthful and to bolster his confidence when he goes job-hunting을 통해 'Max Seddon은 그의 외모를 더 젊게 만들기 위해서 성형수술을 했다'는 것을 알 수 있다.

어휘 economy n. 경제 mainly adv. 주로
 prolong v. 연장하다

49 [2019 한성대]

정답 ④

해설 지문의 빈칸을 채우는 문제이다. 첫 번째 빈칸에 들어갈 do는 목적 보어의 자리이므로 목적어인 cosmetic surgery의 관계를 고려해야 한다. 이때 cosmetic surgery와 do의 관계가 수동 관계이므로, 과거분사인 done이 들어가야 적절하다. 또한 두 번째 빈칸의 이전 부분에서 주름 제거 수술을 더 저렴하게 제공한다고 설명하고 있으므로, 빈칸에는 가격이 낮아진다는 내용이 들어가야 자연스럽다. 따라서 ④번이 정답이다.

50 [2019 한성대]

정답 ②

해석
① ~보다 선호되고 있다
② ~보다 덜 선호되고 있다
③ ~에 가까워지고 있다
④ ~에 덜 가까워지고 있다

해설 밑줄 친 부분의 의미를 추론하는 문제이다. 밑줄 친 are being passed over는 '~보다 무시당하고 있다'라는 의미이다. 주변의 내용을 살펴보면 이것이 구직 시장에서 자격은 갖췄지만 나이가 많은 사람보다 더 젊고 잘생긴 사람이 선택된다는 것임을 알 수 있다. 따라서, 이를 '~보다 덜 선호되고 있다'라고 표현한 ②번이 정답이다.

[51-54]

[A] 세계적인 자원 전쟁에 있어서, 가난한 사람들의 환경 보전 운동은 관청식 경관이 강제로 고장 특유의 경관에 도입될 때 빈번히 일어난다. 고장 특유의 경관은 지역사회가 세대를 걸쳐 고안해 온 정서적이고, 역사적으로 짜인 지도, 명칭과 경로로 가득한 지도, 그리고 중요한 생태학적 특징과 표층 지질학 특징을 알고 있는 지도로 만들어졌다. 고장 특유의 경관은 획일적이지도 않고 명백하지도 않지 만, 저편에 있는 별개의 재생 불능한 자원으로 취급당해 완전히 객관화되는 것보다 지역사회의 사회환경적인 원동력에 필수적이다.

[B] 반대로, 정부, 비정부기구, 기업 또는 이러한 기관들의 조합을 불문하고 관청식 경관은 일반적으로 이러한 이전의 지도들을 염두에 두지 않는 대신, 관료주의적이고, 객관화하고, 무자비하게 도구적인 채취 중심적인 방식으로 지형을 작성한다. 예를 들어, 부유한 국가의 쓰레기와 유독 물질을 아프리카로 내보내려는 Lawrence Summers의 계획은 전혀 드문 일은 아니지만, 대단히 합리화된 관청식 경관의 거창한 한 사례로서 유효한데, 권력 집단의 자원 약탈 측면이든지 유독 화학 약품 처분의 측면이든지 간에 그것은 보통 "마음대로 할 수 있는 시민들"이 거주하는 생태계에 투영되었다.

[C] 전 세계의 지역 고유 자원에 관한 반란의 기하급수적인 급증은 대부분 채취 및 훼손을 하고 떠나기 위해 관청식 경관 지도를 가지고 찾아온 단기적인 이익만을 생각하는 사람들과 생태학적인 여파 속에서 살아야 하기 때문에 시간의 척도에 있어서 부를 다르게 따져보아야 하는 장기적인 이익을 바라보는 사람들 사이의 시간적인 관점의 충돌에서 기인해왔다. 여기에서는 물질적인 부 그 이상이 위태로 워지는데, 간섭하는 관청식 조경사들은 보통 정신적인 의의가 깃든 고장 특유의 경관을 무시하면서, 복잡하게 얽힌 축적된 문화적 의미를 단절하고, 고장 특유의 경관을 마치 살아있는 사람들, 후세의 사람들, 그리고 살아 움직이는 고인들이 살지 않은 곳처럼 취급한다.

---

environmentalism n. 환경 보전 운동 landscape n. 경관
impose v. 도입하다 vernacular adj. 고장 특유의
affective adj. 정서적인 replete adj. 가득한
geological adj. 지질학의 monolithic adj. 획일적인
undisputed adj. 명백한 externalize v. 객관화하다
nonrenewable adj. 재생 불가능한
oblivious adj. 염두에 없는 bureaucratic adj. 관료적인
extraction n. 채취 pitilessly adv. 무자비하게
grandiose adj. 거창한 capture n. 약탈
disposal n. 처분(권) project v. 투영시키다
disposable adj. 마음대로 할 수 있는
exponential adj. 기하급수적인 upsurge n. 급증
rebellion n. 반란 temporal adj. 시간의
despoil v. 훼손하다 depart v. 떠나다
aftermath n. 여파, 영향 weigh v. 따져보다
material adj. 물질적인 discount v. 무시하다
spiritualize v. 정신적 의의를 부여하다 severe v. 단절하다
accumulated adj. 축적된 unborn adj. 후세의

51 [2019 아주대]

정답 ④

해석
① 천연자원을 활용하는 최고의 방법
② 관청식 경관과 고장 특유의 경관 사이의 차이
③ 조경 기술의 장단점
④ 가난한 사람들의 환경 보전 운동과 저항
⑤ 세계화 시대에서 가난한 사람들의 생존

해설 지문의 제목을 묻는 문제이다. 지문 처음에서 가난한 사람들의 환경 보전 운동은 관청식 경관이 강제로 고장 특유의 경관에 도입될 때 빈번히 일어난다고 한 후, 관청식 경관과 고장 특유의 경관 사이의 차이를 설명하면서 이 둘의 관점 충돌로 인해 전 세계의 지역 고유 자원에 관한 반란이 급증한다고 설명하고 있다. 따라서 이 지문의 제목을 '가난한 사람들의 환경 보전 운동과 저항'이라고 표현한 ④번이 정답이다.

어휘 demystify v. 수수께끼를 풀다

52 2019 아주대

정답 ①

해석
① 관청식 — 관청식 — 고장 특유의
② 고장 특유의 — 관청식 — 고장 특유의
③ 고장 특유의 — 고장 특유의 — 관청식
④ 관청식 — 고장 특유의 — 관청식
⑤ 관청식 — 관청식 — 관청식

해설 지문의 빈칸을 채우는 문제이다. 첫 번째 빈칸의 경우, [C] 문단 처음에서 전 세계의 지역 고유 자원에 관한 반란의 급증이 단기적인 이익만을 생각하는 사람과 장기적인 이익을 바라보는 사람들의 충돌에서 기인한다고 했으므로, '_____ 경관 지도를 가지고 찾아온 단기적인 이익만을 생각하는 사람들'이라는 문맥의 빈칸에는 단기적인 이익만을 생각하는 사람들과 관련된 표현이 나와야 적절하다는 것을 알 수 있다. 따라서 '관청식의'가 들어가는 것이 자연스럽다. 두 번째, 세 번째 빈칸의 경우, [C] 문단 두 번째 문장에서 여기에서는 물질적인 부 그 이상이 위태로워진다고 했으므로, '_____ 조경사들은 보통 정신적인 의의가 깃든 _____ 경관을 무시한다'라는 문맥의 빈칸에는 차례대로 '관청식의', '고장 특유의'가 들어가는 것이 자연스럽다. 따라서 ①번이 정답이다.

53 2019 아주대

정답 ④

해석
① 우리가 생태계를 마음대로 할 수 있는 것처럼 취급한다면, 이는 사람들을 마음대로 할 수 있는 것으로 취급하는 것에 해당한다.
② 몇몇 개발업자들은 파괴된 생태계의 장기적인 결과를 생각하지 않는다.
③ 이 세계화 시대에서 심해진 자원에 대한 공격에 맞서는 격렬한 저항이 있다.
④ 고장 특유의 경관은 경관에 대한 토착민들의 변치 않는 합의를 반영하고 있다.
⑤ 부유한 국가의 독성물질을 세계에서 가장 가난한 대륙에 떠넘기려는 계획은 빈번히 제안된다.

해설 지문을 통해 추론할 수 없는 것을 고르는 문제이다. [A] 문단의 두 번째 문장에서 고장 특유의 경관은 지역사회가 세대를 걸쳐 고안해 온 정서적이고, 역사적으로 짜인 지도라고 했으므로, 고장 특유의 경관이 경관에 대한 토착민들의 변치 않는 합의를 반영하고 있다는 것은 추론할 수 없다. 따라서 정답은 ④번이다.

오답 분석
① [B] 문단의 마지막 문장 Lawrence Summers' scheme ~ has often been projected onto ecosystems inhabited by those "disposable citizens."를 통해 '우리가 생태계를 마음대로 할 수 있는 것처럼 취급한다면, 이는 사람들을 마음대로 할 수 있는 것으로 취급하는 것에 해당한다'는 것을 알 수 있다.
② [C] 문단 첫 번째 문장의 the short-termers who arrive ~ and depart를 통해 '몇몇 개발업자들은 파괴된 생태계의 장기적인 결과를 생각하지 않는다'는 것을 알 수 있다.
③ [C] 문단 첫 번째 문장의 The exponential upsurge in indigenous resource rebellion across the globe를 통해 '이 세계화 시대에서 심해진 자원에 대한 공격에 맞서는 격렬한 저항이 있다'는 것을 알 수 있다.
⑤ [B] 문단 마지막 문장의 Lawrence Summers' ~ a grandiose (though hardly exceptional) instance를 통해 '부유한 국가의 독성물질을 세계에서 가장 가난한 대륙에 떠넘기려는 계획은 빈번히 제안된다'는 것을 알 수 있다.

어휘 calculate v. 생각하다   assault n. 공격
agreement n. 합의   offload v. 떠넘기다
propose v. 제안하다

54 2019 아주대

정답 ⑤

해석
① 가득한, 가득 찬
② 염두에 없는, 알지 못하는
③ 기하급수적인, 빠른
④ 여파, 영향
⑤ 살지 않는, 금지된

해설 밑줄 친 단어를 대신할 수 없는 단어를 고르는 문제이다. uninhabited는 '살지 않는'이라는 의미이다. 따라서 '금지된'을 의미하는 prohibited는 uninhabited를 대신할 수 없다. 따라서 정답은 ⑤번이다.

어휘 consequence n. 영향, 결과   prohibit v. 금지하다

[55-59]

16세기에 토머스 모어(Thomas More)경은 자신의 저서 <유토피아(Utopia)>에서 가상의 이상적인 사회를 묘사했다. 그의 유토피아 사람들은 오직 노예들에게만 동물들을 죽일 수 있게 하는데, 그들은 자유 시민이 생물을 죽이는 것과 연관된 잔인함을 경험하는 것을 원하지 않았기 때문이다. 현대식 도축장에서, 소는 종종 많은 불필요한 고통과 함께 도살되고 있다. 즉 동물들이 비참한 두려움과 통증으로 스트레스를 받는다.
유명한 동물 행동 과학자인, 템플 그랜딘(Temple Grandin)은 최고의 전문가이며, 가공처리 공장의 환경을 개선하고, 미국 정부에게 연방의 (고통 없는 도살을 요구하는) '인간적인 도살법'에 대해 조언을 하며, 미국 육류 협회를 위한 가이드라인을 작성한다. [A] 그녀의 실용적 설계의 한 사례는, 소들이 한 줄로 걸어가며 앞에 있는 3마리만 볼 수 있고, 그들을 멈칫하게 만드는 예상치 못한 일을 볼 수 없도록 180도로 굽어지는 통로가 있는 도축장 경사로이다. 높은 벽이 있고, 그림자나 시끄

러운 소음이나 구타 및 발밑에 미끄러짐이 없을 때, 소들은 두려워하지 않고 앞으로 나아가며, 산업 효율성이 개선된다. 비록 많은 동물 복지 옹호자들은 우리가 고기를 먹는 것을 완전히 피해야 한다고 말하지만, 가축은 인간에게 도움이 된다. [B] 그리고 그랜딘은 사람들이 이 동물들에 대해 보살펴주는 역할을 인식해야 한다고 믿고 있다.
동물 권리 활동가들은 또한 사람들에게 소고기 산업의 잔인한 환경에 대한 주의를 환기시켰다. 태어나자마자 어미 소를 빼앗긴, 수컷 송아지는 작은 우리 안에 혼자 넣어지고, 목에 사슬을 채우며, 걸을 수 없게 되는데, 모두 소고기를 아주 부드럽게 하기 위한 것이다. 철분과 섬유질이 부족하고, 화학물질과 항생제 및 호르몬이 가득한, 유동식을 먹으며 길러진 송아지들은 정말로 대략 생후 4개월 정도에 도살장으로 끌려간다. 이제 영국에서는 그런 환경이 금지되어 있으며, 미국의 많은 소비자와 요리사들은 이런 식으로 길러진 소고기를 구매하여 음식 준비를 하는 것에 반대한다. [C]
또한 붉은 고기에서 가금류로 바꾸는 일도 증가하고 있다. 그러나 거대한 공장식 창고 안에 있는 배터리 케이지 안에 빽빽이 갇혀 있는 닭들 또한 항생제와 호르몬을 먹는다. [D] 운송과 도축 환경은 종종 끔찍할 정도다. 결과적으로, 소비자들은 '근심 없는' 계란과 '유기농' 닭만 사용하는 상점에 관심을 갖게 되었다. 추가된 비용에도 불구하고, 그런 동물 처리에 대한 소비자들의 반감과 식품 공급의 산업화에 대한 우려에 의해, 이런 경향은 증가하고 있다.

Sir n. 경(卿), 영국에서 기사나 귀족 작위를 가진 남성의 이름 앞에 붙이는 경칭 imaginary adj. 가상의
slaughterhouse n. 도축장, 도살장
abject adj. 비참한; 비굴한 leading adj. 일류의, 뛰어난
authority n. 권위자 processing plant phr. 가공처리 공장
single file phr. 한 줄로, 1열 종대로 ramp n. 경사로
balk v. 멈칫거리다, 갑자기 멈추다 slippage n. 미끄러짐
underfoot adv. 발밑에, (발아래의) 땅에 livestock n. 가축
serve a purpose phr. 도움이 되다
alert v. 주의를 환기시키다, 경계하게 하다
veal n. 송아지 고기 calf n. 송아지 pen n. 우리, 축사
tender adj. (고기가) 부드러운, 연한 liquid diet phr. 유동식
literally adv. (어구를 강조하여) 정말로, 완전히; 그야말로
drag v. 끌다, 끌고 가다
prepare v. (음식을) 준비하다, 마련하다
switch from A to B phr. A에서 B로 바꾸다, 전환하다
red meat phr. (소·돼지·양 고기 등의) 붉은 고기
poultry n. 가금류 confine v. 감금하다
battery cage phr. 도살하기 전에 닭을 잠시 가두는 우리
warehouse n. 창고
appalling adj. 간담을 서늘하게 하는; 끔찍한
care-free adj. 근심 걱정 없는 disgust n. 혐오감, 역겨움

---

55 2018 세종대

정답 ③

해석
① 템플 그랜딘은 인간이 동물에게 평화로운 죽음을 줘야한다고 믿고 있다.
② 잔인한 환경에서 송아지를 도살하는 것이 오늘날 영국에서는 불법이다.
③ 그랜딘의 발명품은 순전히 이익을 추구하는 것이다.
④ 많은 미국 요리사들은 비인간적인 환경에서 길러진 송아지 고기로 음식 준비하는 것에 반대한다.

해설 지문의 내용과 일치하지 않는 것을 묻는 문제이다. 두 번째 문단의 When there are high walls, ~ and industry efficiency improves.에서 '그랜든이 고안한 도살장에서는 소들은 두려워하지 않고 앞으로 나아가며, 산업 효율성이 개선된다'고 했으므로, 이것이 '순전히 이익을 추구하는 것'이라는 표현은 지문의 내용과 다르다. 따라서 ③번이 지문 내용과 일치하지 않는다.

오답 분석
① 두 번째 문단의 첫 세 문장 Temple Grandine, ~ and industry efficiency improves.를 통해 '템플 그랜딘은 인간이 동물에게 평화로운 죽음을 줘야 한다고 믿고 있다'는 것을 알 수 있다.
② 세 번째 문단의 Such conditions are now banned in Britain을 통해 '잔인한 환경에서 송아지를 도살하는 것이 오늘날 영국에서는 불법'이라는 것을 알 수 있다.
④ 세 번째 문단의 many consumers and chefs in the U.S. resist buying or preparing veal raised in this way를 통해 '많은 미국 요리사들은 비인간적인 환경에서 길러진 송아지 고기로 음식 준비하는 것에 반대한다'는 것을 알 수 있다.

어휘 meticulous adj. 세심한, 꼼꼼한
punctual adj. 시간을 잘 지키는

56 2018 세종대

정답 ③

해석
① 소비자들은 양질의 고기 때문에 송아지보다 닭고기를 점점 더 많이 먹고 있다.
② 유토피아 사람들은 자유인보다 노예가 동물들을 더 효율적으로 죽일 수 있다고 믿었다.
③ 사람들은 그들의 구매력을 이용하여 송아지 산업에 대한 반감을 보여준다.
④ 그랜딘의 발명품은 소들로 하여금 자기 앞에 있는 것을 전혀 볼 수 없게 한다.

해설 지문을 통해 추론할 수 있는 것을 고르는 문제이다. 세 번째 문단의 마지막 문장에서 미국의 많은 소비자들과 요리사들이 비인간적으로 길러진 송아지를 구매하는 것에 저항한다고 했으며, 마지막 문단에서는 붉은 고기에서 가금류로 바꾸는 일이 증가하고 있고 소비자들이 근심 없는 계란과 유기농 닭고기를 사용하는 상점에 관심을 갖게 되었다고 했으므로, '사람

들은 그들의 구매력을 이용하여 송아지 산업에 대한 반감을 보여준다'는 것을 추론할 수 있다. 따라서 ③번이 정답이다.

오답 분석
① 소비자들이 붉은 고기에서 닭고기로 전환하는 것은 고기의 질 때문이 아니라 비인간적인 송아지 산업에 대한 반감 때문이므로, '양질의 고기 때문에 송아지보다 닭고기를 점점 더 많이 먹고 있다'는 것은 지문의 내용과 다르다.
② 첫 문단에서 유토피아 사람들이 노예들에게만 동물들을 죽일 수 있게 한 것은 자유 시민이 생물을 죽이는 것과 연관된 잔인함을 경험하는 것을 원하지 않았기 때문이라고 했으므로, '자유인보다 노예가 동물들을 더 효율적으로 죽일 수 있다고 믿었다'는 것은 지문의 내용과 다르다.
④ 두 번째 문단에서 그랜든이 고안한 도축장 경사로에서는 소들이 자기 앞에 있는 3마리만 볼 수 있다고 했으므로, '앞에 있는 것을 전혀 볼 수 없게 한다'는 것은 지문의 내용과 다르다.

57 2018 세종대

정답 ②

해석
① 참을 수 없는　　② 불충분한
③ 꼴불견인　　　　④ 무능한

해설
밑줄 친 deficient의 동의어를 고르는 문제이다. deficient는 '부족한'이라는 의미이고, ①번 unendurable은 '참을 수 없는', ②번 insufficient는 '불충분한', ③번 unseemly는 '꼴불견인', ④번 incompetent는 '무능한'이라는 의미이다. 따라서 ②번이 정답이다.

어휘 unseemly adj. 꼴불견인, 보기 흉한, 부적절한

58 2018 세종대

정답 ②

해석
① 템플 그랜든의 업적이라는 훌륭한 유산을 강조하기 위해
② 오늘날 도축장에서의 동물들의 비인간적인 환경에 대해 논의하기 위해
③ 가축이 그랜든이 설계한 것에 어떻게 반응하는지를 설명하기 위해
④ 소고기 산업이 고기를 부드럽게 하기 위해 어린 송아지들을 어떻게 기르는지를 보여주기 위해

해설
필자가 이 글을 쓴 목적을 묻는 문제이다. 첫 문단에서는 도살장에서 소가 매우 고통스럽게 도살되고 있다고 언급했고, 두 번째 문단에서는 도살당하는 소의 고통을 줄여주기 위해 템플 그랜든이 설계한 도축장을 소개했으며, 세 번째 문단에서는 소고기 산업에서 송아지가 잔인하게 길러지는 환경을 다시 언급한 다음 이에 대한 소비자들의 반감을 언급했고, 마지막 문단에서는 닭을 사육하는 환경도 잔인하다고 했다. 따라서 이 글의 목적을 '오늘날 도축장에서의 동물들의 비인간적인 환경에 대해 논의하기 위해'라고 표현한 ②번이 정답이다.

어휘 legacy n. 유산

59 2018 세종대

정답 ②

해설
지문의 흐름상 주어진 문장이 들어가기에 가장 적절한 위치를 고르는 문제이다. [A] 뒤의 내용은 템플 그랜든이 설계한 도축장을 앞에 언급한 improving conditions at processing plants ~ and writing guidelines for the American Meat Institute의 예로 든 것이므로 제시문이 들어가기에 적합하지 않다. 제시문에 언급된 these animals는 [B] 앞 문장의 livestock animals를 가리키는 것이며, [B] 뒤에서 송아지가 태어날 때부터 잔인한 환경에서 양육되다가 생후 4개월이 되면 도살장에 끌려간다는 내용을 언급하며, 동물 권리 활동가들은 송아지 고기 산업의 잔인한 환경에 대한 주의를 환기시킨다(즉 caretaking과 관련 있음)고 했으므로, 주어진 문장 '그리고 그랜든은 사람들이 이 동물들에 대해 보살펴주는 역할을 인식해야 한다고 믿고 있다'가 [B] 자리에 들어가야 글의 흐름이 자연스럽게 연결된다. 따라서 ②번이 정답이다.

06 경제·경영

01-52
문제집 p.158

01 ③	02 ③	03 ④	04 ①	05 ⑤
06 ④	07 ④	08 ③	09 ⑤	10 ①
11 ②	12 ④	13 ②	14 ④	15 ④
16 ②	17 ①	18 ①	19 ③	20 ③
21 ③	22 ③	23 ⑤	24 ②	25 ①
26 ③	27 ④	28 ③	29 ③	30 ③
31 ④	32 ③	33 ①	34 ④	35 ②
36 ②	37 ②	38 ②	39 ②	40 ②
41 ②	42 ④	43 ④	44 ①	45 ④
46 ④	47 ②	48 ③	49 ③	50 ③
51 ③	52 ③

---

01 [2019 광운대]
정답 ③

해석 세계 주식시장은 소비가 늘고 투자 심리가 개선되는 시기여서 연말과 연초에 주가가 상승하는 "산타 랠리"를 이어가곤 했다. 그러나, 올해는 "블랙 크리스마스"를 목격했다. 부정적인 경제 전망이 투자 심리를 움츠러들게 했다.
① 따라서 ② 게다가
③ 그러나 ④ 결과적으로
⑤ ~에도 불구하고

해설 빈칸에 적절한 연결어를 넣는 문장이다. 빈칸 앞 문장은 세계 주식시장은 소비가 늘고 투자 심리가 개선되어 연말과 초에 주가가 상승하는 "산타 랠리"를 이어가곤 했다는 내용이고, 빈칸 뒤 문장은 올해는 "블랙 크리스마스"를 목격했는데 이는 부정적인 경제 전망으로, 투자 심리를 움츠러들게 했다는 내용이다. 따라서 대조를 나타내는 연결어인 ③ however(그러나)가 정답이다.

어휘 stock market phr. 주식시장
Santa rally phr. 산타 랠리(크리스마스를 사이에 두고 연말과 연초에 증시가 강세를 보이는 현상) stock price phr. 주가
consumption n. 소비 psychology n. 심리
witness v. 목격하다 outlook n. 전망

02 [2020 가톨릭대]
정답 ③

해석 성공적인 펀딩의 비결은 기업의 초기 성장의 각 단계마다 적합한 유형의 자금을 선택하는 것이다. 신생 기업은 자체 자금조달과 친구, 가족, 그리고 큰 위험을 감수할 준비가 된 사람들로부터의 도움으로 보통 적당하게 시작한다. 크라우드 펀딩 참여자와 비즈니스 엔젤은 기업가를 성공하게 하는 비전문가들인 반면, 벤처기업 투자자는 위험 수위가 낮아지고 상당한 자금 투입한 것에 대한 보상으로 많은 수익을 예상할 수 있을 때 흥미를 갖는다. 증권 거래소 같은 공공시장은 기업의 판매량이 급증하여 성공할 수 있을 것 같을 때 개입할지도 모른다. 모든 단계에서, 투자자는 기업의 부채상환 능력을 평가하기 위한 신용 분석을 실시할 것이다.
① 성공적인 펀딩 신청을 위한 절차들
② 현명한 투자 계획을 세우는 방법
③ 사업의 서로 다른 단계에서의 자금 공급원
④ 펀딩을 찾는 신생 기업들이 따라야 할 사항

해설 지문의 요지를 묻는 문제이다. 지문 처음에서 성공적인 펀딩의 비결은 기업의 최기 성장의 각 단계마다 적합한 유형의 자금을 선택하는 것이라고 하고, 자체 자금 조달, 크라우드 펀딩, 비즈니스 엔젤, 벤처기업 투자자, 증권 거래소 등 각 단계마다 적합한 유형의 자금을 선택하는 방법에 대해 설명하고 있다. 따라서 이 지문의 요지를 '사업의 서로 다른 단계에서의 자금 공급원'이라고 표현한 ③번이 정답이다.

어휘 start-up n. 신생 기업
crowdfunding n. 크라우드펀딩(자금이 없는 벤처사업가나 예술가 등이 자신의 아이디어를 인터넷에 공개하고 다수로부터 투자받는 행위) business angel phr. 비즈니스 엔젤(기업에 재정을 지원해주고 발생한 이익의 몫을 받는 유형의 투자자)
entrepreneur n. 기업가 capitalist n. 자본가
inject v. 투입하다 substantial adj. 상당한
soar v. 급증하다 repay v. 상환하다

03 [2019 가천대]
정답 ④

해석 "뱀파이어 경제"는 정상적인 기업 행동이나 노동을 포함하지 않는 부의 축적을 추구하는 국가, 혹은 다른 회사의 정상적인 경제 활동에 의존해서 살아가는 회사를 말한다. 약 4, 5년 전에, 월스트리트는 한국 경제가 구조조정에 대해 더 엄격했어야 했다는 성명을 발표했고, 한국 경제를 "햇빛을 보는 날에 사라지게 될 나쁜 회사로 가득 찬 뱀파이어 경제"라고 불렀다. 반대로, 진정한 뱀파이어의 소굴은 미국에 존재하는 것으로 밝혀졌다. 지난해의 하반기 초에 전 세계를 휩쓴 금융 위기를 촉발한 대규모의 금융 회사가 서민들의 피를 빨아먹고서 부를 축적했다는 것이 밝혀졌다.
① 즉 ② 더욱이
③ 그에 맞춰 ④ 반대로

해설 지문의 빈칸을 채우는 문제이다. 빈칸의 이전 부분에서는 미국의 월스트리트가 한국 경제를 나쁜 경제인 '뱀파이어 경제'라고 불렀지만, 빈칸의 이후 부분에서 오히려 미국 경제가 진정한 뱀파이어의 소굴이라고 설명하고 있으므로, 빈칸에는 반대의 의미를 가진 부사가 들어가는 것이 적절하다. 따라서, '반대로'라고 한 ④번이 정답이다.

어휘
persue v. 추구하다   accumulation n. 축적
corporate n. 기업   live off phr. ~에 의지하여 살다
statement n. 성명, 진술   restructuring n. 구조조정
den n. 소굴   turn out phr. 밝히다
financial adj. 경제적인, 재정적인   sweep v. 휩쓸다
common people phr. 서민   namely adv. 즉
furthermore adv. 더욱이   accordingly adv. 그에 맞춰
conversely adv. 반대로

[04-06]

신자유주의의 렌즈를 통해 보면, 당신은 복지국가와 마찬가지로, 어떻게 자유시장이 인간의 발명품이 되었는지를 알게 된다. 당신은 오늘날 우리가 우리 자신을 스스로의 재능과 진취력의 소유주로 생각하도록 강요당하는 것이 얼마나 만연한지, 우리가 경쟁하고 적응하도록 당부받는 것이 얼마나 말뿐인 것인지를 알게 된다. 당신은 이전에는 상품 시장(경쟁, 완전정보, 이성적 행동)을 묘사하는 칠판 위의 단순화로 국한되어 있었던 언어가 그것이 우리의 개인적 삶의 티끌까지 침범할 때까지, 사회의 모든 부분에 어느 정도로까지 적용되고 있는지, 그리고 판매 사원의 태도가 어떻게 모든 자기표현 방식 안에 말려들게 되었는지를 알게 된다.

요컨대, "신자유주의"는 단순히 친시장 정책이나 실패한 사회민주당에 만들어진 금융 자본주의에 대한 합의를 위한 이름이 아니다. 그것은 우리가 행하고 생각하는 모든 것들을 조용하게 규제하는 한 전제를 위한 이름인데, 이 전제는 경쟁이 인간의 활동을 위한 유일하게 합법적인 조직 원리라는 것이다. 신자유주의가 현실로서 증명(A)되자마자, 그리고 그것이 시장의 보편적인 위선을 분명히 (A)하자마자, 대중 영합주의자와 권위주의자가 정권을 장악(B)했다.

peer v. 보다, 응시하다   neoliberalism n. 신자유주의
welfare state phr. 복지국가   pervasively adv. 만연하게
proprietor n. 소유주   initiative n. 진취력
glibly adv. 말뿐으로   confine v. 국한하다
chalkboard n. 칠판   simplification n. 단순화
commodity n. 상품   perfect information phr. 완전정보
invade v. 침범하다   grit n. 티끌
enmesh v. 말려들게 하다   pro-market adj. 친시장적인
compromise n. 합의   premise n. 전제
regulate v. 제한하다   legitimate adj. 합법적인
certify v. 증명하다   hypocrisy n. 위선
populist n. 대중 영합주의자   authoritarian n. 권위주의자

04 [2021 경희대]
정답 ①

해석 ① 손익에 타산적인 사람
② 자유 의지의 전달자
③ 신의 은총을 구하는 사람
④ 사업 파트너
⑤ 사치품의 소비자

해설 신자유주의 사회에서 인간을 바라보는 관점을 파악하는 문제이다. 지문 전반에 걸쳐 신자유주의의 관점으로 세상을 바라보면, 단순히 상품 시장을 묘사하는 것으로 여겨졌던 경쟁, 완전정보, 이성적 행동과 같은 경제적 요인들이 실제로는 인간 삶의 아주 작은 측면까지 파고 들어가 있다는 것을 알게 된다는 내용을 설명하고 있으므로, 신자유주의 사회에서는 인간을 이해타산적인 존재 즉, '손익에 타산적인 사람'으로 보고 있음을 알 수 있다. 따라서 ①번이 정답이다.

05 [2021 경희대]
정답 ⑤

해설 문맥상 '신자유주의가 현실로서 증명되자마자, 그리고 그것이 시장의 보편적인 위선을 분명히 하자마자, 대중 영합주의자와 권위주의자가 정권을 장악했다'라는 의미가 되어야 자연스러운데, '~하자마자 …하다'라는 의미는 비교급 표현 관용구인 'no sooner ~ than'을 통해 나타낼 수 있으므로, (A)에는 no sooner가 (B)에는 than이 들어가야 한다. 따라서 ⑤ no sooner — than이 정답이다.

06 [2021 경희대]
정답 ④

해설 주어진 지문에서 '소유주'라는 의미로 사용된 복수명사 proprietors의 동의어를 묻는 문제이다. ①번 conductor는 '지휘자', ②번 creator는 '창조자', ③번 seeker는 '~을 구하는 사람', ④번 owner는 '소유주', ⑤번 designer는 '디자이너'라는 의미이므로, ④번이 정답이다.

[07-08]

그것이 이끈 자본주의와 경제 성장은 20세기의 후반부에 미국을 세계 상위의 초강대국으로 만든 것이었다. 그러나 미국 방식의 자본주의에는 이면이 존재한다. 이 자본주의자와 개인주의적인 경제 체제는 막대한 양의 부를 발생시켰지만, 그것은 또한 돈이 많은 특별한 이익단체에 의해 사로잡혀 있었던 정치 체계에 더해, 사회적 안전망이 부족한 평균적인 미국 노동자를 야기했다. [A] 다시, 이것은 트럼프의 백악관 입성과 함께 갑작스럽게 출현한 새로운 무언가가 아니다. 미국의 자본주의자들은 오랫동안 결과의 불평등을 인정해왔으며, 지난 30년 동안 우리는 기회의 불평등의 증가 또한 점점 더 목격하고 있다. [B] 그리고 그것은 가속화하고 있는 중이다. 30년 전에, 우리가 자본주의에서 실패한 이들에 관해 말할 때, 우리는 대개 자유 무역에 의해 뒤로 밀려난 육체노동자들의 특정 집단을 언급했다. [C] 그러나 오늘날 우리는 자동화와 AI가 사회-경제적 계층을 가로질러 더 넓은 범위의 근로자 집단을 서서히 대체할 것으로 보이는 시점에 다가가고 있다. [D] 이 후자의 형태는 더욱 치명적인데, 사람들은 성공하기는커녕 경쟁할 기회조차 전혀 얻을 수 없다고 느꼈을 때, 분노하기 때문이다. 버니 샌더

스 같은 정치인들의 출현이 보여주듯이, 이것은 정치적 스펙트럼에서 왼쪽에 위치한 유권자들에게도, 오른쪽에 위치한 유권자들에게만큼이나 염려되는 일이다. [E] 그 최종 결과는 더욱 분열된 유권자인데, 그들은 한 집단에서 다른 집단으로 이동할 가능성이 작아진 상태에서, 가진 자들에게는 더 많은 것을 주고 가지지 못한 자들에게는 더 적은 것을 주는 미국의 미래에서 어떻게 살아갈 것인지에 대한 공포로 자극받는다.

capitalism n. 자본주의 drive v. 이끌다
preeminent adj. 상위의 superpower n. 초강대국
flip side phr. 이면 individualist adj. 개인주의적인
tremendous adj. 막대한 capture v. 사로잡다
moneyed adj. 돈이 많은 interests n. 이익단체
inequality n. 불평등 outcome n. 결과
increasingly adv. 점점 더 opportunity n. 기회
accelerate v. 가속화하다 refer v. 언급하다
automation n. 자동화 displace v. 대체하다
electorate n. 유권자 fuel v. 자극하다 prospect n. 전망

07 (2021 경희대)

정답 ④

해석 이 후자의 형태는 더욱 치명적인데, 사람들은 성공하기는커녕 경쟁할 기회조차 전혀 얻을 수 없다고 느꼈을 때, 분노하기 때문이다.

해설 지문의 흐름상 주어진 문장이 들어가기에 가장 적절한 위치를 고르는 문제이다. 주어진 문장은 '이 후자의 형태는 더욱 치명적인데, 사람들은 성공하기는커녕 경쟁할 기회조차 전혀 얻을 수 없다고 느꼈을 때, 분노하기 때문이다'라는 의미이다. 주어진 문장의 This latter form은 30년 전과 달리 오늘날에는 자동화와 AI가 더 넓은 범위의 근로자 집단을 대체하리라는 것을 가리키고 있으므로, [D]의 자리에 주어진 문장이 들어가야 글의 흐름이 자연스럽게 연결된다. 따라서 ④번이 정답이다.

어휘 devastating adj. 치명적인
get a shot to phr. ~할 기회를 얻다
let alone phr. ~하기는커녕

08 (2021 경희대)

정답 ③

해석 ① 기회의 불평등은 지난 30년간 증가해왔다.
② 자본주의적이고 개인주의적인 경제 체제는 돈이 많은 특별한 이익단체에 의해 사로잡히는 정치 체제를 초래한다.
③ 자동화와 AI는 오직 육체노동자의 특정 집단만을 대체할 것이다.
④ 불평등의 가속화는 지금 이 순간 미국이 이렇게 분열된 것을 설명하는 한 이유이다.
⑤ 정치적 스펙트럼에서 양 측면의 미국인 노동자들은 그들의 생존에 대해 걱정하고 있다.

해설 지문의 내용과 일치하지 않는 것을 묻는 문제이다. 지문의 후반에서 오늘날 우리는 자동화와 AI가 사회-경제적 계층을 가로질러 더 넓은 범위의 근로자 집단을 서서히 대체할 것으로 보이는 시점에 다가가고 있다고 했으므로, 자동화와 AI가 오직 육체노동자의 특정 집단만을 대체하리라는 것은 지문의 내용과 다르다. 따라서 ③번이 정답이다.

오답 분석
① in the last thirty years we've increasingly seen the rise of inequality of opportunity as well을 통해 기회의 불평등이 지난 30년간 증가해왔음을 알 수 있다.
② American worker with less of a social safety net, not to mention a political system more prone to capture by moneyed special interests를 통해 자본주의적이고 개인주의적인 경제 체제가 돈이 많은 특별한 이익단체에 의해 사로잡히는 정치 체제를 초래한다는 것을 알 수 있다.
④ 지문 중간에서 불평등이 가속화되고 있다고 했고, 지문의 후반부에서 그로 인한 결과가 분열된 유권자라고 하였으므로 불평등의 가속화가 지금 이 순간 미국이 이렇게 분열된 것을 설명하는 이유라는 것은 지문의 내용과 일치한다.
⑤ 지문 후반에서 정치적 스펙트럼에 있는 양 측면의 사람들이 모두 같은 것을 염려하고 있으며, 그들이 어떻게 살아갈 것인지에 대한 공포로 자극받는다고 했으므로, 정치적 스펙트럼에서 양 측면의 미국인 노동자들은 그들의 생존에 대해 걱정하고 있다는 것은 지문의 내용과 일치한다.

[09-11]

1800년대 후반의 급속한 산업화는 당시의 경제적 호황에 이끌린 많은 시골 지역의 이주민 집단으로 갑작스럽게 밀집한 도시 중심지로 기업들을 집중시켰다. 비록 부동산의 가격이 급격히 올랐지만, 수요가 공급을 앞질렀는데, 이 문제는 수직으로 설계된 건물이라는 전례 없는 발상과 함께 제한된 공간을 최대한 이용함으로써 해결되었다.
초창기에는, 높은 건물의 건설이 특정 높이로 제한되었는데, 이는 더 높은 높이를 감당하기 위한 대부분의 기술이 그저 존재하지 않았기 때문이었다. 먼저, 초기의 엘리베이터 장치는 조악했고, 그래서 수십 층의 계단을 매일 오르내린다는 생각은 바보짓처럼 보였다. 다음으로, 당시의 수압의 힘이 대략 50피트의 높이까지만 물을 퍼 올릴 수 있었고, 이것이 고층의 수도 설비를 몽상으로 만들었다. 마지막으로, 구조적 지지대의 중요성에 대한 제한된 의식은 대부분의 초기 양식이 전적으로 내력벽과 단단한 벽돌의 두꺼운 토대에 의해 지탱되는 것을 의미했다.

rapid adj. 급속한 industrialization n. 산업화
centralize v. 집중시키다 dense adj. 밀집한
teeming adj. 많은 mass n. 집단 migrant n. 이주민
economic boom phr. 경제적 호황
real estate phr. 부동산 outpace v. 앞지르다
conundrum n. 문제, 수수께끼

> vertically-designed adj. 수직으로 설계된 height n. 높이
> accommodate v. 감당하다 elevator n. 엘리베이터
> potency n. 힘 pump v. (물을) 퍼 올리다
> plumbing facility phr. 수도 설비 pipe dream phr. 몽상
> support beam phr. 지지대 solid adj. 단단한
> load-bearing wall phr. 내력벽

09 2021 경희대

정답 ⑤

해석
① 최대한 이용하다 – 환상
② 최소화하다 – 상식
③ 최소화하다 – 환상
④ 최소화하다 – 바보짓
⑤ 최대한 이용하다 – 바보짓

해설 두 개의 빈칸에 들어갈 내용을 묻는 문제이다. 지문의 초반에서 부동산 가격이 올랐음에도, 수요가 공급을 앞질러 문제가 발생했음을 설명하고 있고, 이를 해결하기 위해 수직으로 설계된 건물이라는 전례 없는 발상이 나왔음을 언급하고 있다. 따라서 첫 번째 빈칸에는 '최대한 이용하다'라는 의미의 maximizing이 들어가는 것이 적절하다. 지문의 두 번째 문단은 수직적으로 설계된 건물들이 등장한 초창기에 건물들의 높이가 제한될 수밖에 없었던 이유를 설명하고 있다. 초기의 엘리베이터 장치가 조잡해서, 매일 수십 층의 계단을 오르내린다는 생각이 바보짓처럼 보였다는 내용이 되어야 자연스러우므로, 두 번째 빈칸에는 '바보짓'이라는 의미의 lunacy가 적절하다. 따라서 ⑤ maximizing – lunacy가 정답이다.

10 2021 경희대

정답 ①

해설 주어진 문장에서 '몽상'이라는 의미로 사용된 pipe dream의 동의어를 묻는 문제이다. ①번 fantastic notion은 '실행 불가능한 개념', ②번 financial difficulty는 '재정적 어려움', ③번 technical problem은 '기술적 문제', ④번 structural issue는 '구조적 문제', ⑤번 urban legend는 '도시 전설'이라는 의미이므로, ①번이 정답이다.

어휘 fantastic adj. 실행 불가능한 notion n. 개념
financial adj. 재정적인 structural adj. 구조적인

11 2021 경희대

정답 ②

해석
① 산업화와 부동산
② 고층 건물의 발달
③ 엘리베이터의 발명
④ 도시 중심지의 시골 이주민
⑤ 도시 공간의 이해

해설 주어진 문장의 제목을 묻는 문제이다. 지문의 초반에서는 1800년대에 급속한 산업화로 인해 도시로 사람이 몰리게 되면서 생긴 부동산 문제를 수직적으로 설계된 건물들로 해결했다고 설명하고 있고, 지문의 중간과 후반에서는 최초로 등장한 수직적으로 설계된 건물들의 한계점과 그 이유에 대해 설명하고 있다. 따라서 이 지문의 제목을 '고층 건물의 발달'이라고 표현한 ②번이 정답이다.

오답 분석
① Industrialization and Real Estate는 지문의 초반 내용만 설명할 수 있으므로 답이 될 수 없다.
③ 지문의 엘리베이터가 등장하기는 하였으나, 엘리베이터의 발명에 대해서는 언급되지 않았다.
④ 도시 중심지의 시골 이주민은 지문의 초반에서만 언급되었으므로, 답이 될 수 없다.
⑤ 도시 공간의 이해와 관련된 내용은 지문에서 언급되지 않았다.

어휘 skyscraper n. 고층 건물

[12-13]

> 방글라데시의 경제학자 Muhammad Yunus와 그가 30년 전 설립한 은행은 2006년에 노벨평화상을 공동 수상했다. Yunus는 그의 은행 시스템을 설립해서 아주 적은 융자금이 어떤 시중 은행도 신경 쓰지 않는 수백만 명의 사람들에게 주어질 수 있도록 했는데, 이는 주로 방글라데시 마을의 가난한 시골 사람들이다. 소위 말해서, 저금리 소액융자의 대부분은 여성에게 가고, 여성은 주로 농업, 공예, 혹은 서비스업에서 자신의 수익성 있는 모험적인 사업을 시작하는 데 저금리 소액융자를 사용한다. 가난을 방지하는 데 있어서 Yunus의 은행업 성공은 개발도상국 전체에 걸친 유사한 제도에 영감을 주었다.
>
> economist n. 경제학자 jointly adv. 공동으로
> loan n. 융자금 commercial bank phr. 시중 은행
> low-interest adj. 저금리의 microloan n. 소액융자
> profit-making adj. 수익성 있는
> enterprise n. 모험적인 사업 agriculture n. 농업
> crafts n. 공예 combat v. 방지하다 scheme n. 제도
> developing world phr. 개발도상국

12 2020 가천대

정답 ④

해석
① 편견   ② 소액융자
③ 모험적인 사업   ④ 가난

해설 지문의 빈칸을 채우는 문제이다. 지문의 두 번째 문장에서 Yunus는 그의 은행 시스템을 설립해서 아주 적은 융자금이 주로 방글라데시 마을의 가난한 시골 사람들에게 주어질 수 있도록 했다고 했으므로, 빈칸에는 어떤 것을 방지하는 데 있어서 Yunus의 은행업이 성공했는지에 대한 내용이 나와야 적절하다는 것을 알 수 있다. 따라서 '가난'이라고 한 ④번이 정답이다.

어휘 **prejudice** n. 편견　**microloan** n. 소액융자
enterprise n. 모험적인 사업

13 2020 가천대
정답 ②

해석 ① Yunus는 그의 은행 시스템 혁신으로 노벨상을 받았다.
② 시중 은행 또한 소액융자를 통해 가난한 시골 사람들을 도울 준비가 되어 있었다.
③ 가장 눈에 띄는 수혜자는 가난한 여성인 것으로 밝혀진다.
④ Yunus의 새로운 경제 제도는 국제적으로도 퍼졌다.

해설 지문의 내용과 일치하지 않는 것을 묻는 문제이다. ②번의 키워드인 The commercial bank(시중 은행)가 언급된 지문 주변에서 Yunus는 그의 은행 시스템을 설립해서 아주 적은 융자금이 어떤 시중 은행도 신경 쓰지 않는 수백만 명의 사람들에게 주어질 수 있도록 했는데, 이는 주로 방글라데시 마을의 가난한 시골 사람들이라고 했으므로, 시중 은행 또한 소액 융자를 통해 가난한 시골 사람들을 도울 준비가 되어 있었다는 것은 지문의 내용과 다르다. 따라서 ②번이 지문의 내용과 일치하지 않는다.

오답 ① 지문의 첫 번째 문장 A Bangladeshi economist,
분석　Muhammad Yunus, ~ were jointly awarded the Nobel Peace Prize in 2006.를 통해 'Yunus는 그의 은행 시스템 혁신으로 노벨상을 받았다'는 것을 알 수 있다.
③ 지문의 세 번째 문장 Most of the low-interest microloans ~ go to women을 통해 '가장 눈에 띄는 수혜자는 가난한 여성인 것으로 밝혀진다'는 것을 알 수 있다.
④ 지문의 마지막 문장 Yunus' banking success ~ has inspired similar schemes across the developing world.를 통해 'Yunus의 새로운 경제 제도는 국제적으로도 퍼졌다'는 것을 알 수 있다.

어휘 **innovation** n. 혁신　**commercial bank** phr. 시중 은행
notable adj. 눈에 띄는　**beneficiary** n. 수혜자
scheme n. 제도　**internationally** adv. 국제적으로

[14-15]

경제학자들은 소모된 칼로리나 놓아둔 케이블의 마일과 같은 수량화할 수 있는 대상들을 다루기 때문에 연구에서 사용하는 모델들은 거의 항상 수학적인 개념이다. 그 수학적인 개념들은 단어들로 서술될 수 있지만, 수학이 모델의 구조를 표현하는 대단히 효율적인 방법이다. 더 흥미롭게도, 모델의 결과를 알아내는 점에서 그렇다. 응용 수학자들과 물리학자들은 오랫동안 모델에 대해 알아 왔지만, 경제학자들이 생태학과 같은 지식 분야와 연관 지으면서 뻔뻔스럽게 그 연구 전략을 쓴 것은 단지 20세기 후반뿐이었다. 좋은 모델 제작의 기법은 매우 소수의 요인들에 중점을 두는 것으로부터 많은 이해를 발생시

키는 것이다. 나는 '기법'이라고 하는데, 좋은 모델을 속여서 빼앗는 데 방식이 없기 때문이다. 모델에 대한 엄격한/결정적인/최종적인 테스트 현상에 대한 대체 가능한 설명 중에 구별이 가능한지 아닌지이다. 실험에 근거를 둔 시험에서 살아남은 것들은 그것들에 의문을 제기하는 추가 증거가 나타날 때까지 적어도 한동안 받아들여지는데, 그 경우에는 경제학자들이 더 나은(꼭 더 큰 것은 아닌!) 모델을 만들어 내기 위해 자신들의 화판으로 다시 돌아간다.

quantifiable adj. 수량화할 수 있는
consume v. 소모하다, 소비하다　**construct** n. 개념
enormously adv. 대단히　**structure** n. 구조
interestingly adv. 흥미롭게도　**implication** n. 결과, 영향
mathematician n. 수학자　**physicist** n. 물리학자
brazenly adv. 뻔뻔스럽게　**tactic** n. 전략
discipline n. 지식 분야　**ecology** n. 생태학　**art** n. 기법
causal factor phr. 요인　**discriminate** v. 구별하다
explanation n. 설명　**phenomenon** n. 현상
come along phr. 나타나다
cast doubt on phr. 의문을 제기하다, 의구심을 던지다
drawing board phr. 화판, 제도판

14 2019 국민대
정답 ④

해석 ① 엄격한 시험　　② 결정적인 시험
③ 최종적인 시험　　④ 임의적인 시험

해설 지문의 흐름상 빈칸에 들어갈 수 없는 것을 고르는 문제이다. 삽입될 문장에 들어갈 선택지를 살펴보면 ④번의 arbitrary test를 제외하고 모두 '엄격한/결정적인/최종적인 테스트'의 의미를 담고 있는 단어들이다. 따라서 ④번이 정답이다.

15 2019 국민대
정답 ④

해석 ① 경제 모델은 구두로나 수학적으로 묘사될 수 있다.
② 경제 연구의 대상들은 양적으로 측정될 수 있는 것들이다.
③ 수학은 단지 20세기 후반에만 경제학에서 널리 사용되게 되었다.
④ 좋은 경제 모델은 한 현상을 설명하는 데 있어서 가급적 많은 요인들을 수용한다.

해설 지문의 내용과 일치하지 않는 것을 고르는 문제이다. ④번의 키워드인 good economic model(좋은 경제 모델)과 관련된 지문의 good modelling(좋은 모델 제작) 주변에서 좋은 모델 제작의 기법은 매우 소수의 요인들에 중점을 두는 것으로부터 많은 이해를 발생시키는 것이라고 했으므로, 좋은 경제 모델은 한 현상을 설명하는 데 있어서 가급적 많은 요인들을 수용한다는 것은 지문의 내용과 다르다. 따라서 ④번이 지문의 내용과 일치하지 않는다.

오답분석
① 지문의 두 번째 문장 They can be stated in words, but mathematics is an enormously efficient way to express the structure of a model을 통해 '경제 모델은 구두로나 수학적으로 묘사될 수 있다'는 것을 알 수 있다.
② 지문의 첫 번째 문장 As economists deal with quantifiable objects, ~ the models they use in their researches are almost always mathematical constructs를 통해 '경제 연구의 대상들은 양적으로 측정될 수 있는 것들이다'는 것을 알 수 있다.
③ 지문의 세 번째 문장 but it was only in the second half of the 20th century that economists brazenly adopted that research tactic을 통해 '수학은 단지 20세기 후반에만 경제학에서 널리 사용되게 되었다'는 것을 알 수 있다.

어휘 describe v. 묘사하다, 서술하다   verbally adv. 구두로
quantity n. 양   accommodate v. 수용하다

[16-17]

사업 모델이 아날로그 시대로부터의 유익한 선례를 전혀 갖고 있지 않은 소수의 거대 기업의 성공으로 인해 자본주의 경제가 작동하는 방식에 대한 재평가를 할 수밖에 없다. 전 세계에서 가치가 가장 높은 7대 기업 모두 기술 분야에 있다. (구글을 소유하고 있는) 알파벳과 페이스북 같은 거대기업들이 3차원 공간에는 존재하지 않는 제품들을 전문으로 하고 있다. 애플과 아마존은 상품 콘셉트뿐만 아니라 실제 세계의 물건도 판매하지만, 그들의 재산과 시장 지배력은 모델과 브랜드 및 알고리즘 등의 모호한 개념 위에 만들어져 있다.
부는 더 이상 공장과 파이프라인 또는 소매점에 있지 않다. 그들의 자본은 특정 분야에 고정되어 있지 않다. 그것이 그들을 규제하거나 세금을 부과하기에 어렵게 만든다. 이것들은 디지털 혁명보다 먼저 발생하는 경제적 세계화의 패턴들이다. 소프트웨어와 데이터 같은 일부 무형 자본은 컴퓨터에 매우 의존하지만, 브랜드 같은 다른 무형 자본은 그렇지 않다.
새 시대를 다르게 만드는 것은 가치가 유형의 것으로부터 분리되는 정도이며, 그에 상응하는 사회 경제적 결과이다. 이것이 조나단 해스켈(Jonathan Haskell)과 스티언 웨스틀레이크(Stian Westlake)가 '자본 없는 자본주의'라고 묘사한 역동적인 것이다. 그런 제목을 가진 그들의 책에서, 그 저자들은 무형적인 것의 규모가 시장 경제의 친숙한 메커니즘을 변형시키는 여러 방식들을 보여준다.

a handful of phr. 한 줌의, 소수의   corporate adj. 기업의
powerhouse n. 강자, 강국, 유력 집단
instructive adj. 유익한   precedent n. 선례, 전례
reappraisal n. 재평가, 재검토   titan n. 거인, 거물
specialize in phr. ~을 전문으로 하다, 전공하다
nebulous adj. 모호한   retail outlet phr. 소매점
anchor v. 닻을 내리다, 정박하다

pre-date v. 먼저 형성되다, 먼저 발생하다
intangible adj. 무형의, 실체가 없는   detach v. 떼어내다
tangible adj. 유형의, 실재하는
corresponding adj. 상응하는   deform v. 변형시키다

16 [2018 성균관대]

정답 ②

해석 ① 자본주의 경제의 붕괴
② 무형 자본의 자본주의
③ 기업에서 세계적 네트워크의 중요성
④ 자본주의에서 부의 불평등
⑤ 자본주의에서 유형 자산의 세계적 팽창

해설 밑줄 친 capitalism without capital이 의미하는 것을 추론하는 문제이다. 세계에서 가치가 가장 높은 7대 기업은 모두 기술 분야에 있으며 그들의 재산과 시장 지배력은 모델과 브랜드 및 알고리즘 같은 모호한 개념들 위에 세워져 있다고 했으며, 부는 더 이상 공장이나 파이프라인 또는 소매점에 있지 않다고 했으므로, without capital은 우리가 기존에 친숙한 유형 자본이 없다는 의미이다. 따라서 ②번 '무형 자본의 자본주의'가 정답이다.

17 [2018 성균관대]

정답 ③

해석 ① 자본주의에서 세계화의 필요성
② 자본주의의 세계화
③ 무형 자산의 성공
④ 자본주의의 변화하는 성질
⑤ 새 시대에 성공으로 가는 가이드

해설 지문(사설)의 제목을 묻는 문제이다. 무형 자산을 가진 세계적인 대기업들의 성공을 다루고 있으며 새로운 시대의 자본주의는 기존에 친숙한 유형 자산이 아니라 소프트웨어나 데이터 같은 무형 자산을 토대로 하고 있다고 설명하는 내용이므로, 이 지문의 주제로는 '무형 자산의 성공'이라고 표현한 ③번이 정답이다.

[18-20]

거시경제학은 전체 시장경제에 대한 학문이다. 경제학의 다른 부분들처럼, 거시경제학은 사람들이 희박한 자원으로 목적성 있는 결정을 내린다는 중심 사상을 이용한다. 하지만, 땅콩 시장이든 자전거 시장이든 한 가지 시장의 작동에 초점을 맞추는 대신에 거시경제학은 전체로서의 경제에 초점을 맞춘다. 거시경제학은 큰 그림을 보는데, 경제 성장, 불경기, 실업, 그리고 인플레이션이 그 주제 중에 있다. 거시경제학은 대학을 졸업한 후에 당신이 바람직한 직업을 찾을 기회가 경제 침체기보다 경제 확장기 동안 더 많을 것이기 때문에 당신과 당신의

미래에 더 중요하다. 강력한 경제 성장은 가난을 완화하고, 환경을 정화하기 위한 자원을 확보하며, 그리고 당신 세대를 위한 더 밝은 미래를 가져올 수 있다.

---

macroeconomics n. 거시경제학
purposeful adj. 목적성 있는 **scarce** adj. 희박한, 부족한
recession n. 불경기, 경제 침체 **unemployment** n. 실업
inflation n. 인플레이션 **subject matter** phr. 주제
desirable adj. 바람직한 **expansion** n. 확장
alleviate v. 완화하다 **poverty** n. 가난
free up phr. 확보하다, 풀어주다 **environment** n. 환경
generation n. 세대

---

18 [2019 숙명여대]

정답 ①

해석 ① 전체로서의 ② 부분적으로
③ 상세하게 ④ 목적을 갖고
⑤ 특별한 관점에서

해설 지문의 빈칸을 채우는 문제이다. 빈칸 앞에서 땅콩 시장이나 자전거 시장같이 한 가지 시장에 초점을 맞추는 대신에 거시경제학이 초점을 맞추는 경제의 특성을 설명해야 하므로 빈칸에는 '전체로서의' 경제를 의미하는 as a whole이 적합하다. 따라서 ①번이 정답이다.

어휘 **partially** adv. 부분적으로
specifically adv. 상세하게, 분명히
purposefully adv. 목적을 갖고 **perspective** n. 관점

19 [2019 숙명여대]

정답 ③

해석 ① 암시하다 ② 악화시키다
③ 줄이다 ④ 증가하다
⑤ 불러일으키다

해설 밑줄 친 alleviate의 의미를 추론하는 문제이다. 밑줄이 포함된 문장에서 강력한 경제 성장이 환경을 정화하기 위한 자원을 확보하며, 당신 세대를 위한 더 밝은 미래를 가져올 수 있다고 하였다. 따라서, alleviate의 의미를 '줄이다'라고 한 ③번이 정답이다.

어휘 **allude** v. 암시하다 **aggravate** v. 악화시키다

20 [2019 숙명여대]

정답 ③

해석 ① 거시경제학은 사람들이 결정에 도달하기 위해 충분한 데이터를 사용한다는 생각을 이용한다.
② 거시경제학은 중대한 영역에 초점을 맞춘다는 의미에서 선택적이다.
③ 거시경제학은 우리가 미래 경제의 방향을 더 잘 이해하도록 돕는다.
④ 거시경제학은 경제 침체와 가난을 초래할 수 있다.
⑤ 거시경제학은 언제나 밝은 미래에 대한 청사진을 제공한다.

해설 지문의 내용과 일치하는 것을 묻는 문제이다. 지문에서 거시경제학은 전체로서의 경제에 초점을 맞추며, 경제 성장, 불경기, 실업, 인플레이션과 같은 큰 그림을 본다고 설명하고 있다. 따라서 ③번이 지문의 내용과 일치한다.

오답분석 ① 거시경제학은 사람들이 희박한 자원으로 목적성 있는 결정을 내린다는 중심 사상을 이용한다고 했으므로, 거시경제학은 사람들이 결정에 도달하기 위해 충분한 데이터를 사용한다는 생각을 이용한다는 것은 지문의 내용과 다르다.
② 거시경제학은 전체로서의 경제에 초점을 맞춘다고 했으므로, 거시경제학은 중대한 영역에 초점을 맞춘다는 의미에서 선택적이라는 것은 지문의 내용과 다르다.
④ 거시경제학을 통한 강력한 경제 성장은 가난을 완화하고 환경을 정화하기 위한 자원을 확보한다고 했으므로, 거시경제학은 경제 침체와 가난을 초래할 수 있다는 것은 지문의 내용과 다르다.
⑤ 거시경제학을 통해 다음 세대를 위한 더 밝은 미래를 가져올 수 있다고는 했지만, 거시경제학은 언제나 밝은 미래에 대한 청사진을 제공한다는 것은 지문에서 알 수 없다.

어휘 **reach** v. 달하다, 닿다 **selective** adj. 선택적인
in the sense phr. ~라는 의미에서
critical adj. 중대한; 비판적인 **direction** n. 방향
blue print phr. 청사진

[21-22]

당신이 어떤 통계에 의존하는지에 따라, 미국이 세계 제1의 제조 회사가 될 수도 있고 제2의 제조 회사가 될 수도 있다. 지난 10년 동안, 미국 공장들의 생산량은 인플레이션을 반영하여 3분의 1이 상승했다. 하지만 미국 제조 회사들의 성공은 비용을 들여 얻은 것이었다. 공장들은 수백만 명의 노동자를 기계로 대체했다. 노동 통계는 충격적이다. 미국의 제조업 고용 자료는 1940년대 후반부터 1980년대까지 꾸준한 성장을 보여주었고, 그때 일자리의 숫자가 살짝 감소하였다. 그리고 수준은 1999년까지 고르게 유지되었다. 그 이후로, 그 숫자가 무너졌다. 2009년까지의 10년 동안 공장들은 노동자들을 너무 빠르게 해고하여 지난 70년간 얻어온 거의 모든 노동자를 없앴는데, 대략 6백만 명의 제조 일자리가 사라졌다. 미국 전체에 걸쳐, 많은 공장 작업장이 20년 전에 그랬던 것보다 근본적으로 다르게 보이는데, 훨씬 더 적은 사람들, 훨씬 더 많은 최첨단 기계들, 그리고 남아있는 노동자들에 대해 전체적으로 다른 수요를 가지고 있다.

---

statistics n. 통계, 통계 자료 **manufacturer** n. 제조 회사
output n. 생산량, 산출 **adjust** v. 적응하다, 조정하다

at a cost phr. 비용을 들여   replace v. 대체하다
disturbing adj. 충격적인   employment n. 고용, 취업
steady adj. 꾸준한   slightly adv. 살짝   flat adj. 고른
collapse v. 무너지다   previous adj. 지난, 이전의
roughly adv. 대략   floor n. 작업장, 층
radically adv. 근본적으로   high-tech adj. 최첨단의
entirely adv. 전체적으로

21 2019 한국외대

정답 ③

해석
① 미국 안에서 생산하는 것은 기계의 가격 때문에 큰 비용이 든다.
② 미국의 제조 회사들은 기계를 노동자로 대체해 왔다.
③ 미국 제조업의 성공은 실직으로 인해 생겨났다.
④ 미국에서 사업을 하는 값은 살짝 감소해 왔다.

해설 지문을 통해 추론할 수 있는 것을 고르는 문제이다. 지문 중간에서 미국 제조 회사들의 성공은 비용을 들여 얻은 것이며, 공장들이 수백만 명의 노동자를 기계로 대체했다고 했으므로, 미국 제조업의 성공은 실직으로 인해 생겨났다는 것을 추론할 수 있다. 따라서 정답은 ③번이다.

오답 분석
① 미국 안에서 생산하는 것이 기계의 가격 때문에 큰 비용이 드는지에 대해서는 언급되지 않았다.
② 공장들은 수백만 명의 노동자를 기계로 대체했다고 했으므로, 미국의 제조 회사들은 기계를 노동자로 대체해 왔다는 것은 추론할 수 없다.
④ 미국에서 사업을 하는 값은 살짝 감소해 왔는지에 대해서는 언급되지 않았다.

어휘
costly adj. 큰 비용이 드는   due to phr. ~ 때문에
substitute v. 대체하다, 대신하다
result from phr. ~로 인해 생기다, ~에 기인하다

22 2019 한국외대

정답 ③

해석
① 2009년을 시작으로, 공장들은 노동자를 빠르게 해고했다.
② 1940년대부터 1980년대까지 노동자의 숫자가 무너졌다.
③ 세기가 바뀐 이후로, 공장들은 급격하게 노동력을 줄였다.
④ 현대식 공장들의 근본적인 차이점이 직원의 증가를 요구했다.

해설 지문의 내용과 일치하는 것을 묻는 문제이다. 지문의 중간에서 In the 10 years ending in 2009, factories shed workers so fast의 내용을 통해 세기가 바뀐 이후로, 공장들은 급격하게 노동력을 줄였다는 것을 알 수 있다. 따라서 ③번이 지문의 내용과 일치한다.

오답 분석
① 2009년까지의 10년 동안 공장들은 노동자들을 너무 빠르게 해고했다고 했으므로, 2009년을 시작으로 공장들은 노동자를 빠르게 버렸다는 것은 지문의 내용과 다르다.
② 1940년대 후반부터 1980년대까지 꾸준한 성장을 보여주었고 수준은 1999년까지 고르게 유지되었다고 했으므로, 1940년대부터 1980년대까지 노동자의 숫자가 무너졌다는 것은 지문의 내용과 다르다.
④ 많은 공장 작업장이 남아있는 노동자들에 대해 전체적으로 다른 수요를 가지고 있다고는 했지만, 현대식 공장들의 근본적인 차이점이 직원의 증가를 요구했는지는 알 수 없다.

어휘
commence v. 시작되다   discard v. 버리다, 포기하다
rapidly adv. 빠르게   sharply adv. 급격하게
workforce n. 노동력   staff n. 직원

[23-24]

주식시장에서 성공하기 위한 전략적인 원칙 중의 하나는 기만적인 시장 변동이나 특정한 주가 성과에 자동으로 나오는 반응을 보이는 것을 삼가는 것이다. 급격하게 떨어지는 주식에 다시 투자하기 전에, 분석가와 투자자들은 "짧은 반응"이라고 불리는 하나 이상의 작은 상승추세가 지나가는 것을 기다릴 것이다. 이 용어는 죽은 고양이라도 높은 곳에서 떨어지면 튀어 오를 것이라는 다소 엉성한 생각을 반영한다. 폭락하는 주식이 약간 증가하는 것은 단기 매도, 유발된 매각, 또는 인기 없는 CEO를 교체하는 것과 같이 회사가 만든 변화에 대한 과도하게 낙관적인 반응으로 일어날 수 있다. 이토록 작고 평범한 상승은 보통 기존의 최저치를 뛰어넘는 또 다른 하락으로 이어진다. 이 용어가 대부분 주식 시장에서만 한정으로 관련되어 있지만, 그 용어는 오해의 소지가 있는 전개의 다른 분야를 설명하는 데에도 가끔 사용되는 것이 보인다. 선거일 근처에서 불리해지는 후보의 투표수가 때때로 잠깐 환상에 불과한 급증을 보인다. 스포츠에서, 시즌 중간에 코치를 교체하는 패전 팀들이 때때로 이전의 상태로 돌아가기 전에 한 번 이상의 우승으로 바뀌는 에너지의 작은 급증을 경험한다.

strategic adj. 전략적인   principle n. 원칙
refrain v. 삼가다   knee-jerk adj. 자동 반사의
deceptive adj. 기만적인   fluctuation n. 변동, 오르내림
performance n. 성과   reinvest v. 재투자하다
analyst n. 분석가
dead cat bounce phr. 짧은 반응(주식 시장에서 주가가 대폭 하락한 뒤 잠깐 상승하는 것)   somewhat adv. 다소
crude adj. 엉성한, 대강의   uptick n. 약간의 증가
plummet v. 폭락하다, 급락하다
trigger v. 유발시키다, 촉발시키다   optimistic adj. 낙관적인
unimpressive adj. 평범한   sell-off n. 매각
surpass v. 뛰어넘다
exclusively adv. 한정으로, 배타적으로
occasional adj. 가끔의
misleading adj. 오해의 소지가 있는
candidate n. 후보자   lose ground phr. 불리해지다
surge n. 급증   midseason n. 중간 시즌
translate v. 바꾸다, 옮기다   revert to phr. 되돌아가다

23 [2019 한양대]

정답 ⑤

해석
① "짧은 반등"은 스포츠와 정치에서 관찰될 수 있다.
② "짧은 반등"은 급격한 감소 이후에 주식이 약간 급증하는 것을 말한다.
③ 투자자들은 "짧은 반등"이 일어날 때 보통 다시 투자하기 전에 참아낸다.
④ 회사의 인기 없는 CEO를 교체하는 것은 주식 시장에서 "짧은 반등"의 원인이 될 수 있다.
⑤ "짧은 반등" 이후에 주식의 하락을 기대할 수 있지만, 일반적으로 이전의 최저치를 초과하지는 않는다.

해설 지문의 내용과 일치하지 않는 것을 묻는 문제이다. ⑤번의 키워드인 the previous low point(이전의 최저치)와 관련된 지문의 the previous low(이전의 최저치) 주변에서 작고 평범한 상승은 보통 기존의 최저치를 뛰어넘는 또 다른 하락으로 이어진다고 했으므로, "짧은 반등" 이후에 주식의 하락을 기대할 수 있지만, 일반적으로 이전의 최저치를 초과하지는 않는다는 것은 지문의 내용과 다르다. 따라서 ⑤번이 지문의 내용과 일치하지 않는다.

오답분석
① Poll numbers for a candidate losing ground near an election ~ In sports, losing teams that make midseason coaching changes ~ before the team reverts to form을 통해 '"짧은 반등"은 스포츠와 정치에서 관찰될 수 있다'는 것을 알 수 있다.
② Before reinvesting in a rapidly falling stock, ~ one or more small upward bumps, referred to as "dead cat bounces"를 통해 '"짧은 반등"은 급격한 감소 이후에 주식이 약간 급증하는 것을 말한다'는 것을 알 수 있다.
③ analysts and investors will often wait for the passing of one or more small upward bumps를 통해 '투자자들은 "짧은 반등"이 일어날 때 보통 다시 투자하기 전에 참아낸다'는 것을 알 수 있다.
④ Upticks in a plummeting stock can be caused by ~ overly optimistic reactions to changes made by the company, such as replacing an unpopular CEO를 통해 '회사의 인기 없는 CEO를 교체하는 것은 주식 시장에서 "짧은 반등"의 원인이 될 수 있다'는 것을 알 수 있다.

어휘 practice patience phr. 참아내다
typically adv. 전형적으로

24 [2019 한양대]

정답 ②

해석
① 급격한 ② 환상에 불과한
③ 기대되는 ④ 인상적인
⑤ 설명할 수 없는

해설 지문의 빈칸을 채우는 문제이다. 지문의 전반에 걸쳐 주식이 급격하게 떨어진 후에 등장하는 하나 이상의 작은 상승추세인 "짧은 반등"에 대해 설명하고 있으므로, 빈칸에는 그 상승추세가 실제로는 이전의 상태로 돌아가기 전 잠깐 보이는 것에 불과하다는 내용이 들어가야 한다는 것을 알 수 있다. 따라서 '환상에 불과한'이라고 한 ②번이 정답이다.

어휘 sharp adj. 급격한 illusory adj. 환상에 불과한
expected adj. 기대되는 impressive adj. 인상적인
inexplicable adj. 설명할 수 없는

[25-27]

국제무역과 화물 운송이 발달함에 따라, 수년간에 걸쳐 공통된 행동수칙에 대한 필요성이 인코텀스(Incoterms) 규칙을 만들어냈다. 이 규칙은 1923년 이래로 국제 상공 회의소(ICC)에 의해서 발표되어 오고 있다. (A)인코텀스 규칙은 거래가 실행되는 틀을 만들며 제품의 구매자와 판매자 사이의 의무사항과 비용 및 위험요소를 결정한다. 그때 이후로, 두 당사자 간의 (B)인코텀스 규칙을 따르지 않은 상거래를 찾아 출발지에서 도착지까지 화물을 운송하는 동안 지불과 위험에 대해 누구에게 책임이 있는지를 결정하기 위해 우리는 아주 열심히 찾아보아야 한다. 인코텀스 규칙은 현재의 국제 무역 관행과 (C)인코텀스 규칙이 일치하도록 유지하기 위해 업데이트되며 수정된다. 2011년에 여덟 번째 버전이 발표되었고, 새로운 버전에 대한 협의가 진행 중이며, 2020년에 발표될 예정이다. 인코텀스 규칙은 거래의 두 가지 핵심적 측면을 명시한다. 첫째로, 거래 및 관련 활동들, 예를 들면 수입과 수출에 대한 허가를 받는 것, 상품을 보험에 드는 것 등을 위한 준비와 지불에 대해 구매자와 판매자 중 어느 쪽 당사자가 책임을 져야 하는가? 그리고 둘째로, 운송 중 어느 지점에서 운송에 대한 책임이 판매자에게서 구매자에게로 넘어가는가? 인코텀스 규칙을 이용하기로 동의함으로써, 구매자와 판매자는 (D)그들의 의무와 책임을 정의할 때 정확성과 명확성을 달성한다.

international commerce phr. 국제무역
code of conduct phr. 행동강령, 행동수칙
Incoterms n. 국제적으로 통용되는 무역 용어 해석에 관한 국제 규칙 (international commercial terms의 약칭)
International Chamber of Commerce phr. 국제 상공회의소 (1920년에 창립되었으며 파리에 본부를 두고 있는 국제 경제 협력 기구) framework n. 뼈대, 틀
execute v. 실행하다 obligation n. 의무
transaction n. 거래, 매매 party n. 당사자
destination n. 목적지, 도착지
amend v. (법 등을) 개정(수정)하다
consultation n. 협의, 상의; 회담
specify v. (구체적으로) 명시하다 e.g. phr. 예를 들어
consignment n. 탁송(물), 배송(물)

06 경제·경영 111

25 2018 한국외대

정답 ①

해석 ① 인코텀스 규칙은 모든 당사자의 책임을 명확히 하기 때문에 널리 퍼져있다.
② 국제무역은 인코텀스 없이 일어날 수 없다.
③ 인코텀스 규칙이 매우 유용하기 때문에, 1923년 이래로 바뀌지 않았다.
④ 정확성과 명확성은 더 이상 현재의 무역 관행과 일치하지 않는다.

해설 지문에서 언급되거나 암시된 것을 고르는 문제이다. 첫 문장에서 '국제무역과 화물 운송이 발달함에 따라, 공통된 행동 수칙에 대한 필요성이 인코텀스 규칙을 만들어냈다'고 했으며, 마지막 문장에서 '인코텀스 규칙을 이용하기로 동의함으로써, 구매자와 판매자는 그들의 의무와 책임을 정의할 때 정확성과 명확성을 달성한다'고 했으므로, '인코텀스 규칙은 모든 당사자의 책임을 명확히 하기 때문에 널리 퍼져있다'는 것을 알 수 있다. 따라서 ①번이 정답이다.

오답 분석
② 마지막 문장에서 '인코텀스 규칙을 이용하기로 동의함으로써, 구매자와 판매자는 정확성과 명확성을 달성한다'고 했으므로, '인코텀스 규칙을 이용하기로 동의하지 않는 경우'도 있다는 것을 알 수 있다. 따라서 '국제무역은 인코텀스 없이 일어날 수 없다'는 것은 지문의 내용과 다르다.
③ 지문 중간에서 '인코텀스 규칙은 현재의 국제 무역 관행과 일치하도록 유지하기 위해 업데이트되며 수정된다'고 했으므로, '1923년 이래로 바뀌지 않았다'는 것은 지문의 내용과 다르다.
④ 정확성과 명확성이 현재의 무역 관행과 일치하는지 여부는 언급되지 않았다.

26 2018 한국외대

정답 ③

해석 ① 구매자가 화물에 대한 책임을 떠맡는 시점
② 수출 허가를 획득할 책임이 있는 당사자
③ 상품에 대해 판매자에게 지불해야 할 액수
④ 보험 비용을 감당할 당사자

해설 인코텀스 규칙에 의해 언급되지 않는 거래 요소를 고르는 문제이다. ①, ②, ④번에 대해서는 지문 후반부에 있는 The Incoterms rules specify two key aspects of a transaction. First, ~etc.? And second, ~ to the buyer? 에서 근거를 찾을 수 있다. 그러나 '상품에 대해 판매자에게 지불해야 할 액수'에 대해서는 언급되지 않았다. 따라서 ③번이 정답이다.

어휘 assume v. (책임을) 맡다

27 2018 한국외대

정답 ④

해설 밑줄 친 대명사 중에서 가리키는 것이 나머지 셋과 다른 것을 고르는 문제이다. (A), (B), (C)는 인코텀스 규칙을 가리키지만, 마지막의 (D)는 '구매자와 판매자'를 가리키는 대명사이다. 따라서 ④번이 정답이다.

[28-29]

정치 경제학자 벤자민 프리드먼(Benjamin Friedman)은 과거에 서양 사회를 경제 성장에 의해 바퀴가 계속 돌아가는 안정된 자전거에 비유했다. 혹시라도 앞으로 나아가게 하는 움직임이 느려지거나 중단되면, 우리 사회를 정의하는 기둥들 즉 민주주의와 개인의 자유 그리고 사회적 관용 등이 불안정하게 될 것이다. 우리 세계는 점점 더 추한 곳, 즉 제한된 자원을 놓고 벌어지는 쟁탈전과 바로 옆에 있는 사람들 이외의 사람에 거부로 정의되는 추한 곳이 될 것이다. 혹시라도 우리가 바퀴를 다시 움직이게 할 방법을 찾지 못한다면, 결국 우리는 완전한 사회적 붕괴에 직면할 것이다.
인류 역사에서 그런 붕괴는 여러 번 일어났으며, 어떤 문명도 겉보기에 아무리 위대할지라도 사회를 종말로 이끄는 취약성을 피하지 못한다. 현재 상황이 얼마나 잘 돌아가는지와는 무관하게, 상황은 언제나 바뀔 수 있다. 소행성 충돌, 핵전쟁으로 인한 겨울, 또는 치명적인 세계적 전염병 등과 같은 종을 멸종시킬 정도의 사건들 외에도, 역사는 우리에게 붕괴의 원인이 되는 것은 보통 여러 요인들이라는 것을 말해준다. 그 요인들은 무엇인가 그리고 혹시라도 이미 표면화하기 시작한 요인들이 있다면 어떤 것일까? 인류가 현재 지속 가능하지 않고 불확실한 길 위에 있다는 것은 전혀 놀라운 일이 아니다. 그러나 우리는 돌아올 수 없는 지점까지 얼마나 가까이 온 걸까?

compare A to B phr. A를 B에 비유하다
stable adj. 안정된 cease v. 중단되다
teeter v. 넘어질 듯 불안정하게 서다(움직이다)
scramble n. 서로 밀치기, 쟁탈전
immediate adj. 목전의, (시간적·공간적으로) 아주 가까이에 있는
collapse n. 붕괴
be immune to phr. ~에 면역이 되어 있다, 영향을 받지 않다
vulnerability n. 취약성 put aside phr. ~을 제쳐놓다
asteroid n. 소행성 pandemic n. 전국적인(세계적인) 전염병
plethora n. 과잉, 과다 come as phr. ~이다
unsustainable adj. 지속 가능하지 않은

28 2018 성균관대

정답 ③

해석 ① 행성 간의 충돌
② 핵전쟁 이후의 심각한 기후 변화
③ 화산 분출

④ 경제성장의 멈춤
⑤ 치명적인 전염병의 세계적 확산

해설 우리 세계를 붕괴로 이어지게 하는 것이 아닌 것을 고르는 문제이다. 첫 문단에서 경제성장이 멈추면 우리 사회의 기둥들이 불안정해지고 우리 사회는 추한 곳이 될 것이며 결국엔 완전한 사회적 붕괴에 직면할 것이라고 했다. 그리고 두 번째 문단에서 an asteroid strike, nuclear winter or deadly pandemic을 언급했다. 그러나 화산 분출에 대해서는 언급하지 않았으므로 ③번이 정답이다.

어휘 **interstellar** adj. 행성 간의

29 [2018 성균관대]
정답 ④

해석 ① 경제성장의 취약성
② 현대 서양 사회의 궁극적인 붕괴
③ 생태계 파괴의 잠재적 파국
④ 미래에 일어날 세계 붕괴의 가능성
⑤ 미래 사회를 위한 지속 가능한 모델

해설 지문의 주제를 묻는 문제이다. 첫 문단에서는 경제성장이 멈추면 사회가 붕괴에 직면할 수 있다고 했고, 두 번째 문단에서는 그 외에도 사회가 붕괴할 수 있는 여러 가지 요인들에 대해 언급했다. 그리고 마지막 문장에서는 우리는 돌이킬 수 없는 지점에 얼마나 가까이 왔는가라고 질문을 던지고 있으므로, 이 지문의 주제로는 '미래에 일어날 세계 붕괴의 가능성'이라고 표현한 ④번이 정답이다.

[30-32]

Blue Apron의 주가가 주당 1달러 이하로 무너진 지 며칠 이후로 Weight Watchers International과 시의적절한 제휴는 Blue Apron의 시가총액을 늘려가고 있다. Blue Apron의 주식은 12월 18일 이후 처음으로 주당 1달러 이상으로 다시 급증했다. 그 수준은 투자자들에게 상징적인 의미를 가져오는데, 1달러 수준 아래에서 주식 발행은 보수적인 주주들을 단념시키는 명칭인 투기적 저가주로 간주하기 때문이다. 게다가, 뉴욕 증권거래소는 30일 이상 주당 1달러 이하로 거래되는 주식들의 상장을 폐지한다. Blue Apron 주식의 만회는 12월 21일에 시작되었는데, 그때 회사는 지금은 WW주식회사라고 이름이 바뀐 Weight Watchers를 위한 식자재 세트의 새로운 생산 공정을 만들겠다고 발표하였다.
제휴가 발표되었을 무렵 Blue Apron의 주식은 주당 65센트라는 하한가를 기록했다. 월 스트리트 저널과 같은 간행물들이 새로운 메뉴에 대한 이야기를 쓰기 시작하면서, 주식은 계속해서 상승했다. 오늘 주가 마감 기준으로, Blue Apron의 주식은 최저주가보다 73퍼센트 오른 주당 1.12달러로 올랐지만, 여전히 매출가격이었던 주당 10달러 이하의 89퍼센트에 남아있다. 이번 주의 반응은 회사로 향한 잠재적인 기회를 강조한다. 몇몇 분석가들은 월마트와 같은 대형 체인 식료품점에 Blue Apron의 식자재 세트를 공급하면 주가를 개선할 수 있을 것이라고 말했다.

---

timely adj. 시의적절한, 때맞춘 **partnership** n. 제휴, 동업
fatten up phr. (체중을) 늘리다
market cap phr. 시가총액(market capitalization)
stock n. 주식 **tumble** v. 무너지다, 굴러떨어지다
share n. 주, 주식 **surge** v. 급증하다 **investor** n. 투자자
issue n. 발행 **consider** v. 간주하다
penny stock phr. 투기적 저가주 (1주의 가격이 1달러 미만의 주식) **designation** n. 명칭, 지명
deter v. 단념시키다, 그만두게 하다
conservative adj. 보수적인 **shareholder** n. 주주
delist v. 상장을 폐지하다, 목록에서 빼다
rebound n. 만회, 반등 **announce** v. 발표하다
line n. (생산) 공정, 줄 **publication** n. 간행물
underscore v. 강조하다, 밑줄을 긋다
potential adj. 잠재적인 **ahead for** phr. ~로 향한
analyst n. 분석가 **grocery chain** phr. 체인 식료품점

30 [2019 한국외대]
정답 ③

해석 ① 이름을 바꾸었다.
② Blue Apron의 주가를 올리는 것을 도왔다.
③ 새로운 식자재 세트를 개발했다.
④ Blue Apron과 제휴 관계를 시작했다.

해설 지문을 통해 Weight Watchers에 대해 추론할 수 없는 것을 고르는 문제이다. 첫 번째 단락의 마지막 문장에서 Blue Apron이 Weight Watcher를 위한 식자재 세트의 새로운 생산 공정을 만들겠다고 발표했다고 했지만, 이를 통해 Weight Watchers가 새로운 식자재 세트를 개발했는지는 유추할 수 없으므로 정답은 ③번이다.

오답 분석
① it would create a new line of meal kits for Weight Watchers, now renamed WW Inc을 통해 Weight Watchers가 '이름을 바꾸었다'는 것을 알 수 있다.
② A timely partnership with Weight Watchers International is fattening up Blue Apron's market cap을 통해 Weight Watchers가 'Blue Apron의 주가를 올리는 것을 도왔다'는 것을 알 수 있다.
④ A timely partnership with Weight Watchers International is fattening up Blue Apron's market cap을 통해 Weight Watchers가 'Blue Apron과 제휴 관계를 시작했다'는 것을 알 수 있다.

31 [2019 한국외대]
정답 ④

해석 ① 주가는 12월에 최저가를 기록했다.
② 제휴를 발표한 후에 주식이 급격하게 상승했다.

③ 주식 시장에서 초기 주가는 주당 10달러였다.
④ 월마트에 의해 구입될 것이다.

해설 지문을 통해 Blue Apron에 대해 추론할 수 없는 것을 고르는 문제이다. 지문의 마지막에서 몇몇 분석가들은 월마트와 같은 대형 체인 식료품점에 Blue Apron의 식자재 세트를 공급하면 주가를 개선할 수 있을 것이라고 말했다고 했지만, Blue Apron이 월마트에 의해 구입될 것인지는 유추할 수 없으므로 정답은 ④번이다.

오답분석
① Blue Apron's stock surged back above the $1 a share level for the first time since Dec. 18을 통해 '주가는 12월에 최저가를 기록했다'는 것을 알 수 있다.
② Blue Apron shares had risen to $1.12 a share, or 73% above its low를 통해 '제휴를 발표한 후에 주식이 급격하게 상승했다'는 것을 알 수 있다.
③ but remains 89% below its $10 a share offering price를 통해 '주식 시장에서 초기 주가는 주당 10달러였다'는 것을 알 수 있다.

어휘 sharply adv. 급격하게, 날카롭게   initial adj. 초기의

32 [2019 한국외대]
정답 ③

해석 Blue Apron은 주식 시장에 계속 올라가 있을 수 있었다. 왜냐하면 주식이 30일 이상 주당 1달러 미만에 머물러 있지 않았기 때문이다.
① 그 회사가 곧 거대한 체인 식료품점과 합병될 것이기 때문이다
② 주식이 30일 동안 주당 1달러 미만으로 떨어지지 않았기 때문이다
③ 주식이 30일 이상 주당 1달러 미만에 머물러 있지 않았기 때문이다
④ 월마트와의 제휴 이후로 판매량이 개선되었기 때문이다

해설 지문의 빈칸을 채우는 문제이다. 첫 번째 단락의 중간에서 뉴욕 증권거래소는 30일 이상 주당 1달러 이하로 거래되는 주식들의 상장을 폐지한다고 했으므로, 빈칸에는 Blue Apron의 주식이 30일 이상 주당 1달러 이하로 거래되지 않았다는 내용이 들어가야 한다는 것을 알 수 있다. 따라서 '주식이 30일 이상 주당 1달러 미만에 머물러 있지 않았기 때문이다'라고 한 ③번이 정답이다.

어휘 merge v. 합병하다, 합치다   huge adj. 거대한

[33-35]

자본과 정치는 그 관계가 경제학자, 정치인과 일반 대중이 똑같이 열띤 논쟁을 할 정도로 서로 영향을 준다. 열정적인 자본주의자들은 자본은 자유롭게 정치에 영향을 주어야 하지만, 정치는 자본에 영향을 주도록 허용되어서는 안 된다고 주장하는 경향이 있다. 자본주의자들은 정부가 시장에 개입할 때, 정치적 관심이 시장이 더 느린 성장을 야기하는 현명하지 못한 투자를 하게 한다고 주장한다. 예를 들어, 정부는 경영자들에게 무거운 세금을 부과하고 그 돈을 유권자들에게 인기 있는 넉넉한 실업 수당을 주는 데 사용할 수 있다. 하지만 많은 기업인의 관점에서 보면, 정부가 그 돈을 기업인들에게 남기면 훨씬 더 좋을 것이다. 기업인들은 그들이 그 돈을 새로운 공장을 열고 실업자들을 고용하는 데 쓸 것이라고 주장한다. 이 관점에서, 가장 현명한 경제 정책은 정치를 경제에 영향받지 않게 하고, 세금과 정부 규제를 최소로 줄이고, 시장 원리가 자연스럽게 흘러가도록 무제한의 자유를 허용하는 것이다.

capital n. 자본, 자금   politics n. 정치   relation n. 관계
economist n. 경제학자   politician n. 정치인
general public phr. 일반 대중   alike adv. 똑같이, 비슷하게
ardent adj. 열정적인, 열렬한
capitalist n. 자본주의자, 자본가
interfere in phr. ~에 개입하다
unwise adj. 현명하지 못한, 어리석은   taxation n. 세금
industrialist n. 경영자   lavish adj. 넉넉한, 충분한
unemployment benefit phr. 실업 수당
voter n. 유권자, 투표자   in the view of phr. ~의 관점에서
free rein phr. (행동·결정의) 무제한의 자유

33 [2019 서강대]
정답 ①

해석 ① 기업과 정부 정책이 어떻게 상호 관계를 맺을 수 있는지에 대한 평론을 제시하는 연구원
② 자신의 독자 네트워크에 가장 좋은 투자에 대한 충고를 제공하는 글을 작성하는 블로거
③ 젊은 고객들이 새로운 계좌를 개설하도록 유인하기 위해 안내서를 작성하는 은행 지점장
④ 기업 관리자들이 자신들에게 투표하도록 지지를 호소하는 짧은 선거 연설을 하는 정치인

해설 글쓴이와 유사한 제시 방식을 파악하는 문제이다. 첫 번째 문장에서 자본과 정치는 그 관계가 경제학자, 정치인과 일반 대중이 똑같이 열띤 논쟁을 할 정도로 서로 영향을 준다고 한 뒤, 마지막 문장에서 가장 현명한 경제 정책은 정치를 경제에 영향받지 않게 하고, 세금과 정부 규제를 최소로 줄이고, 시장 원리가 자연스럽게 흘러가도록 무제한의 자유를 허용하는 것이라고 했으므로, 글쓴이와 유사한 제시 방식을 보여주는 것은 '기업과 정부 정책이 어떻게 상호 관계를 맺을 수 있는지에 대한 평론을 제시하는 연구원'이다. 따라서 ①번이 정답이다.

어휘 critique n. 평론, 비평한 글
interrelate v. 상호 관계를 맺다
brochure n. 안내서, 팸플릿   woo v. 지지를 호소하다

34 2019 서강대

정답 ④

해석
① 경영자는 기업체에 낮은 세금을 부과하는 접근법을 채택하는 정치인에게 투표하기 쉽다.
② 자본주의자는 보통 시장이 정치적 개입으로 인해 흐트러지지 않는 것을 바랄 것이다.
③ 규제가 철폐된 시장은 기업체가 이익을 낼 수 있는 가장 좋은 기회를 준다.
④ 정치가 기업체의 영향을 받지 않게 하는 것은 모두에게 항상 일자리가 있을 것임을 보장한다.

해설 지문을 통해 추론할 수 없는 것을 고르는 문제이다. 마지막 문장에서 가장 현명한 경제 정책은 정치를 경제에 영향받지 않게 하고, 세금과 정부 규제를 최소로 줄이고, 시장 원리가 자연스럽게 흘러가도록 무제한의 자유를 허용하는 것이라고는 했지만, 이를 통해 정치가 기업체의 영향을 받지 않게 하는 것은 모두에게 항상 일자리가 있을 것임을 보장하는지는 유추할 수 없으므로 정답은 ④번이다.

오답 분석
① 다섯 번째 문장 But in the view of many business people, ~ if the government left the money with them을 통해 경영자는 기업체에 낮은 세금을 부과하는 접근법을 채택하는 정치인에게 투표하기 쉽다는 것을 알 수 있다.
② 두 번째 문장 Ardent capitalists tend to argue ~ politics should not be allowed to influence capital을 통해 자본주의자는 보통 시장이 정치적 개입으로 인해 흐트러지지 않는 것을 바랄 것이라는 것을 알 수 있다.
③ 마지막 문장 the wisest economic policy is to keep politics out of the economy, ~ and allow market forces free rein to take their course를 통해 규제가 철폐된 시장은 기업체가 이익을 낼 수 있는 가장 좋은 기회를 준다는 것을 알 수 있다.

어휘
adopt v. 채택하다 untroubled adj. 흐트러지지 않은
deregulated adj. 규제가 철폐된
turn a profit phr. 이익을 내다

35 2019 서강대

정답 ②

해설 빈칸에 들어갈 내용을 묻고 있다. 빈칸이 있는 문장 앞에서 열정적인 자본주의자들은 자본은 자유롭게 정치에 영향을 주어야 하지만, 정치는 자본에 영향을 주도록 허용되어서는 안 된다고 주장하는 경향이 있다고 했으므로, 자본주의자들은 정부가 시장에 개입할 때, 정치적 관심이 시장이 더 느린 성장을 야기하는 현명하지 못한 투자를 하게 한다고 주장한다는 내용이 오는 것이 자연스럽다. 따라서 정답은 ②번이다.

[36-38]

기업들은 공개적일 수도 있고 개인적일 수도 있다. 공개 기업의 주식은 일반적인 대중에 의해 매입될 수 있다. [A] 이와는 대조적으로, Gallo Wine, Levi Strauss 혹은 Parcel Service와 같은 개인 기업의 주식은 매우 작은 집단의 사람들만이 소유하고 있고 일반적인 대중에게는 팔리지 않는다. 이런 기업의 지배 주주들은 서로 가족 구성원이거나, 기업의 경영진, 혹은 기업의 직원일 가능성이 높다. [B] 왜냐하면 잘 알려지지 않은 주식은 구매자들의 관심을 끌지 못하는 경향이 있으며, 대부분의 새로운 기업들은 이러한 개인 기업의 형태로 시작하게 되기 때문이다.

기업은 여러 장점을 갖는다. 가장 큰 장점은 유한 책임인데, 투자자의 법적 책임이 개인적으로 그 회사에 투자한 금액으로 한정된다는 것이다. [C] 기업이 도산하는 경우, 법원은 그 회사의 자산을 압수하여 처분할 수 있지만, 마음대로 투자자의 개인적인 소유물을 처분할 수는 없다. 예를 들어, 만약 당신이 1,000달러를 한 회사에 투자했고, 이 회사가 파산하게 되었다고 가정한다면, 당신은 단지 그 금액만큼만 잃게 되는 것이다. 다시 말해서, 1,000달러가 당신이 져야 하는 책임의 한도인 것이다. [D] 또 다른 기업의 장점은 지속성이다. 기업은 법인으로써, 소유주 개인의 생물학적 수명과 분리되어 있기 때문에, 기업은 적어도 이론상으로는 영원히 지속될 수 있다. 예를 들어, 주식은 미래 세대에 상속될 수 있다. 마지막으로, 기업들은 돈을 마련하는 데 우위를 갖는다. 이를테면, 더 많은 주식을 판매함으로써, 기업들은 투자자의 수와 자금의 양을 쉽게 늘릴 수 있다.

public corporation phr. 공개 기업
controlling stockholder phr. 지배 주주
limited liability phr. 유한 책임 failure n. 도산
seize v. 압수하다 dispose of phr. 처리하다
bankrupt adj. 파산한 continuity n. 지속성
inherit v. 상속받다 the upper hand phr. 우세, 우위

36 2020 한성대

정답 ②

해설 지문의 흐름상 주어진 문장이 들어가기에 가장 적절한 위치를 고르는 문제이다. [B]의 앞에서, 개인 기업의 지배 주주가 서로 가족 구성원이거나, 경영진, 혹은 회사의 직원일 가능성이 높다고 이야기하고 있으므로, [B]의 자리에 그 이유를 설명하는 주어진 문장 '왜냐하면 잘 알려지지 않은 주식은 구매자들의 관심을 끌지 못하는 경향이 있으며, 대부분의 새로운 기업들은 이러한 개인 기업의 형태로 시작하게 되기 때문이다'가 오는 것이 자연스럽다. 따라서 ②번이 정답이다.

어휘 attract v. 관심을 끌다 buyer n. 구매자

37 2020 한성대

정답 ②

해석 ① 인생의 다른 모든 것과 마찬가지로
② 적어도 이론상으로는
③ 절대
④ 결코 ~이 아닌

해설 지문의 빈칸을 채우는 문제이다. 빈칸을 포함하는 문장의 앞에서, 기업의 장점 중 하나가 지속성이라고 했으므로, '기업은 법인으로써, 소유주 개인의 생물학적 수명과 분리되어 있기 때문에, _____ 영원히 지속될 수 있다'의 빈칸에는 '절대', '결코 ~이 아닌'과 같은 부정어가 들어갈 수 없으므로, ③번과 ④번은 배제한다. 또한, 기업이 생물학적 수명과 분리되어 있기 때문에 지속될 수 있다는 표현은 인생이 유한함을 의미하고 있으므로, ①번도 답이 될 수 없다. 따라서 ②번이 정답이다.

38 2020 한성대

정답 ③

해석 ① 개인 기업이 주식을 대중에 발행하는 것은 불가능하다.
② 기업 투자자의 책임은 사실상 한계가 없다.
③ 기업은 심지어 최초의 투자자가 죽은 이후에도 지속될 수 있다.
④ 개인 기업의 종업원은 그 회사의 주식을 소유할 수 없게 되어 있다.

해설 지문의 내용과 일치하는 것을 묻는 문제이다. 지문의 두 번째 문단에서, 기업의 두 번째 장점으로 언급된 지속성을 설명하면서 소유주 개인의 생물학적 수명과 분리되어 있는 기업은 적어도 이론적으로는 영원히 지속될 수 있다고 했으므로, 기업은 심지어 최초의 투자자가 죽은 이후에도 지속될 수 있다는 것은 지문의 내용과 일치한다. 따라서 ③번이 정답이다.

오답 분석
① 지문의 첫 번째 문단에서, 개인 기업의 주식은 잘 알려지지 않았기 때문에 구매자의 관심을 끌지 못하는 경향이 있다고 했다. 즉, 대중의 관심을 끌 수 있다면 기업이 주식을 대중에 주식을 발행할 수 있다는 의미이다. 따라서 개인 기업이 주식을 대중에 발행하는 것이 불가능하다는 것은 지문의 내용과 다르다.
② 지문의 두 번째 문단에서, 기업의 장점 중 하나가 유한 책임이며, 유한책임은 투자자가 기업에 투자한 금액만큼만 책임을 지게 된다는 것이므로, 기업 투자자의 책임이 사실상 한계가 없다는 것은 지문의 내용과 다르다.
④ 지문의 첫 번째 문단에서, 개인 기업의 지배 주주는 대개 서로 가족 구성원이거나, 경영진, 혹은 기업의 직원일 가능성이 높다고 했으므로, 개인 기업의 종업원이 그 회사의 주식을 소유할 수 없게 되어 있다는 것은 지문의 내용과 다르다.

어휘 issue stock phr. 주식을 발행하다   virtually adv. 사실상

[39-40]

대부분의 사회 정책은 사회 제도 내의 정해진 소득 분배를 유지하거나 사회를 구성하는 여러 사회 집단 사이에서 소득을 재분배하려는 시도로써 직접 구상되었다. 운이 좋지 않고, 판단력이 떨어지며, 연령과 노쇠함으로 인해 일반적인 수단으로는 적절한 생계 수준을 달성하지 못하는 사람들 사이에 이러한 요소가 항상 존재하기 때문에, 일부 재분배가 반드시 이루어져야 한다는 것은 일반적으로 받아들여져 왔다. 물론, 정확히 얼마나 많은 소득의 재분배가 일어나야 하는지는 다른 시대의 다른 사회가 다른 방식으로 답해온 하나의 윤리적인 문제인데, 이것은 도시 체계에 관한 모든 사회 정책의 수립에서 이루어져야 할 중심적인 윤리적 판단이다. 우리가 선택된 소득 분배를 달성하기 위해서, 먼저 우리는 반드시 소득 불평등을 만드는 메커니즘에 관해 매우 명확한 생각을 가지고 있어야 하는데, 그것은 아마 이러한 메커니즘을 통제하고 조작하는 것을 통해 우리는 주어진 목표를 달성할 수 있을 것이기 때문이다. 이러한 메커니즘을 조사하기 위해 특정한 소득 분배에 관한 선호도를 명시할 필요는 없지만, 아마도 현재 미국이나 영국의 도시 체계에 존재하는 것보다 훨씬 더 평등주의적인 사회 구조에 내가 일반적으로 찬성한다는 점은 다음과 같은 점에서 분명해질 것이다. 복잡한 도시 체계에서 소득 재분배의 "숨겨진 메커니즘"은 보통 불평등을 줄이기보다는 증가시키는 것처럼 보인다. 이것은 숨겨진 재분배의 일반적인 방향성에 대응하기 위해서라면 직접 재분배에서 오버 킬(과도한 수요 억제) 정책의 필요하다는 점을 시사한다는 면에서 사회 정책에 즉각적인 효과를 갖고 있다. 물론, 또 다른 가능성은 재분배를 위한 숨겨진 메커니즘을 통제하거나 이용하려고 하는 것이며, 나는 이것들이 어떻게 이루어질 수 있는지에 관해 약간의 조짐을 보일 것이다. 그러나 내가 가진 사회 정책의 선호도를 고려한 이런 "혼잣말들"은 소득 분배를 통제하는 메커니즘의 직접적인 분석을 방해할 필요가 없다.

---

frame v. 구상하다   distribution n. 분배   frailty n. 노쇠함
adequate adj. 적절한   ethical adj. 윤리적인
formulation n. 수립   with respect to phr. ~에 관한
mechanism n. 메커니즘, 구조   inequality n. 불평등
presumably adv. 아마   manipulate v. 조작하다
investigate v. 조사하다   in favour of phr. ~에 찬성하여
egalitarian adj. 평등주의적인   complex adj. 복잡한
immediate adj. 즉각적인   counteract v. 대응하다
indication n. 조짐   aside n. 혼잣말
interfere v. 방해하다

39 2020 단국대

정답 ④

해석 ① 비록 ~한다 해도   ② ~하도록
③ ~에도 불구하고   ④ ~이기 때문에

해설 빈칸에 적절한 연결어를 넣는 문제이다. 빈칸 앞 문장은 일부 재분배가 이루어져야 한다는 내용이고, 빈칸 뒤 문장은 일부 사람들이 적절한 생계 수준을 달성하지 못한다는 내용이다. 따라서 원인을 나타내는 연결어인 ④ since(~이기 때문에)가 정답이다.

40 [2020 단국대]

정답 ②

해석 ① 사회 정책의 가장 좋은 형태는 미국이나 영국의 진보한 도시 메커니즘에서 찾을 수 있다.
② 직접 재분배의 과도한 정책은 도시 체계의 평등을 달성하기 위해 정당화될 수 있다.
③ 소득의 특정한 분배를 유지하는 것은 대부분의 사회 정책들이 시도하는 것이 아니다.
④ 사회에서 평균보다 더 적은 소득으로 살아가는 사람들은 그들의 삶의 수준을 높이기 위해 더 열심히 노력해야 한다.

해설 지문의 내용과 일치하는 것을 묻는 문제이다. 지문의 중반에서 숨겨진 재분배의 일반적인 방향성에 대응하기 위해서라면 직접 재분배에서 오버 킬(과도한 수요 억제) 정책의 필요하다는 점을 시사한다는 면에서 사회 정책에 즉각적인 효과를 갖고 있다는 내용을 통해 직접 재분배의 과도한 정책은 도시 체계의 평등을 달성하기 위해 정당화될 수 있다는 것을 알 수 있다. 따라서 ②번이 지문의 내용과 일치한다.

오답분석 ① 글쓴이는 현재 미국이나 영국의 도시 체계에 존재하는 것보다 훨씬 더 평등주의적인 사회 구조에 찬성한다고 했으므로, 사회 정책의 가장 좋은 형태는 미국이나 영국의 진보한 도시 메커니즘에서 찾을 수 있다는 것은 지문 내용과 다르다.
③ 대부분의 사회 정책은 사회 제도 내의 정해진 소득 분배를 유지하거나 사회를 구성하는 여러 사회 집단 사이에서 소득을 재분배하려는 시도로써 직접 구상되었다고는 했지만, 소득의 특정한 분배를 유지하는 것은 대부분의 사회 정책들이 시도하는 것이 아니라는 것은 알 수 없다.
④ 일반적인 수단으로는 적절한 생계 수준을 달성하지 못하는 사람들 사이에 이러한 요소가 항상 존재하기 때문에 일부 재분배가 반드시 이루어져야 한다는 것은 일반적으로 받아들여져 왔다고 했으므로, 사회에서 평균보다 더 적은 소득으로 살아가는 사람들은 그들의 삶의 수준을 높이기 위해 더 열심히 노력해야 한다는 것은 지문의 내용과 다르다.

어휘 advanced adj. 진보한 excessive adj. 과도한
justify v. 정당화하다 equality n. 평등

[41-43]

라인강은 중세 시대 유럽인의 교역을 위한 가장 중요한 수로였다. 상선은 신성 로마 제국의 보호책의 대가로 라인강을 따라 각 국가를 지날 때 통행료를 냈다. 하지만 13세기 신성 로마 제국의 쇠퇴(A)와 함께, 남작들은 강변을 수백 개의 성으로 채워 지나가는 선박들로부터 통행료를 요구했다. 그들의 통행료 요구는 너무 (B)대담해져서 상인들은 라인강을 하류에서의 사업을 완전히 포기했다. 라인강을 따라 있던 무역 사업이 실패하면서, 이익을 얻으려 했던 남작들도 그것을 따라 도산했다. 컬럼비아 로스쿨 Michael Heller 교수는 이 효과를 "반공유지의 비극"이라고 칭한다. 주인이 나타나지 않는 소유지의 낭비가 파괴적일 수 있지만, 소유지에 대한 자기 잇속만 차리는 팽창주의적인 싸움은 라인강 사례에서 보듯이 (C)드물게 파멸적일 수 있다. 그의 책 *The Gridlock Economy: How Too Much Ownership Wrecks Markets, Stops Innovation, and Costs Lives*에서, Heller는 너무 분열된 소유권과 광범위한 소유권은 결국 산업과 시장을 (D)막다른 골목에 가둘 수 있다고 주장했다.

현재 생명 공학 산업에서는 특허권이 과다하다. 지난 30년 동안 오로지 DNA와 관련하여 허가를 받은 특허권만 4만 건을 뛰어넘는다. 제약 회사는 많은 특허권 소유자를 거쳐야 하고 신약을 내놓기 전 계약 조건을 협상해야 한다. 많은 실험이 <u>은둔한 특허권 소유자로부터의 소송 반발이 두려워서</u> 실험실을 넘어서지 못한다.

waterway n. 수로 toll n. 통행료
in return for phr. ~의 대가로 in line with phr. ~와 함께
baron n. 남작 riverside n. 강변 audacious adj. 대담한
venture n. (벤처) 사업 collapse v. 실패하다
bring down phr. 도산시키다 sponge v. 얻다, 뜯어내다
common n. 공유지 unclaimed adj. 주인이 나타나지 않는
ruinous adj. 파괴적인
self-serving adj. 자기 잇속만 차리는
expansive adj. 팽창주의적인 disastrous adj. 파멸적인
gridlock n. 정체 ownership n. 소유권
wreck v. 파괴하다 innovation n. 혁신 overly adv. 너무
fragmented adj. 분열된 broad adj. 광범위한
a dead end phr. 막다른 골목 overabundance n. 과다
patent n. 특허권 biotech n. 생명 공학
licensed adj. 허가를 받은
associated with phr. ~와 관련된
pharmaceutical adj. 제약의 numerous adj. 많은
holder n. 소유자 negotiate v. 협상하다
contract term phr. 계약 조건
go beyond phr. ~을 넘어서다 lab n. 실험실

41 [2020 가천대]

정답 ②

해석 ① 라인강 상인과 남작 사이의 갈등
② 소유권과 경제 발전 사이의 충돌
③ 신약 개발의 필요성
④ 특허권 문제와 약의 발달

해설 지문의 제목을 묻는 문제이다. 지문 전체적으로 중세 시대 라인강에서 있었던 사례를 근거로, 너무 분열된 소유권과 광범

위한 소유권은 산업과 시장을 막다른 골목에 가둘 수 있다는 한 교수의 의견을 설명하고 있다. 따라서 이 지문의 제목을 '소유권과 경제 발전 사이의 충돌'이라고 표현한 ②번이 정답이다.

어휘 baron n. 남작 clash n. 충돌 ownership n. 소유권
necessity n. 필요성 patent n. 특허권
progress n. 발달

42 2020 가천대

정답 ③

해설 밑줄 친 낱말의 쓰임이 적절하지 않은 것을 묻는 문제이다. (C) 뒤 문장에서 '너무 분열된 소유권과 광범위한 소유권은 결국 산업과 시장을 막다른 골목에 가둘 수 있다'고 했으므로, '주인이 나타나지 않는 소유지의 낭비가 파괴적일 수 있지만, 소유지에 대한 자기 잇속만 차리는 팽창주의적인 싸움은 라인강 사례에서 보듯이 똑같이(equally) 파멸적일 수 있다'라고 하는 것이 문맥에 알맞다. (B)의 rarely를 equally로 고쳐야 한다. 따라서 ③번이 정답이다.

43 2020 가천대

정답 ④

해석 ① 신약 시장에 대한 정치적 간섭 때문에
② 시장을 지배하기 위한 약사와 의사의 쟁탈전을 야기하는
③ 특허권 소유자의 지나친 요구를 하는 광범위한 소유권에도 불구하고
④ 은둔한 특허권 소유자로부터의 소송 반발이 두려워서

해설 지문의 빈칸을 채우는 문제이다. 마지막 문단 세 번째 문장에서 제약 회사는 많은 특허권 소유자를 거쳐야 하고 신약을 내놓기 전 계약 조건을 협상해야 한다고 했으므로, 빈칸에는 많은 실험이 왜 실험실을 넘어서지 못하는지에 대한 내용이 나와야 적절하다는 것을 알 수 있다. 따라서 '은둔한 특허권 소유자로부터의 소송 반발이 두려워서'라고 한 ④번이 정답이다.

어휘 owing to phr. ~ 때문에 interference n. 간섭
scramble v. 서로 쟁탈하다 pharmacist n. 약사
dominate v. 지배하다 patent n. 특허권
holder n. 소유자 demanding adj. 지나친 요구를 하는
extensive adj. 광범위한 ownership n. 소유권
litigation n. 소송 backlash n. 반발
reclusive adj. 은둔한

[44-46]

월요일에 발표된 자료에서는 한국에서 운영 중인 금융 회사의 모든 최고 경영자 중 한 사람만이 여성인 것을 보였으며, 이 나라의 여성 직원들이 깨기 힘든 유리 천장에 관한 많은 것을 밝히고 있다.

최근 90개의 금융 회사를 기반으로 한 산업 자료에 의하면, 한국 푸르덴셜생명보험의 책임자인 61세의 손병옥 회장은 국내의 모든 금융 회사의 책임자 중 유일한 여성 최고 경영자였다. 손 회장은 그녀가 1996년에 푸르덴셜생명보험에서 일하기 시작한 이전인 1980년대 중반에 체이스맨해튼은행에서 은행원으로 그녀의 경력을 시작했다. 그녀는 여성으로서는 처음으로 2년 전에 서울에 지사를 둔 미국계 보험 회사의 책임을 맡게 되었다.

한편, 자료에 의하면 한국 금융계의 최고 경영자 연령의 평균은 56.4세이다. 증권사의 최고 경영자의 평균은 54.8세로 가장 낮았으며, 생명보험 회사가 55.9세로 그 뒤를 이었다. 금융지주회사는 가장 높은 평균인 59.3세였다.

한국 알리안츠생명보험의 대표이사인 46세의 이명재 회장은 45세의 현대 생명보험 최진환 회장에 이어 이 회사의 지도자가 되며 두 번째로 젊은 사람이 되었다.

한국의 많은 금융 회사의 최고 경영자들은 경제학이나 경영학을 전공했으며, 이는 90명 중 40명을 차지한다고 자료가 밝혔다.

전체 중에서 약 75퍼센트가 서울과 경기 지역에 소재한 대학을 졸업한 반면, 남은 25퍼센트는 다른 지역의 대학을 졸업했다.

chief executive officer phr. 최고 경영자
financial adj. 금융의, 재정적인 operate v. 운영하다
ceiling n. 천장 head n. 책임자 firm n. 회사
clerk n. 직원 take the helm phr. 책임을 맡다
insurance n. 보험 average n. 평균
brokerage n. 증권사
financial holding company phr. 금융지주회사
chairman n. 회장, 의장 economics n. 경제학
business administration phr. 경영학
account for phr. ~를 차지하다

44 2020 단국대

정답 ①

해석 ① 한편 ② 그렇지 않으면
③ 그에 반해서 ④ 정반대로

해설 빈칸에 적절한 연결어를 넣는 문제이다. 빈칸 앞 문장은 손 회장이 2년 전부터 보험 회사의 회장으로 일하게 되었다는 내용이고, 빈칸 뒤 문장은 금융 기업의 최고 경영인 연령의 평균이 54.8세라는 내용이다. 따라서 화제 전환을 나타내는 연결어인 ① Meanwhile(한편)이 정답이다.

45 2020 단국대

정답 ④

해석 ① 한국 금융 회사의 가장 젊은 최고 경영자는 46세였다.
② 한국 금융계에 여성 최고 경영자는 두 명만이 있다.

③ 한국 금융 회사의 최고 경영자 중 40명이 경영학을 전공했다.
④ 한국 금융 회사에서, 여성이 더 높은 직위로 승진하는 것은 어렵다.

해설 지문의 내용과 일치하는 것을 묻는 문제이다. 지문의 처음에서 여성 직원들이 깨기 힘든 유리 천장에 관한 많은 것을 밝히고 있다는 내용을 통해 한국 금융 회사에서, 여성이 더 높은 직위로 승진하는 것은 어렵다는 것을 알 수 있다. 따라서 ④번이 지문의 내용과 일치한다.

오답분석
① 46세의 이명재 회장은 두 번째로 젊은 사람이 되었다고 했으므로, 한국 금융 회사의 가장 젊은 최고 경영자는 46세였다는 것은 지문의 내용과 다르다.
② 손병옥 회장은 국내의 모든 금융 회사의 책임자 중 유일한 여성 최고 경영자였다고 했으므로, 한국 금융계에 여성 최고 경영자는 두 명만이 있다는 것은 지문의 내용과 다르다.
③ 한국의 많은 금융 회사의 최고 경영자들은 경제학이나 경영학을 전공했으며 이는 90명 중 40명을 차지한다고 했으므로, 한국 금융 회사의 최고 경영자 중 40명이 경영학을 전공했다는 것은 지문의 내용과 다르다.

어휘 promote v. 승진시키다

46 (2020 단국대)

정답 ④

해석
① 한국 금융계의 성차별
② 한국 금융 회사들의 최고 경영자들의 대학 전공
③ 한국 금융 회사들의 최고 경영자들의 연령 분포
④ 한국 금융 회사들의 최고 경영자들의 특징

해설 지문의 제목을 묻는 문제이다. 지문의 전반에 걸쳐 한국 금융계의 여성 최고 경영자, 최고 경영자들의 연령과 대학 전공을 포괄적으로 말하고 있다. 따라서 이 지문의 제목을 '한국 금융 회사들의 최고 경영자들의 특징'이라고 표현한 ④번이 정답이다.

어휘 discrimination n. 차별 distribution n. 분포
characteristic n. 특징

[47-48]

규제가 없는 시장의 일반적인 경우는 두 가지 주장에 기초한다. 한 주장은 번영에 관한 것이고, 다른 한 주장은 자유에 관한 것이다. 우선, 시장은 사람들에게 타인이 원하는 제품을 열심히 공급하도록 장려책을 제공하여 사회 전체의 번영을 촉진한다. (일반적인 말로, 번영은 사회 복지의 경제 외적 측면을 포함할 수 있는 더 넓은 개념이기는 하지만, 우리는 보통 번영을 경제적 번영과 동일시한다.) 다음으로, 시장은 개인의 자유를 존중한다. 시장은 재화 및 용역에 특정한 가격을 부과하기보다는, 사람들이 교환하는 물건들에 어떤 가격을 매길지 스스로 선택할 수 있게 한다.

당연히, 부당하게 값을 올리는 것에 대해 규정한 법률의 반대자들은 자유 시장에 대해 이러한 두 개의 비슷한 주장을 언급한다. 부당하게 값을 올리는 것에 대해 규정한 법률의 옹호자들은 어떻게 반응하는가? 첫째로, 옹호자들은 불경기에 청구되는 과도한 가격으로 인해 사회 전체의 번영이 실로 이뤄지지 않는다고 주장한다. 높은 가격이 제품에 대한 더 많은 공급을 불러일으킨다고 하더라도, 이 이득은 이러한 가격이 제품을 살 형편이 가장 안 되는 사람들에게 부과할 부담감과 비교 검토되어야 한다. 부유한 사람들로서는, 폭풍우로 폭등한 1갤런의 휘발유 가격 혹은 모텔 객실 가격을 지불하는 것은 골칫거리가 될 수도 있다. 하지만 가난한 사람들로서는, 이러한 가격이 진정한 어려움을 야기하고, 어려움은 가난한 사람들이 안전한 곳으로 피하기보다 계속 위험한 상황에 남아 있게 할지도 모른다. 부당하게 값을 올리는 것에 대해 규정한 법률의 지지자들은 공공복지에 대한 모든 평가는 비상사태 동안 기본적 필수품에 대해 터무니없이 비싼 가격을 내야 할 수도 있는 사람들의 고통과 괴로움도 포함해야 한다고 주장한다.

두 번째로, 부당하게 값을 올리는 것에 대해 규정한 법률의 옹호자들은 특정한 상황에서 자유 시장은 진정으로 자유롭지 않다고 주장한다. Crist가 지적하듯이, "강압하에 있는 구매자들에게는 자유가 없다. 안전한 거주지와 같은 그들의 필수품 구매는 강요된 것이다." 만약 당신이 허리케인을 피해 가족과 피난하고 있다면, 휘발유와 주거지를 위해 지불하는 과도한 가격은 실제로 자발적인 교환이 아니다. 그것은 강탈에 더 가까운 것이다. 따라서 부당하게 값을 올리는 것에 대해 규정한 법률을 정당화할지 여부를 결정하기 위해, 우리는 사회 번영과 자유에 대한 이 대립하는 설명들을 검토해야 한다.

그러나 우리는 하나의 추가적인 주장을 고려해볼 필요도 있다. 부당하게 값을 올리는 것에 대해 규정한 법률을 향한 많은 대중의 지지는 번영이나 자유보다 더욱 본능적인 것에서 생겨난다. 사람들은 타인의 절박함을 희생물로 하는 "남의 불행을 이용하는 사람들"에게 격분하고, 그들이 처벌받고 초과 이윤을 보상받지 않기를 원한다. 이러한 정서는 보통 공공 정책이나 법에 지장을 주어서는 안 되는 인간 본래의 감정으로 일축된다. Jacoby가 쓴 것처럼, "판매자를 악마로 묘사하는 것은 플로리다의 경제 회복을 촉진하지 않을 것이다." 하지만, 부당하게 값을 올리는 사람들에 대한 격분은 특별한 이유가 없는 분노의 정도로 말하기에 충분하지 않다. 그것은 진지하게 생각해볼 가치가 있는 도덕적 주장을 나타내는 것이다. 격분은 사람들이 받을 만하지 않은 것들을 받고 있다고 생각할 때 당신이 느끼는 특별한 종류의 분노이다. 이 종류의 격분은 부당함에 대한 분노이다.

rest on phr. ~에 기초하다 promote v. 촉진하다
incentive n. 장려책
in common parlance phr. 일반적인 말로
equate v. 동일시하다 prosperity n. 번영
impose v. 부과하다
goods and services phr. 재화 및 용역
gouge v. 값을 부당하게 올리다 invoke v. 언급하다, 들먹이다

exorbitant adj. 과도한 **hard times** phr. 불경기
call forth phr. 불러일으키다
weigh against phr. ~을 비교 검토하다
afford v. 형편이 되다, 여유가 되다 **affluent** adj. 부유한
inflated adj. 폭등한 **annoyance** n. 골칫거리
estimate n. 평가, 추정 **general welfare** phr. 공공복지
price out of phr. 터무니없는 값을 매기다 **duress** n. 강압
lodging n. 거주지 **voluntary** adj. 자발적인
extortion n. 강탈, 강요 **assess** v. 검토하다, 평가하다
visceral adj. 본능적인 **prey on** phr. 희생물로 하다
desperation n. 절박감 **punish** v. 처벌하다
windfall profits phr. 초과 이윤
dismiss v. 일축하다, 묵살하다 **atavistic** adj. 인간 본래의
demonize v. 악마로 묘사하다 **vendor** n. 판매자
mindless adj. 특별한 이유가 없는 **deserve** v. 받을 만하다

47 [2019 중앙대]

정답 ②

해석 ① 비과세의 — 왜냐하면
② 규제가 없는 — ~라 하더라도
③ 억제되지 않은 — ~라는 점에서
④ 아직 손대지 않은 — ~할 때마다

해설 지문의 빈칸을 채우는 문제이다. 첫 번째 빈칸의 경우, 지문의 첫 번째 문단 마지막 문장에서 시장은 재화 및 용역에 특정한 가격을 부과하기보다는, 사람들이 교환하는 물건들에 어떤 가격을 매길지 스스로 선택할 수 있게 한다고 했으므로, 빈칸에는 '규제가 없는'이라는 의미의 unfettered가 들어가는 것이 자연스럽다. 두 번째 빈칸의 경우, 빈칸이 있는 문장은 높은 가격이 제품에 대한 더 많은 공급을 불러일으킨다는 내용이고, 빈칸 뒤 문장은 이 이득은 이러한 가격이 제품을 살 형편이 가장 안 되는 사람들에게 부과할 부담감과 비교 검토되어야 한다는 내용이다. 따라서 양보를 나타내는 연결어인 Even if가 들어가는 것이 자연스럽다. 따라서 ②번이 정답이다.

어휘 **untaxed** adj. 비과세의, 면세의
unfettered adj. 규제가 없는
unrestrained adj. 억제되지 않은
untapped adj. 아직 손대지 않은

48 [2019 중앙대]

정답 ④

해석 ① 부당하게 값을 올리는 것에 대해 규정한 법률의 몇몇 반대자들은 사실 부당이득을 챙기는 것에 격분한다.
② 공공 정책이나 법을 정당화할지 여부를 결정하기 위해, 자연스러운 인간의 감정은 되도록 억제되어야 한다.
③ 부당하게 값을 올리는 것에 대해 규정한 법률의 옹호자들은 시장이 사회 번영을 향상하고 개인 자유를 존중한다고 주장하면서, 자유 시장에 대한 옹호론을 펼친다.
④ 부당하게 값을 올리는 것에 대해 규정한 법률의 지지자들은 사람들이 위기에 경제적 이득을 위해 이웃 사람을 착취하지 않는 좋은 사회를 만들고자 한다.

해설 지문을 통해 추론할 수 있는 것을 고르는 문제이다. 지문 마지막 문단에서 사람들은 타인의 절박함을 희생물로 하는 사람들에게 격분하고, 그들이 처벌받고 초과 이윤을 보상받지 않기를 원한다고 했으므로, 부당하게 값을 올리는 것에 대해 규정한 법률의 지지자들은 사람들이 위기에 경제적 이득을 위해 이웃 사람을 착취하지 않는 좋은 사회를 만들고자 한다는 것을 추론할 수 있다. 따라서 ④번이 정답이다.

오답 분석
① 부당하게 값을 올리는 것에 대해 규정한 법률에 대한 지지자들이 타인의 절박함을 희생물로 하는 사람들이 초과 이윤을 보상받지 않기를 원한다고 했으므로, 법률의 몇몇 반대자들이 사실 부당이득을 챙기는 것에 격분한다는 것은 지문의 내용과 다르다.
② 격분은 보통 공공 정책이나 법에 지장을 주어서는 안 되는 인간 본래의 감정으로 일축된다고 했지만, 공공 정책이나 법을 정당화할지 여부를 결정하기 위해, 자연스러운 인간의 감정이 되도록 억제되어야 하는지는 알 수 없다.
③ 부당하게 값을 올리는 것에 대해 규정한 법률에 대한 반대자들이 자유 시장에 대해 번영과 자유를 언급한다고 했으므로, 법률의 옹호자들이 시장이 사회 번영을 향상하고 개인 자유를 존중한다고 주장하면서 자유 시장에 대한 옹호론을 펼친다는 것은 지문의 내용과 다르다.

어휘 **enrage** v. 격분하게 만들다 **unfair profits** phr. 부당이득
restrain v. 억제하다
make out a case for phr. ~의 옹호론을 펴다
exploit v. 착취하다

[49-50]

1957년에 연설로 시작하여, 이후 1960년에 *The Human Side of Enterprise*라고 하는 획기적인 책에서, McGregor는 기업들이 인간 행동에 관해 잘못된 가정을 바탕으로 운영하고 있다고 주장했다. 대다수의 지도자들은 자신들의 조직에 있는 사람들이 근본적으로 일을 싫어하고 할 수 있으면 일을 피할 것이라고 생각했다. 이러한 정체불명의 아랫사람들은 책임지는 것을 두려워하고, 안전 확보를 열망하고, 지시가 절실하게 필요했다. 결과적으로, "대다수 사람들이 조직 목표의 달성을 향해 충분히 노력하도록 만들기 위해 그들은 강압되고, 통제되고, 지시받고, 처벌로 위협받아야 한다." 그러나 McGregor는 직원에 대해 대체 가능한 관점이 있다고 주장했는데, 그것은 인적 조건에 대한 더 정확한 평가와 기업을 운영하기 위해 더 효과적인 출발점을 제공하는 것이었다. 이 관점은 일에 흥미를 갖는 것이 "놀이를 하거나 쉬는 것처럼 자연스러운" 일이고, 창조성과 독창성은 사람들에게 널리 분포되어 있으며, 적절한 조건하에서 사람들은 책임을 받아들이고, 심지어는 추구하기까지 할 것이라고 간주했다. 이러한 대조적인 견해를 설명하기 위해, McGregor는 알파벳 뒷부분을 사용했

다. 그는 첫 번째 관점을 X 이론, 두 번째 관점을 Y 이론이라고 칭했다. 당신의 출발점이 X 이론이었다면, 당신의 경영 기법은 제한된 결과를 만들어 내거나 심지어는 완전히 실패할 수밖에 없을 것이라고 그는 주장했다. McGregor가 말했듯이, 만약 당신이 "근로자 계급의 평범함"을 믿었다면, 그 후 평범함은 당신이 달성할 수 있는 것에 상한선이 되었을 것이다. 그러나 당신의 출발점이 Y 이론이었다면, 단순히 개인의 잠재력뿐만 아니라, 기업의 최종 결산 결과에 대한 가능성도 방대했다. 따라서, 기업 조직이 더 일을 잘하게 하는 방법은 X 이론에서 벗어나 Y 이론 쪽으로 사고하며 경영 수완을 바꾸는 것이었다.

groundbreaking adj. 획기적인 **operate** v. 운영하다
assumption n. 가정 **organization** n. 조직
minion n. 아랫사람, 부하 **coerce** v. 강압하다
punishment n. 처벌 **put forth an effort** phr. 노력하다
alternative adj. 대체 가능한 **assessment** n. 평가
distribute v. 분포시키다 **managerial** adj. 경영의, 관리의
go awry phr. 실패하다 **mediocrity** n. 평범함, 보통
ceiling n. 상한선, 최대 한계 **potential** n. 잠재력
bottom line phr. 최종 결산 결과

49 [2019 한국항공대]

정답 ③

해석 ① McGregor는 인간 행동에 대한 두 가지의 다른 관점을 제시했다.
② X 이론에서, 관리자들은 직원들이 본질적으로 일을 싫어한다고 생각한다.
③ X 이론에서, 달성은 과업의 특성에 따라 좌우된다.
④ X 이론에서, 직원들은 지시받거나, 심지어는 과업을 수행하도록 강압되어야 한다.

해설 지문의 내용과 일치하지 않는 것을 묻는 문제이다. ③번의 키워드인 achievement(달성)가 그대로 언급된 지문 주변에서 X 이론에서는 대다수 사람들이 조직 목표의 달성을 향해 충분히 노력하도록 만들기 위해 그들은 강압되고, 통제되고, 지시받고, 처벌로 위협받아야 한다고는 했지만, 달성이 과업의 특성에 따라 좌우되는지는 알 수 없다. 따라서 ③번이 지문의 내용과 일치하지 않는다.

오답분석 ① 지문 중간의 He called the first view Theory X and the second Theory Y.를 통해 'McGregor는 인간 행동에 대한 두 가지의 다른 관점을 제시했다'는 것을 알 수 있다.
② 지문의 두 번째 문장 Most leaders ~ they could.를 통해 'X 이론에서, 관리자들은 직원들이 본질적으로 일을 싫어한다고 생각한다'는 것을 알 수 있다.
④ 지문의 네 번째 문장 most people ~ organizational objectives를 통해 'X 이론에서, 직원들은 지시받거나, 심지어는 과업을 수행하도록 강압되어야 한다'는 것을 알 수 있다.

어휘 **distinct** adj. 다른, 뚜렷이 구별되는
inherently adv. 본질적으로

50 [2019 한국항공대]

정답 ③

해석 ① X 이론과 Y 이론은 아랫사람들에 대한 동일한 가정에 기초하고 있다
② Y 이론의 가정은 자기 지시의 발휘를 약화시킨다
③ Y 이론은 근로자 계급의 평범함을 극복할 수 있다
④ X 이론은 직업에 대한 직원의 열의를 최대화할 수 있다

해설 지문을 통해 추론할 수 있는 것을 고르는 문제이다. 지문 후반부에서 X 이론에서는 근로자 계급의 평범함이 달성할 수 있는 것에 상한선이 되었을 것이지만, Y 이론에서는 개인의 잠재력에 대한 가능성이 방대했다고 했으므로, Y 이론은 근로자 계급의 평범함을 극복할 수 있다는 것을 추론할 수 있다. 따라서 정답은 ③번이다.

오답분석 ① X 이론에서 아랫사람들은 책임지는 것을 두려워했다고 한 반면, Y 이론에서는 적절한 조건하에서 사람들은 책임을 받아들이고, 심지어는 추구하기까지 할 것이라고 했으므로, X 이론과 Y 이론이 아랫사람들에 대한 동일한 가정에 기초하고 있다는 것은 지문의 내용과 다르다.
② Y 이론에서 사람들이 일에 흥미를 갖는 것은 자연스럽고, 적절한 조건하에서 사람들은 책임을 받아들이고, 심지어는 추구하기까지 할 것이라고 했으므로, Y 이론의 가정이 자기 지시의 발휘를 약화시킨다는 것은 지문의 내용과 다르다.
④ X 이론에서 지도자들은 자신들의 조직에 있는 사람들이 할 수 있으면 일을 피하고 싶을 것이라고 생각했다고 했으므로, X 이론이 직업에 대한 직원의 열의를 최대화할 수 있다는 것은 지문의 내용과 반대이다.

어휘 **undermine** v. 약화시키다 **exercise** n. 발휘

[51-52]

'세계화'는 여러 가지를 의미할 수 있다. 한편으로는, 세계화는 산업 생산의 현대적 기술의 세계적 확산이며 무역, 자본, 생산 및 정보 등 여러 경계를 가로지르는 온갖 종류의 소통이다. 경계를 넘나드는 이동의 이러한 증가 자체는 새로운 기술이 지금까지도 전근대적인 사회들로 확산된 결과이다. 우리가 세계화 시대에 살고 있다고 말하는 것은 거의 모든 사회가 이제 세계화되었거나 산업화에 착수했다고 말하는 것과 마찬가지다. 세계화는 또한 거의 모든 경제가 전 세계에 걸쳐 다른 경제들과 얽혀있다는 것을 의미한다. 북한처럼, 경제를 세계의 나머지 국가들과 차단시키려는 몇몇 나라들도 있다. 그들은 세계 시장으로부터의 독립을 유지하는 데는 성공했지만, 경제적으로나 인간적으로 큰 대가를 치르고 있다. 세계화는 하나의 역사적 과정이다. 세계화는 전 세계의 경제생활이 똑같이 강

도 높게 통합되기를 요구하지 않는다. 그 주제에 대한 중요한 한 연구가 표현했듯이, "세계화는 단 하나의 어떤 상태가 아니며, 사회 변화의 직선적 과정이나 최종적인 종점도 아니다." 또한 세계화는 모든 경제가 하나로 합쳐지는 최종 상태도 아니다. 세계적인 경제 활동의 똑같이 통합된 보편적 상태는 정확히 말해서 세계화가 아닌 것이다. 그와 반대로, 전 세계의 경제 활동의 상호 연결의 증가는 여러 국가들 간의 고르지 않은 발전을 두드러지게 보여준다. 세계화는 멕시코처럼 '주변적인' 개발도상국들이 미국처럼 '중심부'에 가까운 경제로부터의 투자에 의존하는 것을 강조한다. 비록 더 세계화된 경제의 결과 중 하나는 국가 간의 — 예를 들면 서방 국가들과 중국 간의 — 계층적 경제 관계를 뒤집거나 약화시키는 것이며, 동시에 현존하는 계층적 관계를 강화하거나 새로운 계층적 관계를 만들어낸다.

또한 우리가 심화된 경제생활의 세계화 속에서 빠른 발전을 겪고 있다는 주장이 반드시 어느 사회에서든 경제 활동의 모든 측면이 전 세계의 경제 활동에 대해 상당히 예민해지고 있다는 것을 의미하는 것은 아니다. 세계화가 아무리 진척되더라도, 한 사회의 경제생활의 어떤 측면들은, 시간이 흐름에 따라 바뀌긴 하겠지만, 세계 시장의 영향을 받지 않는다는 것은 언제나 사실이다.

frontier n. 국경, 경계, 한계
hitherto adv. 지금까지; 그때까지
pre-modern adj. 근세의, 전근대적인
embark on phr. ~을 착수하다
intensively adv. 집중(집약)적으로; 강하게
integrate v. 통합시키다 **seminal** adj. 중요한; 영향력 있는
put it phr. 말하다, 표현하다 **singular** adj. 단 하나의; 특이한
linear adj. 직선의 **end-state** n. 최종 상태
converge v. 모여들다, 집중되다
accentuate v. 강조하다, 두드러지게 하다
peripheral adj. 주변적인; 지엽적인
exaggerate v. 강조하다 **overturn** v. 뒤집다
hierarchical adj. 계층의, 서열의
dimension n. 규모, 범위; 차원

51 2018 중앙대

정답 ③

해석 ① 자연스러운 ② 전례가 없는
③ 고르지 않은 ④ 위축되지 않는

해설 지문의 빈칸을 채우는 문제이다. On the contrary가 쓰였으므로, 빈칸 앞 문장에서 단서를 찾아야 한다. 앞 문장에서 세계적인 경제 활동이 똑같이 통합된 보편적 상태는 정확히 말해서 세계화가 아니라고 했으므로, '그와 반대로, 전 세계의 경제 활동의 상호 연결의 증가는 여러 국가들 간의 _____ 발전을 두드러지게 보여준다'는 문맥이므로 똑같이 통합된 보편적 상태의 반대 개념인 uneven이 들어가는 것이 자연스럽다. 따라서 ③번이 정답이다.

어휘 **unforced** adj. 자연스러운, 자발적인
unflinching adj. 위축되지 않는, 불굴의

52 2018 중앙대

정답 ③

해석 ① 세계화는 현대적인 산업 기술의 세계적 확산이다.
② 세계화의 영향을 거부하는 어떤 나라든 그 결정 때문에 큰 대가를 치러야 한다.
③ 세계화는 세계 경제가 똑같이 통합될 것을 필요로 한다.
④ 세계화가 한 사회의 경제생활의 모든 측면에 영향을 미칠 수는 없다.

해설 지문의 내용과 일치하지 않는 것을 찾는 문제이다. equal integration에 대해 언급한 세 번째 문단의 A universal state of equal integration ~ what globalization is not.에서 세계적인 경제 활동의 똑같이 통합된 보편적 상태는 정확히 말해서 세계화가 아니라고 했다. 따라서 ③번이 지문의 내용과 일치하지 않는다.

오답 분석 ① 첫 문단의 On the one hand, ~ industrial production의 내용을 통해 '세계화는 현대적인 산업 기술의 세계적 확산'이라는 것을 알 수 있다.
② 두 번째 문단의 They have succeeded ~ both economic and human.의 내용을 통해 '세계화의 영향을 거부하는 어떤 나라든 그 결정 때문에 큰 대가를 치러야 한다'는 것을 알 수 있다.
④ 마지막 문장 However far globalization proceeds, ~ though these may shift over time.의 내용을 통해 '세계화가 한 사회의 경제생활의 모든 측면에 영향을 미칠 수는 없다'는 것을 알 수 있다.

07 정치·법

01-61

문제집 p.188

01 ③	02 ④	03 ①	04 ④	05 ①
06 ②	07 ②	08 ③	09 ④	10 ②
11 ④	12 ⑤	13 ①	14 ②	15 ①
16 ①	17 ②	18 ②	19 ③	20 ④
21 ①	22 ②	23 ①	24 ②	25 ②
26 ④	27 ①	28 ②	29 ③	30 ①
31 ②	32 ④	33 ④	34 ②	35 ④
36 ⑤	37 ③	38 ③	39 ①	40 ④
41 ①	42 ③	43 ④	44 ①	45 ①
46 ③	47 ②	48 ③	49 ③	50 ④
51 ①	52 ④	53 ①	54 ①	55 ②
56 ②	57 ⑤	58 ③	59 ⑤	60 ④
61 ⑤				

01 2019 광운대

정답 ③

해석 "인공지능을 위한 미-중 경쟁은 무역 경쟁보다 더 많은 우려를 자아낸다. 두 강대국들은 어느 쪽이든 인공지능 기술을 이끄는 쪽이 세계를 지배한다고 믿는다. 인공지능의 등장으로 선진 공업국들이 뒤처지는 국가들을 착취했던 19세기가 21세기에도 되풀이될 수 있다"고 예루살렘 히브리 대학교의 한 강사가 말했다. 그는 민족주의의 부상이 인류에 위협을 가할 수 있다는 그의 우려도 나타냈다.
① 미-중 경쟁은 결국 인류 갈등을 해결할 것이다.
② 미-중 무역전쟁은 인공지능 경쟁보다 더 위험해지고 있다.
③ 인공지능을 위한 미-중 경쟁은 무역 경쟁보다 더 많은 우려를 자아낸다.
④ 개인들은 미-중 시대에서 자신들의 삶을 개선하기 위해 스스로 훈련해야 한다.
⑤ 미국과 중국 모두 상호 협력이 없으면 자국민들을 보호할 수 없다.

해설 지문의 빈칸을 채우는 문제이다. 지문의 중간에서 인공지능의 등장으로 선진 공업국들이 뒤처지는 국가들을 착취했던 19세기가 21세기에도 되풀이될 수 있다고 했으므로, 빈칸에는 인공지능에 있어서의 미국과 중국의 경쟁에 대한 부정적인 내용이 나와야 적절하다는 것을 알 수 있다. 따라서 '인공지능을 위한 미-중 경쟁은 무역 경쟁보다 더 많은 우려를 자아낸다'라고 한 ③번이 정답이다.

어휘 power n. 강대국
industrialized country phr. 선진 공업국
exploit v. 착취하다, 부당하게 이용하다
lag behind phr. 뒤(처)지다 emergence n. 출현
nationalism n. 민족주의 humanity n. 인류
resolve v. 해결하다 trade war phr. 무역전쟁
revamp v. 개조하다, 수리하다

[02-03]

카메라에 친화적인 태도와 외모가 후보자의 성공 가능성을 크게 높인다는 사실을 통해 우리는 대중 매체의 중요성을 확인한다. 카메라에서 편안하게 보이고 행동하는 것은 후보자의 주장을 도울 수 있다. 외모의 중요성에 대한 초기의 징조는 1960년의 케네디와 닉슨 사이의 악명 높은 대통령 선거 토론이었다. 그 토론은 텔레비전으로 방송되었지만, 닉슨은 보좌관들이 추천했던 과한 화장을 하는 것을 거부했다. 카메라에서, 그는 초췌해 보이고 면도를 필요로 하는 것 같았던 반면, 케네디의 젊어 보이고 생기가 넘치는 외모는 그가 했던 방송용 화장의 도움을 받은 것이었다. 외모에서의 이러한 차이의 중요성은 토론 이후 명백해졌다. 여론조사들은 라디오에서 토론을 들은 사람들은 근소한 차이로 닉슨이 이겼을 것으로 생각했지만 텔레비전을 통해 토론을 시청한 사람들도 똑같이 근소한 차이로 케네디에게 우위를 주었다. 이 극적인 사건 이후에, 텔레비전으로 방송되는 토론에서 잘 해내지 못하는 것의 공포가 유력한 대통령 후보들을 너무 두려워하게 만들어서 또 다른 토론이 텔레비전으로 방영되기까지 16년이 걸렸다.

camera-friendly adj. 카메라에 친화적인
enhance v. 높이다 comfortable adj. 편안한
aid v. 돕다 cause n. 주장, 대의 indication n. 징조, 암시
infamous adj. 악명 높은 presidential adj. 대통령 선거의
televise v. 텔레비전으로 방송하다 shave n. 면도
youthful adj. 젊어 보이는 vibrant adj. 생기가 넘치는
significance n. 중요함 apparent adj. 명백한
slim majority phr. 근소한 차이
give the edge to phr. ~에게 우위를 주다
intimidate v. 두려워하게 만들다

02 2021 경희대

정답 ④

해설 주어진 지문에서 '초췌한'의 의미로 사용된 haggard의 동의어를 묻는 문제이다. ①번 angry는 '화가 난', ②번 perplexed는 '당혹한', ③번 dirty는 '더러운', ④번 exhausted는 '고갈된', ⑤번 sleepy는 '졸리운'이라는 의미이므로, ④번이 정답이다.

03 2021 경희대

정답 ①

해석
① 정치인의 외모는 중요하다. 현대의 정치에서 텔레비전에 잘 맞는 것은 중요하다.
② 텔레비전을 통해 토론을 시청한 사람들은 케네디를 선호했는데, 이는 그가 더 나은 연사였기 때문이다.
③ 1960년의 대통령 선거 토론은 성공적이지 않았다.
④ 대통령 선거의 대중 매체 보도는 편향된다.
⑤ 대통령 선거 토론은 그것이 불공평한 결과를 만들어내기 때문에 텔레비전으로 방송되어서는 안 된다.

해설 지문의 요지를 묻는 문제이다. 지문 전반에 걸쳐 '대중 매체에서의 정치인의 외모의 중요성'에 대해 설명하고 있고, 이에 대한 예시로써 1960년의 케네디와 닉슨 사이의 대통령 선거 토론을 라디오를 통해서만 청취한 사람들과 텔레비전 방송을 통해 시청한 사람들에서 차이가 있었음을 들고 있다. 따라서 이 지문의 요지를 '정치인의 외모는 중요하다. 현대의 정치에서 텔레비전에 잘 맞는 것은 중요하다.'라고 설명한 ①번이 정답이다.

오답 분석
② 라디오를 통해 토론을 청취한 이들은 근소한 차이로 닉슨이 이겼다고 생각했다는 내용이 있으므로, 케네디가 더 나은 연사였다는 것은 지문의 내용과 다르다.
③ 1960년의 대통령 선거 토론이 성공적이지 않았다는 내용은 지문에서 언급되지 않았다.
④ 대통령 선거의 대중 매체 보도가 편향된다는 내용은 지문에서 언급되지 않았다.
⑤ 대통령 선거 토론이 불공평한 결과를 만들어 낸다는 내용은 지문에서 언급되지 않았다.

어휘
telegenic adj. 텔레비전에 잘 맞는
contemporary adj. 현대의   prefer v. 선호하다
speaker n. 연사   coverage n. 보도
unfair adj. 불공평한

[04-07]

남북 전쟁 전 남쪽의 위대한 정치인이었던 John C. Calhoun은 소수당이 다수당의 뜻에 복종하도록 (A)강요하지 않고 책임감 있는 입헌 정치를 할 수 있을 것이라고 생각했다. John C. Calhoun은 소수당의 중요한 이익에 (B)영향을 미치는 다수당의 결정에 대하여 소수당에 거부권을 주는 것을 지지했다. 이 해결책(소수당에 다수당의 결정에 대한 거부권을 주는 것)이 가진 문제점은 당연히 모든 중요한 문제에 대해 정부를 무력하게 만들고, 소수당에 다수당의 결정을 무효화하는 최고 권력을 준다는 것이다. 영국의 정치 철학자 John Stuart Mill은 또 다른 해결책을 제시했는데, 그 해결책은 많은 국가들에서 선거 방법의 일부가 된 비례 대표제이다. Mill은 비례 대표제가 소수당이 상당한 표를 얻는 것을 가능하게 하고, 그러면서도 국가 입법 기관에 대표 없이 있을 수 있다는 점을 (C)지적했다. Mill은 "소수 대표제"가 다수결 원칙을 따라야 하고, 소수당이 발언권을 가져야 하지만, 소수당이 최고 권력은 가지는 것은 아니어야 한다고 생각했다. Mill은 또한 더 고등 교육을 받거나 지성이 있는 사람들에게 더 많은 표를 주는 "복수 투표제"를 제안했다. 비례 대표제가 다양한 정치적 신념에 더 공정한 대표성을 부여한다는 점에는 의심할 여지가 없다. 하지만 비례 대표제는 어떤 한 정당도 과반수를 차지할 수 없게 하여 정부를 불안정하게 만드는 (D)경향이 있다. 나는 우리가 모두 다수당이 특정 인권을 빼앗지 않도록 해야 한다는 점에 동의한다고 생각한다. 다수당이 종교적 믿음, 정치적 신념, 혹은 생활 양식을 소수당에 강요(E)하게 해서도 안 된다.

statesman n. 정치인   responsible adj. 책임감 있는
constitutional government phr. 입헌 정치
advocate v. 지지하다, 옹호하다   veto power phr. 거부권
remedy n. 해결책, 치료(약)
ineffective adj. 무력한, 효과 없는
supreme power phr. 최고 권력
electoral procedure phr. 선거 방법
proportional representation phr. 비례 대표제
sizable adj. 상당한   representation n. 대표
lawmaking n. 입법
minority representation phr. 소수 대표제
majority rule phr. 다수결 원칙
plural voting phr. 복수 투표제   conviction n. 신념
unstable adj. 불안정한   impose v. 강요하다

04 2021 숙명여대

정답 ④

해석
① 소수당에 발언권을 주는 것
② 더 고등 교육을 받은 사람들에게 더 많은 표를 주는 것
③ "소수 대표제"에 공감하는 것
④ 비례 대표제를 바로잡는 것
⑤ "복수 대표제"를 제안하는 것

해설 지문의 내용과 일치하지 않는 것을 묻는 문제이다. 지문의 중간에서 Mill이 비례 대표제를 해결책으로 제시했다고는 했지만, Mill이 비례 대표제를 바로잡았는지는 알 수 없다. 따라서 ④번이 지문의 내용과 일치하지 않는다.

오답 분석
① Mill felt ~ that the minority should have a voice를 통해 Mill이 '소수당에 발언권을 주는 것'을 지지했다는 것을 알 수 있다.
② He also suggested ~ which would grant more votes to the more highly educated ~ persons를 통해 Mill이 '더 고등 교육을 받은 사람들에게 더 많은 표를 주는 것'을 제안했다는 것을 알 수 있다.
③ Mill felt that "minority representation" should accompany majority rule, ~ power를 통해 Mill이 '"소수 대표제"에 공감하는 것'을 알 수 있다.
⑤ He also suggested a system of "plural voting"을 통해 Mill이 '"복수 대표제"를 제안하는 것'을 알 수 있다.

어휘 sympathize v. 공감하다 rectify v. 바로잡다

05 2021 숙명여대
정답 ①

해석 지문에 따르면, 정부는 비례 대표제에 의해 불안정해질 수 있다.
① 비례 대표제
② 최고 권력
③ 다수당의 결정
④ 어떤 정치 단체
⑤ 정치 철학자

해설 정부가 무엇 때문에 불안정해질 수 있는지를 파악하는 문제이다. 지문의 후반에서 But it has tended to make governments unstable, with no single party able to attain a majority를 근거로 정부가 '비례 대표제'에 의해 불안정해질 수 있다는 것을 알 수 있다. 따라서 ①번이 정답이다.

06 2021 숙명여대
정답 ②

해석 ① 확인
② 무효화
③ 입증
④ 정화
⑤ 구체화

해설 지문의 빈칸을 채우는 문제이다. 지문의 초반에서 John C. Calhoun이 다수당의 결정에 대하여 소수당에 거부권을 주는 것을 지지했다고 했으므로, 빈칸에는 소수당에 다수당의 결정에 대한 거부권을 주는 것의 문제점이 소수당에 다수당의 결정을 무효화하는 최고 권력을 준다는 것이라는 내용이 나오는 것이 자연스럽다. 따라서 '무효화'라고 한 ②번이 정답이다.

07 2021 숙명여대
정답 ②

해설 ② affects → affect
관계절 내의 동사는 선행사와 수가 맞아야 한다. 선행사 decisions가 복수이므로 단수 동사 affects를 복수 동사 affect로 고쳐야 한다.

오답 분석
① 전치사 without 뒤에 명사 역할을 하는 것이 와야 하므로 동명사 forcing이 올바르게 쓰였다.
③ 종속절의 시제가 과거이며 point out은 '~을 지적하다'라는 의미이므로 과거형 pointed out이 올바르게 쓰였다.
④ 문맥상 과거부터 존재했던 비례 대표제가 현재까지 어떠한 영향이 있는지에 대한 내용이므로 현재완료형 has tended가 올바르게 쓰였다.
⑤ 부정어 nor가 문두로 나가 도치되고 Nor + 조동사(should) + 주어(the majority) + 동사(be) 순서가 되었으므로, 동사 be가 올바르게 쓰였다.

[08-09]

지하디스트가 프랑스에 벌인 최악의 공격은 자생적인 극단주의에 대한 국가의 심각한 문제를 부각했다. 만약 우리가 이 일을 불러일으킨 것이 무엇인지 조사하려고 한다면, 해독하는 것은 까다롭다. 프랑스가 중동과 북아프리카에 상호작용하는 것은 역사적으로 폭력적이었으며, 국내의 무슬림 사회가 프랑스인에 의한 차별적인 관행과 배제를 겪어왔다. 프랑스의 극우세력은 반무슬림, 반이민으로 자주 비판받는 선동적인 미사여구를 사용해 견인력을 얻었다. 프랑스는 북아프리카 이민자들의 소외로 지하디스트 영입이 성행할 수 있는 지역이며, 이슬람국가(IS)가 이것에 대한 실행 가능하고 매력적인 대안을 제시한다.

jihadist n. 지하디스트(이슬람교 시아파의 과격 테러 활동 조직원)
highlight v. 부각시키다, 강조하다
homegrown adj. 자생적인, 지방적인
extremism n. 극단주의 tricky adj. 까다로운, 어려운
decipher v. 해독하다 violent adj. 폭력적인
domestic adj. 국내의 discriminatory adj. 차별적인
practice n. 관행, 관습 exclusion n. 배제, 제외
far-right adj. 극우의 traction n. 견인력
inflammatory adj. 선동적인 rhetoric n. 미사여구
recruiting n. 영입, 모집 thrive v. 성행하다
marginalization n. (사회에서의) 소외
viable adj. 실행 가능한 alternative n. 대안

08 2019 가천대
정답 ②

해석 ① 쌍방의
② 도발적인
③ 눈에 잘 띄는
④ 표면적인

해설 밑줄 친 inflammatory의 의미를 추론하는 문제이다. 밑줄 친 부분이 포함된 문장에서는 프랑스의 우익 세력들이 선동적인 미사여구를 사용해 견인력을 얻었다고 말하고 있다. 따라서, 밑줄 친 단어의 의미를 '도발적인'이라고 한 ②번이 정답이다.

어휘 bilateral adj. 쌍방의 provocative adj. 도발적인
conspicuous adj. 눈에 잘 띄는 ostensible adj. 표면적인

09 2019 가천대
정답 ④

해석 ① 프랑스가 왜 그렇게 자생적인 테러를 많이 가졌는지를 이해하는 것은 복잡하다.
② 프랑스는 중동과 북아프리카의 국가에 대한 추한 역사를 가지고 있다.
③ 극우 세력은 무슬림 이민자에게 적대감을 불러일으키는 언어를 의도적으로 사용한다.
④ 테러에 대한 문제는 무슬림 이민자에 대한 이슬람국가의 무시로 악화해왔다.

해설 지문의 내용과 일치하지 않는 것을 묻는 문제이다. ④번의 키워드인 Islamic State's negligence(이슬람국가의 무시)와 관련된 지문의 Islamic State(이슬람국가) 주변에서 프랑스는 북아프리카 이민자들의 소외로 지하디스트 영입이 성행할 수 있는 지역이며, 이슬람국가(IS)가 이것에 대한 실행 가능하고 매력적인 대안을 제시한다고 했으므로, 테러에 대한 문제는 무슬림 이민자에 대한 이슬람국가의 무시로 악화해왔다는 것은 지문의 내용과 다르다. 따라서 ④번이 지문의 내용과 일치하지 않는다.

오답 분석
① If we try to examine what has caused this, it is tricky to decipher를 통해 '프랑스가 왜 그렇게 자생적인 테러를 많이 가졌는지를 이해하는 것은 복잡하다'는 것을 알 수 있다.
② France's interactions with the Middle East and North Africa have historically been violent를 통해 '프랑스는 중동과 북아프리카의 국가에 대한 추한 역사를 가지고 있다'는 것을 알 수 있다.
③ The French far-right has gained traction, using inflammatory rhetoric that is often criticized as anti-Muslim and anti-immigrant를 통해 '극우 세력은 무슬림 이민자에게 적대감을 불러일으키는 언어를 고의로 사용한다'는 것을 알 수 있다.

어휘 complicated adj. 복잡한 deliberately adv. 고의로
antagonize v. 적대감을 불러일으키다
exacerbate v. 악화하다 negligence n. 무시, 부주의

[10-12]

오바마 대통령은 연방 정부 공무원들이 운전 중에 문자를 보내는 것을 금지했다. [A] 연방 정부의 교통부는 영업용 트럭과 각 주간 이동하는 버스 운전자들에게도 똑같이 적용하려고 계획하고 있다. [B] 그리고 의회 내부에서 주에서 운전 중 문자나 이메일 보내는 것을 금지하는 법안을 제정하는 것이 지지를 얻고 있다. [C] 그렇게 집중을 방해하는 행위는 매년 수만 명의 죽음을 초래한다. 하지만 범죄로 만든다고 해서 사람들이 운전 중에 휴대 전화를 사용하는 것을 막는 방법이 되는 것은 아니다. [D] 너무 많은 운전자들이 안전보다 편리함을 중시하며 자신들이 잡히지 않을 것이라고 가정한다. 더 효과적인 방법은 문자를 보내면서 운전하는 것을 어렵거나 불가능하게 만드는 것이다. [E]

forbid v. 금지하다, 막다 federal adj. 연방 정부의
employee n. 종업원 text v. 문자를 보내다
Transportation Department phr. 교통부
commercial adj. 업무용의, 상업적인
interstate adj. 각 주간의 congress n. 의회
legislation n. 법안, 입법 행위 outlaw v. 금하다, 불법화하다
distraction n. (주의) 집중을 방해하는 것, 오락 (활동)
tens of thousands of phr. 수만이나, 수많은
effective adj. 효과적인 impossible adj. 불가능한

10 [2019 상명대]

정답 ②

해석 ① 수준 ② 범죄
③ 혜택 ④ 변명
⑤ 대리

해설 지문의 빈칸을 채우는 문제이다. 세 번째 문장에서 의회 내부에서 주에서 운전 중 문자나 이메일 보내는 것을 금지하는 법안을 제정하는 것이 지지를 얻고 있다고 했으므로, 빈칸에는 범죄로 만든다고 해서 사람들이 운전 중에 휴대 전화를 사용하는 것을 막는 방법이 되는 것이 아니라는 내용이 나와야 적절하다는 것을 알 수 있다. 따라서 '범죄'라고 한 ②번이 정답이다.

11 [2019 상명대]

정답 ④

해설 지문의 흐름상 주어진 문장이 들어가기에 가장 적절한 위치를 고르는 문제이다. [D]의 앞 문장에서 범죄로 만든다고 해서 사람들이 운전 중에 휴대 전화를 사용하는 것을 막는 방법이 되는 것은 아니라고 했으므로, [D] 자리에 운전자들이 안전보다 편리함을 중시하여 운전 중에 휴대 전화를 사용하더라도 잡히지 않을 것이라고 가정한다고 설명하는 주어진 문장 '너무 많은 운전자들이 안전보다 편리함을 중시하며 자신들이 잡히지 않을 것이라고 가정한다'가 들어가야 글의 흐름이 자연스럽게 연결된다. 따라서 ④번이 정답이다.

어휘 convenience n. 편리함, 편의
assume v. 가정하다, 추측하다

12 [2019 상명대]

정답 ⑤

해석 ① 운전 중에 문자 보내는 것을 금지하는 가장 효과적인 방법은 법으로 막는 것이다.
② 오바마 대통령은 각 주에 운전 중에 휴대 전화를 사용하는 것을 금지하는 것을 요구했다.
③ 운전 중에 문자 메시지를 보내는 것은 불법이다.
④ 운전 중에 전화기를 사용하는 것은 매년 수천 명의 사망자 수를 초래한다.
⑤ 법을 시행하는 것보다 전화기의 기능을 제한하는 것이 더 권장된다.

해설 지문의 내용과 일치하는 것을 묻는 문제이다. 마지막 문장의 더 효과적인 방법이 문자를 보내면서 운전하는 것을 어렵거나 불가능하게 만드는 것이라는 내용을 통해 법을 시행하는 것보다 전화기의 기능을 제한하는 것이 더 권장된다는 것을 알 수 있다. 따라서 ⑤번이 지문의 내용과 일치한다.

오답 분석
① 다섯 번째 문장에서 범죄로 만든다고 해서 사람들이 운전 중에 휴대 전화를 사용하는 것을 막는 방법이 되는 것은 아니라고 했으므로, 운전 중에 문자 보내는 것을 금지하는

가장 효과적인 방법이 법으로 막는 것이라는 것은 지문의 내용과 다르다.

② 첫 번째 문장에서 오바마 대통령이 연방 정부 공무원들이 운전 중에 문자를 보내는 것을 금지했다고는 했지만, 오바마 대통령이 각 주에 운전 중에 휴대 전화를 사용하는 것을 금지하는 것을 요구했는지는 알 수 없다.

③ 세 번째 문장에서 의회 내부에서 주에서 운전 중 문자나 이메일 보내는 것을 금하는 법안을 제정하는 것이 지지를 얻고 있다 했으므로, 운전 중에 문자 메시지를 보내는 것은 불법이라는 것은 지문의 내용과 다르다.

④ 네 번째 문장에서 집중을 방해하는 행위가 매년 수만 명의 죽음을 초래한다고 했으므로, 운전 중에 전화기를 사용하는 것이 매년 수천 명의 사망자 수를 초래한다는 것은 지문의 내용과 다르다.

어휘 prohibit v. 금지하다 prevent v. 막다, 예방하다
illegal adj. 불법의, 위법의 mortality n. 사망자 수, 사망률
limit v. 제한하다 function n. 기능
enforce v. 시행하다, 집행하다

[13-15]

헌신이라는 문제가 하나의 골칫거리가 되는 것은 단지 고통이 연민의 정치학이라는 관점에서 고려될 때이다. 이러한 이유는 연민의 정치학이 이중의 요구를 충족시켜야 한다는 점 때문이다. 하나의 정치학으로서 연민의 정치학은 보편성을 열망한다. 연민의 정치학의 역할은 지엽적인 것으로부터 자신을 떼어내는 것이며 연민을 유발하는 사건들이 일어날 수 있는 그런 필연적으로 지엽적인 상황들로부터 자신을 떼어내는 것이다. 이렇게 하기 위해 정치학은 동등한 가치를 확립하기 위한 기법에 의존하며, 특히 통계적 기법에 의존할 수도 있다. 그러나 연민과 관련하여서는, 연민의 정치학이 특정 사례로부터 완전히 자유로워질 수는 없다. 연민은 일반적인 것들에 의해서는 영감을 받지 못한다. 따라서, 예를 들면, 동등한 가치에 관한 현존 관습에 기초한 양적 지표에 의해 정의되는 절대 빈곤의 모습은 거시경제학 논문에 적합하거나 또한 정치학을 정의하는 데 도움이 될지도 모른다. 하지만 그 모습이 연민의 정치학을 위해 반론의 여지가 없는 감정을 불어넣지는 못할 것이다. 연민을 불러일으키기 위해서는, 고통과 비참한 육체가 운이 좋은 사람들의 감수성에 영향을 줄 수 있는 그런 방식으로 전달되어야 한다. 연민은 비례성이 부족하다는 약점이 있다. 고통받는 아이가 우리의 마음을 슬픔으로 가득 채우지만, 우리는 끔찍한 전투 뉴스를 무관심하게 맞이한다.

standpoint n. 견지, 관점 commitment n. 헌신
aspire v. 열망(염원)하다
generality n. 일반론; 대다수; 보편성
detach v. 떼다, 분리하다 provoke v. 유발하다
compassion n. 연민, 동정심 rely upon phr. ~에 의존하다
equivalence n. 같음, 등가 in particular phr. 특히
in reference to phr. ~에 관하여, ~와 관련하여
by means of phr. ~에 의해, ~을 써서

quantitative adj. 양적인 indicator n. 지표
convention n. 관례, 관습 treatise n. 논문
sentiment n. 감정
indisputable adj. 반론의 여지가 없는, 명백한
arouse v. 불러일으키다, 자아내다
wretched adj. 비참한, 끔찍한
in such a way as to R phr. ~할 만한 그런 방식으로
sensibility n. 감수성 indifference n. 무관심

13 2018 서강대

정답 ④

해석 ① 아이의 죽음은 병사의 죽음보다 더 비극적이다.
② 연민의 정치학에서 통계는 무의미하다.
③ 연민은 공감보다 덜 중요하다.
④ 연민의 정치학은 지엽적인 관심사로부터 벗어나야 한다.

해설 지문의 내용과 일치하는 것을 묻는 문제이다. 네 번째 문장 Its role is to detach itself from the local ~ may arise.를 통해 '연민의 정치학은 지엽적인 관심사로부터 벗어나야 한다'는 것을 알 수 있다. 따라서 ④번이 지문의 내용과 일치한다.

오답 분석
① 마지막 문장에서 '고통받는 아이가 우리의 마음을 슬픔으로 가득 채우지만, 끔찍한 전투 뉴스를 무관심하게 맞이한다'고 했지만 이것은 우리가 타인의 고통에 대해 느끼는 연민의 정도가 다르다는 의미이며, '아이의 죽음이 군인의 죽음보다 더 비극적'이라고 가치 판단을 할 수는 없으므로 이것은 지문의 내용과 다르다.
② 네 번째 문장에서 '정치학은 동등한 가치를 확립하기 위한 기법에 의존하며, 특히 통계적 기법에 의존할 수도 있다'고 했으므로, '연민의 정치학에서 통계는 무의미하다'는 것은 지문의 내용과 다르다.
③ 공감에 대해서는 언급한 내용이 없으므로 '연민이 공감보다 덜 중요한지'는 알 수 없다.

어휘 irrelevant adj. 무관한; 무의미한
empathy n. 공감, 감정이입

14 2018 서강대

정답 ②

해석 ① 고통에 대한 객관적인 견해를 개발하려면, 보편성이 주관적 감정에 오염되지 않아야 한다.
② 연민의 정치학은 폭넓은 시각과 친밀한 정서적 반응 두 가지를 모두 요구한다.
③ 고통을 보는 사람은 통계가 진심 어린 감정을 방해하게 해서는 안 된다.
④ 고통받는 사람들을 동정하려면, 공감을 만들어낼 수 있는 방식으로 통계적 증거를 제한해야 한다.

해설 지문에서 언급한 연민의 정치학이 충족시켜야 할 이중의 요구를 고르는 문제이다. 세 번째 문장 As a politics(정치학으로서)부터 네 번째 문장(~ on statistical techniques in particular)까지는 연민의 정치학이 '정치학'으로서 갖춰야 할 요건에 대해 설명했다. 그리고 다섯 번째 문장 But in its reference to pity(그러나 연민과 관련하여서는)부터는 연민의 정치학이 '연민'으로서 갖춰야 할 요건에 대해 말하고 있다. 즉 정치학으로서는 지엽적인 것에서 벗어나 보편성을 가져야 하며 연민으로서는 고통에 대해 감수성을 불러일으킬 수 있어야 한다고 했다. 따라서 '연민의 정치학은 폭넓은 시각과 친밀한 정서적 반응 두 가지를 모두 요구한다'고 표현한 ②번이 정답이다.

어휘 objective adj. 객관적인 taint v. 오염시키다
subjective adj. 주관적인 intimate adj. 친(밀)한
affective adj. 정서적인 spectator n. 관중
get in the way of phr. 방해하다 heartfelt adj. 진심 어린
sympathize with phr. ~를 동정하다; ~에 공감하다

15 (2018 서강대)

정답 ①

해설 ① 비례성   ② 무기력
③ 무모함   ④ 공감

해설 지문의 빈칸을 채우는 문제이다. 빈칸 다음 문장에서 고통 받는 아이가 우리의 마음을 슬픔으로 가득 채우지만 우리는 끔찍한 전투 뉴스를 무관심하게 맞이한다고 했으므로, '연민은 _____이 부족하다'는 문맥에서 빈칸에는 '비례성'이라고 한 ①번이 정답이다.

어휘 lassitude n. 나른함, 무기력 temerity n. 무모함, 만용

[16-18]

전체주의적인 일방통행 방송에 대한 민주적 대안이 별개의 가두연단을 한 줄로 세워놓는 것이라면, 나는 그 대안이 실행 불가능하며 비합리적이고 인간적으로 매력적이지 않다는 의견을 말하겠다. 그것은 무엇보다도 거짓 대안이다. 누구나 자유롭게 (A)가두 연단을 설치할 수 있고, 강당을 빌려 기꺼이 들어주려는 사람들에게 자기 의견을 자세히 말할 수 있을 때 문명화된 사람들 사이에서 자유가 발전해왔다는 것은 사실이 아니다. 그와 반대로, 오직 다양한 의견이 같은 공간에서 같은 청중에게 설명될 때에만 언론의 자유는 그 본질적 목적을 달성하기 위해 확립된 것이다. 왜냐하면, 말할 권리가 자유의 시작인 반면에, 들어야 할 필요성이 말할 권리를 중요한 것으로 만드는 요인이기 때문이다. 중요한 것은 의견을 말하는 것이 아니다. 중요한 것은 토론에서의 의견 대립이다. (B)모든 바보가 자기가 좋아하는 것을 말해야 한다는 점 깊이 신경 쓰는 사람은 아무도 없다.

alternative n. 대안 totalitarian adj. 전체주의적인
row n. 열, 줄 soapbox n. 가두 연단, 임시연단
submit v. 제출하다; 굴복하다; 의견을 말하다, 제안하다
unworkable adj. 실행(실시) 불가능한

unreasonable adj. 불합리한
above all phr. 특히, 무엇보다도
be free to R phr. 자유롭게 ~하다
set up phr. 설치하다, 세우다 hire v. 빌리다, 세내다
expound v. 자세히 설명하다
utterance n. (말로) 표현함, 발언 confrontation n. 대립

16 (2018 단국대)

정답 ①

해석 ① 자신의 개인 의견을 말하는 것
② 자신의 작은 방을 만드는 것
③ 자신의 세계를 확립하는 것
④ 자신의 극장을 만드는 것

해설 밑줄 친 (A) to set up a soapbox의 의미를 추론하는 문제이다. is free to set up a soapbox와 is free to hire a hall ~ to listen 이 두 개의 어구가 동격을 이루고 있으므로, 비누상자를 설치한다는 것은 공간을 빌려 사람들에게 자신의 의견을 설명한다는 것을 의미한다. 따라서 이를 '자신의 개인 의견을 말하는 것'이라고 표현한 ①번이 정답이다.

17 (2018 단국대)

정답 ②

해석 ① 모든 바보는 존중받아야 한다.
② 다양한 의견에 대해 토론하는 것이 모든 의견을 듣는 것보다 더 중요하다.
③ 모든 사람은 자신이 좋아하는 것을 말할 권리가 있다.
④ 아무도 바보의 의견을 좋아하지 않는다.

해설 밑줄 친 (B) 문장의 의미를 추론하는 문제이다. 이 지문의 요지에 해당하는 내용인데, 앞의 두 문장에서 중요한 것은 의견을 말하는 것이 아니라 토론에서의 의견대립이라고 했으므로, (B)의 의미는 모든 사람의 의견을 (심지어 바보의 의견까지도) 말하고 듣는 것이 중요한 게 아니라 서로 다른 의견을 토론하는 것이 더 중요하다는 의미이다. 따라서 '다양한 의견에 대해 토론하는 것이 모든 의견을 듣는 것보다 더 중요하다'고 표현한 ②번이 정답이다.

18 (2018 단국대)

정답 ②

해석 ① 전체주의적 방송에 대해 사실상의 대안은 없다.
② 표현의 자유를 가지려면, 다양한 의견이 똑같은 조건에서 노출되어야 한다.
③ 별개의 가두 연단이 전체주의의 대안이다.
④ 자신의 의견을 말할 자유를 허용하는 것이 가장 중요하다.

해설 지문의 내용과 일치하는 것을 고르는 문제이다. 네 번째 문장 On the contrary, freedom of speech is established ~

to the same audience.를 통해 '표현의 자유를 가지려면, 다양한 의견이 똑같은 조건에서 노출되어야 한다'는 것을 알 수 있다. 따라서 ②번이 지문의 내용과 일치한다.

오답 분석
① 전체주의적 방송에 대한 '별개의 연단 설치'라는 대안이 잘 못되었음을 지적했을 뿐이므로, '전체주의적 방송에 대해 사실상의 대안은 없다'고 한 것은 지문의 내용과 다르다.
③ 전체주의가 아니라 전체주의적인 방송을 언급한 내용이었으며, 별개의 연단 설치는 잘못된 대안이라고 했으므로, '별개의 가두 연단이 전체주의의 대안'이라는 것은 지문의 내용과 다르다.
④ 모든 사람이 각자의 의견을 따로 말하는 것이 중요한 게 아니라 서로 다른 의견을 같은 조건에서 토론하는 것이 중요하다고 했으므로, '자신의 의견을 말할 자유를 허용하는 것이 가장 중요하다'는 것은 지문의 내용과 다르다.

[19-21]

국가는 반드시 역사적으로 저지른 악행에 대한 책임을 지고 사죄를 해야 하는가? 공개적인 사죄는 주로 불의의 효과가 후손뿐만 아니라 부당한 취급을 받은 사람에게 계속해서 미치고 있음을 인식하고, 과거에 피해를 본 희생자들에게 (A)보상하기 위해 존재한다. 미국에서, 가장 주요한 사죄의 문제는 노예제도의 (B)악행을 둘러싼 것이다. 버지니아주는 가장 노예가 많았던 주였고, 2007년에 노예제도에 대해 제일 먼저 공개적인 (C)참회를 한 주가 되었으며, 그 이후에 다른 몇몇 주들도 그 선례를 따르게 되었다. 그러나, 공화당의 국회의원인 Henry Hyde는 미국이 사과하고 보상해야 한다는 전체적인 생각을 (D)구체화했다. 그는 자신이 결코 개인적으로 노예를 소유한 적이 없었기 때문에, 그가 태어나기도 전의 세대가 했던 행동에 대한 책임을 지지 않아도 된다고 생각했다. 정치적인 보수주의자들이 개인주의적인 입장에서 전체적인 사과에 대한 업신여김을 보여주는 것은 당황스러운 것이다. 결국, 우리는 자신들이 한 행동에 대한 책임만이 있는 개인일 뿐임을 주장하면서, 어떻게 우리의 동포들이 과거에 이룬 업적에 자부심을 가질 수 있겠는가? 애국적인 자부심을 느끼기 위해서 우리는 시대를 초월한 공동체에 어느 정도의 소속감을 느껴야 하며, 그 소속감은 그에 대한 책임감을 가져온다.

accountable for phr. ~에 대해 책임이 있는
historic adj. 역사적인 wrongdoing n. 악행
apologize v. 사죄하다, 사과하다 public adj. 공개적인
acknowledge v. 인정하다, 알아보다 injustice n. 불의
wronged adj. 부당한 취급을 받은 descendant n. 후손
recompense v. 보상하다 victim n. 희생자
primary adj. 주된, 주요한 infamy n. 악행
slavery n. 노예제도 contrition n. 회개, 뉘우침
republican n. (미국) 공화당원 congressman n. 국회의원
substantiate v. 구체화하다 notion n. 생각, 개념
reparation n. 보상 own v. 소유하다
generation n. 세대 prior adj. 앞선
conservative n. 보수주의자 disdain n. 업신여김

collective adj. 집단의 individualist n. 개인주의자
stance n. 입장 accomplishment n. 업적, 성취
countryman n. 동포, 같은 국가의 사람 insist v. 주장하다
belonging n. 소속감, 소속 timeless adj. 시대를 초월한
community n. 공동체, 지역 사회 patriotic adj. 애국적인
pride n. 자부심

19 [2019 가천대]

정답 ③

해석
① 버지니아주는 노예제도에 대해 사죄하기로 한 첫 번째 주이다.
② Henry Hyde가 한 주장의 기반은 개인주의이다.
③ 보수주의적인 정치가들은 자신들 나라의 역사에 자부심을 느끼지 않는다.
④ 사회에 대한 소속감은 과거에 대한 책임감을 요구한다.

해설 지문의 내용과 일치하지 않는 것을 묻는 문제이다. ③번의 키워드인 Conservative politicians(보수주의적인 정치가들)와 관련된 지문의 political conservatives(정치적인 보수주의자들) 주변에서 정치적인 보수주의자들이 개인주의적인 입장에서 전체적인 사과에 대한 업신여김을 보여주는 것은 당황스러운 것이라고는 했지만, 보수주의적인 정치가들이 자신들 나라의 역사에 자부심을 느끼지 않는다는 것은 알 수 없다. 따라서 ③번이 지문의 내용과 일치하지 않는다.

오답 분석
① and in 2007 it became the first state to make public contrition for slavery를 통해 '버지니아주는 노예제도에 대해 사죄하기로 한 첫 번째 주이다'는 것을 알 수 있다.
② For political conservatives to show disdain for collective apologies from an individualist stance is baffling을 통해 'Henry Hyde가 한 주장의 기반은 개인주의이다'는 것을 알 수 있다.
④ One must feel a degree of belonging to a timeless community in order to feel patriotic pride, and that belonging brings with it responsibility를 통해 '사회에 대한 소속감은 과거에 대한 책임감을 요구한다'는 것을 알 수 있다.

어휘 argument n. 주장, 논쟁 individualism n. 개인주의

20 [2019 가천대]

정답 ④

해설 밑줄 친 단어 중에서 문맥상 적절하지 않은 어휘를 고르는 문제이다. Henry Hyde는 자신이 태어나기도 전의 세대가 한 악행에 대해서 책임을 지지 않아도 된다고 생각한 사람이므로 ④번에는 '구체화했다'를 의미하는 substantiated가 아니라 '부정했다'를 의미하는 denied가 들어가는 것이 자연스럽다. 따라서 ④번이 정답이다.

21 2019 가천대

정답 ①

해석 ① 당황스러운 ② 간섭하는
③ 장려하는 ④ 설득하는

해설 지문의 빈칸을 채우는 문제이다. 지문의 후반에서, 글쓴이는 Henry Hyde가 자신이 태어나기도 전의 세대가 한 악행에 대해서 책임을 지지 않아도 된다고 했던 것에 대해 부정적인 견해를 갖고 있으므로, 빈칸에는 Henry Hyde의 의견에 대해 당혹스럽게 생각한다는 의미의 단어가 와야 한다는 것을 알 수 있다. 따라서 '당황스러운'이라고 한 ①번이 정답이다.

어휘 baffling adj. 당황스러운 tampering adj. 간섭하는
encouraging adj. 장려하는 persuading adj. 설득하는

[22-23]

플로리다주에서는 모기와 정치가 뒤엉킨 지 오래되었는데, 일부 카운티는 헌신적인 모기 행정관을 선출한다. 하지만 올해는 지카 바이러스와 그 바이러스를 옮기는 벌레가 선거 경쟁에 영향을 미쳤다. 인정을 받으려는 지나친 활동과 당파적 비난이 확산되는 와중에, 의회의 여름 휴회 기간을 앞두고 의회가 긴급 재정 지원을 통과시키지 못한 것에 대해 모두가 비난한다. 민주당은 플로리다주의 공화당 소속 주지사인 릭 스콧(Rick Scott)을 예전에 주 예산을 삭감한 것에 대해 비난한다. 8월 30일에 있었던 상원의원 예비선거에서의 승자인 패트릭 머피(Patrick Murphy)는 11월 (선거)의 상대 후보로 확정된 공화당의 마르코 루비오(Marco Rubio)를 맹공격한다. 탬파(Tampa) 지역의 일부 정치인들은 유전자 변형 모기의 방출을 요구하고 있는데, 그 모기들은 현재 키스 제도에서 실험이 예정되어 있으며 지카 바이러스를 퍼뜨리는 모기 개체 수를 줄여줄 지도 모른다.
하지만 실제 전쟁에서처럼, 눈길을 끌기 위한 정치적 활동은 사이드 쇼(서커스 등에서 손님을 끌기 위한 소규모 공연)에 불과하다. 진짜 전투원은 모기를 통제하는 작업을 하는 사람들이며, 그들의 도구에는 자신의 몸이 포함되어 있다. 피넬라스(Pinellas) 팀의 롭 크루거(Rob Cruger)는 감시 형태 중 하나는 모기가 윙윙거리는 곳에 서서 1분 만에 그의 몸에 몇 마리의 모기가 앉는지를 보는 것을 포함한다고 말한다. 그의 상사 제이슨 스턱(Jason Stuck)이 예비용 닭들에게서 달걀을 거두어 올 때, "당신은 결국 모기에게 많이 물리게 됩니다."라고 그는 말한다. 플로리다주의 수많은 모기 종에 의해 많은 질병이 옮겨지지만, 지카 바이러스는 유아에게 일으키는 소두증 외에도 관광에 미치는 영향 때문에 걱정의 중심이 되고 있다.

entwine v. 뒤엉키다, 얽히다
dedicated adj. 전념하는, 헌신적인
commissioner n. 지방 행정관 convey v. 전달하다
infect v. 감염시키다 ballot n. 투표, 투표용지
amid prep. ~가운데에, ~중에
epidemic n. 유행병, (유행성) 전염병
hyperactive adj. 활동 과잉의, 매우 활동적인
credit n. 칭찬, 인정 partisan adj. 편파적인, 당파적인
funding n. 자금, 자금(재정) 지원 recess n. 휴회(기간)
assail v. 공격을 가하다, 괴롭히다 victor n. 승리자
senatorial adj. 상원(의원)의 primary n. (미국의) 예비선거
lambast v. 호되게 비난하다 confirm v. 확정하다
agitate for phr. ~을 위한 (정치)운동을 하다; 주장(요구)하다
slate for phr. ~을 계획하다 trial n. 실험
grandstanding n. (사업이나 정치에서) 사람들의 눈길을 끌려는 행위 sideshow n. 부차적인 것, 지엽적 문제
combatant n. 전투원, 전투부대
operative n. (수작업을 하는) 직공; 정보원, 첩보원
squad n. (경찰 등의) ~반, ~계, 팀
recount v. 말하다, 이야기하다 surveillance n. 감시
buzzy adj. 윙윙거리는 end up with phr. 결국 ~되다
reserve n. 예비(비축)물 battalion n. (군대의) 대대, 부대
microcephaly n. 소두증

22 2018 성균관대

정답 ②

해석 ① 모기 물림에 노출되어야 한다
② 모기를 제거할 방법을 알아야 한다
③ 생명공학에 대한 기본 지식을 갖고 있어야 한다
④ 플로리다주의 다른 정치인들을 비난해야 한다
⑤ 최대한 많은 주민들과 친분이 있어야 한다

해설 플로리다주에서 선거를 이기려면 무엇을 해야 하는지를 파악하는 문제이다. 플로리다주에서는 정치와 모기 문제가 얽혀 있으며, 몇몇 카운티는 모기를 담당하는 행정관을 선출한다고 했다. 올해는 지카 바이러스와 그 바이러스를 옮기는 벌레(모기)가 선거에 영향을 미쳤다고 했으며, 일부 정치인들은 유전자 변형 모기를 방출할 것을 요구하고 있다고 했으므로, 플로리다주의 선거에서 이기려면 모기 문제에 대처할 방법을 알아야 한다는 것을 유추할 수 있다. 따라서 ②번이 정답이다.

23 2018 성균관대

정답 ①

해석 ① 그들 자신의 몸 ② 모기의 포식자
③ 생물 무기 ④ 해로운 살충제
⑤ 유전적 돌연변이

해설 지문의 빈칸을 채우는 문제이다. 빈칸 뒤의 문장에서 모기를 감시하는 형태 중 하나는 모기가 윙윙거리는 곳에 서서 1분 만에 자기 몸에 모기가 몇 마리 앉는지 보는 것도 있다고 했으므로, 모기 통제 작업을 하는 사람들의 도구에는 '그들 자신의 몸'도 포함되어 있음을 알 수 있다. 따라서 ①번이 정답이다.

어휘 animate adj. 살아있는, 생물인 insectcide n. 살충제
mutation n. 돌연변이

[24-26]

북한의 국무위원장인 김정은이 이번 주 베이징에서 시진핑 주석을 방문한 다음 가진 연설에서, 대한민국의 문재인 대통령이 다음 정상회담에서 한국전쟁을 공식적으로 종식하는 방법과 평양에 대한 제재 완화에 관해 더 자세한 이야기를 포함할 것이라고 했다. 그는 신년 기자회견에서 "제2차 북미정상회담은 한반도의 평화를 굳건히 할 것"이라고 말했다. 미 대통령은 회담이 이번 달이나 2월에 개최될 수 있지만, 핵무기 개발을 억제하기 위한 북한의 노력과 북한에 대한 국제사회의 제재 완화 중에 무엇이 선행되어야 할지에 관한 논의는 교착 상태에 빠졌다고 말했다.

시진핑 주석이 제2차 북미정상회담을 지지하는 가운데, 중국은 평양의 가장 큰 교역국으로서 한반도에 필수 불가결한 존재로 스스로 자리매김하려 했다고 중국 관영 신화통신이 보도했다. 시진핑 주석은 김 위원장의 방문 후에 "중국은 한반도의 비핵화를 계속해서 고수하는 북한을 지지하며, 북한과 미국이 회담을 하고 성과를 달성하는 것을 지지한다"고 말했다.

summit n. 정상회담 **sanction** n. 제재
relief n. 완화, 경감 **firmly** adv. 굳게, 강하게
solidify v. 굳히다 **peninsula** n. 반도
conference n. 회견, 회담
deadlocked over phr. ~에 대해 교착상태에 빠진
rein v. 억제하다 **nuclear** n. 핵 **lift** v. (제재를) 완화하다
communist state phr. 공산주의 국가
seek to phr. ~하려 노력하다 **cast** v. 역할을 주다
trading n. 교역, 무역 **news agency** phr. (언론의) 통신사
denuclearisation n. 비핵화

24 [2019 한성대]

정답 ②

해석
① 북한과 미국의 지도자들이 이번 달에 만날 예정이다.
② 김정은 국무위원장은 이번 주에 시진핑 주석을 만났다.
③ 미 대통령은 북한에 대한 국제사회의 제재를 곧 완화할 것이다.
④ 중국은 북한과 미국의 두 번째 회담을 좋아하지 않는다.

해설 지문의 내용과 일치하는 것을 묻는 문제이다. 지문의 첫 번째 문장인 Speaking after North Korea leader Kim Jong Un visited President Xi Jinping in Beijing this week의 내용을 통해 김정은 국무위원장은 이번 주에 시진핑 주석을 만났다는 것을 알 수 있다. 따라서 ②번이 지문의 내용과 일치한다.

오답 분석
① 미 대통령은 회담이 이번 달이나 2월에 개최될 수 있다고는 했지만, 북한과 미국의 지도자들이 이번 달에 만날 예정인지는 알 수 없다.
③ 핵무기 개발을 억제하기 위한 북한의 노력과 북한에 대한 국제사회의 제재 완화 중에 무엇이 선행되어야 할지에 관한 논의는 교착 상태에 빠졌다고 했으므로, 미 대통령은 북한에 대한 국제사회의 제재를 곧 완화하리라는 것은 지문의 내용과 다르다.
④ 시진핑 주석이 제2차 북미정상회담을 지지한다고 했으므로, 중국은 북한과 미국의 두 번째 회담을 좋아하지 않는다는 것은 지문의 내용과 다르다.

어휘 **be scheduled to** phr. ~할 예정이다

25 [2019 한성대]

정답 ②

해석
① 중국과 북한 사이의 큰 거래
② 곧 예정된 북미정상회담
③ 김정은 위원장의 미국 방문
④ 미국과 중국의 비핵화

해설 지문의 제목을 묻는 문제이다. 지문의 전체적으로 미국과 북한의 제2차 정상회담이 개최될 것이며, 한반도의 평화를 더 굳건히 할 수 있는 자세한 이야기를 포함할 것이라고 설명하고 있다. 따라서 지문의 제목을 '곧 예정된 북미정상회담'이라고 표현한 ②번이 정답이다.

어휘 **deal** n. 거래

26 [2019 한성대]

정답 ④

해석
① 꼭두각시 — 파견하다
② 필수 불가결한 — 파견하다
③ 꼭두각시 — 고수하다
④ 필수 불가결한 — 고수하다

해설 지문의 빈칸을 채우는 문제이다. 첫 번째 빈칸의 다음에서 중국이 평양의 가장 큰 교역국이라고 설명하고 있으므로 첫 번째 빈칸에는 북한에 중국이 반드시 필요한 존재라는 의미의 단어가 오는 것이 자연스럽다. 또한 두 번째 빈칸의 주변에서 북한이 계속해서 비핵화의 입장을 유지하는 내용이 나와야 흐름이 자연스러우므로, 두 번째 빈칸에는 고수한다는 의미가 와야 한다. 따라서 '필수 불가결한 — 고수하다'라고 한 ④번이 정답이다.

어휘 **puppetry** n. 꼭두각시 **dispatch to** phr. ~로 파견하다
indispensable adj. 필수 불가결한
adhere to phr. ~를 고수하다

[27-29]

언론의 자유는 사상이 단지 입 밖에 낼 뿐 아니라 논쟁의 대상이 되는, 반대되는 의견을 대변하는 의회인 미국 의회나, 발언의 자유가 있는 사람은 대답도 강제로 해야 하는 곳인 영국 의회와 같은 장소를 떠올리면 가장 정확할 것이다. 우리는 자유의 진정한 상태는 증인들이 증언하고 교차 심문을 받으며, 변호사가 같은 판사 앞에서, 그리고 한 명의 배심원이 출석한 상태로 상대편의 변호사와 논쟁하는 법정과 같은 곳에 존재하

는 것처럼 떠올릴 수도 있다. 우리는 자유를 발언자가 질문에 반드시 대답해야 하는 토론회에, 자료, 가설, 그리고 결과가 그 것들을 판단할 권한이 있는 사람에게 제출되는 과학자들의 모임에, 동의하지 않는 사람의 의견을 발행할 뿐만 아니라 그들이 말한 것에 비추어 자신의 의견을 다시 검토하기도 할 명성이 있는 신문에 존재하는 것처럼 떠올릴 수도 있다. 그러므로, 언론의 자유의 본질은 단지 관용 같은 것이 아닌, 관용이 제공하는 토론에 있다. 그것은 의견을 분출하는 것에 있는 것이 아닌, 의견이 대립하는 것에 있다. 이것이 실질적인 실체라는 것은 우리가 다른 보도기관에 의해 제공된 의견의 검열과 규제에 관해 얼마나 다르게 느끼고 행동하는지를 기억할 때 쉽게 이해할 수 있다. 그러면 매체가 토론에서 의견의 대립을 어렵게 만드는 한, 우리는 검열과 규제를 향해 이끌리고 있다는 것을 알게 된다.

---

freedom of speech phr. 언론의 자유
have in mind phr. ~를 떠올리다   assembly n. 의회
opposing adj. 반대되는   utter v. 입 밖에 내다
debate v. 토론하다   compel v. 강요하다
witness n. 증인   testify v. 증언하다   jury n. 배심원
hypothesis n. 가설   conclusion n. 결론
competent adj. 권한이 있는   reputable adj. 명성이 있는
publish v. 발행하다   in the light of phr. ~에 비추어 보아
essence n. 본질   toleration n. 관용   venting n. 분출
confrontation n. 대립   substance n. 실체
readily adv. 쉽게   censorship n. 검열
purvey v. 제공하다   in so far as phr. ~하는 한

---

27 [2020 단국대]

정답 ①

해석 ① 그러므로 ② 대신에
       ③ 이에 반하여 ④ 무관심하게

해설 빈칸에 적절한 연결어를 넣는 문제이다. 빈칸 앞 문장은 언론의 자유는 논쟁하는 법정, 질문에 대답하는 토론회, 제출되는 자료가 판단되는 과학자의 모임, 동의하지 않는 사람의 의견을 다시 검토할 신문에서 찾아볼 수 있다는 내용이고, 빈칸 뒤 문장은 언론의 자유의 본질은 관용이 아니라 관용이 제공하는 토론에 있다는 내용이다. 따라서 결과를 나타내는 연결어인 ① Thus(그러므로)가 정답이다.

28 [2020 단국대]

정답 ②

해설 venting(분출)과 비슷한 의미를 가진 어휘를 묻고 있다. ①번 invention은 '발명', ②번 release는 '방출', ③번 prevention은 '예방', ④번 venture는 '모험'이라는 의미이다. 따라서 ②번이 정답이다.

29 [2020 단국대]

정답 ③

해석 ① 의견의 불일치는 규제가 있을 때는 중요하지 않다.
       ② 관용은 언론의 자유에 관한 토론보다 더 중요하다.
       ③ 관용과 토론은 의견의 자유를 위해 있어야 한다.
       ④ 언론의 자유는 검열이 있을 때만 추천되어야 한다.

해설 지문의 내용과 일치하는 것을 묻는 문제이다. 지문의 중간에서 언론의 자유의 본질은 단지 관용 같은 것이 아닌, 관용이 제공하는 토론에 있다는 내용을 통해 관용과 토론은 의견의 자유를 위해 있어야 한다는 것을 알 수 있다. 따라서 ③번이 지문의 내용과 일치한다.

오답 분석
① 매체가 토론에서 의견의 대립을 어렵게 만드는 한, 우리는 검열과 규제를 향해 이끌리고 있다는 것을 알게 된다고는 했지만, 의견의 불일치는 규제가 있을 때는 중요하지 않은지는 알 수 없다.
② 언론의 자유의 본질은 단지 관용 같은 것이 아닌, 관용이 제공하는 토론에 있다고는 했지만, 관용은 언론의 자유에 관한 토론보다 더 중요한지는 알 수 없다.
④ 우리가 다른 보도기관에 의해 제공된 의견의 검열과 규제에 관해 얼마나 다르게 느끼고 행동하는지를 기억할 때 쉽게 이해할 수 있다고는 했지만, 언론의 자유는 검열이 있을 때에만 추천되어야 한다는 것은 알 수 없다.

어휘 disagreement n. 불일치

[30-31]

뒤르켐(Durkheim)이 몰두한 핵심적인 것들 중에는 무엇이 사회를 결속시키는가라는 문제가 있다. 그의 대답은 이러한 사회적 결속을 촉진하고 유지하는 데 있어서 법의 중요한 역할을 지적한다. 그는, 사회가 종교에서 세속주의로 나아갈 때 그리고 집단주의에서 개인주의로 나아갈 때, 어떻게 법이 처벌보다 보상과 관계를 갖게 되는지를 보여준다. 그러나 처벌은 사회적 결속이 유지되는 집단의 도덕적 태도를 표현하는 데 있어서 중요한 역할을 한다. 그는 자신이 기계적 결속이라고 부르는 것과 유기적 결속이라고 부르는 것을 구분한다. 전자는 획일적인 가치관을 갖고 있고 의미 있는 노동의 분배는 부족한 단순하고 동질적인 사회에 존재한다. 이런 단순한 공동체는 본질적으로 집단화되는 경향이 있다. 그러나 노동의 분배가 존재하는 발전된 사회에서는 고도의 상호의존이 존재한다. 상당한 차이의 인정이 존재하며, 집단주의는 개인주의로 대체된다. 이런 형태의 사회 결속이 법에 반영되어 있다고 그는 주장한다. 즉 법의 다양한 유형을 분류하면 그것에 해당하는 다양한 유형의 사회적 결속을 발견할 것이다. 뒤르켐에 따르면 기계적 결속은 전통적인 소규모 사회에서 작동하는 반면에 유기적 결속은 개인들이 구체적인 과업을 실행하기 위해 서로에게 의존하는 것으로부터 생겨난다.

preoccupation n. 집착, 열중하고 있는 일
secularism n. 세속주의 collectivism n. 집단주의
solidarity n. 연대, 결속 homogeneous adj. 동질적인
uniformity n. 획일성, 통일성 collective adj. 집단의
substantial adj. 상당한; 실질적인
differentiation n. 차별, 차이의 인정
correspond v. 일치하다, 해당하다

30 [2018 한양대]

정답 ①

해석 ① 사회 결속의 유형과 사회의 유형
② 제자리로 돌아오는가? 법과 처벌
③ 노동의 분배: 사회는 어떻게 발전해왔는가
④ 타협을 위한 여지를 만들기: 결속과 개성

해설 지문의 제목을 묻는 문제이다. 지문은 무엇이 사회를 결속시키는가에 대한 뒤르켐의 견해를 소개하고 있다. 따라서 이 지문의 제목을 '사회 결속의 유형과 사회의 유형'이라고 표현한 ①번이 정답이다.

어휘 come full circle phr. 제자리로 돌아오다
compromise n. 타협, 절충 individuality n. 개성

31 [2018 한양대]

정답 ②

해석 ① 유대 — 다양성
② 결속 — 상호의존
③ 결속 — 집단주의
④ 동질성 — 특수성

해설 지문의 빈칸을 채우는 문제이다. 첫 번째 빈칸 앞에서 '무엇이 사회를 결속시키는가(what holds societies together)'라는 문제를 언급했으므로 첫 번째 빈칸에는 '결속'을 의미하는 bond, cohesion, solidarity 등이 들어가는 것이 자연스럽다. 두 번째 빈칸은 유기적 결속이 존재하는 사회를 설명하는 부분인데 마지막 문장에서 유기적 결속은 개인들이 서로 의존하는 것(individuals' reliance on each other)에서 생겨난다고 했으므로 '상호의존'을 의미하는 interdependence가 들어가는 것이 자연스럽다. 따라서 ②번이 정답이다.

[32-34]

신자유주의 국가는 강력한 개인 사유재산권, 법치주의, 그리고 자유롭게 기능하는 시장과 자유 무역의 제도들을 뒷받침해야 한다. 이러한 것들은 개인의 자유를 보장하기 위해 필수적인 것으로 여겨지는 제도적 장치들이다. 따라서 국가는 반드시 무슨 수를 써서라도 이러한 자유를 지키기 위해 폭력 수단에 대한 국가의 독점을 사용해야 한다. 더 나아가, 이런 자유 시장의 자유 무역의 제도적 틀 안에서 사업체와 기업들(법적으로는 개인으로 간주되어짐)이 영업할 수 있는 자유는 근본적인 것으로 간주된다. 민간 기업과 기업가적 자주성은 혁신과 부의 창출의 열쇠로 여겨진다. 지적재산권은 기술 변화를 촉진하기 위해 (예를 들어 특허권을 통해) 보호된다.

신자유주의자들은 특히 자산의 사유화를 추구하는 데에 부지런하다. 울타리 치기와 사유재산권의 배당은 소위 "공유지의 비극"으로부터 보호하기 위한 최선의 방법으로 여겨진다. 이전에 국가에 의해 운영되거나 규제된 부문들은 반드시 민간 영역으로 이관되어야 하며 규제가 철폐되어야만 한다(어떠한 국가의 간섭으로부터든 자유로워야 한다). 경쟁과 결합된 사유화와 규제 철폐는 둘 다 관료적 형식주의를 없애고, 효율성과 생산성을 증가시키고, 질을 향상시키며, 소비자에게 직접적으로는 더 저렴한 상품과 서비스를, 간접적으로는 세금 부담의 감소를 통해 비용을 절감시켜준다고 주장된다.

neoliberal adj. 신자유주의의 favor v. 뒷받침하다, 장려하다
property n. 재산 institution n. 제도
function v. 기능하다 free trade phr. 자유무역
institutional adj. 제도적인 arrangement n. 장치, 제도
essential adj. 필수적인 guarantee v. 보장하다
monopoly n. 독점 mean n. 수단 preserve v. 지키다
at all cost phr. 무슨 수를 써서라도
by extension phr. 더 나아가 legally adv. 법적으로
fundamental adj. 근본적인
private enterprise phr. 민간기업
entrepreneurial adj. 기업가적인, 기업가의
initiative n. 자주성, 진취성 innovation n. 혁신
wealth n. 부 intellectual property phr. 지적재산권
patent n. 특허권 neoliberal n. 신자유주의자
assiduous adj. 부지런한 privatization n. 사유화
asset n. 자산
enclosure n. (공유지를 사유지로 하기 위해) 울타리 치기
assignment n. 배당, 배정
tragedy of the commons phr. 공유지의 비극
deregulate v. 규제를 철폐하다 deregulation n. 규제 철폐
eliminate v. 없애다
bureaucratic red tape phr. 관료적 형식주의
commodity n. 상품 reduction n. 감소

32 [2020 홍익대]

정답 ①

해석 ① 재산권을 정의하기 어려운 상황에서, 국가가 시장 제도를 시행하거나 만들어내는 데에 국가의 힘을 사용하는 것은 권장되지 않는다.
② 개인의 자유가 시장의 자유와 무역의 자유에 의해 보장된다는 가정은 신자유주의 사고의 가장 중요한 특징이다.
③ 계약의 구속력과 행동, 표현, 그리고 선택에 대한 개인의 권리는 반드시 보호되어야 한다.
④ 개인 간의 그리고 회사 간의 경쟁은 기본적인 덕목으로 여겨진다.

해설 지문의 내용과 일치하지 않는 것을 묻는 문제이다. ①번의 키워드인 power to impose or invent market systems(시장 제도를 시행하거나 만들어내는 권력)와 관련된 지문의 첫 번째 문단에서 국가는 반드시 무슨 수를 써서라도 이러한 자유를 지키기 위해 폭력 수단에 대한 국가의 독점을 사용해야 한다고 했다. 따라서 ①번이 지문의 내용과 일치하지 않는다.

오답분석
② 첫 번째 단락 These are the institutional arrangements considered essential to guarantee individual freedoms.를 통해 '개인의 자유가 시장의 자유와 무역의 자유에 의해 보장된다는 가정은 신자유주의 사고의 가장 중요한 특징이다'라는 것을 알 수 있다.
③ 첫 번째 단락 These are the institutional arrangements ~ individual freedoms. The state must therefore ~ to preserve these freedoms at all costs를 통해 '계약의 구속력과 행동, 표현, 그리고 선택에 대한 개인의 권리는 반드시 보호되어야 한다'라는 것을 알 수 있다.
④ 첫 번째 단락 By extension, the freedom of businesses and corporations ~ is regarded as a fundamental good.을 통해 '개인 간의 그리고 회사 간의 경쟁은 기본적인 덕목으로 여겨진다'라는 것을 알 수 있다.

어휘 define v. 정의하다 impose v. 시행하다
invent v. 만들어 내다, 발명하다 assumption n. 가정
cardinal adj. 가장 중요한 feature n. 특징
sanctity n. 구속력 primary adj. 기본적인

33 [2020 홍익대]

정답 ④

해설 ① 경제적 요인에 대한 통제를 공공 부문에서 민간 부문으로 이동시키고자 한다.
② 사생활에 관해 규제가 덜한 국가이다.
③ 시장 경쟁의 효율성과 경제적 성과를 결정하는 데 있어서 개인의 역할을 강조한다.
④ 무슨 수를 써서라도 사회 정의와 재분배를 보호하려고 노력한다.

해설 신자유주의 국가의 특징이 아닌 것을 파악하는 문제이다. 지문의 첫 번째 단락에서 신자유주의 국가는 강력한 개인 사유재산권, 법치주의, 그리고 자유롭게 기능하는 시장과 자유 무역의 제도들을 뒷받침해야 한다고 했으며, 두 번째 단락에서 신자유주의자들은 특히 자산의 사유화를 추구하는 데에 부지런하며, 울타리 치기와 사유재산권의 배당은 소위 "공유지의 비극"으로부터 보호하기 위한 최선의 방법으로 여겨진다고 했으므로, '무슨 수를 써서라도 사회 정의와 재분배를 보호하려고 노력한다'는 점은 신자유주의 국가의 특징이 아니다. 따라서 ④번이 정답이다.

어휘 transfer v. 이동하다, 옮기다 factor n. 요인
regulatory adj. 규제하는 with regard to phr. ~에 관해
emphasize v. 강조하다 efficiency n. 효율성
determine v. 결정하다 economic adj. 경제의

outcome n. 성과 justice n. 정의
redistribution n. 재분배

34 [2020 홍익대]

정답 ②

해설 ① 시장이 불완전하게 성장하여, 사회적 불평등을 초래하는 경향
② 개인이 공공 재산 자원을 무책임하게 이용하는 경향
③ 기업들이 품질 향상 요소에 대해 투자하는 것을 무시하는 경향
④ 사회가 규제받지 않은 시장 교환에 대해 자기 보호를 하려는 경향

해설 밑줄 친 tragedy of the commons의 의미를 추론하는 문제이다. 지문의 두 번째 단락에서 신자유주의자들은 특히 자산의 사유화를 추구하는 데에 부지런하며, 공유지를 사유지로 만들기 위한 울타리 치기와 사유재산권의 배당이 소위 "공유지의 비극"으로부터 보호되기 위한 최선의 방법으로 여겨진다고 했다. 덧붙여, 공유지의 비극(tragedy of the commons)은 누구나 자유롭게 사용할 수 있는 공공자원은 사람들의 남용으로 쉽게 고갈될 수 있다는 이론이다. 따라서 tragedy of the commons의 의미를 '개인이 공공 재산 자원을 무책임하게 이용하는 경향'이라고 한 ②번이 정답이다.

어휘 tendency n. 경향 imperfect adj. 불완전한
inequality n. 불평등 irresponsibly adv. 무책임하게
exploit v. 이용하다, 착취하다 ignore v. 무시하다
invest v. 투자하다 enhance v. 향상시키다, 강화하다
unregulated adj. 규제받지 않은 exchange n. 교환

[35-37]

최근 몇 년 동안 세계가 다수가 아닌 소수를 위해서 재벌, 과두 정치의 지배자, 유착된 정치인에 의해 움직인다는 인상을 주는 많은 요인들이 결합해왔다.
2억 5천만 명의 사람들이 이동하면서 우익 포퓰리스트를 위해 그 어느 때보다도 많은 정보를 제공하는데, 이들은 정치 엘리트들이 이민 관리에 실패하여 일자리, 임금과 사회적 유대를 위협하고 있다고 주장한다.
그동안, 억만장자의 수는 지난 20년 동안 5배 급증하여 2,200명 이상 되며, Forbes지에 따르면, 세계화는 사업가들이 진출할 새로운 시장을 만들어 낸 동시에 세무 당국의 자본, 자산과 수입을 보호하는 것을 가능하게 했다. 전 세계에서 가장 부유한 8명은 가장 가난한 35억 명이 가진 만큼 소유한다. 금융 엘리트들이 얻은 돈의 액수는 10조 파운드나 된다.
하지만 포퓰리즘의 증가에 대한 부분적인 설명을 제공할 수 있는 많은 경제 외적인 요인들도 있다. 엘리트들에 맞서는 문화적 반발, 우리의 정치 배선을 바꾸는 기술 혁명, 지금은 구분이 안 되는 좌익과 우익 정당이 기술주의의 중심에 집중하는 것이다.

a slew of phr. 많은 combine v. 결합하다
impression n. 인상 plutocrat n. 재벌, 부호
oligarch n. 과두 정치의 지배자
semi-detached adj. 한쪽 벽면이 옆집과 붙어 있는, 반쯤 떨어진
politician n. 정치인 ammunition n. 정보, 탄약
right-wing adj. 우익의, 보수파의
populist n. 포퓰리스트, 대중주의자, 인민당원
get a handle on phr. 관리하다, ~을 이해하다
immigration n. 이민, 이주 threaten v. 위협하다, 협박하다
cohesion n. 유대, 단결 billionaire n. 억만장자, 갑부
jump v. 급증하다 fivefold n. 5배
globalization n. 세계화 entrepreneur n. 사업가
tap v. 진출하다 shield v. 보호하다 capital n. 자본
asset n. 자산 income n. 수입, 소득
taxman n. 세무 당국 financial adj. 금융의, 재정의
trillion n. 1조 partial adj. 부분적인
explanation n. 설명 rise n. 증가, 상승
backlash n. 반발 rewire v. 배선을 바꾸다
convergence n. 집중성, 수렴
indistinguishable adj. 구분이 안 되는, 분명하지 않은
technocratic adj. 기술주의의

35 (2019 성균관대)

정답 ④

해석 ① 당신은 포퓰리스트를 어디에서 발견할 수 있는가?
② 포퓰리즘은 무엇인가?
③ 포퓰리스트는 누구인가?
④ 포퓰리스트는 왜 지금 나타나는가?
⑤ 포퓰리스트의 반대는 무엇인가?

해설 지문의 제목을 묻는 문제이다. 첫 번째 문단에서 2억 5천만 명의 사람들이 이동하면서 우익 포퓰리스트를 위해 그 어느 때보다도 많은 정보를 제공하는데, 이들은 정치 엘리트들이 이민 관리에 실패하여 일자리, 임금과 사회적 유대를 위협하고 있다고 주장한다고 하였다. 따라서 이 지문의 제목을 '포퓰리스트는 왜 지금 나타나는가?'라고 표현한 ④번이 정답이다.

어휘 spot v. 발견하다 emerge v. 나타나다, 떠오르다
opposite n. 반대

36 (2019 성균관대)

정답 ⑤

해석 ① 문화적 엘리트주의 ② 탈세
③ 집단 이주 ④ 급증하는 불평등
⑤ 이념적인 대립

해설 마지막 문단에서 포퓰리즘의 증가에 대한 부분적인 설명을 제공할 수 있는 많은 경제 외적인 요인들이 엘리트들에 맞서는 문화적 반발, 우리의 정치 배선을 바꾸는 기술 혁명, 지금은 구분이 안 되는 좌익과 우익 정당이 기술주의의 중심에 집중하는 것이라고 했으므로, 포퓰리즘의 배경을 만들어 냈던 요인으로 지문에서 언급되지 않은 것은 '이념적인 대립'이다. 따라서 ⑤번이 정답이다.

어휘 backdrop n. 배경 elitism n. 엘리트주의
tax evasion phr. 탈세 mass migration phr. 집단 이주
inequality n. 불평등 ideological adj. 이념적인
confrontation n. 대립

37 (2019 성균관대)

정답 ③

해석 ① 우익 정치 엘리트 ② 좌익 정치 엘리트
③ 부패한 엘리트 ④ 사악한 사업가
⑤ 평범한 대중

해설 포퓰리즘이 반대하는 것을 파악하는 문제이다. 첫 번째 문단에서 최근 몇 년 동안 세계가 다수가 아닌 소수를 위해서 재벌, 과두 정치의 지배자, 유착된 정치인에 의해 움직인다는 인상을 주는 많은 요인들이 결합해왔다고 하면서, 사람들이 정치 엘리트들이 이민 관리에 실패하여 일자리, 임금과 사회적 유대를 위협하고 있다고 주장한다고 했으므로, 포퓰리즘이 반대하는 것은 '부패한 엘리트'이다. 따라서 ③번이 정답이다.

어휘 corrupt adj. 부패한, 타락한 wicked adj. 사악한, 못된
ordinary adj. 평범한, 보통의 mass n. 대중

[38-39]

하나의 제품이 그 자체의 성공의 희생양이 되는 것은 가능한 일이다. 제품이 너무 새롭거나, 너무 혁신적이거나, 또는 너무 잘 팔려서 시장과 소비자의 사고방식을 지배할 때, 제품의 상표명과 제품 자체를 연결하는 것은 쉬울 수 있다. 제품의 한 종류가 거의 보편적으로 알려져있거나 그 제품의 한 버전의 상표명으로 불릴 때, 그 상표 이름은 "일반주의"의 희생양이 된다. 아스피린(아세틸살리실산), 에스컬레이터(움직이는 계단), 그리고 포고 스틱(콩콩거리는 장난감)은 모두 이전에는 상표 이름이었는데, 그 성공과 인기가 일반적이고 널리 쓰이는 이름으로 이어지게 해서 발명가나 모회사가 상표권 보호를 유지할 수 없었고, 심지어 한때 최고의 상표 이름이었던 용어로 설명된 비슷한 제품에 대한 경쟁적 우위를 잃어버리게 되었다. 그것에 필요한 모든 것은 믿을 수 있는 상표명이라는 정체성을 벗어나 상표 없는 상품으로 영원히 인정되기 위한 용어에 대한 법원의 판결이다. 이렇게 된다면, 회사는 고객의 의식 속에서 수익을 낼 수 있는 거점을 잃어버리게 될 것이다. 일반주의로의 전환에 따른 수익 손실은 그런 일이 일어나지 않도록 시도하는 데에 회사가 지출하는 다량의 돈으로 악화한다. 법률 및 홍보 캠페인에 수백만 달러를 지출했지만, 킴벌리 클라크사는 사람들이 모든 형태의 티슈를 크리넥스라고 부르는 것을 막기 위해서 힘든 싸움을 계속해오고 있다.

mindset n. 사고방식 associate v. 연결하다, 연관 짓다
universally adv. 보편적으로, 일반적으로

genericism n. 일반주의   hop v. 콩콩 뛰다
widespread adj. 널리 퍼진
parent company phr. 모회사   trademark n. 상표권
term n. 용어   definitive adj. 최고의, 최종적인
court n. 법원   shift away phr. 벗어나다
generic product phr. 상표 없는 상품
profitable adj. 수익을 낼 수 있는   beachhead n. 거점
consciousness n. 의식   revenue n. 수입
be compounded by phr. ~로 인해 악화되다
public relation phr. 홍보   uphill battle phr. 힘든 싸움
tissue n. 티슈; 조직

38 [2019 한양대]

정답 ③

해석 ① 일반주의는 제품에 대한 회사의 성공적인 마케팅의 부산물이다.
② 킴벌리 클라크사는 사람들이 모든 형태의 티슈를 크리넥스라고 부르는 것을 원하지 않는다.
③ 아스피린과 에스컬레이터는 종종 제품의 이름보다 최근에는 오히려 상표명이라고 생각된다.
④ 회사들은 제품이 일반 용어가 되면 보통 그들의 상표권을 지킬 수 없다.
⑤ 회사들은 종종 제품이 일반 용어가 되는 것으로부터 그들의 상표권을 지키기 위해 많은 돈을 지출한다.

해설 지문의 내용과 일치하지 않는 것을 묻는 문제이다. ⑤번의 키워드인 Aspirin and the escalator(아스피린과 에스컬레이터)가 나와 있는 부분에서 모두 이전에는 상표 이름이었는데 그 성공과 인기가 일반적이고 널리 쓰이는 이름으로 이어지게 했다고 했으므로, 아스피린과 에스컬레이터는 종종 제품의 이름보다 최근에는 오히려 상표명이라고 생각된다는 것은 지문의 내용과 다르다. 따라서 ③번이 지문의 내용과 일치하지 않는다.

오답 분석
① whose success and popularity led to such general and widespread use of the names를 통해 '"일반주의는 제품에 대한 회사의 성공적인 마케팅의 부산물이다"'는 것을 알 수 있다.
② Kimberly-Clark has been fighting an uphill battle to keep people from referring to all forms of tissues as Kleenex를 통해 '킴벌리 클라크사는 사람들이 모든 형태의 티슈를 크리넥스라고 부르는 것을 원하지 않는다'는 것을 알 수 있다.
④ When this happens, a company is likely to lose a profitable beachhead within the consumer consciousness를 통해 '회사들은 제품이 일반 용어가 되면 보통 그들의 상표권을 지킬 수 없다'는 것을 알 수 있다.
⑤ The loss of revenue due to a shift to genericism is compounded by the large amounts of money companies spend in an attempt to keep it from happening을 통해 '회사들은 종종 제품이 일반 용어가 되는 것으로부터 그들의 상표권을 지키기 위해 많은 돈을 지출한다'는 것을 알 수 있다.

어휘 by-product n. 부산물   generic term phr. 일반 용어

39 [2019 한양대]

정답 ①

해석 ① 그 자체의 성공의 희생양
② 그것의 품질에 상관없이 인기 있는
③ 그것의 상표명 때문에 인기가 없는
④ 마케팅 전략에 상관없이 큰 성공
⑤ 오직 마케팅 전략 때문에 실패

해설 지문의 빈칸을 채우는 문제이다. 지문의 전반에 걸쳐 성공한 제품의 상표명이 비슷한 제품들의 일반적인 이름이 되어 상표권을 인정받지 못하고 수익이 악화한다고 설명하고 있으므로, 빈칸에는 성공한 제품이 보는 피해에 대한 내용이 들어가야 한다는 것을 알 수 있다. 따라서 '그 자체의 성공의 희생양'이라고 한 ①번이 정답이다.

어휘 victim n. 희생양, 희생자   regardless of phr. ~에 상관없이
strategy n. 전략

[40-42]

임대주는 임차인과 세입자에게 공간을 임대하거나 임차해 준 부동산의 주인이다. [A] 퇴거는 임대주가 세입자를 강제로 내쫓는 과정이다. [B]
퇴거에 관한 법률은 나라와 지역사회마다 다르다. [C] 하지만, 일반적으로 임대주는 서면으로 작성된 통보를 세입자에게 보내야 하고, 새로운 부동산을 찾을 수 있도록 충분한 시간을 허락해야만 한다. [D] 만약 세입자가 서면으로 통보를 한 후에도, 여전히 집을 비우지 않기를 원한다면, 임대주는 소송을 제기해야 하고 법 집행관과 법원이 이 사건을 다룰 수 있도록 해야 한다. 여러 나라에서, 임대주가 세입자가 나가기 전에 전기와 물과 같은 공적인 시설을 차단하거나 자물쇠를 바꾸는 것을 불법으로 간주하고 있다.
임대주는 임대료 미납과 같은 "타당하고 구체적인 이유"에 한해서 세입자를 퇴거시킬 법률적 권리를 갖는다. 또한 많은 지역에서, 임대주는 그 공간을 다른 목적으로 사용하기를 원하는 경우, 그 이상의 별다른 이유 없이도 세입자에게 나가 달라고 요청할 수 있다. 반면, 세입자에게도 법률적 권리가 있다. 대부분의 사법 체계에는 임대 공간이 "주거에 적합한" 공간이어야 한다고 요구하는 법률이 있는데, 다시 말해서, 공간이 합리적으로 안전하고 청결해야 한다는 것이다. 세입자는 임대주에게 어떤 문제에 대해서건 통보해야 하고, 수리를 위한 합리적인 양의 시간을 허락해야 한다. 만약 임대주가 어떤 행동을 취하는 것을 등한시한다면, 세입자는 서면으로 요청서를 작성해야 한다. 그뿐만 아니라, 세입자는 지역 정부 기관에 접촉하여 건축 법안 규제에 대해 알아볼 수 있다.

```
landlord n. 임대주   property n. 부동산
lease v. 임차하다   tenant n. 세입자   eviction n. 퇴거
utility n. 공적 시설   nonpayment n. 미납
jurisdiction n. 사법권, 사법 체계   neglect v. 등한시하다
building code phr. 건축 법안
```

40 2020 한성대

정답 ④

해설 지문의 흐름상 주어진 문장이 들어가기에 가장 적절한 위치를 고르는 문제이다. [D]의 앞 문장에서 임대주는 서면으로 작성된 통보를 세입자에게 보내야 하고, 새로운 부동산을 찾을 충분한 시간을 허락해야만 한다고 했으므로 [D]의 자리에 서면으로 통보한 이후에도, 세입자가 떠나려 하지 않을 때 임대주가 해야 하는 행동을 설명하는 내용의 주어진 문장이 들어가는 것이 자연스럽다. 따라서 ④번이 정답이다.

어휘 vacate the premises phr. 그 집을 비워주다
file v. (소송) 제기하다   lawsuit n. 소송
law enforcement officer phr. 법 집행관   court n. 법원

41 2020 한성대

정답 ①

해석 ① 알아보다   ② 논의하다
③ 노력하다   ④ 융합시키다

해설 지문의 빈칸을 채우는 문제이다. 지문이 포함된 문장은 세입자가 요청한 사항에 대해 임대주가 조치를 취하는 것을 등한시하면, 세입자가 취할 수 있는 행동에 대한 내용이므로, 빈칸에는 정부 기관에 접촉하여 법안 규제에 대해 '알아보다'라는 의미가 되어야 한다. 따라서 ①번이 정답이다.

42 2020 한성대

정답 ③

해석 ① 퇴거 법령은 모든 국가와 지역사회에 걸쳐 표준 규격에 맞춰져 있다.
② 임대주는 세입자를 퇴거시키고 싶을 때, 구두로만 통보해도 된다.
③ 임대주는 법적으로 세입자가 떠나간 이후에야 자물쇠를 바꿀 수 있다.
④ 미납된 임대료는 세입자를 퇴거시키는 데에 충분하지 않다.

해설 지문의 내용과 일치하는 것을 묻는 문제이다. 지문의 두 번째 문단에서, 임대주가 세입자가 나가기 전에 전기와 물과 같은 공적인 시설을 차단하거나 자물쇠를 바꾸는 것을 불법으로 간주하고 있다고 했으므로, 임대주는 법적으로 세입자가 떠나간 이후에야 자물쇠를 바꿀 수 있다는 것은 지문의 내용과 일치한다. 따라서 ③번이 정답이다.

오답 분석
① 지문의 두 번째 문단에서, 퇴거에 관한 법률은 나라와 지역사회마다 다르다고 했으므로, 퇴거 법령이 모든 국가와 지역사회에 걸쳐 표준 규격에 맞춰져 있다는 것은 지문의 내용과 다르다.
② 지문의 두 번째 문단에서, 일반적으로 임대주는 서면으로 작성된 통보를 세입자에게 보내야 한다고 했으므로, 임대주가 세입자를 퇴거시키고 싶을 때, 구두로만 통보해도 된다는 것은 지문의 내용과 다르다.
④ 지문의 세 번째 문단에서, 임대주는 임대료 미납과 같은 타당하고 구체적인 이유에 한해서 세입자를 퇴거시킬 법률적 권리를 갖는다고 했으므로, 미납된 임대료가 세입자를 퇴거시키는 데에 충분하지 않다는 것은 지문의 내용과 다르다.

어휘 standard adj. 표준 규격에 맞춘   verbal adj. 구두의

[43-45]

기계에 대해 가장 영향력 있는 역사가들 중 하나인 고(故) Melvin Kranzberg는 "기술은 좋지도 나쁘지도, 중립적이지도 않다"라고 말했다. 인터넷과 정치에서의 자료 사용도 마찬가지인데, (A)축복도 악도 아니지만, 기술은 영향력을 미친다. 하지만 어떤 영향인가? 그리고, 어떤 것이라면, 기술에 대해 무엇이 되어야 하는가?

"공공권"의 개념을 고안했던 독일의 철학자 Jürgen Habermas는 항상 인터넷에 대해 두 가지 생각을 가지고 있었다. Habermas가 수년 전에 썼던 디지털 통신은 독재주의 국가들에서만 명백한 민주주의적인 장점을 가졌는데, 이 나라들에서 디지털 통신은 그 정부의 정보 독점을 약화시켰다. 하지만 자유주의 정권에서, 매우 다양한 종류의 주제들에 대한 토론을 위한 수백만 개의 공개 토론장들이 있는 온라인 매체는 "대중의 분열"과 "정치의 용해"로 이어질 수 있는데, 이 매체는 민주주의에 (a)유해할 것이다. 미국의 대통령 선거전과 다른 곳의 정치적 동요의 성쇠는 Mr. Habermas의 견해를 (b)뒷받침하는 것처럼 보인다. 사실은, 이 온라인 행동주의가 다른 방법으로 (c)더 낫게 이용될 수 있었던 헛된 정치적인 힘인지 묻는 것은 솔깃하다. 사실은, 많은 온라인 행동의 천문학적인 급상승은 온라인 행동의 (d)동일하게 빠른 소멸을 설명하기 위해 나타난다. 많은 것들은 강력한 조직을 만들 시간을 절대 갖지 못했다. 하지만 (B)온라인 행동주의는 묵살될 수 없다. 몇몇 활동들은 정치적 선전에 대한 사안을 내놓거나 기존의 조직을 장악함으로써 실제적인 영향을 주었다.

```
neutral adj. 중립적인   influential adj. 영향력 있는
historian n. 역사가   philosopher n. 철학자
concept n. 개념   public sphere phr. 공공권
unequivocal adj. 명백한   authoritarian adj. 독재주의의
undermine v. 약화시키다   monopoly n. 독점
liberal adj. 자유주의의   regime n. 정권
forum n. 공개 토론장   fragmentation n. 분열
liquefaction n. 용해   ups and downs phr. 성쇠
```

presidential campaign phr. 대통령 선거전
political turbulence phr. 정치적 동요
activism n. 행동주의 meteoric rise phr. 천문학적인 급상승
robust adj. 강력한 political agenda n. 정치적 선전
take over phr. 장악하다 existing adj. 기존의, 존재하는

43 2019 국민대
정답 ④

해석 ① 저주 ② 악의
③ 적의 ④ 축복

해설 지문의 빈칸을 채우는 문제이다. 지문의 첫 번째 문장에서 한 역사가가 "기술은 좋지도 나쁘지도, 중립적이지도 않다"고 말했다고 했으므로, 빈칸에는 빈칸 뒤의 '악'과 반대되는 단어가 들어가야 한다. 따라서 '축복'이라고 한 ④번이 정답이다.

44 2019 국민대
정답 ①

해설 지문의 문맥에 어울리지 않는 단어를 찾는 문제이다. 지문의 밑줄 (a)harmless의 앞 내용이 '자유주의 정권에서, 매우 다양한 종류의 주제들에 대한 토론을 위한 수백만 개의 공개 토론장들이 있는 온라인 매체는 "대중의 분열"과 "정치의 용해"로 이어질 수 있다'고 했으므로 이것이 민주주의에 좋지 않다는 단어가 나와야 적절하다는 것을 알 수 있다. 따라서 '무해한'이라고 표현한 ①번을 '유해한'으로 고쳐야 한다.

45 2019 국민대
정답 ①

해석 ① 온라인 행동주의는 묵살될 수 없다
② Mr. Habermas의 견해는 항상 옳다
③ 많은 온라인 활동들이 충분히 오래가지 않는다
④ 디지털 통신은 민주주의와 호환되지 않는다

해설 지문의 빈칸을 채우는 문제이다. 지문의 마지막 문장에서 몇몇 활동들이 정치적 선전에 대한 사안을 내놓거나 기존의 조직을 장악함으로써 실제적인 영향을 주었다고 했으므로, 빈칸에는 온라인 행동주의가 묵살될 수 없다는 내용이 나와야 적절하다는 것을 알 수 있다. 따라서 '온라인 행동주의는 묵살될 수 없다'라고 한 ①번이 정답이다.

[46-48]

정치는 어떤 정책 과정을 채택하든, 그리고 그 정책 과정이 아무리 민감하고 그 차이가 존중된다고 해도 억압을 받아서는 안 된다. 다시 말해서, 정치는 끝이 없다. 적절한 기관, 지식, 협의 방법 또는 참여 방법이 의견 충돌을 없앨 수 있다고 생각하는 것은 잘못된 것이다. 모든 종류의 이론은 의견 충돌을 없애기 위해 그것을 처리하거나 관리할 수 있는 방법이 있다는 견해를 (A)장려한다. 그 이론 뒤에 있는 가정은 의견 충돌이 잘못되었고 의견 일치가 (B)바람직한 상태라는 것이다. 사실, 의견 일치는 (C)자주 어떠한 미묘한 강압 형태 없이 나타나고, 의견 충돌을 두려워하지 않고 나타내는 것은 진정한 자유의 근원이다. 논쟁은 보통 의견 충돌이 보다 나은 쪽으로 발전하게 하지만, 긍정적으로 발전하는 논쟁이 꼭 의견 충돌을 줄이는 것은 아니다. 정치에 관한 토의에서 절대 의견 충돌을 억제하는 것이 목표가 되어서는 안 된다. 정치에 관한 의견 충돌이 (D)정상적이지 않다는 의견에 반대하는 방어가 필요하다.

politics n. (국가적인) 정치 suppress v. 억압하다
whichever adj. 어느 ~이든, 어느 쪽(것)을 ~하든
policy process phr. 정책 과정 employ v. 쓰다, 고용하다
respectful adj. 존중하는, 존경심을 보이는
proper adj. 적절한, 제대로 된 institution n. 기관
consultation n. 협의 participatory adj. 참여의, 참가의
mechanism n. 방법
disagreement n. 의견 충돌, 의견 차이
go away phr. 없어지다, 사라지다
manage v. 관리하다, 경영하다 so as to phr. ~를 위해
assumption n. 가정, 추정 consensus n. 의견 일치, 합의
subtle adj. 미묘한, 감지하기 힘든 coercion n. 강압, 강제
absence n. 없음, 결핍, 부재 fear n. 두려움, 공포
source n. 근원 genuine adj. 진짜의
evolve v. 발전하다, 진화하다
for the better phr. 보다 나은 쪽으로
positively adv. 긍정적으로, 분명히
suppression n. 억제, 탄압
deliberation n. 토의, 숙고, 신중함 defense n. 방어, 수비
suggestion n. 의견, 제안

46 2019 단국대
정답 ③

해설 밑줄 친 단어들 중에서 문맥상 적절하지 않은 어휘를 고르는 문제이다. 의견 일치는 어떠한 미묘한 강압 형태 없이 나타나고, 의견 충돌을 두려워하지 않고 나타내는 것은 진정한 자유의 근원이라는 내용이므로 (C)에는 '자주'를 의미하는 often이 아니라 '드물게'를 의미하는 rarely가 들어가는 것이 자연스럽다. 따라서 ③번이 정답이다.

47 2019 단국대
정답 ①

해석 ① 억제 ② 인정
③ 개선 ④ 격려

해설 지문의 빈칸을 채우는 문제이다. 지문의 후반에서 논쟁은 보통 의견 충돌이 보다 나은 쪽으로 발전하게 하지만, 긍정적으로 발전하는 논쟁이 꼭 의견 충돌을 줄이는 것은 아니라고 했

므로, 빈칸에는 정치에 관한 토의에서 의견 충돌을 억제하는 것이 목표가 되어서는 안 된다는 내용이 나와야 적절하다는 것을 알 수 있다. 따라서 '억제'라고 한 ①번이 정답이다.

48 2019 단국대

정답 ③

해석 ① 정치에 관한 상황에서 논쟁 기술을 개발하는 것은 중요하다.
② 사람들은 때때로 합의에 도달하기 위해 그들의 생각을 철회해야 한다.
③ 차이를 허용하는 것은 민주주의 사회의 기본 요건이다.
④ 정치인들은 효과적인 정책을 시행하기 위해 반대 정당과 협상하려고 노력한다.

해설 지문의 내용과 일치하는 것을 묻는 문제이다. 첫 번째 문장에서 정치는 어떤 정책 과정을 채택하든, 그리고 그 정책 과정이 아무리 민감하고 그 차이가 존중된다고 해도 억압을 받아서는 안 된다는 내용을 통해 차이를 허용하는 것이 민주주의 사회의 기본 요건이라는 것을 알 수 있다. 따라서 ③번이 지문의 내용과 일치한다.

오답분석 ① 여덟 번째 문장에서 정치에 관한 토의에서 절대 의견 충돌을 억제하는 것이 목표가 되어서는 안 된다고는 했지만, 정치에 관한 상황에서 논쟁 기술을 개발하는 것이 중요한지는 알 수 없다.
② 여섯 번째 문장에서 의견 일치는 어떠한 미묘한 강압 형태 없이 나타나고, 의견 충돌을 두려워하지 않고 나타내는 것은 진정한 자유의 근원이라고는 했지만, 사람들이 때때로 합의에 도달하기 위해 그들의 생각을 철회해야 하는지는 알 수 없다.
④ 여덟 번째 문장에서 정치에 관한 토의에서 절대 의견 충돌을 억제하는 것이 목표가 되어서는 안 된다고는 했지만, 정치인들이 효과적인 정책을 시행하기 위해 반대 정당과 협상하려고 노력하는지는 알 수 없다.

어휘 cultivate v. 개발하다, 기르다   withdraw v. 철회하다
fundamental adj. 기본적인, 근본적인
requirement n. 요건
democratic society phr. 민주주의 사회
politician n. 정치인   negotiate v. 협상하다
opposite adj. 반대의   party n. 정당, 당
execute v. 수행하다, 실행하다   effective adj. 효과적인

[49-50]

[B] 정치적 안정을 정의하기 위한 시도는 정치와 정치적 구조의 개념을 명확하게 하는 것에서부터 시작한다. 정치적 행위는 사회를 위한 결정을 내리는 권력의 분립 양상에 영향을 미치는 사회 구성원의 행동을 말한다. 정치적 행위는 보편적이다. 사회의 구성원은 사회의 법에 복종하거나 거역하면서 권력 계층 체계를 지지하거나 약화하는 한 정치적으로 행동하는 것이기 때문이다. 따라서 법에 복종하는 것은 선거에서 경쟁하는 것만큼 정치적인 행위인 것이다.

[A] 왜냐하면, 의도하건 그렇지 않건 간에, 법에 대한 복종의 효과는 법이 무엇이어야 하는지 그리고 법이 어떻게 강제되어야 하는지를 결정하는 사람들의 권위를 유지하기 때문이다. 이 권위를 유지하는 것은 사회를 위한 결정을 내리는 권력의 분립 양상을 유지하는 것과 같다. 이와 유사하게, 법을 위반하는 행위 또한 정치적인 행위인데, 모든 법에 대한 저항은 사실 그 자체만으로 이미 제정되어 있던 권위에 대한 저항이기 때문이다. 저항은 사회를 위한 결정을 내리는 권력의 기존 분립 형태를 유지하는 것을 위협한다. 만약 법을 위반하는 사건이 계속 증가하게 되면, 정치적인 권위는 결국 위축되리라는 것은 자명하다.

[C] 우리는 지금까지 특정한 정치적인 행위가 정치적이지 않은 행위로부터 구분된다는 일반적인 의미에서 정치적인 것을 규정하지 않았다. 더불어 우리는 어떤 정의를 내리려는 의도도 갖고 있지 않은데, 그 이유는 정치적인 행동을 그런 방식으로 표현하는 것은 오해의 여지가 다분하기 때문이다. 엄격히 말해서, 심지어 머리를 기르는 것과 같은 사소한 행위를 포함하여, 인간의 행동 중에 본질적으로 비정치적인 행동은 없다. 이것은 어떤 행동의 "정치적임"이 그 행위 자체에 내재하여 있는 어떤 특성을 의미한다기보다 우리가 그 행위에 관해 공부하고, 그 행위가 일어나는 맥락에 따라 그 행위의 특징을 묘사하는 것에서 정의되는 것이기 때문에 사실이다.

[D] 설명을 위해, 우리는 일반적으로 긴 머리를 정치적인 행위의 형태로 간주하지는 않는다. 그러나 어떤 청교도적인 폭군은 긴 머리를 부패한 것으로 결론짓고 결국 모든 사람에게 머리를 짧게 자르라고 명령할 수도 있다. 이 포고령이 널리 강하게 공표된 바로 직후에, 폭군이 초청한 국가 행사에 참석한 모든 이들이 긴 머리로 도착한다고 가정해보라. 이런 상황에서, 우리는 이 사람들이 정치적 불복종이라는 아주 대담한 행위를 하고 있다는 당연한 결론을 내리게 될 것이다.

ubiquitous adj. 아주 흔한, 보편적인
insofar as phr. ~하는 한에 있어서는
undermine v. 약화하다   stratification n. 계층
constitute v. ~라고 여겨지다   uphold v. 지지하다
authority n. 권위   ipso facto phr. 그 사실 자체에 의해
defiance n. 저항   incidence n. 사건
atrophy v. 위축하다   axiomatic adj. 자명한
demarcate v. 분리하다   delineate v. 표시하다
intrinsically adv. 본질적으로   inherent adj. 내재된
characterization n. 특징 묘사   puritanical adj. 청교도의
despot n. 폭군   decree n. 포고, 조례
publicize v. 공포하다   legitimately adv. 도리에 맞게
bold adj. 대담한

49 2020 중앙대

정답 ②

해설 [A], [B], [C], [D]의 적절한 순서를 파악하는 문제이다. 지문 전체적으로 어떤 행위를 정치적인 행위로 정의할 수 있는지 설명하는 글이므로 정치적인 행위의 의미를 설명하는 [B]가 먼저 와야 한다. 그다음, 법을 지키거나 법에 저항하는 행위가 정치적인 행위인 이유를 설명하는 [A]가 와야 하고, 뒤이어 [C]에서 사실상 인간의 모든 행위가 정치적인 행위로 규정될 수 있는 이유를 다루고, 마지막으로 [D]에서 [C]의 내용을 뒷받침할 수 있는 예시를 드는 것이 자연스럽다. 따라서 지문의 적절한 순서는 ② [B] ― [A] ― [C] ― [D]이다.

50 2020 중앙대

정답 ④

해석 ① 조직화 된 사회에서의 개인행동과 집단행동의 심리적 효과
② 정치적 선거와 복종의 개념에 대해 알기
③ 사회 안정화에 대한 문화적 권력의 기여
④ 정치와 정치 구조 사이의 관계에서 정치적 안정을 정의하기

해설 지문의 주제를 묻는 문제이다. 지문의 첫 번째 문단에서, 정치적 안정을 정의하기 위한 시도는 정치와 정치 구조의 개념을 명확히 하는 것에서부터 시작한다고 하였고, 이후 지문 전체적으로 어떤 행위를 정치적인 행위로 정의할 수 있는지 설명하고 있다. 따라서 이 지문의 주제를 '정치와 정치 구조 사이의 관계에서 정치적 안정을 정의하기'라고 표현한 ④번이다.

어휘 **psychological** adj. 심리적인   **contribution** n. 기여

[51-54]

[A] 역사가들은 종종 1898년을 미국이 세계 정치에 부상하는 시점인 과거로부터의 분명한 이탈로 봐왔다. 하지만 그 변화의 정도는 과장될 수 있다. 미국의 힘이 갑자기 증가한 것은 아니지만, 산업화 이후로 미국은 놀라운 잠재적인 강대국이었다. 1898년은 대중의 관심에 갑작스럽고 영구적인 변화를 나타낸 것도 아니었다. 제국주의를 둘러싼 논쟁이 난무하고 난 후, 대부분의 미국인들은 20세기 초반에 그들 국가의 문제에 대한 일상적인 집중을 재개했다. 하지만, 1898년은 미국의 책무에 변화를 가져온 해였다. 이 시점부터, 미국과 유럽의 강대국들 모두가 미국이 세계 위기에 어느 정도 관심을 갖고 있다고 가정했다.

[B] 이러한 변화에 대해 많은 이유가 주어졌다. (A)가장 분명한 제안은 미국 경제가 성숙하게 되었기 때문에 다른 산업 선진국들과 같이 미국도 새로운 원자재와 해외 시장이 필요하게 되었다는 제국주의의 기존 경제 해석을 구체화한다. 많은 역사가들은 미국의 해외 진출과 미국의 내부 경제 발전 사이의 어떠한 연관성도 부정할 것이다. 하지만 이러한 연관성은 국내의 번영과 해외 시장 사이의 관계를 봤던 세기 전환 무렵의 농부와 사업가들에 의해 빈번하게 만들어졌다.

[C] 외교 정책의 새로운 출발에 대한 두 번째 설명은 미국의 "명백한 운명"이라는 기존 사상의 부흥과 재구축이었다. 그러나, 대륙에서 해외 확장정책으로의 변화에는 새로운 정당화가 필요했다. 19세기 말 확장주의자들의 가장 일반적인 주장 중 하나는 앵글로색슨 "인종"의 우월성에 관한 사상이었다. 1980년대에, 일부 사람들이 남부 아프리카계 미국인들과 새로운 이민자들보다 우월함을 주장했다.

[D] 미국 정책 변화의 덜 분명한 또 다른 원인은 큰 정치 권력의 실제 상황이었다. 유럽의 주요 국가들의 제국주의 활동은 이미 미국의 확장 욕구를 (B)자극한 세계의 낙후된 지역에 관한 영토와 영향력의 쟁탈전에 관여했다. 유럽의 강대국들은 아프리카를 나누어 가지고 나서 이제 확장을 위한 남은 두 지역인 근동과 극동 지방에 눈을 돌리고 있었다. 이 지역들이 하나의 강대국으로 전락하기에는 너무 중요했기 때문에, 주도국들은 불안하게 양쪽의 독립을 지지하면서도 경제적 영향력의 영역을 감시했다. 모든 곳에서 상황은 유동적이고 위험했다. 미국의 잠재력이 있는 한 나라가 세계 정치에 관심을 보일 때, 그 나라는 불가피하게 일부 강대국에 위협으로 보였고 다른 국가들의 잠재적인 동맹국으로 간주되었다. 1898년에 일어난 것은 이 모든 권력들을 반영했다. 미국의 의지와는 달리 그것을 많이 깨닫지 못한 채, 미국은 큰 정치 권력에 관여하게 되었다.

---

departure n. 이탈   **emergence** n. 부상   **extent** n. 정도
exaggerate v. 과장하다   **sudden** adj. 갑작스러운
might n. 힘   **industrialization** n. 산업화
potential adj. 잠재적인   **permanent** adj. 영구적인
shift n. 변화   **popular** adj. 대중의
imperialism n. 제국주의   **habitual** adj. 일상적인, 습관적인
concentration n. 집중   **commitment** n. 책무, 헌신
maturity n. 성숙   **raw material** phr. 원자재
expansion n. 확장   **internal** adj. 내부의
frequently adv. 빈번하게   **domestic** adj. 국내의
prosperity n. 번영   **explanation** n. 설명
revival n. 부흥, 부활   **restatement** n. 재구축
manifest adj. 명백한   **destiny** n. 운명
continental adj. 대륙의   **justification** n. 정당화
superiority n. 우월성   **immigrant** n. 이민자
scramble n. 쟁탈   **territory** n. 영토
underdeveloped adj. 낙후된   **appetite** n. 욕구
independence n. 독립   **stake out** phr. 감시하다
sphere n. 영역   **fluid** adj. 유동적인
inevitably adv. 불가피하게   **menace** n. 위협
ally n. 동맹국

51 2020 아주대

정답 ①

해석 ① 미국의 해외 확장
② 미국의 모험의 선구자

③ 미국의 평화와 제국
④ 미국 제국주의의 위험성
⑤ 미국의 성숙한 경제

해설 지문의 주제를 묻는 문제이다. 지문의 전반에 걸쳐 1898년 이후로 미국이 경제적인 이유와 외교적인 이유로 해외 확장에 관여하게 되었다고 설명하고 있다. 따라서 이 지문의 주제를 '미국의 해외 확장'이라고 표현한 ①번이 정답이다.

어휘 forerunner n. 선구자   peril n. 위험성
mature adj. 성숙한

52 2020 아주대

정답 ④

해석 ① 대중들은 미국이 서반구에 특별한 관심을 갖고 있다고 느꼈다.
② 대부분의 사람들은 외국의 위험으로부터의 미국의 자유가 영원하고 자연스러운 것으로 생각했다.
③ 일부 신조들이 유능한 젊은이들의 집단에 의해 큰 힘으로 지지를 받았다.
④ 가장 분명한 제안은 제국주의의 기존 경제 해석을 구체화한다.
⑤ 식민지 확장이 완료되면, 외국 문제에 관한 대중의 관심이 이전의 관심으로 집중된다.

해설 지문의 빈칸을 채우는 문제이다. 빈칸 뒤의 콜론(:)으로 연결된 문장에서 미국 경제가 성숙하게 되었기 때문에 다른 산업 선진국들과 같이 미국도 새로운 원자재와 해외 시장이 필요하게 되었다고 했으므로, 빈칸에는 경제와 관련된 내용이 나와야 적절하다는 것을 알 수 있다. 따라서 '가장 분명한 제안은 제국주의의 기존 경제 해석을 구체화한다'라고 한 ④번이 정답이다.

어휘 hemisphere n. 반구   doctrine n. 신조
able adj. 유능한   suggestion n. 제안
embody v. 구체화하다   interpretation n. 해석
colonial adj. 식민지의

53 2020 아주대

정답 ①

해석 ① 자극하다   ② 슬퍼하다
③ 입증하다   ④ 매달리다
⑤ 빼앗다

해설 지문의 빈칸을 채우는 문제이다. 빈칸이 포함된 문장에서 appetite(욕구)라는 단어가 나왔으므로, 이를 목적어로 취할 수 있는 동사 중에서 어울릴 수 있는 의미의 단어가 와야 한다는 것을 알 수 있다. 따라서 '자극하다'라고 한 ①번이 정답이다.

54 2020 아주대

정답 ①

해석 ① 역사가들은 1898년이 미국의 외교 정책에 구분을 짓는다고 주장해왔다.
② 1898년은 미국 사람들의 관심에 찾아온 갑작스러운 변화를 목격했다.
③ 유럽 국가들은 근동과 극동에 있는 국가들의 독립을 지지하는 것을 중단했다.
④ 앵글로색슨 인종의 우월함에 대한 사상이 1890년대에 부정되었다.
⑤ 많은 역사가들이 미국의 해외 확장이 미국의 경제 위기와 관련 있다고 생각했다.

해설 지문의 내용과 일치하는 것을 묻는 문제이다. 지문의 처음에서 역사가들은 종종 1898년을 미국이 세계 정치에 부상하는 시점인 과거로부터의 분명한 이탈로 봐왔다는 내용을 통해 역사가들은 1898년이 미국의 외교 정책에 구분을 짓는다고 주장해왔다는 것을 알 수 있다. 따라서 ①번이 지문의 내용과 일치한다.

오답 분석
② 1898년은 대중의 관심에 갑작스럽고 영구적인 변화를 나타낸 것도 아니었다고 했으므로, 1898년은 미국 사람들의 관심에 찾아온 갑작스러운 변화를 목격했다는 것은 지문의 내용과 다르다.
③ 주도국들은 불안하게 양쪽의 독립을 지지하면서도 경제적 영향력의 영역을 감시했다고 했으므로, 유럽 국가들은 근동과 극동에 있는 국가들의 독립을 지지하는 것을 중단했다는 것은 지문의 내용과 다르다.
④ 1980년대에 일부 사람들이 남부 아프리카계 미국인들과 새로운 이민자들보다 우월함을 주장했다고 했으므로, 앵글로색슨 인종의 우월함에 대한 사상이 1890년대에 부정되었다는 것은 지문의 내용과 다르다.
⑤ 미국 경제가 성숙하게 되었기 때문에 다른 산업 선진국들과 같이 미국도 새로운 원자재와 해외 시장이 필요하게 되었다고는 했으므로, 많은 역사가들이 미국의 해외 확장이 미국의 경제 위기와 관련 있다고 생각했다는 것은 지문의 내용과 다르다.

어휘 division n. 구분, 분리   witness v. 목격하다
cease v. 중단하다

[55-57]

유럽이 서아프리카에서 아프가니스탄에 이르는 분쟁 지역에서의 전쟁과 박해 및 빈곤에 의해 유발되어 빠르게 악화하고 있는 이민 위기에 직면하여, 심지어 유럽의 고위 관리들조차 명백한 것을 인정하기 시작하고 있다. 유럽의 난민 관리 시스템이 무너졌다. 서유럽에서는, 여러 나라가 1990년대 이후로 가장 큰 파도처럼 밀려오는 망명 신청자들과 난민들을 다루고 있다. 수십만 명의 망명 신청자들이 유럽의 구멍이 숭숭 난 국경을 뚫고 흘러들어오고 있으며, 이탈리아 같은 유럽의 입구

에 해당하는 나라를 떠나 독일 등의 나라로 가고 있는데, 거기서 난민들은 새로운 난제와 긴장을 만들고 있다. 독일은 선진국들 중에서 가장 많은 망명 신청자들을 관리하느라 <u>안간힘을 쓰고 있다.</u>

독일의 정치인들은, 정도는 다르지만, 다정한 사람들과 이민자들의 입국을 차단하기를 원하는 사람들 사이에서 분열된 대중에 직면해 있다. 상당히 많은 이민자들은 시리아에서의 내전이나 남수단에서부터 나이지리아에 이르는 지역의 무장단체들에 의한 공격으로부터 피난 온 사람들이다. 그러나 관리들의 말에 따르면, 대부분은 또한 경제적 이유 때문에 온 사람들이며, 신청 절차가 그들에게 세계에게 가장 부유한 나라에서 이민 생활을 구축할 기회를 제공할지도 모른다는 주사위를 던지고 있는 사람들이다. 인구 8천 2백만의 이 나라가 작년에 유럽의 다른 어느 나라보다 더 많은 망명 신청자들을 받아들여, 17만 3천 명에게 피난처를 제공했다. 너무 많은 망명 신청자가 들어오자 이제 독일은 반(反)이민 운동의 중심지가 된 지역에 있는, 트롤리츠 같은 작은 지역사회에 이민자들을 위한 시설을 찾아야만 한다.

작년에, 난민 센터에서 35건의 방화를 포함하여, 반(反)이민 공격행위들이 상당히 증가했다. "독일은 2차 세계대전에서 너무 많은 난민들을 발생시킨 책임이 있다"고 트롤리츠의 전(前) 시장 마르쿠스 니에르트(Markus Nierth)는 말했다. "이제는 새로운 큰 파도를 이루어 들어오고 있는 난민들에 대한 책임을 우리가 져야 한다." 그러나 니에르트조차도 난민 위기가 트롤리츠 같은 소도시에, 조용하고 동질적인 마을 생활에 익숙한 주민들이 익숙하지 않은 것을 제공하고 있다는 점은 인정한다.

---

confront v. (힘든 상황이) 닥치다, 맞서다
escalate v. 확대(증가)되다; 악화되다
persecution n. 박해   **arc** n. 둥근 (활) 모양
strife n. 갈등, 싸움   **obvious** adj. 명백한
refugee n. 난민, 망명자   **asylum** n. 망명
stream v. 흐르다   **decamp** v. (몰래) 서둘러 떠나다
openhearted adj. 친절한, 다정한
close off phr. 차단(폐쇄)하다
a good number of phr. 상당히 많은
flee v. 달아나다, 도망치다   **roll a dice** phr. 주사위를 던지다
appeals process phr. 항소 절차(과정)
be forced to R phr. ~할 수밖에 없다
accommodation n. 거처, 숙소, 시설
nestled adj. ~에 자리 잡은   **epicenter** n. 진원지, 진앙
arson n. 방화   **concede** v. 인정하다, 수긍하다
used to phr. ~에 익숙한(= accustomed to)
homogeneous adj. 동질적인

---

55   2018 이화여대

정답 ②

해석
① 유럽에서의 박해와 빈곤
② 난민 문제에 대응하는 데 있어서의 새로운 위기
③ 전쟁에 의해 유발된 이민 증가
④ 유럽에서 망명 신청자들을 거부하는 다양한 이유들
⑤ 반(反)이민 운동의 중심지

해설 지문의 제목을 묻는 문제이다. 첫 문단에서 유럽으로 들어오는 난민들이 급증하고 있는 상황을 언급한 후에 독일 등에서 난민들은 새로운 난제와 긴장을 만들고 있다(they are creating new challenges and tensions)고 했으며, 두 번째 문단과 세 번째 문단은 이것에 대한 부연설명이므로, 지문의 제목을 '난민 문제에 대응하는 데 있어서의 새로운 위기'라고 표현한 ②번이 정답이다.

56   2018 이화여대

정답 ②

해석
① 1990년대 이전에는, 유럽의 난민들은 대부분 아프리카와 아프가니스탄으로부터 왔다.
② 일부 난민들은 경제적인 이유 때문에 독일에 왔다.
③ 2차 세계 대전 이후로 트롤리츠에는 다양한 사람들이 살았었다.
④ 독일은 지금까지 8천 2백만 명의 망명 신청자들을 받아들였다.
⑤ 2차 세계대전은 독일에 엄청난 난민 유입을 초래했다.

해설 지문을 통해 추론할 수 있는 것을 고르는 문제이다. 두 번째 문단에서 관리들의 말에 따르면 이민자 대부분은 또한 경제적 이유 때문에 온 사람들이며, 신청 절차가 그들에게 세계에게 가장 부유한 나라에서 이민 생활을 구축할 기회를 제공할지도 모른다는 주사위를 던지고 있는 사람들(But a large portion, officials say, ~ the richest nations in the world)이라고 했으므로, 일부 난민들은 경제적인 이유 때문에 독일에 왔다는 것을 추론할 수 있다. 따라서 ②번이 정답이다.

오답 분석
① 첫 문장의 As Europe confronts ~ from West Africa or Afghanistan에서 유럽이 서아프리카에서 아프가니스탄에 이르는 분쟁 지역에서의 전쟁과 박해 및 빈곤에 의해 유발되어 빠르게 악화하고 있는 이민 위기에 직면하고 있다고 했으므로, 1990년대 이전이라고 한 것은 지문의 내용과 다르다.
③ 마지막 문장의 But even Nierth concedes that ~ used to quiet and homogeneous village life에서 트롤리츠 같은 소도시의 주민들은 과거에 조용하고 동질적인 마을 생활에 익숙했었다고 했으므로, 2차 세계 대전 이후로 트롤리츠에는 다양한 사람들이 살았었다는 것은 지문의 내용과 다르다.
④ 두 번째 문단의 This nation of 82 million absorbed ~ sheltering 173,000.에서 인구 8천 2백만의 이 나라가 작년에 유럽의 다른 어느 나라보다 더 많은 망명 신청자들을 받아들여, 17만 3천 명에게 피난처를 제공했다고 했으므로, 독일이 지금까지 8천 2백만 명의 망명 신청자들을 받아들였다는 것은 지문의 내용과 다르다.

⑤ 세 번째 문단 "Germany was responsible for ~ in World War II"에서 독일은 2차 세계대전에서 너무 많은 난민들을 발생시킨 책임이 있다고 했으므로, 2차 세계대전은 독일에 엄청난 난민 유입을 초래했다는 것은 지문의 내용과 다르다.

어휘 **influx** n. 밀어닥침, 밀려듦, 유입

57 (2018 이화여대)
정답 ⑤

해석 ① 폐쇄된 − 노력하고 있는
② 분열을 초래하는 − 반대하고 있는
③ 충실한 − 길을 찾고 있는
④ 유동적인 − 관찰하고 있는
⑤ 구멍이 숭숭 난 − 안간힘을 쓰고 있는

해설 지문의 빈칸을 채우는 문제이다. 첫 번째 빈칸에는, '수십만 명의 망명 신청자들이 유럽의 _____ 국경을 뚫고 흘러 들어오고 있다'라는 문맥에서, '구멍이 숭숭 난'을 의미하는 porous가 들어가는 것이 자연스럽다. 두 번째 빈칸에는, '독일은 선진국들 중에서 가장 많은 망명 신청자들을 관리하느라 _____하고 있다'라는 문맥에서, '노력하고 있는'을 의미하는 striving 또는 '안간힘을 쓰고 있는'을 의미하는 straining이 들어가는 것이 자연스럽다. 따라서 ⑤번이 정답이다.

어휘 **divisive** adj. 분열을 초래하는   **stalwart** adj. 충실한, 충직한
fluid adj. 부드러운; 유동적인   **porous** adj. 구멍이 숭숭 난
strive v. 노력(분투)하다   **navigate** v. 길을 찾다; 항해하다
strain v. 안간힘을 쓰다, 무리하다

[58-61]

[A] 정의와 모두에게 평등한 기회를 열망하는 자유 사회의 유형에서 감정의 정치적 함양을 위한 두 가지 과제가 있다. 하나는 사회적 재분배, 이전에는 배제되거나 소외되었던 집단의 완전 포용, 환경 보호, 대외 원조, 그리고 국방과 같이 노력과 희생을 요구하는 가치 있는 프로젝트에 대한 강한 의지를 불어넣고 유지하는 것이다. 대부분의 사람은 동정심이 좁은 경향이 있다. 그들은 쉽게 자기도취적인 프로젝트에 가둬져 그들의 좁은 영역 바깥에 있는 사람들의 요구를 잊어버리게 된다. 국가를 향한 감정과 그 목표는 자주 사람들이 더 크게 생각하고 더 큰 공동의 이익에 자신을 다시 헌신하는 데에 크게 도움이 된다.

[B] 공공감정의 함양을 위한 또 다른 관련 과제는 모든 사회에, 궁극적으로는 우리 모두에 숨어있는, 다른 사람을 폄하하거나 경시하는 것을 통해 연약한 우리 자신을 보호하는 경향과 같은 힘의 접근을 막는 것이다. 혐오감과 부러움, 남에게 수치심을 주고 싶은 욕망, 이들 전부가 모든 사회와 모든 개인의 삶에 존재한다. 억제하지 않으면, 그것들은 큰 피해를 불러일으킬 수 있다. 그들이 만드는 피해는 특히 입법이나 사회 형성 과정에서 그것들이 안내하는 역할로서 의존될 때 크다.

[C] 민주주의의 위대한 지도자들은 많은 시대와 장소에서 적절한 감정을 함양하는 것과 사회가 목표를 향해 진보하는 것을 방해하는 것들을 억제하는 것의 중요성을 이해해왔다. 하지만, 자유주의의 정치 철학은 그 주제에 관해 거의 언급하지 않았다. 종교적인 관용을 옹호하는 존 로크는 그의 시대에 영국 안에 존재했던 다른 종교의 구성원들 사이의 널리 퍼진 반감의 문제를 인식하여, 그는 사람들에게 "자선, 너그러움, 그리고 자유 존중"의 태도를 취하도록 촉구했으며, 교회들이 신도들에게 "정교회 사람들처럼 잘못된 사람들뿐만이 아닌 모든 사람들에 대한 평화와 선의의 의무"를 조언할 것을 권유했다.

[D] 하지만, 로크는 편협함의 심리학적 기원을 철저하게 조사하려는 시도는 하지 않았다. 그렇게 해서 그는 나쁜 태도의 본질과 그것이 어떻게 투쟁할 수 있는지에 관해서 거의 안내하지 않았다. 또한 심리적 태도를 형성하기 위한 공식적인 대중적 조치를 권하지도 않았다. 좋은 태도의 함양은 개인과 교회에 남겨졌다. 나쁜 태도가 곪게 된 것은 바로 정확히 교회였다는 점을 감안하면, 로크는 그의 프로젝트를 약하고 불확실한 위치에 남겨둔다. 그러나 그의 관점에서 보면, 자유주의 국가는 스스로를 재산에 대한 사람의 권리 그리고 다른 정치적인 선을 그것들이 해를 입을 때 보호하는 데에 국한시켜야 한다. 동등한 자연적인 권리에 관한 종교적 관용을 기반으로 하는 그의 주장 측면에서, 이것은 한발 늦은 개입이다.

liberal adj. 자유주의의   **aspire** v. 열망하다
cultivation n. 함양   **engender** v. 불어넣다
worthy adj. 가치 있는   **sacrifice** n. 희생
redistribution n. 재분배   **inclusion** n. 포용
excluded adj. 배제된   **marginalized** adj. 소외된
defense n. 방어   **sympathy** n. 동정심
immure v. 가두다   **narcissistic** adj. 자아도취의
keep at bay phr. 접근을 막다   **lurk** v. 숨어있다
tendency n. 경향   **fragile** adj. 약한
denigrate v. 폄하하다   **subordinate** v. 경시하다
disgust n. 혐오감   **inflict** v. 주다, 가하다
unchecked adj. 억제되지 않은   **lawmaking** n. 입법
democratic adj. 민주주의의   **obstruct** v. 방해하다
toleration n. 관용   **acknowledge** v. 인식하다
animosity n. 반감   **bounty** n. 너그러움
erroneous adj. 잘못된   **orthodox** adj. (그리스) 정교회의
delve into phr. 철저하게 조사하다   **combat** v. 투쟁하다
precisely adv. 정확히   **fester** v. 곪다
confine v. 국한시키다   **property** n. 재산
assail v. 해를 주다   **intervention** n. 개입

58 [2020 아주대]

정답 ③

해석 ① 공공의 목표에 대한 좁은 동정심이 끼치는 예상치 못한 영향
② 자유 사회에서 정치적 감정을 함양하는 방법
③ 좋은 자유 사회를 유지하는 데에 있어서 정치적 감정의 역할
④ 자유 사회에 반하는 인간 본성에 대한 자아도취
⑤ 자유주의적 정치 철학과 존 로크의 감정 이론

해설 지문의 제목을 묻는 문제이다. 지문의 전반적으로 감정의 정치적 함양을 위한 두 가지 과제에 관해 언급하면서 좋은 정치적 감정이 자유주의 사회에 어떠한 영향을 끼치는지에 관해 설명하고 있다. 따라서 이 지문의 제목을 '좋은 자유 사회를 유지하는 데에 있어서 정치적 감정의 역할'이라고 표현한 ③번이 정답이다.

어휘 unexpected adj. 예상치 못한

59 [2020 아주대]

정답 ⑤

해석 ① 로크는 올바른 감정이 품위 있는 사회의 설립에 공헌한다는 것을 인정했다.
② 자유주의 정치 철학자들은 정부의 개입하는 역할을 가능한 만큼 엄격하게 제한하기를 원했다.
③ 애국심은 때때로 사람들이 이기심을 극복하고 많은 큰 집단의 사람들을 포함하도록 그들의 동정적인 감정을 넓히도록 돕는다.
④ 로크의 시대에는, 영국의 종교적인 파벌이 적대감의 문화를 넓히는 갈등의 치열한 근원이었다.
⑤ 로크는 교회와 정부가 다른 사람들에 대한 시민들의 관용을 함양하는 데에 동반자가 되어야 한다고 생각한다.

해설 지문의 내용과 일치하지 않는 것을 묻는 문제이다. ⑤번의 키워드인 cultivating citizens' toleration towards others (다른 사람들에 대한 시민들의 관용을 함양하는 것)와 관련된 지문의 The cultivation of good attitudes(좋은 태도의 함양) 주변에서 좋은 태도의 함양은 개인과 교회에 남겨졌다고 했으므로, '로크는 교회와 정부가 다른 사람들에 대한 시민들의 관용을 함양하는 데에 동반자가 되어야 한다고 생각한다'는 것은 지문의 내용과 맞지 않는다. 따라서 ⑤번이 지문의 내용과 일치하지 않는다.

오답 분석
① Great democratic leaders, in many times and places, have understood the importance of cultivating appropriate emotions and discouraging those that obstruct society's progress toward its goals를 통해 '로크는 올바른 감정이 품위 있는 사회의 설립에 공헌한다는 것을 인정했다'는 것을 알 수 있다.
② the liberal state should confine itself to protecting people's rights to property and other political goods, when and if others assail them을 통해 '자유주의 정치 철학자들은 정부의 개입하는 역할을 가능한 만큼 엄격하게 제한하기를 원했다'는 것을 알 수 있다.
③ Emotions directed at the nation and its goals are frequently of great help in getting people to think larger thoughts and recommit themselves to a larger common good을 통해 '애국심은 때때로 사람들이 이기심을 극복하고 많은 큰 집단의 사람들을 포함하도록 그들의 동정적인 감정을 넓히도록 돕는다'라는 것을 알 수 있다.
④ recommended that churches advise their members of "the duties of peace and good-will towards all men, as well towards the erroneous as the orthodox를 통해 '로크의 시대에는, 영국의 종교적인 파벌이 적대감의 문화를 넓히는 갈등의 치열한 근원이었다'는 것을 알 수 있다.

어휘 contribute v. 공헌하다 patriotism n. 애국심
faction n. 파벌 hostility n. 적대감

60 [2020 아주대]

정답 ④

해석 ① 정부가 시민들의 이타주의적인 동기를 북돋을 수 있는 시민 종교를 권장한다.
② 대립하는 두 정당 사이의 적대감이 특정한 문제에 대한 타협 협정에 다다르는 것을 불가능하게 만든다.
③ 사람들의 한 집단이 특정한 과제를 달성하는 데에 능력이 떨어진다는 통계학적 발견은 이러한 사람들을 차별적인 방법으로 대하는 것에 대한 유효한 근거로 사용된다.
④ 사람이 다른 사람들의 집단에 대해 느끼는 혐오감은 이 사람들을 차별적인 방법으로 대하는 것에 대한 유효한 근거로 사용된다.
⑤ 더 젊은 세대는 나이 든 세대가 사람들의 한 집단에 대해 가졌던 증오를 물려받는다.

해설 밑줄 친 The damage they do is particularly great when they are relied upon as guide in the process of lawmaking and social formation에서 the great damage의 예시로 가장 적절한 것이 무엇인지를 묻는 문제이다. '그들이 만드는 피해는 특히 입법이나 사회 형성 과정에서 그것들이 안내하는 역할로서 의존될 때 크다'라는 내용에서 ③번과 ④번에서 언급한 '이러한 사람들을 차별적인 방법으로 대하는 것에 대한 유효한 근거'의 내용과 관련 있음을 알 수 있다. 또한 올바른 공공감정을 함양하는 것은 통계학적 발견과는 관계가 없으므로, ④번이 가장 적절한 예시임을 알 수 있다. 따라서 정답은 ④번이다.

어휘 altruistic adj. 이타적인 antagonism n. 적대감
compromise n. 타협 finding n. 발견 valid adj. 유효한

discriminatory adj. 차별적인   inherit v. 물려받다
hatred n. 증오

61 [2020 아주대]

정답 ⑤

해석
① 감정은 희망을 품고 있지만, 아직 불완전한 정치 문화의 기본적인 원칙을 지지한다.
② 과거의 정치적 자유주의에서 정치의 목표는 정의와 평등을 시행하는 것보다 개인의 자유를 보호하는 것이다.
③ 인간은 다른 사람에 대한 배려보다 자신에 대한 보호를 우선시하는 경향이 있다.
④ 위 단락의 글쓴이는 로크의 이론에 한계가 있어 감정의 역할에 대한 더 많은 강조를 넣어 수정되어야 한다고 생각한다.
⑤ 정치적으로 적절한 감정의 함양은 부정적인 감정의 억압으로 이어지는데, 이것은 모두에게 평등을 보장할 것이다.

해설 지문을 통해 추론할 수 없는 것을 고르는 문제이다. 지문의 전반적인 내용을 통해 정치적으로 적절한 감정의 함양은 부정적인 감정의 억압으로 이어지는데, 이것은 모두에게 평등을 보장할 것이라는 것은 유추할 수 없다. 따라서 정답은 ⑤번이다.

오답분석
① In the type of liberal society that aspires to justice and equal opportunity for all, there are two tasks for the political cultivation of emotion을 통해 '감정은 희망을 품고 있지만, 아직 불완전한 정치 문화의 기본적인 원칙을 지지한다'는 것을 알 수 있다.
② have understood the importance of cultivating appropriate emotions and discouraging those that obstruct society's progress toward its goals와 Liberal political philosophy, however, has said little about the topic을 통해 '과거의 정치적 자유주의에서 정치의 목표는 정의와 평등을 실현하는 것보다 개인의 자유를 보호하는 것이다'는 것을 알 수 있다.
③ ultimately, in all of us: tendencies to protect the fragile self by denigrating and subordinating others를 통해 '인간은 다른 사람에 대한 배려보다 자신에 대한 보호를 우선시하는 경향이 있다'는 것을 알 수 있다.
④ the liberal state should confine itself to protecting people's rights to property and other political goods, when and if others assail them을 통해 '위 단락의 글쓴이는 로크의 이론에 한계가 있어 감정의 역할에 대한 더 많은 강조를 넣어 수정되어야 한다고 생각한다'는 것을 알 수 있다.

어휘 principle n. 원칙   implement v. 시행하다
prioritize v. 우선시하다   preservation n. 보호
emphasis n. 강조   suppression n. 억압

08 문화

01-85

문제집 p.220

01	③	02	⑤	03	②	04	③	05	②
06	③	07	④	08	①	09	③	10	④
11	①	12	④	13	③	14	②	15	③
16	③	17	③	18	②	19	③	20	⑤
21	⑤	22	⑤	23	⑤	24	①	25	④
26	⑤	27	③	28	①	29	③	30	②
31	①	32	③	33	②	34	③	35	①
36	③	37	④	38	③	39	③	40	②
41	①	42	⑤	43	②	44	①	45	③
46	②	47	①	48	③	49	①	50	②
51	①	52	③	53	②	54	②	55	①
56	④	57	③	58	③	59	③	60	①
61	②	62	②	63	④	64	①	65	③
66	①	67	①	68	③	69	①	70	①
71	①	72	③	73	②	74	②	75	③
76	①	77	②	78	⑤	79	③	80	②
81	①	82	③	83	③	84	④	85	③

01 [2020 인하대]

정답 ③

해석 청소년기 동안, 사람들은 나이가 같고 비슷한 관심사를 가진 구성원들이 있는 집단인 또래 집단에 점점 더 관계를 맺게 된다. 또래 집단은 가족 및 학교와 더불어 사회화의 세 가지 주요 요인 중 하나이다. 그러나 또래 집단은 가족 및 학교와는 매우 다르다. [A] 부모와 교사가 어린이와 학생들보다 더 많은 힘을 가지고 있는 반면, 또래 집단은 평등하게 구성된다. [B] 또래 집단은 모든 연령대에서 발생하지만, 특히 청소년의 발달에 있어서 특히 중요하다. [C] 청소년들이 행동하는 방식은 문화마다 차이가 있을 수 있다. [D] 청소년 또래 집단은 그들의 구성원들에게 사교적 기술, 평등한 사람 사이의 우정의 가치를 가르치고 어른들의 권위로부터 독립적으로 되는 것을 가르쳐 준다. [E] 때로 이것은 또래 집단이 그 구성원에게 권위와 어른들에 저항하도록 부추긴다는 것을 의미한다. 그러나 이런 반항적인 행동은 부분적으로 문화적이며 보편적이지는 않다는 것을 유념하는 것이 중요하다.

해설 지문의 흐름과 무관한 문장을 고르는 문제이다. 지문은 또래 집단이 청소년기에 영향을 미친다는 내용이므로, [A] 또래 집단은 평등하게 구성된다, [B] 청소년의 발달에 있어서 또래 집단이 특히 중요하다, [D] 청소년 또래 집단이 구성원들에게 가르쳐 주는 것들이 있다, [E] 청소년 또래 집단에서 배우는 것이 권위와 어른들에 대한 저항을 부추긴다는 것은 모두 지문 내용과 관련이 있다. 그러나 [C]는 '청소년들의 행동 방식이 문화마다 차이가 있다'는 내용이므로, 또래 집단이 청소년기에 영향을 미친다는 내용과 관련이 없다. 따라서 ③번이 정답이다.

어휘 adolescence n. 청소년기   peer group phr. 또래 집단
increasingly adv. 점점 더   involve v. 관계하다
along with phr. ~와 더불어, 함께   agent n. 요인, 동인
socialization n. 사회화   made up of phr. ~로 구성된
particularly adv. 특히   behave v. 행동하다
authority n. 권위   go against phr. ~에 저항하다
rebellious adj. 반항적인   behavior n. 행동
universal adj. 보편적인, 일반적인

[02-03]

아프리카계 미국인에 관한 연구는 흑인 빈곤층의 삶에 대한 조사가 지배적이다. 당대 민족학과 언론의 묘사는 철저히 일탈, 범죄 조직, 마약, 성별 사이의 관계, 성, 좌절된 열망, 그리고 가난한 동네의 가족 형태를 서술했다. 하지만 대다수의 아프리카계 미국인은 가난하지 않다. 흑인들의 중요한 일부 경험들, 즉 노동자 계층과 중산층 흑인들의 일부 경험들은 아직 조사되지 않았다. 우리는 중산층 흑인 동네가 어떤 모습일지 그들의 사회가 어떻게 구성되어 있는지에 대한 정보가 거의 없다.

inquiry n. 조사   contemporary adj. 당대의, 현대의
ethnography n. 민족학   deviance n. 일탈
sexuality n. 성   stymied adj. 좌절된
aspiration n. 열망, 포부

02 [2021 이화여대]

정답 ⑤

해석 ① 대부분의 연구원들은 교육을 잘 받은 사람들이다.
② 부유한 흑인들은 흑인 동네에 살지 않는다.
③ 연구원들은 아프리카계 미국인들의 동네를 방문해서 그런 부정적인 것들을 목격했기 때문에 아프리카계 미국인들의 부정적인 측면에 초점을 맞춘다.
④ 대부분의 흑인들은 교육을 잘 받은 사람들이다.
⑤ 대부분의 연구원들은 흑인들에 대한 고정관념에 따른 추정 하에 연구한다.

해설 지문을 통해 추론할 수 있는 것을 고르는 문제이다. ⑤번 보기의 키워드인 stereotypical assumptions(고정관념에 따른 추정)과 관련된 지문의 초반을 통해, 대부분의 연구원들은 흑인들에 대한 고정관념에 따른 추정 아래 연구한다는 것을 추론할 수 있다. 따라서 정답은 ⑤번이다.

오답분석 ① 대부분의 연구원들이 교육을 잘 받은 사람들인지에 대해서는 언급되지 않았다.

② 부유한 흑인들이 흑인 동네에 살지 않는지에 대해서는 언급되지 않았다.
③ 우리는 중산층 흑인 동네가 어떤 모습일지 그들의 사회가 어떻게 구성되어 있는지에 대한 정보가 거의 없다고 했으므로, 연구원들이 아프리카계 미국인들의 동네를 방문해서 그런 부정적인 것들을 목격했기 때문에 아프리카계 미국인들의 부정적인 측면에 초점을 맞춘다는 것은 지문의 내용과 다르다.
④ 대부분의 흑인들이 교육을 잘 받은 사람들인지에 대해서는 언급되지 않았다.

어휘 **witness** v. 목격하다 **assumption** n. 추정, 가정

03 [2021 이화여대]

정답 ②

해석 ① 신분이 상승하는   ② 가난하지 않은
③ 잘 교육된   ④ 잘 적응한
⑤ 배상금을 청구하는

해설 지문의 빈칸을 채우는 문제이다. 두 번째 문단에서 노동자 계층과 중산층 흑인들의 일부 경험들은 아직 조사되지 않았다고 했으므로, 빈칸에는 대다수의 아프리카계 미국인은 가난하지 않다는 내용이 나오는 것이 자연스럽다. 따라서 '가난하지 않은'이라고 한 ②번이 정답이다.

어휘 **upwardly mobile** phr. 신분이 상승하는
reparation n. 배상금

[04-06]

다양한 방법으로, 대중 매체는 오늘날 우리의 모습을 문화적 조현병 환자들, 즉 바람직하고 가치 있는 여성이 되어야 하는 지배적인 이미지에 저항하면서도 따르는 여성으로 바꾸어 놓았다. 대중 매체는 우리 중 많은 이들에게 일종의 (A)<u>문화적 정체성 위기</u>를 일으켰다. 우리는 한편으로는 여성다움, 다른 한편으로는 페미니즘 이렇게 상반되는 감정을 가진다. 우리는 동등하지만 종속적이라고 말했고, 역사를 바꿀 수 있지만, 역사에 갇혔다고 말하는 등 서로 반대되는 방향으로 끌려갔다. 예를 들어, *Vogue*를 펼칠 때 나는 동시에 (B)<u>격노하면서 매혹된다</u>. 나는 물질주의를 숭배하면서 물질주의를 경멸한다. 나는 아름답게 보이길 원하면서 아름답게 보이길 원하는 것이 당신이 가질 수 있는 가장 말도 안 되는 목표라고 생각한다. *Vogue*는 나의 욕망을 더 부추긴다. *Vogue*는 나의 분노를 일으킨다. 그리고 이는 내가 *Vogue*를 읽을 때만 일어나는 것은 아니며, 언제나 일어난다. 한편으로는, 다른 한편으로는 이는 미국에서 여성이 어떤 존재인지를 보여준다.

schizophrenic n. 조현병 환자
rebel against phr. ~에 저항하다 **prevailing** adj. 지배적인
desirable adj. 바람직한, 호감 가는
worthwhile adj. 가치 있는

engender v. ~을 일으키다, 발생시키다
ambivalent adj. 상반되는 감정을 가진
femininity n. 여성다움 **subordinate** adj. 종속된, 부수적인
simultaneously adv. 동시에
adore v. 숭배하다, 아주 좋아하다
materialism n. 물질주의 **despise** v. 경멸하다
ridiculous adj. 말도 안 되는, 터무니없는
stoke v. (감정을) 더 부추기다
trigger v. 일으키다, 촉발시키다 **bile** n. 분노, 증오

04 [2021 이화여대]

정답 ③

해석 ① 대중 매체는 여성의 낮은 지위에 대한 책임이 있다.
② 매체는 여성다움과 아름다움에 대한 틀에 박힌 이상화된 모습을 영속하게 한다.
③ 여성은 매체에 더 주목해야 한다.
④ 어린 소녀들은 텔레비전을 보면 안 된다.
⑤ 여성들은 자신의 주체성을 키우는 것을 통제하기 위해 도움을 구해야 한다.

해설 지문을 통해 추론할 수 있는 것을 고르는 문제이다. ③번 보기의 키워드인 'media'(매체)가 등장한 지문의 초반을 통해, 여성들이 매체에 더 주목해야 한다는 것을 추론할 수 있다. 따라서 정답은 ③번이다.

오답 분석
① 대중 매체가 여성의 낮은 지위에 대한 책임이 있는지에 대해서는 언급되지 않았다.
② 대중 매체가 여성다움과 페미니즘 이렇게 상반되는 감정을 일으켰다고 했으므로, 매체가 여성다움과 아름다움에 대한 틀에 박힌 이상화된 모습을 영속하게 한다는 것은 추론할 수 없다.
④ 어린 소녀들이 텔레비전을 보면 안 되는지에 대해서는 언급되지 않았다.
⑤ 대중 매체가 많은 이들에게 일종의 문화적 정체성 위기를 일으켰다고는 했지만, 여성들이 자신의 주체성을 키우는 것을 통제하기 위해 도움을 구해야 하는지는 알 수 없다.

어휘 **status** n. 지위, 신분 **perpetuate** v. ~을 영속하게 하다

05 [2021 이화여대]

정답 ②

해석 ① 편향된 기대   ② 문화적 정체성 위기
③ 숨은 기회   ④ 비극적인 무죄
⑤ 고의적인 범죄

해설 지문의 빈칸을 채우는 문제이다. 지문의 초반에서 바람직하고 가치 있는 여성이 되어야 하는 지배적인 이미지에 저항하면서도 따른다고 했으므로, 빈칸 (A)에는 대중 매체가 많은 이들에게 일종의 문화적 정체성 위기를 일으켰다는 내용이 나오는 것이 자연스럽다. 따라서 '문화적 정체성 위기'라고 한 ②번이 정답이다.

어휘 biased adj. 편향된, 치우친　expectation n. 기대
opportunity n. 기회　tragic adj. 비극적인
innocence n. 무죄　willful adj. 고의적인
wrongdoing n. 범죄, 비행

view n. 관점　realism n. 현실주의
proclamation n. 포고, 선언　verisimilitude n. 사실성
redefine v. 재정립하다　altogether adv. 완전히

06 2021 이화여대

정답 ③

해석 ① 역사에 갇힌
② 호기심이 많으면서 소극적인
③ 격노하면서 매혹되는
④ 분하게 생각하면서 혼비백산한
⑤ 과거에 사로잡힌

해설 지문의 빈칸을 채우는 문제이다. 지문의 중간에서 우리는 한편으로는 여성다움, 다른 한편으로는 페미니즘 이렇게 상반되는 감정을 가진다고 했으므로, 빈칸 (B)에는 Vogue를 펼칠 때 나는 동시에 격노하면서 매혹된다는 내용이 나오는 것이 자연스럽다. 따라서 '격노하면서 매혹된'이라고 한 ③번이 정답이다.

어휘 passive adj. 소극적인, 수동적인
infuriated adj. 격노하는, 격분하는　seduced adj. 매혹된
mortified adj. 분하게 생각하는
aghast adj. 혼비백산한, 깜짝 놀란
captivated adj. 사로잡힌

[07-09]

[A] 사진은 많은 방식에 있어서 시각의 기계적인 실현이고, 그림에 대한 그것의 영향은 엄청났다. [B] 세상의 실제적인 이미지들을 만들어 낼 수 있었던 사진기 장치의 개발과 함께, 그림의 사회적 역할은 급격하게 바뀌었다. 서구권 역사 대부분에 걸쳐 그림은 분명히 교회의 세계관을 통한 세계의 이상적인 관점을 만들어 내는 기능을 해왔다 [C] 반면, 원근법의 발명 이후 그것은 점점 더 현실주의의 도구가 되었다. 사진의 발명은 그것의 사실성 포고로 환영받았고, 몇몇 이들은 심지어 그것이 사람의 시각을 완전히 재정립할 것이라고 말했다. [D] 프랑스 작가인 에밀 졸라는 그 당시에 심지어, "우리는 그것이 사진으로 찍히기 전까지 어떤 것도 실제로 보았다고 주장할 수 없다"고 썼다. 따라서 많은 이들은 사진기가 그림보다 세계의 실제적인 이미지들을 만들어 내는 것에 있어서 더 나은 일을 할 수 있다고 느꼈고, 이것이 화가들로 하여금 그림을 고정된 관점의 이데올로기나 현실주의에 항상 묶여있지 않는 새로운 방식으로 생각할 수 있게 했다. [E]

photography n. 사진　mechanical adj. 기계적인
realization n. 실현　perspective n. 시각, 원근법
profound adj. 엄청난　dramatically adv. 급격하게
function v. 기능을 하다　idealized adj. 이상적인

07 2021 경희대

정답 ④

해석 프랑스 작가인 에밀 졸라는 그 당시에 심지어, "우리는 그것이 사진으로 찍히기 전까지 어떤 것도 실제로 보았다고 주장할 수 없다"고 썼다.

해설 지문의 흐름상 주어진 문장이 들어가기에 가장 적절한 곳을 묻는 문제이다. 주어진 문장은 '프랑스 작가인 에밀 졸라는 그 당시에 심지어, "우리는 그것이 사진으로 찍히기 전까지 어떤 것도 실제로 보았다고 주장할 수 없다"고 썼다'라는 의미이다. [D]의 자리에 주어진 문장을 넣으면, 앞 문장의 '몇몇 이들은 심지어 그것이 사람의 시각을 완전히 재정립할 것이라고 말했다'는 내용에서 사람의 시각을 완전히 재정립할 것이라고 말한 몇몇 이들에 대한 예시로 에밀 졸라의 말을 인용할 수 있으므로 글의 흐름이 자연스럽게 연결된다. 따라서 ④번이 정답이다.

08 2021 경희대

정답 ①

해석 ① 현실주의와 사진　② 원근법의 발명
③ 그림과 서양 역사　④ 에밀 졸라와 사진
⑤ 인간 시각의 발달

해설 주어진 지문의 제목을 묻는 문제이다. 지문 전반에 걸쳐 '사진기의 발명과 그것이 그림에 미친 영향'에 관해 설명하고 있다. 지문의 중간에서 원근법이 발명된 이후 그림은 현실주의의 도구가 되었으나, 사진기가 현실적인 이미지들을 만들어 내는 것에 있어서 더 나은 일을 할 수 있게 되자, 화가들은 그림을 고정된 관점의 이데올로기나 현실주의에 항상 묶여있지 않는 새로운 방식으로 생각할 수 있게 되었다고 했으므로, 이 지문의 제목을 '현실주의와 사진'이라고 표현한 ①번이 정답이다.

오답 분석
② 해당 지문은 사진기의 발명과 그것이 그림에 미친 영향에 관한 지문인데, 원근법의 발명은 사진기의 발명과 관련이 없으므로 답이 될 수 없다.
③ 그림과 서양 역사는 지문의 일부 내용만을 설명하는 내용이므로 답이 될 수 없다.
④ 에밀 졸라는 사진이 사람의 시각을 완전히 재정립할 것이라고 말했던 사람들에 대한 예시로 언급되었을 뿐이므로 답이 될 수 없다.
⑤ 인간 시각의 발달과 관련된 내용은 지문에서 언급되지 않았다.

09 2021 경희대

정답 ③

해석 ① 결과적으로 ② ~에도 불구하고
③ 반면 ④ 그러므로
⑤ 그러나

해설 지문의 빈칸에 들어갈 적절한 연결어를 고르는 문제이다. 빈칸을 포함하는 문장은 서구권 역사 대부분에서 그림은 기독교의 이상적인 세계관을 표현하는 역할을 했지만, 원근법이 발명된 이후에는 현실주의의 도구가 되었다는 내용으로, 원근법의 발전 이전과 발전 이후의 그림의 역할의 차이를 대조하고 있다. 따라서 빈칸에는 대조를 나타내는 접속사 Whereas가 들어가야 하므로, ③번이 정답이다.

[10-13]

첫 장맛비가 윈난성 산간 지방을 휩쓰는 5월에, 버섯 채집꾼들은 야생 버섯을 찾기 위해 습기 찬 숲으로 떼를 지어 몰려든다. 할머니들은 소쿠리를 끈으로 등에 묶고, 숲 바닥에 갈퀴질을 하고 야생 버섯을 채집할 막대기를 든다. 동이 트자마자 지역 요리사들, 마을 아이들과 부모들, 그리고 멀리 떨어진 해안 공장들에서 온 몇몇 이주 노동자들이 할머니들과 함께한다.
수천 명의 윈난성 가정에서는 야생 버섯 철에 대부분의 생활비를 버는데, 야생 버섯 철은 10월까지 이어진다. 가난한 남서쪽 지방에서 사람들이 매년 따는 버섯 16만 톤은 약 100억 위안(14억 달러)의 수입을 창출한다. 가장 귀한 버섯은 해외로 수출되어 이탈리아 포시니에서 고기 맛이 나는 송이버섯에 이르기까지 한국인과 일본인에게 중요하게 여겨지는 고급 식사에 오르게 된다. 버섯 바구니에서 식사 자리까지 30시간 이내로 버섯을 전달하기 위해 열차도 운행된다. 작년에 개시된 열차는 "고속 송이버섯 급행열차"라는 별명으로 불려왔다. 신선한 상태로 바로 팔리지 않는 것은 모두 자연 건조되거나, 냉동되거나 렐리시로 만들어진다.
여름에, 버섯 채집꾼들은 산을 샅샅이 뒤지는 것으로 한 달에 4천 위안을 벌 수 있다. 지역 가정들만 채집할 수 있도록 제한되어 경쟁이 덜 치열한 숲 보호 구역에서는, 버섯 따러 다니는 사람들의 한 달 벌이가 1만 위안까지 이를 수 있다. 사람들이 가장 **탐내는** 버섯 종류 중 하나는 "염소 배" 버섯인데, 염소 배 버섯은 버섯 철 후반에 나오면 킬로당 최고 1천 위안에 팔릴 수 있다.

monsoon n. 장마 mountainous adj. 산이 많은
province n. 지방
forager n. 스스로 식량을 구해 찾아다니는 사람
throng v. 떼를 지어 모이다 wield v. 들다, 휘두르다
rake v. 갈퀴질을 하다 at first light phr. 동이 트자마자
migrant adj. 이주하는 far-flung adj. 멀리 떨어진
earn one's living phr. 생활비를 벌다, 밥벌이를 하다
fungus n. 버섯, 균류(pl. fungi)
commandeer v. 징발하다 dub v. 별명을 붙이다
relish n. 렐리시(과일, 채소에 양념을 해서 걸쭉하게 끓인 뒤 차게 식혀 고기, 치즈 등을 얹어 먹는 소스) competition n. 경쟁
fierce adj. 치열한, 극심한 fetch v. (특정 가격에) 팔리다

10 2021 세종대

정답 ④

해석 ① 느슨한 ② 다루기 힘든
③ 지독한 ④ 탐내는

해설 지문의 빈칸을 채우는 문제이다. 지문의 세 번째 문단 마지막에서 염소 배 버섯은 버섯 철 후반에 나오면 킬로당 최고 1천 위안에 팔릴 수 있다고 했으므로, 빈칸에는 사람들이 가장 탐내는 버섯 종류 중 하나가 "염소 배" 버섯이라는 내용이 나오는 것이 자연스럽다. 따라서 '탐내는'이라고 한 ④번이 정답이다.

11 2021 세종대

정답 ①

해석 ① 열차가 한국인과 일본인에게 중요하게 여겨지는 버섯인 송이버섯을 배송하는 것을 전문으로 한다.
② 열차가 윈난성 숲에서부터 고객에게 30시간 이내로 버섯을 배송한다.
③ 열차가 윈난성의 오래된 열차보다 빠른데, 수요가 적은 버섯의 이름을 따서 이름 지어졌다.
④ 열차가 송이버섯이 수확되는 야생 버섯 철 동안에만 운행된다.

해설 새로 개시된 열차가 "고속 송이버섯 급행열차"라고 불리는 이유를 파악하는 문제이다. 지문의 두 번째 문단에서 The most valuable ones ~ prized by South Koreans and Japanese. Trains are commandeered to get the mushrooms를 근거로 새로 개시된 열차가 "고속 송이버섯 급행열차"라고 불리는 이유가 '열차가 한국인과 일본인에게 중요하게 여겨지는 버섯인 송이버섯을 배송하는 것을 전문으로 한다'는 것 때문임을 알 수 있다. 따라서 정답은 ①번이다.

어휘 sought-after adj. 수요가 많은, 인기 있는
harvest v. 수확하다

12 2021 세종대

정답 ④

해석 ① 유럽과 아시아에 있는 해외 시장을 연결하는 연안 항구가 있다.
② 버섯 산업은 윈난성을 중국에서 가장 부유한 지방 중 하나로 만들어 준다.
③ 일 년 내내 강수량이 일정해서, 버섯 재배에 완벽한 기후를 제공한다.
④ 주민들은 숲 보호 구역에서 버섯을 채집하는 데 독점적인 접근권을 가진다.

해설 윈난성에 대해 옳은 것을 파악하는 문제이다. 지문의 세 번째 문단에서 In protected forests, where collecting is limited to local families를 근거로 윈난성의 '주민들은 숲 보호 구역에서 버섯을 채집하는 데 독점적인 접근권을 가진다'는 것을 알 수 있다. 따라서 정답은 ④번이다.

어휘 precipitation n. 강수량   exclusive adj. 독점적인

13 2021 세종대

정답 ③

해석 ① 윈난성의 야생 버섯 철은 5월에서 10월까지 이어진다.
② 야생 버섯 철 동안에 수확되는 일부 버섯들은 신선한 상태로 바로 팔리지 않는다.
③ 윈난성에서는 주민들만 버섯을 채집하는 것이 허용된다.
④ 숲에서 채집된 버섯들은 고속 열차로 배송될 수 있다.

해설 지문의 내용과 일치하지 않는 것을 묻는 문제이다. 지문의 세 번째 문단에서 지역 가정들만 채집이 가능하도록 제한되어 경쟁이 덜 치열한 숲 보호 구역에서는, 버섯 따러 다니는 사람들의 한 달 벌이가 1만 위안까지 이를 수 있다고 했으므로, 윈난성에서 주민들만 버섯을 채집하는 것이 허용된다는 것은 지문의 내용과 다르다. 따라서 ③번이 지문의 내용과 일치하지 않는다.

오답분석 ① 지문의 첫 번째 문단의 In May, ~ wild mushrooms와 두 번째 문단의 Thousands of Yunnanese ~ , which runs until October를 통해 '윈난성의 야생 버섯 철은 5월에서 10월까지 이어진다'는 것을 알 수 있다.
② 지문의 두 번째 문단의 Whatever is not sold fresh is air-dried, frozen or made into a relish를 통해 '야생 버섯 철 동안에 수확되는 일부 버섯들은 신선한 상태로 바로 팔리지 않는다'는 것을 알 수 있다.
④ 지문의 두 번째 문단의 Trains are commandeered to get the mushrooms ~ in under 30 hours를 통해 '숲에서 채집된 버섯들은 고속 열차로 배송될 수 있다'는 것을 알 수 있다.

[14-15]

가부키는 일본 연극의 인기 있는 한 형태이다. 그것은 수 세기 전에 시작되었으며 오늘날 일본 문화의 중요한 부분으로 남아있다. 이러한 이유로, 일본을 찾는 많은 서양인들은 반드시 가부키 공연을 적어도 한 편은 본다. 서양 방문객들은 보통 가부키의 광경이 휘황찬란하다고 말하지만, 그들은 여성 역할을 전문적으로 연기하는 남성 배우를 말하는 '온나가타'라는 전통에 종종 어리둥절해 한다. 한때, '온나가타'의 전통을 버리고 여성을 연기하는 데에 여성이 허용되어야 한다는 말이 있었지만 이 생각은 거부되어왔다. '온나가타'는 가부키 공연의 주역으로 남아있다. 어떤 경우에는 '온나가타'가 엄청난 인기를 끌게 되

어 미국에서 록 뮤지션이나 영화배우가 대접받는 것처럼 대접받을 수도 있다.

spectacle n. 광경   dazzling adj. 휘황찬란한
puzzle v. 어리둥절하게 하다   specialize v. 전문으로 하다
abandon v. 버리다   staple n. 주역

14 2020 단국대

정답 ②

해설 ① 여성 — 여성   ② 남성 — 여성
① 여성 — 남성   ④ 남성 — 남성

해설 지문의 빈칸을 채우는 문제이다. 빈칸이 있는 문장 뒤에서, '온나가타'의 전통을 버리고 여성을 연기하는 데에 여성이 허용되어야 한다는 말이 있었다는 내용이 있으므로, '온나가타'는 남성이 여성을 연기하는 전통임을 알 수 있다. 따라서, '남성 — 여성'이라고 한 ②번이 정답이다.

15 2020 단국대

정답 ③

해석 ① 가부키는 더는 일본의 문화적 현상이 아니다.
② 일부 서양인들이 가부키 공연에 반감을 가졌다.
③ '온나가타'의 전통이 한때 논란이 되었다.
④ '온나가타'는 미국뿐만이 아니라 일본에서 인기가 있다.

해설 지문의 내용과 일치하는 것을 묻는 문제이다. 지문의 중간에서 '온나가타'의 전통을 버리고 여성을 연기하는 데에 여성이 허용되어야 한다는 말이 있었지만, 이 생각은 거부되어왔다는 내용을 통해 '온나가타'의 전통이 한때 논란이 되었다는 것을 알 수 있다. 따라서 ③번이 지문의 내용과 일치한다.

오답분석 ① 가부키는 수 세기 전에 시작되었으며 오늘날 일본 문화의 중요한 부분으로 남아있다고 했으므로, 가부키는 더는 일본의 문화적 현상이 아니라는 것은 지문의 내용과 다르다.
② 서양 방문객들은 보통 가부키의 광경이 휘황찬란하다고 말한다고는 했지만, 일부 서양인들이 가부키 공연에 반감을 가졌는지는 알 수 없다.
④ 서양인들은 여성 역할을 전문적으로 연기하는 남성 배우를 말하는 '온나가타'라는 전통에 종종 어리둥절해 한다고 했으므로, '온나가타'는 미국뿐만이 아니라 일본에서 인기가 있다는 것은 지문의 내용과 다르다.

어휘 phenomenon n. 현상   revolt v. 반감을 갖다
controversial adj. 논란이 되는

[16-17]

혈통은 단순히 개인적인 것이 아니라 대단히 집단적이며, 특히 나 같이 우리 지역의 불행한 다른 나라 출신의 원주민들과 강

한 유대감을 느끼는 라틴 아메리카 사람에게는 더욱더 그렇다. 좌절된 꿈이라는 다루기 힘든 역사는 목적의식과 슬픔, 희망과 회복의 감정을 공유하는 것으로 이어졌는데, 그것은 지리적인 운명이나 국가의 경계를 뛰어넘어 우리를 정서적으로 하나로 만든다. 대형 라틴계 슈퍼마켓의 식료품 판매대를 위아래로 거니는 것은 그 사람들과 땅에 다시 연결되도록 하며, 비록 간접적이지만 지금 이 순간에 남반구 어느 곳에나 있는 수백만 가정이 계획하고 준비하고 있는 식사에 참여하게 된다.

origin n. 혈통, 출신   **merely** adv. 단순히, 단지
especially adv. 특히   **fellowship** n. 유대감
unfortunate adj. 불행한
stubborn adj. 다루기 힘든, 완강한   **thwarted** adj. 좌절된
resilience n. 회복
emotionally adv. 정서적으로, 감정적으로
geographic adj. 지리적인   **boundary** n. 경계
stroll v. 거닐다, 산책하다
grocery isle phr. (대형 매장의) 식료품 판매대
partake v. 참여하다   **vicariously** adv. 간접적으로, 대신에
hemisphere n. 반구

16 2019 가천대

정답 ③

해석 ① 국가의   ② 보편적인
     ③ 집단적인   ④ 공공의

해설 빈칸에 적절한 연결어를 넣는 문제이다. 빈칸 앞에서 personal(개인의)이 나왔고 바로 다음에 역접을 나타내는 접속사인 but으로 연결되었으므로, 빈칸에는 personal의 반대 의미를 갖는 단어가 와야 한다는 것을 알 수 있다. 따라서 '집단적인'이라고 한 ③번이 정답이다.

어휘 **national** adj. 국가의   **universal** adj. 보편적인
     collective adj. 집단적인   **public** adj. 공공의

17 2019 가천대

정답 ③

해석 ① 동료 라틴 아메리카 사람과 식사에 참여하는 것은 그들의 공동체 유대감을 느슨하게 만든다.
     ② 혈통의 역사는 이주의 과정에서 영원히 지워진다.
     ③ 정서적인 연대는 라틴계 사회 안에서 국가적 혹은 지리적인 장벽과 관계없이 만들어진다.
     ④ 국가적 소속은 문화적, 민족적, 그리고 인종적 경험을 뛰어넘은 유대감을 유도할 수 있다.

해설 지문의 내용과 일치하는 것을 묻는 문제이다. 지문의 중간에서 그것은 지리적인 운명이나 국가의 경계를 뛰어넘어 우리를 정서적으로 하나로 만든다는 내용을 통해 정서적인 연대는 라틴계 사회 안에서 국가적 혹은 지리적인 장벽과 관계없이 만들어진다는 것을 알 수 있다. 따라서 ③번이 지문의 내용과 일치한다.

오답 분석
① 대형 라틴계 슈퍼마켓의 식료품 판매대를 위아래로 거니는 것으로 비록 간접적이지만 지금 이 순간에 남반구 어느 곳에나 있는 수백만 가정이 계획하고 준비하고 있는 식사에 참여하게 된다고는 했지만, 동료 라틴 아메리카 사람과 식사에 참여하는 것이 그들의 공동체 유대감을 느슨하게 만드는지는 알 수 없다.
② 라틴 아메리카 사람들은 같은 지역의 불행한 다른 나라 출신의 원주민들과 강한 유대감을 느낀다고는 했지만, 혈통의 역사가 이주의 과정에서 영원히 지워지는지는 알 수 없다.
④ 힘든 역사가 지리적인 운명이나 국가의 경계를 뛰어넘어 라틴 아메리카 사람들을 정서적으로 하나로 만든다고는 했지만, 국가적 소속이 문화적, 민족적, 그리고 인종적 경험을 뛰어넘은 유대감을 유도할 수 있는지는 알 수 없다.

어휘 **fellow** n. 동료   **communal** adj. 공동의
     permanently adv. 영원히, 영구적으로   **migration** n. 이주
     solidarity n. 연대, 결속   **barrier** n. 장벽, 장애물
     induce v. 유도하다   **ethnic** adj. 민족의

[18-19]

모든 사람이 그 애플리케이션을 갖고 있다. 그것은 당신의 홈 화면에서 당신을 조롱하는 애플리케이션이다. 그것은 당신이 그것을 숨기려고 했던 폴더로 당신을 유혹하는 애플리케이션이다. 그것은 당신이 로그아웃하고 삭제했던 애플리케이션이고, 그 결과는 다음 날 아침 다시 다운받을 뿐이다. 그것은 당신이 완전히 그만둘 수 없는 애플리케이션이다.

시애틀에 위치한 첨단기술 마케팅 컨설턴트인 43세 Corey Lewis에게 있어, 그것은 인스타그램이고, 그는 "항상 이유 없이 그것을 끊임없이 스크롤하고 있는 저 자신을 발견했어요"라고 말했다. "제 두뇌가 잠깐 휴식할 때마다 인스타그램을 켜서 제 피드를 획획 넘겨보기 시작하는 잠재의식적인 반응이 꽤 많이 발생했습니다."

사태를 악화시키는 것은 새롭고도 반갑지 않은 어떤 감정이었다. 그는 "저는 제 삶에 전혀 관련 없는 게시글에 실제로 화가 났고, 좀 기묘하면서 별로 저답지 않은 감정을 느끼는 저 자신을 발견했습니다."라고 말했다. 최근, 그의 아기가 그의 주변 세계를 탐험하는 바로 그 순간에도, Lewis 씨는 핸드폰으로 피드를 탐험하는 그 자신을 발견했다.

"저는 아무리 적은 시간이라도 그 시간 모두를 인스타그램으로 가득 채우는 저 자신을 발견했는데, 이것은 완전히 이기적이고 제가 정말 바랐던 가까우면서 개방적이고 곁에 존재하는 부모가 되는 것의 반대입니다."라고 그는 말했다. <u>무언가를 해야 할 시기였다.</u>

mock v. 조롱하다   **lure** v. 유혹하다   **delete** v. 삭제하다
quit v. 그만두다   **constantly** adv. 끊임없이
consultant n. 컨설턴트   **slight** adj. 조금의, 약간의
subconscious adj. 잠재의식적인
thumb through phr. 획획 넘겨보다

unwelcome adj. 반갑지 않은   bearing n. 관련
toddler n. 아기   jam into phr. ~에 가득 채워 넣다

18 [2020 성균관대]

정답 ②

해석 ① 좋은 부모가 되는 방법
② 소셜미디어 중독
③ 연결되는 것의 이점
④ 애플리케이션을 평가하는 방법
⑤ 현대 기술의 위험

해설 지문의 주제를 묻는 문제이다. 첫 번째 문단에서 사람들이 그만둘 수 없는 애플리케이션에 대해 말하고, 뒤 문단들에서 인스타그램에 중독된 Corey Lewis의 경험을 이야기하고 있다. 따라서 이 지문의 주제를 '소셜미디어 중독'이라고 표현한 ②번이 정답이다.

어휘 addiction n. 중독   advantage n. 이점
evaluate v. 평가하다

19 [2020 성균관대]

정답 ⑤

해석 ① 새로운 애플리케이션을 개발하다
② 최신 애플리케이션을 업로드하다
③ 새로운 애플리케이션을 구매하다
④ 그 애플리케이션에 더 많은 시간을 쓰다
⑤ 그 애플리케이션에서 로그아웃하고 그것을 삭제하다

해설 밑줄 친 부분의 의미를 추론하는 문제이다. 밑줄 친 to do something은 '무언가를 해야 할'이라는 의미이다. 주변의 내용을 살펴보면 이것이 가까우면서 개방적이고 곁에 존재하는 부모가 되기 위한 행동임을 알 수 있다. 따라서, 이를 '그 애플리케이션에서 로그아웃하고 그것을 삭제하다'라고 표현한 ⑤번이 정답이다.

어휘 delete v. 삭제하다

20 [2020 인하대]

정답 ⑤

해석 네팔은 전 세계 그 어느 나라보다 작은 제곱 마일 안에 지리적 다양성이 가득하다. 이 땅에 사는 사람들이 이 다양성을 잘 보여준다. 네팔에는 다수의 문화가 존재하지 않는다. 모두 소수이다. 이러한 문화 중 가장 유명한 것은 셰르파이다. 셰르파는 Khumbu로 알려진 지역에 있는 에베레스트산의 남쪽 그림자에 있는 높은 계곡에 산다. 그들은 불교도이고, 문화적으로는 티베트 사람이며, 숫자상으로 인구에서 미미한 부분을 차지한다. 그들의 마을은 주로 10,000~13,000피트 사이 고도의 바위, 얼음 및 눈 위에 위치하고 있으며 좁은 산의 오솔길로 연결되어 있다. 셰르파는 전통적으로 매우 낮은 수준의 기술로 일해왔는데, 감자, 순무, 콜리플라워를 재배하고 손으로 방모 직물을 엮어 만들고 여름에는 야크 떼를 따라 더 높은 초원으로 갔다. 지역 사회 행사는 주로 계절의 흐름에 따라 세워진 양식을 따르며 지역 수도원이 중심이 된다.
① 셰르파의 종교
② 지리의 다양성
③ 셰르파 마을의 위치
④ 소수 문화의 유행
⑤ 고도 기술에 의한 방모 직물 산업

해설 지문에서 네팔에 대해 언급되지 않은 것을 파악하는 문제이다. 여덟 번째 문장에서 셰르파는 전통적으로 매우 낮은 수준의 기술로 일해왔는데, 그중 하나가 손으로 방모 직물을 엮어 만든 것이라고는 했지만, 고도 기술에 의한 방모 직물 산업은 언급되지 않았다. 따라서 정답은 ⑤번이다.

어휘 geographical adj. 지리적인   diversity n. 다양성
square mile phr. 제곱 마일   inhabit v. 살다, 거주하다
mirror v. 잘 보여주다, 반영하다   majority n. 다수
minority n. 소수   Buddhist n. 불교도
culturally adv. 문화적으로   Tibetan n. 티베트 사람
numerically adv. 숫자상으로   insignificant adj. 미미한
population n. 인구   altitude n. 고도
situate v. 위치시키다   footpath n. 오솔길, 좁은 길
traditionally adv. 전통적으로   turnip n. 순무
cauliflower n. 콜리플라워
weave v. 엮어 만들다, 짜서 만들다
woolen cloth phr. 방모 직물   herd n. 떼
pasture n. 초원, 목초지   passage n. 흐름
celebration n. 기념행사
center around phr. ~이 중심이 되다
monastery n. 수도원   geography n. 지리, 지형도
prevalence n. 유행, 널리 퍼짐

[21-22]

라마단은 이슬람력의 아홉 번째 달로, 이슬람 신념에 따라 마호메트에 대한 쿠란의 첫 계시를 기념하기 위한 금식의 한 달로서 전 세계의 이슬람교도들에 의해 지켜진다. 이 연례 의식은 이슬람교의 다섯 가지 지주 중 하나로 여겨진다. 하디스에 수집된 수많은 전기 해석들에 따르면, 이달은 초승달의 시각 관측에 기반하여 29일에서 30일 동안 지속된다. 단어 라마단은 모든 걸 태워 버릴 듯이 더운 열기와 건조함을 의미한다. 금식은 모든 성인 이슬람교도들에게 의무적이나, 병을 앓고 있는 사람, 여행 중인 사람, 노인, 임산부, 모유 수유 중인 사람, 당뇨병이 있는 사람, 만성적으로 아픈 사람 혹은 월경 중인 사람들을 제외한다. 한밤중의 태양이나 극의 밤과 같은 자연적 현상이 있는 지역들에 사는 이슬람교도들은 메카의 일정표를 따라야 하지만, 조금 더 일반적으로 받아들여지는 의견은 그러한 지역의 이슬람교도들은 밤이 낮과 구분될 수 있는 자신들에게 가장 가까운 나라의 일정표를 따라야 한다는 것이다. 새벽부터 일몰까지 금식하는 동안, 이슬람교도들은 음식을 먹는 것, 액

체를 마시는 것, 흡연 그리고 성관계를 삼간다. 이슬람교도들은 또한 자기방어를 제외한 그릇된 발언(모욕하기, 악담, 거짓말 등)과 폭력과 같은 단식의 보상을 무효화하는 죄가 되는 행동을 삼가도록 지시를 받는다.

islamic calendar phr. 이슬람력
observe v. (의식·관습 등을) 지키다
muslim n. 이슬람교도, 회교도   fasting n. 금식
revelation n. 계시   observance n. 의식   pillar n. 지주
crescent moon phr. 초승달   biographical adj. 전기의
account n. 해석   hadith n. 하디스(마호메트의 언행록)
scorching adj. 모든 걸 태워 버릴 듯이 더운
dryness n. 건조 (상태)   obligatory adj. 의무적인
breastfeeding n. 모유 수유   diabetic adj. 당뇨병이 있는
chronically adv. 만성적으로   menstruate v. 월경하다
midnight sun phr. (극지에서 한여름에 볼 수 있는) 한밤중의 태양   polar night phr. 극의 밤   distinguish v. 구분하다
consume v. 먹다, 마시다   refrain from phr. ~을 삼가다
sinful adj. 죄가 되는, 나쁜   negate v. 무효화하다, 부정하다
reward n. 보상   false adj. 그릇된
self-defense n. 자기방어

21 (2019 광운대)

정답 ⑤

해석 ① 준수하기 위한 — 반성하도록
② 간과하기 위한 — 중단하도록
③ 기념하기 위한 — 나타내도록
④ 무시하기 위한 — 돌아다니도록
⑤ 기념하기 위한 — 삼가도록

해설 빈칸에 들어갈 내용을 묻고 있다. 첫 번째 빈칸에는 마호메트에 대한 쿠란의 첫 계시를 무엇하기 위한 금식의 한 달인지가 나와야 하므로, 첫 번째 빈칸에는 '기념하다'라는 의미의 to celebrate와 to commemorate가 적절하고, 두 번째 빈칸에는 단식의 보상을 무효화하는 행동을 무엇하도록 지시받는지가 나와야 하므로, 두 번째 빈칸에는 '삼가도록'이라는 의미의 'to refrain from'이 들어가는 것이 자연스럽다. 따라서 ⑤번이 정답이다.

22 (2019 광운대)

정답 ⑤

해석 ① 라마단과 초승달의 가시성 사이에 관련성이 있다.
② 라마단 중 금식은 특정 조건에서 선택적일 수 있다.
③ 메카의 일정표는 다른 나라에 있는 이슬람교도들에 의해 준수되어왔다.
④ 악담과 싸움은 라마단 중에 금지되지만, 일부 경우에, 그것들은 허용된다.
⑤ 이슬람교도들은 라마단 동안 일몰 후에 절대 음식이나 액체를 섭취하면 안 된다.

해설 지문의 내용과 일치하지 않는 것을 묻는 문제이다. ⑤번의 키워드인 not take food or liquids(음식이나 액체를 섭취하면 안 된다)와 관련된 지문의 refrain from consuming food, drinking liquids(음식을 먹는 것, 액체를 마시는 것을 삼간다) 주변에서 새벽부터 일몰까지 금식하는 동안, 이슬람교도들은 음식을 먹는 것, 액체를 마시는 것, 흡연 그리고 성관계를 삼간다고 했으므로, 이슬람교도들이 라마단 동안 일몰 후에 절대 음식이나 액체를 섭취하면 안 된다는 것은 지문의 내용과 일치하지 않는다. 따라서 ⑤번이 지문의 내용과 일치하지 않는다.

오답 분석
① 지문의 세 번째 문장 The month lasts 29-30 days based on the visual sightings of the crescent moon, ~ in the hadiths를 통해 '라마단과 초승달의 가시성 사이에 관련성이 있다'는 것을 알 수 있다.
② 지문의 다섯 번째 문장 Fasting is obligatory for adult Muslims, except those who are suffering from an illness, travelling, elderly, pregnant, breastfeeding, diabetic, chronically ill or menstruating을 통해 '라마단 중 금식은 특정 조건에서 선택적일 수 있다'는 것을 알 수 있다.
③ 지문의 여섯 번째 문장 Muslims who live in regions with a natural phenomenon such as the midnight sun or polar night should follow the timetable of Mecca, ~를 통해 '메카의 일정표는 다른 나라에 있는 이슬람교도들에 의해 준수되어왔다'는 것을 알 수 있다.
④ 지문의 마지막 문장 Muslims are also instructed to refrain from ~ such as false speech (insulting, cursing, lying, etc.) and fighting except in self-defense를 통해 '악담과 싸움은 라마단 중에 금지되지만, 일부 경우에, 그것들은 허용된다'는 것을 알 수 있다.

어휘 visibility n. 가시성   optional adj. 선택적인
certain adj. 특정한   condition n. 조건
prohibit v. 금지하다

[23-25]

대중 매체에서 아시아계 미국인은 대학교에서 입학 허가를 받는 데 있어 "지나치게, 심지어 도발적으로" 성공한 존재로 묘사되어왔다. 아시아계 미국인 상점 주인들은 그들이 도처에 존재한다는 점과 기업가적 효율성 때문에 비난을 받을 뿐만 아니라 환영도 받았다. 아시아계 미국인이 성공할 수 있다면, 많은 정치인들과 전문가들은 이렇게 묻는다. 왜 아프리카계 미국인은 할 수 없겠는가? (A)그런 비교는 소수 민족들이 서로 싸우게 하고 아시아계 미국인들을 향한 아프리카계 미국인들의 분노를 만들어 낸다. (B)피해자들은 인종 차별과 많은 젊은 아프리카계 미국인 노동자들을 불필요하게 만들어 온 경제보다 자신들의 처지에 대해 비난받는다. 아시아계 미국인들에 대한 찬양은 현실을 보기 어렵게 했다. 예를 들어, 백인들과 비교되는 아시아계 미국인들의 높은 소득에 대한 수치는 오해의 소지가

있다. 대부분의 아시아계 미국인들은 전국 평균보다 소득과 생활비가 더 높은 주인 캘리포니아, 하와이와 뉴욕에 살고 있다.

describe v. 묘사하다, 말하다　media n. 대중 매체
excessively adv. 지나치게, 매우
provocatively adv. 도발적으로, 자극적으로
admission n. 입학, 입장　shopkeeper n. 상점 주인
congratulate v. 환영하다, 축하하다　criticize v. 비난하다
ubiquity n. 도처에 존재함, 편재
entrepreneurial adj. 기업가의
effectiveness n. 효율성, 유효성
make it phr. (자기 분야에서) 성공하다　politician n. 정치인
pundit n. 전문가, 권위자　comparison n. 비교
pit v. 싸우게 하다　minority n. 소수 민족, 소수 집단
resentment n. 분노, 원한　plight n. 처지, 곤경
racism n. 인종 차별　economy n. 경제
worker n. 노동자　superfluous adj. 불필요한
celebration n. 찬양, 축하
obscure v. 보기 어렵게 하다, 모호하게 하다　reality n. 현실
figure n. 수치　earning n. 소득, 수입
Caucasian n. 백인　misleading adj. 오해의 소지가 있는
income n. 소득, 수입　cost of living phr. 생활비
national adj. 전국적인　average n. 평균

23 2019 상명대

정답 ⑤

해석 ① 비용이 높은 지역 대 다른 지역
② 아시아계 미국인 대 백인
③ 백인 대 아프리카계 미국인
④ 백인 대 소수 민족
⑤ 아시아계 미국인 대 아프리카계 미국인

해설 밑줄 친 Such comparisons가 누구(어디)와 누구(어디) 간의 comparison인지를 추론하는 문제이다. 세 번째 문장에서 많은 정치인들과 전문가들은 아시아계 미국인이 성공할 수 있다면, 왜 아프리카계 미국인은 할 수 없겠느냐고 묻는다고 했다. 따라서, Such comparisons를 '아시아계 미국인 대 아프리카계 미국인'이라고 한 ⑤번이 정답이다.

24 2019 상명대

정답 ①

해석 ① 아프리카계 미국인　② 아시아계 미국인
③ 소수 민족　④ 알려지지 않은 사람
⑤ 백인

해설 밑줄 친 victims가 누구를 가리키는지를 추론하는 문제이다. 다섯 번째 문장에서 피해자들이 인종 차별과 많은 젊은 아프리카계 미국인 노동자들을 불필요하게 만들어 온 경제보다 자신들의 처지에 대해 비난받는다고 했다. 따라서, victims를 '아프리카계 미국인'이라고 한 ①번이 정답이다.

어휘 unknown n. 알려지지 않은 사람

25 2019 상명대

정답 ④

해석 ① 통계상으로, 아시아계 미국인들은 백인과 비교하여 높은 소득을 가진다.
② 아시아계 미국인들은 사업과 학업에서 몹시 놀라운 성공을 했다.
③ 대부분의 아시아계 미국인들은 비용이 많이 드는 지역에 거주한다.
④ 모든 소수 민족들은 심지어 성공해도 그들의 처지에 대해 비난받는다.
⑤ 아시아계 미국인들의 성공을 보여주는 수치는 그들의 현실을 보여주지 않는다.

해설 지문의 내용과 일치하지 않는 것을 묻는 문제이다. ④번의 키워드인 minorities(소수 민족)와 관련된 두 번째 문장에서 아시아계 미국인 상점 주인들은 그들이 도처에 존재한다는 점과 기업가적 효율성 때문에 비난을 받을 뿐만 아니라 환영도 받아왔다고 했으므로, 모든 소수 민족들이 심지어 성공해도 그들의 처지에 대해 비난받는다는 것은 지문의 내용과 다르다. 따라서 ④번이 지문의 내용과 일치하지 않는다.

오답 분석
① 일곱 번째 문장 For example, figures on the high earnings of Asian Americans relative to Caucasians are misleading을 통해 '통계상으로, 아시아계 미국인들은 백인과 비교하여 높은 소득을 가진다'는 것을 알 수 있다.
② 첫 번째 문장과 두 번째 문장 Asian Americans have been described ~ successful in gaining admission to universities. Asian American shopkeepers have been congratulated, as well as criticized, ~ entrepreneurial effectiveness를 통해 '아시아계 미국인들은 사업과 학업에서 몹시 놀라운 성공을 했다'는 것을 알 수 있다.
③ 마지막 문장 Most Asian Americans live in ~ states with higher incomes and higher costs of living ~ average를 통해 '대부분의 아시아계 미국인들은 비용이 많이 드는 지역에 거주한다'는 것을 알 수 있다.
⑤ 일곱 번째 문장 For example, figures on the high earnings of Asian Americans relative to Caucasians are misleading을 통해 '아시아계 미국인들의 성공을 보여주는 수치는 그들의 현실을 보여주지 않는다'는 것을 알 수 있다.

어휘 statistics n. 통계　astoundingly adv. 몹시 놀랍게도
academic n. 학문, 학과　reside in phr. ~에 거주하다
reflect v. 보여주다, 반영하다

26 2020 인하대

정답 ⑤

해석 연구 자체가 이 두 가지 기준의 희생자가 되었다. 여성보다 더 많이 말함으로써 남성이 힘을 발휘한다고 주장하는 연구에서, 여성의 침묵은 그들이 힘이 없다는 증거로 언급된다. 동시에 다른 연구에 따르면 남성의 침묵 사용과 말하기를 거부하는 것은 자신의 힘을 보여주는 것이라고 한다. Mirra Komarovsky의 대표적인 연구인 *Blue Collar Marriage*를 통해 진행되는 주제는 인터뷰를 한 많은 아내들이 그들이 남편보다 더 많이 말한다고 이야기했다는 것이다("그는 말을 잘 안 해요"라고 한 여자가 자신의 남편에 대해 말했다. "제 남편은 말하지 않는 훌륭한 습관이 있어요."라고 또 다른 사람이 말했다). 많은 아내들은 문제에 관해 이야기하고 싶어 하며 남편들이 이야기하게 만들고 싶어 한다. 반면에, 많은 남편들은 곤란함, 정서적 스트레스 또는 아내의 "요구"에 직면해 물러난다. 하지만 이 남편들이 그들의 결혼 생활에서 "우세"하다는 데는 의문의 여지가 없다. 과묵 자체는 힘의 수단이 될 수 있다. Komarovsky는 자신의 남편에 대해 이렇게 말한 어머니를 인용한다. "그는 말을 많이 하지 않지만 진심으로 말하며 아이들은 그의 말을 잘 들어요."

① 장황함 ② 경박함
③ 결속 ④ 유창함
⑤ 과묵함

해설 지문의 빈칸을 채우는 문제이다. 지문의 빈칸이 있는 문장 뒤 문장에서 말을 많이 하지 않지만, 진심으로 말하며 아이들이 그 말을 잘 듣는 어느 남편의 예시를 설명했으므로, 빈칸에는 말을 많이 하지 않는 것이 힘의 수단이라는 내용이 나와야 적절하다는 것을 알 수 있다. 따라서 '과묵함'이라고 한 ⑤번이 정답이다.

어휘 fall prey to phr. 피해자가 되다 standard n. 기준, 표준
claim v. 주장하다 exert v. 발휘하다, 행사하다
silence n. 침묵 cite v. 언급하다, 인용하다
evidence n. 증거 refuse v. 거부하다
classic adj. 대표적인 tongue-tied adj. 말이 잘 안 나오는
say of phr. ~에 대해 말하다
withdraw v. 물러나다, 철수하다
in the face of phr. ~에 직면하여
dominant adj. 우세한, 지배적인 instrument n. 수단, 도구
I mean what I say phr. 진심으로 하는 말이다
mind v. ~의 말을 잘 듣다, ~에게 복종하다
prolixity n. 장황함 frivolity n. 경박, 천박
solidarity n. 결속, 연대 volubility n. 유창, 수다
taciturnity n. 과묵

[27-29]

> 오늘날 우리 세계가 현재 인구(소비와 쓰레기를 비롯하여)를 지속할 수 있을 것인지, 심지어 우리 세계의 경제가 현재 수준으로 지속 가능한지에 관한 격렬한 논쟁이 계속 진행되고 있다. 아직 그것들이 가장 큰 위험 요인들은 아니다. 만약, 세계화를 통해, 오늘날 지구에 살고 있는 모든 사람이 미국인 평균의 생활 수준을 달성한다면, 세상에 미치는 영향은 현재의 약 10배는 될 것이고, 분명히 지속 불가능할 것이다.
> 세계화의 첫 번째 물결 동안 문화를 수출하는 나라들이 다른 문화에서 농경 사회의 생활 방식을 받아들이는 것을 기대할 수 없었던 것처럼, 우리는 세상 사람들이 우리의 생활 방식에 맞추고 싶어 하는 것을 막을 수 없다. 하지만 모든 사람들이 제1세계에서 지금 하고 있는 대로 산다면 심지어 현재의 인구도 지속할 수 없기 때문에, 우리에게 모순이 있을 수밖에 없다. 대부분의 분석가들이 생각하듯, 세계화는 막을 수 없다. 하지만 세계화의 결과는 우리를 살게 하는 지구의 능력에 너무 부담을 지울지도 모른다. 그것이 해결해야 하는 모순이다.

vigorous adj. 격렬한, 활발한 debate n. 논쟁, 토론
sustain v. 지속하다, 계속하다 present adj. 현재의
population n. 인구 consumption n. 소비(량)
waste n. 쓰레기 sustainable adj. 지속 가능한
risk n. 위험 요인 globalization n. 세계화
achieve v. 달성하다, 성취하다
standard of living phr. 생활 수준 average adj. 평균의
effect n. 영향 certainly adv. 분명히
unsustainable adj. 지속 불가능한 prevent v. 막다
aspire v. 갈망하다 exporter n. 수출업자, 수출국
embrace v. 받아들이다, 수용하다
First World phr. 제1세계, 부유한 선진국
be left with phr. 가지다, ~이 남다 paradox n. 모순, 역설
analyst n. 분석가
unstoppable adj. 막을 수 없는, 제지할 수 없는
consequence n. 결과
overtax v. 부담을 지우다, 무리하다, 혹사하다
resolve v. 해결하다

27 2019 상명대

정답 ③

해석 ① 인구 과잉으로 초래된 환경 위기
② 미국과 농경 사회 간 생활 수준의 불균형
③ 세계화의 문제
④ 제1세계의 증가하는 생활비
⑤ 지속 가능한 개발을 위한 해결책

해설 지문의 제목을 묻는 문제이다. 첫 문장에서 오늘날 우리 세계가 현재 인구(소비와 쓰레기를 비롯하여)를 지속할 수 있을 것인지, 심지어 우리 세계의 경제가 현재 수준으로 지속 가능한지에 관한 격렬한 논쟁이 계속 진행되고 있다고 하였다. 따라서 이 지문의 제목을 '세계화의 문제'라고 표현한 ③번이 정답이다.

어휘 environmental adj. 환경의 crisis n. 위기
overpopulation n. 인구 과잉 imbalance n. 불균형
problem n. 문제 solution n. 해결책
development n. 발달

28 (2019 상명대)

정답 ①

해설 지문의 빈칸을 채우는 문제이다. 두 번째 문단에서 세계화의 첫 번째 물결 동안 문화를 수출하는 나라들이 다른 문화에서 농경 사회의 생활 방식을 받아들이는 것을 기대할 수 없었던 것처럼, 우리는 세상 사람들이 우리의 생활 방식에 맞추고 싶어 막을 수 없다고 했으므로, 빈칸에는 앞에 prevent와 함께 쓰여 '~하는 것을 막다'라는 의미를 만드는 전치사 from이 나와야 적절하다는 것을 알 수 있다. 따라서 'from'이라고 한 ①번이 정답이다.

29 (2019 상명대)

정답 ⑤

해석
① 지구의 증가하는 인구는 오늘날 가장 시급한 문제이다.
② 세계화의 첫 번째 물결 동안, 문화를 수출하는 나라들은 자신들의 문화를 다른 지역에 퍼뜨리기를 원했다.
③ 현재의 모순은 나라 간의 경제 격차로 야기되었다.
④ 한정된 자원 때문에, 제1세계는 세계화 과정을 규제할 것이다.
⑤ 세계화의 결과로, 세계의 사람들은 미국인 평균 수준까지 그들의 생활 수준을 올리기를 바란다.

해설 지문의 내용과 일치하는 것을 묻는 문제이다. 첫 번째 문단의 만약, 세계화를 통해, 오늘날 지구에 살고 있는 모든 사람이 미국인 평균의 생활 수준을 달성한다면, 세상에 미치는 영향은 현재의 약 10배는 될 것이고, 분명히 지속 불가능할 것이라는 내용을 통해 세계화의 결과로, 세계의 사람들은 미국인 평균 수준까지 그들의 생활 수준을 올리기를 바란다는 것을 알 수 있다. 따라서 ⑤번이 지문의 내용과 일치한다.

오답 분석
① 첫 번째 문단에서 오늘날 우리 세계가 현재 인구를 지속할 수 있을 것인지에 관한 격렬한 논쟁이 계속 진행되고 있지만, 아직 그것들이 가장 큰 위험 요인들은 아니라고 했으므로, 지구의 증가하는 인구가 오늘날 가장 시급한 문제라는 것은 지문의 내용과 다르다.
② 두 번째 문단에서 세계화의 첫 번째 물결 동안 문화를 수출하는 나라들이 다른 문화에서 농경 사회의 생활 방식을 받아들이는 것을 기대할 수 없었다고 했으므로, 세계화의 첫 번째 물결 동안, 문화를 수출하는 나라들이 자신들의 문화를 다른 지역에 퍼뜨리기를 원했다는 것은 지문의 내용과 다르다.
③ 두 번째 문단에서 모든 사람들이 제1세계에서 지금 하고 있는 대로 산다면 현재의 인구도 지속할 수 없기 때문에, 우리에게 모순이 있을 수밖에 없다고는 했지만, 현재의 모순이 나라 간의 경제 격차로 야기되었는지는 알 수 없다.
④ 두 번째 문단에서 모든 사람들이 제1세계에서 지금 하고 있는 대로 산다면 현재의 인구도 지속할 수 없기 때문에, 우리에게 모순이 있을 수밖에 없다고는 했지만, 한정된 자원 때문에 제1세계가 세계화 과정을 규제할 것인지는 알 수 없다.

어휘 urgent adj. 시급한, 긴급한 spread v. 퍼뜨리다, 확산되다
region n. 지역 current adj. 현재의
economic adj. 경제의 gap n. 격차, 간격
limited adj. 한정된 control v. 규제하다, 통제하다
as a result of phr. ~의 결과로서 hope v. 바라다

[30-31]

최근 자조(自助)의 추세는 niksen이라는 것인데, 문자 그대로 아무것도 하지 않거나 시간을 헛되이 보낸다는 네덜란드 단어이다. niksen을 실천하는 것은 단지 주변을 둘러보며 어슬렁거리거나, 아무런 목적 없이 음악을 듣거나, 단순히 의자에 앉아있는 것처럼 단순한 일이다. 명상이 그 순간에 집중하는 것에 관한 것인 반면, niksen은 삶의 작은 일들에 초점을 맞추기보다는 단지 정신을 배회하도록 놓아두고 시간을 보내는 것에 관한 것이다. niksen은 역사적으로 게으름으로 일축돼 왔지만, 세계적으로 스트레스 수준이 증가하고, 극도의 피로처럼, 건강에 치명적인 스트레스의 악영향에 대해 의료계가 인식하기 시작하면서, 아무것도 하지 않는 것이 점점 긍정적이고, 스트레스와 싸우는 전략으로 여겨지기 시작했다. 여유를 갖는 것의 이익에 관한 연구는 설득력이 있는데, 이 연구는 여유를 갖는 것이 마치 불안을 감소시키는 것처럼, 감정적인 특전에서부터 노화 과정을 줄이고 감기와 싸우는 신체 능력을 강화하는 것과 같은 신체적인 장점까지의 이익을 갖는다고 설명하고 있다. 이러한 잠재적인 건강에 대한 긍정적인 영향은 우리 중 가장 바쁘고 많은 부담을 지고 있는 사람들에게조차 niksen을 실천하라고 장려할 수 있을 정도로 충분히 큰 것 같다.

self-help n. 자조(自助) literally adv. 문자 그대로
idle adj. (시간을) 헛되이 보내는
hang around phr. 어슬렁거리다 mindfulness n. 명상
wander v. 배회하다 dismiss v. 일축하다
laziness n. 게으름 crushing adj. 치명적인
burnout n. 극도의 피로 recognition n. 인식
tactic n. 전략 perk n. 특전 hectic adj. 정신없이 바쁜
overburdened adj. 부담이 지나치게 많은

30 (2020 한국외대)

정답 ④

해석
① 바라보다 — 생산하다
② 고정시키다 — 뒤집다
③ 나누다 — 고용하다
④ 배회하다 — 줄이다

해설 지문의 빈칸을 채우는 문제이다. 첫 번째 문장에서, niksen은 아무것도 하지 않고 시간을 헛되이 보내는 것이라고 했으므로, 첫 번째 빈칸에는 그 순간에 집중하는 것인 명상과 달리 niksen은 정신을 어떤 곳에도 집중시키지 않는다는 내용이 들어가야 한다. 두 번째 빈칸이 포함된 문장은 여유를 갖는 것의 장점을 설명하고 있으므로, 두 번째 빈칸에는 노화 과정을

줄인다는 내용이 들어가는 것이 자연스럽다. 따라서 ④번이 정답이다.

31 2020 한국외대

정답 ①

해석
① 전통적으로, *niksen*은 호의적으로 받아들여졌다.
② *Niksen*과 명상은 정신적 과정과 관련이 있다.
③ *niksen*을 실천하는 것에는 신체적인 이득이 있다.
④ *niksen*의 장점은 과학적으로 규명되었다.

해설 지문의 내용과 일치하지 않는 것을 묻는 문제이다. 지문의 네 번째 문장에서 *niksen*은 역사적으로 게으름으로 일축돼 왔다고 했으므로, 전통적으로 *niksen*이 호의적으로 받아들여졌다는 것은 지문의 내용과 다르다. 따라서 ①번이 지문의 내용과 일치하지 않는다.

오답 분석
② 지문의 세 번째 문장에서, 명상은 그 순간에 집중하는 것이고, *niksen*은 정신을 배회하도록 놓아두는 것에 관한 것이라고 했으므로, *niksen*과 명상이 정신적인 과정을 수반한다는 것을 알 수 있다.
③ 지문의 다섯 번째 문장에서, 여유를 갖는 것이 감정적인 특전에서부터 신체적인 이득을 갖는다고 했으므로, *niksen*을 실천하는 것에 신체적인 이득이 있다는 것을 알 수 있다.
④ 지문의 다섯 번째 문장에서, 여유를 갖는 것의 이득에 관한 연구가 설득력이 있다고 했으므로, *niksen*의 장점은 과학적으로 입증되었다는 것을 알 수 있다.

어휘 favorably adv. 호의적으로　establish v. 규명하다

[32-33]

비록 초등학교 단계에서의 독서 능력에 최근 가시적인 진전이 있었지만, 그 모든 진전이 아이들이 십 대가 되자 멈춰 선 것처럼 나타난다. 미국의 십 대 및 성인들의 독서량은 전반적으로 감소하고 있다. 가장 놀랄만한 것은, 대학 졸업자들 사이에서 독서 능력과 일반적인 독서 습관 이 두 가지가 많이 감소했다는 것이다. 이러한 부정적인 추세는 문학의 중요성 그 이상이다. 독서 능력의 감소는 사회, 경제, 문화, 그리고 시민 생활에 분명한 영향을 미친다. 이런 충격적인 이야기를 어떻게 요약할까? 미국인들, 특히 젊은 미국인들은, 독서량이 줄어듦에 따라, 독서 능력도 떨어지고 있다. 그들의 독서 능력이 떨어지기 때문에, 그들은 낮은 수준의 학업 성취도를 가진다. 미국 십 대 중 거의 3분의 1이 학교를 중퇴한다는 부끄러운 사실은 글을 읽고 쓸 줄 아는 능력 및 독해력의 감소와 깊이 관련이 있다. 독서 능력이 낮아짐에 따라, 취업 시장에서 사람들은 저조한 성적을 보인다. 형편없는 독해 능력은 부진한 취업, 낮은 임금, 그리고 승진을 위한 기회의 감소와 연관성이 아주 많다. 그리고 독해 능력이 부족한 독자들은 시민 생활과 문화생활, 가장 현저하게는 자원봉사와 투표에서 적극적으로 될 가능성이 더 작다.

measurable adj. 가시적인　literary adj. 문학의
demonstrable adj. 분명한　disturbing adj. 충격적인
literacy n. 글을 읽고 쓸 줄 아는 능력
comprehension n. 이해력　correlate v. 연관성이 있다
advancement n. 승진　deficient adj. 부족한
notably adv. 현저하게

32 2020 가톨릭대

정답 ③

해석
① 인쇄물 독자의 미래
② 독자 감소 이면의 이유
③ 독서 능력의 감소에 따른 결과
④ 독서 습관과 그것이 학업 수행에 미치는 영향

해설 지문의 제목을 묻는 문제이다. 지문 처음에서 십 대 이후 독서 능력의 진전이 멈춰 선 것처럼 나타난다고 하고, 지문 뒤에서 독서 능력의 감소는 부진한 취업, 낮은 임금, 그리고 승진을 위한 기회의 감소와 연관성이 아주 많다고 했다. 따라서 이 지문의 제목을 '독서 능력의 감소에 따른 결과'라고 표현한 ③번이 정답이다.

어휘 a reason behind phr. ~ 이면의 이유

33 2020 가톨릭대

정답 ②

해석
① 미국의 성인들은 십 대보다 독서를 많이 하는 경향이 있다.
② 심지어 대학 졸업자들도 이전보다 독서를 덜 하는 경향이 있다.
③ 일단 학생이 십 대가 되면, 그들의 독서 능력이 급상승하기 시작한다.
④ 초등학생의 독서 능력은 최근 정체되어 있다.

해설 지문의 내용과 일치하는 것을 묻는 문제이다. 지문의 세 번째 문장 Most alarming, both reading ability and the habit of regular reading have greatly declined among college graduates의 내용을 통해 대학 졸업자들도 이전보다 독서를 덜 하는 경향이 있다는 것을 알 수 있다. 따라서 ②번이 지문의 내용과 일치한다.

오답 분석
① 미국의 십 대 및 성인들의 독서량은 전반적으로 감소하고 있다고 했으므로, 성인들이 십 대보다 독서를 많이 하는 경향이 있다는 것은 지문의 내용과 다르다.
③ 아이들이 십 대가 되자 진전이 멈춰 선 것처럼 나타난다고 했으므로, 십 대가 되면, 독서 능력이 급상승하기 시작한다는 것은 지문의 내용과 다르다.
④ 초등학교 단계에서의 독서 능력에 최근 가시적인 진전이 있었다고 했으므로, 초등학생의 독서 능력은 최근 정체되어 있다는 것은 지문의 내용과 다르다.

어휘 soar v. 급상승하다　standstill n. 정체, 정지

[34-35]

오늘날 전 세계의 대부분의 사람은 대체로 똑같이 옷을 입는다. 같은 청바지, 같은 운동화, 같은 티셔츠가 그것이다. 거대한 의복의 혼합기에 반대하여 저항하는 곳은 단 몇 군데에 불과하다. 그중의 하나가 페루의 지방이다. 안데스산맥에서, 케추아 여성들은 여전히 밝은 색깔의 드레스와 숄, 그리고 경쾌한 각도로 고정되어 있고 그들 부족의 휘장으로 장식된 작은 펠트 모자를 걸친다. 하지만 그것들이 케추아의 전통 의상은 전혀 아니다. 이 드레스와 숄, 그리고 모자는 사실 안달루시아가 기원이며, Túpac Amaru가 패배한 결과로 스페인 총독인 Francisco de Toledo에 의해 1572년에 도입되었다. 실제로 전통적인 안데스산맥의 여성 의복은 허리에 띠로 고정된 튜닉으로 구성되어 있는데, 튜닉 위로는 덮개가 덮여 있으며, 그것은, 투푸 핀으로 단단히 매어졌다. 케추아 여성이 요즘 입는 것은 이 초창기 의복과 그들의 스페인 지배자로부터 입으라고 명령받은 옷의 조합이다. 볼리비아 여성 사이에서 인기 있는 중산모는 나중에 등장했으며, 그때는 영국 노동자들이 볼리비아의 첫 번째 철로를 짓기 위해 도착했을 때였다. 현재 안데스산맥의 남성 사이의 미국식 평상복 패션은 이처럼 그저 의복 서양화의 긴 역사의 최신 장에 불과하다.

hold out phr. 저항하다, 버티다
blending machine phr. 혼합기 **rural** adj. 지방의
shawl n. 숄 (의복의 한 종류) **felt** n. 펠트, 모직
jaunty adj. 경쾌한, 쾌활한 **tribal** adj. 부족의
insignia n. 휘장 **impose** v. 도입하다 **viceroy** n. 총독
in the wake of phr. ~의 결과로
defeat n. 패배; v. 패배시키다 **authentically** adv. 실제로
attire n. 의복 **consist of** phr. ~로 구성되다
secure v. 고정하다 **sash** n. 띠 **mantle** n. 덮개
fasten v. 단단히 매다, 잠그다 **garment** n. 의복
bowler hat phr. 중산모 **merely** adv. 그저, 단지
westernization n. 서양화

34 [2019 서울여대]

정답 ③

해석 ① 사람들이 값싼 옷을 입는 곳
② 사람들이 펑퍼짐한 옷을 싫어하는 곳
③ 사람들이 대량생산된 옷을 거부하는 곳
④ 사람들이 요즘의 패션 동향을 따라 하는 곳

해설 밑줄 친 부분의 의미를 추론하는 문제이다. 밑줄 친 where people hold out against the giant sartorial blending machine은 '거대한 의복의 혼합기에 반대하여 저항하는 곳' 이라는 의미이다. 주변의 내용을 살펴보면 이것이 대체로 사람들이 옷을 똑같이 입는 것에 반대하여 저항한다는 것임을 알 수 있다. 따라서, 이를 '사람들이 대량생산된 옷을 거부하는 곳'이라고 표현한 ③번이 정답이다.

어휘 **baggy** adj. 펑퍼짐한, 헐렁한
mass-produced adj. 대량생산된 **trend** n. 동향, 경향

35 [2019 서울여대]

정답 ①

해석 ① 오늘날 페루 지방의 여성들은 일반적으로 청바지와 티셔츠를 입는다.
② 요즘 많은 안데스산맥의 남자들은 미국식 평상복을 입는다.
③ 현대 케추아 여성들의 의복은 실제로 전통적인 것이 아니다.
④ 스페인 총독이 케추아 여성들에게 안달루시아식의 드레스를 입을 것을 강요했다.

해설 지문의 내용과 일치하지 않는 것을 묻는 문제이다. ①의 키워드인 Today women in rural Peru(오늘날 페루 지방의 여성들)와 관련된 문장 In the mountains of the Andes, ~ with their tribal insignia.에서 케추아 여성들은 여전히 밝은색의 드레스와 숄을 입고 펠트로 된 모자를 쓴다고 했으므로, '일반적으로 청바지와 티셔츠를 입는다'는 것은 지문의 내용과 다르다. 따라서 ①번이 지문의 내용과 일치하지 않는다.

오답분석
② The current fashion among Andean men ~ a long history of sartorial Westernization.을 통해 '요즘 많은 안데스산맥의 남자들은 미국식 평상복을 입는다'는 것을 알 수 있다.
③ Except that these are not traditional Quechua clothes at all.을 통해 '현대 케추아 여성들의 의복은 실제로 전통적인 것이 아니다'는 것을 알 수 있다.
④ The dresses, shawls and hats ~ in the wake of Túpac Amaru's defeat.를 통해 '스페인 총독이 케추아 여성들에게 안달루시아식의 드레스를 입을 것을 강요했다'는 것을 알 수 있다.

어휘 **generally** adv. 일반적으로
contemporary adj. 현대의, 동시대의 **force** v. 강요하다

[36-37]

인도주의의 상업화는 UN 유명인사 지지의 열렬한 재활성화에서 가장 명확한데, 인도주의 장르는 오드리 헵번, 그리고 더 최근에는 앤젤리나 졸리와 같이, 주요 할리우드 우상들과 관련된 성공 역사가 있다. 그러한 스타들의 지지는 항상 인도주의적 담론의 양면적인 수행성에 의존해왔는데, 이것은 타인의 고통에 대한 유명인사의 증언인 "체현"과 이러한 증언에 유명인사 자신의 분명하고 독특한 분위기를 불어넣는 "의인화"를 결합한다. 그러나, 현대의 지지 표현을 과거의 것과 구별하는 것은 유명인사의 "고백적" 의사 전달 구조에 특권을 부여하는 전자(체현)의 경향이다. 유명인사 지지에 대한 초기 형태인 엄격한 격식과는 달리, 고백적 수행성은 "멀리 떨어져 있는 친밀함"에 달려 있고, 이것은 유명인사 삶의 사적인 영역에 대한 간접적 접근을 지칭하는 오늘날 대중문화의 주요 특징인

데, 이는 이 사적인 영역이 유명인사의 공적인 모습의 내재적 측면이 되게 한다.

humanitarianism n. 인도주의 enthusiastic adj. 열렬한
invigoration n. 활성화 celebrity n. 유명인사
advocacy n. 지지 humanitarian adj. 인도주의의
icon n. 우상 rely upon phr. ~에 의지하다
performativity n. 수행성 discourse n. 담론
combine v. 결합하다 impersonation n. 체현
testimony n. 증언 suffering n. 고통
personification n. 의인화 infusion n. 불어넣음, 주입
distinct adj. 분명한 aura n. 독특한 분위기
differentiate v. 구별하다 contemporary adj. 현대의
articulation n. 표현 tendency n. 경향
privilege v. 특권을 주다 confessional adj. 고백의
communicative adj. 의사전달의 formality n. 격식
rest upon phr. ~에 달려 있다 intimacy n. 친밀함
access n. 접근 intimate adj. 사적인 sphere n. 영역
render v. ~이 되게 하다 inherent adj. 내재하는
aspect n. 측면 personae n. (다른 사람들 눈에 비치는, 특히 그의 실제 성격과는 다른, 한 개인의) 모습

36 2020 서강대

정답 ③

해석 ① 유명인사들은 타인의 고통을 대중과 공유한다.
② 유명인사 인도주의는 과거에 더욱 격식을 차렸었다.
③ 오늘날 유명인사들은 죄를 고백하기 위해 공적인 모습을 이용한다.
④ 오늘날 할리우드 우상들은 스타로서 그들의 힘을 증언에 불어넣는다.

해설 지문을 통해 추론할 수 없는 것을 고르는 문제이다. 지문에서 유명인사들이 자신의 죄를 고백하는 것에 대해서는 언급되지 않았으므로, 정답은 ③번이다.

오답 ① 지문의 두 번째 문장 The advocacy of ~ the celebrity's testimony of the suffering of others ~ star aura.를 통해 '유명인사들은 타인의 고통을 대중과 공유한다'는 것을 알 수 있다.
② 지문의 세 번째 문장 What differentiates contemporary ~ celebrity.를 통해 '유명인사 인도주의는 과거에 더욱 격식을 차렸었다'는 것을 알 수 있다.
④ 지문의 두 번째 문장 The advocacy of ~ the infusion of such testimony with the celebrity's own distinct star aura.를 통해 '오늘날 할리우드 우상들은 스타로서 그들의 힘을 증언에 불어넣는다'는 것을 알 수 있다.

어휘 suffering n. 고통 humanitarianism n. 인도주의
formal adj. 격식을 차린 personae n. (다른 사람들 눈에 비치는, 특히 그의 실제 성격과는 다른, 한 개인의) 모습
confess v. 고백하다 guilt n. 유죄 icon n. 우상
infuse v. 불어넣다 testimony n. 증언

37 2020 서강대

정답 ④

해석 ① 전파 — 불투명한 — 열려 있는
② 확산 — 난해한 — 무료의
③ 복합 — 타락한 — 극미한
④ 상업화 — 양면적인 — 간접적인

해설 지문의 빈칸을 채우는 문제이다. 첫 번째 빈칸에는 UN 유명인사 지지의 재활성화가 인도주의의 무엇을 나타내는지에 대한 내용이 나와야 적절하다는 것을 알 수 있다. 따라서 '상업화'라는 내용이 들어가야 자연스럽다. 두 번째 빈칸 뒤에 "체현"과 "의인화"를 결합했다는 내용이 있으므로, 스타들의 지지가 인도주의적 담론의 어떠한 수행성에 의존해왔는지에 대한 내용이 나와야 적절하다는 것을 알 수 있다. 따라서 '양면적인'이라는 내용이 들어가야 자연스럽다. 세 번째 빈칸에는 고백적 수행성은 "멀리 떨어져 있는 친밀함"에 달려 있다고 했으므로, 이것이 유명인사 삶의 사적인 영역에 대한 어떤 접근을 지칭하는 것인지에 대한 내용이 나와야 적절하다는 것을 알 수 있다. 따라서 '간접적인'이라는 내용이 들어가야 자연스럽다. 따라서 ④ commodification — ambivalent — mediated가 정답이다.

어휘 opaque adj. 불투명한 proliferation n. 확산
abstruse adj. 난해한 conglomeration n. 복합
decadent adj. 타락한 minute adj. 극미한
commodification n. 상업화 ambivalent adj. 양면적인
mediated adj. 간접적인

[38-39]

1950년, 도시 지역에 사는 세계 인구의 비율은 30퍼센트였다. 2014년까지, 그 수치는 54퍼센트까지 증가했고 2050년까지 우리 중 3분의 2가 도시에서 살 것이라 예측된다. 이것은 고작 100년 후에 도시 거주자 수가 두 배 이상이 되어있을 것임을 의미한다. 압도적인 이 도시화의 대부분은 아시아와 아프리카에서 일어날 것으로 예상되는데, 사람들이 일자리, 주택, 그리고 의료 및 교육에 대한 더 나은 접근 기회를 찾기 위해 이동하기 때문이다. 런던은 한 세기가 넘는 사이에 백만 명에서 8백만 명 인구가 되었다. 몇몇 아시아 도시들은 50년 이내에 그렇게 되었다. 많은 사람들이 도시 인구의 이러한 급증이 주택 부족과 증가되는 취업 경쟁으로 이어질 것이라고 걱정하지만, 발달의 측면에서는 거의 틀림없이 많은 중대한 이점이 있다. 실제로, 역사는 한 국가에서 눈에 띄는 발전이 도시화 없이 일어날 수 없다는 것을 보여주었다. 따라서 이 글은 개발도상국에서의 도시화가 적극적으로 장려되어야 한다는 것을 주장할 것이다.

predict v. 예측하다 dweller n. 거주자
overwhelming adj. 압도적인 majority n. 대부분, 다수
urbanization n. 도시화 occur v. 일어나다, 발생하다
migrate v. 이동하다 housing n. 주택
access n. 접근권, 접촉 기회 healthcare n. 의료

concern v. 걱정시키다   employment n. 취업, 고용
arguably adv. 거의 틀림없이   significant adj. 중대한
in terms of phr. ~ 면에서는   notable adj. 눈에 띄는

38 [2020 한양대에리카]

정답 ②

해석
① 서서히 제한되다
② 적극적으로 장려되다
③ 강제적으로 시행되다
④ 신중하게 관찰되다

해설 지문의 빈칸을 채우는 문제이다. 지문 마지막에서 도시화는 발달의 측면에서 이점이 있으며, 역사는 한 국가에서 눈에 띄는 발전이 도시화 없이 일어날 수 없다는 것을 보여주었다고 했으므로, 빈칸에는 이 글이 개발도상국에서의 도시화에 대해 어떤 주장을 하는지에 대한 내용이 나와야 적절하다는 것을 알 수 있다. 따라서 '적극적으로 장려되다'라고 한 ②번이 정답이다.

어휘
gradually adv. 서서히   coercively adv. 강제적으로
implement v. 시행하다   observe v. 관찰하다
with caution phr. 신중하게

39 [2020 한양대에리카]

정답 ③

해석
① 도시 거주자들의 비율은 2050년까지 60퍼센트 이하가 될 것이다.
② 많은 아시아인들은 경작할 땅이 충분하지 않아 도시로 이동한다.
③ 일부 아시아 도시들은 런던이 도시화했던 시간의 절반 동안에 도시화되었다.
④ 도시들은 시골 지역과 균형을 깨뜨리지 않기 위해 신중하게 개발되어야 한다.

해설 지문의 내용과 일치하는 것을 묻는 문제이다. 지문의 다섯 번째 문장 Some Asian cities ~의 내용을 통해 일부 아시아 도시들은 런던이 도시화했던 시간의 절반 동안에 도시화되었다는 것을 알 수 있다. 따라서 ③번이 지문의 내용과 일치한다.

오답분석
① 2050년까지 우리 중 3분의 2가 도시에서 살 것이라 예측된다고 했으므로, 도시 거주자들의 비율이 2050년까지 60퍼센트 이하가 될 것이라는 것은 지문의 내용과 다르다.
② 아시아와 아프리카에서 사람들이 일자리, 주택, 그리고 의료 및 교육에 대한 더 나은 접근 기회를 찾기 위해 이동한다고 했으므로, 많은 아시아인들이 경작할 땅이 충분하지 않아 도시로 이동한다는 것은 지문의 내용과 다르다.
④ 도시들은 시골 지역과 균형을 깨뜨리지 않기 위해 신중하게 개발되어야 하는지는 지문에서 언급되지 않았다.

어휘
cultivate v. 경작하다   urbanize v. 도시화하다
rural adj. 시골의

[40-42]

온라인상에서 누구나 이용할 수 있는 무료 공동 제작 백과사전을 통해 "수십 년 전에는 상상도 못 했던 방식으로 많은 사람들이 함께 생각할 수 있게 되었습니다"라고 집단 지성의 어느 연구원이 말한다. "건강관리나 기후 변화와 같이, 사회 집단으로서 우리가 직면하고 있는 문제들을 다루기 위해 필요한 모든 것을 아는 사람은 단 한 사람도 없지만, 전체적으로 우리는 지금까지 우리가 노력한 것보다 훨씬 더 많이 알고 있다." 그러한 생각은 집단 지성에 대한 중요한 사실을 분명히 보여준다. 군중들은 개별 구성원들이 책임감 있게 행동하고 그들 스스로 결정을 내려야 현명하다. 만약 그 구성원들이 서로를 흉내 내거나, 생각 없이 유행을 따르거나, 누군가 그들에게 무엇을 해야 할지 말해주기를 기다린다면, 그 집단은 똑똑하지 않을 것이다. 한 집단이 똑똑하다고 할 때, 개미들로 구성되든 변호사들로 구성되든, 이는 구성원들이 자기 자신의 역할을 하는 것에 달려 있다. 가끔 지구에 대한 우리의 영향을 줄이기 위해 여분의 병을 재활용할 가치가 정말로 있는지 궁금해하는 사람들에게, 사실은 우리가 어떻게 해야 하는지 알 수 없더라도 우리의 행동이 중요하다는 것이다.
"꿀벌은 당신이나 나보다 더 큰 모습을 본 적이 없습니다"라고 한 벌 전문가는 말한다. "우리 중 어느 누구도 사회가 전체적으로 어떤 것을 필요로 하는지 알지 못하지만, 우리는 주위를 둘러보고 말하길, 아, 그들은 학교에서 자원봉사를 하거나, 교회 잔디를 깎거나, 정치 운동을 도울 누군가가 필요하다고 합니다." 복잡한 세상 속에서 롤모델을 찾고 있다면, 개미나 벌 흉내를 내는 것보다 더 나쁜 일을 할 수도 있다.

collaborative adj. 공동 제작의, 합작하는
encyclopedia n. 백과사전   available adj. 이용 가능한
decade n. 10년   collective intelligence phr. 집단 지성
climate n. 기후   collectively adv. 전체적으로, 일괄하여
underline v. 분명히 보여주다, 강조하다
responsibly adv. 책임감 있게   imitate v. 흉내 내다
unthinkingly adv. 생각 없이, 경솔히   fad n. 유행
attorney n. 변호사   lighten v. 줄이다, 덜어 주다
expert n. 전문가   mow v. 깎다   lawn n. 잔디
complexity n. 복잡함

40 [2020 광운대]

정답 ②

해석
① 우리가 알아야 할 드러나지 않은 문제들이 있다.
② 우리는 지금까지 우리가 노력한 것보다 훨씬 더 많이 알고 있다.
③ 다른 사람들과 함께 일하는 것은 쉽지 않을지도 모른다.
④ 개미나 벌은 사람보다 더 똑똑할 수도 있다.
⑤ 개별 구성원들은 독립적으로 일해야 한다.

해설 지문의 빈칸을 채우는 문제이다. 지문의 첫 번째 문장에서 수십 년 전에는 상상도 못 했던 방식으로 많은 사람들이 함께 생각할 수 있게 되었다고 했으므로, 빈칸에는 모든 것을 아는 단 한 사람은 없지만, 집단 지성은 높아졌다는 내용이 나와야 적절하다는 것을 알 수 있다. 따라서 '우리는 지금까지 우리가 노력한 것보다 훨씬 더 많이 알고 있다'라고 한 ②번이 정답이다.

어휘 unseen adj. 드러나지 않은, 보지 못한
independently adv. 독립적으로

41 [2020 광운대]

정답 ①

해석 ① 개별 행동이 전체에 영향을 미치기 때문
② 지성은 단순한 문제일 뿐이기 때문
③ 인간은 실제의 진실을 모르기 때문
④ 벌과 개미는 재활용을 위해 중요하기 때문
⑤ 인간은 벌이나 개미보다 덜 완벽하기 때문

해설 밑줄 친 부분에 대한 예를 들은 이유를 파악하는 문제이다. 빈칸이 있는 지문의 두 번째 문단에서 개별 구성원들이 책임감 있게 행동하고 그들 스스로 결정을 내려야 그 집단이 현명하다고 했으므로, 밑줄 친 recycling에 대한 예를 들은 이유는 '개별 행동이 전체에 영향을 미치기 때문'이다. 따라서 ①번이 정답이다.

어휘 affect v. 영향을 미치다   intelligence n. 지성

42 [2020 광운대]

정답 ⑤

해석 ① 저자는 온라인 공동 제작 백과사전을 집단 지성의 사례로 언급한다.
② 집단 지성은 인간뿐만 아니라 개미나 벌과 같은 곤충에게도 적용된다.
③ 개별 구성원들은 사회가 전체적으로 어떤 것을 필요로 하는지 알지 못하지만, 각각의 사회 활동을 인지한다.
④ 개별 구성원들은 집단 지성을 지적으로 만들기 위해 책임감 있고 창의적이어야 한다.
⑤ 저자는 인간은 사회에서 롤모델이 필요하지만, 개미나 벌의 흉내를 내서는 안 된다고 주장한다.

해설 지문의 내용과 일치하지 않는 것을 묻는 문제이다. ⑤번의 키워드인 role model이 언급된 지문의 주변에서 복잡한 세상 속에서 롤모델을 찾고 있다면, 개미나 벌 흉내를 내는 것보다 더 나쁜 일을 할 수도 있다고 했으므로, 저자는 인간은 사회에서 롤모델이 필요하지만, 개미나 벌의 흉내를 내서는 안 된다고 주장한다는 것은 지문의 내용과 일치하지 않는다. 따라서 ⑤번이 지문의 내용과 일치하지 않는다.

오답 분석
① 지문의 첫 번째 문장 With free collaborative encyclopedias available to anyone online, "it's now possible for huge numbers of people to think together in ways we never imagined a few decades ago,"~를 통해 '저자는 온라인 공동 제작 백과사전을 집단 지성의 사례로 언급한다'는 것을 알 수 있다.
② 지문의 마지막 문장 If you're looking for a role model in a world of complexity, you could do worse than imitate an ant or a bee를 통해 '집단 지성은 인간뿐만 아니라 개미나 벌과 같은 곤충에게도 적용된다'는 것을 알 수 있다.
③ 지문의 마지막 문단 None of us knows what society as a whole needs, but we look around and say, oh, they need someone to volunteer at school~을 통해 '개별 구성원들은 사회가 전체적으로 어떤 것을 필요로 하는지 알지 못하지만, 각각의 사회 활동을 인지한다'라는 것을 알 수 있다.
④ 지문의 두 번째 문단 Crowds are wise only if individual members act responsibly and make their own decisions를 통해 '개별 구성원들은 집단 지성을 지적으로 만들기 위해 책임감 있고 창의적이어야 한다'라는 것을 알 수 있다.

어휘 mention v. 언급하다   responsible adj. 책임감 있는

[43-44]

현재 우리가 '시간'이라고 생각하는 것은 대부분 산업혁명 시대의 발명이다. 공장들과 19세기에 공장을 중심으로 성장한 경제 체제는 낮에서 밤으로 바뀌고 계절과 계절이 바뀌는 자연적인 리듬에서 근로자들의 시간 감각을 분리하는 것에 의존했다. 태양이 뜰 때 거의 깨어 있고 태양이 지고 오래지 않아 잠들고, 수확이 적은 겨울 달에 더 자고, 수확 시기에 덜 자고, 낮잠으로 그들의 하루를 잠시 중단시키는 대신, 노동자들은 공장 종소리에 맞춰 지속적으로 일어나고 그에 따라 휴식 시간을 준비하는 것을 배워야 했다. 여행, 학교, 및 상업을 위한 일정은 획일적인 시계 시간, 즉 계절, 지역, 혹은 직종 전체에 걸쳐 새롭게 동질화된 시간의 산업 패턴을 따랐다. 고용주가 근로자의 너무 많은 시간을 요구하면서 충분한 수면을 빼앗자, 근로자들은 잠을 덜 자기보다는 *더욱* 표준화된 수면을 옹호했다. 그들이 제시했던 것은 오로지 수면을 위해 지정된 시간, 즉 산업이 요구함과 동시에 산업으로 인해 불가능해진 시간이었다. 우리가 알다시피 여덟 시간 노동이라는 이상은 주로 노사 간의 이러한 밀고 당기기의 결과이다.

disconnect from phr. ~에서 분리하다
drop off phr. 잠들다   lean adj. 수확이 적은
harvest n. 수확   punctuate v. 중단시키다, 잠시 그치게 하다
consistently adv. 지속적으로   downtime n. 휴식 시간
commerce n. 상업   homogeneous adj. 동질의, 동종의
profession n. 직종   deprive v. 빼앗다
adequate adj. 충분한   advocate v. 옹호하다
standardize v. 표준화하다   reserved adj. 지정된, 남겨 둔
management and labor phr. 노사

43 2020 서울여대

정답 ②

해석 ① 수면에 대한 연구가 경제 발전에 어떻게 기여했는지
② 현대 산업이 인간의 시간 경험을 어떻게 바꾸었는지
③ 기술이 도시 지역에 사는 사람들의 밤 생활에 어떻게 영향을 미쳤는지
④ 노사 간 싸움이 어떻게 사회적 불안을 이끌었는지

해설 지문의 요지를 묻는 문제이다. 지문 처음에서 현재 우리가 '시간'이라고 생각하는 것은 대부분 산업혁명 시대의 발명이라고 하고, 공장들과 19세기 경제 체제는 자연적인 리듬에서 근로자들의 시간 감각을 분리하는 것에 의존했다고 했다. 따라서 이 지문의 요지를 '현대 산업이 인간의 시간 경험을 어떻게 바꾸었는지'라고 표현한 ②번이 정답이다.

어휘 contribute v. 기여하다 social unrest phr. 사회 불안

44 2020 서울여대

정답 ①

해석 ① 산업 노동자들은 획일적인 시계 시간을 받아들였다.
② 표준화되고 보편적인 시간은 학교에서 산업으로 퍼졌다.
③ 19세기 내내, 근로자들은 보통 여덟 시간을 잤다.
④ 산업혁명 시대 이전에, 근로자들의 취침 시간은 꽤 규칙적이었다.

해설 지문의 내용과 일치하는 것을 묻는 문제이다. 지문의 세 번째 문장에 있는 workers had to learn ~ organize their downtime accordingly의 내용을 통해 산업 노동자들이 획일적인 시계 시간을 받아들였다는 것을 알 수 있다. 따라서 ①번이 지문의 내용과 일치한다.

오답 분석 ② 여행, 학교, 및 상업을 위한 일정이 새롭게 동질화된 시간의 산업 패턴을 따랐다고 했으므로, 표준화되고 보편적인 시간이 학교에서 산업으로 퍼졌다는 것은 지문의 내용과 반대이다.
③ 고용주가 근로자의 너무 많은 시간을 요구하면서 충분한 수면을 빼앗자, 근로자들이 더욱 표준화된 수면을 옹호했다고는 했지만, 19세기 내내, 근로자들이 보통 여덟 시간을 잤는지는 알 수 없다.
④ 산업혁명 시대 이전에 근로자들의 취침 시간이 규칙적이었는지에 대해서는 언급되지 않았다.

어휘 universal adj. 보편적인 regular adj. 규칙적인

[45-46]

장소의 작명은 인식과 의사소통 모두에 필요한 수단일 뿐만 아니라 영토에 대한 권리를 주장하는 기초적인 수단이다. 작명의 과정은 공간의 한 점에 대한 몰가치적인 설명 그 이상인데, 그것은 표현의 한 수단이 되고, 장소에 대한 감각을 조성하며, 이것들을 과거의 선택된 측면과 연결한다. 아일랜드 북부 시골의 예를 이용하여, Reid는 지역 장소의 작명을 통해서 정체성과 기억 사이의 관계를 조사한다. 그녀는 갈라졌거나 분열된 사회에서 특정한 역사적인 서사와 연결되었을 때 작명하는 것이 포함과 배제의 더 넓은 과정 일부일 수 있다고 인정한다. 지역 이름이 다양한 문화적 영향력을 나타낼 수 있지만, 그것은 또한 공간과 장소에 대한 단일 민족의 이해를 위한 연합에서 다원주의의 개념을 거부하는 해석의 대상이 될 수도 있다. 분명히, 이것은 실제 풍경에 지명을 물리적으로 표시하는 것이 민족적 영토권을 더 넓게 주장하는 일부일 수 있는 아일랜드 북부에서 실제로 일어난다. 하지만 북아일랜드의 타운랜드 캠페인에 대한 그녀의 분석에서, Reid는 또한 지역 장소를 표시하는 것에 매우 기초적인 중요성이 남아있어서 그 과정과 관련된 관행들 자체가 이름 붙여진 곳을 보호하고 영속시키기 위해서 분열된 민족이 하나가 될 수 있도록 장려할 수도 있다는 것을 보여준다.

recognition n. 인식 communication n. 의사소통
fundamental adj. 기초적인 territory n. 영토, 영역
value-free adj. 몰가치적인 description n. 설명, 묘사
foster v. 조성하다 rural adj. 시골의, 지방의
acknowledge v. 인정하다 particular adj. 특정한
narrative n. 서사 indicative adj. 나타내는, 지시하는
diverse adj. 다양한 influence n. 영향력
subject n. 대상 interpretation n. 해석
pluralist adj. 다원주의의 consociation n. 연합
in favour of phr. ~를 위해서 singular adj. 단일의
ethnic adj. 민족의 landscape n. 풍경
territoriality n. 영토권 analysis n. 분석
practice n. 관행 perpetuate v. 영속시키다
locality n. 곳, 장소

45 2019 한양대

정답 ③

해석 ① 지명은 여러 가지 자명한 의미로 부여받았다.
② 장소의 작명은 집단의 기념행사의 고의적인 행위로서 이해될 수 없다.
③ 장소를 작명하는 과정은 과거가 어떻게 확인되고 구축되는지와 관련이 있다.
④ 아일랜드 북부의 이름 붙여진 장소는 민족적 단일성의 요구가 증가하면서 시들해졌다.
⑤ 장소에 대한 단일 민족의 이해를 고려하는 것은 다양한 문화적 영향력을 고려하는 것보다 더 중요하다.

해설 지문의 요지를 묻는 문제이다. 지문의 중반에서 Reid는 갈라졌거나 분열된 사회에서 특정한 역사적인 서사와 연결되었을 때 작명하는 것이 포함과 배제의 더 넓은 과정 일부일 수 있다고 인정한다고 하였다. 따라서 이 지문의 요지를 '장소를 작명하는 과정은 과거가 어떻게 확인되고 구축되는지와 관련이 있다'라고 표현한 ③번이 정답이다.

어휘 endow with phr. ~를 부여하다 self-evident adj. 자명한
deliberate adj. 고의적인 collective adj. 집단의, 집합의
commemoration n. 기념행사 associated adj. 관련된

identify v. 확인하다 construct v. 구축하다, 건설하다
wither v. 시들해지다 mount v. 증가하다
consideration n. 고려

46 2019 한양대

정답 ②

해설 지문의 빈칸을 채우는 문제이다. 빈칸이 포함된 문장은 and로 연결된 병치 구문이다. 따라서 빈칸에 들어올 내용의 형태는 and 뒤에 있는 fostering과 linking의 형태와 같아야 한다. 따라서 빈칸에는 현재분사의 형태가 나와야 한다는 것을 알 수 있다. 따라서 ②번이 정답이다.

[47-48]

미국에서 진행 중인 테러에 대한 세계 전쟁에서 점점 더 많은 문학이 계속해서 나오면서, 베트남 전쟁의 문화유산이 아직 미국 군인 사회 내에서 약해지지 않았다는 것이 분명해지고 있다. 오히려, 테러에 대한 세계 전쟁을 하고 있는 군인들은 베트남 전쟁이 자신들이 하는 전쟁의 의미를 분명히 밝히기 위한 노력으로 자신들을 이끌어줄 것이라는 희망을 가지고 베트남 문화에 기대를 걸어온 것처럼 최근 이라크와 아프가니스탄에서의 전쟁과 베트남 전쟁 간의 유사점은 베트남이 지속적으로 관련되어 있다는 것을 확실하게 했다. 철수 전략과 선전포고의 원인으로서 대량 파괴 무기의 합법성에 관한 질문들로 괴로웠던, 테러에 대한 세계 전쟁을 하는 많은 군인들은 이라크와 아프가니스탄에서의 끝이 정해지지 않은 분쟁과 베트남에서의 그들의 아버지의 전쟁 간의 자연스러운 연관성을 보았다. 많은 같은 군인들이 1980년대 중후반에 개봉된 베트남을 주제로 하는 많은 영화를 통해 전투를 보면서 성장했기 때문에, 베트남 전쟁의 문화는 21세기까지 단순히 보존되기만 한 것이 아니었다. 베트남 전쟁은 일부에게, 군인들이 전투에 대한 그들의 생각을 표현할 수 있는 미리 정해져 있는 문화적 청사진이 되었다.

emerge v. 나오다, 나타나다 ongoing adj. 진행 중인
Global War phr. 세계 전쟁 terror n. 테러 (행위·협박)
apparent adj. 분명한 cultural legacy phr. 문화유산
wane v. 약해지다, 줄어들다, 시들해지다 circle n. 사회, 집단
if anything phr. 오히려, 어느 편인가 하면
parallel n. 유사점, 비교, 대비 relevance n. 유사점
in the hope that phr. 희망을 가지고
define v. 분명히 밝히다 plague v. 괴롭히다, 귀찮게 하다
regarding prep. ~에 관하여 exit strategy phr. 철수 전략
legitimacy n. 합법성, 적법성
Weapons of Mass Destruction phr. 대량 파괴 무기
natural adj. 자연스러운 connection n. 연관성, 관련성
open-ended adj. 끝이 정해지지 않은 combat n. 전투
themed adj. ~ 주제의, ~을 특정 주제로 다룬
merely adv. 단순히, 단지 preserve v. 보존하다
frame v. 표현하다, 만들다

47 2019 단국대

정답 ①

해석 ① 미리 정해져 있는 문화적 청사진
② 전후 스트레스 설명서
③ 독특한 향수를 불러일으키는 요소
④ 정확한 군대 암호 첩

해설 지문의 빈칸을 채우는 문제이다. 지문의 후반에서 많은 군인들이 베트남을 주제로 하는 많은 영화를 통해 전투를 보면서 성장했기 때문에, 베트남 전쟁의 문화는 21세기까지 단순히 보존되기만 한 것이 아니었다고 했으므로, 빈칸에는 베트남 전쟁은 군인들이 전투에 대한 그들의 예상을 표현하기 위해 생각해보는 미리 정해져 있는 문화적 청사진이 되었다는 내용이 나와야 적절하다는 것을 알 수 있다. 따라서 '미리 정해져 있는 문화적 청사진'이라고 한 ①번이 정답이다.

어휘 default adj. 내정 값의 blueprint n. 청사진, 계획
after-war adj. 전후의 manual n. 설명서, 안내서
unique adj. 독특한, 특이한
nostalgic adj. 향수를 불러일으키는
momentum n. 요소, 탄력 rigid adj. 정확한, 엄격한
code-book n. 암호 첩

48 2019 단국대

정답 ④

해석 ① 근대의 군인들은 그들이 싸우는 전쟁의 원인을 별로 의심하지 않는다.
② 미국인들은 베트남에서의 비극적인 경험에 대한 기억을 잊으려고 노력한다.
③ 베트남 전쟁 테마의 문화 상품의 양은 줄어드는 경향이 있다.
④ 많은 젊은 군인들은 베트남 전쟁에 관한 영화에 노출되어 왔다.

해설 지문의 내용과 일치하는 것을 묻는 문제이다. 네 번째 문장에서 많은 같은 군인들이 1980년대 중후반에 개봉된 베트남을 주제로 하는 많은 영화를 통해 전투를 보면서 성장했다는 내용을 통해 많은 젊은 군인들이 베트남 전쟁에 관한 영화에 노출되어왔다는 것을 알 수 있다. 따라서 ④번이 지문의 내용과 일치한다.

오답 분석
① 두 번째 문장에서 군인들은 베트남 전쟁이 자신들이 하는 전쟁의 의미를 분명히 밝히기 위한 노력으로 자신들을 이끌어줄 것이라는 희망을 가지고 베트남 문화에 기대를 걸어왔다고 했으므로, 근대의 군인들이 그들이 싸우는 전쟁의 원인을 별로 의심하지 않는다는 것은 지문의 내용과 다르다.
② 첫 번째 문장에서 미국의 진행 중인 테러에 대한 세계 전쟁에서 점점 더 많은 문학이 계속해서 나오면서, 베트남 전쟁의 문화유산이 아직 미국 군인 사회 내에서 약해지지 않았다는 것이 분명해지고 있다고는 했지만, 미국인들이

베트남에서의 비극적인 경험에 대한 기억을 잊으려고 노력하는지는 알 수 없다.
③ 첫 번째 문장에서 미국의 진행 중인 테러에 대한 세계 전쟁에서 점점 더 많은 문학이 계속해서 나오면서, 베트남 전쟁의 문화유산이 아직 미국 군인 사회 내에서 약해지지 않았다는 것이 분명해지고 있다고 했으므로, 베트남 전쟁 테마의 문화 상품의 양이 줄어드는 경향이 있다는 것은 지문의 내용과 다르다.

어휘 modern adj. 근대의   be confident of phr. 의심하지 않다
tragic adj. 비극적인   volume n. 양
decline v. 줄어들다, 감소하다   motion picture phr. 영화

[49-51]

귀여운 것을 좋아하는 최근의 유행은 부분적으로 위협적인 세계에서 벗어나 아이 같은 특성이 보호하는 감정을 불러일으키고, 만족과 위안을 부여하는 순수의 정원으로 가고자 하는 욕구에 의해 자극된다. "귀여움의 단서"는 무력하고, 매력적이고, 순종적인 행동과 큰 머리, 휘둥그래진 눈, 어설픈 움직임 같은 해부학적인 특징들이 포함된다. 아마도 이 귀여움의 단서들에 대한 우리의 반응은 우리가 자식들에게 아이들이 자라는데 필요한 광범위한 보살핌과 양육을 제공하도록 동기 부여하기 위해 발전했을 것이다. 하지만 만약 귀여움이 단지 매력적이고, 순진하고, 위협적이지 않은 것에 불과하거나, 우리가 귀여움에 끌리는 것이 단순히 보호 본능에 의해 자극되는 것뿐이라면, 이것은 보편적인 현상이 아니었을 것이다. 앞의 특징들은 귀여움의 전체 범주에서 우리가 아마 "사랑스러운 것"이라고 부르는 한쪽의 특징만을 이야기하고 있다. 우리가 귀여움의 범주의 또 다른 쪽의 '이상한 것'으로 옮겨가기 시작하면, 사랑스러웠던 귀여움의 단서들은 왜곡되어 어딘지 어둡고, 쉽게 가늠할 수 없으며, 손상된 것으로 변하게 되는데, 여기에는 마치 강력해 보이게, 스테인리스강으로 만들어졌지만, 무력하고, 공허하며, 얼굴이 없는 풍선으로 만든 개 같은 것들이 있다. 귀여움의 범주 사이에 만연한 한정 짓기 어려운 특성과, 아이와 어른 사이같이, 이전에는 구분 지어졌던 영역 간의 경계 침식이 많은 귀여운 대상의 모호해진 성별에 반영되어 있다. 또한 그것은 헬로키티에서도 보이듯이, 인간과 인간이 아닌 것들이 빈번하게 혼합되어 나타나는 귀여운 것들의 형태에도 반영되어 있다.

craze n. 유행   urge n. 욕구
escape from phr. ~로부터 탈출하다
threatening adj. 위협적인   innocence n. 순수
protective adj. 보호하는   bestow v. 주다
contentment n. 만족   solace n. 위안
yielding adj. 순종적인   anatomical adj. 해부학적인
saucer-like eye phr. 휘둥그래진 눈   clumsy adj. 어설픈
merely adv. 단지   instinct n. 본능   spectrum n. 범주
uncanny adj. 이상한   indeterminate adj. 가늠할 수 없는
hollow adj. 공허한   blurred adj. 모호한
blending n. 혼합

49 [2020 한국외대]

정답 ①

해석 ① 귀여움을 규정하고 설명하기 위해
② 귀엽고 매력적인 대상을 홍보하기 위해
③ 귀여운 물건을 생산하는 것의 요점을 설명하기 위해
④ 선호하는 귀여움의 스타일에 관해 논하기 위해

해설 지문의 요지를 묻는 문제이다. 지문 전체적으로 최근의 귀여운 것들에 대한 유행의 이유와 귀여움의 범주에 어떤 것이 포함되는지를 설명하고 있다. 따라서 해당 지문의 요지를 '귀여움을 규정하고 설명하기 위해'라고 표현한 ①번이 정답이다.

어휘 characterize v. 규정하다   promote v. 홍보하다
outline v. ~의 요점을 말하다

50 [2020 한국외대]

정답 ②

해석 ① 성별의 모호함은 귀여움의 애매함의 한 예시이다.
② 쉽게 가늠할 수 없고 손상된 특징은 사랑스러운 대상 사이에서 만연하다.
③ 탈출하고자 하는 욕구는 부분적으로 현재의 귀여움을 추구하는 트렌드를 자극하고 있다.
④ "이상한" 대상에 대한 끌림은 진화 이상의 무언가 때문이다.

해설 지문의 내용과 일치하지 않는 것을 묻는 문제이다. 지문의 여섯 번째 문장에서 귀여움의 범주의 또 다른 쪽의 '이상한 것'으로 옮겨가기 시작하면, 귀여움의 특징이 어딘지 어둡고, 쉽게 가늠할 수 없으며, 손상된 것으로 왜곡되어 변하게 된다고 했으므로, 쉽게 가늠할 수 없고 손상된 특징은 사랑스러운 대상 사이에서 만연하다는 것은 지문의 내용과 다르다. 따라서 ②번이 정답이다.

오답 분석
① 지문의 일곱 번째 문장에서, 귀여움의 범주 사이에 만연한 한정 짓기 어려운 특성과, 아이와 어른 사이같이, 이전에는 구분 지어졌던 영역 간의 경계의 침식이 많은 귀여운 대상의 모호해진 성별에 반영되어 있다고 했으므로 성별의 모호함이 귀여움의 애매함의 한 예시라는 것은 지문의 내용과 일치한다.
③ 지문의 첫 번째 문장에서, 귀여운 것에 대한 유행이 부분적으로 위협적인 세계에서 탈출하고자 하는 욕구에 의해 자극받는다고 했으므로, 탈출하고자 하는 욕구가 현재의 귀여움을 추구하는 트렌드를 자극하고 있다는 것은 지문의 내용과 일치한다.
④ 지문의 네 번째 문장에서, 우리가 귀여움에 대해 갖는 반응이 보호 본능에 의한 것일 뿐이라면, 귀여움을 추구하는 유행은 보편적인 현상이 아니었을 것이라고 했고, 다섯 번째 문장에서, 보호 본능에 의해 자극되는 반응은 귀여움의 범주 중 사랑스러운 대상에만 국한되어 있다는 것을 알 수 있으므로, 이상한 대상에 대한 끌림은 진화 이상의 무언가 때문이라는 것은 지문의 내용과 일치한다.

어휘 vagueness n. 애매함 trend n. 트렌드

51 2020 한국외대
정답 ①

해석
① 우아한 동작
② 크고 동그란 눈
③ 무력한 외모
④ 순종

해설 귀여움의 단서에 포함되지 않는 것이 무엇인지 묻는 문제이다. 지문의 두 번째 문장에서, 귀여움의 단서에는 무력하고, 매력적이고, 순종적인 행동과 큰 머리, 휘둥그레진 눈, 어설픈 움직임 같은 해부학적인 특징들이 포함된다고 했으므로, 우아한 동작은 귀여움의 단서에 포함되지 않는다는 것을 알 수 있다. 따라서 ①번이 정답이다.

[52-54]

현재 형태의 세계화가 확대되면서, 그것에 따라서 일어나는 불평등도 확대된다. 커지는 불평등은 외국인 혐오적이고 고립주의자적인 경향을 촉진하는 인종 편견 확대의 결과를 낳을 수 있다. 예를 들어, 영국과 프랑스의 제국주의 시대에, 인종 편견은 문화 그 자체 내부에 스며들어 있었다. 하지만, 세계 일부 지역에서 보이는 "세계화의 외국인 혐오적 문화"가 확대되면서, 인종 편견의 기미는 여전히 오늘날의 세계화 시대에도 발견된다.
확장되는 세계화와 함께, 특히 북아메리카에서 더 많은 숙련된 노동자들에 대한 요구는 외국인 노동자를 유치하려는 많은 노력으로 이어졌지만, 이는 기술에 근거하여 추려진 사람들이다. 반면에, 이러한 시민들이 선출된 소수의 사람의 일부, 즉 제삼 세계의 비용으로 교육받은 고도로 숙련된 컴퓨터 전문가, 의사와 간호사가 아니라면 더 부유한 국가로 이민하는 것은 더 어렵다. 세계의 이주 관리 전략은 제삼 세계와 구소련 세력권의 가장 숙련되고 교육받은 노동 인구를 선발해 감으로써, 이곳의 경제 활력소를 약화시킨다. 세계화의 관점에서는, 유전자 공급원이 아닌 기술 공급원이 핵심이다.

accompany v. 따라서 일어나다 racial bias phr. 인종 편견
advance v. 촉진하다 xenophobic adj. 외국인 혐오증의
isolationist adj. 고립주의자적인 ingrain v. 스며들게 하다
element n. 기미 filter v. 거르다 immigrate v. 이민하다
migration n. 이주 lifeblood n. 활력소
cream off phr. 추려 가다, 뽑아 가다 perspective n. 관점

52 2019 덕성여대
정답 ③

해석
① 세계화의 장단점
② 세계화가 경제적 불평등과 사회적 부당함과 관련된 문제들을 해결하는 데 어떻게 도움이 되는지
③ 세계화의 결과로 나타난 새로운 유형의 불평등
④ 세계화의 결과로 나타난 부유한 나라들의 이민 정책 강화

해설 지문의 주제를 묻는 문제이다. 지문 처음에서 현재 형태의 세계화가 확대되면서, 그것에 따라서 일어나는 불평등도 확대된다고 하고, 이는 외국인 혐오적이고 고립주의자적인 경향을 촉진하는 인종 편견 확대의 결과를 낳을 수 있다고 했다. 따라서 이 지문의 주제를 '세계화의 결과로 나타난 새로운 유형의 불평등'이라고 표현한 ③번이 정답이다.

어휘 injustice n. 부당함 tighten v. 강화하다

53 2019 덕성여대
정답 ②

해석
① 세계화로 인한 외국 문화의 고립
② 세계화된 사회 내부의 외국 사람들에 대한 지나친 두려움
③ 세계화에 저항하는 문화
④ 세계화를 통해 수입된 문화

해설 밑줄 친 부분의 의미를 추론하는 문제이다. 밑줄 친 xenophobic culture of globalization은 '세계화의 외국인 혐오적 문화'라는 의미이다. 주변의 내용을 살펴보면 이것이 오늘날의 세계화 시대에도 여전히 발견되는 인종 편견의 기미와 관련된 것임을 알 수 있다. 따라서, 이를 '세계화된 사회 내부의 외국 사람들에 대한 지나친 두려움'이라고 표현한 ②번이 정답이다.

어휘 isolation n. 고립 excessive adj. 지나친
resist v. 저항하다 import v. 수입하다

54 2019 덕성여대
정답 ②

해석
① 어느 분야에서든 고도로 훈련받은 러시아 사람
② 어느 나라 출신이든 고도로 훈련받은 컴퓨터 전문가
③ 쿠바 출신의 스타 야구 선수
④ 냉엄한 권위주의적 정권에서 벗어나려고 노력하는 사람

해설 오늘날 미국에 입국하도록 허용될 가능성이 가장 높은 사람이 누구일지 파악하는 문제이다. 두 번째 문단에서 제삼 세계의 비용으로 교육받은 고도로 숙련된 컴퓨터 전문가, 의사와 간호사가 아니라면 더 부유한 국가로 이민하는 것은 더 어렵다고 했으므로, 오늘날 미국에 입국하도록 허용될 가능성이 가장 높은 사람은 '어느 나라 출신이든 고도로 훈련받은 컴퓨터 전문가'이다. 따라서 정답은 ②번이다.

어휘 escape v. 벗어나다 harsh adj. 냉엄한, 가혹한
authoritarian adj. 권위주의적인

[55-57]

의복은 인체를 보호하거나 장식하기 위해 고안된 다양한 피복을 나타내는 전반적인 용어이다. 의복은 동물의 가죽이나 털, 심지어는 "수피(樹皮)"라고 알려진 종류의 종이로 만들어진

직물이나 인공 섬유로 만들어질 수 있다. 구체적으로 말하면, 의복은 널리 퍼진 방식이나 의복의 관례적인 스타일을 의미하는 패션이나 유행과는 구별된다. 현재의 개념으로, 의류는 내구성과 견고함을 내포하고 있으며, 패션은 참신함과 일시성을 내포하고 있다. 예를 들어, 한 어머니가 아이들을 위해서 겨울 옷을 사는데, 이 맥락에서는 그녀가 스타일을 부차적으로 고려할 사항으로 여길 것이 분명하다. 그녀의 주된 관심은 패션보다는 오히려 천의 따뜻함, 착용감, 관리의 용이성, 그리고 아마 합리적인 가격이 제일 중심이 될 것이며, 이러한 것 모두 겨울 옷을 구입하는 데에 (A)관련된 속성들인 것이다.

반면에, 패션은 사건, 환경, 그리고 그 (B)시대의 관습을 반영한다. 그것은 법, 예술, 문화, 그리고 개성에 영향을 받는다. 예를 들어, 여성들이 자신의 남편이 구입할 수 있는 옷보다 더 비싼 옷을 입는 것을 제한했던 뉴잉글랜드 초기 법에서 볼 수 있듯이 법과 규제는 패션에 영향을 끼쳤다. 1914년부터 1918년까지의 의상에 여성적인 개조를 불러일으킨 쇼의 '피그말리온'을 바탕으로 한 엄청나게 성공한 뮤지컬 코미디인 "마이 페어 레이디"에서 (C)예시로 거론되듯이 예술에서의 사건들은 패션에 영향을 끼쳤다. 문화는 강력하게 패션을 조절한다. 르네상스 시대의 화려함은 대상인들의 호화로움을 비단, 새틴, 벨벳, 그리고 보석으로 가져왔다. 프랑스 루이 14세의 화려하고 사치스러운 왕궁에서는 머리 장식이 높이 솟았고 치마는 부풀려졌다. 귀족과 농부, 그리고 상인들을 (D)동화시키는 사치를 규제하는 법이 폐지되고 사회의 모든 계급이 거의 비슷한 옷을 입을 수 있게 된 시절부터 개성은 패션에 큰 영향을 끼쳤다.

---

general adj. 전반적인 **covering** n. 피복
adorn v. 장식하다 **fiber** n. 섬유
distinguished adj. 구별되는 **signify** v. 의미하다
prevailing adj. 널리 퍼진 **customary** adj. 관례적인
connote v. 내포하다, 함의하다 **durable** adj. 내구성이 있는
transitory adj. 일시적인
secondary adj. 부수적인, 부차적인 **primary** adj. 주된
upkeep n. 관리 **reasonable** adj. 합리적인
attribute n. 속성 **era** n. 시대 **personality** n. 개성, 성격
regulation n. 규제 **restrict** v. 제한하다
exemplify v. 예시로 들다 **tremendously** adv. 엄청나게
feminine adj. 여성인 **adaptation** n. 개조, 각색
condition v. 조절하다 **splendor** n. 화려함
magnificence n. 호화로움 **merchant prince** phr. 대상인
fabulous adj. 화려한 **extravagant** adj. 사치스러운
court n. 왕궁 **soar** v. 높이 치솟다
sumptuary adj. 사치를 규제하는 **assimilate** v. 동화시키다
eliminate v. 폐지하다, 없애다

55 [2020 단국대]

정답 ①

해석 ① 견고한 ― 참신한
② 영구적인 ― 혁명적인
③ 상상의 ― 합리적인
④ 강화된 ― 자발적인

해설 지문의 빈칸을 채우는 문제이다. 첫 번째 문단에서 거론된 예시에서, 스타일은 부차적인 고려사항이며 합리적인 가격과 따뜻함, 관리의 용이성이 주된 관심이라고 했으므로, 첫 번째 빈칸에는 실용성과 관련된 의미의 단어가 와야 한다는 것을 알 수 있다. 두 번째 문단에서 거론된 예시에서, 프랑스의 사치스러운 왕궁에서 머리 장식이 높이 솟았고 치마가 부풀려졌다고 했으므로, 두 번째 빈칸에는 이전에 시도되지 않았던 것과 관련된 의미의 단어가 와야 한다는 것을 알 수 있다. 따라서 '견고한 ― 참신한'이라고 한 ①번이 정답이다.

어휘 **substantial** adj. 견고한 **novel** adj. 참신한
permanent adj. 영구적인 **revolutionary** adj. 혁명적인
imaginary adj. 상상의 **reasonable** adj. 합리적인
enforced adj. 강화된 **voluntary** adj. 자발적인

56 [2020 단국대]

정답 ④

해설 밑줄 친 단어들 중에서 문맥상 적절하지 않은 어휘를 고르는 문제이다. 법을 철폐하여 사회의 모든 계급이 거의 비슷한 옷을 입을 수 있게 되었다는 내용이므로 ④번에는 '동화시키다'를 의미하는 assimilating이 아니라 '구별하다'를 의미하는 discriminating이 들어가는 것이 자연스럽다. 따라서 ④번이 정답이다.

57 [2020 단국대]

정답 ④

해석 ① 무엇을 입어야 하는지를 제한하는 법이 있었다.
② 어머니들은 보통 아이들을 위해 실용적인 옷을 고른다.
③ 의복은 천연 재료와 인공 재료로 만들어질 수 있다.
④ 르네상스 시대는 인체와 간소한 의복을 강조했다.

해설 지문의 내용과 일치하지 않는 것을 묻는 문제이다. ④번의 키워드인 The Renaissance(르네상스 시대)와 관련된 지문의 the Renaissance(르네상스 시대) 주변에서 사치스러운 왕궁에서는 머리 장식이 높이 솟았고 치마는 부풀려졌다고 했으므로, 르네상스 시대는 인체와 간소한 의복을 강조했다는 것은 지문의 내용과 다르다. 따라서 ④번이 지문의 내용과 일치하지 않는다.

오답 분석
① when sumptuary laws assimilating nobles, farmers, and tradesmen were eliminated를 통해 '무엇을 입어야 하는지를 제한하는 법이 있었다'는 것을 알 수 있다.
② Her primary concern centers, rather than on fashion, on such matters as warmth of fabric, ~ all of which are attributes relevant to the purchase of winter clothing.을 통해 '어머니들은 보통 아이들을 위해 실용적인 옷을 고른다'는 것을 알 수 있다.

③ It may be made of woven materials or man-made fiber of animal skin or fur or even a type of paper known as "bark-cloth."를 통해 '의복은 천연 재료와 인공 재료로 만들어질 수 있다'는 것을 알 수 있다.

어휘 **practical** adj. 실용적인 **artificial** adj. 인공의
emphasize v. 강조하다

[58-60]

60년 혹은 그 이상의 기간 동안, 미국의 정치 역사는 문화적 전쟁에 의해 이끌려왔다. 문화 전쟁 1.0은 1950년대에 급격히 자유화되고 세속화되는 사회에서 신앙심 깊은 열렬한 지지자들이 기독교의 정신과 영혼을 차지하기 위한 것으로서 시작됐다. 이 첫 번째 전쟁은 대개 종교적 신앙과 가치의 쟁점에 관한 싸움이었는데, 창조설이 생물학적 진화에 관한 이론의 실행 가능한 대안인지 혹은 공적 영역에서 제도화하고 있는 기독교적 가치에 한계가 놓여야 하는지에 대한 것들이었다. 문화 전쟁 2.0은 초자연적 현상, 형이상학, 심지어 종교와 무관한 것이 되어가고 있었다. 문화 전쟁 2.0은 다른 것들 사이에서, 돌고 있었는데, 참여의 새로운 규칙과 같은 것들이었다. 그것들은 어떻게 우리가 우리의 불일치를 다룰 것인가에 연결되어 있었다. 문화 전쟁 1.0에서, 만약 진화론의 생물학자들은 지질학적인 연대 측정 기법을 기반으로 하여 지구의 나이에 대한 대중 강연을 한다면, 창조론자들은 그 강연에 대해 부응하면서, 이런 연대 측정 기법은 믿을 수 없다고 주장하거나, 토론에서 진화론자들에게 이의를 제기하고, 또 질의응답 시간에 날카로운 문제들을 질문했을 것이다. 하지만 문화 전쟁 2.0에서는, 화자와의 불일치는 종종 연설을 단상에서 없애기 위한 시도와 마주치게 되었는데, 연설을 하기 전에 초청장을 취소시키는 소란스러운 캠페인 같은 것들이 여기에 포함되었다. 이 시도가 만약 성공적이지 않다면, 비판적인 사람들은 아마 소리 지르거나 고함을 지르는 것, 소란을 만드는 행위에 참여하는 것, 스피커의 선을 끊어내는 것과 같은 행동들에 의존했을지도 모른다. 이 행동의 목적은 화자가 더 나은 주장을 마주치지 못하게 하거나, 대안적인 관점을 주장하지 못하게 하는 것이 아니라, 단순히 화자가 그녀의 관점을 더 이상 발표하지 못하도록 막는 것에 있었다.

religious adj. 독실한 **enthusiast** n. 열렬한 지지자
liberalize v. ~을 자유주의화하다 **secularize** v. 세속화하다
issue n. 쟁점 **creationism** n. 창조론
viable adj. 실행 가능한 **alternative** n. 대안
institutionalize v. 제도화하다
supernatural n. 초자연적인 현상
metaphysics n. 형이상학 **irrelevant** adj. 무관한
disagreement n. 불일치 **geological** adj. 지질학적인
dating technique phr. 연대 측정법
unreliable adj. 믿을 수 없는 **rowdy** adj. 소란스러운
resort v. 의존하다 **disrupt** v. 방해하다
rip v. 찢다 **argument** n. 주장 **air** v. 발표하다

58 [2020 한국외대]

정답 ②

해석 ① 문화 전쟁에서의 창조론
② 미국의 변화 중인 문화 전쟁
③ 계몽과 문화적 혁명
④ 현대 사회에서의 보수주의 vs 진보주의

해설 지문의 제목을 묻는 문제이다. 지문 전체적으로 미국의 첫 번째 문화 전쟁과 두 번째 문화 전쟁의 차이를 설명하고 있으므로, 이 지문의 주제를 '미국의 변화 중인 문화 전쟁'이라고 표현한 ②번이 정답이다.

어휘 **enlightenment** n. 계몽 **conservatism** n. 보수주의
liberalism n. 진보주의

59 [2020 한국외대]

정답 ③

해석 ① 단결과 다양성 ② 기술과 진화
③ 종교적 신앙과 가치 ④ 관습과 혁신

해설 지문의 빈칸을 채우는 문제이다. 지문의 빈칸이 포함된 문장의 이전 문장에서 문화 전쟁 1.0은 신앙심 깊은 열렬한 지지자들이 기독교의 정신과 영혼을 차지하기 위한 것으로서 시작됐다고 했으므로, 빈칸에는 종교와 관련된 내용이 나와야 적절하다는 것을 알 수 있다. 따라서 '종교적 신앙과 가치'라고 한 ③번이 정답이다.

어휘 **unity** n. 단결

60 [2020 한국외대]

정답 ①

해석 ① 더 폭력적이고 편협한
② 더 정교하고 교활한
③ 덜 친근하지만 더 관대한
④ 덜 치열하지만 더 수용적인

해설 문화 전쟁 1.0과 문화 전쟁 2.0 간의 차이점을 파악하는 문제이다. 지문 전체적으로, 문화 전쟁 1.0에서는 의견의 불일치를 인정하지 못하고 서로를 공격하는 형태의 전쟁이었음을 알 수 있고, 문화 전쟁 2.0은 불일치를 인정하지 않는 것이 아니라 단순히 불일치를 피하고자 그 사람의 관점이나 의견이 발표되기 이전에 강연 등을 취소하는 형태의 전쟁이었음을 알 수 있다. 따라서 문화 전쟁 1.0이 문화 전쟁 2.0에 비해 '더 폭력적이고 편협한' 전쟁이었다고 표현한 ①번이 정답이다.

어휘 **sophisticated** adj. 정교한 **tricky** adj. 교활한
tolerant adj. 관대한 **fierce** adj. 사나운
accommodating adj. 수용적인

[61-63]

학교 시스템은 부르디외에 의해 학문적인 적성과 문화적 전통 간의 숨은 관련성을 통해 정통 문화를 재생산하는 제도로 간주된다. 부르디외는 동등한 기회와 실력주의의 이념에도 불구하고, 지배계급에 의해 정통 문화를 그대로 재생산하고 합법적으로 조작할 수 있는 대리인을 만드는 것 외의 다른 일을 하도록 요구되는 교육 시스템은 거의 없었다고 믿는다.

부르디외는 그것이 학교에서 구현되는 지배 집단의 문화라고 주장해 왔다. 교육적 차이들은 따라서 종종 계급에 기반을 둔 차이가 아닌 개인의 재능에서 비롯된다고 잘못 인식되는데, 학문적 기준에 의해 측정된 능력이 종종 타고난 "재능"이 아니라 "계급 문화적 습관과 교육 시스템의 요구 혹은 교육 시스템 안에서 성공을 정의하는 기준 사이의 더 크거나 작은 관련성"에서 기인한다는 사실을 무시한다.

문화 자본의 개념은 1960년대 초에 중산층 문화에 대한 친숙함을 설명하기 위해 부르디외에 의해 제안되었는데, 중산층 문화의 불평등한 분배는 개인의 재능과 학문적 실력주의의 구실 하에 사회 계급을 유지하는 데 도움을 준다. 이 개념은 습득한 지식(교육적 혹은 그 밖의 것), 문화적 관례, 말하는 방식 등의 것들을 포함하는데, 이는 개인에게 일종의 "아비투스"로 구현되고 문화적 상품들에도 구체화된다.

---

institution n. 제도 reproduction n. 재생산
legitimate adj. 정통의, 합법적인 linkage n. 관련성, 연결
scholastic adj. 학문적인 aptitude n. 적성, 소질
heritage n. 전통 ideology n. 이념 opportunity n. 기회
meritocracy n. 실력주의 dominant adj. 지배적인, 우세한
reproduce v. 재생산하다 manipulate v. 조작하다
legitimately adv. 합법적으로 embody v. 구현하다
misrecognize v. 잘못 인식하다 giftedness n. 재능
ignore v. 무시하다 criteria n. 기준
stem from phr. 기인하다 affinity n. 관련성
define v. 정의하다 notion n. 개념 capital n. 자본
familiarity n. 친숙함 bourgeois adj. 중산층의
unequal adj. 불평등한 distribution n. 분배
conserve v. 유지하다, 보존하다 hierarchy n. 계급, 계층
under the cloak phr. 구실 아래에 academic adj. 학업의
code n. 관례 habitus n. 아비투스(친숙한 사회 집단의 습속·습성 따위를 뜻하는 말로, 프랑스 사회학자 부르디외가 규정한 용어)
objectify v. 구체화하다

---

61 [2020 홍익대]

정답 ②

해석
① 노동자 계급의 학생들은 고등 교육의 중산층 아비투스에서 외부인처럼 느낄 수 있다.
② 개인들은 그들의 사회적 계층을 바탕으로 한 타고난 지능을 보유하는 경향이 있다.
③ 교육 제도들은 지배 계급의 문화 자본의 수익성을 보장한다.
④ 지배 문화는, 스스로를 보편적인 것으로 인식하게 함으로써, 지배 집단의 이익을 정당화한다.

해설 지문의 내용과 일치하지 않는 것을 묻는 문제이다. ②번의 키워드인 innate intelligence(타고난 지능)와 관련된 지문의 두 번째 문단에서 학문적 기준에 의해 측정된 능력이 종종 타고난 "재능"이 아니라 "계급 문화적 습관과 교육 시스템의 요구 혹은 교육 시스템 안에서 성공을 정의하는 기준 사이의 더 크거나 작은 관련성"에서 기인한다는 사실을 무시한다고 했으며 지문에서 말하는 타고난 재능은 사회적 계급에서 기인되지 않은 개인의 선천적 재능을 가리킨다. 따라서 ②번이 지문의 내용과 일치하지 않는다.

오답분석
① 세 번째 문단 The notion of cultural capital was proposed by Bourdieu in the early 1960s ~ under the cloak of individual talent and academic meritocracy를 통해 '노동자 계급의 학생들은 고등 교육의 중산층 아비투스에서 외부인처럼 느낄 수 있다'는 것을 알 수 있다.
③ 세 번째 문단 The notion of cultural capital was proposed by Bourdieu in the early 1960s ~ under the cloak of individual talent and academic meritocracy와 which are embodied as a kind of "habitus" in the individual and are also objectified in cultural goods를 통해 '교육기관은 지배 계급의 문화 자본의 수익성을 보장한다'는 것을 알 수 있다.
④ 세 번째 문단 the unequal distribution of which helps to conserve social hierarchy under the cloak of individual talent and academic meritocracy를 통해 '지배적인 문화는, 스스로를 보편적인 것으로 인식하게 함으로써, 지배 집단의 이익을 정당화한다'는 것을 알 수 있다.

어휘 working-class adj. 노동자 계급의 outsider n. 외부인
middle-class adj. 중산층의 possess v. 보유하다
innate adj. 타고난 intelligence n. 지능
profitability n. 수익성 universal adj. 보편적인
legitimize v. 정당화하다

62 [2020 홍익대]

정답 ②

해석
① 부르디외에 따르면, 모든 문화는 동등하게 평가되고 동등하게 정당하다.
② 부르디외에 따르면, 학교 교육은 기존의 계급 계층화를 촉진하는 특정한 확립된 인지 방법을 만들어 낸다.
③ 부르디외에 따르면, 개인의 효력은 삶의 모든 단계에 걸쳐 통달 된 경험에 의해 가장 강하게 영향을 받는다.
④ 부르디외에 따르면, 문화적 재생산은 사회 경제적 양극화가 일어나는 사소한 메커니즘이다.

해설 지문을 통해 추론할 수 있는 것을 고르는 문제이다. 지문의 첫 번째 단락에서 부르디외는 동등한 기회와 실력주의의 이념에도 불구하고, 지배계급에 의해 정통 문화를 그대로 재생산하고 합법적으로 조작할 수 있는 대리인을 만드는 것 외의 다른

일을 하도록 요구되는 교육 시스템은 거의 없었다고 믿는다고 했으므로, 부르디외에 따르면, 학교 교육은 기존의 계급 계층화를 촉진하는 특정한 확립된 인지 방법을 만들어 낸다는 것을 추론할 수 있다. 따라서 정답은 ②번이다.

오답분석
① 부르디외에 의해 모든 문화는 동등하게 평가되고 동등하게 정당한지에 대해서는 언급되지 않았다.
③ 문화 자본이 습득한 지식(교육적 혹은 그 밖의 것), 문화적 관례, 말하는 방식 등의 것들을 포함하는데, 이는 개인에게 일종의 "아비투스"로 구현되고 문화적 상품들에도 구체화된다고는 했지만, 개인의 효력이 삶의 모든 단계에 걸쳐 통달된 경험에 의해 가장 강하게 영향을 받는지는 알 수 없다.
④ 문화 자본의 개념은 1960년대 초에 중산층 문화에 대한 친숙함을 설명하기 위해 부르디외에 의해 제안되었으며, 중산층 문화의 불평등한 분배는 개인의 재능과 학문적 실력주의의 구실 하에 사회 계급을 유지하는 데 도움을 준다고는 했지만, 이것이 사회 경제적 양극화가 일어나는 사소한 메커니즘인지는 추론할 수 없다.

어휘
entrenched adj. 확립된 foster v. 촉진하다
existing adj. 기존의 stratification n. 계층화
efficacy n. 효력, 효능 mastery n. 통달
trivial adj. 사소한 socioeconomic adj. 사회경제의
polarization n. 양극화

63 2020 홍익대

정답 ④

해석
① 학교 교육에서 개인의 재능의 중요성
② 학교 교육에서의 학생들의 성취의 중요성
③ 학교 교육에서 지배적인 문화의 사회적 책임
④ 학교 교육에서의 불평등의 재생산

해설 지문의 제목을 묻는 문제이다. 지문 첫 번째 단락에서 학교 시스템은 부르디외에 의해 학문적인 적성과 문화적 전통 간의 숨은 관련성을 통해 정통 문화를 재생산하는 제도로 간주되며, 동등한 기회와 실력주의의 이념에도 불구하고, 지배계급에 의해 정통 문화를 그대로 재생산하고 합법적으로 조작할 수 있는 대리인을 만드는 것 외의 다른 일을 하도록 요구되는 교육 시스템은 거의 없었다고 했고, 지문의 세 번째 단락에서 중산층 문화에 대한 친숙함을 설명하기 위해 부르디외에 의해 제안되었는데, 중산층 문화의 불평등한 분배는 개인의 재능과 학문적 실력주의의 구실 하에 사회 계급을 유지하는 데 도움을 준다고 했다. 따라서 이 지문의 제목을 '학교 교육에서의 불평등의 재생산'이라고 표현한 ④번이 정답이다.

어휘 achievement n. 성취

[64-66]

지금까지, 소셜미디어가 매우 잘하는 것처럼 보이는 것들이 있다. 가장 주목할 만한 것은 통합이다. 많은 사람이 정확하게 같은 것을 동시에 하도록 통합하는 것은 어렵기로 알려져 있다. 그 활동이, 가령 예정된 곳에 나타나서 정부에 시위하는 것처럼, 비교적 단순하기만 하다면, 새로운 소셜미디어는 통합에 드는 비용을 대폭 줄여준다. 그러나 소셜미디어가 단순한 행사들을 통합하는 것에 능하기는 하지만, 이제까지 소셜미디어는 정당을 더 큰 규모로 만드는 것에 실패해왔다. 이집트와 튀니지에서, 반정부 시위를 촉진했던 최신 기술에 능통한 청년들은 이미 정치적 단체를 위한 경쟁에서 뒤처지기 시작했다. 이 청년들보다 앞선 이슬람교의 민주주의자들이 있는데, 이들은 수년간 당원들을 끌어모으고, 조직하고, 동원해본 경험이 있는 정치 단체들이다.

왜 페이스북과 트위터는 사회적 단체에는 도움이 되지만 정당에는 그렇지 않을까? 그것을 확실히 알기에는 너무 이르고, 기술이 변화하고 사용자 문화가 발달함에 따라 당연히 소셜미디어에서 더 복잡한 정치 단체가 생겨날 수도 있다. 하지만, 현재로서 그 답은 소셜미디어에는 더 큰 정치적 화합을 만들기 위해 필요한 종류의 관계가 결여됐다는 사실에 있는 듯하다. 사회적 모임에 나타나기 위해, 나는 다른 사람들과 어떠한 친밀한 혹은 반복적인 유대관계도 필요하지 않다. 우리는 모두 사회적 모임에 나타나, 스스로 즐기고 각자의 길을 갈 수 있다. 핵심은 우리의 목적이 복잡하기보다는 단순하다는 것이다. 이와 반대로, 정치 단체는 실로 매우 복잡하다. 성공적인 정치 단체는 세상이 돌아가는 방식과 그 방식이 어떻게 되어야 하는지에 관한 신념을 만들어내야 한다. 그것은 공유된 사회정신이나 도덕성을 반영해야 한다. 무엇보다도, 그것은 어느 정도 공동체 의식을 만들어내야 한다.

remarkable adj. 주목할 만한 coordinate v. 통합하다
notoriously adv. ~으로 소문나서
show up phr. (예정된 곳에) 나타나다 protest v. 시위하다
tech savvy phr. 최신 기술에 능통한
facilitate v. 촉진하다, 조장하다 fall behind phr. 뒤처지다
organization n. 단체 democrat n. 민주주의자
mobilize v. 동원하다 evolve v. 발전하다
cohesion n. 화합 generate v. 만들어내다
ethos n. 사회정신 morality n. 도덕성

64 2019 덕성여대

정답 ①

해석
① 그것을 확실히 알기에는 너무 이르다
② 그것을 확실히 알기는 너무 어렵다
③ 그것을 확실히 알기에는 너무 늦었다
④ 그것을 확실히 모르기에는 너무 이르다

해설 지문의 빈칸을 채우는 문제이다. 빈칸 앞부분에서 왜 페이스북과 트위터는 사회적 단체에는 도움이 되지만 정당에는 그렇지 않은지 묻고 있고, 빈칸 뒤에서 기술이 변화하고 사용자 문화가 발달함에 따라 당연히 소셜미디어에서 더 복잡한

정치 단체가 생겨날 수도 있다고 추측하고 있으므로, 빈칸에는 '그것을 확실히 알기에는 너무 이르다'라는 내용이 나와야 적절하다. 따라서 ①번이 정답이다.

어휘   definitely adv. 확실히

65   2019 덕성여대

정답 ③

해석 ① 이집트에서, 소셜미디어에 아주 능한 청년들이 반정부 시위를 조직했지만, 정당을 더 큰 규모로 만들지는 못했다.
② 소셜미디어의 기술적 변화로부터 더 복잡한 정치 단체가 생겨날 수 있다.
③ 정당은 많은 사람이 정확하게 같은 것을 동시에 하도록 통합하고자 한다면, 소셜미디어에 의존해야 한다.
④ 소셜미디어는 예정된 곳에 나타나 정부에 시위하는 것과 같은 비교적 단순한 활동에 있어서 매우 잘하는 것처럼 보인다.

해설 지문을 통해 추론할 수 없는 것을 고르는 문제이다. 지문의 마지막 부분에서 성공적인 정치 단체는 세상이 돌아가는 방식과 그 방식이 어떻게 되어야 하는지에 관한 신념을 만들어내야 한다고 했지만, 많은 사람이 정확하게 같은 것을 동시에 하도록 통합하기 위해 정당이 소셜미디어에 의존해야 한다는 것은 유추할 수 없으므로 정답은 ③번이다.

오답 ① 첫 번째 문단의 여섯 번째 문장 In Egypt ~ political
분석   organization.을 통해 '이집트에서, 소셜미디어에 아주 능한 청년들이 반정부 시위를 조직했지만, 정당을 더 큰 규모로 만들지는 못했다'는 것을 알 수 있다.
② 두 번째 문단 두 번째 문장에서 of course it is possible ~ social media를 통해 '소셜미디어의 기술적 변화로부터 더 복잡한 정치 단체가 생겨날 수 있다'는 것을 알 수 있다.
④ 첫 번째 문단의 네 번째 문장 So long as ~ the costs of coordination.을 통해 '소셜미디어는 예정된 곳에 나타나 정부에 시위하는 것과 같은 비교적 단순한 활동에 있어서 매우 잘하는 것처럼 보인다'는 것을 알 수 있다.

어휘   organize v. 조직하다   depend on phr. ~에 의존하다
relative adj. 비교적인

66   2019 덕성여대

정답 ①

해석 ① 소셜미디어의 한계
② 소셜미디어 vs. 정당
③ 소셜미디어의 장점
④ 소셜미디어의 사회정신

해설 지문의 제목을 묻는 문제이다. 지문 전체적으로 소셜미디어가 사회적 단체와 같이 비교적 단순한 활동에서 사람들을 통합하는 것에는 도움이 되지만, 정치 단체에는 도움이 되지 않는

다는 내용이다. 따라서 이 지문의 제목을 '소셜미디어의 한계'라고 표현한 ①번이 정답이다.

어휘   limitation n. 한계   advantage n. 장점

[67-69]

[C] 1960년대의 서핑 문화는 주로 10대와 청년들의 관심을 끌었고, 화창한 해변에서 다른 사람과 교제하면서 느끼는 기분 전환과 파도 위에서 해변을 향해 날아오르면서 느끼는 즐거움이 뒤섞여, 낭만과 의무로부터의 해방감을 느낄 수 있다고 강조하고 있었다. [B] 또한, 초창기의 많은 캘리포니아와 호주의 서퍼들은 하와이의 서핑 철학을 받아들였고, 서핑을 자연과 연결되는 방법으로 간주했다. [D] 이 관행이 이상적인 파도를 찾기 위한 시간이 걸리는 일과 결합했을 때, 이것은 "소울 서퍼"라는 생활 방식으로 이어졌으며, 서핑에 전념하는 서퍼들은 이 생활 방식을 따르면서 서핑을 통해 영혼의 안정을 찾는 것에 삶을 집중시키게 되었다. [A] "소울 서퍼"들은 서핑에 대해 논하기 위해 그들만의 별개의 어휘를 만들어내기도 했는데, "stoked" 같은 단어를 큰 파도에서 서핑하는 것을 통해 얻게 되는 불안과 흥분의 조합을 묘사하기 위한 동사로 활용하는 식이었다. 종종, "소울 서퍼"들은 이상적인 서핑 조건을 추구하기 위해 학교나 일과 관련된 책임을 포기하곤 했는데, 이는 몇몇 사람들이 서퍼를 학교나 일에 의해 동기부여 되지 않는 사람으로 여기도록 만들었다.

appeal v. 관심을 끌다   obligation n. 의무
relaxation n. 기분전환   socialize v. 사귀다
launch v. 날아오르다   atop adv. 맨 위에   adopt v. 취하다
time-consuming adj. 시간이 걸리는
demand n. (힘든) 일   dedicated adj. 전념하는
spiritual adj. 영혼의   apprehension n. 불안, 우려

67   2020 한성대

정답 ①

해설 [A], [B], [C] [D]의 적절한 순서를 파악하는 문제이다. 1960년대의 서핑 문화가 10대와 청년들의 관심을 끌었다는 내용의 [C]가 가장 먼저 와야 하고, 이어서 캘리포니아와 호주의 서퍼들이 하와이의 서핑 철학을 받아들였다는 것을 설명하는 [B]가 이어진 다음, 이런 관행이 "소울 서퍼"라는 새로운 생활 방식으로 이어졌다는 내용의 [D]가 오는 것이 자연스럽다. 그리고 마지막으로 [A]에서 "소울 서퍼"들이 그들만의 용어를 만들기도 했다는 내용으로 이어져야 한다. 따라서 [A], [B], [C], [D]의 적절한 순서는 ① [C] — [B] — [D] — [A]이다.

68 [2020 한성대]

정답 ③

해석 ① 학교에서 공부하는 서퍼들
② 교제의 낭만
③ 1960년대의 서핑 문화
④ 캘리포니아의 서퍼 대 호주의 서퍼

해설 지문의 주제를 묻는 문제이다. 지문 전체적으로 1960년대의 서핑 문화인 "소울 서퍼"를 설명하고 있으므로, 이 지문의 주제를 '1960년대의 서핑 문화'라고 표현한 ③번이 정답이다.

69 [2020 한성대]

정답 ④

해석 ① 포기하다 ② 거절하다
③ 포기하다 ④ 떠맡다

해설 문맥상 빈칸에 적절하지 않은 어휘를 고르는 문제이다. 빈칸이 포함된 지문의 내용은 서퍼들이 일과 학교와 관련된 책임을 포기해서, 다른 사람들이 그들을 학교나 일에 의해 동기부여 되지 않는 사람들로 간주하게 되었다는 내용이므로, 빈칸에는 '포기하다'라는 의미가 들어가야 한다. take on은 '~을 떠맡다'라는 의미이므로 ④번이 정답이다.

[70-72]

사람들은 왜 바다 수천 킬로미터를 건너는 <u>모험적인</u> 여행을 하려고 하는 것일까? 개척자들은 왜 대초원 지대, 로키산맥이나 모하비 사막을 건너 미국의 서부에 도달했을까? 사람들은 왜 오늘날에도 몇백만 명이나 계속해서 이주하는 것일까? 많은 이주자들이 직면해 온 위험들은 새로운 곳에 대한 유혹이 얼마나 강한지 그리고 그들의 이전 고향에서의 상황이 얼마나 절망적이었는지를 보여주는 척도이다. 새로운 곳으로의 영구적인 이동은 전통적인 문화적 유대와 한 지역 내 경제 패턴에 지장을 준다. 동시에, 사람들은 이주할 때, 자신들의 언어, 종교, 민족성과 다른 문화적 특성들을 새로운 고향에 가져간다. 대부분의 사람들은 경제적인 이유로 이주한다. 사람들은 취업 기회가 적은 곳에서 이주하는 것에 대해 고려하고, 일자리를 구할 수 있을 것 같은 곳으로 이주해 온다. 경제 개편 때문에, 취업 전망은 보통 나라 간에 다르고, 같은 나라 안에서도 지역 내에서도 달라진다. 미국과 캐나다는 특히 경제 이민을 위한 유망한 <u>목적지</u>였다. 문화적 요소는 특히 사람들을 현재 살고 있는 곳에서 나오게 만드는 강력한 추진 요인이 될 수 있다.

---

adventurous adj. 모험적인, 용기가 필요한
journey n. 여행 **pioneer** n. 개척자, 선구자
Great Plains phr. 대초원 지대
Rocky Mountains phr. 로키산맥
Mojave Desert phr. 모하비 사막
migrate v. 이주하다, 이동하다 **hazard** n. 위험
migrant n. 이주자 **face** v. 직면하다, 마주하다
measure n. 척도, 표준
desperate adj. 절망적인, 필사적인, 절실한
former adj. 이전의, 옛날의 **homeland** n. 고향, 고국
permanent adj. 영구적인 **disrupt** v. 지장을 주다, 방해하다
traditional adj. 전통적인 **cultural** adj. 문화적인
tie n. (강한) 유대(관계) **economic** adj. 경제의
pattern n. 패턴, 양상 **region** n. 지역
at the same time phr. 동시에 **language** n. 언어
religion n. 종교 **ethnicity** n. 민족성 **trait** n. 특성, 특징
reason n. 이유 **emigrate** v. 이주하다, 이민하다
opportunity n. 기회 **immigrate** v. 이주해 오다
available adj. 이용할 수 있는 **restructuring** n. 개편, 개혁
job prospects phr. 취업 전망 **vary** v. 달라지다, 다양하다
region n. 지역 **especially** adv. 특히
promising adj. 유망한, 장래성 있는
economic migrant phr. 경제 이민(일자리를 구하거나 더 나은 삶의 질을 위해 이주하는 사람) **compelling** adj. 강력한
factor n. 요인 **present** adj. 현재의

70 [2019 상명대]

정답 ①

해석 ① 이주하는 이유
② 이주의 위험을 극복하는 법
③ 사람들이 이주하도록 만드는 문화적 요소
④ 미국 내 증가하는 이주자의 수
⑤ 전통적인 문화에 대한 이주의 영향

해설 지문의 제목을 묻는 문제이다. 지문 초반에서 사람들이 왜 오늘날에도 몇백만 명이나 계속해서 이주하는 것인지 물은 뒤, 이주하는 이유에 관한 내용이 이어지고 있다. 따라서 이 지문의 제목을 '이주하는 이유'라고 표현한 ①번이 정답이다.

어휘 overcome v. 극복하다

71 [2019 상명대]

정답 ①

해설 adventurous(모험적인)와 비슷한 의미를 가진 어휘를 묻고 있다. ①번 perilous는 '위험한', ②번 hilarious는 '유쾌한', ③번 spontaneous는 '자발적인', ④번 parsimonious는 '인색한', ⑤번 monetary는 '통화의'라는 의미이다. 따라서 ①번이 정답이다.

72 [2019 상명대]

정답 ③

해석 ① 잠깐 들르는 곳 ② 저장고
③ 도착지 ④ 피난처
⑤ 출발지

해설 지문의 빈칸을 채우는 문제이다. 지문의 후반에서 경제 개편 때문에, 취업 전망은 보통 나라 간에 다르고, 같은 나라 안에서도 지역 내에서도 달라진다고 했으므로, 빈칸에는 미국과 캐나다가 특히 경제 이민을 위한 유망한 목적지였다는 내용이 나와야 적절하다는 것을 알 수 있다. 따라서 '목적지'라고 한 ③번이 정답이다.

어휘
stopover n. 잠깐 들르는 곳   storage n. 저장고
destination n. 도착지   refuge n. 피난처
starting point phr. 출발지

[73-75]

패션 산업은 현대의 산물이다. 19세기 중반 이전에, 사실상 모든 옷은 개인용으로 가정에서 만들어지거나 재봉사나 재단사에게 주문하여 손으로 만들어졌다. [A] 20세기 초까지, 재봉틀과 같은 새로운 기술 및 세계 자본주의의 출현과 공장 생산 시스템의 발달, 백화점과 같은 소매점의 확산과 함께 옷은 점점 더 표준 사이즈로 대량 생산되고 고정 가격에 판매되었다. [B] 패션 산업이 처음엔 유럽과 미국에서 발달하긴 했지만, 오늘날 패션 산업은 옷이 보통 한 나라에서 디자인되고, 다른 나라에서 제조되고, 제3국에서 판매됨에 따라 국제적이고 매우 세계화된 산업이다. [C] 예를 들어, 미국의 한 패션 회사는 중국에서 직물을 얻어서 옷이 베트남에서 제조되고, 이탈리아에서 완성되고, 국제적으로 소매점에 유통되기 위해 미국에 있는 창고로 운송되게 할 수 있다. 미국에서 패션 산업은 오랫동안 가장 큰 고용 기업들 중 하나이고, 21세기까지 여전히 그대로이다. 그러나, 제조가 점점 더 해외, 특히 중국으로 옮겨가면서 고용은 상당히 감소했다. 패션 산업에 대한 자료가 일반적으로 국가 경제를 위해 보고되고 산업의 많은 독립된 부문 면에서 나타나기 때문에, 세계에서 생산되는 직물과 옷의 합계 수치는 얻기 어렵다. 그러나, 틀림없이, 패션 산업은 논쟁의 여지가 없이 세계 경제 생산의 상당량을 차지한다. [D] 패션 산업은 네 단계로 이루어져 있는데, 주로 섬유와 직물, 또한 가죽과 모피 원료의 생산, 디자이너, 제조사, 하청업자와 다른 이들에 의한 패션 상품의 생산, 소매 판매, 다양한 형태의 광고와 판촉 활동이다. 이 단계들은 독립되었지만, 상호의존적인 많은 부문들로 이루어지는데, 모두 패션 산업에서 참가자들이 이익을 남기고 운영할 수 있도록 하기 위한 환경에서 의류에 대한 소비자 수요를 충족시키려는 목표에 전념한다.

handmade adj. (기계가 아니라) 손으로 만든
dressmaker n. 재봉사   tailor n. 재단사
sewing machine phr. 재봉틀
global capitalism phr. 세계자본주의
proliferation n. 확산, 급증   retail outlet phr. 소매점
increasingly adv. 점점 더
mass-produced adj. 대량 생산의
international adj. 국제적인
manufacture v. 제조하다, 생산하다
employer n. 고용 기업, 고용주   employment n. 고용
considerably adv. 상당히   in terms of phr. ~ 면에서
sector n. 부문   aggregate n. 합계   figure n. 수치
textile n. 직물
by any measure phr. 틀림없이, 아무리 따져 보아도
inarguably adv. 논쟁의 여지가 없이, 명백히
account for phr. (부분·비율을) 차지하다
consist of phr. ~으로 이루어지다   raw material phr. 원료
principally adv. 주로   fibre n. 섬유
contractor n. 하청업자   advertising n. 광고
promotion n. 판촉 활동
interdependent adj. 상호의존적인   apparel n. 의류
participant n. 참여자   at a profit phr. 이익을 남기고

73 [2019 홍익대]

정답 ②

해석
① 재봉틀의 도입
② 외부 위탁 관행의 확대
③ 소매점의 확대
④ 세계 자본주의의 출현

해설 패션 산업에서 대량 생산의 발달에 기여한 요소가 아닌 것을 파악하는 문제이다. 지문의 세 번째 문장에서 20세기 초까지, 재봉틀과 같은 새로운 기술 및 세계 자본주의의 출현과 공장 생산 시스템의 발달, 백화점과 같은 소매점의 확산과 함께 옷은 점점 더 표준 사이즈로 대량 생산되고 고정 가격에 판매되었다고 했으므로, 패션 산업에서 대량 생산의 발달에 기여한 요소가 아닌 것은 '외부 위탁 관행의 확대'이다. 따라서 정답은 ②번이다.

어휘
introduction n. 도입   expansion n. 확대, 확장
outsourcing n. 외부 위탁, 외주 제작   practice n. 관행
rise n. 출현, 오름

74 [2019 홍익대]

정답 ②

해석
① 광고와 판촉 활동   ② 고용과 교육
③ 원료의 생산   ④ 패션 상품의 생산

해설 패션 산업의 단계가 아닌 것을 파악하는 문제이다. 지문의 마지막에서 두 번째 문장에서 패션 산업은 주로 섬유와 직물, 또한 가죽과 모피 원료의 생산, 디자이너, 제조사, 하청업자와 다른 이들에 의한 패션 상품의 생산, 소매 판매, 다양한 형태의 광고와 판촉 활동 단계로 이루어져 있다고 했으므로, 패션 산업의 단계가 아닌 것은 '고용과 교육'이다. 따라서 정답은 ②번이다.

75 [2019 홍익대]

정답 ③

해설 지문의 흐름상 주어진 문장이 들어가기에 가장 적절한 위치를 고르는 문제이다. [C]의 앞 문장에서 오늘날 패션 산업은

옷이 보통 한 나라에서 디자인되고, 다른 나라에서 제조되고, 제3국에서 판매됨에 따라 국제적이고 매우 세계화된 산업이라고 했으므로, [C] 자리에 다양한 나라를 거치는 패션 산업의 예시를 주는 주어진 문장 '예를 들어, 미국의 한 패션 회사는 중국에서 직물을 얻어서 옷이 베트남에서 제조되고, 이탈리아에서 완성되고, 국제적으로 소매점에 유통되기 위해 미국에 있는 창고로 운송하게 할 수 있다'가 들어가야 글의 흐름이 자연스럽게 연결된다. 따라서 ③번이 정답이다.

어휘 source v. (특정한 곳에서 무엇을) 얻다 fabric n. 직물, 천
warehouse n. 창고 distribution n. (상품의) 유통
internationally adv. 국제적으로

[76-78]

지도의 경우, 포괄의 규칙은 표현을 위해 선택된 현상의 측면을 상징하는 데에 쓰이는 전략과 형식적인 장치도 결정한다. 특히 여기에 정당한 지배적 이해관계에 사용되는 구상주의적 전략이 있다. 주된 정당화 전략은 공간의 계층화에 기초하는데, 공간은 등방성으로, 즉 어느 곳에서나 동등한 가치를 가지는 것으로 인식되지 않기 때문이다. 공간은 이방성으로 인식되기 때문에, 시각적 요소의 배치는 특별한 의미를 부여하는 방법이 된다. 특별한 의미의 위치를 결정하는 것은 다양한 방법으로 영향을 받을 수 있다. '중앙집중화'를 통한 특별한 의미 부여는 지도제작학 문헌에서 주목을 피하지 못했다. 따라서, 여전히 하나의 표준인 메르카토르의 15세기 지도 제작 체계는, 설계자의 고향인 독일을 지도의 중앙에 놓았으며, 유럽 중심적인 관습은 전 대륙에 걸쳐 빠르게 받아들여졌다.

특별한 의미를 부여하는 것은 또한 지도의 조직 구조의 위계적인 표시에서 볼 수 있듯이, 높은 계급의 직원들이 나머지 사람들보다 위쪽에 위치하는 것처럼 위쪽에 배치하는 것으로 영향을 받을 수 있다. Mumby(1986)에 의하면, "계층의 개념은 조직의 구조가 하향식으로 '자연스럽게' 일어나는 것으로 받아들여지는 지점에서 구상되어 왔다"고 한다. 실제로, 북반구의 독자들은 호주의 아이들이 자신들의 대륙을 종종 지도의 위쪽에 위치한다고 배우는 것을 안다면 놀랄 것이다.

마지막으로, 특별한 의미 부여는 순서 조정을 통해 연속적으로 영향을 받았는데, 순서 조정에서는 첫 번째 요소가 구분을 받게 된다. Wood(1987)는, 예를 들어 Goode의 세계 전도에서 지도 순서의 효과에 대해 "국가가 개체발생적으로 지도의 물리적 환경의 앞부분인 처음에 오는 것으로 특별한 의미의 위치를 받게 된다"고 썼다. Wood는 이 특별한 의미 부여의 결과를 "이 나라들이 지형과 기후와 같은 발전 상태를 가지고 있기 때문에 사람의 운명에서 비와 바람과는 다른 방법으로는 연관되지 않는다는 인상을 준다"는 자연화라는 용어를 사용하여 평가한다.

inclusion n. 포함 strategy n. 전략
symbolize v. 상징하다 aspect n. 측면
phenomena n. 현상 legitimate adj. 정당한
dominant adj. 우세한 hierarchization n. 계층화

perceive v. 인식하다 isotropically adv. 등방성으로
anisotropically adv. 이방성으로 impart v. 부여하다
privilege n. 특별한 의미, 특권
cartographic adj. 지도제작학의 literature n. 문헌
standard n. 표준 convention n. 관습
continent n. 대륙 echelon n. 계급 personnel n. 직원
reify v. 구체화하다 hemisphere n. 반구
distinction n. 구분, 구별
ontogenetically adv. 개체발생적으로
physical adj. 물리적인 appraise v. 평가하다
consequence n. 결과 impression n. 인상
landform n. 지형 climate n. 기후
implicatable adj. 연관 지을 수 있는 fate n. 운명

76 2020 이화여대
정답 ①

해석 ① 2차원에 표시된 지리학적 공간의 그림
② 개념이나 사상의 상징적인 시각적 표현의 모든 형태
③ 사물들의 자연적 관계에 관한 설계자의 인식을 반영하는 그림
④ 헤게모니 가치 체계를 강화하는 유럽 중심적 관습
⑤ 국가의 정치적 경계를 보여주는 전통적인 표현

해설 지문에서 언급된 예시들을 바탕으로 단어 "map"의 정의로 가장 알맞은 것을 묻는 문제이다. 지문에서는 세 가지 예시를 보여주는데, 특별한 의미를 부여하기 위한 지역을 지도의 중앙, 상단, 첫 부분에 위치시키는 예시에 관해 각각 설명하고 있다. 이 점으로 보아, 지도는 지역을 평면에 지역을 위치시키는 것이라고 볼 수 있다. 따라서 단어 "map"의 정의를 '2차원에 표시된 지리학적 공간의 그림'이라고 표현한 ①번이 정답이다.

어휘 geographical adj. 지리학적인 dimension n. 차원
perception n. 지각 border n. 경계

77 2020 이화여대
정답 ②

해석 ① 중국의 고대 지도는 유럽이 아닌 중국을 세계의 중심에 위치시켰다.
② 한국에서 지하철역 인근 지도는 독자가 위를 향하도록 방향을 놓는다.
③ 기금 모금 행사에서 자리 배치도는 내빈의 테이블을 상단에 배치한다.
④ 파리에서 출판된 유럽 식당 안내서는 첫 번째 장에 프랑스의 식당들 목록을 넣는다.
⑤ 한 회사의 내선 전화번호 안내는 회장의 이름을 제일 상단에 놓는다.

해설 지문의 요지를 나타내지 못하는 예시를 찾는 문제이다. 지문에서는 한 지역을 지도의 중심, 상단, 처음에 놓아 그 지역에

상대적으로 특별한 의미를 주는 '계층화'를 통해 일종의 구상주의적 전략을 펼치고 있다는 것을 요지로 하고 있다. 지하철역 인근 지도에서 독자가 위를 향하도록 방향을 놓는 것은 독자를 배려하기 위함으로 계층화와는 관계가 없다. 따라서 ②번이 정답이다.

어휘 neighborhood n. 인근 fundraising n. 기금 모금
guest of honor phr. 내빈, 귀빈 directory n. 안내(표)

78 2020 이화여대

정답 ⑤

해석
① 조직에서 일부 사람들이 다른 사람들이 가진 것보다 더 많은 권력을 가지는 것은 자연스러운 것이다.
② 지도를 만드는 사람이 지배적인 이익을 정당화하는 것은 불가능하다.
③ 무엇이 자연스러운지 아닌지에 관한 개념은 등방성 요소와 이방성 요소 모두에게서 보일 수 있다.
④ 지도의 요소에는 중심 위치를 둘러싼 특별한 의미를 규정하는 위계가 있다.
⑤ 지도에서 시각적 요소들이 일부 항목에서 다른 것들보다 특별한 의미를 받는 것은 불가피하다.

해설 지문에 의해 뒷받침되지 않는 진술을 찾는 문제이다. 지문의 처음에서 공간은 어느 곳에서나 동등한 가치를 가지는 것으로 인식되지 않기 때문에 특별한 의미를 부여하는 시각적 요소의 배치가 정당한 전략이라고 말하고 있다. 따라서 지문에 의해 뒷받침되지 않는 진술을 '지도에서 시각적 요소들이 일부 항목에서 다른 것들보다 특별한 의미를 받는 것은 불가피하다'라고 표현한 ⑤번이 정답이다.

어휘 unavoidable adj. 불가피한

[79-81]

자메이카에서, 대부분의 영국인과 미국인은 문화, 좋은 날씨, 아름다운 건물, 또는 여행하는 사람들이 찾는 다른 것들의 소비자로서 관광업을 접한다. 나는 학생으로서 한 해 동안 자메이카에 살면서 카리브해 지역을 여행 다닐 때, 관광업으로 먹고사는 사람들의 눈을 통해 관광업을 보았고, 경제적 생존을 위해 관광업에 의존하는 문화에서 관광업의 부패한 영향들을 목격했다.
내가 사람들에게 자메이카에서 장학금으로 살았다고 말하면, 그들은 눈을 희번덕거리며 나의 행운에 놀랐는데, 이는 그들이 텅 빈 해변, 맑은 파란 하늘과 가끔 미소 짓는 흑인들의 얼굴을 보여주는 자메이카 관광업에 대한 광고를 보아왔기 때문이다. 나는 어떻게 반응해야 할지 몰랐는데, 내가 살았고 일부 관광객들에게만 볼 수 있는 특권을 줬던 자메이카는 경찰관부터 간자(마리화나) 밀매인까지 대부분의 사람들이 자신들의 여가와 거의 독점적으로 호텔 주인들과 정부 관리들의 소수 엘리트들에게 가는 자신들의 돈을 두고 관광객들을 원망하는 가난하고, 붐비고, 폭력적인 곳이었기 때문이다.
방문객들의 돈을 차지하기 위해 고개를 숙이고, 구걸하고, 팔거나 훔쳐야 하는 나머지 사람들 사이에서, 관광업은 소매치기와 사기꾼을 만들어 낸다.
관광객들이 그들의 모습에서 너무 <u>유난히 두드러진</u> 게 아니라면 이야기가 다를 수도 있다. 옷, 언어, 외모와 같이 많은 것들로 관광객들과 현지인들을 구별할 수 있다. 자메이카에서, 관광객들을 구별하는 것은 피부색인데, 자메이카인의 95퍼센트가 흑인이고, 대부분의 관광객들은 백인이기 때문이다. 자메이카 거리에 있는 낯선 백인은 관광객으로 간주되고, 그래서 그 사람은 자질구레한 장신구, 기념품 또는 마약을 사는 데 관심이 있는 것으로 간주된다.

encounter v. 접하다, 마주치다 tourism n. 관광업
the Caribbean phr. 카리브해 지역 witness v. 목격하다
corrupting adj. 부패한, 타락한
economic survival phr. 경제적 생존
scholarship n. 장학금
roll one's eyes phr. 눈을 굴리다, 눈을 희번덕거리다
marvel at phr. ~에 놀라다 occasional adj. 가끔의
privilege v. 특권을 주다 crowded adj. 붐비는
violent adj. 폭력적인 peddler n. (마약 등의) 밀매인, 행상인
resent v. 원망하다, 분개하다, 괘씸하게 생각하다
exclusively adv. 독점적으로, 오로지
official n. 관리, 관계자 bow v. 고개를 숙이다
beg v. 구걸하다 pickpocket n. 소매치기
impostor n. 사기꾼 appearance n. 모습, 외모
distinguish from phr. ~와 구별하다
set apart phr. 구별하다 stranger n. 낯선 사람
assume v. 간주하다, 추정하다 trinket n. 자질구레한 장신구
souvenir n. 기념품 drug n. 마약

79 2019 단국대

정답 ③

해석
① 긍정적인, 낙관적인   ② 온화한, 순한
③ 유난히 두드러진   ④ 우울한

해설 지문의 빈칸을 채우는 문제이다. 세 번째 문단에서 옷, 언어, 외모와 같이 많은 것들로 관광객들과 현지인들을 구별할 수 있다고 했고, 자메이카인의 95퍼센트가 흑인이고 대부분의 관광객들은 백인이라고 했으므로, 빈칸에는 관광객이 그들의 모습에서 유난히 두드러진 게 아니라면 이야기가 다를 수도 있다는 것에 대한 내용이 나와야 적절하다는 것을 알 수 있다. 따라서 '유난히 두드러진'이라고 한 ③번이 정답이다.

80 2019 단국대

정답 ③

해석
① 신이 난   ② 낙관적인
③ 분석적인   ④ 미적인

해설 필자의 어조를 묻는 문제이다. 첫 번째 문단에서 필자가 학생으로서 한 해 동안 자메이카에 살면서 관광업으로 먹고사는 사람들의 눈을 통해 관광업을 보았고, 경제적 생존을 위해 관광업에 의존하는 문화에서 관광업의 부패한 영향들을 목격했다고 하였다. 따라서 필자의 어조를 '분석적인'이라고 표현한 ③번이 정답이다.

81 2019 단국대

정답 ①

해석 ① 자메이카 관광업의 현실
② 관광객을 자메이카의 관광지로 유인하는 것
③ 자메이카의 인종 차별과 사회 분열
④ 자메이카에서 장학생으로 공부하는 것

해설 지문의 주제를 묻는 문제이다. 첫 번째 문단에서 필자가 학생으로서 자메이카에 살면서 경제적 생존을 위해 관광업에 의존하는 문화에서 관광업의 부패한 영향들을 목격했다고 하였다. 따라서 이 지문의 주제를 '자메이카 관광업의 현실'이라고 표현한 ①번이 정답이다.

어휘 luring n. 유인하는 것   racism n. 인종 차별
social division phr. 사회 분열

[82-85]

미국 원주민의 전통 의식 춤인 태양 춤의 형식은 항상 지역 사회마다 달랐다. 하지만, 그 춤에는 많은 부족이 공유하는 특정한 특징이 있다. 종종, 그 춤은 대부에 의해서 시작되어야 하는데, 대부란 걱정이 해소되거나, 다가올 해에 축복받기를 바라면서 맹세를 하는 사람이다. [A] 그것은 거의 항상 하지 무렵에 실시된다. 대부분의 태양 춤은 엄숙하게 선택하고 잘라낸 중앙 기둥 주변으로 원형의 천막집을 세우는 것으로 시작한다. 그다음 사흘에서 나흘 동안, 춤을 추는 기간에 노래와 북을 곁들이는 휴식과 명상의 시간을 가진다. 춤추는 사람들은 춤을 추는 기간 내내 먹거나 마시지 않지만, 일부 사람은 입안에 수분을 유지하기 위해 천궁이라는 풀을 씹는다. 춤의 마지막이 다가오면, 참가자들은 환상을 경험하고 축복을 받게 된다. [B] 초기 유럽인들은 이런 의식에서 스스로 고행의 길을 걷는 일부 부족들의 관습에 거부감을 느꼈다. [C] 춤추는 남성들은 가슴이나 등에 꼬챙이를 꿰고 중앙에 있는 천막집 기둥에 매어졌다. 그들은 춤을 추면서 밧줄로 팽팽하게 잡아당기다가, 마침내 꼬챙이에서 떨어져 나왔다. 이러한 의식을 통해, 참가자들은 지역 사회를 대신하여 말 그대로 고통을 겪고 신을 불러내어 자신들을 불쌍히 여기고 자신들의 맹세를 이행할 수 있게 도와달라고 요청한다. [D] 의식의 이러한 측면이 1870년대 말에서 1935년 사이에 연방 공무원들이 의식을 금지한 주된 이유이다. 하지만, 이러한 금지에도 불구하고, 많은 부족이 계속해서 자신들의 보호 구역에서 떨어진 지역에서 은밀하게 태양 춤을 유지하거나 불쾌한 요소를 빼고 공연한다.

---

ceremonial adj. 의식의   feature n. 특징
tribe n. 부족, 종족   initiate v. 시작하다
sponsor n. 대부(代父)   relieve v. 해소하다, 경감하다
summer solstice phr. 하지(夏至)   erection n. 설치, 건립
lodge n. 천막집, 오두막   solemnly adv. 엄숙하게, 경건하게
accompany v. 동반하다, 함께하다
intersperse v. 배치하다   meditation n. 명상
bear root phr. 천궁(약초의 일종)   participant n. 참가자
repulsed adj. 거부감이 드는, 메스꺼운
mortification n. 고행, 금욕   strain v. (팽팽하게) 잡아당기다
eventually adv. 결국   skewer n. 꼬챙이   ritual n. 의식
on behalf of phr. ~를 대신하여   call upon phr. 불러내다
pity v. 불쌍히 여기다   fulfillment n. 이행
federal adj. 연방의   surreptitiously adv. 은밀하게, 숨어서
reservation n. (원주민) 보호구역
enact v. 공연하다, 시행하다   objectionable adj. 불쾌한

82 2019 세종대

정답 ③

해석 ① 그러므로   ② 그런 이유로
③ 하지만   ④ 반면에

해설 빈칸에 적절한 연결어를 넣는 문제이다. 빈칸 앞 문장은 태양 춤이 지역 사회마다 다르다는 내용이고, 빈칸 뒤 문장은 많은 부족이 공유하는 태양 춤의 특징이 있다는 내용이다. 따라서 역접을 나타내는 연결어인 ③ Nevertheless(하지만)가 정답이다.

83 2019 세종대

정답 ③

해설 지문의 흐름상 주어진 문장이 들어가기에 가장 적절한 위치를 고르는 문제이다. [C]의 이전 문장에서 초기 유럽인들이 태양 춤의 의식에서 스스로 고행의 길을 걷는 일부 부족들의 관습에 거부감을 느꼈다고 했으므로, [C] 자리에 거부감을 느낀 이유에 관해 설명하는 주어진 문장 '춤추는 남성들은 가슴이나 등에 꼬챙이를 꿰고 중앙에 있는 천막집 기둥에 매어졌다'가 들어가야 글의 흐름이 자연스럽게 연결된다. 따라서 ③번이 정답이다.

어휘 breast n. 가슴   back n. 등

84 2019 세종대

정답 ④

해석 ① 춤을 추는 사람들은 입안의 수분을 유지하기 위해 특정한 식물의 뿌리를 씹는 것이 허용된다.
② 한 개인은 대부로서 태양 춤을 시작할 수 있다.
③ 태양 춤의 일부 측면들은 많은 부족에 공통적이다.
④ 태양 춤은 금지된 동안 실행되지 않았다.

08 문화 175

| 해설 | 지문의 내용과 일치하지 않는 것을 묻는 문제이다. ④번의 키워드인 prohibition period(금지된 기간)와 관련된 지문의 ban(금지) 주변에서 많은 부족이 계속해서 자신들의 보호 구역에서 떨어진 지역에서 은밀하게 태양 춤을 유지하거나 불쾌한 요소를 빼고 공연한다고 했으므로, 태양 춤은 금지된 기간 동안 실행되지 않았다는 것은 지문의 내용과 다르다. 따라서 ④번이 지문의 내용과 일치하지 않는다. |

| 오답분석 | ① some do chew on bear root to keep their mouths moist를 통해 '춤을 추는 사람들은 입안의 수분을 유지하기 위해 특정한 식물의 뿌리를 씹는 것이 허용된다'는 것을 알 수 있다.
② the dance must be initiated by a sponsor를 통해 '한 개인은 대부로서 태양 춤을 시작할 수 있다'는 것을 알 수 있다.
③ there are certain features of the dance that many tribes share를 통해 '태양 춤의 일부 측면들은 많은 부족에 공통적이다'는 것을 알 수 있다. |

| 어휘 | **bite** v. 물다, 씹다　**moisten** v. 적시다, 촉촉하게 하다 |

85　2019 세종대

| 정답 | ③ |

| 해석 | ① 참가자들이 육체적 고통을 견딜 수 있는 한계를 시험하기 위해서
② 지역 사회를 도울 수 있는 참가자들의 용기와 결의를 보이기 위해서
③ 신을 설득하여 참가자들이 자신들의 맹세를 이행하는 것을 돕도록 하기 위해서
④ 부족의 미래에 대한 환상과 신을 향한 참가자들의 동정심을 경험하기 위해서 |

| 해설 | 스스로 고행을 하는 주된 목적을 파악하는 문제이다. 두 번째 문단의 중반에서 태양 춤의 참가자들은 지역 사회를 대신하여 말 그대로 고통을 겪고 신을 불러내어 자신들을 불쌍히 여기고 자신들의 맹세를 이행할 수 있게 도와달라고 요청한다고 설명하고 있다. 따라서 정답은 ③번이다. |

| 어휘 | **endure** v. 견디다, 참다　**physical** adj. 육체적인, 신체적인
courage n. 용기　**determination** n. 결의 |

09 교육

01-22
문제집 p.266

01 ②	02 ④	03 ④	04 ②	05 ②
06 ④	07 ③	08 ①	09 ①	10 ①
11 ⑤	12 ④	13 ①	14 ①	15 ①
16 ③	17 ①	18 ①	19 ①	20 ①
21 ②	22 ④			

01 2018 한양대
정답 ②

해석 초기의 교사 양성에 대한 어떤 접근 방법에서든 핵심 문제들 중의 하나는 훈련과 교육 사이에서 맞춰져야 하는 균형이다. [C] 그렇긴 하지만, 전자(training)는 지난 몇 년간 적어도 교사를 교육하는 사람들 사이에서는 다소 인기를 잃었다. [B] 예를 들면, 자격 있는 교사 지위를 수여 하고 대학 졸업자들을 공립학교에서 근무하도록 허가하는, 영국 PGCE 프로그램의 초보 교사들은 오늘날 흔히 'trainee teachers'보다는 'student teachers'라고 불린다. [A] 명명법에서의 이런 변화는 'trainee'와 'training'이 암시한다고 여겨지는, 대체로 백지상태로 간주되는 초보자들에게 미리 정해져 있는 일련의 행동을 전달한다는 함축된 의미와의 부정적인 연상을 피하려는 것이다.

해설 주어진 지문 다음에 이어질 [A], [B], [C]의 적절한 순서를 파악하는 문제이다. 주어진 지문은 '초기의 교사 양성에서 훈련과 교육의 균형을 잡는 것이 중요한 문제'라고 했는데, '훈련(training)과 교육(education) 중에서 전자인 training이라는 용어가 인기를 잃었다'고 언급한 [C]가 먼저 와야 한다. 그런 [C]의 내용을 student teachers와 trainee teachers의 예를 들어 설명하는 [B]가 이어지는 것이 자연스럽다. 그리고 '이러한 변화(This change)는 trainee와 training이라는 말이 함축하고 있는 부정적인 연상을 피하려는 것이라고 설명한 [A]가 그 뒤에 이어지는 것이 자연스럽다. [A]의 지시어 This change와 [B]의 연결어 For example 등이 문장의 순서를 정하는데 단서가 된다. 따라서 주어진 지문 다음에 이어질 순서는 ② [C] - [B] - [A]이다.

어휘 teacher preparation phr. 교사 양성
that said phr. 그렇긴 하지만, 그렇다고는 하지만
out of favor phr. 눈 밖에 난, 인기를 잃은
novice n. 초보자 PGCE n. 교사 자격 인증 석사
(Postgraduate Certificate in Education phr. 영국에서 일반 대학 졸업생이 석사 과정을 통해 취득할 수 있는 교사 자격증)
confer v. (학위·자격을) 수여 하다, 부여하다
qualified adj. 자격이 있는
refer to A as B phr. A를 B라고 부르다

nomenclature n. 명명법 association n. 연관, 연상
imply v. (넌지시) 나타내다, 풍기다
connotation n. 함축(된 의미) transmission n. 전파, 전달
blank slate phr. 백지상태

[02-03]

19세기 후반의 미국 대학들은 수학과 고전에 중점을 둔 규율, 도덕성, 그리고 교과과정을 교회 학교의 신학에서 윤리와 미사여구와 함께 주입하려고 시도했다. 역사, 현대 언어와 문학, 그리고 일부 과학 수업은 용인되었지만, 실험실 연구는 보통 수업에서 교수가 시범을 보이는 것으로 제한되었다. 대학 교사는 일시적인 피난처를 찾는 젊은 사람이나 안전한 은신처를 찾는 쇠진한 전도사인 경향이 많았다. 1871년에 한 작가가 전형적인 교수를 "별 특징이 없고, 측량과 라틴어 웅변을 가르칠 준비가 되어 있으며, 대학 울타리를 하얗게 칠하기 위해 그의 급여가 삭감되지 않으면 감사할 사람"이라고 불렀다.

seek to phr. ~하려고 시도하다 instill v. 주입하다
discipline n. 규율 morality n. 도덕성
curriculum n. 교과과정 theology n. 신학
ethics n. 윤리 rhetoric n. 미사여구
tolerate v. 용인하다, 참다 laboratory n. 실험실
demonstration n. 시범 be apt to phr. ~하는 경향이 있다
temporary adj. 일시적인 refuge n. 피난처
preacher n. 전도사 harbor n. 은신처, 항구
typical adj. 전형적인 nondescript adj. 별 특징 없는
surveying n. 측량 eloquence n. 웅변
salary n. 급여, 봉급 be docked phr. 삭감되다, 깎이다
whitewash v. 하얗게 칠하다

02 2019 가천대
정답 ④

해석 ① 연설가   ② 변덕스러운 사람
       ③ 잡일꾼   ④ 특색 없음

해설 밑줄 친 nondescript의 의미를 추론하는 문제이다. 밑줄 친 부분이 포함된 문장의 이전 문장에서 대학 교사는 일시적인 피난처를 찾는 젊은 사람이나 안전한 항구를 찾는 망가진 전도사인 경향이 많았다고 말하고 있다. 따라서, 밑줄 친 단어의 의미를 '특색 없음'이라고 한 ④번이 정답이다.

어휘 orator n. 연설가, 웅변가 chameleon n. 변덕스러운 사람
handyman n. 잡일꾼, 잡역부
anonymity n. 특색 없음, 익명

03 2019 가천대
정답 ④

해석 ① 19세기 후반에, 미국의 대학은 고전보다 현대 언어와 문학에 우선순위를 두었다.

② 장비를 많이 갖춘 실험실에서, 학생들은 스스로 실험을 수행하도록 장려되었다.
③ 대부분의 대학 교사들은 신학을 전공한 명성 높은 노인들이었다.
④ 교수들은 세속적인 보상으로부터 자신을 멀리하는 것 같지 않았다.

해설 지문의 내용과 일치하는 것을 묻는 문제이다. 지문의 마지막 문장에서 대학 울타리를 하얗게 칠하기 위해 그의 급여가 삭감되지 않으면 감사할 사람이라는 내용을 통해 교수들은 세속적인 보상으로부터 자신을 멀리하는 것 같지 않았다는 것을 알 수 있다. 따라서 ④번이 지문의 내용과 일치한다.

오답분석
① 19세기 후반의 미국 대학들은 수학과 고전에 중점을 둔 규율, 도덕성, 그리고 교과과정을 교회 학교의 신학에서 윤리와 미사여구와 함께 주입하려고 시도했다고 했으므로, 19세기 후반에, 미국의 대학은 고전보다 현대 언어와 문학에 우선순위를 두었다는 것은 지문의 내용과 다르다.
② 실험실 연구는 보통 수업에서 교수가 시범을 보이는 것으로 제한되었다고 했으므로, 장비를 많이 갖춘 실험실에서, 학생들은 스스로 실험을 수행하도록 장려되었다는 것은 지문의 내용과 다르다.
③ 대학 교사는 일시적인 피난처를 찾는 젊은 사람이나 안전한 항구를 찾는 망가진 전도사인 경향이 많았다고 했으므로, 대부분의 대학 교사들은 신학을 전공한 명성 높은 노인들이었다는 것은 지문의 내용과 다르다.

어휘 priority n. 우선순위 equipped adj. 장비를 갖춘
prestige adj. 명성 높은
hold oneself aloof phr. 자신을 멀리하다
worldy adj. 세속적인

04 (2017 서강대)

정답 ②

해석 중등과정 이후의 기관들은 의무교육 연령이 지난 학생들에게 교육을 제공한다. 미국에서, 중등과정 이후의 학생들은 매우 다양한 전통적 연령 및 비전통적 연령의 학생들인데 그 학생들의 목표는 아주 구체적인 직업 교육에서부터 교양 교육 습득과 같은 더 일반적인 목표에 이르기까지 그리고 추가적인 전문적 연구를 위해 고도로 전문화된 준비에 이르기까지 다양하다. 그러한 각각의 학생 집단을 위해 준수되는 이중 언어 방식의 역할과 범위는 상당히 다양하다. 미국에서 성인들을 위한 일부 이중 언어 프로그램은 특별한 정부 지원을 받을 자격을 갖춘 난민들처럼 특수한 사람들을 위해 단기적이고 매우 집중적인 직업 교육을 제공하기 위해 개발되어왔다. 같은 모국어를 공유하는 영어 학습자들이 많은 곳에서는, 참가자들로 하여금 가능한 한 빨리 일자리를 찾도록 도와주는 것을 목표로 한 비교적 단기적인 프로그램의 일부로서 모국어로 하는 교육이 포함될 수도 있다.
① 하지만, 그 기관들은 완전한 학위 수여 프로그램이 영어와 스페인어 둘 다를 이용해 제공된다는 점에서 사실은 이중 언어를 사용한다.
② 모국어를 이용한 교육을 포함한 이러한 이중 언어 프로그램은 최근 이민자들이 가장 많이 정착한 지역에서 발견되는 경향이 있다.
③ 최근의 한 연구는 영어 학습자들의 대부분이 학교를 영어 습득을 위해 정기적으로 이용하는 곳으로 간주한다는 것을 보여준다.
④ 학위 수여 프로그램에 등록된 중등과정 이후의 학생들은 제2의 언어로 제공되는 학문 교육을 이용할 것이다.

해설 주어진 지문의 뒤에 올 내용을 고르는 문제이다. 마지막 두 문장에서 '성인들을 위한 일부 이중 언어 프로그램은 특별한 정부 지원을 받을 자격을 갖춘 난민들처럼 특수한 사람들을 위해 단기적이고 매우 집중적인 직업 교육을 제공하기 위해 개발되어왔다'고 했으며, '같은 모국어를 공유하는 영어 학습자들이 많은 곳에서는, 그들의 모국어로 하는 교육이 포함될 수도 있다'고 했다. 즉 요약하면 '일부 이중 언어 프로그램은 난민들을 위해 영어뿐만 아니라 그들의 모국어로도 직업 교육을 제공한다'는 것이다. 따라서 '모국어를 이용한 교육을 포함한 이러한 이중 언어 프로그램은 최근 이민자들이 가장 많이 정착한 지역에서 발견되는 경향이 있다'는 내용이 지문의 뒤에 나올 것임을 알 수 있다. 따라서 ②번이 정답이다.

어휘 post-secondary adj. 중등과정 이후의
institution n. 기관, 시설; 제도
compulsory adj. 강제적인, 의무적인
occupational adj. 직업의, 직업과 관련된
liberal education phr. 일반교양 교육
approach n. (접근) 방법
bilingual adj. 이중 언어를 사용하는
observe v. 지키다, 준수하다   vocational adj. 직업의
qualify for phr. ~의 자격을 얻다
enroll v. 등록하다; 등록시키다   access n. 이용, 접근

[05-07]

미국인들이 1970년대 후반 교사의 무능력을 재발견했을 때, 언론은 교사 양성에 대한 문제점을 찾는 데 힘을 모았다. 미국인들이 반복적으로 들었듯이, 예비 교사들은 전문대와 대학교에서 가장 성적이 가장 안 좋은 학생들 가운데 존재했었다. 많은 시민들이 하락한 대학교 입학시험 점수에 분개했을 때, 시민들은 장래의 교사가 될 학생들의 시험 성적이 다른 학생들의 성적에 비하여 더 빠르게 떨어졌다는 것을 깨달았다. 교사 희망 학생들의 대학 진학 능력 기초시험(SAT)과 미국 대학 입학 시험(ACT)을 가지고 다른 학부생들과 비교하여 등급을 매겼을 때, 사범대에 다니는 학생들은 지속적으로 성적 하위권에서 있었으며, 오로지 농업이나 가정학과 같은 영역을 전공으로 삼는 학생들보다만 앞서 있었다. 사범대 교수들은 비난의 대부분을 떠안았으며, 언론은 책망했는데, 그 사범대 교수들은 1970년대 사범대 등록 저조에 맞춰서, 그들의 기준점을 예전에 낮췄기 때문이다.

rediscover v. 재발견하다 incompetency n. 무능력
join v. 힘을 합치다 trace v. 추적하다
prospective adj. 예비의 undergraduate adj. 학부의
bottom n. 밑바닥 major in phr. ~을 전공으로 삼다
charge v. 비난하다, 책망하다 enrollment n. 등록

05 2017 국민대

정답 ②

해석
① 그리고 ② 때문에
③ 반면에 ④ 그럼에도 불구하고

해설 빈칸에 적절한 연결어를 넣는 문제이다. 빈칸 앞은 사범대 교수들이 비난을 받고, 언론은 이를 책망했다는 내용이고, 빈칸 뒤는 이에 대한 이유로 교수들이 예전에 입학 기준을 낮췄었다는 내용이다. 따라서 병치가 가능한 등위 상관 접속사이자 이유와 원인을 나타내는 연결어인 ② for(~때문에)가 정답이다.

06 2017 국민대

정답 ④

해석
① 언론의 악영향
② 사범대 등록의 감소
③ 대학 입학시험에서 낮아지는 점수
④ 예비 교사들의 학업 능력의 저조

해설 지문의 주제를 묻는 문제이다. 지문의 처음에 교사들의 무능함을 재발견하고 이에 대한 원인을 규명하는 내용으로 글이 시작되며, 순차적으로 인과 관계를 따져서 교사들의 무능함의 원인을 밝혀내는 내용으로 전개가 된다. 따라서 이 지문의 주제를 '예비 교사들의 학업 능력의 저조'라고 표현한 ④번이 정답이다.

07 2017 국민대

정답 ③

해석
① 사람들은 교사들이 필요 이상의 학력이나 능력을 가졌다고 생각했다.
② 언론은 사범대 교수들에게 교수들의 기준을 낮추라고 요구했었다.
③ 예비 교사들은 종종 다른 전공을 가진 학생들보다 낮은 SAT 점수를 가지고 있었다.
④ 사범대 교수들은 자신들의 학생들로부터 매우 높은 학업 능력을 기대했었다.

해설 지문의 내용과 일치하는 것을 묻는 문제이다. 지문의 중간 Ranked against ~ in near the bottom의 내용을 통해 예비 교사들은 종종 다른 전공을 가진 학생들보다 낮은 SAT 점수를 가지고 있었다는 것을 알 수 있다. 따라서 ③번이 지문의 내용과 일치한다.

오답분석
① 사람들은 교사가 무능하다고 생각했으므로, 필요 이상의 학력이나 자격 등을 갖췄다고 생각했다는 것은 지문의 내용과 다르다.
② 언론은 교수들에게 입학점수를 낮춘 이유를 추궁한 것이므로, 언론이 기준을 낮추라고 요구했다는 것은 지문의 내용과 다르다.
④ 지문의 마지막에 등록 저조 때문에 기준을 낮췄다고 했으므로, 학생들에게 높은 학업 능력을 기대했다는 것은 지문의 내용과 다르다.

[08-10]

신경 다양성에 대한 생각은 정말로 우리가 특수교육에서 아이들을 어떻게 생각하는지에 대한 인식체계의 전환이다. 이 학생들을 결손, 질병, 기능 장애로 고생하고 있다고 여기는 대신에, 신경 다양성은 우리가 그들의 강점에 대해 말하도록 제안한다. <u>신경 다양성은 우리가 뇌의 다양성에 대해 우리가 생물 다양성과 문화 다양성에 대해 말할 때 이용하는 것과 같은 종류의 담론을 이용하여 논의하도록 촉구한다.</u> 우리는 컬러 백합이 "꽃잎 결손 장애"가 있다고 말하는 것으로 병리적으로 진단하지 않는다. 우리는 단순히 그 꽃의 독특한 아름다움을 감상한다. 우리는 우리와 다른 피부색을 가지고 있는 개인을 "색소 기능 장애"로 고생하고 있다고 진단하지 않는다. 그것은 인종차별적일 것이다. 이처럼, 우리는 다른 종류의 뇌와 다른 방식의 사고와 학습을 가지고 있는 아이들을 병리적으로 진단하면 안 된다.

neurodiversity n. 신경 다양성
paradigm shift phr. (획기적인) 인식체계의 전환
special education phr. 특수교육
regard v. 여기다, 간주하다 suffer v. 고생하다, 고통받다
deficit n. 결손 disease n. 질병
dysfunction n. 기능 장애 strength n. 강점
urge v. 촉구하다 discuss v. 토론하다 brain n. 뇌
discourse n. 담론, 대화 employ v. 이용하다
biodiversity n. 생물 다양성
cultural diversity phr. 문화 다양성
pathologize v. 병리적으로 진단하다 petal n. 꽃잎
disorder n. 장애 appreciate v. 감상하다
unique adj. 독특한 diagnose v. 진단하다
individual n. 개인 pigmentation n. 색소
racist adj. 인종 차별주의의 similarly adv. 이처럼, 비슷하게
ought to phr. ~해야 한다

08 2019 숙명여대

정답 ①

해석
① 신경 다양성과 인식체계의 전환
② 신경 다양성과 생물다양성과의 관계
③ 개인 특성을 진단하기 위한 방법으로서의 신경 다양성
④ 아이들의 강점과 가치를 개인화하기 위한 신경 다양성
⑤ 임상 치료의 근원으로서의 신경 다양성

해설 지문의 제목을 묻는 문제이다. 지문의 초반에서 신경 다양성은 특수교육에서 아이들을 어떻게 생각하는지에 대한 커다란 인식체계의 변환이 될 것이라고 말하였다. 따라서 이 지문의 제목을 '신경 다양성과 인식체계의 전환'이라고 표현한 ①번이 정답이다.

어휘 characteristic n. 특징   individualize v. 개인화하다
clinical adj. 임상의   treatment n. 치료

09 [2019 숙명여대]

정답 ①

해석 ① 진단하다   ② 동정하다
③ 동화되다   ④ 평가하다
⑤ 비판하다

해설 밑줄 친 pathologize의 의미를 추론하는 문제이다. 밑줄이 포함된 문장들을 보면, 우리는 컬러 백합이나 피부색이 다른 사람들을 보면서 "꽃잎 결핍 장애"나 "색소 기능 장애"라고 말하면서 'pathologize'하지 않는다고 설명하고 있다. 따라서, pathologize의 의미를 '진단하다'라고 한 ①번이 정답이다.

어휘 diagnose v. 진단하다   sympathize v. 동정하다
assimilate v. 동화되다   evaluate v. 평가하다
criticize v. 비판하다

10 [2019 숙명여대]

정답 ①

해석 ① 우리가 생물 다양성과 문화 다양성을 위해 사용하는 공통의 원칙은 뇌 다양성의 분야에도 적용되어야 한다.
② 담론 분석은 이 모든 세 영역에서 공통으로 사용될 수 있는 유용한 도구이다.
③ 신경 다양성은 우리의 집중을 생물 다양성과 문화 다양성의 영역으로 되돌린다.
④ 생물 다양성과 문화 다양성은 더 진보한 지식의 영역이다.
⑤ 생물 다양성과 문화 다양성은 심리학적 치료의 모델로서 사용된다.

해설 밑줄 친 Neurodiversity urges us ~ and cultural diversity의 의미를 추론하는 문제이다. 밑줄 친 문장 다음에 컬러 백합과 피부색이 다른 사람을 예시로 들면서 뇌의 다양성도 병리학적으로 진단하지 말아야 한다는 것을 설명하고 있다. 따라서, Neurodiversity urges us ~ and cultural diversity의 의미를 '우리가 생물 다양성과 문화 다양성을 위해 사용하는 공통의 원칙은 뇌 다양성의 분야에도 적용되어야 한다'라고 한 ①번이 정답이다.

어휘 common adj. 공통의, 흔한   apply v. 적용하다; 지원하다
area n. 영역, 구역   helpful adj. 유용한, 도움이 되는
tool n. 도구   bring back phr. 되돌리다
attention n. 집중   advanced adj. 진보한
knowledge n. 지식   model n. 모델, 견본
psychological adj. 심리학의

11 [2018 인하대]

정답 ⑤

해석 교육의 중요성이 점점 커진 것이 별도의 청년 문화가 등장하는데 기여했다. 20세기에는 개인의 삶에서 구별되는 기간으로서의 청소년기에 대한 개념은 대개 생소한 것이었다. 그것은 어느 정도 프로이트 심리학이 영향을 미친 결과였다. 그러나, 그것은 또한 젊은이가 직장에 들어갈 준비가 되기 전에 더 긴 기간의 훈련과 준비가 필요하다고 사회가 인식한 결과였다. 학교와 대학은 청소년들에게 그들 자신의 사교적 방식, 자신의 습관 그리고 자신의 관심과 활동을 개발할 수 있는 환경을 제공했다. 점점 더 많은 학생들이 학교를 단지 학문적인 교육을 위한 곳일 뿐만 아니라 체계적인 운동, 다른 과외 활동, 동아리, 남학생과 여학생의 사교 클럽 등을 위한 곳 — 즉, 그들에게 더욱 또래 집단의 관점에서 자신을 정의할 수 있게 해주는 기관 — 으로 간주했다.
① 젊은이들로 하여금 보수가 낮은 직업을 찾게 하는
② 현대 경제에서 요구되는 전문 기술을 가르치는 것을 전문으로 하는
③ 많은 사람들로 하여금 가족을 부양하기 위해 더 많은 돈을 벌도록 도와주는
④ 전통적인 학문 분야에서 교육과 서비스를 둘 다 제공하는
⑤ 그들에게 더욱 또래 집단의 관점에서 자신을 정의할 수 있게 해주는

해설 지문의 빈칸을 채우는 문제이다. 빈칸 앞 문장에서 '학교와 대학은 청소년들에게 그들 자신의 사교적 방식, 취미, 관심과 활동 등을 개발할 수 있는 환경을 제공했다'고 했으며, 빈칸 바로 앞에서는 학생들이 학교를 체계적인 운동, 다른 과외 활동, 동아리, 사교클럽 등을 위한 곳으로 간주한다고 했다. 따라서 이것을 부연하는 that is 뒤에 나온 빈칸에는 청소년들만의 독특한 문화(첫 문장에서 말한 a separate youth culture)를 형성할 수 있게 되었다는 내용이 나와야 적절하다는 것을 알 수 있다. 따라서 ⑤번이 정답이다.

어휘 adolescence n. 청소년기   distinct adj. 구별되는, 별개의
in some measure phr. 어느 정도, 약간
extended adj. 길어진, 늘어난
athletics n. 육상경기, 운동경기
extracurricular adj. 정규 교과 이외의, 과외의
fraternity n. (직종·이해관계·신념이 같은 사람들의) 협회, 조합; (미국 대학의) 남학생 사교 클럽
sorority n. (미국 대학의) 여학생 클럽
discipline n. 규율, 기강; 징계; 훈련, 수양; 학과목, 학문 분야

[12-13]

현재의 교육 제도는 훈련과 교육 사이의 차이를 얼버무려왔다. 대부분의 대학과 대학교의 행정부는 현대의 기업을 거울삼아 그들의 기관을 세움으로써 예산 제약과 (A)불안정한 고용 시장으로 인해 야기된 경제적 그리고 문화적 불확실성에 대응해 왔다. 그 결과, 많은 이들이 훈련을 전면에 내밀고 그것을 교육

이라 부른다. 학생들을 사회화하는 통일된 국가 문화와 독립 과정을 안내할 수 있는 (B)교육 철학이 결여된 채, 교육 제도는 전반적으로 학생들에게 졸업과 동시에 취업 준비를 요구하는 (C)시장 논리에 사로잡혀 있다. 이러한 의무 아래에서 대학과 대학교들은 학생들에게 (D)경쟁적인 취업 시장에 준비시키는 교육 프로그램을 시행할 수 없다. 대신, 교육계 지도자들은 "우수함"이라는 주문을 외치는데, 이는 대학교의 모든 부분이 "시행함"을 의미하며, 그들은 기업 경제에 지식과 자격을 갖춘 노동력을 얼마나 잘 전달하고, 행정부가 이 제도를 유지하는 데 필요한 채용과 자금 목표를 얼마나 잘 달성하는가에 따라 판단된다.

---

academic adj. 교육의, 학교의   fudge v. 얼버무리다
distinction n. 차이   administration n. 행정부
uncertainty n. 불확실성   provoke v. 야기하다
budget constraint phr. 예산 제약   volatile adj. 불안정한
construct v. 세우다, 건설하다   institution n. 기관
on the model of phr. ~을 거울삼아   corporation n. 기업
consequently adv. 그 결과, 따라서
thrust v. 내밀다, 밀어붙이다   to the fore phr. 전면에
unified adj. 통일된   socialize v. 사회화하다
philosophy n. 철학   steer v. 안내하다, 이끌다
imperative n. 의무, 책무   implement v. 시행하다
chant v. 외치다   mantra n. 주문, 기도
qualified adj. 자격을 갖춘   labor n. 노동력
fulfill v. 달성하다, 이행하다   recruitment n. 채용

12 2020 국민대
정답 ④

해설 밑줄 친 단어 중에서 문맥상 적절하지 않은 어휘를 고르는 문제이다. 대학교들이 학생들에게 취업에 대비하는 훈련만을 내세우고 있다는 점을 지적하고 있으므로 (D)에는 '경쟁적인 취업 시장'을 의미하는 the competitive job market이 아니라 '사회화'를 의미하는 socialization 또는 '독립'을 의미하는 independence가 들어가는 것이 자연스럽다. 따라서 ④번이 정답이다.

13 2020 국민대
정답 ①

해석 ① 대신   ② 사전에
③ 다행스럽게도   ④ 그렇기는 하지만

해설 빈칸에 적절한 연결어를 넣는 문제이다. 빈칸 앞 문장은 대학교들이 학생들에게 국가 문화와 교육 철학을 교육하는 데 실패한다는 내용이고, 빈칸 뒤 문장은 대학교 우수함의 판단 기준이 취업과 경영이라는 내용이다. 따라서 그 중간의 연결어로는 '대신'을 의미하는 Instead가 들어가는 것이 자연스럽다. 따라서 ①번이 정답이다.

어휘   proactively adv. 사전에, 적극적으로
nevertheless adv. 그렇기는 하지만, 그럼에도 불구하고

[14-15]

고등교육에서는, 우리는 교사의 요건에 집중하는 경향이 있는데, 교사는 어떤 교수법을 가져야 하는지, 많은 학생들을 가르치는 데 우리는 얼마나 많은 교사들이 필요한지, 교사가 되기 위해 필요한 능력을 구성하는 것이 무엇인지가 있다. 그리고 우리가 기술에 기반을 둔 교수법을 생각할 때, 우리는 (A)이분법으로 반응하는 경향이 있다. 우리는 온라인 교육과 다양한 형태의 인공 지능을 보았고, 이런 사실이 교사와 학생들 사이의 인간적 접촉의 가치에 위협이 되는 것을 포함할지도 모르기 때문에 우리는 기술에 반대하여 설교를 하거나, 기술이 우리를 다른 방식으로 사회화해 주는 것으로 간주하기 때문에, 알고리즘을 받아들인다. 어떤 식으로든 고등교육에서 가르치는 것이 무엇을 의미하는지 생각할 때, 우리는 사회적인 부분과 기술적인 부분을 서로 분리시키기 위해 매우 열심히 노력하는 경향이 있다. (B)그러나 앞으로 20년 또는 50년 동안의 과제는 교사가 알고리즘이 되고 알고리즘이 교사가 되는 시기를 생각하는 것이다. 지금 이 순간, 나는 우리가 그 문제(C)를 크게 다루기 시작했다고 생각하지 않는다.

---

needs n. 욕구, 요구, 필요한 것   constitute v. 구성하다
practice n. 관행; 능력, 기술   preach v. 설교하다
embrace v. 포용하다, 받아들이다
algorithm n. 알고리즘, 계산법, 수식
one way or another phr. 어떤 식으로든
grapple with phr. ~을 해결하려고 노력하다, 다루다, 처리하다

14 2018 숙명여대
정답 ①

해석 ① 이분법의   ② 부정적인
③ 차분한   ④ 긍정적인
⑤ 예상치 못한

해설 지문의 빈칸을 채우는 문제이다. 지문의 빈칸 (A)의 뒤에서 기술(알고리즘)에 대해 반대하거나 받아들인다고 했으므로, 빈칸에는 반대되는 입장을 표현해주는 단어가 나와야 적절하다는 것을 알 수 있다. 따라서 '이분법의'라고 한 ①번이 정답이다.

15 2018 숙명여대
정답 ①

해설 빈칸에 적절한 연결어와 전치사를 넣는 문제이다. 빈칸 (B)의 앞에 내용은 기술과 사회적인 부분에 대한 분리를 말하고 있지만, 빈칸의 뒤에서는 교사와 알고리즘의 구분이 없어지는 반대되는 내용이 나와 있다. 따라서 역접을 나타내는 연결어인 ①번의 However와 ②번의 Nevertheless가

가능하지만, 빈칸 (C)의 경우 앞에 나온 동사 grapple의 용법에 맞는 전치사를 골라야 하므로 '(문제 등) ~을 다루다, 처리하다, 해결하다'의 의미를 나타내는 with를 선택해야 하므로, ① However — with가 정답이다.

[16-18]

> 동아시아 국가들에서 가장 근시인 사람들이 모두 수학 성적표와 관련 있다는 것은 우연의 일치가 아니다. Hammond 교수는 "이 아이들은 아주 어린 나이부터 매우 집중적인 교육으로 몰아붙여 지고 많은 시간을 실내에서 가까이에 있는 것을 공부하면서 보내고 바깥에서는 아주 조금의 시간만 보냅니다. [A] 그래서 걱정되는 것은 스마트폰을 가지고 노는 것과 같이 모든 가까이에서 하는 것들이 그 아이들이 더 근시가 되도록 만들 가능성이 있다는 것입니다."라고 말한다.
> [B] 그러면 우리는 스마트폰 화면을 보지 못하게 막거나 제한해야 할까? [C] 음, 말하기는 쉽지만, 행동으로 옮기기는 쉽지 않다! 어떤 부모라도 아이들이 그들이 가장 사랑하는 휴대폰에 관해서라면 뼈다귀를 가진 개들과 같다는 것을 알 것이다. [D] 아이들에게서 그 기기를 떼어놓으려고 하는 것을 훨씬 더 불가능하며, 확실히 엄청난 말다툼 없이는 더 그렇다.
> 세 아이의 어머니인 Dr. Dahlmann-Noor는 스마트폰 화면을 보지 못하게 막는 것은 아마 비현실적인 목표라고 말한다. Dr. Dahlmann-Noor는 "당신은 그 아이들에게 스마트폰이 눈을 근시로 만들 수 있고 아이들이 스마트폰을 하고 싶은 만큼 많이 사용해서는 안 된다고 말할 수밖에 없어요. [E] 하지만, 가슴에 손을 얹고, 저는 저희가 스마트폰으로부터 벗어날 수 있을 거라고 생각하지 않는데, 아이들은 학교 숙제를 노트북 컴퓨터와 iPad로 해야 하기 때문이에요. 그래서 저는 저희가 실제로 장래에 스마트폰 화면을 보는 것을 줄일 거라고 생각하지 않아요."라고 말한다.
>
> coincidence n. 우연의 일치   myopic adj. 근시안의
> correlate with phr. ~와 관련 있다
> league table phr. 성적표   intensive adj. 집중적인
> potential n. 가능성   short-sighted adj. 근시의
> youngster n. 아이, 청소년   beloved adj. 가장 사랑하는
> device n. 기기, 장치   massive adj. 엄청난, 거대한
> argument n. 말다툼, 언쟁, 논쟁   probably adv. 아마
> unrealistic adj. 비현실적인
> aspiration n. 목표, 염원의 대상

16 [2019 성균관대]

정답 ③

해설 지문의 흐름상 주어진 문장이 들어가기에 가장 적절한 위치를 고르는 문제이다. [C]의 앞 문장에서 스마트폰 화면을 보지 못하게 막거나 제한해야 하는지 묻고, 뒤 문장에서 어떤 부모라도 아이들이 그들이 가장 사랑하는 휴대폰에 관해서라면 뼈다귀를 가진 개들과 같다는 것을 알 것이라고 했으므로, [C]의 자리에 스마트폰 화면을 보지 못하게 막거나 제한하는 것이 말하기는 쉽지만, 행동으로 옮기기는 쉽지 않다는 것을 설명하는 주어진 문장 '음, 말하기는 쉽지만, 행동으로 옮기기는 쉽지 않다!'가 들어가야 글의 흐름이 자연스럽게 연결된다. 따라서 ③번이 정답이다.

17 [2019 성균관대]

정답 ①

해석 ① 진심으로   ② 두드러지게
③ 지체 없이   ④ 계속적으로
⑤ 연합하여

해설 밑줄 친 hand on heart의 의미를 추론하는 문제이다. 세 번째 문단에서 저는 저희가 스마트폰으로부터 벗어날 수 있을 거라고 생각하지 않는다며, 아이들은 학교 숙제를 노트북 컴퓨터와 iPad로 해야 하기 때문이라고 했다. 따라서, hand on heart의 의미를 '진심으로'라고 한 ①번이 정답이다.

18 [2019 성균관대]

정답 ④

해석 ① 노트북 컴퓨터를 사용하는 학교 숙제
② 스마트폰 사용
③ 과도한 수학 공부
④ 햇빛 노출
⑤ 많은 시간 동안 실내에서 공부하는 것

해설 동아시아 아이들의 근시에 대한 원인이 아닌 것을 파악하는 문제이다. 첫 번째 문단과 세 번째 문단에서 학교 숙제를 노트북 컴퓨터로 해야 하는 것, 스마트폰을 가지고 노는 것, 수학 성적표와 관련 있는 것, 많은 시간을 실내에서 공부하면서 보내는 것이 동아시아 국가들에서 아이들의 근시에 대한 원인이라고 했으므로, 동아시아 아이들의 근시에 대한 원인이 아닌 것은 '햇빛 노출'이다. 따라서 ④번이 정답이다.

어휘 excessive adj. 과도한

[19-22]

> [A] 교과서 종류는 그것이 어떤 학문과 관련 있는지와 관계없이, 학문적인 맥락에서 공통의 목적에 맞는데, 이것은 교과서 종류의 많은 일반적인 특징에 반영되어 있다. 교과서는 학문 중심적 지식을 전파함과 동시에, 다소 동등하지 않은 저자와 독자 간의 관계를 보여주는데, 저자는 그 학문의 전문가이며, 독자는 그 학문을 접해보지 않은 초보자이다. 하지만, 입문자들을 위한 명백한 지식을 전파하려는 이 노력은 가끔 '최첨단' 이론이라고 주장되는 것을 제공하려는 시도로 인해 위태로워진다. 그럼에도 불구하고 교과서는 보고, 질문, 상급 표시, 그리고 열거와 같은 다양한 수사적 기교를 빈번히 사용함으로써 많은 독자가 받아들이기 쉬운 '성문화된 지식의 저장소'로 여겨진다.

[B] 하지만, 전 학문에 걸친 교과서의 이러한 공통된 특징에도 불구하고, 학문의 문화는 여러 차원에서 다른데, 이 중 일부는 구성 양식의 제약, 지식 구조와 질문 규범에서의 차이, 표현, 전문 어휘 및 담론의 일반적 형태와 관련 있는 수사적인 상세한 지식의 대표적 양식, 그리고 이러한 학문을 가르치는 별개의 접근법을 포함한다.

[C] 학문적 지식이 구성되고 교육적 맥락에서 전달되는 방법을 비교하기 위해 법학과 경제학, 두 개의 학문으로 시작해보겠다. 표면적으로는, 두 학문은 모두 수사적인 측면, 절차, 그리고 결과 간의 관계를 강화하는 경향이 있다는 점에서 비슷한 것처럼 보인다. 마찬가지로, 두 학문은 또한 통합된 개념의 복잡성을 만들고 표현하며, 특정한 독자를 위해 문법적인 비유를 사용하여 학문적 지식을 정리한다. 비록 경영학에서는 사실과 수치가 절댓값을 지니고, 법학에서는 사실과 수치가 사회법률적 관계 내에서 얽힌 인간 행위로 구성되어 있긴 하지만, 두 학문은 사실과 수치를 언급하여 여러 개념 간 상호관계를 설명해야 하는 방식을 공유하기도 한다.

[D] 다른 여러 방식으로, 그 두 학문은 매우 다른 것처럼 보이는데, 특히 두 학문이 지식을 구성하기 위해 사용하는 수사적 전략 측면에서 그렇다. 경영학은 대체로 담론을 구성하는 방식에 있어서 적극적인 혁신에 의존한다. 실제로, 지난 수십 년간, 다른 여러 전문적인 글 맥락의 전달 방식에 있어서 혁신의 대부분은 경영학 분야의 전달 방식 변화에 의해 영감을 받은 것인데, 이것은 경제학 교과서에도 나타나 있다. 반면에, 법학은 담론을 구성하는 방식에 있어서 극도의 보수주의를 따른다. 이것은 그 분야의 다른 표현 형태에도 영향을 미쳤다. 법학 교과서 집필은 이런 점에서 예외가 없다.

---

irrespective of phr. ~와 관계없이   discipline n. 학문
associate with phr. 관련시키다
disseminate v. 전파하다   initiate v. 접하게 하다
novice n. 초보자   uncontested adj. 명백한
compromise v. 위태롭게 하다   cutting edge phr. 최첨단
repository n. 저장소   codify v. 성문화하다
accessible adj. 받아들이기 쉬운
rhetorical adj. 수사적인, 수사학의   enumeration n. 열거
constraint n. 제약   intimacy n. 상세한 지식
instructional adj. 교육적인   reinforce v. 강화하다
formulate v. 표현하다   integrated adj. 통합적인
interrelationship n. 상호관계
numerical value phr. 절댓값   entangle v. 얽히게 하다
aggressive adj. 적극적인   discourse n. 담론
communicative adj. 전달의   inspire v. 영감을 주다
conservatism n. 보수주의

---

19 [2019 아주대]

정답 ①

해석 ① 전 학문에 걸친 교과서의 이러한 공통된 특징에도 불구하고
② 기술적 개념의 정의와 설명과 관계없이
③ 많은 공통적인 학문의 차이와 관련하여
④ 서로 다른 학문의 유사하면서 광범위한 실제에 의하여
⑤ 종류와 전문 학문 간의 보편적인 관계 외에도

해설 지문의 빈칸을 채우는 문제이다. 빈칸 앞부분에서 교과서 종류는 어떤 학문과 관련 있는지와 관계없이, 학문적인 맥락에서 공통의 목적에 맞다고 하고, 빈칸 뒤에서 하지만(However) 학문 분야로서의 문화는 여러 차원에서 다르다는 서로 반대되는 내용이므로, 빈칸에는 '전 학문에 걸친 교과서의 이러한 공통된 특징에도 불구하고'가 들어가는 것이 자연스럽다. 따라서 ①번이 정답이다.

어휘 clarification n. 설명
with reference to phr. ~와 관련하여   variation n. 차이
by means of phr. ~에 의하여   discursive adj. 광범위한

20 [2019 아주대]

정답 ①

해석 ① 교과서 종류는 최신 정보를 제공한다.
② 교과서 종류는 학문 특유의 지식을 포함한다.
③ 교과서 종류는 다양한 수사적 전략을 사용한다.
④ 교과서 종류는 저자와 독자 간의 계층적 관계를 보여준다.
⑤ 교과서 종류는 한정된 독자 집단을 겨냥한 정보를 포함한다.

해설 교과서 종류의 특징으로 언급되지 않은 것을 파악하는 문제이다. [A] 문단 세 번째 문장에서 교과서는 입문자들을 위한 명백한 지식을 전파하려 노력하지만, 가끔 '최첨단' 이론이라고 주장되는 것을 제공하려는 시도로 인해 입문자들을 위한 지식을 전파하려는 노력이 위태로워진다고 했으므로, 교과서 종류의 특징으로 언급되지 않은 것은 '교과서 종류는 최신 정보를 제공한다'는 것이다. 따라서 정답은 ①번이다.

어휘 state-of-the-art adj. 최신의   involve v. 포함하다
hierarchical adj. 계층적인

21 [2019 아주대]

정답 ②

해석 ① 복잡하게 통합된 개념이 구성될 수 있다.
② 사실과 수치의 절댓값이 강조될 수 있다.
③ 학문 중심적 정보를 전달하기 위해 비유가 사용될 수 있다.
④ 개념의 연관성을 분명히 보여주기 위해 사실과 수치가 사용될 수 있다.
⑤ 수사학적인 측면, 절차, 그리고 결과 간의 관계가 강화될 수 있다.

해설 경제학과 법학의 공통된 특징이 아닌 것을 파악하는 문제이다. [C] 문단의 마지막 문장에서 경영학에서는 사실과 수치가 절댓값을 지니고, 법학에서는 사실과 수치가 사회법률적 관계 내에서 얽힌 인간 행위로 구성된다는 차이점을 언급했

으로, 경제학과 법학의 공통된 특징이 아닌 것은 '사실과 수치의 절댓값이 강조될 수 있다'는 것이다. 따라서 정답은 ②번이다.

어휘 complicatedly adv. 복잡하게   emphasize v. 강조하다
convey v. 전달하다   illustrate v. 분명히 보여주다
association n. 연관성   consolidate v. 강화하다, 굳히다

22   2019 아주대

정답 ④

해석 ① 교과서는 이러한 두 개의 목적에 따라 만들어진다.
② 이 두 개의 표현은 법률과 관련된 교과서가 집필되는 방식에 영향을 주었다.
③ 이 두 개의 표현은 학문적 지식이 전달되는 중요한 방법이다.
④ 그 두 표현은 경영학과 법학 각각에 대한 특유의 성질이다.
⑤ 교과서는 보수주의에서 혁신으로 그것의 초점을 바꾸었다.

해설 "적극적인 혁신"과 "극도의 보수주의"라는 표현이 언급된 이유를 파악하는 문제이다. [D] 문단 첫 번째 문장에서 경영학과 법학은 지식을 구성하기 위해 사용하는 수사적 전략 측면에서 매우 다르게 보인다고 했으므로, 두 표현이 언급된 이유는 '그 두 표현은 경영학과 법학 각각에 대한 특유의 성질'이기 때문이다. 따라서 정답은 ④번이다.

어휘 pivotal adj. 중요한   properties n. 속성
characteristic adj. 특유의

10 심리

01-77

문제집 p.278

01	④	02	③	03	③	04	①	05	⑤
06	③	07	④	08	②	09	⑤	10	①
11	④	12	②	13	①	14	①	15	②
16	③	17	④	18	③	19	④	20	④
21	①	22	②	23	③	24	②	25	③
26	⑤	27	①	28	②	29	④	30	①
31	③	32	②	33	②	34	③	35	④
36	②	37	④	38	②	39	③	40	③
41	④	42	②	43	②	44	①	45	②
46	⑤	47	③	48	③	49	③	50	④
51	④	52	②	53	③	54	①	55	④
56	③	57	①	58	①	59	④	60	②
61	④	62	②	63	④	64	③	65	③
66	①	67	②	68	②	69	③	70	①
71	①	72	②	73	②	74	④	75	④
76	①	77	②						

01 [2020 인하대]

정답 ④

해석 심리학자들이 매우 창의적인 사람들의 삶을 볼 때, 그들이 발견한 것은 생각을 교환하고 생각을 발전시키는 데 능숙한 사람들이지만 심각하게 내향적인 경향이 있는 사람들도 있다. 그리고 이는 고독이 종종 창의성에 있어서 결정적인 요소이기 때문이다. 찰스 다윈은 숲속에서 혼자서 오랫동안 산책을 하였고 저녁 파티 초대를 단호하게 거절했다. Steve Wozniak은 당시 그가 일하고 있었던 Hewlett-Packard사의 좁은 방에 홀로 앉아 최초의 애플 컴퓨터를 발명했다. 그리고 그는 그가 자라면서 너무 내성적이라서 집을 떠날 수 없지 않았다면 처음에는 그런 전문가가 되지 않았을 것이라고 말한다.
① 조화 — 외로운
② 고독 — 외향적인
③ 완고함 — 외향적인
④ 고독 — 내향적인
⑤ 완고함 — 내향적인

해설 지문의 빈칸을 채우는 문제이다. 지문의 첫 번째 문장에서 창의적인 사람들의 삶을 볼 때, 심각하게 내향적인 경향이 있다고 했고, 두 번째 빈칸 앞 문장에서 Steve Wozniak이 좁은 방에 홀로 앉아 애플 컴퓨터를 발명했다고 했으므로, 첫 번째와 두 번째 빈칸 모두에는 내향성과 관련 있는 내용이 나와야 적절하다는 것을 알 수 있다. 따라서 ④ solitude(고독) — introverted(내향적인)가 정답이다.

어휘 psychologist n. 심리학자 streak n. 경향, 기질
introversion n. 내향성 crucial adj. 결정적인, 중대한
ingredient n. 요소 emphatically adv. 단호하게
turn down phr. 거절하다 cubicle n. 좁은 방
solitude n. 고독 extroverted adj. 외향적인, 사교적인
stubbornness n. 완고함, 완강함
introverted adj. 내향적인, 내성적인

02 [2020 건국대]

정답 ③

해석 사회학자들과 심리학자들은 어떻게 인간의 성격이 형성되는지에 대해 수 세기 동안 논쟁을 벌여왔다. 이 논쟁은 두 가지 (A)상반된 이론을 설명하는 '본성 대 양육'으로 오랫동안 알려져 왔다. 첫 번째 이론은 태어나기 전에 성격이 (B)유전적으로 형성된다고 말한다. 이 이론에 따르면, 본성이 유전적 특성을 통해 어떤 사람이 될 것인지 결정한다고 한다. 이와는 반대로, 다른 이론에서는 신생아는 어떤 (C)부족한 성격도 가지지 않는다고 말한다. 아이들의 성격은 그 혹은 그녀가 자라면서 발달하고, 이 성격의 발달은 아이의 가족과 사회적인 환경에 (D)영향을 받아 형성된다는 것이다. 따라서 두 번째 이론에 따르면, 가장 (E)중요한 것은 문화적, 사회적 요인들이다.

해설 밑줄 친 단어 중에서 문맥상 적절하지 않은 어휘를 고르는 문제이다. 양육 이론에서는 신생아에게 확실한 성격적 특성을 가지고 태어나지 않는다는 내용이므로 (C)에는 '부족한'을 의미하는 deficient가 아니라 '확실한'을 의미하는 definite가 들어가는 것이 자연스럽다. 따라서 ③번이 정답이다.

어휘 nature n. 본성 opposing adj. 상반된
genetically adv. 유전적으로 deficient adj. 부족한

[03-04]

연구는 예를 들어 현실 관계에서 눈과 눈을 마주치는 것의 중요성을 보여주며, 한 사람이 눈을 마주치는 패턴의 특성이, 다른 사람의 눈을 똑바로 쳐다보든지 혹은 곁눈질을 하거나 시선을 좌우로 옮기든지 간에 중요한 역할을 할 수 있다는 것을 나타낸다. 하지만, 특정한 어린이 프로그램에서 사람들이 아이들에게 직접 말을 하도록 의도하고, 카메라가 촬영되고 있는 사람에 직접 초점을 맞춤으로 이러한 착각을 만들어낸다고 하더라도, 아이들이 텔레비전을 보는 관계에서 눈을 마주친다는 것은 가능하지 않다. 이러한 현실 관계의 왜곡이 아이들의 신뢰, 개방, 그리고 다른 '실제' 사람들과 좋은 관계를 맺는 능력의 발달에 어떻게 영향을 줄 수 있을까? 텔레비전 화면에서 오는 따뜻한 언어적 의사소통과 소위 텔레비전 인격체라고 감정적으로 깊이 호소하는 것에 하루의 대부분을 수동적으로 듣도록 가르침을 받고 조건화되어온 아이들은 숙련된 배우에게보다 감정이 훨씬 덜 생기기 때문에 종종 실제 사람들에 반응하기 어렵다.

indicate v. 나타내다 squarely adv. 똑바로
gaze n. 곁눈질 significant adj. 중요한
purport v. 의도하다 illusion n. 착각 distortion n. 왜곡
verbal adj. 언어적인

03 2020 단국대

정답 ③

해석 ① 대신에   ② 따라서
③ 하지만   ④ 더욱이

해설 빈칸에 적절한 연결어를 넣는 문제이다. 빈칸 앞 문장은 눈을 마주치는 것이 중요하다는 내용이고, 빈칸 뒤 문장은 아이들이 텔레비전을 보면서 눈을 마주치는 것은 불가능하다는 내용이다. 따라서 역접을 나타내는 연결어인 ③ However(하지만)가 정답이다.

04 2020 단국대

정답 ①

해석 ① 눈을 마주치는 다양한 방법들이 있다.
② 텔레비전 시청자들은 숙련된 배우에게 어떻게 눈을 맞춰야 하는지를 배워야 한다.
③ 실제 사람들은 텔레비전 화면에 있는 사람보다 더 많은 감정을 생기게 한다.
④ 텔레비전 화면에 있는 사람에게 초점을 맞추는 것은 아이들이 다른 사람들과 관계를 더 잘 맺을 수 있게 한다.

해설 지문의 내용과 일치하는 것을 묻는 문제이다. 지문의 처음에서 한 사람이 눈을 마주치는 패턴의 특성이, 다른 사람의 눈을 똑바로 쳐다보든지 혹은 곁눈질을 하거나 시선을 좌우로 옮기든지 간에 중요한 역할을 할 수 있다는 것을 나타낸다는 내용을 통해 눈을 마주치는 다양한 방법들이 있다는 것을 알 수 있다. 따라서 ①번이 지문의 내용과 일치한다.

오답 ② 아이들이 텔레비전을 보는 관계에서 눈을 마주친다는 것
분석 은 가능하지 않다고 했으므로, 텔레비전 시청자들은 숙련된 배우에게 어떻게 눈을 맞춰야 하는지를 배워야 한다는 것은 지문의 내용과 다르다.
③ 아이들은 숙련된 배우에게보다 감정이 훨씬 덜 생긴다고 했으므로, 실제 사람들은 텔레비전 화면에 있는 사람보다 더 많은 감정을 생기게 한다는 것은 지문의 내용과 다르다.
④ 하루의 대부분을 텔레비전 화면에서 오는 따뜻한 언어적 의사소통을 수동적으로 듣도록 가르침을 받아온 아이들은 숙련된 배우에게보다 감정이 훨씬 덜 생긴다고 했으므로, 텔레비전 화면에 있는 사람에게 초점을 맞추는 것은 아이들이 다른 사람들과 관계를 더 잘 맺을 수 있게 한다는 것은 지문의 내용과 다르다.

어휘 diverse adj. 다양한

[05-07]

나는 최근에 유명 대학의 교수인 친구와 이야기를 나누었다. 내 친구는 빈번하게 여행을 다니고 종종 술집, 식당, 그리고 공항에서 낯선 이들과 대화를 나눈다. 그 친구는 다양한 경험을 통해 이와 같은 대화에서 절대 그의 교수라는 직업을 사용하지 않아야 한다는 것을 배웠다고 말한다. 그는 그가 그렇게 하면, 그 대화의 성격이 바로 변한다고 전한다. 30분 전만 해도 즉흥적이고 흥미로운 대화 상대였던 사람이 공손해지고, 수용적이 되며, 지루해지는 것이다. 이전이라면 활발한 교환을 만들었을지 모르는 그의 의견들은 이제 대개 동의에 의한 연장된 서술을 만들어 낸다. 그는 "나는 여전히 30분 전에 그들과 대화를 나누었던 똑같은 사람인데 말이야, 그렇지?"라고 말한다. 내 친구는 이제 그와 같은 상황에서 그의 직업에 대해 철저히 거짓말을 한다.

faculty member phr. 교수, 교수진   chat v. 대화를 나누다
conversation n. 대화 spontaneous adj. 즉흥적인
respectful adj. 공손한 dull adj. 지루한
extended adj. 연장된 statement n. 서술
accord n. 동의 occupation n. 직업

05 2021 경희대

정답 ⑤

해석 ① 낯선 사람을 만났을 때 당신의 직업을 자랑하지 말라.
② 술집, 식당 그리고 공항에서 낯선 사람들과 대화를 나눌 때 개인 정보에 대해 말하는 것은 위험하다.
③ 대화 중에 당신의 직함을 사용함으로써 당신은 사람들을 불쾌하게 만들 수 있다.
④ 심지어 흥미로운 대화들도 30분이 지나면 지루해질 수 있다.
⑤ 우리의 행동은 흔히 그 직함을 가지고 있는 사람의 천성보다 직함 자체에 의해 더 영향을 받는다.

해설 지문의 요지를 묻는 문제이다. 지문 전반에 걸쳐 교수인 화자의 친구가 술집, 식당, 공항에서 만난 사람들과 대화를 할 때, 자신의 직업을 밝히면, 대화 상대의 태도가 바뀐다는 내용을 설명하고 있고, 지문의 후반에 "나는 여전히 30분 전에 그들과 대화를 나누었던 똑같은 사람인데 말이야, 그렇지?"라고 화자의 친구가 언급한 내용이 있다. 따라서 이 지문의 요지를 '우리의 행동은 흔히 그 직함을 가지고 있는 사람의 천성보다 직함 자체에 의해 더 영향을 받는다'라고 표현한 ⑤번이 정답이다.

오답 ① 화자의 친구가 낯선 사람들과의 대화에서 자신의 직업을
분석 밝히지 않는다고는 했지만, 이것이 직업을 자랑해서는 안 된다는 것을 의미하지는 않는다.
② 술집, 식당 그리고 공항에서 낯선 사람들과 대화를 나눌 때 개인 정보에 대해 말하는 것이 위험하다는 내용은 지문에서 언급되지 않았다.
③ 대화 중에 직함을 사용하는 것이 사람들을 불쾌하게 만들 수 있다는 내용은 지문에서 언급되지 않았다.

④ 흥미로운 대화들도 30분이 지나면 지루해질 수 있다는 내용은 지문에서 언급되지 않았다.

어휘 boast v. 뽐내다 personal information phr. 개인 정보
offend v. 불쾌하게 만들다

06 [2021 경희대]
정답 ③

해설 주어진 지문에서 '성격'이라는 의미로 사용된 tenor의 동의어를 묻는 문제이다. ①번 burden은 '부담', ②번 evaluation은 '평가', ④번 theme은 '주제', ⑤번 purpose는 '목적'이라는 의미이므로 답이 될 수 없다. 반면 ③번 atmosphere는 '분위기'라는 의미인데, 대화의 성격은 대화의 분위기와 비슷한 의미를 갖는다고 할 수 있으므로 ③번이 정답이다.

07 [2021 경희대]
정답 ④

해석 ① 몹시 화가 난   ② 슬픈
③ 매우 기뻐하는   ④ 당황한
⑤ 감상적인

해설 주어진 지문의 밑줄 친 부분에 나타난 어조를 묻는 문제이다. 직업을 밝혔을 때, 대화를 나누던 상대의 태도가 갑자스럽게 변화했다고 했으므로, "나는 여전히 30분 전에 그들과 대화를 나누었던 똑같은 사람인데 말이야, 그렇지?"라는 표현에는 당황스러움이 담겨 있음을 추론할 수 있다. 따라서 ④번이 정답이다.

[08-09]

공상에 잠기는 것처럼, 혼잣말하는 것은 당신이 생각을 정리하는 데 도움이 되고, 당신이 특정 목표를 실현하는 것에도 도움이 될 수 있다. Dr. Schneberger는 "때때로 사람들이 있는 데서 혼잣말을 하다가 갑자기 멈추게 되는데, 우리는 '미친' 것처럼 보이고 싶지 않기 때문에 당황스러울 수 있지만, 그것은 완전히 정상적인 거예요. 모두가 그렇게 하거든요."라고 말한다. Dr. Schneberger는 큰소리로 혼잣말하는 것이 "우리 주위를 살피는 데 대한 거르지 못한 무의식적인 반응"이라고 설명하는데, 이때 당신은 마치 당신이 말을 고쳐야 하거나 다른 사람들로부터 평가받아야 하는 것처럼 아무런 생각 없이 당신이 무슨 생각을 하는지를 전달하는 것이다. Dr. Breur는 동의하면서, 혼잣말하는 것은 당신이 살아가면서 직면하는 많은 책임감과 압박감을 해결하는 데 도움이 될 수 있다고 덧붙인다. Dr. Breur는 그렇지만 부정적인 자기 대화는 주의하라고 말한다. "나는 너무 멍청해"와 같은 말은 감정적으로 해로울 수 있으므로, 그런 표현은 더 긍정적인 것으로 대신하려고 노력해라. 스스로에게 너무 심하게 대하지 않도록 하는 몇 가지 방법이 있다.

daydream v. 공상에 잠기다
talk to oneself phr. 혼잣말하다 thought n. 생각
certain adj. 특정한 in public phr. 사람들이 있는 데서
normal adj. 정상적인, 평범한
unfiltered adj. 거르지 못한, 여과되지 않은
unconscious adj. 무의식적인 survey v. 살피다
convey v. 전달하다 alter v. 고치다, 바꾸다
judge v. 판단하다, 여기다
sort out phr. 해결하다, ~을 정리하다
responsibility n. 책임감 pressure n. 압박감
face v. 직면하다, 향하다
be mindful of phr. ~에 잘 주의하다
negative adj. 부정적인, 나쁜 self-talk n. 자기 대화
phrase n. 말, 구절
emotionally adv. 감정적으로, 정신적으로
damaging adj. 해로운, 불리한
replace v. 대신하다, 대체하다 statement n. 표현, 진술
positive adj. 긍정적인

08 [2019 성균관대]
정답 ②

해석 ① 모두가 특별하다
② 당신은 혼자가 아니다
③ 예외 없는 규칙은 없다
④ 아름다움은 피상적이다
⑤ 아무리 안 좋은 상황에서도 한 가지 긍정적인 측면은 있다

해설 Dr. Schneberger의 요점을 파악하는 문제이다. 두 번째 문장에서 Dr. Schneberger는 "때때로 사람들이 있는 데서 혼잣말을 하다가 갑자기 멈추게 되는데, 우리는 '미친' 것처럼 보이고 싶지 않기 때문에 당황스러울 수 있지만, 그것은 완전히 정상적인 거예요. 모두가 그렇게 하거든요."라고 말한다고 했으므로, Dr. Schneberger의 요점은 '당신은 혼자가 아니다'이다. 따라서 ②번이 정답이다.

어휘 exception n. 예외 skin deep phr. 피상적인
every cloud has a silver lining phr. 아무리 안 좋은 상황에서도 한 가지 긍정적인 측면은 있다

09 [2019 성균관대]
정답 ⑤

해석 ① 다른 사람들을 욕하는 것
② 입에 담을 수 없는 말을 하는 것
③ 다른 사람들의 이야기를 방해하는 것
④ 항상 혼자 노는 것
⑤ 자신에게 모든 책임을 지우는 것

해설 사람들이 있는 데서 혼잣말하는 것은 괜찮지만, 어떤 것은 괜찮지 않은지를 파악하는 문제이다. 지문의 후반에서 부정적인 자기 대화는 주의하라고 하면서, 스스로에게 너무 심하게

대하지 않도록 하는 몇 가지 방법이 있다고 했으므로, 사람들이 있는 데서 혼잣말하는 것은 괜찮지만, '자신에게 모든 책임을 지우는 것'은 괜찮지 않다는 것을 알 수 있다. 따라서 ⑤번이 정답이다.

어휘 curse v. ~을 욕하다, 저주하다
dirty word phr. 입에 담을 수 없는 말, 금기 어구

[10-12]

사회적 존재로서, 우리가 다른 사람들과 잘 지내는 것은 자연스럽다. 우리의 생존과 성공은 다른 사람들과 잘 지내는 것에 달려 있다. 하지만, 건전한 사회적 행동과 상습적으로 눈치 보는 것으로 인해 감정 소모를 경험하는 것 사이에는 적정선이 있다. 상습적으로 눈치를 보는 것의 흔한 조짐들과 상습적으로 눈치 보는 것을 극복하기 위한 몇 가지 방법들이 있다. [A] 사회 심리학자 Susan Newman에 따르면, 눈치 보는 사람들은 주변에 있는 모든 사람들이 행복하기를 바라고, 주변 모든 사람들이 행복해하는 것을 유지하기 위해 자신들이 부탁받는 것은 무엇이든 할 것이다. 눈치 보는 사람들은 흔히 누군가가 자신에게 도움을 요청할 때 <u>된다</u>고 말해야 할 것 같다고 느낀다. 도움 요청을 승낙하는 것은 눈치 보는 사람들이 자신을 중요한 사람이라고 느끼게 하고 자신이 다른 사람의 삶에 기여하고 있다고 느끼게 한다. 눈치 보는 사람들은 자신이 <u>안 된다</u>고 말할 때 다른 사람들이 자신들을 어떻게 볼지 걱정한다. 사람들은 게으르거나, 이기적이거나, 완전히 자기중심적인 것처럼 보이고 싶어 하지 않는다. 사람들은 자신들이 친구들, 가족 혹은 직장 동료든지 간에 환영받지 못하고 그 그룹으로부터 단절될 것을 두려워한다. [B] 눈치 보는 사람들은 외부로부터의 검증을 몹시 받고 싶어 한다. 임상 심리학자 Linda Tillman은 눈치 보는 사람들 개인의 안전하다는 느낌과 자신감은 다른 사람들의 인정을 받는 것에 기초한다고 말했다. Linda Tillman은 따라서 눈치 보는 사람들이 마음속으로 자신감이 부족하다고 말했다. [C] 눈치 보는 많은 사람들이 깨닫지 못하고 있는 것은 눈치 보는 것에 심각한 위험 요소들이 있을 수 있다는 것이다. 눈치 보는 것은 눈치 보는 사람들에게 많은 압박을 가하고 스트레스를 줄 뿐만 아니라, 근본적으로 눈치 보는 사람들이 너무 눈치를 보는 바람에 자신을 병들게 만들 수도 있다. [D] <u>당신이 눈치 보는 사람이 되지 않도록 도와줄 많은 전략들이 있다. 누군가 당신에게 부탁할 때마다 당신에게는 항상 안 된다고 말할 선택권이 있다는 것을 기억해라. 당신의 우선순위를 정해라. 당신의 우선순위와 가치를 아는 것은 당신이 눈치 보는 것을 멈추도록 도와줄 것이다.</u>

depletion n. 소모, 고갈 chronic adj. 상습적인, 만성적인
overcome v. 극복하다, 이기다 selfish adj. 이기적인
egocentric adj. 자기중심적인
yearn v. 몹시 ~하고 싶어 하다, 갈망하다 validation n. 검증
at the core phr. 마음속에서

10 [2021 세종대]

정답 ①

해석 ① 된다 - 안 된다 ② 된다 - 된다
③ 안 된다 - 안 된다 ④ 안 된다 - 된다

해설 지문의 빈칸을 채우는 문제이다. 세 번째 문단 중간에서 도움 요청을 승낙하는 것은 눈치 보는 사람들이 자신을 중요한 사람이라고 느끼게 하고 자신이 다른 사람의 삶에 기여하고 있다고 느끼게 한다는 것으로 보아, 첫 번째 빈칸에는 눈치 보는 사람들은 누군가가 자신에게 도움을 요청할 때 된다고 말해야 할 것 같다고 느낀다는 내용이 나와야 하므로, '된다'라는 의미의 yes가 들어가는 것이 자연스럽다. 또한, 세 번째 문단 끝에서 사람들은 친구들, 가족 혹은 직장 동료 그룹으로부터 단절될 것을 두려워한다는 것으로 보아, 두 번째 빈칸에는 눈치 보는 사람들은 자신이 안 된다고 말할 때 다른 사람들이 자신들을 어떻게 볼지 걱정한다는 내용이 나와야 하므로, '안 된다'라는 의미의 no가 들어가는 것이 자연스럽다. 따라서 ① yes - no가 정답이다.

11 [2021 세종대]

정답 ④

해석 당신이 눈치 보는 사람이 되지 않도록 도와줄 많은 전략들이 있다. 누군가 당신에게 부탁할 때마다 당신에게는 항상 안 된다고 말할 선택권이 있다는 것을 기억해라. 당신의 우선순위를 정해라. 당신의 우선순위와 가치를 아는 것은 당신이 눈치 보는 것을 멈추도록 도와줄 것이다.

해설 지문의 흐름상 주어진 단락이 들어가기에 가장 적절한 위치를 고르는 문제이다. 주어진 단락은 '당신이 눈치 보는 사람이 되지 않도록 도와줄 많은 전략들'에 관한 내용이다. 이 단락을 [D] 자리에 넣는다면, 눈치 보는 것이 사람들에게 많은 압박을 가하고 스트레스를 주고, 자신을 병들게 만들 수 있으므로 눈치 보는 사람이 되지 않도록 도와줄 전략들을 알려준다는 내용이 되므로 글의 흐름이 자연스럽게 연결된다. 따라서 ④번이 정답이다.

어휘 a slew of phr. 많은

12 [2021 세종대]

정답 ④

해석 ① 눈치 보는 것은 사회적 존재로서 인간의 건전한 사회적 행동의 하나이다.
② Susan Newman은 눈치 보는 사람들이 계속 행복할 수 있는 몇 가지 팁을 주었다.
③ Linda Tillman에 따르면, 낮은 자신감은 상습적으로 눈치 보는 것의 유일한 원인이다.
④ 눈치 보는 사람들은 스스로 많은 압박을 가하고 스트레스를 주는 경향이 있다.

해설 지문을 통해 추론할 수 있는 것을 고르는 문제이다. ④번 보기의 키워드인 'pressure and stress'(압박과 스트레스)가 등장한 지문의 후반을 통해, 눈치 보는 사람들은 스스로 많은 압박을 가하고 스트레스를 주는 경향이 있다는 것을 추론할 수 있다. 따라서 정답은 ④번이다.

오답 분석
① 사회적 존재로서 우리가 다른 사람들과 잘 지내는 것은 자연스럽다고는 했지만, 눈치 보는 것이 사회적 존재로서 인간의 건전한 사회적 행동 중 하나인지에 대해서는 언급되지 않았다.
② Susan Newman이 눈치 보는 사람들은 주변에 있는 모든 사람들이 행복하기를 바라고 이를 유지하기 위해 자신들이 부탁받는 것은 무엇이든 할 것이라고는 했지만, 눈치 보는 사람들이 계속 행복할 수 있는 몇 가지 팁을 주었는지는 알 수 없다.
③ Linda Tillman이 눈치 보는 사람들은 마음속으로 자신감이 부족하다고 말했다고는 했지만, 낮은 자신감이 상습적으로 눈치 보는 것의 유일한 원인인지는 알 수 없다.

[13-15]

가면 증후군은 학교와 직장 모두에서 개인이 자신의 업적을 의심하고 사기꾼으로 발각되는 것에 대해 끊임없이 반복되는 내면화된 공포를 가지는 심리적 패턴이다. 개인의 능력에 대한 외적 증거에도 불구하고, 이 현상(가면 증후군)을 겪는 사람들은 여전히 자신들이 사기꾼이라고 확신하고 있고 자신들이 이룬 모든 것들을 받을 자격이 없다고 생각한다. 가면 증후군을 앓고 있는 개인들은 자신들의 성공을 운 때문이라고 잘못 생각하거나 자신들의 성공은 다른 사람들을 속여서 자신들이 스스로 인지하는 것보다 더 똑똑하다고 생각하게 한 결과라고 여긴다. [A] 초기 연구가 높은 성과를 올리는 여성들 사이에서 널리 퍼진 것에 초점을 맞춘 데 반해, 가면 증후군은 남성과 여성 모두에게 동등하게 영향을 미치는 것으로 여겨졌다. [B] 가면 현상이라는 용어는 1978년에 Pauline R. Clance 박사와 Suzanne A. Imes 박사에 의해 소개되었다. Pauline R. Clance 박사와 Suzanne A. Imes 박사는 가면 현상을 스스로 인지한 지적 허위 혹은 사기에 대한 개인적 경험으로 정의했다. 연구원들은 높은 성과를 올리는 여성 150명 샘플을 인터뷰함으로써 이 내적 경험이 널리 퍼진 것에 대해 조사했다. [C] 모든 참가자들은 공식적으로 자신들이 업무적으로 뛰어나다는 것을 직장 동료들에게 인정받았고, 자신들이 받은 학위와 표준화된 시험 점수를 통해 학업 성취도를 보여주었다. 일관된 외부 검증에 의한 증거 앞에서도, 높은 성과를 올리는 이 여성들은 자신의 업적을 스스로 인정하지 못했다. 참가자들은 다른 사람들이 자신들의 지능과 능력을 과대평가하는 동안 자신들의 성공이 어떻게 운에 따른 것이었는지 설명했다. Clance와 Imes는 가면 현상에 대한 이 정신 구조가 성 고정관념, 초기의 가족 역학 관계, 문화, 그리고 귀인 양식과 같은 요인에서 발전했다고 믿었다. 연구원들은 가면 현상을 경험했던 여성들이 우울증, 일반화된 불안, 그리고 낮은 자신감과 관련된 증상을 보였다는 것을 알아냈다. [D]

---

imposter syndrome phr. 가면 증후군(자신의 성공이 노력이 아니라 순전히 운으로 얻어졌다고 생각하며 불안해하는 심리)
accomplishment n. 업적
persistent adj. 끊임없이 반복되는   fraud n. 사기꾼
competence n. 능력   phenomenon n. 현상
prevalence n. 널리 퍼진 것   phoniness n. 허위, 엉터리
validation n. 검증   overestimate v. 과대평가하다

13 [2021 세종대]

정답 ①

해석
① 외부의   ② 허구의
③ 헌법의   ④ 내부의

해설 지문의 빈칸을 채우는 문제이다. 지문의 첫 번째 문단에서 가면 증후군을 겪는 사람들은 자신들이 사기꾼이라고 확신하고 있고 자신들이 이룬 것들을 받을 자격이 없다고 생각한다고 했으므로, 빈칸에는 개인의 능력에 대한 외적(외부의) 증거에도 불구하고, 가면 증후군을 겪는 사람들은 여전히 자신들이 사기꾼이라고 확신하고 자신들이 이룬 것들을 받을 자격이 없다고 생각한다는 내용이 나오는 것이 자연스럽다. 따라서 '외부의'라고 한 ①번이 정답이다.

14 [2021 세종대]

정답 ③

해석 모든 참가자들은 공식적으로 자신들이 업무적으로 뛰어나다는 것을 직장 동료들에게 인정받았고, 자신들이 받은 학위와 표준화된 시험 점수를 통해 학업 성취도를 보여주었다.

해설 지문의 흐름상 주어진 문장이 들어가기에 가장 적절한 위치를 고르는 문제이다. 주어진 문장은 '모든 참가자들은 공식적으로 자신들이 업무적으로 뛰어나다는 것을 직장 동료들에게 인정받았고, 자신들이 받은 학위와 표준화된 시험 점수를 통해 학업 성취도를 보여주었다'라는 의미이다. 이 문장을 [C] 자리에 넣는다면, [C]의 뒤 문장인 '일관된 외부 검증에 의한 증거 앞에서도, 높은 성과를 올리는 이 여성들은 자신의 업적을 스스로 인정하지 못했다'는 내용에서 '일관된 외부 검증'이 무엇인지를 주어진 문장이 설명해 줄 수 있으므로 글의 흐름이 자연스럽게 연결된다. 따라서 ③번이 정답이다.

어휘 excellence n. 뛰어남, 탁월함

15 [2021 세종대]

정답 ②

해석 ① 가면 증후군은 높은 성과를 올리는 여성들에 대한 직장 동료들의 의혹에 의해 야기된다.

10 심리 189

② 여성들뿐만 아니라 남성들도 가면 현상을 겪을 수 있다.
③ 높은 성과를 올리는 여성 참가자 150명 모두는 가면 증후군을 극복했다.
④ 높은 자신감을 가지고 있는 사람들은 가면 증후군을 발현시키는 경향이 있다.

해설 지문의 내용과 일치하는 것을 묻는 문제이다. 지문의 첫 번째 문단 마지막의 impostor syndrome has been recognized to affect both men and women equally라는 내용을 통해 여성들뿐만 아니라 남성들도 가면 현상을 겪을 수 있다는 것을 알 수 있다. 따라서 ②번이 지문의 내용과 일치한다.

오답 분석
① 높은 성과를 올리는 여성들은 자신의 업적을 스스로 인정하지 못했다고는 했지만, 가면 증후군이 높은 성과를 올리는 여성들에 대한 직장 동료들의 의혹에 의해 야기되는지는 알 수 없다.
③ 연구원들이 높은 성과를 올리는 여성 150명 표본을 인터뷰했다고는 했지만, 높은 성과를 올리는 여성 참가자 150명 모두가 가면 증후군을 극복했는지는 알 수 없다.
④ 연구원들이 가면 현상을 경험했던 여성들이 낮은 자신감과 관련된 증상을 보였다는 것을 알아냈다고 했으므로, 높은 자신감을 가지고 있는 사람들이 가면 증후군을 발현시키는 경향이 있다는 것은 지문의 내용과 다르다.

[16-17]

> 방해의 두 번째 기본 유형은 순향 억제이다. 순향 억제는 선행 학습이 나중의 학습을 방해할 때 발생한다. 예를 들어, 당신이 심리학 시험 벼락치기 공부를 하고 나서 같은 날 밤에 역사 시험 벼락치기 공부를 한다면, 두 번째로 공부한 역사에 대한 당신의 기억은 역사만 공부했을 때보다 덜 정확할 것이다. 순향 억제는 특히 이전 학습이 새로운 학습과 충돌할 때 발생하기 쉽다. 이동식 주택이 붙어 있는 차를 후진시키는 것을 배우는 것은 좋은 예이다. 보통은 당신이 차를 후진시킬 때, 자동차 핸들은 당신이 가고자 하는 방향을 향한다. 이것은 보통 운전할 때도 똑같기 때문에 쉽게 익힐 수 있다. 하지만, 이동식 주택이 있으면, 자동차 핸들은 이동식 주택이 가고자 하는 방향과 반대 방향을 향해야 한다. 이는 자리를 잡은 운전 습관을 방해하는 원인이 되고 이동식 주택을 후진시키는 것을 어렵게 만든다.
>
> **interference** n. 방해, 간섭
> **proactive inhibition** phr. 순향 억제(선행 학습으로 인해 방해받는 일) **cram for** phr. ~을 대비해서 벼락치기 공부를 하다
> **psychology** n. 심리학 **accurate** adj. 정확한, 정밀한
> **conflict with** phr. ~와 충돌하다, 모순되다
> **back a car** phr. 차를 후진시키다 **trailer** n. 이동식 주택
> **steering wheel** phr. (자동차의) 핸들 **direction** n. 방향
> **master** v. ~을 완전히 익히다, 숙달하다
> **established** adj. 자리를 잡은, 정해진

16 [2019 단국대]

정답 ③

해설 빈칸에 적절한 연결어를 넣는 문제이다. 빈칸 앞 문장은 차를 후진시킬 때, 자동차 핸들은 당신이 가고자 하는 방향을 향하고, 운전할 때도 똑같기 때문에 쉽게 익힐 수 있다는 내용이고, 빈칸 뒤 문장은 이동식 주택이 있으면, 자동차 핸들은 이동식 주택이 가고자 하는 방향과 반대 방향을 향해야 하므로, 운전 습관을 방해하는 원인이 되고 이동식 주택을 후진시키는 법을 어렵게 만든다는 내용이다. 따라서 역접을 나타내는 연결어인 ③ However(하지만)가 정답이다.

17 [2019 단국대]

정답 ④

해석
① 영어를 하는 사람이 영어 문법을 중국어에 적용하기 때문에 중국어를 배우는 데 더 큰 어려움을 느낄 수도 있다.
② 쇼핑하는 마트의 통로가 바뀌면, 당신은 무의식적으로 이전 선반을 향해 걷기 시작한다.
③ 당신은 새로운 곳으로 이사해서 자신이 편지에 이전 주소를 쓰고 있는 것을 발견한다.
④ 몇몇 사람들은 최근에 자동 변속기 차량을 운전하기 시작하면서, 수동 변속기 차량을 다시 운전하는 데 어려움을 겪는다.

해설 순향 억제의 예가 아닌 것을 파악하는 문제이다. 두 번째 문장에서 순향 억제는 선행 학습이 나중의 학습을 방해할 때 발생한다고 했으므로, 순향 억제의 예가 아닌 것은 '몇몇 사람들은 최근에 자동 변속기 차량을 운전하기 시작하면서, 수동 변속기 차량을 다시 운전하는 데 어려움을 겪는다'이다. 따라서 ④번이 정답이다.

어휘 apply v. 적용하다 aisle n. 통로, 복도
instinctively adv. 무의식적으로, 본능적으로
stick shift phr. (차량의) 수동 변속기

18 [2020 중앙대]

정답 ③

해석 1950년대에, Festinger는 사회적 비교와 인지적 부조화에 관한 이론을 발표했는데, 이 이론은 어떤 이가 의견과 욕구를 발전시키는 과정에서 타인이 부조화된 인지의 감소만큼이나 (A)중요한 역할을 한다고 제안하고 있다. 이 이론은 사람들이 그들이 처한 환경에서 그들의 의견, 믿음, 사고방식 등을 평가하기 위해 다른 사람들을 바라본다는 사실에 초점을 맞추고 있다. 이 과정을 통해 한 사람은 자신과 비슷한 이들로 구성된 적절한 비교 집단의 태도와 의견에 대한 준거 기준을 가지고 스스로가 어디에 서 있는지를 평가할 수 있게 된다. 능력에 관해서도, 어떤 이는 주어진 업무에 대한 자신의 실적을 (B)기준과 비교한다.(예를 들어, 누가 얼마나 빨리 1마일을 뛸 수 있는 가는 같은 연령의 주자들의 평균 시간과 비교될 수 있다). 하지만, 개인의 의견과 사고방식에 대한 평가는 (C)양

립할 수 없는 준거 기준을 갖게 되므로, 오로지 그 개인이 선택한 비교집단에 의해 만들어지는 정신적 지주에게만 관련된 정보를 산출한다. 본질적으로, 연구자들은 개인이 그들과 비슷한 타인을 통해 의견, 믿음, 사고방식을 평가한다고 결론짓고, 부분적으로 이 결론을 근거로 삼아, 사회적 지지가 사회적 비교 과정에 의해 (D)이끌린다고 주장하고 있다. 조금 더 세부적으로 들어가자면, 사회적 비교와 관련된 가정은 사회적 지지라는 유익한 행위를 근거로 제공하는 것이 가능하다는 것이다.

해설 지문의 흐름에 적합하지 않은 것을 고르는 문제이다. 지문은 어떤 개인이 자신의 의견, 믿음, 사고방식 등을 평가하기 위해 자신과 비슷한 타인으로 구성된 비교집단을 활용한다는 내용이므로, (A) 어떤 이가 의견과 욕구를 발전시키는 과정에서 타인이 '중요한' 역할을 한다는 것, (B) 자신의 능력을 파악하기 위해 명확한 '기준'을 사용한다는 것, (D) 개인이 다른 사람을 기준으로 하여 의견을 발전시키기 때문에, 사회적 지지가 사회적 비교 과정에 의해 '이끌린다'는 것은 모두 지문의 흐름에 적합하다. 그러나 (C) 개인의 의견과 사고방식에 대한 평가가 '양립할 수 없는 준거 기준'을 갖게 된다는 내용은 그에 대한 근거가 지문에서 설명되어 있지 않기 때문에 지문의 흐름에 적합하지 않다. 따라서 ③번이 정답이다.

어휘 social comparison phr. 사회 비교
cognitive dissonance phr. 인지 부조화
dissonant adj. 부조화된   reference n. 준거 기준
appropriate adj. 적절한
be composed of phr. ~로 구성되어 있다
incompatible adj. 양립할 수 없는   yield v. 산출하다
finding n. 연구 결과   proposition n. 주장, 제안

[19-20]

나는 일반적으로 전문가의 의견과는 별개로, 큰 문제나 작은 문제에서나 다른 사람의 의견에 대해 너무 많은 존중이 가해진다고 생각한다. 굶주림을 피하고 감옥에 들어가지 않기 위해 필요한 한에 있어서는 여론을 존중해야 하지만, 이를 넘어선 것은 무엇이든 불필요한 횡포에 자발적으로 굴복하는 것이며, 온갖 방법으로 행복을 방해할 가능성이 높다. 예를 들어, 지출 문제를 들어보자. 아주 많은 사람들이 단지 그들 이웃의 존경심이 좋은 차를 소유하고 훌륭한 저녁 식사를 대접하는 능력에 달려 있다고 생각하기 때문에 그들의 타고난 취향이 요구하는 것과는 꽤 다른 방식으로 돈을 쓴다. 사실, 분명히 차를 살 여유가 되지만 여행이나 좋은 서재를 진정으로 선호하는 사람은 결국 그가 다른 모든 사람들과 똑같이 행동했을 때보다 훨씬 더 존경받을 것이다. 물론 의도적으로 여론을 무시하는 것은 의미가 없다. 거꾸로 된 방식이긴 하지만, 여전히 여론의 지배하에 있어야 한다. 그러나 여론에 진정으로 무관심하는 것은 강인함과 행복의 원천이다.

apart from phr. 별도로, 제외하고   expert n. 전문가
opinion n. 의견   public opinion phr. 여론

in so far as phr. ~하는 한에 있어서는
starvation n. 굶주림   keep out of phr. ~에 들어가지 않다
prison n. 감옥   voluntary adj. 자발적인
submission n. 굴복, 복종   tyranny n. 횡포, 폭정
expenditure n. 지출   enjoin v. 요구하다, 명령하다
depend upon phr. ~에 달려 있다, 의존하다
possession n. 소유   obviously adv. 분명히, 당연히
afford v. ~할 여유가 되다   genuinely adv. 진정으로, 진실로
behave v. 행동하다   deliberately adv. 의도적으로, 고의로
flout v. 무시하다, 어기다   domination n. 지배, 우세
topsy-turvy adj. 역의, 거꾸로의   indifferent adj. 무관심한

19 [2020 국민대]

정답 ④

해석 ① 탐닉하다   ② 가입하다
③ 이겨내다   ④ 방해하다

해설 지문의 빈칸을 채우는 문제이다. 빈칸이 있는 문장에서 필요한 정도를 넘어선 여론 존중은 불필요한 횡포에 굴복하는 것이라고 했으므로, 빈칸에는 행복이 제약을 받는다는 내용이 나와야 적절하다는 것을 알 수 있다. 따라서 '방해하다'라고 한 ④번이 정답이다.

어휘 indulge in phr. ~에 탐닉하다
affiliate with phr. ~에 가입하다, ~와 제휴하다
triumph over phr. ~을 이겨내다
interfere with phr. ~을 방해하다

20 [2020 국민대]

정답 ④

해설 enjoin(요구하다)과 비슷한 의미를 가진 어휘를 묻고 있다. ①번 alter는 '바꾸다', ②번 refuse는 '거부하다', ③번 replace는 '교체하다', ④번 demand는 '요구하다'라는 의미이다. 따라서 ④번이 정답이다.

[21-22]

공포는 엄청난 동기 요인이다. 공포는 아마 다른 어떤 것보다도 많은 사람들에게 동기를 부여할 것이다. 유감스럽게도, 공포는 대부분의 사람들이 망설이고, 스스로를 의심하고, 할 수 있었던 것보다 (A)훨씬 많이 성취하고, 실제로 어떤 사람인지를 숨기도록 동기를 부여한다.
당신의 잠재력에 도달하는 데 가장 큰 장애물 중 하나는 아마 자신의 개인적인 공포일 것이다. 만약 두렵다면, 당신만 그런 것이 아니다. (B)모든 사람들이 공포를 가지고 있다. 그러나, 우리의 공포는 학습된다. 아기였을 때, 당신에게는 두 가지 공포가 있었는데, 이는 떨어지는 것에 대한 공포와 시끄러운 소음에 대한 공포이다. 나이가 들어가면서, 당신은 아마 당신의 공포 목록을 (C)늘렸을 것이다. 그리고 당신이 대부분의 사람

들과 같다면, 스스로에게 "시도해봤다가 실패하면 어쩌지?"라는 것들을 말하면서 당신의 공포가 삶의 일부를 (D)지배하게 둘 것이다.

공포에 관한 한 당신에게는 두 가지 선택권이 있다. 당신은 공포가 당신의 삶을 지배하게 둘 수도 있고, 당신이 정말로 성취하고 싶은 것들에 초점을 맞출 수도 있으므로, 공포를 (E)잊어버리고, 해보아라. 자신의 분야에서 가장 성공한 사람들은 두려웠지만 사람들의 성취하려는 욕구가 더 컸기 때문에 공포를 극복했다고 말할 것이다. Barbra Streisand는 연기할 때 무대 공포증으로 신체적으로 구역질이 났지만, 이 공포에 맞서서 우리 시대의 가장 인기 있는 연예인 중 한 명으로서 자신의 자리를 지키고 있다.

---

fear n. 공포, 두려움
motivator n. 동기 요인, 동기를 부여하는 것
hold back phr. 망설이다, 기다리다
accomplish v. 성취하다, 해내다 **obstacle** n. 장애물, 장애
potential n. 잠재력, 가능성 **dominate** v. 지배하다
put A behind phr. A를 잊어버리다, A를 고려하지 않다
go for it phr. 해보다, 힘내다 **overcome** v. 극복하다
physically adv. 신체적으로, 육체적으로
nauseate v. 구역질 나다 **stage fright** phr. 무대 공포증
perform v. 연기하다, 공연하다

21 [2019 건국대]

정답 ①

해설 (A)의 다음 문장에서 '당신의 잠재력에 도달하는 데 가장 큰 장애물 중 하나는 아마 자신의 개인적인 공포일 것이다'고 했으므로 '대부분의 사람들이 망설이고, 스스로를 의심하고, 할 수 있었던 것보다 훨씬 적게(much less) 성취하고, 실제로 어떤 사람인지를 숨기도록 동기를 부여한다'고 하는 것이 문맥에 맞다. (A)의 much more를 much less로 고쳐야 한다. 따라서 ①번이 정답이다.

22 [2019 건국대]

정답 ④

해석 ① 사람들은 공포에 직접적으로 맞설 필요가 없다
② 사람들의 잠재력은 충분히 강하다
③ 사람들은 더 이상 선택권이 없다.
④ 사람들의 성취하려는 욕구가 더 컸다
⑤ 공포는 사람들이 맞서는 가장 큰 장애물이 아니다

해설 지문의 빈칸을 채우는 문제이다. 빈칸 다음 문장에서 'Barbra Streisand는 연기할 때 무대 공포증으로 신체적으로 구역질이 났지만, 이 공포에 맞서서 우리 시대의 가장 인기 있는 연예인 중 한 명으로서 자신의 자리를 지키고 있다'고 했으므로, '자신의 분야에서 가장 성공한 사람들은 두려웠지만 _____기 때문에 공포를 극복했다고 말할 것이다'라는 문맥에서 빈칸에는 '사람들의 성취하려는 욕구가 더 컸다'라는

의미의 their desire to achieve is greater가 들어가는 것이 자연스럽다. 따라서 ④번이 정답이다.

어휘 **directly** adv. 직접적으로 **potential** n. 잠재력, 가능성
desire n. 욕구, 갈망

[23-24]

일부 사회심리학자들에 의한 한 연구에서, 참가자들은 두 개의 과업에 참여하도록 요청받았다. 첫 번째 과업에서, 그들은 제공되는 일련의 단어들로 문장을 만들도록 요구받았다. 그다음, 가정상 다른 연구인 것의 일환으로서, 참가자들은 경제 관련 게임을 했는데, 그 게임에서 참가자들은 1달러 동전 열 개를 받았고 그들 자신과 다음 참가자 간에 그 동전들을 나눌 것을 요청받았다. 다음 참가자만이 그들이 결정한 것을 알 수 있었으며, 그 참가자는 동전을 준 사람이 누구였는지는 알 수 없었다. 당신이라면 이 상황에서 어떻게 할 것인지 잠깐 생각해 보라. 여기에는 10달러를 빠르게 벌 기회가 있고, 모든 동전을 갖고 싶은 강한 유혹이 있다. 하지만 당신은 모든 돈을 비축하고 다음 사람을 위해 아무것도 남겨두지 않는 것에 대해 약간의 죄책감을 느낄 것이다. 이것은 한쪽 어깨에 악마가 있고 ("어리석게 굴지 말고, 모두 가져라!") 다른 어깨에는 천사가 있는 ("남에게 대접받고자 하는 대로 남을 대접하라.") 상황 중 하나이다. 즉, 사람들은 돈을 원하지만, 이것은 남을 잘 대하려는 그들의 목표와 모순된다. 어떤 목표가 이길까?

그것은 어느 정도 최근에 어떤 목표가 미리 주어졌는가에 따라 좌우된다. 사람들이 처음에 했던 문장 완성 과업을 기억하는가? 그 과업에서, 참가자의 절반은 신과 관련된 단어(정신, 신성한, 신, 성스러운, 예언자)를 받았고, 이것들은 이웃에게 친절히 행동하라는 목표를 세우기 위해 고안되었다. 그 밖의 참가자 절반은 중립적인 단어를 받았다. 중요한 세부사항은 참가자들이 문장 완성 과업과 경제 관련 게임 간의 연관성을 만들지 못했다는 것이고, 그들은 두 과업이 완전히 관련이 없는 것으로 생각했다. 그렇기는 하지만, 신과 관련이 있는 단어로 문장을 만든 사람들은 중립적인 단어를 얻은 사람들이 남긴 것보다 (평균 2.56달러) 다음 참가자를 위해 상당히 더 많은 돈을 남겨두었다 (평균 4.56달러).

---

supposedly adv. 가정상, 아마 **buck** n. 달러
temptation n. 유혹 **hoard** v. 비축하다, 저장하다
conflict with phr. ~와 모순되다 **win out** phr. 이기다
completion n. 완성 **divine** adj. 신성한
sacred adj. 성스러운 **prophet** n. 예언자
neutral adj. 중립적인 **unrelated** adj. 관련 없는
significantly adv. 상당히

23 [2019 가톨릭대]

정답 ③

해석 ① 당신이 자신을 위해 세운 개인적 목표
② 사람들이 신을 믿는지 아닌지

③ 최근에 어떤 목표가 미리 주어졌는가
④ 주류 사회의 지배적 규범

해설 지문의 빈칸을 채우는 문제이다. 지문의 두 번째 문단에서 전체적으로, 문장 완성 과업에서 이웃에게 친절히 행동하라는 목표를 세우기 위해 고안된 단어를 받은 참가자들이 중립적인 단어를 받은 참가자들이 남긴 돈보다 더 많이 남겨두었다는 연구의 결과가 제시되어 있으므로, 빈칸에는 돈을 얻으려는 목표와 남을 잘 대하려는 목표가 어떤 것에 따라 좌우되는지에 대한 내용이 나와야 적절하다는 것을 알 수 있다. 따라서 그것(어떤 목표가 이길지)은 '최근에 어떤 목표가 미리 주어졌는가'에 따라 좌우된다고 한 ③번이 정답이다.

어휘 **prime** v. 미리 주다 **prevailing** adj. 지배적인, 우세한
mainstream adj. 주류의

24 2019 가톨릭대

정답 ②

해석 ① 모든 참가자는 일련의 같은 단어를 받았다.
② 다음 참가자에게 돈을 남긴 사람은 받는 사람에게 계속 알려지지 않았다.
③ 참가자들은 주어진 두 과업 간 연관성을 잘 알고 있었다.
④ 참가자들에게 모든 돈을 가질 것인지, 아니면 다음 사람에게 절반을 줄 것인지의 두 가지 선택권이 주어졌다.

해설 지문의 내용과 일치하는 것을 묻는 문제이다. 지문 첫 번째 문단의 네 번째 문장 Only the next participant ~ who the givers were.의 내용을 통해 다음 참가자에게 돈을 남긴 사람은 받는 사람에게 계속 알려지지 않았다는 것을 알 수 있다. 따라서 ②번의 내용이 지문의 내용과 일치한다.

오답 분석 ① 과업에서 참가자의 절반은 신과 관련된 단어를 받았고, 다른 참가자 절반은 중립적인 단어를 받았다고 했으므로, 모든 참가자가 일련의 같은 단어를 받았다는 것은 지문의 내용과 다르다.
③ 참가자들은 문장 완성 과업과 경제 관련 게임 간의 연관성을 만들지 못했다고 했으므로, 참가자들이 주어진 두 과업 간 연관성을 잘 알고 있었다는 것은 지문의 내용과 다르다.
④ 참가자들은 그들 자신과 다음 참가자 간에 동전을 나눌 것을 요청받기는 했지만, 참가자들에게 모든 돈을 가질 것인지, 아니면 다음 사람에게 절반을 줄 것인지의 두 가지 선택권이 주어진 것은 아니므로 지문의 내용과 다르다.

어휘 **recipient** n. 받는 사람

[25-26]

우리들 대부분은 노골적으로 공격적인 사람들을 잘 포착한다. 누군가가 당신을 모욕하거나, 비판하거나, 또는 업신여길 때 기분이 좋지 않지만, 적어도 당신은 왜 당신이 왜 상처받고 있는지를 알 수 있다. 하지만 때때로 가까운 가족, 친구, 그리고 동료를 포함한 우리 주변의 사람들이 우리를 불편하게 만들 때도 있지만, 우리는 딱히 왜인지를 설명하지 못한다. 예를 들어, 당신의 친구가 한 주에 세 번이나 복도에서 당신에게 인사를 하지 못할 수도 있다. 당신은 그것이 아마도 실수라고 생각하는 척하겠지만, 당신은 무엇인가 잘못되었다고 느낄 것이다. 만약에 이것이 당신의 삶에서 한 사람이나 그 이상의 사람에게서 자주 일어난다면, 당신은 수동적 공격성을 발견한 것일지도 모르는데, 이는 노골적으로 공격적인 행동보다 훨씬 더 감지하기 어렵다. 수동적 공격성이란 교묘한 모욕, 언짢은 듯한 행동, 완고함, 또는 요청받은 업무를 완료하지 못하는 고의적인 실패와 같은 행동들을 통해 은연중에 내포된 적대감의 표현에 관여하는 성향이다. 수동적 공격성은 은연중에 내포되기 때문에, 당신이 심리적인 영향을 느끼고 있을 때조차 알아차리기 어려울 수 있다. 당신이 이러한 종류의 행동을 식별하는 것을 돕기 위해서, 아래에 다섯 가지 사례를 서술하였다. 이러한 사람들 모두가 수동적 공격성을 갖고 있다는 것은 아니지만, 그것들은 가장 일반적이다.

spot v. 포착하다 **overtly** adv. 노골적으로, 겉으로
aggressive adj. 공격적인 **insult** v. 모욕하다
belittle v. 업신여기다
cannot put a finger on phr. 딱히 설명하지 못하다
greet v. 인사하다 **hallway** n. 복도
make believe phr. ~인 척하다 **slip** n. 실수, 지나침
amiss adj. 잘못된 **frequently** adv. 자주, 빈번히
passive-aggressive behavior phr. 수동적 공격성
detect v. 감지하다 **tendency** n. 경향
engage in phr. ~에 관여하는 **hostility** n. 적대감
sullen adj. 언짢은 듯한, 시무룩한 **stubbornness** n. 완고함
deliberate adj. 고의적인 **consequence** n. 영향, 결과
identify v. 식별하다, 확인하다 **instance** n. 사례
common adj. 일반적인, 흔한, 공통된

25 2019 인하대

정답 ③

해석 ① 대담한   ② 순진한
③ 은연중에 내포된   ④ 정직한
⑤ 외설적인

해설 지문의 빈칸을 채우는 문제이다. 지문의 두 번째 단락의 두 번째 문장에서 교묘한 모욕, 언짢은 듯한 행동, 완고함, 고의적인 실패와 같은 행동들이 적대감을 이렇게 표현하는 것이라고 했으므로, 빈칸에는 노골적으로 행동하는 것이 아닌 것에 대한 내용이 나와야 적절하다는 것을 알 수 있다. 따라서 '은연중에 내포된'이라고 한 ③번이 정답이다.

어휘 **bold** adj. 대담한 **naive** adj. 순진한
implicit adj. 은연중에 내포된, 함축적인 **honest** adj. 정직한
obscene adj. 외설적인

26 [2019 인하대]

정답 ⑤

해석
① 공격적인 행동 비교
② 수동적 공격성의 원인
③ 수동적 공격성을 다루는 방법
④ 수동적 공격성의 효과
⑤ 수동적 공격성의 예시

해설 주어진 지문의 뒤에 올 내용을 고르는 문제이다. 지문의 마지막에서 두 번째 문장에서 아래에 다섯 가지 사례를 서술하였다고 했으므로, '수동적 공격성의 예시'에 대한 내용이 지문의 뒤에 나올 것임을 알 수 있다. 따라서 ⑤번이 정답이다.

어휘 comparison n. 비교

[27-29]

자신에 대해 조소할 수 있는 능력은 대단히 귀중한 선물이다. 자신의 업적을 과시하는 사람은 지루하지만, 자신의 실수에 대해 남들과 함께 웃고 떠들기를 청하는 사람은 주변에 두기에 즐거운 사람이다. 당신이 높은 자리에 오르고 있을 때, 자기 비하적인 유머는 질투와 부러움을 물리친다. 그리고 일이 마음대로 되지 않을 때는, (A)이것은 당신의 관점과 유머 감각을 유지할 수 있도록 도움을 주게 된다. 그래서 (B)자기 비하적인 유머는 종종 신비한 무형의 매력의 필수적인 요소가 된다. 만약 당신이 (C)이 유머를 전업으로 활용한다면, 이것은 심지어 당신을 부자로 만들 수도 있는데, Bob Hope에게 물어보라! 해가 지나갈수록, 매력적인 Mr. Hope는 대중의 즐거움을 위해 기꺼이 자신을 비하했다. 그래서 청중은 그를 질려 하지 않았다. 그들은 그를 끝없이 좋아했다. Hope가 최근 텔레비전 프로그램에 게스트로 나타났을 때, 프로 권투에 관한 이야기가 프로그램의 주제였다. Mr. Hope는 "제가 어렸을 때, 복싱을 했어요."라고 넋이 빠진 얼굴로 먼 곳을 쳐다보며 말했다. "제 고향에서 저는 유일하게 백미러와 싸운 사람이었어요. 또 저는 유일하게 (D)경기장에 들려 올라갔다가 들려 내려온 사람이었지요."

poke v. 조소하다 priceless adj. 매우 귀중한
brag v. 자랑하다 accomplishment n. 업적
ride high phr. 높은 자리에 오르다, 잘 나가다
self-deprecating adj. 자기 비하적인
perspective n. 관점 essential adj. 필수적인
ingredient n. 요소 mysterious adj. 신비한
intangible adj. 무형의 charm n. 매력
full-time adv. 전업으로 get enough of phr. 질려 하다
adore v. 좋아하다 prize fighting phr. 프로 권투
rapt adj. 넋이 빠진 faraway adj. 먼 곳을 바라보는
rear-view mirror phr. 백미러

27 [2020 한성대]

정답 ①

해석
① Bob Hope는 재산이 많았다.
② 자기 비하적인 유머는 모욕적이다.
③ 자신의 업적을 자랑하는 사람들은 가까이 두기에 즐거운 사람들이다.
④ 자신에 대해 조소하는 것은 질투와 부러움을 자초한다.

해설 지문을 통해 추론할 수 있는 것을 고르는 문제이다. 지문의 첫 번째 문단에서, 만약 당신이 자기 비하적인 유머를 전업으로 활용한다면, 이것은 심지어 당신을 부자로 만들 수도 있다고 설명하며, 예시로 Bob Hope를 제시하고 있으므로 Bob Hope가 재산이 많았음을 추론할 수 있다. 따라서 ①번이 정답이다.

오답 분석
② 지문의 첫 번째 문단에서, 자신에 대해 조소할 수 있는 능력은 대단히 귀중한 선물이라고 했으므로, 자기비하적인 유머가 모욕적이라는 것은 지문의 내용과 다르다.
③ 지문의 첫 번째 문단에서, 자신의 업적을 자랑하는 사람들은 지겹다고 했으므로, 자신의 업적을 사람들이 가까이 두기에 즐거운 사람이라는 것은 지문의 내용과 다르다.
④ 지문의 첫 번째 문단에서, 자신에 대해 조소하는 자기 비하적인 유머가 질투와 부러움을 물리친다고 했으므로, 자신에 대해 조소하는 것이 질투와 부러움을 자초한다는 것은 지문의 내용과 다르다.

어휘 offensive adj. 모욕적인

28 [2020 한성대]

정답 ④

해설 (A)~(D) 가운데 의미하는 바가 다른 것을 파악하는 문제이다. (A), (B), (C)는 모두 자기 비하적인 유머를 의미하는데, (D)는 경기장을 의미하므로 (A)~(D) 가운데 의미하는 바가 다른 것은 (D)이다. 따라서 ④번이 정답이다.

29 [2020 한성대]

정답 ④

해석
① 기쁨
② 재미, 우스움
③ 기쁨, 즐거움
④ 원통함

해설 문맥상 빈칸에 적절하지 않은 어휘를 묻는 문제이다. 지문 전체적으로 자신에 대해 조소할 수 있는 능력, 즉 자기 비하적인 유머의 장점에 관해 설명하고 있으므로, Mr. Hope가 대중의 '원통함'을 위해 기꺼이 자신을 비하했다는 문맥상 자연스럽지 않다. 따라서 ④번이 정답이다.

[30-31]

당신이 행복을 살 수 없다는 생각은 반복해서 근거 없는 믿음인 것으로 드러났다. 더 부유한 국가는 가난한 국가보다 더 행복하다. 더 부유한 국가의 더 부유한 사람 또한 더 행복하다. 그 증거는 분명하다: 돈은 당신을 행복하게 만든다. 당신은 돈으로 무엇을 해야 할지 알기만 하면 된다.

심리학자 Daniel Gilbert는 몇 년 전 한 인터뷰에서 너무 많은 물건을 사는 것을 멈추고, 경험에 더 많은 돈을 소비하기 위해 노력하라고 말했다. 우리는 경험이 재밌을 수는 있지만, 경험이 우리에게 보여줄 만한 성과를 남겨주지 않는다고 생각한다. 하지만 그것은 좋은 것으로 판명되었다. 대다수의 사람들에게, 행복은 타인과 경험을 공유하는 것으로부터 오는데, 경험은 보통 발생할 때 처음으로 공유되고 그 후 우리가 친구들에게 이야기할 때 몇 번이고 공유된다.

반면, 물건은 너무 오래되면 싫증이 난다. 만약 당신이 융단을 정말 좋아한다면, 그것을 살 것이다. 당신은 그것을 처음에 몇 번 보면, 그것을 감탄하며 바라보고 행복을 느낄 것이다. 하지만 시간이 흐르며, 아마 융단은 그저 하나의 융단이라는 것이 드러날 것이다. 오래된 가구 한 점이 언제 당신을 마지막으로 황홀하게 만들었는지 기억해보라.

expose v. 드러내다 **myth** n. 근거 없는 믿음
unequivocal adj. 분명한 **psychologist** n. 심리학자
wear out one's welcome phr. 너무 오래 묵어 미움을 사다
admire v. 감탄하며 바라보다 **reveal itself** phr. 드러나다
ecstatic adj. 황홀해하는

30 2020 서울여대
정답 ①

해석 ① 물건보다는 경험을 사라.
② 타인에게 친절히 해라.
③ 삶을 의미 있는 방식으로 바꿔라.
④ 이미 가진 것에 만족하라.

해설 지문의 요지를 묻는 문제이다. 지문 중간에서 한 심리학자가 너무 많은 물건을 사는 것을 멈추고, 경험에 더 많은 돈을 소비하기 위해 노력하라고 말했다고 하고, 융단을 구매했을 시의 예시를 보여주고 있다. 따라서 이 지문의 요지를 '물건보다는 경험을 사라'라고 표현한 ①번이 정답이다.

어휘 meaningful adj. 의미 있는 satisfied adj. 만족하는

31 2020 서울여대
정답 ③

해석 ① 우리는 나쁜 기분에서 벗어나는 해결 수단을 살 수 있다.
② 물건은 대개 경험보다 선호된다.
③ 물건을 사는 것으로부터 얻는 우리의 행복은 시간과 함께 감소한다.
④ 우리는 보통 우리가 필요한 것보다는 원하는 것을 산다.

해설 밑줄 친 부분의 의미를 추론하는 문제이다. 밑줄 친 objects wear out their welcome은 '물건은 너무 오래되면 싫증이 난다'라는 의미이다. 주변의 내용을 살펴보면 이것이 몇 번이고 공유되는 경험으로부터 오는 행복과 반대되는 것임을 알 수 있다. 따라서, 이를 '물건을 사는 것으로부터 얻는 우리의 행복은 시간과 함께 감소한다'라고 표현한 ③번이 정답이다.

어휘 decline v. 감소하다

[32-33]

*Act of Creation*에서 심리학자 Arthur Koestler는 연결되지 않는 생각들이 동시에 발생함을 의미하는 '이합'이라는 용어를 창안하여, 인간의 창조 과정에 관한 자신의 광범위한 연구 내용을 요약했다. Arthur Koestler는 창조 행위란 모순되지는 않지만 늘 양립할 수 없는 두 개의 준거 틀 내에서 어떤 상황이나 개념인 L을 인지하는 것이라고 설명했다. L이라는 사건 속에서 그 두 개의 준거 틀이 교차하고, 이를테면 L은 두 개의 다른 사고에서 동시에 진동을 일으키게 된다. 이런 상태가 지속되는 동안, L은 단순히 한 쪽의 연상적 상황에만 연결되는 것이 아니라, 두 쪽에 이합된다. 우리가 창의적 아이디어들에서 가치 있게 여기는 것은 확실한 참신함만은 아니다. 참신함은 새롭게 연결되는 방향이나 분야를 만들어내는 데에 영향을 주기 때문에 인지적 면에서 자극을 유발하고, 이는 엄청난 에너지의 분출을 필요로 할 것이다. 하지만 이런 경험을 갖더라도 자극은 오래가지 못할 수도 있는데, 이는 일단 자극이 시작되면 그 방향은 다시는 똑같은 방식으로 열리지 않기 때문이다. 더 다양한 창조 행위는 복잡하고 지대한 영향을 미칠 새로운 길, 전혀 다른 개념들을 연결하는 길을 만드는 과정 속에 있고, 그 길이 많을수록 자극의 정도도 커지는데 Koestler의 용어에 따르면 하나가 이합을 증대시킨다. 만약 우리의 감각이 최소한 부분적으로라도 활발한 정신세계의 존재에 의존한다면 더 활발한 정신세계가 더 광범위한 자각력과 존재감을 만들어 낸다고 볼 수 있다. 정신세계가 어느 때고 더 다양하고 복잡할수록 그 세계를 오가기 위해서 그에 상응하는 더 많은 에너지가 필요하고, 그에 따라 신체적 활기도 더 높아진다.

convey v. 의미하다 **coincidence** n. 동시 발생
discontinuous adj. 끊어진 **perceive** v. 인지하다
self-consistent adj. 자기모순이 없는 **habitually** adv. 늘
incompatible adj. 양립할 수 없는
wavelength n. 사고방식 **novelty** n. 참신함
cognitive adj. 인지의 **medium** n. 환경
disparate adj. 전혀 다른 **multiply** v. 늘리다
traverse v. 오락가락하다 **exhilaration** n. 활기

32 2020 한국항공대
정답 ②

해석 ① 이합된 활기의 부정적인 영향
② 참신함과 자극의 발생

③ 인지적 매개와 결합적 상황
④ 에너지의 복합적인 물리적 특징들

해설 지문의 제목을 묻는 문제이다. 지문의 중간에서 참신함은 새롭게 연결되는 방향이나 분야를 만들어내는 데에 영향을 주기 때문에 인지적 면에서 자극을 유발한다고 했으며, 이를 설명하기 위해 '이합'이라는 용어를 언급하고 있다. 따라서 이 지문의 제목을 '참신함과 자극의 발생'이라고 표현한 ②번이 정답이다.

어휘 associative adj. 결합의

33 (2020 한국항공대)

정답 ②

해석 ① 연결되지 않는 생각들을 연결하는 인간의 능력은 한계가 있다.
② 창조성은 완전히 새로운 무언가의 생성에만 반드시 있는 것은 아니다.
③ 파괴는 창조의 정반대 극이다.
④ 창의적인 사고 자체는 과학적으로 측정되지 않는 한 쓸모가 없다.

해설 지문을 통해 추론할 수 있는 것을 고르는 문제이다. 지문의 초반에서 Arthur Koestler는 창조 행위란 모순되지는 않지만 늘 양립할 수 없는 두 개의 준거 틀 내에서 어떤 상황이나 개념인 L이라는 사건을 인지하는 것이라고 설명했다고 했으므로, 창조성은 완전히 새로운 무언가의 생성에만 반드시 있는 것은 아니라는 것을 추론할 수 있다. 따라서 정답은 ②번이다.

오답 분석
① 더 다양한 창조 행위는 복잡하고 지대한 영향을 미칠 새로운 길, 전혀 다른 개념들을 연결하는 길을 만드는 과정 속에 있다고는 했지만, 연결되지 않는 생각들을 연결하는 인간의 능력은 한계가 있다는 것은 알 수 없다.
③ 파괴는 창조의 정반대 극이라는 것은 지문에서 알 수 없다.
④ 창의적인 사고 자체는 과학적으로 측정되지 않는 한 쓸모가 없다는 것은 지문에서 알 수 없다.

[34-35]

부부가 신혼여행의 기분을 계속 이어갈 수 있도록 할 수 있는 무언가가 있을까? 연구가인 Arthur Aron은 새로운 관계의 흥분이 사라진 후에, 새롭고 자극적인 활동에 함께 참여하는 것으로 파트너들이 지루함을 이겨낼 수 있다고 말한다. 한 실험에서, 그는 임의로 선택된 부부를 실험실로 데려와서, 바닥을 가로질러 체육용 매트를 깔고, 파트너의 손들을 손목에서 함께 묶고, 방의 한쪽 끝에서 다른 쪽 끝까지 손과 무릎으로 기어서 장애물을 넘어가도록 했다. 이것을 하는 내내 그들의 몸 사이에 베개를 끼워 가져오도록 했다. 다른 부부들은 한 번에 한 사람씩 매트를 가로질러 공을 굴리는 더 간단한 일을 받았다. 세 번째 그룹은 아무런 과제를 받지 않았다. 그 후에, 모든 참가자가 그들의 관계에 대해 설문조사를 받았다. Aron이 예상한 대로, 신선하고 자극적인 활동을 통해 그들만의 방식대로 몸부림치고 웃었던 부부들이 다른 부부들보다 <u>그들의 관계의 질에 더 만족하는</u> 것으로 보고되었다.

honeymoon n. 신혼여행 thrill n. 흥분
wear off phr. 사라지다, 닳다 combat v. 싸우다
boredom n. 지루함 engage in phr. ~에 참여하다
arousing adj. 자극적인 experiment n. 실험
randomly adv. 임의로, 무작위로 laboratory n. 실험실
gymnasium n. 체육관 wrist n. 손목 crawl v. 기어가다
barrier n. 장애물 pillow n. 베개 assignment n. 과제
afterward adv. 그 후에 struggle v. 몸부림치다, 투쟁하다

34 (2019 한국외대)

정답 ③

해설
① 즐겁고 신나는 움직임을 더 기꺼이 시도하는
② 그들의 운동 일정에 대해 더 열정적인
③ 그들의 관계의 질에 더 만족하는
④ 더 불안한 결혼생활을 할 것 같은

해설 지문의 빈칸을 채우는 문제이다. 지문의 처음에서 Aron이 새롭고 자극적인 활동에 함께 참여하는 것으로 파트너들이 지루함을 이겨낼 수 있다고 말했으므로, 빈칸에는 부부의 관계에 대해 긍정적인 내용이 나와야 적절하다는 것을 알 수 있다. 따라서 '그들의 관계의 질에 더 만족하는'이라고 한 ③번이 정답이다.

어휘 willing to phr. 기꺼이 ~하는 enthusiastic adj. 열정적인
routine n. 일정, 습관 troubled adj. 불안한

35 (2019 한국외대)

정답 ④

해설
① 행복하지 않은 결혼의 신호
② 결혼한 부부에게 실시된 세 가지 실험
③ 많은 결혼이 이혼으로 끝나는 이유
④ 당신의 결혼을 신선하게 유지하는 방법

해설 지문의 주제를 묻는 문제이다. 지문의 처음에서 부부가 신혼여행의 기분을 계속 이어갈 수 있도록 할 수 있는 무언가가 있을까 하고 질문으로 시작했다. 따라서 이 지문의 주제를 '당신의 결혼을 신선하게 유지하는 방법'이라고 표현한 ④번이 정답이다.

어휘 conduct v. (실험, 조사를) 실시하다 divorce n. 이혼

[36-37]

한 세기 전, Gustave Le Bon은 사람들이 군중을 이루기 위해 모였을 때 작동된 불가사의한 힘에 대해 글을 썼다. 그는

군중 내 일원임을 느끼는 것은 자부심의 확장(권력 의식), 충동 방출, *전염 의식*, 그리고 피암시성 강화의 원인이 되었다고 주장했다. Le Bon은 이러한 심리적 특징이 개인의 정체성을 군중의 정체성으로 통합하는 것에서 비롯되었다고 주장했다. Le Bon은 효과적인 군중 지도자가 행동을 직접적으로 가리키는 간결하고 이미지 같은 사상을 확인하고, 그리고 이러한 이미지 같은 사상을 반복하는 것에 의존했다고 추론했다: 확언은 이미지를 떠올리게 하고, 이미지는 감정을 불러오며, 감정은 행동을 이끈다. 군중 속 개인은 지도자의 행위를 모방하고, 이 모방은 한번 시작되면 속한 모든 사람들을 변화시킨다. Le Bon은 본질적으로 정서 전염에 관심이 없었지만, 군중 행동에 대한 그의 관찰은 정서 전염에 가장 영향받기 쉬운 개인의 일부 특징에 대한 단서를 포함하고 있을 수도 있다.

operate v. 작동되다   congregate v. 모이다
membership n. 일원임   contribute v. ~의 원인이 되다
enlargement n. 확장   ego n. 자부심   impulse n. 충동
contagion n. 전염, 감염   heighten v. 강화하다
suggestibility n. 피암시성(내부 또는 외부로부터 투입되는 자극을 암시로 받아들이는 경향성)
psychological adj. 심리적인   derive v. 비롯되다
absorption n. 통합   identity n. 정체성
rely on phr. ~에 의존하다   affirmation n. 확언
evoke v. 떠올려 주다, 불러내다   sentiment n. 감정, 정서
mimic v. 모방하다   mimicry n. 모방, 흉내
initiate v. 시작하다   inflect v. 변화시키다
per se phr. 본질적으로   observation n. 관찰
mob behavior phr. 군중 행동
susceptible adj. 영향받기 쉬운

36 [2020 서울여대]

정답 ②

해석 ① 말없이 행동하다
② 이미지 같은 사상을 제공하다
③ 같은 행위를 반복하다
④ 민중의 목소리를 듣다

해설 Le Bon이 주장하는 효과적인 군중 지도자의 특징을 파악하는 문제이다. 지문 중간에서 효과적인 군중 지도자가 간결하고 이미지 같은 사상을 확인하고, 그리고 이러한 이미지 같은 사상을 반복하는 것에 의존했다고 했으므로, Le Bon에 의한 효과적인 군중 지도자의 특징은 '이미지 같은 사상을 제공한다'는 것이다. 따라서 정답은 ②번이다.

37 [2020 서울여대]

정답 ④

해석 ① 그들은 스스로 영향력 있다고 느낀다.
② 그들은 서로의 감정에 감염되기 쉽다.
③ 그들은 집단 정체성에 지배되는 경향이 있다.
④ 그들은 지도자를 모방하기 전 서로를 모방한다.

해설 군중 속 개인에 대해 사실이 아닌 것을 파악하는 문제이다. 지문 중간에서 군중 속 개인은 지도자의 행위를 모방한다고 했으므로, '그들이 지도자를 모방하기 전 서로를 모방한다'는 것은 군중 속 개인에 대한 사실이 아니다. 따라서 정답은 ④번이다.

어휘 catch v. 감염되다, 걸리다   dominate v. 지배하다
collective adj. 집단의

[38-39]

지난 10년간 행동학자들은 몇몇 아주 흥미로운 통찰을 제안했다. 상류층을 대상으로 한 캘리포니아의 식료품점에 의해 실시된 한 가지 획기적인 실험에서, 연구원들은 잼을 진열한 시식 테이블을 설치했다. 첫 번째 테스트에서, 그들은 24개의 서로 다른 맛의 잼을 매력적인 배열로 내놓았고, 다른 날에는 6개만 진열했다. 시식에 참여했던 쇼핑객들은 가게에서 동일 브랜드의 어떤 잼이라도 살 수 있는 할인 쿠폰을 받았다. 더 많은 쇼핑객들이 24개의 잼이 있었을 때 진열대에 멈춘 것으로 드러났다. 하지만 이후 구매에 있어서, 6개의 잼이 있는 테이블에 멈춘 쇼핑객 중 무려 30퍼센트가 잼을 구매하는 단계로 넘어갔고, 24개의 선택권과 마주한 쇼핑객들 중 단 3퍼센트만이 구매한 것과 대비된다.

선택권이 크게 증가함에 따라, 선택 가능한 것들 사이에서 현명하게 구별할 수 있도록 하는 충분한 정보를 얻기 위해 필요한 노력이 추가적인 선택권을 가진 소비자에게 주는 혜택을 능가하는 지점이 있을 수도 있다. 이 지점에서, 선택은 더 이상 소비자를 자유롭게 해주는 것이 아니라, 압제한다. 즉, 몇 개의 선택이 좋다는 사실이 더 많은 선택이 더 좋다는 것을 반드시 의미하지는 않는다. 소비자들은 너무 많은 선택권이 정보 습득의 스트레스와 결합되어 심신을 피곤하게 만든다고 생각하는데, 이는 오해와 판단 착오의 위험, 이용 가능한 대안을 오해할 위험, 자신의 취향을 오해할 위험, 찰나의 변덕에 굴복하여 나중에 후회할 위험 때문이다.

behavioral adj. 행동의   intriguing adj. 아주 흥미로운
insight n. 통찰   landmark n. 획기적인 사건
upmarket adj. 상류층을 대상으로 한   sampling n. 시식
tempting adj. 매력적인   voucher n. 쿠폰
merely adv. 단지   selection n. 선택
multiply v. 크게 증가하다   sensibly adv. 현명하게
alternative n. 선택 가능한 것, 대안   outweigh v. 능가하다
liberate v. 자유롭게 해주다   tyrannize v. 압제하다
debilitating adj. 심신을 쇠약하게 하는
misperception n. 오해   miscalculation n. 판단 착오
misreading n. 오해   yield v. 굴복하다   whim n. 변덕
acquisition n. 습득

38 [2020 성균관대]

정답 ②

해석
① 선택과 자유 민주주의
② 선택의 역설
③ 자유 선택과 경제 성장
④ 정보와 인간 행동
⑤ 소비 사회에서 인간이 되는 것

해설 지문의 제목을 묻는 문제이다. 두 번째 문단에서 선택권이 크게 증가함에 따라, 선택 가능한 것들 사이에서 현명하게 구별할 수 있도록 하는 충분한 정보를 얻기 위해 필요한 노력이 추가적인 선택권을 가진 소비자에게 주는 혜택을 능가하는 지점이 있을 수도 있다고 하고, 소비자들은 너무 많은 선택권이 정보 습득의 스트레스와 결합되어 심신을 피곤하게 만든다고 생각한다고 했다. 따라서 이 지문의 제목을 '선택의 역설'이라고 표현한 ②번이 정답이다.

어휘 liberal adj. 자유주의의 democracy n. 민주주의
paradox n. 역설 consumer society phr. 소비 사회

39 [2020 성균관대]

정답 ③

해석
① 사람들은 완벽한 선택이 있다고 믿는다
② 쇼핑객들은 더 많은 선택에 의해 방해받지 않는다
③ 너무 많은 선택은 의욕을 꺾는다
④ 만약 당신이 24가지 종류의 모든 것을 가질 수 있다면, 결정하는 것은 쉬운 일이 된다
⑤ 물건이 더 비쌀수록, 결정이 어려워진다

해설 캘리포니아 식료품점의 쇼핑객들을 대상으로 한 실험이 무엇을 드러내는지 파악하는 문제이다. 마지막 문장에서 소비자들은 여러 오해와 판단 착오 등의 위험 때문에 너무 많은 선택권이 심신을 피곤하게 만든다고 생각한다고 했으므로, 실험이 드러낸 것은 '너무 많은 선택은 의욕을 꺾는다'는 것이다. 따라서 정답은 ③번이다.

어휘 put off phr. 방해하다 demotivate v. 의욕을 꺾다
variety n. 종류, 품종 daunting adj. 어려운

[40-42]

최근에, 영국 의사인 Lord Robert Winston은 런던에서 맨체스터로 가는 기차를 탔고, 자신이 자꾸 격분하고 있다는 것을 깨달았다. 한 여성이 전화를 받고 큰소리로 대화를 하기 시작했는데, 이 대화는 믿기 어렵게도 한 시간이나 지속되었다. 몹시 화가 나서, Winston은 그 여성에 대해 트위터로 메시지를 전달하기 시작했고, 그녀의 사진을 찍어서 4만 명이 넘는 팔로워들에게 그 사진을 보냈다. 기차가 목적지에 도착했을 때, Winston은 달아났다. 언론에서 그 여성을 기다리고 있었고 그녀에게 Lord의 메시지를 보여주었다. 그녀는 Winston의 행동을 단 한 단어로 무례하다고 말했다.

연구들은 무례함은 거의 보통 감기와 같이 빠르게 그리고 (A)바이러스처럼 퍼진다는 것을 보여주었다. 단지 무례함을 목격하는 것만으로도 우리는 결국 나중에 무례해질 가능성이 훨씬 더 크다. 일단 감염되면, 우리는 더 공격적이고, 덜 창의적이며, 일을 더 못하게 된다. 성격의 그러한 요소를 없애는 유일한 방법은 그렇게 하기 위해 (B)의식적인 결정을 하는 것이다. 우리는 서로 얼굴을 맞대고 큰 소리로 말하는 용기가 있어야 한다. 우리는 "그만 하세요."라고 말해야 한다. Winston의 경우는 여성에게 다가가서 정중하게 그녀에게 더 조용히 얘기하거나 다른 때에 전화하는 것을 부탁하는 것이다.

우리가 낯선 사람의 무례한 행동에서 느끼는 분노와 부당함은 우리가 이상한 행동을 하도록 만들 수 있다. 2천 명의 성인을 조사한 한 연구에서, 사람들이 했던 보복 행위는 범위가 터무니없는 것("저는 그들의 자동차 앞 유리에 감자튀김을 문질렀어요.")에서 충격적인 것("저는 회사에서 그들을 고의로 방해했어요.")까지 이르렀다.

우리는 정면으로 무례함을 방지하기 위해 싸워야 한다. 우리는 상점에서 무례한 일이 일어나는 것을 보면, 나서서 무슨 말을 해야 한다. 동료에게 무례한 일이 일어난다면, 우리는 그것을 지적해야 한다. 우리는 가장 친한 친구들을 지키는 것과 같은 방법으로 낯선 사람을 지켜야 한다. 하지만 우리는 공격적이지 않고 스스로에게 무례하지 않으면서 품위 있게 그렇게 할 수 있다. 무례한 사람들은 다른 사람들의 눈을 통해 자신들의 행동을 볼 수 있기 때문에, 스스로 자신의 성격에서 그 무례한 요소를 없앨 가능성이 훨씬 더 높다. <u>이런 무례함의 경향이 많아지면서, 문명사회는 정중함을 필요로 한다.</u>

---

steadily adv. 자꾸, 끊임없이 **enrage** v. 격분하다
pick up phr. 전화를 받다 **unbelievable** adj. 믿기 어려운
furious adj. 몹시 화가 난 **destination** n. 목적지, 도착지
bolt v. 달아나다, 도망치다 **press** n. 언론
rudeness n. 무례함 **common** adj. 보통의
witness v. 목격하다 **in turn** phr. 결국
later on phr. 나중에 **infect** v. 감염시키다
aggressive adj. 공격적인
strain n. (성격·태도상의 특별한) 요소, 부담
conscious adj. 의식적인, 의도적인
have the guts to do phr. ~하는 용기가 있다
face to face phr. 서로 얼굴을 맞대고
at another time phr. 다른 때에 **rage** n. 분노, 격노
injustice n. 부당함, 불평등 **behavior** n. 행동
stranger n. 낯선 사람
drive v. (사람을 특정한 방식의 행동을 하도록) 만들다
odd adj. 이상한 **revenge** n. 보복, 원한
ridiculous adj. 터무니없는, 말도 안 되는, 웃기는
disturbing adj. 충격적인, 불안감을 주는
sabotage v. 고의로 방해하다, 사보타주하다
combat v. (방지하기 위해) 싸우다 **colleague** n. 동료
point out phr. 지적하다 **defend** v. 지키다, 옹호하다
grace n. 품위 **trace** n. 흔적 **aggression** n. 공격성

40 [2019 단국대]

정답 ③

해설 (A)virally(바이러스처럼)와 비슷한 의미를 가진 어휘를 묻고 있다. ①번 slovenly는 '단정치 못하게', ②번 virtually는 '사실상', ③번 contagiously는 '전염적으로', ④번 heretically는 '이단으로'라는 의미이다. 따라서 ③번이 정답이다.

41 [2019 단국대]

정답 ④

해석
① 공격적인 트위터 메시지
② 지나친 부당함
③ 터무니없는 행동
④ 예의 바른 요청

해설 밑줄 친 (B) conscious decision의 의미를 추론하는 문제이다. 두 번째 문단에서 우리는 서로 얼굴을 맞대고 큰 소리로 말하는 용기가 있어야 한다고 하며, 예시로 Winston의 경우는 여성에게 다가가서 정중하게 그녀에게 더 조용히 얘기하거나 다른 때에 전화하는 것을 부탁하는 것이라고 했다. 따라서, (B) conscious decision의 의미를 '예의 바른 요청'이라고 한 ④번이 정답이다.

어휘 **outrageous** adj. 지나친, 터무니없는
ludicrous adj. 터무니없는
decent adj. 예의 바른, 품위 있는

42 [2019 단국대]

정답 ④

해석 ① 당신이 낯선 사람을 만날 때 정중함은 가장 좋은 행동이다.
② 우리 시대의 소셜 미디어는 무례함을 증가시킨다.
③ 다른 사람들을 칭찬하는 것은 당신이 그들에게 우월감을 가질 수 있게 한다.
④ 이런 무례함의 경향이 많아지면서, 문명사회는 정중함을 필요로 한다.

해설 지문의 빈칸을 채우는 문제이다. 네 번째 문단에서 우리는 정면으로 무례함을 방지하기 위해 싸워야 한다고 하고, 공격적이지 않고 스스로에게 무례하지 않으면서 품위 있게 그렇게 할 수 있다고 했으므로, 빈칸에는 무례함의 경향이 많아지면서, 문명사회가 정중함을 필요로 한다는 내용이 나와야 적절하다는 것을 알 수 있다. 따라서 '이런 무례함의 경향이 많아지면서, 문명사회는 정중함을 필요로 한다'라고 한 ④번이 정답이다.

어휘 **policy** n. 행동, 수단, 정책 **compliment** v. 칭찬하다
feel superior to phr. 우월감을 갖다 **tide** n. 경향, 흐름
civilization n. 문명사회 **civility** n. 정중함, 예의 바름

[43-45]

한 실험에서 참가자들은 이야기의 도식을 암시하는 제목이 앞에 붙은 이야기를 읽었다. 예를 들어, 한 이야기는 "40층에서 평화의 행진 바라보기"라는 제목이 붙었다. 그 이야기의 대부분은 돌아다니는 군중들, 텔레비전 카메라, 그리고 연설에 관한 이야기였다. 하지만, 그 이야기의 중간에 "착륙은 온화했고, 대기권은 어떠한 특별한 옷도 입을 필요가 없을 정도였다."는 것과 같이 이상한 문장이 있었다. 그 문장을 읽은 대부분의 사람은 평화의 행진에 대한 그들의 나머지 도식에 그 문장을 맞출 수가 없었기 때문에 그 문장을 전혀 이해하지 못했다. (A)그 결과, 사람들이 나중에 그 이야기를 기억해내라는 요청을 받았을 때, 그들은 그 특정한 문장을 기억하지 못했다. 또 다른 참가자 집단은 같은 이야기를 읽었지만, 그 이야기의 제목이 "사람이 거주하는 행성으로의 우주여행"이라고 들었다. 이 집단은 그 이상한 문장을 그들이 읽었을 때 완벽하게 이해할 수 있었고, 또한 평화의 행진에 대해 읽고 있다고 생각한 참가자들보다 그 이야기를 더 잘 기억해내는 것 같았다. 당신이 이야기를 읽거나 들을 때, 그리고 당신이 삶에서 사건을 경험할 때, 당신은 그것들을 당신이 시간에 걸쳐 발달시킨 도식에 비추어 이해한다. 이 도식들은 사건의 어떤 부분이 당신에게 이해가 되도록 만드는가에 영향을 끼치는 것뿐만이 아닌, 당신이 그 사건에 대해 무엇을 기억하는지에도 영향을 준다. 당신은 (B)당신이 가진 도식에 일관된 세부사항들을 기억하려는 경향이 있다. 들어맞지 않는 것들은 종종 기억에서 떨어져 나오게 된다.

participant n. 참가자 **precede** v. 앞에 나오다, 선행하다
schema n. 도식 **landing** n. 착륙
atmosphere n. 대기권; 분위기
recall v. 기억해내다, 떠올리다 **particular** adj. 특정한
inhabited adj. (사람이) 거주하는 **experience** v. 경험하다
in light of phr. ~에 비추어 **make sense** phr. 이해가 되다
drop out of phr. ~에서 떨어져 나오다, ~에서 낙오하다

43 [2019 한국외대]

정답 ②

해석 ① 행성 착륙: 잊혀진 이야기
② 정신적 도식: 기억의 결정 요소
③ 독서 실험: 밝혀지는 인간의 수수께끼
④ 정신의 힘: 평화의 행진과 우주 탐사의 대결

해설 지문의 제목을 묻는 문제이다. 지문의 후반에서 당신이 이야기를 읽거나 들을 때, 그리고 당신이 삶에서 사건을 경험할 때, 당신은 그것들을 당신이 시간에 걸쳐 발달시킨 도식에 비추어 이해한다고 하였다. 따라서 이 지문의 제목을 '정신적 도식: 기억의 결정 요소'라고 표현한 ②번이 정답이다.

어휘 **determinant** n. 결정 요소 **unravelling** adj. 밝혀지는
exploration n. 탐사

44 2019 한국외대

정답 ①

해석 ① 그 결과　　② 대조적으로
③ 그럼에도 불구하고　　④ 그러나

해설 빈칸에 적절한 연결어를 넣는 문제이다. 빈칸 앞 문장은 사람들이 접한 이상한 문장을 이미 갖고 있는 도식에 맞출 수 없었다는 내용이고, 빈칸 뒤 문장은 사람들이 그 문장을 기억해내지 못했다는 내용이다. 따라서 결과를 나타내는 연결어인 ① As a result(그 결과)가 정답이다.

45 2019 한국외대

정답 ②

해석 ① 정신 안에서 즐거운
② 당신이 가진 도식에 일관된
③ 뒤따르는 문장과 비슷한
④ 당신에게 흥미롭고 기억할 만한

해설 지문의 빈칸을 채우는 문제이다. 지문의 마지막에서 도식들은 사건의 어떤 부분이 당신에게 이해가 되도록 만드는가에 영향을 끼치는 것뿐만이 아닌, 당신이 그 사건에 대해 무엇을 기억하는지에도 영향을 준다고 했으므로, 빈칸에는 세부사항들이 도식에 들어맞거나 연결되는 것에 대한 내용이 나와야 적절하다는 것을 알 수 있다. 따라서 '당신이 가진 도식에 일관된'이라고 한 ②번이 정답이다.

어휘 enjoyable adj. 즐거운　consistent adj. 일관된
in line with phr. ~와 비슷한
following adj. 뒤따르는, 그다음의
memorable adj. 기억할 만한

[46-47]

내가 하품 전염을 연구하기 시작했을 때, 나에게는 이미 사회적 억제에 대한 실험적 증거가 있었고, 그 증거는 실험에서 자기 보고의 사용에 대한 근거를 제공했다. 내 하품 연구가 주의를 끌면서(대중 매체가 이 주제에 대한 이야기에 몹시 집착하는 성향을 가지고 있다), 나는 하품에 대한 억제가 발생하는 것을 보는 경험을 했다.
어느 날 텔레비전 뉴스 프로그램 팀이 한 부분을 녹화하기 위해 나타났다. 내 조언에 맞서, 그 프로그램의 제작자는 큰 강의를 듣는 학생들의 절반은 딸꾹질에 관한 억제 구절을 읽은 반면 절반은 하품에 관한 글을 읽었던 내 실험을 재현하는 것에 착수했다. 보통은 하품의 영향에 관한 글은 확고하고, 다른 대학교에서 수업 시간에 전염의 증거로 사용되어왔다.
내가 예상했던 대로, 그 전염의 증거는 국영 네트워크 텔레비전 팀에 의한 정밀 조사를 직접적으로 견뎌 내지 못했다. 학생들이 읽고 있을 때 카메라가 돌아가자, 평소 하품하는 양의 아주 적은 일부만 관찰되었다. 영상 팀은 하품에 대한 사회적 억제의 강력한 영향을 보여주는 나의 원래 연구로부터 무심코 한 것 치곤 유익했던 변형된 연구를 수행했다. 국영 텔레비전에 자원할 정도로 매우 의욕을 가지고 있던 하품을 많이 하는 사람들조차도 카메라 앞에 앉자 하품하는 것을 멈췄다. 하품의 사회적 억제가 무의식적으로 발생했고, 사회적 억제가 하품하는 사람이 무례하거나 부적절한 행동을 억제하려는 자발적인 현상이 아니었다는 것은 주목할 만하다. 사회적으로 중요한 행동은 무의식적인 과정에 의해 야기될 수도 혹은 억제될 수도 있다.

---

experimental adj. 실험적인
social inhibition phr. 사회적 억제, 사회적 금지
yawning n. 하품　contagion n. 전염, 감염
self-reporting n. 자기 보고
voracious adj. 몹시 집착하는, 매우 열심인
appetite n. 성향, 욕구　magazine n. (라디오·텔레비전에서 특정 화제에 대한) 프로그램, 잡지
turn up phr. 나타나다, 도착하다　tape v. 녹화하다, 녹음하다
segment n. 부분　re-create v. 재현하다
control n. 억제, 통제　passage n. 구절
hiccupping n. 딸꾹질　robust adj. 확고한, 튼튼한
demonstration n. 증거, 증명, 실물 설명
up-close-and-personal adv. 직접적으로, 상세하게, 친밀히
scrutiny n. 정밀 조사, 철저한 검토
roll v. (기계가) 돌아가다, 작동되다　fraction n. 일부, 부분
observe v. 관찰하다　motivated adj. 의욕을 가진
prolific adj. 많은　notable adj. 주목할 만한
unconsciously adv. 무의식적으로
voluntary adj. 자발적인　suppress v. 억제하다
inappropriate adj. 부적절한

46 2019 이화여대

정답 ⑤

해석 ① 단언하다, 주장하다　② 제거하다, 없애다
③ 흉내 내다　　④ 없애다, 지우다
⑤ 견뎌 내다

해설 지문의 빈칸을 채우는 문제이다. 빈칸 뒤에서 국영 네트워크 텔레비전 팀에서 나의 연구로부터 변형된 연구를 수행했는데, 하품의 사회적 억제가 무의식적으로 발생했고, 사회적 억제가 하품하는 사람이 무례하거나 부적절한 행동을 억제하려는 자발적인 현상이 아니었다고 했으므로 '내가 예상했던 대로, 그 전염의 증거는 국영 네트워크 텔레비전 팀에 의한 정밀 조사를 직접적으로 _____지 못했다'는 문맥에서 빈칸에는 '견뎌 내다'를 의미하는 'survive'가 들어가는 것이 자연스럽다. 따라서 ⑤번이 정답이다.

47 2019 이화여대

정답 ⑤

해석 ① 당신이 관찰될 수도 있다는 강렬한 자기 인식은 하품을 억제한다.

② 사회 과학 공동체에서 당신이 자신의 실험을 객관적으로 보고할 수 있는지 아닌지에 대한 의혹이 있다.
③ 하품에 관한 구절을 읽는 사람들은 딸꾹질에 관한 구절을 읽는 사람들보다 하품할 가능성이 더 크다.
④ 텔레비전 프로그램 제작자에 의해 수행된 실험은 무의식적으로 통제된 행동의 사회적 억제에 대한 강력한 증거를 제공한다.
⑤ 다른 사람들과 공감하는 능력이 부족한 사람들은 전염되는 하품에 가장 영향을 받기 쉽다.

해설 지문을 통해 추론할 수 없는 것을 고르는 문제이다. 하품 전염이 사회적 억제에 영향을 받는다는 내용이므로, 다른 사람과 공감하는 능력이 부족한 사람들은 전염되는 하품에 가장 영향을 받기 쉬운지는 유추할 수 없다. 따라서 ⑤번이 정답이다.

오답 분석
① 세 번째 문단의 With the cameras rolling as the students read, only a tiny fraction of the usual amount of yawning was observed를 통해 당신이 관찰될 수도 있다는 강력한 자기 인식은 하품을 억제한다는 것을 알 수 있다.
② 두 번째 문단의 Against my advice, the show's producer ~ about hiccupping을 통해 사회 과학 공동체에서 당신이 자신의 실험을 객관적으로 보고할 수 있는지 아닌지에 대한 의혹이 있다는 것을 알 수 있다.
③ 두 번째 문단의 Against my advice, the show's producer ~ about hiccupping. Normally the effect of the yawning article is robust, ~ a demonstration of contagion in classes at other universities를 통해 하품에 관한 구절을 읽는 사람들은 딸꾹질에 관한 구절을 읽는 사람들보다 하품할 가능성이 더 크다는 것을 알 수 있다.
④ 세 번째 문단의 It is notable that ~ the yawner to suppress a rude or inappropriate act를 통해 텔레비전 프로그램 제작자에 의해 수행된 실험은 무의식적으로 통제된 행동의 사회적 억제에 대한 강력한 증거를 제공한다는 것을 알 수 있다.

어휘 self-awareness n. 자기 인식
objectively adv. 객관적으로
deficient adj. 부족한, 결핍된   empathize v. 공감하다
be susceptible to phr. ~에 영향을 받기 쉽다

[48-50]

1874년에 영국의 (A)박식가인 Francis Galton은 미국의 과학자들의 표본을 분석했고 막대한 다수가 맨 먼저 태어난 아들이라는 점을 알아냈다. 이것은 Galton이 맨 먼저 태어난 아이들이 자신이 지적으로 잘 자랄 수 있게 해준 부모로부터 특별한 수준의 관심을 받는 것을 즐겼다고 추측하는 것으로 이어졌다. 반세기 후에, 오스트리아의 심리학자인 Alfred Adler는 성격에 관하여 비슷한 주장을 했다. Adler가 생각하기에, 맨 먼저 태어난 아이들은 더 성실한 반면, 늦게 태어난 아이들은 더 외향적이고 정서적으로 안정적이었다. [A] 그 이후의 많은 연구들이 이 개념들을 분석해왔지만, 연구의 결과들은 분명하지 않았는데, 일부는 개념들을 지지했고 일부는 인정하지 않았다. 이제 독일에 있는 라이프치히 대학교의 Stefan Schmukle이 이끄는 팀에서 현재까지 이 문제에 대해 가장 포괄적인 증거를 모아 오고 있다. 그 결론은 Adler는 틀렸지만, Galton은 옳았을 수도 있었다는 것이다.

Schmukle이 이끄는 팀이 알아낸 출생 순서는 성격에 영향을 미치지 않았다: 맨 먼저 태어난 아이들은 어린 형제자매보다 성실하거나 외향적이거나 신경과민인 것이 그 이상도 이하도 아니었다. 하지만 출생 순서가 지능에는 영향을 미쳤다. [B] 두 명의 아이가 있는 가정에서, 우연히 예상되는 50퍼센트가 아니라 그 당시의 60퍼센트는 첫째 아이가 둘째보다 더 똑똑했다. 평균적으로, 이 60퍼센트는 첫째와 둘째 형제자매 사이에서 1.5 IQ 점수의 차이를 의미한다. [C] 그 수치는 이전의 연구들로부터의 대다수의 의견과 일치하며, 그러므로 확인된 것으로 보인다. 그럼에도 불구하고, 1.5 IQ 점수 차이는 꽤 작은 차이이고, 이 차이가 Galton의 최초 의견의 이유가 되기에 충분한지 아닌지는 (B)논의할 여지가 있다. 아무튼, 이 차이는 분명히 결정론적이진 않다. [D] Galton은 9명 중 막내였다.

analyze v. 분석하다   vast adj. 막대한   majority n. 다수
first-born adj. 맨 먼저 태어난   speculate v. 추측하다
attention n. 관심   thrive v. 잘 자라다
intellectually adv. 지적으로   psychologist n. 심리학자
argument n. 주장   personality n. 성격
conscientious adj. 성실한, 양심적인
extrovert adj. 외향적인   emotionally adv. 정서적으로
stable adj. 안정적인   subsequent adj. 그 이후의, 다음의
explore v. 분석하다, 탐구하다
finding n. (조사·연구 등의) 결과
comprehensive adj. 포괄적인, 종합적인
evidence n. 증거   conclusion n. 결론
no more, no less phr. 그 이상도 이하도 아닌
sib n. 형제자매   neurotic adj. 신경과민의
intelligence n. 지능   by chance phr. 우연히
translate v. 의미하다   difference n. 차이   figure n. 수치
consensus n. 대다수의 의견   confirmed adj. 확인된
account for phr. ~의 이유가 되다
observation n. 의견, 관찰   deterministic adj. 결정론적인

48 2019 국민대

정답 ③

해설 (A) polymath(박식가)와 비슷한 의미를 가진 어휘를 묻고 있다. ①번 a man of great ability in mathematics는 '수학에 뛰어난 재능을 가진 사람', ②번 a man of good taste in food and clothes는 '음식과 옷에 좋은 취향을 가진 사람', ③번 a man of much learning in various fields는 '다양한 분야에서 많이 유식한 사람', ④번 a man of huge wealth with good manners는 '좋은 매너가 있는 막대한 부를 가진 사람'이라는 의미이다. 따라서 ③번이 정답이다.

어휘 **mathematics** n. 수학　**taste** n. 취향
various adj. 다양한　**field** n. 분야

49 [2019 국민대]

정답 ③

해설 (B) moot(논의할 여지가 있는)와 비슷한 의미를 가진 어휘를 묻고 있다. ①번 useless는 '쓸모없는', ②번 verified는 '확인된', ③번 debatable은 '논란의 여지가 있는', ④번 insignificant는 '사소한'이라는 의미이다. 따라서 ③번이 정답이다.

50 [2019 국민대]

정답 ④

해설 지문의 흐름상 주어진 문장이 들어가기에 가장 적절한 위치를 고르는 문제이다. [D]의 앞부분에 출생 순서가 성격에 영향을 미치지 않았으나 지능에는 영향을 미쳤다는 내용이 나오고, [D] 앞 문장에서 이 차이가 Galton의 최초 의견의 이유가 되기에 충분한지 아닌지는 논의할 여지가 있고 결정론적이지 않다고 했으므로, [D] 자리에 주어진 문장 'Galton은 9명 중 막내였다'가 들어가야 글의 흐름이 자연스럽게 연결된다. 따라서 ④번이 정답이다.

[51-53]

충고에 관해 흥미로운 것은 우리가 종종 충고를 잘못된 사람으로부터 받게 된다는 것이다. 다르게 이야기하면, 우리는 대체로 평범한 사람들의 조언을 과소평가하는 반면, 자격이 있는 전문가의 조언은 과대평가하고 있다. 조언을 받는 것이 문제가 되는 한 가지 이유는 자격이 꽤 큰 문제가 된다는 것이다. 인식의 기벽인, 낙관주의 편향은 우리 중 대다수가 우리에게 불리한 역경이 계속 쌓여감에도 모든 것들이 잘 풀릴 것이라는 일반적인 희망을 품게 한다. 여러 연구에 따르면, 충고를 해주는 사람이 전문가로 보일 때 낙관주의 편향은 점차 증가하게 된다. 따라서 우리가 전문가의 말을 듣게 된다면, 심지어 전문가가 틀렸다는 것이 종종 입증되었음에도 불구하고, 전문가의 조언은 성공에 대한 기대감을 높이게 된다.

우리 대부분은 다른 누군가의 조언을 받는 것에 익숙하지 않다. 우리는 일반적으로 다른 사람의 의견에 비해 우리 자신의 의견에 더 많은 지분을 두게 된다. 이것이 자기중심적 편향이라 불리는 또 다른 인식의 맹점이다. 우리를 비판하는 사람이 옳다고 인정하기보다는, 그들이 우리의 천재성을 이해하기에는 너무 우둔하다거나, 단순히 질투를 느끼고 있다거나, 어떤 숨겨진 의도가 있다고 믿기가 쉽다고 생각된다. 겸손을 위해 요구되는 도약은 너무 거대한 난관인 것이다. 한 가지 도움이 되는 요령이 동양철학에서 발견된다. 한국의 선종 스님인, 혜민 스님에 따르면, 다른 사람이 우리에게 충고하려 할 때, 바로 그때가 자신에 대한 방어를 높이지 않고, 낮춰야 하는 시간이다.

undervalue v. 과소평가하다　**input** n. 조언
overvalue v. 과대평가하다　**credentialed** adj. 자격이 있는
problematic adj. 문제가 있는　**optimism** n. 낙관주의
bias n. 편향　**cognitive** adj. 인지의　**quirk** n. 기벽
odds n. 역경　**stack** v. 쌓다　**ratchet up** phr. 증가하다
enhance v. 높이다　**adept** adj. ~에 익숙한
blind spot phr. 맹점　**egocentric** adj. 자기중심적인
grasp v. 이해하다　**leap** n. 도약　**humility** n. 겸손
zen n. 선종　**precisely** adv. 바로　**defense** n. 방어

51 [2020 한성대]

정답 ④

해석 ① 혜민 스님은 자기중심적 편향을 믿는다.
② 스님은 방어를 올리는 것을 좋아한다.
③ 사람들은 자신의 의견보다 다른 사람의 의견을 더 가치 있게 생각한다.
④ 충고를 받아들이는 것은 도전일 수 있다.

해설 지문의 내용과 일치하는 것을 묻는 문제이다. 지문의 두 번째 문단에서, 우리 대부분은 다른 누군가의 조언을 받는 것에 익숙하지 않다고 했으므로, 충고를 받아들이는 것이 도전일 수 있다는 것은 지문의 내용과 일치한다. 따라서 ④번이 정답이다.

오답 분석
① 지문의 두 번째 문단에서, 자기중심적 편향을 줄이기 위한 요령을 동양철학에서 발견할 수 있다고 하면서, 그 예시로 혜민 스님의 이야기를 제시하고 있으므로, 혜민 스님이 자기중심적 편향을 믿는다는 것은 지문의 내용과 다르다.
② 지문의 두 번째 문단에서, 혜민 스님은 남들이 충고하려 할 때, 자신을 보호하는 방어를 높이지 말고 내려야 한다고 했으므로, 스님이 방어를 올리는 것을 좋아한다는 것은 지문의 내용과 다르다.
③ 지문의 두 번째 문단에서, 우리는 일반적으로 남들에 의견보다 자신의 의견에 더 많은 지분을 두게 된다고 했으므로, 사람들은 자신의 의견보다 다른 사람의 의견을 더 가치 있게 생각한다는 것은 지문의 내용과 다르다.

어휘 **value** v. 가치 있게 생각하다

52 [2020 한성대]

정답 ①

해석 ① 다수의 사람들은 누군가로부터 충고를 받는 것에 능숙하다.
② 평범한 사람의 충고는 때때로 과소평가된다.
③ 충고가 항상 적절한 사람들에 의해 주어지는 것은 아니다.
④ 전문가의 충고는 보통 과대평가된다.

해설 지문의 내용과 일치하지 않는 것을 묻는 문제이다. 지문의 두 번째 문단에서 우리 대부분은 다른 누군가의 조언을 받는 것에 익숙하지 않다고 했으므로, 다수의 사람들이 누군가로부터 충고를 받는 것에 능숙하다는 것은 지문의 내용과 다르다. 따라서 ①번이 정답이다.

오답 분석
② 지문의 첫 번째 문단에서, 우리는 항상 평범한 사람의 충고를 과소평가한다고 했으므로, 평범한 사람의 충고가 때때로 과소평가된다는 것은 지문의 내용과 일치한다.
③ 지문의 첫 번째 문장에서, 충고에 관해 흥미로운 것은 그것이 때때로 잘못된 사람으로부터 주어진다는 것이라고 했으므로, 충고가 항상 적절한 사람들에 의해 주어지는 것이 아니라는 것은 지문의 내용과 일치한다.
④ 지문의 첫 번째 문단에서, 우리는 평범한 사람의 충고를 과소평가하는 반면, 전문가의 충고는 과대평가한다고 했으므로, 전문가의 충고가 보통 과대평가된다는 것은 지문의 내용과 일치한다.

어휘 proficient adj. 능숙한 appropriate adj. 적절한

53 [2020 한성대]
정답 ③

해석
① 의제
② 의도
③ 확장
④ 동기

해설 문맥상 빈칸에 적절하지 않은 어휘를 묻는 문제이다. 빈칸이 포함된 문장은 자기중심적 편향 때문에 사람들은 자신을 비판하는 사람들이 옳다고 생각하기보다는, 그들이 자신의 천재성을 이해할 수 없을 정도로 우둔하거나, 질투를 느끼거나, 혹은 어떤 의도 혹은 목적을 가지고 있기 때문에 비판하는 것이라 믿게 된다는 내용이므로, '확장'이라는 의미의 extensions는 빈칸에 적절하지 않다. 따라서 ③번이 정답이다.

[54-56]

어디에서나 사회적인 윤활유 역할을 하는 거짓 미소의 정체가 새로운 연구에 의해 드러났는데, 그 연구에서 진정한 기쁨을 나타내는 특정한 근육 패턴이 불쾌함을 감추기 위한 미소의 패턴과 다르다는 것을 구별해냈다. 심리학자 Ekman 박사와 그의 동료들은 사람이 감정을 바꿀 때 나타나는 100개 이상의 얼굴 근육 패턴을 분석하기 위한 기술을 발전시켰다. 그 방법을 통해, 그들은 얼굴이 주어진 감정 표현을 떠맡게 되었을 때 어떤 근육이 활동 중인지 정확하게 판단할 수 있었다.
거짓말에 대한 연구에서, 진짜 미소는 불행한 감정을 숨기는 미소와 두 가지 사항이 달랐다. 자연스럽게 생긴 미소에서는, 볼이 올라가고 눈 주위의 근육이 팽팽해지며, 눈꼬리로부터 뻗어 나온 선인 잔주름을 만들고, 눈썹 주위의 피부가 눈 쪽을 향해 살짝 아래로 쳐진다. 하지만, 거짓 미소에서는 얼굴이 소위 행복의 표현이라는 것과는 별개로 보이는 미소 뒤의 불행한 감정의 자취를 드러내는데, 예를 들어, 눈썹 사이의 근육을 약간 찡그리는 것이 있다. 미소가 특별하게 넓지 않다면 눈은 잔주름을 만들지 않을 것이다. 그리고 심지어 그때에도, 가장 하기 힘든 눈썹 주변 피부의 숨길 수 없는 처짐이 나타나지 않을 것이다. 이 연구는 누군가 미소라는 가면 뒤에서 신체적인 고통, 감정적인 괴로움, 또는 사악한 의도를 숨기는 때를 알기 위해 때때로 미묘한 신호에 의존할 필요가 있는 사람에게 특히 중요할 수 있다.

---

ubiquitous adj. 어디에나 존재하는   lubricant n. 윤활유
unmask v. 정체를 드러내다   differentiate v. 구별하다
displeasure n. 불쾌함   psychologist n. 심리학자
precisely adv. 정확하게   at play phr. 활동 중인
differ from phr. ~와 다르다
on ~ counts phr. ~가지 사항에서
spontaneous adj. 자연스럽게 생기는, 자발적인
tighten v. 팽팽하게 하다   crow's feet phr. (눈가의) 잔주름
eyebrow n. 눈썹   droop v. 처지다
apart from phr. ~와는 별개로   supposed adj. 소위
furrow v. 찡그리다   tell-tale adj. 숨길 수 없는
feign v. 가장하다   emerge v. 나타나다   subtle n. 미묘한
cue n. 신호   anguish n. 괴로움

54 [2019 한국외대]
정답 ①

해석
① 진짜 미소와 가짜 미소의 해부학
② 얼굴 표현과 근육의 움직임
③ 감정의 얼굴 표현 읽기
④ 누군가가 거짓말을 하고 있는지 구별하는 방법

해설 지문의 제목을 묻는 문제이다. 지문의 전반에 걸쳐 진짜 미소와 거짓된 미소에서 근육과 피부의 움직임이 어떻게 다른지에 대해 설명하고 있다. 따라서 이 지문의 제목을 '진짜 미소와 가짜 미소의 해부학'이라고 표현한 ①번이 정답이다.

어휘 anatomy n. 해부학 fake adj. 가짜의, 모조의
tell v. 구별하다

55 [2019 한국외대]
정답 ④

해석
① 주름진 눈꺼풀
② 찡그려진 눈썹
③ 길어진 눈썹의 선
④ 쳐진 눈썹

해설 진짜 미소의 신호인 것을 찾는 문제이다. 지문 중간에서 자연스럽게 생긴 미소에서는 볼이 올라가고 눈 주위의 근육이 팽팽해지며, 눈꼬리로부터 뻗어 나온 선인 잔주름을 만들고, 눈썹 주위의 피부가 눈 쪽을 향해 살짝 아래로 쳐진다고 설명하고 있다. 따라서 정답은 ④번이다.

어휘 wrinkled adj. 주름진 eyelid n. 눈꺼풀

56 [2019 한국외대]

정답 ③

해석 ① 진짜 미소에서는 볼이 위로 움직인다.
② 얼굴 근육은 100개 이상이 있다.
③ 이 연구는 범죄자 수사를 위해 사용될 수 있다.
④ 거짓으로 미소 짓는 것은 흔한 관례이다.

해설 지문을 통해 추론할 수 없는 것을 고르는 문제이다. 지문의 마지막에서 이 연구는 누군가 미소라는 가면 뒤에서 신체적인 고통, 감정적인 괴로움, 또는 사악한 의도를 숨기는 때를 알기 위해 때때로 미묘한 신호에 의존할 필요가 있는 사람에게 특히 중요할 수 있다고는 했지만, 이를 통해 이 연구는 범죄자 수사를 위해 사용될 수 있는지는 유추할 수 없으므로 정답은 ③번이다.

오답 분석
① In spontaneous smiles, the cheeks move up and the muscles around the eyes tighten을 통해 '진짜 미소에서는 볼이 위로 움직인다'는 것을 알 수 있다.
② Psychologist Dr. Ekman and his colleagues ~ for analyzing more than 100 muscle patterns of the face as a person changes expression을 통해 '얼굴 근육은 100개 이상이 있다'는 것을 알 수 있다.
④ The false smile, a ubiquitous social lubricant를 통해 '거짓으로 미소 짓는 것은 흔한 관례이다'라는 것을 알 수 있다.

어휘 criminal n. 범죄자 investigation n. 수사
falsely adv. 거짓으로 practice n. 관례, 관습

[57-59]

만약 당신이 미국에 있는 누군가, 혹은 영국에서 사업을 하는 누군가에게 그 사람의 생활 속 기쁨을 가장 방해하는 것이 무엇인지 물어본다면, 그 사람은 "생존 경쟁"이라고 말할 것이다. 그 사람은 정말 진심으로 생존 경쟁이라고 말할 것이고, 그렇다고 믿을 것이다. 보기에 따라서는, 그게 사실이지만, 다른 매우 중요한 의미에서는, 완전히 틀렸다. 생존 경쟁은 물론, 일어나는 것이다. 생존 경쟁은 우리가 운이 나쁘면 우리 중 누구에게나 일어날 것이다. 예를 들어, 생존 경쟁은 Conrad의 영웅 Falk에게 일어났는데, 그는 깨닫고 보니 버려진 배에 있었고, 다른 사람들 말고는 먹을 게 없는 화기를 소유하고 있었던 선원들 사이의 두 명 중 하나였다. 두 사람이 식사를 마치고 나자, 진짜 생존 경쟁이 시작되었다. Falk가 이겼지만, 그 뒤 쭉 채식주의자가 되었다. 이제 생존 경쟁은 영국의 그 사업가가 "생존 경쟁"(A)에 대해 말할 때 의미했던 것이 아니다. 생존 경쟁은 본래 사소한 것의 품위를 높이기 위해 그가 고른 부정확한 관용구이다. 사업가에게 삶에서 그의 계층에서 아는 사람 중에 굶어 죽은 사람이 얼마나 많이 있었는지 물어보아라. 그의 친구들이 파멸된 후에 무슨 일이 일어났는지 물어보아라. 모든 사람은 파멸할 기회를 가질 만큼 부유해본 적이 한 번도 없는 사람보다 파멸한 사업가가 아직까지 물질적 위안과 관련

있기 때문에 (B)형편이 더 낫다는 것을 알고 있다. 그러므로, 사람들이 생존 경쟁에 대해 의미하는 것은 실제로 성공을 위한 경쟁이다. 그 경쟁에 참여했을 때 사람들이 두려워하는 것은 다음 날 아침에 아침 식사를 못 하는 게 아니라, (C)자신들의 주변 사람보다 더 뛰어나지 못하는 것이다.

in business phr. 사업을 하는
interfere v. 방해하다, 간섭하다 enjoyment n. 기쁨, 즐거움
existence n. 생활, 생계
the struggle for life phr. 생존 경쟁
in all sincerity phr. 정말 진심으로, 진정으로
in a certain sense phr. 보기에 따라서는
profoundly adv. 완전히 false adj. 틀린
occur v. 일어나다, 발생하다
unfortunate adj. 운이 나쁜, 불행한
find oneself phr. (깨닫고 보니) ~에 있다
derelict adj. 버려진, 유기된 possess v. 소유하다
firearm n. (소지가 가능한 권총 등의) 화기
vegetarian n. 채식주의자
inaccurate adj. 부정확한, 오류가 있는
phrase n. 관용구, 구절 dignity n. 품위, 존엄
essentially adv. 본래, 근본적으로 trivial adj. 사소한, 하찮은
die of phr. ~로 죽다 hunger n. 굶주림, 기아
so far phr. 아직까지 material comfort phr. 물질적 위안
chance n. 기회, 가능성

57 [2019 국민대]

정답 ①

해석 ① Falk는 버려진 배에서 무기를 가지고 있었다.
② Falk는 깨닫고 보니 버려진 섬에 있었다.
③ Falk와 다른 선원들은 결국 살아남았다.
④ Falk는 배에 있던 채식주의자를 쫓고 있었다.

해설 Conrad의 영웅 Falk에 대해 사실인 것을 파악하는 문제이다. 지문의 여섯 번째 문장에서 Falk가 버려진 배에 있었고 화기를 소유하고 있었던 선원들 사이의 두 명 중 하나였다고 했으므로, Falk에 대해 사실인 것은 'Falk는 버려진 배에서 무기를 가지고 있었다'이다. 따라서 정답은 ①번이다.

어휘 weapon n. 무기 deserted adj. 버려진 chase v. 쫓다

58 [2019 국민대]

정답 ①

해설 지문의 빈칸을 채우는 문제이다. 첫 번째 빈칸에 들어갈 '~에 대해 말하다'라는 동사구는 speak of, 두 번째 빈칸에 들어갈 '형편이 더 낫다'라는 의미의 동사구는 better off이다. 따라서 ① of – off가 정답이다.

어휘 better off phr. 형편이 더 낫다

59 2019 국민대

정답 ④

해석
① 재난에서 살아남다
② 스스로 계속 살아 있다
③ 치명적인 사고를 막다
④ 자신들의 주변 사람보다 더 뛰어나다

해설 지문의 빈칸을 채우는 문제이다. 지문의 후반에서 사람들이 생존 경쟁에 대해 의미하는 것은 실제로 성공을 위한 경쟁이라고 했으므로, 빈칸에는 경쟁에 참여했을 때 사람들이 두려워하는 것은 다른 사람보다 뛰어나지 못한 것이라는 내용이 나와야 적절하다는 것을 알 수 있다. 따라서 '자신들의 주변 사람보다 더 뛰어나다'라고 한 ④번이 정답이다.

어휘 calamity n. 재난, 재앙   outshine v. ~보다 더 뛰어나다

[60-63]

성가시다, 약 오르다, 화나다, 귀찮다, 짜증 나다와 같이 당신이 그 감정을 어떻게 말하든, 화가 난다는 것은 그 누구도 즐기지 않을 감정이다. 하지만 분노를 경험하는 것은 완전히 정상적이고 인간적인 반면에, 우리가 감정을 건강한 방법으로 처리하지 않을 때 문제가 나타나기 시작할 수 있다. 분노는 시기적절한 방법으로 적절하게 다뤄지지 않으면 매우 현실적이고 만성적인 문제가 될 수 있다. 당신은 작은 것에도 화를 내는 자신을 발견할 것이며, 발끈해서 나중에 후회할 만한 행동이나 말을 하게 될 것이다. 여기에 당신의 화를 처리하는 몇 가지 건강한 방법을 소개한다.
바보같이 들릴지도 모르겠지만, 열을 세는 것(진짜로 화가 났다면 백을 세는 것)은 쌓인 긴장을 어느 정도 풀어줄 수 있는 즉각적인 좋은 방법이다. 왜 그럴까? 그것은 자신에게 먼저 신경을 쓰는 특정한 일에 정신을 집중하기 때문이다.
많은 것들이 화를 불러올 수 있지만, 그런 문제들 또한 당신이 정면으로 대처하고자 한다면 해결할 수 있다. 당신의 10대 자녀들이 잘못 행동하거나, 직장 동료가 당신을 짜증 나게 하거나, 또는 특정한 문제에 대해 당신의 배우자가 눈을 마주치지 않을 때, 화를 쏟아내고 자리를 박차고 나가는 것 보다 문제의 근원을 파악하는 데 힘써라. 다른 사람들이 존중을 받는다고 느낄 수 있도록 하는 방법으로 다음을 논의하는 것과 당신이 아끼는 사람이 당신이 어떤 감정인지를 알도록 하는 것은 모든 인간이 할 수 있는 일이다.

tick off phr. 귀찮게 하다   peeve v. 약 올리다
irritate v. 화나게 하다   annoy v. 짜증 나게 하다
chronic adj. 만성적인   properly adv. 적절하게
timely adj. 시기적절한   blow up phr. 화를 쏟아붓다
in the heat of the moment phr. 발끈해서, 욱해서
immediately adv. 즉시   build up phr. 쌓아 올리다
be willing to phr. 기꺼이 ~하려 하다
meet head-on phr. 정면으로 대처하다
storm off phr. 자리를 박차고 떠나다
misbehave v. 잘못된 행동을 하다   spouse n. 배우자
be capable of phr. ~를 할 수 있다

60 2019 세종대

정답 ②

해설 지문의 흐름상 주어진 문장이 들어가기에 가장 적절한 위치를 고르는 문제이다. 두 번째 문단의 시작부터 쌓인 긴장을 풀어줄 방법을 소개하고 있으므로, 첫 번째 문단의 마지막 자리에 주어진 문장 '여기에 당신의 화를 처리하는 몇 가지 건강한 방법을 소개한다'가 들어가야 글의 흐름이 자연스럽게 연결된다. 따라서 ②번이 정답이다.

61 2019 세종대

정답 ④

해석
① 무슨 일이 있어도   ② 그래서
③ 똑같이   ④ 반면에

해설 빈칸에 적절한 연결어를 넣는 문제이다. 빈칸 앞 문장은 분노를 경험하는 것이 정상적이고 인간적이라는 내용이고, 빈칸 뒤 문장은 분노에 적절하게 대처하지 않으면 문제가 된다는 내용이다. 따라서 역접을 나타내는 연결어인 ④ while(반면에)이 정답이다.

62 2019 세종대

정답 ②

해석
① 스스로 진정할 시간을 주어라
② 문제를 해결하라
③ 체육관을 다녀라
④ 견딜 수 있는 방법을 찾아라

해설 세 번째 문단의 제목을 묻는 문제이다. 세 번째 문단의 중간에서 화를 쏟아내고 자리를 박차고 나가는 것 보다 문제의 근원을 파악하는 데 힘쓰라고 말하고 있다. 따라서 세 번째 문단의 제목을 '문제를 해결하라'라고 표현한 ②번이 정답이다.

어휘 meet v. 충족하다, 만족하다   enthusiasm n. 열정
motivation n. 동기 부여

63 2019 세종대

정답 ④

해석
① 분노는 적절하게 다뤄지면 만성적인 문제가 될 것이다.
② 당신의 배우자가 눈을 똑바로 바라보지 않을 때, 당신은 화를 내고 자리를 박차고 나가도 된다.
③ 문제의 근원을 파악하는 것은 당신이 아끼는 사람에게 당신이 어떤 감정인지 알도록 할 수 있다는 것을 의미하지 않는다.

④ 인간으로서, 당신은 관련된 모든 사람이 존중받고 있다고 느낄 수 있도록 하는 방법으로 다름을 논의할 수 있는 능력을 지니고 있다.

해설 지문의 내용과 일치하는 것을 묻는 문제이다. 지문의 후반에서 Discussing differences in a way that all parties involved feel respected and letting someone you care about know how you feel are things every human being is capable of doing의 내용을 통해 인간으로서, 당신은 관련된 모든 사람이 존중받고 있다고 느낄 수 있도록 하는 방법으로 다름을 논의할 수 있는 능력을 지니고 있다는 것을 알 수 있다. 따라서 ④번이 지문의 내용과 일치한다.

오답 분석
① 분노는 시기적절한 방법으로 적절하게 다뤄지지 않으면 매우 현실적이고 만성적인 문제가 될 수 있다고 했으므로, 분노는 적절하게 다뤄지면 만성적인 문제가 될 것이라는 것은 지문의 내용과 다르다.
② 당신의 배우자가 눈을 마주치지 않을 때, 화를 쏟아내고 자리를 박차고 나가는 것 보다 문제의 근원을 파악하는 데 힘쓰라고 했으므로, 당신의 배우자가 눈을 똑바로 바라보지 않을 때, 당신은 화를 내고 자리를 박차고 나가도 된다는 것은 지문의 내용과 다르다.
③ 다른 사람들이 존중을 받는다고 느낄 수 있도록 하는 방법으로 다름을 논의하는 것과 당신이 아끼는 사람이 당신이 어떤 감정인지를 알도록 하는 것은 모든 인간이 할 수 있는 일이라고 했으므로, 문제의 근원을 파악하는 것은 당신이 아끼는 사람에게 당신이 어떤 감정인지 알도록 할 수 있다는 것을 의미하지 않는다는 것은 지문의 내용과 다르다.

어휘 straight adv. 똑바로   concerned adj. 관련 있는

[64-65]

우리는 끊임없이 무의식적으로 우리의 현재 요구에 기반을 두고 기억을 고르고 선택한다. 이것은 '모니터링 시스템'이라고 불리는 심리학적 기제에 의해 수행된다. 당신이 무엇인가를 기억해낼 때, 당신의 모니터링 시스템이 당신에게 이 기억이 얼마나 자세하고 감성적인가에 근거한 기억처럼 느껴지는지, 그리고 그 기억이 얼마나 그럴듯한지에 근거한 자신의 현재 생각에 들어맞는지 아닌지를 말해준다. 만약 들어맞는다면, 그것은 당신 이야기의 일부가 되고, 그렇지 않다면 방치될 것이다. 하지만 경우에 따라서, 우리의 '기억'은 단순한 추억이 아닌, 발명일 수도 있다. 한 연구에서는 20퍼센트의 참가자가 적어도 일어났다고 더 이상 믿지 않는 하나의 기억을 갖고 있다는 것을 알았다. 이 거짓된 기억은 실제로 일어났거나 완전히 만들어진 무엇인가에 근거하여 가능한 시나리오를 상상하는 두뇌 능력의 결과이다. 이 심상의 생생함과 감정적 강렬함은 모니터링 시스템이 그 심상을 실제라고 잘못 명명하도록 속인다. 그래서 우리가 기억하는 과거가 전적으로 정직한 것은 아니다. 하지만, 이것이 나쁜 것은 아니다. 기억은 우리가 인생을 헤쳐 나갈 수 있게 도와주는 자아에 대한 일관된 감각을 제공한다. 그리 신뢰할 만하지 않은 과거는 이 목표를 달성했다. 문제는 개인적 서사와 실제 사이에 극도의 불일치가 존재할 때에만 일어난다. 우리 대부분은 우리의 선택적인 기억과 함께 매우 잘 살아가고 있다.

---

constantly adv. 끊임없이
subconsciously adv. 무의식적으로
carry out phr. 수행하다   psychological adj. 심리학적인
mechanism n. 기제, 메커니즘   recall v. 기억해내다
recollection n. 기억, 추억   detailed adj. 자세한
plausible adj. 그럴듯한   neglected adj. 방치된
at least phr. 적어도   vividness n. 선명함
intensity n. 강렬함, 강도   mental image phr. 심상
trick v. 속이다
mislabel v. 잘못 명명하다, 라벨을 잘못 붙이다
truthful adj. 정직한   consistent adj. 일관된
self n. 자아   go through life phr. 삶을 헤쳐나가다
discrepancy n. 불일치, 괴리   narrative n. 서사, 서술
selective adj. 선택적인

---

64 [2019 한국외대]

정답 ③

해석
① 우리는 우리의 자아에 극도의 불일치를 설정하기 위해 우리의 과거를 날조한다.
② 연구는 기억의 20퍼센트가 만들어진 것이라는 것을 밝혀냈다.
③ 사실과 닮아있는 허구의 기억들이 반드시 우리에게 해로운 것은 아니다.
④ 오로지 새로운 시나리오를 상상하는 두뇌의 능력이 기억의 원인이 된다.

해설 지문의 내용과 일치하는 것을 묻는 문제이다. 지문의 중간에서 So, the past we remember is not entirely truthful. But this is no bad thing의 내용을 통해 사실과 닮아있는 허구의 기억들이 반드시 우리에게 해로운 것은 아니라는 것을 알 수 있다. 따라서 ③번이 지문의 내용과 일치한다.

오답 분석
① 문제는 개인적 서사와 실제 사이에 극도의 불일치가 존재할 때에만 일어난다고는 했지만, 우리가 우리의 자아에 극도의 불일치를 설정하기 위해 우리의 과거를 날조하는지는 알 수 없다.
② 한 연구에서 20퍼센트의 참가자가 적어도 일어났다고 더 이상 믿지 않는 하나의 기억을 갖고 있다는 것을 알았다고는 했지만, 연구가 기억의 20퍼센트가 만들어진 것이라는 것을 밝혀냈는지는 알 수 없다.
④ 거짓된 기억은 실제로 일어났거나 완전히 만들어진 무엇인가에 근거하여 가능한 시나리오를 상상하는 두뇌 능력의 결과라고는 했지만, 오로지 새로운 시나리오를 상상하는 두뇌의 능력이 기억의 원인이 되었는지는 알 수 없다.

어휘 fabricate v. 날조하다 establish v. 설정하다, 설립하다
fictitious adj. 허구의 resemble v. 닮다
injurious adj. 해로운, 손상을 주는 solely adv. 오로지
responsible adj. ~의 원인이 되는, 책임이 있는

65 2019 한국외대

정답 ③

해석 ① 고의적인 위조는 기억되는 많은 것들의 특징이다.
② 선택적인 기억은 규칙적으로 불행한 곤경을 일으킨다.
③ 모니터링 시스템은 한 사람의 자아 인식을 반영하는 기억을 만든다.
④ 범죄 목격자의 기억은 객관적이고 믿을 수 있다.

해설 지문을 통해 추론할 수 있는 것을 고르는 문제이다. 지문의 후반에서 기억은 우리가 인생을 헤쳐나갈 수 있게 도와주는 자아에 대한 일관된 감각을 제공한다고 했으므로, 모니터링 시스템은 한 사람의 자아 인식을 반영하는 기억을 만든다는 것을 추론할 수 있다. 따라서 정답은 ③번이다.

오답 분석
① 고의적인 위조가 기억되는 많은 것들의 특징인지에 대해서는 언급되지 않았다.
② 우리 대부분은 우리의 선택적인 기억과 함께 매우 잘 살아가고 있다고 했으므로, 선택적인 기억은 규칙적으로 불행한 곤경을 일으킨다는 것은 추론할 수 없다.
④ 우리가 기억하는 과거가 전적으로 정직한 것은 아니라고 했으므로, 범죄 목격자의 기억은 객관적이고 믿을 수 있다는 것은 추론할 수 없다.

어휘 deliberate adj. 고의적인 falsification n. 위조
hallmark n. 특징 regularly adv. 규칙적으로
unfortunate adj. 불행한 predicament n. 곤경
self-perception n. 자아 인식 witness n. 목격자
objective adj. 객관적인 reliable adj. 믿을 수 있는

[66-67]

많은 부모들이 벌을 받고 자라서, 부모들이 벌에 의존하는 것을 이해할 수 있다. 하지만 벌은 갈등을 심화시키고 학습을 억제시키는 경향이 있다. 벌은 싸움이나 도피 반응을 끌어내는데, 이는 전두엽의 복잡한 생각이 정지하고 기본적인 방어 기제가 나타난다는 것을 의미한다. 벌은 우리를 반항하고, 수치심을 느끼게 하거나 화나게 하며 우리의 감정을 억누르게 하거나 잘못이 걸리지 않는 방법을 알아내게 한다. 이런 경우에, 완전히 성장한 네 살배기의 반항이 최고조에 달할 것이다.
그렇다면 보상이 긍정적인 선택이지 않겠는가? 아직 이르다. 수십 년에 걸쳐, 심리학자들은 보상이 우리의 자연스러운 동기 부여와 즐거움을 감소시킬 수 있다고 말했다. 예를 들어, 실험 조건 아래에서, 그림 그리는 것을 좋아하면서 그림을 그릴 때마다 돈을 받는 아이들은, 돈을 받지 않는 아이보다 그림을 덜 그렸다. 이것은 심리학자들이 "과잉 정당화 이론"이라고 부르는 것인데, 외적 보상이 아이들의 내적 동기를 무색하게 만든다는 것이다.
보상은 또한 창의성을 저하시키는 것과도 연관되어 있다. 한 고전적인 일련의 연구에서, 사람들은 재료 세트(핀 상자, 양초, 그리고 성냥 한 갑)를 받고, 벽에 양초를 붙일 수 있는 방법을 알아내도록 요청받았다. 그 해결법은 재료들을 그것들의 목적과는 관계없는 방법으로 보는 (상자를 양초 받침으로 보는) 혁신적인 사고를 요구한다. 이 딜레마를 풀면 보상을 받게 된다고 들었던 사람들은 평균적으로 그것을 알아내는 데 더 오래 걸렸다. 보상은 우리의 시야를 좁힌다. 우리의 뇌는 자유롭게 생각하는 것을 멈춘다. 우리는 깊게 생각하고 가능성을 보는 것을 멈춰버린다.
별과 보상의 전체적인 개념은 아이들이 우리들에 의해 통제되고 정해져야만 하며 그들은 좋은 의도를 갖고 있지 않다는 아이들에 대한 부정적인 추정에 근거하고 있다. 하지만 우리는 아이들을 유능하고 공감, 협동, 팀 정신, 그리고 근면과 밀접한 관계가 있는 것으로 여기기 위해 이 관점을 뒤집을 수 있다. 그런 관점이 우리가 아이들에게 강력한 방법으로 어떻게 말하는지를 바꾼다. 보상과 별은 조건적이지만, 우리의 사랑과 아이들에 대한 긍정적인 관심은 무조건적이다. 실제로, 우리가 공감으로 이끌고 진심으로 아이들을 들으면, 아이들도 더 우리를 들을 것이다.

punishment n. 벌 escalate v. 심화시키다, 확대시키다
elicit v. 끌어내다 flight response phr. 도피 반응
sophisticate adj. 복잡한, 정교한, 세련된
frontal cortex phr. 전두엽 go dark phr. 정지하다, 멈추다
defense mechanism phr. 방어 기제
kick in phr. 나타나다 rebel v. 반항하다
repress v. 억누르다 full-fledged adj. 완전히 성장한
resistance n. 반항 peak n. 최고조, 꼭대기
psychologist n. 심리학자
overjustification n. 과잉 정당화
overshadow v. 무색하게 만들다, 빛을 잃게 만들다
attach v. 붙이다, 첨부하다 dilemma n. 딜레마, 진퇴양난
puzzle v. (머리를 짜내어) 생각하다 assumption n. 추정
shape v. 정하다, 형성하다 flip v. 홱 뒤집다
wire v. ~과 밀접한 관계가 있다 empathy n. 공감
cooperation n. 협동 perspective n. 관점

66 2019 인하대

정답 ①

해석 ① 보상은 또한 창의성을 저하시키는 것과도 연관되어 있다
② 하지만, 보상은 아이들을 부모에게 더 집중하도록 만든다
③ 보상은 또한 창의력을 향상시키는 것과도 연관되어 있다
④ 보상과 벌은 창의력을 향상시키는 데 필수적이다
⑤ 보상은 창의력을 향상하는 데 벌보다 더 효과적이었다

해설 지문의 빈칸을 채우는 문제이다. 지문의 세 번째 단락의 마지막 세 개의 문장에서 보상은 우리의 시야를 좁히고 뇌가 자유롭게 생각하는 것을 멈추게 하며, 우리는 깊게 생각하고 가능

성을 보는 것을 멈춰버린다고 했으므로, 빈칸에는 창의성의 저하에 대한 내용이 나와야 적절하다는 것을 알 수 있다. 따라서 '보상은 창의성을 저하시키는 것과도 연관되어 있다'라고 한 ①번이 정답이다.

어휘 associated with phr. ~와 연관된
attentive adj. 집중하는   enhance v. 향상하다
vital adj. 필수적인

67 2019 인하대

정답 ①

해석 ① 보상과 벌 둘 다 좋은 해결책이 아니다.
② 처음에는 벌을 주고 나서 보상을 주는 것이 더 좋은 해결책이다.
③ 처음에는 보상을 주고 나서 벌을 주는 것이 더 좋은 해결책이다.
④ 더 많은 보상과 적은 벌이 좋은 해결책이다.
⑤ 더 많은 벌과 적은 보상이 더 좋은 해결책이다.

해설 지문의 내용과 일치하는 것을 묻는 문제이다. 지문의 마지막 단락의 첫 번째 문장에서 벌과 보상의 전체적인 개념이 아이들에 대한 부정적인 추정에 근거하고 있다는 내용을 통해 보상과 벌이 둘 다 좋은 해결책이 아니라는 것을 알 수 있다. 따라서 ①번이 지문의 내용과 일치한다.

오답 분석
② 보상과 벌의 순서와 효과성의 관계는 지문에서 언급되지 않았다.
③ 보상과 벌의 순서와 효과성의 관계는 지문에서 언급되지 않았다.
④ 보상은 창의성을 저하한다고 했으므로, 더 많은 보상과 적은 벌이 좋은 해결책이라는 것은 지문의 내용과 다르다.
⑤ 벌은 갈등을 심화시키고 학습을 중단시킨다고 했으므로, 더 많은 벌과 적은 보상이 좋은 해결책이라는 것은 지문의 내용과 다르다.

[68-69]

인적 오류는 "적절한" 행동에서의 모든 일탈로 정의된다. 많은 상황에서, 적절한 행동은 알려진 것이 아니거나 사후에만 결정되는 것이기 때문에 적절하다는 단어는 따옴표로 묶여 있다. 그러나 여전히, 오류는 일반적으로 용인되는 옳거나 적절한 행동에서의 일탈로 정의된다. 오류는 모든 잘못된 행위를 이르는 보편 명사이다. 오류에는 두 가지 주요 부류가 있는데, 이는 실수와 착오이다. 실수는 더 나아가 두 가지의 주요 부류로 나뉘고 착오는 세 가지로 나뉜다. 이러한 오류의 범주는 모두 의도에 대해 다른 결과를 가진다. 나는 이제 이러한 오류의 분류와 의도의 결과를 더 자세히 들여다보겠다. 실수는 사람이 한 행위를 의도하고 결국 다른 것을 하게 되었을 때 일어난다. 실수가 있으면, 수행된 행위는 의도되었던 행위와 같은 것이 아니다. 실수에는 두 가지의 주요 부류가 있는데, 이는 행위기반 실수와 건망증이다. 행위기반 실수에서는, 잘못된 행위가 수행된다. 건망증에서는, 기억이 없어져서, 의도된 행위가 수행되지 않거나 행위의 결과가 평가되지 않는다. 행위기반 실수와 건망증은 그것들의 원인에 따라 더 분류될 수 있다. 착오는 잘못된 목표가 확립되거나 잘못된 계획이 형성되었을 때 일어난다. 그 이후에는, 행위가 적절히 수행되더라도, 행위 자체가 부적절하기 때문에 그것들은 오류의 일부이고, 잘못된 계획의 일부이다. 착오가 있으면, 수행되는 행위는 계획과 일치하지만, 그것은 잘못된 계획이다. 착오에는 세 가지의 주요 부류가 있는데, 이는 규칙 기반 착오, 지식기반 착오, 그리고 건망증이다. 규칙 기반 착오에서, 사람은 알맞게 상황을 진단했지만, 그다음에 잘못된 행동 방향으로 결정하여 잘못된 규칙이 뒤따라온다. 지식기반 착오에서는, 잘못되거나 불완전한 지식으로 인해 문제가 오진된다. 건망증에 따른 착오는 목표, 계획, 혹은 평가의 단계에서 망각이 있을 때 발생한다.

deviance n. 일탈   appropriate adj. 적절한, 적합한
after the fact phr. 사후에   general term phr. 보편 명사
slip n. 실수   implication n. 결과   design n. 의도, 계획
intend v. 의도하다   evaluate v. 평가하다
establish v. 확립하다   execute v. 수행하다
diagnose v. 진단하다   forgetting n. 망각

68 2019 한국항공대

정답 ④

해석 ① 오류에는 두 가지의 주요한 형태가 있다.
② 실수는 목표가 올바르지만, 요구되는 행위가 적절히 행해지지 않을 때 일어난다.
③ 건망증은 실수나 착오 중 하나로 이어질 수 있다.
④ 실수는 결과에 따라 더 분류될 수 있다.

해설 지문의 내용과 일치하지 않는 것을 묻는 문제이다. ④번의 키워드인 can be further divided(더 분류될 수 있다)와 관련된 지문의 can be further classified(더 분류될 수 있다) 주변에서 행위기반 실수와 건망증은 그것들의 원인에 따라 더 분류될 수 있다 했으므로, 실수가 결과에 따라 더 분류될 수 있다는 것은 지문의 내용과 다르다. 따라서 ④번이 지문의 내용과 일치하지 않는다.

오답 분석
① 지문의 다섯 번째 문장 There are two major classes of error: slips and mistakes.를 통해 '오류에는 두 가지의 주요한 형태가 있다'는 것을 알 수 있다.
② 지문의 아홉 번째 문장 A slip occurs when a person intends to do one action and ends up doing something else.를 통해 '실수는 목표가 올바르지만, 요구되는 행위가 적절히 행해지지 않을 때 일어난다'는 것을 알 수 있다.
③ 지문의 열한 번째 문장 There are ~ memory-lapse.와 지문 마지막에서 네 번째 문장 Mistakes have ~ memory-lapse.를 통해 '건망증은 실수나 착오 중 하나로 이어질 수 있다'는 것을 알 수 있다.

69 [2019 한국항공대]

정답 ③

해석
① 지식기반 착오
② 건망증에 따른 착오
③ 행위기반 실수
④ 건망증에 따른 실수

해설 지문을 통해 추론할 수 있는 것을 고르는 문제이다. 지문 중간에서 실수는 사람이 한 행위를 의도하고 결국 다른 것을 하게 되었을 때 일어난다고 하고, 그중 행위기반 실수에서는 잘못된 행위가 수행된다고 설명하고 있다. 커피에 우유를 붓고 나서 커피를 냉장고에 집어넣음으로써 커피를 마시고자 하는 의도와 다른 것을 하게 되었기 때문에 착오가 아닌 실수임을 추론할 수 있고, 커피를 냉장고에 집어넣은 행위는 건망증이 아니라 잘못된 행위를 수행한 것임을 추론할 수 있다. 따라서 정답은 ③번이다.

오답 분석
① 지식기반 착오에서는 잘못되거나 불완전한 지식으로 인해 문제가 오진된다고 했으므로, 문제에 나온 행위는 지식기반 착오에 해당하지 않는다.
② 건망증에 따른 착오는 목표, 계획, 혹은 평가의 단계에서 망각이 있을 때 발생한다고 했으므로, 문제에 나온 행위는 건망증에 따른 착오에 해당하지 않는다.
④ 건망증에 따른 실수에서는, 기억이 없어져서, 의도된 행위가 수행되지 않거나 행위의 결과가 평가되지 않는다고 했으므로, 문제에 나온 행위는 건망증에 따른 실수에 해당하지 않는다.

[70-72]

킬로그램을 없애는 것은 늘리는 것보다 더 어려운데, 이는 체중 감량 업계가 그렇게 큰 이유이다. 최근의 대표적인 예는 참가자들이 목표 체중을 정하고 목표 체중을 향한 참가자들의 경과를 감시할 수 있는, 살찐 사람들을 위한 소셜 네트워크인 온라인 체중 관리 사이트이다.

[A] 다른 소셜 네트워크를 이용할 때처럼, 그들은 같은 사이트에 가입한 현실의 사람들이든 인터넷에서 친구가 된 디지털을 쓰는 다른 사람들이든 어느 한 쪽의 친구들로부터 그들의 도움을 받을 수도 있다. 그 우정은 중요해질 가능성이 있다. 체중 감량 프로그램에 대한 다른 연구들은 지원을 받는 것이나 친구들이 성가시게 괴롭히는 것이 사람들이 식단과 운동 관리 체제를 고수하도록 돕는다는 것을 시사한다.

[D] 그러나, 그 연구들은 모두 현실 세계에서 서로를 알았던 사람들의 그룹들로 진행되어 왔다. 일리노이주 노스웨스턴대학교의 Julia Poncela-Casanovas가 이끄는 연구원 팀은 사이버 공간에 있는 그룹들에서도 마찬가지인지 확인하기로 결정했다. 결과들은 그렇다는 것을 시사한다.

[B] 그러나 그녀와 그녀의 동료들은 이 경우엔 친구들과 체중 감량이라는 두 가지가 연관성이 있다는 것을 제외하고는 정착할 수 있다는 것을 지적하는 것이 빠르다. 그것은 어떤 것이 어떤 것을 초래하는지를 보여 주지는 못한다. 이것을 알아내는 것은 통제된 실험을 필요로 한다.

[C] 그렇다 하더라도, 그것들의 결과들은 고무적이다. 체중 관리 웹사이트들은 더욱이 많은 사람들에게 현실의 지원 그룹들이 하는 것보다 훨씬 더 저렴하게 도달할 가능성을 갖고 있다. 더욱이, 우정 네트워크가 체중 감량을 위한 마술 지팡이라는 것이 밝혀지면, 그다음에 사람들이 실제로 땀 나게 하는 체육관에서 서로를 만나야 하는 것보다 전자적으로 그런 네트워크 쪽으로 조금씩 움직이는 것이 더 쉬워질 수 있다. 비만 수준의 증가에 대한 의학 결과를 고려해 볼 때, 웹사이트들은 훨씬 해 볼 가치가 있을 것이다.

---

put on phr. 늘리다　**weight-loss** n. 체중 감량
manifestation n. 표현, 명시
weight-management n. 체중 관리　**plump** adj. 살찐
target n. 목표　**monitor** v. 감시하다　**progress** n. 경과
real-life adj. 현실의　**befriend** v. 친구가 되다
stick to phr. 고수하다　**regime** n. 관리 체제
the same is true of phr. ~에서도 마찬가지다
cyberspace n. 사이버 공간　**colleague** n. 동료
point out phr. 지적하다　**only that** phr. ~을 제외하고는
controlled adj. 통제된　**experiment** n. 실험
encouraging adj. 고무적인　**potential** n. 가능성, 잠재력
magic wand phr. 마술 지팡이
electronically adv. 전자적으로　**sweaty** adj. 땀나게 하는
consequence n. 결과　**obesity** n. 비만

70 [2019 국민대]

정답 ①

해석
① 없애다
② 통제하다
③ 늘리다
④ 계산하다

해설 지문의 빈칸을 채우는 문제이다. 지문의 빈칸 다음의 내용은 소셜 네트워크인 온라인 체중 관리 사이트에 관한 내용이며 빈칸 뒤의 내용에서 킬로그램을 늘리는 것보다 더 어려운 것이라고 했으므로, 빈칸에는 킬로그램을 없앤다는 내용이 나와야 적절하다는 것을 알 수 있다. 따라서 '없애다'라고 한 ①번이 정답이다.

71 [2019 국민대]

정답 ①

해설 chivy(성가시게 괴롭히다)와 비슷한 의미를 가진 어휘를 묻고 있다. ①번 nag는 '계속 괴롭히다', ②번 praise는 '칭찬하다', ③번 embrace는 '받아들이다', ④번 recommend는 '추천하다'라는 의미이다. 따라서 ①번이 정답이다.

72 [2019 국민대]

정답 ②

해설 주어진 지문 다음에 이어질 [A], [B], [C], [D]의 적절한 순서를 파악하는 문제이다. 주어진 지문은 체중 감량 업계가 크

고 있고, 소셜 네트워크인 온라인 체중 관리 사이트에 대한 내용이므로, 이 사이트에 가입한 사람들이 어떤 도움을 받는지에 관해 설명한 [A]가 먼저 와야 한다. 그다음에 [D]에서 사이트 가입자들이 서로 현실에서 알았던 사람들이어서 노스웨스턴대학교의 연구원 팀에서 사이버 공간에 있는 그룹들에서도 마찬가지인지 확인한다는 내용이 오고, [B]에서 그 연구원 팀이 발견한 내용과 통제된 실험이 필요하다는 내용이 나오고, 마지막으로 [C]에서 실험 결과들이 고무적이며 웹사이트를 통한 체중 감량의 긍정적인 면을 설명하는 것이 자연스럽다. 따라서 주어진 지문 다음에 이어질 순서는 ② [A] — [D] — [B] — [C]이다.

[73-74]

Dave Balter는 광고 분야에서 일했고, 그는 대부분의 사람이 광고를 싫어한다는 것을 알았다. 사람들은 광고를 보거나, 읽거나, 또는 듣는 것을 피한다. 또한, 그는 사람들이 알고 있는 상품이나 서비스에 대한 것을 들을 때 잘 집중한다는 것을 알았다. 그래서 그는 스스로 "아무도 광고에 집중하지 않지만 친구와 가족의 의견에는 집중을 잘한다면, 그 점에 초점을 맞추어보자."라고 스스로에게 말했다. Balter가 제안한 것은 소비자들이 무료 제품을 받을 수 있도록 등록할 수 있는 웹사이트였다. 그 대신에, 사람들이 그 제품을 마음에 들어 한다면 친구들에게 말하겠다고 약속했다. 대부분의 경우에, 지원자들은 친구들에게 전해줄 수 있는 쿠폰도 받았다. Balter가 요청한 것은 그들이 제품에 대해 어떻게 생각하는지와 그 제품에 대해 누구에게 말했는지의 두 가지 질문에 응답해 달라는 것이 전부였다.
4년 후에, Balter는 제품을 체험하고 그들이 좋아한 제품에 대해 사람들에게 말해주는 65,000명의 지원자를 갖게 되었다. 그리고 한 기자가 Balter의 아이디어에 대해 듣고 주요 잡지에 그 이야기를 썼다. 그 자체도 무료 광고인 것이다! 그 이야기가 나온 지 1년도 안 되어, Balter는 13만 명의 지원자를 갖게 되었다. 오늘날, 그가 시작한 회사는 백만 명 이상의 사람들이 폭넓은 제품들에 대하여 말을 퍼뜨리고 있다. 그들은 입소문으로 광고를 하는 것인데, 아마도 최고의 광고 수단이 아닐까 싶다. 하지만, *구전 마케팅의 비밀*의 저자인 George Silverman에 의하면, 입소문으로 광고를 하는 데에는 위험이 있을 수도 있다. 그 위험은 무엇일까? 연구 결과는 한 제품이나 서비스를 마음에 들어 하는 고객은 평균 3명의 사람에게 그것에 대해 말하라는 것을 보여준다. 하지만, 마음에 들지 않는다면, 평균 11명에게 마음에 들지 않는다고 말할 것이다.

pay attention phr. 집중하다
volunteer n. 지원자, 자원봉사자
report back phr. 응답하다, 보고하다
appear v. 나오다, 나타나다
spread the word phr. 말을 퍼뜨리다
a wide variety of phr. 폭넓은, 다양한
word-of-mouth adj. 입소문의, 구전의

73 [2019 한양대에리카]

정답 ②

해석 ① 비슷하게 ② 그 대신에
③ 결과적으로 ④ 사실은

해설 빈칸에 적절한 연결어를 넣는 문제이다. 빈칸 앞 문장은 사람들이 웹사이트에 등록하여 무료로 제품을 받는다는 내용이고, 빈칸 뒤 문장은 사람들이 그 제품이 마음에 들면 친구들에게 그 제품에 대해 말하겠다고 약속했다는 내용이다. 따라서 조건을 나타내는 연결어인 ② In return(그 대신에)이 정답이다.

어휘 **similarly** adv. 비슷하게 **in return** phr. 그 대신에
consequently adv. 결과적으로

74 [2019 한양대에리카]

정답 ④

해석 ① 대부분의 사람이 광고를 좋아하지 않지만, 제품에 대한 친구의 의견에는 집중한다.
② Balter는 무료 제품을 얻기 위해 목록에 자신의 이름을 올릴 수 있는 웹사이트를 설치했다.
③ 잡지에 그의 이야기가 나온 지 1년도 안 되어, Balter는 이전보다 두 배 많은 지원자를 얻었다.
④ Silverman의 연구는 불만족한 고객이 만족한 고객보다 더 적은 사람에게 말하라는 것을 알아냈다.

해설 지문의 내용과 일치하지 않는 것을 묻는 문제이다. ④번의 키워드인 Silverman's studies(Silverman의 연구)와 관련된 지문의 according to George Silverman(George Silverman에 따르면) 주변에서 제품을 마음에 들어 하는 고객은 그것을 평균 3명의 사람에게 말하지만 그렇지 않은 고객은 평균 11명의 사람에게 말할 것이라고 했으므로, Silverman의 연구는 불만족한 고객이 만족한 고객보다 더 적은 사람에게 말하라는 것을 알아냈다는 것은 지문의 내용과 다르다. 따라서 ④번이 지문의 내용과 일치하지 않는다.

오답 분석
① They avoid watching them, reading them, or listening to them. He also knew that people do pay attention when they hear about goods and services from people they know를 통해 '대부분의 사람이 광고를 좋아하지 않지만, 제품에 대한 친구의 의견에는 집중한다'는 것을 알 수 있다.
② What Balter came up with was a website where consumers could sign up to receive free products를 통해 'Balter는 무료 제품을 얻기 위해 목록에 자신의 이름을 올릴 수 있는 웹사이트를 설치했다'는 것을 알 수 있다.
③ Balter had 65,000 volunteers trying products and telling people about the ones they liked와 Within a year after that story appeared, Balter had 130,000 volunteers를 통해 '잡지에 그의 이야기

가 나온 지 1년도 안 되어, Balter는 이전보다 두 배 많은 지원자를 얻었다'는 것을 알 수 있다.

어휘 dissatisfied adj. 불만족한　satisfied adj. 만족한

[75-77]

정상이거나 건강하다는 말은 두 가지 방식으로 정의될 수 있다. 첫째로, 기능 사회의 관점에서, 한 사람은 특정한 사회 내에서 맡은 사회적 역할을 이행할 수 있으면 정상이거나 건강하다고 할 수 있다. 더 구체적으로, 이것은 그 사람이 특정한 사회에서 요구되는 방식으로 일할 수 있고, 더 나아가 그 사람이 가족을 꾸릴 수 있는 사회의 재생산에 참여할 수 있음을 의미한다. 두 번째로, 개인의 관점에서, 우리는 건강이나 정상 상태를 성장의 최적 조건 및 개인의 행복으로 간주한다. 하나의 특정한 사회 구조가 개인의 행복을 위한 최적의 가능성을 제공한 그런 사회였다면, 두 관점이 부합했을 것이다. 하지만, 우리 자신의 사회를 포함하여, 우리가 알고 있는 대부분의 사회에서는 그렇지 않다. 사회가 개인 성장의 목표를 촉진하는 정도는 다르지만, 사회의 원활한 기능과 개인 성숙의 목적 사이에는 차이가 있다. [A] 이 사실은 건강의 두 가지 개념을 반드시 뚜렷이 구별해야 하는 것으로 만든다. 하나는 사회적 필요성에 의해 지배되고, 다른 하나는 개인적 존재의 목적에 관련된 가치와 규범에 의해 지배된다. 안타깝게도, 이 구별은 흔히 무시된다. [B] 대다수 정신과 의사들은 그들 자신의 사회 구조를 너무 당연한 것으로 받아들여 그들에게 사회에 잘 적응하지 못한 사람은 덜 가치 있다는 오명을 가지고 있다. 반대로, 사회에 잘 적응한 사람은 인간의 가치 척도 측면에서 더 가치 있는 사람으로 생각된다. 만약 우리가 정상과 신경과민이라는 두 개념을 구별한다면, 다음과 같은 결론이 날 것이다. 잘 적응한다는 측면에서 정상인 사람은 보통 인간의 가치 측면에서 신경이 과민한 사람보다 덜 건강하다. 보통, 사람은 자신이 될 것으로 기대된다고 생각하는 그만저만한 사람이 되기 위해 자아를 포기해가는 희생만으로 사회에 잘 적응한다. [C] <u>모든 진실된 개성과 자발성은 상실되었을지도 모른다.</u> 반면, 신경이 과민한 사람은 자아를 위한 싸움에서 완전히 포기할 준비가 안 되었던 사람으로 특징지어질 수 있다. [D] 분명히, 자신의 개별적 자아를 구하고자 한 그 사람의 노력은 성공하지 못했고, 자아를 생산적으로 표출하는 대신에 그 사람은 신경증적인 징후를 통해, 상상 속의 삶으로 떠남으로써 구원을 추구했다. 그럼에도 불구하고, 인간 가치의관점에서, 그 사람은 개성을 모두 상실한 정상적인 유형의 사람보다 덜 무능력하다.

functioning n. 기능　fulfill v. 이행하다
reproduction n. 재생산　normalcy n. 정상 상태
optimum n. 최적 조건; adj. 최적의
coincide v. 부합하다, 일치하다　promote v. 촉진하다
discrepancy n. 차이　full development phr. 성숙
imperative adj. 반드시 ~해야 하는, 필수의
govern v. 지배하다　neglect v. 무시하다
psychiatrist n. 정신과 의사

neurotic adj. 신경과민의, 신경증의
at the expense of phr. ~을 희생하고
surrender v. 포기하다　salvation n. 구원, 구제
withdraw v. 떠나다, 철수하다　crippled adj. 무능력한
individuality n. 개성

75 2019 한국항공대

정답 ④

해석 ① 신경과민은 인간의 행복과 자아실현에 큰 위협이다.
② 사회에 자신을 적응시키는 것은 건강한 사람이 되기 위한 안정적인 기반을 제공한다.
③ 기능 사회에서, 신경이 과민한 사람들과 정상인 사람들 간의 갈등은 매우 유용하다.
④ 흔히 신경과민이라고 불리는 사람들은 인간의 가치 측면에서 중요할 수 있다.

해설 지문의 내용과 일치하는 것을 묻는 문제이다. 지문의 마지막 문장 Nevertheless, from the standpoint of human values ~의 내용을 통해 인간 가치의 관점에서, 그 사람(신경이 과민한 사람)은 개성을 모두 상실한 정상적인 유형의 사람보다 덜 무능력하다는 것을 알 수 있다. 따라서 ④번이 지문의 내용과 일치한다.

오답 분석
① 신경이 과민한 사람은 자아를 위한 싸움에서 완전히 포기할 준비가 안 되었던 사람으로 특징지어질 수 있다고 했으므로, 신경과민은 인간의 행복과 자아실현에 큰 위협이라는 것은 지문의 내용과 다르다.
② 정상인 사람은 보통 인간의 가치 측면에서 신경이 과민한 사람보다 덜 건강하고, 자아를 포기해가는 희생만으로 사회에 잘 적응하는 것이라고 했으므로, 사회에 자신을 적응시키는 것은 건강한 사람이 되기 위한 안정적인 기반을 제공한다는 것은 지문의 내용과 다르다.
③ 정상과 신경과민이라는 두 개념을 구별하고는 있지만, 기능사회에서, 신경이 과민한 사람들과 정상인 사람들 간의 갈등이 매우 유용한지는 알 수 없다.

어휘 self-realization n. 자아실현　stable adj. 안정적인
invaluable adj. 매우 유용한　label v. ~을 부르다

76 2019 한국항공대

정답 ①

해석 ① 건강에 대한 두 가지 정의 사이의 차이, 그리고 신경이 과민한 사람들의 의의
② 건강하면서 정상적인 사람들과 비교한 신경이 과민한 사람들의 기능 장애
③ 정상 사회에서 정상적인 사람, 건강한 사람, 그리고 신경이 과민한 사람들의 조화로운 관계
④ 비정상적인 사회에서 개성에 관하여 건강하지 않은 사람과 신경이 과민한 사람들에 대한 지나친 단순화

10 심리　211

해설 지문의 요지를 묻는 문제이다. 지문 처음에서 정상이거나 건강하다는 말은 두 가지 방식으로 정의될 수 있다고 하고, 지문 후반부에서 신경이 과민한 사람들이 인간 가치의 관점에서 덜 무능력하다고 하였다. 따라서 이 지문의 요지를 '건강에 대한 두 가지 정의 사이의 차이, 그리고 신경이 과민한 사람들의 의의'라고 표현한 ①번이 정답이다.

어휘 significance n. 의의   malfunction n. 기능 장애
harmonious adj. 조화로운
reductionism n. 지나친 단순화, 환원주의

77 [2019 한국항공대]

정답 ③

해설 지문의 흐름상 주어진 문장이 들어가기에 가장 적절한 위치를 고르는 문제이다. [C]의 뒤 문장에서 반면, 신경이 과민한 사람은 자아를 위한 싸움에서 완전히 포기할 준비가 안 되었던 사람으로 특징지어질 수 있다고 했으므로, [C] 자리에 이와 반대로 잘 적응하는 사람들의 특징을 설명하는 주어진 문장 '모든 진실된 개성과 자발성은 상실되었을지도 모른다'가 들어가야 글의 흐름이 자연스럽게 연결된다. 따라서 ③번이 정답이다.

어휘 spontaneity n. 자발성

11 인류학

01-22
문제집 p.324

01 ⑤	02 ③	03 ③	04 ③	05 ②
06 ①	07 ④	08 ②	09 ③	10 ③
11 ④	12 ③	13 ④	14 ③	15 ②
16 ②	17 ③	18 ③	19 ①	20 ①
21 ③	22 ④			

01 [2019 광운대]
정답 ⑤

해석 사피엔스는 유일하게 다수와 유연하게 협력할 수 있는 동물이기 때문에 세계를 지배하게 되었다. 선사시대의 사피엔스는 네안데르탈인과 같은 다른 인류 멸종의 주요 원인이었다. 다수와 협력할 수 있는 사피엔스의 능력은 신, 국가, 돈 그리고 인권과 같은 순전히 상상 속에 존재하는 것들을 믿는 독특한 능력에서 비롯된다. 종교, 정치구조, 무역망 그리고 법률기관들을 포함하는 모든 대규모의 인간 협력 시스템들은 허구에 대한 사피엔스의 독특한 인지 능력의 출현 덕분이다.
① 접근하다, 들어가다 — 인정하다, 고맙게 여기다
② 거주하다 — 처리하다
③ 지배하다 — 소비하다
④ 조화를 이루다, 잘 어울리다 — 확보하다
⑤ 협력하다 — 덕분이다

해설 빈칸에 들어갈 내용을 묻고 있다. 첫 번째 빈칸에는 사피엔스가 다수와 유연하게 무엇할 수 있는 동물인지가 나와야 하므로, 첫 번째 빈칸에는 '조화를 이루다'라는 의미의 harmonize와 '협력하다'라는 의미의 cooperate가 적절하고, 두 번째 빈칸에는 허구에 대한 사피엔스의 독특한 인지 능력의 출현이 대규모 인간 협력 시스템에 어떤 영향을 준 것인지가 나와야 하므로, 두 번째 빈칸에는 '덕분이다'라는 의미의 'owe'가 들어가는 것이 자연스럽다. 따라서 ⑤번이 정답이다.

어휘 dominate v. 지배하다 cooperate v. 협력하다
flexibly adv. 유연하게, 융통성 있게
extinction n. 멸종, 소멸 capacity n. 능력
purely adv. 순전히, 오직 institution n. 기관, 단체
emergence n. 출현, 발생 distinctive adj. 독특한
cognitive adj. 인지의, 인식의 capacity n. 능력
fiction n. 허구

02 [2020 가천대]
정답 ③

해석 인류학을 어떻게 실세계에 적용할까? 이것은 신인류학자에 의해 자주 제기되는 질문이다. 한 가지 실질적인 적용은 서로 다른 문화 집단 출신의 여러 사람들이 (A)이동되어야 하는 때인 자연 재앙의 여파에 있다. 이 과정에서, 서로 전혀 다른 배경과 가치를 지닌 지역 사회는 종종 (B)충돌이 발생하는 채로 공존할 수밖에 없다. 신인류학자는 이러한 상황을 (C)악화하기 위해 그들의 지식과 통찰력을 줄 수 있다. 그들의 가치는 한 문화 체계가 얼마나 역동적일 수 있는지 설명하는 데 있으며, 동시에 (D)회복력 있으면서 융통성 있는 혼합 문화를 지닌 지역 사회를 위한 길을 연다.

해설 밑줄 친 낱말의 쓰임이 적절하지 않은 것을 묻는 문제이다. (C) 앞 문장에서 '서로 전혀 다른 배경과 가치를 지닌 지역 사회는 종종 충돌이 발생한다'고 했으므로, '신인류학자는 이러한 상황을 개선하기(improve) 위해 그들의 지식과 통찰력을 줄 수 있다'고 하는 것이 문맥에 알맞다. (C)의 aggravate를 improve로 고쳐야 한다. 따라서 ③번이 정답이다.

어휘 anthropology n. 인류학 anthropologist n. 인류학자
application n. 적용
in the aftermath of phr. ~의 여파로
catastrophe n. 재앙 relocate v. 이동하다
disparate adj. 서로 전혀 다른 value n. 가치
co-exist v. 공존하다 clash n. 충돌
insight n. 통찰력 aggravate v. 악화하다
pave the way for phr. ~을 위해 길을 열다
resilient adj. 회복력 있는 adaptable adj. 융통성 있는

03 [2019 인하대]
정답 ③

해석 모든 인류의 이주에서 가장 중요한 사건은 약 5만 년 전 마지막 빙하기 동안 시작되었다. 호모 사피엔스가 유라시아의 본토 전체에 정착하고 아메리카 대륙으로 육교를 건너가기 전까지, 그 시기에 아프리카 바깥으로 호모 사피엔스의 확산이 일어났다. 호모 사피엔스는 또한 카누나 뗏목을 타고 열대의 수역을 완전히 익혔는데, 이는 호모 사피엔스가 뉴기니와 호주로 이동해 가는데 도움을 주었다. 세계를 식민지화하는 것은 의도적인 계획은 아니었지만, 사냥할 새로운 동물, 채집할 새로운 식량 작물, 그리고 새로운 살 공간을 위한 그들의 끊임없는 탐색의 결과였다. 그들이 새로운 공간으로 이주하고 나서, 그들은 편하게 지낼 수 있었다. 하나의 종으로서 호모 사피엔스의 적응성은 그들이 광대한 범위의 새로운 환경을 이용할 수 있도록 만들었다.
① 흉포함   ② 독점
③ 적응성   ④ 부동성
⑤ 소심함

해설 지문의 빈칸을 채우는 문제이다. 지문의 빈칸이 있는 문장의 이전 문장에서 호모 사피엔스가 새로운 공간으로 이주하고

나서 편하게 지낼 수 있었다고 했으므로, 빈칸에는 새로운 공간에서도 편하게 지낼 수 있는 성질에 대한 내용이 나와야 적절하다는 것을 알 수 있다. 따라서 '적응성'이라고 한 ③번이 정답이다.

어휘
significant adj. 중요한 migration n. 이주, 이동
mainland n. 본토 land bridge phr. 육교, 해륙 수송
master v. 완전히 익히다, 통달하다 raft n. 뗏목
drift v. 이동하다, 표류하다 colonize v. 식민지화하다
deliberate adj. 의도적인, 고의적인
consequence n. 결과 ceaseless adj. 끊임없는
make oneself at home phr. 편하게 지내다
exploit v. 이용하다, 활용하다, 착취하다
vast adj. 광대한, 광활한 ferocity n. 흉포함
exclusivity n. 독점 adaptability n. 적응성
immovability n. 부동성 meticulousness n. 소심함

[04-06]

현상학이란 무엇인가? 그리고 왜 인류학자들을 비롯하여 역사, 심리학, 교육학, 혹은 정치경제학 학자들이 관심을 가져야만 하는가? 철학 내에서 현상학은 그것에 종사하는 사람들만큼이나 다양하다. 실제로, 현상학의 철학적 전통에 대한 한 입문서는 독자들에게 현상학이 어느 정도 "합의된 방법으로 결합하거나, 하나의 이론적 견해, 혹은 의식, 지식, 그리고 세계에 대한 철학적 논지들의 한 경향을 받아들인다."고 과장해서는 안 된다고 경고하는 것이 중요하다는 것을 발견했다. 이 다양성 중 일부는 현상학의 인류학적 사용의 특성으로 이어진다. 그렇지만 우리는 또한 현상학의 의미 범위의 경험적 축소에 대해 찬성하는 주장을 한다. 우리는 현상학의 잠재적 적용 가능성을 넓혀, 그것을 결합된 지식 분야들을 비롯하여 인류학에 더욱 유익하게 만들기 위해 그렇게 주장한다. 현상학의 사용을 넓히기 위해 의미를 제한하는 것이 역설처럼 보일 수 있지만, 이것은 사실 현상학 고유의 가르침을 계속하는 것이다. 임시 용도로, 우리는 현상학의 쓸 만한 정의를 제안하는데, 그것은 현상학이 인간이 유아기에 물려받고 그들이 사는 사회적이고 실질적으로 결합된 세계를 인간이 어떻게 인식하고, 경험하고, 이해하는지에 대한 연구라는 것이다.

이 방식에 맞춰, 인류학 안의 현상학은 모든 사회에서 모든 남성, 여성, 그리고 아이들에게 적용되는 인식과 경험에 관한 이론이다. 그러한 것으로서, 현상학은 인류학자들이 들락날락하는 현장 연구 장소들의 현지인들뿐만 아니라, 인류학자들과 철학자들 자신의 지역 생활하고도 관련이 있으며, 모든 사람들과 모든 장소처럼 인간과 비인간이라는 중요한 의미를 갖는 다른 것들에 의해 둘러싸여 있다. 따라서 현상학은 확실히 보편적 관점을 가진다. 하지만 현상학은 확고하게 배타주의적이기도 하다. 우리가 특권을 주는 현상학은 사회적이고 관습적인 일들을 통해 어떻게 경험과 지각이 구성되는지 보여주는 것에 착수한다. 사람들의 활동과 관심사에 대한 현상학적 서술은 현세적이고 누적되는 관점이고, 이것이 우리 몸에 서식하면서 사람들의 행동과 관점을 이끄는 방향들에 대한 현상학의 미묘한 단어에서 가장 깊이 나타난다.

phenomenology n. 현상학 anthropologist n. 인류학자
practitioner n. 종사하는 사람, 전문직
overstate v. 과장하다 cohere v. 결합하다, 일관성이 있다
consciousness n. 의식, 자각
heuristic adj. 경험적인, 체험적인
applicability n. 적용 가능성 instructive adj. 유익한
aligned adj. 결합된, 제휴한 discipline n. 지식 분야, 규율
preliminary adj. 임시의, 서문의 serviceable adj. 쓸 만한
materially adv. 실질적으로 inherit v. 물려받다, 상속받다
infancy n. 유아기 pertain v. 적용하다
fieldwork n. 현장 연구 regional adj. 지역의
decidedly adv. 확실히
universalistic adj. 보편적인, 전반의
determinedly adv. 확고하게, 결연히
particularistic adj. 배타주의적인
set out phr. 착수하다, 준비하다
constitute v. ~을 구성하다, 여겨지다
cumulative adj. 누적되는
phenomenological adj. 현상학적인
profoundly adv. 깊이 subtle adj. 미묘한
orientation n. 방향, 지향

04 2021 홍익대

정답 ③

해석
① 어떻게 현상학과 인류학을 구분할 수 있는가
② 어떻게 우리가 현상학에서의 인류학적 접근을 확인할 수 있는가
③ 어떻게 현상학적 방법들이 인류학에 적용될 수 있는가
④ 어떻게 사회과학이 현상학과 같은 비 경험적 방법론을 무시할 수 있는가

해설 지문의 주제를 묻는 문제이다. 지문 전반에 걸쳐 '인류학 안의 현상학'에 대해 설명하고 있고, 지문의 초반에 현상학과 현상학의 인류학적 사용에 대해 설명하고 있으며, 지문의 후반에 인류학에서의 현상학적 관점에 대해 설명하고 있다. 따라서 지문의 제목을 '어떻게 현상학적 방법들이 인류학에 적용될 수 있는가'라고 표현한 ③번이 정답이다.

오답 분석
① 지문에서 현상학과 인류학을 구분하는 내용은 언급되지 않았으므로 정답이 될 수 없다.
② 현상학에서의 인류학적 접근을 확인하는 것이 아니라 현상학적 방법들을 인류학에 적용하는 것에 대한 내용이므로 정답이 될 수 없다.
④ '어떻게 사회과학이 현상학과 같은 비 경험적 방법론을 무시할 수 있는가'라는 내용은 지문 초반의 '그리고 왜 인류학자들을 비롯하여 역사, 심리학, 교육학, 혹은 정치경제학 학생들이 흥미로워할까?'의 내용으로 보아 지문의 내용과 다르므로 정답이 될 수 없다.

어휘 empirical adj. 경험적인, 실험상의
methodology n. 방법론

05 [2021 홍익대]

정답 ②

해석
① 현상학은 통일된 방법론에 근거하여 철학적 지식의 한 분야로 정의될 수 있다.
② 현상학은 사람들의 인식, 경험, 그리고 세계에 대한 이해에 주로 집중한다.
③ 현상학적 방법론을 인류학에 적용함으로써, 연구원들은 제한적으로 현장 연구의 현지인들에 집중한다.
④ 현상학적 인류학은 특정한 양상을 고려하지 않고, 인간 삶의 보편적인 측면을 강조한다.

해설 지문의 내용과 일치하는 것을 묻는 문제이다. 지문 중간의 phenomenology is an investigation ~의 내용을 통해 현상학은 사람들의 인식, 경험, 그리고 세계에 대한 이해에 주로 집중한다는 것을 알 수 있다. 따라서 ②번이 지문의 내용과 일치한다.

오답분석
① "현상학이 합의된 방법으로 결합하거나, 하나의 이론적 견해, 혹은 의식, 지식, 그리고 세계에 대한 철학적 논지들의 한 경향을 받아들인다"고 과장해서는 안 된다고 경고하는 것이 중요하다는 내용이 있으므로 현상학이 통일된 방법론에 근거하여 철학적 지식의 한 분야로 정의될 수 있다는 것은 지문의 내용과 다르다.
③ 인류학 안의 현상학은 모든 사회에서 모든 사람들에게 적용되는 이론으로, 현장 연구 장소의 현지인들뿐만 아니라 연구원 자신의 지역 생활하고도 관련이 있다고 했으므로 현상학적 방법론을 인류학에 적용함으로써, 연구원들은 현장연구에서 제한적으로 현지인들에 집중한다는 것은 지문의 내용과 다르다.
④ 현상학은 확실히 보편적인 관점을 가지지만 배타주의적으로 사회적이고 관습적인 일들을 통해 경험과 지각이 어떻게 구성되는지를 보여주는 것에 착수한다고 했으므로 현상학적 인류학이 특정한 양상을 고려하지 않고, 인간 삶의 보편적인 측면을 강조한다는 것은 지문의 내용과 다르다.

어휘 unified adj. 통일된 adopt v. 적용하다, 채택하다; 입양하다

06 [2021 홍익대]

정답 ①

해설 지문의 흐름상 'not'이 들어가기에 가장 적절한 위치를 고르는 문제이다. 'not'을 [A] 자리에 넣는다면, 현상학은 그것에 종사하는 사람들만큼이나 다양하므로 그것이 "합의된 방법으로 결합하거나 하나의 이론적 견해, 혹은 의식, 지식, 그리고 세계에 대한 철학적 논지들의 한 경향을 받아들인다."고 과장하지 않는 것이 중요하다고 설명할 수 있으므로 글의 흐름이 자연스럽게 연결된다. 따라서 ①번이 정답이다.

[07-08]

전 세계의 정글에서 얼마나 많은 사람의 부족들이 문명과 접촉하지 않고 생존하는지를 추정하는 것은 불가능하다. 전문가들의 가장 좋은 추측은 대략 100여 개의 작은 집단들이 대부분 아마존의 열대우림에 남아있다는 것이다.

이러한 부족들 중에서 얼마나 많은 부족들이 진정으로 현대 세계를 인지하지 못하는지 또한 알려져 있지 않다. 그러나 확실한 것은 접촉은 항상 재앙으로 끝난다는 것이다. 10년 전에, 페루의 정글 지대에서 살고 있는 Murunahua 부족에게 "최초의 접촉"이 이루어졌다.

그들은 총을 쏘아서 죽이는 불법적인 벌목꾼들에 의해서 강제로 접촉되었다. 일부는 총에 맞아서 죽었지만, 대부분은, 서구인들은 독감에 대한 자연적인 방어가 있지만, 항상 고립되어서 살아온 부족들에게는 치명적일 수 있는 독감과 같은 질병으로 죽었다.

calculate v. 추정[산정, 계산]하다
uncontacted adj. (문명과) 접촉하지 않은
survive v. 생존하다   rainforest n. (열대)우림
genuinely adv. 진정으로   disaster n. 재앙
forcibly adv. 강제적으로   illegal adj. 불법적인
logger n. 벌목꾼   fatal adj. 치명적인
isolation n. 격리, 고립

07 [2017 한성대]

정답 ④

해석
① 전문가들은 현재 전 세계에 약 100개의 문명과 접촉하지 않은 부족들이 있다고 대충 추정한다.
② 얼마나 많은 그러한 부족들이 실제로는 현대 세계와 전혀 접촉을 안 했는지는 확실하지 않다.
③ Murunahua 부족은 바깥 세계와의 첫 번째 접촉을 자진해서 한 것이 아니었다.
④ 불법적인 벌목꾼들의 총격은 많은 Murunahua 부족들이 사망한 가장 큰 이유였다.

해설 지문의 내용과 일치하지 않는 것을 묻는 문제이다. ④번의 키워드인 the biggest reason for the deaths(사망에 대한 가장 큰 이유)와 관련된 지문의 세 번째 문단에서 일부는 총격으로 죽었지만, 대부분은 독감과 같은 질병으로 죽었다고 했다. 따라서 ④번이 지문의 내용과 일치하지 않는다.

오답분석
① 지문의 두 번째 문장 The best guess of experts is that around 100 small groups remain을 통해 '전문가들은 현재 전 세계에 약 100개의 문명과 접촉하지 않은 부족들이 있다고 대충 추정한다'는 것을 알 수 있다.
② 지문의 두 번째 문단 첫 문장 How many of these tribes are genuinely unaware of the modern world is also unknown을 통해 '얼마나 많은 부족들이 진정으로 현대 세계와 전혀 접촉을 안 했는지는 확실하지 않다'는 것을 알 수 있다.

③ 지문의 세 번째 문단 첫 문장 They were forcibly contacted by illegal loggers를 통해 'Murunahua 부족은 바깥 세계와의 첫 번째 접촉을 자진해서 한 것이 아니었다'는 것을 알 수 있다.

08 2017 한성대

정답 ②

해석 ① 무기　② 면역
③ 질병　④ 우림

해설 밑줄 친 natural defenses의 의미를 추론하는 문제이다. 지문의 마지막 문장에서 서구인들은 독감에 대한 자연적인 방어가 있다고 했다. 따라서 natural defenses의 의미를 '면역'이라고 한 ②번이 정답이다.

[09-10]

수렵과 채집에서 농경으로의 전환은 인류 역사라는 커다란 체계 안에서는 매우 급격했지만, 농부 개개인의 관점에서는 점진적인 것이었다. 왜냐하면 야생 작물과 재배되는 작물 사이가 구분 없는 연속체를 이루는 것처럼 완전한 수렵-채집인과 완전한 경작인 사이에는 어느 정도 점진적인 범위가 존재하기 때문이다. 수렵-채집인들은 식량의 이용 가능성을 증가시키기 위해 때때로 생태계를 조작한다. 비록 그런 행동이 우리가 농경이라고 부르는 의도적인 대규모 경작에는 훨씬 못 미치지만 말이다. 예를 들어, 땅을 개간하고 새로운 성장을 촉진시키기 위해 불을 사용하는 것은 최소 35,000년 전으로 거슬러 올라가는 행위이다. 현대까지 살아남은 얼마 안 되는 수렵-채집 그룹들 중 하나인 호주 원주민들은 식량의 이용 가능성을 증가시키기 위하여, 그들이 몇 달 후에 특정 장소로 돌아올 때는, 가끔 씨앗을 심는다. 이것을 농경이라고 부르는 것은 과장일 것이다. 왜냐하면 그런 식량은 그들의 음식에서 아주 작은 부분만을 구성하기 때문이다. 그러나 의도적인 생태계의 조작은 그들이 전적으로 수렵-채집인인 것도 아니라는 사실을 의미한다.

farming n. 농사, 농업　**perspective** n. 관점, 시각
scheme n. 제도, 체계　**domesticate** v. 사육하다, 재배하다
continuum n. 연속체　**fall short of ~** phr. ~에 못 미치다
cultivation n. 경작, 재배　**prompt** v. 촉진시키다
aborigine n. 원주민　**on occasion** phr. 가끔
exaggeration n. 과장　**make up** phr. 구성하다
fraction n. 부분　**deliberate** adj. 의도적인
exclusively adv. 전적으로, 오로지

09 2018 서울여대

정답 ③

해석 ① 그들 식량의 대부분은 재배된 작물에서 온다.
② 그들은 땅을 개간하고 새로운 성장을 촉진시키기 위해 불을 사용한다.
③ 그들은 때때로 의도적으로 생태계를 조작한다.
④ 그들은 수렵과 채집에서 농경으로 급격하게 진화해 왔다.

해설 지문의 내용과 일치하는 것을 묻는 문제이다. 지문의 마지막 문장 the deliberate manipulation of the ecosystem ~ 의 내용을 통해 때때로 호주 원주민들은 의도적으로 생태계를 조작한다는 것을 알 수 있다. 따라서 ③번이 지문의 내용과 일치한다.

오답분석 ① 호주 원주민들은 농경에서 식량의 일부분만을 얻는다고 했으므로 식량의 대부분이 재배된 작물에서 온다는 것은 지문의 내용과 다르다.
② 땅을 개간하고 새로운 성장을 촉진시키기 위하여 불을 사용하는 것은 호주 원주민에 해당하는 내용이 아니다.
④ 호주 원주민은 수렵-채집에서 농경으로의 변화가 점진적으로 일어난 예로서 나온 내용이므로, 그들이 수렵과 채집에서 농경으로 급격하게 진화해 왔다는 것은 지문의 내용과 다르다.

10 2018 서울여대

정답 ③

해석 ① 호주 원주민들의 긴 역사를 강조하기 위하여
② 호주 원주민들이 유목 생활을 한다는 것을 사람들에게 알리기 위하여
③ 수렵-채집과 농경이 연속성을 가진다는 것을 보여주기 위하여
④ 농약에 의해 야기되는 환경 문제들을 사람들에게 경고하기 위하여

해설 호주 원주민들을 저자가 지문에서 언급한 이유를 묻는 문제이다. 첫 번째 문장에서 수렵-채집에서 농경으로의 변화가 점진적이었다는 저자의 중심 생각을 밝히고 나서, 부연 설명으로서 호주 원주민의 예를 드는 글의 구조이므로, 저자가 호주 원주민을 언급한 이유는 '수렵-채집과 농경이 연속성을 가진다는 것을 보여주기 위하여'이다. 따라서 정답은 ③번이다.

어휘 **agricultural** adj. 농업의　**chemicals** n. 화학 약품

[11-12]

글은 우리가 생각을 기록하고 전달하도록 도와준다. 그것은 일상적인 인간의 경험의 결정적이고 필수적인 부분이다. 우리가 쇼핑목록을 쓰든 장편소설을 쓰든지 간에, 우리는 그것이 없으면 우리 자신들이 고립되어 있다고 느끼는 (글이라는) 도구를 사용한다. 글이 없으면, 우리는 정치적인 의견의 표현, 응급상황에 대한 묘사, 그리고 일기와 편지에서 우리의 감정에 대한 고찰과 같은 필수적인 과정으로부터 우리 자신을 고립시키게 된다.

글은 많은 문화를 넘나든다. 우리가 유서 깊은 동굴 그림을 고찰하든 세계무역센터 참사 후의 팩스 메시지의 전송을 고찰하

든 간에, 우리는 다른 사람들에게 전달하려는 인간의 본능적인 증거를 발견한다.
[A] 과거에는, 글이 변화를 야기했다. [B] 흑인 노예들은 빈번하게 읽거나 쓰는 것을 배우는 것을 금지당했지만, 일부는 어쨌든 읽고 쓰는 능력을 얻기 위한 방법을 그럭저럭 찾았다. [C] 노예의 삶에 대한 그들의 이야기는 노예 폐지 운동에 불을 지피는 데 도움이 되었다. 19세기에 살았던 여성들은 참정권이라는 대의명분을 진전시키기 위해서 글을 이용했고, 열정적인 연설과 신문에 낸 기사로 투표권을 획득했다. [D] 이민자들은 신대륙에서 더 나은 삶을 찾기 위해서 영어를 배우려고 몸부림쳤다. [E]

communicate v. (의사)소통하다(with); 전달하다
definitive adj. 결정적인, 최후적인(= conclusive, determining); 명확한(= absolute)   isolate v. 고립[격리]시키다
isolated adj. 고립된, 격리된
cut A off from B phr. A를 B에서 고립[단절]시키다
process n. 과정, 절차
emergency n. 응급[위급](사태, 상황)
examination n. 고찰, 검토; 조사, 검사; 심사; 시험
cross v. 넘나들다, 횡단하다, 가로지르다
historic adj. 유서 깊은, 역사적으로 유명한[중요한]
cave n. 동굴   drawing n. 그림, 스케치
transmission n. 전송, 전달
disaster n. 재앙, 재해, 재난, 참사   instinct n. 본능
bring about phr. 야기하다, 발생시키다(= cause, generate, trigger, give rise to)   forbid v. 금(지)하다
manage to R phr. 그럭저럭[가까스로] ~하다
literacy n. 읽고 쓰는 능력
anyway adv. 어쨌든, 하여튼; 어떻게 해서든
advance v. 진전[진척, 촉진]시키다
cause n. 대의명분; 원인   suffrage n. 참정권, 투표(권)
article n. 기사   immigrant n. 이민자
struggle v. 버둥거리다, 몸부림치다, 노력하다

11   2016 상명대

정답   ④

해석   ① 우리는 무엇인가를 쓸 때, 다른 사람들로부터 떨어진 채로, 대개는 혼자 있는 상태가 된다.
② 노예제도의 폐지 이전에는, 어떠한 흑인들도 읽거나 쓸 수 없었다.
③ 그림이 다양한 문화를 가로질러서 보편적인 의사소통 도구인 반면에, 글은 어떤 문화에 제한된다.
④ 19세기 이전에 여성들은 투표하도록 인정받지 못했다.
⑤ 짤막한 쪽지나 긴 산문을 쓰기 위해서, 우리는 도구가 필요하다.

해설   본문의 후반부 '19세기에 살았던 여성들은 참정권이라는 대의명분을 진전시키기 위해서 글을 이용했고, 열정적인 연설과 신문에 낸 기사로 투표권을 획득했다.'를 통해서 정답을 유추할 수 있다.

오답분석   ① 1문단 세 번째 문장 '~ 그것이 없으면 우리 자신들이 고립되어 있다고 느끼는 (글이라는) 도구를 사용한다.'에서 글이라는 도구가 없으면 고립된다고 느낀다고 했기 때문에 보기와는 내용이 다르다.
② 3문단 두 번째 문장 '흑인 노예들은 빈번하게 읽거나 쓰는 것을 배우는 것을 금지당했지만, 일부는 어쨌든 읽고 쓰는 능력을 얻기 위한 방법을 그럭저럭 찾았다.'를 통해서 보기의 'none'이 틀렸음을 알 수 있다.
③ 2문단 첫 줄 '글은 많은 문화를 넘나든다.'에서 보기의 내용일치가 틀렸음을 알 수 있다.
⑤ 1문단 세 번째 문장 '~ 그것이 없으면 우리 자신들이 고립되어 있다고 느끼는 (글이라는) 도구를 사용한다.'에서 본문의 tool은 '(글이라는) 도구'이고, 보기의 tool은 '(연필이나 펜 등의) 도구'를 의미하기 때문에 내용일치가 틀렸다.

어휘   abolition n. 폐지, 철폐   slavery n. 노예제도
universal adj. 보편적인   prose n. 산문

12   2016 상명대

정답   ③

해석   문맥상 주어진 문장의 Their는 3문단 두 번째 문장의 African American slaves를 받아 온다. 그리고 slave life는 3문단 두 번째 문장 '흑인 노예들은 빈번하게 읽거나 쓰는 것을 배우는 것을 금지당했지만, 일부는 어쨌든 읽고 쓰는 능력을 얻기 위한 방법을 그럭저럭 찾았다.' 부분을 받는다. 그러므로 [C]가 가장 적당한 자리이다.

어휘   fire v. ~에 불을 붙이다, 자극하다, 격앙시키다
abolition n. 노예 (제도) 폐지

[13-15]

포스트휴먼의 대상은 혼합물이고, 여러 다른 종류들로 이루어진 요소들의 모음이자, 그 영역이 지속적으로 구성되고 재건되는 물질적인 정보를 제공하는 존재이다. 포스트휴먼 체제의 전형적인 시민인 6백만 달러짜리 남자를 생각해보아라. 그 남자의 6백만 달러짜리라는 이름이 암시하듯이, 그는 자신의 일부가 실제로 누군가에 소유된 것이지만, 그 일부에 대한 소유권은 시장에서의 관계보다 우선하는 자연적인 조건이라서가 아니라, 그 사람이 구매되었기 때문에 정확하게 말해서 그는 소유된 것이라고 볼 수 있다. 이와 유사하게, 포스트휴먼에서는 매개물과 욕망 혹은 다른 사람들의 의지와 분명히 구별되는 자신의 의지가 존재한다는 가정이 약화되는데, 그 이유는 포스트휴먼에서 공통적인 여러 다른 종류들로 이루어진 특성은 서로 전혀 다른 부분에 위치한 광범위한 인식을 암시하기 때문이다. 포스트휴먼의 광범위한 인식이 개개의 매개물을 어떻게 복잡하게 만드는지 이해하기 위해서는 로보캅의 프로그램된 명령을 방해하는 메모리 플래시를 생각해보면 된다. 만약 인간의

본질이 다른 사람들의 의지에서 벗어나 있는 상태라면, 포스트휴먼은 어쩔 수 없이 자유가 없기 때문이 아니라, 다른 사람의 의지와 분명히 구별되는 자신의 의지를 확인할 연역적인 방법이 없기 때문에 "포스트(다음의)"이다. 이러한 예시들은 포스트휴먼의 인공 두뇌학적 측면을 특히 중시하지만, 포스트휴먼의 구성은 그 대상이 문자 그대로 사이보그가 되는 것을 요구하지 않는다는 점을 아는 것이 중요하다. 신체에 개입이 있었든 아니든 간에, 인지 과학과 인공 생명과 같은 분야에서 나온 주관성을 나타내는 새로운 모델들은 생물학적으로 이전과 똑같은 호모 *사피엔스*조차도 포스트휴먼으로 간주된다는 것을 암시한다. 본질적인 의미를 규정하는 그 특성들은 비생물학적인 요소들의 존재가 아니라, 주관성의 구성을 포함한다.

posthuman n. 포스트휴먼(로봇 공학 및 다른 기술로 유전적 구조를 조작하고 자기 몸을 확대·증대하여 인간에서 진화한 상상의 인류; 이러한 인류의 미래 시대)
amalgam n. 혼합물, 결합물
heterogeneous adj. 여러 다른 종류들로 이뤄진
component n. (구성) 요소, 부품
informational adj. 정보를 제공하는   **entity** n. 존재, 실체
boundary n. 영역, 경계
continuous adj. 지속적인, 계속적인
reconstruction n. 재건
paradigmatic adj. 전형적인, 모범의
regime n. 체제, 제도, 정권   **indeed** adv. 실제로
precisely adv. 정확히   **preexist** v. ~보다 전에 존재하다
presumption n. 가정, 추정   **agency** n. 매개
desire n. 욕망   **distinguish** v. 구별하다
undercut v. 약화시키다
collective adj. 공동의, 공통의, 집단의   **cognition** n. 인식
disparate adj. 서로 전혀 다른, 이질적인
interfere v. 방해하다   **programmed** adj. 프로그램된
directive n. 명령, 지시   **complicate** v. 복잡하게 만들다
freedom from phr. ~에서 벗어나 있는 상태
necessarily adv. 어쩔 수 없이, 필연적으로
priori adj. 연역적인, 원인에서 결과로
foreground v. 특히 중시하다
cybernetic adj. 인공 두뇌학의   **aspect** n. 측면
literal adj. 문자 그대로의   **intervention** n. 개입, 조정, 중재
subjectivity n. 주관성
cognitive science phr. 인지 과학(정신적 작업의 질과 그것을 가능케 하는 뇌의 기능을 연구)   **artificial life** phr. 인공 생명
biologically adv. 생물학적으로
unaltered adj. 이전과 똑같은, 변하지 않은
count as phr. ~이라 간주되다
defining adj. 본질적인 의미를 규정하는
characteristic n. 특성, 특징
nonbiological adj. 비생물학적인

13 2019 홍익대

정답 ④

해석 ① 혼합물 구성 요소의 존재
② 광범위한 인식의 매개물
③ 새로운 주관성 모델
④ 생물학적으로 변한 부분들의 종

해설 포스트휴먼의 특징이 아닌 것을 파악하는 문제이다. 지문의 여덟 번째 문장에서 생물학적으로 이전과 똑같은 호모 사피엔스조차도 포스트휴먼으로 간주된다고 했으므로, 포스트휴먼의 특징이 아닌 것은 '생물학적으로 변한 부분들의 종'이다. 따라서 정답은 ④번이다.

어휘 hybrid n. 혼합물

14 2019 홍익대

정답 ③

해석 ① 포스트휴먼에서 절대 약화되지 않는다는 인간주의의 가정이 존재한다.
② 포스트휴먼은 신체의 개입을 통해서만 나타난다.
③ 포스트휴먼 주관성의 구성이 완전히 인공적인 것은 아니다.
④ 포스트휴먼은 호모 *사피엔스*의 생물학적 측면으로 대체된다.

해설 지문을 통해 추론할 수 있는 것을 고르는 문제이다. 지문의 여덟 번째 문장에서 주관성을 나타내는 새로운 모델들은 생물학적으로 이전과 똑같은 호모 *사피엔스*조차도 포스트휴먼으로 간주된다는 것을 암시한다고 했으므로, 포스트휴먼 주관성의 구성이 완전히 인공적인 것은 아니라는 것을 추론할 수 있다. 따라서 정답은 ③번이다.

오답 분석
① 포스트휴먼에서는 매개물과 욕망 혹은 다른 사람들의 의지와 분명히 구별되는 자신의 의지가 존재한다는 가정이 약화된다고 했으므로, 포스트휴먼에서 절대 약화되지 않는다는 인간주의의 가정이 존재한다는 것은 지문의 내용과 다르다.
② 신체에 개입이 있었든 아니든 간에, 인지 과학과 인공 생명과 같은 분야에서 나온 주관성을 나타내는 새로운 모델들은 생물학적으로 이전과 똑같은 호모 사피엔스조차도 포스트휴먼으로 간주된다는 것을 암시한다고 했으므로, 포스트휴먼이 신체의 개입을 통해서만 나타난다는 것은 지문의 내용과 다르다.
④ 생물학적으로 이전과 똑같은 호모 사피엔스조차도 포스트휴먼으로 간주된다고는 했지만, 포스트휴먼이 호모 *사피엔스*의 생물학적 측면으로 대체되는지는 알 수 없다.

어휘 give way to phr. ~로 대체되다

15 2019 홍익대

정답 ②

해석 ① 인공 지능의 구조를 강조하기 위해
② 인식이 광범위하고 복잡하다는 것을 설명하기 위해
③ 최근 시장에서의 관계에 대한 예시를 추가로 주기 위해
④ 사람들이 포스트휴먼에 대해 갖는 불안감을 면밀히 분석해주기 위해

해설 글쓴이가 로보캅을 언급하는 이유를 파악하는 문제이다. 지문의 다섯 번째 문장에서 포스트휴먼의 광범위한 인식이 개개의 매개물을 어떻게 복잡하게 만드는지 이해하기 위해서는 로보캅의 프로그램된 명령을 방해하는 메모리 플래시를 생각해보면 된다고 했으므로, 글쓴이가 로보캅을 언급하는 이유는 '인식이 광범위하고 복잡하다는 것을 설명하기 위해'이다. 따라서 정답은 ②번이다.

어휘 put emphasis on phr. ~을 강조하다, ~에 역점을 두다
mechanism n. 구조, 방법
put the case phr. 사정을 설명하다, 가정하다
in-depth adj. 면밀한, 상세한   analysis n. 분석
anxiety n. 불안(감), 염려

[16-17]

인간의 불행은 두 종류로 나눌 수 있다: 첫 번째는 인간이 아닌 환경에 의해 가해지는 불행이며, 두 번째는 다른 인간에 의해 가해지는 불행이다. 인류가 지식과 기술에서 발전함에 따라, 두 번째 종류의 불행이 전체 불행에서 차지하는 비중이 점점 더 증가하고 있다. 예를 들면, 옛날에는 기근이 자연의 원인 때문이었으며, 사람들이 기근과 최선을 다해 싸워도, 많은 사람들이 아사(餓死)했다. 현재는 세계의 여러 지역이 기근의 위협에 직면해 있지만, 비록 자연적 원인이 그 상황에 기여한다 하더라도, 주된 원인은 사람이다.

오랫동안 전 세계의 문명화된 여러 나라들이 서로를 죽이는 일에 전념했으며, 그들은 갑자기 서로를 살리는 일로 전환하기가 어렵다고 생각한다. 이제 인간의 최악의 적은 인간이다. 여전히 인간은 죽는다는 것이 자연의 섭리지만, 의학의 발전 덕분에 사람들이 천수를 누릴 때까지 사는 경우가 더욱더 흔해질 것이다. 우리는 영원히 살기를 소망하며 끝없는 천국의 즐거움을 고대하는 것으로 생각된다. 그러나 사실은, 만약 당신이 더 이상 젊지 않은 어느 솔직한 사람에게 물어본다면, 아마도 그는 당신에게 이 세상에서의 삶을 맛보니 다음 세상에서 새로 또 삶을 시작하고 싶지는 않다고 말해줄 것이다. 따라서 미래에는 인류가 고려해야 할 가장 중요한 악은 인간들이 어리석음이나 증오심 때문에 또는 그 두 가지 모두 때문에 서로에게 가하는 악이라고 간주될 것이다.

inflict v. (고통 등을) 가하다   famine n. 기근; 기아
starvation n. 기아, 굶주림
switch over to phr. ~로 바꾸다, 전환하다
see to it that ~ phr. ~하도록 조처하다, 주의하다

mortal adj. 죽을 운명인
have one's fill of phr. ~을 실컷 맛보다, 즐기다
for ever phr. 영원히   candid adj. 솔직한
malevolence n. 악의, 증오

16 2018 중앙대

정답 ②

해석 ① 자연의 수호자   ② 인간의 최악의 적
③ 환경의 친구   ④ 문명의 창조자

해설 지문의 빈칸을 채우는 문제이다. 첫 문단에서 인간이 겪는 불행 중에 인간에 의한 불행이 점점 커지고 있다고 했으며, 빈칸 앞 문장에서는 문명국가들이 서로를 죽이는 일에 전념했으며 갑자기 서로를 살리는 일로 전환하기가 어렵다고 했으므로, 강조 구문의 빈칸에는 '이제 인간의 최악의 적은 인간이다'라는 의미가 되도록 man's worst enemy가 들어가는 것이 자연스럽다. 따라서 ②번이 정답이다.

17 2018 중앙대

정답 ③

해석 ① 인간 자신에 의해서 만들어지는 인간의 문제들이 다른 모든 문제들보다 더 많다.
② 비록 우리 모두 언젠가는 죽지만, 의학은 사람들이 예전보다 더 오래 사는 것을 가능하게 했다.
③ 기회가 주어진다면 다음 세상에서 다시 새로운 삶을 시작할 기회를 거부할 사람은 없다.
④ 미래에 인간에게 가장 중요한 문제는 아마도 인간의 적대감과 지혜 부족 때문에 인간 자신일 것이다.

해설 지문의 내용과 일치하지 않는 것을 찾는 문제이다. 다음 세상에 대해 언급한 후반부의 But in fact, if you question ~ as a 'new boy' in another.에서 '만약 당신이 더 이상 젊지 않은 어느 솔직한 사람에게 물어본다면, 아마도 그는 당신에게 이 세상에서의 삶을 맛보니 다음 세상에서 새로 또 삶을 시작하고 싶지는 않다고 말해줄 것이라고 했다. 따라서 ③번이 지문의 내용과 일치하지 않는다.

오답 분석 ① 첫 문단의 As mankind have progressed ~ of the total.의 내용을 통해 '인간 자신에 의해서 만들어지는 인간의 문제들이 다른 모든 문제들보다 더 많다'는 것을 알 수 있다.
② 두 번째 문단의 Nature, it is true, still ~ until they have had their fill of life의 내용을 통해 '비록 우리 모두 언젠가는 죽지만, 의학은 사람들이 예전보다 더 오래 사는 것을 가능하게 했다'는 것을 알 수 있다.
④ 마지막 문장 For the future, ~ stupidity or malevolence or both.의 내용을 통해 '미래에 인간에게 가장 중요한 문제는 아마도 인간의 적대감과 지혜 부족 때문에 인간 자신일 것'이라는 것을 알 수 있다.

어휘   **exceed** v. (수나 양을) 초과하다, 넘어서다
       maliciousness n. 악의, 적의

[18-20]

이성적인 의견과 이성적인 행동을 하는 인류 사이에 우세함이 있다면, 그것은 사람의 실수는 고쳐질 수 있다는 인간 정신의 질, 다시 말해 지적 존재로서나 도덕적 존재로서의 인간에게서 존경할 수 있는 모든 것의 원천이기 때문이다. 인간은 자신의 실수를 토론과 경험을 통해 바로잡을 수 있다. 경험만을 가지고 바로잡을 수는 없다. 경험이 어떻게 해석되는지를 보여주기 위해서는 반드시 토론이 있어야 한다. 잘못된 의견과 관행도 점차적으로 사실과 논쟁에 굴복하지만, 마음에 어떠한 영향을 미치기 위해서는 반드시 그 전에 사실과 논쟁을 가져와야 한다. 그것들의 의미를 꺼내기 위한 논평 없이, 자신의 이야기를 말할 수 있는 사실은 거의 없다. 그러고 나서, 그것을 올바르게 설정할 수단을 지속적으로 가까이해야 인간 판단의 전체적인 힘과 가치에 의존할 수 있다. 정말 신뢰할 만한 판단을 가진 사람의 경우는 어떻게 그렇게 된 것일까? 그의 의견과 행동에 대한 비판에 대해 그가 마음을 열어놓았기 때문이다. 자신의 의견을 다른 사람들의 의견에 분석하여 수정하고 완성하는 꾸준한 습관은 그것에 대한 적절한 의존을 위한 흔들리지 않는 유일한 기반이다. 적어도 분명하게, 그에 반대한다고 말할 수 있는 모든 것을 인지하고 모든 반대자들에게 맞서 그의 위치를 유지하면서, 그는 비슷한 과정을 거치지 않은 어떠한 다른 사람이나 대중들보다 그의 판단이 더 낫다고 생각할 권리가 있기 때문이다.

---

preponderance n. 우세함   **rational** adj. 이성적인
conduct n. 행동   **respectable** adj. 존경할 수 있는
intellectual adj. 지적인   **corrigible** adj. 고칠 수 있는
rectify v. 바로잡다   **interpret** v. 해석하다
gradually adv. 점진적으로   **comment** n. 논평
reliance n. 의존   **confidence** n. 신뢰, 자신감
collate v. 분석하다   **foundation** n. 기반
cognisant adj. 인지하고 있는   **multitude** n. 대중

18 [2020 단국대]

정답 ③

해설   preponderance(우세함)와 비슷한 의미를 가진 어휘를 묻고 있다. ①번 criticism은 '비평', ②번 rationality는 '이성', ③번 superiority는 '우월함', ④번 reflection은 '반성'이라는 의미이다. 따라서 ③번이 정답이다.

19 [2020 단국대]

정답 ①

해석   ① 반대자   ② 지지자
       ③ 숭배자   ④ 변절자

해설   지문의 빈칸을 채우는 문제이다. 빈칸이 포함된 문장에서 그에 반대한다고 말할 수 있는 모든 것을 인지한다고 했으므로, 반대와 관련된 의미의 단어가 와야 한다는 것을 알 수 있다. 따라서 '반대자'라고 한 ①번이 정답이다.

어휘   **gainsayer** n. 반대자   **supporter** n. 지지자
       votary n. 숭배자   **apostate** n. 변절자

20 [2020 단국대]

정답 ①

해석   ① 사실은 의견의 의존도를 결정할 것이다.
       ② 의견은 토론이 되지 않고서는 신뢰할 수 없다.
       ③ 비평은 의견의 신뢰도를 높이기 위해서는 피하면 안 된다.
       ④ 인간 정신의 지적인 질은 오류를 고치는 능력에서 찾을 수 있다.

해설   지문의 내용과 일치하지 않는 것을 묻는 문제이다. ①번의 키워드인 the reliance of opinions(의견의 의존도)와 관련된 지문의 just reliance(적절한 의견) 주변에서 자신의 의견을 다른 사람들의 의견에 분석하여 수정하고 완성하는 꾸준한 습관은 그것에 대한 적절한 의존을 위한 흔들리지 않는 유일한 기반이라고 했지만 사실이 의견의 의존도를 결정할 것이라는 것은 알 수 없다. 따라서 ①번이 지문의 내용과 일치하지 않는다.

오답분석
② There must be discussion, to show how experience is to be interpreted를 통해 '의견은 토론이 되지 않고서는 신뢰할 수 없다'라는 것을 알 수 있다.
③ he has kept his mind open to criticism of his opinions and conduct를 통해 '비평은 의견의 신뢰도를 높이기 위해서는 피하면 안 된다'는 것을 알 수 있다.
④ the source of everything respectable in man either as an intellectual or as a moral being, namely, that his errors are corrigible을 통해 '인간 정신의 지적인 질은 오류를 고치는 능력에서 찾을 수 있다'는 것을 알 수 있다.

[21-22]

개미의 군집 내에서, 각각의 일개미들은 자신의 적절한 역할을 수행한다. 그 군집에는 독립된 병사 계급도 있을 수 있다. 매우 특수한 일부 개체들은 왕이나 여왕의 역할을 수행한다. 만약 인류가 이런 군집 체계를 본보기로 취한다면 사람들은 파시스트 국가에서 살아갈 것이고, 그 국가에서는 이상적으로 각 개인은 출생부터 적당한 직업을 갖도록 결정되며, 그 국가의 지도자들은 영원히 지도자이고 군인들은 영원히 군인이고 농부들은 농부일 뿐이고 노동자는 노동자로 운명이 정해진다. 인간 계급에 대해 개미를 모델로 하는 파시스트의 염원은 개미의 본성과 사람의 본성 모두에 대한 깊은 오해에서 비롯된다. 나는 곤충의 신체적 발달이야말로 곤충이 근본적으로 무지하고 학

습한 것을 잊어버리며, 크게 변형될 수 없는 틀 내에서 역할이 정해진 존재가 되게 한다는 점을 지적하고 싶다. 나는 또한 어떻게 이러한 생리학적 조건들이 곤충을 한 번 쓰이고 버려지는 종이로 된 파이 접시보다도 개별적 가치가 없는 저렴하고 대량 생산된 것들 중 하나로 만드는지에 대해 말하고 싶다. 반면에, 나는 인생의 거의 절반을 차지할 수도 있는 방대한 학습과 연구가 가능한 인간은 개미와 달리 그러한 학습 능력을 위해 신체적으로 갖춰져 있음을 알리고 싶다. 다양성과 가능성은 다름 아닌 인체의 체계가 차지하고 있기 때문에 인간의 지각 기관에 내재되어 있고, 참으로 인간의 숭고한 비상의 비결이다. 우리가 개미를 능가하여 갖는 이러한 엄청난 이점을 버리고 인류에 파시스트적인 개미의 계급을 만드는 것이 가능할지라도, 나는 정말로 이는 인간의 본성에 대한 비하이고 경제적 측면에서 인간이 가진 위대한 가치의 낭비라고 생각한다.

community n. (동물의) 군집 caste n. 계급
pattern n. 본보기 condition v. 결정하다
peasant n. 농부 doom v. 운명을 짓다
aspiration n. 염원 mold n. 틀
physiological adj. 생리학의 inherent adj. 내재하는
sensorium n. 지각 기관 flight n. 비상
degradation n. 비하

21 2020 한국항공대

정답 ③

해석 ① 개미 군집은 인간의 추론으로 제대로 분석될 수 없는 이해하기 어려운 조직 구조를 가지고 있다.
② 개미의 조직 구조는 인간을 이해하는 데에 널리 이용될 수 있다.
③ 개미의 본성과 인간의 본성에 대한 오해는 파시스트적인 인간 사회를 만들 수도 있다.
④ 개미는 인간보다 더 많은 발달상의 가능성과 잠재력을 갖는다.

해설 지문의 내용과 일치하는 것을 묻는 문제이다. 지문의 중간에서 인간 계급에 대해 개미를 모델로 하는 파시스트의 염원은 개미의 본성과 사람의 본성 모두에 대한 깊은 오해에서 비롯된다는 내용을 통해 개미의 본성과 인간의 본성에 대한 오해는 파시스트적인 인간 사회를 만들 수도 있다는 것을 알 수 있다. 따라서 ③번이 지문의 내용과 일치한다.

오답 분석
① 우리가 개미를 능가하여 갖는 이러한 엄청난 이점을 버리고 인류에 파시스트적인 개미의 계급을 만드는 것이 가능할 수도 있다고 했으므로, 개미 군집은 인간의 추론으로 제대로 분석될 수 없는 이해하기 어려운 조직 구조를 가지고 있다는 것은 지문의 내용과 다르다.
② 정말로 이는 인간의 본성에 대한 비하이고 경제적 측면에서 인간이 가진 위대한 가치의 낭비라고 생각한다고 했으므로, 개미의 조직 구조는 인간을 이해하는 데에 널리 이용될 수 있다는 것은 지문의 내용과 다르다.

④ 나는 곤충의 신체적 발달이야말로 곤충이 근본적으로 무지하고 학습한 것을 잊어버리며, 크게 변형될 수 없는 틀 내에서 역할이 정해진 존재가 되게 한다는 점을 지적하고 싶다고 했으므로, 개미는 인간보다 더 많은 발달상의 가능성과 잠재력을 갖는다는 것은 지문의 내용과 다르다.

어휘 intimate adj. 밀접한 presuppose v. 전제로 하다

22 2020 한국항공대

정답 ④

해석 ① 인간 본성에 대한 비하
② 인류의 취약함
③ 개미와 인간에서 발견되는 기이한 일과 사건의 회오리
④ 인간에게 내재된 숭고한 체계

해설 지문의 제목을 묻는 문제이다. 지문의 후반에서 다양성과 가능성은 다름 아닌 인체의 체계가 차지하고 있기 때문에 인간의 지각 기관에 내재되어 있고, 참으로 인간의 숭고한 비상의 비결이라고 말하고 있다. 따라서 이 지문의 제목을 '인간에게 내재된 숭고한 체계'라고 표현한 ④번이 정답이다.

어휘 quirk n. 기이한 일 eddy n. 회오리

12 의학·건강

01-50
문제집 p.338

01 ③	02 ②	03 ③	04 ⑤	05 ②
06 ②	07 ①	08 ②	09 ①	10 ①
11 ④	12 ②	13 ⑤	14 ③	15 ①
16 ⑤	17 ①	18 ④	19 ①	20 ④
21 ④	22 ①	23 ③	24 ④	25 ②
26 ④	27 ②	28 ②	29 ①	30 ②
31 ①	32 ①	33 ②	34 ②	35 ④
36 ①	37 ②	38 ②	39 ①	40 ④
41 ②	42 ①	43 ③	44 ①	45 ③
46 ④	47 ①	48 ③	49 ②	50 ①

01 [2018 서강대]
정답 ③

해석 [C] 섬유질이 풍부한 음식들로 구성된 식단은 당뇨병, 심장병 그리고 관절염에 걸릴 위험을 줄여준다.
[A] 정말로, 섬유질의 이점에 대한 증거는 특정 질환에 국한되지 않는다.
[D] 그것이 바로 전문가들이 언제나 음식물의 섬유질이 우리에게 얼마나 좋은지를 말하는 이유이다.
[B] 그러나 이점들이 명확한 반면에, 섬유질이 왜 그렇게 훌륭한지는 별로 분명하지 않다.

해설 주어진 문장의 적절한 순서를 파악하는 문제이다. 섬유질이 풍부한 음식이 3가지 질병에 걸릴 위험을 줄여준다고 한 [C]가 먼저 오고 그다음에 섬유질의 이점은 특정 질환에 국한되지 않는다고 한 [A]가 오는 것이 자연스럽다. 그리고 이렇게 이점이 많기 때문에 전문가들이 항상 섬유질이 얼마나 좋은지를 말하고 있다고 한 [D]로 이어지는 것이 자연스럽다. 그리고 섬유질의 이점과 다른 내용인 [B]가 마지막에 오는 것이 자연스럽다. 따라서 주어진 문장의 올바른 순서는 ③번의 [C] — [A] — [D] — [B]이다.

어휘 fiber n. 섬유질 ailment n. 질병, 질환 diet n. 식단
diabetes n. 당뇨병 arthritis n. 관절염
dietary adj. 음식물의, 식이요법의

02 [2020 인하대]
정답 ②

해석 냉동식품 저녁 식사는 미국인 식단의 일부가 되었다. [A] 소비자들은 매년 40억 달러를 그것에 소비하고 있으며 식품 제조업체들은 끊임없이 새로운 종류의 상품을 만들어 내고 있다. [B] 건강을 고려하는 소비자들의 과제는 어느 것이 영양가 높은 식단에 확실히 적합한지를 알아내는 것이다. 냉동식품에 대한 연구에서, 필수 비타민과 미네랄을 포함하면서 지방, 열량 및 나트륨 섭취는 제한하기를 원하는 사람들에게 적합한 주요 요리를 확인하는 데 엄격한 기준이 사용되었다. [C] 결과는 고무적이었다. [D] 총 173개 냉동 음식이 20퍼센트 미만의 지방 열량을 함유하였고, 73개는 100칼로리당 200밀리그램 미만의 나트륨을 함유하고, 50개는 비타민A 또는 비타민C의 일일영양소권장량의 최소 30퍼센트를 가지고 있었다. [E] 몇몇 식사는 일부 영양소가 부족할 수 있으므로 보완할 음식이 추가되어야 한다.

해설 지문의 흐름상 주어진 문장이 들어가기에 가장 적절한 위치를 고르는 문제이다. [B]의 뒤 문장에서 건강한 영양 섭취를 원하는 사람들을 위한 냉동식품을 연구했다고 했으므로, [B] 자리에 건강을 고려하는 소비자들에 대해 설명하는 주어진 문장 '건강을 고려하는 소비자들의 과제는 어느 것이 영양가 높은 식단에 확실히 적합한지를 알아내는 것이다'가 들어가야 글의 흐름이 자연스럽게 연결된다. 따라서 ②번이 정답이다.

어휘 challenge n. 과제, 도전
health-conscious adj. 건강을 고려하는
determine v. 알아내다, 밝히다
fit into phr. 적합하다, 어울리다 easily adv. 확실히, 물론
nutritious adj. 영양가가 높은 manufacturer n. 제조업체
constantly adv. 끊임없이, 계속
turn out phr. ~을 만들어 내다, 생산하다
line n. (상품의) 종류 strict adj. 엄격한 criteria n. 기준
entrees n. 주요 요리 suitable for phr. ~에 적합한
intake n. 섭취 calorie n. 열량 sodium n. 나트륨
essential adj. 필수의
encouraging adj. 고무적인, 장려하는
at least phr. 최소한, 적어도
recommended daily allowance phr. 일일영양소권장량
deficient adj. 부족한 nutrient n. 영양소
compensate v. 보완하다, 보상하다

[03-04]

노년의 사람들이 한 칵테일 파티에서 이름들을 더 이상 기억하지 못할 때, 그들은 그들의 지적 능력이 감퇴하고 있다고 생각하는 경향이 있다. 그러나 점점 더 많은 연구들이 이러한 추정이 대개 틀렸다는 것을 시사한다. <u>대신에</u>, 그 연구는 노화된 두뇌가 종종 장기적인 이익을 위해 단지 더 많은 데이터를 취하고 뒤죽박죽인 정보를 가려내려고 시도한다는 것을 발견했다. 몇몇 두뇌는 늙어감에 따라 약화된다. <u>예를 들어</u>, 알츠하이머병은 65세 이상의 미국인들 중 13퍼센트에 발병한다. 그러나 대개의 노년층 사람들에게, 발생하는 일의 대부분은 점진적으로 주의력의 초점이 넓어져 이름이나 전화번호와 같은 <u>단순한 한 가지 사실을 이해하는</u> 것을 더 어렵게 만드는 것이라고 저자는 말한다. 비록 그것이 불만스러울 수는 있지만, 때때로는 유용하다.

tend to phr. ~하는 경향이 있다   brainpower n. 지적 능력
declining adj. 감퇴하는   assumption n. 추정
sift v. 가려내다, 체로 걸러내다   clutter n. 뒤죽박죽, 난잡
deteriorate v. 약화되다
Alzheimer's disease phr. 알츠하이머병
strike v. 발병하다   widen v. 넓어지다   focus n. 초점
attention n. 주의력   latch onto phr. 이해하다
frustrating adj. 불만스러운

03 2021 건국대

정답 ③

해석 ① 즉 - 그에 반해서
② 게다가 - 그러나
③ 대신에 - 예를 들어
④ 설상가상으로 - 마지막으로
⑤ 그러므로 - 그러나

해설 두 개의 빈칸에 적절한 연결어를 넣는 문제이다. 첫 번째 빈칸 앞 내용은 노년의 사람들은 그들의 지적 능력이 감퇴하고 있다고 생각하지만, 이러한 추정이 대개 틀렸다는 내용이고 빈칸 뒤 내용은 연구가 노화된 두뇌가 장기적인 이익을 위해 더 많은 데이터를 취하고 뒤죽박죽인 정보를 가려내려고 시도한다는 것을 발견했다는 내용이므로, 연구가 밝혀낸 사실과 앞서 추정이 서로 대조적이라는 것을 알 수 있다. 따라서 첫 번째 빈칸에는 '대조'를 나타내는 연결어인 Instead가 적절하다. 두 번째 빈칸의 경우, 빈칸 앞 문장은 몇몇 두뇌가 늙어감에 따라 약화된다는 내용이고, 빈칸 뒤 문장은 알츠하이머병이 65세 이상의 미국인들 중 13퍼센트에 발병한다는 내용이므로, 빈칸 뒤 문장이 앞 문장의 예시임을 알 수 있다. 따라서 두 번째 빈칸에는 '예시'를 나타내는 연결어인 for example이 적절하다. 따라서 ③ Instead - for example이 정답이다.

04 2021 건국대

정답 ⑤

해설 주어진 지문에서 '이해하다'라는 의미로 사용된 latch onto의 동의어를 묻는 문제이다. ①번 ignore는 '무시하다', ②번 forget은 '잊다', ③번 overstate는 '과장하다', ④번 minimize는 '축소하다', ⑤번 comprehend는 '이해하다'라는 의미이므로, ⑤번이 정답이다.

[05-07]

극심한 우울증은 사람들이 스스로 울혈성 심부전, 신장병, 또는 담석에서 벗어날 수 있는 것처럼 그들 스스로 벗어날 수 있는 것이 아니다. 울혈성 심부전이 있는 환자들이 호흡 곤란을 일으킬 때, 그들은 보통 고통을 덜어 주는 (A)치료를 감사하게 여긴다. 그 환자들은 심장이 뛰는 것을 통제한다는 느낌이 없기 때문에 그들 스스로 이런 병을 감당할 수 있을 것이라고 거의 믿지 않는다. 우리는 또한 뇌의 작용을 느끼지 못하지만, 우리의 정신은 통제하고 있다고 느낀다. 이 정신을 통제하고 있다는 느낌은 우울증이 있는 사람들이 자신을 극심한 우울증에서 벗어날 수 있다고 믿게 한다. 나의 경험상 일단 우울증이 뇌의 병이고, 그들이 통제할 수 있는 것이 아니라는 것을 노인들이 깨달으면, 그들은 (A)치료를 고려하는 것을 더 쉽게 받아들인다. 환자들이 그들의 문제를 더 이상 감당하지 못하는 것이 아니라, 오히려 그들의 뇌가 기대를 저버리는 것이다. 나는 종종 나의 환자들에게, (B)"당신이 아니라, 당신의 뇌입니다."라고 말한다.

congestive heart failure phr. 울혈성 심부전
kidney disease phr. 신장병   gallstones n. 담석
distress n. 고통   consider v. 고려하다
let down phr. ~의 기대를 저버리다, 실망하게 하다

05 2021 동국대

정답 ②

해석 ① 것보다 적은   ② 것처럼
③ 것일 뿐   ④ 것에 못지않게

해설 지문의 빈칸을 채우는 문제이다. 지문의 중간에서 정신을 통제하고 있다는 느낌은 우울증이 있는 사람들이 자신을 우울증에서 벗어날 수 있다고 믿게 한다고 했으므로, 빈칸에는 울혈성 심부전, 신장병, 또는 담석에서 벗어날 수 있는 것처럼 스스로 벗어날 수 있는 것이 아니라는 내용이 나오는 것이 자연스럽다. 따라서 '것처럼'이라고 한 ②번이 정답이다.

06 2021 동국대

정답 ②

해석 ① 만족   ② 치료
③ 휴식   ④ 요구

해설 지문의 빈칸을 채우는 문제이다. 지문의 초반에서 그들은 고통을 덜어 주는 이것을 감사하게 여긴다고 했고, 지문의 후반에서 노인들이 우울증이 뇌의 병이면서 그들이 통제할 수 있는 것이 아니라는 것을 깨달으면 이것을 고려하는 것을 더 쉽게 받아들인다고 했으므로, 첫 번째 (A)의 빈칸에는 그들은 고통을 덜어주는 치료를 감사하게 여기고, 두 번째 (A)의 빈칸에는 그들이 통제할 수 있는 것이 아니라는 것을 깨달으면 치료를 고려하는 것을 더 쉽게 받아들인다는 내용이 나오는 것이 자연스럽다. 따라서 '치료'라고 한 ②번이 정답이다.

07 2021 동국대

정답 ①

해석 ①"당신이 아니라, 당신의 뇌입니다."
②"당신의 뇌가 아니라, 당신입니다."

③ "당신이 아니라, 당신의 우울증입니다."
④ "당신의 우울증이 아니라, 당신입니다."

해설 지문의 빈칸을 채우는 문제이다. 지문의 후반에서 환자들이 그들의 문제를 더 이상 감당하지 못하는 것이 아니라, 오히려 그들의 뇌가 기대를 저버리는 것이라고 했으므로, 빈칸에는 지문의 화자가 종종 그의 환자들에게 (우울증의 원인은) 환자 자신이 아니라 환자의 뇌라고 말한다는 내용이 나오는 것이 자연스럽다. 따라서 "당신이 아니라, 당신의 뇌입니다."라고 한 ①번이 정답이다.

[08-09]

많이 먹고 나서 곧바로 공부하는 것은 현명하지 못하다. 이때에는 소화기관이 많은 부담을 가지고 있기 때문에 뇌와 몸의 다른 부분으로부터 많은 양의 혈액 공급을 받는다. 그리고, 두 군데에서 동시에 적절한 혈액의 공급이 일어날 수 없기 때문에, 소화기관이 혈액 공급을 빼앗기게 되어 소화작용이 제대로 일어나지 않는 결과를 초래하게 되거나, 또는 뇌가 상당히 저하되어 일을 제대로 할 수 없을 것이다. 이러한 이유로 많이 먹은 후에 적어도 30분 정도는 음악을 듣거나 가벼운 독서, 또는 알맞고 쉬운 신체적인 운동을 하는 데 써야 한다.

wise adj. 현명한   digestive adj. 소화의   organ n. 기관
heavily adv. 많이, 상당히   burdened adj. 부담을 가진
supply n. 공급   proper adj. 적절한
rob v. 빼앗다, 강탈하다   digestion n. 소화
carry out phr. 수행하다
impoverished adj. 저하된, 빈곤한   physical adj. 신체적인

08 [2019 한국외대]

정답 ②

해설 ① 식사 후에 뇌가 강렬히 활동적으로 되는 것
② 두 가지 기관을 위한 충분한 혈액이 없는 것
③ 소화 기능이 심하게 손상된 것
④ 혈액 공급이 예정에 따라서만 이루어지는 것

해설 밑줄 친 For this reason의 의미를 추론하는 문제이다. 밑줄 이전의 문장에서 두 군데의 기관에서 동시에 혈액 공급이 일어날 수 없다고 했다. 따라서, For this reason의 의미를 '두 가지 기관을 위한 충분한 혈액이 없는 것'이라고 한 ②번이 정답이다.

어휘 acutely adv. 강렬히, 절실히   function n. 기능
severely adv. 심하게
handicapped adj. 손상된, 장애가 있는
schedule n. 예정, 일정

09 [2019 한국외대]

정답 ①

해석 ① 알맞고 쉬운
② 힘들고 땀이 나는
③ 친숙하지만 힘든
④ 정신적인 것뿐만 아니라

해설 지문의 빈칸을 채우는 문제이다. 빈칸이 포함된 문장에서 적어도 30분 정도는 음악을 듣거나 가벼운 독서를 해야 한다고 했으므로, 빈칸에는 음악을 듣거나 가벼운 독서를 하는 것과 같이 가벼운 종류의 활동이 나와야 한다는 것을 알 수 있다. 따라서 '알맞고 쉬운'이라고 한 ①번이 정답이다.

어휘 agreeable adj. 알맞은   sweaty adj. 땀이 나는
familiar adj. 친숙한   demanding adj. 힘든

10 [2019 건국대]

정답 ①

해석 낙관론자들은 최후의 승리를 얻고 낙관론자들의 심장은 불평가들의 것보다 더 오래 건강을 유지한다. 10년 전에 자신을 매우 낙관적이라고 묘사했던 사람들은 심혈관질환으로 인한 사망률이 더 낮았고 전반적인 사망률도 강한 비관주의자들보다 낮았다. 9년 전 65세에서 85세의 남녀 999명의 연구 집단이 건강, 자기 존중, 사기, 낙관주의, 관계에 관한 설문지에 답했다. 그 이후에, 연구 집단 중 397명이 사망했다. 낙관적인 참가자들은 모든 원인으로 인한 사망 위험이 55퍼센트 낮았고 심부전으로 인한 사망 위험이 23퍼센트 낮았다. 이 연구는 비관적인 사람들은 흡연, 비만, 그리고 고혈압과 같이 삶을 단축할 수 있는 습관과 문제들이 생기기 더 쉬울 수 있다는 것에 주목한다. 낙관주의에 대한 성향은 다른 경우라면 비교적 짧은 기대 수명을 가진 대상에게 생존 이익을 주는 것처럼 보였다.

해설 지문의 빈칸을 채우는 문제이다. '낙관론자들이 최후의 승리를 얻고 낙관론자들의 심장은 불평가들의 것보다 더 오래 건강을 유지한다'고 했으므로 '자신을 매우 _____이라고 묘사했던 사람들은 심혈관질환으로 인한 사망률이 더 낮았'고, '_____ 참가자들은 모든 원인으로 인한 사망 위험 및 심부전으로 인한 사망 위험이 낮았'으며, '이 연구는 _____ 사람들은 삶을 단축할 수 있는 습관과 문제들이 생기기 더 쉬울 수 있다는 것에 주목한다'는 문맥에서 첫 번째 빈칸에는 '낙관적인'을 의미하는 optimistic, 두 번째 빈칸에는 '낙관적인'을 의미하는 Optimistic, 그리고 세 번째 빈칸에는 '비관적인'을 의미하는 pessimistic이 들어가는 것이 자연스럽다. 따라서 ①번이 정답이다.

어휘 optimist n. 낙관론자, 낙천주의자
get the last laugh phr. 최후의 승리를 얻다
grump n. 불평가   describe v. 묘사하다, 말하다
cardiovascular disease phr. 심혈관질환
pessimist n. 비관주의자   questionnaire n. 설문지
self-respect n. 자기 존중   morale n. 사기, 의욕
optimism n. 낙관주의   relationship n. 관계

participant n. 참가자　heart failure phr. 심부전
be prone to phr. ~하기 쉽다　cut short phr. 단축하다
obesity n. 비만　hypertension n. 고혈압
predisposition n. 성향, 경향
relatively adv. 비교적, 상대적으로
life expectancy phr. 기대 수명

[11-12]

(A)연구원들은 최근에 신경과학의 기반이 되는 교리를 뒤집을 일련의 발견을 발표했다. 수십 년 동안 (B)완전히 성장한 뇌는 새로운 뉴런을 발달시킬 수 없다고 이해되었다. 사람이 성년에 이르면, 뇌가 뉴런을 얻기보다 잃기 시작한다고 생각되었다. 그러나 사실 (C)성인의 뇌가 새로운 뉴런을 만들어 낼 수 있다는 증거가 쌓이고 있었다. 특히 쥐를 대상으로 한 (D)놀랄 만한 한 실험에서, 과학자들은 단순히 쳇바퀴를 달리는 것이 해마, 즉 기억과 관련된 뇌 구조에서 새로운 뉴런의 탄생으로 이어진다는 것을 발견했다. 그 이후, 다른 연구들은 또한 운동이 인간의 뇌에, 특히 우리가 나이가 들어감에 따라 긍정적인 영향을 미친다는 것과 운동이 알츠하이머병과 다른 신경병성 질환에 걸릴 위험을 줄이는 데도 도움이 될 수 있다는 것을 확증했다.

incapable adj. ~을 할 수 없는　neuron n. 뉴런
individual n. 사람　adulthood n. 성년
generate v. 만들어 내다　particularly adv. 특히
hippocampus n. 해마　establish v. 확증하다
neurodegenerative adj. 신경병성의　condition n. 질환

11 [2020 서강대]

정답 ④

해석
① 인간의 — 연세가 드신 — 급작스러운
② 포유동물 — 미숙한 — 믿기 어려운
③ 청소년 — 충분히 성장된 — 확정적인
④ 완전히 성장한 — 성인의 — 놀랄 만한

해설 지문의 빈칸을 채우는 문제이다. 빈칸 (B) 뒤 문장에서 사람이 성년에 이르면, 뇌가 뉴런을 얻기보다 잃기 시작한다고 생각되었다고 했으므로, 빈칸 (B)에는 수십 년 동안 어떤 뇌가 새로운 뉴런을 발달시킬 수 없다고 이해되었는지에 대한 내용이 나와야 적절하다는 것을 알 수 있다. 따라서 '완전히 성장한'이라는 내용이 들어가야 자연스럽다. 빈칸 (C) 앞부분에 대조의 의미를 나타내는 But(그러나)이 있으므로, 빈칸 (C)에는 사실 어떤 뇌가 새로운 뉴런을 만들 수 있다는 증거가 쌓이고 있었는지에 대한 내용이 나와야 적절하다는 것을 알 수 있다. 따라서 '성인의'라는 내용이 들어가야 자연스럽다. 빈칸 (D) 뒤에서 과학자들이 단순히 쳇바퀴를 달리는 것이 새로운 뉴런의 탄생으로 이어진다는 새로운 내용을 발견했다는 내용이 있으므로, 이것이 어떠한 실험인지에 대한 내용이 나와야 적절하다는 것을 알 수 있다. 따라서 빈칸 (D)에는 '놀랄 만한'이라는 내용이 들어가야 자연스럽다. 따라서 ④ mature — adult — striking이 정답이다.

어휘 precipitous adj. 급작스러운　mammal n. 포유동물
immature adj. 미숙한　astounding adj. 믿기 어려운
adolescent n. 청소년　definitive adj. 확정적인
mature adj. 완전히 성장한　striking adj. 놀랄 만한

12 [2020 서강대]

정답 ②

해석
① 최근 연구는 우리가 오랫동안 뇌에 대해 사실인지 의심해 왔던 것이 사실임을 보여준다.
② 연구원들은 최근에 신경과학의 기반이 되는 교리를 뒤집을 일련의 발견을 발표했다.
③ 연구원들은 최근에 신경병성 질환에 대한 흥미로운 새 치료법을 발견했다.
④ 최근 연구는 운동이 새로운 뉴런을 만들어 냄으로써 성인 뇌의 총질량을 두 배로 만들 수 있다는 것을 시사한다.

해설 지문의 빈칸을 채우는 문제이다. 지문 앞부분에서 사람이 성년에 이르면, 뇌가 뉴런을 얻기보다 잃기 시작한다고 생각되었지만, 성인의 뇌가 새로운 뉴런을 만들어 내고 있다는 증거가 쌓이고 있었다고 하고, 뒷부분에서 운동이 인간의 뇌에 긍정적인 영향을 미친다는 새로운 발견을 언급하고 있으므로, 빈칸 (A)에는 이러한 새로운 내용들을 소개할 수 있는 문장이 나와야 적절하다는 것을 알 수 있다. 따라서 '연구원들은 최근에 신경과학의 기반이 되는 교리를 뒤집을 일련의 발견들을 발표했다'라고 한 ②번이 정답이다.

어휘 confirm v. 사실임을 보여주다　suspect v. 의심하다
upend v. 뒤집다　bedrock n. 기반　tenet n. 교리
neuroscience n. 신경과학
neurodegenerative adj. 신경병성의　condition n. 질환
generate v. 만들어 내다　neuron n. 뉴런

[13-14]

마야(Maya) 같은 젊은 여성이 반복적으로 오진을 받는 일은 드물지 않다. 자폐증이 여자아이들보다는 남자아이들에게 최소한 3배나 흔하기 때문에, 과학자들은 연구에 늘 남자아이들만 포함한다. 그 결과 우리는 놀랍게도 자폐증이 남자아이들과 여자아이들에게서 차이가 있는지 그리고 어떻게 차이가 나는지에 대해 잘 알지 못한다. 우리가 알고 있는 것은 형편없는 수준인데, 평균적으로, 약한 자폐 증상을 갖고 있는 여자아이들이 진단을 받는데 남자아이들보다 2년이 더 걸린다. 왜 이렇게 되는지에 대해서는 약간의 논란이 있다. 애초부터, 여자아이들의 제한적인 관심이 — 아마도 열차 시간표보다는 인형이나 책 등의 — 관심이 사회적으로 더 허용되며 그래서 (자폐 증상이 있다는 것을) 알아채지 못한 채 넘어갈 수도 있다. 그러나 진단 테스트가 자폐증이 있는 남자아이들에 대한 관찰에 기초하고 있다는 사실이 오진과 (진단) 지연의 원인이 되는 것이 거의 확실하다.
10대에 진입하면서, 여자아이들은 사회적 관계의 복잡한 규

칙을 따라잡으려고 노력한다. 무슨 말을 해야 할지 그리고 어떻게 말해야 할지에 대한 쪽지를 베끼면서, 많은 여자아이들은 조화를 이루기 위해 노력하지만, 내면의 자아에 큰 대가를 치른다. 청소년기부터, 그들은 우울증과 불안감의 비율이 높아진다. 몇몇 연구는 또한 흥미롭게도 자폐증과 거식증 같은 식사 장애가 겹친다는 것을 발견했지만, 연구가 너무 적어 얼마나 많은 여성들이 그 두 가지를 갖고 있는지는 추정할 수 없다.

misdiagnose v. 오진하다   autism n. 자폐증
routinely adv. 일상적으로, 늘
grim adj. (질적으로) 형편없는
acceptable adj. 용인(허용)되는
contribute to phr. ~의 원인이 되다
keep up with phr. ~을 따라잡다, 뒤처지지 않다
elaborate adj. 정교한, 복잡한   crib v. 베끼다, 표절하다
blend in phr. 조화를 이루다, 섞여들다
adolescence n. 청소년기   intriguing adj. 흥미로운
overlap n. 겹침   anorexia n. 신경성 무식욕증, 거식증

13 2018 성균관대

정답 ⑤

해석 ① 자폐증이 있는 여자아이들이 많지 않아서
② 자폐증이 있는 여자아이들의 부모가 아이들을 숨겨서
③ 남자아이들의 자폐증과 다르지 않아서
④ 자폐증이 있는 여자아이들이 집에만 있어서
⑤ 여자아이들의 자폐증은 관심을 많이 받지 못해서

해설 여자아이들의 자폐증이 잘 알려져 있지 않은 이유를 묻는 문제이다. 첫 문단에서 자폐증이 여자아이들보다 남자아이들에게 3배나 많이 발생하기 때문에, 과학자들이 남자아이들만 연구에 포함시킨다고 했다. 그 결과 여자아이들의 자폐증에 대해서는 알려진 것이 없으며 오진과 진단 지연의 원인이 된다고 했다. 따라서 여자아이들의 자폐증이 잘 알려져 있지 않은 이유로 '여자아이들의 자폐증은 관심을 많이 받지 못해서'라고 표현한 ⑤번이 정답이다.

14 2018 성균관대

정답 ③

해석 ① 우울증   ② 불안감
③ 체중 증가   ④ 마른 체형
⑤ 적은 식사

해설 십 대 여자아이들의 자폐증 증상이 아닌 것을 고르는 문제이다. 두 번째 문단에서, 여자아이들은 청소년기부터 우울증과 불안감의 비율이 높아진다고 했다. 그리고 자폐증과 거식증 같은 식사 장애가 겹친다고 했다. 하지만 십 대 여자아이들의 자폐증 증상으로 '체중 증가'는 언급되지 않았으므로 ③번이 정답이다.

[15-16]

우울증은 심각한 문제이다. 그 원인은 업무 또는 학업의 압박감, 환경 영향, 가족력 및 질병/약물 부작용 등을 포함한다. 음식은 우울증의 예방과 치료에 한몫을 한다. 이 질병은 호르몬 불균형이나 비타민 결핍으로 인해 발생할 수 있다. 이러한 상황을 예방하기 위해, 비타민이 풍부한 음식을 더 많이 포함하도록 당신의 식단을 바꾸는 것이 이로울 것이다. 예를 들어, 브라질너트, 현미 그리고 해산물은 셀레늄이 풍부한데, 이 성분은 유리기로부터 보호해주고 우울증 발병 가능성을 감소시킬 수 있다. 뿐만 아니라, 비타민B는 뇌에서 우울증을 방지하는 중요한 화학 물질을 생성하는 데 도움이 되는 것으로 나타났다. 비타민B의 음식물 공급원에는 우유, 바나나, 잎이 많은 녹색 채소, 계란 및 조개가 포함된다. 커피나 술과 같이 피하는 게 좋을 음식이 있다. 카페인은 뇌를 활동적으로 유지시켜 줄 수 있지만, 불안이나 긴장을 증가시킬 수도 있는 반면 술은 항우울제 약물을 방해하여 그 효과를 떨어뜨릴 수 있다.

depression n. 우울증   include v. 포함하다
academic adj. 학업의, 학문의   pressure n. 압박, 압력
environmental adj. 환경의   impact n. 영향
medication n. 약물, 약   side effect phr. 부작용
play a role phr. 한몫을 하다, 역할을 맡다
prevention n. 예방   treatment n. 치료
occur v. 발생하다   hormonal adj. 호르몬의
imbalance n. 불균형   deficiency n. 결핍, 부족
beneficial adj. 이로운, 유익한   brown rice phr. 현미
element n. 성분, 요소
free radical phr. 유리기(동식물의 체내 세포들의 대사과정에서 생성되는 산소화합물인 활성산소)   likelihood n. 가능성
furthermore adv. 뿐만 아니라, 게다가
chemical n. 화학 물질   combat v. 방지하다, 싸우다
dietary adj. 음식물의   leafy adj. 잎이 많은, 무성한
green n. 녹색 채소   clam n. 조개   anxiety n. 불안
nervousness n. 긴장, 초조
interfere with phr. ~을 방해하다
antidepressant n. 항우울제, 우울증 치료제

15 2020 인하대

정답 ①

해석 ① 음식   ② 가족
③ 운동   ④ 호르몬
⑤ 약물

해설 지문의 빈칸을 채우는 문제이다. 지문의 다섯 번째 문장에서 우울증 예방을 위해 비타민이 풍부한 음식으로 식단을 구성하는 것의 이로움에 대해 설명한 뒤, 그다음 문장들에서 우울증 예방에 도움이 되는 음식 속 성분들을 소개하고 있으므로, 빈칸에는 음식이 우울증 예방과 치료에 한몫을 한다는 내용이 나와야 적절하다는 것을 알 수 있다. 따라서 '음식'이라고 한 ①번이 정답이다.

16 [2020 인하대]

정답 ⑤

해석
① 우울증은 유전자에 의해 유발될 수 있다.
② 우울증을 예방하기 위해 호르몬 균형이 맞아야 한다.
③ 브라질너트와 현미는 우울증 예방에 도움이 될 수 있다.
④ 바나나, 계란 그리고 조개는 우울한 사람들에게 좋다.
⑤ 커피와 술은 우울증 치료에 사용될 수 있다.

해설 지문을 통해 추론할 수 없거나 지문의 내용과 일치하지 않는 것을 묻는 문제이다. ⑤번의 키워드인 Coffee and Alcohol(커피와 술)과 관련된 지문의 마지막에서 커피와 술은 피하는 게 좋은 음식이라고 한 뒤, 카페인과 술이 우울증에 미치는 부정적인 영향에 대해 설명했으므로, 커피와 술은 우울증 치료에 사용될 수 있다는 것은 지문의 내용과 다르다. 따라서 ⑤번이 지문의 내용과 일치하지 않는다.

오답 분석
① Its causes include ~ family history ~를 통해 '우울증은 유전자에 의해 유발될 수 있다'는 것을 알 수 있다.
② The disease may occur due to hormonal imbalances or vitamin deficiencies를 통해 '우울증을 예방하기 위해 호르몬 균형이 맞아야 한다'는 것을 알 수 있다.
③ ~ Brazil nuts, brown rice and seafood are high in selenium, an element that ~ may decrease the likelihood of developing depression을 통해 '브라질너트와 현미는 우울증 예방에 도움이 될 수 있다'는 것을 알 수 있다.
④ B vitamins have been shown to help produce important chemicals in the brain that combat depression. Dietary sources of B vitamins include milk, bananas, leafy greens, eggs and clams를 통해 '바나나, 계란 그리고 조개는 우울한 사람들에게 좋다'는 것을 알 수 있다.

어휘 gene n. 유전자

[17-18]

먹으면 안 되는 것, 나중에 후회하게 될 것, 나쁘고 위험하게 유혹하고 건강하지 않은 것과 같이 우리는 음식에 대해 부정적으로 얘기한다. (A)이것의 효과는 과도한 양의 "나쁜 음식"이 될 수 있는 어떤 것보다도 더 사악하다. 음식에 대해 조바심을 냄으로써, 우리는 편안함과 기쁨을 위한 기회를 두려움과 걱정의 근원으로 바꾼다. 그리고 우리가 어떠한 음식을 피할 때, 우리는 대개 다른 음식을 많이 섭취하는 것으로 보상한다. 이 모든 것이 과학이라는 껍질 아래 일어난다. 하지만 우리의 음식에 대한 두려움 이면의 연구를 자세히 들여다보면 악마로 묘사되는 대부분의 많은 음식은 실제로 우리에게 괜찮다는 것을 알 수 있다. 소금을 생각해보자. 고혈압을 가진 사람이 많은 소금을 섭취하면 그것은 심장마비와 같은 심혈관계 질환으로 이어질 수 있다는 것은 사실이다. 가공식품에 소금이 과다하게 사용된다는 것도 사실이다. 하지만 평균적인 미국인은 하루에 나트륨을 3g이 살짝 넘는 정도로 섭취하는데, 이는 실제로 건강에 가장 좋은 정도이다. 소금을 거의 섭취하지 않는 것은 너무 많이 섭취하는 것만큼 위험할 수도 있다. 이것은 특히 고혈압을 갖고 있지 않은 대부분의 사람에게 사실이다. 어떻든지, (B)전문가들은 계속해서 더 낮은 권고안을 추천한다. 특정 음식을 피하라고 추천하는 (C)많은 의사와 영양학자들은 그 위험성의 규모를 올바르게 설명하지 못한다. 몇몇 연구에서, 대량의 가공된 붉은 고기는 암 발생에 상대적인 위험의 증가와 관련이 있다. 하지만, 절대적인 위험은 보통 상당히 작다.

tempt v. 유혹하다   insidious adj. 사악한
overindulgent adj. 과도한; 무관심한   fret v. 조바심을 내다
occasion n. 기회; 행사   anxiety n. 걱정, 근심
compensate v. 보상하다   consume v. 섭취하다, 소비하다
guise n. 껍질, 겉모습   demonize v. 악마로 묘사하다
blood pressure phr. 혈압
cardiovascular event phr. 심혈관계 질환
heart attack phr. 심장마비   overuse v. 과다하게 사용하다
processed adj. 가공된   sodium n. 나트륨, 소듐
sweet spot phr. 가장 좋은 정도, 구간
recommendation n. 권고안, 추천
nutritionist n. 영양학자   properly adv. 올바르게, 적합하게
magnitude n. 규모   associate v. 관련짓다, 연관시키다
relative adj. 상대적인   absolute adj. 절대적인

17 [2019 서울여대]

정답 ①

해석
① 음식 공포의 효과
② "나쁜 음식"의 효과
③ 너무 많이 먹는 것의 효과
④ 가공식품을 먹는 것의 효과

해설 밑줄 친 The effects의 의미를 추론하는 문제이다. 지문의 처음에서 우리가 음식에 대해서 부정적으로 얘기한다고 했다. 따라서 The effects의 의미를 '음식 공포의 효과'라고 한 ①번이 정답이다.

18 [2019 서울여대]

정답 ④

해석
① (B)와 (C) 모두 동의한다
② (B)에는 동의하지만, (C)에는 동의하지 않는다
③ (C)에는 동의하지만, (B)에는 동의하지 않는다
④ (B)와 (C) 모두 동의하지 않는다

해설 지문을 통해 작가가 동의하는 것을 추론하는 문제이다. 지문의 밑줄 친 (B)와 (C)의 이전에서 소금을 거의 섭취하지 않는 것은 너무 많이 섭취하는 것만큼 위험할 수 있다고 했으며, 밑줄 친 (B)와 (C)는 소금을 거의 섭취하지 않도록 경고하는

사람들을 지시하므로, (B)와 (C) 모두 동의하지 않는다는 것을 추론할 수 있다. 따라서 정답은 ④번이다.

[19-20]

'키홀 수술'이라고 알려진 수술 기법은 최근 몇 년 동안 더 널리 알려지게 되었다. 이 기법은 외과 전문의가 큰 규모의 절개를 할 필요를 없애준다. 그 대신에, 수술 부위 주변에 각각 1센치미터 정도로 측정되는 두서너 개의 작은 규모의 절개가 이루어진다. 약간 젓가락처럼 보이는 기다란 도구들이 아주 작은 절개 부분을 통해 삽입되어 환자의 신체로 들어간다. 이 도구들의 끝부분에는 표준 수술용 도구와 유사한 작은 도구들이 있다. 내시경이라고 불리는 조그마한 카메라도 절개 부분 중 한 곳을 통해 신체로 삽입된다. 카메라는 환자 신체 내부에서 어떤 일이 일어나고 있는지에 대한 사진을 대형 컴퓨터 모니터로 전달하기 때문에, 의사들은 어떤 일이 진행되고 있는지, 그리고 도구를 어디에 놓아야 하는지 확인할 수 있다. 키홀 수술에서 주의를 요하는 부분은 그것이 직관에 어긋난다는 것이다. 한 외과 전문의가 도구를 왼쪽으로 옮기고 싶으면, 그 의사는 도구를 오른쪽으로 밀어야 하며, 반대 또한 그렇다.

keyhole surgery phr. 키홀 수술(환자의 몸을 아주 조금만 절개한 후 레이저 광선을 이용해서 하는 수술)
eliminate v. 없애다 surgeon n. 외과 전문의
incision n. 절개 operate on phr. ~을 수술하다
insert v. 삽입하다 endoscope n. 내시경
relay v. 전달하다 awkward adj. 주의를 요하는
counterintuitive adj. 직관에 어긋나는

19 [2019 단국대]

정답 ①

해석 ① 그 대신에 ② 그러나
③ 마찬가지로 ④ 특히

해설 빈칸에 적절한 연결어를 넣는 문제이다. 빈칸 앞 문장은 키홀 수술 기법이 큰 규모의 절개를 할 필요를 없애준다는 내용이고, 빈칸 뒤 문장은 수술 부위 주변에 두서너 개의 작은 규모의 절개가 이루어진다는 내용이다. 따라서 그 중간의 연결어로는 '그 대신에'를 의미하는 Instead가 들어가는 것이 자연스럽다. 따라서 ①번이 정답이다.

20 [2019 단국대]

정답 ④

해석 ① 키홀 수술은 길고, 가느다란 도구와 작은 카메라를 사용해야 한다.
② 의사는 컴퓨터 화면으로 환자의 신체 내부를 본다.
③ 키홀 수술은 보다 작은 상처를 남길 것이다.
④ 키홀 수술에서는 긴 젓가락이 절개 부분을 통해 삽입되어야 한다.

해설 키홀 수술에 관해 사실이 아닌 것을 파악하는 문제이다. 지문 중간에서 약간 젓가락처럼 보이는 기다란 도구들이 아주 작은 절개 부분을 통해 삽입되어 환자의 신체로 들어간다고는 했으므로, 키홀 수술에 관해 사실이 아닌 것은 '키홀 수술에서는 긴 젓가락이 절개 부분을 통해 삽입되어야 한다'는 것이다. 따라서 정답은 ④번이다.

어휘 scar n. 상처

[21-22]

만약 당신이 손에 마비, 저림, 또는 약해짐을 느끼고 있다면, 의사에게 손목 터널 증후군을 검사해 달라고 요청하는 것을 고려해 보아라. 그것은 당신의 중앙 신경에 가해지는 압력으로 유발되는데, 그 신경은 팔의 길이만큼 뻗어있고, 손목 터널이라고 불리는 손의 통로를 통해 가며, 손에서 끝난다. 그 중앙 신경은 엄지손가락의 움직임과 감각을 통제하고, 또한 새끼손가락을 제외한 모든 손가락의 움직임도 통제한다. 손목 터널은 보통 부어오름으로 생기는 중앙 신경에 대한 압력의 결과로 좁아진다. 손목 터널 증후군은 타이핑과 같이 계속해서 수행하는 움직임과 같은 반복적인 동작 때문에 일어날 수 있다. 이것은 특히 당신의 손이 손목보다 낮은 위치에 있을 때 일어나는 행동에 대해서도 해당한다. 그것이 더 심해지면, 손의 근육이 줄어들기 때문에 당신의 악력은 더 낮아질지도 모른다. 이것을 예방하기 위해서, 당신은 손목을 일자로 뻗고, 일하는 도중에 더 자주 휴식을 가져야 한다. 특정한 스트레칭이나 운동 또한 도움이 된다.

numbness n. 마비 tingling n. 저림, 얼얼함
carpal tunnel syndrome phr. 손목 터널 증후군
pressure n. 압력 median nerve phr. 중앙 신경
passage n. 통로 wrist n. 손목 pinky n. 새끼손가락
swell v. 부어오르다, 부풀다 perform v. 수행하다
type v. 타이핑하다, 키보드를 치다 especially adv. 특히
be true of phr. ~에 대해 해당하다 severe adj. 심한
grip strength phr. 악력 shrink v. 줄어들다, 오그라들다
prevention n. 예방 straight adv. 똑바로, 곧바로
frequent adj. 자주, 빈번한 break n. 휴식
stretch v. 스트레칭하다, 뻗다

21 [2019 한국외대]

정답 ④

해석 ① 손목 터널 증후군의 증상은 손의 마비와 저림을 포함한다.
② 엄지손가락의 움직임과 감각은 중앙 신경이 통제한다.
③ 손목 터널 증후군은 손의 근육을 줄어들게 만들 수 있다.
④ 손목 위로 손을 계속 위치시키는 것은 손목 터널 증후군의 가능성을 높인다.

해설 지문의 내용과 일치하지 않는 것을 묻는 문제이다. ④번의 키워드인 above the wrist(손목 위로)와 관련된 지문의 lower than your wrist(손목보다 아래로) 주변에서 손목 터널 증후군의 원인은 당신의 손이 손목보다 낮은 위치에 있을 때 일어

나는 행동에 대해서도 해당한다고 했으므로, 손목 위로 손을 계속 위치시키는 것은 손목 터널 증후군의 가능성을 높인다는 것은 지문의 내용과 다르다. 따라서 ④번이 지문의 내용과 일치하지 않는다.

오답 분석
① If you are feeling numbness, tingling, or weakness in your hand, consider asking your doctor to check you for carpal tunnel syndrome을 통해 '손목 터널 증후군의 증상은 손의 마비와 저림을 포함한다'는 것을 알 수 있다.
② The median controls the movement and feeling of your thumb을 통해 '엄지손가락의 움직임과 감각은 중앙 신경이 통제한다'는 것을 알 수 있다.
③ As it becomes more severe, you may have less grip strength because the muscles in your hand shrink를 통해 '손목 터널 증후군은 손의 근육을 줄어들게 만들 수 있다'는 것을 알 수 있다.

22 [2019 한국외대]

정답 ①

해석
① 반복적인 동작   ② 느린 수축
③ 극소의 굽힘   ④ 불규칙한 두드리기

해설 지문의 빈칸을 채우는 문제이다. 빈칸이 포함된 문장에서 손목 터널 증후군은 타이핑과 같이 계속해서 수행하는 동작으로 일어날 수 있다고 했으므로, 빈칸에는 계속해서 수행하는 동작에 대한 내용이 나와야 적절하다는 것을 알 수 있다. 따라서 '반복적인 동작'이라고 한 ①번이 정답이다.

어휘 repetitive adj. 반복적인 contraction n. 수축
minuscule adj. 극소의 flexing n. 굽힘, 휨
irregular adj. 불규칙한

[23-24]

비타민 D는 우리가 햇볕에 노출되어 있을 때 우리 몸에 의해 생산되기 때문에 '햇볕 비타민'으로도 알려져 있다. 충분한 양의 비타민 D를 소비하는 것이 건강에 중요하다. 비타민 D는 건강한 뼈와 치아를 유지하도록 도와주며, 또한 우리의 면역체계와 뇌 그리고 신경계를 지탱시켜 준다. 게다가, 비타민 D는 또한 암, 당뇨, 경화증 같은 여러 질병으로부터 우리를 보호해준다. 비록 우리가 그 이름에 속을 수도 있지만, 비타민 D는 사실은 비타민이 아니라 일종의 프로호르몬이다. 비타민은 몸에 의해 생산되지 못하며 식단을 통해 획득해야 하는 영양소라고 정의된다. 하지만, 우리 몸은 일주일에 두세 번 5~10분 정도 태양 직사광에 노출되면 '비타민' D를 생산할 수 있다. 일반적으로 우리가 햇볕에 덜 노출되는 겨울에는, 비타민 D가 아주 빠르게 분해될 수 있다고 전문가들은 경고한다. 저장해 놓은 것이 고갈되는 것을 막기 위해, 우리는 음식이나 영양 보충제를 통해 비타민 D의 섭취를 증가시킬 것을 전문가들은 권장한다.

vital adj. 중요한 immune system phr. 면역체계
nervous system phr. 신경계 sclerosis n. 경화증
store n. 비축(저장)량 run low phr. 고갈되다, 부족해지다
intake n. 섭취(량) supplement n. 보충(물), 보충제

23 [2018 한국외대]

정답 ③

해석
① 건강한 골격 구조를 위해 충분한 양의 비타민 D가 필요하다.
② 비타민 D는 우리 몸에 의해 생산될 수 있는 프로호르몬의 일종이다.
③ 충분한 비타민 D를 생산하려면 햇볕에 매일 노출되는 것이 필요하다.
④ 겨울에는 비타민 D의 영양 보충제가 권장된다.

해설 지문의 내용과 일치하지 않는 것을 찾는 문제이다. 지문의 일곱 번째 문장 However, our bodies are ~ a week.에서 '우리 몸은 일주일에 두세 번 5 ~ 10분 정도 태양 직사광에 노출되면 비타민 D를 생산할 수 있다'고 했으므로, '매일 노출되어야 한다'고 한 ③번은 지문의 내용과 일치하지 않는다.

오답 분석
① 지문의 세 번째 문장 Vitamin D helps us ~ nervous system.을 통해 '건강한 골격 구조를 위해 충분한 양의 비타민 D가 필요하다'는 것을 알 수 있다.
② 지문의 다섯 번째 문장 Though we may be fooled ~ a type of pro-hormone.과 일곱 번째 문장 However, our bodies are ~ a week.를 통해 '비타민 D는 우리 몸에 의해 생산될 수 있는 프로호르몬의 일종'이라는 것을 알 수 있다.
④ 지문의 마지막 두 문장 Experts warn ~ very quickly.와 They recommend ~ through food or nutritional supplements.를 통해 '겨울에는 비타민 D의 영양 보충제가 권장된다'는 것을 알 수 있다.

어휘 skeletal adj. 뼈대(골격)의

24 [2018 한국외대]

정답 ④

해석
① 비타민일 뿐만 아니라
② 희귀한 유형의 비타민(이지만)
③ 몇 가지 다른 형태를 갖고 (있지만)
④ 사실은 비타민이 아니라

해설 지문의 빈칸을 채우는 문제이다. 빈칸 앞의 부사절에서 '우리가 그 이름에 속을 수도 있다'고 했으며, 다음 문장에서는 '비타민은 우리 몸에 의해 생산되지 못하는 것'이라고 정의되는데 '우리 몸이 비타민 D를 생산할 수 있다'고 했으므로, 빈칸에는 빈칸 뒤에 있는 but a type of pro-hormone과 함께

not A but B 구문이 되어 '사실은 비타민이 아니라 프로호르몬'이라는 내용이 들어가야 적절하다는 것을 알 수 있다. 따라서 ④번이 정답이다.

[25-28]

최근까지 민주화된 건강 분야 혁신의 개척자들은 생체의학 연구와 규제 기관의 주변부에 있었다. 하지만 겨우 지난 2개월 동안, 두 사람이 규제받지 않는 유전자 치료제를 자신에게 주사하고 있는 비디오를 널리 공유했다. 조시아 자이너(Josiah Zayner)는 자기 몸에 실험한 그 두 명 중 한 명이며, 가정용 유전자 편집 장비를 판매하는 신규업체인 오딘(Odin)의 경영자이다. [A] 유전자 편집 기술로 자기 몸에 실험하는 것을 우리는 '허가받지 않은' 혁신의 새로운 형태로 홍보해야 할까? 아니면 자칭 바이오 해커라는 자들이 규제의 틀을 시험해 봄으로써, 생체의학 혁신에 기여하는 시민들의 신흥 생태계에 해를 끼치는 것인가? [B] 유전자 치료법을 자신에게 실험하는 것은 감염과 면역 반응의 가능성에서부터 관련된 위험에 대한 이해의 부족과 환자들로부터의 비현실적인 기대에 이르기까지 골치 아픈 안전 및 윤리 문제를 제기한다. 그러나 유전자 편집 장비의 판매를 금지하는 것은 단지 나약하고 일시적인 해법일 뿐이다. 우리에게 필요한 것은 전통적인 연구 기관들 밖에도 책임감 있는 혁신의 기풍을 조성하는 것이다. 우리는 새로운 형태의 건강 연구를 위하여 합법성뿐만 아니라 안성 맞춤형의 규제 관련 지원을 구축해야 할 필요성이 시급하다는 것을 인식해야 한다. [C] 앞으로 가야 할 길은 급진적인 제멋대로의 과학을 촉진하는 것이 아니라 시민, 환자, 윤리학자 및 당국자들로 하여금 다시 생각해보고 적절한 관리 체계를 설계하게 해줄 참여 채널을 개발하는 것이다. [D]

pioneer n. 개척자, 선구자
margin n. (주류에 포함되지 않는) 주변부
biomedical adj. 생물(생체) 의학의
regulatory adj. 규제(단속) 권한을 가진
establishment n. 기관, 시설
unregulated adj. 규제받지 않는
start-up n. 신규업체, 신생기업   kit n. (도구·장비) 세트
herald v. 알리다, 발표하다
self-proclaimed adj. 자기 혼자 주장하는
emerging adj. 신흥의, 최근 생겨난
foster v. 조성하다; 기르다   ethos n. 기풍, 정신
urgent adj. 긴급한, 시급한   legitimacy n. 합법성
tailored adj. 맞춤 제작된

25 [2018 서강대]

정답 ②

해석 ① 초국가적인 — 더욱이
② 민주화된 — 그러나
③ 생태학적인 — 예를 들면
④ 최적의 — 그럼에도 불구하고

해설 지문의 빈칸을 채우는 문제이다. 첫 번째 빈칸의 경우, 다음 문장에서 규제받지 않는 유전자 치료제를 자기 몸에 주사하고 있는 두 사람을 예로 들었으므로, 규제에서 벗어났다는 의미에서 '민주화된'이라고 표현한 democratized가 들어가는 것이 자연스럽다. 그리고 두 번째 빈칸의 경우에는, 앞 문장에서 바이오 해커들이 해로운 것일 수 있음을 언급한 후에 단지 금지하는 것은 일시적인 해결책이라고 했으므로, '역접'을 나타내는 연결어 Yet이 들어가는 것이 자연스럽다. 따라서 ②번이 정답이다.

어휘 transnational adj. 초국가적인, 국가를 초월한
optimal adj. 최적의

26 [2018 서강대]

정답 ④

해석 ① 학자적 분석을 제공하는 연구자
② 뉴스 기사에 대해 보도하고 있는 일간신문 기자
③ 영감을 주는 이야기를 하며 동기를 부여하는 강연자
④ 윤리적 딜레마에 관한 의견을 제시하고 있는 대중적 지식인

해설 필자의 태도 및 어조를 파악하여 필자가 어떤 사람인지를 유추하는 문제이다. 앞부분에서는 두 명의 바이오 해커에 대해 새로운 형태의 혁신으로 홍보해야 하는가 아니면 그들은 혁신에 기여하는 시민들에게 해를 끼치는 것인가라는 딜레마에 대해 언급하고, 후반부에서는 앞으로 나아갈 방향을 제시하고 있으므로, 필자를 '윤리적 딜레마에 관한 의견을 제시하고 있는 대중적 지식인'이라고 표현한 ④번이 정답이다.

어휘 entrepreneur n. 기업가
clerk n. (회사) 사무원, (의회나 법원의) 서기, (상점) 점원
aristocrat n. 귀족   beggar n. 거지

27 [2018 서강대]

정답 ②

해석 ① 생명공학은 개인이 가정에서 유전자 치료를 실험할 수 있을 정도까지 발전했다.
② 미국 정부는 최근에 전통적인 연구기관 밖에서의 전문가들에 의한 자기 실험을 승인했다.
③ 건강 분야 연구에서 최근의 발달은 기업가 정신과 관련이 있다.
④ 시민들이 의료 관행의 바깥에서 주도적인 역할을 할 가능성이 있음에도 불구하고, 많은 윤리적 문제들은 여전히 해결되지 않았다.

해설 지문을 통해 추론할 수 없는 것을 고르는 문제이다. 여덟 번째 문장 We must recognize the urgent need to build legitimacy, ~ of health research.에서 우리는 새로운 형태의 건강 연구를 위하여 합법성뿐만 아니라 안성 맞춤형의 규제 관련 지원을 구축해야 할 필요성이 시급하다는 것을 인식해야 한다고 했으므로, '미국 정부가 최근에 전통적인 연구

기관 밖에서의 전문가들에 의한 자기 실험을 승인했다'고 유추할 수는 없다. 따라서 정답은 ②번이다.

오답분석
① 두 번째 문장 Yet in the last two months alone, ~ with unregulated gene therapies.와 세 번째 문장 Josiah Zayner is ~ for home use.를 통해 '생명공학은 개인이 가정에서 유전자 치료를 실험할 수 있을 정도까지 발전했다'는 것을 알 수 있다.
③ 세 번째 문장 Josiah Zayner is ~ for home use.를 통해 '건강 분야 연구에서 최근의 발달은 기업가 정신과 관련이 있다'는 것을 알 수 있다.
④ 다섯 번째 문장의 the emerging ecosystem of citizens who contribute to biomedical innovation 등의 표현을 통해 '시민들이 의료 관행의 바깥에서 주도적인 역할을 할 가능성이 있음에도 불구하고, 많은 윤리적 문제들은 여전히 해결되지 않았다'는 것을 유추할 수 있다.

어휘
biotechnology n. 생명공학
practitioner n. (의사·변호사 등의) 전문가
proactive adj. 상황을 앞서서 주도하는

28 (2018 서강대)

정답 ②

해석 유전자 치료법을 자신에게 실험하는 것은 감염과 면역 반응의 가능성에서부터 관련된 위험에 대한 이해의 부족과 환자들로부터의 비현실적인 기대에 이르기까지 골치 아픈 안전 및 윤리 문제를 제기한다.

해설 지문의 흐름상 주어진 문장이 들어가기에 가장 적절한 위치를 고르는 문제이다. [B]의 앞에 두 문장에서 일명 바이오 해커 두 명이 유전자 치료법을 자신에게 실험한 것이 이로운 것인가 해로운 것인가라는 질문을 던졌고, 제시문은 이 질문에 대한 필자의 의견이므로 [B] 자리에 들어가는 것이 자연스럽다. 따라서 ②번이 정답이다.

어휘 immunological adj. 면역의, 면역학의

[29-30]

의학은 인류만큼 오래되었다. 5만 년도 더 전에, 석기 시대에 동굴에서 살던 인간들은 치유적인 특성을 위해 약초를 처음으로 분쇄하고 우렸다. 유감스럽게도, 기술된 역사에만 알려져 있는 일부 전통적인 의학의 형태는 아프리카의 사막과 정글에서 북아메리카의 평원, 남아메리카의 열대 우림과 온화한 태평양 섬까지 모든 대륙에서 발달했다. 서아시아, 중동, 북아프리카, 중국과 인도의 최초 기록 문서에는 무수한 질병, 치유에 쓰이는 식물과 외과 수술이 기록되어 있다. 고대 이집트인은 그들의 종교적 믿음에 통합되는 복잡하고, 계층적인 의학적 방법을 가지고 있었다. 신과 영혼은 치명적인 질병을 맡고, 성직자 의사는 인간의 고통을 덜어 주기 위해 초자연적 영역을 중재했다. 성직자 의사 Imhotep은 의학사상의 첫 위인들 중 하나이다. 그리스와 로마 문명에는 각각 히포크라테스와 갈레노스라는 의학계 거인이 있었다. 히포크라테스는 오늘날까지 지속되는 환자 돌봄, 의사의 태도와 철학에 관한 기준을 세웠다. 갈레노스는 이론과 실무 경험을 너무 광범위하고 권위적으로 써서 유럽에서 1,400년 동안 유사 종교적 지위를 얻었고 사실상 의학적 진보를 늦췄다. 로마 제국이 끝난 후에, 연금술, 마법, 귀신 쫓아내기, 기적적인 치료제의 비밀스러운 기술들이 서유럽에서 번성했다. 고대 인도와 중국에서도 수준 높은 의학 체계가 뛰어난 공헌자들과 함께 발달했다. 인도에서는, 히포크라테스 전후 세기에 Susruta와 Chakara가 아유르베다 의학에 대한 박식한 책을 썼다. 갈레노스와 동시대 사람인 중국의 의사 Zhang Zhongjing도 수백 개의 질병을 기술하고 수천 개의 치료법을 제시하는 책을 편찬했다.

---

crush v. 분쇄하다, 으스러뜨리다
infuse v. (약·차 등을) 우리다   herb n. 약초
curative adj. 치료의, 치유적인   property n. 특성, 도구
traditional adj. 전통적인   sadly adv. 유감스럽게도, 슬프게
continent n. 대륙   rain forest phr. 열대 우림
balmy adj. 온화한   Pacific adj. 태평양의
myriad adj. 무수한   surgical adj. 외과의
procedure n. 수술   hierarchical adj. 계층적인
integrate into phr. ~에 통합되다, 흡수되다   belief n. 믿음
in charge of phr. ~을 맡아서, 담당해서
mortal adj. 치명적인, 대단히 심각한   mediate v. 중재하다
supernatural adj. 초자연적인   realm n. 영역
suffering n. 고통   civilization n. 문명
respective adj. 각각의, 각자의
giant n. (어떤 분야에서 재능이 아주 뛰어난) 거인
physician n. 의사   philosophy n. 철학
persist v. 지속하다, 계속하다
extensively adv. 광범위하게, 널리
authoritatively adv. 권위 있게, 명령조로
attain v. 얻다, 달성하다   quasi- adj. 유사-, 준-, 반-
stall v. 늦추다, 지연시키다   empire n. 제국
murky adj. 비밀스러운, 어두운   alchemy n. 연금술
sorcery n. 마법   exorcism n. 귀신 쫓아내기
cure n. 치료제, 치료   flourish v. 번성하다, 번창하다
sophisticated adj. 수준 높은, 정교한
outstanding adj. 뛰어난, 현저한   contributor n. 공헌자
encyclopedic adj. 박식한   Ayurvedic adj. 아유르베다의
contemporary n. 동시대의 사람
compile v. 편찬하다, 편집하다
prescribe v. 제시하다, 처방하다   remedy n. 치료법, 치료

29 (2019 명지대)

정답 ①

해석 ① 의학은 인류만큼 오래되었다
② 좋은 약은 항상 더 쓰다
③ 의학과 종교는 결국 하나로 통합된다
④ 의료업은 예전 같지 않다

해설 지문의 빈칸을 채우는 문제이다. 두 번째 문장에서 5만 년도 더 전에, 석기 시대에 동굴에서 살던 인간들은 치유적인 특성을 위해 약초를 처음으로 분쇄하고 우렸다고 했으므로, 빈칸에는 의학이 인류만큼 오래되었다는 내용이 나와야 적절하다는 것을 알 수 있다. 따라서 '의학은 인류만큼 오래되었다'라고 한 ①번이 정답이다.

어휘 **medicine** n. 의학, 의료, 약 **humankind** n. 인류
taste v. ~ 맛이 나다 **bit** adj. 쓴
converge v. 하나로 통합되다 **after all** phr. 결국
medical profession phr. 의료업

30 2019 명지대

정답 ②

해석 ① 고대 이집트의 성직자 의사는 의학사에서 인정받았다.
② 갈레노스의 실무 경험은 로마 제국의 멸망 이후에 의학을 발전시켰다.
③ 과거에, 의학은 신앙의 문제에 묶여있는 것으로 생각되었다.
④ 유럽과 중국은 같은 시기에 의료 체계를 발달시켰다.

해설 지문의 내용과 일치하지 않는 것을 묻는 문제이다. ②번의 키워드인 Galen's practices(갈레노스의 실무 경험)와 관련된 아홉 번째 문장에서 갈레노스는 이론과 실무 경험을 너무 광범위하고 권위적으로 써서 사실상 의학적 진보를 늦췄다고 했으므로, 갈레노스의 실무 경험이 로마 제국의 멸망 이후에 의학을 발전시켰다는 것은 지문의 내용과 다르다. 따라서 ②번이 정답이다.

오답 분석
① 여섯 번째 문장 Gods and spirits were in charge of mortal disease, and priest-physicians ~ mediated with the supernatural realm to ease human suffering을 통해 '고대 이집트의 성직자 의사는 의학사에서 인정받았다'는 것을 알 수 있다.
③ 다섯 번째 문장 Ancient Egyptians ~ medicine integrated into their religious beliefs를 통해 '과거에, 의학은 신앙의 문제에 묶여있는 것으로 생각되었다'는 것을 알 수 있다.
④ 마지막 문장 Chinese physician Zhang Zhongjing, a contemporary of Galen, ~ prescribed thousands of remedies를 통해 '유럽과 중국은 같은 시기에 의료 체계를 발달시켰다'는 것을 알 수 있다.

어휘 **faith** n. 신앙(심)

[31-32]

페니실린은 여러 심각한 박테리아 감염에 효과가 있다. 스코틀랜드의 과학자 Alexander Fleming은 1928년에 페니실린을 발견했다. 그러나 자신이 발견한 것을 곧바로 이해하지는 못했다. 그 당시 그는 박테리아를 파괴할 수 있는 여러 가지 곰팡이를 관찰하고 있었다. 그러나 Fleming은 그다지 깔끔한 과학자는 아니었다. 그는 종종 그의 연구실 주변에 박테리아 트레이를 그대로 두고 갔다. 1928년 8월, 그는 휴가를 떠났다. 그가 돌아왔을 때, 그는 트레이들 중 하나에서 이상한 일이 일어났다는 것을 알았다. 곰팡이가 박테리아에서 자라나 그것들을 죽였다. 처음에 Fleming은 왜 이런 일이 일어났는지 이해하지 못했지만, 나중에 자신이 발견한 것을 깨달았다. 그는 그 곰팡이가 강력하고 박테리아 감염을 치료하는데 유용할 수 있다는 것을 깨달았지만 여전히 그것이 얼마나 중요한 것인지는 이해하지 못했다. 그는 이 곰팡이가 인간의 몸 안에서 박테리아를 죽일 만큼 충분히 오랫동안 효과적일 수 있을지를 의심했다. 처음 몇 년 동안 그가 키운 페니실린은 효과가 너무 느려서, 그는 그것에 공들이기를 그만두었다. 몇 년 후, 그는 다시 그 일을 시작했다. Fleming과 다른 과학자들은 이 물질이 더 빠르게 작용하도록 하는 방법을 발견했고, 그것은 곧 현존하는 가장 효과적인 항생제가 되었다. 이 발견은 수백만 명의 생명을 구했다.

bacterial adj. 박테리아의, 세균의 **infection** n. 감염
discover v. 발견하다 **immediately** adv. 곧바로, 즉시
observe v. 관찰하다 **fungi** n. fungus(곰팡이)의 복수형
neat adj. 깔끔한, 단정한 **doubt** v. 의심하다
work on phr. ~에 공들이다, 작업하다 **rapidly** adv. 빠르게
antibiotic n. 항생제 **in existence** phr. 현존하는

31 2020 국민대

정답 ①

해석 ① 물질
② 대체물
③ 부속물
④ 반응을 일으키기에 불충분한

해설 지문의 빈칸을 채우는 문제이다. 빈칸 앞 문장에서 페니실린의 효과가 너무 느려서 연구를 그만두었다가 다시 시작했다고 했으므로, 빈칸에는 페니실린을 다시 연구한 내용이 나와야 적절하다는 것을 알 수 있다. 따라서 '물질'이라고 한 ①번이 정답이다.

어휘 **substance** n. 물질 **substitute** n. 대체물, 대용품
subsidiary n. 부속물, 부가물
subthreshold adj. 반응을 일으키기에 불충분한

32 2020 국민대

정답 ①

해석 ① 우연한 발견 ② 값비싼 발견
③ 재앙적인 발견 ④ 논란이 많은 발견

해설 지문의 제목을 묻는 문제이다. 지문 중간에서 과학자 Alexander Fleming이 박테리아 트레이를 치우지 않고 휴가를 다녀오는 바람에 그 위에서 자란 곰팡이인 페니실린을

발견하게 되었다고 설명하고 있다. 따라서 이 지문의 제목을 '우연한 발견'이라고 표현한 ①번이 정답이다.

어휘 accidental adj. 우연한, 돌발적인
catastrophic adj. 재양의, 파멸적인
controversial adj. 논란이 많은

[33-35]

필라델피아 주의 펜실베이니아 대학 병원에서, 17살의 Amy Salinger와 그녀의 부모는 신장 전문의인 Dr. Smith의 진단을 들었다. Smith는 그들 가족에게 Amy가 급성 신염이라고 알려진 흔치 않은 염증을 가지고 있다는 이야기와 Amy의 신장의 95퍼센트 정도가 파괴되었다는 이야기를 했다. 이 끔찍한 소식을 들은 Amy의 얼굴은 얼이 빠진 듯했다. 몇 분이 지난 후, Amy는 자신을 조금 누그러뜨린 이후에 치료 방법에 대해 질문했다. 의사는 그녀에게 그녀의 상태가 이미 되돌릴 수 없는 지경이며, 그녀가 곧 신장 투석을 받아야 할 것이라고 이야기했다. Amy는 다시 충격에 빠졌다. 하지만, Dr. Smith는 여전히 Amy에게 희망이 있음을 언급했다. 적합한 기증자가 발견된다면, 이식수술이 수행될 수 있다는 것이었다.
얼마간의 시간이 지나고, Dr. Smith는 은밀히 Amy의 부모와 상담을 하면서 그들에게 시신의 신장을 구하는 데 3년 이상이 걸릴 것이기 때문에 이식을 받을 방법이 제한되고 있다고 설명했다. 불행하게도, Amy의 양부모는 Amy를 입양한 이후 Amy의 친부모가 어디에 사는지 알 수 없었다. 또한, 비극적이게도, 양부모 모두 적합한 기증자가 아니었다. Dr. Smith는 Amy의 부모에게 Amy가 살 수 있는 가능성을 가지려면, 그들이 Amy의 친부모를 가능한 한 빨리 찾아야만 한다고 이 일이 정말 긴요한 일이라고 이야기했다.

diagnosis n. 진단 kidney n. 신장 specialist n. 전문의
inflammation n. 염증 acute nephritis phr. 급성 신염
compose v. 누그러뜨리다 dialysis n. 신장 투석
compatible adj. 적합한, 호환이 되는 donor n. 기증자
transplant n. 이식 privately adv. 은밀히
cadaver adj. 시신의 foster parents phr. 양부모
tragically adv. 비극적으로 imperative adj. 긴요한

33 2020 한성대

정답 ②

해석 ① 되돌릴 수 있는 ― 불행하게도
② 되돌릴 수 없는 ― 불행하게도
③ 되돌릴 수 없는 ― 운 좋게도
④ 되돌릴 수 있는 ― 운 좋게도

해설 빈칸에 들어갈 내용을 묻고 있다. 지문 전체적으로 Amy가 급성 신염으로 인해 신장의 95퍼센트가 파괴되었을 정도로 상태가 좋지 않고 신장 이식 수술이 필요하지만, 시신의 신장을 기다리는 데에 너무 오래 걸려 친부모를 빠르게 찾아야 한다는 내용이므로, 첫 번째 빈칸에는 문맥상 '되돌릴 수 없는'

이라는 의미의 irreversible이 들어가는 것이 자연스럽고, 두 번째 빈칸에는 '불행하게도'라는 의미의 unfortunately가 들어가는 것이 자연스럽다. 따라서 ②번이 정답이다.

34 2020 한성대

정답 ②

해석 ① Amy는 20대이다.
② Amy의 양부모는 이상적인 기증자가 아니다.
③ 시신의 신장은 이미 준비되어 있다.
④ Dr. Smith는 간 이식만을 전문으로 한다.

해설 지문의 내용과 일치하는 것을 묻는 문제이다. 지문의 두 번째 문단에서, Amy의 양부모는 적합한 기증자가 아니었다고 했으므로, Amy의 양부모가 이상적인 기증자가 아니라는 것은 지문의 내용과 일치한다. 따라서 ②번이 정답이다.

오답 ① 지문의 첫 번째 문단에서, Amy는 17살이라고 했으므로, Amy가 20대라는 것은 지문의 내용과 다르다.
분석 ③ 지문의 두 번째 문단에서, Dr. Smith가 Amy의 양부모와 은밀히 상담하면서 시신의 신장을 구하는 데 3년 이상이 걸릴 것이라 이야기했다고 했으므로, 시신의 신장이 이미 준비되어 있다는 것은 지문의 내용과 다르다.
④ 지문의 첫 번째 문단에서, Dr. Smith는 신장 전문의라고 했으므로, Dr Smith가 간 이식을 전문으로 한다는 것은 지문의 내용과 다르다.

어휘 ideal adj. 이상적인 liver n. 간

35 2020 한성대

정답 ④

해석 ① Amy의 입양   ② 급성 신염의 역사
③ 진단을 기다리는 것   ④ Amy 구하기

해설 지문의 제목을 묻는 문제이다. 지문 전체적으로 Amy가 급성 신염으로 위급한 상태임에도 불구하고, 이식받을 신장을 찾는 데 어려움을 겪고 있다는 내용이므로, 지문의 제목을 'Amy 구하기'라고 표현한 ④번이 정답이다.

[36-37]

2006년, Cornell 대학교의 연구원들은 1980년대의 텔레비전 재편성에 대한 몇 가지 가설을 포함한 장기 연구 결과를 발표했다. 이 연구 프로젝트는 매우 어린 아이들의 텔레비전 시청과 자폐증 사이의 상관관계를 제안하기 위해 자료를 모았다. 자폐증 연구에서 가장 시급한 문제 중의 하나는 1980년대 중후반에 시작된 자폐증 빈도의 놀랍고 이례적인 증가를 설명하는 것이었다. 2500명 중 1명꼴로 자폐증이 발생한 때인 1970년대 후반부터, 발병률이 급격하게 높아지면서, 지금으로부터 몇 년 전, 약 150명 중 1명꼴로 영향을 미쳤으며, 안정될 기미

를 보이지 않았다. 분명히, 텔레비전은 1950년대부터 북아메리카 가정에 널리 보급되어왔다. 그렇다면 왜 1980년대 초부터 현저하게 다른 결과를 가져온 것일까? 이 연구는 그 10년 동안 새로운 요인들, 특히 케이블 TV의 광범위한 가용성, 어린이 전용 채널과 비디오테이프의 증가, 그리고 VCR의 인기, 뿐만 아니라 2대 혹은 그 이상의 TV 수상기를 가진 가정의 커다란 증가와 같은 요인들의 결합이 일어났다고 제안한다. 따라서 매우 어린 아이들이 매일 장기간에 걸쳐 텔레비전에 노출될 수 있는 조건이 갖추어져 있었고, 앞으로도 계속 그럴 것이다. 그들의 구체적인 결론은 상대적으로 조심스럽다. 세 살 미만의 나이에 계속된 텔레비전 시청이 "위험한 상태의" 아이들에게 장애의 시작을 촉발할 수 있다.

---

release v. 발표하다 hypothesis n. 가설
reorganization n. 재편성 assemble v. 모으다, 조립하다
correlation n. 상관관계 autism n. 자폐증
urgent adj. 시급한, 긴급한
extraordinary adj. 놀라운; 비범한
anomalous adj. 이례적인 frequency n. 빈도; 주파수
incidence n. 발병, 발생
approximately adv. 약, 대략적으로, 어림잡아
level off phr. 안정되다
pervasive adj. 보급된, 널리 퍼진, 만연한
markedly adv. 현저하게 consequence n. 결과
coalescence n. 결합, 융합 widespread adj. 광범위한
availability n. 가용성
dedicated adj. 전용의; 헌신하는, 전념하는
household n. 가정 exposure n. 노출
on a daily basis phr. 매일 relatively adv. 상대적으로
cautious adj. 조심스러운 extended adj. 계속된, 길어진
trigger v. 촉발하다; 방아쇠를 당기다; n. 방아쇠
onset n. 시작 disorder n. 장애

36 2019 서울여대

정답 ①

해석 ① 1980년대의 자폐증 사례의 증가
② 1950년대의 텔레비전 수상기의 전국적인 확산
③ VCR과 같은 새로운 시각 도구의 출현
④ 텔레비전과 자폐증 사이 관계의 새로운 증거

해설 Cornell 대학의 연구원들이 텔레비전에 관심을 갖게 된 원인을 파악하는 문제이다. 지문의 중간에서 1980년대에 TV의 보급, 어린이 전용 채널의 증가 등의 요인들이 나타난 이후로 자폐증의 사례가 증가했다고 했으므로, 연구원들이 텔레비전에 관심을 갖게 된 원인은 '1980년대의 자폐증 사례의 증가'이다. 따라서 정답은 ①번이다.

어휘 take interest in phr. ~에 관심을 갖다
nationwide adj. 전국적인
instrument n. 도구, 기구; 악기

37 2019 서울여대

정답 ②

해석 ① 북아메리카에서는, 어린이 전용 채널이 이미 1950년대에 인기 있었다.
② 1970년대 후반에, 어린이 자폐증 발병률이 2500명 중의 1명꼴보다 높지 않았다.
③ 장시간 동안 TV를 보는 것은 어린이뿐만 아니라 어른들에게도 자폐증을 유발하는 경향이 있다.
④ 몇 년 전에, 어린이 자폐증 발병률이 약 150명 중의 1명꼴로 걸린 정도로 안정화되었다.

해설 지문의 내용과 일치하는 것을 묻는 문제이다. 지문의 중간에서 2500명 중 1명꼴로 자폐증이 발생한 때인 1970년대 후반부터 발병률이 급격하게 높아졌다는 내용을 통해 1970년대 후반에 어린이 자폐증 발병률이 2500명 중 1명꼴보다 높지 않았다는 것을 알 수 있다. 따라서 ②번이 지문의 내용과 일치한다.

오답 분석 ① 북아메리카 가정에 텔레비전이 1950년대부터 보급되어 왔다고 했으므로, 어린이 전용 채널이 이미 1950년대에 인기 있었다는 것은 지문의 내용과 다르다.
③ 세 살 미만의 나이에 계속된 텔레비전 시청이 아이들에게 장애의 시작을 촉발할 수 있다고는 했지만, 어린이뿐만 아니라 어른들에게도 자폐증을 유발하는 경향이 있는지는 알 수 없다.
④ 몇 년 전에 150명 중 1명꼴로 영향을 미쳤고, 안정될 기미를 보이지 않았다고 했으므로, 어린이 자폐증 발병률이 약 150명 중의 1명꼴로 걸린 정도로 안정화되었다는 것은 지문의 내용과 다르다.

어휘 as well as phr. ~뿐만 아니라

[38-40]

"정신 질환"은 더 이상 자아의 파괴가 아니라 자아와는 별개이지만 자아에 일어나는 신경 화학의 사건이다. 고혈압처럼, 우리의 세포 내에서 일어나고, 우리는 그것을 없애기 위해 약을 삼킨다. 내가 13살에 강박 장애로 진단받은 후 몇 년 동안 어른들은 거의 내가 어디가 아픈지에 대해 이렇게 이야기했다. 나는 임상적으로 신경 쇠약자였고 나의 두려움 중 많은 것은 나 자신의 정신 변화에 관한 것이었다. 내가 미쳤던 건가? 내가 운이 안 좋았던 건가? 이 사람이 정말 나였던 건가? 치료사들과 우리 부모님은 내가 겪는 것이 세로토닌 때문에 우연히 일어난 일이고, 독감이나 햇볕으로 인한 화상에 지나지 않는 정도의 설명하기는 힘들지만 고칠 수 있는 "불균형"이라는 말로 나를 안심시켰다. 나는 약물치료를 하는 것을 망설였고, 약물치료가 나를 변하게 할까 봐 걱정했다. 나는 "당신은 병에 걸렸고, 이것은 그냥 그 병을 낫게 할 약일 뿐이에요. 당뇨병에 걸린 것 같은 거죠. 당신은 '진짜' 몸 상태가 당뇨병에 걸린 거니까 인슐린을 거부하지 않을 거잖아요."라고 들었다. 결국, 나는 공황 발작을 참을 수 없어서 Prozac을 복용했고 그 약을 가지

고 나는 무슨 일이 일어나고 있는지 이해했다. <u>그것은 효과가 있었다.</u> 그 약은 내 손을 떨게 했지만, 내 정신은 내가 기억하는 다시 거의 건강하고 안정적인 상태로 바뀌었다.

(*Prozac: 우울증, 강박 장애 등에 듣는 약)

mental illness phr. 정신 질환, 정신병
breach n. 파괴, 위반   neurochemical adj. 신경 화학의
hypertension n. 고혈압   swallow v. 삼키다
OCD n. 강박 장애   obsessive adj. 강박적인
compulsive adj. 강박적인, 조절이 힘든
disorder n. 장애, 무질서   clinically adv. 임상적으로
nervous wreck phr. 신경 쇠약자
transformation n. 변화, 변질
insane adj. 미친, 정신 이상의
doomed adj. 불운한, 운이 다한   therapist n. 치료사
reassurance n. 안심시키는 말(행동)
serotonin n. 세로토닌
mysterious adj. 설명하기 힘든, 신비한
correctable adj. 정정할 수 있는, 교정 가능한
imbalance n. 불균형   balk at phr. ~에 망설이다
take medication phr. 약물치료를 하다
diabetes n. 당뇨병   authentic adj. 진짜의, 확실한
panic attack phr. 공황 발작   stable adj. 안정적인

38 2019 성균관대

정답 ③

해석 ① 모두가 일종의 질환을 앓고 있다
② 모든 인간은 불운하다
③ 글쓴이의 병이 치료될 수 있다
④ 감이나 햇볕으로 인한 화상에는 치료법이 없다
⑤ 글쓴이가 자라면 병이 없어질 것이다

해설 글쓴이 주위의 어른들이 무엇을 확신했는지를 파악하는 문제이다. 여덟 번째 문장에서 치료사들과 우리 부모님은 내가 겪는 것이 세로토닌 때문에 우연히 일어난 일이고, 독감이나 햇볕으로 인한 화상에 지나지 않는 정도의 설명하기는 힘들지만 고칠 수 있는 "불균형"이라는 말로 나를 안심시켰다고 했으므로, 글쓴이 주위의 어른들은 '글쓴이의 병이 나을 수 있다'고 확신했다는 것을 알 수 있다. 따라서 ③번이 정답이다.

어휘 cure v. 치료하다; n. 치료법

39 2019 성균관대

정답 ①

해석 ① 그것은 효과가 있었다
② 그것은 큰 실수이다
③ 나는 그런 뜻이 아니었다
④ 내가 틀렸다
⑤ 안타깝다

해설 지문의 빈칸을 채우는 문제이다. 마지막 문장에서 그 약은 내 손을 떨게 했지만, 내 정신은 내가 기억하는 다시 거의 건강하고 안정적인 상태로 바뀌었다고 했으므로, 빈칸에는 약이 효과가 있었다는 내용이 나와야 적절하다는 것을 알 수 있다. 따라서 '그것은 효과가 있었다'라고 한 ①번이 정답이다.

40 2019 성균관대

정답 ④

해석 ① 의학적 치료를 몹시 싫어했다
② 의사들을 믿지 않았다
③ 약물의 부작용을 알았다
④ 원래 그녀의 모습대로 남아 있기를 원했다
⑤ 자신이 이겨 내지 못할까 봐 두려워했다

해설 글쓴이가 약을 먹는 것을 망설였던 이유를 파악하는 문제이다. 아홉 번째 문장에서 나는 약물치료를 하는 것을 망설였고, 약물치료가 나를 변하게 할까 봐 걱정했다고 했으므로, 글쓴이가 약을 먹는 것을 망설였던 이유는 '원래 그녀의 모습대로 남아 있기를 원했기' 때문이다. 따라서 ④번이 정답이다.

어휘 side-effect n. (약 등의) 부작용

[41-43]

페이스북(Facebook)의 최고경영자 마크 저커버그(Mark Zuckerberg)는 '모든 질병을 치료하고, 관리하고, 예방하기 위해' 최소 30억 달러를 투자하겠다고 약속했다. 다른 많은 이들이 부화뇌동하여, 유전자 변형을 엄청 강조하며 보건 의료 영역에서 과거의 유산(다윈의 진화론)을 추구하고 있다. 그러나 (그들 사이에는) 연결되는 것이 없다. 몸을, 유전자 조작 도구에 의해 오류가 해결되어 완성되는, 기계에 비유하는 것은 찰스 다윈의 진화론과 모순된다: 기계와 컴퓨터는 진화하지 않지만, 생물은 진화한다. 한 가지 기능을 손상시키는 몇 개의 유전암호가 종종 다른 기능을 향상시키거나 환경이 바뀌면 새로운 기능을 위해 고쳐질 수도 있다. 진화에서는, 모든 것이 자신의 목적을 고수한다. 망가진 부분들이 다음엔 최고의 것이 될 수도 있다. 진화에서는, 아무것도 그냥 생겨나는 것은 없다. 스트레스는 독창성을 촉발시킬 수도 있고 많은 만성질환을 악화시킬 수도 있다. 낭포성 섬유증을 유발하는 유전자 변형체가 콜레라로부터 보호해줄 수도 있다. 유전자 이식은 한 개의 잘못된 유전자에 의해 유발된 질병을 효과적으로 치료할 수 있다. 그러나, 질병에 영향을 미치는 이 유전자의 현존하는 위험 변종은 종종 시간이 지나면서 이점들을 제공하기 때문에 사라지지 않을 것이다. 다윈의 관점으로부터, 우리는 더 완벽한 형태로 발전한 것이 아니라 지엽적인 환경에 적응한 것이다. 만약 인간이 기계라면, 우리는 간단하게 고장 난 부분을 수리할 수 있다. 그러나 우리는 기계가 아니며, 단순한 생물학적 메커니즘 보다 생명의 위기에 더욱 근본적인 무언가가 있다. 따라서 위험 및 위험 요소는 <u>언제나 우리와 함께 있을</u> 것이다.

pledge	v. 약속(맹세)하다
follow suit	phr. 방금 나온 패와 같은 패를 내다; 부화뇌동하다
legacy	n. 유산 **realm** n. 영역, 범위; 왕국
gene modification	phr. 유전자 변형, 유전자 조작
bug	n. 오류; (가벼운) 질병
conflict with	phr. ~와 상충하다, ~와 모순되다
organism	n. 유기체, 생물
code	n. (생물의 특징을 결정하는) 유전암호
compromise	v. 타협하다; 손상시키다
repurpose	v. 다른 용도에 맞게 고치다
grasp for	phr. ~을 단단히 붙잡다; 파악하다
compound	v. 악화시키다, 더욱 심하게 하다
a raft of	phr. 많은 **chronic** adj. 만성적인
maladie	n. 질환, 질병 **variant** n. 변종
cystic fibrosis	phr. (선천성) 낭포성 섬유증
gene transfer	phr. 유전자 이식
errant	adj. 잘못된, 정도를 벗어난
exiting	adj. 기존의, 현존하는

41 2018 한국외대

정답 ②

해석 ① 유전자 변형 치료는 진화의 개입보다 더 큰 비용이 든다.
② 유리한 진화론적 특징들에는 불리한 특징들이 수반된다.
③ 모든 생물은 극단적으로 긴 진화 과정의 산물이다.
④ 진화 과정은 생물 쪽에서는 엄청난 노력이 필요하다.

해설 밑줄 친 부분의 의미를 추론하는 문제이다. 밑줄 친 In evolution, nothing comes for free.는 '진화에서는, 아무 것도 그냥 생겨나는 것은 없다'는 의미이다. 다음 문장에서 '스트레스는 독창성을 촉발시킬 수도 있고 많은 만성질환을 악화시킬 수도 있다'고 했으므로, '유리한 진화론적 특징들에는 불리한 특징들이 수반된다'는 것을 알 수 있다. 따라서 ②번이 정답이다.

어휘 **intervention** n. 개입, 간섭 **accompany** v. 동반(동행)하다

42 2018 한국외대

정답 ①

해석 ① 언제나 우리와 함께 있다
② 결코 다시는 나타나지 않는다
③ 완전히 근절된다
④ 규모에 있어서 무시해도 될 정도이다

해설 지문의 빈칸을 채우는 문제이다. 이 지문은 유전자 변형(이식)을 통해 질병을 치료하려는 사람들에게 너무 낙관적으로 판단하지 말고 부작용이 있을 수 있음을 경계하라는 내용이다. 따라서 '위험 및 위험 요소는 _____할 것이다'라는 문맥에서 risk and an element of danger will _____.의 빈칸에는 '언제나 우리와 함께 있다'라는 말이 들어가야 적절하다는 것을 알 수 있다. 따라서 ①번이 정답이다.

어휘 **eradicate** v. 근절하다, 뿌리 뽑다
negligible adj. 무시해도 될 만한
magnitude n. 규모, 중요도

43 2018 한국외대

정답 ③

해석 ① 결함이 있는 유전자를 확인하는 것이 최우선으로 할 일이다.
② 유전자를 고치는 것은 오래 걸리지만 바람직한 과정이다.
③ 유전자 변형 방식은 성공하지 못할 것이다.
④ 적응할 수 있는 유전자 상호작용을 분류하는 것이 시급하다.

해설 필자의 태도를 묻는 문제이다. 필자는 유전자 변형(이식)을 통해 질병을 치료하려고 노력하는 사람들에 대해 우리는 기계가 아니기 때문에 생명과 질병에 대해 생물학적 메커니즘의 관점에서만 접근할 수는 없다는 부정적 태도를 취하고 있다. 따라서 필자의 태도를 '유전자 변형 방식은 성공하지 못할 것'이라고 표현한 ③번이 정답이다.

어휘 **defective** adj. 결함이 있는
catalog v. 목록을 작성하다; 분류하다
adaptive adj. 적응할 수 있는 **interaction** n. 상호 작용
imperative adj. 반드시 해야 하는, 긴요한

[44-47]

나이가 들면서, 쥐젖이라고 불리는 작은 혹들이 당신의 몸에 튀어나오기 시작할 수 있다. 쥐젖은 밑 부분이 더 얇고 위로 갈수록 더 넓어지기 때문에 그것을 알아볼 수 있을 것이다. 쥐젖이 암이 되는 사마귀처럼 아프거나 위험하지는 않지만, 당신이 그것을 제거하기를 원하는 매우 합당한 이유가 있다. 의학 박사이자 피부과 의사인 Rossi 씨는 사람들이 온갖 이상한 방법으로 자신이 가진 쥐젖을 제거하려고 했다고 말한다. 그는 사람들이 쥐젖 주변으로 실을 묶고, 태우고, 손가락으로 그것을 뽑으려 하고, 심지어는 책으로 쥐젖을 내리치기까지 하는 사람들에 대해 들었다. 반면에, 피부과 의사는 쥐젖을 빠르고 깔끔하게 제거할 수 있다.

먼저, 피부과 의사들은 살균된 기구를 가지고 있지만, 당신이 가진 것을 사용하는 것은 감염을 일으킬 수 있다. [A] 게다가, 피부과 의사들은 국소 마취를 사용하고 출혈을 멈출 수 있는 비품들이 있지만, 당신이 집에서 사용하는 방법으로는 감당할 수 없을 정도로 출혈이 생길 수 있다. [B] 쥐젖을 녹인다고 주장하는 병원의 약품도 나쁠 수 있다고 Rossi 씨는 말한다. 그는 "당신은 피부에 화상이나 흉터를 남길 수 있고, 의도하지 않은 결과가 생길 수 있습니다."라고 말한다.

하지만, 전문가를 찾아가야 할 훨씬 더 큰 이유가 있다. [C] 피부과 의사가 혹을 제거하고 나면, 그 혹을 현미경으로 들여다본다. Rossi 씨는 "쥐젖처럼 보이지만 암이 될 수 있는 것들이 있죠."라고 말한다. 그것은 쥐젖을 찾을 때마다 겁을 먹어야 한다는 뜻은 아니다. [D] 대부분의 쥐젖은 양성이지만, 당신이

물어보기 전까지 확실히 알 수는 없을 것이다. 게다가, 쥐젖을 검사하는 것은 의사가 당신의 나머지 몸에 피부암과 비정형 종양, 혹은 악성 종양이 있는지를 확인하도록 하는 "좋은 구실"이 된다고 Rossi 씨는 말한다.

growth n. 혹, 종양
skin tag phr. 쥐젖(피부에 조그맣게 튀어나오는 양성 섬유종)
pop up phr. 튀어나오다
cancerous adj. 암이 되는, 암의 성질을 가진
mole n. (피부의) 사마귀 dermatologic adj. 피부과의
string n. 실, 줄 slam v. 내려치다, 세게 닫다
dermatologist n. 피부과 의사 sterile adj. 살균된, 소독된
instrument n. 기구, 도구 infection n. 감염
anesthesia n. 마취 supply n. 비품
uncontrollably adv. 감당할 수 없게, 통제할 수 없게
at-home adj. 집에 있는 medication n. 약품
dissolve v. 녹이다 mark n. 흉터, 자국
unintended adj. 의도하지 않은 consequence n. 결과
microscope n. 현미경 freak out phr. 겁을 먹다
atypical adj. 이형의, 이례적인 malignant adj. 악성의

44 2019 한성대

정답 ①

해석 ① 쥐젖을 처리하는 방법
② 쥐젖의 결과
③ 쥐젖을 집에서 처치하는 것의 이점
④ 쥐젖의 원인

해설 지문의 제목을 묻는 문제이다. 지문의 전체적으로 쥐젖을 집에서 처리하는 것보다 피부과 의사를 방문하여 제거하는 것이 훨씬 바람직하다고 설명하고 있다. 따라서 지문의 제목을 '쥐젖을 처리하는 방법'이라고 표현한 ①번이 정답이다.

어휘 handle v. 처리하다, 다루다

45 2019 한성대

정답 ③

해석 ① 쥐젖은 원뿔 모양이다.
② 사람들은 쥐젖을 제거하기 위해 다양한 방법을 시도한다.
③ 쥐젖 대부분은 암이 될 수 있다.
④ 쥐젖이 발견되었다면 몸을 검사받는 것이 좋다.

해설 지문의 내용과 일치하지 않는 것을 묻는 문제이다. ②번의 키워드인 cancerous(암이 되는)와 관련된 지문의 cancerous mole(암이 되는 사마귀) 주변에서 쥐젖이 암이 되는 사마귀처럼 아프거나 위험하지는 않다고 했으므로, 쥐젖 대부분이 암이 될 수 있다는 것은 지문의 내용과 다르다. 따라서 ③번이 지문의 내용과 일치하지 않는다.

오답 ① they're thinner at the base and get wider at the
분석 top을 통해 '쥐젖은 원뿔 모양이다'라는 것을 알 수 있다.

② People have used all kinds of crazy methods to try removing skin tags on their own을 통해 '사람들은 쥐젖을 제거하기 위해 다양한 방법을 시도한다'는 것을 알 수 있다.
④ checking a skin tag is a "good excuse" to get your doctor to check the rest of your body for skin cancer and atypical or malignant growths를 통해 '쥐젖이 발견되었다면 몸을 검사받는 것이 좋다'는 것을 알 수 있다.

어휘 circular adj. 원형의 cone n. 뿔

46 2019 한성대

정답 ④

해석 대부분의 쥐젖은 양성이지만, 당신이 물어보기 전까지 확실히 알 수는 없을 것이다.

해설 지문의 흐름상 주어진 문장이 들어가기에 가장 적절한 위치를 고르는 문제이다. [D]의 앞 문장에서 쥐젖처럼 보이지만 암이 될 수 있는 것들이 있으며, 그렇다고 해서 쥐젖을 찾을 때마다 겁을 먹어야 할 필요는 없다고 했으므로, [D] 자리에 왜 겁을 먹어야 할 필요가 없는지를 설명하는 주어진 문장 '대부분의 쥐젖은 양성이지만, 당신이 물어보기 전까지 확실히 알 수는 없을 것이다'가 들어가야 글의 흐름이 자연스럽게 연결된다. 따라서 ④번이 정답이다.

어휘 benign adj. 양성의

47 2019 한성대

정답 ①

해석 ① 좋은 구실   ② 위험한 과정
③ 쓸모없는 방법   ④ 필요악

해설 지문의 빈칸을 채우는 문제이다. 빈칸의 주변 부분에서 쥐젖을 검사받는 과정에서 자신의 몸에 피부암이나 다른 종양이 있는지를 확인할 수 있다고 했으므로, 빈칸에는 긍정적인 의미의 단어가 들어가는 것이 적절하다. 따라서 '좋은 구실'이라고 한 ①번이 정답이다.

어휘 excuse n. 구실 necessary evil phr. 필요악

[48-50]

오래 건강하게 사는 삶을 위한 여러 전문가적인 정보들이 있다. 먼저, 식사이다. 체중 감량은 더 낮은 혈압이나 더 나은 혈당량과 같은 많은 긍정적인 변화를 설명할 것 같다. 하지만 몇몇 전문가들은 단식도 신체를 스트레스에 더 저항력이 있게 만들어 준다고 추측하는데, 단식은 세포 수준에 유익한 영향을 줄 수 있다. 한 전문가는 "식사는 노화와 나이와 관련된 질병들을 늦추기 위한 틀림없이 가장 강력한 치료이다."라고 말한다.

과거 몇 년 동안, 과학자들은 하루 종일 앉아있는 것처럼 (A)몸을 많이 움직이지 않는 행동이 예상보다 이른 죽음의 위험 인자라는 것을 보여주었다. 과학자들은 앉아서 보내는 시간들이 2형 당뇨병과 무알코올 성 지방간 질환의 증가된 위험과 연관된다는 것을 알아냈다. 당신은 운동만으로 너무 많이 앉아 있는 것의 모든 나쁜 영향들을 없앨 수는 없다. 하지만 좋은 소식은 가만히 앉아 있는 것 이외의 심지어 꼼지락거리는 것도 포함하여 무엇이든 하는 것은 도움이 될 수 있다는 것이다. 최소한의 신체 활동을 기록했던 사람들은 다음 10년 동안 심장과 관련된 사건에 대한 가장 높은 위험이 있었는데, 이 사실은 놀랍지 않다. 하지만 연구원들을 놀라게 했던 것은 집 주변의 잡일을 하는 것 같이 단지 하루 동안 조금만 더 움직이는 것만으로 심장과 관련된 질환의 발생 위험을 낮추기에 충분했던 것이었다.

이제 과학자들에게 우리의 감정이 생명 활동에 영향을 준다는 것은 명확하다. 연구들은 수년 동안 분노와 스트레스가 아드레날린과 같은 스트레스 호르몬을 우리의 핏속으로 방출할 수 있고, 이 호르몬이 심장을 더 빠르고 더 세게 뛰도록 유발한다는 것을 보여 주었다. 스트레스는 심지어 우리의 뇌가 알츠하이머병에 맞서 얼마나 잘 견디는지에 영향을 미칠 수도 있다. 연구원들은 젊을 때 노화에 대해 더 부정적인 생각을 가졌던 사람들이 손실이 알츠하이머병과 연관되는 뇌 부분인 해마 용량에서 더 큰 손실이 있었다는 것을 알아냈다. 연구가 (B)우리가 노화에 대해 어떻게 느끼는지가 어떻게 나이 드는지에 영향을 미칠 수 있다는 것을 시사했던 것은 이번이 처음이 아니다.

pro adj. 전문가적인 diet n. 식사
blood pressure phr. 혈압
blood-sugar level phr. 혈당량
speculate v. 추측하다, 짐작하다
resistant adj. 저항력 있는 beneficial adj. 유익한
cellular adj. 세포의 by far phr. 틀림없이
intervention n. 치료, 간섭 risk factor phr. 위험 인자
Type 2 diabetes phr. 2형 당뇨병
nonalcoholic fatty liver disease phr. 무알코올 성 지방간 질환 anything but phr. 이외의 무엇이나, 결코 ~가 아닌
fidget v. 꼼지락거리다, 가만히 못 있다
count v. 포함되다, ~으로 간주되다 log v. 기록하다
chore n. 잡일 emotion n. 감정
Alzheimer's disease phr. 알츠하이머병
hippocampus n. (대뇌 측두엽의) 해마

48 [2019 국민대]

정답 ③

해석 ① 활동적인, 적극적인
② 갑작스러운
③ 몸을 많이 움직이지 않는, 주로 앉아서 하는
④ 시끄러운

해설 지문의 빈칸을 채우는 문제이다. 지문의 중간에서 과학자들은 앉아서 보내는 시간이 각종 질환에 대한 위험과 연관된다고 했으므로, 빈칸 (A)에는 몸을 많이 움직이지 않는 행동이 예상보다 이른 죽음의 위험 인자라는 내용이 나와야 적절하다는 것을 알 수 있다. 따라서 '몸을 많이 움직이지 않는, 주로 앉아서 하는'이라고 한 ③번이 정답이다.

49 [2019 국민대]

정답 ②

해석 ① 오랫동안 가만히 앉아 있지 않은 것
② 과도한 운동을 하는 것
③ 식사의 식이요법을 유지하는 것
④ 낙관적인 태도를 갖는 것

해설 오래 건강하게 사는 삶을 위한 전문가적인 정보가 아닌 것을 고르는 문제이다. 지문의 중간에서, 운동만으로 너무 많이 앉아 있는 것의 모든 나쁜 영향들을 없앨 수는 없다고 했으므로, 과도한 운동을 하는 것은 오래 건강하게 사는 삶을 위한 정보가 아니다. 따라서 정답은 ②번이다.

어휘 excessive adj. 과도한 regimen n. 식이요법
optimistic adj. 낙관적인 attitude n. 태도

50 [2019 국민대]

정답 ①

해석 ① 우리가 노화에 대해 어떻게 느끼는지가 어떻게 나이 드는지에 영향을 미칠 수 있다
② 스트레스와 운동은 서로 밀접한 관계가 있다
③ 알츠하이머병은 노화에 대한 긍정적인 생각과 연관된다
④ 분노와 스트레스는 알츠하이머병과 직접적인 관련이 없다

해설 지문의 빈칸을 채우는 문제이다. 지문의 후반에서 과학자들에게 우리의 감정이 생명 활동에 영향을 준다는 것은 명확하다고 했으므로, 빈칸 (B)에는 여러 연구에서 우리가 노화에 대해 어떻게 느끼는지가 어떻게 나이 드는지에 영향을 미칠 수 있다는 것을 시사했다는 내용이 나와야 적절하다는 것을 알 수 있다. 따라서 '우리가 노화에 대해 어떻게 느끼는지가 우리가 어떻게 나이 드는지에 영향을 미칠 수 있다'라고 한 ①번이 정답이다.

13 물리·화학·기술·건축

01-58
문제집 p.364

01 ③	02 ①	03 ①	04 ③	05 ②
06 ④	07 ①	08 ③	09 ①	10 ④
11 ④	12 ②	13 ①	14 ④	15 ②
16 ④	17 ①	18 ③	19 ③	20 ④
21 ③	22 ④	23 ②	24 ③	25 ②
26 ①	27 ①	28 ⑤	29 ③	30 ②
31 ①	32 ③	33 ①	34 ④	35 ①
36 ③	37 ②	38 ④	39 ④	40 ②
41 ①	42 ①	43 ①	44 ③	45 ①
46 ④	47 ①	48 ①	49 ③	50 ③
51 ③	52 ②	53 ②	54 ③	55 ④
56 ④	57 ②	58 ④		

[01-02]

아리스토텔레스의 전통은 한 사람이 순수한 생각으로 우주를 지배하는 모든 법칙을 알아낼 수 있으며, 이것은 관찰을 통해 확인될 필요가 없다고 주장했다. 그래서 갈릴레오 이전까지는 누구도 실제로 다른 무게의 물체가 다른 속도로 떨어지는지를 알아보기 위해 애를 쓰지 않았다. 갈릴레오는 기울어진 피사의 탑에서 무거운 것들을 떨어뜨림으로써 아리스토텔레스의 믿음이 잘못되었다는 것을 입증했다고 말해진다. 이 이야기는 거의 확실히 사실이 아니지만, 갈릴레오는 이에 상당하는 무언가를 행했는데, 그것은 그가 다양한 무게의 공들을 매끄러운 경사면에 굴렸다는 것이다. 이 상황은 무거운 물체가 수직적으로 떨어졌을 때의 상황과 유사하지만, 관찰하기에는 훨씬 더 용이한데, 이는 속도가 더 작기 때문이다. 갈릴레오의 측정은 각각의 물체가 그것의 무게와는 관계없이 동등한 비율로 속도를 증가시킨다는 것을 보여주었다. 예를 들어, 만약 매 10미터마다 1미터씩 급경사를 이루는 경사면에 공 하나를 놓으면, 그 공은 1초 뒤에는 1초당 1미터의 속도로, 2초 뒤에는 1초당 2미터의 속도 등으로 경사면 아래로 이동할 것이다.

Aristotelian adj. 아리스토텔레스의 govern v. 지배하다
pure adj. 순수한 observation n. 관찰
bother v. 애를 쓰다 weight n. 무게
demonstrate v. 입증하다 leaning adj. 기울어진
certainly adv. 확실히 roll v. 굴리다
smooth adj. 매끄러운 slope n. 경사면
vertically adv. 수직적으로 measurement n. 측정
indicate v. 보여주다

01 2021 한양대

정답 ③

해석 ① 한 물체는 동일한 가속도로 떨어진다.
② 기울어진 피사의 탑에 관한 이야기는 아마도 사실이 아니다.
③ 무거운 물체는 그것의 무게에 정비례해서 가벼운 물체보다 빠르게 떨어진다.
④ 갈릴레오의 실험에서, 경사면이 떨어지는 물체를 측정하기 위해 사용되었다.
⑤ 아리스토텔레스의 전통에서, 과학적인 법칙은 관찰보다는 순수한 생각의 결과이다.

해설 지문의 내용과 일치하지 않는 것을 묻는 문제이다. 지문의 후반부에서 갈릴레오의 측정은 각각의 물체가 그것의 무게와는 관계없이 동등한 비율로 속도를 증가시킨다는 것을 보여주었다고 했으므로, 무거운 물체가 그것의 무게에 정비례하여 가벼운 물체보다 빠르게 떨어진다는 것은 지문의 내용과 다르다. 따라서 ③번이 지문의 내용과 거리가 멀다.

오답분석 ① 갈릴레오의 측정은 각각의 물체가 그것의 무게와는 관계없이 동등한 비율로 속도를 증가시킨다는 것을 보여주었다고 했으므로, 지문의 내용과 일치한다.
② It is said that Galileo demonstrated that Aristotle's belief was false by dropping weights from the leaning tower of Pisa를 통해 기울어진 피사의 탑에 관한 이야기가 사실이 아님을 알 수 있다.
④ 갈릴레오가 다양한 무게의 공들을 매끄러운 경사면에 굴렸다고 했으므로, 지문의 내용과 일치한다.
⑤ The Aristotelian tradition held that one could work out all the laws that govern the universe by pure thought를 통해 아리스토텔레스의 전통에서, 과학적인 법칙은 관찰보다는 순수한 생각의 결과임을 알 수 있다.

어휘 acceleration n. 가속도
in direct proportion to phr. ~에 정비례해서
inclined plane phr. 경사면

02 2021 한양대

정답 ①

해석 ① 속도가 더 작다
② 다양한 무게의 물체가 사용되었다
③ 물체는 다양한 비율로 가속화한다
④ 물체는 똑같은 높이에서 떨어진다
⑤ 물체가 떨어지는 속도는 질량에 의존한다

해설 지문의 빈칸을 채우는 문제이다. 빈칸 앞에서 경사면에 공을 굴리는 상황이 무거운 물체가 수직적으로 떨어졌을 때의 상황과 유사하지만 관찰하기에는 더 용이했다고 언급하고 있으므로, 빈칸에는 물체가 수직적으로 떨어질 때에 비해 경사면에서 굴렀을 때 관찰하기가 더 용이한지에 대한 이유가 나와

야 한다. 따라서 지문의 빈칸에는 '속도가 더 작다'라는 내용의 관찰이 용이한 이유가 나와야 하므로, ①번이 정답이다.

[03-04]

"cybernetic organism(인공두뇌 생물체)"의 축약형인 '사이보그'라는 단어는 우주여행에 관한 1960년도 논문에서 처음 사용되었다. 사이보그는 "새로운 환경에 적응할 목적으로 외부 요소가 덧붙여진" 생물체로 정의되었다. 이러한 정의에 따르면, 우주복을 입은 우주 비행사는 사이보그의 한 예시인데, 이는 우주복이 우주비행사들로 하여금 우주라는 새로운 환경에 적응하도록 돕기 때문이다. 더 최근에, 그 단어(사이보그)는 사람들을 인간 이상으로 만들어주는 기계식 신체 기관을 가진 인간을 가리키는 것으로 그 의미가 확장되었다.

비록 로보캅과 같은 초인간은 아직까지 실제로 존재하는 것이 아니지만, 현실의 사이보그 기술의 발전은 일부 사람들이 그들이 잃어버린 능력을 보완하게 해주고, 다른 사람들에게 새롭고 특별한 능력을 준다. 한 예시는 영화감독 Rob Spence와 그의 생체 공학으로 만들어진 눈이다. Spence는 사고로 그의 한쪽 눈을 다쳤다. 그의 손상된 눈을 일반적인 의안으로 교체하는 것 대신에, Spence는 그의 안와에 카메라가 심어진 인공 눈을 착용했다. 그 눈은 Spence의 두뇌나 시신경에는 연결되어있지 않지만, Spence가 보는 것을 녹화할 수 있다. Spence는 그의 카메라 눈을 생체 공학적 신체 기관을 가진 사람들에 관한 다큐멘터리를 위해 인터뷰를 녹화하는 데 사용해왔다.

---
cybernetic adj. 인공두뇌의 **external** adj. 외부의
component n. 요소 **super-human** n. 초인간
compensate v. 보완하다 **bionic** adj. 생체 공학의
glass eye phr. 의안 **prosthetic** adj. 인공의
implant v. 심다 **eye socket** phr. 안와, 눈구멍
optic nerve phr. 시신경

03 [2021 단국대]

정답 ①

해석 ① ~ 대신에   ② ~ 덕분에
③ ~에 더하여   ④ ~에도 불구하고

해설 지문의 빈칸을 채우는 문제이다. 빈칸 앞에서 Spence가 사고로 그의 한쪽 눈을 잃었다고 했으므로, 빈칸에는 Spence가 일반적인 의안 대신에 안와에 카메라가 심어진 인공 눈을 착용했다는 내용이 나오는 것이 자연스럽다. 따라서 '~ 대신에'라고 한 ①번이 정답이다.

04 [2021 단국대]

정답 ③

해설 ① Spence는 그의 인공 눈 덕분에 사물을 볼 수 있다.
② Spence는 사고로 그의 두 눈을 다쳤다.
③ 우주복을 입은 우주 비행사는 사이보그로 생각될 수 있다.
④ 초인간은 요즘 실제로 존재한다.

해설 지문의 내용과 일치하는 것을 묻는 문제이다. 지문 초반의 A cyborg was defined as an organism ~의 내용을 통해 우주복을 입은 우주비행사가 사이보그로 생각될 수 있다는 것을 알 수 있다. 따라서 ③번이 지문의 내용과 일치한다.

오답분석 ① 인공 눈은 Spence의 두뇌나 시신경에는 연결되어 있지 않지만, Spence가 보는 것을 녹화할 수 있다고 했고, Spence는 사고로 한쪽 눈만 다쳤다고 하여 그에게 다치지 않은 다른 눈이 있는 것이므로, 그가 인공 눈 덕분에 사물을 볼 수 있다는 것을 알 수 있으므로 지문의 내용과 다르다.
② Spence는 사고로 그의 한쪽 눈을 다쳤다고 했으므로, 그가 사고로 그의 두 눈을 다쳤다는 것은 지문의 내용과 다르다.
④ 로보캅과 같은 초인간은 아직 실제로 존재하는 것이 아니라고 했으므로, 초인간이 요즘 실제로 존재한다는 것은 지문의 내용과 다르다.

[05-06]

연소는 화학 반응의 여러 다른 유형 중 하나의 예시일 뿐이다. 그밖에 다른 세 개는 분해, 결합, 그리고 치환이다. 분해가 일어나는 동안, 물질 안의 복합체는 분열하여 더 조그만 복합체나 심지어는 개별적 요소를 형성한다. 결합의 경우, 정반대의 과정이 일어나는데, 여기에서는 복합체가 서로 만나 새로운 복합체를 만들어낸다. 치환 화학 반응에서는, 하나 또는 더 많은 복합체가 분열하고 다른 것과 일부를 교환한다. 모든 화학 반응에서, 물질은 만들어지거나 파괴되지 않는다는 것을 이해하는 것이 중요하다. 물질은 그저 한 형태에서 또 다른 것으로 변화하는 것이다.

---
combustion n. 연소 **chemical reaction** phr. 화학 반응
decomposition n. 분해 **combination** n. 결합
replacement n. 치환 **compound** n. 복합체, 혼합물
split v. 분열하다 **take place** phr. 일어나다
swap v. 교환하다

05 [2019 덕성여대]

정답 ②

해석 ① 에너지가 열과 빛의 형태로 방출된다.
② 복합체가 더 조그만 복합체로 분리된다.
③ 분자가 서로 만나 새로운 복합체를 형성한다.
④ 물질이 분열하고 일부를 교환한다.

해설 분해에서 일어나는 과정이 무엇인지를 파악하는 문제이다. 지문의 세 번째 문장에서 분해가 일어나는 동안, 물질 안의 복합체는 분열하여 더 조그만 복합체나 심지어는 개별적 요소를 형성한다고 했으므로, 분해에서 일어나는 과정은 '복합

체가 더 조그만 복합체로 분리된다'는 것이다. 따라서 정답은 ②번이다.

어휘 release v. 방출하다　separate v. 분리되다
molecule n. 분자　substance n. 물질

06 2019 덕성여대

정답 ④

해석
① 물질은 화학 반응이 일어나는 동안 만들어진다.
② 물질은 화학 반응이 있을 때 발견할 수 있다.
③ 물질은 화학 반응이 일어나는 동안 파괴된다.
④ 물질은 화학 반응이 일어나는 동안 한 형태에서 또 다른 것으로 변화된다.

해설 물질에 대한 저자의 설명에 관해 사실인 것을 파악하는 문제이다. 지문 마지막 문장에서 물질은 그저 한 형태에서 또 다른 것으로 변화하는 것이라고 했으므로, 물질에 대한 저자의 설명은 '물질은 화학 반응이 일어나는 동안 한 형태에서 또 다른 것으로 변화된다'는 것이다. 따라서 정답은 ④번이다.

어휘 detectable adj. 발견할 수 있는

[07-08]

DNA의 이중 나선 구조의 발견이 처음에는 높게 평가되었지만, 현재는 불확실한 미래의 문을 연 것으로 생각된다. 과학자들은 새로운 DNA의 일부를 살아있는 세포에 주입할 수 있었으며, 그 즉시, 그런 활동은 의심스럽게 생각되었다. 인류 문명이 세포의 형태로 조작될 수 있는 일부 질병으로 인해 파멸할 수 있다고 여겨졌다. 사람들은 그러한 연구를 통제할 수 있는 엄격한 규제가 만들어져야 할 필요가 있다는 것을 깨달았다. 이 때문에, 과학자들이 재조합형 DNA 기술을 발견하기까지 시간이 걸렸다. 다행히 통제 규제는 행동으로 옮겨지지 않았고, DNA 기술에 대한 두려움이 근거가 없게 되자, 규제를 위한 모든 시도도, 심지어는 온건한 시도조차도 사라지게 되었다.

double-helical adj. 이중 나선의
revered adj. 높게 평가되는, 존경받는
uncertain adj. 불확실한　immediately adv. 즉시
civilization n. 문명　engineer v. (유전자를) 조작하다
recombinant-DNA n. 재조합형 DNA
put into action phr. 행동으로 옮기다
unfounded adj. 근거가 없는　regulation n. 규제
moderate adj. 온건한, 온화한
dissipate v. 사라지다, 소멸하다

07 2019 가천대

정답 ①

해석 ① 의심스럽게　② 호의적으로
③ 공정하게　④ 만족스럽게

해설 지문의 빈칸을 채우는 문제이다. 빈칸이 포함된 문장 다음에서 DNA의 일부를 살아있는 세포에 주입하는 기술은 세포의 형태로 조작된 질병이 인류 문명을 파괴하도록 만들 수 있다고 설명하고 있으므로, 빈칸에는 이 기술에 대해 못마땅한 의미의 단어가 와야 한다는 것을 알 수 있다. 따라서 '의심스럽게'라고 한 ①번이 정답이다.

어휘 suspiciously adv. 의심스럽게
favorably adv. 호의적으로　impartially adv. 공정하게
approvingly adv. 만족스럽게

08 2019 가천대

정답 ③

해석
① DNA 기술을 규제하기 위한 성공적인 시도
② 생명과학 기술의 비신뢰성
③ DNA 기술에 대한 근거 없는 두려움
④ 생물학적인 진보의 잠재력

해설 지문의 요지를 묻는 문제이다. 지문의 마지막에서 DNA 기술에 대한 두려움 때문에 규제를 만들려고 했으나, 재조합형 DNA 기술의 발견으로 이러한 두려움이 근거가 없다는 것이 밝혀져 규제를 만들려는 시도가 사라졌다고 하였다. 따라서 이 지문의 주제를 'DNA 기술에 대한 근거 없는 두려움'이라고 표현한 ③번이 정답이다.

어휘 unreliability n. 신뢰할 수 없음
biology n. 생명과학, 생물학　groundless adj. 근거 없는
potential n. 잠재력　advance n. 진보, 발전

[09-10]

뉴턴이 살았던 18세기는 그 의구심을 무시했지만, 사실은 뉴턴의 연구에서 암시되는 중요한 통계학적 의구심이 있었다. 물리적 측정은 절대로 정확하지 않고, 기계나 다른 역학 시스템과 관련하여 우리가 말해야만 하는 것은 최초의 위치와 운동량이 아주 정확하게 주어졌을 때 (이는 절대 일어나지 않는다) 우리가 예상해야 하는 것이 아니라 최초의 위치와 운동량이 이를 수 있는 정도로 정확하게 주어졌을 때 우리가 예상할 수 있는 것에 정말로 관련된다. 이는 단지 우리가 최초의 완전한 상태가 아니라 그들의 구분에 대한 무언가를 안다는 것을 의미한다. 다른 말로 하자면, 물리학에서 물리학에 적용되는 요소는 사건의 불확실성과 우연성을 고려하는 것을 피할 수 없다. 처음으로 이 우연성을 고려하는 명확한 과학적 방식을 제시한 것은 기브스의 공로였다. 이 과학사학자는 단 하나의 진전도 하지 못한 것처럼 보인다. 기브스의 연구는 잘 오려졌지만 잘못 꿰매졌고, 그가 시작한 일을 다른 사람들이 마무리하도록 남겨졌다.

reservation n. 의구심　implicit adj. 암시된
dynamic adj. 역학의　momentum n. 운동량

attainable adj. 이룰 수 있는   merit n. 공로
in vain phr. 헛되이

09 2020 한국항공대

정답 ①

해석 ① 뉴턴의 시대에서 통계 자료의 암시는 완전히 밝혀지지 않았다.
② 물리학의 적용은 사건의 우연성 및 정확성과 무관하다.
③ 물리학의 적용은 기브스의 최초의 완전한 상태를 발견하는 명확한 도구에 크게 의존한다.
④ 뉴턴의 시대에서 동일한 물리적 법칙이 다양한 시스템에 적용되지 않았다.

해설 지문을 통해 추론할 수 있는 것을 고르는 문제이다. 지문의 첫 번째 문장에서 뉴턴이 살았던 18세기는 그 의구심을 무시했지만 사실은 뉴턴의 연구에서 암시되는 중요한 통계학적 의구심이 있었다고 했으므로, 뉴턴의 시대에서 통계 자료의 암시는 완전히 밝혀지지 않았다는 것을 추론할 수 있다. 따라서 정답은 ①번이다.

오답 분석
② 물리학에서 물리학에 적용되는 요소는 사건의 불확실성과 우연성을 고려하는 것을 피할 수 없다고 했으므로, 물리학의 적용은 사건의 우연성 및 정확성과 무관하다는 것은 지문의 내용과 다르다.
③ 기브스의 연구는 잘 오려졌지만 잘못 꿰매졌고, 그가 시작한 일을 다른 사람들이 마무리하도록 남겨졌다고는 했으므로, 물리학의 적용은 기브스의 최초의 완전한 상태를 발견하는 명확한 도구에 크게 의존한다는 것은 지문의 내용과 다르다.
④ 뉴턴의 시대에서 동일한 물리적 법칙이 다양한 시스템에 적용되지 않았다는 것은 지문에서 알 수 없다.

어휘 irrelevant adj. 무관한

10 2020 한국항공대

정답 ④

해석 ① 역학 시스템의 완전성
② 뉴턴의 물리학적 기여
③ 뉴턴의 이론의 뒤집을 수 없는 입장
④ 기브스 이론의 이익

해설 지문의 제목을 묻는 문제이다. 지문의 후반에서 기브스의 연구가 처음으로 이 우연성을 고려하는 명확한 과학적 방식을 제시했다고 말하고 있다. 따라서 이 지문의 제목을 '기브스 이론의 이익'이라고 표현한 ④번이 정답이다.

어휘 irreversible adj. 뒤집을 수 없는

[11-12]

천문학자에게 가장 중요한 과학적 도구는 망원경이다. 이것은 태양계와 관련한 최초의 중요한 갈릴레오의 발견이 망원경 발명과 동시에 일어났다는 사실에 의해 입증된다. 수 세기에 걸쳐 망원경의 배율이 증가하면서, 망원경은 천문학자들이 우주의 특성에 대한 더 많은 발견을 하도록 했다. 최초의 망원경은 빛을 집중시키기 위해 유리 렌즈를 사용했지만, 가장 현대의 망원경은 이제 주요 집광기로서 거울을 사용한다. 렌즈 망원경에서, 빛은 렌즈를 통과해야 하므로 렌즈는 온전히 완전해야 한다. 그러나 거울 망원경에서, 빛은 그저 거울에서 튕겨 나간다. 이는 거울의 표면만 완전하면 된다는 것을 의미하고, 이는 큰 거울을 만드는 것을 훨씬 수월하게 한다. 점점 더 큰 망원경용 거울을 만드는 것은 중요한데, 이는 망원경의 배율이 거울의 크기에 정비례하기 때문이다. 따라서, 천문학자들의 주요 관심사는 그들의 망원경에 적절한 가장 큰 거울을 얻는 것이다.

astronomer n. 천문학자   telescope n. 망원경
prove v. 입증하다   accompany v. 동시에 일어나다
power n. 배율   bounce off phr. 튕기다
manufacture v. 만들다   proportional adj. 비례하는
concern n. 관심사

11 2019 덕성여대

정답 ④

해석 ① 렌즈 망원경은 만들기 쉬웠다.
② 렌즈 망원경은 더 배율이 높았다.
③ 렌즈 망원경은 빛을 더 효과적으로 포착한다.
④ 렌즈에 흠이 없어야 한다.

해설 렌즈 망원경에 대해 사실인 것을 파악하는 문제이다. 지문 중간에서, 렌즈 망원경에서 빛은 렌즈를 통과해야 하므로 렌즈는 온전히 완전해야 한다고 했으므로, 렌즈 망원경에 대해 사실인 것은 '렌즈에 흠이 없어야 한다'는 것이다. 따라서 정답은 ④번이다.

어휘 powerful adj. 배율이 높은   capture v. 포착하다
flawless adj. 흠 없는

12 2019 덕성여대

정답 ②

해석 ① 현대에, 거울은 렌즈 대신에 빛을 모으는 데 사용된다.
② 렌즈 망원경을 만드는 데에는 어떤 문제도 생기지 않는다.
③ 거울 망원경은 완전한 표면을 가진 거울을 필요로 한다.
④ 거울 망원경의 배율은 거울의 크기와 함께 증가한다.

해설 지문의 내용과 일치하지 않는 것을 묻는 문제이다. ②번의 키워드인 Lens telescopes(렌즈 망원경)가 언급된 지문 주변을 보면, 렌즈 망원경에서, 빛은 렌즈를 통과해야 하므로 렌즈는 온전히 완전해야 한다고 했으므로, 렌즈 망원경을 만드는

데에는 어떤 문제도 생기지 않는다는 것은 지문의 내용과 다르다. 따라서 ②번이 지문의 내용과 일치하지 않는다.

오답 분석
① 지문 네 번째 문장의 most modern telescopes now use mirrors as their major light collectors를 통해 '현대에, 거울은 렌즈 대신에 빛을 모으는 데 사용된다'는 것을 알 수 있다.
③ 지문의 일곱 번째 문장 This means that only the surface of the mirror must be perfect, making ~ mirrors.를 통해 '거울 망원경은 완전한 표면을 가진 거울을 필요로 한다'는 것을 알 수 있다.
④ 지문의 여덟 번째 문장 Making larger and larger mirrors for telescopes is important because a telescope's power is directly proportional to the size of its mirror.를 통해 '거울 망원경의 배율은 거울의 크기와 함께 증가한다'는 것을 알 수 있다.

어휘 present v. (곤란 등을) 생기게 하다

[13-15]

가상현실과 자율 주행 자동차가 최근 몇 년 동안 많이 거론되고 있으며, 올해에도 여전히 거론될 것이다. 하지만 이 두 기술은 아직 초창기이며 너무 이르다. 지난 2년 동안, 페이스북, 구글, 그리고 삼성 같은 기술 회사는 가상현실 헤드셋과 수많은 소프트웨어와 게임을 시장에 넘쳐나게 했다. 하지만 아직 사람들이 그 제품들을 꼭 받아들인 것은 아니다. eMarketer라는 연구 회사의 분석가인 Martin Kabila는 최근 게시물에서 "이 산업이 고가의 장비, (A)멀미, 흥미로운 콘텐츠의 부족, 전반적인 소비자의 관심 부족 등으로 고전하고 있습니다."라고 말했다.
자율 주행 자동차 또한 주류가 되기에는 아직 멀다. 캘리포니아, 애리조나, 그리고 다른 곳의 일부 회사가 자율 주행 자동차를 시험할 수 있는 허가를 받았지만, 구글과 아마존 같은 이 기술의 선두를 달리고 있는 몇몇 회사가 자율 주행 자동차의 출시일을 밝히는 것을 꺼려 왔다. Kabila는 "자동차의 기술에 대한 많은 논란이 (B)있겠지만, 독특하거나 특별할 것은 없을 것입니다."라고 말했다.

virtual reality phr. 가상현실
self-driving car phr. 자율 주행 자동차
nascent adj. 초창기의
premature adj. (시기보다) 이른, 조숙한
flood v. 넘치게 하다, 잠기게 하다
embrace v. 받아들이다, 껴안다
be plagued by phr. ~에 고생하다, ~에 시달리다
high-cost adj. 고가의   analyst n. 분석가
mainstream n. 주류   autonomous adj. 자율적인
refrain v. 꺼리다, 삼가다   commit v. (의사를) 밝히다
release n. 출시, 발표   noise n. 논란, 잡음
automotive adj. 자동차의   distinct adj. 독특한, 구별되는

13 [2019 한성대]

정답 ①

해석
① 첨단 기술로 가기 위한 여전히 먼 길
② 첨단 기술의 밝은 미래
③ 투자하기 좋은 분야
④ 가상현실과 자율 주행 자동차의 장점

해설 지문의 제목을 묻는 문제이다. 지문의 첫 번째 문단에서는 가상현실 기술이 많은 소프트웨어와 게임을 만들었지만 소비자들에게 외면받고 있다고 설명하고 있으며, 두 번째 문단에서는 자율 주행 자동차 기술의 선두주자인 구글과 아마존이 자율 주행 자동차의 출시일 발표를 꺼리고 있다고 설명하고 있다. 따라서 지문의 제목을 '첨단 기술로 가기 위한 여전히 먼 길'이라고 표현한 ①번이 정답이다.

어휘 high-tech n. 첨단 기술   advantage n. 장점, 이점

14 [2019 한성대]

정답 ④

해석
① 멀미
② 흥미로운 콘텐츠의 부족
③ 전반적인 소비자의 관심 부족
④ 여러 가지 편리한 도구들

해설 지문의 흐름상 빈칸에 들어갈 수 없는 것을 고르는 문제이다. 빈칸 (A)가 포함된 문장에서, 가상현실 기술이 고가의 장비로 인해 고전하고 있다고 설명하고 있으므로, '고가의 장비'와 같이 가상현실 기술이 가진 단점에 관한 표현이 들어가야 할 것이다. ④번의 a series of convenient utilities는 '여러 가지 편리한 도구들'의 의미가 있으므로, 단점에 관한 표현과는 거리가 멀다. 따라서 ④번이 정답이다.

어휘 motion sickness phr. 멀미
dearth n. 부족   compelling adj. 흥미를 끄는
utility n. 도구

15 [2019 한성대]

정답 ②

해석
① 그렇지 않으면   ② 하지만
③ 그래서   ④ 그러면

해설 빈칸에 적절한 연결어를 넣는 문제이다. 빈칸 (B) 앞 문장은 자동차의 기술에 대한 많은 논란이 있을 것이라는 내용이고, 빈칸 뒤 문장은 독특하거나 특별할 것은 없을 것이라는 내용이다. 따라서 대조를 나타내는 연결어인 ② but(하지만)이 정답이다.

[16-18]

1902년 하노이의 쥐 대학살은 우리가 왜 빅 데이터에 경계해야 할 필요가 있는지를 상기시키는 고전적인 예다. 도시 전역에 걸친 설치류의 확산에 불안해한 그 당시의 프랑스 식민지 정부는, 지역의 쥐잡이꾼들에게 그들이 잡은 동물 각각에 현상금을 제공했다. 정부는 제거의 증거로서 제출된 쥐의 꼬리마다 1센트를 지급했다. 초기에는, 쥐를 죽였다고 상당한 수의 보고가 들어왔기 때문에 그 데이터는 조짐이 좋아 보였지만, 그 계획은 빗나가게 되었다. 교활한 베트남의 기업가들은 그들의 수입을 늘리기 위해서 설치류 농장을 세웠다. 곧, 흑사병이 하노이에 발생하였다.

오늘날 우리가 스마트폰에서 만들어내는 데이터는 하노이에서의 쥐의 침입에 대한 식민지의 통계 수치와는 동떨어진 것처럼 보일지 모르지만, 데이터를 잘못 해석하는 것의 위험성은 똑같이 남아있다. 장려책은 변함없이 이득을 위해 부당하게 조작될 소지가 있다. 상관관계는 때때로 비논리적이다. 빅 데이터와 강력한 데이터 사이의 차이점은 중요하기 때문에, 맥락을 빼앗긴다면 데이터는 오해의 소지가 있을 수 있다. 통계적 모형이 반드시 다른 맥락에 걸쳐 적용되는 것은 아니다. "표절하는 학생도 사기를 저지르는 것이 되는가?" 다른 요소들이 표절로 이어질지라도, 통계는 긍정적인 관계를 추정할 수 있다. 그러므로 미래의 사례에서도 같은 모형을 이용하는 것은 문제가 될 것이다.

rat n. 쥐 massacre n. 대학살 classic adj. 고전적인
reminder n. 상기시키는 것 wary adj. 경계하는
colonial adj. 식민지의 alarmed adj. 불안해하는
rodent n. 설치류 bounty n. 현상금 elimination n. 제거
initially adv. 초기에는, 처음에는
promising adj. 조짐이 좋은, 유망한
substantial adj. 상당한 awry adj. 빗나간
crafty adj. 교활한 entrepreneur n. 기업가
boost v. 늘리다, 신장시키다
bubonic plague phr. 흑사병, 림프절 페스트
break out phr. 발생하다, 발발하다
generate v. 만들어내다, 생성하다
far removed from phr. ~와 동떨어진 statistics n. 통계
infestation n. 침입 misinterpret v. 잘못 해석하다
incentive n. 장려책 invariably adv. 변함없이
be gamed phr. 개인적인 이득을 위해 부당하게 조작되다
correlation n. 상관관계 spurious adj. 비논리적인, 거짓된
strip of phr. ~를 빼앗다 context n. 맥락
misleading adj. 오해의 소지가 있는
significant adj. 중요한 plagiarize v. 표절하다
commit v. 저지르다 fraud n. 사기
lead to phr. ~로 이어지다 problematic adj. 문제가 되는

16 2019 한국외대

정답 ④

해석 ① 데이터는 오해의 소지가 있기 때문에, 우리는 그것을 생략해야 한다.
② 스마트폰으로부터 온 데이터는 강력한 데이터와 비슷하다.
③ 설치류 농장은 수익성이 있는 시도였다.
④ 예측을 위한 데이터의 이용은 맥락의 고려를 요구한다.

해설 지문의 주제를 묻는 문제이다. 지문의 후반에서 맥락을 빼앗긴다면 데이터는 오해의 소지가 있을 수 있다고 하였다. 따라서 이 지문의 주제를 '예측을 위한 데이터의 이용은 맥락의 고려를 요구한다'라고 표현한 ④번이 정답이다.

어휘 dispense with phr. ~를 생략하다
profitable adj. 수익성이 있는 endeavor n. 시도, 노력
prediction n. 예측 consideration n. 고려

17 2019 한국외대

정답 ②

해석 ① 게임은 좋은 데이터를 제공할 것이다.
② 쥐를 죽이는 것에 관한 데이터는 오해의 소지가 있다.
③ 행정가들이 기업가에 의해 불안해했다.
④ 쥐잡이꾼들이 그들이 죽인 각각의 쥐에 대금을 지불했다.

해설 지문의 내용과 일치하는 것을 묻는 문제이다. 지문의 중간에서 Stripped of context, data can be misleading because there is a significant difference between Big Data and strong data의 내용을 통해 쥐를 죽이는 것에 관한 데이터는 오해의 소지가 있다는 것을 알 수 있다. 따라서 ②번이 지문의 내용과 일치한다.

오답분석 ① 게임이 좋은 데이터를 제공하리라는 것은 지문에서 언급되지 않았다.
③ 그 당시의 프랑스 식민지 정부가 도시 전역에 걸친 설치류의 확산에 불안해했다고는 했지만, 행정가들이 기업가에 의해 불안해했는지는 알 수 없다.
④ 정부가 지역의 쥐잡이꾼들에게 그들이 잡은 동물 각각에 현상금을 제공했다고 했으므로, 쥐잡이꾼들이 그들이 죽인 각각의 쥐에 대금을 지불했다는 것은 지문의 내용과 다르다.

어휘 provide v. 제공하다 regarding prep. ~에 관한
administrator n. 행정가

18 2019 한국외대

정답 ③

해석 ① 쥐잡이꾼들이 보상 체계를 이용했다.
② 빅 데이터와 강력한 데이터의 차이는 중요하다
③ 스마트폰 데이터를 이용한 예측의 모형은 정확하다.
④ 현상금을 지급하는 것은 하노이의 쥐 문제를 해결하지 못했다.

해설 지문의 내용과 일치하지 않는 것을 묻는 문제이다. ③번의 키워드인 smartphone data(스마트폰 데이터)와 관련된 지문의 our smartphones today(오늘날 우리의 스마트폰) 주변에서 오늘날 우리가 스마트폰에서 만들어내는 데이터는 하노

이에서의 쥐의 침입에 대한 식민지의 통계 수치와는 동떨어진 것처럼 보일지 모르지만, 데이터를 잘못 해석하는 것의 위험성은 똑같이 남아있다고 했으므로, 스마트폰 데이터를 이용한 예측의 모형은 정확하다는 것은 지문의 내용과 다르다. 따라서 ③번이 지문의 내용과 일치하지 않는다.

오답 분석
① Crafty Vietnamese entrepreneurs set up rodent farms to boost their income을 통해 '쥐잡이꾼들이 보상 체계를 이용했다'는 것을 알 수 있다.
② because there is a significant difference between Big Data and strong data를 통해 '빅 데이터와 강력한 데이터의 차이는 중요하다'는 것을 알 수 있다.
④ Initially, the data looked promising because substantial numbers were reported killed, but the plan went awry를 통해 '현상금을 지급하는 것은 하노이의 쥐 문제를 해결하지 못했다'는 것을 알 수 있다.

어휘 take advantage of phr. ~를 이용하다
reward n. 보상   accurate adj. 정확한

[19-20]

오늘날 우리는 자신을 관찰의 대상으로 보는 행동을 위한 확장되는 일련의 기술적 수단에 맞서있다. 첩보 기관에 의해 사용되는 감시와 데이터 분석의 가장 진보한 형태는 이제 큰 사업체의 마케팅 전략에 있어 똑같이 필수적이다. 널리 사용되는 것은 눈의 움직임을 추적하는 스크린이나 화면의 다른 형태인데, 그뿐만 아니라 시각 자료의 순서나 흐름에 따른 시각적 관심의 지속시간이나 고정도 포함된다. 한 사람이 하나의 웹 페이지를 속독하는 것도 어떻게 눈이 훑어보고, 멈추고, 움직이고, 다른 부분보다 어떤 부분에 집중의 우선순위를 주는지 분 단위로 분석되고 수량화될 수 있다. 심지어 큰 백화점의 보행 공간 안에서도, 시선 추적 스캐너는 예를 들어, 어떤 사람이 그가 사지 않은 물품을 얼마나 오랫동안 보았는지를 알아내는 것과 같은, 개인의 행동에 대한 자세한 정보를 제공한다. 폭넓게 지원된 시각 인체공학의 연구 분야는 한동안 유지되어 왔다. 수동적이고 때때로 자발적으로, 사람들은 이제 자신의 감시와 데이터 마이닝에 협력한다.

---

confront v. 맞서다   expand v. 확장시키다
array of phr. 일련의   surveillance n. 감시
intelligence agency phr. 첩보 기관, 정보국
indispensable adj. 필수적인, 없어서는 안 될
strategy n. 전략   track v. 추적하다   duration n. 지속시간
fixation n. 고정   sequence n. 순서   stream n. 흐름
casual perusal phr. 속독   quantify v. 수량화하다
attentive adj. 집중의, 집중하는   priority n. 우선순위
optical adj. 시각의, 빛의   passively adv. 수동적으로
voluntarily adv. 자발적으로   collaborate v. 협력하다
data-mining n. 데이터 마이닝(겉으로는 보이지 않는 데이터들 간의 상호 관계를 분석함으로써 데이터들 속에 숨어 있던 새로운 정보를 추출해 내는 작업)

19 [2019 서울여대]
정답 ③
해석 ① 생산 과정에서의 기술 혁신
② 경영 과학에서의 데이터 분석의 새로운 방법론
③ 관찰자가 관찰의 대상으로 바뀌는 방법
④ 수감자의 시각 활동을 이용한 교도소 감시 체계

해설 지문의 주제를 묻는 문제이다. 지문의 처음에서 우리가 맞서 있는 기술적 수단이 그것들 자신을 관찰의 대상으로 보는 행동을 하기 위함이라고 하였다. 따라서 이 지문의 주제를 '관찰자가 관찰의 대상으로 바뀌는 방법'이라고 표현한 ③번이 정답이다.

어휘 innovation n. 혁신   methodology n. 방법론
observer n. 관찰자   observation n. 관찰
inmate n. 수감자

20 [2019 서울여대]
정답 ④
해석 ① 인터넷 검색 습관
② 사람들의 쇼핑 행동
③ 눈의 움직임을 추적하기 위한 도구
④ 첩보 기관을 위한 정부 자금

해설 지문에서 언급되지 않은 것을 파악하는 문제이다. 지문의 마지막에서 시각 인체공학에 대한 폭넓은 지원이 있었다고 했지만, 첩보 기관을 위한 지원에 대해서는 찾아볼 수 없으므로, 지문에서 언급되지 않은 것은 '첩보 기관을 위한 정부 자금'이다. 따라서 정답은 ④번이다.

어휘 instrument n. 도구, 기구

[21-22]

21세기 미국에 있어 중요한 문제 중 하나는 비 연안 도시와 지방 지역 사회들이 디지털 혁명에 참여할 수 있을 것인가이다. 우리는 거의 모든 미국인들이 기술의 열렬한 소비자이지만, 많은 미국인들에게 우리의 디지털 경제에 활기를 불어넣는 창조적인 활동을 할 기회가 부족하다는 것을 안다. (A)수백만 명의 존엄성이 위태롭다. 향후 10년 이내에, 일자리의 약 60퍼센트는 업무의 3분의 1이 인공지능에 의해 자동화될 수 있다. 많은 전통적 산업들이 디지털화되어가고 있다. 최근에, 한 호텔 전무는 그의 사업이 본질적으로 디지털 사업이라고 설명하면서, 그의 이윤 폭이 소프트웨어 설계자들의 실효성 여하에 달려있었다고 설명했다. 오늘날의 서비스업 종사자들, 꼼꼼한 농부들 그리고 전기 기술자들은 디지털 작업에 상당한 시간을 할애한다. 경제학자들은 우리의 디지털 미래에 소외된 사람들에게 과학기술의 중심으로 움직이라고 계속 말한다. 만약 경제학자들이 네브래스카주의 링컨이나 워싱턴주의 터코마와 같은 장소를 방문한다면, 그들은 그곳의 많은 사람들이 동요하지 않는다

는 것을 알게 될 것이다. 그곳의 사람들은 자신들의 소도시의 가치들을 자랑스러워하며 가족과 가까이 지내는 것을 즐긴다. 소도시의 사람들은 자신들의 소도시에 많은 신호등이 필요하지 않다고 자랑한다. (B)소도시들이 직면하는 선택은 양자택일이어서는 안 되는데, 그 선택은 "과학기술의 중심지가 되는 것 혹은 과학기술의 미래를 놓치는 것"이면 안 된다.

noncoastal adj. 비 연안의 **rural** adj. 지방의
avid adj. 열렬한 **fuel** v. ~에 활기를 불어넣다
at stake phr. 위태로운 **dignity** n. 존엄성
automate v. 자동화하다
artificial intelligence phr. 인공지능
profit margin phr. 이윤 폭
contingent on phr. ~의 여하에 달린
effectiveness n. 실효성, 유효성
hospitality adj. 접객업의, 접대용의
vendor n. 노점상, 행상인 **precision** adj. 정밀한
hub n. 중심 **small-town** adj. 소박한, 시골 소도시의
brag v. 자랑하다 **binary** adj. 양자택일의
adopt v. 도입하다, 채택하다 **miss out on** phr. ~을 놓치다

21 [2019 광운대]

정답 ③

해석
① 경제가 회복되기 시작했지만 지방 지역에 있는 많은 수의 사람들이 실업자가 되었다.
② 미국인들은 인공지능을 가진 최신 기술을 구입하기 위해 너무 많은 돈을 소비한다.
③ 비록 미국이 기술 발전을 겪고 있지만, 많은 사람들이 그러한 변화로 생산적이지 못하다.
④ 기업들이 전통적인 인간 노동력을 인공지능을 가진 현대 기술로 열심히 대체하기 시작했다.
⑤ 미국의 기업들이 다른 지역으로 이전하면서, 이동할 수 없는 많은 사람들이 일자리를 잃을 수 있다.

해설 밑줄 친 (A)의 원인을 파악하는 문제이다. 밑줄 친 (A) 앞 문장에서 거의 모든 미국인들이 기술의 열렬한 소비자이지만, 많은 미국인들에게 우리의 디지털 경제에 활기를 불어넣는 창조적인 활동을 할 기회가 부족하다고 했고, 밑줄 친 (A)의 수백만 명은 디지털 경제에 활기를 불어넣는 창조적 활동을 할 기회가 부족한 많은 미국인들을 가리킨다. 이 많은 미국인들의 삶이 존엄하지 못하고 위태로워질 수 있는 원인은 그들이 디지털화되고 있는 경제에 적응하지 못하고 생산적인 활동을 하지 못하기 때문이다. ④번의 경우, 밑줄 친 (A) 문장 뒤에서 향후 10년 이내에, 일자리의 약 60퍼센트는 업무의 3분의 1이 인공지능에 의해 자동화될 수 있다고 하였지만, 전통적인 인간 노동력을 인공지능을 가진 현대 기술로 대체하여도 사람들이 이러한 디지털화 되고 있는 경제에 잘 적응한다면 이 점이 수백만 명의 존엄성을 위협하지는 않을 것이다. 따라서 정답은 ③번이다.

어휘 **unemployed** adj. 실업자인 **recover** v. 회복되다
latest adj. 최신의 **productive** adj. 생산적인
avidly adv. 열심히 **relocate** v. 이전하다

22 [2019 광운대]

정답 ④

해석
① 소도시들은 과학기술의 중심지가 되거나 과학기술의 미래를 놓쳐야 한다.
② 소도시들은 사람들이 이동하는 것을 막기 위해 성장의 한계를 정해야 한다.
③ 소도시들은 과학기술의 중심으로 변화하면서 디지털 미래를 향해 나아갈 수 있다.
④ 소도시들은 그곳의 다양한 과학기술직들을 창출함으로써 그들의 지역사회 가치를 지켜낼 수 있다.
⑤ 소도시들은 그들의 주민들이 디지털 경제에 더 많이 인식할 수 있도록 장려해야 한다.

해설 밑줄 친 부분의 의미를 추론하는 문제이다. 밑줄 친 The choice facing small towns should not be binary — it should not be "adopt the Silicon name or miss out on the tech future."는 '소도시들이 직면하는 선택은 양자택일이어서는 안 되는데, 그 선택은 "과학기술의 중심지가 되는 것 혹은 과학기술의 미래를 놓치는 것"이면 안 된다'라는 의미이다. 주변의 내용을 살펴보면 이것이 소도시의 가치를 버리고 과학기술의 중심지로 변화하는 것 혹은 과학기술을 전혀 받아들이지 않는 것인 두 가지의 극단적인 선택안 중 하나를 고르면 안 되며, 소도시가 전면적으로가 아닌 점진적으로 전통적 산업들을 디지털화해 나가야 한다는 내용임을 알 수 있다. 따라서, 이를 '소도시들은 그곳의 다양한 과학기술직들을 창출함으로써 지역사회 가치를 지켜낼 수 있다'라고 표현한 ④번이 정답이다.

어휘 **delimit** v. 한계(범위)를 정하다 **population** n. 인구, 사람들

[23-25]

세계에서 가장 아름다운 건축물 중 하나인 인도에 있는 타지마할의 이야기에는 전설과 역사가 섞여 있다. 1631년, 무굴 황제인 Shah Jahan이 사랑했던 세 번째 아내인 Mumtaz Mahal이 열네 번째 아이를 낳다가 세상을 떠났다. 황제가 슬픔에서 벗어나게 되었을 때, 그는 아내를 위한 웅장한 묘지를 지었는데, 그것이 타지마할이다.

1632년부터 1653년까지, 흰 대리석의 무덤이 아그라에 있는 야무나강둑에 세워졌다. 2만 명의 장인들이 건축가들의 지휘 아래에서 대칭적인 돔 구조로 되어 있는 건물과 정원들을 만들었다. 그것은 세심하게 건축된 걸작이었다. 예를 들어, 중앙 건물의 측면에 있는 높은 탑이 살짝 밖으로 치우쳐있지만, 시각적인 착시로 인해 똑바로 세워져 있는 것처럼 보인다.

그 후에, 건물을 세운 장인들이 다시는 경쟁적인 건물을 지을 수 없도록 손을 잘라내고 눈을 파냈다는 이야기가 생겨났다.

다른 이야기에서는, 실의에 빠진 황제가 야무나강둑의 반대편에 블랙 타지마할이라는 타지마할과 똑같이 생긴 어두운 무덤을 건설했다고 전해진다. 이 이야기 중 아무것도 사실로 입증되지 않았다. 사실인 것은 황제가 자기 아들에 의해 말년을 아그라 요새에 있는 감옥에서 보냈다는 것인데, 그곳에서 그는 타지마할을 바라볼 수는 있었지만 다시는 들어갈 수 없었다.

beloved adj. 사랑하는 **emperor** n. 황제
give birth phr. 아이를 낳다
emerge from phr. ~에서 벗어나다
mourning n. 슬픔, 애도 **tomb** n. 무덤 **marble** n. 대리석
mausoleum n. 묘지 **bank** n. 둑 **artisan** n. 장인
architect n. 건축가 **assemble** v. 만들다, 조립하다
symmetrical adj. 대칭적인 **masterpiece** n. 걸작
flank v. 측면에 위치하다 **strike off** phr. 잘라내다
gouge out phr. 파내다, 도려내다
brooding adj. 침울한, 음울한 **substantiate** v. 입증하다
imprisoned adj. 수감된, 감금된 **gaze** v. 바라보다

23 [2019 한성대]

정답 ②

해석 ① 타지마할은 황제의 무덤이다.
② 주 건물 주변의 탑들은 수직으로 세워져 있는 것처럼 보인다.
③ 타지마할을 짓기 위해 장인들은 독립적으로 작업했다.
④ Mahal은 그의 아내를 기리기 위해 타지마할을 지었다.

해설 지문의 내용과 일치하는 것을 묻는 문제이다. 두 번째 문단의 마지막 문장인 the tall towers that flank the central building lean outward slightly but appear to be upright in a feat of optical trickery의 내용을 통해 주 건물 주변의 탑들은 수직으로 세워져 있는 것처럼 보인다는 것을 알 수 있다. 따라서 ②번이 지문의 내용과 일치한다.

오답 분석
① 황제가 아내를 위해 웅장한 묘지를 지었다고 했으므로, 타지마할을 황제의 무덤이라는 것은 지문의 내용과 다르다.
③ 2만 명의 장인들이 건축가들의 지휘 아래에서 건물과 정원들을 만들었다고 했으므로, 타지마할을 짓기 위해 장인들은 독립적으로 작업했다는 것은 지문의 내용과 다르다.
④ 아내를 기리기 위해 웅장한 묘지를 지은 황제의 이름은 Shah Jahan이라고 했으므로, Mahal은 그의 아내를 기리기 위해 타지마할을 지었다는 것은 지문의 내용과 다르다.

어휘 **vertically** adv. 수직으로 **independently** adv. 독립적으로
in honor of phr. ~를 기리기 위해

24 [2019 한성대]

정답 ③

해석 ① 색상 효과 ② 웅장한 무덤
③ 시각적인 착시 ④ Mumtaz Mahal

해설 지문의 빈칸을 채우는 문제이다. 빈칸이 포함된 문장에서 탑이 실제로는 밖으로 살짝 치우쳐 있지만, 똑바로 세워져 있는 것처럼 보인다고 설명하고 있으므로, 빈칸에는 실제로 그렇지 않은 것이 주변 환경으로 인해 그렇게 보이는 것에 대한 내용이 나오는 것이 적절하다. 따라서 '시각적인 착시'라고 한 ③번이 정답이다.

어휘 **optical** adj. 시각적인 **trickery** n. 착시

25 [2019 한성대]

정답 ②

해설 ① 이야기에 따르면, 장인들은 건물을 완성하고 나서 눈이 멀게 되었다.
② 이야기에 따르면, 블랙 타지마할이 야무나강 위에 세워졌다.
③ 블랙 타지마할에 대해 증명된 증거는 존재하지 않는다.
④ Shah Jahan은 아그라 요새에서 시간을 보냈다.

해설 지문의 내용과 일치하지 않는 것을 묻는 문제이다. ②번의 키워드인 Black Taj(블랙 타지마할)와 관련된 지문의 Black Taj(블랙 타지마할) 주변에서 블랙 타지마할이 야무나 강독의 반대편에 세워졌다고 했으므로, 블랙 타지마할이 야무나 강 위에 세워졌다는 것은 지문의 내용과 다르다. 따라서 ②번이 지문의 내용과 일치하지 않는다.

오답 분석
① Stories arose that afterward, the building's artisans had their hands struck off and their eyes gouged out so that they would never be able to raise a rival building을 통해 '이야기에 따르면, 장인들은 건물을 완성하고 나서 눈이 멀게 되었다'라는 것을 알 수 있다.
③ Neither of these stories has been substantiated를 통해 '블랙 타지마할에 대해 증명된 증거는 존재하지 않는다'는 것을 알 수 있다.
④ What is true is that the emperor spent his last years imprisoned by his own son in Agra Fort를 통해 'Shah Jahan은 아그라 요새에서 시간을 보냈다'는 것을 알 수 있다.

어휘 **blind** adj. 눈이 먼 **verify** v. 증명하다, 입증하다
evidence n. 증거

[26-28]

많은 분야들이 가상현실로 인해 그들의 분야가 크게 달라지고 있음을 발견할 것이다. 우선 하나의 예로, 교육자들은 지식을 전달할 광범위한 새로운 기회들을 제공받을 것이다. 향후 5년에서 10년 이내에 교사들은 교과서나 평면 스크린, 심지어는 교실 그 자체에서 완전히 벗어나, 몰입형 지도 및 학습 영역으로 나아갈 수 있게 할 것이다. 한 예를 들면, 역사를 공부하는 학생들은 세계 최대의 전쟁과 갈등의 중심지로 가서 승리의 책

략을 직접 경험하고 이해할 수 있다. 의대생들은 마치 그들이 혈구 크기인 것처럼 인체를 여행할 수 있는 기회를 제공받을 수 있으며, 정맥과 동맥 혹은 신경계가 어떻게 상호 연결되었는지에 대한 그들의 이해력을 쌓을 수 있다. 음악을 공부하는 학생들은 가상현실 오케스트라가 지역 공연장 또는 심지어는 시드니 오페라 하우스든 자신이 선택한 장소에서 새로운 작곡을 공연하는 것을 볼 수 있을 것이다. 표준 중국어를 공부하는 학생은 언젠가 현지 원어민들과 대화하고, 지역의 발음을 연습하며 베이징의 거리를 '걸을' 수 있게 될 것이다.

landscape n. 분야, 풍경 **alter** v. 달라지다, 변하다
virtual adj. 가상의 **immersive** adj. 몰입형의
epicenter n. 중심지, 핵심 **conflict** n. 갈등
machination n. 책략 **first-hand** adj. 직접 경험한
comprehension n. 이해 **vein** n. 정맥 **artery** n. 동맥
nerve system phr. 신경계 **interconnect** v. 상호 연결하다
perform v. 공연하다 **composition** n. 작곡, 작품
venue n. 장소 **Mandarin** n. 표준 중국어
converse v. 대화하다 **native** adj. 현지의
regional adj. 지역의 **pronunciation** n. 발음

26 (2020 상명대)

정답 ①

해석 ① 가상현실이 어떻게 교육을 변화시킬 수 있는가?
② 가상현실의 미래
③ 가상현실이 학생들에게 어떻게 도움을 주는가
④ 가상현실과 학생에 대한 사례 연구들
⑤ 오늘날의 몰입형 교육!

해설 지문의 제목을 묻는 문제이다. 지문 처음에서 우선 하나의 예로, 교육자들은 지식을 전달할 광범위한 새로운 기회들을 제공받을 것이며, 향후 5년에서 10년 이내에 교사들은 교과서나 평면 스크린, 심지어는 교실 그 자체에서 완전히 벗어나, 몰입형 지도 및 학습 영역으로 나아갈 수 있게 할 것이라고 하였으며, 이어지는 내용에서 가상현실이 역사, 의학, 음악, 언어 등의 교육방식에 어떤 변화가 있을지 설명하고 있다. 따라서 이 지문의 제목을 '가상현실이 어떻게 교육을 변화시킬 수 있는가?'라고 표현한 ①번이 정답이다.

27 (2020 상명대)

정답 ⑤

해석 ① ~에 대해 ② ~부터
③ ~에 ④ ~처럼
⑤ ~ 이내에

해설 지문의 빈칸을 채우는 문제이다. 지문의 빈칸이 있는 문장에서 향후 5년에서 10년이라는 미래의 특정 기간을 말하고 있으므로, 특정 기간을 나타내는 전치사가 나와야 적절하다는 것을 알 수 있다. 따라서 '~ 이내에'라고 한 ⑤번이 정답이다.

28 (2020 상명대)

정답 ⑤

해석 ① 중국어를 배우는 학생들
② 의사가 되기 위해 공부하는 학생들
③ 역사를 공부하는 학생들
④ 새로운 음악을 작곡하는 학생들
⑤ 발레를 배우는 학생들

해설 지문에서 언급되지 않은 예시를 파악하는 문제이다. 지문의 중간 부분부터 역사를 공부하는 학생들, 의대생들, 음악을 공부하는 학생들 그리고 표준 중국어를 공부하는 학생들을 예시로 들고 있으므로, 지문에서 언급되지 않은 예시는 '발레를 배우는 학생들'이다. 따라서 정답은 ⑤번이다.

어휘 **compose** v. 작곡하다

[29-32]

[A] 컴퓨터 기술의 발전은 과학자들이 AI에 있어서 엄청난 진보를 할 수 있게 해주었지만, 그런데도 여전히 인간의 뇌를 가상으로 복원하는 일은 도달하기 어려운 일이다. [B] 사람들은 인간의 행동을 하는 기계는 모습도 인간처럼 보여야 한다고 생각한다. [C] 예를 들어, 혼다는 2010년에 ASIMO라는 130cm 크기의 휴머노이드 로봇을 공개했다. Advanced Step in Innovative Mobility를 의미하는 ASIMO는 이동이 불편한 사람들이 일상적으로 평범한 일들을 수행하는 데 도움을 주기 위해 만들어졌다. ASIMO는 두 발로 걷고, 계단 같은 평평하지 않은 지역도 돌아다닐 수 있으며, 최대 시속 6km까지 낼 수 있다. 두 개의 카메라 "눈"을 가진, 이 로봇은 방향과 거리를 확인하고, 사람의 몸짓에 반응하며, 최대 10명까지의 사람을 인식하고 이름을 부를 수 있도록 프로그램되어 있다. [D] <u>과학에 대한 흥미를 유발하기 위해, ASIMO는 종종 대중 앞에 등장하게 되는데, 그럴 때마다 ASIMO는 춤을 추고, 그가 음성 명령을 이해할 수 있다는 것을 보여준다.</u>
하지만, 사람의 특징을 소유할 수 있는 기계를 만들 것이라는 전망은 많은 공포와 불안을 발생시키기도 했다. 1968년 출간된 Philip K. Dick의 *Do Androids Dream of Electric Sheep?*이라는 제목의 디스토피아 소설에서, 안드로이드는 인간의 외형을 하고 있고 인간의 기억을 이식받았지만, <u>공감 능력이 없는</u> 존재이다. 그들은 사람들 <u>대신에</u> 위험하고 어려운 일을 하도록 강요받는다. 그러다가 6명의 안드로이드가 반란을 시작하자, 현상금 사냥꾼들은 안드로이드를 추적하여 파괴할 것을 요청받는다. 이 소설은 몇 개의 질문을 하게 만드는데, "무엇이 인간과 기계를 구분하는가?"와 "자신을 인간이라 믿는 기계를 파괴하는 것은 윤리적인가?" 같은 질문들이다.

simulated adj. 가상의 **reconstruction** n. 복원
unattainable adj. 도달할 수 없는 **expect** v. 생각하다
stand for phr. ~을 의미하다 **bipedal** adj. 두 발로 걷는
terrain n. 지형 **ascertain** v. 확인하다
engender v. 발생시키다 **anxiety** n. 불안

dystopian	adj. 디스토피아의	implant	v. 이식하다
devoid of	phr. ~이 없는	empathy	n. 공감, 감정이입
rebellion	n. 반란	bounty hunter	phr. 현상금 사냥꾼
beg the question	phr. 질문을 하게 만들다		
distinguish	v. 구별하다	moral	adj. 도덕적인

29 [2020 한성대]

정답 ④

해설 지문의 흐름상 주어진 문장이 들어가기에 가장 적절한 위치를 고르는 문제이다. [D]의 앞 문장에서, 혼다가 공개한 휴머노이드 로봇인 ASIMO가 지닌 기능을 통해 할 수 있는 일을 설명하고 있으므로 [D]의 자리에 ASIMO가 때때로 대중 앞에 등장하여 과학에 대한 흥미를 유발한다는 내용의 주어진 문장이 들어가는 것이 자연스럽다. 따라서 ④번이 정답이다.

어휘 choreographed dance phr. 안무

30 [2020 한성대]

정답 ④

해석 ① 안드로이드가 도덕을 가지고 있다고 독자들을 설득하기 위해
② 공감 능력이 안드로이드의 가장 중요한 특징이라고 주장하기 위해
③ 인간이 아닌 지능에 관한 Philip K. Dick의 서술을 비판하기 위해
④ 무엇이 인간과 안드로이드를 구분하는지 지적하기 위해

해설 저자가 'but are devoid of empathy'를 언급한 이유에 대해 추론하는 문제이다. Philip K. Dick의 디스토피아 소설이 '무엇이 인간과 기계를 구분하는가?'와 같은 질문을 하게 만들었다고 했고 이 소설에서 묘사되는 안드로이드와 인간의 유일한 차이는 공감 능력의 유무이므로, 저자가 'but are devoid of empathy'를 언급한 이유를 무엇이 인간과 안드로이드를 구분하는지 지적하기 위함이라고 추론할 수 있다. 따라서 ④번이 정답이다.

어휘 morals n. 도덕   depiction n. 묘사
characteristic n. 특징

31 [2020 한성대]

정답 ①

해석 ① 사람들은 일반적으로 사람과 유사한 능력을 가진 기계는 사람과 닮은 외형을 가지고 있다고 생각한다.
② ASIMO의 디자인은 Philip K. Dick의 소설에 나오는 안드로이드의 디자인을 근간으로 하고 있다.
③ 이식된 인간의 기억은 사람과 ASIMO와 같은 로봇을 구분하는 중요한 요소이다.
④ Philip K. Dick가 가진 ASIMO의 제작에 대한 불안은 공감 능력을 지닌 안드로이드의 출현으로 인해 존재하게 되었다.

해설 지문의 내용과 일치하는 것을 묻는 문제이다. 지문의 첫 번째 문단에서, 사람들은 인간의 행동을 하는 기계는 모습도 인간처럼 보여야 한다고 생각한다고 했으므로, 사람들은 일반적으로 사람과 유사한 능력을 가진 기계가 사람과 닮은 외형을 가지고 있다고 생각한다는 것은 지문의 내용과 일치한다. 따라서 ①번이 정답이다.

오답 분석
② 지문의 첫 번째 문단에서 ASIMO는 130cm 크기의 휴머노이드라고 했고, 두 번째 문단에서, Philip K. Dick의 소설에 나오는 안드로이드는 인간과 똑같은 외형을 가지고 있다고 했으므로, ASIMO의 디자인이 Philip K. Dick 소설에 나오는 안드로이드의 디자인을 근간으로 하고 있다는 것은 지문의 내용과 다르다.
③ 지문의 두 번째 문단에서, Philip K. Dick의 소설 속 안드로이드는 인간의 외형을 하고, 인간의 기억을 이식받았지만, 공감 능력이 없는 존재이다. 여기에서 인간과 안드로이드를 구분하는 차이는 공감 능력의 유무이므로, 이식된 인간의 기억이 사람과 ASIMO 같은 로봇을 구분하는 중요한 요소라는 것은 지문의 내용과 다르다.
④ 공감 능력을 지닌 안드로이드가 출현했다는 내용은 지문에서 근거를 찾을 수 없고, Philip K. Dick이 ASIMO의 제작에 대해 불안을 느꼈다는 내용도 지문에서 찾아볼 수 없는 내용이므로, Philip K. Dick가 가진 ASIMO의 제작에 대한 불안은 공감 능력을 지닌 안드로이드의 출현으로 존재하게 되었다는 것은 지문의 내용과 다르다.

32 [2020 한성대]

정답 ③

해석 ① ~의 대신에
② ~의 대신에
③ ~의 희망을 가지고
④ ~의 대신에

해설 문맥상 빈칸에 적절하지 않은 것을 묻는 문제이다. 빈칸이 포함된 문장은 사람 대신 안드로이드가 위험하고 어려운 일을 하도록 강요받았다는 내용이므로, 빈칸에는 '~의 대신에'라는 의미가 들어가야 한다. in hopes of는 '~의 희망을 가지고'라는 의미이므로 ③번이 정답이다.

[33-34]

Strivr는 360도 카메라와 소프트웨어로 빠르게 만들어진 후 모든 직원들이 상점, 경기장 또는 어딘가 완전히 다른 곳에서 적용될 수 있는 실력을 기르는 것을 돕는 데 사용될 수 있는 개인이 원하는 대로 할 수 있는 가상 체험을 만들기 위해 회사들과 함께 일한다. Facebook 본사와 Menlo 공원의 붐비는 모

퉁이에 있는 Stanford 중간에 있는 Strivr는 요즘 축구의 범위를 훨씬 넘어서 새로운 분야로 진출했다. Walmart와 다양한 NFL과 다른 스포츠팀에 더하여, Strivr는 United Rentals, 두 곳의 자동차 제조 회사와 다수의 고객들과도 함께 일하고 있다. Walmart에서, 적어도 디지털 운영 부서의 선임 이사인 Brock McKeel은 이것이 도움이 된다고 생각한다. Brock McKeel은 그 회사가 세 가지 종류의 교육을 위해 약 187개의 직원 교육 센터에서 Strivr를 사용한다고 말하는데, 세 가지 교육은 블랙 프라이데이나 상점에서 시뮬레이션을 설정할 수 없는 비상사태와 같은 상황을 위해 준비하는 것, 고객 서비스를 배우는 것, 농산물이 어떻게 쌓이고 정리되어야 하는지와 같은 운영 방식을 가르치는 것이다. 미래에, Strivr는 더 많은 종류의 일자리에 초점을 맞추기를 원한다고 회사의 최고 기술 책임자인 Brian Meek이 말한다. Brian Meek은 공감과 이해력과 같은 소위 부드러운 기술들을 가르치는 것뿐만 아니라 위험한 상황을 어떻게 처리하는지에 대해 가상현실(VR)에서 직원들을 교육하는 것을 구상한다. Strivr는 또한 최근에 안전의 기본 원리를 포함하여 공사 현장에서 일하는 것이 어떤지를 보여주는 VR 체험을 만들기 위해 기술 대학과도 함께 일하고 있다. Meek은 그것이 곧 출시될 것이라고 말한다.

personalized adj. 개인이 원하는 대로 할 수 있는
virtual adj. (컴퓨터를 이용한) 가상의 **hone** v. 연마하다
playing field phr. 경기장, 운동장
somewhere adv. 어딘가에 **midway** adv. 중간에
headquarters n. 본사
branch out phr. (새로운 분야로) 진출하다 **director** n. 이사
emergency n. 비상사태 **operational** adj. 운영상의
stack v. 쌓다 **chief** adj. 최고의
envision v. 구상하다, 계획하다, 상상하다
virtual reality phr. 가상현실 **hazardous** adj. 위험한
so-called adj. 소위, 이른바 **empathy** n. 공감, 감정이입
hospitality n. 이해력, 수용력, 환대
construction site phr. 공사 현장 **basic** n. 기본 원리
roll out phr. (신상품을) 출시하다

33 [2019 명지대]

정답 ①

해석 ① VR 방식으로 사람들을 교육하기
② Strivr의 불안정한 미래
③ Walmart의 구조 작업에 온 Strivr
④ 위치와 VR 사용법 사이의 상관관계

해설 지문의 제목을 묻는 문제이다. 지문 초반에서 Strivr가 다른 회사들과 가상 체험을 만드는 일을 함께한다고 하고, 가상현실(VR)에서 직원들을 교육하는 것에 관한 이야기가 계속되고 있다. 따라서 이 지문의 제목을 'VR 방식으로 사람들을 교육하기'라고 표현한 ①번이 정답이다.

어휘 **uncertain** adj. 불안정한, 불확실한 **rescue** n. 구조 작업
correlation n. 상관관계, 연관성

34 [2019 명지대]

정답 ④

해석 ① 축구는 Strivr의 고객층에서 원래 큰 부분이다.
② Walmart는 상점에서 물품들을 어떻게 배열하는지를 가르치기 위해 Strivr를 사용한다.
③ Strivr는 직원들에게 위험한 상황들을 어떻게 처리하는지를 가르칠 수 있다.
④ Strivr 덕분에, 로봇은 이제 인간의 감정을 흉내 낼 수 있다.

해설 지문의 내용과 일치하지 않는 것을 묻는 문제이다. ④번의 Strivr 덕분에, 로봇은 이제 인간의 감정을 흉내 낼 수 있다는 것에 대해서는 언급되지 않았다. 따라서 ④번이 정답이다.

오답 분석
① 두 번째 문장 These days Strivr ~ has branched out far beyond football을 통해 '축구가 Strivr의 고객층에서 원래 큰 부분이다'라는 것을 알 수 있다.
② 다섯 번째 문장 He says the company uses Strivr in about 187 employee training centers, ~ and teaching operational stuff like how produce should be stacked and arranged를 통해 'Walmart가 상점에서 물품들을 어떻게 배열하는지를 가르치기 위해 Strivr를 사용한다'는 것을 알 수 있다.
③ 일곱 번째 문장 He envisions training employees in virtual reality (VR) on how to deal with hazardous situations ~ empathy and hospitality를 통해 'Strivr가 직원들에게 위험한 상황들을 어떻게 처리하는지를 가르칠 수 있다'는 것을 알 수 있다.

어휘 **customer base** phr. 고객층 **simulate** v. 흉내 내다

[35-37]

Fermat은 자신의 최단 시간의 원리를 바탕으로 광학에 관한 연구를 진행했는데, 최단 시간의 원리란 빛이 진행 과정의 가장 가까운 구간을 지나 가로지르는데 최소한의 시간이 걸리는 경로를 따른다는 것이다. Huygens는 빛이 원천으로부터 퍼져 나오고 그 원천 주위에 최초의 원천과 같이 빛을 전파하는 이차적 원천으로 구성된, 작은 구와 같은 것을 결과적으로 형성한다고 밝힘으로써, 현재 "하위헌스의 원리"라고 알려진 것의 초기 형태를 발전시켰다. 한편, Leibnitz는 전체 세계를 "모나드"라고 불리는 개체의 집합으로 보았는데, 모나드의 활력은 신에 의해 정해져서 이미 확립된 조화에 근거하여 다른 모나드를 인식하는 것에서 나오고, Leibnitz가 이 상호작용을 주로 광학적 용어들에서 생각해냈다는 것은 매우 분명하다. 이 견해 외에도, 모나드는 "창"이 없어서 Leibnitz의 관점에서 모든 물리적 상호작용은 사실 광학적 상호작용의 형언하기 어려운 결과에 지나지 않는다. Leibnitz의 일부 철학에서 매우 분명하게 드러나는 광학과 통신에의 몰두는 그의 철학 전체에 퍼져 있다. 그의 몰두는 Leibnitz의 가장 초기의 관념들 중 두 가지에서 중요한 역할을 하는데, 그 관념들은 *Characteristica Universalis*에서의 것, 즉 세계 공통의 과학 언어, 그리고

*Calculus Ratiocinator*에서의 것, 즉 논리적 계산법이다. 그 자체로는 불완전하지만, Calculus Ratiocinator는 현대의 수학적 논리의 직접적인 원형이다. 통신에 대한 개념들에 사로잡힌 Leibniz는 기계 계산이나 자동 장치에도 관심이 있었기 때문에 한 가지 이상의 방면에서 이지적인 선구자이다. 나의 관점은 Leibniz적인 것과는 거리가 매우 멀지만, 내가 관심을 갖는 문제들은 대부분 확실하게 Leibniz적이다. Leibniz의 계산기는 그가 생각하는 논리적 계산 논법인 컴퓨터 언어에 대한 그의 관심의 파생적 결과이자 완전한 인공 언어에 대한 그의 개념 확장일 뿐이었다.

> **further** v. 진행시키다 **optics** n. 광학
> **primitive** adj. 초기의 **sphere** n. 구
> **secondary** adj. 이차적인 **in turn** phr. 결과적으로
> **propagate** v. 전파하다 **lay down** phr. 정하다
> **preoccupation** n. 몰두 **subtle** adj. 이해하기 어려운
> **run through** phr. ~ 속으로 퍼지다 **calculus** n. 계산법
> **ancestor** n. 원형 **automaton** n. 자동 장치
> **offshoot** n. 파생적 결과 **indication** n. 조짐
> **aside** n. 혼잣말 **interfere** v. 방해하다

35 [2020 한국항공대]

정답 ①

해석 ① Fermat과 달리 Leibniz는 광학에 관심이 있었다.
② 모나드에 관한 Leibniz의 관념은 이미 형성된 신의 조화에 근거한다.
③ Leibniz에 따르면, 모나드는 광학적으로 상호 작용을 한다.
④ Leibniz 이후에, 일부 과학자들은 기계 계산을 연구했다.

해설 지문의 내용과 일치하지 않는 것을 묻는 문제이다. ②번의 키워드인 Ulike Fermat(Fermat과 달리)과 관련된 지문의 Fermat 주변에서 Fermat은 자신의 최단 시간의 원리를 바탕으로 광학에 관한 연구를 진행했다고 했으므로 Fermat과 달리 Leibniz는 광학에 관심이 있었다는 것은 지문의 내용과 다르다. 따라서 ①번이 지문의 내용과 일치하지 않는다.

오답분석
② Leibnitz, in the meantime, saw the whole world as a collection of beings called "monads" whose activity consisted in the perception of one another on the basis of a pre-established harmony laid down by God을 통해 '모나드에 관한 Leibniz의 관념은 이미 형성된 신의 조화에 근거한다'는 것을 알 수 있다.
③ the monads had no "windows," so that in his view all mechanical interaction really becomes nothing more than a subtle consequence of optical interaction을 통해 'Leibniz에 따르면, 모나드는 광학적으로 상호 작용을 한다'는 것을 알 수 있다.
④ Leibnitz is an intellectual ancestor in more than one way, for he was also interested in machine computation and in automata를 통해 'Leibniz 이후에, 일부 과학자들은 기계 계산을 연구했다'라는 것을 알 수 있다.

어휘 **gift** n. (천부적인) 재능 **observation** n. 관찰
combination n. 결합, 조합
abstain from phr. ~를 삼가다

36 [2020 한국항공대]

정답 ③

해석 ① 논리적 계산 논법의 불완전함
② 컴퓨터 언어의 불안정한 특성들
③ 광학과 컴퓨터 언어 간의 관계
④ 자동 장치에 있어서의 Leibnitz의 부정적인 영향

해설 지문의 제목을 묻는 문제이다. 지문 전반적으로 Leibnitz의 관점에서 본 모든 물리적 상호작용은 광학적 상호작용의 결과이며, 그 개념은 논리적 계산 논법인 컴퓨터 언어에 대한 관심의 파생적 결과이자 완전한 인공 언어에 대한 개념의 확장이라고 말하고 있다. 따라서 이 지문의 제목을 '광학과 컴퓨터 언어 간의 관계'라고 표현한 ③번이 정답이다.

어휘 **irreversible** adj. 뒤집을 수 없는

37 [2020 한국항공대]

정답 ②

해석 ① 따라서, 외부 세계와의 관계에 의해 통제되는 기계는 우리와 공존하고 이전부터 그래왔다.
② 따라서, 그의 계산기에서도 Leibnitz의 몰두는 대부분 언어적이고 통신적이었다.
③ 따라서, 효율적으로 사는 것은 충분한 정보를 가지고 사는 것이다.
④ 따라서, 의사소통과 통제는 인간의 영적 생활의 본질에 속한다.

해설 주어진 지문의 뒤에 올 내용을 고르는 문제이다. 지문의 마지막 문장에서 Leibnitz의 계산기는 컴퓨터 언어에 대한 관심의 파생적 결과이자 완전한 인공언어에 대한 개념 확장이라고 했으므로, 'Leibnitz의 계산기도 인공언어와 같은 성질을 가지고 있을 것이다'는 맥락의 내용이 지문의 뒤에 나올 것임을 알 수 있다. 따라서 ②번이 정답이다.

어휘 **adequate** adj. 충분한 **inner life** phr. 영적 생활

[38-40]

> 어떤 여성들은 임신과 출산을 즐겁고, 자연스럽고, 성취감을 주는 일로 경험하는 반면, 다른 여성들은 임신으로 자궁 속에 아이가 살면서 생기는 신체적 부담으로 인한 공포와 출산의 잠재적인 잔혹성에 의해서 움츠러드는 자신을 발견하게 된다. 일부 여성들은 피와 땀, 눈물을 필수적이고 피할 수 없는 삶의 일

부로 여길지도 모른다. 하지만 다른 어떤 여성들은 이 과정을 "야만적인" 것으로 보는 다소 관대하지 않은 관점으로 생각한다. 대다수는 이 (A)두 입장 사이에서 흔들리거나, 그렇지 않으면 중간 사이의 어딘가에 위치한다. 임신의 "당연함"에 대한 문제에서 누군가의 입장이 무엇이건 간에, 인공 자궁 기술의 발전이 이 논의를 급격하게 바꾸리라는 것은 부인할 수 없다. 먼저, 인공 자궁 기술이 제공하는 치료상의 이점이 있다. 임신이 위험할 수 있는 여성들은 태아를 인공 자궁으로 옮길 수 있을 것이고, 그렇게 함으로써 태아의 성장이 여성의 신체적 건강에 거의 지장을 주지 않은 채 유지될 수 있게끔 만들 수 있다. 마찬가지로, 조산의 위험에 놓인 태아들도 인공 자궁으로 옮겨져 그들에게 필요한 성장을 완료할 수 있다. 피와 땀, 눈물은 임신이라는 과정에서 본질적인 것이 아니게 될 수도 있는 것이다. 두 번째로, 이 기술은 여성에게 중요한 사회적 장점을 준다. 인공 자궁은 (B)번식 과정에서의 심한 성적 차별이 반영된 역할을 무효화시킴으로써, 현재의 여성에 대한 억압을 보장하던 주요한 여건을 제거할 수 있을 것이다. 그러나 만약 태아가 인공 자궁에서 성장하게 되면, 여성은 마침내 자유롭게 그들의 흥미와 욕구를 추구할 수 있을 것이다.

pregnancy n. 임신 **childbirth** n. 출산
recoil v. 움찔하다 **brutality** n. 잔혹성
forgiving adj. 관대한 **barbaric** adj. 야만적인
oscillate v. 흔들리다 **naturalness** n. 당연함
deny v. 부인하다 **artificial-womb** n. 인공 자궁
therapeutic adj. 치료의 **fetus** n. 태아
fetal adj. 태아의 **premature birth** phr. 조산
eliminate v. 제거하다 **ensure** v. 보장하다
oppression n. 압박 **neutralize** v. 무효화하다
gendered adj. 성별을 반영한

38 (2020 한국외대)

정답 ④

해석 ① 집안일로부터 여성의 해방
② 여성의 정신적 신체적 건강
③ 계획적인 임신과 신체적 건강
④ 인공 자궁 기술의 잠재적인 이점

해설 지문의 주제를 묻는 문제이다. 지문 전체적으로 인공 자궁 기술이 갖는 두 가지 장점에 관해 설명하고 있다. 첫 번째는 인공 자궁 기술이 여성의 신체적 건강에 해롭지 않게 태아가 성장할 수 있다는 것이고, 두 번째는 이 기술이 여성에게 사회적 혜택을 주리라는 것이다. 따라서 이 지문의 제목을 '인공 자궁 기술의 잠재적인 이점'이라고 표현한 ④번이 정답이다.

어휘 **liberation** n. 해방

39 (2020 한국외대)

정답 ④

해석 ① 인공 자궁에 관한 찬반양론
② 임신에 대한 잔혹하고 두려운 관점
③ 인공 자궁과 생체 자궁의 지지자들
④ 임신과 출산에 관한 긍정적인 관점과 부정적인 관점

해설 밑줄 친 two positions의 의미를 추론하는 문제이다. 지문의 두 번째 문장과 세 번째 문장에서, 일부 여성들은 임신이라는 과정에서 피와 땀, 눈물은 필수적이고 피할 수 없는 삶의 일부로 여기고, 또 다른 어떤 여성들은 임신 과정에서의 피와 땀, 눈물을 야만적인 것으로 바라본다고 했다. 따라서 밑줄 친 two positions의 의미를 '임신과 출산에 관한 긍정적인 관점과 부정적인 관점'이라고 표현한 ④번이 정답이다.

어휘 **pros and cons** phr. 찬반양론 **proponent** n. 지지자

40 (2020 한국외대)

정답 ①

해석 ① 번식을 위해 여성들에게 가해지는 사회적 압력
② 분만과 양육의 건강과 관련된 위험
③ 여성에 대한 자녀 양육 요구
④ 여성에 대한 직장 내 장애물

해설 밑줄 친 부분의 의미를 추론하는 문제이다. 밑줄 친 'the heavily gendered roles played in reproduction'은 '번식 과정에서의 심한 성적 차별이 반영된 역할'이라는 의미이다. 주변의 내용을 살펴보면 이와 같은 임신과 출산 과정에서 여성에게만 부과되는 역할이 여성에 대한 사회적 억압을 보장하는 주요한 여건과 관계되어 있음을 알 수 있다. 따라서 ①번이 정답이다.

[41-44]

[D] 일부 평범한 선글라스는 당신의 눈을 해로운 자외선, 청색광, 그리고 반사광에 노출해 당신의 시력을 흐리게 만들 수 있다. [A] 또한 당신이 잘 볼 수 있도록 빛을 가려주기도 한다. [C] 하지만 이제, NASA의 제트 추진 연구소의 과학자들이 진행한 독자 연구는 태양 복사광의 해로운 영향으로부터 인간의 시력을 보호하는 데 도움을 주는 획기적인 기술을 내놓았다. [B] 이 뛰어난 렌즈 기술은 NASA의 과학자들이 눈을 보호하기 위한 뛰어난 방법을 찾기 위해 자연을 관찰했을 때, 특히 고도로 예리한 시각을 가지고 있다고 알려진 독수리의 눈을 연구함으로써 최초로 발견되었다.

이 발견은 현재 Eagle Eyes라고 알려진 것을 만들었다. Eagle Eyes는 지금까지 만들어진 것 중에 가장 진보된 눈 보호 기술을 특징으로 한다. 그것은 삼중 편광 필터를 제공하여 청색광으로부터 눈을 보호하는 효과를 더한 것뿐만 아니라 장파장과 중파장의 자외선을 99.9퍼센트 막아준다. Eagle

Eyes는 이러한 놀라운 기술로 우주 인증 프로그램에서 공식적인 인증을 <u>획득한</u> 유일한 광학 기술이다.

darken v. 어둡게 하다 **superior** adj. 뛰어난
specifically adv. 특히 **acuity** n. 예리함
independent research phr. 독자 연구
conduct v. (실험이나 연구를) 하다
ground-breaking adj. 획기적인 **eyesight** n. 시력, 시야
solar adj. 태양의 **radiation** n. (열에너지의) 복사
obscure v. 흐리게 하다 **UV** n. 자외선
reflective adj. 반사되는 **advanced** adj. 진보한
triple-filter n. 삼중 필터 **polarization** n. 편광
UVA n. 장파장 자외선 **UVB** n. 중파장 자외선
optic adj. 광학의 **recognition** n. 인정, 인증
certification n. 인증 **remarkable** adj. 놀라운

41 [2019 한성대]

정답 ①

해설 [A], [B], [C], [D]의 적절한 순서를 파악하는 문제이다. [A]와 [B]는 이전에 나온 내용을 지칭하는 지시사인 they와 this로 시작하며, [C]는 접속사 but으로 시작하기 때문에 앞에 다른 문장이 없이 시작할 수 없다. 문장 [D]가 먼저 와야 한다. 그다음에 [A]에서 눈에 해를 끼칠 수 있는 일부 선글라스와 다르게 보는 것을 도와주는 선글라스도 있다고 설명하고, 그다음에 [C]에서 NASA의 제트 추진 연구소에서 획기적인 기술을 만들었다고 설명하고, 마지막으로 [B]에서 이 뛰어난 기술이 나올 수 있게 된 배경에 관해 설명하는 것이 자연스럽다. 따라서 주어진 지문 다음에 이어질 순서는 ① [D] — [A] — [C] — [B]다.

42 [2019 한성대]

정답 ①

해설 ① 훌륭한 렌즈 기술 ② 태양 복사광
③ 청색광 보호 ④ NASA의 과학자들

해설 지문의 제목을 묻는 문제이다. 지문의 첫 번째 문단에서는 NASA의 과학자들이 독수리의 눈을 보고 태양 복사광의 해로운 영향으로부터 눈을 보호할 수 있는 뛰어난 렌즈 기술을 만들었다고 설명하고 있으며, 두 번째 문단에서는 이 기술을 사용한 Eagle Eyes가 눈에 해로운 빛을 막아주며, 우주 인증 프로그램에서 인증을 <u>획득한</u> 유일한 광학 기술이라고 설명하고 있다. 따라서 지문의 제목을 '훌륭한 렌즈 기술'이라고 표현한 ①번이 정답이다.

어휘 **splendid** adj. 훌륭한

43 [2019 한성대]

정답 ①

해석 ① 일부 선글라스는 위험할 수 있다.
② 독수리는 시각적 예리함이 부족하다.
③ Eagle Eyes는 모든 빛을 완벽하게 차단한다.
④ 청색광은 자외선보다 더 해롭다.

해설 지문의 내용과 일치하는 것을 묻는 문제이다. 밑줄 친 ⓓ의 문장인 Some ordinary sunglasses can obscure your vision by exposing your eyes to harmful UV rays, blue light, and reflective glare의 내용을 통해 일부 선글라스는 위험할 수 있다는 것을 알 수 있다. 따라서 ①번이 지문의 내용과 일치한다.

오답 분석
② 뛰어난 렌즈 기술이 특히 고도로 예리한 시각을 가지고 있다고 알려진 독수리의 눈을 NASA의 과학자들이 연구함으로써 최초로 발견되었다고 했으므로, 독수리는 시각적 예리함이 부족하다는 것은 지문의 내용과 다르다.
③ Eagle Eyes는 삼중 편광 필터를 제공하여 청색광으로부터 눈을 보호하는 효과를 더한 것뿐만 아니라 장파장과 중파장의 자외선을 99.9퍼센트 막아준다고 했으므로, Eagle Eyes는 모든 빛을 완벽하게 차단한다는 것은 지문의 내용과 다르다.
④ 일부 평범한 선글라스는 눈을 해로운 자외선, 청색광, 그리고 반사광에 노출해 시력을 흐리게 만들 수 있다고는 했지만, 청색광이 자외선보다 더 해로운지는 알 수 없다.

44 [2019 한성대]

정답 ③

해설 지문의 흐름상 빈칸에 들어갈 수 없는 것을 고르는 문제이다. 삽입될 문장에 들어갈 선택지를 살펴보면 ③번의 has qualified를 제외하고 모두 '얻다, 받다, 획득하다'의 의미를 담고 있는 단어들이다. 따라서 ③번이 정답이다.

어휘 **garner** v. 얻다, 모으다 **qualify** v. 자격을 주다
attain v. 획득하다

[45-46]

표현주의 건축 양식을 특징짓기는 특히 어렵다. 표현주의에 관해 말하자면, Ian Boyd Whyte는 "이 운동은 종종 그것이 무엇인지보다 이성주의자, 기능주의자 등과 같이 그것이 아닌 측면에서 정의되어왔다". 어떤 명확한 정의의 (A)결여에도 불구하고, 그 운동의 관심사는 분명하다. 관심사는 고뇌의 표현, 내적 경험의 상징적 표현을 지지하여 객관성과 사실주의에 대한 경시, 추상적 개념, 그리고 모더니즘에 관하여 중요한 위치이다. 주관적 혹은 감정적 영향으로 현실을 왜곡하려는 욕망은 모든 예술 형태에서 나타난다. 모든 예술의 기저가 되는 목적은 새로우면서 공상적인 차원을 달성하는 것인데, 이는 표현주

의가 다른 대부분의 아방가르드 운동보다 더 추구했던 것이다. 그림 예술에서, 그 운동은 강렬한 색, 역동적인 구도, 형식적 왜곡, 그리고 표현을 향한 열망을 통해 생생한 반응을 포착하는 데 집중했다. (B)반면에, 건축 양식에서 표현주의는 형태, 추상적 개념, 현대풍 이성주의적 이상에 대한 거부, 그리고 전통 고전 양식의 틀을 강조했다. 되풀이되는 형식적 테마들은 종종 동굴, 크리스털, 바위, 그리고 유기적이고 비기하학적 형태와 같은 (C)자연 현상에 영감을 받은 것이었다. 기하학적인 것보다 유기적인 것에 관심을 둔 이유는 움직임과 감정, 분위기, (D)고전주의, 그리고 전면적 변화가 있는 건축 양식을 만들어내기 위해서였다. 이것은 미학적으로 보기 좋은 소재를 재현하는 것보다 주관적 해석의 표현을 장려했다. 디자인 제약의 감소는 바로 이전의 (건축 양식의) 해체가 불가피함을 나타냈다.

expressionist adj. 표현주의의
architecture n. 건축 양식, 건축학
characterize v. 특징짓다   rationalist n. 이성주의자
functionalist n. 기능주의자   patent adj. 분명한
subordination n. 경시   objectivity n. 객관성
abstraction n. 추상적 개념   impulse n. 욕망
distort v. 왜곡하다   subjective adj. 주관적인
exhibit v. 나타내다   visionary adj. 공상적인
dimension n. 차원
avant-garde adj. 아방가르드의, 전위적인
pictorial adj. 그림의   composition n. 구도, 구성
repudiation n. 거부, 거절
classical adj. 고전 양식의, 고전의
recurring adj. 되풀이되는   organic adj. 유기적인
geometric adj. 기하학적인   ambiance n. 분위기
reproduction n. 재현, 재생산
aesthetically adv. 미학적으로   restraint n. 제한, 억제
dismantle v. 해체하다, 없애다

45 2019 중앙대

정답 ①

해석 ① 표현주의 건축 양식의 특징과 주관성
② 예술 복고주의 양식의 대변동
③ 예술계에 있어서 선례의 권위의 중요성
④ 표현주의의 역사적인 궤적: 과거와 미래

해설 지문의 제목을 묻는 문제이다. 지문 첫 번째 문단에서 표현주의 건축 양식을 특징짓기는 어렵지만, 주관적 혹은 감정적 영향으로 현실을 왜곡하려는 욕망은 표현주의가 다른 대부분의 아방가르드 운동보다 더 추구했던 것이라고 설명하고 있다. 따라서 이 지문의 제목을 '표현주의 건축 양식의 특징과 주관성'이라고 표현한 ①번이 정답이다.

어휘 subjectivity n. 주관성   upheaval n. 대변동
revivalist n. 복고주의자   precedent n. 선례, 전례
authority n. 권위   trajectory n. 궤적, 궤도

46 2019 중앙대

정답 ④

해설 지문의 흐름에 적합하지 않은 것을 고르는 문제이다. 지문은 표현주의 건축 양식이 특징짓기는 어렵지만, 고뇌의 표현, 내적 경험의 상징적 표현, 추상적 개념, 모더니즘에서의 위치 등에 관심사를 두었다는 내용이므로, (A) 표현주의 건축 양식에 대한 명확한 정의의 '결여', (B) 그림 예술에서의 표현주의 특징에 대비되는 건축 양식에서의 표현주의, (C) 유기적이고 비기하학적 형태와 같은 '자연 현상'에 영감을 받은 표현주의 건축 양식에 대한 내용은 모두 지문의 흐름에 적합하다. 그러나 (D)는 표현주의 건축 양식이 '고전주의'를 만들어내려 했다는 내용이므로, 모더니즘에 관하여 중요한 위치를 관심사로 삼는 표현주의 건축 양식의 특징에 적합하지 않다. 따라서 ④번이 정답이다.

[47-50]

[A] 뫼비우스의 띠라고 불리는 물체는 1858년 독일의 수학자인 어거스트 뫼비우스에 의해 발견된 이래로 환경 운동가, 예술가, 기술자, 수학자, 그 외에도 많은 이들의 마음을 사로잡았다. 뫼비우스는 꼭짓점, 가장자리, 납작한 면으로 구성된 입체도형인 다면체의 기하학적 이론에 관한 연구를 하면서 뫼비우스의 띠를 접하게 된 것으로 보인다. (A) 뫼비우스의 띠는 종이 띠를 가지고, 띠를 홀수만큼 반 비틀고 나서, 양 끝을 테이프로 결합하여 고리를 형성하여 만들어질 수 있다. 만약 당신이 연필을 가지고 띠의 중앙을 따라 선을 그리면, 당신은 그 선이 고리의 양면을 따라 이어지는 것을 확인할 것이다.

[B] 한 면만 가진 물체라는 개념은 네덜란드의 그래픽 디자이너 M.C. Escher와 같은 예술가들에게 영감을 주었는데, Escher의 목판화 "Möbius Strip Ⅱ"는 붉은 개미들이 차례로 뫼비우스의 띠를 따라 기어가는 것을 보여준다. (B) 뫼비우스의 띠는 단 하나의 놀라운 특성 그 이상을 지니고 있다. 예를 들어, 가위를 가지고 당신이 그렸던 선을 따라 띠를 반으로 가르는 것을 시도해 보라. 당신에게 두 개의 더 작은 한 면만 가진 뫼비우스의 띠가 아니라, 그 대신 하나의 긴 두 개의 면을 가진 고리가 남겨지는 것을 발견하고 깜짝 놀랄 수도 있다.

[C] (C) 뫼비우스의 띠가 확실히 시각적인 매력을 갖고 있기는 하지만, 그것의 가장 큰 영향은 수학에서였는데, 위상기하학이라고 불리는 전 분야의 발달에 박차를 가하는 데 도움을 주었다. 위상기하학자는 물체가 이동되고, 구부러지고, 늘려지거나 비틀어질 때, 절단하거나 조각을 함께 붙이지 않아도 보존되는 물체의 특성을 연구한다. 예를 들어, 뒤얽힌 한 쌍의 초소형 헤드폰은 위상기하학적 의미에서 얽히지 않은 헤드폰과 같은 것인데, 이는 한 물체에서 다른 물체로 변하는 것이 오직 이동, 구부림, 그리고 비틀림만을 필요로 하기 때문이다. 위상기하학적으로 같은 또 다른 물체의 쌍은 커피잔과 도넛이다. (D) 두 물체

에는 모두 하나의 구멍만 있기 때문에, 늘림과 구부림만을 통해 한 물체가 다른 것으로 변형될 수 있다. 물체에 있는 구멍의 수는 절단과 붙임을 통해서만 변형될 수 있는 특성이다. 이 특성은 물체의 "종수"라고 불리는데, 도넛은 하나의 구멍을 가진 반면 한 쌍의 초소형 헤드폰에는 구멍이 없기 때문에, 우리가 한 쌍의 초소형 헤드폰과 도넛은 위상기하학적으로 다르다고 주장할 수 있도록 한다. [D] 유감스럽게도, 전형적인 실리콘 의식 팔찌처럼, 뫼비우스의 띠와 두 개의 면을 가진 고리는 둘 다 하나의 구멍을 가지고 있는 것처럼 보이기 때문에, 이 특성은 적어도 위상기하학자의 관점에서 봤을 때 그 둘을 구별하기에 불충분하다. 그 대신에, 뫼비우스의 띠를 두 개의 면을 가진 고리로부터 구별 짓는 특성은 <u>가향성</u>이라고 불린다. 구멍의 개수처럼, 한 물체의 가향성은 절단이나 붙임을 통해서만 바뀔 수 있다. (E) 속이 다 비치는 표면에 당신 자신에게 메모를 작성하고 나서, 그 표면 주위를 걷는다고 상상해 보아라. 만약 당신이 산책에서 돌아왔을 때 그 메모를 항상 읽을 수 있다면, 그 표면은 가향적이다. 비가향적 표면에서, 당신은 산책에서 돌아와 보니, 당신이 적었던 말이 명백히 거울에 비치는 상으로 변해서 오른쪽에서 왼쪽으로만 읽힐 수 있다는 것을 발견할 것이다. 두 개의 면을 가진 고리에서, 그 메모는 당신의 행로가 어디였든지 간에 항상 같은 것을 나타낼 것이다. 두 개의 면을 가진 고리는 가향적인 반면, 뫼비우스의 띠는 비가향적이기 때문에, 이것들은 위상기하학적으로 서로 다르다.

encounter v. 접하다, 마주치다   polyhedra n. 다면체
solid figure phr. 입체도형   compose v. 구성하다
vertex n. 꼭짓점   inspire v. 영감을 주다
woodcut n. 목판화   crawl v. 기어가다
preserve v. 보존하다   tangled adj. 뒤얽힌
topological adj. 위상기하학의   insufficient adj. 불충분한
tell apart phr. 구별하다   apparently adv. 명백히

47 [2019 아주대]

정답 ①

해석 ① 뫼비우스 띠와 한 면만 가진 다른 물체들의 수학적 의미
② 한 면만 가진 물체와 두 면을 가진 물체 간의 결정적인 차이점들
③ 뫼비우스 띠의 학문적 유용성
④ 뫼비우스 띠 발견의 뜻밖의 결과
⑤ 뫼비우스 띠와 한 면만 가진 다른 물체들의 구별되는 특징

해설 지문의 제목을 묻는 문제이다. 지문 전체적으로 한 면만 가진 물체인 뫼비우스의 띠를 소개하며, 이것이 수학, 특히 위상기하학 발달에 영향을 주었다고 설명하고 있다. 따라서 이 지문의 제목을 '뫼비우스 띠와 한 면만 가진 다른 물체들의 수학적 의미'라고 표현한 ①번이 정답이다.

어휘 implication n. 의미, 영향   usability n. 유용성
unexpected adj. 뜻밖의
distinguishing adj. 다른 것과 구별되는

48 [2019 아주대]

정답 ①

해석 ① 변형되는   ② 일치되는
③ 수행되는   ④ 미리 형성되는
⑤ 열 성형되는

해설 지문의 빈칸을 채우는 문제이다. [C] 문단 세 번째 문장에서 위상기하학적으로 같은 또 다른 물체의 쌍은 커피잔과 도넛이라고 했으므로, 빈칸에는 늘림과 구부림만을 통해 커피 또는 도넛이 어떻게 되는지에 대한 내용이 나와야 적절하다는 것을 알 수 있다. 따라서 '변형되는'이라고 한 ①번이 정답이다.

어휘 deform v. 변형시키다   conform v. 일치시키다
preform v. 미리 형성하다   thermoform v. 열성형하다

49 [2019 아주대]

정답 ③

해석 ① 두 면을 가진 고리는 가향적이다.
② 한 무리의 물체의 "종수"가 될 수 있다.
③ 물체를 비트는 것은 물체의 가향성에 영향을 미칠 수 있다.
④ 그것은 주로 위상기하학 분야에서 조사되어왔다.
⑤ 그것은 뫼비우스 띠로부터 실리콘 의식 팔찌를 구별 지을 수 있다.

해설 '가향성'에 대해 사실이 아닌 것을 파악하는 문제이다. [D] 문단의 세 번째 문장에서 구멍의 개수처럼, 한 물체의 가향성은 절단이나 붙임을 통해서만 바뀔 수 있다고 했으므로, '가향성'에 대해 사실이 아닌 것은 '물체를 비트는 것은 물체의 가향성에 영향을 미칠 수 있다'는 것이다. 따라서 정답은 ③번이다.

어휘 investigate v. 조사하다   distinguish v. 구별 짓다

50 [2019 아주대]

정답 ③

해설 지문의 흐름상 주어진 문장이 들어가기에 가장 적절한 위치를 고르는 문제이다. (C)의 뒤 문장에서 위상기하학자는 물체가 이동되고, 구부러지고, 늘려지거나 비틀어질 때 절단하거나 조각을 함께 붙이지 않아도 보존되는 물체의 특성을 연구한다고 했으므로, (C) 자리에 뫼비우스의 띠가 위상기하학과는 어떤 관계인지 설명하는 주어진 문장 '뫼비우스의 띠가 확실히 시각적인 매력을 갖고 있기는 하지만, 그것의 가장 큰 영향은 수학에서였는데, 위상기하학이라고 불리는 전 분야의 발달에 박차를 가하는 데 도움을 주었다'가 들어가야 글의 흐름이 자연스럽게 연결된다. 따라서 ③번이 정답이다.

어휘 appeal n. 매력, 호소   spur v. 박차를 가하다

[51-52]

나는 내가 언제 처음으로 특이점 시대를 알아차렸는지 잘 모르겠다. 나는 특이점 시대를 알아차린 것이 혁신적인 자각이었다고 말해야 할 것 같다. 내가 컴퓨터 및 관련 기술에 몰두했던 약 반세기 동안, 나는 내가 목격했던 여러 수준의 반복되는 대변동의 의미와 목적을 이해하기 위한 시도를 했다. 서서히, 나는 21세기 전반기에 어렴풋이 나타난 변혁적 사건을 알아차리게 되었다. 우주의 블랙홀이 사상의 지평선으로 물질과 에너지를 급속히 이동시키면서 그것들의 패턴을 크게 바꾸는 것처럼, 우리 미래에 곧 닥칠 이 특이점 시대는 점차 모든 규칙과 성적 특질부터 정신성까지 이르는 인간 생활의 양상을 변형시키고 있다. 그렇다면, 특이점 시대란 무엇인가? 특이점 시대는 기술 변화 속도가 아주 빠르고, 기술 변화의 영향이 너무 강해서, 인간 생활이 돌이킬 수 없을 정도로 변형될 미래 시대이다. 이 시대는 이상적이지도 음울하지도 않지만, 우리가 사업 모델부터 죽음 그 자체를 포함하는 인간 생애 주기에 이르기까지, 삶에 의미를 부여하기 위해 필요로 하는 개념을 변형시킬 것이다. 특이점 시대를 이해하는 것은 우리의 과거와 미래 결과의 중요성에 대한 관점을 바꿀 것이다. 진정으로 특이점 시대를 이해하는 것은 전반적인 삶과 자신의 특정한 삶에 대한 한 사람의 관점을 본질적으로 변화시킨다. 나는 특이점 시대를 이해하고 자신의 삶에 미치는 특이점 시대의 영향을 되돌아본 사람을 "특이점 주의자"로 여긴다.

나는 많은 목격자들이 내가 수확 가속의 법칙(생물학적 진화의 연속처럼 기술적 발전에서 일어나는 발전 속도의 고유 가속)이라고 불렀던 것의 명백한 영향을 선뜻 받아들이지 않는 이유를 알 수 있다. 어쨌든, 바로 내 앞에 있던 것을 알아차릴 수 있게 되는 데 40년이 걸렸으며, 나는 여전히 그것의 모든 결과에 완전히 만족스럽다고 말할 수 없다.

곧 닥칠 특이점 시대의 <u>기저가 되는</u> 핵심 개념은 인간이 만든 기술의 변화 속도가 <u>빨라지고</u> 있고 기술의 세력이 기하급수적인 속도로 <u>확장되고</u> 있다는 것이다. 기하급수적 발전은 믿을 수 없다. 발전은 거의 알아차릴 수 없게 시작되고 나서 갑자기 예상치 못하게 격렬해지는데, 예상치 못하다는 것은 즉, 만약 한 사람이 지난 발전되어온 경로를 뒤따르는 데 신경 쓰지 않는다면 그럴 것이다.

progressive adj. 혁신적인 awakening n. 자각
immerse v. 몰두시키다 continual adj. 반복되는
upheaval n. 대변동, 격변 transform v. 변형시키다
loom v. 어렴풋이 나타나다 alter v. 바꾸다
accelerate v. 빠르게 하다, 가속하다
event horizon phr. 사상의 지평선(블랙홀의 외연(外緣))
impending adj. 곧 닥칠, 임박한 sexuality n. 성적 특질
spirituality n. 정신성
irreversibly adv. 돌이킬 수 없을 정도로
utopian adj. 이상적인 dystopian adj. 음울한
epoch n. 시대 perspective n. 관점, 시각
significance n. 중요성 ramification n. 결과, 영향
inherently adv. 본질적으로
reflect on phr. ~을 되돌아보다 implication n. 영향, 의미
inherent adj. 고유의 evolution n. 발전, 진화
continuation n. 연속 consequence n. 결과
exponential adj. 기하급수적인
deceptive adj. 믿을 수 없는
imperceptibly adv. 알아차릴 수 없게
explode v. 갑자기 ~하다, 폭발하다 fury n. 격렬
trajectory n. 지나온 경로

51 [2019 중앙대]

정답 ③

해석 ① 빨라지는 — 기저가 되는 — 확장되는
② 빨라지는 — 확장되는 — 기저가 되는
③ 기저가 되는 — 빨라지는 — 확장되는
④ 기저가 되는 — 확장되는 — 빨라지는

해설 빈칸에 들어갈 내용을 묻고 있다. 지문의 두 번째 문단 처음에서, 특이점 시대는 기술 변화 속도가 아주 빠르고, 기술 변화의 영향이 너무 강해서 인간 생활이 변형될 미래 시대라고 했으므로, 빈칸에는 특이점 시대의 핵심 개념에 대한 내용이 나와야 적절하다는 것을 알 수 있다. 따라서 첫 번째 빈칸에는 '기저가 되는'이라는 의미의 underlying, 두 번째 빈칸에는 '빨라지는'이라는 의미의 accelerating, 세 번째 빈칸에는 '확장되는'이라는 의미의 expanding이 들어가는 것이 자연스럽다. 따라서 ③번이 정답이다.

어휘 underlie v. 기저가 되다 expand v. 확장되다

52 [2019 중앙대]

정답 ③

해석 ① 특이점 시대에서, 인간은 기술에 의해 되돌릴 수 없는 인류로 진화할 것이다.
② 저자는 기술 발전과 함께 음울한 미래가 나타날 것을 걱정한다.
③ 과거와 미래에 대한 전통적 개념은 우리가 특이점 시대를 이해한다면 바뀔 수 있다.
④ 기술의 빠른 발전에도 불구하고, 저자는 곧 닥칠 특이점 시대에 회의적이다.

해설 지문을 통해 추론할 수 있는 것을 고르는 문제이다. 지문 두 번째 문단에서 특이점 시대를 이해하는 것은 우리의 과거와 미래 결과의 중요성에 대한 관점을 바꿀 것이라고 했으므로, 과거와 미래에 대한 전통적 개념은 우리가 특이점 시대를 이해한다면 바뀔 수 있다는 것을 추론할 수 있다. 따라서 정답은 ③번이다.

오답 분석 ① 특이점 시대는 인간 생활이 돌이킬 수 없을 정도로 변형될 미래 시대라고는 했지만, 인간이 기술에 의해 되돌릴 수 없는 인류로 진화할 것인지는 추론할 수 없다.
② 저자는 특이점 시대가 이상적이지도, 암울하지도 않다고 했으므로, 저자가 기술 발전과 함께 음울한 미래가 나타날 것을 걱정한다는 것은 지문의 내용과 다르다.

④ 저자는 특이점 시대를 알아차린 것이 혁신적인 자각이었다고 말했으므로, 저자가 곧 닥칠 특이점 시대에 회의적이라는 것은 지문의 내용과 다르다.

어휘 evolve v. 진화시키다 irreversible adj. 되돌릴 수 없는
comprehend v. 이해하다 skeptical adj. 회의적인

[53-56]

[A] 아이스크림 제조회사에서 내부 용기를 둘러싼 물이 크림을 얼게 할 정도로 충분히 차가워지게 하기 위해 소금이 종종 사용된다. 소금은 물이 얼음으로 변하기 전에 화씨 32도 (섭씨 0도)보다 더 차가워질 수 있도록 어는점을 (A)낮추는 효과가 있다. 사실, 소금을 함유한 물은 거의 화씨 영하 6도까지 도달할 수 있다.

[B] 아이스크림을 만들 때, 크림을 통 안에 넣어 얼음 욕조 안에서 회전을 시킨다. 만약 얼음 욕조에 소금을 첨가하지 않으면, 욕조가 도달할 수 있는 가장 낮은 온도는 화씨 32도. 크림이 이 온도에서도 얼 수 있지만, 더 낮은 온도에서는 더 빠르게 얼 수 있다. 얼음 욕조에 소금(아이스크림 제조 시에는 대개 암염)이 첨가되면, 소금은 녹고 있는 얼음의 표면에 있는 물의 얇은 막과 접촉하게 된다. 그 소금이 녹아 물은 소금물이 된다. 이 소금물은 더 낮은 어는점을 갖게 되며, 따라서 얼음 욕조의 온도가 훨씬 더 차가워지며 아이스크림을 더 빠르게 얼게 한다.

[C] 소금이 물의 어는점을 낮추는 원리는 겨울에 도로를 안전하게 유지하기 위해 종종 사용된다. 눈이 내리고 얼음이 생기는 동안, 트럭들이 도로 위에 소금의 얇은 막을 뿌린다. 이것이 눈과 얼음을 얼게 하는 게 아니라 충격에 녹게 하며 도로를 빙판이 되어 위험하게 되는 게 아니라 젖은 상태가 되게 한다. 하지만, 물이 얼기 전에 얼마나 차가워질 수 있는가에는 한계가 있다. 극도로 추운 온도에서는, 마찰을 증가시키기 위해 도로에 모래를 뿌리는 것이 소금을 뿌리는 것보다 더 유용하다. 더 추운 온도에서는 염화나트륨 이외에 다른 유형의 소금이 사용될 수 있다. 예를 들면, 염화칼슘과 염화마그네슘은 낮은 온도에서 얼음을 녹일 수 있다. 하지만 이런 혼합물들 중 일부는 환경에 해로울 수 있으며 단지 가끔 사용될 뿐이다.

[D] 소금을 첨가하는 것이 물의 끓는점을 낮출까? 소금이 물의 어는점을 낮추지만, 끓는점을 낮추지는 않는다. 사실은, (B)소금물이 더 높은 온도에서 끓는다. 물에 소금을 첨가하는 것은 끓는점 상승이라 불리는 현상을 유발한다. 물의 끓는점이 약간 상승하지만, 당신이 그 온도 차이를 알아챌 정도는 아니다.

freezing point phr. 어는점   Fahrenheit n. 화씨
Celsius n. 섭씨   canister n. 통, 금속용기
rock salt phr. 암염   frigid adj. 몹시 추운
apply v. 바르다, 뿌리다   friction n. 마찰
sodium chloride phr. 염화나트륨
compound n. 화합물, 혼합물   detrimental adj. 해로운

boiling point phr. 끓는점
result in phr. (어떤 결과를) 초래하다

53 [2018 아주대]

정답 ②

해석 ① 왜 소금물이 가장 가치 있는가?
② 소금은 물에 어떤 작용을 하는가?
③ 우리는 일상생활에서 소금을 어떻게 이용할 수 있는가?
④ 소금에 의해 가능해지는 과학적 효과는 무엇인가?
⑤ 온도와 물의 물리적 상태는 어떻게 관련되어 있는가?

해설 지문의 제목을 묻는 문제이다. [A] 문단과 [B]에서는 아이스크림 제조사들이 아이스크림을 사용하는 이유를 설명하고 있는데 소금이 물의 어는점을 낮추기 때문이다. [C] 문단에서는 겨울에 도로의 결빙을 막기 위해 소금이 물의 어는점을 낮추는 원리를 이용한다고 언급했다. 그리고 마지막 [D] 문단에서는 소금이 물의 끓는점을 높이는 효과가 있음을 설명하고 있으므로, 이 지문의 제목을 '소금은 물에 어떤 작용을 하는가?'이라고 표현한 ②번이 정답이다.

54 [2018 아주대]

정답 ③

해설 지문의 빈칸 (A)에 들어갈 수 없는 단어를 묻고 있다. 빈칸 뒤의 문장에서 소금을 함유한 물은 거의 화씨 영하 6도까지 도달할 수 있다고 했으므로, '소금은 물의 어는점을 _____하는 효과가 있다'라는 문맥의 빈칸에는 '낮추다'라는 의미의 단어가 들어가는 것이 자연스럽다. 따라서 '팽창시키다'를 의미하는 ③번 distend는 빈칸에 들어갈 수 없다.

어휘 depress v. 하락시키다, 떨어뜨리다
distend v. 팽창시키다

55 [2018 아주대]

정답 ④

해석 ① 소금은 끓는점에 영향을 미치지 않는다
② 소금은 끓는점 상승을 방해한다
③ 소금물은 더 낮은 온도에서 끓는다
④ 소금물은 더 높은 온도에서 끓는다
⑤ 소금은 끓는점을 상당히 증가시킨다

해설 빈칸에 들어갈 내용을 묻고 있다. 빈칸 다음 문장에서 물에 소금을 첨가하는 것이 끓는점 상승이라는 현상을 유발한다고 했고, 마지막 문장에서는 끓는점이 약간 상승하지만, 당신이 알아챌 정도는 아니라고 했다. 따라서 '소금물은 더 높은 온도에서 끓는다'라고 한 ④번이 정답이다.

56 2018 아주대

정답 ④

해석 ① 염화나트륨은 물을 더 차갑게 할 수 있다.
② 염화나트륨은 물의 어는점을 낮출 수 있다.
③ 염화나트륨은 물의 끓는점을 높일 수 있다.
④ 염화나트륨은 마찰을 일으키는 데 모래보다 더 효과적이다.
⑤ 염화나트륨과 염화마그네슘은 호환적으로 사용될 수 있다.

해설 지문의 내용과 일치하지 않는 것을 묻는 문제이다. [C] 문단에서 극도로 추운 온도에서는 마찰을 증가시키기 위해 도로에 모래를 뿌리는 것이 소금을 뿌리는 것보다 더 유용하다(in extremely frigid temperatures, applying sand to the roads to increase friction is more useful than applying salt)고 했으므로, ④번은 지문 내용과 일치하지 않는다.

오답 분석
① [A] 문단의 Salt works ~ so the water can become colder than 32 degrees Fahrenheit를 통해 '염화나트륨은 물을 더 차갑게 할 수 있다'는 것을 알 수 있다.
② [B] 문단의 This salt water has a lower freezing point를 통해 '염화나트륨은 물의 어는점을 낮출 수 있다'는 것을 알 수 있다.
③ [D] 문단의 Adding salt to water results in a phenomenon called boiling point elevation.을 통해 '염화나트륨은 물의 끓는점을 높일 수 있다'는 것을 알 수 있다.
⑤ [C] 문단의 Types of salt other than sodium chloride ~ in colder temperatures. Calcium chloride and magnesium chloride ~ at low temperatures.를 통해 '염화나트륨과 염화마그네슘은 호환적으로 사용될 수 있다'는 것을 알 수 있다.

어휘 interchangeably adv. 호환적으로, 서로 바꿔가며

[57-58]

플라스틱 빗으로 머리를 빗은 후, 당신은 빗이 작은 종잇조각들을 끌어당기는 것을 발견할 것이다. 인력은 보통 종이를 빗에 매달 정도로 충분히 강력하고, 전 지구의 중력을 거스른다. 유리와 경질 고무와 같은 다른 문질러진 물질들로도 같은 효과가 발생한다. 또 다른 간단한 실험은 부푼 풍선을 모직에 문지르는 것이다. 건조한 날에, 문질러진 풍선은 보통 몇 시간 동안 방의 벽에 붙어있을 것이다. 이 물질들은 전하를 띠게 되었다. 당신은 신발을 모직 깔개에 강하게 문지르거나 자동차 좌석을 미끄러지듯 움직임으로써 당신의 몸에 전하가 생기게 할 수 있다. 그다음에 당신은 팔에 가벼운 접촉으로 당신 자신과 희생자 모두에게 가벼운 충격을 주어, 친구나 동료를 놀라거나 짜증 나게 할 수 있다. 이러한 실험들은 과도한 수분이 전하의 유출을 촉진할 수 있기 때문에 건조한 날에 가장 효과가 있다. 또한 실험들은 두 가지 유형의 전하가 있음을 증명하는데, 벤저민 프랭클린은 이를 양전하와 음전하로 명명했다. 털에 문질러진 경질 고무나 플라스틱 막대는 줄 한 가닥에 매달린다. 비단에 문질러진 유리 막대를 고무 막대 가까이 가져오면, 그 고무 막대는 유리 막대 쪽으로 끌린다. 전기를 띠는 두 개의 고무 막대나 두 개의 유리 막대를 서로 가까이 가져오면, 그것들 간의 힘은 서로를 밀어낸다. 이러한 관찰은 고무와 유리 막대가 서로 다른 종류의 과잉 전하를 획득했다고 가정함으로써 설명될 수 있다. 우리는 프랭클린이 제시한 관례를 이용하는데, 거기에서 유리 막대에 있는 과잉 전하는 양전하로, 고무 막대에 있는 것은 음전하로 불린다. 이러한 관찰에 근거하여, 우리는 같은 전하는 서로 밀어내고 다른 전하는 서로 끌어당긴다고 결론 내린다. 물체는 보통 같은 양의 양전하와 음전하를 포함하고, 물체들 간의 전력은 물체가 순음전하나 순양전하를 갖고 있을 때 발생한다. 자연의 기본적인 양전하 운반체는 양성자인데, 양성자는 중성자와 함께 원자핵에 위치한다. 핵은 약만 배 더 큰 넓이로 음전하를 띠는 전자 무리에 의해 둘러싸여 있다. 전자는 양성자와 같은 크기의 전하를 갖고 있지만, 반대의 부호를 갖고 있다. 1그램의 물질에는 음전하를 띤 전자만큼이나 많은 대략 1023개의 양전하를 띤 양성자가 있어서, 순전하는 0이다. 원자핵이 고체 안 공간에 단단하게 유지되어 있기 때문에, 양성자는 절대 한 물질에서 다른 물질로 이동하지 않는다. 전자는 양성자보다 훨씬 가볍기 때문에 힘에 의해 더 쉽게 속도가 붙는다. 뿐만 아니라, 전자는 원자의 바깥 영역을 차지한다. 그 결과, 물체는 전자를 얻거나 잃음으로써 전기를 띠게 된다. 전하는 한 유형의 물질에서 다른 물질로 쉽게 이동한다. 두 물질을 함께 문지르는 것은 접촉 부분을 늘려, 이동 과정을 용이하게 한다. 전하의 중요한 특징은 항상 보존된다는 것이다. 전하는 두 중성 물체가 함께 문질러질 때 만들어지지 않는다. 반대로, 음전하가 한 물체에서 다른 물체로 이동되기 때문에 물체가 전기를 띠는 것이다. 한 물체는 다른 물체가 같은 양의 음전하를 잃어서 순양전하로 남겨지면서 음전하를 얻는다. 유리 막대를 비단과 문지를 때, 전자는 막대에서 비단으로 옮겨진다. 결과적으로, 유리 막대는 순양전하를, 비단은 순음전하를 갖게 된다. 마찬가지로, 고무를 털과 문지를 때, 털에서 고무로 전자가 옮겨진다.

comb n. 빗 attractive force phr. 인력
defy v. 거역하다 gravitational pull phr. 중력
electric charge phr. 전하 facilitate v. 촉진하다
suspend v. 매달다 repulsive adj. 밀어내는
repel v. 밀어내다 proton n. 양성자 neutron n. 중성자
electron n. 전자 magnitude n. 크기
conserve v. 보존하다

---

57 2019 한국항공대

정답 ②

해석 ① 그에 반해서 ② 그 결과
③ 그러나 ④ 그럼에도 불구하고

해설 빈칸에 적절한 연결어를 넣는 문제이다. 빈칸 앞부분은 양성자는 물질 간에 이동하지 않지만, 전자는 양성자보다 가벼워 쉽게 속도가 붙을 뿐만 아니라 원자의 바깥 영역을 차지한다

는 내용이고, 빈칸 뒤 문장은 물체는 전자를 얻거나 잃음으로써 전기를 띤다는 내용이다. 따라서 결과를 나타내는 연결어인 ② Consequently(그 결과)가 정답이다.

58 [2019 한국항공대]

정답 ④

해석 ① 음전하를 띠는 고무 막대는 양전하를 띠는 유리 막대에 끌린다.
② 음전하를 띠는 고무 막대는 음전하를 띠는 유리 막대에 밀어내진다.
③ 고무가 털에 문질러지면, 털은 순양전하로 남게 된다.
④ 유리 막대가 비단에 문질러지면, 전자와 양성자는 유리에서 비단으로 옮겨진다.

해설 지문의 내용과 일치하지 않는 것을 묻는 문제이다. ④번의 키워드인 a glass rod is rubbed with silk(유리 막대가 비단에 문질러지다)가 그대로 언급된 지문 주변에서 유리 막대를 비단과 문지를 때, 전자는 막대에서 비단으로 옮겨진다고 했으므로, 유리 막대가 비단에 문질러지면, 전자와 양성자가 유리에서 비단으로 옮겨진다는 것은 지문의 내용과 다르다. 따라서 ④번이 지문의 내용과 일치하지 않는다.

오답 분석
① 지문 중간의 we conclude that like charges repel one another and unlike charges attract one another를 통해 '음전하를 띠는 고무 막대는 양전하를 띠는 유리 막대에 끌린다'는 것을 알 수 있다.
② 지문 중간의 we conclude that like charges repel one another and unlike charges attract one another를 통해 '음전하를 띠는 고무 막대는 음전하를 띠는 유리 막대에 밀어내진다'는 것을 알 수 있다.
③ 지문의 마지막 문장 Likewise, when rubber is rubbed with fur, electrons are transferred from the fur to the rubber.를 통해 '고무가 털에 문질러지면, 털은 순양전하로 남게 된다'는 것을 알 수 있다.

14 생물

01-83
문제집 p.396

01 ①	02 ④	03 ①	04 ⑤	05 ①
06 ④	07 ①	08 ⑤	09 ②	10 ③
11 ④	12 ③	13 ④	14 ②	15 ④
16 ①	17 ③	18 ⑤	19 ③	20 ③
21 ②	22 ②	23 ②	24 ②	25 ①
26 ④	27 ①	28 ②	29 ③	30 ①
31 ③	32 ②	33 ③	34 ①	35 ③
36 ④	37 ①	38 ③	39 ①	40 ③
41 ②	42 ③	43 ①	44 ④	45 ④
46 ①	47 ③	48 ③	49 ①	50 ①
51 ①	52 ③	53 ①	54 ④	55 ⑤
56 ①	57 ②	58 ③	59 ③	60 ④
61 ②	62 ③	63 ③	64 ①	65 ④
66 ②	67 ②	68 ④	69 ④	70 ②
71 ③	72 ④	73 ④	74 ②	75 ②
76 ①	77 ②	78 ④	79 ③	80 ④
81 ④	82 ②	83 ⑤		

01 [2019 인하대]

정답 ①

해석 질병 유전자를 제거하기 위하거나 또는 인간 증강을 위한 인간 유전체 수정에 대한 논의는 새로운 것이 아니며 1980년대에 인간 유전체 배열에 관한 첫 논의가 이루어진 이후로 아주 흔한 일이 되어왔다. 많은 생명 윤리학자들이 인간 유전체 배열에 관한 논의들로 그들의 경력을 만들어 왔으며, 현재 Amazon에는 우리의 유전자를 수정하는 것이 인류의 종말로 이끌 것이라고 예측하는 주제들을 포함한 인간 증강의 주제에 대한 광범위한 책들이 수십 권이 있다.
① 생명 윤리학자
② 산부인과 의사
③ 물리학자
④ 치과 교정 의사
⑤ 방사선과 의사

해설 지문의 빈칸을 채우는 문제이다. 지문의 첫 번째 문장에서 질병 유전자를 제거하거나 인간 증강을 위해서 유전체 수정에 대해 논의가 이루어지고 있다고 했으므로, 빈칸에는 질병 유전자 혹은 유전체 수정에 관련된 직업이 나와야 적절하다는 것을 알 수 있다. 따라서 '생명 윤리학자'라고 한 ①번이 정답이다.

어휘 genome n. 유전체, 게놈 modification n. 수정
eliminate v. 제거하다
human enhancement phr. 인간 증강(사람의 인지와 몸의 성능을 높이기 위한 기술)
commonplace n. 아주 흔한 일, 진부한 것
sequencing n. 배열 dozens of phr. 수십의
bioethicist n. 생명 윤리학자
gynecologist n. 산부인과 의사 physicist n. 물리학자
orthodontist n. 치과 교정 의사
radiologist n. 방사선과 의사

02 [2019 서강대]

정답 ④

해석 [D] 환경 운동가들은 유전자 조작 연어를 먹으면 건강에 좋지 않을 수 있다는 점을 걱정한다.
[C] 만약 이 연어가 자연으로 탈출한다면, 그것들은 자연적인 연어와 함께 번식하고 자연적인 연어의 유전자 공급원을 오염시킬지도 모른다.
[A] 유전자 조작 연어는 또한 자연에서 살아남는 데 유리할 수도 있는데, 이는 그것들이 더 빠르게 자라서 모든 자연적인 연어가 멸종되는 것을 야기할 수도 있기 때문이다.
[B] 일부 양어장 경영자들은 또한 이 새로운 연어를 업계에 불필요한 위험 요소로 보는데, 이는 이미 세계 시장에 연어가 너무 많기 때문이다.

해설 주어진 문장의 적절한 순서를 파악하는 문제이다. 환경 운동가들이 유전자 조작 연어를 먹으면 건강에 좋지 않을 수 있다는 점을 걱정한다는 [D]가 먼저 오고 그다음에 이 연어들이 자연으로 탈출한다면 자연적인 연어와 함께 번식하면서 자연적인 연어의 유전자 공급원을 오염시킬지도 모른다고 한 [C]가 오는 것이 자연스럽다. 그리고 이 유전자 조작 연어는 또한 자연에서 살아남는 데 유리할 수도 있다고 한 [A]로 이어지는 것이 자연스럽다. 마지막으로 일부 양어장 경영자들은 이미 세계 시장에 연어가 너무 많기 때문에 새로운 연어를 불필요한 위험 요소로 본다는 내용인 [B]가 오는 것이 자연스럽다. 따라서 주어진 문장의 올바른 순서는 ④번 [D] − [C] − [A] − [B]이다.

어휘 environmentalist n. 환경 운동가
genetically engineered phr. 유전자 조작의
salmon n. 연어 unhealthy adj. 건강에 좋지 않은
breed with phr. 번식하다 pollute v. 오염시키다
gene pool phr. 유전자 공급원 die out phr. 멸종되다
unnecessary adj. 불필요한 risk n. 위험 요소

[03-04]

진화 생물학은 항상 논란이 많았다. 이는 다윈의 이론이 종교적 전통에 뿌리를 내린 인간의 기원에 대한 초자연적인 설명들을 직접적으로 부정하고 초자연적인 설명들을 완전히 자연적인 것들로 대체했기 때문이다. 철학자 Daniel Dennett은 거

의 모든 전통적인 개념들을 부식시키고, 뒤이어 혁신적인 세계관을 남기는 일종의 "보편적인 산"으로 진화를 설명했으며, 이는 대부분의 오래된 두드러진 특색들은 여전히 알아볼 수 있되, 본질적인 방식으로 변형되게 한다. 이 부식성의 사상을 두려워한, 미국의 진화론 반대 측은 창세기에 기술된 것처럼 하나님이 생명을 오늘날의 형태로 창조했다고 믿었던 보수파의 복음주의 기독교인들로부터 비롯되었다.

evolutionary biology phr. 진화 생물학
controversial adj. 논란이 많은
contradict v. 부정하다, 반박하다
supernatural adj. 초자연적인 account n. 설명
root v. 뿌리 내리다 universal adj. 보편적인
acid n. 산 revolutionize v. 혁신을 일으키다
world-view n. 세계관 recognizable adj. 알아볼 수 있는
fundamental adj. 본질적인, 근본적인
right-wing adj. 보수파의, 우익의
evangelical adj. 복음주의의
Genesis n. 창세기(구약 성서의 제1권)

03 2019 광운대

정답 ①

해석 ① 부식성의 ② 구성주의의
③ 공동의 ④ 현대의
⑤ 경멸하는

해설 지문의 빈칸을 채우는 문제이다. 빈칸 앞 문장에서 Daniel Dennett이 거의 모든 전통적인 개념들을 부식시키고, 뒤이어 혁신적인 세계관을 남기는 일종의 "보편적인 산"으로 진화를 설명했다고 했으므로, 빈칸에는 "보편적인 산"을 다루는 어떠한 사상에 대한 내용이 나와야 적절하다는 것을 알 수 있다. 따라서 '부식성의'라고 한 ①번이 정답이다.

04 2019 광운대

정답 ⑤

해석 ① 미국의 기독교인들은 더 이상 다윈이 옳다고 믿지 않는다.
② 다윈은 한동안 보수파의 복음주의 전도사들에 의해 높이 찬양받았다.
③ Dennett은 화학을 통해 인간 존재의 기원을 설명했다.
④ 다윈의 이론은 인간 기원의 초자연적인 설명을 뒷받침하는 것으로 밝혀졌다.
⑤ Dennett에 따르면, "보편적인 산"은 오래된 개념들을 완전히 새로운 세계관으로 변화시킨다.

해설 지문의 내용과 일치하는 것을 묻는 문제이다. 지문의 세 번째 문장 The philosopher Daniel Dennett has described evolution as a sort of "universal acid" that "eats through just about every traditional concept, ~ , but transformed in fundamental ways."의 내용을 통해 Dennett에 따르면, "보편적인 산"은 오래된 개념들을 완전히 새로운 세계관으로 변화시킨다는 것을 알 수 있다. 따라서 ⑤번이 정답이다.

오답분석
① 미국의 보수파의 복음주의 기독교인들로부터 진화론 반대 측이 비롯되었다고 했으므로, 미국의 기독교인들이 더 이상 다윈을 옳다고 믿지 않는다는 것은 지문의 내용과 다르다.
② 미국의 진화론 반대 측은 보수파의 복음주의 기독교인들로부터 비롯되었다고 했으므로, 다윈이 한동안 보수파의 복음주의 전도사들에 의해 높이 찬양받았다는 것은 지문의 내용과 다르다.
③ Dennett이 진화를 일종의 "보편적인 산"에 빗대어 설명했다고 했지만, Dennett이 화학을 통해 인간 존재의 기원을 설명했다는 것은 지문의 내용과 다르다.
④ 다윈의 이론은 초자연적인 설명들을 직접적으로 부정하고 초자연적인 설명들을 완전히 자연적인 것들로 대체했다고 했으므로, 다윈의 이론은 인간 기원의 초자연적인 설명을 뒷받침하는 것으로 밝혀졌다는 것은 지문의 내용과 다르다.

어휘 praise v. 찬양하다, 칭찬하다 evangelist n. 전도사
account for phr. 설명하다 turn out phr. 밝혀지다

[05-08]

인간은 자연스럽게 반복되는 행동과 주로 입수한 지식을 모델로 하는 사고방식을 발달시킨다. 이러한 사고방식은 우리가 비슷하거나 익숙한 상황에서 같은 행동과 지식을 빠르게 적용하도록 돕지만, 우리가 문제를 보고, 이해하고, 그리고 해결하는 새로운 방식에 빠르고 쉽게 접근하거나 발달시키는 것을 막을 가능성도 있다. 이 사고방식은 종종 스키마라고 불리는데, 스키마는 조직화된 정보 및 우리가 여러 환경적 자극들을 접할 때 인간 내면에서 활성화되면서 시작되는 상황, 행동과 생각 사이의 관계를 나타낸다. 하나의 스키마에는 막대한 양의 정보가 들어갈 수 있다. 예를 들어, 우리는 다리 4개, 털, 날카로운 이빨, 꼬리 1개, 발, 그리고 많은 다른 눈에 띄는 특징들을 포함하는 개에 대한 스키마가 있다. 환경적 자극들이 이 스키마와 일치할 때, 심지어 보잘것없는 관련성만 있거나 아주 소수의 특징들만 있을 때, 똑같은 사고 패턴이 머릿속에 떠오른다. 이 스키마는 무의식적으로 활성화되기 때문에, 그 상황에 더 맞는 생각을 방해하거나 어떤 면에서는 새로운 문제 해결 전략을 가능하게 하는 방식으로 문제를 보지 못하게 막을 수 있다.

repetitive adj. 반복되는 potential n. 가능성
schema n. 스키마(정보를 통합하고 조직화하는 인지적 개념 또는 틀), 도식 stimulate v. 활성화시키다
stimulus n. 자극(pl. stimuli) vast adj. 막대한
encompass v. ~을 포함하다 presence n. 있음, 존재
paw n. 발 perceptible adj. 눈에 띄는, 인지할 수 있는
characteristic n. 특징
automatically adv. 무의식적으로, 자동적으로
obstruct v. 방해하다 enable v. 가능하게 하다

05 [2021 숙명여대]

정답 ①

해설 지문의 빈칸을 채우는 문제이다. 첫 번째 빈칸은 동사 model과 함께 쓰이는 전치사 자리이다. 동사 model은 전치사 on과 함께 model on(~을 모델로 하다, 본뜨다)의 형태로 쓰이므로 전치사 on을 써야 한다. 두 번째 빈칸은 동사 bring과 함께 쓰이는 전치사 자리이다. 동사 bring은 전치사 into와 함께 bring into(~로 이동시키다)의 형태로 쓰이므로 전치사 into를 써야 한다. 따라서 ① on – into가 정답이다.

06 [2021 숙명여대]

정답 ④

해설 주어진 지문에서 '보잘것없는'이라는 의미로 사용된 tenuous의 동의어를 묻는 문제이다. ①번 circumspect는 '신중한', ②번 implacable은 '확고한', ③번 reckless는 '무모한', ④번 weak은 '약한', ⑤번 stout은 '튼튼한'이라는 의미이므로, ④번이 정답이다.

07 [2021 숙명여대]

정답 ①

해석
① 깊이 몸에 밴 사고방식의 문제점
② 비판적 사고의 교육 패턴
③ 전통적인 문제 해결 연습의 이점
④ 전체론적 접근 방식으로 창의적인 아이디어 내기
⑤ 스키마를 교육과 학습에 적용하는 방법

해설 지문의 제목을 묻는 문제이다. 지문 전반에 걸쳐 '스키마'에 대해 설명하고 있고, 지문의 초반에서 스키마는 우리가 비슷하거나 익숙한 상황에서 같은 행동과 지식을 빠르게 적용하도록 돕지만 새로운 방식에 빠르고 쉽게 접근하거나 발달시키는 것을 막을 가능성도 있다고 하였다. 따라서 이 지문의 제목을 '깊이 몸에 밴 사고방식의 문제점'이라고 표현한 ①번이 정답이다.

오답분석
② 비판적 사고의 교육 패턴은 지문에서 언급되지 않았으므로 정답이 될 수 없다.
③ 전통적인 문제 해결 연습의 이점은 지문에서 언급되지 않았으므로 정답이 될 수 없다.
④ 전체론적 접근 방식으로 창의적인 아이디어 내기는 지문에서 언급되지 않았으므로 정답이 될 수 없다.
⑤ 스키마를 교육과 학습에 적용하는 방법은 지문에서 언급되지 않았으므로 정답이 될 수 없다.

어휘 ingrained adj. 깊이 몸에 밴, 타고난
conventional adj. 전통적인, 관습적인
holistic adj. 전체론적인

08 [2021 숙명여대]

정답 ⑤

해석
① 인간에 의해 자연스럽게 발달된다.
② 문제를 해결하는 것을 방해할 가능성이 있다.
③ 극단적으로 많은 양의 정보는 일부일 뿐이다.
④ 스키마는 의도적인 목적 없이 만들어진다.
⑤ 우리가 문제를 해결하는 새로운 방법을 개발하도록 장려한다.

해설 지문의 내용과 일치하지 않는 것을 묻는 문제이다. 지문 후반에서 스키마는 무의식적으로 활성화되기 때문에 새로운 문제 해결 전략을 가능하게 하는 방식으로 문제를 보지 못하게 막을 수 있다고 했으므로, 우리가 문제를 해결하는 새로운 방법을 개발하도록 장려한다는 것은 지문의 내용과 다르다. 따라서 ⑤번이 지문의 내용과 일치하지 않는다.

오답분석
① Humans naturally develop patterns of thinking을 통해 '인간에 의해 자연스럽게 발달된다'는 것을 알 수 있다.
② As these schemas are stimulated automatically, this can obstruct ~ prevent us from seeing a problem in a way ~ a new problem-solving strategy를 통해 '문제를 해결하는 것을 방해할 가능성이 있다'는 것을 알 수 있다.
③ A single schema can contain a vast amount of information을 통해 '극단적으로 많은 양의 정보는 일부일 뿐이다'는 것을 알 수 있다.
④ Humans naturally develop patterns of thinking을 통해 '스키마는 의도적인 목적 없이 만들어진다'는 것을 알 수 있다.

어휘 interfere v. 방해하다   conscious adj. 의도적인, 의식적인
intention n. 목적

[09-12]

파키린쿠스 바구미는 동태평양에 있는 대부분의 섬에서 발견된다. 이 바구미들이 날 수 있다면, 바구미가 동태평양에 있는 대부분의 섬에서 발견된다는 것이 놀랍지는 않았을 것이다. 하지만 바구미들은 날지 못한다. 그래서 바구미들이 왜 그렇게 널리 퍼진 것인지는 수수께끼이다. 하지만 대만에 있는 국립자연과학박물관의 Wen-San Huang은 자신이 그 수수께끼를 풀었다고 생각한다. 1923년으로 거슬러 올라가는 한 가지 이론은, 딱정벌레가 바깥 껍질 아래에 각자가 가지고 있는 아주 작은 기포에 의해 떠서 이곳저곳을 이동하는데, 이러한 이동은 그 곤충, 즉 딱정벌레가 떠다닐 수 있게 해준다는 것이다. Huang 박사가 딱정벌레가 떠다니는지 실험했을 때, 그는 실제로 딱정벌레가 떠다닌다는 것을 발견했다. 하지만, 바닷물에서 떠다니는 것은 딱정벌레에게 별로 좋지 않았다. Huang 박사가 시험했던 모든 57마리의 성충들은 2일 안에 죽었다. 분명히, 성충 바구미들은 좋은 선원들은 아니다.

하지만, 성충 바구미들이 좋은 선원들이 아니라는 것이 어린 바구미들도 좋은 선원들이 아니라는 것을 의미하지는 않는다. [A] 파키린쿠스 바구미는 어독 나무라고 불리는 맹그로브 거주 식물의 열매 안에 알을 낳는 것을 좋아한다. 어독 나무는 열매를 바다에 빠뜨리는데, 바다는 열매를 이동 시켜 멀리 떨어져 있는 해변에서 싹 트게 한다. 어독 나무 열매에 있는 화학 물질들은 배고픈 해양 생물이 열매를 먹지 않도록 열매를 보호해준다. [B]
Huang 박사는 바구미 유충들이 바닷물에 떠다니는 열매 안에 깊숙이 있다면 어떻게 살아가는지 궁금해했다. 그래서 Huang 박사는 바구미 유충들이 바닷물에 떠다니는 열매 안에 깊숙이 있을 때 어떻게 살아가는지도 실험했다. Huang 박사의 실험은 바구미 유충들이 소금기가 있는 환경을 잘 견뎌 내는지를 밝혔다. [C] <u>분명히, 한 열매 안에 있던 바닷물에 던져진 18개의 유충 중에서, 2개가 6일 동안 살아남았다.</u> 게다가, 이 유충들은 건강한 성충으로 성장했다. [D]

weevil n. 바구미 **buoy** v. 뜨다 **air cavity** phr. 기포
predilection n. 좋아함 **germinate** v. 싹 트다
larvae n. 유충 **fare** v. 살아가다, 지내다
tolerant adj. 잘 견디는 **saline** adj. 소금기가 있는

09 [2021 세종대]

정답 ②

해석 ① 단호한 ② 널리 퍼진
③ 퇴보하는 ④ 약삭빠른

해설 지문의 빈칸을 채우는 문제이다. 지문의 첫 번째 문단에서 바구미가 날지 못하는데 동태평양에 있는 대부분의 섬에서 발견된다고 했으므로, 빈칸에는 바구미들이 왜 그렇게 널리 퍼진 것인지는 수수께끼라는 내용이 나오는 것이 자연스럽다. 따라서 '널리 퍼진'이라고 한 ②번이 정답이다.

10 [2021 세종대]

정답 ③

해석 분명히, 한 열매 안에 있던 바닷물에 던져진 18개의 유충 중에서, 2개가 6일 동안 살아남았다.

해설 지문의 흐름상 주어진 문장이 들어가기에 가장 적절한 위치를 고르는 문제이다. 주어진 문장은 '분명히, 한 열매 안에 있던 바닷물에 던져진 18개의 유충 중에서, 2개가 6일 동안 살아남았다'라는 의미이다. 이 문장을 [C] 자리에 넣는다면, Huang 박사의 실험에서 바구미 유충들이 소금기가 있는 환경을 잘 견뎌 내는지를 밝혔다는 내용을 뒷받침하고 뒤에서 이 유충들이 건강한 성충으로 성장했다는 내용이 이어지므로 글의 흐름이 자연스럽게 연결된다. 따라서 ③번이 정답이다.

어휘 **grub** n. 유충

11 [2021 세종대]

정답 ④

해석 ① 파키린쿠스 바구미는 전 세계에 있는 대부분의 열대 섬에서 발견된다.
② 파키린쿠스 바구미 유충은 섬 사이를 수영할 수 있지만, 성충은 수영하지 못한다.
③ 어독 나무는 해양 생물로부터 물리적으로 보호할 수 있다.
④ 딱정벌레는 다 자라면 남은 생애 동안 같은 섬에 계속 머무른다.

해설 지문을 통해 추론할 수 있는 것을 고르는 문제이다. ②번 보기의 키워드인 'matures'(다 자라다)와 관련된 'adult weevils'(성충)가 등장한 지문의 두 번째 문단을 통해, 성충은 수영을 하지 못하므로 다 자라면 남은 생애 동안 같은 섬에 계속 머무른다는 것을 추론할 수 있다. 따라서 정답은 ④번이다.

오답분석 ① 파키린쿠스 바구미가 동태평양에 있는 대부분의 섬에서 발견된다고는 했지만, 전 세계에 있는 대부분의 열대 섬에서 발견되는지는 알 수 없다.
② 유충들이 바닷물에 떠다니는 열매 안에 있다고는 했지만, 수영을 하는 것이 아니라 열매를 배처럼 타고 이동하는 것이므로 파키린쿠스 비구미 유충이 섬 사이를 수영할 수 있는지는 추론할 수 없다.
③ 어독 나무 열매에 있는 화학 물질들이 배고픈 해양 생물이 열매를 먹지 않도록 열매를 보호해준다고는 했지만, 어독 나무가 해양 생물로부터 물리적으로 보호할 수 있는지는 추론할 수 없다.

12 [2021 세종대]

정답 ③

해석 ① 어독 나무는 동태평양 섬 한 곳 이상에서 발견될 수 있다.
② 어독 나무의 열매는 소금기가 있는 물에서 뜰 수 있다.
③ 어독 나무 열매의 화학 물질은 성충 딱정벌레에게는 유독하지만, 딱정벌레 유충에게는 유독하지 않다.
④ 어독 나무의 열매는 파키린쿠스 바구미가 뚫고 들어갈 수 있다.

해설 지문을 통해 추론할 수 없는 것을 고르는 문제이다. 지문의 세 번째 문단 마지막에서 어독 나무 열매에 있는 화학 물질들이 배고픈 해양 생물이 열매를 먹지 않도록 열매를 보호해준다고는 했지만, 이를 통해 어독 나무 열매의 화학 물질이 성충 딱정벌레에게는 유독하지만, 딱정벌레 유충에게는 유독하지 않다는 내용은 추론할 수 없으므로 정답은 ③번이다.

오답분석 ① 보기의 키워드인 'fish-poison tree'(어독 나무)와 관련된 'Pachyrhynchus weevil'(파키린쿠스 바구미)이 등장한 첫 번째 문단을 통해, 어독 나무는 동태평양 섬 한 곳 이상에서 발견될 수 있다는 것을 추론할 수 있다.
② 보기의 키워드인 'saline water'(소금기가 있는 물)와 관련된 'seawater'(바닷물)가 등장한 네 번째 문단을 통해,

어독 나무의 열매가 소금기가 있는 물에서 뜰 수 있다는 것을 추론할 수 있다.
④ 보기의 키워드인 'fruit'(열매)이 등장한 지문의 세 번째 문단을 통해, 파키린쿠스 바구미는 어독 열매 안에 알을 낳으므로, 어독 나무의 열매는 파키린쿠스 바구미가 뚫고 들어갈 수 있다는 것을 추론할 수 있다.

어휘 penetrate v. 뚫고 들어가다, 침투하다

[13-16]

[A] 기근 이후에, 두 번째로 큰 인류의 적은 역병과 전염병이었다. 끊임없는 상인, 관리, 그리고 순례자들로 연결된 북적거리는 도시들은 인류 문명의 기반일 뿐만 아니라 병원균을 위한 이상적인 환경이었다. 그래서 사람들은 자신들이 다음 주에 병에 걸려 죽을지도 모른다는 것, 혹은 전염병이 갑자기 발생해서 자신의 가족 모두를 한 번에 파멸시킬지도 모른다는 것을 알면서도 고대 아테네 혹은 중세 피렌체에서 살았다.

가장 유명한 소위 흑사병의 발생은, 벼룩에 감염된 세균인 'Yersinia pestis'가 벼룩에 물린 사람들을 감염시키기 시작했을 때, 동아시아 혹은 중앙아시아 어딘가에서, 1330년대에 시작되었다. [B] 동아시아 혹은 중앙아시아 어딘가에서부터, 쥐와 벼룩 무리에 탄 역병은 빠르게 아시아, 유럽 그리고 북아프리카 전역으로 퍼졌고, 대서양 해안까지 닿는 데 20년도 채 걸리지 않았다. [C] 7천 5백만 명에서 2억 명 사이의 사람들이 죽었다. 영국에서는, 10명 중 4명이 죽었다. 피렌체시에서는 10만 명의 주민 중 5만 명을 잃었다.

[D] 당국은 재앙 앞에서 완전히 무력했다. 기도하는 사람들을 모으고 행진을 준비하는 것 외에, 사람들은 그 전염병(흑사병)의 치료법은 물론이고 병의 확산을 막을 방법도 생각할 수 없었다. 근대까지도, 사람들은 병을 나쁜 공기, 심술궂은 악마와 화난 신들 탓으로 돌렸고, 세균과 바이러스의 존재는 의심하지 않았다. 사람들은 천사와 요정들의 존재는 선뜻 믿었지만, 아주 작은 벼룩이나 물 한 방울이 치명적인 전염병 포식자의 전체 함대를 저지할 수도 있다는 것은 상상도 하지 못했다.

---

famine n. 기근   plague n. 역병, 전염병
infectious adj. 전염병의   bustling adj. 북적거리는, 부산한
ceaseless adj. 끊임없는   merchant n. 상인
pilgrim n. 순례자   bedrock n. 기반
breeding ground phr. 환경, 번식지   pathogen n. 병원균
fall ill phr. 병에 걸리다   epidemic n. 전염병, 유행병
outbreak n. 발생, 발발   flea n. 벼룩
Yersinia pestis phr. 페스트균   procession n. 행진, 행렬
malicious adj. 심술궂은, 악의 있는   demon n. 악마
existence n. 존재, 실재   armada n. 함대
deadly adj. 치명적인

13 [2021 세종대]

정답 ④

해석 ① 감탄하기 위해   ② 격려하기 위해
③ 설득하기 위해   ④ 알려 주기 위해

해설 지문의 목적을 묻는 문제이다. 지문의 첫 번째 문단에서 기근 이후로 두 번째로 큰 인류의 적이 역병과 전염병이라고 하였고, 두 번째 문단과 세 번째 문단에서 전염병 사례로 흑사병을 들면서 흑사병이 시작된 시기와 사망자 수 등에 대해 설명하고 있다. 따라서 이 지문의 목적을 '알려 주기 위해'라고 표현한 ④번이 정답이다.

14 [2021 세종대]

정답 ②

해석 ① 혼자만   ② ~은 물론
③ ~보다는   ④ ~보다 많이

해설 지문의 빈칸을 채우는 문제이다. 지문의 세 번째 문단에서 사람들이 흑사병에 대해 기도하는 사람들을 모으고 행진을 준비하는 것밖에 하지 못했다고 했으므로, 빈칸에는 사람들이 흑사병의 치료법은 물론이고 병의 확산을 막을 방법도 생각할 수 없었다는 내용이 나오는 것이 자연스럽다. 따라서 '~은 물론'이라고 한 ②번이 정답이다.

15 [2021 세종대]

정답 ④

해석 당국은 재앙 앞에서 완전히 무력했다.

해설 지문의 흐름상 주어진 문장이 들어가기에 가장 적절한 위치를 고르는 문제이다. 주어진 문장은 '당국은 재앙 앞에서 완전히 무력했다'라는 의미이다. 이 문장을 [D] 자리에 넣는다면, [D]의 뒤 문장인 '기도하는 사람들을 모으고 행진을 준비하는 것 외에, 사람들은 그 전염병(흑사병)의 치료법은 물론이고 병의 확산을 막을 방법도 생각할 수 없었다'는 내용에서 당국이 재앙(전염병) 앞에서 어떻게 무력했는지를 설명해주고 있으므로 글의 흐름이 자연스럽게 연결된다. 따라서 ④번이 정답이다.

어휘 calamity n. 재앙, 재난

16 [2021 세종대]

정답 ①

해석 ① 피렌체시 주민들의 절반이 흑사병으로 죽었다.
② 인류가 직면한 가장 심각한 문제는 역병과 전염병이었다.
③ 소위 흑사병은 쥐에 물린 사람들에서 비롯되었다.
④ 근대까지, 사람들은 천사와 요정의 존재를 의심했다.

해설 지문의 내용과 일치하는 것을 묻는 문제이다. 지문의 두 번째 문단 마지막의 The city of Florence lost 50,000 of its

100,000 inhabitants라는 내용을 통해 피렌체시 주민의 절반이 흑사병으로 죽었다는 것을 알 수 있다. 따라서 ①번이 지문의 내용과 일치한다.

오답 분석
② 기근 이후 두 번째로 큰 인류의 적이 역병과 전염병이었다고 했으므로, 인류가 직면한 가장 심각한 문제가 역병과 전염병이었다는 것은 지문의 내용과 다르다.
③ 흑사병의 발생은 벼룩에 감염된 세균인 'Yersinia pestis'가 벼룩에 물린 사람들을 감염시키면서 시작되었다고 했으므로, 소위 흑사병이 쥐에 물린 사람들에서 비롯되었다는 것은 지문의 내용과 다르다.
④ 근대까지도 사람들이 천사와 요정들의 존재는 선뜻 믿었다고 했으므로, 근대까지 사람들이 천사와 요정의 존재를 의심했다는 것은 지문의 내용과 다르다.

[17-18]

왜 우리는 숨 쉴 산소나 마실 물이 바닥나지 않는가? 많은 유기체가 광합성이라고 불리는 과정을 진행하는 동안 산소를 생산하는데, 광합성은 모든 유산소 생물들이 소비하는 산소를 끊임없이 다시 채워준다. 생명이 의존하는 물리적 물질은 현재 지구상에 있는 것으로 제한되어 있다. 예를 들면, 물은 자연 상태에서 대기로부터 지표면으로 그리고 먹이사슬을 통해 다시 대기로 순환한다. 질소, 탄소 그리고 다른 중요한 물질들도 비슷한 방식으로 순환한다. 자연의 과정에 의해 대체되거나 재생되는 천연자원은 재생 가능한 자원이라고 불린다. 재생 가능한 자원의 다른 사례에는 식물, 동물, 농작물, 햇빛, 그리고 토양 등이 있다.

run out of phr. ~을 다 써버리다, ~이 다 떨어지다
organism n. 유기체, 생물   **photosynthesis** n. 광합성
constantly adv. 끊임없이
replenish v. 다시 채우다, 보충하다   **aerobic** adj. 유산소의
food web phr. 먹이사슬

17 2017 건국대

정답 ③

해석 ① 자연 과정의 한계
② 보존 또는 소비
③ 천연자원 재활용
④ 산소가 바닥나면 어떻게 될까
⑤ 생명에 중요한 물질

해설 지문의 제목을 묻는 문제이다. 생명이 의존하는 물질은 현재 지구상에 있는 것으로 제한되어 있고 모든 유기체가 계속 소비하는데도 바닥나지 않는 이유, 즉 순환을 포함한 천연자원의 재활용에 대한 내용이다. 따라서 이 지문의 제목을 '천연자원 재활용'이라고 표현한 ③번이 정답이다.

18 2017 건국대

정답 ⑤

해설 지문의 빈칸을 채우는 문제이다. 빈칸 앞 문장에서 '물이 자연 상태에서 순환하는 과정'을 설명했고, 빈칸 뒷 문장에서는 '자연 과정에 의해 대체되거나 재생되는 천연자원은 재생 가능한 자원이라고 불린다'고 했으므로, 그 중간에 있는 문장에서는 '질소, 탄소 그리고 다른 중요한 물질도 비슷한 방식으로 순환한다'는 내용이 나와야 적절하다는 것을 알 수 있다. 따라서 '비슷한'이라고 한 ⑤번이 정답이다.

어휘 **transitive** adj. (다른 것으로) 이행하는, 과도적인

[19-20]

최근 생겨난 신경과학 분야는 한 사람의 감정이 다른 사람들의 감정에 어떻게 영향을 미칠 수 있는지에 관한 것이다. 이 분야에 중심이 되는 것은 "거울 신경 세포"인데, 이는 우리가 다른 사람들이 느낄 수 있는 것을 감지하는 것을 돕기 위해 나타나는 뇌세포 부류이다. 우리가 다른 사람의 감정이나 심지어 의도를 인지 및 감지할 때, 이 세포들은 우리가 인지 및 감지하는 것과 관련된 뇌 부위를 자극한다. 어느 정도, 다른 사람의 행동은 이러한 세포들에 의해 우리의 정신에서 복제되거나 "반영된다". 거울 신경 세포는 우리의 공감과 다른 사람들의 감정에 대한 우리의 이해를 설명할 수 있다.

emerging adj. 최근 생겨난   **neuroscience** n. 신경과학
concern v. ~에 관한 것이다
mirror neuron phr. 거울 신경 세포   **perceive** v. 인지하다
associated adj. 관련된   **in a way** phr. 어느 정도
replicate v. 복제하다   **empathy** n. 공감

19 2020 가천대

정답 ③

해석 ① 체포하다   ② 엉기다
③ 자극하다   ④ 반사하다

해설 지문의 빈칸을 채우는 문제이다. 지문의 두 번째 문장에서 "거울 신경 세포"는 우리가 다른 사람들이 느낄 수 있는 것을 감지하는 것을 돕기 위해 나타나는 뇌세포 부류라고 했으므로, 빈칸에는 우리가 다른 사람의 감정이나 의도를 인지할 때, 거울 신경 세포가 하는 역할에 대한 내용이 나와야 적절하다는 것을 알 수 있다. 따라서 '자극한다'라고 한 ③번이 정답이다.

어휘 **arrest** v. 체포하다   **congeal** v. 엉기다

20 2020 가천대

정답 ②

해석 ① 뇌가 공감에 대하여 어떻게 작동하는지 연구하는 것은 최근에 생겨난 분야이다.

② 사람들은 거울 신경 세포를 통해 다른 사람들의 감정을 제어한다.
③ 신경과학자들은 사람들이 다른 사람들의 감정에 어떻게 영향을 받는지에 많은 관심이 있다.
④ 거울 신경 세포는 우리가 다른 사람과 공감하도록 도울 수 있다.

해설 지문의 내용과 일치하지 않는 것을 묻는 문제이다. ②번의 키워드인 mirror neurons(거울 신경 세포)가 언급된 지문 주변에서 거울 신경 세포는 우리가 다른 사람들이 느낄 수 있는 것을 감지하는 것을 돕기 위해 나타난다고 했고, 우리의 공감과 다른 사람들의 감정에 대한 우리의 이해를 설명할 수 있다고 했으므로, 사람들이 거울 신경 세포를 통해 다른 사람들의 감정을 제어한다는 것은 지문의 내용과 다르다. 따라서 ②번이 지문의 내용과 일치하지 않는다.

오답 분석
① 지문의 첫 번째 문장 An emerging field of ~ affect another's.를 통해 '뇌가 공감에 대하여 어떻게 작동하는지 연구하는 것은 최근에 생겨난 분야이다'라는 것을 알 수 있다.
③ 지문의 첫 번째 문장 An emerging field of ~ affect another's.를 통해 '신경과학자들은 사람들이 다른 사람들의 감정에 어떻게 영향을 받는지에 많은 관심이 있다'는 것을 알 수 있다.
④ 지문의 마지막 문장 Mirror neurons may explain our feelings of empathy ~를 통해 '거울 신경 세포는 우리가 다른 사람과 공감하도록 도울 수 있다'는 것을 알 수 있다.

어휘 empathy n. 공감 emerging adj. 최근 생겨난
mirror neuron phr. 거울 신경 세포
neuroscientist n. 신경과학자
be concerned with phr. ~에 관심이 있다
empathize v. 공감하다

[21-22]

아프리카 남동부 해안가에 최종적으로 정착하기에 앞서, 8천~1억만 년 전에 인도에서 분리된 마다가스카르는 많은 점에서 별도의 지구이다. 마다가스카르의 동물들과 식물들이 완전히 독창적인 형태로 진화했듯이, 지리적으로 고립되었던 모든 시간이 마다가스카르를 진화론의 활동 영역으로 만들었다. 대략 이 섬의 식물들의 90퍼센트와 동물들의 70퍼센트는 이 지역에만 있는 (A)고유한 것인데, 즉 이 동식물들은 오로지 마다가스카르에서만 발견된다는 의미이다. 그러나 이 섬의 생물을 특별하게 만들어주는 것이 독특하게도 생물을 (B)취약하게 만들기도 한다. 만약에 우리가 마다가스카르에서 이 동물들을 잃게 된다면, 그들은 영원히 사라지게 된다.

separate v. 분리되다 settle off phr. 정착하다, 자리 잡다
apart adj. 별도의 isolation n. 분리
Darwinian adj. 진화론의 playground n. 활동 영역

edible adj. 먹을 수 있는
endemic adj. 풍토의, (지역에) 고유한
prolific adj. 많은, 다작의 carnivorous adj. 육식의
sacred adj. 신성한 vulnerable adj. 취약한, 약점이 있는
flourishing adj. 번창하는
prestigious adj. 일류의, 명성이 있는

21 2017 국민대
정답 ②

해석 ① 먹을 수 있는
② 풍토의, (지역에) 고유한
③ 많은, 다작의
④ 육식의

해설 지문의 빈칸을 채우는 문제이다. 빈칸 뒤에 meaning이라는 분사구문이 나와서 빈칸에 들어갈 단어를 설명해주고 있으며, 마다가스카르에서만 발견된다고 했으므로 빈칸에는 이를 표현하는 내용이 나와야 적절하다는 것을 알 수 있다. 따라서 '(지역에) 고유한'이라고 한 ②번이 정답이다.

22 2017 국민대
정답 ②

해석 ① 신성한
② 취약한, 약점이 있는
③ 번창하는
④ 일류의, 명성이 있는

해설 지문의 빈칸을 채우는 문제이다. 지문의 마지막 문장을 보면 마다가스카르에서 동물이 없어지면, 영원히 사라지는 것이라고 했으므로, 빈칸 역시 이에 대한 내용이 나와야 적절하다는 것을 알 수 있다. 따라서 '취약한'이라고 한 ②번이 정답이다.

23 2018 건국대
정답 ②

해석 뇌와 학습에 관한 몇 가지 흥미로운 점들이 여기 있다. 운동의 이면에 있는 핵심적인 생각은 뇌에 적절한 양의 산소를 가져다준다는 것이다. 이것은 또한 숨쉬기 운동을 통해서도 행해질 수 있다. 시험을 보기 전에 또는 숙제를 시작하기 전에 몇 분 동안 시간을 내서 깊이 그리고 천천히 호흡하는 것이 집중과 동기부여에 긍정적인 영향을 줄 수도 있다. 이것이 당신의 아이가 숙제를 시작하기 전에 약간의 운동을 하게 하는 것이 좋은 아이디어인 이유이다. 껌을 씹는 것이 뇌를 운동시키는 또 하나의 방법이다. 연구들은 운동과 마찬가지로, 껌에 당분이 너무 많지만 않다면, 껌을 씹는 것이 뇌 속의 혈액 순환을 향상시키고, 기억력을 증가시키고, 걱정은 감소시킨다는 것 또한 보여준다. 이런 이유 때문에, 집중력에 문제가 있는 일부 아이들은 수업 중에 껌을 씹도록 조정을 받는다.

해설 지문의 빈칸을 채우는 문제이다. 운동을 통해 뇌에 산소를 공급하는 것이 학습에 도움이 된다는 내용을 서술하고 빈칸 앞 문장에서 '껌을 씹는 것이 뇌를 운동시키는 또 하나의 방법'이라고 했으므로 '껌을 씹는 것은 뇌 속의 혈액 순환을 _____하고, 기억력을 _____하고, 걱정을 _____한다'는 문맥에서 첫 번째 빈칸에는 '향상시키다'를 의미하는 improves, 두 번째 빈칸에는 '증가시키다'를 의미하는 increases, 그리고 세 번째 빈칸에는 '감소시키다'를 의미하는 decreases가 들어가는 것이 자연스럽다. 따라서 ②번이 정답이다.

어휘 have an impact on phr. ~에 영향을 미치다
motivation n. 동기부여   leap into phr. ~에 뛰어오르다
chew v. 씹다   circulation n. 순환
as long as phr. ~하는 한, ~하기만 하다면
attention n. 주의(집중), 주목
accommodation n. 합의; 조정, 조절
deteriorate v. 악화되다, 더 나빠지다

[24-25]

연구에 따르면, 최근 수십 년간 일어난 야생동물의 '생물학적 전멸'은 지구의 역사에서 여섯 번째 대량 멸종이 진행 중이며 이전에 두려워했던 것보다 더 심각하다는 것을 의미한다. 과학자들은 흔한 종과 희귀종 모두 분석하여 수십억 개의 지역 개체군이 사라졌다는 것을 발견했다. 그들은 인간의 인구과잉과 과소비 때문에 그 위기가 왔다고 생각하며 그것은 인류 문명의 생존을 위협하며, 대처할 수 있는 시간이 얼마 없다고 경고한다.

이전의 연구에 따르면 종들은 전에 수백만 년 동안 멸종되었던 것보다 상당히 빠른 속도로 멸종되고 있지만, 멸종이 비교적 드물어서 생물 다양성이 점진적으로 감소하고 있다는 인상을 주었다. 새로운 연구는 그 대신에 더 폭넓은 견해를 취하여, 서식지가 줄어들기 때문에 세계적으로 개체 수가 줄고 있지만 다른 어딘가에 여전히 존재하는 많은 흔한 종들을 평가한다.

annihilation n. 전멸
under way phr. 진행 중인, 이미 시작된
window n. 시간(대), 기간   even so phr. 그렇기는 하지만
assess v. 평가하다   range n. (서식) 범위
shrink v. 줄어들다

24 2018 성균관대

정답 ②

해석 ① 그것은 부분적으로 인간의 인구과잉에 의해 유발된다.
② 그것은 진행 중이지만, 속도는 더 느려지고 있다.
③ 그것은 전 세계에서 심각하게 발생하고 있다.
④ 그것은 인류 문명의 지속을 위태롭게 한다.
⑤ 그것은 지역의 생물 종이 지구로부터 사라지는 것을 의미한다.

해설 '여섯 번째 대량 멸종'에 관하여 옳지 않은 것을 묻는 문제이다. 첫 문단에서 이전에 두려워했던 것보다 더 심각하다 (more severe than previously feared)고 했으며 두 번째 문단에서는 종들은 전에 수백만 년 동안 멸종되었던 것보다 상당히 빠른 속도로 멸종되고 있다(species are becoming extinct at a significantly faster rate than for millions of years before)고 했으므로, '진행 속도가 더 느려지고 있다'고 한 ②번은 지문 내용과 일치하지 않는다.

오답분석 ① 첫 문단의 They blame human overpopulation ~ for the crisis를 통해 '그것은 부분적으로 인간의 인구과잉에 의해 유발된다'는 것을 알 수 있다.
③ 두 번째 문단의 many common species which are losing populations all over the world as their ranges shrink를 통해 '그것은 전 세계에서 심각하게 발생하고 있다'는 것을 알 수 있다.
④ 첫 문단의 They blame ~ and warn that it threatens the survival of human civilization을 통해 '그것은 인류 문명의 지속을 위태롭게 한다'는 것을 알 수 있다.
⑤ 첫 문단의 Scientists analyzed both common and rare species and found billions of regional or local populations have been lost. 통해 '그것은 지역의 생물 종이 지구로부터 사라지는 것을 의미한다'는 것을 알 수 있다.

어휘 continuation n. 계속, 지속, 연속

25 2018 성균관대

정답 ①

해석 ① 생물 다양성의 점진적인 상실
② 생물 종이 갑자기 사라짐
③ 인류의 완전한 멸종
④ 생물학적 유형의 일부 종말
⑤ 생물학적 다양성의 지속적인 연속성

해설 지문의 빈칸을 채우는 문제이다. 역접의 접속사 but 앞에서 생물 종들은 수백만 년 동안 멸종되었던 것보다 상당히 빠른 속도로 멸종되고 있다고 했지만, but 뒤에서는 '멸종이 비교적 드물어서 _____라는 인상을 준다'고 했으므로, 빈칸에 실제로는 매우 빠른 속도로 멸종되고 있다는 것과 반대되는 내용이 적합하다. 따라서 '생물 다양성의 점진적 상실'이라고 표현한 ①번이 정답이다.

어휘 gradual adj. 점진적인   partial adj. 부분적인
enduring adj. 오래가는, 지속적인
continuity n. 지속성, 연속성

[26-27]

오늘날 우리는 뇌를 신경계를 통제하는 기관으로 생각하는데, 이 10개 정도의 상호 작용하는 기능 체계 중 하나는 골격계, 순환계, 소화계 등과 마찬가지로 생물학자에 의해 나누어져 있다. 신경계는 두 가지 기능 때문에 탁월하다. 첫째, 이것은 한편

으로는 행동을 통제하고, 다른 한편으로는 눈, 귀, 코, 혀, 그리고 피부를 통해 주위의 감각 정보를 처리함으로써, 인체의 상호 작용을 외부 세계와 함께 통제한다. 사고나 인지는 환경과 신경계의 상호작용에 있어서 뇌의 기본적인 기능이다. 그리고 둘째로, 신경계는 신체의 내부 상태를 통제하고 심장, 위, 생식기 등에서 본능적인 감각 정보를 처리한다. 느낌이나 감정은 신경계에 의한 오장육부의 조절에 있어서 뇌의 기본적인 기능이다. 요컨대, 뇌는 신경계 전체의 생물학적 기관이고, 정신은 뇌 활동의 산물이며, 사고와 느낌은 마음의 요소이다.

organ n. 기관   control v. 통제하다
nervous system phr. 신경계   or so phr. ~정도, ~쯤
interact v. 상호 작용을 하다   functional adj. 기능의
biologist n. 생물학자   skeletal system phr. 골격계
circulatory system phr. 순환계
digestive system phr. 소화계
preeminent adj. 탁월한, 뛰어난
direct v. 통제하다, 감독하다   interaction n. 상호작용
behavior n. 행동   environmental adj. 주위의, 환경의
sensory adj. 감각의   cognition n. 인지, 인식
visceral adj. 본능적인   genitals n. 생식기, 성기
affect n. 감정   viscera n. 오장육부
biological adj. 생물학적인   component n. 요소

26 [2020 국민대]

정답 ③

해석 ① 안정적인 — 불안정한
② 감각의 — 수용적인
③ 외부의 — 내부의
④ 구체적인 — 추상적인

해설 지문의 빈칸을 채우는 문제이다. 첫 번째 빈칸이 있는 문장에서 신경계가 눈, 귀, 코, 혀, 그리고 피부를 통해 주위의 감각 정보를 처리한다고 했으므로, 첫 번째 빈칸에는 인체의 상호 작용을 신체 밖의 정보와 함께 통제한다는 내용이 나와야 적절하다는 것을 알 수 있다. 따라서 '외부의'가 들어가야 한다. 두 번째 빈칸이 있는 문장에서 신경계는 심장, 위, 생식기 등에서 본능적인 감각 정보를 처리한다고 했으므로 두 번째 빈칸에는 신체 내의 상태를 통제한다는 내용이 나와야 적절하다는 것을 알 수 있다. 따라서 '내부의'가 들어가야 한다. 따라서 ③ external(외부의) — internal(내부의)이 정답이다.

어휘 unstable adj. 불안정한   receptive adj. 수용적인
concrete adj. 구체적인   abstract adj. 추상적인

27 [2020 국민대]

정답 ①

해석 ① 뇌는 무엇을 하는가?
② 무엇이 신체 체계를 구성하는가?
③ 신체와 정신은 어떻게 경쟁하는가?
④ 생각과 느낌은 어떻게 다른가?

해설 지문의 요지를 묻는 문제이다. 지문 전반에 걸쳐 뇌는 신경계를 통제하는데, 그 신경계를 두 가지 기능으로 나누어 설명하고 있다. 따라서 이 지문의 요지를 '뇌는 무엇을 하는가?'라고 표현한 ①번이 정답이다.

어휘 constitute v. 구성하다

[28-29]

형질의 지위는 기준점에 좌우된다. 예를 들면, 유인원의 경우 다른 영장류 모두 손톱을 갖고 있기 때문에 손톱은 다른 영장류에 비해 원시적인 것으로 간주된다. 따라서 유인원을 예로 들었을 때 손톱은 원숭이와 구분하는 데 도움이 되지 않을 것이다. 하지만, 다른 어떤 포유류도 손톱이 없기 때문에, 손톱은 영장류 전체의 파생된 특성이다. 따라서 손톱은 영장류를 다른 포유류와 구분하는 데 도움이 된다. 여기에 설명되어 있는 두 번째 형질인 눈두덩은 오직 사람과(科) 유인원에게서만 발견되며, 다른 영장류에서는 발견되지 않기에 따라서 사람과(科) 유인원을 위해 파생된 것이다. 이 형질은 유인원과 원숭이를 구분 짓는다. 하지만, 침팬지의 경우, 눈두덩은 다른 사람과(科) 유인원에 비해 원시적인 것으로 간주된다. 즉, 그 형질은 침팬지를 예로 들었을 때 고릴라와 구분 지어 주지 않는다.

status n. 지위; 상태, 상황
character trait phr. 형질 (생물의 고유한 특징)
reference point phr. (판단·비교용) 기준, 참고점
ape n. 유인원   primitive adj. 원시적인
in relation to phr. ~와 비교하여   primate n. 영장류
illustrate v. 설명하다, 분명히 보여주다
brow ridge phr. 눈두덩, 눈 위의 뼈가 융기한 부분
hominoid n. 사람과(科) 유인원(고릴라, 오랑우탄, 침팬지, 사람 등)
with respect to phr. ~에 관하여; ~에 비하여

28 [2017 한양대에리카]

정답 ③

해석 ① 종의 상대적 지위   ② 종의 절대적 지위
③ 형질의 상대적 지위   ④ 형질의 절대적 지위

해설 지문의 제목을 묻는 문제이다. 지문은 어떤 생물 고유의 특징인 형질(character)에 관한 내용이며, 손톱이라는 형질을 기준으로 하면 유인원과 원숭이는 구분되지 않지만, 영장류와 포유류를 구분할 수 있다고 했다. 그리고 눈두덩이라는 형질을 기준으로 하면 유인원 중에서도 사람과(科) 유인원을 구분하는 기준이 된다고 했다. 따라서 이 지문의 제목을 '형질의 상대적 지위'라고 표현한 ③번이 정답이다.

29 2017 한양대에리카

정답 ③

해석 ① 모든 영장류는 손톱을 갖고 있다.
② 일부 영장류는 눈두덩을 갖고 있다.
③ 유인원과 원숭이 둘 다 사람과(科) 유인원에 속하지 않는다.
④ 침팬지와 고릴라 둘 다 사람과(科) 유인원에 속한다.

해설 지문의 내용과 일치하지 않는 것을 묻는 문제이다. ③의 Neither apes nor monkeys belong to hominoids(유인원과 원숭이 둘 다 사람과(科) 유인원에 속하지 않는다)와 관련된 지문의 후반부에서 눈두덩은 사람과(科) 유인원에게서만 발견되고 다른 영장류에서는 발견되지 않는다고 했으며, 이 형질이 유인원과 원숭이를 구분 짓는다(This character distinguishes apes from monkeys)고 했다. 따라서 ③번이 지문의 내용과 맞지 않다.

오답 분석
① 두 번째 문장에서 다른 모든 영장류가 손톱을 갖고 있다(all other primates have fingernails)고 했으므로, '모든 영장류는 손톱을 갖고 있다'는 것을 알 수 있다.
② 여섯 번째 문장에서 눈두덩은 사람과(科) 유인원에게서만 발견되며 다른 영장류에서는 발견되지 않는다(is found only in hominoids, not in other primates)고 했으므로, '일부 영장류는 눈두덩을 갖고 있다'는 것을 알 수 있다.
④ 마지막 문장에서 그 형질(눈두덩)은 침팬지와 고릴라를 구분 지어 주지 않는다(the character would not distinguish a chimpanzee from a gorilla)고 했으므로, '침팬지와 고릴라 둘 다 사람과(科) 유인원에 속한다'는 것을 알 수 있다.

[30-31]

쓰여진 자료들을 글자에서 단어로, 문장으로, 이야기로 처리하는 것은 뉴런들이 모든 정보를 전송하는 작업을 시작할 때 재빨리 주의를 기울이게 한다. 그것은 우리가 구어를 처리할 때에도 일어나지만, (A)읽기의 본성 자체는 뇌가 더 열심히 더 잘 작동하도록 장려한다. "보통, 읽을 때, 생각할 시간이 더 많이 있습니다,"라고 로스앤젤레스의 Dyslexia UCLA 센터의 책임자인 Maryanne Wolf는 말한다. "읽는 것은 당신에게 이해와 통찰을 위한 독특한 일시 정지 버튼을 줍니다. (B)하지만, 당신이 영화를 보거나 테이프를 들을 때와 같은 구어에 대해서 당신은 일반적으로 정지 버튼을 누르지 않습니다."

letter n. 글자, 문자　snap v. 재빨리 움직이다
neuron n. 뉴런, 신경 단위　transmit v. 전송하다
spoken language phr. 구어
typically adv. 보통, 일반적으로　director n. 책임자, 관리자
comprehension n. 이해　insight n. 통찰, 간파
oral adj. 구어의, 구두의　pause n. 정지 버튼, 멈춤
in general phr. 일반적으로, 대개

30 2020 국민대

정답 ①

해석 ① 읽기　② 배우기
③ 보기　④ 말하기

해설 지문의 빈칸을 채우는 문제이다. 지문의 첫 번째 문장에서 쓰여진 자료들을 글자에서 단어로, 문장으로, 이야기로 처리하는 것은 뉴런들이 모든 정보를 전송하는 작업을 시작할 때 재빨리 주의를 기울이게 한다고 했으므로, 빈칸 (A)에는 쓰여진 정보들을 읽는 것에 관한 내용이 나와야 적절하다는 것을 알 수 있다. 따라서 '읽기'라고 한 ①번이 정답이다.

31 2020 국민대

정답 ③

해석 ① 마찬가지로　② 정확히 말하면
③ 하지만　④ 게다가

해설 빈칸에 적절한 연결어를 넣는 문제이다. 빈칸 (B) 앞 문장은 읽기의 경우 이해하는 데 생각할 시간이 주어진다는 내용이고, 빈칸 (B) 뒤 문장은 구어를 처리하는 경우에는 시간이 주어지지 않는다는 내용이므로, 대조를 나타내는 연결어인 However가 들어가야 한다. 따라서 ③ However(하지만)가 정답이다.

[32-33]

최근까지, 과학자들은 인간의 뇌가 세 살 때 완전히 발달됐다고 믿었다. 이 이론에 따르면, 부모를 가장 걱정시키는 십 대의 행동들, 예를 들어 위험 부담, 그들의 행동이 그들 자신과 타인들에 얼마나 영향을 미칠지에 대한 세심함 결여, 증가된 공격성, 줄어든 정신 집중, 또는 부정적인 사고방식이 잘못된 육아나 신체의 화학 반응 변화 때문이라고 생각되었다. 하지만, 새로운 기술은 연구자들이 작용하고 있는 건강한 뇌를 조사할 수 있도록 했고, 그들이 발견한 것은 당신을 놀라게 할지도 모른다. 그 건강한 뇌는 세 살이 지나고도 계속 성장할 뿐만 아니라, 십 대의 뇌는 성인의 뇌보다 더 크다.

십 대의 뇌는 청소년기에 화학 물질로 가득 차 있기 때문에, 뇌가 성장한다. 하지만, 동시에, 더 많이 쓰이는 뇌세포는 덜 쓰이는 뇌세포와 경쟁한다. 가장 많이 쓰이는 세포들과 그것들 사이의 연결부만이 그 경쟁에서 살아남을 것이다. 덜 쓰이는 세포들은 뇌가 성인 크기에 이르기까지 소멸하기 시작한다.

theory n. 이론　concern v. 걱정시키다
risk-taking n. 위험 부담　sensitivity n. 세심함
aggression n. 공격성　attitude n. 사고방식
parenting n. 육아　chemistry n. 화학 반응
examine v. 조사하다, 검토하다　at work phr. 작용하여
flood v. 가득 차게 하다　chemical n. 화학 물질
adolescence n. 청소년기　die off phr. 소멸하다

32 [2020 한양대에리카]

정답 ②

해석
① 그들을 걱정하게 만든다
② 당신을 놀라게 할지도 모른다
③ 그들에게 실망스럽다
④ 당신이 이해하도록 만들지도 모른다

해설 지문의 빈칸을 채우는 문제이다. 지문의 첫 번째 문단 끝에서 과학자들이 최근까지 믿었던 바와 달리 뇌는 세 살이 지나고도 계속 성장하고, 십 대의 뇌는 성인의 뇌보다 더 크다고 했으므로, 빈칸에는 연구자들이 발견한 것이 어떠한지에 대한 내용이 나와야 적절하다는 것을 알 수 있다. 따라서 '당신을 놀라게 할지도 모른다'라고 한 ②번이 정답이다.

어휘 fear v. 걱정하다   disappointing adj. 실망스러운

33 [2020 한양대에리카]

정답 ③

해석
① 인간의 뇌는 세 살 이후에 발달을 멈춘다.
② 십 대의 나쁜 행동은 대부분 잘못된 부모에 의해 초래된다.
③ 뇌의 크기는 십 대에 가장 커진다.
④ 가장 활발하게 쓰이는 뇌세포는 사용되지 않는 세포들을 없앤다.

해설 지문의 내용과 일치하는 것을 묻는 문제이다. 첫 번째 문단의 마지막 문장 Not only does the brain ~의 내용을 통해 뇌는 세 살이 지나고도 계속 성장할 뿐만 아니라, 십 대의 뇌는 성인의 뇌보다 더 크다는 것을 알 수 있다. 따라서 ③번이 지문의 내용과 일치한다.

오답 분석
① 뇌는 세 살이 지나고도 계속 성장한다고 했으므로, 인간의 뇌는 세 살 이후에 발달을 멈춘다는 것은 지문의 내용과 다르다.
② 부모를 걱정시키는 십 대의 행동들이 잘못된 육아나 신체의 화학 반응의 변화 때문이라고 생각되었다고는 했지만, 십 대의 나쁜 행동은 대부분 잘못된 부모에 의해 초래되는지는 알 수 없다.
④ 덜 쓰이는 세포들은 뇌가 성인 크기에 이르기까지 소멸한다고 했으므로, 가장 활발하게 쓰이는 뇌세포가 사용되지 않는 세포들을 없앤다는 것은 지문의 내용과 다르다.

어휘 unused adj. 사용되지 않는

[34-35]

침입종은 과학적 수수께끼다. 인간은 동식물을 그들이 처음 진화한 곳으로부터 수천 마일 이동시킨다. 그런 종들 중의 다수는 새로 온 곳에서 하나씩 죽어간다. 일부가 가까스로 근근이 살아간다. 그러나 일부는 생태학적 악몽이 되며 토종 생물들보다 경쟁력이 뛰어나다. 과학자들은 이런 종들이 원산지로부터 아주 먼 곳에서 우수한 것으로 판명되는 이유를 잘 알지 못하며, "토종 생물이 환경에 적응해 있고 외래종이 다른 곳에서 온 것인데, 왜 그것들(외래종)은 (토종을) 침입할 수 있는 것인가?"라고 질문한다. 생태학자들은 미국 북동부의 많은 외래종이 동아시아로부터 침입했다는 것을 관찰했다. 그러나 그 반대의 경우는 사실이 아니다(미국의 생물 종이 동아시아로 침입하지는 않았다). 이것은 우연의 일치가 아니다. 그것은 침입종들이 진화하는 서식지와 관련이 있다. 세계의 일부 지역은, 다른 환경에서 번성하도록 준비된 우수한 경쟁자들을 생산하는, 진화론적 인큐베이터라는 증거가 있다. 침입 식물은 서로 경쟁하고 있는 아주 다양한 종들이 있는 서식지에서 진화할 가능성이 더 크다. 이런 종들은 계속해서 더 다양해지며, 계속 진화하여, 결국에는 침입할 준비가 된 더 우수한 경쟁자가 된다.

invasive species phr. 침입종(외부에서 들어와 다른 생물의 서식지를 점유하고 있는 생물), 외래 유입종
die off phr. 하나씩 죽어가다
eke out phr. 간신히 버티다, 근근이 살아가다
existence n. 존재; 생활(생계)   ecological adj. 생태학적인
outcompete v. ~보다 경쟁력이 뛰어나다
be adapted to phr. ~에 적응하다
exotic adj. 외국의, 이국적인; n. 외래종
coincidence n. 우연의 일치; 동시 발생
have to do with phr. ~와 관련이 있다   habitat n. 서식지
incubator n. (조산아 등의) 인큐베이터, 보육기; 부화 장치
prime v. 대비(준비)시키다

34 [2018 한국외대]

정답 ①

해석
① 그것은 외래종이 어디서 진화했느냐에 달려있다.
② 그것은 서식지에 있는 천적과 관련이 있다.
③ 외래종은 우수한 유전자 구성으로 돌연변이가 되는 경향이 있다.
④ 외래종은 새로운 환경으로 가는 도중에 빠르게 진화한다.

해설 밑줄 친 질문에 대한 답이 될 수 있는 것을 고르는 문제다. 밑줄 친 질문은 '토종 생물이 환경에 적응해 있고 외래종이 다른 곳에서 온 것인데, 왜 그것들(외래종)은 (토종을) 침입할 수 있는 것인가?'라는 의미이다. 그다음 내용을 보면 '미국 북동부의 많은 외래종이 동아시아로부터 침입한 것이지만 그 반대의 경우는 사실이 아니며(미국의 생물 종이 동아시아로 침입하지는 않았으며) 이것은 침입종들이 진화하는 서식지와 관련이 있다'고 했다. 따라서 외래종이 어디서 진화했느냐에 달려 있다는 것을 알 수 있다. 따라서 ①번이 정답이다.

35 [2018 한국외대]

정답 ③

해석
① 곧 멸종 (된다)
② 진화론적 틈새가 (된다)
③ 우수한 경쟁자가 (된다)
④ 너무 복잡해서 생존할 수 없게 (된다)

해설 지문의 빈칸을 채우는 문제이다. 빈칸의 앞 문장에서 '침입 식물은 서로 경쟁하고 있는 아주 다양한 종들이 있는 서식지에서 진화할 가능성이 더 크다'고 했으므로, '이런 종들은 결국 _____가 된다'라는 문맥에서 빈칸에는 '더 강해진다'는 내용이 들어가야 적절하다는 것을 알 수 있다. 따라서 '우수한 경쟁자들'이라고 표현한 ③번이 정답이다.

어휘 extinct adj. 멸종된   in no time phr. 곧, 머지않아
niche n. 적소 (꼭 맞는 자리·역할·일); 틈새(시장)

[36-37]

시조새는, 19세기 독일에서 많은 이빨과 깃털이 있는 상태로 발견된 화석, 생명의 역사상 아주 중요한 순간 — 곧 공룡이 하늘을 날고 이로 인해 조류가 탄생한 순간 — 을 시사해준다. [A] 이에 필적할 수 있는 진화 과정은 많지 않은데, 몇몇 작은 육생 포유동물의 자손에 의해 이루어진 육생 포유동물이 크릴새우를 먹는, 수염고래라고 불리는 거대한 수생동물로 변한 진화 과정이 바로 그 과정이다. [B] 북아메리카에서 새롭게 발견된 많은 이빨과 지느러미가 있는 고래수염 화석을 분석하면 이런 놀라운 진화 과정의 한 부분을 설명할 수 있을 것으로 보인다. 수염고래는 많은 양의 물을 빨아들인다. 그리고 나서 고래수염판이라고 알려진 섬유질이 뻗어 나온 부분으로 빨아들인 물을 작은 먹이들을 먹기 위하여 몸(입) 밖으로 다시 내보낸다. [C] 이 수염판은 다른 포유동물들의 이빨이 나는 곳에 위치하지만 치아의 주성분인 튼튼한 상아질로 되어있는 것과는 달리 머리카락과 손톱을 구성하는 부드러운 물질인 케라틴으로 구성되어 있다. [D] 일부 연구자들은 고래가 빨아들임(흡입)과 내보냄(여과)을 통하여 먹이를 먹는 것은 다 함께 같이 걸러서 단순한 체를 만들 수 있는 이빨에서부터 시작되었으며, 그 후 시간이 흐르고 나서 고래수염으로 대체되었다는 이론을 제시한다.

archaeopteryx n. 시조새
toothy adj. 많은 이가 있는; 뻐드렁니의, 이를 드러낸
feathered adj. 깃이 있는; 깃을 단; 깃털로 장식된; 깃 모양을 한; 날개 있는, 새처럼 나는, 빠른
hint at phr. ~을 암시하다, 시사하다
rival v. ~에 필적하다, ~와 경쟁상대가 되다
evolutionary adj. 진화론의, 진화의
descendant n. 후예, 자손
terrestrial adj. 지구(상)의; 지상의, 뭍으로 된; 흙의, 토질의
gigantic adj. 거인 같은, 거대한; 아주 큰; 엄청나게 큰
(= colossal, enormous)   aquatic adj. 수생의; 수종의
baleen whale phr. 수염고래   finned adj. 지느러미가 있는
illuminate v. 비추다, 분명히 하다, 설명하다, 해명하다
fibrous adj. 섬유질의, 섬유 모양의
outgrowth n. 자연적인 발전, 결과; 부산물(= by-product)
filter out phr. ~을 걸러 내다   robust adj. 튼튼한, 강건한
ingredient n. 재료, 성분; 구성 요소
flexible adj. 융통성이 있는, 유연한
theorize v. 이론을 세우다, 이론화하다   gnash v. 이를 갈다
sieve n. 체 (가루 등을 거르는 데 쓰는 부엌 도구)
subsequently adv. 그 후, 뒤에, 계속해서

36 [2018 한양대에리카]
정답 ②

해설 지문의 흐름상 주어진 문장이 들어가기에 가장 적절한 위치를 고르는 문제이다. 문장삽입의 전형적인 문제로 지시어를 활용하여 풀어야 한다. 주어진 문장의 내용과 지시어 this에 유의하면, 주어진 문장 앞에는 고래의 진화에 대한 내용이 나와야 적절하다는 것을 알 수 있다. 그러므로 주어진 문장 '북아메리카에서 새롭게 발견된 많은 이빨과 지느러미가 있는 고래수염 화석을 분석하면 이런 놀라운 진화 과정의 한 부분을 설명할 수 있을 것으로 보인다'가 [B] 자리에 들어가야 글의 흐름이 자연스럽게 연결된다. 따라서 ②번이 정답이다.

37 [2018 한양대에리카]
정답 ①

해석 ① 액체에서 고체를 분리하는 그물망
② 치근 주변의 단단한 실
③ 고체를 갈아 가루로 만드는 장치
④ 먹이를 물어뜯고 씹는 데 사용되는 뼈 구조

해설 밑줄 친 부분의 의미를 추론하는 문제이다. 단어 추론 문제는 일반적으로 직접적인 의미도 물어보지만, 글의 전체적인 문맥에서 답을 찾아야 함에 유의하여야 한다. 제시된 단어 'sieve'는 가루나 알갱이를 거르는 데 쓰는 부엌 도구인 '체'를 뜻하는 단어로, 주어진 지문에서는 '액체에서 고체를 분리하는 그물망'의 의미로 쓰였다. 따라서 ①번이 정답이다.

[38-39]

적십자사는 매년 미국에서 680만 명이 헌혈을 하고 있고, 대략 1360만 통의 혈액을 공급하고 있다고 추산한다. 가장 먼저 알려진 인간 대 인간의 헌혈은 1818년에 인간이 혈액형이라는 것이 무엇인지 알기 전에 이루어졌는데, 그 당시에 산부인과 의사인 James Blundell이 아이를 막 출산한 여성에게 혈액을 이동했다. Blundell은 많은 환자가 출산 중에 사망하는 것을 보고, 그의 실험적인 절차가 그 자신의 무력함에 느끼는 끔찍함에서 기인했다고 적었다. 남은 세기 동안, 과학자들은 혈액 이동을 실험했다. 이런 생각 모두가 성공적인 것은 아니었는데, 일부는 인간에게 젖소의 우유를 주입하는 것을 지지했으며, 이것이 실제 혈액보다 더 우월하다고 여겼다. 1873년부터 1880년에 걸쳐, 우유로 혈액을 공급하는 추세가 미국 전역을 휩쓸었다. 다행히도, 곧이어 오스트리아의 한 생물학자가 모든 것을 바꿀 수 있는 발견을 이루었다. 1901년에, Karl Landsteiner는 인간 대 인간 혈액 이동 중에 헤모글로빈에 의해 인간의 혈류에서 이물질이 분열되었다는 것을 깨달았다.

1909년에, Landsteiner가 처음으로 인간의 혈액을 유형으로 분류했을 때, 그의 연구는 실제로 시작되었다. 이 그룹들은 오늘날 A, B, AB, O로 알려져 있다.

The Red Cross phr. 적십자사
estimate v. 추산하다, 어림잡다
donate v. 헌혈하다, 기부하다   approximately adv. 대략
blood type phr. 혈액형   obstetrician n. 산부인과 의사
transfer v. 이동하다, 전송하다   give birth phr. 출산하다
childbirth n. 출산, 분만   experimental adj. 실험적인
procedure n. 절차, 과정   stem from phr. ~에서 기인하다
appalled adj. 끔찍해 하는   helplessness n. 무력함
advocate v. 지지하다   infuse v. 주입하다
superior adj. 우월한, 우수한   sweep v. 휩쓸다
thankfully adv. 다행히도   biologist n. 생물학자
discovery n. 발견   foreign body phr. 이물질
bloodstream n. 혈류   hemoglobin n. 헤모글로빈
classify v. 분류하다   take off phr. 시작하다, 이륙하다

38 [2019 한국외대]

정답 ③

해석 ① 거의 1,400만 명의 미국인이 매년 헌혈을 한다.
② Landsteiner는 이동을 발전시키기 위해 1909년에 연구를 시작했다.
③ Blundell은 여성이 출산 중에 사망하는 것을 막을 수 없는 자신의 무능함에 경악했다.
④ 혈액 이동은 현재 Landsteiner가 발견한 그룹들을 무시한다.

해설 지문의 내용과 일치하는 것을 묻는 문제이다. 지문의 중간에서 Having watched many patients ~ stemmed from being appalled at his own helplessness의 내용을 통해 Blundell은 여성이 출산 중에 사망하는 것을 막을 수 없는 자신의 무능함에 경악했다는 것을 알 수 있다. 따라서 ③번이 지문의 내용과 일치한다.

오답분석 ① 적십자사는 매년 미국에서 680만 명이 헌혈을 하고 있다고 추산한다고 했으므로, 거의 1,400만 명의 미국인이 매년 헌혈을 한다는 것은 지문의 내용과 다르다.
② 1909년에, Landsteiner가 처음으로 인간의 혈액을 유형으로 분류했을 때, 그의 연구가 실제로 시작되었다고는 했지만, 그가 이동을 발전시키기 위해 1909년에 연구를 시작했는지는 알 수 없다.
④ Landsteiner가 처음으로 인간의 혈액을 유형으로 분류했다고는 했지만, 혈액 이동이 현재 Landsteiner가 발견한 그룹들을 무시하는지는 알 수 없다.

어휘 nearly adv. 거의   develop v. 발전시키다, 개발하다
aghast adj. 경악한   inability n. 무능함
prevent v. 막다, 예방하다   currently adv. 현재
disregard v. 무시하다

39 [2019 한국외대]

정답 ①

해석 ① 헤모글로빈이 혈액에서 비정상적인 것을 파괴한다.
② 성공적인 혈액 이동은 혈액형에 달려있다.
③ 혈액은 수혈에서 우유보다 우월하다.
④ 혈액 이동은 헤모글로빈을 분열시킨다.

해설 밑줄 친 discovery의 의미를 추론하는 문제이다. 지문의 밑줄 친 단어가 있는 문장의 다음 문장에서 Karl Landsteiner는 인간 대 인간 혈액 이동 중에 헤모글로빈에 의해 인간의 혈류에서 이물질이 분열되었다는 것을 깨달았다고 했다. 따라서, discovery의 의미를 '헤모글로빈이 혈액에서 비정상적인 것을 파괴한다'라고 한 ①번이 정답이다.

어휘 unnatural adj. 비정상적인   transfusion n. 수혈

[40-42]

지구에서 인간이 가장 개체 수가 많은 포유동물이기 때문에, 사람이 가장 큰 유전적 가변성을 가지고 있다고 예상할 수 있다. 역설적으로, 인간은 살아있는 가장 가까운 친척이라고 할 수 있는 영장류에 비해서, 훨씬 작은 유전적 가변성을 가지고 있다. 이 놀라운 발견은 많은 과학자가 오늘날의 모든 인간이 상대적으로 작은 유전자 풀에서 나왔으며, 이 유전자 풀은 개체군 병목현상이나 선구자 효과에 의한 결과일 것이라는 결론짓도록 만들었다.
[A] 개체군 병목현상은 홍수, 남획 혹은 기근과 같은 재앙적인 사건이 한 종의 전체 개체 수를 상당히 감소시킬 때 일어난다. [B] 예를 들어, 남획은 20세기 초에 아메리카들소 같은 동물의 개체 수를 1,000마리 밑으로 떨어뜨렸다. 이런 사건들이 한 개체의 집단을 무작위로 죽게 만들기 때문에, 대립 유전자 빈도가 변하게 되고, 이것이 중요한 유전적 변형이 일어날 가능성을 커지게 만든다. [C] 일부 연구자들은 Toba 재앙 때 인간이 개체군 병목현상을 경험했다고 주장한다. [D] 대략 7만 년 전에, 인도네시아 Toba 호수에 위치한, 엄청난 화산의 폭발이 지구가 10년 동안 이어진 "화산 겨울" 상태로 돌입하게 했을지도 모른다. 이 시기 동안 화산재는 햇빛을 가렸고, 지구 위의 많은 동식물의 개체 수를 말살했다. 추정된 것에 따르면 화산 폭발 직후 인간의 개체 수는 대략 3천 명에서 만 명 사이의 어딘가에 위치해 있다. 그러므로, 인류의 현재의 유전적 다양성은 폭발 이후 지구에서 다시 번성하기 위해 제한된 유전자 풀에서 생겨난 작고, 고립된 집단들에 의한 결과일 수 있는 것이다.

---

populous adj. 인구가 많은   mammal n. 포유동물
variance n. 가변성   paradoxically adv. 역설적으로
primate n. 영장류   startling adj. 대단히 놀라운
gene pool phr. 유전자 풀
population bottleneck phr. 개체군 병목현상
founder effect phr. 선구자 효과
catastrophic adj. 재앙적인   overhunting n. 남획
famine n. 기근   allele frequency phr. 대립 유전자 빈도
plunge into phr. ~에 돌입하다   repopulate v. 다시 살다

40 [2020 한성대]

정답 ③

해석 ① 다른 영장류가 그들의 환경에 더 잘 적응했다고 주장하기 위해
② 이전 문장의 내용을 요약하기 위해
③ 인간의 유전자에 관한 놀라운 사실을 지적하기 위해
④ 인간과 영장류의 유사한 특성을 비교하기 위해

해설 저자가 Paradoxically라는 단어를 사용한 이유에 대해 추론하는 문제이다. 지문의 첫 번째 문단은 전체적으로 인간이 지구에서 가장 개체 수가 많은 동물이기 때문에, 가장 큰 유전적 가변성을 가지고 있다고 예측하기 쉽지만, 놀랍게도 사람이 가장 가까운 친척이라 할 수 있는 영장류에 비해서도 더 적은 가변성을 가지고 있다는 것을 설명하는 내용이므로, 저자가 Paradoxically라는 단어를 사용한 이유를 '인간의 유전자에 관한 놀라운 사실을 지적하기 위해'라고 표현한 ③번이 정답이다.

어휘 summarize v. 요약하다

41 [2020 한성대]

정답 ②

해설 지문의 흐름상 주어진 문장이 들어가기에 가장 적절한 위치를 고르는 문제이다. [B]의 앞 문장에서, 홍수, 남획, 기근과 같은 재앙적인 사건이 한 종의 전체 개체 수를 상당히 감소시킬 때, 개체군 병목현상이 일어난다고 하였으므로, [B]의 자리에 20세기 초, 남획이 아메리카들소 같은 동물의 개체 수를 떨어뜨렸다는 내용의 예시가 들어가는 것이 자연스럽다. 따라서 ②번이 정답이다.

어휘 American bison phr. 아메리카들소

42 [2020 한성대]

정답 ②

해석 ① 살아남은 인간들은 자원 때문에 빈번하게 들소들과 싸웠다.
② 대부분의 사람들은 부족한 식량 공급으로 인해 죽었다.
③ 인도네시아는 폭발에 영향을 받지 않았다.
④ 대립 유전자 빈도는 바뀌지 않았다.

해설 Toba catastrophe의 결과로 추론할 수 있는 것을 묻는 문제이다. 지문의 두 번째 문단에서, 인도네시아의 Toba 호수 근처의 거대한 화산이 폭발하면서 화산재가 햇빛을 가려 "화산 겨울"이 시작되었고, 많은 동식물이 죽게 되었다고 했으므로, 대부분의 사람들이 부족한 식량 공급으로 인해 죽었다는 것을 추론할 수 있다. 따라서 ②번이 정답이다.

오답 분석
① 지문의 두 번째 문단에서, 아메리카들소는 남획으로 한 종의 개체 수가 감소할 수 있음을 보여주는 사례였고, 20세기 초 인간의 남획에 의해 개체 수가 감소하였다고 했으므로, 살아남은 인간들과 들소들이 자원 때문에 빈번하게 싸웠다는 것은 지문의 내용과 다르다.
③ 지문 내에서 다뤄진 화산 폭발은 인도네시아의 Toba Lake의 근처의 화산이 폭발한 사건이므로, 인도네시아가 폭발에 영향을 받지 않았다는 것은 지문의 내용과 다르다.
④ 지문의 두 번째 문단에서, 몇몇 연구자들이 Toba catastrophe 이후 인간의 대립 유전자 빈도가 변화했다고 주장한다고 했으므로, 대립 유전자 빈도가 바뀌지 않았다는 것은 지문의 내용과 다르다.

어휘 survivor n. 살아남은 사람 insufficient adj. 부족한

[43-44]

1890년대 후반에 두 명의 독일 심리학자 게오르그 뮐러(Georg Müller)와 알폰스 필제커(Alfons Pilzecker)는 뇌 속에 기억이 자리를 잡는데, 즉 '강화되는데' 약 1시간이 걸린다는 것을 알아냈다. 그다음의 연구들은 단기 기억과 장기 기억이 존재한다는 것을 확인했으며 단기 기억이 장기 기억으로 전환되는 강화 국면이 중요하다는 추가 증거를 제공했다. 1960년대에 펜실베이니아 대학교의 신경학자 루이스 플렉스너(Louis Flexner)는 특히 흥미로운 발견을 했다. 쥐에게 세포로 하여금 단백질 생산을 못 하게 하는 항생제를 주사한 후에, 그는 쥐가 장기 기억을 형성하지는 못하지만 계속해서 단기 기억을 저장할 수 있다는 것을 발견했다. 그 의미는 명백하다: 장기 기억은 단지 단기 기억의 강화된 형태일 뿐이다. [A] 그 두 가지 유형의 기억은 서로 다른 생물학적 과정을 수반한다. 장기 기억을 저장하는 것은 새로운 단백질의 합성을 필요로 한다. 단기 기억을 저장하는 것은 그렇지 않다. 더욱 최근의 연구는 단기 기억과 장기 기억의 물리적 작용이라는 문제를 다루었다. [B] 실험 결과는 경험이 여러 번 반복될수록, 그 경험에 대한 기억은 더욱더 오래 지속된다는 것을 발견했다. 반복은 강화를 부추긴다. 특히, 연구자들이 반복이 신경 신호에 미치는 생리학적 영향을 조사했을 때, 그들은 놀라운 것을 발견했다. [C] 시냅스 내에 있는 신경전달물질의 농도가 변화하여 뉴런 사이에 존재하는 연결부의 힘을 바꾸었을 뿐만 아니라, 뉴런들은 완전히 새로운 시냅스 터미널을 성장시켰다. 다시 말해서, 장기 기억의 형성은 생화학적 변화뿐만 아니라 해부학적 변화도 수반한다. [D] 그것은 기억 강화가 새로운 단백질을 필요로 하는 이유를 설명해준다. 단백질은 세포 내에 구조적 변화를 일으키는 데 중요한 역할을 한다.

consolidate v. 굳히다, 강화하다
subsequent adj. 그다음의, 그 이후의
neurologist n. 신경학자 intriguing adj. 흥미로운
antibiotic n. 항생제, 항생물질
implication n. 함축(내포)된 의미 synthesis n. 종합, 합성
physiological adj. 생리학적인
neuronal adj. 뉴런의, 신경 단위의
neurotransmitter n. 신경전달물질
synapse n. 신경 접합부, 시냅스
anatomical adj. 해부학상의

43 2017 중앙대

정답 ①

해석 그 두 가지 유형의 기억은 서로 다른 생물학적 과정을 수반한다.

해설 지문의 흐름상 주어진 문장이 들어가기에 가장 적절한 위치를 고르는 문제이다. [A] 뒤에서 '장기 기억을 저장하는 것은 새로운 단백질의 합성을 필요로 하지만 단기 기억을 저장하는 것은 그렇지 않다'고 했으므로, [A] 자리에 주어진 문장 '그 두 가지 유형의 기억은 서로 다른 생물학적 과정을 수반한다'가 들어가야 글의 흐름이 자연스럽게 연결된다. 따라서 ①번이 정답이다.

어휘 entail v. ~을 수반하다

44 2017 중앙대

정답 ④

해석 ① 항생제 약물의 사용은 사람으로 하여금 아주 최근의 일도 기억하지 못하게 한다.
② 단기 기억은 우리가 강화된 정보를 활발하게 얼마나 오래 기억할 수 있느냐에 대한 핵심적인 예측 도구이다.
③ 장기 기억이 형성될 때 비교적 더 적은 신경전달물질이 뇌의 시냅스 내에 배출되는 것으로 예상된다.
④ 정보를 뇌 속에 더 오랫동안 기억하는 것은 시냅스의 해부학적 변화를 수반할 가능성이 매우 높다.

해설 지문을 통해 추론할 수 있는 것을 고르는 문제이다. 지문의 후반에서 '장기 기억의 형성은 생화학적 변화뿐만 아니라 해부학적 변화도 수반한다(The formation of long-term memories, in other words, involves not only biochemical changes but anatomical ones)'고 했으므로, '정보를 뇌 속에 더 오랫동안 기억하는 것은 시냅스의 해부학적 변화를 수반할 가능성이 매우 높다'는 것을 추론할 수 있다. 따라서 정답은 ④번이다.

오답 분석 ① 네 번째 문장에서, '쥐에게 세포로 하여금 단백질 생산을 못하게 하는 항생제를 주사했더니 쥐가 장기 기억을 형성하지는 못하지만 계속해서 단기 기억을 저장할 수 있다는 것을 발견했다(After injecting mice with an antibiotic drug ~)'고 했으므로 '항생제 약물의 사용은 사람으로 하여금 아주 최근의 일도 기억하지 못하게 한다'는 것은 지문 내용과 상반되는 추론이다.
② '단기 기억이 장기 기억에 대한 핵심적인 예측 도구'라는 것은 추론할 근거가 없다.
③ [C]의 뒤에서 시냅스 내에 있는 신경전달물질의 농도가 변화한다고 언급했지만 '비교적 더 적은 신경전달물질이 배출되는지'는 알 수가 없다.

어휘 predictor n. 예측 도구
in an active manner phr. 활발하게
retain v. 보유하다, 기억하다
be accompanied by phr. ~을 동반하다

[45-47]

[C] 세균은 자라나서 유기체로 발달할 수 있는 작은 생명체이다. 세균은 질병을 포함하여 많은 문제를 일으킬 수 있다. 사람들을 아프게 만드는 세균은 어느 곳에나 존재한다. 보이진 않지만, 세균은 그곳에 존재한다. 세균은 책상 위에 있다. 세균은 컴퓨터 키보드에 숨어 있다. 심지어는 당신이 숨 쉬는 공기 속에도 있다.

[B] 세균에는 두 가지 종류가 있다: 바이러스와 박테리아다. 바이러스는 살아가고 증식하기 위해서 동물이나 식물 내부에 있는 세포를 이용한다. 바이러스는 독감이라고 불리는 인플루엔자 같은 질병을 일으킨다. 박테리아는 매우 작은 생명체이다. 일부 박테리아는 좋다. 그것들은 당신의 위장에서 음식을 소화하도록 돕는다. 다른 박테리아는 좋지 않다. 그것들은 목을 따갑게 하거나 귀에 감염을 일으킬 수 있다.

[A] 이러한 작은 침입자들이 당신을 아프게 하는 것을 막을 수 있을까? 당신의 피부가 세균을 막아내는 첫 번째 방어막이다. 일부 질병을 예방하기 위한 가장 쉬운 방법의 하나는 바로 비누와 물로 손을 씻는 간단한 것이다. 하지만 세균은 여전히 피부의 작은 상처나 입, 눈, 그리고 코를 통해 몸 안으로 들어올 수 있다.

tiny adj. 매우 작은 invader n. 침입자
defense n. 방어물, 방어 시설 germ n. 세균
prevent v. 예방하다 cut n. 상처 bacteria n. 박테리아
multiply v. 증식하다, 복제하다
influenza n. 인플루엔자, 독감 creature n. 생명체
stomach n. 위장 digest v. 소화하다
sore throat phr. 인후염 infection n. 감염
organism n. 유기체

45 2019 한성대

정답 ③

해설 [A], [B], [C]의 적절한 순서를 파악하는 문제이다. 세균에 대한 정의와 세균이 어디에나 존재한다는 사실을 알려주는 [C]가 먼저 와야 한다. 그다음에 [B]에서 세균에 바이러스와 박테리아의 두 가지 종류가 있으며 그것들이 질병을 일으킨다는 사실을 설명하고, 마지막으로 [A]에서 세균이 이러한 질병을 일으키는 것을 예방하기 위한 방법에 관해 설명하는 것이 자연스럽다. 따라서 주어진 지문 다음에 이어질 순서는 ③ [C] — [B] — [A]다.

46 2019 한성대

정답 ①

해석 ① 세균은 우리 눈으로 보기에는 매우 작다.
② 일부 바이러스는 인간의 신체에 긍정적인 영향을 준다.
③ 박테리아는 독감이라고 불리는 인플루엔자 같은 질병을 일으킨다.
④ 박테리아는 살아있는 세포에서만 성장하고 증식할 수 있다.

해설 지문의 내용과 일치하는 것을 묻는 문제이다. 지문의 첫 번째 문단의 How can you stop these tiny invaders from making you sick의 내용과 세 번째 문단의 You can't see them, but they're there의 내용을 통해 세균은 우리 눈으로 보기에는 매우 작다는 것을 알 수 있다. 따라서 ①번이 지문의 내용과 일치한다.

오답분석
② 일부가 좋고 다른 것은 좋지 않다고 한 것은 박테리아라고 했으므로, 일부 바이러스는 인간의 신체에 긍정적인 영향을 준다는 것은 지문의 내용과 다르다.
③ 인플루엔자와 같은 질병을 일으킬 수 있는 것은 바이러스라고 했으므로, 박테리아는 독감이라고 불리는 인플루엔자 같은 질병을 일으킨다는 것은 지문의 내용과 다르다.
④ 살아가고 증식하기 위해서 동물과 식물 안에 있는 세포를 이용하는 것은 바이러스라고 했으므로, 박테리아는 살아있는 세포에서만 성장하고 증식할 수 있다는 것은 지문의 내용과 다르다.

어휘 impact n. 영향

47 [2019 한성대]
정답 ③

해석
① 피부를 보호하는 방법
② 피부, 방어의 첫 번째 전선
③ 매우 작은 침입자들
④ 세균 산업

해설 지문의 제목을 묻는 문제이다. 지문의 전체적으로 바이러스와 박테리아와 같은 세균에 대한 정의와 그 세균들이 질병을 일으킨다는 사실, 그리고 질병을 예방하기 위한 방법에 대해 포괄적으로 설명하고 있다. 따라서 지문의 제목을 '매우 작은 침입자들'이라고 표현한 ③번이 정답이다.

어휘 protect v. 보호하다 line n. 전선(戰線)
industry n. 산업

[48-51]

고통을 느낄 수 있는 능력은 인간과 나머지 동물에게 주어진 자연의 선물 중 하나이다. 이 능력이 없다면, 우리는 뜨거운 물건을 만졌을 때 반사적으로 움찔하지 않을 것이고, 맨발로 깨진 유리를 밟는 것을 피할 줄 모를 것이기 때문이다. 통증에 대한 즉각적이거나 기억에 의한 경험으로 촉진되는 이러한 행동들은 우리가 신체적 위험을 축소할 수 있도록 만들어 준다. 우리는 고통을 느끼도록 진화해 왔는데 이는 고통을 느끼는 감각이 자기 보호를 위해 필수적인 경고 체계의 역할을 하기 때문이다.
이 체계의 보초 역할을 하는 것은 통각 수용기라 불리는 특별한 감각 신경 세포의 범주인데, (A)이것은 피부, 폐, 내장을 비롯하여 몸의 다른 부위까지 확장하는 섬유 조직을 가지고, 척추 근처에 위치해 있다. (B)통각 수용기는 자상, 타는 듯한 산성, 녹아내리는 밀랍의 열과 같은 다양한 종류의 해로운 자극을 느끼기 위한 장비를 갖추고 있다. 통각 수용기가 어떤 위협을 감지했을 때, (C)그들은 척수에 전기 신호를 보내게 되는데, 이때 척수는 이 (D)전기 신호를 다른 신경 세포를 통해 뇌로 올려보낸다. 그리고 이 상향 고통 경로의 다음 목적지인 피질 속 상위 세포들은 전기 신호를 입력받은 고통의 지각으로 변환시킨다. 통증을 인식하자마자, 뇌는 통증에 대응하기 위한 시도를 한다. 뇌 안에 위치한 신경망은 전기적 신호를 다시 우리가 하향 고통 경로라 부르는 길을 따라 내려 보내는데, 이것이 엔도르핀과 다른 자연적인 오피오이드의 방출을 촉발하는 것이다. 이러한 생화학적 물질은 상향 고통 경로를 억제하여, 효과적으로 고통의 양을 줄이게 된다.

---

humankind n. 인류 recoil v. 움츠러들다
barefoot adv. 맨발로 minimize v. 축소하다
sensation n. 감각 vital adj. 필수적인
self-preservation n. 자기 보호 sentry n. 보초
sensory neuron phr. 감각 신경 세포
nociceptor n. 통각 수용기 spine n. 척추
spinal cord phr. 척수 transmit v. 옮기다
cortex n. 피질 register v. 인식하다
counteract v. 대응하다 neural network phr. 신경망
trigger v. 촉발시키다 endorphin n. 엔도르핀
opioid n. 오피오이드 biochemical n. 생화학 물질

48 [2020 한성대]
정답 ③

해석
① 고통을 느끼는 것은 생존을 위한 신체의 핵심 기능이다.
② 뇌 안의 특정한 신경 세포가 없다면, 우리는 고통을 인식할 수 없을 것이다.
③ 통각 수용기는 외부 고통의 침입으로부터 우리를 보호해주는 경호원과 같다.
④ 통증 신호는 신경 세포의 망을 통해 몸의 위아래로 이동한다.

해설 지문의 내용과 일치하지 않는 것을 묻는 문제이다. 지문의 두 번째 문단에서, 통각 수용기는 고통을 감지하여 뇌로 전달하는 일종의 보초 역할을 한다고 했으므로, 통각 수용기가 외부 고통의 침입으로부터 우리를 보호해주는 경호원과 같은 역할을 한다는 것은 지문의 내용과 다르다. 따라서 ③번이 정답이다.

오답분석
① 지문의 첫 번째 문단에서, 사람이 고통을 느낄 수 있기 때문에 뜨거운 물건을 만졌을 때 몸을 움츠리고, 깨진 유리 조각을 맨발로 밟지 않을 수 있다고 설명하고 있으므로, 고통을 느끼는 것이 생존을 위한 신체의 핵심 기능이라는 것은 지문의 내용과 일치한다.
② 지문의 두 번째 문단에서, 뇌의 피질에서 전기 신호의 입력값을 고통의 지각으로 변환시킨다고 했으므로, 뇌 안의 특정 신경 세포가 없다면, 우리는 고통을 인식할 수 없으리라는 것은 지문의 내용과 일치한다.

④ 지문의 마지막 문단에서, 고통을 전달하는 전기적 신호는 상향 고통 경로와 하향 고통 경로를 통해 몸 안에서 이동한다고 했으므로, 통증 신호가 신경 세포의 망을 통해 몸의 위아래로 이동한다는 것은 지문의 내용과 일치한다.

어휘 **key function** phr. 핵심 기능　**infiltration** n. 침입
external adj. 외부의

49 [2020 한성대]

정답 ④

해석
① 생각에 잠겨 — 효과적으로
② 생각에 잠겨 — 감정적으로
③ 반사적으로 — 감정적으로
④ 반사적으로 — 효과적으로

해설 지문의 빈칸을 채우는 문제이다. 첫 번째 빈칸이 포함된 문장은 고통을 느끼는 감각이 없다면 뜨거운 물건에 손을 대더라도 반사적으로 움츠러들지 않을 것이라는 문맥이 자연스러우므로, '반사적으로'를 의미하는 reflexively가 들어가야 한다. 두 번째 빈칸에는 엔도르핀과 오피오이드와 같은 생화학 물질들이 효과적으로 인식되는 고통의 양을 줄인다는 문맥이 자연스러우므로 '효과적으로'라는 의미의 effectively가 들어가야 한다. 따라서 ④번이 정답이다.

50 [2020 한성대]

정답 ④

해설 (A)~(D) 가운데 의미하는 바가 다른 것을 파악하는 문제이다. (A), (B), (C)는 모두 '통각 수용기'를 의미하는데, (D)는 '전기 신호'를 의미하므로 (A)~(D) 가운데 의미하는 바가 다른 것은 (D)이다. 따라서 ④번이 정답이다.

51 [2020 한성대]

정답 ①

해석
① 우리의 신체가 어떻게 고통을 다루는가
② 어떻게 고통을 줄이는가
③ 고통 신호의 마지막 목적지
④ 오피오이드의 발전

해설 지문의 제목을 묻는 문제이다. 지문 전체적으로 고통을 겪게 됐을 때 일어나는 신체 내부의 활동을 설명하고 있다. 따라서 이 지문의 제목을 '우리의 신체가 어떻게 고통을 다루는가'라고 표현한 ①번이 정답이다.

어휘 **handle** v. 다루다

[52-55]

[A] 유전학의 큰 발전은 우리에게 밝은 전망과 함께 곤경도 제공한다. 밝은 전망은 우리가 곧 심신을 쇠약하게 하는 수많은 질병을 치료하고 예방할 수 있을 것이라는 점이다. 곤경은 새로 발견된 우리의 유전학 지식은 또한 우리의 근육과 기억력 그리고 기분을 향상시키고, 자녀의 성별과 키 그리고 다른 유전적 특질들을 선택하고, 우리의 신체 능력과 인지 능력을 개선하며, 우리 자신을 '건강한 상태 이상으로 더 건강하게' 만드는 등, 우리로 하여금 우리 자신의 본성을 조작할 수 있게 한다는 점이다. 대부분의 사람들은 적어도 몇 가지 형태의 유전공학을 불안감을 조성하는 것으로 생각한다. 그러나 우리의 불안감의 원천을 명확하게 말하기는 쉽지 않다. 도덕적 담론과 정치적 담론의 익숙한 용어들은 우리의 본성을 개량하는 것이 뭐가 잘못인지 말하기 어렵게 만든다.

[B] 복제 문제를 다시 생각해보자. 1997년의 복제 양 돌리(Dolly)의 탄생은 복제 인간에 대한 전망에 관하여 엄청난 우려를 갖게 하였다. 걱정할 만한 충분한 의학적 이유가 있다. 대부분의 과학자들은 복제가 안전하지 않으며 심각한 기형과 선천적 장애를 가진 자손을 생산할 가능성이 있다는 점에 동의한다. 돌리는 때 이른 죽음을 맞이했다. 그러나 그런 위험이 자연스러운 임신의 위험보다 더 크지 않은 정도까지 복제 기술이 향상된다고 가정해보자. 그래도 인간 복제가 (A)반대할 만한 것인가? 자기 부모와 유전적으로 쌍둥이인 아이를 만드는 것이 정확하게 뭐가 잘못인가?

[C] 어떤 이들은 복제가 아이의 자율성에 대한 권리를 침해하기 때문에 잘못이라고 말한다. 미리 아이의 유전적 구성을 선택함으로써, 부모는 아이를 먼저 살다간 누군가의 그림자 속의 삶을 살게 하는 것이며, 따라서 그 아이에게서 여러 가능성이 열려있는 미래에 대한 권리를 박탈하는 것이다. (B)자율성에 근거한 반대는 복제에 대해서 뿐만 아니라 부모로 하여금 자녀의 유전적 특성을 선택할 수 있게 하는 생명공학의 어떤 형태에 대해서도 제기될 수 있다.

breakthrough n. 돌파구; 큰 발전
promise n. 밝은 전망, 장래성　**predicament** n. 곤경, 궁지
a host of phr. 많은
debilitating adj. (심신을) 쇠약하게 하는
manipulate v. 다루다, 조작하다
enhance v. 높이다, 향상시키다
disquieting adj. 불안을 조성하는
articulate v. 똑렷이 말하다; 분명히 표현하다
unease n. 불안(감), 우려　**discourse** n. 담론
reengineer v. 재설계하다, 개량하다
torrent n. 급류, 마구 쏟아짐, 빗발침　**offspring** n. 자식, 자손
abnormality n. 기형, 이상　**birth defect** phr. 선천적 장애
objectionable adj. 반대할만한, 불쾌한
autonomy n. 자치권, 자율성
consign v. (어디에) 놓다, 두다; (어떤 상황에) 처하게 하다
bioengineering n. 생명공학

52 ⓐ 2018 아주대

정답 ③

해석 ① 유전공학의 큰 발전과 유전공학의 장래성 있는 미래
② 우리의 본성을 개량하는 것을 도덕적 담론이 뒷받침해야 할 필요성
③ 유전공학에 대한 우리의 우려를 분명히 표현하기
④ 자녀 양육에서 자율성과 부모의 보살핌의 의미
⑤ 심신을 쇠약하게 하는 질병의 확산으로 인한 의료산업의 성장

해설 지문의 제목을 묻는 문제이다. [A] 문단에서는 유전공학의 발전이 사람들을 불안하게 하지만, 불안감의 원천을 명확하게 말하기는 쉽지 않다고 했다. [B] 문단에서는 복제 문제를 언급하며 걱정할 만한 충분한 의학적 이유가 있다고 했다. 문단 [C]에서는 복제로 태어난 아이의 자율성이 침해된다는 점을 근거로 한 복제 반대를 소개하고 있다. 따라서 이 지문의 제목으로 '유전공학에 대한 우리의 우려를 분명히 표현하기'라고 표현한 ③번이 정답이다.

어휘 proliferation n. 급증, 확산

53 ⓐ 2018 아주대

정답 ①

해석 ① 때 이른 ② 더없이 행복한
③ 갈망하는 ④ 차분한
⑤ 용서할 수 있는

해설 지문의 빈칸을 채우는 문제이다. 빈칸 앞에서 대부분의 과학자들은 복제가 안전하지 않으며 심각한 기형과 선천적 장애를 가진 자손을 생산할 가능성이 있다는 점에 동의한다고 했으므로, 복제 양 돌리 또한 정상적이지 않은 죽음을 맞이했다는 것을 알 수 있다. 따라서 ①번이 정답이다.

어휘 premature adj. 정상(예상)보다 이른, 때 이른
covetous adj. 탐내는, 갈망하는
placid adj. 차분한, 잔잔한
excusable adj. 변명이 되는, 용서할 수 있는

54 ⓐ 2018 아주대

정답 ②

해석 ① 치유 가능한 ② 달갑지 않은
③ 이해할 수 있는 ④ 운용(실행) 가능한
⑤ 이해할 수 있는

해설 밑줄 친 (A) objectionable을 대신할 수 있는 동의어를 고르는 문제이다. objectionable은 '반대할 만한, 불쾌한'이라는 의미이다. 따라서 '달갑지 않은, 불쾌한'을 의미하는 ②번 undesirable이 정답이다.

55 ⓐ 2018 아주대

정답 ⑤

해석 ① (유리한 유전적 향상조차도) '맞춤형 아이들'을 모든 질병에 면역이 있는 완벽한 존재로 만들기 (때문에)
② (유리한 유전적 향상조차도) '맞춤형 아이들'에게 깊이 생각하며 잘 짜인 인생 계획을 만들어낼 능력을 심어줄 수 없기 (때문에)
③ (유리한 유전적 향상조차도) '맞춤형 아이들'에게 타인의 자율성을 존중하지 않고 주류 사회의 가치관과 규범에 따르도록 강요하기 (때문에)
④ (유리한 유전적 향상조차도) '맞춤형 아이들'을 자신의 자율성에 반대하게 하고 끊임없이 부모의 도움에 의존하게 하기 (때문에)
⑤ (유리한 유전적 향상조차도) 특정한 인생 선택을 향해 방향을 정해주며, 스스로 인생 계획을 선택할 권리를 침해하기 (때문에)

해설 [C] 문단의 (B)자율성에 근거한 반대에 따르면 유전공학의 문제점이 무엇인지 고르는 문제이다. [C] 문단에 의하면 자율성에 근거한 반대는 미리 아이의 유전적 구성을 선택함으로써 부모는 아이를 먼저 살다간 누군가의 그림자 속의 삶을 살게 하는 것이며, 따라서 그 아이에게서 여러 가능성이 열려있는 미래에 대한 권리를 박탈하기 때문에 복제는 잘못된 것이라고 주장하는 입장이다. 따라서 문제의 '심지어 유리한 유전적 향상조차도 _____ 때문에 맞춤형 아이들이 완전히 자유롭지는 않다'라는 문맥에서 빈칸에는 ⑤번의 '특정한 인생 선택을 향해 방향을 정해주며, 스스로 인생 계획을 선택할 권리를 침해하기 (때문에)'라는 표현이 들어가는 것이 적합하다.

어휘 inculcate in phr. (생각 등을 머릿속에) 심어주다
reflect v. 깊이 생각하다, 성찰하다

[56-57]

척추동물의 신경계는 머리 부분에서 뇌로 확대되어 끝나는 속이 비어있는 등의 신경 코드를 특징으로 한다. 심지어 가장 원시적인 형태에서도 이 코드와 그것에 붙어있는 신경은 진화 과정의 전문화의 결과이며 하등 척추동물로부터 고등 척추동물로의 진화는 완전히 이해되지 못하고 있는 과정이다. 그럼에도 불구하고, 기본적인 배치는 모든 척추동물에게 유사하며, 하등 동물에 대한 연구는 고등 동물 신경계의 형태와 구조에 대한 통찰력을 제공한다. 더욱이 어떤 종이든, 신경계의 발생학 상의 발달에 대한 연구는 성체 형태를 이해하기 위해 필수적이다. 어떤 척추동물에서든 신경계의 두 개 주요 부분이 구별될 수 있다. 이것들(그 두 부분)은 뇌와 척수로 구성되는 중추신경계와 두개골의 신경, 척추 신경, 말초신경 그리고 그것들의 운동신경과 감각신경 종말로 구성되는 말초신경계이다. '자율신경계'라는 용어는 심장 근육과 입 근육 그리고 많은 분비선에 공급을 하고 조절을 하는 중추신경계와 말초신경계의 여러 부분들을 나타낸다. 신경계는 수많은 신경과 교질 세포 그리고

혈관과 소량의 연결 조직으로 구성되어 있다. 신경세포 즉 '뉴런'은 여러 과정을 특색으로 하며 감수성과 전도성이라는 현상을 상당한 정도로 보여준다는 점에서 특화되어 있다. 중추신경계의 교질 세포는 '신경교'라고 통칭되는 세포들을 유지시키고 있다. 그것들은 뉴런, 혈관 및 연결 조직과 특별한 관계를 맺고 있는 짧은 과정들을 특색으로 한다. 말초신경계의 비슷한 세포들은 '신경초' 세포라는 용어로 불린다.

vertebrate n. 척추동물 hollow adj. (속이) 빈
dorsal adj. (동물의) 등에 있는 nerve n. 신경
enlargement n. 확대(확장)한 것 insight n. 통찰력
embryological adj. 발생학(상)의
indispensable adj. 없어서는 안 될, 필수적인
morphology n. 형태학 spinal cord phr. 척수, 등골
peripheral adj. 주변적인, 지엽적인
peripheral nervous system phr. 말초신경계
cranial adj. 두개골의 spinal adj. 척추의
motor n. 운동신경 sensory ending phr. 감각신경 종말
autonomic nervous system phr. 자율신경계
cardiac adj. 심장의 gland n. (분비)선
glial cell phr. 교질 세포 irritability n. 자극 감수성, 과민성
conductivity n. 전도성 neuroglia n. 신경교
comparable adj. 비교할만한, 비슷한
neurilemmal adj. 신경초의

56 2018 한양대

정답 ③

해석 ① 신경 세포의 진화
      ② 생명공학의 발전
      ③ 척추동물의 신경계
      ④ 자율신경계의 기능

해설 지문의 주제를 묻는 문제이다. 첫 문장에서 '척추동물의 신경계'는 속이 비어있는 등의 신경 코드를 특징으로 한다고 언급한 이후에 척추동물의 신경계를 구성하는 중추신경계와 말초신경계 그리고 자율신경계 등에 관한 설명으로 이어진다. 따라서 지문의 주제를 '척추동물의 신경계'라고 표현한 ③번이 정답이다.

57 2018 한양대

정답 ②

해석 ① 다른 종에서의 똑같은 구조에 대한 향상된 연구
      ② 완전히 발달된 구조에 대한 더 나은 이해
      ③ 과학자들이 신경질환을 진단할 수 있는 방법
      ④ 부진한 발달이 교정될 수 있는 방법을 발견하는 것

해설 배아의 생물학적 구조를 신중하게 연구하면 어떤 결과로 이어질지를 고르는 문제이다. 네 번째 문장 Moreover, for any species, the study of the embryological development ~ understanding of adult morphology.에서 '더욱이 어떤 종이든, 신경계의 발생학상의 발달에 대한 연구는 성체 형태를 이해하기 위해 필수적'이라고 했으므로, 배아의 생물학적 구조에 대한 연구의 결과는 '완전히 발달된 구조에 대한 더 나은 이해'라는 것을 알 수 있다. 따라서 ②번이 정답이다.

어휘 embryo n. 배아

[58-60]

먹이사슬에서 인류의 위치는 최근까지 확실히 중간이었다. 수백만 년 동안, 더 큰 포식자들에게 사냥을 당하는 동안 인간은 더 작은 생명체를 사냥했고, 그들이 모을 수 있는 것을 모았다. 몇몇 종의 인간이 정기적으로 거대한 사냥감을 사냥하기 시작한 것은 불과 40만 년 전이었으며, 불과 10만 년에 걸쳐 호모 사피엔스의 출현과 함께 인간은 먹이 사슬의 정상으로 갑자기 뛰어올랐다.

중간에서 정상으로 오른 이 극적인 도약에는 엄청난 결과가 있었다. 사자와 상어와 같이 피라미드의 상위에 있는 다른 동물들은 그 위치로 매우 점진적으로, 수백만 년에 걸쳐 진화했다. 이것은 사자와 상어가 생태계에 너무 큰 피해를 입히지 않도록 생태계가 견제와 균형의 원리를 발달할 수 있게 했다. 사자가 더 치명적으로 됨에 따라, 가젤은 더 빠르게 뛰고, 하이에나는 더 잘 협동하고, 코뿔소는 더 성미가 까다롭게 진화했다. 반대로, 인류는 정상으로 너무 빠르게 올라가서 생태계가 적응할 충분한 시간이 주어지지 않았다. 게다가, 인간 자신들도 적응하지 못했다. 지구의 가장 상위 포식자들은 장엄한 생명체이다. 수백만 년간의 지배는 포식자들을 자신감으로 가득 차게 했다. 그에 반해서 현 인류는 바나나 공화국의 독재자와 더 유사하다.

predator n. 포식자 game n. 사냥감
spectacular adj. 극적인 enormous adj. 엄청난
consequence n. 결과 evolve v. 진화하다
wreak v. 입히다, 가하다 havoc n. 큰 피해
deadly adj. 치명적인 bad-tempered adj. 성미가 까다로운
ascend to phr. ~로 올라가다 adjust v. 적응하다
majestic adj. 장엄한 confidence n. 자신감
banana-republic n. 바나나 공화국(해외 원조로 살아가는 가난한 나라)

58 2019 단국대

정답 ③

해석 ① 성향과 번식   ② 경쟁과 공존
      ③ 견제와 균형   ④ 특권과 규제

해설 지문의 빈칸을 채우는 문제이다. 빈칸 뒤 문장에서 사자가 더 치명적으로 됨에 따라, 가젤은 더 빠르게 뛰고, 하이에나는 더 잘 협동하고, 코뿔소는 더 성미가 까다롭게 진화했다고 했으므로, 빈칸에는 사자와 상어가 생태계에 너무 큰 피해를 입히지 않도록 생태계가 어떤 것을 발달시켰는지에 대한 내용이

나와야 적절하다는 것을 알 수 있다. 따라서 '견제와 균형'이라고 한 ③번이 정답이다.

어휘 disposition n. 성향 reproduction n. 번식
privilege n. 특권 regulation n. 규제

59 2019 단국대

정답 ③

해석 ① 현 인류는 처음에 유인원에서 진화했으며, 주식 작물인 바나나에 의존했다.
② 호모 사피엔스는 특유의 정치적 구조를 기반으로 막강한 지배력을 이루어냈다.
③ 인간은 그들의 위치에 불안해하는데, 이것은 인간을 잔혹하고 위험하게 만든다.
④ 인류는 최초의 부유한 사회를 만들기 위해 농업 혁명을 이루어냈다.

해설 밑줄 친 부분의 의미를 추론하는 문제이다. 밑줄 친 'Sapiens by contrast is more like a banana-republic dictator.'는 '그에 반해서 현 인류는 바나나 공화국의 독재자와 더 유사하다.'라는 의미이다. 주변의 내용을 살펴보면 이것이 인간은 그들의 위치에 불안해하는데, 이것은 인간을 잔혹하고 위험하게 만든다는 것을 의미함을 알 수 있다. 따라서 ③번이 정답이다.

어휘 dependent adj. 의존하는 staple food phr. 주식
brutal adj. 잔혹한 agricultural adj. 농업의

60 2019 단국대

정답 ④

해석 ① 호모 사피엔스는 40만 년 전에 동물을 길들이고 식물을 재배하여 생활했다.
② 사자와 상어는 수백만 년 동안 먹이사슬의 중간에 있다.
③ 가장 상위 포식자들은 다른 동물을 사냥함으로써 생태계를 파괴했다.
④ 생태계는 포식자가 더 강력하게 진화함에 따라 변했다.

해설 지문의 내용과 일치하는 것을 묻는 문제이다. 두 번째 문단의 네 번째 문장 As lions became deadlier ~를 통해 생태계는 포식자가 더 강력하게 진화함에 따라 변했다는 것을 알 수 있다. 따라서 ④번이 지문의 내용과 일치한다.

오답분석 ① 불과 10만 년에 걸쳐 호모 사피엔스의 출현과 함께 인간은 먹이 사슬의 정상으로 갑자기 뛰어올랐다고 했으므로, 호모 사피엔스는 40만 년 전에 동물을 길들이고 식물을 재배하여 생활했다는 것은 지문의 내용과 다르다.
② 사자와 상어와 같이 피라미드의 상위에 있는 다른 동물들은 그 위치로 매우 점진적으로, 수백만 년에 걸쳐 진화했다고 했으므로, 사자와 상어가 수백만 년 동안 먹이사슬의 중간에 있다는 것은 지문의 내용과 다르다.
③ 생태계는 사자와 상어와 같은 포식자가 생태계에 너무 큰 피해를 입히지 않도록 견제와 균형의 원리를 발달시켰다고 했으므로, 가장 상위 포식자들이 다른 동물을 사냥함으로써 생태계를 파괴했다는 것은 지문의 내용과 다르다.

어휘 subsist v. 생활하다 domesticate v. 길들이다, 재배하다

[61-62]

프로그램이 사라진 컴퓨터의 행동방식을 관찰하고 분석하는 사람은 원칙적으로 그 프로그램 또는 그것과 기능적으로 동등한 것을 복원할 수 있을 것이다. 그러나 그 프로그램이 원래 어떤 언어로 쓰였었는지를 알 방법은 없다. 최종 결과는 어떤 경우에서든 똑같다: 컴퓨터는 제곱근을 계산하는 것과 같은 일부 유용한 일을 실행한다. 동물을 관찰하는 생물학자는 사라진 프로그램을 실행하는 컴퓨터를 관찰하는 엔지니어와 다소 똑같은 입장에 처한다. 그 동물은, 마치 어떤 프로그램 즉 질서정연한 일련의 긴요한 지시사항을 따르고 있는 것처럼, 조직적이고 목적의식이 있는 것처럼 보이는 방식으로 행동하고 있다. 그 동물의 프로그램은, 작성된 적이 없기 때문에, 사실은 사라진 것이 아니다. 오히려, 자연도태는 연속으로 여러 세대의 신경계가 작동하도록 변경시키는 돌연변이를 선호함으로써, 하드웨어에 내장된 기계어 프로그램에 상응하는 것을 <u>대충 꿰맞추었다</u>. 그럼에도 불구하고, 우리는 동물을 영어처럼 쉽게 이해되는 언어로 '쓰여진' 어떤 프로그램을 '따르는' 것으로 생각하는 것이 편리하다. 그러면 우리가 할 수 있는 일들 중의 하나는, 그 개체군의 신경계에서 '컴퓨터 시간'을 갖기 위해 서로 '경쟁하는' 대체 프로그램이나 하위 루틴을 상상하는 것이다.

in principle phr. 원칙적으로, 대체로
reconstruct v. 복원(재건)하다
equivalent n. 상당(대응)하는 것 square root phr. 제곱근
purposeful adj. 목적의식이 있는 orderly adj. 질서정연한
sequence n. 순서, 차례
imperative adj. 반드시 해야 하는, 긴요한
natural selection phr. 자연도태, 자연 선택
cobble together phr. 대충 꿰맞추다
hard-wired adj. 하드웨어에 내장된
machine code phr. 기계어, 기계언어
successive adj. 연속적인, 잇따른

61 2018 한양대

정답 ②

해석 ① 자연도태는 많은 대체 프로그램이나 하위 루틴에 작용한다.
② 동물의 프로그램이 원래 어떤 유전자에 작성되어 있었는지를 알 수 있는 방법이 많다.
③ 동물은 마치 프로그램을 따르는 것처럼 분명히 효과적이고 잘 계획된 방식으로 행동한다.
④ 동물의 행동 방식을 설명할 때, 필자는 사라진 프로그램을 실행하고 있는 컴퓨터에 비유한다.

해설   지문의 내용과 일치하지 않는 것을 찾는 문제이다. 두 번째 문장 But there is no way of knowing in which language the program was originally written.에서 '그러나 그 프로그램이 원래 어떤 언어로 쓰였었는지를 알 방법은 없다'고 했으므로, '동물의 프로그램이 원래 어떤 유전자에 작성되어 있었는지를 알 수 있는 방법이 많다'는 것은 지문의 내용과 다르다. 따라서 ②번이 지문의 내용과 일치하지 않는다.

오답 분석
① 마지막 세 문장에서 '자연도태는 돌연변이를 선호함으로써 하드웨어에 내장된 프로그램에 상응하는 것을 대충 꿰맞추었다'고 했으며, '우리는 동물을 어떤 프로그램을 따르는 것으로 생각하는 것이 편리하며, 그러면 우리가 할 수 있는 일들 중의 하나는 서로 경쟁하는 대체 프로그램이나 하위 루틴을 상상하는 것'이라고 했으므로, '자연도태는 많은 대체 프로그램이나 하위 루틴에 작용한다'는 것을 알 수 있다.
③ 다섯 번째 문장 The animal is behaving in what appears to be an organized, purposeful way, as if it was obeying a program, an orderly sequence of imperative instructions.를 통해 '동물은 마치 프로그램을 따르는 것처럼 분명히 효과적이고 잘 계획된 방식으로 행동한다'는 것을 알 수 있다.
④ 네 번째 문장 A biologist looking at an animal is somewhat the same position as an engineer looking at a computer running a lost program.을 통해 동물의 행동 방식을 설명할 때, 필자는 사라진 프로그램을 실행하고 있는 컴퓨터에 비유한다는 것을 알 수 있다.

어휘   **analogy** n. 비유; 유사점

62 [2018 한양대]

정답 ③

해설
① 확고히 고정된
② 영구히 사라진
③ 유용하지만 완벽하지는 않은
④ 일련의 규칙으로 해석되는

해설   화자가 'cobbled together'라는 어구를 사용한 의도를 파악하는 문제이다. cobbled together가 포함된 문장에서 '자연도태는 연속으로 여러 세대의 신경계가 작동하도록 변경시키는 돌연변이를 선호함으로써'라고 했으므로, '자연도태가 만든 하드웨어에 내장된 기계어 프로그램은 유용하지만 완벽하지는 않다'는 것을 나타내기 위해서라는 것을 알 수 있다. 따라서 정답은 ③번이다.

[63-64]

어떤 한 유기체의 행동이라는 것은 그 유기체가 처한 특정상황이나 자극에서 특별한 방식으로 반응하는 경향이다. 그러나 모든 하나의 동물은 일관된 지속적인 방식으로 행동할지도 모르지만, 서로 다른 개체군들은 행동이 다른 경향이 있다. 이런 다양성을 알아보기 위해서는, 당신의 마당에 있는 다람쥐에게 다가가기만 하면 된다. 어느 지점에서 당신은 다람쥐에게 너무 가까이 다가서게 될 것이고, 그러면 다람쥐는 재빠르게 나무 위로 달아날 것이다. 이제 또 다른 다람쥐에게 다가가라. 그리고 또 다른 다람쥐에게도 다가가면 그 다람쥐도 달아날 것이다. 당신은 어떤 다람쥐들은 당신이 가까이 오도록 허용하는 반면, 다른 다람쥐들은 재빠르게 달아난다는 것을 알게 될 것이다. 이러한 차이는 동물들 안에 어디에서나 있다. 어떤 개체군은 다른 개체들보다 더 공격적이다. 어떤 개체들은 더 호기심이 많다. 어떤 개체들은 빨리 반응하지만 어떤 개체들은 주저한다. 이런 행동의 다양성은 생명이나 죽음을 의미하기도 한다. 대담한 다람쥐는 결국 코요테의 점심거리가 될지도 모른다. 겁이 많은 다람쥐는 겨울에 살아남기 위한 충분한 먹이를 찾지 못할지도 모른다. 그러므로 이런 행동의 다양성에 대한 표출(표현방식)은 개체의 적합성에 영향을 미친다.

---

fashion n. 방법, 방식; 유행   **stimulus** n. 자극
vary v. 가지각색이다, 다르다; 변하다
variation n. 변화, 차이, 변동
bolt n. 빗장, 자물쇠청, 걸쇠; (총의) 노리쇠; 볼트, 나사못;
v. 내닫다, 뛰다; 달아나다, 도망치다
ubiquitous adj. (동시에) 도처에 있는, 편재하는
(= omnipresent); 여기저기 모습을 나타내는
aggressive adj. 공격적인, 적극적인
inquisitive adj. 호기심이 많은, 캐묻기를 좋아하는, 꼬치꼬치 캐어묻는, 듣고 싶어 하는, 탐구적인
hold back phr. 저지하다, 억제하다; 망설이다
bold adj. 용감한, 대담한
fitness n. 적당, 적절; 적합성, 타당성(= propriety); 건강; 체력

63 [2018 한양대에리카]

정답 ③

해설
① 다람쥐들의 특별한 행동
② 행동과 개체의 적합성
③ 개체들의 행동 불일치
④ 공격성과 생존 가능성

해설   지문의 제목을 묻는 문제이다. 특정 동물, 본문에서는 다람쥐를 예로 들면서 행동의 불일치에 대해서 예로 들어 설명하고 있다. 따라서 이 지문의 제목을 '개체들의 행동 불일치'라고 표현한 ③번이 정답이다.

64 [2018 한양대에리카]

정답 ①

해설
① 호기심이 많은   ② 무관심한
③ 의심스러운   ④ 방어적인

해설 밑줄 친 부분의 의미를 추론하는 문제이다. 단어 추론 문제는 일반적으로 직접적인 의미도 물어보지만 글의 전체적인 문맥에서 답을 찾아야 함에 유의한다. inquisitive는 '호기심이 많은, 탐구적인'이란 뜻이므로, ① curious가 정답이다.

[65-66]

수천 년 동안, 계절에 따른 바이칼호의 장기적인 결빙은 호수에 있는 대부분의 동식물 상이 얼음 위와 아래에서의 삶에 적응하도록 했다. 담수나 염수 환경에서 사는 미생물인 식물성 플랑크톤은 바이칼호 먹이 그물의 토대이다. 바이칼호는 지배적인 제1차 생산자(식물성 플랑크톤)와 상위 포식자(바이칼 물범) 모두가 번식을 위해 얼음이 있어야 하는 전 세계에서 유일한 호수이다.

바이칼호의 식물성 플랑크톤은 녹조를 포함하는데, 며칠에서 몇 주간 지속하여 만개하면서 폭발적으로 자랄 수 있다. 얼음의 두께와 투명도는 물에 도달하는 빛의 양을 결정하는데, 이는 식물성 플랑크톤의 성장에 중요한 요소이다. 이러한 독특한 조류가 특정한 얼음 아래의 환경에 적응해왔기 때문에, 따뜻해지고 있는 대기 온도에 의해 초래된 최근 얼음의 변화는 조류 성장률을 감소시켰고, 봄에 일어나는 조류 대 증식을 둔화했다. 이 감소의 영향은 이후 먹이 사슬의 위쪽으로 옮겨가는데, 조류를 먹는 많은 아주 작은 갑각류 동물부터 그 갑각류를 먹는 물고기 및 물고기를 주 식량원으로 삼는 바다표범까지 이른다.

바이칼 물범은 세계 물범 중 가장 작으면서 담수에서만 사는 유일한 종인데, 바이칼호에서 짝짓기를 하고 출산을 한다. 바이칼 물범은 초봄에 은신처로서 얼음이 필요하다. 만약 얼음이 녹는 것이 일찍 발생한다면, 물범은 물로 들어가야만 하고, 이로 인해 추가적인 에너지가 소모되는 것은 암컷의 생식능력과 양육 능력에 영향을 미친다.

prolonged adj. 장기적인   seasonal adj. 계절에 따른
flora and fauna phr. 동식물 상
phytoplankton n. 식물성 플랑크톤
microscopic organism phr. 미생물
food web phr. 먹이 그물   dominant adj. 지배적인
primary producer phr. 제1차 생산자   predator n. 포식자
reproduction n. 번식   green algae phr. 녹조
explosively adv. 폭발적으로   transparency n. 투명도
algal bloom phr. 조류 대 증식   crustacean n. 갑각류 동물
expend v. (많은 돈·시간·에너지를) 쏟다, 들이다
fertility n. 생식능력   nurture v. 양육하다

65 2019 가톨릭대
정답 ④

해석 ① 지구 온난화가 세계의 일부 지역에 이로운 변화로 이어질 수도 있다는 것
② 생물체는 환경적 변화에도 불구하고 놀라운 회복력을 보여준다는 것
③ 동식물 상이 기후 변화로부터 담수 환경을 보호하는 방법
④ 대기의 변화가 수권과 생물권의 변화와 연결되는 방식

해설 주어진 문장의 빈칸을 채우는 문제이다. 지문의 두 번째 문단 중간에서 따뜻해지고 있는 대기 온도에 의해 초래된 최근 얼음의 변화는 조류 성장률을 감소시켰고, 봄에 일어나는 조류 대 증식을 둔화했다고 했으므로, 빈칸에는 최근 바이칼호의 수온과 얼음 변화가 무엇을 예증하는지에 대한 내용이 나와야 적절하다는 것을 알 수 있다. 따라서 '대기의 변화가 수권과 생물권의 변화와 연결되는 방식'이라고 한 ④번이 정답이다.

어휘 exemplify v. 예증하다   beneficial adj. 이로운
remarkable adj. 놀라운   resilience n. 회복력
in the face of phr. ~에도 불구하고   atmosphere n. 대기
hydrosphere n. 수권   biosphere n. 생물권

66 2019 가톨릭대
정답 ②

해석 ① 바이칼호의 얼음은 조류가 번식하는 데 중요한 환경을 만든다.
② 최근의 따뜻한 날씨는 바이칼호에 사는 식물성 플랑크톤의 증가를 초래했다.
③ 바다표범 중에서, 바이칼 물범은 염수가 아닌 물에서만 사는 독특한 종이다.
④ 예상보다 이른 얼음 용해는 바이칼 물범의 번식력을 감소시킨다.

해설 지문의 내용과 일치하지 않는 것을 묻는 문제이다. ②번의 키워드인 warm weather(따뜻한 날씨)와 관련된 지문의 warming air temperature(따뜻해지고 있는 대기 온도) 주변에서 따뜻해지고 있는 대기 온도에 의해 초래된 최근 얼음의 변화는 조류 성장률을 감소시켰고, 봄에 일어나는 조류 대 증식을 둔화했다고 했으므로, 최근의 따뜻한 날씨가 바이칼호에 사는 식물성 플랑크톤의 증가를 초래했다는 것은 지문의 내용과 다르다. 따라서 ②번의 내용이 지문의 내용과 일치하지 않는다.

오답분석
① 첫 번째 문단의 세 번째 문장 Lake Baikal is ~ require ice for reproduction.을 통해 '바이칼호의 얼음은 조류가 번식하는 데 중요한 환경을 만든다'는 것을 알 수 있다.
③ 세 번째 문단의 첫 번째 문장 The Baikal seal ~ the only species exclusively living in freshwater ~ ice.를 통해 '바다표범 중에서, 바이칼 물범은 염수가 아닌 물에서만 사는 독특한 종이다'라는 것을 알 수 있다.
④ 세 번째 문단의 세 번째 문장 If ice melt occurs early ~ nurturing ability.를 통해 '예상보다 이른 얼음 용해는 바이칼 물범의 번식력을 감소시킨다'는 것을 알 수 있다.

어휘 reproduce v. 번식하다   premature adj. 예상보다 이른

[67-70]

[A] 포유류와 조류는 정기적으로 짝 선호를 나타내고 짝 선택을 한다. 포유류 사이에서의 짝 선택에 관한 자료는 이 행동 '유인 체계'는 도파민에 반응하는 뇌의 보상 경로와 관련 있다는 것을 암시한다. 많은 문화에 걸쳐 인간의 보편적 특성인 열렬하고 낭만적인 사랑은 이 유인 체계가 발전된 형태라는 것이 제시되었다.

[B] 인간의 낭만적인 끌림과 관련 있는 신경 기제를 밝혀내기 위해, 우리는 기능적 자기 공명 기록법(fMRI)을 사용하여 강렬하게 '사랑에 빠진' 17명의 사람을 연구했다. 사랑에 빠진 사람들에게 특수한 활성화가 뇌간 우복측 피개부와 우후배측 미상핵체에서 나타났다. 이러한 결과와 그 밖의 결과들은 도파민에 반응하는 보상 및 동기 부여 경로가 낭만적인 사랑의 양상에 한 원인이 된다는 것을 시사한다.

[C] 또한 우리는 기능적 자기 공명 기록법을 사용하여 사랑에서 거부당했던 15명의 남녀를 연구했다. 예비 분석은 불확실한 큰 손익이 있는 화폐 도박과 연관 있는 보상 체계 관련 부위와 최근 절제하는 코카인에 중독된 사람들에게서 드러난 마음 이론, 강박적/충동적 행동, 그리고 분노 조절과 연관 있는 측면 안와전두피질 부위에서 사랑에 빠진 사람들에게서 나타나는 특수한 작용을 보여주었다.

[D] 이러한 자료는 낭만적인 사랑이 조류와 포유류 종에서 직접적인 번식을 위해 진화한 세 가지의 주요한 뇌 체계 중 하나라는 우리의 견해에 기여한다. 성욕은 개체가 다양한 짝짓기 상대를 찾도록 동기를 부여하기 위해 진화했고, 유인은 개체가 특정한 상대를 선호하고 추구하도록 동기를 부여하기 위해 진화했으며, 애착은 개체가 종 특유의 새끼를 돌보는 의무를 완수할 수 있을 정도로 오랜 시간 함께 있도록 동기를 부여하기 위해 진화했다. 이 세 개의 행동 목록은 크게 구별되지만 밀접한 관계에 있는 뇌 체계에 기반을 둔 것으로 보이고, 뇌 체계는 호르몬과 모노아민 모두를 사용하여 번식을 조정하기 위해 특정한 방식으로 상호작용 한다. 인간, 그리고 다른 포유류 종의 선조에서 나타나는 낭만적인 끌림은 중요한 역할을 하는데, 이 신경 기제는 개체가 특정한 다른 상대에게 구애 에너지를 쏟도록 동기 부여함으로써, 귀중한 시간과 대사 에너지를 보존하고, 짝 선택을 용이하게 한다.

---

attraction n. 유인, 끌림
dopaminergic adj. 도파민에 반응하는
universal n. 보편적 특성 neural adj. 신경의
mechanism n. 기제 brainstem n. 뇌간
contribute v. (~의) 한 원인이 되다, 기여하다
preliminary adj. 예비의 gambling n. 도박
obsessive adj. 강박적인 compulsive adj. 충동적인
abstinent adj. 절제하는 evolve v. 진화하다
avian adj. 조류의 reproduction n. 번식
attachment n. 애착, 애정 repertoire n. 목록
interrelated adj. 밀접한 관계에 있는 orchestrate v. 조정하다
antecedent n. 선조, 조상 courtship n. 구애
metabolic adj. 대사의

67 [2019 아주대]

정답 ②

해석 ① 낭만적인 사랑: 절대적인 인간의 능력
② 낭만적인 사랑: 짝 선택을 위한 포유류의 뇌 체계
③ 낭만적이지 않은 사랑: 짝 선택에 있어서 뇌가 속이는 것
④ 낭만적이지 않은 사랑: 성욕의 다른 말
⑤ 수수께끼가 풀린 인간의 뇌

해설 지문의 제목을 묻는 문제이다. [A] 문단에서 인간의 낭만적인 사랑은 동물의 '유인 체계'가 발전된 형태라고 하고, [B], [C] 문단에서 이를 뒷받침하는 연구 결과를 제시한 후, [D] 문단에서 인간 및 포유류의 선조에서 나타나는 낭만적인 끌림은 중요한 역할을 하고 있다고 설명하고 있다. 따라서 이 지문의 제목을 '낭만적인 사랑: 짝 선택을 위한 포유류의 뇌 체계'라고 표현한 ②번이 정답이다.

어휘 faculty n. 능력   demystify v. 수수께끼를 풀다

68 [2019 아주대]

정답 ④

해석 ① 포유류가 짝을 선택할 때, 뇌에서 도파민이 나올 확률이 높다.
② 기능적 자기 공명 기록법은 우리가 뇌 활동을 측정하고 나타내도록 돕는다.
③ 사랑에서 거부당한 사람들의 뇌는 마약 중독자의 뇌와 유사한 양상을 보여준다.
④ 낭만적인 사랑은 번식을 제어하는 포유류의 뇌와 관련되어 있다.
⑤ "애착"이라는 단어는 "유인"이라는 단어보다 영속성의 의미를 더 함축하고 있다.

해설 지문의 내용과 일치하지 않는 것을 묻는 문제이다. ④번의 키워드인 reproduction(번식)이 그대로 언급된 지문의 세 번째 문단 첫 번째 문장에서 낭만적인 사랑이 포유류 종에서 직접적인 번식을 위해 진화한 세 가지의 주요한 뇌 체계 중 하나라고 했으므로, 낭만적인 사랑이 번식을 제어하는 포유류의 뇌와 관련되어 있다는 것은 지문의 내용과 다르다. 따라서 ④번의 내용이 지문의 내용과 일치하지 않는다.

오답 분석
① [A] 문단의 두 번째 문장 Data on mate choice ~ with dopaminergic reward pathways in the brain.을 통해 '포유류가 짝을 선택할 때, 뇌에서 도파민이 나올 확률이 높다'는 것을 알 수 있다.
② [B] 문단의 첫 번째 문장 To begin to determine the neural mechanisms associated with romantic attraction in humans, we used functional magnetic resonance imaging (fMRI) ~을 통해 '기능적 자기 공명 기록법은 우리가 뇌 활동을 측정하고 나타내도록 돕는다'는 것을 알 수 있다.
③ [C] 문단의 두 번째 문장 Preliminary analysis showed ~ revealed in recently abstinent cocaine-dependent

individuals.를 통해 '사랑에서 거부당한 사람들의 뇌는 마약 중독자의 뇌와 유사한 양상을 보여준다'는 것을 알 수 있다.
⑤ [D] 문단 두 번째 문장의 attachment evolved to motivate individuals to remain together long enough to complete species-specific parenting duties를 통해 '"애착"이라는 단어는 "유인"이라는 단어보다 영속성의 의미를 더 함축하고 있다'는 것을 알 수 있다.

어휘 map v. 나타내다, 보여주다
connote v. (어떤 의미를) 함축하다   durability n. 영속성

69 2019 아주대

정답 ④

해석 ① 그들이 삶에서 더 중요한 것들에 집중할 수 있도록 돕다.
② 짝 선택을 방해하다.
③ 그들이 삶에서 더 중요한 것들에 집중할 수 없게 하다.
④ 짝 선택을 용이하게 하다.
⑤ 그들이 사랑에 빠지도록 돕다.

해설 지문의 빈칸을 채우는 문제이다. [D] 문단 마지막 문장에서 인간, 그리고 다른 포유류 종의 선조에서 나타나는 낭만적인 끌림은 중요한 역할을 한다고 했으므로, 빈칸에는 어떠한 역할을 하는지에 대한 구체적인 내용이 나와야 적절하다는 것을 알 수 있다. 따라서 '짝 선택을 용이하게 하다'라고 한 ④번이 정답이다.

어휘 interfere with phr. ~을 방해하다   prevent v. 막다
facilitate v. 용이하게 하다

70 2019 아주대

정답 ③

해석 ① 도파민으로 유도된 행복을 느끼다.
② 그것들의 관계를 더 안정적인 방향으로 완전하게 하다.
③ 그것들의 자녀를 기르는 데 협력하다.
④ 그들 자신을 적대적 환경에 맞서 보호하다.
⑤ 부부의 행복을 경험하다.

해설 어떤 동물들이 짝과 오랜 시간 동안 함께 있는 주된 이유를 파악하는 문제이다. [D] 문단 중간에서 애착은 개체가 종 특유의 새끼를 돌보는 의무를 완수할 수 있을 정도로 오랜 시간 함께 있도록 동기를 부여하기 위해 진화했다고 했으므로, 동물들이 짝과 오랜 시간 동안 함께 있는 주된 이유는 '그것들의 자녀를 기르는 데 협력'하기 위해서다. 따라서 정답은 ③번이다.

어휘 induced adj. 유도된   consummate v. 완전하게 하다
cooperate v. 협력하다   hostile adj. 적대적인
marital adj. 부부의   bliss n. 행복, 축복

[71-73]

당신은 자동차나 기차 또는 비행기로 타고 갈 때 속이 메스꺼울 수도 있다. 만약 그렇다면, 당신이 느끼는 메스꺼움은 당신의 뇌가 제대로 기능하고 있다는 것을 보여주는 것이므로 안도해도 될 것이다. 멀미 연구자들은 우리가 움직이는 동안, 뇌는 몸에 독이 들어왔을 때와 똑같이 반응한다는 것을 발견했다. 고속의 이동은 최근에 와서야 인간 행동에 추가된 것이기 때문에, 뇌가 아직 그것에 적응하지 못한 것 같다. 당신이 고속으로 이동할 때, 대개 당신은 앉아있을 것이다. 뇌는 발과 엉덩이 그리고 허리를 포함한 몸으로부터 당신이 정지해있다는 신호를 받는다. 그러나 뇌는 또한, 귀 안쪽의 작은 액체 관인, 균형 감지기관으로부터 당신이 빠른 속도로 앞으로 이동하고 있다는 신호를 받는다. 이렇게 뒤섞인 메시지가 뇌로 하여금 당신이 부정확하게 사물을 인지하고 있다는 부정확한 가정에 이르게 하며, 자연 세계에서 당신을 부정확하게 인식하도록 만들 수 있는 유일한 것은 바로 독이다. 그래서 당신이 중독되었다고 믿는 몸은, 단지 안전해지기 위해, 자동으로 독을 씻어내려고 노력하는 것이다. 요약하자면, 당신은 메스꺼워진다. 하지만, 만약 당신이 창밖을 주시한다면, 증가된 시각적 자극이 뇌에게 당신이 사실은 움직이고 있는 것이라고 말해줄 것이며, 이것이 메스꺼움을 사라지게 할 것이다.

feel sick phr. 곧 토할 것 같다, 속이 메스껍다
take comfort phr. 위안을 얻다, 안도하다
queasiness n. 메스꺼움   motion sickness phr. 멀미
adapt to phr. ~에 적응하다   buttock n. 엉덩이
stationary adj. 정지한, 움직이지 않는
flush out phr. 쫓아내다, 씻어내다
nausea n. 구역질, 메스꺼움

71 2017 한국외대

정답 ③

해석 ① 달팽이관을 자극하는 것
② 해독제를 먹는 것
③ 창밖을 내다보는 것
④ 무언가를 마시는 것

해설 이 지문에서 언급한 멀미에 대한 치료법을 파악하는 문제이다. 마지막 문장에서 '만약 창밖을 주시한다면, 시각적 자극이 증가하여 뇌에 사실은 움직이고 있다는 올바른 정보를 주어 메스꺼움이 사라질 것이다(if you stare out the window, ~ the nausea pass)'라고 했으므로, 지문에서 언급된 멀미에 대한 치료법은 '창밖을 내다보는 것'이다. 따라서 정답은 ③번이다.

어휘 balance tube phr. (몸의 균형을 감지하는) 달팽이관
antidote n. 해독제

72 [2017 한국외대]

정답 ④

해석 ① 뇌가 이동에 적응했다.
② 몸이 이동으로 인해 너무 약해졌다.
③ 당신이 독이 있는 액체에 의해 중독되었다.
④ 몸이 자연스럽게 기능하고 있다.

해설 멀미를 한다는 것이 무엇을 의미하는가 하는 지문의 세부 정보를 파악하는 문제이다. 두 번째 문장에서 '당신이 느끼는 메스꺼움은 당신의 뇌가 제대로 기능하고 있다는 것을 보여주는 것(the queasiness ~ functioning properly)'이라고 했으므로, 멀미를 한다는 것은 '몸이 자연스럽게 기능하고 있다'는 것이다. 따라서 ④번이 정답이다.

어휘 toxic adj. 유독한, 독이 있는

73 [2017 한국외대]

정답 ④

해석 ① 정신과 몸은 완전한 조화 속에서 작동한다.
② 병은 창밖을 주시한 결과이다.
③ 차멀미는 적응에 의해 유발된 오래된 문제이다.
④ 감지기관의 상충하는 정보가 차멀미를 유발한다.

해설 지문의 내용과 일치하는 것을 묻는 문제이다. 다섯 번째 문장(As you travel at high speed, ~)부터 여덟 번째 문장(The mixed messages lead ~)까지의 내용을 보면 당신이 자동차 등에 앉아서 고속으로 이동할 때 몸은 당신이 정지해있다고 신호를 뇌에 보내지만, 균형 감지기관은 당신이 빠르게 이동하고 있다는 신호를 보낸다. 그래서 이렇게 뒤섞인 메시지가 뇌로 하여금 당신이 독에 중독되어 부정확한 인지를 하고 있다는 그릇된 추정에 이르게 한다는 것이다. 따라서 정답은 ④번이다.

오답분석
① 지문에 따르면 발과 엉덩이 그리고 허리 등은 뇌에 정지해 있다는 신호를 보내지만, 균형 감지기관은 빠르게 움직이고 있다는 신호를 보내므로 뇌는 몸이 독에 중독되었다는 잘못된 추정을 하게 된다. 따라서 '정신과 몸은 완전한 조화 속에서 작동한다'는 것은 지문의 내용과 다르다.
② 마지막 문장에서 창밖을 내다보는 것이 멀미의 해결책이라고 했으므로, '병은 창밖을 주시한 결과이다'라는 것은 지문의 내용과 다르다.
③ 네 번째 문장에서 고속의 이동은 인간 행동에 최근에 추가된 것이며, 뇌는 아직 적응을 하지 못했다고 했으므로, '차멀미는 적응에 의해 유발된 오래된 문제이다'라는 것은 지문의 내용과 다르다.

어휘 coordination n. 조화 conflicting adj. 상충하는, 모순되는

[74-76]

오늘날 전형적인 미국인의 집에서 아기의 방에 들어가 본다면, 당신은 아마 봉제 동물 인형과 아기 바로 위에 매달려 있는 색색의 장난감들이 가득 찬 아기용 침대를 보게 될 것이다. 이 장난감 중 일부는 빛이 나거나, 움직이고, 또는 노래가 나올 수도 있다. 당신은 아기에게 보고 갖고 놀 수 있는 것을 이렇게나 많이 제공하는 이면에 담긴 부모의 논리가 무엇이라고 추측하는가? 아기들이 이 장난감들을 즐기고 긍정적인 반응을 보이는 것 같다는 사실과는 별개로, 대부분의 부모는 최적의 두뇌 발달을 위해 자극적인 환경이 아이에게 필요하다고 믿는다. 특정한 경험이 두뇌에 물리적인 변화를 만들어 내는지에 대한 문제는 몇 세기 동안 과학자들 사이에서 연구의 주제가 되어왔다. 1785년에, 해부학자인 Vincenzo Malacarne는 같은 배에서 나온 강아지 한 쌍과 같은 알 묶음에서 나온 한 쌍의 새를 연구했다. 각 쌍에 대해, 하나는 오랜 기간에 걸쳐 훈련을 시켰지만 다른 하나는 동일하게 보살핌받았지만 훈련받지는 않았다. 나중에 동물들을 부검한 결과, 그는 훈련받은 동물들의 뇌가 더 복잡하고 많은 수의 주름과 틈이 있었다는 것을 알게 되었다. 19세기에, 인간의 머리둘레와 한 사람이 경험한 학습의 양 사이를 관계 짓기 위한 시도가 많이 있었다. 일부 초기의 발견이 그러한 관계를 주장했지만, 후기의 연구는 이것이 두뇌 발달의 유효한 척도가 아님을 밝혀냈다.

---

typical adj. 전형적인   crib n. 아기용 침대
stuff v. 속을 채우다   dangle v. 매달리다
infant n. 아기, 유아   reasoning n. 논리, 추리
stimulating adj. 자극적인   environment n. 환경
optimal adj. 최적의   development n. 발달, 개발
physical adj. 물리적인, 신체의
litter n. (동물의) 한 배에서 난 새끼들   batch n. 묶음, 집단
train v. 훈련하다   participant n. 참가자
autopsy n. 해부   complex adj. 복잡한   fold n. 주름
fissure n. 틈   circumference n. 둘레, 원주
determine v. 밝히다, 알아내다, 결정하다   valid adj. 유효한
measure n. 척도, 기준

74 [2019 세종대]

정답 ②

해석 ① 물리학자   ② 해부학자
③ 검안사   ④ 생물 통계학자

해설 지문의 빈칸을 채우는 문제이다. 빈칸의 다음 부분에서 Vincenzo Malacarne가 동물들에 실험한 후 뇌를 관찰하기 위하여 부검했다고 설명하고 있으므로, 빈칸에는 부검과 관련된 의미의 단어가 와야 한다는 것을 알 수 있다. 따라서 '해부학자'라고 한 ②번이 정답이다.

어휘 physicist n. 물리학자   anatomist n. 해부학자
optometrist n. 검안사   biostatistician n. 생물 통계학자

75 (2019 세종대)

정답 ②

해석
① 아기들이 그것들을 좋아하는 것 같기 때문에
② 부모들이 아기들은 최적의 두뇌 발달을 무시한다고 믿기 때문에
③ 아기들이 그것들에 긍정적으로 반응하는 것 같기 때문에
④ 부모들이 아기들에게 자극적인 환경이 필요하다고 추측하기 때문에

해설 아기의 방에서 봉제 동물 인형과 색색의 장난감을 찾을 수 있는 이유가 아닌 것을 파악하는 문제이다. 첫 번째 문단의 마지막 부분에서 아기들이 이 장난감들을 즐기고 긍정적인 반응을 보이는 것 같다는 내용과 대부분의 부모는 최적의 두뇌 발달을 위해 자극적인 환경이 아이에게 필요하다고 믿는다는 내용을 언급하고 있지만, 부모들이 아기들은 최적의 두뇌 발달을 무시한다고 믿는다는 것은 본문에서 찾을 수 없다. 따라서 정답은 ②번이다.

어휘 disregard v. 무시하다 affirmatively adv. 긍정적으로 surrounding n. 환경

76 (2019 세종대)

정답 ①

해석
① 하나의 과학 연구를 소개하기 위해
② 아이들을 위한 새로운 종류의 장난감을 광고하기 위해
③ 부모들에게 최고의 아이 훈육 관습에 대해 조언하기 위해
④ 문제가 있는 사회의 현상을 보고하기 위해

해설 지문의 목적을 묻는 문제이다. 두 번째 문단에서 Vincenzo Malacarne가 동물들을 대상으로 특정 경험과 뇌의 물리적인 변화에 대해 연구를 했다는 것을 설명하고 있다. 따라서 이 지문의 목적을 '하나의 과학 연구를 소개하기 위해'라고 표현한 ①번이 정답이다.

어휘 introduce v. 소개하다 scientific adj. 과학의, 과학적인 advertise v. 광고하다 child-rearing n. 아이를 훈육하는 것 practice n. 관습 problematic adj. 문제가 있는 phenomenon n. 현상

[77-79]

많은 사람들은 Dolly라는 이름의 양에 대해 읽기 전까지는 "복제"라는 단어를 들어본 적이 없었다. 전 세계 신문들이 과학자들이 어떻게 Dolly를 실험실에서 성공적으로 복제했는지에 대한 기사를 실었을 때, 모든 사람들이 복제 이야기를 하고 있는 것처럼 보였다. 사람들은 복제에 대해, 마치 전에 없던 완전히 새로운 것처럼 얘기했다. 사실, 과학자들이 Dolly를 복제하기 (A)전에, 이미 연구 실험실에서는 소규모 복제 성공이 많이 있었다. Dolly를 다르게 만든 것은 과학자들이 그녀를 (B)배아 세포가 아닌 성인 양 세포에서 복제했다는 것이다.

사람들이 Dolly의 복제에 대해 알았을 때, 그들은 그 생각이 매우 논쟁의 여지가 있다고 생각했다. 복제가 좋은 것인지 아닌지에 대한 논쟁이 시작되었다. Dolly가 태어났을 때, 대부분의 사람들은 Mary Shelley의 프랑켄슈타인 같은 책에서 누군가가 실험실에서 생명을 만든다는 이야기를 들었을 뿐이었다. 하지만 Dolly가 태어나자마자, 사람들은 복제가 장차 무엇을 의미할지 매우 열심히 생각해 보아야 했다.

Dolly가 2003년에 죽었을 때, 그녀는 겨우 6년을 살았지만, 죽을 (C)때까지, 아버지가 없다는 것을 제외하고는 완전히 정상적인 양이었다!

clone n. 복제; v. 복제하다 laboratory n. 실험실
completely adv. 완전히
controversial adj. 논쟁의 여지가 있는

77 (2020 국민대)

정답 ②

해석
① 비록 ― 후에   ② 전에 ― ~때까지
③ 비록 ― ~때까지   ④ 전에 ― 후에

해설 지문의 빈칸을 채우는 문제이다. (A) 앞 문장은 사람들이 마치 복제를 새로운 것처럼 얘기한다는 내용이고, 빈칸 뒤 문장은 복제에 성공한 경우가 많이 있었음을 언급하는 내용이므로, 빈칸 (A)에는 Dolly의 복제 전에 이미 복제가 있었다는 내용이 나와야 적절하다는 것을 알 수 있다. 따라서 '전에'가 들어가야 한다. 빈칸 (C)가 있는 문장에서 Dolly가 죽었을 때 아버지가 없다는 것 외에는 정상적인 양이었다고 했으므로 빈칸 (C)에는 Dolly가 죽을 때까지 정상이었다는 내용이 나와야 적절하다는 것을 알 수 있다. 따라서 '~때까지'가 들어가야 한다. 따라서 ② before(전에) ― by the time(~때까지)이 정답이다.

78 (2020 국민대)

정답 ④

해석
① 감정을 자극하는   ② 휘말린
③ 진정시키는   ④ 배아의

해설 지문의 빈칸을 채우는 문제이다. 빈칸 (B)가 있는 문장에서 Dolly가 이전의 복제와 다른 점은 성인 양 세포에서 복제했다는 것이라고 했으므로, 빈칸에는 성인 세포와는 반대되는, Dolly 이전의 복제에서 사용한 세포가 무엇인지에 대한 내용이 나와야 적절하다는 것을 알 수 있다. 따라서 '배아의'라고 한 ④번이 정답이다.

어휘 emotive adj. 감정을 자극하는
embroiled adj. 휘말린, 끌려든 emollient adj. 진정시키는
embryonic adj. 배아의, 초기의

79 2020 국민대

정답 ③

해석
① Dolly는 복제의 첫 번째 성공담이 아니었다.
② Dolly의 탄생으로 사람들은 복제의 미래에 대해 생각하게 되었다.
③ Dolly는 실험실 밖에서 만들어졌기 때문에 특이했다.
④ 모든 사람들이 생물체를 복제한다는 생각을 환영하지는 않았다.

해설 지문의 내용과 일치하지 않는 것을 묻는 문제이다. ③번의 키워드인 laboratory(실험실)가 나온 지문 주변에서 Dolly를 실험실에서 성공적으로 복제했다고 했으므로, Dolly는 실험실 밖에서 만들어졌기 때문에 특이했다는 것은 지문의 내용과 다르다. 따라서 ③번이 지문의 내용과 일치하지 않는다.

오답 분석
① Actually, before scientists cloned Dolly, there had already been a lot of small cloning successes in research laboratories를 통해 'Dolly는 복제의 첫 번째 성공담이 아니었다'는 것을 알 수 있다.
② As soon as Dolly was born, however, people had to think very hard about what cloning might mean in the future를 통해 'Dolly의 탄생으로 사람들은 복제의 미래에 대해 생각하게 되었다'는 것을 알 수 있다.
④ A debate began about whether cloning is a good thing to do or not을 통해 '모든 사람들이 생물체를 복제한다는 생각을 환영하지는 않았다'는 것을 알 수 있다.

어휘 duplicate v. 복제하다, 복사하다

[80-83]

[A] 최초의 뇌는 약 5억 년 전에 지구상에 나타났으며, 초기 영장류의 뇌로 진화하는 데 찬찬히 4억 3000만 년의 시간이 걸렸고, 최초 원시인의 뇌로 진화하는 데에는 또 다른 7천만 년의 시간이 들었다. 그러고 나서, 어떤 일이 일어났는데, 곧 인간의 것으로 진화할 뇌 2백만 년이 조금 넘는 기간에 질량을 두 배 이상으로 늘려, 1.25파운드의 호모 하빌리스 뇌를 약 3파운드의 호모 사피엔스 뇌로 탈바꿈한 전례 없는 급성장을 겪었다. (A)

[B] 그런데 당신이 만약 핫퍼지 식단을 먹게 되어 아주 단기간에 당신의 무게를 두 배로 늘렸다면, 우리는 당신의 여러 신체 부분 모두가 무게 증가에 있어서 똑같이 몫을 나누었을 거라 예상하지 않을 것이다. (B) <u>당신의 혀와 발가락이 비교적 호리호리하고 영향을 받지 않은 상태로 남아있는 반면, 복부와 엉덩이는 아마 새로 획득된 군살을 받아들이는 주요한 부분이 될 것이다.</u> 마찬가지로, 인간의 뇌 크기에 있어서 극적인 증가는 현대 사람들이 구조적으로 이전의 뇌와 똑같고, 더 크기만 한 새로운 뇌를 갖게 되도록 모든 부분의 질량을 평등하게 두 배로 늘리지 않았다. 오히려, 성장의 불균형적인 지분은 전두엽이라고 알려진 뇌의 특정 부분에 집중되었다. (C)

[C] 과학자들은 전두엽 손상이 있는 환자들이 보통 표준 지능 검사에서 잘 수행하기는 하지만, 계획을 수반하는 모든 검사에서 심각한 결함을 나타냄을 알아챘다. 환자들은 심지어 그들이 오후 이후에 무엇을 할지 말하는 것도 사실상 불가능하다는 것을 알았다. (D) 이 결과는 전두엽이 우리로 하여금 현재를 떠나 미래가 발생하기 전에 미래를 경험할 수 있게 하는 타임머신이라고 추정하는 데 도움이 된다. 다른 어떤 동물도 우리와 같은 전두엽을 갖고 있지 않은데, 이는 우리가 생각하듯이 미래에 대해 생각하는 유일한 동물인 이유이다. (E) 전두엽에 대한 이야기가 우리에게 어떻게 사람들이 가상의 미래를 마음속에 그려내는지 알려주더라도, 그것은 우리에게 이유를 알려주진 않는다.

evolve v. 진화하다 **primate** n. 영장류
protohuman n. 원시인 **unprecedented** adj. 전례 없던
identical adj. 똑같은 **disproportionate** adj. 불균형의
impairment n. 결함, 손상 **vacate** v. 떠나다, 비우다
conjure v. 마음속에 그려내다

80 2019 아주대

정답 ④

해석
① 인간 뇌의 꾸준한 진화
② 뇌 크기의 중요성
③ 인간의 놀라운 지적 능력의 수수께끼가 풀리다
④ 미래를 계획하는 뇌 영역
⑤ 뇌 손상이 시간 개념에 미치는 영향

해설 지문의 제목을 묻는 문제이다. [A] 문단에서 최초의 뇌가 질량을 늘리면서 인간의 뇌로 전례 없던 급성장을 했다고 하고, [B] 문단에서 뇌는 모든 부분의 질량을 평등하게 늘린 것이 아니라, 전두엽에 성장이 집중되었다고 한 후, [C] 문단에서 전두엽의 성장은 우리가 미래에 대해 생각하는 유일한 동물인 이유라고 설명하고 있다. 따라서 이 지문의 제목을 '미래를 계획하는 뇌 영역'이라고 표현한 ④번이 정답이다.

어휘 demystify v. 수수께끼를 풀다

81 2019 아주대

정답 ④

해석
① 원시인 뇌의 크기는 인간 뇌 크기의 절반 이하이다.
② 무엇이 인간 뇌의 급격한 성장을 일으켰는지 여전히 알려지지 않았다.
③ 인간의 뇌는 불균형적으로 발전했다.
④ 전두엽 손상이 있는 환자들은 시간이 어떻게 가는지 이해하지 못한다.
⑤ 인간의 뇌는 크기뿐만 아니라 구조에서도 다른 뇌와 다르다.

해설 지문을 통해 추론할 수 없는 것을 고르는 문제이다. [C] 문단의 두 번째 문장에서 전두엽 손상이 있는 환자들은 심지어 그들이 오후 이후에 무엇을 할지 말하는 것도 사실상 불가능했다고 했지만, 환자들이 시간이 어떻게 가는지 이해하지 못하는지는 유추할 수 없으므로 정답은 ④번이다.

오답분석
① [A] 문단 두 번째 문장의 the soon-to-be-human brain ~ more than doubled its mass를 통해 '원시인 뇌의 크기는 인간 뇌 크기의 절반 이하이다'라는 것을 알 수 있다.
② [A] 문단의 두 번째 문장 Then, something happened ~ brain of Homo sapiens.를 통해 '무엇이 인간 뇌의 급격한 성장을 일으켰는지 여전히 알려지지 않았다'는 것을 알 수 있다.
③ [B] 문단의 마지막 문장 Rather a disproportionate ~ the frontal lobe.를 통해 '인간의 뇌는 불균형적으로 발전했다'는 것을 알 수 있다.
⑤ [C] 문단의 네 번째 문장 No other animals have a frontal lobe quite like our를 통해 '인간의 뇌는 크기뿐만 아니라 구조에서도 다른 뇌와 다르다'는 것을 알 수 있다.

어휘 proceed v. 가다, 계속하다

82 [2019 아주대]

정답 ②

해설 지문의 흐름상 주어진 문장이 들어가기에 적절한 위치를 고르는 문제이다. (B)의 앞 문장에서 당신이 단기간에 무게를 두 배로 늘렸다면, 신체 부분 모두가 무게 증가에 있어서 똑같이 몫을 나누지 않았을 거라고 했으므로, (B) 자리에 어떤 부분에 무게가 더 집중되었는지 설명하는 주어진 문장 '당신의 혀와 발가락이 비교적 호리호리하고 영향을 받지 않은 상태로 남아있는 반면, 복부와 엉덩이는 아마 새로 획득된 군살을 받아들이는 주요한 부분이 될 것이다'가 들어가야 글의 흐름이 자연스럽게 연결된다. 따라서 ②번이 정답이다.

어휘 belly n. 복부   buttock n. 엉덩이   flab n. 군살
svelte adj. 호리호리한   unaffected adj. 영향을 받지 않은

83 [2019 아주대]

정답 ⑤

해석 ① 왜 우리는 인간의 뇌를 연구해야 하는가.
② 왜 사람들은 예측치 못한 미래를 대비해야 하는가.
③ 왜 동물의 뇌는 인간의 뇌와 다르게 작동하는가.
④ 왜 심각하게 손상된 전두엽은 쉽게 치료될 수 없는가.
⑤ 왜 사람들은 행동의 결과에 대해 미리 생각해야 하는가.

해설 주어진 지문 뒤에 논의될 내용을 고르는 문제이다. 지문의 마지막 문장에서 '전두엽에 대한 이야기가 우리에게 어떻게 사람들이 가상의 미래를 마음속에 그려내는지 알려주더라도, 그것이 우리에게 이유를 알려주진 않는다고 했으므로, 지문 뒤에는 사람들이 미래를 그려내는 이유와 관련된 '왜 사람들은 행동의 결과에 대해 미리 생각해야 하는가.'에 대한 내용이 지문 뒤에 논의될 것임을 알 수 있다. 따라서 ⑤번이 정답이다.

어휘 prepare v. 대비하다   consequence n. 결과
in advance phr. 미리, 사전에

15 지구과학·천문학·환경

01-51
문제집 p.440

01 ⑤	02 ③	03 ②	04 ④	05 ⑤
06 ③	07 ②	08 ③	09 ①	10 ①
11 ③	12 ④	13 ②	14 ①	15 ③
16 ②	17 ④	18 ⑤	19 ③	20 ①
21 ⑤	22 ③	23 ④	24 ④	25 ①
26 ①	27 ⑤	28 ③	29 ③	30 ②
31 ④	32 ②	33 ③	34 ①	35 ②
36 ④	37 ③	38 ③	39 ③	40 ④
41 ③	42 ①	43 ④	44 ③	45 ①
46 ②	47 ③	48 ③	49 ③	50 ④
51 ④				

01 2019 인하대

정답 ⑤

해석 사막화는 부적합한 토지 사용과 혹독한 기후의 영향의 축적된 결과이다. 인간의 네 가지 활동이 가장 즉각적인 원인을 나타낸다: 지나친 경작이 토양을 고갈시키고, 과도한 방목이 토양의 침식을 방지하는 식생 피복을 제거하고, 삼림 벌채가 흙을 토지에 고정하는 나무를 파괴하며, 그리고 잘 배수되지 않는 관개 시설은 경작지를 소금기가 있게 바꾼다. 게다가, 교육과 지식의 부족, 전쟁 시에 난민들의 이동, 개발도상국의 불리한 무역 조건과 다른 사회경제적이고 정치적인 요소들이 이 사막화의 영향을 강화한다. 그 원인은 여러 가지이고 복잡한 방식으로 상호작용한다.
① 대조적으로
② 결과적으로
③ 예를 들어
④ 그 대신에
⑤ 게다가

해설 빈칸에 적절한 연결어를 넣는 문제이다. 빈칸 앞 문장은 사막화를 불러일으키는 인간의 네 가지 활동에 대한 내용이고, 빈칸 뒤 문장은 사막화의 영향을 강화하는 요소에 대한 내용이다. 따라서 부연 설명을 나타내는 연결어인 ⑤ Moreover(게다가)가 정답이다.

어휘 desertification n. 사막화
accumulated adj. 축적된, 누적된
ill-adapted adj. 부적합한   immediate adj. 즉각적인
over-cultivation n. 지나친 경작
overgraze v. 과도하게 방목하다
vegetation cover phr. 식생 피복, 초목 커버
erosion n. 침식   deforestation n. 삼림 벌채
bind v. 고정하다, 묶다   drain v. 배수하다
irrigation n. 관개   cropland n. 경작지   refugee n. 난민
unfavourable adj. 불리한, 순조롭지 못한
socio-economic adj. 사회경제적인
consequently adv. 결과적으로   in return phr. 그 대신에

02 2019 한양대에리카

정답 ③

해석 항행은 자신의 위치를 정확하게 알아내고 나서 경로를 계획하고 따라가는 과학이다. 항행의 가장 초기의 형태는 육로 항행이었다. 이것은 한 곳에서 다른 곳으로 가는 여정을 기록하기 위해 물리적인 지형지물에 의존했다. 땅에서 멀어지면, 사람은 성공적으로 항해하기 위해 다른 표시를 사용해야 한다. [C] 이것을 위한 다른 현대적인 한 방법은 위도와 경도를 이용하여 자신의 위치를 계속 추적하는 것이다. [B] 이것들은 지구를 보여주는 지도나 지구본 위에 그려진 두 종류의 가상의 선이다. [A] 위도는 적도로부터 북쪽 또는 남쪽으로의 거리이다. 경도는 북극으로부터 영국 그리니치를 지나 남극으로 뻗어있는 가상의 선인 그리니치 자오선으로부터 동쪽 또는 서쪽으로의 거리이다.

해설 주어진 지문 중간에 나오는 [A]~[C]의 적절한 순서를 파악하는 문제이다. 지문의 앞부분에 주어진 것은 땅과는 다르게 성공적으로 항해하기 위해서 물리적인 지형지물이 아닌 다른 것을 이용해야 한다는 내용이므로, 물리적인 지형지물이 아닌 위도와 경도를 이용한다는 내용인 [C]가 먼저 와야 한다. 그다음에 [B]에서 위도와 경도가 무엇인지에 대해 설명하고, 그다음에 [A]에서 위도의 정의를 설명한 후, 지문의 뒷부분에서 경도의 정의에 관해 설명하는 것이 자연스럽다. 따라서 주어진 지문 중간에 나오는 순서는 ③ [C] – [B] – [A]다.

어휘 navigation n. 항행(航行), 항해
accurately adv. 정확하게
determine v. 알아내다, 결정하다   landmark n. 지형지물
chart v. 기록하다   longitude n. 경도   latitude n. 위도
imaginary adj. 가상의   represent v. 보여주다, 나타내다
equator n. 적도   meridian n. 자오선
North Pole phr. 북극   South Pole phr. 남극

[03-04]

도시 홍수는 놀라울 만큼 어김없이 뉴스거리가 된다. 바로 지난 몇 달 동안, 허리케인 Harvey는 휴스턴을 물에 잠기게 했고, 계절성 장마는 남아시아에 있는 도시들을 무력하게 만들었다. 갈수록 더 심해지는 폭풍으로 만들어진 극적인 홍수는 인적 그리고 재정적으로, 엄청난 비용을 수반하고, 기후 변화로 그 문제는 더 악화되기만 할 것이다. 도시화는 홍수가 초래한 치명적인 사상자 수에 대한 가장 큰 원인들 중 하나이다.
도시가 발달하면서, 숲이나 습지대 위로 수 마일에 달하는 불침투성 보도가 놓여지고, 시내, 지하로 흐르는 하천, 또는 습지대 같은 자연적인 홍수 관리 시스템을 대체한다. 사람이 전혀

살지 않는 지형에서, 강우는 네 가지 다른 방법들로 자연 물순환에 흡수된다. 지면을 완전히 흠뻑 적셔서 지하수가 되고, 계곡을 따라 수역으로 흘러 들어가서 결국 바다에 도달하고, 식물에 흡수되거나 그냥 증발한다. 포장된 도로, 고속도로와 주차장으로 불규칙하게 퍼져나가는 도시나 교외에서, 물은 갈 곳이 없어서 모든 폭우는 홍수가 될 수 있는 것이다.

하지만 이제 빗물이 수 마일의 보도를 통해 흘러가 해로운 홍수를 야기하도록 두는 대신 빗물을 흡수할 수 있는 더 스마트하고 "더 스펀지 같은" 도시를 건설하기 위한 전 세계적 움직임이 있다. 아이오와에서 버몬트까지 그리고 샌프란시스코에서 시카고까지, 도시 기반 시설은 다시 시동을 걸고 있다.

더 나은 폭우 관리 시스템을 만드는 것은 도시 계획에서 환경친화적인 기반 시설 요소들을 이용하는 것과 도시화에 밀려 잃어버린 빗물 저장 능력 일부를 되찾는 것을 필요로 한다. 이 요소들은 대략 두 가지 범주로 나누어질 수 있고, 이 두 가지는 인공으로 가공된 자연 물길과 도시가 발달하기 전에 존재했던 원래 물길의 복원이다.

make (the) news phr. 뉴스거리가 되다
with regularity phr. 어김없이, 규칙대로
submerge v. 물에 잠기게 하다   monsoon n. 장마
urbanization n. 도시화   culprit n. 원인   toll n. 사상자 수
wreak v. 초래하다   impervious adj. 불침투성의
wetland n. 습지대   displace v. 대체하다
creek n. 시내, 개울   uninhabited adj. 사람이 살지 않는
groundwater n. 지하수   evaporate v. 증발하다
sprawl v. 불규칙하게 퍼지다   infrastructure n. 기반 시설
reboot n. 재시동   stormwater n. 폭우   element n. 요소
restore v. 되찾다

03 2021 이화여대

정답 ②

해석 ① 사람이 살지 않는 지역   ② 빗물 저장 능력
③ 자연 수화 작용   ④ 지하수의 양
⑤ 생태계의 가치

해설 지문의 빈칸을 채우는 문제이다. 지문의 후반에서 빗물을 흡수할 수 있는 더 스마트하고 "더 스펀지 같은" 도시를 건설하기 위한 전 세계적 움직임이 있다고 했으므로, 빈칸에는 더 나은 폭우 관리 시스템을 만드는 것은 도시 계획에서 환경친화적인 기반 시설 요소들을 이용하는 것과 도시화에 밀려 잃어버린 빗물 저장 능력 일부를 되찾는 것을 필요로 한다는 내용이 나오는 것이 자연스럽다. 따라서 '빗물 저장 능력'이라고 한 ②번이 정답이다.

어휘 retention n. 저장, 보유   hydration n. 수화 작용
ecosystem n. 생태계

04 2021 이화여대

정답 ④

해석 ① 도시 생활을 더 환경친화적으로 만드는 방법
② 무고한 생명을 죽이는 도시화의 문제점
③ 성급한 기술적 도시화에 대한 보상 방법
④ 도시를 더 스펀지 같이 만들어서 도시 홍수 문제를 해결하는 방법
⑤ 인공 재해: 도시화의 결과

해설 지문의 제목을 묻는 문제이다. 지문 전반에 걸쳐 '도시 홍수'에 대해 설명하고 있고, 지문의 후반에서 빗물이 수 마일의 보도를 통해 흘러가 해로운 홍수를 야기하도록 두는 대신 빗물을 흡수할 수 있는 더 스마트하고 "더 스펀지 같은" 도시를 건설하기 위한 전 세계적 움직임이 있다고 하였다. 따라서 이 지문의 제목을 '도시를 더 스펀지 같이 만들어서 도시 홍수 문제를 해결하는 방법'이라고 표현한 ④번이 정답이다.

오답분석 ① '도시 생활을 더 환경친화적으로 만드는 방법'은 지문에서 언급되지 않았으므로 정답이 될 수 없다.
② '무고한 생명을 죽이는 도시화의 문제점'은 첫 번째 문단밖에 설명하지 못하기 때문에 정답이 될 수 없다.
③ '성급한 기술적 도시화에 대한 보상 방법'은 지문에서 언급되지 않았으므로 정답이 될 수 없다.
⑤ '인공 재해: 도시화의 결과'는 두 번째 문단밖에 설명하지 못하기 때문에 정답이 될 수 없다.

어휘 ecofriendly adj. 환경친화적인   innocent adj. 무고한
rash adj. 성급한   consequence n. 결과

[05-07]

당신이 큰 수역에 물고기가 몇 마리 있는지 알고 싶어 한다고 가정해보자. 당연히 당신은 그 물고기를 다 셀 수는 없다. 당신은 낚싯대를 가지고 릴을 감아 물고기를 끌어 올려 꼬리표를 붙이고, 놓아준 뒤, 그 물고기가 헤엄쳐 갈 동안 시간을 준다. 그리고 나서 당신은 또 다른 물고기를 잡고, 꼬리표를 붙이고 놓아주고, 다음에 또 다른 물고기에게도 그렇게 하면서, 각각의 물고기가 당신이 전에 잡았던 것인지 아닌지 확인한다. 수역에 물고기가 조금 있다면, 어느 순간에 당신은 그 많지 않은 똑같은 물고기를 되풀이해서 잡고 있을 것이다. 수역에 물고기가 엄청나게 많다면, 당신이 끌어올리는 대부분의 물고기는 전에 잡혔던 물고기가 아닐 것이다. 만약 물고기 수가 제한이 없거나 본래 (A)무한하다면, 즉 만약 물고기의 번식 속도가 당신이 물고기를 잡는 속도보다 빠르다면, 당신은 절대 똑같은 물고기를 두 번 잡지 않을 것이다. 수많은 시도 끝에, 당신은 당신이 한 번 잡았던 물고기의 수, 두 번 잡았던 물고기의 수 등을 적을 수 있다. 한 번만 잡혔던 물고기의 어획량 비율이 높을수록, 당신은 (B)물에 더 많은 물고기가 있다고 결론을 내릴지도 모른다.

rob n. 낚싯대   reel v. 릴을 감아 끌어 올리다
tag v. 꼬리표를 붙이다
open-ended adj. 제한이 없는, 조정이 가능한
essentially adv. 본래, 본질적으로   breed v. 번식하다
proportion n. 비율   conclude v. 결론을 내리다

05 2021 숙명여대

정답 ⑤

해석 ① 완전한   ② 끝에서 두 번째의
③ 분명한   ④ 궁극적인
⑤ 무한한

해설 지문의 빈칸을 채우는 문제이다. 지문의 중간에서 만약 물고기의 번식 속도가 당신이 물고기를 잡는 속도보다 빠르다면 절대 똑같은 물고기를 두 번 잡지 않을 것이라고 했으므로, 빈칸 (A)에는 만약 물고기 수가 제한이 없거나 본래 무한하다면 절대 똑같은 물고기를 두 번 잡지 않을 것이라는 내용이 나오는 것이 자연스럽다. 따라서 '무한한'이라고 한 ⑤번이 정답이다.

06 2021 숙명여대

정답 ③

해석 ① 장기적으로 적지 않은 물고기가 잡힐 것이다.
② 꼬리표가 붙여진 물고기는 잡기 쉽다.
③ 수역에 있는 총 물고기 수는 적다.
④ 수역에는 잡힌 것과 똑같은 수만큼의 물고기가 있을 것이다.
⑤ 위 보기 중 아무것도 해당 없음

해설 일부 물고기가 반복적으로 잡힐 경우, 가장 가능성 있는 것을 파악하는 문제이다. 지문의 중간에서 If the body of water contains a small number of fish, ~ you'll keep catching the same few fish again and again을 근거로 일부 물고기가 반복적으로 잡힐 경우, 가장 가능성 있는 것은 '수역에 있는 총 물고기 수는 적다'임을 알 수 있다. 따라서 정답은 ③번이다.

07 2021 숙명여대

정답 ②

해석 ① 더 많은 물고기가 더 빠르게 잡힌다
② 물에 더 많은 물고기가 있다
③ 물고기가 살아있을 가능성이 더 희박해진다
④ 물에 더 적은 물고기가 번식할 것이다
⑤ 꼬리표가 붙여진 물고기가 덜 나타난다

해설 지문의 빈칸을 채우는 문제이다. 지문의 중간에서 물고기가 엄청나게 많다면 당신이 끌어올리는 대부분의 물고기는 전에 잡혔던 물고기가 아닐 것이라고 했으므로, 빈칸에는 한 번만 잡혔던 물고기의 어획량 비율이 높을수록, 물에 더 많은 물고기가 있다고 결론을 내릴지도 모른다는 내용이 나오는 것이 자연스럽다. 따라서 '물에 더 많은 물고기가 있다'라고 한 ②번이 정답이다.

어휘 slim adj. (가능성 등이) 희박한

[08-09]

환경에 대한 관심이 높은 이 시대의 자원 산업은 지속 가능한 개발을 현재의 철학으로 하고 있다. 그것의 주된 전제는 자연 환경의 요구가 충족되고 있는지를 보장함과 동시에 오늘날과 미래의 인류에게 충분한 자원이 있는지를 확실하게 만드는 것이다. 이를 위해서, 회사들은 소비하는 에너지를 줄이고, 탄소 발자국을 줄이며, 다른 종류의 폐기물을 최소화하기 위한 새로운 방법을 찾기 위해 항상 경계하고 있다. 지속 가능한 발전을 통해서 사회적으로 책임을 져야 한다는 생각으로 더욱 장기적으로 이윤을 바라보는 관점을 가진 회사는 정부의 지원과 상품을 사는 소비자들에 의해 보상받고 있다.

sustainable development phr. 지속 가능한 개발
current adj. 현재의   philosophy n. 철학
resource n. 자원   industry n. 산업
environmental adj. 환경의   concern n. 관심, 걱정
premise n. 전제   concurrently adv. 동시에, 함께
ensure v. 보장하다   meet v. 충족하다
on the lookout phr. 경계하여
carbon footprint phr. 탄소 발자국
minimize v. 최소화하다
responsible adj. 책임을 지는, 책임이 있는

08 2019 가천대

정답 ③

해석 ① 이윤   ② 정직성
③ 명제   ④ 선전

해설 밑줄 친 premise의 의미를 추론하는 문제이다. 밑줄 친 부분이 포함된 문장은 앞에 언급되었던 지속 가능한 개발이 이루어지기 위한 전제 조건에 대해서 말하고 있다. 따라서, 밑줄 친 단어의 의미를 '명제'라고 한 ③번이 정답이다.

어휘 profit n. 이윤, 수익   probity n. 정직성
proposition n. 명제   propaganda n. 선전

09 2019 가천대

정답 ①

해석 ① 보상받다   ② 반박되다
③ 비난받다   ④ 처벌받다

해설 지문의 빈칸을 채우는 문제이다. 빈칸이 포함된 문장에서, 지속 가능한 발전을 위해서 사회적 책임을 다하고 있는 회사에

는 정부가 지원해주고 고객들이 제품을 산다고 설명하고 있으므로, 빈칸에는 긍정적인 의미의 단어가 와야 한다는 것을 알 수 있다. 따라서 '보상받다'라고 한 ①번이 정답이다.

어휘 reward v. 보상하다, 사례하다 counter v. 반박하다
denounce v. 비난하다, 고발하다 penalize v. 처벌하다

[10-11]

당신이 적도 근처에 있을수록, 날씨는 더욱 변하지 않고 여름의 날씨가 된다. 일 년 내내 꽃과 초록빛의 잎이 자라있는데, 이것이 열대 지방이 많은 사람에게 일종의 낙원이라고 생각되는 이유이다. 생각해보라. 만약 우리가 북쪽의 겨울 동안 열대 섬으로 탈출할 수 있다면, 우리는 지구의 둥근 모양과 옆으로 기울어진 덕에 휴가를 갈 수 있는 것이다. 왜 그럴까? 북반구와 남반구는 서로 굽어 있기 때문에 지구의 기울어짐을 정면으로 견뎌낼 수 있다. 일 년 중 일부 동안, 뉴욕은 햇볕이 내리쬔다. 또 다른 일부 동안은 많은 눈과 얼어붙는 비바람에 떤다. 그 사이에, 뉴욕은 봄과 가을의 더 온화한 날씨를 즐긴다. 하지만, 지구의 불룩한 가운데 부분 가까이 사는 사람은 기울임의 영향을 받지 않는다. 지구의 중간 부분에서는 일 년의 어느 부분은 태양으로부터 급격히 멀어져 기울어진다거나 태양 쪽을 향해 기울어지지 않는다. 적도 주변의 지역들은 연중 강한 햇빛을 받는다.

equator n. 적도 permanently adv. 변하지 않고
summery adj. 여름의 tropics n. 열대 지방
paradise n. 낙원 sideways adv. 옆으로 tilt n. 기울어짐
hemisphere n. 반구 curve v. 곡선을 그리다
bear the brunt of phr. ~를 정면으로 견뎌내다
a load of phr. 많은 broil v. 내리쬐다 shiver v. 떨다
bulging adj. 튀어나온 lean v. 기울다, 기대다

10 2020 단국대
정답 ①

해석 ① 하지만 ② 그러므로
③ 게다가 ④ 비슷하게

해설 빈칸에 적절한 연결어를 넣는 문제이다. 빈칸 앞 문장은 뉴욕에 덥고 춥고 온화한 모든 날씨가 있다는 내용이고, 빈칸 뒤 문장은 적도 주변에서는 연중 강한 햇빛을 받는다는 내용이다. 따라서 역접을 나타내는 연결어인 ① However(하지만)가 정답이다.

11 2020 단국대
정답 ③

해석 ① 열대 지방은 몹시 추운 날씨가 자주 있을 수 있다.
② 온화한 지역은 많은 사람들에게 낙원으로 여겨진다.
③ 매우 더운 지역은 변하지 않고 여름과 같은 날씨이다.
④ 뉴욕의 날씨는 연중 비교적 변하지 않는다.

해설 지문의 내용과 일치하는 것을 묻는 문제이다. 지문의 처음에서 당신이 적도 근처에 있을수록, 날씨는 더욱 변하지 않고 여름의 날씨가 된다는 내용을 통해 매우 더운 지역은 변하지 않고 여름과 같은 날씨인 것을 알 수 있다. 따라서 ③번이 지문의 내용과 일치한다.

오답분석 ① 당신이 적도 근처에 있을수록, 날씨는 더욱 변하지 않고 여름의 날씨가 된다고 했으므로, 열대 지방은 몹시 추운 날씨가 자주 있을 수 있다는 것은 지문의 내용과 다르다.
② 이것이 열대 지방이 많은 사람에게 일종의 낙원이라고 생각되는 이유라고 했으므로, 온화한 지역은 많은 사람들에게 낙원으로 여겨진다는 것은 지문의 내용과 다르다.
④ 일 년 중 일부 동안 뉴욕은 햇볕이 내리쬐고 또 다른 일부 동안은 많은 눈과 얼어붙는 비바람에 떤다고 했으므로, 뉴욕의 날씨는 연중 비교적 변하지 않는다는 것은 지문의 내용과 다르다.

어휘 frequently adv. 자주 temperate adj. 온화한
torrid adj. 매우 더운 relatively adv. 비교적
invariable adj. 변하지 않는

[12-14]

새들은 어디에나 있다. 우리는 매일 새들이 우리의 머리 위를 날아다니거나 뒷마당에서 깡충깡충 뛰어다니는 모습을 목격한다. 그러나 과학자들은 새들의 개체 수가, 특히 북미지역에서, 빠르게 감소하고 있는 중이라고 이야기한다. 1970년 이래로 북미 대륙의 전체 새의 수 중 대략 29퍼센트가 사라지고 있다. 게다가, 참새와 찌르레기 같은 평범한 새의 종들이 심지어 희귀종의 새들보다도 빠르게 걱정스러운 속도로 사라지고 있다는 사실이 발견되었다. 새로운 연구에 따르면, 거의 모든 종의 새들이 곤경에 처하고 있는 중이라고 한다. 목초지 조류의 수는 엄청난 손실을 겪고 있으며, 53퍼센트 수준까지 감소하고 있는 중이다. 목초지 조류보다 그 수가 많은, 숲에 거주하는 새들 또한 매우 빠르게 사라지고 있는 중이다. 10억 마리의 새가 사라지고 있다. 지구의 반구를 이주하며 돌아다니는 해안가의 새들도 급격하고, 지속적인 개체 수의 감소를 보여주고 있다. 심지어, 때때로 다양한 환경에서 적응할 수 있는, 외래 침입종의 새들도 이 운명에서 벗어날 수 없을 것 같다. 새들은 그들의 평안함이 생태계 전반의 건강을 나타낼 수 있는, 지표동물이기 때문에, 과학자들은 이와 같은 엄청난 개체 수 손실을 북미 지역 전반의 생태계 상태에 대한 경고로 받아들여야 한다고 이야기한다.

hop v. 깡충깡충 뛰다 backyard n. 뒷마당
decline v. 감소하다 rapidly adv. 빠르게
especially adv. 특히 approximately adv. 대략
continent n. 대륙 sparrow n. 참새
blackbird n. 찌르레기 disappear v. 사라지다
alarming adj. 걱정스러운 rate n. 속도 rare adj. 희귀한
forest-dwelling adj. 숲에 사는
outnumber v. ~보다 수가 많다

shorebird n. 바닷가에 사는 새	migrate v. 이동하다
hemisphere n. 반구	sharp adj. 급격한
consistent adj. 지속적인	invasive adj. 침습성의
environment n. 환경	indicator animal phr. 지표동물
well-being n. 평안	reflect v. 나타내다
massive adj. 엄청난	warning n. 경고
ecosystem n. 생태계	in general phr. 전반적으로

12 [2020 경기대]

정답 ④

해석
① 마침내 ② 그러므로
③ 그러나 ④ 게다가

해설 빈칸에 적절한 연결어를 넣는 문제이다. 빈칸 앞 문장은 1970년 이래로 북미 대륙의 새의 수 중 대략 29퍼센트가 사라지고 있다는 내용이고, 빈칸 뒤 문장은 참새와 찌르레기 같은 평범한 새의 종들이 심지어 희귀종의 새들보다도 빠르게 사라지고 있다는 사실이 발견되었다는 내용이므로, 내용의 추가를 나타내는 연결어인 ④ Moreover(게다가)가 들어가야 한다.

어휘 appropriate adj. 적절한

13 [2020 경기대]

정답 ③

해석
① 바닷가에 사는 새
② 외래종의 새
③ 목초지 새
④ 숲에 거주하는 새

해설 북미 지역에서 어떤 종류의 새들이 비율적으로 가장 크게 줄었는지를 파악하는 문제이다. 일곱 번째 문장의 Grassland bird populations ~ by 53%에서 최상급 표현인 the greatest loss를 확인할 수 있으므로, 정답은 ③번이다.

어휘 percentage n. 비율

14 [2020 경기대]

정답 ①

해석
① 새들의 운명은 다른 동물들을 향해 제기된 잠재적인 위협을 암시한다.
② 새의 종은 주로 외래종의 종들 때문에 감소하는 중이다.
③ 가장 일반적인 새의 종은 가장 잘 적응할 수 있다는 것을 증명하고 있는 중이다.
④ 새의 수가 일반적인 새의 이주 경로를 따라 가장 많이 감소하고 있는 중이다.

해설 지문을 통해 추론할 수 있는 것을 고르는 문제이다. 지문의 끝부분에서 새들이 지표 동물이기 때문에 과학자들이 새들 개체 수의 손실을 북미 지역 생태계 상태에 대한 경고로 받아들여야 한다고 이야기한다(As birds are indicator animals ~ the state of North American ecosystems in general)고 했으므로, 새들의 운명은 다른 동물들을 향해 제기된 잠재적인 위협을 암시한다는 것을 추론할 수 있다. 따라서 ①번이 정답이다.

오답 분석
② 열한 번째 문장의 Even invasive species ~ this fate에서 침습성의 조류들 또한 다른 종의 새들처럼 수가 감소하고 있다는 내용을 확인할 수 있으므로, 새의 종이 침습성의 종들 때문에 감소하고 있다는 것은 지문의 내용과 다르다.

③ 마찬가지로, 열한 번째 문장의 Even invasive species ~ this fate에서 환경에 적응할 수 있는 새의 종은 침습성의 조류들임을 확인할 수 있으므로, 가장 일반적인 새의 종이 가장 잘 적응할 수 있다는 것을 증명한다는 것은 지문의 내용과 다르다.

④ 일곱 번째 문장의 Grassland bird ~ disappearing fast에서 가장 많은 수의 손실이 있는 새의 종류는 목초지 새임을 확인할 수 있고, 여덟 번째 문장의 Shorebirds ~ population losses에서 이주하는 종류의 새들은 바닷가에 사는 새들임을 확인할 수 있으므로, 새의 수가 새의 이주 경로를 따라 가장 많이 감소하고 있다는 것은 지문의 내용과 다르다.

어휘 point to phr. 암시하다 potential adj. 잠재적인
threat n. 위협 prove v. 입증하다 migration n. 이주

15 [2019 명지대]

정답 ③

해석 Northern Lights라고도 알려진 북극광은 태양풍 입자가 지구를 향해 돌진하고 대기에 있는 화학 물질들과 상호 작용하면서 발생되는 굉장한 자연 현상이다. 잘 알려지지는 않았지만 동일하게 멋진 남극광(또는 Southern Lights)도 있는데, 남반구의 최남단 지역에서 보인다. 북극광(과 남극광)이 오로지 극지방 주변에서만 존재하는 이유는 지구의 자기장 때문인데, 이 자기장은 태양 입자가 최북단과 최남단 지대에 모이는 것을 야기한다. 여기서, 태양 입자는 산소와 질소 입자와 섞이고, 유명한 활기 넘치는 무지개 색깔의 극광을 형성하는 광자를 방출한다. 질소와의 상호 작용이 자줏빛을 띤 빨간색, 보라색 과 (조금 덜 빈번하게는) 파란색이 되는 데 반해, 산소와의 상호 작용은 일반적으로 노란색이나 초록색 빛 중 하나를 발생시킨다. 어떤 한 시간의 빛의 밝기는 태양풍 입자와 진동하는 자기장 선의 움직임의 연관성을 보여준다.
① 태양 입자는 보라색 극광을 형성하기 위해 산소와 섞인다.
② 남극광은 북극에서 관찰될 수 있다.
③ 태양 입자는 지구의 자기장 때문에 극지방에 모인다.
④ 지구의 자기장 선은 잘 정돈되고 안정적이다.

해설 지문의 내용과 일치하는 것을 묻는 문제이다. 지문의 중반에서 북극광(과 남극광)이 오로지 극지방 주변에서만 존재하는 이유는 지구의 자기장 때문이고, 이 자기장은 태양 입자가 최

북단과 최남단 지대에 모이는 것을 야기한다고 했으므로, 태양 입자가 지구의 자기장 때문에 극지방에 모인다는 것을 알 수 있다. 따라서 ③번이 지문의 내용과 일치한다.

오답분석
① 다섯 번째 문장에서 태양 입자가 질소와 상호 작용했을 때 보라색이 된다고 했으므로, 태양 입자가 보라색 극광을 형성하기 위해 산소와 섞인다는 것은 지문의 내용과 다르다.
② 두 번째 문장에서 남극광은 남반구의 최남단 지역에서 보인다고 했으므로, 남극광이 북극에서 관찰될 수 있다는 것은 지문의 내용과 다르다.
④ 세 번째 문장에서 북극광과 남극광이 극지방 주변에서만 존재하는 이유가 지구의 자기장 때문이라고는 했지만, 지구의 자기장 선이 잘 정돈되고 안정적인지는 알 수 없다.

어휘
aurora n. 북극광   aka adj. ~라고도 알려진(also known as)
Northern Lights phr. 북극광
spectacular adj. 굉장한, 장관인
natural phenomenon phr. 자연 현상
particle n. 입자, 미립자   solar wind phr. 태양풍
hurtle v. 돌진하다   interact with phr. ~와 상호 작용하다
atmosphere n. 대기   trippy adj. 멋진, 기분이 좋은
aurora australis phr. 남극광
Southern Lights phr. 남극광
visible from phr. ~에서 보이는
southernmost adj. 최남단의   hemisphere n. 반구
exclusively adv. 오로지, 독점적으로   pole n. 극
magnetic field phr. 자기장   converge v. 모이다
northernmost adj. 최북단의   latitude n. 지방, 지대
mingle with phr. 섞다   nitrogen n. 질소
photon n. 광자(빛의 입자)   famously adv. 유명하게
exuberant adj. 활기 넘치는   aurora n. 극광, 오로라
interaction n. 상호 작용
typically adv. 일반적으로, 전형적으로
whereas conj. ~하는 반면   result in phr. 결국 ~이 되다
purplish adj. 자줏빛을 띤   slightly adv. 조금, 약간
frequently adv. 빈번하게   correlate v. 연관성을 보여주다
oscillating adj. 진동하는

[16-17]

Carl Bosch는 거대한 양의 암모니아를 생산하는 것을 가능하게 했는데, 그 암모니아 중의 많은 양이 질소가 풍부한 질산암모늄 비료로 만들어진다. 세심한 추정에 따르면 합성 비료는 전 세계 인구의 절반 정도를 먹여 살린다고 한다. 식물은 단백질과 DNA를 합성하는데 질소 화합물에 의존한다. 자연에서, 질산염은 부패하는 식물과 동물 물질, 그리고 공기에서 질소를 고정하는 특정한 박테리아에서 나온다. 하지만, Bosch의 영속적인 유산은 양날의 검이다. 인공 비료는 수백만 명을 굶주림으로부터 구했지만, 암모니아의 대량 생산이 가능하게 된 1910년에 약 18억 명에서 한 세기 후에 약 70억 명이라는 인구의 큰 증가는 세계의 자원에 큰 부담을 주었다. 합성 비료들의 제조는 세계의 총 에너지 소비의 약 1퍼센트를 차지하고, 그

것들의 사용은 오염을 일으킨다. 농지의 유출수가 호수와 하구에 여분의 질소로 인한 '해로운 녹조'를 만들어낸다.

ammonia n. 암모니아
ammonium nitrate phr. 질산암모늄
fertilizer n. 비료   estimate n. 추정
synthetic adj. 합성의   population n. 인구
nitrogen n. 질소   compound n. 혼합물
protein n. 단백질   decay v. 부패하다
lasting adj. 영속적인, 오래 가는   legacy n. 유산
double-edged adj. 양날의 검 같은, 두 가지로 해석될 수 있는
artificial adj. 인공의   starvation n. 굶주림, 기근
strain n. 부담, 압박   account for phr. ~를 차지하다
agricultural run-off phr. 농지 유출수
algal bloom phr. 녹조   estuary n. 하구, 어귀

16 (2019 서울여대)

정답 ②

해석 ① 수질 오염을 줄이는 것
② 합성 비료를 생산하는 것
③ 물에서 질소를 얻는 것
④ 녹조가 생성되는 것을 막는 것

해설 Carl Bosch가 가능하게 만든 것을 파악하는 문제이다. 지문의 처음에서 Bosch는 암모니아를 생산하는 것을 가능하게 했고 그것이 질산암모늄 비료로 만들어진다고 했으므로, Carl Bosch가 가능하게 만든 것은 '합성 비료를 생산하는 것'이다. 따라서 정답은 ②번이다.

어휘 manufacture v. 생산하다

17 (2019 서울여대)

정답 ④

해석 ① 농지 유출수는 동물이 섭취하면 박테리아 감염을 일으킨다.
② Carl Bosch는 기근 구제 기금을 설립하는 데 적극적으로 관여했다.
③ 부패하는 식물과 동물 물질은 호수 오염의 주요 원인이다.
④ 암모니아의 생산은 대규모로 비료의 제조를 가능하게 했다.

해설 지문의 내용과 일치하는 것을 묻는 문제이다. 지문의 처음에서 Carl Bosch가 암모니아를 대량으로 생산하는 것을 가능하게 했으며, 그것으로 질산암모늄 비료를 만든다는 내용을 통해 암모니아의 생산은 대규모로 비료의 제조를 가능하게 했다는 것을 알 수 있다. 따라서 ④번이 지문의 내용과 일치한다.

오답분석 ① 농지 유출수가 호수와 하구에 녹조를 만든다고는 했지만, 농지 유출수를 동물이 섭취했을 때 박테리아 감염이 일어나는지는 알 수 없다.

② Carl Bosch가 가능하게 한 암모니아의 대량 생산으로 합성 비료를 만든다고는 했지만, Carl Bosch가 기근 구제 기금을 설립하는 데 적극적으로 관여했는지는 알 수 없다.
③ 부패하는 식물과 동물 물질에서 질산염이 나온다고는 했지만, 부패하는 식물과 동물 물질이 호수 오염의 주요 원인인지는 알 수 없다.

어휘   infection n. 감염   relief fund phr. 구제 기금

[18-19]

아레시보에 있는 Puerto Rico 대학교 교수 Abel Mendez는 "우리가 '잠재적으로 주거할 수 있는' 태양계 밖에 있는 행성을 말하면, 그것은 주거할 수 있는 조건을 위해 필요한 행성의 측정할 수 있는 특성을 나타내는 용어이."라고 말한다. 그래서, 이 행성들은 장래성이 있는 대상이지만, 아무것도 보장되지 않는다. 하지만 두 가지 기준은 행성의 주거성에 대한 대중의 토론에서 우위를 차지한다: 첫째는, 행성이 지구의 일반적인 크기 범위 내에 있는지 아닌지 (그래서 바위처럼 될 가능성을 가지는지) 그리고, 두 번째로 행성이 주거할 수 있는 지역으로 알려진 곳에 있는지 아닌지이다.
이것은 행성의 표면에서 물을 액체 상태로 유지할 만큼 충분한 별빛이 있는 주인 항성 주변의 거리 범위이다. 항성에 너무 가까이 가면, 그 열은 물이 증발하게 할 것이다. 너무 멀어진다면 어떤 물이든 얼 것이다.
이것들은 유용한 경험 법칙이지만, 많은 요인들은 행성이 얼마나 살기에 알맞은지에 영향을 준다. 그리고 일부 요인들은 기술의 한계 때문에 논의 대상에서 제외된다.

potentially adv. 잠재적으로, 가능성 있게
habitable adj. 주거할 수 있는, 살 수 있는
exoplanet n. 태양계 외 행성
measurable adj. 잴(측정할) 수 있는
promising adj. 장래성이 있는, 기대되는
guarantee v. 보장하다   criterion n. 기준 (pl. criteria)
dominate v. 우위를 차지하다, 좌우하다
planetary adj. 행성의   habitability n. 주거성, 살 수 있음
range n. 범위   rocky adj. 바위로 된
reside v. 있다, 거주하다   starlight n. 별빛   liquid n. 액체
boil off phr. 증발하다   freeze v. 얼다   factor n. 요인, 인자
hospitable adj. 알맞은, 쾌적한   conversation n. 대화
limitation n. 한계, 제한

18 2019 성균관대

정답 ⑤

해석 ① 물   ② 크기
     ③ 거리   ④ 별빛
     ⑤ 태양

해설 지문의 중후반에서 행성이 지구의 일반적인 크기 범위 내에 있는지, 행성의 표면에서 물을 액체 상태로 유지할 만큼 충분한 별빛이 있는 주인 항성 주변의 거리 범위인 살 수 있는 지역에 있는지가 행성의 주거성 기준이라고 했으므로, 태양계 밖에 있는 주거할 수 있는 행성을 위해 필요한 조건이 아닌 것은 '태양'이다. 따라서 ⑤번이 정답이다.

19 2019 성균관대

정답 ①

해석 ① 실제적인 경험을 기반으로 하는 기준
     ② 이론적인 추론으로 도출해 낸 방법
     ③ 과학적인 관찰로 초래된 최고의 규칙
     ④ 지출을 기반으로 하는 주요 기준
     ⑤ 정교한 계산으로 만들어진 쉬운 절차

해설 밑줄 친 rules of thumb의 의미를 추론하는 문제이다. 세 번째 문단에서 항성에 너무 가까이 가면, 그 열은 물이 증발하게 할 것이고, 너무 멀어진다면 어떤 물이든 얼 것이라고 했다. 따라서, rules of thumb의 의미를 '실제적인 경험을 기반으로 하는 기준'이라고 한 ①번이 정답이다.

어휘 practical adj. 실제적인   procedure n. 방법
     theoretical adj. 이론적인   inference n. 추론
     induce v. 유발하다   observation n. 관찰
     prime adj. 주요한   expenditure n. 지출, 소비
     procedure n. 절차, 방법   elaborate adj. 정교한
     calculation n. 계산

[20-21]

Lancet Planetary Health 저널의 최근 연구에 따르면 평균 기온이 상승함에 따라 전 세계적으로 공기로 운반되는 꽃가루 수가 증가하고 있다. 조사된 17개 장소 중 대다수는 20년이 넘는 동안 꽃가루 양의 증가와 꽃가루 계절이 길어진 것으로 보였다. 기후 변화가 빠를수록 더 악화된다. 이것이 전 세계 평균보다 두 배 빠르게 따뜻해지고 있는 알래스카의 주민들이 특히 높은 알레르기 위험에 직면한 이유이다.
장기적으로 종합해 생각해 볼 때, 계절성 알레르기는 지구 온난화가 건강에 대한 위험을 증가시키는 방법 중 가장 강력한 사례 중 하나이다. 알레르기는 이미 주된 건강 부담이며, 경제를 더욱 고갈시키는 것이 될 것이다.
"이건 정말 강력합니다. 사실, 저는 반박할 수 없는 자료가 있다고 생각합니다."라고 알래스카의 알레르기, 천식 및 면역학 센터의 이사인 Jeffrey Demain은 말했다. "그것은 기후 변화가 건강에 미치는 영향의 모델이 되었습니다." 그리고 많은 사람들이 피해를 보고 있기 때문에 — 일부 추정치에 따르면, 최대 5천만 명의 미국인이 코 알레르기가 있다고 말한다 — 과학자들과 보건 당국자들은 증가한 꽃가루 사태 이후 약간의 경감을 일으킬 희망으로 이러한 위험을 초래하는 기후 요인들을 알아내려고 현재 애쓰고 있다.

airborne adj. 공기로 운반되는   pollen n. 꽃가루
average adj. 평균의   temperature n. 기온

climb v. 오르다   majority n. 대다수, 다수   site n. 장소
climate n. 기후   resident n. 주민   allergy n. 알레르기
take together phr. 하나로 합쳐서 생각하다
long term phr. 장기   seasonal adj. 계절적인
global warming phr. 지구온난화
robust adj. 강력한, 튼튼한   burden n. 부담
drain n. 고갈시키는 것, 낭비   director n. 이사
asthma n. 천식   immunology n. 면역학
afflict v. 피해를 입히다, 괴롭히다   estimate n. 추정치
up to phr. 최고~, ~까지   nasal adj. 코의
official n. 당국자, 관계자   tease out phr. 알아내려고 애쓰다
relief n. 경감, 완화   in the wake of phr. ~이후, ~여파로
avalanche n. 사태

20 2020 인하대

정답 ①

해석 ① 기후 변화   ② 도덕적 해이
③ 경제 위기   ④ 감소하는 꽃가루 수
⑤ 환경 파괴

해설 지문의 빈칸을 채우는 문제이다. 지문의 두 번째 단락 첫 번째 문장에서 계절성 알레르기는 지구 온난화가 건강에 대한 위험을 증가시키는 가장 강력한 사례 중 하나라고 했으므로, 빈칸에는 지구 온난화와 관련된 내용이 나와야 적절하다는 것을 알 수 있다. 따라서 '기후 변화'라고 한 ①번이 정답이다.

어휘 moral hazard phr. 도덕적 해이   crisis n. 위기
decreasing adj. 감소하는   environmental adj. 환경의
destruction n. 파괴

21 2020 인하대

정답 ⑤

해석 ① 알레르기가 방지될 것이다.
② 꽃가루를 막을 수 없게 되고 있다.
③ 알래스카는 꽃가루 알레르기로 고통받기에는 너무 춥다.
④ 계절성 알레르기는 국가 경제에서 중요한 역할을 한다.
⑤ 꽃가루 알레르기의 계절은 기온이 상승함에 따라 더 길고 극심해진다.

해설 지문의 요지를 묻는 문제이다. 지문의 처음에서 평균 기온이 상승함에 따라 전 세계적으로 꽃가루 양이 증가하고 꽃가루 계절이 길어졌다고 설명하고 있다. 따라서 이 지문의 요지를 '꽃가루 알레르기의 계절은 기온이 상승함에 따라 더 길고 극심해진다'라고 표현한 ⑤번이 정답이다.

어휘 control v. 방지하다, 막다
play an important role in phr. ~에서 중요한 역할을 하다
intense adj. 극심한, 강렬한

[22-23]

경관 생태학은 조망 규모에서 생태계 관계에 초점을 맞춘다. 생태학자 Richard Forman과 Michel Godron에 따르면, 경관 생태학은 '상호 작용을 하는 생태계로 구성된 여러 다른 종류들로 이뤄진 면적에서의 구조, 기능, 변화에 관한 연구'이다. 유럽과학자들은 미국의 과학자들에 앞서 경관생태학을 진보시켰다. 유럽의 경관은 북아메리카에서보다 더 밀집하여 정리되었고, 그 결과, 인간의 영향력이 유럽 과학자들에 의해 빠르게 인정되었다. 미국 생태학자들은 비교적 원시적인 경관을 연구하는 데 더 익숙하다. 전국적으로 증가한 교외의 스프롤 현상과 관련된 경관 생태학 분야의 개선은 더 많은 미국의 생태학자들이 자연계와 인간의 상호작용을 인정하면서 이 상황을 바꿔왔다. 경관 생태학은 유럽, 미국, 호주의 원인들 간의 다양한 상호 작용을 통해 발전해왔기 때문에, 새롭고 강력한 것으로 구체화해왔다. Richard Forman은 거주지가 경관에 대해 모자이크와 같은 양식을 형성하고 이 지역 모자이크 광경이 그 경관을 기꺼이 과학자들, 특히 생태학자들이 접근하기 쉽도록 해주는 것을 보았다.

ecological adj. 생태계의
landscape scale phr. 조망 규모, 지형 규모
ecologist n. 생태학자
heterogeneous adj. 여러 다른 종류들로 이뤄진
ecosystem n. 생태계   advance v. 진보시키다
counterpart n. 상대방   settle v. 정리하다, 결정하다
influence n. 영향력
be accustomed to phr. ~에 익숙하다
relatively adv. 비교적
pristine adj. 원시적인, 자연 그대로의   refinement n. 개선
discipline n. 학문의 분야   suburban adj. 교외의
sprawl n. (도시의) 스프롤 현상(무계획적인 팽창 현상)
interaction n. 상호작용   evolve v. 발전하다
contributor n. 원인, 기여   crystallize v. 구체화하다
readily adv. 기꺼이

22 2019 건국대

정답 ③

해석 ① 완벽하게   ② 안전하게
③ 밀집하여   ④ 가볍게
⑤ 정확하게

해설 지문의 빈칸을 채우는 문제이다. 빈칸 앞 문장에서 '유럽과학자들은 미국의 과학자들에 앞서 경관 생태학을 진보시켰다'고 했으므로, '유럽의 경관은 북아메리카에서보다 더 정리되었고, 그 결과, 인간의 영향력이 유럽 과학자들에 의해 빠르게 인정되었다'라는 문맥에서 빈칸에는 '밀집하여'라는 의미의 densely가 들어가는 것이 자연스럽다. 따라서 ③번이 정답이다.

23 2019 건국대

정답 ④

해설 지문의 내용과 일치하지 않는 것을 찾는 문제이다. '인간과 자연의 독립성'과 관련된 지문은 중반부에 The refinement of the landscape ecology discipline, coupled with increased suburban sprawl nationwide, has changed this situation as more American ecologists acknowledge human interactions with natural systems에서 확인할 수 있다. '전국적으로 증가한 교외의 스프롤 현상과 관련된 경관 생태학 분야의 개선은 더 많은 미국의 생태학자들이 자연계와 인간의 상호작용을 인정하면서 이 상황을 바꿔왔다'라고 했으므로 ④번은 지문의 내용과 일치하지 않는다.

오답 분석
① 지문의 세 번째 문장 European scientists advanced landscape ecology before their American counterparts를 통해 '유럽 과학자들은 미국 과학자들에 앞서 경관 생태학을 발전시켰다'는 것을 알 수 있다.
② 지문의 네 번째 문장 The landscapes of Europe have been more densely settled than in North America, and, as a result, the human influence was recognized quickly by European scientists를 통해 '유럽 과학자들은 자연에 미치는 인간의 영향력을 일찍이 인식하였다'는 것을 알 수 있다.
③ 지문의 다섯 번째 문장 American ecologists are more accustomed to studying relatively pristine landscapes를 통해 '미국 생태학자들은 비교적 원시적 경관을 연구하는 데 더 익숙하다'는 것을 알 수 있다.
⑤ 지문의 마지막 문장 Richard Forman observes that human settlements form mosaic-like patterns on landscapes and that this land mosaic vision makes the landscape readily accessible to scientists, especially ecologists를 통해 '생태학자들은 땅의 모자이크식 패턴 덕분에 경관에 쉽게 접근한다'는 것을 알 수 있다.

[24-25]

Gervase는 그의 책에서 1178년 6월 캔터베리의 한 수도승 집단이 초승달을 바라보면서 한밤중에 밖에서 어떻게 있었는지를 묘사한다. 그것을 보고 있을 때, (A)초승달의 한쪽 끝이 둘로 갈라지는 것처럼 보였다. 그곳에서 화염과 불꽃이 터졌고 달의 나머지 부분도 흔들리는 것처럼 보였다.
Gervase는 스스로 그 사건을 보지 못했지만, 실제로 본 일부의 사람들에 의해 그것을 들었다고 인정하고 있다. 그는 그 사람들이 진실을 말하는 것을 맹세했다고 말한다.
여러 해 동안 역사가들은 수도승들이 본 것이 무엇인지를 골똘히 생각해왔다. 일부는 그것이 달 앞으로 지나가는 구름같이 단순한 것이었을 것으로 생각한다. 다른 사람들은 그것이 실제로 일어난 일이 아니라 단지 이야기일 뿐이라고 믿는다.

하지만, Jack Hartung 박사라는 한 과학자는 그가 답을 찾았을지도 모른다고 믿는다. Hartung 박사가 Gervase의 설명을 읽었을 때, 그는 달의 표면에서 무언가 폭발하는 소리가 났다고 생각했다. 그는 만약에 (B)달의 표면에 유성이 충돌했다면, 지구에서 본 광경은 수도승들이 봤던 사건과 비슷하리라 생각했다.

---

describe v. 묘사하다 **monk** n. 수도승, 승려
split v. 갈라지다, 나뉘다 **flame** n. 화염 **spark** n. 불꽃
burst v. 터지다, 폭발하다 **swear** v. 맹세하다
historian n. 역사가 **puzzle over** phr. 골똘히 생각하다
account n. 설명 **explosion** n. 폭발 **surface** n. 표면
view n. 광경

24 2019 한양대에리카

정답 ④

해석
① 하현 ② 반
③ 보름 ④ 초승

해설 지문의 빈칸을 채우는 문제이다. 빈칸 (A) 이전의 문장에서 수도승들이 한밤중에 새로운 달(초승달)을 보았다고 말하고 있다. 따라서 빈칸 (A)에는 초승달을 설명하는 단어가 와야 한다는 것을 알 수 있다. 따라서 ④번이 정답이다.

어휘 **waning moon** phr. 그믐달 **half moon** phr. 반달
full moon phr. 보름달 **crescent moon** phr. 초승달

25 2019 한양대에리카

정답 ①

해석
① 달의 표면에 유성이 충돌했다
② 다른 행성의 외계인이 달을 침략했다
③ 지구의 중력이 평소보다 강했다
④ 달이 우연히 궤도에서 벗어났다

해설 지문의 빈칸을 채우는 문제이다. 빈칸 (B) 이전의 문장에서 Hartung 박사가 달의 표면에서 무언가 폭발하는 소리가 났다고 생각했다고 설명하고 있으므로, 빈칸 (B)에는 폭발의 원인이 될 수 있는 내용이 와야 한다는 것을 알 수 있다. 따라서 '달의 표면에 유성이 충돌했다'라고 한 ①번이 정답이다.

어휘 **meteor** n. 유성, 운석 **alien** n. 외계인
invade v. 침략하다, 침범하다 **gravity** n. 중력
than usual phr. 평소보다 **by accident** phr. 우연히

[26-27]

지진의 영향은 진원지를 둘러싼 넓은 구역에서 제일 강하다. 수평과 수직 방향으로 몇 야드씩이나 움직이면서 지표면의 균열이 종종 발생한다. 그런 움직임은 보통 대지진 중에는 일어나지 않는데, '지층 변형'이라고 불리는 주기적인 경미한 움직

임은 느낄 수 없을 정도로 너무 작은 미세지진에 동반될 수 있다. 지진의 진동과 그에 따른 지역의 피해 규모는 부분적으로 땅의 특성에 의존한다. 예를 들어, 지진의 진동은 제대로 다져지지 않은 매립지나 하천 침전물 같이 굳어있지 않은 표면 물질에서 더 오래 지속하고 더 큰 파동의 진폭이 발생하고, 기반 지역은 영향을 덜 받는다. 가장 심한 피해는 구조물들이 심한 흔들림에 버틸 수 있도록 지어지지 않은 인구 밀집 도시 지역에서 발생한다.

> earthquake n. 지진 surround v. 둘러싸다
> epicenter n. 진원지, 진앙 surface ground phr. 지표면
> crack v. 갈라지다 horizontal adj. 수평의, 가로의
> vertical adj. 수직의, 세로의 displacement n. 이동
> major earthquake phr. 대지진 slight adj. 경미한
> periodic adj. 주기적인 fault creep phr. 지층 변형
> accompany v. 동반하다 extent n. 규모, 정도
> vibration n. 진동 subsequent adj. 그에 따른, 그다음의
> partly adv. 부분적으로 dependent adj. 의존하는
> characteristic n. 특성 amplitude n. 진폭
> unconsolidated adj. 굳어있지 않은 material n. 물질
> compact v. (땅을) 다지다 deposit n. 침전물
> bedrock n. 기반
> densely populated area phr. 인구 밀집 지역
> structure n. 구조물 withstand v. 버티다

26 2019 숙명여대

정답 ①

해석 ① 대지진 동안, 보통 수평과 수직 방향으로 지진이 일어난다.
② 땅의 특성이 지진의 진동 규모에 부분적으로 영향을 준다.
③ 인구 밀집 도시 지역은 가장 심한 피해를 볼 수 있다.
④ 수평과 수직 방향의 지진은 보통 대지진 동안에 일어나지 않는다.
⑤ 지진의 진동은 굳어있지 않은 표면 물질보다 굳어있는 쪽에서 더 짧게 지속할 것이다.

해설 지문의 내용과 일치하지 않는 것을 묻는 문제이다. 지문의 초반에 수평과 수직 방향으로 몇 야드씩이나 움직이면서 지표면의 균열이 종종 발생하며, 그런 움직임은 보통 대지진 중에는 일어나지 않는다고 했으므로, 대지진 동안, 보통 수평과 수직 방향으로 지진이 일어난다는 것은 지문의 내용과 다르다. 따라서 ①번이 정답이다.

오답 분석
② 지문의 The extent of earthquake vibration and subsequent damage to a region is partly dependent on characteristics of the ground를 통해 땅의 특성이 지진의 진동 규모에 부분적으로 영향을 준다는 것을 알 수 있다.
③ 지문의 The worst damage occurs in densely populated urban areas를 통해 인구 밀집 도시 지역이 가장 심한 피해를 볼 수 있다는 것을 알 수 있다.
④ 지문의 Surface ground cracking often occurs, with horizontal and vertical displacements of several yards. Such movement does not usually occur during a major earthquake를 통해 수평과 수직 방향의 지진은 보통 대지진 동안에 일어나지 않는다는 것을 알 수 있다.
⑤ 지문의 earthquake vibrations last longer and are of greater wave amplitudes in unconsolidated surface material을 통해 지진의 진동은 굳어있지 않은 표면 물질보다 굳어있는 쪽에서 더 짧게 지속할 것이라는 것을 알 수 있다.

어휘 affect v. 영향을 주다 consolidated adj. 굳어있는

27 2019 숙명여대

정답 ⑤

해석 ① ~와 같은 – 명백하게
② ~와 같은 – 드물게
③ ~에 관해 – 희박하게
④ 예를 들어 – 희박하게
⑤ ~와 같은 – 빽빽하게

해설 지문의 빈칸을 채우는 문제이다. 첫 번째 빈칸의 경우 빈칸 뒤에 나오는 단어들이 앞의 unconsolidated surface material의 예시를 들고 있으므로, '~와 같은'이라는 의미의 such as가 적합하다. 두 번째 빈칸의 경우 가장 심한 피해가 도시 지역에서 일어난다고 했으므로, '인구가 _____ 모인 도시 지역'이라는 문맥에서 두 번째 빈칸에는 '빽빽하게'를 의미하는 densely가 적합하다. 따라서 ⑤번이 정답이다.

어휘 clearly adv. 명백하게 rarely adv. 드물게
scarcely adv. 희박하게 densely adv. 빽빽하게

[28-29]

> 비닐봉지가 400마리가 넘는 바다 장수거북의 소화기계에서 발견되었다. 바다 장수거북은 위태롭게 멸종 위기에 처한 종이다. 해파리는 바다 장수거북의 주식이다. 해류에 떠다니는 비닐봉지가 증가하면서, 바다 장수거북이 이 비닐봉지를 해파리로 오해하고 먹어서 피해를 입는 경우가 발생하고 있다. 비닐 봉지는 모든 해양 쓰레기의 12퍼센트를 차지하고, 플라스틱병과 플라스틱 뚜껑도 각각 6퍼센트와 8퍼센트로 널리 퍼져 있다. 해양 쓰레기는 세계의 바다와 수로를 괴롭히는 가장 만연하고 해결할 수 있는 오염 문제들 중 하나이다. 비닐봉지 문제에 대한 간단한 해결책은 재사용할 수 있는 장바구니이다. 비닐봉지가 주는 영향에 대한 인식이 증가하면서 많은 주와 나라들에서 비닐봉지와 관련된 법률을 시행하도록 야기해왔다. 예를 들어, 아일랜드가 소비자에 의해 사용되는 각 비닐봉지에 요금을 부과했을 때, 일회용 비닐봉지 소비는 90퍼센트 떨어졌다.

> plastic bag phr. 비닐봉지
> digestive system phr. 소화기계

leatherback turtle phr. 바다 장수거북
critically adv. 위태롭게
endangered adj. 멸종 위기에 처한   species n. 종
jellyfish n. 해파리   drift v. 떠다니다, 표류하다
current n. 해류, 기류   account for phr. 차지하다
debris n. 쓰레기   cap n. 뚜껑   lid n. 뚜껑
prevalent adj. 널리 퍼져 있는   respectively adv. 각각
litter n. 쓰레기   pervasive adj. 만연한
solvable adj. 해결할 수 있는   plague v. 괴롭히다
waterway n. 수로   reusable adj. 재사용할 수 있는
awareness n. 인식, 의식   impose v. 부과하다
single-use adj. 일회용의   consumption n. 소비

28 2019 건국대

정답 ②

해석
① 비닐봉지의 유용성을 강조한다
② 비닐봉지와 관련된 법률을 시행한다
③ 많은 멸종 위기에 처한 동물들의 상태를 인지한다
④ 더 나은 환경을 위한 시민권을 인정한다
⑤ 제조사들이 플라스틱 제품들을 생산하는 것을 금지한다

해설 지문의 빈칸을 채우는 문제이다. 빈칸 다음 문장에서 '예를 들어, 아일랜드가 소비자에 의해 사용되는 각 비닐봉지에 요금을 부과했을 때, 일회용 비닐봉지 소비는 90퍼센트 떨어졌다'고 했으므로, '비닐봉지가 주는 영향에 대한 인식이 증가하면서 많은 주와 나라들에서 도록 야기해왔다'라는 문맥에서 빈칸에는 '비닐봉지와 관련된 법률을 시행한다'라는 의미의 implement plastic bag related legislation이 들어가는 것이 자연스럽다. 따라서 ②번이 정답이다.

어휘
emphasize v. 강조하다   usefulness n. 유용성
implement v. 시행하다   legislation n. 법률, 입법 행위
civil right phr. 시민권   ban v. 금지하다
manufacturer n. 제조사

29 2019 건국대

정답 ④

해설 지문의 내용과 일치하지 않는 것을 찾는 문제이다. '해양 오염의 해결'과 관련된 지문은 중반부에 Marine litter is one of the most pervasive and solvable pollution problems plaguing the world's oceans and waterways에서 확인할 수 있다. '해양 쓰레기는 세계의 바다와 수로를 괴롭히는 가장 만연하고 해결할 수 있는 오염 문제들 중 하나이다'라고 했으므로 ④번은 지문의 내용과 일치하지 않는다.

오답분석
① 지문의 첫 번째 문장 Plastic bags were found in the digestive systems of more than 400 leatherback turtles를 통해 '바다 장수거북의 소화기관에서 플라스틱이 발견되었다'는 것을 알 수 있다.

② 지문의 두 번째 문장 The leatherback turtle is a critically endangered species를 통해 '바다 장수거북은 멸종 위기종에 속한다'는 것을 알 수 있다.
③ 지문의 다섯 번째 문장 Plastic bags account for 12 percent of all marine debris, and plastic bottles and plastic caps and lids are also prevalent at six and eight percent respectively를 통해 '플라스틱병은 전체 해양 쓰레기의 6퍼센트를 차지한다'는 것을 알 수 있다.
⑤ 지문의 마지막 문장 For example, when Ireland imposed a fee on each plastic bag used by consumers, single-use plastic bag consumption dropped by 90 percent를 통해 '아일랜드에서는 플라스틱 봉투를 사용할 때 수수료를 내야 한다'는 것을 알 수 있다.

[30-32]

지속가능한 삶은 할 수 있는 한 최대한으로 자신이 사용한 것을 재활용하게 함으로써 천연자원에 대한 사람들의 수요를 감소시키도록 하는 관행과 관련이 있다. 때때로 그것은 지속가능성을 촉진하지 않는 관행을 이용해 만든 제품을 소비하지 않는 것을 의미할 수도 있고, 또 때때로는 사람들이 어떻게 행동하는지를 변화 시켜, 그들이 삶의 순환에서 더 활동적인 역할을 시작할 수 있도록 하는 것을 의미하기도 한다.

사람들은 지구 온난화, 기후 변화, 오존층의 고갈, 혹은 자원의 감소가 실제적이고 이것들이 인간과 동물의 삶에 미치는 영향이 비극적일 수 있다는 것을 알고 있다. 이제는 사람들이 자신의 생활 방식을 바꿈으로써 지속가능한 삶을 위한 행동을 취해야만 할 때이다. 예를 들어, 대중교통을 조금 더 자주 이용하고, 에너지 소비를 줄이며, 더 환경친화적인 사람이 되는 것과 같은 기본적인 조치가 사람들의 환경적 영향을 축소하고 지구를 안전하고 깨끗한 곳으로 만드는 데 큰 영향을 미칠 수 있다.

sustainable adj. 지속가능한   practice n. 관행, 실천
ensure v. ~하게 하다   promote v. 촉진하다
sustainability n. 지속가능성   depletion n. 고갈, 소모
catastrophic adj. 비극적인   adopt v. 취하다
eco-friendly adj. 환경친화적인   minimize v. 축소하다

30 2020 한성대

정답 ②

해석
① 지속가능한 삶은 환경적 영향을 축소하기 위해 삶의 방식을 바꾸는 것을 포함한다.
② 지속가능한 삶은 많은 물건들을 구매함으로써 더 많은 천연자원을 사용하는 것을 포함한다.
③ 지속가능한 삶은 최대한으로 자신이 사용한 것을 재활용하도록 애쓰는 것을 포함한다.
④ 지속가능한 삶은 에너지를 덜 사용하는 것을 포함한다.

해설 지문과 일치하지 않는 것을 묻는 문제이다. 지문의 첫 번째 문장에서, 지속가능한 삶은 할 수 있는 한 최대한으로 자신이 사용한 것을 재활용하게 함으로써 천연자원에 대한 사람들의 수요를 감소시키는 관행과 관련이 있다고 했으므로, 지속가능한 삶이 많은 물건들을 구매함으로써 더 많은 천연자원을 사용하는 것을 포함한다는 내용은 지문의 내용과 다르다. 따라서 ②번이 정답이다.

오답 분석
① 지문의 두 번째 문단에서, 생활 방식을 바꿈으로써 지속가능한 삶을 위한 행동을 취해야 한다고 했고, 생활 방식을 바꾸는 기초적인 조치들이 사람들이 초래하는 환경적 영향을 축소할 수 있다고 했으므로, 지속가능한 삶이 인간의 환경적 영향을 축소하기 위해 삶의 방식을 바꾸는 것을 포함한다는 것은 지문의 내용과 일치한다.
③ 지문의 첫 번째 문단에서, 지속가능한 삶은 할 수 있는 한 최대한으로 자신이 사용한 것을 재활용하게 함으로써 천연자원에 대한 사람들의 수요를 감소시키도록 하는 관행과 관련이 있다고 했으므로, 지속가능한 삶이 최대한 사용한 것을 재활용하도록 애쓰는 것을 포함한다는 것은 지문의 내용과 일치한다.
④ 지문의 두 번째 문단에서, 에너지 소비를 줄이는 것이 사람들의 환경적 영향을 축소하는 데에 큰 영향을 미칠 수 있다고 했으므로, 지속가능한 삶이 에너지를 덜 사용하는 것을 포함한다는 것은 지문의 내용과 일치한다.

31 2020 한성대

정답 ④

해석 ① 출근하기 위해 더 자주 걷거나 자전거를 타는 것을 통해 지속가능성의 촉진을 도울 수 있다.
② 전구보다 자연광을 더 많이 사용함으로써 에너지 소비를 줄일 수 있다.
③ 물건을 재사용하거나 고쳐 용도를 변경함으로써 환경친화적이 될 수 있다.
④ 세계에 자신의 발자취를 늘림으로써 탄소 발자국을 줄일 수 있다.

해설 지문을 통해 추론할 수 없는 것을 고르는 문제이다. 지문 전체적으로 지속가능한 삶이 의미하는 바와 지속가능한 삶을 위해 사람들이 그들의 생활 방식을 바꿔야 할 필요성에 관해 설명하고 있지만, 세계에 발자취를 늘림으로써 탄소 발자국을 줄일 수 있는지는 유추할 수 없으므로 정답은 ④번이다.

오답 분석
① 출근하기 위해 더 자주 걷거나 자전거를 타는 행위는 에너지 소비를 줄이는 행위이므로 이 행위들이 지속가능성의 촉진을 도울 수 있다는 것을 알 수 있다.
② 전기가 필요한 전구에 비해 자연광을 이용하는 것이 에너지 소비를 줄이는 데 도움이 되리라는 것은 자명한 사실이므로, 전구보다 자연광을 더 많이 사용함으로써 에너지 소비를 줄일 수 있다는 것을 알 수 있다.
③ 두 번째 문단에서, 재활용, 환경친화적인 사람이 되는 것과 같은 생활 방식의 기초적인 변화가 지속가능한 삶의 예시로 나타나고 있으므로 두 행위가 서로 연결되어 있음을 알 수 있다. 따라서 물건을 재사용하거나 고쳐 용도를 변경함으로써 환경친화적이 될 수 있다는 것은 추론할 수 있다.

어휘 natural light phr. 자연광
repurpose v. 다른 용도에 맞게 고치다   use n. 용도

32 2020 한성대

정답 ②

해석 ① 소비하다 – 영향을 미치다
② 소비하다 – 영향
③ 상담하다 – 영향을 미치다
④ 상담하다 – 영향

해설 지문의 빈칸을 채우는 문제이다. 지문 전체적으로 지속가능한 삶을 위해 삶의 방식을 변경해야 한다는 것을 설명하고 있으므로, 첫 번째 빈칸에는 지속가능성을 촉진하지 않는 관행으로 만들어진 제품을 소비하지 않는다는 내용이 들어가는 것이 자연스럽다. 두 번째 빈칸은 their라는 한정사 뒤의 명사 자리이므로 명사 형태의 impact가 들어가야 한다. 따라서 ②번이 정답이다.

[33-36]

태양계를 거쳐 3억 마일을 여행한 후, NASA의 우주선인 InSight가 화성의 하늘을 통해 내려가 엘리시움 평원의 매끄러운 표면에 안전하게 착지했다. [A] 항공 우주국의 탐사선과는 다르게, InSight는 오로지 한 지점에서 행성 전체를 연구하기 위해 설계된 착륙선이다. 로봇 팔을 사용하여, 착륙선은 먼저 화성의 표면에 초감도 지진계를 설치할 것이며, 그곳에서 지진계가 운석 충돌과 화성의 지진을 감지하려 귀를 기울일 것이다. [B] 이러한 사건들로 인한 지진파는 과학자들에게 행성의 내부 구조에 대한 더 분명한 그림을 제시할 것이다. 그러고 나면 Insight는 열 탐사선을 내보낼 것인데, 이 탐사선들은 스스로 16인치의 못을 두드려 몇 주에 걸쳐 16피트 깊이까지 파고 들어갈 것이다. 이 기구는 화성 내부에서 얼마만큼의 열이 빠져나가는지를 측정하게 되는데, 이것은 화성에 포함된 열을 만들어내는 방사성 원소의 양과 이 행성이 오늘날 얼마나 지질학적으로 활동하는가를 밝혀낼 것이다. [C] 또한 이 우주선에는 갑판 위에 RISE라고 불리는 두 개의 X 대역 안테나를 가지고 있는데, 이것이 세 번째 기기를 구성한다. [D] RISE로부터 나오는 무전 신호는 화성 궤도의 흔들림을 추적하기 위해서 사용될 것이다. 이것은 연구원들이 화성 핵의 크기와 상태를 이해할 수 있게 도울 것이다. 더불어, 이 실험들은 화성을 열어 과학자들이 수십 년간 찾아 헤맸던 행성의 비밀을 밝혀낼 것이다.

solar system phr. 태양계   spacecraft n. 우주선
descend v. 내려가다   Martian adj. 화성의

lander n. 착륙선 super-sensitive adj. 초감도의
seismometer n. 지진계 meteorite n. 운석
Marsquake n. 화성의 지진 seismic adj. 지진의
internal adj. 내부의 structure n. 구조 probe n. 탐사선
nail n. 못 burrow down phr. 파고 내려가다
instrument n. 기구, 도구 radioactive adj. 방사성의
element n. 원소
X-band adj. X 대역의(5,200~10,900MHz 주파수 사이의)
deck n. 갑판 radio adj. 무전의 signal n. 신호, 표시
wobble n. 흔들림 orbit n. 궤도 planetary adj. 행성의

33 [2019 세종대]

정답 ③

해석 ① 화성의 내부 구조와 열을 생산하는 방사성 원소에 대해 논의하기 위해서
② 긴 여정 끝에 InSight가 안전하게 착륙했다는 것을 강조하기 위해서
③ 화성의 비밀을 밝히기 위해 InSight가 수행하게 될 실험에 관해 설명하기 위해서
④ 화성이 자전하면서 생기는 흔들림이 어떻게 자기장과 관련이 있는지를 보여주기 위해서

해설 지문의 목적을 묻는 문제이다. 지문의 마지막에서 이러한 실험들이 화성의 비밀을 밝혀낼 것이라고 설명하고 있다. 따라서 이 지문의 목적을 '화성의 비밀을 밝히기 위해 InSight가 수행하게 될 실험에 관해 설명하기 위해서'라고 표현한 ③번이 정답이다.

어휘 emphasize v. 강조하다 journey n. 여정
rotation n. 자전, 회전 magnetic field phr. 자기장

34 [2019 세종대]

정답 ①

해설 지문의 흐름상 주어진 문장이 들어가기에 가장 적절한 위치를 고르는 문제이다. [A]의 다음 문장에서 InSight가 행성을 연구하기 위해서 수행하는 여러 가지 실험에 관해 설명하고 했으므로, 자리에 여러 가지 실험을 수행하는 InSight에 대해 소개하는 주어진 문장 '항공 우주국의 탐사선과는 다르게, InSight는 오로지 한 지점에서 행성 전체를 연구하기 위해 설계된 착륙선이다'가 들어가야 글의 흐름이 자연스럽게 연결된다. 따라서 ①번이 정답이다.

어휘 space agency phr. 항공 우주국 rover n. 탐사선

35 [2019 세종대]

정답 ②

해석 ① 천문학적으로 ② 지질학적으로
③ 기하학적으로 ④ 우주 비행으로

해설 지문의 빈칸을 채우는 문제이다. 빈칸의 이전 부분에서 열 탐사선이 화성 표면으로부터 16피트 깊이까지 파고 들어가 화성 내부를 조사한다고 설명하고 있으므로, 빈칸에는 땅의 내부와 관련된 의미의 단어가 와야 한다는 것을 알 수 있다. 따라서 '지질학적으로'라고 한 ②번이 정답이다.

어휘 astronomically adv. 천문학적으로
geologically adv. 지질학적으로
geometrically adv. 기하학적으로
astronautically adv. 우주 비행으로

36 [2019 세종대]

정답 ④

해석 ① NASA는 화성의 표면에 우주선을 간신히 안전하게 착륙시키는 데에 세 번 성공했다.
② 우주선 InSight의 갑판에는 화성의 비밀을 밝힐 수 있는 기구가 총 다섯 개가 있다.
③ 화성이 자전할 때 생기는 흔들림을 추적하는 데에 지진파가 사용될 것이다.
④ 스스로 두드리는 못이 화성 내부로부터 나오는 열의 양을 측정할 것이다.

해설 지문의 내용과 일치하는 것을 묻는 문제이다. 지문의 두 번째 문단에서 InSight will then release its heat probe, a self-hammering 16-inch nail that will burrow down as deep as 16 feet over the course of several weeks. The instrument will measure how much heat escapes from Mars' interior, which will reveal the amount of heat-producing radioactive elements it contains의 내용을 통해 스스로 두드리는 못이 화성 내부로부터 나오는 열의 양을 측정할 것이라는 것을 알 수 있다. 따라서 ④번이 지문의 내용과 일치한다.

오답분석 ① NASA의 우주선인 InSight가 화성의 하늘을 통해 내려가 엘리시움 평원의 매끄러운 표면에 안전하게 착륙했다고는 했지만, NASA는 화성의 표면에 우주선을 간신히 안전하게 착륙시키는 데에 세 번 성공했는지는 알 수 없다.
② 우주선에는 갑판 위에 RISE라고 불리는 두 개의 X 대역 안테나를 가지고 있는데, 이것이 세 번째 기기를 구성한다고는 했지만, 우주선 InSight의 갑판에는 화성의 비밀을 밝힐 수 있는 기구가 총 다섯 개가 있는지는 알 수 없다.
③ RISE로부터 나오는 무전 신호는 화성 궤도의 흔들림을 추적하기 위해서 사용될 것이라고 했으므로, 화성이 자전할 때 생기는 흔들림을 추적하는 데에 지진파가 사용될 것이라는 것은 지문의 내용과 다르다.

어휘 manage to phr. 간신히 ~하다

[37-38]

지구 온난화에 대한 과학적 합의는 기후 변화에 관한 정부 간 협의체(IPCC)에서 생겨난다. 이 협의체는 기후 변화의 과학을 평가하고, 기후 변화가 환경과 사회에 미치는 영향을 밝히고, 이에 대응할 전략을 만들어내기 위해 세계기상기구와 유엔환경계획에 의해 1988년에 설립되었다. 40개국의 900명이 넘는 과학자들이 1995년 출간된 IPCC 최신 보고서의 저자 혹은 전문 검토 위원으로 참여해왔다.

"그것은 기술적 수준, 즉 우리가 기후 체계에 대해 아는 것을 살펴보는 것입니다"라고 보고서 챕터 중 하나에 대한 주요 필자인 미국 국립기상연구소의 Gerald Meehl은 말한다. 실제로 수천 명의 사람이 이것들을 읽게 되었는데요... 이것은 관여하기로 한 거의 모든 사람의 합의된 견해입니다." 6월에, 2,400여 명의 과학자들은 그 조사 결과들을 승인한다고 하는 공식 문서에 서명했다.

지구 온난화의 기본적인 원리는 단순하다. 이산화탄소와 메탄 가스를 비롯한 소위 온실가스라고 하는 것이 대기에 쌓인다. 이산화탄소는 인간 활동으로 발생하는 온실가스에서 가장 중요하다. 온실가스는 창문이 닫힌 채로 햇볕 아래 주차된 자동차처럼 태양열을 가둔다. 이 사실을 대기에 있는 이산화탄소의 양은 약 1750년경 산업화 이전 시대 이래로 30퍼센트가 증가했다는 기본적인 사실과 연관하여 생각해보라. 그 의미는 기온이 상승하고 있다는 것이고, 그것이 바로 IPCC가 연구를 담당했던 것이다.

consensus n. 합의   **establish** v. 설립하다
assess v. 평가하다   **formulate** v. 만들어내다
reviewer n. 검토 위원
the state of the art phr. 어떤 시점에서의 기술적 수준
wind up phr. 처하게 되다   **involve** v. 관여시키다
atmosphere n. 대기   **generate** v. 발생시키다
couple v. 연관하여 생각하다   **implication** n. 의미
charge v. 담당시키다

37 [2019 단국대]

정답 ③

해석 ① 지구 온난화에 대한 과학적 및 사회적 합의
② 지구 온난화의 원인과 결과
③ IPCC 보고서와 지구 온난화의 기본적인 원리
④ 지구 온난화에 대한 IPCC의 정치적 견해

해설 지문의 주제를 묻는 문제이다. 첫 번째, 두 번째 문단에서 IPCC에서 출간한 보고서에 관해 설명하고, 마지막 문단에서 지구 온난화의 기본적인 원리를 예를 들어 설명하고 있다. 따라서 이 지문의 주제를 'IPCC 보고서와 지구 온난화의 기본적인 원리'라고 표현한 ③번이 정답이다.

38 [2019 단국대]

정답 ①

해석 ① 승인했다   ② 반박했다
③ 질책했다   ④ 비난했다

해설 지문의 빈칸을 채우는 문제이다. 빈칸 앞 문장에서 보고서는 관여하기로 한 거의 모든 사람의 합의된 견해라고 했으므로, 빈칸에는 과학자들이 어떤 내용의 공식 문서에 서명했는지에 대한 내용이 나와야 적절하다는 것을 알 수 있다. 따라서 '승인했다'라고 한 ①번이 정답이다.

어휘 **endorse** v. 승인하다   **dispute** v. 반박하다
rebuke v. 질책하다   **denounce** v. 비난하다

[39-40]

전 세계의 천문학자들은 1993년 8월이 다가올 때 흥분하여 기다리고 있었다. 미국의 우주선 Mars Observer호는 화성 주위의 궤도로 이동할 예정이었고, 지구로 다시 새로운 정보를 보내기 시작했다. 행성을 보여주는 것뿐 아니라, Mars Observer호는 화성의 대기와 표면을 연구할 예정이었다.

(A)유감스럽게도, 과학자들은 8월 24일에 Mars Observer호와 연락이 끊겼다. 8억 4500만 달러가 든 Mars Observer호 우주 비행은 실패했다.

그에 반해서, 미국의 (B)이전의 화성으로의 우주 비행은 대단한 성공이었다. 1976년에, 두 대의 미국 우주선이 생명체의 흔적을 찾기 위해 화성에 착륙했다. 그 Viking 착륙선들이 수행했던 실험들은 부정적인 결과를 낳았다. 그러나, 과학자들은 우주에 있는 우리의 가까운 이웃에 대해 여전히 의문을 가졌다. 과학자들은 화성에 있는 생명체의 가능성에 대해 더 조사하고 싶어 했다. 이것은 Mars Observer호 우주 비행의 목적이었다.

과학자들은 Viking 우주 비행에 (C)만족했다. 그 우주선이 착륙했던 두 장소는 안전한 착륙장을 제공했으나, 특별히 흥미로운 장소들은 아니었다. 과학자들은 화성에 생명체를 살게 하는 지구의 특정 장소들과 유사한 다른 지역이 있을 거라고 믿는다. 예를 들어, 남극 대륙에 있는 지역으로, 얼음으로 뒤덮이지 않은 남부의 빅토리아 지역은 화성의 한 지역과 (D)유사하다. 남부 빅토리아 지역의 건곡에서, 평균 기온은 영하지만, 생물학자들은 바위와 얼어붙은 호수에서 단순한 생물 형태를 발견했다. 아마 화성의 지역에서도 해당할 것이다.

과학자들은 화성에서의 또 다른 조사를 원한다. 과학자들은 그 행성의 표면의 지도를 만들고 더 장래성이 있는 장소에 우주선을 착륙시키고 싶어 한다. 과학자들은 고대 생명체의 유해인 화석을 찾고 싶어 한다. 만약 생명체가 화성에 산 적이 있었다면, 과학자들은 미래의 우주 비행은 모래 속, 혹은 얼음 안에서 생명체의 기록을 찾을 수도 있다고 믿는다. 과학자들은 Mars Observer호 우주 비행의 실패에 매우 (E)실망했고 새로운 우주 비행을 시작하고 싶어 한다.

astronomer n. 천문학자　**spacecraft** n. 우주선
map v. 보여주다, 발견하다, ~의 지도를 만들다
Martian adj. 화성의, 화성에서 온　**atmosphere** n. 대기
surface n. 표면, 표층
lose contact with phr. ~와 연락이 끊기다
mission n. 우주 비행, 임무　**sign** n. 흔적, 징후
lander n. 착륙선　**investigate** v. 조사하다
site n. 장소, 위치　**particularly** adv. 특별히, 특히
specific adj. 특정한　**support** v. 살게 하다, 부양하다
Antarctica n. 남극 대륙　**resemble** v. 유사하다
dry valley phr. 건곡　**promising** adj. 장래성이 있는

39 [2019 건국대]

정답 ③

해설 밑줄 (C)의 다음 문장에서 '그 우주선이 착륙했던 두 장소는 안전한 착륙장을 제공했으나, 특별히 흥미로운 장소들은 아니었다'고 했으므로 '과학자들은 Viking 우주 비행에 만족하지 않았다(not satisfied)'고 하는 것이 문맥에 맞다. (C)의 satisfied를 not satisfied로 고쳐야 한다. 따라서 ③번이 정답이다.

40 [2019 건국대]

정답 ①

해석 ① 생명체를 찾기 위한 화성으로의 우주 비행
② Mars Observer의 재앙
③ 화성에서 천문학자들의 도전
④ 지구와 화성은 어떻게 유사한가
⑤ 우주여행을 위한 미래의 우주선

해설 지문의 제목을 묻는 문제이다. 일곱 번째 문장 In 1976, two American spacecraft landed on Mars in order to search for signs of life에서 생명체의 흔적을 찾기 위해 두 대의 우주선을 보냈다는 것을 알 수 있고, 아홉 번째 문장부터는 과학자들이 화성에 있는 생명체의 가능성에 대해 더 조사하고 싶어 했다는 이 지문의 요지를 파악할 수 있다. 따라서 이 지문의 제목을 '생명체를 찾기 위한 화성으로의 우주 비행'이라고 표현한 ①번이 정답이다.

어휘 **disaster** n. 재앙, 불행　**challenge** n. 도전

[41-43]

수년 동안, 온실가스의 최대 배출국인 중국의 역할과 1인당 배출이 최대 배출국 중 하나인 미국의 역할에 관심이 집중되었다. 2014년 11월에 두 나라는 처음으로 온실가스 배출에 대한 실질적인 한도를 약속했다; 중국은 2030년 이후에 이산화탄소 배출량을 떨어뜨릴 것을 약속했고, 미국은 거의 같은 기간 안에 이산화탄소 배출량을 4분의 1보다 더 줄이기로 서약했다. 사실, 중국의 배출량은 지난해에 빠르게 떨어져서 많은 사람들은 중국이 예정보다 빨리 목표를 이룰 수도 있다고 믿고 있는데, 이것이 아직 기후 변화에 맞서는 이 다툼에서 가장 큰 진전이다.

대조적으로, 인도의 탄소 배출량은 다른 어떤 나라보다도 빠르게 증가하고 있다. 이 추세가 계속되고 그럴 것이라는 근거가 있다면, 인도는 25년 내에 중국을 뛰어넘어 세계 최대 배출국이 될 것이다. 아마, 인도의 증가하는 배출량은 나머지 나라들의 모든 삭감 노력을 상쇄하고, 대참사로 이어질 수 있을 것이다. 국제 기후 캠페인의 시에라 클럽 이사인 John Coequyt는 "인도는 가장 큰 퍼즐 조각이에요. 지금까지보다 재생 가능 에너지를 더 많이 사용해서 그렇게 빠르게 성장하면서도 사람들을 가난에서 벗어나게 할 방법이 있을까요? 아니면 오염에 대한 법적 규제를 하지 않고 그들이 가지고 있는 것을 더 지을까요?"라고 말한다. John Coequyt는 물론 후자가 "모두에게 엄청난 불행"이 될 것이라고 말한다.

emitter n. 방사체　**green house gas** phr. 온실가스
per capita phr. 1인당　**substantial** adj. 실질적인, 상당한
emission n. 배출　**pledge** v. 약속하다
carbon dioxide phr. 이산화탄소　**vow** v. 서약하다
stride n. 진전　**climate change** phr. 기후 변화
carbon n. 탄소　**surpass** v. 뛰어넘다, 능가하다
conceivably adv. 아마, 생각할 수 있는 바로는, 상상컨대
offset v. ~을 상쇄하다　**curtailment** n. 삭감, 단축
catastrophe n. 대참사, 재난
Sierra Club phr. 시에라 클럽(미국의 자연환경 보호 단체)
renewable energy phr. 재생 가능 에너지
pollution n. 오염　**latter** n. (둘 중에서) 후자
disaster n. 엄청난 불행, 대참사

41 [2019 성균관대]

정답 ③

해석 ① 중국은 미국과의 약속을 지키는 것을 주저하고 있다
② 미국은 중국이 국제적인 규칙에 따르도록 압력을 가했다
③ 인도는 온실가스 최대 배출국이 될 것이다
④ 미국은 중국과 경쟁해야 했다
⑤ 인도는 중국의 방식을 따를 것이다

해설 지문을 통해 추론할 수 있는 것을 고르는 문제이다. 두 번째 문단 두 번째 문장에서 이 추세가 계속되고 그럴 것이라는 근거가 있다면, 인도는 25년 내에 중국을 뛰어넘어 세계 최대 배출국이 될 것이라고 했으므로, 인도는 온실가스 최대 배출국이 될 것이라는 것을 추론할 수 있다. 따라서 ③번이 정답이다.

오답 분석
① 첫 번째 문단에서 2014년 11월에 두 나라는 처음으로 온실가스 배출에 대한 실질적인 한도를 약속했다고는 했지만, 중국이 미국과의 약속을 지키는 것을 주저하고 있는지는 알 수 없다.
② 미국은 중국이 국제적인 규칙에 따르도록 압력을 가했는지에 대해서는 언급되지 않았다.

④ 미국이 중국과 경쟁해야 했는지에 대해서는 언급되지 않았다.
⑤ 두 번째 문단에서 인도는 25년 내에 중국을 뛰어넘어 세계 최대 배출국이 될 것이라고는 했지만, 인도가 중국의 방식을 따를 것인지는 알 수 없다.

어휘 be reluctant to phr. ~을 주저하다, 망설이다

42 2019 성균관대

정답 ①

해석 ① 대조적으로 ② 하지만
③ 한편으로는 ④ 사실은
⑤ 그런데

해설 빈칸에 적절한 연결어를 넣는 문제이다. 빈칸 앞 문장은 중국의 배출량이 빠르게 떨어진다는 내용이고, 빈칸 뒤 문장은 인도의 탄소 배출량은 빠르게 증가하고 있다는 내용이다. 따라서 '대조'를 나타내는 연결어인 ① by contrast(대조적으로)가 정답이다.

43 2019 성균관대

정답 ④

해석 ① 태양 에너지 ② 풍력
③ 수소 에너지 ④ 석탄 발전소
⑤ 재식림 프로젝트

해설 "그들이 가진 것"의 예를 파악하는 문제이다. 지문의 후반에서 오염에 대한 법적 규제를 하지 않고 그들이 가지고 있는 것을 더 짓는다면 모두에게 엄청난 불행이 될 것이라고 했으므로, "그들이 가진 것"의 예는 '석탄 발전소'이다. 따라서 ④번이 정답이다.

어휘 reforestation n. 재식림

[44-47]

자연은 질병, 날씨, 그리고 기근을 통한 여러 가지 방법으로 인간을 시험한다. 해안을 따라서 사는 사람에게, 재앙과도 같은 파괴를 가능하게 하는 한 가지 흔치 않은 현상은 바로 쓰나미다. 쓰나미란 충격의 요동으로 인해 수역에서 생성되는 일련의 파도이다. 지진, 산사태, 화산 분출, 폭발, 그리고 운석의 충돌조차도 쓰나미를 생성할 수 있다. 바다에서 시작된 쓰나미는 천천히 육지로 접근하면서 하부의 마찰과 난류를 통해 높이는 높아지고 에너지는 잃어버리게 된다. 그렇지만, 다른 파도와 마찬가지로, 쓰나미는 해안 위로 쏟아져 내리면서 엄청난 에너지를 방출한다. 쓰나미는 상당한 침식 가능성을 가지고 있기 때문에, 모래사장을 긁어내고, 나무의 아래쪽을 약하게 만들며, 내륙 수백 미터까지 물에 잠기게 만든다. 쓰나미는 자동차, 주택, 초목, 그리고 충돌하는 것이면 무엇이든지 손쉽게 파괴할 수 있다. 쓰나미의 파괴를 최소화하기 위해, 과학자들은 더 정확하고 신속하게 쓰나미를 예측하기 위해 꾸준히 노력하고 있다. 삶을 위협하는 쓰나미가 만들어지는 데에 여러 가지 요소가 관계되어 있기 때문에, 그것을 예견하기는 쉽지 않다. 이러한 점에도 불구하고, 기상학 연구원들은 쓰나미의 움직임을 계속해서 연구하고 예측하고 있다.

famine n. 기근 phenomenon n. 현상
catastrophic adj. 재앙의, 파멸의 destruction n. 파괴
generate v. 생성하다, 만들다
impulsive adj. 충격의, 충동적인
disturbance n. 요동, 소란; 방해 earthquake n. 지진
landslide n. 산사태 volcanic adj. 화산의
eruption n. 분출 explosion n. 폭발 meteorite n. 운석
friction n. 마찰 turbulence n. 난류, 격변
unleash v. 풀다, 놓다; 촉발시키다
tremendous adj. 엄청난, 굉장한
plunge v. (아래로) 쏟아져 내리다, 급락하다
erosion n. 침식, 부식 potential n. 가능성, 잠재력
strip v. 긁어내다 undermine v. 약하게 만들다
vegetation n. 초목, 식물
collide with phr. ~와 충돌하다, ~와 부딪치다
devastation n. 파괴, 손상
constantly adv. 계속해서, 꾸준히 anticipate v. 예측하다
foresee v. 예견하다 meteorology n. 기상학
persevere v. (인내하고) 계속하다
behavior n. 움직임, 행동

44 2019 경기대

정답 ③

해석 ① 쓰나미는 나쁜 날씨로 인해 발생하기 때문에
② 쓰나미는 날씨 현상보다 더 파괴적이기 때문에
③ 파괴적인 자연의 힘을 보여주는 하나의 예시로서
④ 해안가의 폭풍이라는 주제의 도입으로서

해설 글쓴이가 첫 문장에서 날씨를 언급한 이유를 파악하는 문제이다. 지문 전체적으로 쓰나미가 엄청난 파괴적인 힘을 갖고 있음을 설명하고 있으므로, 첫 문장에서 글쓴이는 쓰나미 이외의 다른 파괴적인 힘을 지닌 자연의 예시를 들고 있다. 따라서 정답은 ③번이다.

어휘 destructive adj. 파괴적인 force n. 힘
introduction n. 도입, 소개 coastal adj. 해안의

45 2019 경기대

정답 ①

해석 ① 방출하다 ② 소모하다
③ 포함하다 ④ 지속하다

해설 밑줄 친 unleash의 의미와 비슷한 단어를 찾는 문제이다. 밑줄이 포함된 문장은 육지로 접근한 쓰나미가 해안가에 쏟아

져 내리며 엄청난 에너지를 방출한다는 내용이다. 따라서, 밑줄 친 단어의 의미를 '방출하다'라고 한 ①번이 정답이다.

어휘 **release** v. 방출하다, 놓다　**consume** v. 소모하다
contain v. 포함하다　**sustain** v. 지속하다

46　2019 경기대

정답　②

해석　① ~와 함께　　　　　② ~에도 불구하고
　　　③ ~와는 반대로　　　④ ~에 비해서

해설　빈칸에 적절한 연결어를 넣는 문제이다. 빈칸 앞 문장은 쓰나미를 예측하기는 쉽지 않다는 내용이고, 빈칸 뒤 문장은 기상학 연구원들이 쓰나미의 움직임을 계속해서 연구하고 예측하고 있다는 내용이다. 따라서 양보를 나타내는 연결어인 ② Despite(~에도 불구하고)가 정답이다.

47　2019 경기대

정답　③

해석　① 쓰나미는 가까운 미래에 이용 가능한 에너지의 새로운 원천이 될 수 있다.
　　　② 쓰나미는 홍수보다 육지에 끼치는 피해가 더 크다.
　　　③ 쓰나미는 특히 해안 지방에 재앙과도 같은 영향을 준다.
　　　④ 과학자들은 상당한 수준의 정확성으로 쓰나미를 예측하고 추측할 수 있어서 쓰나미의 잠재적인 영향을 줄일 수 있다.

해설　지문의 요지를 묻는 문제이다. 지문의 중간에서 쓰나미는 해안 위로 쏟아져 내리면서 엄청난 에너지를 방출하며, 그 에너지로 인해 쓰나미가 자동차, 주택, 초목, 그리고 충돌하는 것이면 무엇이든지 손쉽게 파괴할 수 있다는 것을 보여주고 있다. 따라서 이 지문의 요지를 '쓰나미는 특히 해안 지방에 재앙과도 같은 영향을 준다'라고 표현한 ③번이 정답이다.

어휘　**damage** v. 피해를 주다　**flooding** n. 홍수, 범람
track v. 추적하다　**a fair degree of** phr. 상당한 수준의
accuracy n. 정확성

[48-51]

Dr. Pickett이라는, 캐나다 곤충학자와 그의 동료들은 더 독성이 강해지는 화학물질인 도깨비불을 계속 추구한 다른 곤충학자들에 동의하는 것 대신 새로운 길을 개척했다. [A] Dr. Pickett과 그의 동료들은 자연에 강한 동맹이 있다는 것을 인식하여, 자연의 통제력을 최대한 활용하고 살충제를 최소한으로 사용하는 프로그램을 고안해냈다. 살충제를 살포할 때마다 최소 투여량 즉, 유익한 종에게 피할 수 있는 해를 입히지 않으면서 해충을 겨우 박멸할 수 있는 만큼만, 사용하는 것이다. 적절한 시기 또한 고려된다. [B] 따라서, 만약 사과꽃이 분홍색으로 변한 이후가 아닌 이전에 니코틴 황산염을 살포하면 중요한 포식자(해충) 중의 하나는 살아남게 되는데, 아마도 그 해충이 아직 알 속에 있는 단계이기 때문일 것이다.

이 프로그램은 얼마나 효과가 있었을까? Dr. Pickett의 완화된 살포 프로그램을 따르던 노바스코샤의 과수 재배자들은 강한 화학약품을 사용하는 사람들만큼이나 높은 비율로 일 등급 과일을 생산하고 있다. 또한 과수 재배자들은 높은 생산량을 만들어내고 있다. 게다가, 그들은 상당히 더 저렴한 비용으로 이러한 결과를 얻고 있다. [C]

이러한 훌륭한 결과 보다 더 중요한 것은 Dr. Pickett의 프로그램이 자연의 균형에 해를 끼치지 않는다는 사실이다. [D] 그것은 G. C. Ullyett가 십 년 전에 언급한 철학을 잘 실현해나가는 중에 있다. G. C. Ullyett 는 "우리는 우리가 가진 철학을 바꿔야만 하고, 인간이 우월하다는 우리의 태도를 버려야 하며, 우리가 스스로 할 수 있는 것보다 더 경제적인 방법으로 유기체의 개체 수를 제한하는 방법들을 자연환경의 여러 경우에서 찾아야 하는 것을 인정해야 합니다."라고 말했다.

---

entomologist n. 곤충학자　**associate** n. 동료
strick out phr. (방법을) 생각해내다, (새로운 길을) 개척하다
go along with phr. ~에 동의하다　**pursue** v. 추적하다
will-o'-the-wisp n. 도깨비불; 사람을 호리는 것
toxic adj. 독성의, 유독의　**chemical** n. 화학제품
ally n. 동맹(국), 연합국; 협력자　**devise** v. 고안하다
insecticide n. 살충제　**dosage** n. 투약, 조제
pest n. 해충　**beneficial** adj. 유익한, 이익을 가져오는
orchardist n. 과수 재배업자　**proportion** n. 비율; 조화, 균형
substantially adv. 상당히
do violence to phr. ~를 해치다, 위반하다
abandon v. (계획, 습관 등을) 단념하다, 그만두다
superiority n. 우월, 우위, 탁월
economical adj. 경제적인, 실속 있는

48　2020 세종대

정답　④

해석　① 비옥한 — 탄력 있는
　　　② 단조로운 — 다양한
　　　③ 조심성 없는 — 신중한
　　　④ 완화된 — 강한

해설　지문의 빈칸을 채우는 문제이다. 지문의 첫 번째 문단 처음에서 Dr. Pickett과 그의 동료들이 살충제를 최소한으로 사용하는 프로그램을 고안해냈다고 했으므로, 첫 번째 빈칸에는 살충제를 최소한으로 사용한 결과에 관한 내용이 나와야 적절하다는 것을 알 수 있다. 따라서 '완화된'이 들어가는 것이 자연스럽다. 두 번째 빈칸에는 완화된 살포 프로그램을 따르던 노바스코샤의 과수 재배자들과 비교되는 대상으로 반대의 내용이 나와야 적절하다는 것을 알 수 있다. 따라서 '강한'이 들어가는 것이 자연스럽다. 따라서 '완화된'과 '강한'이라고 한 ④번이 정답이다.

49 [2020 세종대]

정답 ②

해석 한 포식자(해충) 중의 하나는 살아남게 되는데, 아마도 그 해충이 아직 알 속에 있는 단계이기 때문일 것이다.

해설 지문의 흐름상 주어진 문장이 들어가기에 가장 적절한 위치를 고르는 문제이다. [B]의 앞 문장에서 적절한 시기 또한 고려된다고 했으므로, [B] 자리에 시기를 고려하여 살충제를 살포한 내용인 주어진 문장 '따라서, 만약 사과꽃이 분홍색으로 변한 이후가 아닌 이전에 니코틴 황산염을 살포하면 중요한 포식자(해충) 중의 하나는 살아남게 되는데, 아마도 그 해충이 아직 알 속에 있는 단계이기 때문일 것이다'가 들어가야 글의 흐름이 자연스럽게 연결된다. 따라서 ②번이 정답이다.

어휘 sulphate n. 황산염 predator n. 포식자

50 [2020 세종대]

정답 ④

해석 ① 최대한의 투여량과 적절한 시기
② 적절한 투여량과 이른 시기
③ 충분한 투여량과 이른 시기
④ 최소한의 투여량과 적절한 시기

해설 Dr. Pickett의 프로그램에서 살충제를 살포하는 데 가장 중요한 두 가지 요소를 파악하는 문제이다. 지문의 첫 번째 문단의 두 번째 문장 Recognizing that they ~ 의 내용을 통해 Dr. Pickett의 프로그램에서는 최소한의 살충제를 사용한다는 것을 알 수 있다. 또한, 네 번째 문장 Proper timing also enters in.의 내용을 통해 적절한 시기 또한 고려된다는 것을 알 수 있으므로, 살충제를 살포하는 데 가장 중요한 두 가지는 '최소한의 투여량과 적절한 시기'이다. 따라서 정답은 ④번이다.

51 [2020 세종대]

정답 ④

해석 ① Dr. Pickett과 그의 동료들은 그들이 자연에 강한 동맹을 가지고 있다고 믿었다.
② Dr. Pickett의 프로그램이 가진 장점 중 하나는 더 적은 비용으로 긍정적인 결과를 만들어냈다는 것이다.
③ G. C. Ullyett와 Dr. Pickett은 자연을 사용하는 방법에 대해 의견이 일치했다.
④ Dr. Pickett과 그의 동료들은 유기체의 개체 수를 제한할 필요성을 믿지 않았다.

해설 지문을 통해 추론할 수 없는 것을 고르는 문제이다. 지문의 세 번째 문단의 네 번째 문장에서 Dr. Pickett의 프로그램이 G. C. Ullyett의 철학을 잘 실현해나가고 있다고 했고, 다섯 번째 문장에서 G. C. Ullyett은 유기체의 개체 수를 제한하는 방법들을 자연환경의 여러 경우에서 찾아야 하는 것을 인정해야 한다고 말했지만, 이를 통해 Dr. Pickett과 그의 동료들은 유기체의 개체 수를 제한할 필요성을 믿지 않았는지는 유추할 수 없으므로 정답은 ④번이다.

오답 분석
① 지문의 두 번째 문장 Recognizing that they had a strong ally in nature를 통해 'Dr. Pickett과 그의 동료들은 자연에 강한 동맹을 가지고 있다고 믿었다'는 것을 알 수 있다.
② 지문의 일곱 번째 문장 They are getting these results, moreover, at a substantially lower cost.를 통해 'Dr. Pickett의 프로그램이 가진 장점 중 하나는 더 적은 비용으로 긍정적인 결과를 만들어냈다'라는 것을 알 수 있다.
③ 지문의 아홉 번째 문장 It is well ~ a decade ago를 통해 'G. C. Ullyett와 Dr. Pickett은 자연을 사용하는 방법에 대해 의견이 일치했다'는 것을 알 수 있다.

어휘 see eye to eye phr. 의견이 일치하다

16 동·식물

01-23

문제집 p.466

01 ①	02 ④	03 ③	04 ⑤	05 ③
06 ②	07 ④	08 ①	09 ③	10 ①
11 ④	12 ①	13 ②	14 ③	15 ④
16 ②	17 ①	18 ②	19 ①	20 ④
21 ③	22 ②	23 ②		

[01-02]

해변에서 햇볕을 너무 오래 쬐면서 긴 하루를 보낸 후, 많은 사람은 햇볕에 탄 것을 식히기 위해서 피부 진정 로션을 찾는다. 이런 연고들의 주요 재료는 보통 알로에 베라인데, 이것은 인간이 사용한 역사가 오래되고 문서로 잘 정리된 아프리카가 원산인 식물이다. 알로에 베라는 299종의 알로에 중 하나이며, 그 수만큼이나 사용법도 많다. 알로에 베라는 장미꽃 모양을 이루는 풍성하고 넓고 살집이 두꺼운 잎을 가지고 있으며, 건조한 지역뿐만 아니라 열대 지방에서도 자란다. 알로에 베라는 약효가 있는 특성이 증명되었으며 외부와 내부에서 모두 사용할 수 있다. 알로에 베라는 햇볕에 탄 피부에 즉각적인 진정 효과를 줄 뿐만 아니라, 상처 위로 감염을 막아줄 수 있는 얇은 막을 제공하기도 한다.

soothing adj. 진정시키는 **ingredient** n. 재료, 요소
ointment n. 연고 **indigenous** adj. 원산의
well-documented adj. 문서로 잘 정리된
abundant adj. 풍성한, 풍부한 **fleshy** adj. 살집이 두꺼운
comprise v. 이루다, 구성하다 **rosette** n. 장미 모양
tropical adj. 열대 지방의 **arid** adj. 건조한
medicinal adj. 약효가 있는 **property** n. 특성
externally adv. 외부에서 **internally** adv. 내부에서
immediate adj. 즉각적인 **infection** n. 감염

01 (2019 가천대)

정답 ①

해석 ① 토착의 ② 진짜의
 ③ 스며든 ④ 깨끗한

해설 밑줄 친 indigenous의 의미를 추론하는 문제이다. 밑줄 친 부분이 포함된 문장의 다음 문장에서 알로에 베라는 열대 지방뿐만 아니라 건조한 지역에서도 자란다고 언급되었으므로, 의미상 알로에 베라가 아프리카에서 유래했다는 의미가 되어야 할 것이다, 따라서, 밑줄 친 단어의 의미를 '토착의'라고 한 ①번이 정답이다.

어휘 **aboriginal** adj. 토착의, 원주민의

genuine adj. 진짜의, 정품의
infiltrated adj. 스며든, 침투한
immaculate adj. (티 없이) 깨끗한

02 (2019 가천대)

정답 ④

해석 ① 악화 ② 발단
 ③ 인질 ④ 진정

해설 지문의 빈칸을 채우는 문제이다. 빈칸이 포함된 문장에서, 알로에 베라는 또한 상처에 감염을 막아줄 수 있는 얇은 막을 제공한다고 설명하고 있으므로, 빈칸에는 햇볕에 탄 피부에 도움을 주는 의미의 단어가 와야 한다는 것을 알 수 있다. 따라서 '진정'이라고 한 ④번이 정답이다.

어휘 **aggravation** n. 악화 **incipience** n. 발단, 초기
hostage n. 인질 **relief** n. 진정, 경감

03 (2018 명지대)

정답 ③

해석 태국의 야생동물 관리 당국은 수요일에 호랑이 사원의 냉동고에서 40마리의 죽은 호랑이 새끼를 발견했으며, 그 시체들이 사원의 불법 야생동물 거래에 연루의 증거인지 아닌지를 조사하고 있었다. 이번 발견은 태국의 야생동물 관리자들이 사원이 멸종 동물 종들을 밀매하고 있다는 불평 사항들을 접수한 후에 그 관광 지구를 폐쇄하기 위한 노력의 일환으로 사원으로부터 어른 호랑이를 제거하고(옮기고) 있었을 때 이루어졌다. 사원은 오랫동안 환경 보호론자들과 동물 보호 운동가들에 의해 동물을 이용하고 학대한다는 것으로 비난받고 있었고, 이러한 비난 내용을 사원은 부인해왔다. 야생동물 관리인들은 수요일에 발견된 죽은 새끼의 한 마리만이 법으로 요구된 대로 정부에 보고되었다고 말했다. 판매에 있어서는 불법인 호랑이 신체 일부들은 아시아에서 전통적인 약의 용도로 수요가 많다. 지난달 이들(냉동된 새끼 호랑이들) 네 마리를 배달하는 베트남 남성이 체포되었듯이, 여전히 냉동된 새끼 호랑이를 판매하는 시장도 존재한다.
① 냉동고에서 발견된 새끼 호랑이의 시체 수
② 태국의 야생동물 관리자들이 어른 호랑이를 옮기고 있었던 이유
③ 호랑이 사원이 호랑이 새끼들을 얻게 된 방법
④ 호랑이의 신체 일부가 왜 아시아에서 높은 가치가 있는지

해설 지문의 내용과 일치하지 않는 것을 묻는 문제이다. ③번의 호랑이 사원이 호랑이 새끼들을 얻게 된 방법은 본문에서 언급되지 않았다. 따라서 ③번이 지문의 내용과 일치하지 않는다.

오답 분석 ① The Thai wildlife authorities found 40 dead tiger cubs in a freezer on Wednesday at the Tiger Temple~을 통해 '냉동고에서 발견된 새끼 호랑이의 시체 수'를 알 수 있다.

③ ~in an effort to shut down the attraction after receiving complaints that the temple was trafficking in endangered species~를 통해 '불평사항을 접수하고 관광 지구를 폐쇄하기 위해 어른 호랑이를 옮기고 있었다.'라는 것을 알 수 있다.
④ Tiger parts, while illegal to sell, are in high demand in Asia for use in traditional medicine을 통해 '호랑이의 신체 일부가 왜 아시아에서 높은 가치가 있는지'를 알 수 있다.

어휘 tsar n. 황제, 전제군주, 독재자 carcass n. 시체, 짐승의 사체
trafficking n. (마약 등의) 밀매
abuse v. 학대하다, 남용하다, 모욕하다; n. 남용, 학대, 욕
accusation n. 고소, 고발, 비난, 비난의 말

04 [2018 건국대]

정답 ⑤

해석 크랜베리는 덤불에서 자라는 북아메리카 과일이다. 1600년대에 잉글랜드에서 온 정착민들이 그 열매를 좋아했는데 학(cranes)이라고 불리는 새들이 그 열매를 먹었기 때문에 그 열매를 'crane berries'라고 불렀다. 크랜베리 덤불이 미국의 모든 곳에서 자라는 것은 아니다. 사실, 그것은 겨우 다섯 개 주에서만 자란다. 이 주들은 크랜베리 덤불에 필요한 특별한 조건들을 갖고 있다. 날씨가 추워지기 시작할 때 크랜베리 열매가 익는다. 가을에는 상점에서 크랜베리를 볼 수 있다. 크랜베리 재배자들은 최고의 크랜베리와 나머지 것들을 구분한다. 그냥 보기만 해서는 최고의 크랜베리를 알아보기 어렵다. 그래서 크랜베리 재배자들은 특별한 방법을 이용한다. 그들은 크랜베리를 구분하기 위해 일곱 계단 테스트를 이용한다. 최고의 크랜베리는 일곱 개의 계단을 통통 튕겨 내려가는 것들이다!

해설 지문의 내용과 일치하지 않는 것을 찾는 문제이다. '육안으로 구별하는 것'과 관련된 지문은 후반부에 It's hard to recognize the best cranberries just by looking에서 확인할 수 있다. '단지 보는 것만으로는 최고의 크랜베리를 알아보기 어렵다'고 했으므로 ⑤번은 지문의 내용과 일치하지 않는다.

오답 분석
① 지문의 첫 문장 The cranberry is a North American fruit that grows on a bush를 통해 '덤불에서 자라는 북아메리카 과일'이라는 것을 알 수 있다.
② 지문의 두 번째 문장 The settlers from England ~ because birds called cranes ate them을 통해 '이름의 유래가 그것을 먹는 새와 관련이 있다'는 것을 알 수 있다.
③ 지문의 네 번째 문장 In fact, it grows in only five states를 통해 '미국의 5개 주에서만 자란다'는 것을 알 수 있다.
④ 지문의 여섯 번째 문장 Cranberries ripen when the weather starts to become cold를 통해 '날씨가 추워지기 시작하면 열매가 익는다'는 것을 알 수 있다.

어휘 bush n. 관목, 덤불 crane n. 학, 두루미
ripen v. 익다; 익히다 bounce v. 튀다, 튀어 오르다

[05-06]

자이언트 판다는 대나무에 대한 식욕을 만족할 줄 모른다. 전형적인 동물은 하루 24시간 중 12시간을 꽉 채워, 하루 반나절 동안 먹고 하루에 수십 차례 볼일을 본다. 자이언트 판다의 하루 식욕을 만족시키기 위해서는 28파운드의 대나무가 필요하고, 엄지손가락과 같은 기능을 하는 가늘고 긴 손목뼈로 대나무줄기를 탐욕스럽게 뜯어 먹는다. 판다는 가끔 새나 설치류 또한 먹곤 한다.
야생 판다는 중국 중부의 외진, 산악 지역에만 산다. 이렇게 높은 대나무 숲은 시원하고 습한데, 판다가 이런 환경을 좋아한다. 야생 판다는 여름철 고지대에서 먹을 것을 먹기 위해 13,000피트의 높이만큼 오르기도 한다. 판다는 나무에 오르는 데 능숙하며 수영에 실력이 있다.
자이언트 판다는 혼자 있기를 좋아한다. 판다는 매우 잘 발달된 후각을 가지고 있는데 수컷은 서로를 피하고 봄철 짝짓기를 할 암컷을 찾는 데에 후각을 사용한다. 5개월간의 임신 기간을 거친 뒤, 암컷은 한 마리 혹은 두 마리의 새끼를 낳는데, 암컷은 쌍둥이를 다 돌보지는 못한다. 눈도 뜨지 못한 새끼 판다는 단지 무게가 5온스에 불과하고 생후 3개월이 될 때까지는 기어 다닐 수도 없다. 그들은 하얀색 털을 갖고 태어나는데, 나중에는 사람들이 많이 좋아하는 색으로 발달한다.

insatiable adj. 만족할 줄 모르는 appetite n. 식욕
relieve v. 볼일을 보다 dozens of phr. 수십의, 많은
dietary adj. 음식물의, 식이 요법의
hungrily adv. 게걸스럽게, 탐욕스럽게
pluck v. (꽃, 잡초 따위를) 뽑아내다 stalk n. (식물의) 줄기
elongated adj. (비정상적으로) 가늘고 긴
rodent n. 설치류 remote adj. 외진
solitary adj. 혼자 있기를 좋아하는 cub n. (동물의) 새끼
crawl v. (엎드려) 기다

05 [2020 가톨릭대]

정답 ③

해석 ① 음식   ② 서식지
    ③ 개체 수   ④ 번식

해설 지문에서 언급되지 않은 것을 파악하는 문제이다. 지문의 처음에서 자이언트 판다는 하루에 28파운드의 대나무를 먹으며 가끔 새나 설치류 또한 먹는다고 했고, 지문의 중간에서 이들은 중국 중부의 외진, 산악 지역에 산다고 했고, 마지막에서 봄철 짝짓기를 위해 후각을 사용하여 암컷을 찾는다고 했지만, 개체 수에 대해서는 찾아볼 수 없으므로, 지문에서 언급되지 않은 것은 '개체 수'이다. 따라서 정답은 ③번이다.

오답 분석
① 지문의 세 번째 문장 It takes 28 pounds of bamboo to satisfy a giant panda's daily dietary needs를 통해 자이언트 판다가 먹는 '음식'에 대한 것을 알 수 있다.

② 지문의 다섯 번째 문장 Wild pandas live only in remote, mountainous regions in central China를 통해 자이언트 판다가 서식하는 '서식지'에 대한 것을 알 수 있다.
④ 지문의 열 번째 문장 They have a ~ in the spring을 통해 자이언트 판다의 '번식' 방식에 대한 것을 알 수 있다.

어휘 reproduction n. 번식

06 2020 가톨릭대

정답 ②

해석
① 자이언트 판다는 오직 식물만 먹는다.
② 자이언트 판다는 무리 지어 살지 않는다.
③ 자이언트 판다는 태어날 때 사물이 흑백으로만 보인다.
④ 자이언트 판다는 검은색과 하얀색 털을 가지고 태어난다.

해설 지문의 내용과 일치하는 것을 묻는 문제이다. 세 번째 지문의 첫 번째 문장 Giant pandas are solitary의 내용을 통해 자이언트 판다는 무리 지어 살지 않는다는 것을 알 수 있다. 따라서 ②번이 지문의 내용과 일치한다.

오답 분석
① 자이언트 판다는 새와 설치류도 먹는다고 했으므로, 오직 식물만 먹는다는 것은 지문의 내용과 다르다.
③ 자이언트 판다는 혼자 있기를 좋아한다고는 했지만, 무리 지어 살지 않는지는 알 수 없다.
④ 자이언트 판다는 하얀색 털을 갖고 태어난다고 했으므로, 검은색과 하얀색 털을 가지고 태어난다는 것은 지문의 내용과 다르다.

[07-09]

내 옆집에 사는 이웃은 코기를 가지고 있었는데, 그는 이 코기로부터 새끼를 얻을 계획을 하고 있었지만, 한 폭스테리어가 이 과정에 끼어들었고, 오래 지나지 않아 5마리의 코기-폭스테리어 강아지가 한배에서 태어났다. 나는 이 강아지 중 한 마리를 분양받을 수 있는 행운을 얻게 되었는데, 내가 그 강아지들을 보러 갔을 때, 한 마리가 비틀거리면서 내 다리로 다가와 정면으로 머리를 다리에 올려두었다. 그래서 나는 이 강아지를 원하게 되었다. 그리고 나는 결국 그 강아지에게 Max라는 이름을 지어주게 되었다.
머리와 가슴 쪽에 하얀 반점을 가진, Max는 곧 우리 가족의 필수적인 부분이 되었다. 그는 내 아내와 두 아들에게 수년간 행복과 즐거움을 주었지만, 오랜 시간이 지난 이후에는 관절염이 발병하여 움직일 때마다 극도로 고통스러워했다. 수의사는 아무 소용이 없었던 약을 처방해주었고, 그래서 나는 비록 Max를 잃는다는 것이 괴로운 일이기는 했지만, 그의 고통을 연장시키지 않기 위해 Max를 안락사시킬 때가 되었다고 결심하게 되었다. 하지만, 수의사는 우리가 다른 약을 써보기를 추천했고, 나는 거기에 동의했다. 새로운 약은 놀라운 효과를 입증했고 Max는 2주 만에 어떠한 고통의 신호 없이 뛰고 놀기 시작했다. 처음에 Max에게 약을 먹이는 것은 힘든 일이었지만, Max는 이내 약이 자신에게 이로움을 준다는 것을 깨달았다. 그래서 내가 단순히 "이리와 Max, 약 먹을 시간이야"라고만 이야기해도 그는 빠르게 다가와 누운 후, 등을 대고 구르면서 입을 열어 내가 약을 넣어주었을 때 약을 삼켰다. 그러고 난 뒤, 그는 환한 미소로 일어나곤 했다.

---

breed v. 새끼를 낳다   a litter of phr. 한 배에서 난 ~의 새끼
totter v. 비틀거리다   squarely adv. 정면으로, 똑바로
blaze n. 반점   integral adj. 필수적인   arthritis n. 관절염
vet n. 수의사   prescribe v. 처방하다
be of no use phr. 아무 소용이 없는
euthanize v. 안락사시키다   trot v. 빨리 걷다
swallow v. 삼키다   grin n. 웃음

07 2020 한성대

정답 ④

해석
① 줄이다
② 짧게 하다
③ 축소하다
④ 연장하다

해설 지문의 빈칸을 채우는 문제이다. 빈칸 앞에서 Max가 관절염으로 움직일 때마다 고통스러워했고, 수의사가 처방한 약이 소용이 전혀 없었기 때문에, 그를 안락사시키기로 결정했다고 했으므로 빈칸에는 '고통을 연장시키지 않기 위해'라는 의미가 들어가는 것이 자연스럽다. 따라서 ④번이 정답이다.

08 2020 한성대

정답 ①

해석
① Max는 순종 코기이다.
② Max는 뛰어다니며 노는 것을 좋아했다.
③ Max에게 약을 주는 것이 항상 쉬운 일은 아니었다.
④ Max를 영원히 잠들게 하는 것은 Max의 주인이 깊이 생각해 본 선택지 중 하나였다.

해설 지문의 내용과 일치하지 않는 것을 묻는 문제이다. 지문의 첫 번째 문단에서, Max는 코기와 폭스테리어 사이에서 태어난 다섯 마리의 강아지 중 한 마리였다고 했으므로, Max가 순종 코기였다는 것은 지문의 내용과 다르다. 따라서 ①번이 정답이다.

오답 분석
② 지문의 두 번째 문단에서, Max가 새로운 약을 먹고 건강을 되찾자 다시 뛰어다니며 놀았다고 했으므로, Max는 뛰어다니며 노는 것을 좋아했다는 것은 지문의 내용과 일치한다.
③ 지문의 두 번째 문단에서, 처음 Max에게 약을 먹이는 것은 힘든 일이었다고 했으므로, Max에게 약을 주는 것이 항상 쉬운 일은 아니었다는 것은 지문의 내용과 일치한다.
④ 지문의 두 번째 문단에서, 처음 수의사가 처방한 약이 소용이 없어, Max가 계속 고통스러워하자, 그 고통을 연장시키지 않기 위해 Max를 안락사시키기로 결정했다고

했으므로, Max를 영원히 잠들게 하는 것이 Max의 주인이 깊이 생각해 본 선택지 중 하나였다는 것은 지문의 내용과 일치한다.

어휘 **for good** phr. 영구히　**ponder** v. 깊이 생각하다

09 2020 한성대

정답 ③

해석 ① 암으로부터 회복
② 어떻게 순종을 입양하는가
③ Max의 두 번째 삶의 기회
④ 올바른 개를 선택하는 것

해설 지문의 제목을 묻는 문제이다. 지문 전체적으로 Max라는 강아지가 관절염 때문에 고통받고 약도 소용이 없자, Max를 안락사시키려고 했지만, 새로운 약을 먹은 이후에 Max가 다시 건강을 되찾을 수 있었다는 내용이므로, 이 지문의 제목을 'Max의 두 번째 삶의 기회'라고 표현한 ③번이 정답이다.

[10-12]

다음에 폭풍우 동안 당신의 강아지가 왔다 갔다 하기 시작하거나, 당신이 하루 동안 떠나 있어야 하고 강아지에게 분리 불안이 뒤이어 일어날 수 있다는 것을 안다면, 라디오나 음향 장치를 켜는 것을 고려해보아라. 사람의 목소리 음향은 애완동물의 불안감을 없애줄 수 있어서, 당신은 토크쇼로 채널을 맞추면 된다. 하지만, 새로운 스코틀랜드의 연구에 따르면, 개들도 음악을 좋아하는데, 특히 레게와 소프트 록 음향을 좋아한다. 연구에서, Glasgow 대학교의 연구원들은 개들이 머무르게 하기 위해 다섯 가지 다른 장르(클래식, 소프트 록, 레게, 팝과 모타운 사운드)의 음악을 여섯 시간 동안 들려주었다. 개들이 음악을 듣고 있는 동안, 연구원들은 스트레스 레벨을 판단하는 개들의 심박 수 가변성, 코르티솔 레벨과 짖거나 눕는 것과 같은 행동들에 주목했다.
개들이 음악을 들었을 때 일반적으로 '덜 스트레스를 받는' 것으로 밝혀졌고, 레게나 소프트 록을 들을 때 가장 차분했다. 모타운 사운드는 많이는 아니지만, 개들이 발을 아래에 두게 했다.
하지만, 인간처럼, 개들도 아마 개개의 음악 선호도를 가진 것처럼 보였는데, 연구에서 다른 개들이 특정 음악 종류에 다르게 반응했기 때문이다. 그 결과에 기반하여, 보호소와 개 주인들은 스트레스를 많이 받는 상황에서 그들의 개들에게 음악을 들려주는 것으로 도움을 받을 수 있다.
같은 팀에 의해 진행되었던 개들에게 미치는 클래식 음악의 영향에 관한 이전 연구는 개들이 덜 짖고 다른 위안의 신호를 보여준다는 것을 알아냈다. 하지만, 클래식 음악을 6일 동안 들려준 후에 개들은 가만히 있지 못하게 되었다. 해결책은 무엇인가? 당신이 개에게 들려줄 음악 연주곡 목록을 섞으면 된다.

pup n. 강아지　**thunderstorm** n. 폭풍우, 뇌우
pace v. (규칙적으로) 왔다 갔다 하다
separation anxiety phr. 분리 불안
ensue v. 뒤이어 일어나다　**sound system** phr. 음향 장치
reassuring adj. 불안감을 없애 주는
tune into phr. ~로 채널을 맞추다
Scottish adj. 스코틀랜드의　**reggae** n. 레게
soft rock phr. 소프트 록(섬세한 록 음악)
researcher n. 연구원
Motown n. 모타운 사운드(1960년대와 1970년대 사이에 디트로이트시에 근거를 둔 흑인 음반 회사가 유행시킨 음악 형태)
shelter v. 머물게 하다, 보호하다
take note of phr. ~에 주목하다　**heart rate** phr. 심박 수
variability n. 가변성, 다양성
cortisol n. 코르티솔(부신 피질에서 생기는 스테로이드 호르몬의 일종)　**behaviour** n. 행동, 행위　**bark** v. 짖다
lie down phr. 눕다　**paw** n. (동물의 발톱이 달린) 발
possibly adv. 아마　**differently** adv. 다르게
benefit from phr. ~의 도움을 받다　**canine** n. 개
high-stress adj. 스트레스를 많이 받는　**situation** n. 상황
effect n. 영향　**discover** v. 알아내다, 발견하다
relaxation n. 위안, 휴식, 완화
restless adj. 가만히 있지 못하는, 만족하지 못하는

10 2019 국민대

정답 ①

해설 ensue(뒤이어 일어나다)와 비슷한 의미를 가진 어휘를 묻고 있다. ①번 follow는 '~의 뒤에 일어나다', ②번 growl은 '(개 등이) 으르렁거리다', ③번 descend는 '내려오다', ④번 disappear는 '사라지다'라는 의미이다. 따라서 ①번이 정답이다.

11 2019 국민대

정답 ④

해석 ① 독특한 목소리 특성　② 훌륭한 후각
③ 특이한 인생 경험　④ 개개의 음악 선호도

해설 지문의 빈칸을 채우는 문제이다. 빈칸 뒤에서 연구에서 다른 개들이 특정 음악 종류에 다르게 반응했다고 했으므로, 빈칸에는 인간처럼 개들도 개개의 음악 선호도를 가진 것처럼 보인다는 내용이 나와야 적절하다는 것을 알 수 있다. 따라서 '개개의 음악 선호도'라고 한 ④번이 정답이다.

어휘 **superb** adj. 훌륭한, 최고의　**olfactory sense** phr. 후각
unusual adj. 특이한　**individual** adj. 개개의, 개인의
preference n. 선호도

12 2019 국민대

정답 ①

해석
① 음악: 개를 진정시키는 방법
② 모타운 사운드: 개가 가장 좋아하는 음악
③ 분리 불안: 소리 없이 개를 죽이는 것
④ 클래식 음악: 개를 위한 스트레스 완화 장치

해설 지문의 제목을 묻는 문제이다. 지문 처음에서 강아지가 분리 불안을 느끼지 않게 하기 위해 라디오나 음향 장치를 켜는 것을 고려해보라고 한 뒤, 2문단에서 개들이 음악을 들었을 때 일반적으로 '덜 스트레스를 받는' 것으로 밝혀졌다고 하였다. 따라서 이 지문의 제목을 '음악: 개를 진정시키는 방법'이라고 표현한 ①번이 정답이다.

어휘 reliever n. 완화 장치

13 2020 인하대

정답 ②

해석 당신이 올해 진짜 크리스마스트리를 사려 한다면 예전보다 더 열심히 찾아봐야 할 수도 있다. 지난 5년간 미국의 많은 지역에서 크리스마스트리 부족이 보고되었다.

[B] 한 가지 요인은 2008년 불경기 기간 동안과 그 이후에 재배자들이 땅을 매각해 나무를 적게 심었다는 것이다. 크리스마스트리의 수명에 있어서 2008년부터 현재까지의 10년은 대략 한 세대의 재배이다. 그러나 농업과 식품 체계에 대한 인간 관점에서의 나의 연구에서는 다른 요인도 작용하고 있는 것을 볼 수 있다.

[D] 크리스마스트리는 다 자라기까지 6년에서 12년이 걸리며, 소비자 선호는 종종 농부들이 조정할 수 있는 것보다 더 빠르게 변한다. 기후 변화는 기온과 강우 패턴을 바꾸고 있는데, 이는 질 높은 나무를 생산하는 재배자의 능력과 소비자들이 찾는 품종에 심각하게 영향을 미친다.

[A] 전체적으로, 이러한 추세는 크리스마스트리 애호가, 재배자 또는 업계에 좋은 징조가 아니다. 그러나 젊은 농부들이 풀타임 또는 파트타임으로 이 시장에 진입할 수 있는 기회가 있다.

[C] 새로운 시작 단계의 재배자가 적합한 환경 조건이 있는 지역에 산다면, 크리스마스트리는 농민들이 자신들의 사업을 다양화하고 비수기 수입을 제공하는 데 이용할 수 있는 고품질 대체 작물이다.

해설 주어진 지문 다음에 이어질 [A], [B], [C], [D]의 적절한 순서를 파악하는 문제이다. 주어진 지문은 크리스마스트리 부족 현상에 관한 내용이므로, 크리스마스트리 부족의 요인에 대해 설명하는 [B]가 먼저 와야 한다. 그다음에 [D]에서 또 다른 요인에 대해 설명하고, 그다음에 [A]에서 이러한 추세의 부정적인 면과 새로운 기회에 대해 제시하고, 마지막으로 [C]에서 크리스마스트리 재배의 이점에 관해 설명하는 것이 자연스럽다. 따라서 주어진 지문 다음에 이어질 순서는 ② [B] − [D] − [A] − [C]다.

어휘
collectively adv. 전체적으로, 집합적으로
bode well for phr. 좋은 징조, 조짐   opportunity n. 기회
grower n. 재배자, 양식자   sell off phr. 매각하다
recession n. 불경기   lifespan n. 수명
roughly adv. 대략   generation n. 세대
dimension n. 관점, 차원   appropriate adj. 적합한, 적절한
environmental adj. 환경의
high-quality adj. 고품질의, 질 높은
complementary adj. 대체하는, 보완하는   crop n. 작물
diversify v. 다양화하다   operation n. 사업, 작업
off-season n. 비수기   mature adj. 다 자란
preference n. 선호   alter v. 바꾸다   rainfall n. 강우
severely adv. 심각하게   variety n. 품종, 종류

[14-15]

고래를 보호하는 데에 관심이 증가하는 한 가지 이유는 많은 사람이 고래를 직접 관찰할 수 있는 기회를 가져보았기 때문이다. 사실, 고래 관람은 해안 지역에서 중요한 관광 기업이 되었다. 매사추세츠주 보스턴에서 선박을 타고 쉽게 접근할 수 있는 Stellwagen 둑은 매년 7,800만 달러의 가치가 있다고 추산되는 미국의 고래 관람 산업의 중심지가 되었다. 봄부터 가을에 걸쳐 운영하면서, 수많은 선박이 둑을 너머로 모여드는 고래를 관람하기 위해 매일 앞바다로 모험을 떠난다. 많은 혹등고래가 관광객을 즐겁게 하는 것을 즐기는 것처럼 보이며, 때로는 몇 시간 동안 선박 옆에서 즐겁게 헤엄치며 놀기도 한다. 미적인 가치와 오락적인 가치를 가지고 있는 것 외에, 고래 관람은 과학적인 가치도 갖고 있다. 고래 관람 여행 선박은 보통 고래의 종을 식별하고 관광객을 위한 경험을 설명하는 생물학자를 싣는다. 생물학자들은 종종 Stellwagen 둑의 고래들을 연구하고 혹등고래에 대한 많은 논문을 발행해온 연구원 무리와 연관되어 있다.

firsthand adv. 직접   indeed adv. 사실
tourist enterprise phr. 관광 기업   coastal adj. 해안의
bank n. 둑   estimate v. 추산하다
worth adj. ~의 가치가 있는   annually adv. 매년
operate v. 운영하다, 가동하다   scores of phr. 수많은
venture v. 모험하다   offshore adj. 앞바다의
congregate v. 모이다   humpback whale phr. 혹등고래
frolic v. 즐겁게 뛰놀다   alongside prep. ~의 옆에
aesthetic adj. 미적인   biologist n. 생물학자
interpret v. 설명하다, 해석하다
associated with phr. ~와 연관된   publish v. 발행하다
paper n. 논문

14 2019 한국외대

정답 ③

해석
① 고래 관람의 인기
② 미국의 고래 관람 산업의 가치
③ 혹등고래의 멸종 위기 상태
④ 고래 관람 여행에서 생물학자의 역할

해설 지문에서 언급되지 않은 것을 찾는 문제이다. 지문 중간에서 많은 혹등고래가 관광객을 즐겁게 하는 것을 즐기는 것처럼 보이며, 때로는 몇 시간 동안 선박 옆에서 즐겁게 헤엄치며 놀기도 한다고 했지만, 이 외에 혹등고래의 멸종 위기 상태에 대해서는 언급하지 않았다. 따라서 정답은 ③번이다.

어휘 endangered adj. 멸종 위기에 처한

15 [2019 한국외대]

정답 ④

해석 ① 소중한 관광 목적지
② 매사추세츠주 보스턴과 가깝다
③ 수백만 달러 산업의 중심지
④ 겨울에 고래 관람을 운영한다

해설 Stellwagen 둑에 대해 지문에서 언급되지 않은 것을 찾는 문제이다. 지문 중간에서 봄부터 가을에 걸쳐 운영하면서, 수많은 선박이 둑을 너머로 모여드는 고래를 관람하기 위해 매일 앞바다로 모험을 떠난다고 했으므로, Stellwagen 둑에서 겨울에 고래 관람을 운영한다는 것은 지문에서 언급하지 않았다. 따라서 정답은 ④번이다.

어휘 dispense with phr. ~를 생략하다
profitable adj. 수익성이 있는   endeavor n. 시도, 노력
prediction n. 예측   consideration n. 고려

[16-18]

대나무는 세상에서 가장 중요한 식물 중의 하나이다. 한 가지 예를 들자면, 대나무 숲은 같은 크기의 나무숲보다 35퍼센트 더 많은 산소를 우리 대기 중으로 방출함으로써 인간에게 이로움을 준다. 대나무는 또한 많은 양의 이산화탄소를 흡수함으로써 대기를 깨끗하게 한다. 게다가, 대나무는 매우 강하며 빠르게 자라는 식물이다. 일부 대나무의 종은 한 시간에 2인치의 속도로 자라며, 그래서 그것들은 벌채된 지역을 빠르게 다시 푸르게 만들어 토양의 침식을 막고 태양으로부터 보호를 제공해 줄 수 있다. 연강의 능가하는 내구성에 덧붙여, 이 식물의 놀랄 만한 성장 속도는 대나무를 훌륭한 건축 재료로 만든다. 그리고 대나무는 또한 인간에게 식량과 약부터 종이와 연료까지 광범위한 다른 생산물들도 제공해왔다. 토머스 에디슨은 그의 첫 전구에 대나무 필라멘트를 사용했는데, 그것은 워싱턴 DC에 있는 스미스소니언 박물관에 아직도 켜져 있으며, 알렉산더 그레이엄 벨의 첫 축음기 바늘도 대나무로 만들어졌다.

stand n. (나무로 된) 숲   atmosphere n. 대기
cleanse v. 깨끗하게 하다   a great deal of phr. 많은 양의
carbon dioxide phr. 이산화탄소   hardy adj. 강한, 견고한
deforest v. (삼림을) 벌채하다   erosion n. 침식
fuel n. 연료   filament n. 필라멘트   bulb n. 전구
phonograph n. 축음기

16 [2020 단국대]

정답 ②

해석 ① 극복하다   ② 능가하다
③ 강화하다   ④ 소멸하다

해설 지문의 빈칸을 채우는 문제이다. 빈칸이 포함된 문장에서 대나무가 훌륭한 건축 재료가 된다고 했으므로, 연강의 내구성과 비슷하거나 더 좋다는 의미의 단어가 와야 한다는 것을 알 수 있다. 따라서 '능가하다'라고 한 ②번이 정답이다.

어휘 overcome v. 극복하다   surpass v. 능가하다
reinforce v. 강화하다   dissipate v. 소멸하다

17 [2020 단국대]

정답 ③

해석 ① 대나무는 지구에서 가장 빨리 자라는 식물 중의 하나이다.
② 대나무는 토양 손실을 막기 위한 주요한 역할을 할 수 있다.
③ 대나무는 에디슨의 전구와 벨의 전화기에 사용되었다.
④ 대나무는 동등한 양의 나무숲보다 더 많은 산소를 방출한다.

해설 지문의 내용과 일치하지 않는 것을 묻는 문제이다. ③번의 키워드인 Bell's telephones(벨의 전화기)와 관련된 지문의 Alexander Graham Bell's(알렉산더 그레이엄 벨) 주변에서 최초의 축음기의 바늘로 대나무를 사용했다고 했지만, 전화기에서 대나무를 사용했는지는 알 수 없다. 따라서 ③번이 지문의 내용과 일치하지 않는다.

오답 분석
① bamboo is a very hardy, fast-growing plant를 통해 '대나무는 지구에서 가장 빨리 자라는 식물 중의 하나이다'라는 것을 알 수 있다.
② preventing damaging erosion and providing protection from the sun을 통해 '대나무는 토양 손실을 막기 위한 주요한 역할을 할 수 있다'는 것을 알 수 있다.
④ by releasing into our atmosphere 35 percent more oxygen than a stand of trees the same size를 통해 '대나무는 동등한 양의 나무숲보다 더 많은 산소를 방출한다'는 것을 알 수 있다.

어휘 major adj. 주요한, 큰   equivalent adj. 동등한

18 [2020 단국대]

정답 ②

해석 ① 녹색 해결책으로서의 대나무
② 왜 대나무인가?
③ 대나무 심기
④ 매력적인 대나무 식품들

해설 지문의 제목을 묻는 문제이다. 지문의 전반에 걸쳐 대나무의 산소 방출 능력, 녹지 재생 능력, 건축 재료로서의 탁월함, 인간에게 요긴한 생산물들에 대해 언급하며 대나무가 중요한

식물이라는 것을 말하고 있다. 따라서 이 지문의 제목을 '왜 대나무인가?'라고 표현한 ②번이 정답이다.

어휘 fascinating adj. 매력적인

[19-23]

비버는 분주하기로 유명하며, 비버는 자신의 재능을 풍경을 재설계하는 일에 사용하는데, 이런 일을 할 수 있는 다른 동물은 거의 없다. 이용 가능한 터가 있으면, 비버는 강과 호수의 둑에 굴을 판다. 그러나 비버는 또한 댐을 건설함으로써 덜 적합한 서식지를 변형시킨다. 강한 이빨과 강력한 턱으로 나무들을 쓰러뜨리고 갉아, 비버는 거대한 통나무와 나뭇가지 및 진흙 구조물을 만들어 개울물을 막고 들과 숲을 비버가 좋아하는 큰 연못으로 만든다. [A]
lodge라고 불리는, 돔처럼 생긴 비버의 집 또한 나뭇가지와 진흙으로 만들어진다. 그 집들은 종종 연못의 가운데에 전략적으로 위치해 있으며 오직 물속의 입구를 통해서만 도달할 수 있다. 이 집들은 일부일처제를 지키는 부모와 어린 새끼들 그리고 지난봄에 태어난 한 살배기들로 구성된 대가족의 보금자리이다. [B]
비버는 덩치가 가장 큰 설치류에 속한다. 비버는 초식동물이며 잎사귀, 나무껍질, 나뭇가지, 뿌리 및 수생 식물을 먹는 것을 좋아한다.
이 큰 설치류 동물이 육지에서는 볼품없이 뒤뚱뒤뚱 움직이지만 물속에서는 우아하며, 물갈퀴가 있는 큰 뒷발을 잠수용 핀처럼 사용하고, 노 모양의 꼬리를 방향타처럼 사용한다. [C] 이러한 속성들은 비버로 하여금 시속 5마일에 이르는 속도로 헤엄칠 수 있게 한다. 비버는 수면 위로 나오지 않고 15분 동안 수중에 있을 수 있으며, 마치 고글처럼 기능하는 투명한 눈꺼풀을 갖고 있다. 비버의 털은 선천적으로 기름기가 있으며 방수가 된다.
비버는 놀라거나 두려울 때 위험 신호를 내는 것으로 알려져 있다. 헤엄치던 비버는 넓은 꼬리로 물을 강하게 찰싹 치면서 빠르게 잠수를 한다. 이것은 비버가 물을 철썩거리는 큰 소음을 낸다는 것을 의미하며, 그것은 물 위에서나 아래에서나 먼 거리에서도 들을 수 있다. 이런 비버의 경고 소음은 그 지역에 있는 비버들에게 경고하는 역할을 한다. [D] 일단 한 마리 비버가 이런 위험 신호를 내면, 인근에 있는 비버들은 잠수를 하고 한동안 돌아오지 않는다.
두 종류의 비버가 있는데, 둘 다 북아메리카와 유럽 그리고 아시아의 숲에서 발견된다. 이 동물들은 겨우내 활동하며, 심지어 얼음층이 표면을 덮고 있을 때조차도 그들의 연못에서 헤엄을 치고 먹이를 찾아다닌다.

reengineer v. 재설계하다, 개량하다　burrow v. 굴을 파다
bank n. 둑, 제방　habitat n. 서식지
fell v. (나무를) 베어 쓰러뜨리다　gnaw v. 쏠다, 갉아먹다
stream n. 개울, 시내　lodge n. 오두막; 비버의 굴(집)
construct v. 건설하다; 구성하다
entrance n. 입구, 문; 입장, 등장　dwelling n. 주거(지), 주택

monogamous adj. 일부일처의
kit n. 새끼 고양이, 새끼 여우 등　yearling n. 한 살배기 동물
rodent n. 설치류　herbivore n. 초식동물
bark n. 나무껍질　twig n. 나뭇가지
aquatic adj. 물속(물가)에 사는, 수생의
ungainly adj. (움직임이) 어색한, 볼품없는
waddle n. (오리처럼) 뒤뚱뒤뚱 걷기
webbed adj. 물갈퀴가 있는　rear adj. 뒤쪽의
paddle n. (작은 배의) 노; 주걱　rudder n. (배의) 키, 방향타
transparent adj. 투명한
waterproof adj. 방수의, 방수가 되는　forage v. 먹이를 찾다

19 [2018 세종대]

정답 ①

해석 ① 야생동물 잡지
② 금융 보고서
③ 환경 팸플릿
④ 잡식동물에 관한 논문

해설 이 글이 실리기에 적합한 것을 고르는 문제이다. 이 글은 비버의 습성과 특성에 관한 내용이므로 야생동물에 관한 잡지에 실리기에 적합하다. 따라서 ①번이 정답이다.

어휘 omnivore n. 잡식동물

20 [2018 세종대]

정답 ④

해석 ① 분노한　　　② 동정하는
③ 무관심한　　　④ 애정 어린

해설 비버에 대한 필자의 태도를 묻는 문제이다. 전체적으로는 객관적인 설명이지만, 비버의 습성을 설명하며 다른 동물들은 이런 일을 할 수 없다(as few other animals can)고 했으며 비버가 헤엄치는 모습이 우아하다(graceful)고 언급한 것으로 보아 필자가 비버에 대해 호감을 갖고 있다는 것을 알 수 있다. 따라서 '애정 어린'이라고 표현한 ④번이 정답이다.

어휘 indignant adj. 분개하는, 분노한
uninterested adj. 무관심한
adore v. 흠모(사모)하다; 아주 좋아하다

21 [2018 세종대]

정답 ③

해설 지문의 흐름상 주어진 문장이 들어가기에 가장 적절한 위치를 고르는 문제이다. 제시문에 있는 지시어 these attributes(이런 속성들)가 가리키는 것을 찾아야 한다. [C]의 앞 문장에서 '비버는 물갈퀴가 있는 큰 뒷발을 잠수용 핀처럼 사용하고, 노 모양의 꼬리를 방향타처럼 사용한다'고 했으므로, 주어진 문장 '이러한 속성들은 비버로 하여금 시속 5마일에 이르는

속도로 헤엄칠 수 있게 한다'가 [C] 자리에 들어가야 글의 흐름이 자연스럽게 연결된다. 따라서 ③번이 정답이다.

22 [2018 세종대]

정답 ②

해석 ① 양도할 수 없게 ② 전략적으로
③ 무분별하게 ④ 말로 형언할 수 없이

해설 지문의 빈칸을 채우는 문제이다. 빈칸이 포함된 문장에서 비버의 집은 연못의 한 가운데에 위치해 있으며 물속에 있는 입구를 통해서만 도달할 수 있다고 했으므로, 빈칸에는 '전략적으로'를 의미하는 strategically가 들어가는 것이 자연스럽다. 따라서 ②번이 정답이다.

어휘 indiscreetly adv. 무분별하게, 몰지각하게, 경솔하게
indescribably adv. 형언할 수 없이, 말로 다 할 수 없이

23 [2018 세종대]

정답 ②

해석 ① 비버는 모든 식물과 뿌리를 먹는 중간 크기의 설치류다.
② 비버는 노 모양의 꼬리를 이용해 물을 철썩 치는 큰 소리를 낼 수 있다.
③ 한 살배기 비버들은 봄에 영원히 집을 떠난다.
④ 비버는 연못 표면이 얼음에 덮여있을 땐 헤엄치지 않는다.

해설 지문의 내용과 일치하는 것을 묻는 문제이다. 다섯 번째 문단의 A swimming beaver will rapidly dive while forcefully slapping the water with its broad tail.을 통해 '비버는 노 모양의 꼬리를 이용해 물을 철썩치는 큰 소리를 낼 수 있다'는 것을 알 수 있다. 따라서 ②번이 지문의 내용과 일치한다.

오답 분석
① 세 번째 문단에서 비버는 가장 큰 설치류에 속한다(Beavers are among the largest of rodents.)고 했으므로, '중간 크기의 설치류'라는 표현은 지문의 내용과 다르다.
③ 두 번째 문단에 지난봄에 태어난 한 살배기들(the yearlings born in the previous spring)이라는 표현이 나올 뿐이며 이들이 언제 집을 떠나는지는 알 수 없다.
④ 마지막 문단에서 심지어 얼음층이 표면을 덮고 있을 때도 비버는 헤엄을 치고 먹이를 찾아다닌다(These animals are active all winter, swimming and foraging in their ponds even when a layer of ice covers the surface.)고 했으므로 '연못 표면이 얼음에 덮여있을 땐 헤엄치지 않는다'는 것은 지문의 내용과 다르다.

17 기타

01-78
문제집 p.478

01	②	02	③	03	①	04	④	05	①
06	④	07	②	08	①	09	④	10	②
11	②	12	④	13	③	14	③	15	⑤
16	①	17	③	18	①	19	④	20	②
21	①	22	③	23	②	24	①	25	⑤
26	④	27	⑤	28	②	29	①	30	④
31	③	32	③	33	④	34	②	35	①
36	①	37	②	38	④	39	④	40	③
41	①	42	②	43	②	44	④	45	④
46	③	47	⑤	48	⑤	49	⑤	50	②
51	③	52	③	53	①	54	④	55	⑤
56	②	57	④	58	②	59	④	60	②
61	④	62	④	63	①	64	②	65	①
66	①	67	①	68	③	69	②	70	①
71	③	72	②	73	②	74	②	75	②
76	⑤	77	④	78	④				

01 2019 명지대

정답 ②

해석 축구의 큰 매력은 특별한 장비 없이 할 수 있다는 점이다.
[B] 어디에 있든지 아이들은 빈 깡통, 몇몇 싸맨 누더기 또는 다른 스포츠의 공이 전부 충분히 찰 수 있다는 것을 알고 있다. 이 교묘한 발명품은 사람들이 동물의 방광이 부풀려지고 매듭으로 묶음으로써 가볍고 탄력성 있는 공이 될 수 있다는 점을 발견했던 수백 년 전에 처음 나타났다.
[A] 당연히, 방광만으로는 오래가지 않았고, 시간이 가면서 사람들은 가죽으로 바꾸기 위해 적절히 보존 처리가 된 동물의 피부로 만들어진 껍데기로 방광을 보호하기 시작했다.
[C] 이 디자인은 잘 적용되어서 오늘날에도 여전히 쓰이고 있지만, 동물 제품보다는 현대의 합성 물질과 함께 쓰이고 있다.

해설 주어진 문장 다음에 이어질 [A], [B], [C]의 적절한 순서를 파악하는 문제이다. 주어진 문장은 축구의 큰 매력은 특별한 장비 없이 할 수 있다는 내용이므로, 아이들이 장비 없이 축구를 어떻게 했는지, 수백 년 전에 동물의 방광을 공으로 썼다는 내용이 있는 [B]가 먼저 와야 한다. 그다음에 [A]에서 동물의 방광을 어떻게 공으로 활용했는지 계속해서 설명하고, 마지막으로 [C]에서 오늘날에도 동물의 방광 디자인을 적용하여 합성 물질로 만든 공이 사용되고 있다고 설명하는 것이 자연스럽다. 따라서 주어진 문장 다음에 이어질 순서는 ② [B] – [A] – [C]이다.

어휘 appeal n. 매력 equipment n. 장비
tin can phr. 빈 깡통 rag n. 누더기, 헝겊
entirely adv. 전부 satisfyingly adv. 충분히, 만족스럽게
ingenuity n. 교묘한 발명품 display v. 보이다, 드러내다
discover v. 발견하다 bladder n. 방광 inflate v. 부풀다
knot v. 매다 bouncy adj. 탄력성 있는
understandably adv. 당연히, 당연하게도
properly adv. 적절히 cure v. 보존 처리를 하다, 치료하다
synthetic adj. 합성의, 인조의 rather than phr. ~보다는

[02-03]

국제 언론은 우리에게 YAP("프라하의 젊은 미국인")이라는 별명을 붙였다. 저렴한 생활비, 많은 취업 기회, 그리고 열광적인 분위기는 1989년 혁명 이후로 수만 명의 젊은 미국인들과 다른 서양인들을 끌어모았다. 상대적으로 부유한 프라하의 서양인들은 도시 중심부에 거주할 형편이 되고, 훌륭한 대중교통 체계를 이용할 수 있으며, 사람들이 우글거리는 거리를 돌아다닐 수 있다. 당신은 프라하의 서쪽과 동쪽 모든 도시의 출입구에서 흔히 볼 수 있는 걸인들을 찾아볼 수 없다. 밤에 이 도시를 걸어 다니는 것은 안전하다. 우리는 새 건물들이 지어지고 오래된 건물들의 때가 제거되는 것을 봤다. 우리는 프라하에서 되살아난 카페 중심의 상류층 모임, 아르누보 건축의 화려함, 재즈 클럽, 오페라 극장에 빠져들었다. 우리는 최소 하나의 일자리를 찾는 데 어떠한 어려움도 겪지 않았으며, 우리 중 많은 사람들은 두 개 혹은 세 개의 직업을 가지고 있다. 우리가 체코어 실력은 부족하지만, 우리가 정직하고, 유능하며, 성실하기 때문에, 주요 서양 기업들은 체코 평균보다 높은 임금으로 YAP들을 기꺼이 고용해오고 있다. 1990년대 초반에, 경력 없는 젊은 미국인이 다른 어디에서 세계의 정상급 광고 회사나 법률 사무소에 걸어 들어가 이력서도 보여주지 않고 채용될 수 있었겠는가?

dub v. ~라는 별명을 붙이다 electric adj. 열광적인
teeming adj. (사람들이) 우글거리는, 많은
clear of phr. ~을 제거하다, 없애다 grime n. 때
soak up phr. 빠져들다, 흡수하다 revive v. 되살아나게 하다
inexperienced adj. 경력 없는, 미숙한

02 2021 단국대

정답 ③

해석 ① ~ 이든지   ② ~ 하도록
③ ~ 하지만   ④ ~ 이후로

해설 빈칸에 적절한 연결어를 넣는 문제이다. 빈칸 앞 내용은 주요 서양 기업들이 평균보다 높은 임금을 주면서 YAP들을 기꺼이 고용한다는 내용이고, 빈칸 뒤 내용은 '우리(YAPs)'가 체코어 실력이 부족하다는 내용으로, 양보를 나타내고 있다는 것을

알 수 있다. 따라서 '양보'를 나타내는 연결어인 ③ though (~하지만)가 정답이다.

03 2021 단국대

정답 ①

해석 ① 체코의 회사들은 유능함과 근면성 때문에 젊은 미국인들을 기꺼이 채용하려고 했다.
② 일반적으로 프라하에 사는 젊은 미국인들은 그 도시의 분위기와 저렴한 생활비를 좋아했다.
③ 1980년대 말에 체코슬로바키아에서 혁명이 있었다.
④ 프라하에 사는 꽤 많은 수의 젊은 미국인들이 하나 이상의 일자리를 얻을 수 있었다.

해설 지문의 내용과 일치하지 않는 것을 묻는 문제이다. 지문 후반에서 주요 서양 기업들이 YAP들을 그들의 정직함, 유능함, 그리고 근면성 때문에 체코 평균보다 높은 임금을 주면서 기꺼이 고용했다고 했지만, 체코 회사들도 그러한 이유로 YAP들을 기꺼이 고용했는지는 알 수 없다. 따라서 ①번이 지문의 내용과 일치하지 않는다.

오답 분석
② The cheap cost of living, the many job opportunities, and the electric atmosphere have attracted ~를 통해 '일반적으로 프라하에 사는 젊은 미국인들은 그 도시의 분위기와 저렴한 생활비를 좋아했다'는 것을 알 수 있다.
③ The cheap cost of living ~ since the 1989 revolution을 통해 '1980년대 말에 체코슬로바키아에서 혁명이 있었다'는 것을 알 수 있다.
④ We have not had any difficulty ~ many of us have two or three를 통해 '프라하에 사는 꽤 많은 수의 젊은 미국인들이 하나 이상의 일자리를 가질 수 있었다'는 것을 알 수 있다.

[04-06]

북미 원주민이 오염된 강을 따라 걸어가는 것을 보여주는 70년대의 오래된 텔레비전 광고가 있다. 그 원주민의 뺨을 따라 눈물이 흘러내리면서 쓰레기가 강 수면과 강둑 위로 떠 오른다. 그 남자는 아무 말도 하지 않지만, 한때 그의 조상의 것이었던 아름다운 땅에 우리가 저지른 일에 대해 그가 부끄럽고 얼이 빠져있는 것은 분명하다. 매일, 우리는 우리의 행동이 미래에 영향을 미친다는 것을 인식하지 못한다. 만약 우리가 <u>이사를 해서</u> 가족이 플로리다로 이주한다면, 그들은 뉴잉글랜드 사람이 아닌 남부지방 사람으로 자랄 것이다. 그 가족은 눈과 추위가 전혀 없는 세상에서 살 것이고 그들의 쾌적함을 위해 선풍기와 에어컨에 의지할 것이다. 만약 당신이 하루 18시간 동안 일하고 당신의 아이가 보모나 다른 보육 서비스 제공자들에 의해 길러진다면, <u>그들이 자라나서 될 사람들</u>에 놀라지 마라. 모든 행동에는 반응이 있다. 그것을 오늘 당신이 인식하지 못할 수 있지만, 미래에 누군가는 인식할 것이다.

> river bank phr. 강둑   appalled adj. 얼이 빠진
> devoid adj. 전혀 없는   child care phr. 보육

04 2021 동국대

정답 ④

해석 ① 모험을 해서   ② 돈을 모두 투자해서
③ 땅을 복구해서   ④ 이사를 해서

해설 밑줄 친 부분의 의미를 추론하는 문제이다. pull up our stakes의 의미로 미루어보아, 밑줄 친 부분은 지문의 중간에서 언급된 '가족이 플로리다로 이주한다면'과 동일한 의미의 '이사를 하다'라는 의미임을 추론할 수 있다. 따라서 ④번이 정답이다.

05 2021 동국대

정답 ①

해석 ① 그들이 자라나서 될   ② 그들이 미래에 만날
③ 아름다운 자연을 다루는   ④ 날씨에 적응하는

해설 지문의 빈칸을 채우는 문제이다. 지문의 후반에서 모든 행동에는 반응이 있고 오늘 당신이 인식하지 못할 수 있지만, 미래에 누군가는 인식할 것이라고 했으므로, 빈칸에는 당신의 아이가 다른 사람들의 손에서 길러진다면 그들이 자라나서 될 사람들에 놀라지 말라는 내용이 나오는 것이 자연스럽다. 따라서 '그들이 자라나서 될'이라고 한 ①번이 정답이다.

06 2021 동국대

정답 ④

해석 ① 우리는 더 늦기 전에 자연을 보호해야 한다.
② 우리는 기상 상태의 지배를 받는다.
③ 당신이 아이를 기를 때는 조심해야 한다.
④ 미래의 결과들은 필연적으로 현재의 행동에 의해 형성된다.

해설 지문의 요지를 묻는 문제이다. 지문 전반에 걸쳐 '오늘날의 행동은 미래에 영향을 미친다'는 것에 대해 설명하고 있고, 지문의 후반에서 모든 행동에는 반응이 있고 이를 당신이 오늘 인식하지 못하더라도 미래에 누군가는 인식할 것이라고 하였다. 따라서 이 지문의 요지를 '미래의 결과들은 필연적으로 현재의 행동에 의해 형성된다'고 표현한 ④번이 정답이다.

오답 분석
① '우리는 더 늦기 전에 자연을 보호해야 한다'는 내용은 지문 초반의 예시밖에 설명하지 못하기 때문에 정답이 될 수 없다.

② '우리는 기상 상태의 지배를 받는다'는 내용은 지문 중간에 언급된 예시의 일부분밖에 설명하지 못하기 때문에 정답이 될 수 없다.
③ '당신이 아이를 기를 때는 조심해야 한다'는 것은 지문에서 언급되지 않았으므로 정답이 될 수 없다.

어휘   be subject to phr. ~의 지배를 받다
consequence n. 결과, 결론, 중요성
inevitably adv. 필연적으로, 반드시

해설 지문의 빈칸을 채우는 문제이다. 빈칸이 포함된 문장에서 that is 뒤의 내용은 앞의 내용을 정리하는 역할을 한다. that is의 앞에서 좋은 책을 읽을 때는 얼마나 많은 책이 당신에게 전달되는지가 더 중요하다고 했으므로, 빈칸에는 좋은 책의 내용이 자신의 머릿속에 들어온다는 내용이 나와야 한다는 것을 알 수 있다. 따라서 '당신의 것으로 만들다'라고 한 ①번이 정답이다.

어휘 recall v. 불러오다, 회상하다   limited adj. 한정된, 제한된

[07-08]

우리들 대부분은 독서의 속도가 지능의 척도라고 잘못 생각한다. 똑똑한 독서를 위한 올바른 속도 같은 것은 존재하지 않는다. 어떤 것은 빠르고 쉽게 읽어야 하고, 어떤 것은 느리고 주의 깊게 읽어야 한다. 독서에서 지능의 표시는 가치에 따라 다른 것을 다르게 읽을 수 있는 능력이다. 좋은 책을 읽는 경우에, 중요한 것은 당신이 얼마나 많은 책을 읽어낼 수 있는지를 보는 것이 아니라 오히려 얼마나 많은 책이 당신에게 전달되는지, 즉 얼마나 많은 책을 당신의 것으로 만들 수 있는지를 보는 것이다. 천 명의 지인보다 적은 친구가 더 낫다. 이것이 당신의 목표라면, 물론 그렇게 해야 하겠지만, 당신은 신문을 읽을 때보다 위대한 책을 읽기 위해 더 많은 시간과 노력이 들어도 조급해하면 안 될 것이다.

mistakenly adv. 잘못하여, 실수로   measure n. 척도, 기준
intelligence n. 지능   effortlessly adv. 쉽게, 노력하지 않고
get through phr. 끝내다, 전달되다   acquaintance n. 지인
impatient adj. 조급한, 참을성 없는

07 2019 한국외대
정답 ②

해석 ① 좋은 책을 고르는 방법
② 위대한 책들을 읽는 방법
③ 독서 속도를 빠르게 하는 방법
④ 책의 질을 측정하는 방법

해설 지문의 주제를 묻는 문제이다. 지문의 중반에서 좋은 책을 읽는 경우에 중요한 것은 얼마나 많은 책을 당신의 것으로 만들 수 있는지를 보는 것이라고 하였다. 따라서 이 지문의 주제를 '위대한 책들을 읽는 방법'이라고 표현한 ②번이 정답이다.

08 2019 한국외대
정답 ①

해석 ① 당신의 것으로 만들다
② 기억에서 불러오다
③ 자신만의 책을 쓰다
④ 한정된 시간 안에 읽다

[09-10]

이력서의 목적은 취업 면접을 보는 것이다. 고용주들은 원하지 않거나 호감이 덜 가는 후보를 가려내기 위해 이력서를 이용한다. 당신의 이력서는 당신의 능력과 경력을 요약하고 당신을 고용함으로써 얻을 가치에 대해 고용주들을 설득해야 한다. 이것은 당신 자신을 위한 광고인데, 모든 광고와 마찬가지로, 이것은 흥미를 일으키고 읽는 이를 자극해야 한다.
이력서를 준비하기 전에 잠시 시간을 내어 당신의 시장성 있는 능력들을 생각해 보아라. 당신이 찾고 있는 직책과 관련 있는 강점과 성과를 찾아보고, 가능한 한 간결하고 명확하게 그것들을 제시해라. 당신은 이 모든 정보를 읽기 쉽고 매력적인 형식으로 2페이지 이내로 정리할 필요가 있을 것이다. 이 이상 이력서 작성에 관해 명확한 규칙은 없다.

resume n. 이력서   employer n. 고용주, 고용인
undesirable adj. 원하지 않는, 달갑지 않은
desirable adj. 호감이 가는, 바람직한   candidate n. 후보
summarize v. 요약하다   convince v. 설득하다
advertisement n. 광고   as with phr. 마찬가지로, ~처럼
generate v. 일으키다, 발생시키다
motivate v. 자극하다, 유발하다   prepare v. 준비하다
marketable adj. 시장성이 있는   Identify v. 찾다, 발견하다
strength n. 강점   accomplishment n. 성과, 업적
relevant adj. 관련 있는   succinctly adv. 간결하게
clearly adv. 명확하게   organize v. 정리하다, 조직하다
attractive adj. 매력적인
hard-and-fast adj. 명확한, 엄중한

09 2020 국민대
정답 ④

해석 ① 해고하다   ② 고용하다
③ 이해하다   ④ 가려내다

해설 지문의 빈칸을 채우는 문제이다. 빈칸 뒤의 문장에서 이력서는 당신을 고용함으로써 얻을 가치에 대해 고용주를 설득해야 한다고 했으므로, 빈칸에는 후보를 가려낸다는 내용이 나와야 적절하다는 것을 알 수 있다. 따라서 '가려내다'라고 한 ④번이 정답이다.

어휘 put out phr. 해고하다, 내쫓다
take on phr. 고용하다, 떠맡다

catch on phr. 이해하다, 인기를 얻다
screen out phr. 가려내다, 거르다

10 [2020 국민대]

정답 ②

해석 ① 이력서의 목적
② 이력서 형식의 변화
③ 이력서에서 필요한 내용
④ 이력서 작성 원칙 안내

해설 지문에서 언급되지 않은 것을 파악하는 문제이다. 지문의 마지막에서 이력서는 읽기 쉽고 매력적인 형식으로 정리되어야 한다고는 했지만, 이력서 형식의 변화는 언급되지 않았다. 따라서 정답은 ②번이다.

어휘 variation n. 변화   content n. 내용
principle n. 원칙, 원리

[11-12]

유도의 독특한 특징은 상대방의 힘을 역이용한다는 것이다. 예를 들면, 공격해오는 상대방을 전속력으로 끌어안아, 당신의 몸을 지렛대 삼아, 상대방을 당신의 어깨 너머로 바닥에 내던질 수 있다. 이것이 덩치가 작은 유도선수들이 더 큰 선수들을 이기는 방식이며, 그것이 유도의 진수다. 상대방이 공격을 시작하려 할 때, 당신은 몸을 수그려 그들을 균형을 잃게 할 수 있다. 다윗이 골리앗을 이겼듯이, 유도에서 덩치가 큰 선수들은 작은 선수들에 의해 기습을 당할 수 있으며, 5분간의 시합을 하는 동안 많은 전술적 싸움을 가능하게 한다. 예를 들면, 공격에 전력을 다하는 것은 반격에 취약해지게 한다. 그러나 <u>또한 항상 물러서 있을 여유는 없다.</u> 소극적인 접근은 경고를 받게 하며 점수를 잃을 수도 있다. 이것이 유도가 신체적 운동임에도 불구하고 재치 싸움으로 알려진 이유이다.

judo n. 유도   opponent n. 상대, 적
bear-hug v. 힘껏 포옹하다   charge v. 돌격(공격)하다
lever n. 지렛대   judoka n. 유도선수
essence n. 본질; 정수, 진수
mount an attack phr. 공격을 개시하다
duck v. (머리나 몸을) 휙 수그리다   surprise v. 기습하다
ensure v. 확실하게 하다, 보장하다
tactical adj. 작전(전술)의, 전략적인
go all out phr. 전력을 다하다   vulnerable adj. 취약한
counterattack n. 반격, 역습
sit back phr. 편안히 앉다; 물러나다   approach n. 접근 방법
for all phr. ~임에도 불구하고
physicality n. 물질적임; 신체적임

11 [2018 한국외대]

정답 ②

해석 ① 각 한 판이 끝난 후에는 앉아있어야 한다.
② 공격적이면서 방어적이어야 한다.
③ 서 있는 자세를 유지해야 한다.
④ 앞자리로 바꾸는 것이 더 낫다.

해설 밑줄 친 부분의 의미를 추론하는 문제이다. 밑줄 친 you can't afford to sit back all the time은 '당신은 항상 물러서 있을 여유는 없다'는 의미이다. 앞 문장에서 '공격에 전력을 다하는 것은 반격에 취약해지게 한다'고 했으며, 뒤 문장에서는 '소극적인 접근은 경고를 받게 되며 점수를 잃을 수도 있다'고 했으므로, 밑줄 친 문장은 '공격도 해야 하고 방어도 해야 한다'는 의미라는 것을 알 수 있다. 따라서 ②번이 정답이다.

12 [2018 한국외대]

정답 ④

해석 ① 시간문제   ② 힘의 전쟁
③ 운으로 하는 게임   ④ 재치 싸움

해설 지문의 빈칸을 채우는 문제이다. 빈칸의 앞부분에서 '유도에서는 덩치 큰 선수가 작은 선수에게 기습을 당할 수 있으며, 많은 전략적 싸움을 가능하게 한다'고 했으며, 마지막 문장에서는 '신체적 운동임에도 불구하고(for all its physicality)'라고 했으므로, 빈칸에는 '머리를 쓰는 전략적인 싸움'이라는 내용이 들어가야 적절하다는 것을 알 수 있다. 따라서 '재치 싸움'이라고 표현한 ④번이 정답이다.

13 [2019 가톨릭대]

정답 ③

해석 초콜릿의 역사는 고대 마야족으로 거슬러 올라갈 수 있다. 마야족은 초콜릿을 먹었을 뿐만 아니라, 그것을 숭배하기도 했다. 마야족에 대해 저술된 역사에서는 기념행사에 사용되고 중요한 거래를 마무리하는 데 사용된 초콜릿 음료를 언급한다. 마야족 문화에서 초콜릿의 중요성에도 불구하고, 그것은 부유층이나 권력자를 위해 따로 남겨진 것이 아니었고 거의 모든 사람이 쉽게 구할 수 있는 것이었다. 여러 마야족 가정에서, 초콜릿은 매 식사와 함께 곁들여졌다. 마야족의 초콜릿은 걸쭉하고, 거품이 떠 있으면서, 종종 매운 고추, 꿀, 혹은 물과 합쳐졌다.
아즈텍족은 또 다른 차원으로 초콜릿을 찬양했다. 그들은 카카오가 그들의 신에 의해 주어진 것이라고 믿었다. 마야족처럼, 그들은 화려하게 장식한 용기에 담긴 강한 맛이 나는 뜨거운 혹은 차가운 초콜릿 음료의 카페인이 함유된 자극적인 맛을 즐겼지만, 그들은 카카오 열매를 식품이나 다른 물품을 사기 위한 화폐로 사용하기도 했다. 아즈텍 문화에서, 카카오 열매는 금보다 더 가치 있는 것으로 여겨졌다. 아즈텍족의 초콜릿은 대부분 상위층의 사치품이었던 반면, 하위층은 결혼식이나 다른 기념행사에서 이따금 초콜릿을 즐겼다.

① 마야에서는, 사회 각계각층의 사람들이 초콜릿을 먹었다.
② 초콜릿은 아스텍 문화에서 신성하게 여겨졌다.
③ 마야와 아스텍에서 마시는 초콜릿 음료는 상당히 달랐다.
④ 아즈텍족은 카카오 열매를 돈으로 사용했다.

해설 지문의 내용과 일치하지 않는 것을 묻는 문제이다. ③번의 키워드인 Chocolate beverages(초콜릿 음료)가 그대로 언급된 지문의 주변에서 마야족처럼, 그들은 화려하게 장식한 용기에 담긴 강한 맛이 나는 뜨거운 혹은 차가운 초콜릿 음료의 카페인이 함유된 자극적인 맛을 즐겼다고 했으므로, 마야와 아스텍에서 마시는 초콜릿 음료가 상당히 달랐다는 것은 지문의 내용과 다르다. 따라서 ③번이 지문의 내용과 일치하지 않는다.

오답분석
① 첫 번째 문단의 네 번째 문장 Despite chocolate's importance in Mayan culture ~ available to almost everyone.을 통해 '마야에서는, 사회 각계각층의 사람들이 초콜릿을 먹었다'는 것을 알 수 있다.
② 두 번째 문단의 두 번째 문장 They believed cacao was given to them by their gods.를 통해 '초콜릿은 아스텍 문화에서 신성하게 여겨졌다'는 것을 알 수 있다.
④ 두 번째 문단의 세 번째 문장 Like ~ they also used cacao beans as currency to buy food and other goods.를 통해 '아즈텍족은 카카오 열매를 돈으로 사용했다'는 것을 알 수 있다.

어휘 be traced to phr. ~로 거슬러 올라가다
consume v. 먹다, 마시다   revere v. 숭배하다
celebration n. 기념행사   finalize v. 마무리하다
transaction n. 거래   reserve v. 남겨 두다
available adj. 구할 수 있는   frothy adj. 거품이 떠 있는
combine v. 결합하다   admiration n. 찬양
caffeinated adj. 카페인이 함유된   kick n. 자극성, 쏘는 맛
spiced adj. 강한 맛이 나는   ornate adj. 화려하게 장식한
currency n. 화폐, 통화   extravagance n. 사치(품)
occasionally adv. 이따금   divine adj. 신성한
considerably adv. 상당히

[14-15]

> 나는 평생 시험에서 우수한 점수를 기록해 왔으며, 그래서 나는 자신이 상당히 똑똑하다는 안일한 느낌이 들게 되었다. 하지만, 실제로 그러한 점수는 단순히 내가 그 지능 시험을 작성하는 사람들, 즉 나와 비슷한 지적 취향을 가진 사람들에 의해 답변할 가치가 있다고 여겨지는 학문적인 종류의 문제에 답변을 잘한다는 것을 의미하는 것뿐이지 않을까?
> 나의 학문적인 훈련과 언어적 능력을 사용할 수 없는 세상이라면, 나는 성적이 좋지 않을 것이다. 그렇다면, 나의 지성은 절대적인 것이 아니라 내가 살아가는 사회와 그 사회의 작은 부분이 사회의 나머지에 자신을 지능 문제의 심판이라고 속여온 사실이 작용한 것이다.

> register v. 기록하다, 등록하다
> exceptional adj. 우수한, 뛰어난
> complacent adj. 안일한, 자기만족의
> intelligent adj. 똑똑한   academic adj. 학문적인, 학술적인
> worthy of phr. ~할 만한   intellectual adj. 지적인
> bent n. 취향   verbal adj. 언어의, 말의
> do poorly phr. 성적이 좋지 않다   absolute adj. 절대적인
> subsection n. (세부적인) 부분   foist v. 속이다

14 2019 가천대

정답 ③

해석 ① 자질   ② 투자
     ③ 성향   ④ 속성

해설 밑줄 친 bent의 의미를 추론하는 문제이다. 밑줄 친 부분이 포함된 구(people with an intellectual bent similar to mine)는 그 앞의 구(people making up intelligence test)와 비슷한 의미를 가져야 하므로, '지능 시험을 작성하는 사람들'이라는 의미와 비슷한 맥락의 의미임을 알 수 있다. 따라서, 밑줄 친 단어의 의미를 '성향'이라고 한 ③번이 정답이다.

어휘 endowment n. 자질, 재능   investment n. 투자
propensity n. 성향, 경향   property n. 속성, 특성

15 2019 가천대

정답 ②

해석 ① 비전문가   ② 심판
     ③ 반대자   ④ 은둔자

해설 지문의 빈칸을 채우는 문제이다. 첫 번째 단락에서 시험에서 받은 점수를 통해 단지 학문적인 종류의 문제에 답변을 잘한다는 것만을 의미한다고 설명하고 있으므로, 빈칸에는 시험이 한 사람의 지능 문제를 판단하는 것에 관한 내용이 와야 한다는 것을 알 수 있다. 따라서 '심판'이라고 한 ②번이 정답이다.

어휘 layman n. 비전문가   judge n. 심판, 판사
dissenter n. 반대자   recluse n. 은둔자

[16-17]

> 안녕하세요, Kathy. 오늘 아침에 주고받은 채팅은 유익했습니다. 약속드린 바와 같이, 우리가 당신을 대신하여 중재인에게 제출한 기밀 중재 서류의 사본을 첨부해드립니다. 중재 회의는 시애틀시의, 1200 유니버시티 가, 스위트 700, 유니온 플라자에 위치한 조정 & 중재 서비스 센터에서 오전 9시부터 오후 1시까지 열릴 예정입니다. 당신의 담당 변호사, Mr. Rawlins가 거기서 당신을 만나 뵐 것입니다. 혹시 당신이 궁금해하실까 봐 말씀드리는데, 복장은 "비즈니스 캐쥬얼"로 입으

시길 바랍니다. 중재 회의에 오실 때 읽을거리 혹은 다른 전자기기(태블릿, 노트북) 휴대하셔도 좋은데, 회의가 진행되는 동안 중간 휴식 시간이 길어질 것으로 예상되기 때문입니다. 또한, 가벼운 다과가 제공될 예정입니다. 만약 중재 회의 전에 다른 질문이 있으시다면 저에게 알려주시기를 바랍니다.

Sandra 드림

Sandra J. Kelly, 소송 담당 변호사 보조원
J. Rawlins 법률 단체

---

confidential adj. 기밀의 **mediation** n. 조정, 중재
on one's behalf phr. ~를 대신하여
arbitration n. 조정, 중재 **attorney** n. 변호사
interval n. 중간 휴식 시간 **refreshment** n. 다과
litigation n. 소송 **paralegal** n. 법률가 보조원

16 [2020 가톨릭대]

정답 ①

해석 ① 법률 사무소 — 의뢰인
② 법정 — 중재인
③ 원고 — 피고
④ 검사 — 피고인

해설 지문을 통해 보낸 이와 받는 사람의 관계를 추론하는 문제이다. 지문 중간에서 보낸 이가 받는 사람에게 중재 회의에서 담당 변호사를 만나게 될 것이라고 했고, 편지의 마지막 부분에 자신을 소송 담당 변호사 보조원이라고 밝혔으므로, 보낸 이와 받는 사람의 관계는 '법률 사무소와 의뢰인'이라는 것을 추론할 수 있다. 따라서 정답은 ①번이다.

어휘 **plaintiff** n. 원고 **defendant** n. 피고
prosecutor n. 검사 **the accused** phr. 피고인

17 [2020 가톨릭대]

정답 ③

해석 ① 첨부된 문서는 대중에게 공개되어 있다.
② 중재 회의는 엄격한 복장 규정이 정해진 공식 행사이다.
③ 중재 회의는 도중에 쉬지 않는 격렬한 회의를 하지는 않을 것이다.
④ 음식물은 중재 회의에서 제공되지 않을 것이다.

해설 지문의 내용과 일치하는 것을 묻는 문제이다. 지문의 여섯 번째 문장 You may wish to bring with ~의 내용을 통해 중재 회의는 도중에 쉬지 않는 격렬한 회의를 하지는 않을 것임을 알 수 있다. 따라서 ③번이 지문의 내용과 일치한다.

오답 분석 ① 첨부된 문서는 중재인에게 제출한 기밀 중재 서류라고 했으므로, 첨부된 문서가 대중에게 공개되어 있다는 것은 지문의 내용과 다르다.

② 복장 규정은 "비즈니스 캐쥬얼"이라고 했으므로, 엄격한 복장 규정이 정해져 있다는 것은 지문의 내용과 다르다.
④ 중재 회의에서 가벼운 다과가 제공될 예정이라고 했으므로, 음식물이 제공되지 않을 것이라는 것은 지문의 내용과 다르다.

어휘 **unlikely** adj. ~할 것 같지 않은 **intense** adj. 격렬한

[18-20]

내 모국인 캐나다에서 Johnson 대학에 온 지 여러 해가 지난 후에도 나는 여전히 가르친다는 것이 숭고한 소명이며 교수는 학생을 위해 봉사할 의무가 있다고 믿는다. 그러나, 어떠한 교수도 모든 학생의 마음에 들 수는 없기 때문에, 자신의 포부를 현실적으로 누그러뜨릴 준비를 해야 한다. 나에게, 이런 균형을 잡는 행동은 유능한 학교 선생님과 훌륭한 연구원이 되기 위해 노력함으로써 주로 외국어로서의 영어 듣기와 말하기 실력을 발달시키는 데에 학생들을 돕는 나의 교직 생활에 더 집중할 수 있게 해주었다. 교실에서, 나는 그들이 달성하기에 비현실적인 목표를 설정하지 않고도 그들이 가진 영어의 한계를 뛰어넘을 수 있도록 학습자에게 동기를 부여하는 것의 중요성을 이해한다. 만약 내가 이성을 버리고, 실용적이지 못한 학습 목표를 설정한다면, 결과는 실패로 돌아갈 것이고, 그것은 결국 부정적인 효과의 동기부여가 될 것이다. 그래서 나는 학생들에게 가지고 있는 기대에 대해서 현실적인 태도를 취함과 동시에, 학생들에게 배움의 열정을 불러일으키도록 노력해왔다.

---

native adj. 모국의, 원산지의 **noble** adj. 숭고한, 고귀한
calling n. 소명 **be obligated to** phr. ~할 의무가 있다
be all things to phr. ~의 마음에 들게 행동하다
temper v. 누그러뜨리다 **aspiration** n. 포부, 열망
practicality n. 현실성, 실용성 **balance** v. 균형을 잡다
primarily adv. 주로 **assist** v. 돕다
development n. 발달 **endeavor** v. 노력하다
researcher n. 연구원 **motivate** v. 동기를 부여하다
exceed v. 넘다, 초과하다
unreasonable adj. 비현실적인, 비합리적인
abandon v. 버리다 **impractical** adj. 비실용적인
seek to phr. ~하도록 추구하다 **invoke** v. 불러일으키다
passion n. 열정 **expectation** n. 기대

18 [2019 경기대]

정답 ①

해석 ① 글쓴이는 학생들에 대해 하나의 목표를 가지고 있다.
② 교수가 모든 학생의 요구를 충족할 수 있는 것은 아니다.
③ 글쓴이는 영어 학습에 있어 학생들의 열정을 높이려고 노력했다.
④ 실패는 동기 부여를 감소시킨다.

해설 지문의 내용과 일치하지 않는 것을 묻는 문제이다. ③번의 키워드인 a singular aim(하나의 목표)과 관련된 지문의 impractical learning goals(실용적이지 못한 학습 목표) 주

변에서 이성을 버리고, 실용적이지 못한 학습 목표를 설정한다면 결과는 실패로 돌아갈 것이라고는 했지만, 글쓴이가 학생들에 대해 하나의 목표를 가지고 있다는 것은 알 수 없다. 따라서 ①번이 지문의 내용과 일치하지 않는다.

오답분석
② no professor can be all things to all students를 통해 '교수가 모든 학생의 요구를 충족할 수 있는 것은 아니다'는 것을 알 수 있다.
③ I have sought to invoke passion in my students for learning을 통해 '글쓴이는 영어 학습에 있어 학생들의 열정을 높이려고 노력했다'는 것을 알 수 있다.
④ the result would likely be failure, which would in turn negatively impact motivation을 통해 '실패는 동기 부여를 감소시킨다'는 것을 알 수 있다.

어휘 singular adj. 하나의 meet v. 충족하다, 만족하다
enthusiasm n. 열정 motivation n. 동기 부여

19 [2019 경기대]
정답 ④

해석
① 버리다 ② 조사하다
③ 당혹하게 만들다 ④ 완화하다

해설 밑줄 친 temper의 의미를 추론하는 문제이다. 밑줄 친 부분이 포함된 문장 바로 다음에서 이것이 균형을 잡는 행동이라고 했으며, 지문 마지막에서 학생들에게 가진 기대에 대해 현실적인 태도를 취한다고 했다. 따라서, 밑줄 친 단어의 의미를 '완화하다'라고 한 ④번이 정답이다.

어휘 examine v. 조사하다 confound v. 당혹하게 만들다
moderate v. 완화하다

20 [2019 경기대]
정답 ②

해석
① 학술적 맥락에서의 균형
② 현실성은 효과적인 지도의 핵심
③ 가르치는 것은 신성한 직업
④ Johnson 대학에서의 일상

해설 지문의 제목을 묻는 문제이다. 지문의 마지막에서 이성을 버리고 실용적이지 못한 학습 목표를 설정한다면, 결과는 실패로 돌아갈 것이고, 그것은 결국 부정적인 효과의 동기부여가 될 것이라고 했으며, 그래서 글쓴이는 학생들에게 가지고 있는 기대에 대해서 현실적인 태도를 취했다고 설명하고 있다. 따라서 이 지문의 요지를 '현실성은 효과적인 지도의 핵심'이라고 표현한 ②번이 정답이다.

어휘 academic adj. 학술적인, 학업의 context n. 맥락
instruction n. 지도, 설명 profession n. 직업

[21-22]

돼지에 관해 말하자면, 그것들은 이미 완벽하게 읽고 쓸 수 있었다. 개는 웬만큼 읽는 것을 배웠지만, 7계명 이외에는 어떤 것도 읽는 데 관심이 없었다. 염소 Muriel은 개보다 다소 잘 읽을 수 있었고, 때때로 저녁에 다른 동물들에게 책을 읽어주곤 했다. Benjamin은 어떤 돼지와도 마찬가지로 잘 읽었지만, 그의 능력을 절대 발휘하지 않았다. 그가 알고 있는 한, 읽을 만한 것은 없다고 그는 말했다. Clover는 알파벳 전체를 배웠지만, 단어를 함께 합치지 못했다. Boxer는 알파벳 D 이상을 넘기지 못했다. 그는 큰 발굽으로 먼지 속에서 A, B, C, D를 그리고 나서, 그 알파벳들을 응시하며 서 있곤 하며, 온 힘을 다해 다음에 오는 것을 기억하려고 노력했지만 절대 성공하지 못했다. 실은, 그는 몇 차례나 E, F, G, H를 배웠지만, 그가 그것들을 안 무렵에는, A, B, C, D를 까먹었다는 것을 항상 깨달았다. 마침내 그는 처음 네 개의 알파벳에 만족하기로 했고, 매일 한두 번 그의 기억을 되살리기 위해 그것들을 써내곤 했다.

Commandment n. (성경의 십계명 중 한) 계명
exercise v. 발휘하다 faculty n. 능력
trace out phr. ~을 그리다 hoof n. 발굽 might n. 힘
refresh v. 기억을 되살리다

21 [2020 가천대]
정답 ①

해석
① 만족하는 ② 중립적인
③ 무관심한 ④ 단호한

해설 지문의 빈칸을 채우는 문제이다. 빈칸 앞 문장에서 Boxer가 알파벳을 네 개 이상 외우지 못하는 내용이 나와 있으므로, 빈칸에는 마침내 Boxer가 무엇을 결정했는지에 대한 내용이 나와야 적절하다는 것을 알 수 있다. 따라서 처음 네 개의 알파벳에 '만족하기로' 했다고 한 ①번이 정답이다.

어휘 content adj. 만족하는 neutral adj. 중립적인
indifferent adj. 무관심한 resolute adj. 단호한

22 [2020 가천대]
정답 ③

해석
① 개는 학습에서 어느 정도 영리하다.
② Benjamin은 학습 욕구가 없다.
③ Clover는 Boxer보다 학습에서 더 느리다.
④ Boxer는 근면한 학습자이다.

해설 지문의 내용과 일치하지 않는 것을 묻는 문제이다. ③번의 키워드인 Clover가 언급된 지문 주변에서 Clover는 알파벳 전체를 배웠지만, 단어를 함께 합치지 못했고, Boxer는 알파벳 D 이상을 넘기지 못했다고 했으므로, Clover가 Boxer보다 학습에서 더 느리다는 것은 지문의 내용과 다르다. 따라서 ③번이 지문의 내용과 일치하지 않는다.

오답 분석
① 지문의 두 번째 문장 The dogs learned to read fairly well을 통해 '개는 학습에서 어느 정도 영리하다'는 것을 알 수 있다.
② 지문의 다섯 번째 문장 So far as he knew, he said, there was nothing worth reading.을 통해 'Benjamin은 학습 욕구가 없다'는 것을 알 수 있다.
④ 지문의 여덟 번째 문장 He would trace out ~ succeeding.을 통해 'Boxer는 근면한 학습자이다'라는 것을 알 수 있다.

어휘 motivation n. 욕구, 동기 부여 industrious adj. 근면한

[23-24]

*The Newbury House Dictionary of American English*에 따르면, 소문은 "다른 사람의 행동이나 삶에 대한 이야기나 글 또는 때로는 거짓인 것"이라고 한다. 예를 들어, 누군가가 친구가 우는 것을 보고 다른 사람에게 그 친구가 울고 있고 감정적인 문제가 있다고 말하면, 이것은 소문이다. 처음에, 소문은 나쁘지 않아 보일지도 모른다. 한 사람은 두 번째 사람에게 다른 사람에 대한 사적인 것을 말하고, 그 두 번째 사람은 세 번째 사람에게 말하는 등등이다. 그 정보는 사람에게서 사람에게로 전달된다. (A)하지만, 소문은 단순한 정보 그 이상이다. 소문이 자라서 변할 수 있다. 사람들은 종종 모든 사실을 알지 못한다. 그들은 고의든 아니든 뭔가 사실이 아닌 것을 첨가할 수도 있다. (B)그 결과, 소문의 대상이 되는 사람은 상처를 받을 수도 있다. 그 결과가 그 사람을 기분 나쁘게 하는 것에서부터 그 사람의 경력을 망치는 것까지 (C)다양하기 때문에, 소문은 단순히 "말이나 글"보다 훨씬 더 나쁘다.

gossip n. 소문, 험담 untruthful adj. 거짓의, 진실이 아닌
private adj. 사적인, 사사로운 and so on phr. 기타 등등
untrue adj. 사실이 아닌, 허위의
on purpose phr. 고의로, 일부러 subject n. 대상, 주제
destroy v. 망치다, 파괴하다 career n. 경력, 커리어

23 2020 국민대
정답 ③

해석 ① 하지만 — 게다가
② 게다가 — 예를 들어
③ 하지만 — 그 결과
④ 게다가 — 그건 그렇고

해설 빈칸에 적절한 연결어를 넣는 문제이다. (A) 앞 문장은 정보에 대한 내용이고, 빈칸 뒤 문장은 소문은 단순한 정보 그 이상이라고 하며 정보와 소문의 차이를 언급하는 내용이므로, 대조를 나타내는 연결어인 However가 들어가야 한다. (B) 앞 문장은 사실이 아닌 것이 첨가되는 소문의 특성에 관한 내용이고, 빈칸 뒤 문장은 소문의 대상이 상처를 받을 수 있다는 내용이므로, 결과를 나타내는 연결어인 As a result가 들어가야 한다. 따라서 ③ However — As a result가 정답이다.

24 2020 국민대
정답 ①

해석 ① 다양하다   ② 데리고 가다
③ 연결하다   ④ 교체하다

해설 지문의 빈칸을 채우는 문제이다. 빈칸 (C)가 있는 문장에서 그 결과가 그 사람을 기분 나쁘게 하는 것에서부터 그 사람의 경력을 망치는 것까지라고 했으므로, 빈칸 (C)에는 다양하다는 내용이 나와야 적절하다는 것을 알 수 있다. 따라서 '다양하다'라고 한 ①번이 정답이다.

어휘 range from A to B phr. A에서 B까지 다양하다
alternate v. 교체하다, 교대로 하다

25 2019 인하대
정답 ⑤

해석 세팍타크로는 동남아시아에서 인기 있는 스포츠이다. 그것은 등나무로 만든 공을 사용하고, 선수들이 높은 그물망 위로 공을 닿아서 넘기기 위해 그들의 발, 무릎, 가슴, 그리고 머리만을 사용하도록 허용한다는 점만 뺀다면 배구와 비슷하다. 이 경기는 "공을 차다"라는 의미의 용어인 츄슈라는 중국의 경기를 기반으로 했을 수도 있다. 1400년대 초반까지 이 경기는 무역을 통해 말레이시아와 태국으로 들어왔다. 그 당시에는 주로 남자와 소년들이 원형으로 서서 공을 그들 사이에 앞뒤로 차면서 경기가 진행되었다. 그 경기는 수백 년 동안 원형 모양으로 남아있었고, 세팍타크로의 현대판은 1800년대 초반 언제부턴가 형태를 갖춰가기 시작했다. 1829년에 시암 체육협회가 첫 번째 규칙의 초안을 작성하고, 배구식의 그물망을 도입했다. 몇 년 안으로, 세팍타크로는 태국과 말레이시아 학교의 교과과정에 도입되었으며, 두 나라의 독립을 축하하는 행사의 한 부분으로서 전시회가 개최될 정도로 사랑받는 지역 관습이 되었다. 1940년대에, 이 경기는 동남아시아 전역에 퍼졌으며, 오늘날 국제 세팍타크로 연맹에 의해 경기가 주최되고 있다.
① 배구와의 차이점
② 세팍타크로가 인기 있는 지역
③ 중국 경기인 츄슈와의 연결점
④ 처음으로 규칙을 정립한 기구
⑤ 학교 교과과정에 도입된 이유

해설 지문에 언급되지 않은 것을 고르는 문제이다. 지문의 마지막에서 두 번째 문장에서 세팍타크로가 태국과 말레이시아 학교의 교과과정에 도입되었다고는 했지만, 그 이유는 서술되어 있지 않으므로, 지문에 언급되지 않은 내용은 '학교 교과과정에 도입된 이유'이다. 따라서 정답은 ⑤번이다.

어휘 resemble v. 비슷하다, 닮다
rattan adj. 등나무로 만든, 등나무의
back and forth phr. 앞뒤로
take shape phr. 형태를 갖추다 association n. 협회
draft v. 초안을 작성하다 curriculum n. 교육과정
cherished adj. 사랑받는 exhibition n. 전시회

stage v. 개최시키다, 무대에 올리다
celebration n. 축하 행사, 기념식
independence n. 독립   throughout adv. 전역에
govern v. 주최하다; 지배하다   federation n. 연맹

[26-28]

십 대 때 나는 숙제를 하면서 베아 바르토(Béa Bartó)의 현악 4중주곡을 듣는 습관을 갖게 되었는데, 나는 그 곡들이 약간 불협화음이라고 생각했지만 그래도 즐거웠다. 왠지 그 불협화음을 무시하는 것이 내가 수산화암모늄의 화학 방정식에 집중하는 데 도움이 되었다.

몇 년 후에, 내가 마감 시한에 맞춰 뉴욕 타임스를 위한 기사를 쓰고 있을 때, 나는 바르토를 무시하던 예전의 그 훈련이 기억났다. 뉴욕 타임스에서 나는 과학 담당 부서의 한 가운데서 열심히 일하고 있었는데, 그 당시에 그 부서는 12명 정도의 과학 담당 기자와 6명의 편집자들을 위한 책상들을 쑤셔 넣은 교실 크기의 동굴 같은 공간을 차지하고 있었다. 언제나 바르토 스타일의 불협화음을 흥얼거리는 소리가 있었다. 근처에는 서너 명이 수다를 떨고 있고, 기자들이 취재원과 인터뷰를 할 때 여러 통의 전화 대화가 끝나가는 소리를 우연히 들릴 것이다. 편집자들은 기사가 언제 준비되냐고 묻기 위해 사무실을 가로질러 소리를 질러댔다. 설령 있다 하더라도, 고요함은 거의 없었다. 하지만 나를 포함한 우리 과학 기자들은 날마다 편집할 준비가 된 사본을 바로 제시간에 확실하게 전달을 하곤 했다. 아무도 모두 조용히 좀 해달라고 애원하지 않았으며, 그래서 우리는 집중할 수 있었다. 우리 모두 단지 집중력을 배가시켰으며, 고함소리는 무시했다.

소음의 한 가운데서의 그런 집중은 선택적 집중력, 즉 들어오는 자극들을 무시하면서 단 하나의 목표물에만 집중하는 신경계의 능력을 보여준다.

string quartet phr. 현악 4중주 곡
cacophonous adj. 불협화음의, 귀에 거슬리는
somehow adv. 어떻게든; 왠지
tune out phr. ~을 듣지 않다, 무시하다
discordant adj. 조화를 이루지 못하는; 불협화음의
equation n. 방정식
ammonium hydroxide phr. 수산화암모늄
drill n. 반복연습, 훈련
labor away phr. 꾸준히(끊임없이) 일하다
cavern n. 동굴, 어두운 방   cram v. 밀어 넣다, 쑤셔 넣다
hum n. 흥얼거림   overhear v. (남의 대화 등을) 우연히 듣다
source n. 취재원   reliably adv. 신뢰할 수 있게, 확실하게
copy n. 복사본   day after day phr. 매일같이, 날마다
plead v. 애원하다, 간청하다   redouble v. 배가(강화)하다
roar n. 포효, 함성   din n. (계속되는 크고 불쾌한) 소음
indicate v. (사실이거나 존재한다는 것을) 보여주다
neural adj. 신경(계통)의   beam v. (빛을) 발하다, 비추다

26 2018 이화여대

정답 ④

해석
① 소음이 생산성에 왜 그렇게 중요한가
② 소음이 심한 기자의 작업 환경
③ 일상의 소음을 견디는 법
④ 집중력을 향상시키는 소음의 기능
⑤ 조용함은 우리의 집중력에 왜 해로운가

해설 지문의 제목을 묻는 문제이다. 첫 문단에서는 불협화음의 음악을 들으며 그 불협화음을 무시하는 것이 화학 방정식에 집중하는데 도움이 되었다고 했으며, 두 번째 문단에서는 기자가 되어 굉장히 시끄러운 환경 속에서 소음을 무시함으로써 집중력을 배가시켰다고 했다. 그리고 마지막 문단에서는 이런 소음 속에서의 집중력이 선택적 주의력이라고 결론을 짓고 있다. 따라서 지문의 제목을 '집중력을 향상시키는 소음의 기능'이라고 표현한 ④번이 정답이다. 참고로 소음이 오히려 집중력을 높이는 데 도움이 되었다는 내용이므로 소음이 생산성에 중요하다고 유추할 수도 있겠지만 그 이유(why)에 대한 내용은 없으므로 ①번을 고르면 함정에 빠지는 것이다.

어휘 crucial adj. 중대한, 결정적인

27 2018 이화여대

정답 ⑤

해석
① 위에 묘사된 기자들의 작업 공간은 크다.
② 기자들의 일반적인 작업 환경은 생산성을 증가시키고 싶은 사람들에게 적합하다.
③ 기자들은 대개 그들에게 들리는 소음에 괴로워하지 않는다.
④ 바르토는 그의 음악의 질이 형편없다는 것으로 악명이 높다.
⑤ 음악은 당신의 일에 집중하도록 도와주는 소음으로 사용될 수 있다.

해설 지문을 통해 추론할 수 있는 것을 고르는 문제이다. 첫 문단에서 필자는 학창 시절에 베아 바르토의 현악 4중주곡을 듣는 습관을 갖게 되었는데 그 곡들이 약간 불협화음이라고 생각했지만 오히려 그 불협화음을 무시하는 것이 공부에 집중하는 데 도움이 되었다고 했으므로, 음악이 당신의 일에 집중하도록 도와주는 소음으로 사용될 수 있다고 추론할 수 있다. 따라서 정답은 ⑤번이다.

오답분석
① 두 번째 문단에서 그 부서는 12명 정도의 과학 담당 기자와 6명의 편집자들을 위한 책상들을 쑤셔 넣은 교실 크기의 동굴 같은 공간을 차지하고 있었다(which in those years occupied a classroom-sized cavern ~ a half dozen editors)고 했으므로, '위에 묘사된 기자들의 작업 공간은 크다'는 것은 지문의 내용과 다르다.
② 필자가 근무했던 환경이 매우 시끄러웠지만, 오히려 집중력을 높이는 데 도움이 되었다는 것일 뿐이므로, 이런 환경이 생산성을 증가시키고 싶은 사람들에게 적합한지는 알 수 없다.

③ 필자가 근무했던 곳의 기자들은 소음에 개의치 않았지만, 이것으로 기자들은 대개 그들에게 들리는 소음에 괴로워하지 않는다고 일반화시켜 추론할 수는 없다.
④ 필자는 바르토의 현악 4중주곡이 불협화음이라고 생각했다고 했지만, 바르토가 그의 음악의 질이 형편없다는 것으로 악명이 높은지는 알 수 없다.

어휘   attentive   adj. 주의 깊은
be notorious for   phr. ~로 악명이 높다

28   2018 이화여대

정답 ②

해석 ① 받은 정보를 처리하면서
② 들어오는 자극들을 무시하면서
③ 소음의 소리를 올림으로써
④ 주의력의 수준을 증가시키면서
⑤ 동료들과 건강한 동료애를 유지하면서

해설 지문의 빈칸을 채우는 문제이다. 첫 번째 문단에서 학창시절에는 바르토의 음악을 들으며 불협화음을 무시하는 것(tuning out those discordant tones)이 화학 방정식에 집중하는 데 도움이 되었다고 했으며, 두 번째 문단에서는 굉장히 시끄러운 신문사 사무실에서 소음을 무시하면서(tuning out the roar) 집중력을 배가했다고 했으므로, 선택적 집중력(selective attention)과 동격을 이루는 the neural capacity to beam in on just one target while _____의 빈칸에는 '들어오는 자극들을 무시하면서'를 의미하는 ignoring incoming stimuli가 들어가는 것이 자연스럽다. 따라서 ②번이 정답이다.

어휘   turn up   phr. (소리 등을) 높이다, 올리다

[29-30]

과학은 두 가지 이유로 작동한다. 우선, 과학의 결과는 실험에 기초한 것이다. 즉 안락의자에 앉아 철학적인 이야기를 함으로써가 아니라 지구에 직접 물어봄으로써 지구의 비밀을 얻는다. 개방성과 복제의 문화는 과학자들이 동료들에게 점검을 받는다는 것을 의미한다. 과학 논문들은 다른 이들이 실험을 반복하여 같은 결론에 도달한다는 것을 확인할 수 있도록 (실험)방법들에 관한 부분들을 포함하고 있다.
적어도, 이론적으로는 그렇다. 실제로는, 오래된 (실험)결과를 확인하는 것이 흥미로운 새로운 결과를 발표하는 것보다 과학자의 경력에는 별로 좋지 않다. 그런 확인이 없으면, 부실한 결과가 문헌에 들어갈 수 있다. 최근 몇 년간 의학, 심리학 그리고 유전학은 현미경 아래 놓였는데(자세히 살펴보았는데) 부실한 것으로 판명되었다. 예를 들어, 작년에 발표된 100편의 심리학 논문에 대한 한 분석은 그 연구 결과 중 겨우 36퍼센트만을 재연할 수 있었다. 그리고 미국의 제약 회사인 암젠(Amgen)에 의해 2012년에 행해진 한 연구는 그것이 검토한 53편의 논문들 중 겨우 11퍼센트만 재연할 수 있었다.

extract   v. 뽑다(얻다), 추출하다
armchair   n. 안락의자; adj. (책이나 텔레비전 등을 통해) 간접적으로 아는, (실제는 모르는) 탁상공론식의
replication   n. 복제   police   v. 감시하다, 단속하다
dodgy   adj. 의심스러운, 부실한
sneak   v. 살금살금(몰래) 가다
wanting   adj. 부족한, 모자라는   replicate   v. 복제하다

29   2018 성균관대

정답 ①

해석 ① 과학 논문에서 교차 확인의 중요성
② 과학 논문과 사설 간의 차이점
③ 과학 논문을 쓰는 방법
④ 무엇이 최고의 과학 실험을 만드나
⑤ 무엇이 인간의 과학 연구에 동기를 부여하는가

해설 지문의 주제를 묻는 문제이다. 첫 문단에서 과학이 효과적으로 작동하는 이유는 실험에 기초하기 때문이며 또한 다른 이들에 실험에 의해 확인되기 때문이라고 했다. 그러나 두 번째 문단에서 실제로는 과학자들이 다른 이의 실험 결과를 확인하는 것보다는 새로운 결과를 발표하는 것이 경력에 더 이롭기 때문에 '연구 결과에 대한 확인이 부실해지고 있다'는 점을 지적하고 있다. 따라서 지문의 주제를 '과학 논문에서 교차 확인의 중요성'라고 표현한 ①번이 정답이다.

30   2018 성균관대

정답 ④

해석 ① 실험을 완수할 수 없기 (때문에)
② 원하는 결과를 얻을 수 없기 (때문에)
③ 동료 과학자들을 오도할 수 있기 (때문에)
④ 그 과학 실험을 증명할 수 없기 (때문에)
⑤ 신뢰할 수 없는 결과를 얻기 (때문에)

해설 실험 방법이 중요한 이유 즉 실험 방법이 없으면 어떻게 되는지를 묻는 문제이다. 첫 문단의 마지막 문장에서 다른 이들이 실험을 반복하여 같은 결론에 도달한다는 것을 확인할 수 있도록 과학 논문에는 실험 방법에 관한 부분들이 포함된다고 했으므로, 실험 방법이 중요한 이유는 그 과학 실험의 결과가 타당한지를 확인(증명)하기 위해 필요하기 때문이라고 할 수 있다. 따라서 실험 방법이 없으면 '그 과학 실험을 증명할 수 없기' 때문에 중요하다고 표현한 ④번이 정답이다.

어휘   mislead   v. 오도(호도)하다   verify   v. 입증(증명)하다

[31-33]

펩시와 코카콜라는 아마도 지금까지 가장 논란이 많은 음료 논쟁 중 하나일 것이다. 코카콜라만을 고집하는 사람들과 펩시에 열광하는 사람들의 뚜렷한 구분은 언제나 존재했다. 하지만, 두 음료는 캐러멜 시럽의 색상부터 재료까지 모든 면에서 실제로 동일하다. 두 음료 모두 나트륨, 설탕, 탄산수, 액상과당, 인산, 카페인, 그리고 천연 향료가 들어간다.

두 음료는 수많은 유사점이 있지만, 펩시와 코카콜라는 여전히 사람들에게 두 가지 다른 맛의 경험을 가져다주는데, 그것이 왜 사람들이 둘 중 하나를 더 선호하는지를 설명한다. 작가이자 기자인 Malcolm Gladwell이 의사결정과 사고에 대해 저술한 Blink라는 책에서, 그는 "펩시가 코카콜라보다 더 달고 코카콜라의 건포도와 바닐라 맛과는 다르게 펩시는 강한 감귤류의 향을 가진 것이 특징이다."라고 서술했다. 실제로, 12온스의 펩시 캔에는 코카콜라에 들어있지 않은 한 가지 재료인 구연산이 들어간다. 게다가, 펩시는 코카콜라보다 설탕이 2g 더 많이 들어간다. 이 두 가지의 미세한 차이점이 사람들이 좋아할 수도 싫어할 수도 있는 펩시의 단맛과 감귤류의 향을 만든다. 또한, 한 캔의 코카콜라에 더 들어가 있는 15mg의 나트륨이 <u>부드러워진</u> 단맛을 가진 탄산수의 맛이 나는 이유를 설명해줄지도 모른다.

controversial adj. 논란이 많은
diehard adj. 고집하는, 보수적인
enthusiast n. 열광적인 지지자   practically adv. 실제로
identical adj. 동일한   ingredient n. 재료
sodium n. 나트륨   carbonated water phr. 탄산수
high fructose corn syrup phr. 액상과당
phosphoric acid phr. 인산
numerous adj. 수많은   similarity n. 유사점
journalist n. 기자   characterize v. 특징으로 하다
citrusy adj. 감귤류의   raisiny adj. 건포도 같은
citric acid phr. 구연산   subtle adj. 미세한
loathe v. 싫어하다, 혐오하다   club soda phr. 탄산수

31 [2019 한성대]

정답 ③

해석 ① 나트륨과 설탕의 이점
② 더 달콤한 펩시
③ 펩시와 코카콜라 사이의 맛의 차이점
④ 탄산음료의 재료

해설 지문의 제목을 묻는 문제이다. 두 번째 문단에서 펩시와 코카콜라 사이에 구연산, 설탕, 그리고 나트륨의 함량이 달라서 맛이 다르다고 설명하고 있다. 따라서 지문의 제목을 '펩시와 코카콜라 사이의 맛의 차이점'이라고 표현한 ③번이 정답이다.

어휘 benefit n. 이점

32 [2019 한성대]

정답 ④

해석 ① 코카콜라는 펩시보다 더 풍미가 강하다.
② 코카콜라를 고집하는 사람들이 펩시보다 더 많다.
③ 코카콜라는 펩시만큼 달다.
④ 코카콜라에 열광하는 사람은 감귤류의 향을 좋아하지 않는다.

해설 지문의 내용과 일치하는 것을 묻는 문제이다. 지문의 마지막에서 두 번째 문장인 These two subtle differences give Pepsi its sweet, citrus-like flavor that people either love or loathe의 내용을 통해 코카콜라에 열광하는 사람은 감귤류의 향을 좋아하지 않는다는 것을 알 수 있다. 따라서 ④번이 지문의 내용과 일치한다.

오답분석 ① 코카콜라는 건포도와 바닐라 향이 강하다고는 했지만, 코카콜라는 펩시보다 더 풍미가 강한지는 알 수 없다.
② 코카콜라를 고집하는 사람과 펩시에 열광하는 사람에 뚜렷한 구분이 있다고는 했지만, 코카콜라를 고집하는 사람들이 펩시보다 더 많은지는 알 수 없다.
③ 펩시에는 코카콜라보다 2g의 설탕이 더 들어가 있다고 했으므로, 코카콜라는 펩시만큼 달다는 것은 지문의 내용과 다르다.

어휘 flavorful adj. 풍미가 강한

33 [2019 한성대]

정답 ②

해석 ① 강한   ② 부드러워진
③ 신맛의   ④ 감귤류 같은

해설 지문의 빈칸을 채우는 문제이다. 빈칸의 이전 부분에서 펩시가 코카콜라보다 한 캔에 설탕이 2g 더 들어가 있다고 설명하고 있으므로, 빈칸에는 코카콜라의 단맛이 덜하다는 의미의 단어가 들어가는 것이 적절하다. 따라서 '부드러워진'이라고 한 ②번이 정답이다.

어휘 sour adj. (맛이) 신

[34-36]

1970년대 후반, 1980년대, 1990년대 초반에 지어진 스포츠 시설들은 일상적으로 시설 내 경험을 높이기 위해 설계되었으나 일상적으로 가까운 토지에서 이루어질 수 있었던 관련된 경제 활동을 (A)<u>이용하는</u> 것에 대한 가능성은 무시되었다. 이 기간 동안 지어진 시설들은 상당한 공공 투자로 건설되었다. 부동산 가치를 (B)<u>깎아내리고</u> 그 장소 내에서 이루어지는 경제 활동을 활용하는 데 실패한 것은 새로운 장소를 확보하기 위한 팀의 노력을 지지하는 그 결정에 대해 상당한 수준의 불만을 발생시켰다. <u>그 결과</u>, 그 장소에 있는 건물로부터의 모든 혜

택은 팀 소유주와 그 스포츠 산업과 연관된 다른 사람들에게 (C)발생했다. 공공 부문 협력 업체에 간 재정 수익은 거의 없었다. 팀 소유주가 이 새로운 최신 시설이 만들어졌던 수익원의 전부는 아니지만, 대부분을 (D)보유하도록 허용되자 상황은 더 심각해졌다.

---

facility n. 시설　**routinely** adv. 일상적으로, 관례대로
enhance v. 높이다　**potential** n. 가능성
harness v. 활용하다, 이용하다　**associated** adj. 관련된
take place phr. 이루어지다, 발생하다
adjacent adj. 가까운, 인접한　**real estate** phr. 토지, 부동산
substantial adj. 상당한
public investment phr. 공공 투자
diminish v. 깎아내리다, 줄어들다
property level phr. 부동산 가치
capitalize on phr. ~을 활용하다, 기회로 삼다
venue n. 장소　**discontent** n. 불만　**secure** v. 확보하다
accrue v. 발생하다　**financial** adj. 재정　**return** n. 수익
public sector phr. 공공 부문　**partner** n. 협력 업체
retain v. 보유하다　**revenue** n. 수익, 세입
state-of-the-art adj. 최신의, 최근의

34 [2019 단국대]

정답 ②

해설 밑줄 친 단어들 중에서 문맥상 적절하지 않은 어휘를 고르는 문제이다. 부동산 가치를 높이고 그 장소 내에서 이루어지는 경제 활동을 활용하는 데 실패했다는 내용이므로 (B)에는 '깎아내리다'를 의미하는 diminish가 아니라 '높이다'를 의미하는 increase가 들어가는 것이 자연스럽다. 따라서 ②번이 정답이다.

35 [2019 단국대]

정답 ①

해설 빈칸에 적절한 연결어를 넣는 문제이다. 빈칸 앞 문장은 부동산 가치를 높이고 그 장소 내에서 이루어지는 경제 활동을 활용하는 데 실패한 것이 새로운 장소를 확보하기 위한 팀의 노력을 지지하는 결정에 대한 상당한 수준의 불만을 발생시켰다는 내용이고, 빈칸 뒤 문장은 그 장소에 있는 건물로부터의 모든 혜택은 팀 소유주와 그 스포츠 산업과 연관된 다른 사람들에게 생겼다는 내용이다. 따라서 인과관계를 나타내는 연결어인 ① As a result(그 결과)가 정답이다.

36 [2019 단국대]

정답 ①

해석 ① 새로운 스포츠 시설을 짓는 것의 혜택은 공평하게 나누어지지 않는다.
② 스포츠팀이 새로운 시설을 찾는 것은 어렵다.
③ 현대 스포츠 산업에서는 재무 관리가 가장 중요하다.
④ 팀 소유주는 공공의 투자를 받은 스포츠 산업의 발전에 기여했다.

해설 지문의 내용과 일치하는 것을 묻는 문제이다. 마지막 문장에서 팀 소유주가 새로운 최신 시설이 만들어졌던 수익원의 대부분을 보유하도록 허용되었다는 내용을 통해 새로운 스포츠 시설을 짓는 것의 혜택은 공평하게 나누어지지 않는다는 것을 알 수 있다. 따라서 ①번이 지문의 내용과 일치한다.

오답 분석
② 첫 번째 문장에서 1970년대 후반, 1980년대, 1990년대 초반에 지어진 스포츠 시설들은 일상적으로 시설 내 경험을 높이기 위해 설계되었다고는 했지만, 스포츠팀이 새로운 시설을 찾는 것이 어려운지는 알 수 없다.
③ 네 번째 문장에서 그 장소에 있는 건물로부터의 모든 혜택은 팀 소유주와 그 스포츠 산업과 연관된 다른 사람들에게 생겼다고는 했지만, 현대 스포츠 산업에서 재무 관리가 가장 중요한지는 알 수 없다.
④ 네 번째 문장에서 그 장소에 있는 건물로부터의 모든 혜택은 팀 소유주와 그 스포츠 산업과 연관된 다른 사람들에게 생겼다고는 했지만, 팀 소유주가 공공의 투자를 받은 스포츠 산업의 발전에 기여했는지는 알 수 없다.

어휘 **fairly** adv. 공평하게　**distribute** v. 나누어 주다, 분배하다
financial management phr. 재무 관리
significant adj. 중요한　**development** n. 발전, 발달

[37-38]

타임 디프닝의 특별한 경우는 멀티태스킹이다. 멀티태스킹(그리고 멀티프로세싱)이라는 용어는 원래 동시에 한 가지 이상의 업무나 프로그램을 수행하는 컴퓨터의 능력에 쓰였다. 현대의 언어에서 그것은 업무를 수행하는 타임 디프닝의 개념으로 쓰인다. 멀티태스킹은 전형적으로 통화, 이메일, 인스턴트 메시지, 그리고 컴퓨터 작업을 더 생산적으로 하기 위해 동시에 곡예하듯이 하는 것을 포함한다. 그러나, 몇몇 연구 결과는 멀티태스킹이 실제로 생산성을 높이지 않는다는 증거를 제공한다. 신경과학자, 심리학자, 그리고 경영학 교수들의 연구 결과는 멀티태스킹이 당신을 느리게 만들고 실수의 가능성을 증가시킨다고 말한다. 한 번에 한 가지 이상의 업무를 하는 것은 우리의 능력이 정보를 처리하지 못하게 한다. 사회적인 통념에 따르면, 젊은 사람들이 가장 능숙한 멀티태스킹 하는 사람들인데, 동시에 이메일을 보내고, 인스턴트 메시지를 보내고, iPod에서 음악을 듣고, 공부도 한다. 하지만, 마이크로소프트 사의 젊은 직원들에 대한 최근의 연구에서, 직원들이 수신 받는 이메일이나 인스턴트 메시지에 답장한 후에, 보고서나 컴퓨터 코드를 작성하는 것과 같이 머리를 써야 하는 만만치 않은 과제를 다시 시작할 수 있기까지 15분이 걸렸다. 미국 경제에 미치는 그러한 생산성 손실의 비용은 일 년에 거의 6500억 달러로 추정된다.

---

time deepening phr. 타임 디프닝 (세밀한 시간 관리를 통해 짧은 시간에 더 많은 일을 하거나 동시에 여러 가지 일을 하는 것)

multitasking n. 멀티태스킹 (여러 가지 일을 동시에 하는 것)
term n. 용어 **apply** v. 쓰다, 적용하다; 지원하다
execute v. 수행하다, 실행하다
contemporary adj. 현대의, 동시대의
parlance n. 언어, 말투 **typically** adv. 전형적으로
juggle v. 곡예 하듯 하다
instant message phr. 인스턴트 메시지 (인터넷으로 이루어지는 텍스트를 즉각적으로 교환하는 시스템, 메신저)
productive adj. 생산적인, 생산성이 있는
productivity n. 생산성 **prohibit** v. 못하게 하다, 금지하다
conventional wisdom phr. 사회적인 통념
adept adj. 능숙한 **estimate** v. 추정하다, 어림잡다

37 2019 인하대

정답 ②

해석 ① 멀티태스킹을 독려하는 방법에 대한 팁
② 업무 생산성에 대한 멀티태스킹의 효과
③ 시간 절약에 대한 멀티태스킹의 긍정적인 영향
④ 멀티태스킹을 하는 사람들을 컴퓨터 작업에 연결하는 것의 중요성
⑤ 기술이 주도한 의사소통이 일터에서 성행하는 방법

해설 지문의 주제를 묻는 문제이다. 지문의 중간에서 몇몇 연구 결과가 멀티태스킹이 실제로 생산성을 높이지 않는다는 것을 보여준다고 한 뒤, 멀티태스킹이 생산성을 높이지 못한 연구 결과와 사례를 설명하였다. 따라서 이 지문의 주제를 '업무 생산성에 대한 멀티태스킹의 효과'라고 표현한 ②번이 정답이다.

어휘 **encourage** v. 독려하다, 격려하다 **influence** n. 영향
technology-enabled adj. 기술이 주도한
thrive v. 성행하다, 번창하다 **workplace** n. 일터, 직장

38 2019 인하대

정답 ④

해석 ① 그러나 ─ 비슷하게
② 예를 들어 ─ 그 결과
③ 그러므로 ─ 그렇기는 하지만
④ 그러나 ─ 하지만
⑤ 예를 들어 ─ 반대로

해설 빈칸에 적절한 연결어를 넣는 문제이다. 첫 번째 빈칸 앞 문장은 멀티태스킹은 작업을 더 생산적으로 하기 위한다는 내용이고, 빈칸 뒤 문장은 멀티태스킹이 실제로 생산성을 높이지 않는다는 내용이므로, 대조를 나타내는 연결어인 however가 들어가야 한다. 두 번째 빈칸 앞 문장은 젊은 사람들이 능숙하게 멀티태스킹을 해낸다는 내용이고, 빈칸 뒤 문장은 젊은 사람들이 여러 가지 과제로 전환하는 데에 시간이 오래 걸린다는 내용이므로, 대조를 나타내는 연결어인 Yet이 들어가야 한다. 따라서 ④ however ─ Yet이 정답이다.

[39-40]

아이디어가 합리적인지 아닌지를 진짜로 알기 위한 유일한 방법은 그것을 시험하는 것이다. 각각의 가능성 있는 방안에 대한 즉각적인 원형 혹은 실물 모형을 만들어라. 이 과정의 초기 단계에서, 실물 모형은 연필 스케치, 발포 고무와 판지 모형, 혹은 간단한 그리기 도구로 만들어진 단순한 그림이 될 수 있다. 나는 스프레드시트와 파워포인트 슬라이드로, 그리고 색인카드나 스티커 메모에 한 스케치로 실물 모형을 만들어왔다. 특히 당신이 원형을 만들기 어려운 서비스나 자동화 체제를 개발하고 있다면, 때때로 아이디어는 많은 기법으로 잘 전달된다. 한 가지 유명한 원형 기법은 "오즈의 마법사"라고 불리는데, L. Frank Baum의 고전 도서인 The Wonderful Wizard of Oz에 나온 마법사에서 따온 것이다. 그 마법사는 사실상 평범한 사람일 뿐이었지만, 교묘한 속임수를 사용하여 그가 신비하고 전능하게 보이도록 했다. 다시 말해서, 그것은 모두 속임수였다. 그 마법사에게는 특별한 힘이 없었다. 오즈의 마법사 방법은 거대하고, 효과적인 체제를 만들기 전에 그것을 모방하는 데 사용될 수 있다.

reasonable adj. 합리적인
prototype n. 원형; v. 원형을 만들다 **mock-up** n. 실물 모형
potential adj. 가능성 있는 **convey** v. 전달하다
smoke and mirrors phr. 교묘한 속임수

39 2019 한국항공대

정답 ④

해석 ① 그것이 만들어지자마자
② 그것의 제작 시간을 고려하지 않고
③ 그것이 만들어진 후에
④ 그것을 만들기 전에

해설 지문의 빈칸을 채우는 문제이다. 지문 처음에서 아이디어가 합리적인지 아닌지를 알기 위해 즉각적인 원형 혹은 실물 모형을 만들라고 했으므로, 빈칸에는 그것이 언제 사용되는 것인지에 대한 내용이 나와야 적절하다는 것을 알 수 있다. 따라서 '그것을 만들기 전에'라고 한 ④번이 정답이다.

40 2019 한국항공대

정답 ③

해석 ① 원형을 만드는 것은 전능한 그림을 만드는 초기 단계에서 매우 효과적이다.
② 자동화 체제는 파워포인트 슬라이드를 통해 표현될 수 있다.
③ 원형을 만드는 방법은 아이디어의 유효성을 확인하는 검사 시스템이다.
④ 오즈의 마법사 기법은 실물 상품의 실제 효력을 보여준다.

해설 지문의 내용과 일치하는 것을 묻는 문제이다. 지문의 첫 번째 문장 The only way to really know whether an idea is reasonable is to test it.의 내용을 통해 아이디어가 합리적

인지 아닌지를 진짜로 알기 위한 유일한 방법은 그것을 시험하는 것임을 알 수 있다. 따라서 ③번이 지문의 내용과 일치한다.

오답분석
① 실물 모형을 만드는 초기 단계에서, 실물 모형은 간단한 그리기 도구로 만들어진 단순한 그림이 될 수 있다고 했으므로, 원형을 만드는 것은 전능한 그림을 만드는 초기 단계에서 매우 효과적이라는 것은 지문의 내용과 다르다.
② 원형을 만들기 어려운 자동화 체제 개발 시 사용할 수 있는 오즈의 마법사 기법을 소개하고 있으므로, 자동화 체제가 파워포인트 슬라이드를 통해 표현될 수 있다는 것은 지문의 내용과 다르다.
④ 오즈의 마법사 방법은 거대하고, 효과적인 체제를 만들기 전에 그것을 모방하는 데 사용될 수 있다고 했으므로, 오즈의 마법사 기법이 실물 상품의 실제 효력을 보여준다는 것은 지문의 내용과 다르다.

어휘
remarkably adv. 매우   omnipotent adj. 전능한
represent v. 표현하다, 보여주다   validity n. 유효성, 타당성
virtual adj. 실제의

[41-42]

국경 없는 의사회(MSF)는 국제적인 의료 인도주의 단체이다. MSF에서 일하는 의사, 간호사, 그리고 다른 의학 전문가들은 인종, 종교, 또는 정치적 소속과 관계없이 위기의 상황에 있는 사람들을 도와주는 데에 전념한다. 1971년부터, MSF 팀은 양질의 의료 관리를 약 60개국에 제공하는 것을 담당하고 있다. 그 팀들은 어렵고, 심지어는 위험한 환경에서 일하는 것에 익숙한 우수한 자격을 갖춘 전문가들을 갖고 있으며, MSF 국제 구호원의 대부분은 위기 상황이 일어나고 있는 지역 사회 출신이다. MSF 팀의 업무는 직접적인 의료 관리를 제공하는 것에만 국한되지 않고, 또한 그들이 돕는 사람들이 겪는 위기의 목격자 역할을 하는 것에 대한 헌신을 공유한다. 하지만, 하나의 기구로서 MSF는 중립적이다. 무력 충돌에서 편을 들지 않고 오로지 필요를 기반으로 하는 보살핌에 신경을 쓰는 것으로 명성을 갖고 있다. 정부나 다른 당사자와는 독립적으로 운영하고 독립적으로 자금을 후원받는다는 이 신념은 도움을 지원하는 행동 능력의 핵심이다.

international adj. 국제적인
humanitarian adj. 인도주의적인
organization n. 단체, 조직   specialist n. 전문가
be dedicated to phr. ~에 전념하다
regardless of phr. ~에 관계없이   race n. 인종
political affiliation phr. 정치적 소속
be responsible for phr. ~를 담당하다, ~에 책임이 있다
quality adj. 양질의   be familiar with phr. ~에 익숙하다
circumstance n. 환경   aid worker phr. 국제 구호원
community n. 지역 사회   commitment n. 헌신
witness n. 목격자   reputation n. 명성
take side phr. 편을 들다   armed adj. 무장한, 무기를 갖춘

conflict n. 충돌, 갈등   on the basis of phr. ~를 기반으로
operate v. 운영하다, 작동하다
independently adv. 독립적으로   government n. 정부
party n. 당사자, 정당   conduct v. 행동하다, 수행하다

41 [2019 한양대에리카]

정답 ①

해석
① 중립적인   ② 공격적인
③ 전문적인   ④ 인도주의적인

해설 지문의 빈칸을 채우는 문제이다. 빈칸 다음의 문장에서 MSF가 무력 충돌에서 편을 들지 않는다고 설명하고 있으므로, 빈칸에는 중립적인 자세를 유지한다는 내용이 와야 한다는 것을 알 수 있다. 따라서 '중립적인'이라고 한 ①번이 정답이다.

어휘 neutral adj. 중립적인   aggressive adj. 공격적인
professional adj. 전문적인
humanitarian adj. 인도주의적인

42 [2019 한양대에리카]

정답 ②

해석
① MSF는 위기에 처한 사람들을 위해 자격을 갖춘 의료 관리를 제공하는 것을 목표로 한다.
② 대부분의 MSF 구성원은 평화로운 상황의 지역 사회에서 온 자원봉사자다.
③ MSF는 정부나 다른 당사자와는 독립적으로 자금을 후원받는 것을 목표로 한다.
④ MSF는 직접적인 의료 관리를 제공하지만, 정치적 문제에서는 멀리 떨어져 있다.

해설 지문의 내용과 일치하지 않는 것을 묻는 문제이다. ③번의 키워드인 communities in peaceful situation(평화로운 상황의 지역 사회)과 관련된 지문의 aid workers are from the communities(지역 사회에서 온 국제 구호원) 주변에서 MSF 국제 구호원 다수는 위기가 일어나고 있는 지역 사회에서 왔다고 했으므로, 대부분의 MSF 구성원은 평화로운 상황의 지역 사회에서 온 자원봉사자라는 것은 지문의 내용과 다르다. 따라서 ②번이 지문의 내용과 일치하지 않는다.

오답분석
① MSF teams have been responsible for providing quality medical care in nearly 60 countries를 통해 'MSF는 위기에 처한 사람들을 위해 자격을 갖춘 의료 관리를 제공하는 것을 목표로 한다'는 것을 알 수 있다.
③ This belief in operating independently of government or other parties and obtaining independent funding is the key to MSF's ability to conduct its aid efforts를 통해 'MSF는 정부나 다른 당사자와는 독립적으로 자금을 후원받는 것을 목표로 한다'는 것을 알 수 있다.

④ It has a reputation for not taking sides in armed conflicts and for being concerned with providing care on the basis of need alone을 통해 'MSF는 직접적인 의료 관리를 제공하지만, 정치적 문제에서는 멀리 떨어져 있다'는 것을 알 수 있다.

어휘 stay away from phr. ~에서 떨어져 있다

[43-45]

Marti 이모는 오늘 밤에 집에 있는 나에게 전화해서 내가 무엇을 하고 있는지 묻는다. 나는 "그냥 책을 때리고 있어요(열심히 공부하고 있어요)."라고 말한다. 그건 잘 넘어가지 못할 것이다. Marti 이모는 "때리다"라는 단어는 사용할 필요가 없다면서 폭력적인 비유를 쓴다고 나를 꾸짖는다. 나는 "알았어요, 저는 책에 조심스러운 지압 요법을 실시하고 있어요."라고 말한다. Marti 이모는 그 표현을 더 좋아하는 것처럼 보인다. 나는 Marti 이모를 좋아하지만, Marti 이모와의 대화는 항상 내가 무엇을 잘못하고 있는지와 무엇을 잘못 말하고 있는지, 그리고 그것이 남성 중심의 권력 구조를 어떻게 지지하는지를 포함한다. Marti 이모는 몇몇 생각을 가지고 있다. 진보적인 사람이 있고, 진짜 진보적인 사람도 있고, 그리고 이보다 더 급진적인 Marti 이모가 있다. Berkeley가 이모에게 너무 파시스트적이긴 하지만, Marti 이모는 Berkeley 근처에서 충분히 적당한 거리 밖에서 살고 있다.

[B] 나는 Julie가 임신한 이후로 Marti 이모와 얘기하지 않았다. 나는 내가 할 수 있는 한 최대한 부드럽게 Marti 이모에게 소식을 전했고, 인구 과잉 문제에 기여한 것에 대해 이모에게 사과했다. Marti 이모는 "괜찮아."라고 말했다. Marti 이모는 나를 용서할 것이다. 하지만, Marti 이모는 내가 아이를 엄격한 채식주의자로 길러서 환경에 피해를 최소화하는 것을 도울 수 있다고 지적했다.

[C] Marti 이모 자신은 엄격한 채식주의자를 넘어섰다. 동물의 권리 보호는 Marti 이모의 열정이고(이모는 권리 보호라는 개념이 너무 서구적이라고 생각하긴 하지만), 이모는 전국을 바쁘게 돌아다니며 채식주의자 학회에 참석하면서 한 해의 대부분을 보낸다. 나는 Marti 이모가 먹지 않는, 물론 고기와 닭고기, 생선, 달걀, 유제품(이모는 아이스크림을 "굳어진 점액"이라고 부르는 것을 좋아한다)과 같은 것을 열거하는 데 꽤 많은 시간을 쓸 수 있다. 꿀도 이모가 안 먹는 것인데, 이모는 벌이 최저 임금 같은 것도 못 받고 억압받는다고 생각한다.

[A] 당신은 Marti 이모가 콩을 좋아할 거라고 생각하겠지만, 이모는 콩 산업이 부패했다고 생각한다. Marti 이모는 최근에 날 식품 애호가가 되면서 식단을 새로운 수준으로 바꾸었는데, 그것은 이모가 더 자연적이기 때문에 날것만 먹는다는 것을 의미한다.

---

hit the book phr. 열심히 공부하다, 벼락치기 공부하다
scold v. 꾸짖다, 야단치다   violent adj. 폭력적인, 난폭한
metaphor n. 비유, 은유   gentle adj. 조심스러운, 온화한

acupressure n. 지압 (요법)   conversation n. 대화, 회화
phallocentric adj. 남성 중심의
power structure phr. 권력 구조
liberal adj. 진보적인, 자유민주주의적인
appropriately adv. 적당하게, 알맞게
fascist adj. 파시스트적인   pregnant adj. 임신한
break the news phr. 소식을 전하다, (~에게) 처음으로 알려주다
overpopulation n. 인구 과잉   problem n. 문제
forgive v. 용서하다   point out phr. 지적하다, 언급하다
minimize v. 최소화하다   damage n. 피해
vegan n. 엄격한 채식주의자, 절대 채식주의자
animal rights phr. 동물의 권리 보호 (운동)
a good part of phr. ~의 대부분
fly around phr. 바삐 돌아다니다
vegetarian adj. 채식주의자의   conference n. 학회, 회의
take up phr. (시간·공간을) 쓰다   dairy n. 유제품
solidified adj. 굳어진   mucus n. (동물의) 점액
oppressed adj. 억압당하는, 탄압받는
union scale phr. 최저 임금   soy n. 콩, 간장
uncooked adj. 날것의, 요리되지 않은

43 2019 명지대

정답 ②

해설 주어진 지문 다음에 이어질 [A], [B], [C]의 적절한 순서를 파악하는 문제이다. 주어진 지문은 급진적인 Marti 이모와의 대화가 어떠한지에 관한 내용이므로, Marti 이모와의 대화의 또 다른 예시인 임신과 채식주의자에 관해 설명하는 [B]가 먼저 와야 한다. 그다음에 [C]에서 Marti 이모가 엄격한 채식주의자 이상이며, 채식주의자로서 어떤 활동을 하는지 설명하고, 마지막으로 [A]에서 Marti 이모가 최근에는 식단을 새롭게 바꾸어서 날것을 먹는다는 내용이 오는 것이 자연스럽다. 따라서 주어진 지문 다음에 이어질 순서는 ② [B] - [C] - [A]이다.

44 2019 명지대

정답 ④

해석 ① 화가 나고 놀란
② 차분하고 태연한
③ 흥분하지만 비판적인
④ 유머러스하지만 솔직한

해설 필자의 태도를 묻는 문제이다. 첫 번째 문단에서 '책을 때린다'는 표현을 폭력적이라고 꾸짖는 내용이 나오고, ⑧ 문단에서 임신한 것을 인구 과잉 문제라고 사과하자 아이를 엄격한 채식주의자로 길러서 환경에 피해를 최소화하는 것을 도울 수 있다고 하였다. 따라서 필자의 태도를 '유머러스하지만 솔직한'이라고 표현한 ④번이 정답이다.

어휘 demeanor n. 태도, 품행   enraged adj. 화가 난, 격분한
flabbergasted adj. 놀란, 당황스러운   calm adj. 차분한

nonchalant adj. 태연한, 무심한
critical adj. 비판적인, 비난하는   candid adj. 솔직한

45 2019 명지대

정답 ④

해석 ① Marti 이모는 Berkeley의 왼쪽에 있는 도시에 산다.
② Marti 이모의 딸은 지금 임신 중이다.
③ Marti 이모는 글쓴이의 말이 완곡하다고 생각한다.
④ Marti 이모는 극도의 채식주의자의 생활 방식을 지지한다.

해설 지문의 내용과 일치하는 것을 묻는 문제이다. ⓒ 문단에서 Marti 이모 자신은 엄격한 채식주의자를 넘어섰고, 전국을 바쁘게 돌아다니며 채식주의자 학회에 참석하면서 한 해의 대부분을 보낸다는 내용을 통해 Marti 이모가 극도의 채식주의자의 생활 방식을 지지한다는 것을 알 수 있다. 따라서 ④번이 지문의 내용과 일치한다.

오답 분석 ① 첫 번째 문단에서 Marti 이모가 Berkeley 근처에서 충분히 적당한 거리 밖에서 살고 있다고는 했지만, Berkeley의 왼쪽에 있는 도시에 사는지는 알 수 없다.
② [B] 문단에서 나는 Julie가 임신한 이후로 Marti 이모와 얘기하지 않았다고는 했지만, Marti 이모의 딸이 지금 임신 중인지는 알 수 없다.
③ 첫 번째 문단에서 내가 폭력적인 비유를 쓴다고 Marti 이모가 나를 꾸짖는다고 했으므로, Marti 이모가 글쓴이의 말이 완곡하다고 생각한다는 것은 지문의 내용과 다르다.

어휘 at the moment phr. 지금, 바로 그때
euphemistic adj. 완곡한   advocate v. 지지하다
extreme adj. 극도의

[46-48]

제인 월든(Jane Walen)의 눈이 커졌다. "당신, 마이크(Mike)가 그 일과 관련이 있을 것이라고 의심하는 건 아니죠?"
"음, 제인, 왠지, 경보기를 해제할 수 없는 누군가가 그 경보 시스템을 해제했어요. 당연히 그 암호에 접근할 수 있는 사람에게 의심이 가는 거죠."
제인 월든은 울음을 터뜨릴 듯 보였지만, 그러다 마음을 가라앉혔다. "마이크는 나이가 거의 칠십이에요." "그렇다면 그는 아마도 약간의 비상금이 필요하겠죠. 내가 당신에게 말해주는 것을 가장 엄격하게 비밀로 유지해야 한다는 거 이해하시죠." 그녀는 고개를 끄덕였고 동시에 코를 닦았다. 손대지 않았던 커피를 빠르게 조금씩 홀짝거리며 마셨다.
프랭크(Frank)는 말을 이어갔다. "그리고 누군가가 그 보안 시스템에 어떻게 접근했는지 나에게 설명할 수 있을 때까지, 나에게 가장 타당성 있는 길들을 조사해야 할 겁니다."

have to do with phr. ~와 관련이 있다
disarm v. 무장을 해제하다
have access to phr. ~에 접근할 수 있다, ~을 이용할 수 있다

code n. 암호, 부호, 코드
compose oneself phr. 심란한 마음을 가라앉히다
nest egg phr. 비상금, 밑천   strict adj. 엄격한
confidence n. 신뢰, 자신감, 확신; 비밀
sip v. (음료를) 홀짝이다, 조금씩 마시다
burst n. 갑자기 ~함, 한바탕 ~함
make sense phr. 이치에 맞다, 말이 되다

46 2018 성균관대

정답 ③

해석 ① 용의자   ② 원고
③ 형사   ④ 강도
⑤ 피고

해설 지문에 등장하는 프랭크의 직업이 무엇인지 유추하는 문제이다. 프랭크는 마이크가 경보 시스템을 해제했을 것으로 의심하고 있으며, 마지막 문장에서도 어떻게 보안 시스템에 접근했는지를 조사할 것이라고 했으므로 '형사'라는 것을 알 수 있다. 따라서 ③번이 정답이다.

47 2018 성균관대

정답 ②

해석 ① 피해자를 유혹하기 위한 미끼
② 미래를 위해 저축한 약간의 돈
③ 의지할 만한 가까운 친구
④ 둥지에 남겨 놓은 중요하지 않은 알
⑤ 전에 본 적이 없는 새로운 장치

해설 밑줄 친 nest egg의 의미를 유추하는 문제이다. nest egg는 '비상금, 밑천, 노후 대비를 위해 모은 돈'을 의미하는 관용표현이다. 따라서 ②번이 정답이다.

어휘 bait n. 미끼   sum n. 액수, 금액
marginal adj. 미미한, 중요하지 않은; 주변부의
gadget n. 장치

48 2018 성균관대

정답 ⑤

해석 ① 행위의 이유를 정당화하다
② 사건을 밝혀내다
③ 증거에 반하는 증언을 하다
④ 새로운 목격자를 찾다
⑤ 가능성을 조사하다

해설 밑줄 친 explore the avenues의 의미를 유추하는 문제이다. 어떻게 보안 시스템을 해제했는지 조사하고 있는 형사에게 '여러 개의 길을 탐구하다'라는 말은 '여러 가지 가능성을 조사하다'라는 의미로 볼 수 있다. 따라서 ⑤번이 정답이다.

[49-51]

몇천 년 전에, 사람들은 고대에 존재했던 종류인 밀과 다른 곡물을 납작한 빵을 만들기 위해 모닥불로 달군 뜨거운 바위 위에서 사용했다. 그리고 어느 때엔가, 초기의 요리사들이 그 빵을 접시처럼 이용해서 그 위에 다른 재료들을 얹기 시작했다. 그것이 바로 세계 최초의 피자 크러스트였다!

시간이 흘러, 피자는 우리가 오늘날 알고 있는 음식처럼 보이기 시작했다. 유럽인 탐험가들이 아메리카 대륙에 도착했을 때, 그들은 아메리카 원주민들이 토마토를 먹고 있는 것을 보았다. 하지만, 그들이 (A)그것을 다시 유럽으로 가져갔을 때, 그곳의 사람들은 (B)그것을 먹지 않았다. 유럽인들은 토마토를 먹는 것이 (C)그들을 아프게 만들 수 있다고 생각했다.

하지만, 점차 유럽인들은 토마토가 맛있고 먹어도 안전하다는 것을 알게 되었다. 이탈리아의 도시인 나폴리의 요리사들은 납작한 빵 위에 (D)그것을 올려놓기 시작했다. 진정한 세계 최초의 피자 가게가 1830년 나폴리에 개장했다. 사람들은 피자를 점심과 저녁 식사로 먹었다. 심지어 그들은 피자를 아침 식사로도 먹었다.

ancient adj. 고대의   **grain** n. 곡물, 곡식
flat adj. 납작한, 평평한   **campfire** n. 모닥불
plate n. 접시

49 [2019 한성대]

정답 ②

해석 ① 햄버거   ② 피자
③ 파스타   ④ 샌드위치

해설 지문의 빈칸을 채우는 문제이다. 첫 번째 빈칸의 이전 부분에서 빵을 그릇처럼 사용하여 빵 위에 여러 가지 재료를 올려놓는다고 설명하고 있다. 따라서 '피자'라고 한 ②번이 정답이다.

50 [2019 한성대]

정답 ③

해석 ① 피자는 아메리카 원주민들에게 처음으로 소개되었다.
② 피자는 아메리카 원주민들이 처음으로 만들었다.
③ 토마토는 유럽인들이 아메리카 대륙에 넘어간 다음에야 피자에 넣기 시작했다.
④ 나폴리의 사람들은 아침 식사로 피자를 선호했다.

해설 지문의 내용과 일치하는 것을 묻는 문제이다. 지문의 두 번째 문단과 세 번째 문단에서 When European explorers arrived in the Americas, ~ Cooks in Naples, an Italian city, began putting them on their flat bread 의 내용을 통해 토마토는 유럽인들이 아메리카 대륙에 넘어간 다음에야 피자에 넣기 시작했다는 것을 알 수 있다. 따라서 ③번이 지문의 내용과 일치한다.

오답 분석
① 세계 최초의 피자 가게가 1830년 나폴리에 개장했다고 했으므로, 피자는 아메리카 원주민들에게 처음으로 소개되었다는 것은 지문의 내용과 다르다.
② 나폴리의 요리사들이 납작한 빵 위에 토마토를 올려놓기 시작했다고 했으므로, 피자는 아메리카 원주민들이 처음으로 만들었다는 것은 지문의 내용과 다르다.
④ 나폴리의 사람들이 피자를 심지어 아침 식사로도 먹는다고는 했지만, 나폴리의 사람들은 아침 식사로 피자를 선호했는지는 알 수 없다.

어휘 **introduce** v. 소개하다   **invent** v. 발명하다
prefer v. 선호하다

51 [2019 한성대]

정답 ③

해설 지문에서 지시하는 대상이 다른 것을 고르는 문제이다. 지문의 는 유럽인이며 나머지 (A), (B), (D)는 모두 토마토를 지칭한다. 따라서 유럽인을 나타내는 ③번 (C)가 정답이다.

[52-54]

Louise는 근육위축병으로 고통받고 있다. 어느 날 기차역을 빠져나가기를 시도하던 중에, Louise는 그녀 자신이 에스컬레이터나 엘리베이터가 없는 곳에서 엄청난 높이의 한 줄로 이어진 계단을 마주했음을 발견했다. 울음이 터져 나오려 했지만, Louise는 한 여자가 갑자기 나타나 Louise의 가방을 들고, 친절하게 그녀가 계단을 올라갈 수 있도록 도와주는 것을 목격했다. Louise가 그녀에게 고마움을 표하기 위해 돌아섰을 때, 그녀는 이미 사라졌었다. Michael은 회의에 늦은 상황이었다. 이미 깨져버린 관계로 인해 스트레스를 받고 있던, Michael은 오로지 터진 타이어로 인해 런던의 차량들과 싸움을 시작하고 있었다. 그는 어찌해 볼 수도 없이 빗속에서 서 있었는데, 한 남자가 군중에게서 나와, 트렁크를 열고, 차를 잭으로 들어 올리더니, 타이어를 바꿨다. Michael이 고마움을 표하기 위해 돌아섰을 때, 그는 이미 사라졌었다. 이런 신비한 도움을 주는 사람은 누구인가: 친절한 낯선 사람일까 아니면 그 이상의 무엇일까? 우리가 천사에 대해 가지고 있는 날개가 있고 밝게 빛나는 사람이라는 대중적인 이미지는 반만 사실이다. 일부는 이런 방식으로 나타나지만, 또 다른 몇몇은 더러운 발과 함께 나타나 일반 사람들이 오해하기 쉽게 만든다. 우리는 Louise와 Michael을 도운 사람들이 천사인지 아닌지 알 수 없지만, 그들은 천사일 수도 있었다. 천사들은 지금 일을 하고 있고, 그들은 길 위의 사람들만큼이나 평범한 모습일 수 있다.

muscular dystrophy phr. 근육위축병
a flight of stairs phr. 한 줄로 이어진 계단
on the verge of phr. 막 ~하려는   **suddenly** adv. 갑자기
traffic n. (특정 시간대의) 차량들
flat tire phr. 바람 빠진 타이어

helplessly adv. 어찌할 수도 없이
jack up phr. 잭으로 들어 올리다   mysterious adj. 신비한
radiant adj. 빛이 나는   winged adj. 날개가 있는
creature n. 사람, 생물   mistake v. 오해하다

52 [2020 한국외대]

정답 ③

해석 ① 악마들은 괴로움을 가지고 오고, 천사들은 그것들을 없앤다.
② 사회가 변화함에 따라, 천사에 대한 개념도 변화한다.
③ 천사들은 우리의 일상생활에 아주 다양한 형태로 나타난다.
④ 천사들은 고통의 순간에 나타나는 빛나는 사람이다.

해설 지문의 주제를 묻는 문제이다. 지문 전체적으로 우리가 천사에 대해 가지고 있는 대중적인 이미지와는 달리, 천사는 길 위의 일반적인 사람들과 같은 모습으로 나타나 사람을 돕는 존재임을 알 수 있다. 따라서 이 지문의 주제를 '천사들은 우리의 일상생활에 아주 다양한 형태로 나타난다'고 표현한 ③번이 정답이다.

어휘 distress n. 고통   concept n. 개념

53 [2020 한국외대]

정답 ①

해석 ① 초자연적인 존재로서
② 좋은 소식의 전조로써
③ 고통을 받는 이들을 돕는 존재로서
④ 인간과 비인간의 후원자로서

해설 밑줄 친 this way의 의미를 추론하는 문제이다. 밑줄 this way가 있는 문장의 앞에서 우리가 천사에 대해 가지고 있는 날개가 있고 빛나는 사람이라는 대중적인 이미지에 관해 설명하고 있다. 따라서 this way의 의미를 '초자연적인 존재로서'라고 한 ①번이 정답이다.

어휘 supernatural adj. 초자연적인   herald n. 전조
benefactor n. 후원자

54 [2020 한국외대]

정답 ③

해석 ① 광채가 빛날 수 있을 만큼 빛나는
② 누군가 천사들을 보기를 바라는 만큼 종종
③ 길 위의 사람들만큼 평범한
④ 종교적인 성서에서 이야기될 만큼 기적적인

해설 지문의 빈칸을 채우는 문제이다. 빈칸이 포함된 지문의 앞 문장에서 어떤 천사들은 더러운 발과 함께 나타나 일반 사람들이 오해하기 쉽게 만든다고 했으므로, 사람들의 오해를 살 수 있을 만큼 천사들이 평범한 모습일 수 있다는 것을 알 수 있다. 따라서 '길 위의 사람들만큼 평범한'이라고 한 ③번이 정답이다.

어휘 ordinary adj. 평범한   miraculously adv. 기적적으로
religious adj. 종교적인   scripture n. 성경

[55-56]

예비 학회 행사
고성능 직물 섬유 개별 지도 시간
3월 6일, 화요일 오후 2시~5시 15분
발표자: 텍사스 테크 대학교 부직포&신소재 연구소 및 신소재학과 교수 Seshardri Ramkumar 박사
고성능 직물은 기본적으로 의류 소재의 일반적인 특성에 더하여 직물에 부가 가치를 주는 기능성 직물이다. 그 기능은 시재료인 섬유, 구조적 측면, 그리고 최종 생성물로 전해지는 마무리 과정으로 획득된다.
이 개별 지도 시간에는 가장 기본이 되는 특징에 초점을 맞출 것인데, 이것은 신 섬유제품의 원자재이다. 세미나는 특히 직물과 공업용 직물에 대한 기초적인 이해가 있는 사람들뿐만 아니라 이 분야의 초보자들에게도 맞춰져 있다. 다룰 주제 영역은 고성능 직물의 개요, 섬유의 분류, 서로 다른 기능을 제공하는 섬유, 이성분 섬유, 지속 가능성 측면, 미세와 나노 구조의 섬유 등과 같은 3차원 구조의 섬유가 제공하는 기능을 포함할 것이다.
개별 지도 시간은 학회 등록에 포함되지 않는다. 학회에 참석하는 사람들은 할인된 개별 지도 시간 등록비로 이용 가능할 것이다.

conference n. 학회   high performance phr. 고성능
nonwoven n. 부직포   laboratory n. 연구소
functional adj. 기능성의   attribute n. 특성
impart v. 전하다   pillar n. 기본적인 특징
industrial adj. 공업용   sustainability n. 지속 가능성
registration n. 등록

55 [2019 단국대]

정답 ②

해석 ① 의류 회사의 회계사
② 섬유재 연구자
③ 에너지 공장에서 일하는 근로자
④ 유치원에서 일하는 선생님

해설 이 정보에 가장 흥미를 느낄 사람이 누구인지 파악하는 문제이다. 지문 전체적으로 고성능 직물 섬유에 관한 개별 지도 시간을 안내하고 있으므로, 이 정보에 가장 흥미를 느낄 사람은 '섬유재 연구자'이다. 따라서 정답은 ②번이다.

어휘 accountant n. 회계사   engage in phr. ~에 종사하다

56 2019 단국대

정답 ②

해석
① 개별 지도는 학회 이후에 이루어질 것이다.
② 학회 참가자들은 개별 지도에 대해 정식 요금보다 적게 청구될 것이다.
③ 예비 학회 행사는 이틀 동안 열릴 것이다.
④ 사람들은 개별 지도 행사와 학회 발표 모두에 참여할 수 없다.

해설 지문의 내용과 일치하는 것을 묻는 문제이다. 지문의 마지막 문장 A discounted ~ the conference의 내용을 통해 학회 참가자들은 개별 지도에 대해 정식 요금보다 적게 청구될 것임을 알 수 있다. 따라서 ②번이 지문의 내용과 일치한다.

오답분석
① 예비 학회 행사라고 했으므로, 개별 지도는 학회 이후에 이루어진다는 것은 지문의 내용과 다르다.
③ 3월 6일, 화요일 오후 2시~5시 15분에 진행된다고 했으므로, 예비 학회 행사가 이틀 동안 열린다는 것은 지문의 내용과 다르다.
④ 학회에 참석하는 사람들은 할인된 개별 지도 시간 등록비로 이용 가능할 것이라고 했으므로, 사람들이 개별 지도 행사와 학회 발표 모두에 참여할 수 없다는 것은 지문의 내용과 다르다.

어휘 charge v. 청구하다   take part in phr. 참여하다

[57-58]

간 소고기는 아주 옛날부터 빵의 어떠한 형태든지 함께 제공되었을 수도 있지만, 그것을 햄버거라고 하지는 않는다. 햄버거는 소고기 패티같이 생긴, 일반적으로 "햄버거 번"이라고 불리는 의도적으로 구워진 빵을 사용하는 것에 의해서 정의된다. 당신은 이 조합에 원하는 만큼 많은 토핑을 추가하거나 무수한 방법으로 소고기를 요리할 수 있으며, 그렇게 하더라도 그것은 여전히 햄버거일 것이다. 하지만 빵을 바꾸거나 다른 종류의 고기를 사용한다면 당신은 햄버거가 아닌 다른 무엇인가를 먹게 된다.
우리가 오늘날 즐기고 있는 현대의 햄버거는 1916년에 캔자스주의 위치타에서 Walter A. Anderson이 소고기 패티와 그것을 사이에 끼우기 위해 만들어진 주문 제작한 빵을 조합하면서 처음으로 시작되었다. 사실, Anderson이 Edgar Waldo Ingram과 제휴하여 White Castle을 창립한 1921년까지 그 요리는 단지 다른 종류의 샌드위치에 불과했다.
이 식당에서는 햄버거가 분명하고 일반적으로 분간이 가는 미국 요리로 상품화되고 표준화되었다. 현대의 햄버거를 만드는 것 외에도, White Castle은 모든 패스트푸드 체인점이 등장할 수 있도록 청사진을 만들면서 최초의 패스트푸드 "체계"를 마련하였다. 햄버거는 White Castle 이전에도 식당 메뉴에 존재했지만, 그것은 샌드위치 구역 안에 적혀있었다. White Castle 이후에, 햄버거는 메뉴에 그것 자체의 구역을 가지고 다른 샌드위치들과 분리되었고 구분되게 되었다.

첫 번째 햄버거는 크기가 작았는데, 소고기는 2에서 3온스 정도였다. 하지만 그것은 발전이 없는 채로 남아있지 않았다. 혁신은 신속하고 빠르게 찾아왔다. 통설로는 최초의 치즈버거는 캘리포니아주의 패서디나에 있는 Rite Spot에서 "치즈 햄버거"로서 1926년에 만들어졌다.
제2차 세계 대전 후, 국가는 값싼 소고기와 값싼 강철뿐만 아니라 급성장하는 주와 주 사이의 고속도로 체계의 폭발적인 증가를 누렸다. 이것은 햄버거가 공업단지를 벗어나 시내 중심가로 이동할 수 있게 했다. 전쟁 후에 등장한 햄버거는 그것이 더 커지고 더 다양해짐으로써 미국의 급속한 성장을 말해 주었다.

grind v. 갈다, 빻다
since time immemorial phr. 아주 옛날부터
purposefully adv. 의도적으로, 목적성 있게
universally adv. 일반적으로, 보편적으로   **bun** n. 번, 빵
patty n. 패티, 고기 반죽   **combination** n. 조합
a myriad of phr. 무수한, 수많은
conceive v. 시작하다, 일으키다   **encapsulate** v. 압축하다
partner v. 제휴하다; n. 동반자, 짝   **found** v. 설립하다
commoditize v. 상품화하다   **standardize** v. 표준화하다
recognizable adj. 분간이 가는, 인식 가능한
blueprint n. 청사진   **ounce** n. 온스 (무게의 단위)
stagnant adj. 발전이 없는, 침체된
reputedly adv. 통설로는, 소문에 의하면
explosion n. 폭발적인 증가, 폭발   **burgeon** v. 급성장하다
interstate adj. 주와 주 사이의, 주간의
industrial park phr. 공업단지
emerge v. 등장하다, 나타나다

57 2019 인하대

정답 ④

해석
① 유행에서 뒤처진
② 좀 더 유럽적인
③ 지역적이고 고립된
④ 더 크고 더 다양한
⑤ 햄버거와는 다른 무언가

해설 지문의 빈칸을 채우는 문제이다. 지문의 마지막에서 두 번째 단락에서 햄버거는 발전이 없는 채로 남아있지 않고 혁신이 신속하게 찾아왔으며 최초로 치즈버거가 만들어졌다고 했으므로, 빈칸에는 햄버거의 모습이 혁신적으로 바뀌는 내용이 나와야 적절하다는 것을 알 수 있다. 따라서 '더 크고 더 다양한'이라고 한 ④번이 정답이다.

어휘 out of fashion phr. 유행에서 뒤처진, 구닥다리의
isolated adj. 고립된, 격리된

58 2019 인하대

정답 ②

해석
① 옥수수빵 위에 닭가슴살을 얹은 것은 햄버거라고 불릴 수 있다.

② White Castle은 햄버거의 역사상 중요한 부분을 차지하고 있다.
③ 햄버거는 1916년에 메뉴에서 햄버거 구역에 적혀있었다.
④ Walter A. Anderson과 Edgar Waldo Ingram이 최초의 치즈버거를 만들었다.
⑤ 미국 사람들은 전쟁 후에 가난하고 굶주렸다.

해설 지문의 내용과 일치하는 것을 묻는 문제이다. 지문의 두 번째 단락의 마지막 문장 문장에서 Anderson이 Edgar Waldo Ingram과 함께 제휴를 맺어 White Castle을 설립하기 이전까지는 햄버거가 단지 다른 종류의 샌드위치에 불과했다는 내용을 통해 White Castle이 햄버거의 역사상 중요한 부분을 차지하고 있다는 것을 알 수 있다. 따라서 ②번이 지문의 내용과 일치한다.

오답 분석
① 소고기 패티와 햄버거 번이 아닌 다른 종류의 고기와 빵을 사용한다면 햄버거가 아니라고 했으므로, 옥수수 식빵 위에 닭가슴살을 얹은 것이 햄버거라고 불릴 수 있다는 것은 지문의 내용과 다르다.
③ 1921년에 White Castle이 창립되고 나서 햄버거가 다른 샌드위치들과 분리되어 적혔다고 했으므로, 햄버거가 1916년에 메뉴에서 햄버거 구역에 적혀있었다는 것은 지문의 내용과 다르다.
④ 최초의 치즈버거는 1926년 캘리포니아주의 패서디나에 있는 Rite Spot에서 만들었다고 했으므로, Anderson과 Ingram이 최초의 치즈버거를 만들었다는 것은 지문의 내용과 다르다.
⑤ 제2차 세계 대전 후에 미국이 값싼 소고기와 값싼 강철의 폭발적인 증가를 누렸다고 했으므로, 미국 사람들이 전쟁 후에 가난하고 굶주렸다는 것은 지문의 내용과 다르다.

어휘 **chicken breast** phr. 닭가슴살 **starved** adj. 굶주린

[59-61]

월드컵 경기 중, 인기 축구선수 Alex Morgan의 차 마시기 승리의 춤에 대한 논쟁은 차츰 잦아들었지만, 그것은 영국의 두 번째로 고지식한 신문인 *The Times of London*지 구독자들 사이에서 영국인들을 오랫동안 괴롭혀온 문제에 대한 논쟁을 재점화했다: 차를 찻잔에 부을 때, 무엇을 먼저 부어야 하는가? 차인가? 아니면 우유인가?
편집장에게 보내진 결투 편지는 7월 4일에 시작하였는데, 브라이턴에 사는 Bob Maddams는 미국의 축구 선수인 Ms Morgan이 우유를 먼저 붓는지 아닌지에 대해 말로 나타내며 골똘히 생각했다. 이것은 서리에 사는 Tom Howe의 답장을 이끌었고, 이것은 7월 5일에 다음과 같이 실렸다:
"편집장님, 여자 월드컵에서 *Alex Morgan*의 차 마시기 세리머니에 대한 *Bob Maddams*의 편지(7월 4일)는 우유를 먼저 넣는 것이 옳다는 것을 암시합니다. 저는 우유가 첫 번째냐 두 번째냐에 대한 질문은 본래 사회적 지위의 표시였다고 항상 믿게 되었습니다. 값싼 자기는 뜨거운 차가 부어지면 갈라졌기 때문에, 우유가 온도를 낮추고 그러한 참사를 피하기 위해 먼저 부어져야 했죠."

Mr Howe의 편지는 독자들을 매우 폭발시켰다. 7월 6일 *The Times*지는 한 개가 아닌 네 개의 답장을 실었다. 레스터셔에 사는 Peter Sergeant는 "차는 자기를 얼룩지게 하므로, 우유를 먼저 넣으면 이것이 완화됩니다."라고 적었다. 두 번째 답장은 옥스퍼드에서 왔으며, 우유가 얼마나 필요한지 결정하기 위해 차가 먼저 부어져야 한다고 주장했다. 세 번째 답장은 보스턴 차 사건을 언급했다. 그리고 서리에 사는 Catherine Money에게서 온 네 번째 답장은 "우유 먼저"의 약어뿐만 아니라, 사회적 계급의 중요한 문화적 맥락을 제공했다.

그녀는 "편집장님, *Tom Howe*는 차를 붓기 전 컵에 우유를 붓는 것으로 전해지는 메시지를 기억한 점에서 옳습니다. 누군가를 "*오히려 MIF*"라고 묘사하는 것은 알아야 할 모든 것을 말해줬죠."라고 썼다.

영국 신문들에서 편지란은 민감한 도구인데, 이것은 국가의 중심지에서 나오는 실망의 물결을 감지하는 데 사용될 수 있다. 예를 들어, 옥스퍼드 주간 신문의 편집장은 올봄에 편집장에게 보내는 편지의 호칭 형태인 "Sir"를 단계적으로 없애기로 했고, 험악한 편지들이 너무 쇄도하여 그는 즉시 <u>그 결정</u>을 되돌렸다.

controversy n. 논쟁 **die down** phr. 차츰 잦아들다
reignite v. 재점화하다 **starchy** adj. 고지식한
broadsheet n. 보통 사이즈의 신문 **duel** n. 결투
muse v. 골똘히 생각하다 **standing** n. 지위
porcelain n. 자기 **disaster** n. 참사
set off phr. ~을 폭발시키다 **stain** v. 얼룩지게 하다
mitigate v. 완화시키다 **context** n. 맥락
acronym n. 약어 **recollection** n. 기억 **dismay** n. 실망
emanate from phr. ~에서 나오다 **heartland** n. 중심지
phase out phr. 단계적으로 폐지하다 **address** n. 호칭
inundate with phr. ~가 쇄도하다 **promptly** adv. 즉시
reverse v. 되돌리다

59 [2020 성균관대]

정답 ③

해석 ① Bob Maddams ② Tom Howe
③ 두 번째 답장 ④ 네 번째 답장
⑤ Peter Sergent

해설 '우유 먼저' 넣는 것이 옳지 않다고 주장한 사람을 파악하는 문제이다. 네 번째 문단에서 두 번째 답장은 우유가 얼마나 필요한지 결정하기 위해 차가 먼저 부어져야 한다고 주장했다고 했으므로, '우유 먼저' 넣는 것이 옳지 않다고 주장한 사람은 '두 번째 답장'을 쓴 사람이다. 따라서 정답은 ③번이다.

60 [2020 성균관대]

정답 ②

해석
① 우유를 먼저 붓는 것
② "Sir" 표현을 사용하지 않는 것
③ 편집장에게 보내는 편지란을 없애는 것
④ 편지 작성자들 중 한 명의 편을 들지 않기
⑤ 편집장에게 보내는 편지에 답장하지 않기

해설 밑줄 친 the decision의 의미를 추론하는 문제이다. 지문의 마지막 문장에서 옥스퍼드 주간 신문의 편집장은 편집장에게 보내는 편지의 호칭 형태인 "Sir"를 단계적으로 없애기로 했고, 험악한 편지들이 너무 쇄도하여 그는 즉시 그 결정을 되돌렸다고 했다. 따라서, the decision의 의미를 '"Sir" 표현을 사용하지 않는 것'이라고 한 ②번이 정답이다.

어휘 take sides phr. 편을 들다

61 [2020 성균관대]

정답 ④

해석
① 예의를 알고 있던 상류층
② 차 문화를 즐길 여유가 있던 부자들
③ 중국식 자기를 사용하던 왕실
④ 값싼 찻잔을 사용하던 빈민들
⑤ 우유보다 차를 더 많이 마시던 중산층

해설 Catherine Money에 따르면, 소위 MIF는 무엇을 지칭하는 것인지 파악하는 문제이다. 세 번째 문단에서 값싼 자기는 뜨거운 차가 부어지면 갈라졌기 때문에, 우유가 온도를 낮추고 그러한 참사를 피하기 위해 먼저 부어져야 했다고 했으므로, 소위 MIF는 '값싼 찻잔을 사용하던 빈민들'을 지칭한다. 따라서 정답은 ④번이다.

어휘 upper class phr. 상류층   royal family phr. 왕실
porcelain n. 자기   middle class phr. 중산층

[62-64]

고독을 느끼기 위해, 인간은 사회뿐 아니라 자신만의 공간에서도 물러날 필요가 있다. 나는 내가 글을 읽고 쓰는 동안 아무도 나와 함께 있지 않아도 외롭지 않다. 하지만 만약 혼자 있으려고 하는 사람이 있다면, 그 사람에게 별을 보게 해주어라. 하늘로부터 내려오는 별빛은 그 사람과 그가 만지는 것을 떨어지게 해줄 것이다. 누군가는 영원한 숭고함의 존재인 천체가 인간에게 주려는 의도로 대기를 투명하게 했다고 생각할지도 모른다. 만약 그 별들이 천 년에 한 번만 나타난다면, 사람들은 어떻게 믿음을 가지고 그것을 숭배할 것이며, 많은 세대 동안 신이 보여준 신의 도시에 대한 추억을 간직할 것인가! 하지만 이 아름다움의 특사인 별은 매일 밤 나와서, 타이르는 듯한 미소를 띤 채로 우주를 비춘다.

그 별들은 항상 존재하지만 접근하기는 어렵기 때문에 숭배하는 마음을 일깨운다. 하지만 모든 자연물들은 우리가 그것들의 신비로운 힘을 순순히 받아들일 때 비슷한 느낌을 준다. 자연은 절대 인색한 모습을 하지 않는다. 가장 지혜로운 사람은 자연의 비밀을 빼앗는 것이 아니며, 자연의 완벽함을 발견하여 자신의 호기심을 잃는 것도 아니다. 자연은 절대 지혜로운 사람에게 장난감 같은 존재가 되지 않았다. 꽃, 동물, 산은 지혜로운 사람의 어린 시절을 즐겁게 했으며, 그의 가장 좋은 시기에 그에게 지혜를 보여주었다.

우리가 자연에 대해 이런 식으로 말하면, 우리는 마음속에 분명하면서도 시적인 감각을 가지게 된다. 우리는 여러 가지 자연물로 만들어진 완전한 상태를 의미하는 것이다. 그것은 나무꾼의 나무 한 토막과 시인의 나무를 구별해주는 것이다. 내가 오늘 아침에 봤던 멋진 풍경은 틀림없이 20-30개의 농장으로 이루어진 것이었다. Miller가 이 농장을 소유하고, Locke는 저 농장, Manning은 그 너머에 삼림 지대를 소유한다. 하지만 Miller, Locke, Manning 중 아무도 그 멋진 풍경을 소유한 것은 아니다. 그 범위 내에 모든 부분들을 완성할 수 있는 눈을 가진 사람, 즉 시인의 것을 제외하고는 아무도 가질 수 없는 소유물이 존재한다. 이 풍경은 이 사람들의 농장에서 가장 좋은 부분이지만, 그들의 하자 담보 증서와 같은 토지 관련 계약서에는 이 땅에 대한 소유권이 나와 있지 않다.

---

solitude n. 고독, 외로움   retire v. 물러나다
chamber n. 공간   whilst conj. ~ 동안
solitary adj. 외로운, 혼자의   ray n. 빛
heavenly adj. 하늘의   separate v. 떨어지다, 분리하다
atmosphere n. 공기, 대기
transparent adj. 투명한, 빛을 통과시키는
design n. 의도, 계획   heavenly body phr. 천체
perpetual adj. 영원한, 끊임없이 계속되는
presence n. 존재   sublime n. 숭고한 것
adore v. 숭배하다, 아주 좋아하다   preserve v. 간직하다
generation n. 세대   remembrance n. 추억
envoy n. 특사, 사절   admonish adj. 타이르는
reverence n. 숭배   inaccessible adj. 접근하기 어려운
natural object phr. 자연물   kindred adj. 비슷한
impression n. 느낌, 인상
be open to phr. ~을 순순히 받아들이다
influence n. (별의) 신비로운 힘, 영향
mean adj. 인색한, 비열한   extort v. 빼앗다, 강탈하다
perfection n. 완벽, 완성   spirit n. 사람, 영혼
delight v. 즐겁게 하다   simplicity n. 순박함, 소박함, 단순함
childhood n. 어린 시절   in this manner phr. 이런 식으로
distinct adj. 분명한, 뚜렷한   poetical adj. 시적인
integrity n. 완전한 상태, 진실성, 온전함
manifold adj. 여러 가지의   distinguish v. 구별하다
wood-cutter n. 나무꾼
indubitably adv. 틀림없이, 의심할 여지 없이
woodland n. 삼림 지대   beyond adv. 그 너머에
property n. 소유물, 재산   horizon n. 범위, 지평선
integrate v. 완성하다, 통합하다
warranty-deed n. 하자 담보 증서
title n. (특히 부동산) 소유권

62 [2019 홍익대]

정답 ③

해석
① 별을 보기 위한 혼자만의 시간을 갖는 것
② 시인의 관찰력을 갖기 위해 자신을 훈련하는 것
③ 자신이 여러 개의 농장을 소유하도록 보장하는 것
④ 자연의 완벽함에 대한 호기심을 유지하는 것

해설 자연을 감상하는 방법이 아닌 것을 묻는 문제이다. ③번의 키워드인 farms(농장)와 관련된 지문의 세 번째 문단에서 이 풍경은 이 사람들의 농장에서 가장 좋은 부분이지만, 그들의 하자 담보 증서와 같은 토지 관련 계약서에는 이 땅에 대한 소유권이 나와 있지 않다고 했으므로, 자신이 여러 개의 농장의 소유하도록 보장하는 것이 자연을 감상하는 방법인지는 알 수 없다. 따라서 ③번이 지문의 내용과 일치하지 않는다.

오답분석
① 첫 번째 문단 But if a man would be alone, let him look at the stars를 통해 '별을 보기 위한 혼자만의 시간을 갖는 것'이 자연을 감상하는 방법이라는 것을 알 수 있다.
② 세 번째 문단 When we speak of nature in this manner, we have a distinct but most poetical sense in the mind를 통해 '시인의 관찰력을 갖기 위해 자신을 훈련하는 것'이 자연을 감상하는 방법이라는 것을 알 수 있다.
④ 두 번째 문단 Neither does the wisest man extort her secret, and lose his curiosity by finding out all her perfection을 통해 '자연의 완벽함에 대한 호기심을 유지하는 것'이 자연을 감상하는 방법이라는 것을 알 수 있다.

어휘 possession n. 소유

63 [2019 홍익대]

정답 ①

해석
① 별들은 아름다움의 특사에 비유된다.
② 지혜로운 사람은 자연을 장난감 같은 것으로 여긴다.
③ 시인의 나무는 나무꾼의 나무만큼 소중하다.
④ 별들은 접근하기 더 어려울수록, 더 숭고해진다.

해설 지문의 내용과 일치하는 것을 묻는 문제이다. 첫 번째 문단에서 아름다움의 특사인 별은 매일 밤 나와서, 타이르는 듯한 미소를 띤 채로 우주를 비춘다는 내용을 통해 별들이 아름다움의 특사에 비유된다는 것을 알 수 있다. 따라서 ①번이 지문의 내용과 일치한다.

오답분석
② 첫 번째 문단에서 자연은 절대 지혜로운 사람에게 장난감 같은 존재가 되지 않았다고 했으므로, 지혜로운 사람이 자연을 장난감 같은 것으로 여긴다는 것은 지문의 내용과 다르다.
③ 세 번째 문단에서 나무꾼의 나무 한 토막과 시인의 나무를 구별해주는 것이라고는 했지만, 시인의 나무가 나무꾼의 나무만큼 소중한지는 알 수 없다.
④ 두 번째 문단에서 별들은 항상 존재하지만 접근하기는 어렵기 때문에 숭배하는 마음을 일깨운다고는 했지만, 별들이 접근하기 더 어려울수록, 더 숭고해지는지는 알 수 없다.

어휘 liken to phr. ~에 비유하다 valuable adj. 소중한, 귀중한 inaccessible adj. 접근하기 어려운

64 [2019 홍익대]

정답 ④

해석
① 독자들에게 천체의 감춰진 규칙을 알려주기 위해
② 독자들이 조용히 은거하도록 설득하기 위해
③ 독자들이 환경 운동에 참여하도록 장려하기 위해
④ 독자들에게 자연의 경이로운 가치를 상기시키기 위해

해설 지문의 목적을 묻는 문제이다. 지문 초반에서 고독을 느끼기 위해, 인간은 사회뿐 아니라 자신만의 공간에서도 물러날 필요가 있다고 하면서, 별과 같은 자연물을 예찬하고 있다. 따라서 이 지문의 목적을 '독자들에게 자연의 경이로운 가치를 상기시키기 위해'라고 표현한 ④번이 정답이다.

어휘 hidden adj. 감춰진, 비밀의
go into retirement phr. 은거하다, 은퇴하다
movement n. 운동

[65-67]

Annette Poitras가 숨이 차고 멍한 상태로 정신이 들었을 때, 두 쌍의 개의 눈이 다시 그녀의 눈을 자세히 들여다보고 있었다. 몇 분 전인가, 아니면 몇 시간 전인가? 그 전문 개 산책 도우미는 그녀의 집에서 10분 거리에 있는 이글 산을 가로질러 굽이치는 익숙한 자갈길을 따라 열심히 나아가고 있었다. 그녀는 세 마리를 담당이 있었는데, Roxy(독일종의 개 복서), Bubba(13살짜리 퍼글) 그리고 Chloe이다. 4인조가 그 몸통이 맥주 통처럼 굵고, 흠뻑 젖은 이끼가 1미터 아래까지 광활하게 뻗어있는 쓰러진 나무를 우연히 마주쳤을 때 Poitras는 그것을 건너가기 위해 기어올랐다. 그날 아침, 빗속을 산책한 후, 그녀는 흠뻑 젖은 등산화를 고무장화와 바꿔 신었었다. 그녀는 미끄러운 나무를 발로 밟으면서 통나무에 쾅 하고 부딪히며 미끄러졌다. 내려가는 길에 머리를 부딪쳐 Poitras는 아래쪽의 숲 바닥으로 곤두박질쳐 있었다.

이제, 그녀가 땅바닥에 누워 있을 때 왼쪽 겨드랑이에서부터 종아리까지 줄곧 통증이 뿜어져 나왔고 그녀는 갈비뼈에 금이 갔는지 어지러울 정도로 궁금했다. 그녀는 일어서서 다시 단단한 지형에 오를 수 있었기 때문에 허리는 부러지지 않았다고 생각했다. 그녀의 옆쪽에 가죽끈이 풀어져 있는 Roxy와 Chloe를 지나 주위를 둘러보며, Poitras는 Bubba가 달아났다는 것을 깨달았다. 그녀는 지금이 몇 시인지, 얼마 동안이나 의식을 잃고 있었는지 몰랐다. 하지만 산을 내려오기 전에 그 퍼글을 찾아야 한다는 것은 알고 있었다. 그녀는 그 개들을 아주 좋아했고 한 마리를 두고 가는 것은 상상도 할 수 없는 일이었다.

```
winded    adj. 숨이 찬, 바람을 쐰     dazed    adj. 멍한, 아찔한
canine    adj. 개의      peer into    phr. 자세히 들여다보다
professional    adj. 전문적인
dog-walker    n. 개를 산책시키는 사람
work one's way    phr. 일하면서 나아가다    gravel    n. 자갈
trail    n. 오솔길    snake    v. (길 등이) 굽이치며 이어지다
charge    n. 담당, 임무, 과제    quartet    n. 4인조
come across    phr. 우연히 마주치다    barrel    n. 통, 맥주 통
soggy    adj. 흠뻑 젖은    moss    n. 이끼
clamber    v. 기어오르다, 기어가다    gum-boot    n. 고무장화
tread on    phr. 밟다    slick    adj. 미끄러운
slip    v. 미끄러지다    slam into    phr. ~에 쾅 하고 충돌하다
log    n. 통나무    plummet    v. 곤두박질치다, 떨어지다
armpit    n. 겨드랑이    all the way    phr. 줄곧, 처음부터 끝까지
calf    n. 종아리    wonder    v. 궁금해하다
dizzily    adv. 어지럽게, 아찔하게    crack    v. 금이 가게 하다
figure    v. 생각하다, 판단하다    terrain    n. 지형, 지대
unleash    v. ~의 가죽끈을 풀다, 해방하다
look around    phr. 주위를 둘러보다, 돌아보다
bolt    v. 달아나다    knock out    phr. 의식을 잃게 만들다
adore    v. 아주 좋아하다    leave behind    phr. 두고 가다
unthinkable    adj. 상상도 할 수 없는
```

65 [2020 국민대]

정답 ①

해설 지문의 빈칸에 들어갈 수 없는 것을 고르는 문제이다. 지문의 후반에서 그녀는 얼마 동안이나 의식을 잃고 있었는지 모른다고 했으므로, 빈칸에는 의식이 돌아왔다는 내용이 나와야 적절하다는 것을 알 수 있다. 따라서 '~을 맡아 하다'라는 의미의 ①번이 정답이다.

어휘 come to   phr. 의식을 회복하다, 정신이 들다
come round   phr. 정신이 돌아오다, 바꾸다

66 [2020 국민대]

정답 ①

해석 ① 젖은 — 묶이지 않은
② 그슬린 — 남겨진
③ 견고한 — 해방된
④ 닳아서 해진 — 안도한

해설 soaked(흠뻑 젖은)와 비슷한 의미를 가진 어휘를 묻고 있다. ①번 wet은 '젖은', ②번 seared는 '그슬린', ③번 sturdy는 '견고한', ④번 worn out은 '닳아서 해진'이라는 의미이다. unleashed(가죽끈이 풀어진)와 비슷한 의미를 가진 어휘를 묻고 있다. ①번 untied는 '묶이지 않은', ②번 left는 '남겨진', ③번 set loose는 '해방된', ④번 relieved는 '안도한'이라는 의미이다. 따라서 ①번이 정답이다.

67 [2020 국민대]

정답 ①

해석 ① Poitras의 사고를 일으킨 것은 그녀의 장화였다.
② Poitras는 그녀가 갈비뼈에 금이 간 것을 깨닫지 못했다.
③ Poitras가 의식을 잃은 동안, 그녀 소유의 개는 도망쳤다.
④ Poitras의 직업윤리는 그녀가 실종된 개 없이는 내려오지 못하게 했다.

해설 지문의 내용과 일치하는 것을 묻는 문제이다. 지문의 중간에서 그날 아침에 Poitras가 등산화를 고무장화로 바꿔 신었고, 미끄러운 나무를 밟아 미끄러졌다는 내용을 통해 Poitras의 사고를 일으킨 것은 그녀의 장화였다는 것을 알 수 있다. 따라서 ①번이 지문의 내용과 일치한다.

오답분석
② 갈비뼈에 금이 갔는지 어지러울 정도로 Poitras가 궁금했다고는 했지만, 그녀가 갈비뼈에 금이 간 것을 깨닫지 못했는지는 알 수 없다.
③ Poitras가 전문 개 산책 도우미라고 했으므로, 도망친 개가 그녀의 소유라는 것은 지문의 내용과 다르다.
④ Poitras가 그 개들을 아주 좋아했고 한 마리를 두고 가는 것은 상상도 할 수 없는 일이었다고 했으므로, 직업윤리가 실종된 개 없이는 그녀가 내려오지 못하게 했다는 것은 지문의 내용과 다르다.

어휘 unconscious   adj. 의식을 잃은   ethic   n. 윤리, 도덕

[68-69]

*Knorr*는 280피트짜리 선박으로, 교대 근무 하는 동료들, 재정상의 후원자들뿐만 아니라 30명의 기술자, 과학자, 그리고 학자들이 거기에 머물고 있으며, 보기 좋지는 않더라도 임시적으로 사용하고 있는 거처인데, 연구 비자가 없어 지정된 임무를 하지 못한 채, 터키 북부의 도시 Sinop의 부두에 지난 48시간 동안 묶여있다. 미국 선박과 선원들은 고대의 난파선을 조사하기 위해 흑해로 왔지만, 현지 언론은 회의적이다. 기자들 무리는 낮 동안 돌로 된 부두를 오르락내리락 움직이면서 부르면 닿을 듯한 거리에 있는 갑판 위의 아무에게나 카메라를 들이밀고 질문을 한다.
"여기에 정말로 왜 오신 거죠? 기름을 찾고 있는 건가요? 미군의 비밀 임무를 맡으셨나요? 노아의 방주를 찾는 건가요?" 수백 명의 주민들이, 직접 보고 싶어서, 그들의 역사상 유명한 성곽 도시의 만에서 떴다 잠겼다 하는 첨단 기술의 하이테크 제품으로 채워진 큰 배에 경탄하며 멋진 7월 말의 저녁에 팔짱 끼고 물가를 거닌다.
하지만 프로젝트에 하루에 4만 달러를 쓰면서 귀중한 연구 시간을 잃어버리고 있는, 즉 최신식의 원격으로 조종되는 잠수정, 심해 고해상도 카메라, 그리고 미래적인 광대역 위성 통신 시스템에 수백만 달러를 투자해 온 탐험대장인 Robert D. Ballard에게는, 부두에서 밤마다 하는 축제에 대해 마법 같은 것은 아무것도 없다.

"우리는 과다 출혈로 죽을 지경이에요. 돈을 출혈하고 있죠." 라고 Ballard가 말한다.

그리고 이 최근의 지연은 여름의 유일한 실패가 아니었다. Ballard의 원래 일정은 이집트에 가라앉은 2700년 전의 페니키아 난파선 한 쌍으로 이동하기 전에, 불가리아와 터키에 가라앉은 그리스와 비잔틴의 여러 난파선들에 그의 기계들을 시험해 볼 필요가 있었다. 하지만 몇 주 앞서, Knorr가 메사추세츠주 Woods Hole의 모항을 떠나기 직전, 불가리아 과학원과의 협상에서 생긴 문제들이 Ballard가 현재로는 항해의 일부를 취소하도록 강요했다. 후에, 탐사가 시작되고 나서, Ballard는 또한 이집트 방위부가 페니키아 배를 탐사하기 위한 허가를 거부했다는 통지를 받았다.

---

vessel n. 선박 temporary adj. 임시적인
harmonious adj. 보기 좋은, 조화로운
rotating adj. 교대 근무를 하는, 회전하는
roster n. 명부, 등록부 financial adj. 재정적인, 금전적인
lash v. 묶다 pier n. 부두 appointed adj. 지정된, 정해진
investigate v. 조사하다 shipwreck n. 난파선
skeptical adj. 회의적인 packs of phr. ~의 무리
journalist n. 기자 scramble v. (빠르게) 움직이다
dock n. 부두 deck n. 갑판
earshot n. 부르면 닿는 (가까운) 거리
Noah's ark phr. 노아의 방주 resident n. 주민
stroll v. 거닐다 arm in arm phr. 팔짱을 낀 채로
waterfront n. 물가 marvel v. 경탄하다, 감탄하다
high-tech adj. 최첨단의
wizardry n. 하이테크 제품, 마법, 묘기
bob v. (배가) 떴다 잠겼다 하다, 위아래로 흔들리다
but for phr. ~이 아니었다면, ~가 없었더라면
expedition n. 탐험대, 탐험 priceless adj. 귀중한
invest v. 투자하다 state-of-the-art adj. 최신식의
remotely adv. 원격으로 submersible n. 잠수정
high-definition adj. 고해상도의
futuristic adj. 미래적인, 초현대적인
high-bandwidth adj. 광대역의 satellite n. 위성
carnival n. 축제
hemorrhage v. 출혈하다, (돈을) 손실하다
delay n. 연기 setback n. 실패, 차질 itinerary n. 여정
a series of phr. 일련의 wreck n. 난파선
home port phr. 모항, 소속된 항구
complication n. 문제, 합병증 negotiation n. 협상
cruise n. 항해, 순항 under way phr. 시작된, 진행 중인
get words phr. 통지를 받다, 말을 듣다
security n. 방위부, 보안 explore v. 탐사하다

68 2019 인하대

정답 ③

해석 ① 기름을 찾기 위해
② 군사 임무를 완수하기 위해
③ 고대 난파선을 조사하기 위해
④ 노아의 방주의 잔해를 찾기 위해
⑤ 침몰한 배에서 선원을 구조하기 위해

해설 배 Knorr가 터키에 온 이유를 파악하는 문제이다. 지문의 첫 번째 단락의 두 번째 문장에서 미국 선박과 선원들이 고대의 난파선을 조사하기 위해 흑해로 왔다고 했으므로, 배 Knorr가 터키로 온 이유는 '고대 난파선을 조사하기 위해'이다. 따라서 정답은 ③번이다.

어휘 accomplish v. 완수하다, 성취하다
military adj. 군사적인, 군사의 remain n. 잔해
rescue v. 구조하다 sunken adj. 침몰한, 가라앉은

69 2019 인하대

정답 ②

해석 ① 터키에 들어가기 위한 연구 비자 없음
② 터키인 기자들과의 문제
③ 프로젝트를 위한 많은 지출
④ 이집트로부터 난파선 탐사에 대한 허가 없음
⑤ 불가리아 과학원과의 협상에서의 어려움

해설 Ballard가 처한 문제점이 아닌 것을 파악하는 문제이다. 지문의 첫 번째 단락에서 현지 언론들이 회의적이고 기자들이 갑판에 있는 사람들에게 카메라를 들이밀고 질문을 한다고 하였지만, Ballard와 문제가 있거나 갈등을 겪고 있는 모습은 찾아보기 어려우므로, Ballard가 처한 문제점이 아닌 것은 '터키인 기자들과의 문제'이다. 따라서 정답은 ②번이다.

어휘 expenditure n. 지출

[70-74]

아인슈타인(Einstein)은 아이작 뉴턴(Isaac Newton)의 연구 이후로 거의 300년간 과학자들에게 받아들여졌던 물리학의 기본 원리들 중 일부에 도전한 물리학자였다. 그는 또한 뛰어난 작가였으며, 바이올린 연주자였으며 20세기에 가장 정치적 영향력이 큰 목소리를 낸 사람들 중 하나였다.
(A)하지만, 그가 살아있는 동안 그리고 그의 사후에, 보통 사람들이 아인슈타인에 대해 가장 좋아했던 점은 그의 이론과 다른 업적들보다는 그의 전설적인 이미지이다. 예를 들면, 그의 다소 헝클어진 모습이 — 크게 뜬 눈과 지저분한 머리 및 부주의한 옷차림 등 — 사람들의 관심을 끌었다. 사실, 그의 특이한 성격과 행동을 둘러싼 많은 이야기들이 있다. 그가 아직 소년이었을 때, 그의 학교 선생님은 그의 아버지에게 말했다. "이 아이가 어떤 분야로 들어가는가는 중요하지 않습니다. 그는 결코 어떤 일이든 성공하지 못할 거예요." 대학 다닐 때는, 그의 아내와 친한 친구들이 그에게 계속 기본적인 것들, 밥을 먹는다든가 수업에 들어간다든가 하는 것들을 계속 상기시켜 줘야만 했다. 그가 유명해진 후에는, 그에게 사인해달라고 요청하는 사람들에게 값을 청구하기 시작했다. 그는 사인해주기 전에 1달러를 요구하고 그 돈을 자선단체에 기부하곤 했다.

또 하나의 전설적인 일이 그의 (B)건망증을 더 잘 보여주었다. 프린스턴 대학에서 어느 날, 아인슈타인은 점심을 먹고 사무실로 돌아가는 중이었다. 걸어가다가, 그는 조용히 앉아 그가 가장 좋아하는 소재들 중 두 개인 시간과 공간이라는 문제에 대해 생각을 하기 시작했다. 그가 사무실로 돌아왔을 때, 그는 자신이 써놓은 "점심 먹으러 갔습니다. 10분 후에 돌아옵니다."라는 메모를 보았다. 나중에 그는 자기 사무실 밖에서 자신이 돌아오기를 기다리며 앉아 있는 모습이 동료 교수들에 의해 발견되었다.

accomplished adj. 기량이 뛰어난
legendary adj. 전설적인   accomplishment n. 업적, 공적
somewhat adv. 다소, 약간   disorganized adj. 흐트러진
messy adj. 지저분한, 엉망인
intrigue v. 흥미롭게 하다, 관심을 끌다   charge v. 청구하다
autograph n. (유명인의) 사인   incident n. 일, 사건

70 [2018 세종대]

정답 ①

해석 ① 하지만   ② 그러므로
     ③ 마찬가지로   ④ 결과적으로

해설 지문의 빈칸을 채우는 문제이다. 빈칸 (A) 앞의 첫 문단에서는 아인슈타인이 얼마나 뛰어난 사람이었는지를 언급했는데, 빈칸 (A) 뒤에서는 일반 사람들이 아인슈타인에 대해 좋아하는 점으로 그의 훌륭한 업적이 아니라 그의 특이한 모습과 건망증 등에 관한 기행을 언급하고 있으므로, 빈칸 (A)에는 '역접'을 나타내는 접속부사 However가 들어가는 것이 자연스럽다. 따라서 ①번이 정답이다.

71 [2018 세종대]

정답 ③

해석 ① 사람들은 아인슈타인의 흥미로운 외모를 비난했다.
     ② 아인슈타인은 어렸을 때 다른 어느 분야보다 야외 스포츠에서 실력이 형편없었다.
     ③ 아이작 뉴턴이 확립한 물리학의 원리들 중 일부는 아인슈타인의 도전을 받았다.
     ④ 보통 사람들은 아인슈타인의 물리학 이론에 관심이 없었다.

해설 지문을 통해 추론할 수 있는 것을 고르는 문제이다. 첫 문단의 Einstein was a physicist who challenged some of basic principles of physics ~ of Isaac Newton.을 통해 아이작 뉴턴이 확립한 물리학의 원리들 중 일부는 아인슈타인의 도전을 받았다는 것을 추론할 수 있다. 따라서 ③번이 정답이다.

오답분석 ① 두 번째 문단의 For instance, his somewhat disorganized appearance ~ intrigued people.에서 그의 다소 헝클어진 외모가 사람들의 흥미를 끌었다고 했으므로, 사람들은 아인슈타인의 흥미로운 외모를 비난했다는 것은 지문의 내용과 다르다.
② 아인슈타인이 어렸을 때 야외 스포츠를 잘하지 못했는지에 대해서는 언급되지 않았다.
④ 두 번째 문단의 what ordinary people enjoyed most about Einstein was ~ other accomplishments.에서 보통 사람들이 아인슈타인에 관해 좋아했던 점은 그의 이론과 다른 업적들보다는 그의 전설적인 이미지였다고 했는데, 이것은 보통 사람들이 아인슈타인의 전설적인 이미지에 더 관심을 가졌다는 의미일 뿐이며, 이것을 근거로 보통 사람들이 아인슈타인의 물리학 이론에 관심이 없었다고 추론할 수는 없다.

72 [2018 세종대]

정답 ②

해석 ① 아인슈타인은 사인해준 후에 1달러를 요구했다.
     ② 아인슈타인은 대학 때 수업 시간에 들어가는 것을 잊어버리곤 했다.
     ③ 아인슈타인은 평생 동안 자선단체에 돈을 기부했다.
     ④ 아인슈타인은 일을 할 때 꼼꼼하며 시간을 잘 지켰다.

해설 아인슈타인에 관하여 지문의 내용과 일치하는 것을 묻는 문제이다. 두 번째 문단의 During his college years, his wife and best friends had to keep reminding him to do basic things, such as to eat and go to class.를 통해, '아인슈타인은 대학 때 수업 시간에 들어가는 것을 잊어버리곤 했다'는 것을 알 수 있다. 따라서 ②번이 지문 내용과 일치한다.

오답분석 ① 두 번째 문단 He would ask for a dollar before signing에서 사인하기 전에 1달러를 요구하곤 했다고 했으므로, '사인해준 후에 1달러를 요구했다'는 것은 지문의 내용과 다르다.
③ 두 번째 문단 He would ask for a dollar ~ and gave the money to charities.에서 사인을 해주면서 받은 1달러를 자선단체에 기부했다고 했지만, '평생 동안' 기부했는지는 알 수 없다.
④ 두 번째 문단과 마지막 문단에서 아인슈타인은 건망증이 심했다고 했으므로, '일을 할 때 꼼꼼하며 시간을 잘 지켰다'는 것은 지문의 내용과 다르다.

어휘 meticulous adj. 세심한, 꼼꼼한
     punctual adj. 시간을 잘 지키는

73 [2018 세종대]

정답 ②

해석 ① 천재성   ② 건망증
     ③ 무기력함   ④ 명성

해설 지문의 빈칸을 채우는 문제이다. 빈칸 (B) 뒤에서 언급하고 있는 일화는 아인슈타인이 프린스턴 대학에 있을 때 어느 날 점심을 먹으러 나가면서 '잠깐 점심 먹고 오겠다'는 메모를 붙이고 갔는데 점심을 먹고 한참 다른 생각에 몰두해 있다가 돌아와서는 그 메모를 다른 사람이 붙인 것으로 착각하고는 자기 사무실 앞에서 한참을 기다렸다는 내용이다. 이것은 아인슈타인의 '건망증'을 보여주는 사례이므로, ②번 forgetfulness가 정답이다.

어휘 languidness n. 나른함, 무기력함

74 [2018 세종대]

정답 ②

해석 ① 아인슈타인은 자신의 사무실을 다른 사람의 사무실로 착각했다.
② 아인슈타인은 다른 사람의 사무실을 자신의 사무실로 착각하여 그 사무실 밖에서 기다렸다.
③ 아인슈타인은 문에 붙인 메모를 읽고 사무실 주인이 자리를 비웠다고 생각했다.
④ 아인슈타인은 문에 붙인 메모를 쓴 사람이 자신이라는 것을 깨닫지 못했다.

해설 프린스턴 대학에서 있었던 일을 묘사하고 있지 않은 것을 고르는 문제이다. 세 번째 문단은 아인슈타인이 프린스턴 대학에 있을 때 어느 날 점심을 먹으러 나가면서 사무실 문 앞에 '잠깐 점심 먹고 오겠다'는 메모를 붙이고 갔는데 한참 후에 돌아와서 그 메모를 다른 사람이 붙인 것으로 착각하고는 자기 사무실 앞에서 한참을 기다렸다는 내용이므로, '프린스턴 대학에서 있었던 일이 아닌 것'은 아인슈타인이 '다른 사람의 사무실을 자신의 사무실로 착각'한 것이다. 따라서 ②번이 정답이다.

어휘 mistake A for B phr. A를 B로 착각하다

[75-78]

[A] 스티브 잡스(Steve Jobs)와 리 클로우(Lee Clow)는 애플이, 감정적 호소력 면에서 아마도 5위 안에 드는, 세계의 훌륭한 브랜드들 중 하나라는 점에는 동의했지만, 애플에 관하여 독특한 점이 무엇인지 사람들에게 상기시켜줄 필요가 있다. 그래서 그들은 상품을 주인공으로 하는 일련의 광고가 아니라 브랜드 이미지 광고를 원했다. 광고는 컴퓨터가 무엇을 할 수 있는지가 아니라 창의적인 사람들이 컴퓨터를 가지고 무엇을 할 수 있는지를 찬양하도록 설계되었다. "이것은 프로세서의 속도나 메모리에 관한 것이 아니었어요."라고 잡스는 회상했다. "그것은 창의성에 관한 것이었습니다. 그것이 그 광고의 기원이었습니다."

[B] 클로우와 그의 팀은 '다르게 생각하는' '미친 녀석들'을 찬양하는 다양한 접근 방법을 시도했다. 결국 그들은 스스로 문구를 써야 할 필요가 있다고 결정했다. 그들의 초안은 '미친 녀석들을 위하여'로 시작했다. 원래의 60초 버전의 문구는 다음과 같았다; 미친 녀석들을 위하여. 부적응자들. 반역자들. 말썽꾸러기들. 사각형 구멍 안의 둥근 말뚝들. 사물을 다르게 보는 사람들. 그들은 규칙을 좋아하지 않는다. 그리고 그들은 현재 상황을 존중하지 않는다. 당신은 그들을 인용할 수도 있고, 그들에게 동의하지 않을 수도 있고, 그들을 찬미할 수도 비난할 수도 있다. 당신이 할 수 없는 거의 유일한 일은 그들을 무시하는 것이다. 그들이 세상을 바꾸기 때문이다. 그들은 인류를 앞으로 나아가게 한다. 그리고 어떤 이들은 그들을 미친 녀석들로 간주하겠지만 우리는 천재로 간주한다. 자기가 세상을 바꿀 수 있다고 생각할 정도로 충분히 미친 사람들이 바로 그렇게 하는 사람들이다.

[C] 잡스는 각각의 이러한 정서와 동질감을 느낄 수 있었으며 자신도 '그들은 인류를 앞으로 나아가게 한다'를 포함한 몇 개의 문구를 적었다. 8월 초에 보스턴 맥월드 엑스포가 개최될 때까지 그들은 이미 대략적인 버전을 만들었다. 그들은 그것이 아직 준비되지 않았다는 점에 동의했지만, 잡스는 거기서 행한 기조연설에서, 그 개념들과 '다르게 생각하라(think different)'라는 구절도 사용했다. 그때 그는 "거기에는 빛나는 아이디어의 싹이 있어요."라고 말했다. "애플은 고정관념의 틀을 깨는 사람들, 즉 컴퓨터가 그들이 세상을 변화시킬 수 있게 도와주도록 컴퓨터를 사용하는 사람들과 관련이 있습니다."

[D] 그들은 문법적 문제에 대해 토론을 했다. 만약 'different'가 동사 'think'를 수식해야 한다면, 그것은 'think differently'에서처럼 부사가 되어야 한다. 그러나 잡스는 'think victory' 또는 'think beauty'에서처럼 'different'가 명사로 사용되기를 원한다고 주장했다. 그것은 또한 'think big'에서처럼, 구어체의 용례를 따라 한 것이었다. 잡스는 나중에 설명했다. "우리는 그것(광고)을 실행하기 전에 그 표현이 정확한 것인지 토론했습니다. 만약 당신이 우리가 무엇을 말하려고 하는지에 대해 생각한다면, 그것은 문법적으로 맞습니다. 그것은 똑같은 것을 생각하는 것이 아니라 *다른 것*을 생각하는 것입니다. 조금 다른 것을 생각하라, 많이 다른 것을 생각하라, 다른 것을 생각하라. 나에게는 'Think differently'가 그 의미를 정확하게 맞추지 못합니다."

emotional appeal phr. 감정적 호소(력)
distinctive adj. 구별되는, 독특한   celebrate v. 찬양하다
Here's to ~ phr. ~을 위하여 건배   misfit n. 부적응자
rebel n. 반역자, 반대자   peg n. 말뚝
be fond of phr. ~을 좋아하다   status quo phr. 현재 상황
quote v. 인용하다, (말을) 옮기다
glorify v. 미화하다, 찬미하다   vilify v. 비난(비방)하다
sentiment n. 정서, 감정
Macworld Expo phr. 미국 IDG 사가 주최하는 매킨토시에 관련된 하드웨어, 소프트웨어 등의 전시회
keynote speech phr. 기조연설
germ n. 세균, 미생물; 기원; (생물의) 싹

think outside the box phr. 새로운 사고를 하다, 고정관념의 틀을 벗어나다 **modify** v. 수식하다 **verb** n. 동사 **adverb** n. 부사 **noun** n. 명사 **colloquial** adj. 구어체의 **genesis** n. 기원; 발생

75 (2018 아주대)

정답 ②

해석
① 완성
② 시작
③ 장엄함
④ 중단
⑤ 최후

해설 밑줄 친 genesis를 대신할 수 있는 동의어를 고르는 문제이다. genesis는 '기원, 발생'이라는 의미이다. 따라서 '시작, 개시'를 의미하는 ②번 origination이 정답이다.

76 (2018 아주대)

정답 ⑤

해석
① 경쟁자들
② 중재자들
③ 지지자들
④ 청교도들
⑤ 일반적 관행을 따르지 않는 사람들

해설 밑줄 친 The round pegs in the square holes를 대신할 수 있는 동의어를 고르는 문제이다. 밑줄 친 부분은 부적응자들, 반역자들, 말썽꾸러기들과 함께 열거된 표현이므로 '일반적 관행을 따르지 않는 사람들'을 의미하는 ⑤번 the nonconformists가 정답이다.

77 (2018 아주대)

정답 ④

해석
① 경제적 수익을 내는 측면에서 최고인 컴퓨터를 생산하는 것을 목표로 하는 사람들
② 상자 산업 역사에서 가장 멋있는 금속 상자를 발명하기를 열망하는 사람들
③ 계산 능력, 메모리, 저장 능력을 극적으로 향상시키려고 시도하는 사람들
④ 컴퓨터가 그들이 세상을 변화시킬 수 있게 도와주도록 컴퓨터를 사용하는 사람들
⑤ 기술이 인간보다 우수함을 증명하는 슈퍼컴퓨터를 만들기를 열망하는 사람들

해설 지문의 빈칸을 채우는 문제이다. 이들의 광고는 컴퓨터가 무엇을 할 수 있는지가 아니라 창의적인 사람들이 컴퓨터를 가지고 무엇을 할 수 있는지를 찬양하도록 설계되었다(It was designed to celebrate ~ what creative people could do with the computers.)고 했으며, 광고 문구에서도 자기가 세상을 바꿀 수 있다고 생각할 정도로 충분히 미친 사람들이 바로 그렇게 하는 사람들(Because the people who are crazy enough to think they can change the world are the ones who do.)이라고 했으므로, 고정관념을 깨는 사람들(who think outside the box)과 동격으로 쓰인 빈칸에는 '컴퓨터를 이용해 세상을 변화시키려는 사람들'이 들어가는 것이 자연스럽다. 따라서 ④번이 정답이다.

어휘 **second to none** phr. 최고 **long** v. 열망하다 **aspire** v. 열망하다

78 (2018 아주대)

정답 ④

해석
① 그는 문법적인 문제는 무시하면서 동료들의 조언은 묵살하는 매우 독단적인 리더였다
② 그는 'think different'가 구어체적 용례에 맞지 않다는 것을 깨달았지만 'think differently'보다 'think different'를 선호했다
③ 그는 정통 문법 규칙을 따르는 데 있어서 매우 예민하고 꼼꼼했다
④ 그것이 그 자체로 'think different'의 좋은 사례이다
⑤ 강력한 광고 문구를 쓰기 위해서는 광고 설계자들이 전통적인 문법 규칙을 위반하는 것이 절대적으로 필요하다

해설 스티브 잡스가 애플 광고에서 핵심적인 구절로 'Think Different'를 고르기로 결정한 방식이 무엇을 증명하는지 고르는 문제이다. [D] 문단 마지막의 인용문에서 스티브 잡스는 '만약 당신이 우리가 무엇을 말하려고 하는지에 대해 생각한다면, 그것은 문법적으로 맞습니다(It's grammatical, if you think about what we're trying to say). 그것은 똑같은 것을 생각하는 것이 아니라 다른 것을 생각하는 것입니다(It's not think the same, it's think different). 나에게는 'Think differently'가 그 의미를 정확하게 맞추지 못합니다('Think differently' wouldn't hit the meaning for me)."라고 직접 설명했다. 즉 Think Different라는 표현이 정통 문법에는 맞지 않지만 이 광고가 전하고자 하는 '기존의 틀에서 벗어나 다르게 생각하라'는 메시지를 고려하면 think different 자체가 think different의 가장 훌륭한 예라고 할 수 있다. 따라서 ④번이 정답이다.

어휘 **dogmatic** adj. 독단적인 **conform to** phr. ~을 따르다 **fastidious** adj. 세심한, 꼼꼼한; 까다로운 **orthodox** adj. 정통(파)의, 전통적인 **violate** v. 위반하다, 침해하다 **compelling** adj. 눈을 뗄 수 없는, 매우 흥미로운, 설득력 있는

종로 특별반 **최종합격률 100%**
최상위권 진학에 특화된
해커스편입 특별반

전과목 1타
스타강사진 지도

상위권으로만 구성된
선발고사 필수반

매달 최대 2,000제의
상위권 전용문제로 수업

심층 토론 스터디로
학습능률 극대화

[100%] 2019년 12월 종각 본원 특별반 등록생 기준 16명 중 16명 합격
[강우진 1위] 해커스편입 강남/종각/수원 편입논리 강의평가 평균 1위(2020년 1월~6월)
[공재웅 1위] 해커스편입 종각 본원 편입문법 강의평가 평균 1위(2020년 3월~6월)
[유익재 1위] 해커스편입 수원역캠퍼스 편입독해 독해 수강생 수 1위(2020년 3월~6월)

성적우수자 장학 혜택! 선발고사 무료 응시하기 ▶

상담 및 문의전화
[종 각 본원] 02-735-1881
[강남역캠퍼스] 02-522-1881
[수원역캠퍼스] 031-243-3333

해커스편입 HackersUT.com